SUPERVISORY MECHANISMS
IN INTERNATIONAL
ECONOMIC ORGANISATIONS

SUPERVISORY MECHANISMS IN INTERNATIONAL ECONOMIC ORGANISATIONS

IN THE PERSPECTIVE OF A RESTRUCTURING OF THE INTERNATIONAL ECONOMIC ORDER

P. van Dijk

General Editor

G. J. H. van Hoof & K. de Vey Mestdagh

Assistant-Editors

KLUWER
Law and Taxation Publishers
Deventer/Netherlands
ANTWERP · BOSTON · FRANKFURT ·
LONDON

T.M.C. ASSER INSTITUUT
The Hague

Distribution in U.S.A. and Canada
Kluwer Law and Taxation
190 Old Derby Street
Hingham MA 02043 U.S.A.

Interuniversitair Instituut voor Internationaal Recht T.M.C. Asser Instituut
20–22 Alexanderstraat, 2514 JM The Hague, Phone (0)70-630900, Telex 34273 asser nl

Director: C.C.A. Voskuil

Deputy Director: J.A. Wade; Heads of Departments: M. Sumampouw (Private International Law), Ko Swan Sik (Public International Law), A.E. Kellermann (Law of the European Communities, General Secretary); Office Manager: G.J. de Roode.

The T.M.C. Asser Instituut was founded in 1965 by the Dutch universities offering courses in international law to promote education and research in the fields of law covered by the departments of the Institute: Private International Law, including International Commercial Arbitration, Public International Law and Law of the European Communities. The Institute discharges this task by the establishment and management of documentation and research projects, in some instances in co-operation with non-Dutch or international organisations, by the dissemination of information deriving therefrom and by publication of monographs and series. In addition, the Institute participates in the editing of the Yearbook Commercial Arbitration and in the editing and publishing of, *inter alia*, the Netherlands International Law Review and the Netherlands Yearbook of International Law.

D/1984/2664/75

ISBN 90 6544 076 3

PREFACE

The research project of which the present book contains the results, was a common undertaking of a group of experts in the law of international organisations, who at the moment of the preparation of their contributions all formed part of the staff of the Europa Institute, University of Utrecht. As is explained in the General Introduction, they have thus made a next step to what they hope will become a Utrecht tradition in the field of comparative international law.

As the whole project took several years, quite some time elapsed between the moment when some of the individual reports were completed and the finalisation of the comparative and concluding part. Up-dating during the proof-reading phase was possible only to a very limited extent. However, in our opinion this fact has in no way detracted from the topical relevance of the results of this study, since recent developments in the field of research concerned have not shown major changes from the point of view of the object of study.

The authors owe much gratitude to the many persons and institutions who with their advice, assistance or financial support formed essential links in the chain of the project.

The advice and assistance is gratefully acknowledged of the following persons: Mr. D. W. Caulfield, Mr. G. Courage, Professor J. H. Jackson, Mr. J. de Jong, Mr. H. Kindred and Mr. W. A. Smit. Much help was also received from staff-members of the Permanent Mission of the Netherlands with the OECD and of the Secretariats of the OECD and the IEA, the GATT and the TSB, the IMF and the World Bank.

Completion of the project would not have been possible without the very generous financial support of the University of Utrecht, which provided the general editor with an assistant for a period of four years. Part III was prepared with the financial support of the Dutch Government in the form of the 'Bi-centennial Scholarship'. For Part VII support was received from the Twente University of Technology. Part IX was partly prepared in the framework of an exchange programme between the J. F. Kennedy Institute in Tilburg and the Polish Institute of International Affairs in Warsaw. Research for several elements of Part X was conducted at Columbia University and the University of Michigan on the basis of a Fulbright Scholarship for Advanced Research and a research grant from the University of Michigan Law School.

Since English is the mother language of only one of the authors, revision of the manuscripts in that respect was very important. This was done in a most experienced way by Mr. A. D. Stephens, then of the staff of the T.M.C. Asser Instituut, and for Part X by Professor H. Hovenkamp. This revision was made possible through a grant from the Legatum Visserianum.

Furthermore, the stimulating and co-operative assistance of the T.M.C. Asser Instituut is highly appreciated by the authors.

The voluminous manuscripts have been typed and retyped in their various versions with much patience and admirable accuracy by Ms. M. Kiel, who deserves the authors' appreciation for that. Finally, the attention and care are gratefully acknowledged which Messrs. R. J. Kasteleyn, M. Nieuwenhuis and A. Vonk of Kluwer Law and Taxation Publishers have devoted to the publication of the book.

Bilthoven, June 1984
P. van Dijk
Professor of the law of
International Organisations
University of Utrecht

TABLE OF CONTENTS

LIST OF ABBREVIATIONS

AFDI	Annuaire Français de Droit International
AJIL	American Journal of International Law
BISD	Basic Instruments and Selected Documents (GATT)
CILJ	Cornell International Law Journal
CJTL	Columbia Journal of Transnational Law
FD	Finance and Development
IA	International Affairs (Moscow)
IJIL	Indian Journal of International Law
IL	The International Lawyer
IO	International Organization
JIE	Journal of International Economics
JWTL	Journal of World Trade Law
NILR	Netherlands International Law Review
PASIL	Proceedings of the American Society of International Law
PCIJ Series A	Permanent Court of International Justice, Collection of Judgments
PCIJ Series B	Permanent Court of International Justice, Collection of Advisory Opinions
PYIL	Polish Yearbook of International Law
RCDAI	Recueil des Cours de L'Académie de Droit International
RGDIP	Recueil Général de Droit International Public
YBWA	Year Book of World Affairs
ZaöRV	Zeitschrift für ausländisches und öffentliches Recht und Völkerrecht

GENERAL INTRODUCTION

by P. van Dijk

The book on 'The Changing Structure of International Economic Law' by
Pieter VerLoren van Themaat, published in 1981,[1] was the result of a
research project in which several international lawyers of the universities of
Utrecht and Leyden participated. The principal aim of the project was to
contribute to a general theory of international economic organisations on
the basis of an extensive comparative law study, and to integrate the
conclusions drawn from this study in a general theory of international
economic law.[2] When writing his book, VerLoren van Themaat could draw
upon 29 reports on the existing international economic organisations and
new problem areas, written by the other participants.[3] These individual
studies, and the project in general, focused on the institutional characteristics
of the international economic organisations as well as on their characteristics
from the point of view of their substantive law. Special attention has been
paid to the relationship between the economic and political infrastructure of
the international economic organisations on the one hand and the institutional structure and legal instruments necessary for the realisation of their
objectives on the other, as well as to the correlation between objectives,
institutional structure and legal instruments. One of the instruments available
to international organisations for the realisation of their objectives is the
supervision of the conduct of their Member States in terms of these objectives
and of the standards and rules laid down in the founding treaties and
subsequent decisions of the organisations. This instrument has been dealt
with in the afore-mentioned project in an implied and summary way only
and referral was made to the present project, which had already been,
started.[4]

In that respect, among others, the research project of which this book
contains the results may be regarded as a continuation of the project
supervised by VerLoren van Themaat. However, not all the organisations
dealt with in 'The Changing Structure of International Economic Law' have
also been included in this 'Stage II'. A selection has been made of the most
important economic and financial organisations, worldwide and regional,
while the International Atomic Energy Agency has been added because of
the very special features of its supervisory mechanism. The European
Communities are not dealt with in a separate report, because a fairly recent
comprehensive study of the supervision in these organisations was available,
of which an updated second edition is to be published soon.[5] In spite of the
selection thus made, we are of the opinion that the conclusions based upon
a comparison of these organisations are of a sufficiently general character to
have relevance for the supervision in other international economic organisations and economic arrangements as well.

As was the case of VerLoren van Themaat's study, the present study, in addition to the principal aim mentioned above, purports to enhance the contribution of legal theory to the discussion of the restructuring of the international economic order. At a moment on which that discussion seems to have reached an almost complete stalemate in the political fora, and the original demands put forward by the developing countries seem to be further removed than ever from full realisation, reflection on some of the legal aspects of the required structural changes of the international economic order and of the ways and means towards their effectuation, which did not receive sufficient attention in the heat of the fight, may be especially appropriate and fruitful. The assumption that supervisory mechanisms in international economic organisations may very well form part of the required restructuring and at the same time provide the ways and means towards the carrying out of other structural changes, and for that reason deserve a comparative analysis from a theoretical and practical point of view, was the main incentive to our research.

The foregoing does not mean that the desirability of restructuring the international economic order was the dominating perspective for the examination and evaluation of the separate supervisory mechanisms. The individual reports deal with these mechanisms in their present regulation and functioning, and assess their effectiveness in relation to the purposes of the organisation concerned. The issue of a 'new' international economic order is not expressly discussed there. That is done to a certain extent in this general introduction and in a more detailed way in the final part of the book. In that context, references to the New International Economic Order in capital initials or to the acronym NIEO allude to the concept of a new international economic order as laid down in the pertinent resolutions of the General Assembly of the United Nations and other UN bodies, whereas the use of small capitals refers to the issue of restructuring the international economic order in general. The difference is not unimportant, since our own research, and discussions with experts inside and outside the organisations dealt with, lead us to conclude that the NIEO concept in its entirety and the scheme incorporated in it may very well still perform a useful function as a general frame of reference to the ultimate desiderata of, especially, the Third World countries, but that the feasibility of an integral realisation is very low in the short term. Therefore, any legal analysis must also take less far-reaching structural changes into consideration as possible steps towards a more just and equitable international economic order.

Before more information is given on the way in which the individual reports were prepared and on the scheme of analysis followed by the participants, some observations are made here concerning the relevance of institutional and supervision issues for the accomplishment of certain changes in the international economic order and on the institutional framework within which these changes can best be effectuated. These observations and the conclusion drawn from them serve as further arguments for the comparative approach opted for in this project.

I. THE RELEVANCE OF INSTITUTIONAL AND SUPERVISION ISSUES FOR THE ACCOMPLISHMENT OF STRUCTURAL CHANGES IN THE INTERNATIONAL ECONOMIC ORDER

> Effective multilateral machinery for negotiating a new order is not a sufficient condition for the realisation of that new order, but it is very probably a necessary condition.

With these words Robert W. Gregg, in his study on the issue of venue for negotiating a New International Economic Order (NIEO),[6] indicates the important bearing which institutional aspects have, not only upon the NIEO itself, but also upon the negotiations towards the establishment of the NIEO. And in one of his other studies he stresses the same point in the following words:

> The institutional context within which the NIEO is planned and negotiated will presumably affect the content of a new order, the manner and speed of its coming into being, and the legitimacy it enjoys.[7]

These words can be fully endorsed. Although the institutional framework in which negotiations take place will in general not be decisive for the outcome of these negotiations, it may influence this outcome to a large extent. Recognition of the importance of the institutional framework of negotiations has been, and still is, of course, one of the reasons for the establishment of international organisations: to create a permanent forum in which a certain group of States can conduct their negotiations towards the accomplishment of certain common goals, assisted by the secretariat of the organisation and using the other facilities the organisation has to offer. The large number of conventions that have resulted from the functioning of organisations such as the International Labour Organisation and the Council of Europe, finds part of its explanation in the effective treaty-making machinery these organisations provide.

An appropriate institutional framework is of the utmost importance, not only for the negotiation of structural changes in the international economic order, but also for the implementation of the principles and rules ensuing from these negotiations. It is remarkable that institutional issues have often been treated as points of secondary importance during negotiations leading to the establishment of international organisations. Moreover, they tend to receive less attention than the substantive provisions when the organisation is in operation. In our opinion this shows a lack of appreciation of the close connection between the institutional structure of an organisation and the goals it has to achieve.[8] We are inclined, with Professor Jackson and a number of other specialists, 'to view the question of institutional improvement and evolution as one of the most important aspects today of our current international economic problems'.[9]

It is the very launching and subsequent discussion of the NIEO concept which has directed attention, especially where global international organisations are concerned, to those institutional arrangements which, according to the developing countries, have been shaped in such a way that they serve mainly the interests of the economically more powerful Western States. Therefore, the demand for a more equitable allocation of voting rights and a more representative composition of organs of restricted membership has become an issue that occupies a prominent place in the NIEO debate.[10] These two aspects of the voting procedure will determine the impact of each individual State on the decision-making, and on the contents and development of the international economic order. This is why one could indeed state that 'the central issue in the NIEO relates to international decision-making'.[11] As Gregg puts it quite descriptively:

> The developing countries seek not only a larger share of the pie, but also control of the knife that cuts the pie.[12]

To a large extent, the same holds good for supervisory mechanisms. They are not the centre of attention, neither in the discussions leading to the establishment of international organisations, nor in those concerning their functioning and development. Indeed, sometimes one cannot help having the impression that they are regarded—and treated—as an inconvenient and costly ritual, rather than a device for the collective assessment of the fulfilment of the obligations undertaken by the participating states.[13] Since the compulsory value of principles and rules depends, *inter alia*, on the question of whether the possibility exists to check their implementation, it is of vital importance to the gradual restructuring of the international economic order that the acceptance of principles and rules constituting the basis of such a restructuring and giving shape to it, is accompanied by the creation of procedures for supervising their implementation.

Contrary to what has been said above about institutional issues, it is not the developing countries that take the lead in emphasising the need for the restructuring or introduction of supervisory mechanisms. In particular the new States seem to fear that these mechanisms will undermine their sovereign rights, regarding them as a neo-colonial form of Western interference. It may well be, however, that the acceptance of some sort of supervisory mechanism by the developing countries will turn out to be instrumental in obtaining the approval of the developed countries for certain procedural and substantive changes, since the latter then wish to have in exchange some sort of collective supervision over the internal and external policy of the developing countries.

Both issues – the appropriate institutional structures and the appropriate supervisory mechanisms – still do not receive the attention they deserve in the discussions and studies concerning the international economic relations. This situation seems to be changing gradually, however. The present study, together with VerLoren van Themaat's book mentioned at the beginning of this introduction and other publications, *e.g.* those by John Jackson, to which reference will repeatedly be made in Parts II, III and X, purport *inter alia* to bring about an awareness of the pertinence of precisely these issues.

II. *INSTITUTIONAL FRAMEWORK FOR RESTRUC-TURING THE INTERNATIONAL ECONOMIC ORDER*

What is the most appropriate institutional framework for negotiating a restructuring of the international economic order and implementing the relevant principles and rules agreed upon? The original NIEO documents do not deal with this question at all. In this respect, too, they are a political manifesto rather than an outlined programme of action or a blueprint for a future organisational set-up. Nevertheless, the question is a pertinent one that demands further discussion because the opinions of the developing and developed countries seem to differ quite substantially on this issue.

The Western countries are basically in favour of a pluralistic system of negotiations leading to the incorporation of new rules into those of the numerous already existing global and regional economic organisations. They argue that because of their structure and aims, these organisations are best suited to deal with individual NIEO issues such as the level of official development aid, technical assistance, debt renegotiations, removal of tariff barriers, development of an international food programme, commodity pricing, special drawing rights, transfer of technology, regulation of activities of transnational corporations, and consultation on industrialisation.[14] The developing countries, however, stress that all negotiations should take place under the aegis of the General Assembly of the United Nations with its egalitarian and majoritarian voting-procedure, which, in their opinion, will best guarantee their full participation in debates and decision-making. As Weintraub rightly puts it, 'each group of countries will wish to negotiate issues of importance to it in the institutions that it dominates' and 'dialogue is useful, but control is crucial in how different groups view the various international organisations'.[15] In any case, practice makes it sufficiently clear that this important issue has not been settled by Resolution 32/174 of December 19, 1977, of the General Assembly, which states 'that all negotiations of a global nature relating to the establishment of the New International Economic Order should take place within the framework of the United Nations system'. Negotiations have continued and will continue in different fora, also outside the UN-system *stricto sensu,* depending on the concrete issues in question.[16]

To what extent does the General Assembly offer the most appropriate forum? The establishment of a new international economic order constitutes a *political* plan de campagne and a detailed programme of *economic* measures at the same time. Consequently, the negotiations require a political forum where political positions can be brought into effect, but it is equally important that the forum can rely on sufficient economic and technical competence among both government representatives and secretariat personnel.

Those who are familiar with the functioning of the General Assembly of the United Nations through practical experience, will agree that the first condition is better met than the second one. As far as the first condition is concerned, the representatives who participate in the plenary meetings and

Committee meetings act according to the instructions of their governments and consequently will not agree with the text of a resolution dealing with important issues that does not have the political support of their governments. As to the second condition, however, the composition of the national delegations changes so often, and the amount of attention devoted by individual delegates to the preparation of the meetings and to the discussions during the meetings often seems to be so haphazardly inconsistent, that they can hardly be classified as meetings of experts. Moreover, the Secretariat would seem to be not quite adequately staffed with respect to the number and scope of the items on the agendas of the seven Committees, and tends to be very reluctant to influence and structure the discussion by bringing its special expertise to bear upon it. Besides, economic expertise would seem to be not the most distinctive feature of the UN Secretariat if one compares it to those of other international institutions.[17] This is bound to hamper in particular the General Assembly as a *forum of discussion* on economic matters. Its appropriateness as a *system of effective economic action* is open to even more serious doubt. As VerLoren van Themaat observes:

> The United Nations' objectives and its authority in the field of peace and security, and in the social sector, also results in full justice being done, in principle, to the interdependence between economic, social, military and general political problems within this universal worldwide organisation. However, this is offset in the economic sphere by the fact that the extremely diverse economic situations and economic and political systems of the Member States, as well as the existence of numerous international economic organisations specialised according to function and general coverage, impose great limitations on the possibility of effective action.[18]

Turning the General Assembly of the United Nations into the primary forum for negotiating the restructuring of the international economic order might have the negative effect that other institutions do not take the NIEO resolutions, adopted by the General Assembly, into consideration, when undertaking activities that are closely connected to that issue. Indeed, the binding character of those resolutions is denied by most Western countries, because of the institutional setting in which they have been negotiated and adopted. It would seem, therefore, that here, too, as was the case with other developments towards new forms of co-operation and organisation, a pluralistic rather than a centralised approach might lead to the best possible results in the near future, while a centralised system can be only a long-term solution.[19]

The argument sometimes put forward,[20] namely that only the United Nations organs carry a mandate broad enough to negotiate and implement the NIEO programme as a whole, is not very convincing, because this line of thought does not take into account, it seems, the perhaps more successful alternative of partial negotiation and implementation by other organisations in their respective fields of competence. Moreover, one cannot overlook the fact that neither the General Assembly, nor ECOSOC, and not even UNCTAD, have been very effective so far in using their broad competence for the implementation of a NIEO; they have functioned mainly as a discussion forum. All the manpower spent, the meetings held, the resolutions adopted and the studies devoted to the NIEO concept in these fora have not prevented the concept from becoming an almost dead or at least deadlocked issue in present negotiations. It has hardly transcended its initial role of a political manifesto of the Third World.[21] In specific economic and financial organisations, however, negotiations for a restructuring of the economic order are more likely to lead to concrete results – modest as these may be, when measured against the Third World demands – because the costs and profits of specific elements of such a restructuring are much more manifest and direct in such a context.[22]

The plea for a decentralised system, at least as an intermediate approach, cannot be refuted by the argument that the essence of the NIEO concept implies that the required international economic order can only be realised in an institutional context with universal membership and an egalitarian voting procedure which excludes the most relevant specialised and all regional organisations for not fulfilling both conditions. In the long run it is certainly desirable, if not necessary, that all States participate in the process, with a fair share in the decision-making involved. However, it is precisely the egalitarian and majority voting procedure which has created a tradition of '"resolution therapy", in which the majority passes resolutions which the minority frequently ignores'.[23] Since, as a rule, the minority is composed of the Western industrialised nations, this 'therapy' may very well offer a useful massage of the minds of those in power in these nations and of public opinion, but it is not suited for the creation of the law that is needed. Thus, when Mohammed Bedjaoui, a well-known spokesman for the Third World, says that 'the Third World possesses for the first time . . . a "right to the creation of law" thanks to the strength of its numbers',[24] the question remains whether the United Nations have proved to be the right forum to effectuate that 'right' for the Third World. One may well wonder whether the changes in functions and powers which would be required for the transformation of the United Nations into such a forum, are not more difficult to realise in a short term than the equally necessary adaptation of the structures and procedures of certain economic organisations to the justified demands of a more just and equitable international economic order. The rather disappointing efforts to restructure the economic and social sectors of the United Nations do not give rise to optimism in this respect. In any case, it is very doubtful whether the developed market economy States will approve of any substantial amendment of the powers of the United Nations in the economic field, concerned as they are that this will lead to circumventing the role of the economic and financial organisations.

However, it is clear that, if one opts for a short-term process of functional and decentralised reshaping of the international economic relations, there is a strong need for co-ordination of the decentralised activities as part of this process, and of the procedures for monitoring the results achieved and their implications for the activities of the other organisations and for the economic order in general. The United Nations – and especially its General Assembly – seems to be the most appropriate forum for this co-ordination and for defining the overall policy, given its universal membership, the annual discussions of the NIEO issues during its plenary meetings and meetings of its Second Committee and other Committees, the promoting and co-ordinating role of its Special Sessions and last but not least the fact that the UN Charter provides a well-defined legal basis for co-ordination activities.[25] However, in this forum emphasis should be placed on general debates, the adoption of guidelines and the assessment of the progress made, rather than on the discussion and decision of specific issues. As Gregg rightly observes:

> The General Assembly, in spite of its alleged advantages as a forum where political will can more readily be brought to bear, is much better suited to the airing of grievances than it is to bargaining about an economically complex agenda.[26]

To remedy some of the deficits of the UN structure, the composition has been suggested of a small but politically powerful group of high officials, who meet regularly *in camera* in order to try and break log-jams that impede the negotiating process.[27] It is doubtful, however, whether such a formula would really work in practice. At present, a small but politically powerful group of high officials who meet regularly *in camera* can be found in the annual Summits of the Ten: meetings of the Heads of Government of the ten economically most important countries. Needless to say, this institution can hardly be expected to give new impetus to the restructuring of the international economic order into a direction the Third World will agree with. If the Group of Ten could be enlarged to include some of the recognised spokesmen of the Third World for the discussion of the NIEO issues, the group would still remain small and would still consist of politically powerful officials, but it, too, would not be able to break log-jams and give new impetus, as a *collectivum,* to the NIEO debate, because the discussion and decision-making would in all probability be a mere reflection of their equivalents in the plenary bodies. After all, the deadlock has not been caused primarily by the number of delegates that participate in the discussion, but by differences of opinion, and by the lack of political will to compromise.

This is not to deny, of course, that a small group is more likely to negotiate effectively than a large group. However, no State wants to be kept out of the negotiations concerning such a fundamental issue as the NIEO. It would therefore be advisable that the actual negotiations be held in working groups of a restricted but representative membership, in so far as negotiations are held within the UN framework, while the results of these negotiations are reviewed by Committee II of the General Assembly or by a Committee of the Whole.[28] However, as said before, even these negotiations are likely to be effective only to the extent that they are directed towards defining the overall policy and the formulation of general principles and norms concerning the restructuring of the international economic order, rather than towards reaching agreement on specific technical aspects of that restructuring.

III. *EXISTING INTERNATIONAL ECONOMIC ORGANISATIONS AS A POINT OF DEPARTURE*

The above observations lead to the provisional conclusion that, at least in an intermediate perspective, the specific economic and financial organisations have a vital role to play in any effective restructuring of the international economic order.

This is all the more likely because of the fact that these organisations are important channels through which international economic relations are co-ordinated and regulated, and because they constitute the main instruments for developing and elaborating modern international economic law. It is very unlikely, as one of the leading authors on international economic law observes, 'that a totally new international economic order will be set up on the ruins of the existing order. For many reasons it is more likely that new developments will take place on the basis of the experiences of the past and the present, making use of the existing international organisations.'[29] And in the words of another leading author: 'It [the establishment of a NIEO; *v.D.*] is not a question of "revolutionary" destruction of existing international economic law but rather a gradual substantive evolution and adjustment of new realities'.[30] This means that it is important to study the various international economic and financial organisations in view of the contribution they can make to changing the structure of the economic order, both individually and co-ordinatedly. Moreover, a comparative analysis of these organisations may lead to the formulation of certain general features of the law of international economic organisations as part of a general theory of international economic law, from which conclusions may be drawn as to the legal structure and contents of the existing international economic order and concerning the question of which changes are needed to make it a more just and equitable order which benefits all States. As previously mentioned, this was the purpose of the research project carried out under the supervision of VerLoren van Themaat. The present study may be considered to be a continuation of that project, focusing on the role which the supervisory mechanisms in these organisations may play in that respect.[31]

Supervision of the fulfilment of those obligations which serve the interests of the individual members of a given society as well as the common interest, is of vital importance to the existence and functioning of that society. The same holds good for the international society and for the separate international organisations forming part of it.[32] As will be set out in more detail in Part I of the present book,[33] international supervision is characterised by the fact that it is carried out by a great variety of organs and through many different procedures and instruments. This makes systematic analysis difficult. On the other hand, it is evident that such a systematic analysis is indispensable to any conclusive comparative study. In order to facilitate such an analysis of the individual organisations, a uniform scheme of analysis has been developed, which was taken into consideration by the individual participants in the project in preparing their reports. Moreover, the introductory study on international supervision, its nature, functions, modalities, forms and instruments, and its effectiveness, which constitutes Part I of the present book, was available as a general theoretical background paper before the other participants started their research.

The uniform scheme of analysis, mentioned above, reads as follows:

1. *Introduction*
2. *Scope of Activities and Institutional Structure of the Organisation*
3. *Legal Instruments of the Organisation*
   3.1. Decision making
   3.2. Legal character of the decisions
4. *Supervision within the Organisation*
5. *Effectiveness of the Organisation's Supervision.*

Within the framework of this global scheme each participant was to distinguish and discuss the different functions, modalities, forms and instruments of supervision as set out in the introductory study mentioned above, to the extent that they were relevant to the organisation concerned.

Only supervision of *State* behaviour by the *organisations* is dealt with in the present book. Supervision of acts or failures to act *on the part of the organs of the organisation* by the *Member States* is not covered, although that kind of supervision is of course also important in respect of the realisation of an organisation's objectives. Supervision of State behaviour by *other States or private persons,* and supervision of the behaviour of *private persons* is also not taken into consideration, unless these kinds of supervision are directly connected to the supervision of State behaviour by the organisation.

The theory and practice of supervision within the individual organisations have been studied on the basis of the relevant documents of these organisations and the leading legal writing dealing with the organisations and their supervisory mechanisms. Moreover, the participants have consulted one or more experts from within and/or outside the organisation concerned to familiarise themselves with the practice of the organisation and to exchange views on the evaluation of the effectiveness of that organisation's supervision. It is fully recognised by all participants that, even after such consultations, a complete and in all respects balanced evaluation can hardly be made by an outsider, no matter how meticulously and intelligently the available information is collected and studied. It is, therefore, with due modesty that they present the results of their studies and the general observations and conclusions based thereon.

NOTES

1. Pieter VerLoren van Themaat, *The Changing Structure of International Economic Law* (The Hague/Boston/London, 1981).
2. Preface to the book mentioned in the preceding note, p. xvii.
3. For a list of the individual reports, see *ibid.,* pp. 379–380. They have been published in Dutch only: P. VerLoren van Themaat, ed., *Studies over internationaal economisch recht* (Studies on International Economic Law), 5 vols. (Alphen a/d Rijn, 1977–78).
4. *Op. cit.,* note 1, p. 32 and note 90.
5. H. A. H. Audretsch, *Supervision in European Community Law* (Amsterdam, 1977).
6. Robert W. Gregg, 'Negotiating a New International Economic Order: The Issue of Venue', in: Rüdiger Jütte & Annemarie Grosse-Jütte, eds., *The Future of International Organization* (London, 1981), pp. 51–69 at p. 67.
7. Robert Gregg, 'UN Decision-Making Structures and the Implementation of the NIEO', in: Ervin Laszlo & Joel Kurtzman, eds., *Political and Institutional Issues of the New International Economic Order* (New York, etc., 1981), pp. 103–132.
8. For this connection, see Pieter VerLoren van Themaat, *op. cit.,* note 1, pp. 108–114.
9. John H. Jackson, 'The Crumbling Institutions of the Liberal Trade System' (1978) 12 *Journal of World Trade Law* 93 at 101. See also the report of the Panel on International Trade Policy and Institutions of the American Society of International Law: 'Re-Making the System of World Trade; A Proposal for Institutional Reform' 12 *Studies in Transnational Legal Policy* (Washington D.C., 1976).
10. See *e.g.* Programme of Action on the Establishment of a New International Economic Order, GA Res. 3202 (S-VI), May 1, 1974, Chapter II, section 1(d) and (g) and Chapter IX, section 5.
11. Sidney Weintraub, 'The Role of the United Nations in Economic Negotiations', in: David A. Kay, ed., *The Changing United Nations; Options for the United States,* Proceedings of The Academy of Political Science (New York, 1977), p. 93 at p. 96.
12. Robert Gregg, 'The New International Economic Order as a Political Manifesto', *UNITAR News,* Vol. XI (1979), p. 21 at p. 22.
13. *Cf.* John H. Jackson, *loc. cit.,* note 9, p. 102, who states that: 'with so many pressing substantive issues that are more readily understood by political interests back home, governments tend to downplay the importance of the more remotely related procedural questions such as dispute settlement'.
14. On these and other NIEO issues, see Ervin Laszlo *et al., The Objectives of the New International Economic Order* (New York, etc., 1978).
15. *Loc. cit.,* note 11, p. 97.
16. See GA Res. 34/138 of December 14, 1979, providing that global negotiations 'should not involve any interruption of, or having any adverse effect upon, the negotiations in other United Nations forums but should reinforce and draw upon them'.
17. *Ibidem,* p. 116. The creation of the post of Director-General for Development and International Economic Co-operation, though in itself an important step, thus far has not had the all-penetrating impact on the Secretariat as a whole as to attention for and competence in economic matters, that many had hoped it would, especially because of lack of clarity as to mandate and powers. In this connection, see the 1981 Report of the Joint Inspection Unit on 'Relationships between the Director-General for Development and International Economic Co-operation and entities of the United Nations Secretariat', and the comments of the Secretary-General on this report; A/36/419 and Addendum 1.
18. *Op. cit.,* note 1, p. 79.
19. Compare the functional and decentralised approach to Western European integration. See *e.g.* A. H. Robinson, *European Institutions; Co-operation: Integration: Unification* (3rd ed., London, 1973), pp. 1–35.
20. See *e.g.,* Robert W. Gregg, *loc. cit.,* note 7, p. 109.
21. *Ibidem,* p. 104.
22. For a comparable plea to converge the NIEO discussion and negotiation to issues directly relevant for technical rule-making rather than on basic values and principles with a strong political element, see Norbert Horn, 'Normative Problems of a New International Economic Order' (1982) 16 *Journal of World Trade Law* 338 at 349–350.
23. Robert Gregg, *loc. cit.,* note 7, p. 112, with reference to Andrew Boyd. At. p. 115 Gregg speaks of a 'majority steamroller'.

24. Mohammed Bedjaoui, *Towards a new international economic order*, (UNESCO, Paris, 1979), p. 142.

25. See, especially, Arts. 58, 62–64 and 70. On the co-ordination role, see: 'Report of the Secretary-General on restructuring of the economic and social sectors of the United Nations System: implementation of section VIII of the annex to General Assembly resolution 32/197 and section IV of Assembly resolution 33/202', A/35/527, December 19, 1979, Part B: Interagency co-ordination.

26. *Loc. cit.* note 6, p. 59.

27. See Robert Gregg, *loc. cit.*, note 7, p. 126, who endorses a recommendation in that direction by Jahangir Amuzegar.

28. *Cf.* 'A New United Nations Structure for Global Economic Co-operation', Report of a Group of Experts on the Structure of the United Nations System, E/AC.62/9. See also Johan Kaufmann, 'Decision-Making for the New International Economic Order', in: Antony J. Dolman & Jan van Ettinger, eds., *Partners in Tomorrow; Strategies for a New International Order* (New York, 1978), pp. 174–181 at p. 178.

29. Pieter VerLoren van Themaat, *op. cit.*, note 1, p. xvii.

30. Milan Bulajic, 'Legal Aspects of a New International Economic Order', in: Kamal Hossain, ed., *Legal Aspects of the New International Economic Order* (London, 1980), p. 45. See also Norbert Horn, *loc. cit.*, note 22, pp. 344–346.

31. See the beginning of this Introduction.

32. In more detail, *infra*, pp. 4–7.

33. *Infra*, pp. 7–10.

PART I

MECHANISMS OF INTERNATIONAL SUPERVISION

MECHANISMS OF INTERNATIONAL SUPERVISION

by G. J. H. van Hoof & K. de Vey Mestdagh

CONTENTS

I. THE CONCEPT OF SUPERVISION

1.1 Introduction

In any society members have to commit themselves to certain behaviour in the interest of other members and in the common interest of society at large. Members' obligations *vis-à-vis* other members and society at large are laid down in written and/or unwritten regulations. These regulations have to be observed if the society is to be at all viable. Therefore, supervision of the observance of obligations is an inherent feature of any society. This is true for the national society (the State), as well as for international society (the community of States). Compared to most national societies, international society has far fewer and much less effective mechanisms for ensuring that the law regulating relations between States is observed. In national societies supervision is entrusted to an institution, *i.e.* the State, with authority *over* the individual members; in international society supervision still rests mainly *with* the individual Member States themselves.

Since the First World War the situation regarding international supervision has gradually developed. International relations have become more numerous and complex and this development has made supervision more important, but at the same time more difficult. Although the sovereign States are still the highest authorities, they have delegated an increasing number of functions to international institutions, including parts of their supervisory function. Accordingly, international supervision has gained in importance, and has acquired a much more diverse and complex character. In the light of this development, it is remarkable that international supervision has not received more attention from scholars in international law. While supervision within the context of certain international organisations such as the ILO and the European Communities has been dealt with on a wider scale, writing on the issue as such is relatively scarce.[1] This might be due to the nature of the phenomenon of international supervision itself. It has a number of characteristics which make it very elusive.

In the first place international supervision is sometimes opaque or, at first sight, not visible at all. For instance, with regard to diplomatic relations between States, it cannot always be established with certainty by outsiders whether supervision is exercised in one way or another, and, if so, to what extent. Similarly, activities of international organisations which are not among the supervisory functions of the organisation in the strict sense may, on closer inspection, contain elements of supervision. The mere discussion of a topic within an organ of the organisation may cause a State to alter its point of view on that matter, thereby bringing that State's behaviour into accordance with the relevant rules of international law. In such a case the observance of the law has been attained which is one of the main goals of supervision.

Secondly, international supervision can take many different forms. If international supervision at this moment had to be tensely characterised, the key-word would undoubtedly be *diversity*. At the international level supervision is marked by a great variety of organs, procedures and instruments. Moreover, the nature of international supervision renders it very hard to classify the different types and to deal with it in a systematic fashion. Classification and systematisation, however, are necessary if the factors affecting the degree of effectiveness of international supervision in a given field of international law are to be explored and explained on a comparative basis. The diverse character of the phenomenon is further complicated by the fact that international supervision, like international law itself, is still in the process of development. One has constantly to bear in mind that changes may occur of one kind or another.

Finally, international supervision is a highly complex phenomenon. In national societies with a more or less full-fledged legal system, the machinery for supervising the observance of the law is already very complicated. This is even more the case at international level. For, as will be shown in more detail below, because of the specific features of international society, international supervisory bodies do not only have to operate in less favourable conditions than those usually prevailing in a national context, but they also have a broader function than national supervisory bodies.[2] Circumstances are less favourable, because at international level there is no authority like the State with its power of enforcement. International supervisory bodies have to carry out a broader function as a result of the weakness of the international legislative machinery and of executive-type institutions. Functions which in national societies are performed by the legislature and the executive have, internationally, to be exercised sometimes by supervisory bodies.

For all these reasons international supervision raises many problems which the scholar finds hard to tackle. On the other hand, a thorough study of the subject becomes all the more indispensable. After what has been observed above about the nature of the phenomenon of international supervision, it goes without saying that it is impossible to cover all the different aspects of international supervision within one single study. The present introduction aims to contribute to the characterisation and classification of international supervision and thereby to lay the foundations for further study of the topic. In this introductory study we shall confine ourselves to the most important international supervisory mechanisms that have been set up within the framework of international organisations.

Supervision within international organisations is of course not the only form of international supervision. It is clear that outside this framework, too, States can exercise supervision over each other in many different ways. These latter types of supervision will be referred to in the following as diplomatic, or inter-State supervision.[3] Although diplomatic supervision originated earlier than supervision within international organisations there are good reasons for focusing attention on the latter type of supervision.

First of all, the activities of international organisations cover an ever-growing part of international relations. As a consequence, supervision within international organisations is still expanding. In quantitative terms, therefore, supervision within international organisations is of substantial importance and can be expected to become even more important in the future. Furthermore, the effectiveness of supervision is enhanced once this supervision is collectivised, organised and/or institutionalised in one way or another. Therefore, in a qualitative sense, supervision within international organisations is of special significance. Finally, an advantage incidental to the study of supervision within the framework of international organisations is that, within these organisations, the political configuration is to a certain extent formalised and institutionalised. Thus, the impact of political factors on supervision can be taken into account more easily than in the case of supervision outside the framework of international organisations, where the political configuration is usually more amorphous. With regard to the foregoing, however, it should be borne in mind that the *direct* influence of States upon each other also constitutes a basic element of supervision *within* international organisations.

Another major limitation of the scope of the present study concerns the object of supervision. Here we shall discuss only the supervisory mechanisms which relate to the obligations incumbent upon *States* under international law. The observance of international obligations incumbent upon other subjects of international law, for example (the organs of) international organisations and private parties, such as companies and individuals, will be

6

left out of consideration. Although the acts and omissions of these other subjects are coming more and more within the purview of international law,[4] it can hardly be doubted that the behaviour of States is still to a large extent the decisive factor in international relations.

The purpose of the present study is to set the stage for an analysis of international supervision as it occurs within various international economic organisations and other arrangements of an economic character. Obviously, such an analysis can best be conducted on the basis of a clear understanding of the phenomenon of international supervision as such. In the following, therefore, we will first discuss the nature of international supervision in general. Subsequently, we will try to set out the specific features of international supervision in more detail by analysing its functions, modalities, forms and instruments. On the basis of these various functions, modalities, forms and instruments the final section constitutes an effort to answer the question what factors govern the effectiveness of international supervision.

1.2. The nature of international supervision

1.2.1. Introduction

The few authors who have dealt with the problem of international supervision so far have all produced their own definitions.[5] Although these definitions have some elements in common, they differ in many respects. The reason is to be found in the hybrid nature of international supervision itself. It is very hard indeed to capture the various aspects of international supervision in one definition without this definition being so general and abstract as to lack all distinctive capacity.

For a description of the nature of the phenomenon of supervision the reader is referred to the study of Kaasik, which was not only one of the first, but is still also one of the most profound studies on this topic.[6] Kaasik has characterised supervision (French: contrôle) as follows:

> The supervisory function is an essential part of the legal technique. It performs a function which is absolutely necessary to the existence and progress of any society, of any social organisation. The main object of this function is to ensure respect for the law and the realization of rules of law as well as the regular functioning of public service within the limits laid down in these rules of law. Supervision is an organic function which makes it possible for errors (either in the assessment of a situation or in taking action) which might jeopardize the stability and security of social existence to be rectified. It therefore serves to ensure public order.[7]

On the basis of this general definition by Kaasik the nature of international supervision can be clarified by briefly tracing its development during the present century and by contrasting international supervision with the more or less full-fledged supervisory procedures that may be found in some national legal systems.

1.2.2. Origin and development of international supervisory mechanisms

In the period before the First World War the contacts between States in times of peace were more incidental and less all-embracing and complex than at present.[8] As the nature and development of the law is closely linked to the structure of the society in which it has to operate, this state of affairs was reflected in international law. The function of traditional international law consisted mainly of the delimitation of powers between the different sovereign States. It was, therefore, a relatively simple body of law in the sense that, with regard to many subjects, it did not provide for substantive rules, but confined itself to designating the competent State.[9] It is not surprising that in such a situation international supervision did not reach a very high stage of development.

At the outset, States exercised supervision over each other through the intermediary of their diplomatic organs. This so-called diplomatic or inter-State supervision has all the characteristics and disadvantages of a subjective form of supervision: its exercise may contain a high degree of partiality and arbitrariness and its effectiveness is usually dependent upon the strength of the supervising party in relation to that of the party over whom supervision is exercised.

Today international society has acquired a considerably different character. From the end of the First World War changes began to take place and, after the Second World War, this process of change dramatically accelerated. International relations in the political, economic, technical, social and cultural fields have become much more frequent and intensive. In general, this process can be described as one of a growing interdependence. The main reason for this growing interdependence is that States are more and more dependent upon each other for the solution of the problems facing international society.

All this of course has not left international law unaffected. From the many examples of the changes that have taken place, two should be singled out here as being of special importance for the present study, *i.e.* the proliferation of multilateral treaties with a law-making character, and the steady growth in the number and activities of international organisations. Both factors are symptomatic of the general pattern of change in international law which can be described as a development towards a greater 'density'. This means, first, that international law today, compared to the traditional system, covers a considerably greater number of relations within international society and, secondly, that the way in which the issues covered are regulated is much more penetrating and detailed. It is not surprising that this steady expansion of international law both horizontally and vertically has made the matter of supervision more significant. The more States become dependent upon each other for the solution of international problems, the more crucial it becomes that States ensure mutual compliance with their obligations under international law in order to keep the international society viable. States are, of course, expected to live up to the rules of international law binding upon them. This idea is embodied in one of the most fundamental principles of international law, as contained in the maxim *pacta sunt servanda*, which, so far as treaties are concerned, is laid down in the 1969 Vienna Convention on the Law of Treaties.[10]

In the changed circumstances described above, however, it was not sufficient merely to rely on this principle and the defective diplomatic supervision. An increasing need was felt for mechanisms that could ensure, or at least enhance and promote, the observance by States of their international obligations. Within the framework of international organisations this need has been satisfied to a certain extent. After the First World War a number of supervisory mechanisms were instituted, for example in the Mandate-system[11]; in relation to the protection of minorities[12]; and within the International Labour Organisation.[13] Since 1945 international supervision has even constituted one of the major issues of many international problems such as the non-proliferation of nuclear arms,[14] atomic energy,[15] the use of outer space,[16] the protection of human rights[17] and international economic relations.[18] While international supervision used to be exercised exclusively by individual States on a reciprocal basis, nowadays it is also entrusted to collective international bodies.

1.2.3. *Difference between national and international supervision*

Although there have been some remarkable changes in the last century, international law cannot be equated with a more or less fully fledged system of national law. According to a classical definition international law is the body of customary and conventional rules which are considered legally binding by States in their relations with each other.[19] This is still a fairly accurate description of international law. For the most part international law is still not only State-orientated, but also State-made and State-dominated. The States are essentially the decisive factor in international law.

As a result of this predominant role of the States international supervision in many respects differs from supervision in the most developed national legal systems. In the latter, a master-organisation in the form of the State is superimposed on the subjects of the law. By way of typology the make-up of this master-organisation can be described as follows: a democratically elected legislator, a politically responsible executive branch of government and an independent judicial power, whose judgments can be enforced, if necessary, by coercive measures imposed by the States.

In essence, these characteristics of the organisational structure of the nation State are lacking at the international level. Internationally there is no central legislative body. Apart from the very few cases where organs of international organisations have been given the power to take binding decisions, the principal subjects of international law – the States – determine themselves if, and by what norms, they wish to regulate their international relations. Compared to the subjects of national legal systems States still have the status of a *homo liber*.[20] Therefore, to establish whether a rule is a binding rule of international law, it is generally considered that 'It is the will of States, their consent or consensus, which has to be ascertained, revealed or discovered'.[21]

Without discussing in detail here whether or not rules of international law derive their binding force only from the consent of States, one cannot deny that, in general, the importance of this consent with regard to the creation of rules of international law can hardly be exaggerated. The consent of States is also decisive with regard to other functions at international level. In the light of the subject-matter of the present study the most important of these functions are the execution of the rules of law drawn up by the 'legislator', their application to concrete cases and the supervision of their observance. In national societies these functions are usually exercised by the executive and judicial branches of the State. It is often very difficult to attribute the exercise of each of these functions in national legal systems precisely to the one branch or the other. Generally, both the executive and the judicial branch help to exercise the functions mentioned. For our purpose it is not necessary to establish a clear-cut division between the two branches of government. It is sufficient to indicate, that in national societies these functions are exercised by bodies superimposed on the subjects of the law and that the situation in international law is quite different.

Under international law States are, as a rule, not answerable to any higher authority. There are no international judicial bodies comparable to national courts whose jurisdiction is of a compulsory character. The jurisdiction of international tribunals is, as a rule, of a voluntary character. Even in cases in which States have, in one way or another, accepted the jurisdiction of an international tribunal, there is no certainty that those States will also implement its judgment. Although acceptance of jurisdiction implies an obligation to do so, in general no authority exists with the power to enforce such an obligation.

The development towards centralisation of governmental power and towards a separation of functions within that centralised power, which can be discerned in most national societies, has, in international society, at best only just started. International society is still highly decentralised, *i.e.* the (governmental) power is still predominantly in the hands of the members of that society. This is one of the most manifest consequences of the sovereignty of States. In principle, sovereignty does not prevent States from transferring powers to a supra-national or inter-governmental institution. However, it is precisely as a result of their sovereignty that States enjoy complete freedom to do so or not. In practice, States are not inclined to confer powers upon international institutions without retaining a decisive influence for themselves. Therefore, neither the horizontal and vertical expansion of international law nor even the rise and development of international organisations has transformed the essential features of international law. Nevertheless, international organisations have made a substantial contribution to enhancing the capacity of international society to solve the problems with which it is confronted. It is for this and other reasons that the present study focuses on supervision within the framework of international organisations.[22]

10

II. FUNCTIONS, MODALITIES, FORMS AND INSTRU-MENTS OF INTERNATIONAL SUPERVISION

2.1. The functions of international supervision

In view of the preceding discussion of the nature of international supervision, its functions will be dealt with in this section. Three functions of international supervision may be discerned, *i.e.* the review function, the correction function and the creative function.

2.1.1. The review function

In general, review means measuring or judging something against a standard. Within a legal context review consists of the judging of behaviour for its conformity to a rule of law. The review function of international supervision in relation to States, therefore, can be said to be exercised whenever the behaviour of States is judged against a rule of international law by a supervisory body with an international status. The supervision is exercised either by one or more States or by an institution created by or in virtue of a treaty.[23] The review function results in the determination of whether or not the behaviour reviewed is or was in conformity with international law. In the case of a positive decision, international supervision has reached its goal with the completion of the review function.

2.1.2. The correction function

The correction function is mainly relevant where a situation has been found to be contrary to international law. Nevertheless, correction may also be of a preventive character, when States conform to rules of international law as a result of the mere existence or threat of correction mechanisms. The ultimate goal of international supervision is to assure the observance of the rules of international law. Infringements, therefore, should be corrected. Apart from cases in which the infringing State remedies its infringements of its own accord, compliance with international legal obligations has to be ensured through outside persuasion or pressure. This constitutes the correction function of international supervision, which is usually referred to as the enforcement function.[24] A problem which arises in this context is that of sanctions in international law, to which we will return later.[25]

2.1.3. The creative function

The review and the correction function can be considered as the hard core of supervision. Indeed, these are inherent in the very concept of supervision, national as well as international. It is submitted, however, that with the description of review and correction, the functions of supervision are not exhausted; supervision often fulfils also a creative function. This applies particularly to international supervision.

11

As a result of the present configuration of international society (its low degree of organisation and, notably, the absence of an executive and a judicial type of institution) the functions of international supervisory bodies are not limited to review and correction. Legislative measures are quite often very vague and abstract. In many cases they contain only very broad directives with respect to the subject-matter which is to be regulated. These directives need to be elaborated into more specific norms before they can be applied in practice. With regard to review, too, this elaboration is necessary, because review and, therefore, also correction might be impossible if the norm which has to be used as a standard is too abstract and vague.

This task of further specifying general norms is, in national legal systems, performed partly by the legislature itself, partly by the judicial branch, but mainly by the executive branch of the State. The legislature can, of course, draw up new, more specific norms; the executive can further specify the norm through its own 'legislative' measures, and by interpreting general norms and individualising them through legal acts of an individual character. The result of the process just described is that national supervisory bodies *pur sang* (judges and judicial tribunals) are usually confronted with norms of a reasonably specified character. Of course, the work of the national supervisor is not purely mechanical. A judgment does not simply result from putting side by side a norm on the one hand and the behaviour reviewed on the other. Some interpretation is always required. Moreover, a national supervisor, too, might find himself in a situation in which the applicable norm is vague or in which there are no directly applicable norms at all. The pronouncement of the judge may in such a case result in so-called judge-made law.

In general, however, it seems that the role which this aspect (the specification of general and vague norms) plays in the work of the national judge is a minor one compared to that of international supervisory bodies. First of all, rules of international law are often even more general and vague than national legislation. For although custom has been replaced by treaties as the main source of international law,[26] it is clear that even treaty-making cannot be put on the same level as national legislation. The legislative machinery of international society is less monolithic because States act collectively as the international legislature. Moreover, international legislation is not always performed by the same group of States. The composition of the international legislature differs with the subject-matter or with the international organisation concerned. The cohesion of the international legislature is therefore a matter of degree, because it can vary with different international organisations. For instance, the EEC and, to a lesser extent, the ILO are equipped with a legislative machinery (a constitutional basis and legislative procedures on a permanent and institutionalised basis) comparable to national legal systems. In general, however, multilateral (law-making) treaties are concluded on an *ad hoc* basis, and constitute the highest common denominator. The international legislator is not always a permanently functioning body. Legislative organs of international organisations sometimes function only on a periodic basis. Their products, therefore, are

12

sometimes an *ad hoc* reaction to a current problem. Furthermore, organs of international organisations are, in general, only competent to adopt non-binding resolutions. While this kind of 'soft' law is undoubtedly of value with regard to the elaboration and the progressive development of 'hard' international law, it cannot in this respect be equated with real legislative action. In short, it is submitted that the international legislative machinery contributes to the specification of more general norms of international law to a far smaller degree than does the national legislature with regard to national law.

Secondly, the specification function as performed by an executive type of institution is even less impressive in international society. In national societies the executive branch of government is the most important symbol of the centralised organisation of the State. A comparable institution is not available in international society. The executive function is also performed by States, but this time in an even less organised way than is the case with the legislative function. The executive organs of most international organisations resemble the executive branch of national government only in a marginal way at best. As a matter of fact, in a number of instances the executive function is hardly performed at all, due to the lack of a sufficiently common basis of agreement between the States on the realisation of the purposes of the organisation. It is one thing to reach an agreement on one or more very abstract objectives laid down in a number of general and vague norms; it is another to reach agreement on the ways and means by which those objectives are to be realised in practice. It is clear that in such a case supervision is hardly feasible. If a supervisory mechanism is, nevertheless, instituted, its results will be very poor.

But even in cases where the situation is better in this respect, the task of further specifying general and vague norms is often postponed to the supervisory phase, *c.q.* unloaded upon the supervisory organs. Of course this places an extra burden on these organs. The task of the supervisory organs *pur sang* (judicial or technical) is, however, sometimes partly alleviated by the fact that the legislative and/or executive organs (of the organisation) participate in the supervisory procedure within the organisation. Especially in cases in which the basis of consensus within the organisation is weak, this co-operation between different types of organs for the purpose of supervision can hardly be avoided. For, in these cases the supervisory organ *pur sang* lacks the necessary basis upon which a final decision could be based. Such a basis has then to be found in a politically representative organ, exercising a creative function.

It is difficult to describe the content and scope of this creative function of international supervision precisely, but some indication for this has been given in the foregoing. In general it is the elaboration of already existing norms which are not specific enough to be applied in practice. Therefore, the creative function often consists of interpretation. As such, it sometimes coincides with the review function. It is not always easy to draw a clear dividing line between the creative function and the review function: elements of the former are interwoven within the latter. However, the creative function can go further than what can still be considered interpretation. In such cases it amounts to an elaboration of the purposes of the organisation and/or the principles underlying the legal order concerned. In this sense the creative function can be said to contribute to the realisation of the legal order.[27]

2.2. Modalities of supervision

In studying the problem of international supervision, a distinction can be made between specific supervision and general supervision.[28]

2.2.1. Specific supervision

In the case of specific supervision, the behaviour of States is subjected to supervision for its conformity with certain obligations only in particular and well-defined circumstances. This supervision is ordinarily triggered by the alleged existence of a state of facts inconsistent with these obligations, or on the basis of indications that make it likely that such a state of facts will arise.

Specific supervision is usually exercised in situations of a certain importance and as a rule deals with individual cases which are judged on their own merits. Sometimes specific supervision is preceded by a suspicion, or even accusation, of a violation of the obligation concerned.[29]

2.2.2. General supervision

General supervision on the other hand, is initiated in terms of the international obligation itself. As a rule, it is exercised on a periodic basis, and independent of particular circumstances. Its permanency may contribute much to its effectiveness because the surveillance is not restricted to a narrowly defined set of facts; even smaller incidents may be observed. As far as general supervision is concerned there is no need for an accusation or suspicion *expressis verbis*.[30]

Whereas specific supervision proceeds from the specific case to the general situation, general supervision proceeds from the general to the specific. From the information on the general situation, this latter modality of supervision may proceed into the details of specific cases. General supervision has an inquisitorial rather than accusatorial character; supervision is not exercised over any particular State, but over all States concerned.

2.2.3. Modalities in forms and instruments

General and specific supervision both have their characteristic form and instruments for monitoring the behaviour of States. The most characteristic form of specific supervision is the judicial type of surveillance. As regards judicial supervision it is the only modality possible given the necessarily accusatorial character of international judicial supervision. Quasi-judicial

14

supervision also seems to be of a mainly specific nature. Non-judicial supervision, however, may take on the specific as well as the general modality.

Proceedings of a general character often make use of the reporting system as an instrument, while specific supervision mostly is exercised by means of an investigation on the basis of a complaint or petition. This does not mean, however, that each instrument belongs exclusively to general or specific procedures respectively. As will be pointed out in the following, modalities and instruments might also be of a mixed nature, depending upon the particular case.

2.3. Forms of supervision

The forms of supervision refer to the three main manifestations of supervision within international organisations, *i.e.* judicial, quasi-judicial and non-judicial supervision. A distinction between these three forms will be made according to the differences in organs, procedures, and decisions. These forms may involve various procedures ranging from highly structured to extremely subtle ones. It should be emphasised that only institutionalised forms of international supervision will be dealt with here. Political or economic pressure and *ad hoc* consultations are left out of consideration in the present section. Yet, it should be borne in mind that these subsidiary forms of supervision have sometimes proved to be well established and highly effective.

2.3.1 Judicial supervision

Judicial supervision is supervision exercised by independent and impartial persons or bodies that are competent to give, on the basis of facts determined by due process, legally binding judgments. This form of supervision is mainly confined to a determination of the facts and their legality. The essential task of the judge is to apply the rule of law to the facts of the case brought before him. Through judicial supervision the rule of law is individualised by judging the legality of the challenged action or inaction. The most well-known international judicial supervisory organs are the International Court of Justice, the Court of Justice of the European Communities and the European Court of Human Rights.[31]

2.3.1.1. Organs

The elements that characterise an organ of judicial supervision are the independence and impartiality of its members.[32] Although governments do play a role in the nomination and election of judges their influence formally ends upon the selection of a judge. Thereafter, the judges are not under the instruction of any government; they are obliged to work independently and impartially throughout the course of their term.[33] Yet, in particular with

15

regard to the World Court, the political influences, or rather political *'Vorverständnis'*, cannot be disregarded.[34]

Unlike the Court of Justice of the European Communities and the European Court of Human Rights, which consist of at least as many judges as there are Member States,[35] the International Court of Justice, due to its universal character, must necessarily be of limited composition. Nevertheless, the litigant States may appoint a judge *ad hoc* if a judge of their own nationality is not represented on the bench.[36]

2.3.1.2. Procedures

The rules of procedure of international courts are based on principles which are also familiar to many national courts. Thus, with respect to international judicial supervision, one finds procedural regulations influenced by notions of due process, such as the public character of hearings.[37]

As far as *locus standi* before and jurisdiction of international judicial organs are concerned, a number of observations should be made. Except for the fact that the organs of the UN and its specialised agencies may request an advisory opinion,[38] in which case one cannot speak of judicial supervision *stricto sensu* (no binding decision, no parties), the International Court of Justice is exclusively a court for the settlement of disputes between States.[39] However, one State cannot automatically summon another before the Court in case of dispute. The Court is competent to hear a dispute only if the respondent State has accepted the jurisdiction of the Court, by a specific declaration recognising the compulsory jurisdiction beforehand (the optional clause), by treaty, by compromise, or unilaterally on an *ad hoc* basis.[40]

The Court of Justice of the European Communities has broader competences and may decide disputes between Member States,[41] or between a Member and the Community[42] and it can review the legality of Community acts at the request of a Community Institution, a Member State or an individual.[43] The Court also exercises some control over the interpretation and application of community law within the national legal order by giving preliminary rulings.[44]

Under the European Convention on Human Rights a case may be referred to the European Court of Human Rights, by the Commission or any of the States concerned provided that the complaint has been declared admissible by the Commission and the efforts to reach a friendly settlement have failed.[45] The State against which the complaint has been lodged must have accepted the jurisdiction of the Court.[46]

2.3.1.3. Decisions

As a rule, decisions take the form of a judgment. The judgments are legally binding on the parties involved.[47] The execution of the judgment is usually left to the litigating parties themselves. However, some supervision over the execution is guaranteed with respect to judgments of the International Court of Justice by the Security Council,[48] of the Court of Justice of the European Communities by the European Commission,[49] and of the European Court of

16

Human Rights by the Committee of Ministers of the Council of Europe.[50] Nevertheless, there are virtually no sanctions available to enforce a judgment.[51]

If it considers that the rights which form the subject of its application are in immediate danger, either party to a conflict generally may request a judicial organ to indicate interim measures of protection. As a rule, the organ may also indicate these provisional measures, as they are otherwise known, of its own motion. Such measures are binding decisions which are meant to have a 'containment effect' in order to forestall a conflict from becoming worse.[52]

2.3.1.4. Exursus: international arbitration

International arbitration is usually dealt with under judicial supervision, but is somewhat different from the subject as treated above. The distinction between judicial settlement in the strict sense and arbitration lies neither in the nature of the procedure, nor in the character of the decision, but in the composition of the adjudicating body. In 1958 the International Law Commission defined arbitration as 'the procedure for the settlement of disputes between States by a binding award on the basis of law and as the result of an undertaking voluntarily accepted'.[53] The initial undertaking to arbitrate, whether in the form of an *ad hoc* agreement ('compromise') or of a pre-existing general arbitration treaty, is essentially a *pactum de contrahendo, i.e.* an imperfect obligation that becomes effective only when the obligation to set up a tribunal and its terms of reference have been fulfilled.[54]

It is generally conceded that modern arbitration began with the 1794 Jay Treaty between Great Britain and the United States. Since that time *ad hoc* arbitral bodies have been, basically, of three types: the single arbitrator, the joint commission, and the 'mixed' commission. The single arbitrator, chosen by mutual agreement, would frequently be a foreign sovereign or head of State, or a collegiate chief of State. As to the joint commission, the tribunal would consist of a plurality of persons, but they would all be of a highly 'representative' character. Here, the supervising process approximates that of the negotiation of a compromise; and, the risk of failure to reach an agreement is high. This risk is lessened by the practice adopted in the 1794 Jay Treaty of choosing an 'odd' (although not neutral) member by agreement or by lot. The 'mixed' commission type of arbitral body represents a further and substantial improvement over the joint commission, because a 'neutral element' is employed. In this context, a neutral member is one with a decisive vote who is not a national of either party.[55]

Arbitration has seldom been provided for in case of settlement of disputes between an international organisation and its Member States. Sometimes institutional facilities and/or procedural rules are established by or in the framework of an organisation in order to settle disputes by arbitration among Member States, between Member States and individuals or even between individuals.[56]

2.3.2. Quasi-judicial supervision

Quasi-judicial supervision is a form of surveillance falling between judicial and non-judicial supervision. Here too, an organ relatively independent from State influences applies rules of law to facts established by due process. The finding, however, can be either binding or non-binding, but cannot be subjected to political reconsideration. Essential to this rather broad circumscription of quasi-judicial supervision is the notion of due process and the finality of the decision. All the rest remains in the 'quasi' sphere, and much depends on the criteria used. Hence, the interpretation of what is quasi-judicial as compared to judicial and non-judicial for the most part depends on these criteria. An example of quasi-judicial supervision can be found in the procedures for the protection of human rights, as instituted by the European Convention on Human Rights. The European Commission of Human Rights, as an independent organ, gives – on the basis of facts established by due process – a binding decision in respect of the admissibility of the complaint. On the merits, however, the Commission can only give its opinion, and must leave the final decision to the Committee of Ministers of the Council of Europe, or the European Court of Human Rights.[57] In the case that neither the Commission nor the State or States involved refer the case to the Court,[58] a decision has to be taken by the Committee of Ministers. We must regard such a procedure on the whole as non-judicial according to the definition given in the following section. Should the case be referred to the Court, then the ultimate procedure is one of judicial supervision.

2.3.3. Non-judicial supervision

Non-judicial supervision is supervision exercised, in the last resort, by a politically dependent organ of an international organisation, which by way of a procedure which is, in general, not well-defined comes to a binding decision or non-binding recommendation, depending on the constitutional powers of the organ.

Unlike judicial supervision, non-judicial supervision not only judges the legality of the behaviour of States, but may also take into consideration its expediency. Within non-judicial supervisory mechanisms two phases can often be distinguished: frequently there is a technical phase, which precedes the political phase. In the technical phase organs of restricted composition, mostly consisting of (independent or dependent) experts, fulfil an investigatory function.[59] Their task consists for the most part of fact-finding and inquiry. They generally lay down their findings in a report, which may or may not be supplemented by a tentative opinion. This task of data-processing might also be fulfilled by secretariat personel,[60] but then the result is produced in a much more mechanical way, without evaluation.

In the political phase, in which representatives of all the States Members to the organisation usually participate, decisions are taken as a rule on the basis of the outcome of the technical phase, along the political lines of confrontation, debates, conciliation, concessions, etc.[61]

2.3.3.1. Organs

At the outset it was the States themselves which, as contracting parties to a treaty, exercised reciprocally the supervision required through their diplomatic agents.[62] However, diplomacy usually results in a *'surveillance de façade'*,[63] which means that the degree of effectiveness of observation is highly dependent upon the cooperation of the local authorities, at least for the official gathering of data. Hence, this method of supervision is often organised in a more indirect, camouflaged way.[64] International supervision exercised by individual States still exists, and cannot be underestimated. In particular much of what happens outside the official sessions of supervisory organs of international organisations, within the setting of conference diplomacy, might be considered as falling within this category.

However, especially since the rise of international organisations after the First World War, States have increasingly delegated supervisory powers to international organs. Governments and their traditional diplomatic agents, as foreign affairs generalists, proved to be generally insufficiently prepared, particularly in view of the growing permanency of supervision. Moreover, supervision became more technical which required experts. Nevertheless, States mostly retained a political surveillance over this delegated supervision through the institution of a body consisting of representatives of all the countries concerned. Hence as was observed above, many supervisory mechanisms within international organisations show a distinction between a technical and political phase.[65]

As to the composition of non-judicial supervisory organs there is often a technical supervisory organ of restricted composition alongside a political supervisory organ composed of representatives of all Member States.[66] The technical supervisory organs can be composed in three different ways: in the first place they may consist of national officials who are experts and who are under instructions from their governments. These so-called 'para-diplomats'[67] are to be found in particular within technical organisations.[68] Secondly, one may find supervisory organs composed of independent experts, appointed by international organisations. To this group belong in the first place the international civil servants, who are, however, not experts in the strict sense. Nevertheless, they often play an important role in reviewing the work of the organisation and the behaviour of the Member States.[69] On the other hand, many international organisations seek the advice of independent experts, who serve either as consultants *ad hoc*, or as members of an expert commission on a permanent or *ad hoc* basis.[70] Lastly, there are the organs where the composition is mixed. Here one may think of organs composed of official governmental representatives and independent experts. The independent experts in this case are sometimes representatives of national non-governmental organisations, like trade unions and federations of employers. Although they are State representatives, they are not governmental representatives, *i.e.* they are not under any instruction from their government.[71]

In addition (independent) experts being representatives of non-governmental organisations may take part in supervision in a different capacity.[72]

Sometimes non-governmental organisations, if recognised as such, and if a specific status is granted to them, are empowered to furnish supervisory organs with reports on their own motion or on request.

Commissions composed of (independent) experts should be considered as representing the common interest of the organisation within which they function, and thus the collectivity of the States as a whole. They have no authority to take decisions.[73] This competence, i.e. to take binding decisions within non-judicial supervisory procedures, is, as a rule, the prerogative of the political supervisory organs.[74]

The political organs of supervision for the most part are the principal or plenary organs of the international organisations in which all the States, as members of a particular organisation, participate. In these organs the political influence of individual States counts most.[75] Sometimes, a political organ deals with supervisory questions and takes decisions without referring them first to a technical body.[76] In such cases supervision can be regarded as being exclusively political.

2.3.3.2. Procedures

No particular procedure is prescribed for international supervision of a non-judicial character. On the contrary, procedural regulations regarding, for instance, due process or *locus standi*, which are inherent in any judicial supervisory procedure, are lacking in respect of non-judicial supervision. Within non-judicial supervisory mechanisms international organisations are free to adopt their own procedures for the purpose of supervising the behaviour of the Member States. This explains why – contrary to judicial supervision, in which the necessarily accusatorial procedure can only be initiated by a complaint – in the case of non-judicial supervision one may find apart from the complaint procedure,[77] also the petition,[78] an action by the supervisory organ *prorio motu*,[79] or periodical supervision.[80]

2.3.3.3. Decisions

Depending on the provisions in the constitution of the international organisations concerned, decisions may be of a binding character (decisions *stricto sensu*) or in the form of non-binding recommendations. Clear examples of both may be found in, for instance, the United Nations. The Security Council is competent to take a binding decision in order to maintain or restore international peace and security.[81] The General Assembly, on the other hand, is usually only in the position of adopting recommendations,[82] although it can take decisive action such as excluding a member who has persistently violated the principles laid down in the Charter.[83]

2.4. Instruments of supervision

The instruments of supervision are the ways and means used within the different forms of supervision to effectuate the three functions of international supervision, *i.e.* the review function, the correction function and the creative function. Hence, in dealing with the instruments of supervision, a distinction must be made between the instruments of these three functions.

2.4.1. Instruments of the review function

For the review function, the gathering of information is of primary import-ance. Regardless of which instruments of review we take, their usefulness depends on the extent to which exact knowledge of the facts has been obtained. What conditions any instrument of review are the sources of information.[84] The effectiveness of review depends largely on the information gathered, but, on the other hand, the instruments of the review function are decisive for the sort of information required. As has been explained above the modality of supervision (*i.e.* general or specific) to some extent deter-mines the instruments to be used.[85] The review instruments of general supervision as a rule will be used at regular intervals, and hence will provide the reviewing body with information on a regular basis. The instruments of specific supervisory review do not ensure a continuous and regular flow of information. As a rule, they only reveal the facts of the incorrect situations the existence of which provoked the coming into operation of the supervisory mechanism. The instruments will thus be of irregular use and will be conditioned by particular circumstances.

2.4.1.1. Exchange of information

Before dealing with general or specific instruments of supervision in the institutional sphere, an instrument of the review function has to be mentioned which is primarily of a non-institutional character. As stated above, the members of the international community themselves often supervise the application of international rules by other members.[86] This 'primitive' form of international supervision is still widespread in international society and exists alongside more developed supervisory procedures within international organisations. The instrument of review of this type of supervision, referred to above as diplomatic or inter-State supervision,[87] can be described as an exchange of information between States concerning their intentions, formu-lated policies or the execution thereof.[88] Such exchanges can become more meaningful by extending them to preconcerted consultation.

Exchange of information may easily become institutionalised if an inter-national organisation renders some kind of (secretariat) support to its Member States. The main difference, however, between this instrument of review and reporting (to be dealt with in the following section) is that exchange of information generally is voluntary and takes place on the initiative of a State, while reporting is often of an obligatory character and constitutes an instrument provided for by the constitution of the organisation.

2.4.1.2. Reporting

The main review instrument of general supervision is the reporting proce-dure, according to which reports have to be drawn up periodically[89] by the

States concerned on the implementation of the obligations they have undertaken. An instrument of a more specific character may be found in *ad hoc* reporting procedures.[90] One other instrument can be distinguished here, *viz.* automatic reporting or notification. Notification results from an obligation to report automatically, *a priori* or *a posteriori,* in case certain circumstances occur.

The advantage of periodical reports is that they ensure permanency and continuity of supervision. Moreover, States often have to report on the basis of questionnaires drawn up by the organisation. This system guarantees at least a certain degree of uniformity and, if the questions are well-defined, is likely to result in a fairly precise and reliable picture, which facilitates comparison of the behaviour of the various States involved. This holds true in particular, if, as is generally the case, the possibility of requiring complementary information is provided for.[91]

Frequently reports, whether in a processed form or otherwise, are subject to publication and are given a wide dissemination. Besides, the contents of the reports might be subject to public discussion in the principle organs of the institutions.[92] Depending upon the organisation, the discussion may take place in a plenary organ (general assembly or council) or in a restricted organ (executive council). In some cases a special organ or committee is created to study the reports supplied by States, and to discuss them in the presence of a representative of the government concerned.[93]

2.4.1.3. Complaints and petitions

The instrument of the review function used pre-eminently in specific supervision is investigation on the basis of a complaint or a petition. The main difference between a complaint and a petition is that a complaint gives the right to a hearing of the case after the complaint is lodged, whereas the right of petition does not include the *right* to have the case placed on the agenda of the competent organ. An instrument of review related to the complaint is the facility conferred upon States to request consultations in case the policy of another member adversely affects their interests.[94]

Complaints by States are communciations lodged with the supervisory organ to the effect that another State is not fulfilling its obligations.[95] Sometimes, the State complaint is based on the idea, that the regularity of the behaviour of States is in the interest of the international community at large; in such cases any State can act against an assumed irregularity. This so-called *actio popularis* has as a characteristic that no relation is required between the violated rights and the individual interests of the complaining party or its nationals.[96]

Complaints and petitions by individuals have the same ultimate purpose as complaints by States: they are intended to draw the attention of the reviewing organ to the non-fulfilment by a contracting State of its obligation, and to that end to initiate the supervisory procedures. There are a few cases in which individuals and non-governmental organisations have a right to present such a complaint or petition, asking for an investigation and conclusion by an organ through a prescribed procedure.[97]

2.4.1.4. Fact-finding and inspection

Mention should also be made of two instruments of review which most actively involve the international organisation itself, *i.e.* fact-finding and inspection. The notion of fact-finding is, unlike other forms of gathering of information (*e.g.* clearing-house), as a rule strictly related to the supervisory functions of an international organisation. It consists of the collection of data in the widest sense of the word and from all sources of information available. This instrument of supervision can be used at the organisation's own initiative. Fact-finding is different from (*ad hoc*) reporting in that the latter is based on an obligation of the Member States, whereas fact-finding belongs to the competences of the international organisation. Secretariat studies of many organisations are usually based on reporting as well as fact-finding.

International inspection is supervision on the spot and can be defined as investigation or observation exercised on the spot by persons invested with international supervisory powers with a view to verifying the conformity of certain acts, a situation or the exercise of competences, with a rule, an engagement or the requirements of the international order.[98] Inspection can be of a general as well as of a specific character.[99]

Inspection is sometimes carried out for the purpose of investigating a factual situation with a view to elucidating controversial points of fact without questioning in advance the information furnished by a State. In ascertaining the underlying circumstances and facts of a dispute, fact-finding by way of inspection may resolve conflicts based on different views of the facts by the parties.

There are domains where unilateral interpretations of international obligations carry too many risks – where reports or comments upon complaints cannot be considered as a reliable source of information. In particular, this is the case with collective security measures (conventional as well as in the field of non-proliferation), but also in respect of the production of atomic energy and regarding the non-occupied territories under international supervision. In these cases supervision on the spot is often inevitable, or at least a very important additional source of information. The opposition of States to this instrument of supervision is easy to explain: because of the direct action by international supervisory organs on the territory of States, surveillance on the spot constitutes a sensitive infringement of the conception of absolute State-sovereignty. Hence, this instrument of the review function can, as a rule, only be used with the *ad hoc* consent of the State on the territory of which the supervision is to be exercised.

2.4.2. *Instruments of the correction function*

The three main instruments of the correction function of supervision as exercised within international organisations are political discussion, friendly settlement and sanctions.

2.4.2.1. Political discussion

Following the technical or factual review phase, the political discussions are mostly held in a plenary organ. During these discussions criticisms can be formulated with respect to the defective behaviour of States. A discussion may be followed by decisions or recommendations which, through their legal or moral pressure, may contribute to the correction of the behaviour of States. Apart from this repression, the discussion itself may also be an instrument of correction, preventive of character. Inherent in a plenary discussion of shortcomings of a State is the so-called 'mobilisation of shame', which can harm the international reputation of that State if public opinion is alerted by measures of publicity in appropriate cases. This external publicity may be preceded by internal publicity, *i.e.* publicity within the circle of governments represented in the organisation (*e.g.* the GATT), in which case the public at large is not informed – governments inform each other, or are informed, and thus have a chance to react.

A special form of political discussion which might serve as a corrective element regarding State behaviour is exercised within so-called 'groups' of countries, the members of which have found among each other a common basis for action. Essential to negotiating in groups is that among the members of the different groups standpoints are prepared in advance, and that the individual member will act accordingly. The formulation of these standpoints mostly takes place in regional (*e.g.* the EC) or functional organisations (*e.g.* OECD, OPEC or the Group of '77'). An example of an organisation in which group negotiations are more or less institutionalised is the United Nations Conference on Trade and Development (UNCTAD).[100]

Finally, mention should be made of a far-fetched form of political discussion, the so-called confrontation technique, which is of a highly structured character and normally takes place in more restricted fora. A confrontation procedure implies that the policy, with respect to well-defined matters, of one country is confronted with comments and criticism regarding that policy of other countries. Briefly the confrontation technique generates in the following manner. A country report is called for, sometimes by issuing a detailed questionnaire; the replies are studied by other Member States and the secretariat, and a critical analysis is prepared. The country under 'examination' which prepared a reply then is obliged to defend its 'case' against a well-briefed 'opposition' which may be, and frequently is, unanimously and vigorously expressed.[101]

2.4.2.2. Friendly settlement

Friendly settlement as an instrument of the correction function can be subdivided into consultation, good offices, mediation and conciliation. Consultation as such constitutes a corrective instrument primarily used by States *inter se*, without there being any supervisory role for international organisations. Hence, consultation is in the first place an instrument of correction which belongs to diplomatic or inter-State supervision.[102] Nevertheless, consultation as a means to settle a dispute must sometimes be employed before the dispute is referred to an international organisation.

The notion of consultation is often translated into negotiation[103] or renegotiation. The renegotiation, under the aegis of an organisation, of existing obligations is a common practice which is usually closely linked with supervision (GATT, Comecon, etc.). If mandatory consultation or the possibility to request consultation is provided for within the framework of supervision by an international organisation, as a rule secretariat or conference facilities are included.

Good offices and mediation, obviously leave room for a certain role, albeit passive, to be played by the international organisation. These two forms of assistance were once clearly distinguished, in that good offices consisted of employing the third party as a messenger between the disputants, or as the deviser of possible solutions, without the parties being compelled to enter into direct contact. Mediation was rather a form of help in bringing direct negotiations between the two to a satisfactory result. In the practice of international organisations, however, there is hardly any difference between the two institutions.[104] Good offices and mediation, for which the secretariat of an organisation is particularly qualified because of its multinational composition and its independence of national governments, can play a role in the general supervisory work of the organisation.

Conciliation – as an instrument of correction in which the organisation is much more actively involved – is more specifically related to international supervisory procedures. Conciliation may be provided for in recommendations adopted, or treaties concluded within the framework of an international organisation. The Security Council of the UN can be considered as a permanent conciliation commission for situations likely to endanger international peace and security. Other examples of institutionalised forms of conciliation provided for in a treaty can be found in, *inter alia*, GATT and the Multi-Fibre Arrangement.[105]

2.4.2.3. Sanctions

Whenever the pressure emanating from political discussion and/or one or more of the procedures of friendly settlement do not succeed, the organisation might be left with the *ultimum remedium* of sanctions as a response to the deviant behaviour of a State. The notion 'sanction' is used here in a broad sense, developed as it has within the framework of international organisations. Not only traditional sanctions, like suspension of membership-rights or exclusion, are to be taken into consideration. Also such forms as the 'mobilisation of shame' as a result of publicity, or the sanction of non-participation, *i.e.* exclusion from common endeavours and facilities through the refusal to elect a particular State to subsidiary organs, the withholding of a favour to a State (for instance a loan), or attaching conditions to certain services, may under certain circumstances turn out to be important instruments to correct a recalcitrant party.

The traditional sanctions used by international organisations are usually mentioned specifically in the constitution of an organisation. These include: suspension of voting rights, mostly as a sanction for non-compliance with contribution obligations,[106] suspension of representation,[107] suspension of services of the organisation,[108] authorisation of retaliation[109] and expulsion.[110] Next to these expressly formulated sanctions, the constitutions of some organisations provide for the possibility of sanctions which are not specified. General conferences are sometimes invested with the power to take measures deemed appropriate, or to suspend, in general, the rights of membership.[111]

Even if sanctions are not provided for at all they may be imposed in the fields where the organisation has discretionary powers. 'Suspension' of admission, or suspension of representation have been used several times. An implied basis may sometimes be found in the power of each organ to approve the credentials of the delegates of the Member States.[112] When a constitution does not provide for expulsion the same result may in fact be reached by exerting pressure for voluntary withdrawal.[113]

The Security Council of the UN, according to its primary responsibility for the maintenance of international peace and security,[114] is invested with exceptional enforcement powers. On the basis of Arts. 41 and 42 of the Charter, the Council may decide what measures are to be taken to give effect to its decisions. These measures may be of a non-military (*e.g.* economic or diplomatic) character (Art. 41), or in case of inadequacy (of these) of a military character. These sanctions are different from those dealt with above to the extent that the organisation is completely dependent upon the co-operation of its members with regard to the execution of the economic as well as military measures.

2.4.3. Instruments of the creative function

As has been submitted previously, the plenary organ is, as a rule, the organ in which the formulation of recommendations and conventions takes place. Similarly, it has been shown that in respect of supervision of these recommendations or conventions, the same plenary organ, as the highest political body, often plays a decisive role. Only in rare instances is the power to take the final supervisory decision delegated to an independent judicial or quasi-judicial body.

If these bodies, in exercising their supervisory functions, reach the conclusion that the convention or recommendation must be specified or interpreted in a certain way, they are the organs pre-eminently competent to do so. Hence, the politically dependent plenary organs, and, albeit less often, the independent (quasi-) judicial bodies, necessarily fulfil an important role in the creative function of international supervision.

Apart from deliberations *in camera* as an instrument of the creative function used in (quasi-) judicial supervisory procedures, the most frequently used instrument of the creative function is the political discussion held in the plenary organs of the international organisations whether or not on the basis of an expert report. Hence, the political discussion acts as an instrument of the correction function as well as of the creative function. It not only serves to establish the deviations committed, but also to discover (in particular if the discussion is based on solidly established information) the causes of and the reasons for deviations, and the difficulties met by a particular State. This may often result in a more liberal interpretation or even modification of the rules concerned.[115] Sometimes these results are caused by more extensive political discussions which take the form of renegotiations (GATT, CMEA). Henceforth, political discussion and renegotiation are two sides of the same coin.

Reports supplied by States and comments by committees of experts can be efficient elements of information in this context. They provide the supervisory organ with the material sources in order to oversee the effects of a norm, and they draw attention to necessary and possible improvements, which would escape a less penetrating observation.[116]

III. EFFECTIVENESS OF INTERNATIONAL SUPERVISION

3.1. Effectiveness in general

The question of effectiveness is of course the crux of the whole matter of international supervision. At the same time, effectiveness is the most difficult aspect of international supervision to evaluate. It has been contended that the measurement of the effectiveness of international supervision is an immense and highly delicate undertaking, which can only be performed on a long-term basis and by those who are familiar with the practice and development of international institutions.[117] It is beyond doubt that the most reliable picture of the effectiveness of international supervision would be obtained by a systematic analysis over an extensive period of time of the supervisory practice of various international organisations on the basis of which the effectiveness of international supervision could be evaluated comparatively. However, analyses of such a scope and character are still lacking for most international organisations.[118]

Bearing this reservation in mind, some provisional observations of a general character on the effectiveness of international supervision can be made. In the following sections the subject will be discussed according to the modalities, the forms and the functions of international supervision set out above. Before dealing with effectiveness in these different respects, something has to be said about effectiveness of international supervision as such.

First of all, the question what is meant by effectiveness arises. Effectiveness is closely related to the purpose or the goal aimed at. The more international supervisory mechanisms contribute to the realisation of the goals for which they have been set up, the more effective they are. From this it follows that in order to be able to determine the degree of effectiveness of international supervision in each case, one has to know the purpose of the rule or set of rules which has to be supervised. In many cases this purpose can be deduced simply from the rule concerned, although differences of opinion may arise with regard to its application in concrete cases. However, as has been stated above, sometimes the norms laid down in rules of international law are – and increasingly so – of an abstract and vague character which makes their purpose difficult to determine.[119] In such cases, one is inclined to read one's own conception into the rule concerned. Therefore, the determination of the purpose is to a high degree subjective.

It is obvious that in such a situation the evaluation of the effectiveness of international supervision can become very subjective as well. To avoid this subjectivity as much as possible, the evaluation has to begin by investigating, if possible on the basis of the *travaux préparatoires*, the original purpose which the drafters of the rule in question had in mind. Next, it has to be established whether this purpose has changed during the period in which the norm has found application. At the same time it has to be established to what extent this 'collective' purpose is in accordance with the intentions of the individual States, since consent or consensus as to the purpose of the norm has an enormous impact on the effectiveness of international supervision.[120] The term consent will be used hereinafter to designate the agreement *of* one State to the purpose of a given rule, whereas by consensus the agreement *among* more States is meant.

In addition to this consent of or consensus among the States concerned the effectiveness of international supervision is influenced by the adequacy of the rule in question. By adequacy is meant the capacity of the rule to achieve the purpose for which it has been enacted. While in the case of consent the factors influencing the effectiveness of supervision are situated outside the rule of law concerned, in the case of adequacy these are embodied in (the charactersistics of) the rules themselves. There is a close relationship between consent or consensus and adequacy. The greater the consensus between the States as to what they want to achieve, the greater the guarantee of adequacy of the rule of law enacted for that purpose. The consensus among States as to the purpose of a rule of law should find expression in the clarity of its contents and in the consent of each individual State to that rule, *e.g.* through ratification of or adherence to a treaty.[121] This consent makes a rule binding upon the State concerned.[122] After the rule has become binding the measure of consent can be deduced from the record of the implementation of the rule. Both the original and the subsequent consent are relevant factors in the determination of the effectiveness of the supervision.[123]

It is, therefore, of primary importance to know what elements influence the consent of States in the period before the rule concerned was accepted. This period can be called the gestation period. Effectiveness is usually discussed with regard to the time after the gestation period, when the rules have become operative. In this period too, however, the consequences can sometimes still be felt of what happened in the gestation period. If the acceptance by a State of a set of rules is not based upon its free will as expressed in the gestation period, that State can be expected to obstruct the functioning of those rules once they become operative.[124]

28

When a text is drawn up within the framework of an international organisation of which a State is a member, the State in question might feel compelled (*e.g.* for reasons of political prestige) to accept that text without wholeheartedly consenting. This, too, might detract from a State's willingness to co-operate in the implementation of the rule. The same holds true if a State voluntarily consented to a rule but no longer fully agrees with its implementation, without being willing or able to withdraw. In that situation, too, the State concerned will try to change the rule or impede its implementation.

Because the differences between the elements of consent in the gestation period and in the operative period[125] are only slight, these elements can be dealt with at the same time. The elements which determine the consent of States can be divided into two categories, *i.e.* national and international elements. In the national category the most important element is the basic attitude of a State towards, or its interest in, the subject-matter in question. This attitude varies both with the State concerned and the subject-matter dealt with. Indonesia (as an island State), for instance, will have a different attitude towards the direction in which the international law of the sea should develop than Czechoslovakia (as a landlocked State). Furthermore, Indonesia will show a greater interest in international regulations regarding the régime of the high seas than those concerning polar régimes. It is clear, therefore, that no general statements can be made on whether a State's basic attitude is favourable or not with regard to the effectiveness of international supervision. This has to be established in each concrete case. In general, this basic attitude is modified in a less favourable direction by the insistence of States upon their sovereignty. States are very reluctant to transfer parts of their sovereign powers in favour of a more effective international regulation. Other elements, however, can influence the basic attitude of a State in a direction favourable to effectiveness. Public opinion in a State, for instance, may be strongly in favour of or strongly against the acceptance of international obligations with regard to a certain subject-matter. The pressure emanating from public opinion is sometimes so powerful that it is impossible for the government to resist it. The involvement of public opinion is often initiated, or at least strengthened by the activities of national pressure-groups (labour unions, organisations of employers, human rights activists, environmental groups, etc.). There are sufficient examples in practice to support the submission that those elements can have a considerable impact, positive as well as negative, on a government's policy in international matters. (Action groups in the U.S. calling for the observance of the boycott against Rhodesia, Norway's refusal to join the EEC as result of a referendum, U.S. withdrawal from the ILO resulting from pressure by both employers and employees, activities of groups monitoring the implementation of the Helsinki Final Act.)

Finally, an element should be mentioned here which can be called the 'integration-mindedness' of a State. This element is always instrumental, never detrimental to the effectiveness of international supervision and is therefore to be considered as the counterpart of sovereignty pretensions: a

State's unwillingness to allow encroachments upon attributes of its sovereignty is sometimes counteracted by its willingness to co-operate internationally based upon its awareness of interdependence. Although in a concrete case integration-mindedness can predominate over the pretensions of sovereignty, it is clear from international practice that in general the situation is the other way around.

Integration-mindedness is an element of consent from *within* a State. From the outside too pressure can be brought to bear on States in order to talk (or even force) them into accepting supervisory mechanisms or into being more co-operative in the operative period. Here we enter into the category of international elements determining the consent of States. Outside pressure can emanate from governmental or from private circles, *i.e.* international pressure groups. Well-known examples of the latter in, *e.g.* the field of human rights are Amnesty International and The World Council of Churches, in economic affairs the international associations of labour unions, multinational corporations and a movement like the Club of Rome. However, at present the quantitatively and qualitatively most important pressure exerted on a State is that stemming from other States. The ways in which States can influence each other are manifold. The possibilities range from diplomatic persuasion to downright coercion. As far as the outcome of this process of influencing is concerned the possibilities (in a negative as well as a positive direction) are also numerous depending upon the relative power of the States involved. Therefore, no general statements can be made in this matter.

The same holds true for the process of influencing or putting pressure on States within international organisations, because the same power relations between States have their impact there. However, international organisations add a special dimension to the above-mentioned process. They sometimes constitute a kind of social constraint for States. This can make it very difficult for a State to escape supervision. In the operative period a State cannot fly from supervision without leaving the organisation, a step which is, as a general rule, out of the question. In the gestation period it might prove very hard for a Member State not to accept a supervisory mechanism elaborated within the framework of the organisation.

As has been stated already, the second factor determining the effectiveness of supervision, namely, adequacy of the rule, is in its turn closely linked to the consent of States. The higher the degree of consent, the more adequate the rules of law will be to realise its purpose. Next to this consent the adequacy of rules is also determined by their technical, juridical adaptation to the instrument in the context of which they have to be applied. This applies in particular to the procedural rules. As far as the substantive rules are concerned, they seem to be conditioned to a larger extent by the consent.

In this respect attention should be focused on an issue, which has, for the most part, been left out of discussion above, *viz.* the difference between formally binding and non-binding rules containing a substantive norm. International supervision can be exercised with regard to formally non-binding rules too. Practice shows examples of this, which have been very successful indeed.[126] It has even been contended that the legal nature of a rule is not decisive with regard to the effectiveness of international supervision, as long as there is a high degree of consent of the States concerned.[127] This, however, looks like putting things upside down. Consent determines to a large extent the legal nature of the rule. If the degree of consent is high with regard to a subject matter, States are probably prepared to accept formally binding obligations in respect of this matter. The fact that a subject can only be regulated through formally non-binding rules, is a sign of a defective consent. Therefore, apart from some exceptional cases supervision of a formally binding rule can be expected to be more effective, just because it concerns a rule which is considered to be a result of a high level of consent. Of course it remains possible that a high degree of consent, as expressed in a formally binding rule, decreases over a period of time, and that the rule loses its binding character. Similarly, an originally non-binding rule can become binding as a result of a growing consensus.

As far as the effectiveness of supervision is concerned no absolute distinction between binding and non-binding can be made. Between them there is a grey area of rules, which are more or less binding or non-binding. Moreover, all formally binding rules, on the one hand, or the non-binding ones on the other, cannot be put on the same line. In practice, a wide variety in degrees of consent or consensus may exist, as expressed in different types of rules. A completely accurate description of all the differences in this respect is impossible, but the problem can be clarified on the basis of a rough classification of the levels of consent or consensus.

Apart from the case where there is really no agreement at all, three basic grades of consensus can be discerned. As the first level can be taken the moment when a problem is identified, and a general feeling (or even agreement) exists that it should be solved. This does not imply, however, that the consensus is strong enough to serve as the basis for international legal obligations for the realisation of a common purpose. Such a situation seems in general still to prevail with regard to the problem of disarmament. Although it is generally considered desirable to put a stop to, or at least to reduce the arms race, it has until now proved impossible to work out a more or less all embracing regulation to that effect.[128]

A second level of consensus presents itself where States agree on a common purpose to the extent that the elaboration of rules on the subject matter would in principle be possible. However, at this stage agreement on the methods and means to realise this purpose is still lacking. In our view, the international attempts to solve the problems of the developing countries might serve as an example for this second level. The rules in this field are usually not formally binding and/or have a merely indicative character, in the sense that they set goals which the States undertake to realise as much as possible before a certain date.[129] Non-compliance with such norms, therefore, does not constitute the violation of a legal obligation. Another possibility is that, although the rules have a formally binding character, they are so abstract and/or vague, that ways for realising the common purpose

31

cannot be clearly deduced from them. In such a case the solution of a problem is hindered by a sharp disagreement on the nature of that solution.

On the third level, there is consensus with regard to both the purpose underlying the rule and the methods and means to realise that purpose. Within this category many different degrees of perfection can be found. In the more technical fields the best results are usually achieved. An early and well-known example is the regulation regarding narcotic drugs.[130] In such cases supervision is, as a rule, highly effective. In the following sections the binding or non-binding character of the rule to be supervised will not be dealt with explicitly. It should be kept in mind, however, that it constitutes an important factor with regard to the effectiveness of international supervision.

3.2. Effectiveness of specific and general supervision

In the second part of this study the two different modalities of international supervision, *i.e.* specific and general supervision were briefly discussed.[131] Here, the advantages and disadvantages of specific and general supervision have to be considered in more detail in relation to the question of their effectiveness. It might be recalled that specific supervision is strongly related to particular and well-defined cases, while general supervision is exercised regularly and is independent of specific facts and circumstances. The most important disadvantage attached to specific supervision is the fact that it is often exercised under difficult psychological circumstances. It implies in many cases a preceding suspicion with regard to the State against which it is initiated. In cases of complaints or petitions, the initiative even takes the form of an accusation; an accusation in face of which a State will instinctively try to exculpate itself, because it feels that its prestige is at stake. Hence, the procedure often takes on a political character with the risk that there is an increase in international tension, or at least that the case is not dealt with purely on its merits.[132]

General supervision, on the other hand, is initiated in the international agreement itself and, in addition, it is as a rule exercised on a more or less regular basis. Therefore, neither a preceding suspicion or accusation, nor certain specific facts are needed to put this supervisory mechanism into motion.

As a result of the mostly regular character of general supervision, it is a mechanism which is meant not only to determine and redress, but also to anticipate violations, while at the same time it presents a more comprehensive way of surveillance over State behaviour. Moreover, general supervision is carried out in a less isolated and incidental way than is the case with specific supervision, and a possible infringement can be considered in a much wider context.

The absence of any need for a suspicion or accusation, coupled with the fact that it is exercised equally over all the States subjected to the supervisory mechanism, means that general supervision, at least at the outset, is less hurtful than specific supervision to the political feelings of the State concerned. Lastly, general supervision, more than its specific counterpart, may play a preventive role, because of the certainty that surveillance will be exercised at regular intervals.[133]

Yet, specific supervision is in many respects more attractive to States than general supervision. The fact that the initiative rests with the States – at least in those cases in which only States have the right to lodge a complaint – is of great importance with regard to the acceptability of specific supervision. It is in the first instance up to the States to judge whether or not other States fulfil their obligations and States themselves decide whether it is expedient or not to start a supervisory procedure. Therefore – and more especially because in inter-State relations complaints are considered as unfriendly acts, and for that reason are very seldom lodged – States are inclined to prefer specific to general supervision. The less effective supervision is likely to be in the operative period, the more acceptable it generally is in the gestation period. Moreover, the complaint procedure, as the pre-eminent instrument of specific supervision, is an optional one, while the reporting system as a rule is not. Finally, general supervision obviously loads the State apparatus with much more administrative action on a regular basis.

However, specific supervision is not very attractive in the case of complaints or petitions by individuals. Individuals lack much of the diffidence shown by States. Hence, the State is permanently threatened by complaints or petitions to which it has to react, even if they are manifestly ill-founded. If specific supervision instigated by individuals is more effective than general supervision, this also explains why the complaint procedure is optional and sometimes even regulated in a separate protocol. In the operative period, specific supervision can pay attention to infringements which might escape notice in the process of general supervision. The interested parties, as such, can be better informed, which counts as well for States in their traditional international relations, as for individuals. In particular, private persons or bodies might bring infringements to the attention of an international organisation in cases in which a State would not readily be inclined to do so. However, the role of the individual in specific supervision must not be overestimated. There are only a few cases in which individuals or non-governmental organisations have a right to present a complaint or petition.[134]

3.3 Effectiveness of judicial and non-judicial supervision

In order to deal with the effectiveness of supervision systematically, we shall now take a closer look at the advantages and disadvantages attached to the different forms of supervision.[135] In this chapter quasi-judicial supervision will not be treated separately, because it is necessarily of hybrid character. Much of what holds true for, on the one hand, judicial and, on the other hand, non-judicial supervision counts equally, as the case may be, for quasi-judicial supervision.

There are a number of reasons preventing judicial supervision from being widely used in international practice. A very important obstacle to the development of judicial supervision in international society is the scanty influence States can exert on the composition of judicial organs.[136] Moreover, States are reluctant to restrict their sovereign power to take decisions on matters concerning their international relations, and to subject themselves to the possibility – ever lying in wait – of an unpredictable and sometimes untoward, but in any case binding result of judicial proceedings. The fear of a definitive and possibly untoward result encroaching upon their national interests and national ambition prompts governments to pursue by all available political means their aim of safeguarding such interests, and this prevails over their concern that substantive justice be done.[137] Contrary to the finality of judicial settlement, political decisions can be re-adjusted at any moment.

The problem of safeguarding the impartiality and disinterestedness of an international tribunal is also an important question with regard to the acceptability of judicial supervision. It is obvious that in the international field the number of possible litigants is much smaller than within the State, and so the judges can hardly be ignorant of the position of the parties and be impartial in the cases brought before them.[138]

Another negative factor finds its base mainly in the fact that, although the possibility of *ex aequo et bono* decisions is sometimes provided for (a possibility which in the case of the International Court of Justice has never been used), judicial organs are only competent to judge the legality of an action or omission, disregarding political complications. Consequently, the belief of States that not all conflicts of interests are capable of being solved by judicial techniques within an existing legal framework restricts the use made of judicial supervision. Apart from this national interpretation of what are legal or justiciable and what are political or non-justiciable disputes, there are, of course, many conflicts that are of such a predominantly political character that they are not susceptible at all to judicial settlement.[139] Moreover, recourse to a judicial procedure can be hindered by the fact that instituting such proceedings might be considered an unfriendly act.

Most obstacles to the broadening of the international judicial function find their explanation in the individualistic character of the society of nations, the unequal distribution of power among those nations and the predominantly political character of their mutual relations. Consequently, the settlement of disputes between States is not comparable to the settlement of disputes between individuals, to whom a judicial decision is as a rule the impersonal application of legal rules which embrace almost the whole of the social spectrum in society.[140]

Lastly, as far as institutionalised international society is concerned, the possibility for judicial supervision is reduced by the fact that most international organisations cannot take binding decisions. In these circumstances, governments who consider a given decision to be illegal can disregard it, and do not need its judicial annulment or a declaratory judgment as to its legality.[141]

Next, some of the major differences between judicial and non-judicial supervision have to be emphasised. First, there is the difference just mentioned that within a non-judicial supervisory mechanism the supervisory organ may take expediency questions into account. At least it can discuss political implications expressly and at length, whereas a judicial procedure is restricted to the application of the law. It has been submitted that the essential feature of non-judicial supervision is that it is ultimately exercised by a politically dependent organ, which will give full weight to the political aspects of a question.[142] Of course, just as political arguments also play some role in judicial supervision, juridical aspects too, will generally be taken into consideration in political supervision.[143]

Another important difference between judicial and non-judicial supervision is that in judicial supervision the Court always lacks the power to initiate the procedure itself. Organs in non-judicial supervisory mechanisms, on the other hand, sometimes have the right to start the supervisory procedure *proprio motu*.[144] This also means that supervision can be exercised on a permanent basis, since no complaint or petition has to be waited for.

Finally, it should be emphasised that judicial supervision leads to a binding decision; this is not always the case in non-judicial supervision. However, the difference between a binding decision and a non-binding recommendation can, in practice, be considerably smaller than would seem at first sight. The effectiveness of any decision following upon a supervisory procedure is frequently not only determined by its legally binding nature, but also by the cogency emanating from the inquiry and the authority given to the conclusion by a form of consensus.

The foregoing should, however, not lead us to conclude that judicial supervision is qualitatively inferior to its non-judicial counterpart. On the contrary, it might be said that judicial supervision is a more developed form of international surveillance, reflecting a high degree of integration where it functions in practice. Yet, it cannot be denied that non-judicial supervision is better suited to the requirements, or rather shortcomings, of international society as it is at present. In that society, the willingness to accept international supervision depends mainly on the degree of encroachment upon national sovereignty resulting therefrom. By accepting the jurisdiction of a court, the State formally limits its sovereignty to a degree which it is prepared to do only in rare cases and under special circumstances. By delegating national powers to international political bodies the State remains in the position of exerting influence on the use of these powers.

3.4. Effectiveness of the review function

With regard to the effectiveness of the review function of international supervision, first of all we must consider the adequacy of the supervisory organ and procedures in relation to this review function. This raises the question of whether, or to what extent, supervisory organs are able to determine the degree of conformity of a State's behaviour with international norms (given the supervisory instruments at their disposal). Thus, the abilities of collecting and verifying information have to be studied. It goes without saying that hardly any instrument of supervision can be used effectively if governments do not co-operate in supplying information. The availability of the necessary information is, as stated above, a *conditio sine qua non*, and as such the preliminary problem to every exercise of supervision.[145]

As was indicated in the preceding sections of this study there is a great variety of instruments for the various functions of supervision. This diversity is even one of the main characteristics of supervision within international organisations.[146] In each case the most appropriate instruments have to be chosen, taking into account all the different elements of the subject-matter to be supervised. Nothing seems more contrary to the practice of international organisations than to advocate the general use of a certain instrument, only because it has had good results in a certain context, without investigating if the subject-matter to which one wants to extend it is of a similar character.

In respect of the data-collecting instruments of the review function some of the problems which relate to the characteristics of present international society should first be discussed. The reporting procedure is problematical in the way that the number of responses handed in may often vary, while many reports are sent in too late.[147] Moreover, depending on whether or not the obligations in question have been fulfilled, the answers are often superficial or flattering, and hence do not give a realistic picture of the situation. Experience has shown that reporting by States often offers a sufficient basis for efficient supervision only if the States are encouraged and guided by the organisation. The secretariats often play an activating role in this context alongside special review committees.[148] Apart from the drawing up of questionnaires, which by means of a strict formulation can enhance the adequacy of reporting, the possibility of asking for supplementary information can also contribute to greater efficiency.

Complaints and petitions, on the other hand, are for the most part quite reliable sources of information because of the involvement of the informant parties, and also because of the contradictory character of (complaint) procedures.[149]

The disadvantage attached to supervision on the spot, *i.e.* inspection, is that it must be carried out within the territory of one or more of the parties concerned. Consequently, the consent of States is of vital importance in respect of the effective exercise of inspection. Only in rare cases have States given their consent for an indefinite duration through a provision in a treaty, by virtue of which a mechanism of inspection could be set up.[150]

Apart from the collection of information by using one or more of the instruments of the review function, something remains to be said about the assessment of the data collected, *i.e.* the review in the strict sense. The effectiveness of this assessment depends on how the supervisory organs are composed. In highly political matters one can imagine that the effectiveness of supervision is enhanced if the decisions of the supervisory organs are taken by politically dependent persons representing the whole political constellation of the organisation concerned. The more technical a matter to be supervised becomes, however, the more experts are needed. In the latter case experts might be under the instructions of their government, or take part as independent experts, either to the exclusion of State representatives or together with them.

The reasons for choosing a particular form of composition may vary. Within the many specialised agencies – working in a politico-technical field – a compromise between the traditional diplomatic representation and expert representation is attempted. Governments are required to appoint technically qualified representatives, while the supervising organ has to exercise its functions on behalf of the plenary organ rather than on behalf of the individual States which the members represent.[151]

With judicial organs like the International Court of Justice, the reason is to secure an independent body of experts capable of looking at international law objectively, and representing the principal legal systems of the world rather than specific States.[152]

A factor relevant to the composition of supervisory organs but quite different from the ones mentioned is to be found in the recognition that individuals may represent a set of interests, distinct from State interests, which ought to be represented in the organisation if the organisation is to achieve its purpose. Hence the tripartite system of representation in the Conference and Governing Body of the ILO is a recognition of the necessity to represent the interests of workers and employers separately from the interests represented by the governmental delegates.[153]

3.5. Effectiveness of the correction function

The question of the effectiveness of the correction function is different from that discussed above, in that it deals with the problem of whether, and to what extent, supervision can promote or has promoted compliance with international obligations. The correction function in this sense is of importance for the prevention as well as for the redress of deviant behaviour by States. In fact, these two aspects are closely interrelated, since an effective exercise of redress will have a positive impact on the prevention of similar behaviour in the future. In other words, one could speak of a self-stoking cycle stemming from the (intrinsic) dynamics of the correction function.

Even if supervisory organs of an international organisation have the power to take binding decisions, they can hardly attach adequate sanctions to these decisions.[154] Hence, they are almost forced to act by way of deliberation and persuasion. Their conclusions have to be convincing and acceptable for the States in question, and most cases must impose themselves *eo ipso*. For this purpose the politically dependent organs within non-judicial supervisory mechanisms play an important role. The political discussion in plenary organs is the possibility *par excellence* to effectuate social constraint.

However, it is not always enough that States are convinced by the observations of supervisory organs. Sometimes there is need for additional pressure, national or international, on governments who manifest hesitations or meet with difficulties in carrying out the conclusions of the supervisory organs. This pressure can take different forms, but the publication of those conclusions, if other means fail, is an essential element of such pressure.[155] In general, governments are concerned about their international reputation, and a 'mobilisation of shame' can, by alerting public opinion in an appropriate case, be very effective. Hence, publicity is often considered a sanction or quasi-sanction which international bodies have at their disposal.

Preceding a reflection in more detail on the effectiveness of sanctions, something should be said about friendly settlement. As an instrument of the correction function friendly settlement is an attempt by the supervisory organ to redress the recalcitrant party's behaviour, without using the *ultimum remedium* of sanctions. To this end the international organisation can fulfil a more passive (good offices and mediation) or a more active (conciliation) function.[156] In both cases much depends not only on the willingness of the parties concerned to find a reasonable solution and on the earlier mentioned social constraint, but also and to a large extent, on the diplomatic abilities and inventiveness of the intermediary organ.

Be this as it may, correcting unlawful behaviour often requires the possible imposition of sanctions. A sanction can be described as a social procedure destined to ensure the enforcement of a rule of law, through the repression of its violations.[157] It is, of course, not correct to think of a sanction as *the* characteristic of law. Law exists even in the absence of sanctions. However, the enforcement of law, and hence the correction of unlawful behaviour, is unquestionably closely related to the availability and the threat of sanctions. Sanctions are not widespread in international law, and if they have been provided for at all, they find their strength more often in considerations of national interest (reciprocity) than in an authority of an international character.

In international institutionalised society, however, sanction mechanisms have been developed. One should bear in mind that the application of sanctions to independent States cannot be compared with sanctions on individuals and collectivities subordinated to a State. Sanctions provided for within international institutions are usually measures such as suspension or refusal of material aid (with financial consequences), suspension of membership-rights and expulsion.[158] Apart from pecuniary measures, international organisations have hardly any means to execute sanctions. Suspension of membership-rights and, particularly, expulsion are methods of the last resort and usually do not harmonise with the regionality or universality striven after by international organisations. Expulsion is a token of impotence, and the more primitive the legal system, the more evident this lack of power will be. The member that cannot be controlled is expelled from the community.[159] Consequently, the effective exercise of the correction function of supervision depends, all things considered, to a large extent on the acceptance by the governments of the findings and recommendations of supervisory organs and, in general, on the recognition by States of the inviolability of international legal norms, embodied in the general principle of *pacta sunt servanda*.

3.6. Effectiveness of the creative function

When a supervisory organ applies a general and/or vague rule to a particular set of facts it sometimes asserts a new rule of a more specific character. In this sense, the so-called creative function of international supervision has strong law-making characteristics. This makes the question of the effectiveness of this function particularly difficult to answer without dealing with the effectiveness of the functioning of international organisations in general. Some of the difficulties attached to that question have already been referred to.[160] According to that analysis, the effectiveness of the creative function is dependent upon the political cohesion of, and the consensus within, the organisation concerned. The degree of cohesion of an organisation is, *inter alia*, reflected in the functions and powers formally attributed to the supervisory organs and in the extent to which these organs can actually exercise these functions and powers.

A high degree of cohesion underlies the instititution of a system of judicial (and usually also quasi-judicial) supervision. If the cohesive character of an organisation makes it possible to entrust supervision to independent and impartial persons or bodies, clothed with the competence to take binding decisions, there is at the same time the guarantee that the creative function within this form of supervision will be exercised in an effective way due to the authority of the organ concerned. Yet, in spite of this, judicial supervisory organs do not need, or are not even allowed, to take into account questions of political expediency; they are concerned principally with the law. However, the creative function plays an important role precisely in cases with a high political impact. As the large majority of the issues subject to international supervision are of a predominantly political and not of a legal character, international judicial supervision has only a limited area of application.[161]

With regard to non-judicial supervision, the situation is more or less the reverse. Non-judicial supervisory organs are numerous, and are *eo ipso* competent to consider the political aspects of a case; however, the effectiveness of their creative function is not self-evident. The effectiveness of the creative function of non-judicial supervision depends on the same conditions which determine effectiveness in general.[162] As cohesion varies from organisation to organisation and consensus even from issue to issue, so do the functions and powers of the organs concerned and the effectiveness of these functions and powers. If a minimum degree of cohesion exists, the creative function will be made effective through the political discussion in the plenary organ.[163] If cohesion is lacking, the political discussion in the plenary organ will not result in an authoritative clarification of specification of the norm, but can at best serve to enhance this cohesion. This, however, is no longer to be considered part of the creative function of supervision.

NOTES

1. The following studies have been used as a frame of reference: M. Kaasik, *Le contrôle en droit international* (Paris, 1933); E. Bernath, *Die internationale Kontrolle* (Zurich, 1935); P. Berthoud, *Le contrôle international de l'exécution des conventions collectives* (Geneva, 1946); L. Kopelmanas, 'Le contrôle international' (1950-II) 77 *Recueil des Cours de l'Académie de Droit International* 59–147; H. Hahn, 'Internationale Kontrollen' (1958–1959) 7 *Archiv des Völkerrechts* 88–113; M. Merle, 'Le contrôle exercé par les organisations internationales sur les activités des Etats Membres', *Annuaire Français de Droit International* (1959), pp. 411–431; F. van Asbeck, 'Quelques aspects du contrôle international non-judiciaire de l'application par les gouvernements de conventions internationales' in *Liber Amicorum in Honour of J. P. A. François* (Leiden, 1959), pp. 27–41; R. Monaco, 'Le contrôle dans les organisations internationales' in *Festschrift für Walter Schätzel* (Dusseldorf, 1960), pp. 329–339; J. Rideau, *Juridictions internationales et contrôle du respect des traités constitutifs des organisations internationales* (Paris, 1969); M. Schwebel, ed., *The Effectiveness of International Decisions* (New York/Leiden, 1971); N. Valticos, 'Aperçu de certains grands problèmes du contrôle international (spécialement à propos des conventions internationales du travail)' in *Mélanges Maridakis* (Athens, 1964), Vol. III, pp. 543–586; E. Landy, *The Effectiveness of International Supervision (Thirty Years of ILO Experience)* (London/New York, 1966); N. Valticos, 'Une système de contrôle international: La mise en oeuvre des conventions internationales du travail' (1968–I) 123 *Recueil des Cours de l'Académie de Droit International* 311–407; H. A. H. Audretsch, *Supervision in European Community Law* (Amsterdam, 1977); G. Fischer & D. Vignes, eds., *L'inspection internationale* (Brussels, 1976).
2. See *infra*, p. 9 *et seq.*
3. See also H. A. H. Audretsch, *op. cit.*, *supra*, note 1, p. 1.
4. See on this subject in general: C. Nørgaard, *The Position of the Individual in International Law* (Copenhagen, 1962).
5. See Audretsch, *op. cit.*, *supra*, note 1, pp. 3–5; Van Asbeck, *loc. cit.*, *supra*, note 1, pp. 28–29; Bernath, *op. cit.*, *supra*, note 1, p. 12; Berthoud, *op. cit.*, *supra*, note 1, p. 6; Hahn, *loc. cit.*, *supra*, note 1, p. 96; Kaasik, *op. cit.*, *supra*, note 1, p. 7; Landy, *op. cit.*, *supra*, note 1, p. 210; Merle, *loc. cit.*, *supra*, note 1, pp. 411–412; Monaco, *loc. cit.*, *supra*, note 1, pp. 329–332; Rideau, *op. cit.*, *supra*, note 1, p. 65; Valticos, *loc. cit.*, *supra*, note 1, p. 579.
6. See *supra*, note 1.
7. 'La fonction de contrôle est une partie essentielle de la technique juridique, une des fonctions absolument nécessaires à la vie et du progrès de toute société, de toute organisation sociale. Le but principal de cette fonction est d'assurer le respect et la réalisation du droit normatif, ainsi que le fonctionnement régulier d'une service public dans des conditions tracées par le droit constructif. Le contrôle est une fonction organique qui permet de faire rectifier les erreurs, soit d'appréciation, soit d'action, qui pourraient compromettre la stabilité et la sécurité de la vie sociale. Il sert donc à assurer l'ordre public nécessaire.' Kaasik, *op. cit.*, *supra*, note 1, p. 7.
8. See in general on the changes in international law W. Friedmann, *The Changing Structure of International Law* (London, 1964).
9. As a result, the so-called *domaine reservé* (domestic jurisdiction) of States at that time was considerably larger than today. The process of the growing importance of international law coincides to a large extent with the shrinking of the *domaine reservé* of the States. See in this context the Permanent Court of International Justice in the Tunis-Morocco Nationality Decrees of 1923, where it was upheld that 'The question whether a certain question is or is not solely within the jurisdiction of a State is essentially a relative question; it depends upon the development of international relations.' (PCIJ, series B, No. 4 (1923), pp. 23–24.)
10. See Art. 26.
11. For the mandate system in general and for the texts of the Mandates, see Q. Wright, *Mandates under the League of Nations* (Chicago, 1930).
12. See P. van Dijk, *Judicial Review of Governmental Action and the Requirement of an Interest to Sue* (Alphen aan den Rijn, 1980), p. 440 *et seq.*
13. Art. 22, 24, 25 and 26 Constitution ILO.
14. B. Boskey & M. Willrich, eds., *Nuclear Proliferation: Prospects for Control* (New York, 1970).
15. Art. XII.A, para. 6 IAEA; Article 77 *et seq.* Euratom.
16. N. Mateesco Matte, *Aerospace Law. From Scientific Exploration to Commercial Utilization* (Toronto/Paris, 1977), in particular Part III at p. 153.

17. L. B. Sohn & Th. Buergenthal, *International Protection of Human Rights* (Indianapolis, 1973).
18. The reader is referred to the different studies of this research project.
19. See for instance the definition by L. Oppenheim, *International Law* (6th ed., by H. Lauterpacht, London, 1947).
20. See M. Bos, 'Old Germanic law analogies in international law, or the State as homo liber', *Netherlands International Law Review*, Vol. XXV, 1978/1, pp. 51–62.
21. M. Lachs, 'Some reflections on substance and form in international law' in *Transnational Law in a Changing Society, Essays in Honor of Philip C. Jessup* (New York/London, 1972), p. 110.
22. Also *supra*, p. 6 *et. seq.*
23. See also H. Audretsch, *op. cit., supra*, note 1.
24. *E.g.* H. G. Schermers, *International Institutional Law* (Leiden, 1972), Vol. II, p. 557 *et seq.*
25. *Infra*, p. 25.
26. See A. Verdross, *Die Quellen des Völkerrechts* (Freiburg, 1973), p. 38.
27. In our view this creative function is also hinted at by Merle, *loc. cit., supra,* note 1, p. 413 and Kopelmanas, *loc. cit., supra,* note 1, p. 67.
28. See in this context the distinction made by Khol between 'individuelle Verfahren' and 'generelle Verfahren', in *Zwischen Staat und Weltstaat* (Vienna, 1969), p. 409 *et seq.* Some authors distinguish between 'occasional' and 'permanent' supervision; see *e.g.* Berthoud, *op. cit., supra*, note 1, p. 66 *et seq.*
29. *E.g.* GATT Arts. XII and XIII.
30. *E.g.* UNCTAD supervision ex Board resolution 19(II); OECD supervision of the Member States' economic policy by the Economic and Development Review Committee; World Bank supervision of projects.
31. For a more exhaustive list, see H. H. Schermers, *International Institutional Law* (Leiden, 1972) Vol. I, p. 245 *et seq.* See also the proposed International Tribunal for the Law of the Sea, Draft Convention A/Conf.62/WP.10/rev.3, Art. 287.
32. Arts. 2 and 20 Statute ICJ; Art. 3 Rules of Procedure of the European Court of Human Rights; Art. 167 EEC and Art. 2 Protocol of the Court of Justice of the European Communities.
33. Nine years in the case of the ICJ, Art. 13 Statute, and the European Court of Human Rights, Art. 40 Convention; six years in the case of the Court of Justice of the EC, Art. 167 EEC.
34. See also Il Roh Suh, 'Voting behaviour of national judges in international courts', 63 *American Journal of International Law* (1969) 224–236; and R. P. Anand, *Compulsory Jurisdiction of the International Court of Justice* (London, 1961), pp. 101–116.
35. Art. 38 European Convention of Human Rights (see, however, also Art. 43); Art. 165 EEC.
36. Art. 31 Statute ICJ.
37. See Arts. 39–65 Statute ICJ; Arts. 18 and 35 ff. Rules of Procedure of the European Court of Human Rights; Arts. 17–46 Protocol of the Court of Justice of the EC.
38. Art. 96 Charter UN.
39. Art. 93 Charter UN, *j*° Art. 34 Statute ICJ.
40. See P. van Dijk, *op. cit., supra,* note 12, p. 367.
41. Art. 170 EEC.
42. Art. 169 EEC.
43. Arts. 173, 175, 184 EEC.
44. Art. 177 EEC.
45. See for more details under quasi-judicial supervision, *infra*, p. 18.
46. Art. 48 European Convention of Human Rights.
47. Arts. 59, 60 Statute ICJ; Art. 94–1 Charter UN; Art. 171 EEC; Arts. 52, 53 European Convention of Human Rights.
48. Art. 94–2 Charter UN.
49. Art. 169 EEC.
50. Arts. 32 and 54 European Convention of Human Rights.
51. See under Effectiveness of the correction function, *infra*, p. 37.
52. Art. 41 Statute ICJ; Art. 34 Rules of Procedure of the European Court of Human Rights; Art. 83 Protocol of the Court of Justice of the EC.
53. Report of the ILO concerning the work of its Tenth session, 1958, General Assembly Official Records, Thirteenth session, Suppl. No. 9 (A/3859).
54. See D. W. Bowett, *The Law of International Institutions* (London, 1975), p. 231.
55. *Ibid.* pp. 232–233.

56. *E.g.* the International Centre for the Settlement of Investment Disputes (ICSID) of the World Bank; and the mandatory arbitration for the settlement of disputes between individual enterprises within the context of COMECON.

57. Art. 32 European Convention of Human Rights.

58. Art. 32, *j* ° Art. 48 European Convention of Human Rights.

59. See *e.g.* the Committee of Experts of the ILO, ex. Art. 22 Constitution ILO; the UN Committee, ex Art. 8 of the Convention on the Elimination of All Forms of Racial Discrimination; and the Economic and Development Review Committee of the OECD.

60. See *e.g.* the work done by the secretariats of *inter alia* UNCTAD, GATT or COMECON.

61. Compare most of the plenary organs of international organisations.

62. Kaasik, *op. cit., supra* note 1, pp. 309 and 318–319, where he speaks of 'la communauté international amorphe'.

63. *Ibid.* p. 347.

64. Van Asbeck, *loc. cit., supra,* note 1, p. 28.

65. See *supra,* p. 18.

66. Berthoud, *op. cit., supra,* note 1, p. 303, distinguishes in this context respectively 'representation' and 'participation'.

67. Labeyrie-Menahem, *Des institutions spécialisées* (Paris, 1953) pp. 99–100.

68. *E.g.* the World Meteorological Organization: the members of its Congress are to be representatives of Member States, amongst whom one should be the director of its meteorological service, as its principal delegate.

69. Arts. 97–101 Charter UN; and the reports prepared by the secretariats of *inter alia* GATT, UNCTAD and OECD.

70. *E.g.* the ILO Committee of Experts on the Application of Conventions and Recommendations, also the Commissions of Inquiry set up under Art. 26 of the ILO Constitution; formally the Human Rights Committee, provided for in the Covenant on Civil and Political Rights, Art. 28, para. 3; the Inspector of the IAEA, ex Art. XII of the State.

71. Art. 3, para. 1 and 5, Art. 4, para. 1 Constitution ILO; Panels for investigation within the GATT system; the Textile Surveillance Body in relation to the Multi-Fibre Arrangements; see also Khol, *Zwischen Staat und Weltstaat,* pp. 132 *et. seq.* and p. 441.

72. *E.g.* the International Commission of Jurists in Geneva, or Amnesty International in London.

73. Exceptions are found in some quasi-judicial procedures, *supra* p. 18.

74. Van Asbeck, *loc. cit., supra,* note 1, p. 37.

75. See *e.g.* UNCTAD, GATT, World Bank, ILO, FAO, UNESCO, WHO; this repository of power with the plenary organ is well worth the attention of those who, familiar with the UN, tend to think of the organ of limited composition as the organ with the most explicit and effective power.

76. Arts. 10 and 11 Charter UN, regarding the General Assembly; and Arts. 39, *j* ° 41 and 42 Charter in respect of the Security Council.

77. *E.g.* GATT, Art. XXIII; UNCTAD Principles and Rules for the control of restrictive business practices, section F, para. 4; Art. 41 Covenant on Civil and Political Rights.

78. *E.g.* Art. 87 Charter UN.

79. *E.g.* Art. 26 para. 4 ILO Constitution.

80. *E.g.* UNCTAD supervision on Tungsten; Project supervision by the World Bank; Art. 9 Convention on the Elimination of All Forms of Racial Discrimination.

81. Arts. 39, *j* ° 41 and 42 UN.

82. Arts. 10 and 11 Charter UN.

83. Art. 6 Charter UN.

84. Kaasik, *op. cit., supra,* note 1, p. 366; Berthoud, *op. cit., supra,* note 1, p. 331; see also Audretsch, *op. cit., supra,* note 1, pp. 141–142, the author distinguishes three sources of information: official journals, complaints and questions, primarily through third parties, and information given by the general publicity media.

85. See *supra* p. 14/15.

86. See *supra* p. 19.

87. See *supra* p. 6.

88. Berthoud, *op. cit., supra,* note 1, p. 332.

89. See the ILO Constitution, Art. 22; the FAO Constitution, Art. XI; Project supervision by the World Bank; Arts. 32 and 33 of the OECD/IEA Agreement on an International Energy Programme; and the Convention on the Elimination of All Forms of Racial Discrimination, Art. 9.

90. *E.g.* The majority of GATT's specific supervisory procedures; Art. 16 Covenant on Economic, Social and Cultural Rights; Art. 40 Covenant on Civil and Political Rights; and Art. 57 European Convention on Human Rights.
91. *E.g.* the Commission of Experts of the ILO; the confrontation technique within OECD.
92. See *infra*, p. 25/26.
93. *E.g.* Art. 23 Constitution ILO; the Economic and Development Review Committee, and the Development Assistance Committee of OECD.
94. See for example *inter alia* supervisory procedures within GATT and OECD.
95. *E.g.* GATT, Art. XXIII.
96. See Art. 41 International Covenant on Civil and Political Rights, regarding the competence of the Human Rights Committee (which must be recognised by parties to the covenant) 'to receive and consider communications to the effect that a State Party claims that another State Party is not fulfilling its obligations under the present Covenant'; see also Art. 11 Convention on the Elimination of All Forms of Racial Discrimination; Art. 26 ILO Constitution; and the Protocol to the UNESCO Convention Against Discrimination in Education.
97. See Art. 87 Charter UN, regarding petitions within the Trusteeship system: Arts. 24 and 25 ILO Constitution concerning representation of employers' associations and trade unions; and Art. 26 of the Constitution with respect to complaints by employers' and workers' representatives in the Assembly; Art. 14 of the Racial Discrimination Convention; and Art. 25 of the European Convention on Human Rights with regard to individual complaints (it must be noticed that, although there is talk of 'petition' in Art. 25 Convention, a complaint – as distinguished from petition – is meant).
98. Fisher and Vignes, *op. cit., supra,* note 1, p. 7.
99. General: Art. 87 Charter UN; Art. XII A, para. 6 IAEA; Art. 77 ff. Euratom; and Art. VII of the Antarctic Treaty of December 1, 1959; Project supervision by the World Bank; Specific: Art. 26 Constitution ILO and Art. 28(a) European Convention of Human Rights.
100. For a more detailed approach, see J. Kaufmann, *Conference Diplomacy* (Leiden, 1968) p. 144 *et seq*; and B. Gosovic, *UNCTAD, Conflict and Compromise* (Leiden, 1972), p. 267 *et seq.*
101. This technique is mainly applied in the OECD (*e.g.* by the Economic and Development Review Committee, and the Development Assistance Committee) and the OECD affiliated International Energy Agency.
102. See *supra*, p. 6.
103. Art. 33 Charter UN.
104. J. H. W. Verzijl, *International Law in Historical Perspective* (Leiden, 1976), vol. III, p. 49.
105. See *e.g.* Arts. XXII and XXIII of GATT; also Art. 28, para. (b) ECHM.
106. Art. 19 Charter UN; Arts. 13–14 Constitution ILO; Art. XIX(A) IAEA; Art. IV-8(b) UNESCO; Art. VI section 2 IBRD.
107. Art. 9 Statute of the Council of Europe.
108. Art. VI section 5 IBRD; Art. XII-7(c) IAEA.
109. Art. XXIII GATT.
110. Art. 6 Charter UN; Art. VI section 2 IBRD, similar provisions are found in the Articles of Agreement of the IMF, IFC and IDA; Art. 8 Statute Council of Europe.
111. Art. 5 Charter UN; Art. XIX(B) IAEA; Art. 33 ILO.
112. H. G. Schermers, *op. cit., supra,* note 36, Vol. II, pp. 586/587.
113. H. G. Schermers, *ibid.,* Vol. I, p. 59.
114. Art. 24, *j* ≗ 25 Charter UN.
115. Merle, *loc. cit., supra,* note 1, pp. 427–428.
116. Kaasik, *op. cit., supra,* note 1, p. 374.
117. See Merle, *loc. cit., supra,* note 1, pp. 430–431.
118. Notable exceptions are the International Labour Organisation and the European Communities. The effectiveness of the supervisory mechanisms of these organisations has been investigated thoroughly by Landy, *op. cit., supra,* note 1 and Audretsch, *op. cit., supra,* note 1.
119. See *supra*, p. 12; also Landy, *op. cit., supra,* note 1, p. 210.
120. See also Valticos, *loc. cit., supra,* note 1, p. 323.
121. A more advanced technique with regard to acceptance by States of draft rules of international law is the 'opting-out' procedure of the World Health Organisation, see Bowett, *The Law of International Institutions* (3rd ed., London, 1975), p. 130.
122. Apart from the fact this acceptance is needed before the rule can be held against the State concerned, many treaties require a minimum number of ratifications before they enter into force at all.

123. The importance of the original consensus is illustrated by the history of both UN Covenants. The work on the Covenants started in 1948. Their texts were adopted by the General Assembly in 1966, and subsequently it took ten more years before they entered into force.

124. The mandate system and the system for the protection of minorities were more or less forced upon the State concerned and this is considered to be the main reason for the hindrance by those States of the effective exercise of the supervision. See Kohl, *op. cit., supra,* note 34, p. 166.

125. *Idem,* p. 573 *et seq.*

126. A well-known example is the institution in 1961 of the so-called Committee of Twenty-Four within the framework of the United Nations. The official name of this Committee indicates its task: Special Committee on the Situation with Regard to the Implementation of the Declaration on the Granting of Independence to Colonial Countries and peoples. See L. M. Goodrich, *The United Nations in a Changing World* (New York/London, 1974) p. 191 *et seq.*

127. See Kohl, *op. cit., supra,* note 34, p. 592.

128. See in this respect Hoffman, 'Three Essential Ingredients for Disarmament' in *The International Lawyer,* Vol. 12, no. 2, p. 439 *et seq.*

129. See for instance the one per cent norm in respect of development aid and the 0·7 per cent ODA-norm, which were adopted by the general Assembly of the UN as targets for the Second Development Decade (GA.Res.2626 XXV).

130. See Kopelmanas, *loc. cit., supra,* note 1, p. 60.

131. See *supra,* p. 14.

132. See also Berthoud, *op. cit., supra,* note 1, pp. 269–270.

133. *Ibid.* pp. 271–273.

134. See *supra,* p. 22.

135. See *supra,* p. 15 *et. seq.*

136. See *supra,* p. 15.

137. Verzijl, *op. cit., supra,* note 102, Vol. VIII, p. 114.

138. R. P. Anand, *Compulsory Jurisdiction of the International Court of Justice* (London, 1961), p. 102.

139. Verzijl, *op. cit., supra,* note 102, Vol. VIII, pp. 5–27 and 90–105.

140. R. P. Anand, *op. cit., supra,* note 138, p. 92.

141. Also H. G. Schermers, *op. cit., supra,* note 36, Vol. I, p. 242.

142. See *supra* p. 18.

143. In this context it should be pointed out, that the political organs of most organisations related to the UN, may base their decision concerning a violation of their laws on an advisory opinion of the International Court of Justice, ex Art. 96 Charter UN.

144. Especially in those cases in which the rights and interests not of States but of private persons who as a rule lack *locus standi* to institute proceedings, are at stake, this possibility on the part of the supervisory organ to take the initiative itself might be essential. *E.g.* Art. 26, para. 4, Constitution ILO.

145. See *supra,* p. 21.

146. Rideau, *op. cit., supra,* note 1, p. 65.

147. *E.g.* the response to questionnaires in case of supervision by UNCTAD and the Textile Surveillance Body.

148. H. G. Schermers, *op. cit., supra,* note 3b, vol. II, pp. 562–563.

149. GATT supervision ex Arts. XXII and XXIII, and in the field of subsidies, dumping and government procurement. The right to complain granted to individuals is still a very delicate subject. States are not readily inclined to be supervised in one way or another by individuals. Examples can be found in the right to petition, ex. Art. 25 of the European Convention of Human Rights, which is still not granted by Cyprus, Greece, Malta and Turkey, and the right to communicate violations of human rights as set forth in the Covenant on Civil and Political Rights on the basis of the Optional Protocol. Yet, if the right to lodge a complaint or petition has been granted at all, the use of these instruments of information is often hampered by the fact that proceedings often turn out to be lengthy, costly, and complicated, which is very discouraging in particular for private persons. Moreover, the ignorance of the private parties as to their right of complaint or petition often forms an impediment in this respect.

150. By way of example one can point to the Antarctic Treaty (Art. VII), the IAEA (Art. XII-A, para. 6) and the European Convention on Human Rights (Art. 28.a).

151. This is the case with the UNESCO, WHO, ITU, and to a lesser extent UPU and the financial agencies.

152. Whether this ideal is achieved through a system of election of judges by the political organs of the United Nations is another matter.

153. See also Bowett, *op. cit., supra,* note 121, pp. 353–355.

154. See *supra,* p. 25.

155. Valticos, *loc. cit.., supra,* note 1, p. 434.

156. See *supra* p. 24/25.

157. L. Cavare, 'L'idée de sanction et sa mise en oeuvre en droit international public', *Recueil Général de Droit International Public* (1937), p. 388.

158. See *supra,* p. 25/26.

159. H. G. Schermers, *op. cit., supra,* note 36, vol. I, p. 55.

160. See *supra,* p. 11 *et. seq.*

161. See *supra,* p. 33.

162. See *supra,* p. 27.

163. See *supra,* p. 26.

PART II

SUPERVISION WITHIN THE GENERAL AGREEMENT ON TARIFFS AND TRADE

SUPERVISION WITHIN THE GENERAL AGREEMENT ON TARIFFS AND TRADE

by I. H. Courage-van Lier

CONTENTS

I. INTRODUCTION

1.1. The gestation of GATT

During the interwar period, international economic relations were far from optimal. Nation-States erected high trade restrictions against imports; there was no free currency exchange and exchange rates fluctuated strongly. Nevertheless, international conferences, such as the 1920 monetary and financial conference in Brussels and the 1927 World Economic Conference in Geneva, were held during this period. In October 1927, the League of Nations called a diplomatic conference to attack quantitative restrictions as part of an effort to reduce all import restrictions.[1] These conferences resulted in the adoption of texts recommending trade liberalisation and amelioration of international economic relations; these texts did not contain binding obligations, nor did they provide for mechanisms of supervision concerning their implementation. In practice these conferences had no effect, except to bring trade policy officials from the major trading nations together to exchange ideas.

In 1943 trade policy experts from the United Kingdom and the United States met informally in Washington to compare ideas about postwar economic policy being developed in the two countries. It was during this informal seminar that the foundations were laid for the later discussions with regard to an International Trade Organisation and a General Agreement on Tariffs and Trade, since the experts of these two powerful countries found themselves in agreement about most of the substantive policy issues.[2]

At the first session of the ECOSOC,[3] in February 1946, a resolution was adopted[4] calling for the convening of a UN Conference on Trade and Employment, with the purpose of drafting a charter for an International Trade Organisation and pursuing negotiations for reductions in world wide tariffs. Pursuant to this resolution a preparatory committee was set up to draft rules and proposals for the Conference.[5] Before the Committee met, the U.S. prepared the first draft charter for an International Trade Organisation. The Preparatory Committee met twice: once during October and November 1946 in London and once from April to November 1947 in Geneva. A Drafting Committee, set up by the Preparatory Committee met in New York during January and February 1947. The actual UN Conference on Trade and Employment was held in Havana from November 1947 to March 1948. During this conference the final text of the so-called Havana Charter, the Charter of the ITO was drafted. It was the central purpose of the Havana Charter to contribute to the improvement of living standards all around the world by promoting the expansion of international trade on a basis of multilateralism and non-discrimination, by fostering stability in production and employment by encouraging the economic development of backward areas.[6] It consisted of 106 articles grouped in nine chapters dealing with:

1. Purpose and objectives
2. Employment and economic activity
3. Economic development and reconstruction
4. Commercial policy
5. Restrictive business practices
6. Inter-governmental commodity agreements in general
7. The International Trade Organisation's institutional structure and functions
8. Settlement of disputes
9. General provisions.[7]

The attention of the conference was focused primarily on the second and fourth chapters. However, the chances of ITO coming into force disappeared, when in December 1950 U.S. President Truman announced that he would not resubmit the ITO Charter to Congress for approval.[8]

During its London session, the Preparatory Committee added as Annex 10 to the draft ITO Charter, a report on Procedures to give effect to certain Provisions of the Charter of the ITO by means of a General Agreement on Tariffs and Trade (GATT) and established a Drafting Committee to formulate a detailed draft of GATT. In early 1947 the Drafting Committee developed the first full draft of such a General Agreement. It was meant to provide for rules applicable to the tariff negotiations to be held in Geneva until the ITO Charter became effective. The GATT is based on Chapter IV of the ITO, concerning trade policy.

From April to October 1947 the Preparatory Committee met for the second time to complete the draft of the ITO Charter and to negotiate national commitments as to maximum tariffs on particular items. A set of rules had to be laid down to guide these negotiations. This set of rules was based on the existing GATT draft and contained many articles of the ITO Charter. It was developed into what is now known as the GATT.[9]

The mandates of most of the delegations concerned tariff negotiations only. They could not commit their home countries to binding rules concerning other trade restrictions or general matters. Therefore the Conference could not decide which parts of the draft ITO Charter had not yet reached its final form. Nevertheless, the Conference wanted to establish GATT, since a framework agreement regarding the implementation and supervision of the results of the tariff negotiations was necessary. This problem was solved by the adoption of a Protocol of Provisional Application on October 30, 1947.[10]

The governments of the States which have signed this Protocol apply Parts I and III of the GATT in their entirety, and Part II to the extent its provisions are inconsistent with existing legislation. According to this Protocol, a withdrawal shall take effect upon the expiration of 60 days from the day on which written notice of such withdrawal is received by the Secretary General of the UN. According to the GATT text itself, it shall take effect after six months.[11] By the terms of this Protocol, the GATT has been in effect since January 1, 1948. The relationship between GATT and ITO is dealt with in Article XXIX.[12]

Most countries that have acceded on a later date have done so by means of a Protocol of Provisional Application. Haiti is the only one that has accepted GATT in accordance with Article XXVI,6.[13] Although the requirement that the GATT must be accepted by governments, the territories of which account for 85 per cent. of world trade has only been fulfilled recently, the GATT has been applied *de facto* since 1948.[14]

1.2. GATT's legal character

What is GATT? Is it an international governmental organisation, or just a trade agreement? The answer to this question depends, among other things, on one's definition of an international organisation. According to Schermers[15] an organisation must fulfil three requirements to be recognised as an international governmental organisation under public international law:

(1) it must be established by international agreement,
(2) it must have organs, and
(3) it must be established under international law.

Other authors[16] add other requirements to these such as:

(4) it must aim at a lasting co-operation and
(5) its members must have a common purpose to be established by the organisation.

Once an international organisation is established, it is likely to pursue its own policy to realise the common purpose. Where such a common policy is absent, the existence of a true international organisation must be doubted.

The GATT is based on an international agreement. However, this agreement was never meant to be the constitution of an international organisation. The contracting parties have obviously shown by denouncing the ITO charter and the Organisation for Trade Co-operation (OTC) that they did not want to create an international trade organisation. There is thus an agreement, but not one meant to create an international organisation. Therefore, one cannot say that the General Agreement establishes an international organisation. So the first requirement is not fulfilled.

Within GATT, organs have gradually been established. They have derived their competence from the GATT itself, from customary law, or as a result of decisions by competent existing GATT organs. Therefore, the second requirement has been fulfilled.

The GATT has been established under international law, for the GATT itself is an international agreement, as are the subsequent agreements concluded within GATT. The co-operation within GATT is lasting and the contracting parties espouse the same purposes, so that the other requirements are fulfilled as well. However, since the international agreement has not been concluded to establish an international organisation, the GATT cannot be regarded as such *de lege*; the non-fulfilment of the first requirement is prohibitive of that. On the other hand, GATT is more than just a new trade agreement.

Some conceive the issue as to whether GATT is an international organisation as a highly academic one. However, recognition as an international organisation may be important for the organisation itself, and for those who want to make use of it, since such recognition affects its legal status and therefore its capacity to act under international law. The GATT provides in the first place for a framework for actions by the contracting parties. Moreover, since the GATT has organs and a permanent secretariat that function well, one cannot deny its existence. On the other hand the GATT does not pursue its own policy. Considering these factors the GATT would qualify as a *de facto* international organisation.

1.3. GATT and the international economic order

Together with IMF, GATT is one of the most important pillars of the international economic order as a creation of the so-called Bretton Woods period following the Second World War. However, since the establishment of GATT, the international economic order as well as GATT itself has changed significantly. What then are the actual functions of GATT? How effective is it in performing these functions? What, if any, will be its place in tomorrow's international economic order?

To answer the first two questions, knowledge about GATT and how it has developed as well as about the present state of the international economic order and state practice are essential. The answer to the third question largely depends on one's views concerning a New International Economic Order.

The present study does not pretend to give the final answers to these questions, but rather purports to contribute to the discussion by providing some data concerning GATT, its mechanisms of supervision and their functioning in practice. To this end, the next two sections will deal with the scope, the institutional structure, the budget and the legal instruments of

GATT. Section IV will deal with mechanisms of supervision and evaluate them along the scheme devised by Van Hoof and de Vey Mestdagh in the General Introduction. Section V focuses on the effectiveness of GATT as it is and gives some indications into what direction GATT may develop and what its place in a New International Economic Order might be.

II. SCOPE, INSTITUTIONAL STRUCTURE AND BUDGET

2.1. Objectives

The objectives of GATT are to be found in its preamble and include:
1. raising standards of living;
2. ensuring full employment;
3. ensuring a large and steadily growing volume of real income and effective demand;
4. developing the full use of the resources of the world; and
5. expanding the production and exchange of goods.

The contracting parties are desirous of contributing to these objectives by entering into reciprocal and mutually advantageous arrangements directed to the substantial reduction of tariffs and other barriers to trade and to the elimination of discriminatory treatment in international commerce.[17] These are the so-called intermediate objectives.

These purposes have been refined by the addition of Article XXXVI to Part IV of GATT which became effective on June 27, 1966. In this article, the contracting parties recall that the basic objectives of GATT include the raising of standards of living and the progressive development of all contracting parties and consider that the attainment of these objectives is particularly urgent for less-developed contracting parties. They consider the importance international trade might have for the development of these countries and note that there is a wide gap between standards of living in less-developed countries and in other countries. They recognise that individual and joint action is essential to further the development of the economies of less-developed countries and they allow for discrimination in favour of less-developed countries.

2.2. Guiding principles

2.2.1. Reciprocity[18]

Pursuant to Article XXVIII*bis*, the negotiations are to be held on a reciprocal and mutually advantageous basis. However, in practice this objective cannot always be realised. The value of a Concession is often hard to determine, especially when non-tariff Concessions are involved. The Concessions made by socialist countries usually consist of promises to increase imports. These are hardly comparable with tariff Concessions made by western countries. In addition, countries with high tariffs hold a stronger bargaining position than those with low tariffs.[19] Developing countries having a low national income, and therefore low imports,[20] can offer little, if anything, to obtain Concessions from other countries. However, Concessions are necessary for the increases in exports that are essential for the economic development of the developing countries. In addition to these difficulties, developing countries are unable to make Concessions because of balance-of-payments problems or the need to protect newly established industries. Finally, the implementation of this guiding principle is difficult since the lack of criteria for reciprocity thwarts the bargaining process.[21]

2.2.2. Most-Favoured-Nation treatment

According to the Most-Favoured-Nation (MFN) principle, a Concession given by country A to country B is also given to the other countries, who need to give something in return. They receive the benefits of the so-called 'bonus effect', which is in conflict with the principle of reciprocity, and which gives rise to free rider and hold-out problems.[22] To counteract this bonus effect, the rule of the principal supplier has developed which states that countries need only make Concessions with regard to a certain item to its principal supplier.[23] Another way of dealing with this problem is multilateralism. In that case, contracting parties to the GATT (cps) only make Concessions if they receive other Concessions of like value in return from cps that would otherwise benefit from the bonus effect. In practice, however, the cps focus their attention mainly on the principal supplier.[24]

2.2.3. Preferences

In a number of cases cps have to give preferences to developing countries. This practice is in conflict with the principle of reciprocity, as well as with that of Most-Favoured-Nation treatment. In 1958 Article XXVIII bis, 3 (b) was added to the GATT, which requires the cps to take into account the needs of less-developed countries for a more flexible application of tariff protection to assist their economic development and their special needs to maintain tariffs for revenue purposes. Also, since the introduction of Article XXXVI, 8 in 1966, developed cps no longer expect reciprocity for commitments made by them in trade negotiations to reduce or remove tariffs and other barriers to the trade of less-developed cps. Under Article XXXVII, 1 (a) developed cps have to accord high priority to the reduction and elimination of barriers to trade facing less-developed countries. On November 28, 1979 the GATT Member States adopted an agreement regarding differential and more favourable treatment, reciprocity and fuller participation of developing countries,[25] also referred to as 'the enabling clause'. Under this agreement, developing country members of GATT are given more favourable treatment and the least developed countries are given special treatment notwithstanding the MFN provisions of GATT Article I.

2.3. The structure of the Agreement

The GATT text has been divided in four parts:

1. The first part, containing Articles I and II, deals with general Most-Favoured-Nation treatment and its consequences or schedules of concessions provided for in GATT;
2. The second part, containing Articles III to XXIII, includes the substantive rights and obligations of the contracting parties to GATT;
3. The third part, containing Articles XXIV to XXXV, deals with implementation and procedures; and
4. The fourth part, containing Articles XXXVI to XXXVIII deals with the special position of less-developed countries.

Nine annexes have been added to the GATT text. They form an integral part of GATT, as do the Schedules.[26] Within GATT a number of separate agreements have been concluded, which can change rights and obligations or elaborate them in some more detail.

2.4. The scope of GATT ratione personae

As at February 1981, there are 85 contracting parties to the GATT,[27] hereafter referred to as 'cp' in the singular and 'cps' in the plural. But for Liechtenstein and Andorra, all Western countries, 27 in number, have become cps. In addition to these, 6 socialistic and 51 developing countries have adopted GATT. Accession to GATT is dealt with in Article XXXIII. The Contracting Parties[28] decide on this issue by two-thirds majority after negotiations with the government of the applicant. Since this might be a prolonged affair and since the acceding government may also need some time to adjust its international trading practices to bring them into conformity with the obligations that it will undertake in GATT, the practice has developed of new countries undertaking a series of stages of participation. The last stage before the accession itself is provisional accession. Provisionally acceded countries participate in the work of GATT, but do not have the right to vote.[29] As of February 15, 1980, two countries had acceded provisionally. There are 30 countries to whose territories the GATT had formerly been applied and which now, as independent states, maintain a *de facto* application of the GATT pending final decisions as to their future commercial policy.[30] All these countries together account for 85 per cent. of world trade. China and the U.S.S.R. are not among the countries which participate in GATT. Certain GATT negotiations are attended by countries that do not participate in GATT on a regular basis.[31]

Full sovereignty is not a requirement for becoming a cp; a separate customs territory[32] possessing full autonomy in the conduct of its external commercial relations and of the other matters provided for in the GATT is eligible for accession. Besides original membership, accession is possible for countries whose governments did not participate in the first rounds of negotiations.[33] Article XXVI, 5(c) provides for acquisition of membership by customs territories in respect of which a cp has accepted the GATT. Such territories can only become cps to the GATT if they possess full autonomy in the conduct of their external commercial relations and of the other matters provided for in the Agreement, or if they will acquire such autonomy. The EEC cannot be a cp formally, because it has no full autonomy in the conduct of its external commercial relations and of the other matters provided for in the GATT. However, it is represented permanently in Geneva by a delegation that participates in the work of GATT.

The GATT establishes a régime creating different rights and obligations for different cps. In the first place, the Agreement, or alternatively Article II, need not apply between all cps, since the GATT does not apply between cps that have not entered into tariff negotiations with each other and since all cps, including acceding ones, may withhold their consent to such application in case of accession.[34]

Secondly, cps which have not accepted amendments to the Agreement that have become effective upon acceptance by two-thirds of the cps, are not bound by such amendments, whereas those who accepted them are.[35] Finally, cps are allowed to deviate from Part II of the Agreement, if this part is inconsistent with national legislation existing at the time they undertook to apply the GATT provisionally.[36]

2.5. The scope of GATT, ratione materiae

2.5.1. Most-Favoured-Nation treatment

All trade between cps must be based on the Most-Favoured-Nation principle. This is to say that any cp must give to all cps the same advantage as it has given to any other cp, free of any conditions whatsoever. The general Most-Favoured-Nation (MFN) treatment is dealt with in Article I, which applies to:

(a) customs duties and charges of any kind imposed on or in connection with: importation, exportation, and international transfer of payments for imports or exports;
(b) the method of levying such duties and charges;
(c) all rules and formalities in connection with importation and exportation; and
(d) all matters referred to in Article III paragraphs 2 and 4 with regard to products, but not such intangible matters as business rights.[37]

Most-Favoured-Nation treatment is also referred to in many other provisions.[38]

2.5.2. Schedules of concessions

The most important obligation of GATT is the Tariff Concession, which is a commitment by a cp to levy no more than a stated tariff on a particular item. All concessions to which a cp agrees constitute its Schedule. According to Article II,7, the Schedules are made an integral part of Part I of the GATT. The items in the Schedules are termed 'bound' items and the individual commitment is sometimes termed a 'binding'.

In addition to the general GATT obligations a number of special obligations apply to bound items. These commitments are mentioned in Article II and include the paragraph 3 commitment against altering the method of valuing goods, the commitment of paragraph 6 against using a currency revaluation to effectively change specific tariff rates, the commitment of paragraph 5 regarding impairment of the value of a concession because of the classification of a product under a party's tariff laws, the commitment of paragraph 5 regarding consultation and the commitment in paragraphs 1 (b) and (c) against imposing additional duties or charges on bound products.[39]

Occasionally, a Schedule will contain tariff quota. In that case, a given amount of the product per year may enter at one tariff rate, and all in excess of that amount will enter at a higher rate.[40] The Schedule of a cp with a socialist economy may contain a commitment to increase purchases from abroad, since tariff concessions are not likely to be of much influence on the quantity imported in countries with such an economy. Concessions other than on tariffs are permitted in general and are included in the Schedules.[41]

Each party's concessions are constantly changing through rounds of negotiations, rectifications, suspension of their application pursuant to Article XXIII, waivers or other GATT procedures, like the application of the escape clause. Since these changes are usually not inserted into the Schedules, one cannot conclude from the Schedules which bindings are effective. Furthermore, should a concession be lowered, any already existing concession remains effective, unless it is explicitly withdrawn. Consequently, when a more recent concession is withdrawn, a cp is bound by a previous higher concession, that remains, as it were, slumbering.

2.5.3. Non-tariff barriers

Although in principle, the GATT only allows import control by means of tariffs, a number of exceptions to the general principles are permitted. These include the following:

1. According to Article III, internal taxes and other internal charges, and laws, regulations and requirements affecting internal trade and production should not be applied to imported or domestic products so as to afford protection to domestic production. However, according to paragraph 8 of this Article, governmental agencies procuring products purchased for governmental purposes and not with a view to commercial resale or with a view to use on the production of goods for commercial sale, are allowed to discriminate.

2. Quantitative regulations relating to exposed cinematograph films are, under certain conditions, allowed pursuant to Articles III,10 and IV.
3. Article V calls for freedom of transit via the routes most convenient for international transit, without unnecessary delay and without distinction based on the 'nationality' of the means of transport or the goods transported. An impediment of transport constitutes a trade restriction as well.
4. Measures about anti-dumping[42] and countervailing duties are permitted under certain conditions mentioned in Article VI.
5. Administrative barriers to trade are restricted as much as possible pursuant to Articles VII, VIII and IX.
6. According to Article X, the cps are obliged to publicise national laws, regulations, judicial decisions and administrative rulings of general application with regard to a certain product. Lack of information constitutes a non-tariff barrier, since it prevents full competition.
7. Quantitative restrictions on imports and exports are generally eliminated by Article XI. However, restrictions concerning agricultural products, restrictions to safeguard the balance of payments and restrictions on behalf of the new industries in less-developed countries are permitted under certain conditions inserted in Articles XI to XV and XVIII.
8. Under special conditions, subsidies are permitted according to Article XVI.
9. The existence of State trading enterprises may give rise to non-tariff barriers, too. This is permitted under certain conditions according to Article XVII. Pursuant to the Protocols of Provisional Application these provisions are applicable only if not inconsistent with legislation existing on the date of the protocol.

2.5.4. Exceptions to GATT obligations

Under certain circumstances deviations from fundamental GATT rules are possible:

1. Articles XX and XXI name a number of general exceptions.
2. Under certain circumstances a cp is allowed to take emergency measures in case any product is being imported into the territory of that cp in such increased quantities and under such conditions as to cause or threaten serious injury to domestic producers. This is provided for in Article XIX, the so-called escape clause.[43]
3. Pursuant to Article XXIV cps are under certain conditions allowed to deviate from GATT if they are forming a customs union or a free trade area or if they are entering into an interim agreement leading to the formation of such a union or area.[44]
4. Less-developed countries are sometimes allowed to deviate from GATT according to Article XVIII and Part IV.[45]
5. The provisions of Article XXV,5 make it possible to grant waivers to cps to prevent violations of GATT obligations.[45]

2.5.5. Other provisions

Articles XXII and XXIII provide for[47] central dispute settlement procedure.[48] Procedural and institutional matters are dealt with in Articles XXV to XXVII and XXIX to XXXV.

2.6. Institutional Structure

The GATT was drafted to contain the results of the first round of negotiations within the ITO. An institutional and administrative structure was provided for in the ITO Charter, which, however, has never entered into force. For this reason, the GATT does not provide a solid base for such a structure. Nevertheless in practice the GATT has obtained its own institutions and its own administrative staff. In 1955, attempts were made to provide for a formal institutional structure for GATT, by establishing an Organisation for Trade Operation (OTC). The OTC, however, met the same fate as the ITO: stillbirth through the failure of the Congress of the United States to ratify the underlying agreement.[49]

2.6.1. The Contracting Parties

The original GATT text provides for one institutional body, the Contracting Parties acting jointly, hereafter referred to as the CP.[50] The GATT confers several powers on the CP, such as the authority to consult with respect to any matter; the authority to request information, reports and consultation; the authority to investigate matters referred; to consult, to make recommendations and to authorise the suspension of obligations and concessions; the waiver authority; authorities regarding negotiations and renegotiations; the authority to specify an amendment as important enough that non-signers shall be free to withdraw, or to remain a cp with the consent of the CP; authorities regarding anti-dumping and countervailing measures; the authority to co-operate with and perform some functions of the IMF; the authority to review quantitative restrictions; the authority to request information regarding, and review of, domestic administrative review relating to customs matters; authorities regarding non-tariff barriers, import restrictions for balance of payments reasons and regional integration; and the authority to enter into agreements for the accession of new governments.[51]

According to Article XXV,1 the CP shall meet from time to time for the purpose of giving effect to those provisions of the GATT which involve joint action, and generally with a view to facilitating its operation and furthering its objectives; in other words to exercise their powers as described *supra*. These meetings are called sessions and are generally held once a year. The CP have adopted rules of procedure for their sessions.[52] Each cp has one vote in every session. Decisions are taken by a simple majority, except when otherwise provided for in the GATT.[53] At first, this had to be the majority of the votes cast, but subsequently the procedure was changed into a simple majority of all cps.[54] Voting by post is permitted as appears from the preparatory work.[55] The CP have adopted special rules for airmail and telegraphic ballots.[56]

2.6.2. The Council of Representatives

Soon the need arose for an institution to deal with matters arising between sessions of the CP. At first a number of committees were established with increasing powers.[57] In 1960 it was decided to establish the Council of Representatives,[58] further referred to as 'The Council'. Its functions are:

(1) To consider matters arising between sessions of the CP which require urgent attention, and to report thereon to the CP with recommendations as to any action to be taken by the CP at their next session or by postal ballot;
(2) to supervise the work of subsidiary bodies of the CP;
(3) to undertake preparation for sessions of the CP; and
(4) to deal with such other matters with which the CP may deal at their sessions, and to exercise such additional functions with regard to matters referred to above, as may be expressly delegated to it by the CP, including action on behalf of the CP in performing functions under the provisions of the GATT, other than granting waivers under paragraph 5 of Article XXV, and under decisions and other formal actions taken by the CP.

The Council is composed of the representatives of cps willing to accept the responsibilities of membership and to make arrangements for active participation. Membership in the Council is also open to governments which have acceded provisionally to the General Agreement. The Council may establish subsidiary bodies and instruct intersessional bodies of the CP. Decisions of the Council must be taken by a majority of all cps, including those who are not members of the Council or who are absent.[60] Rules of Procedure have not yet been drafted. If a cp considers itself adversely affected by the exercise by the Council of any of its functions, it may suspend the operation of any such action by the Council through the submission of a written appeal to the CP. If no appeal has been lodged within a specified reasonable period, the CP may provide that recommendations, determinations or decisions of the Council shall become final.[61] At the moment the Council is one of the most important institutions of GATT.

2.6.3. The Consultative Group of Eighteen

On July 11, 1975, the Council decided to establish a Consultative Group of Eighteen.[62] The group was given the task to facilitate the carrying out, by the CP, of their responsibilities, particularly with respect to:

a. Following international trade developments with a view to the pursuit and maintenance of trade policies consistent with the objectives and principles of the General Agreement;

b. the forestalling, whenever possible, of sudden disturbances that could represent a threat to the multilateral trading system and to international trade relations generally and action to deal with such disturbances if they in fact occur; and

c. the international adjustment process and the co-ordination, in this context, between the GATT and the IMF.

The Group cannot take over any of the powers or functions of other GATT bodies.

The Group is composed of representatives of 18 members chosen in a balanced and broadly representative way. Each member has to provide for the attendance of alternates. One seat is in fact taken by a representative of the European Communities and each of their member states,[63] so in fact the group does not consist of 18 but of 44 members and an EC representative, which is more than half of the cps. The group may invite observers. It meets periodically as necessary and reports to the Council. The group was established for a period of one year, after which its tasks, composition and terms of reference were reviewed by the Council. Its mandate has been prolonged every year up until 1979. In November 1979 the Council decided to make it a permanent body.[64] The first year of the Group as a permanent GATT body was 1980. The Group met three times in that year to discuss the prevalent economic situation and its implications for trade policies, the link between structural adjustment and trade policy, the trade policy aspects of the North-South dialogue, and the future work of the Group itself.

The Group's influence has increased considerably.[65] In addition to the tasks given to it in 1975 the Group now functions as a high-level group representing the diverse economic and commercial interest of the 85 cps, while being small enough to permit early, specific and frank discussion of international trade problems. The Group thus will lay the ground for major decisions by GATT member states; for instance, the Group prepared GATT's future work programme which was adopted at the annual CP session in 1979.[66] During its fourteenth meeting in March 1981 the Group discussed the international trading system as it relates to agricultural trade.[67]

2.6.4. The Secretariat

The Interim Commission for the ITO (ICITO) originally rendered secretariat services for GATT, among other functions, on behalf of ITO. After the failure of ITO, this was the only remaining function of the ICITO.[68] In the beginning years of GATT it consisted of three experts and a number of typists. Today it is much bigger, but compared to Secretariats of other international organisations it still is rather small. The Secretariat is divided into three major departments as well as the Director's office and the International Trade Centre. The three departments are: the Department of Conference Affairs, Liaison and Administration; the Department of Trade Policy; and the Department of Trade and Development. The head of the Secretariat has been called the Director-General since March 23, 1965.

Before that date he was called the Executive Secretary.[69] The International Trade Centre was established by GATT in 1964,[70] and is charged with the responsibility of assisting less-developed countries in promoting and finding markets for their products. Since 1968 GATT and UNCTAD have sponsored and financed this centre jointly.[71] The Secretariat has no official status under the GATT: formally it is still the ICITO.

2.6.5. Subsidiary Bodies

The CP and the Council have established several *ad hoc* committees to deal with certain issues. For example, for each round of tariff negotiations a Tariff Negotiations Committee is established to facilitate the negotiations.[72] Furthermore, standing committees have been established, like the Balance-of-Payments Committee,[73] the Committee on Trade and Development,[74] the Agricultural Committee,[75] and the Committee on Industrial Products.[76] Committees have also been established by means of special agreement outside of the CP or the Council. Examples are the Textiles Committee[77] and the Committee on Anti-dumping Practices.[78]

In addition to these Committees the CP and the Council have established Working Parties, further referred to as WPs, to deal with specific questions often concerning disputes. A WP consists of representatives of countries appointed by the CP. The national governments decide which persons will be members. Another subsidiary body is the Panel, which is composed of persons in their individual capacities. Although they are usually government representatives to GATT, they do not act as representatives of their country, but as experts or 'objective' judges of particular matters. Sometimes in practice the distinction between Committees, WPs and Panels is not crystal clear.

2.7. Budget

No formal structure of financial regulations exists in GATT. The practice has developed that finances are conducted along the United Nations' pattern and that the Director-General reports any departure from this to the CP or their committee. The Secretariat internally develops its budget for the forthcoming year and proposes the figures it wishes to recommend to a Committee on Budget and Finance, set up by the CP, which reviews it and might add some changes before it recommends the budget to the CP. The CP adopt the budget at their session.

The CP also allocate the amount that each country must pay to GATT to finance the Secretariat and Conference activities. This allocation is based upon relative percentages of international trade.[79] The contributions of the cps are the only source of income of GATT. Compared to other international organisations the GATT budget is small. The budget for 1977 totalled 36,633,000 Swiss francs.[80]

The budget of ITU for 1977 was 74,034,000 Swiss francs[81] and the Council draft budget for the EEC for 1977 was $11,925,647,580 in U.S. currency.[82]

III. MEANS TO REALISE GATT'S PURPOSES

3.1. Exchange of information

One of the most important functions of GATT is to collect and examine information concerning restrictions to trade and general trends in trade policies and international trade. This information is used to make reports, mostly by the Secretariat or one of the subsidiary organs. These reports constitute a basis for action by the CP or one of the cps and can play an important part during negotiations.

In a number of provisions of the GATT text itself, cps are obliged to provide information. For example, pursuant to Article X, all cps are required to publish promptly any laws, regulations, judicial decisions and administrative rulings of general application as well as agreements pertaining to or affecting trade. In several provisions, the CP are authorised to ask the cps for specific information.[83] In a number of provisions, the cps are obliged to give notice to the CP before or after certain actions.[84]

In 1964 the CP adopted a resolution in which they recommended that the cps forward promptly to the Secretariat copies of the laws, regulations, decisions, rulings and agreements of the kind described in paragraph 1 of Article X of the General Agreement together with such other information they consider relevant to the objectives of this recommendation.[85] Exchange of information also takes place by means of bilateral contacts. However, much information is restricted and is to be read by governments and their administrative staff only.

3.2. Consultations and negotiations

Consultations and negotiations constitute the most important mechanisms of GATT. The Concessions are determined by means of negotiations; the CP consult together during their yearly sessions. In several provisions,[86] the CP are given the competence to invite cps to consult with them or with each other. Consultations and negotiations are part of several procedures for dispute settlement.[87] Sometimes a cp is obliged to consult before it is allowed to act or after taking certain actions.[88]

Negotiations and consultations may lead to the creation of new rules or commitments or to a change of existing ones. They can also be a part of mechanisms of supervision which shall be dealt with in Part IV of this study. The distinction between these two functions is not always crystal clear. For example, Concessions are determined during negotiations. These can be original negotiations or renegotiations. Original negotiations take place in the form of rounds of negotiations between the CP or negotiations with a view to accession by a new cp. Their primary function is to create new obligations. Renegotiations can be aimed at modification or rectification of Concessions.[89] They also take place if a Customs Union, a free trade area or an Interim Agreement leading to the formation of either one is created,[90] and when a developing country wants to modify or withdraw Concessions to promote the establishment of a particular industry.[91] Finally, a cp must consult with other cps that have a substantial interest in a product if a Concession is negotiated with a government that has not become or has ceased to be a cp.[92] The primary function of renegotiations is supervision and so will be dealt with in Chapter 4.3.

3.2.1. Rounds of negotiations

Most of the Concessions have been established during the so-called rounds of (tariff) negotiations. Rounds are multilateral conferences on which Concessions are negotiated. During the first round which was held in 1947 in Geneva, the GATT text was adopted.[93] The second round was held in Annecy in 1949, the third in Torquay in 1951 and the fourth in Geneva in 1955. The fifth round, the 'Dillon Round', and the sixth round, the 'Kennedy Round', have been held from 1960 to 1961 and 1964 to 1967 respectively in Geneva. The seventh round, the 'Tokyo Round', was started in 1973 in Geneva and the negotiations were terminated in April 1979.[94]

Since GATT was meant to contain the results of the first round, it did not provide for rules or guidelines for the rounds; these were to be laid down in the ITO Charter. Hence a provision concerning tariff negotiations was added as Article XXVIII*bis* in 1957.

A preparatory phase precedes the rounds. During this phase a declaration of ministers is adopted which contains the aims of the round-to-be, its procedures, the methods of negotiations and the subjects that will be dealt with. For the Tokyo Round a Trade Negotiations Committee was established, to elaborate and put into effect detailed trade negotiating plans and to establish appropriate negotiating procedures, including special procedures for the negotiations between developed and developing countries and to supervise the progress of the negotiations.[95]

The second and third rounds were primarily designed to facilitate the accession of countries that had not participated in the Geneva Round, but at Torquay, original cps also negotiated *inter se*. Reduction of tariffs was the primary goal of the following three rounds.[96] During the Tokyo Round, the attention of the participants was focused on the elimination or reduction of non-tariff barriers, the multilateral safeguard system and certain sectors of internal trade. This round resulted in the adoption of: the 1979 Geneva Protocol to the GATT and the Supplementary Protocol thereto, containing tariff concessions, an Agreement on Technical Barriers to Trade, an Agreement on Government Procurement, a Code on Subsidies and Countervailing Duties, a Code on Customs Valuation, an Agreement on Import Licensing Procedures, an anti-dumping code together with two understandings, an Agreement on Trade in Civil Aircraft, an arrangement on Bovine Meat,

International Dairy arrangements and four texts on the framework for conduct of international trade.[97]

3.2.1.1. Negotiation techniques

During the first five rounds negotiations were held on a product-by-product basis. This meant that tariffs were considered per product. During the Kennedy Round the cps tried to reduce tariffs as a whole by a single negotiated percentage. This is the so-called linear method. However, this method was not carried through consistently. Agricultural products, among others, were exempted from the uniform tariff reductions. Therefore, a number of cps which export agricultural products did not agree with the application of the linear method.[98] During the Tokyo Round attention was not only focused on the linear method to reduce tariffs, but also on the modalities of so-called tariff harmonisation. This technique aims at reductions of levels of tariffs on a certain product in such a way that those levels become closer to each other. Higher tariffs are reduced more than lower ones on an item. By means of differentiation per country, the tariffs are harmonised. This can also be done for groups of products.[99]

3.2.1.2. The results of the rounds

As a result of these rounds a considerable reduction of tariffs on industrial products has been accomplished. As far as agricultural and other primary products are concerned, the rounds have only been moderately successful. Tariff reductions are not the only results of these negotiations. During the Kennedy Round, for example, agreement was reached on a World Grains Arrangement and the so-called Anti-Dumping Code was drafted. During the Tokyo Round non-tariff barriers, and other measures that impede or distort world trade, were discussed, as well as the multilateral safeguard system and the international framework for the conduct of world trade. Since tariff barriers have been reduced for the most part, non-tariff barriers constitute the main impediments to world trade. These remain to be eliminated or reduced in the future. With regard to tariff reductions the Tokyo Round was quite successful as well. The total value of trade affected by most favoured nation tariff reductions and bindings of prevailing tariff rates amounts to $155 billion measured on MFN imports in 1976 or 1977, excluding petroleum. As a result of the harmonising effect of the tariff-cutting formula the difference in the tariff levels of the 17 most industrialised nations will be reduced by 25 per cent.

3.2.2. Negotiations with a view to accession

Pursuant to Article XXXIII, a government may accede to the GATT, on terms to be agreed upon between it and the CP, who decide by a two-thirds majority. The negotiations aim at the establishment of a certain equilibrium between the Concessions already made by the cps and those to be made by the applicant since it too will benefit from all Concessions made by the cps because of the Most-Favoured-Nation principle. One could say that the applicant has to buy itself into the GATT. Major concessions are usually required from applicants with a strong position in world trade to prevent them from taking too strong a position during future GATT negotiations. According to Article XXV, 1(b) the GATT or Article II do not apply as between two cps if either of them, at the time either becomes a cp, does not consent. When Japan acceded to GATT many cps invoked this provision.

3.3. Decisions (binding)[100]

GATT organs rarely take binding decisions. This is one of the consequences of the fact that the GATT is not set up as a formal international organisation. The GATT text contains binding norms and provides for a framework for negotiations. These norms are changed through negotiations leading to amendments of the GATT or the Schedules or to side agreements concluded by the cps themselves. There is hardly a body of secondary GATT law created by the GATT organs, as is the case in the EEC for instance. The CP are authorised to take binding decisions only to allow for deviations from GATT.[101] As the granting of waivers requires a decision that takes the specific circumstances of the particular case into account, there must be a body, competent to make binding decisions.

3.4. Financial Stimuli

Within the GATT system, no use can be made of financial stimuli. The budget is too small for that. Also, the GATT does not provide the means for any action or project other than services of the Secretariat, negotiations and meetings of GATT bodies. Furthermore, the GATT is dependent on contributions from the cps and does not collect its own funds.

IV. SUPERVISION IN GATT

4.1. Supervision in general

The GATT text as well as other related agreements provide for several mechanisms of supervision. In the first place, supervision is aimed at the realisation of the intermediate purposes of GATT, such as protecting existing Concessions, keeping benefits balanced and counteracting discrimination. There is much less supervision on the realisation of the purpose of preferences for developing countries provided for in Part IV. An act or omission conflicting with GATT is likely to conflict with its purposes, too. A cp that infringes a technical rule of GATT, such as a failure to report, will not necessarily violate its purposes, however.

Certain mechanisms of supervision consist of dispute settlement procedures. In practice, cps have never submitted a dispute concerning GATT rules to an international judicial organ like the International Court of Justice in The Hague, or to an arbitral tribunal. Conflict resolution takes place within GATT itself.

The provisions on supervision are mingled with the substantive ones and are to be found in many places in GATT. Many times the cps are obliged or invited to provide information. There are a great number of provisions obliging or inviting cps to consult with one another or with the CP. The GATT rules themselves are created by means of negotiations and consultations. Therefore, the borderline between the creation of rules and supervision of their implementation is not always clear. Furthermore, in several provisions the cps are authorised to withdraw or change a given Concession, for the purpose of compensation or as a sanction.

The mechanisms of supervision are elaborated either by supplementary decisions of the CP or the Council, or by their interpretations, usually in conformity with a proposal made by a Committee, a WP or a Panel. The mechanisms of supervision are distinguishable as either central procedures, applicable to the GATT system as a whole, or specific procedures,[102] which deal with only one subject. The existence of a specific procedure does not exclude the use of a central procedure. They can be complementary.

4.1.1. Central procedures of supervision

According to Article X the cps are obliged to publish national measures pertaining to international trade. This gives rise to objective general supervision. Review takes place by means of reports, and correction by means of the mobilisation of shame. In addition, the reports constitute a basis for other mechanisms of supervision:

- Article XXII contains the central consultation provision, which will be dealt with in section 4.2.
- The protection of benefits against nullification and impairment is provided for in Article XXIII, which will also be dealt with in section 4.2.

4.1.2. Specific procedures of supervision

Supervision of existing Concessions is provided for in Articles II,5; XVIII,7; XXIV,6; XXVII and XXVIII, and will be discussed in section 4.3.

Supervision of anti-dumping and countervailing duties is based on Article VI and also, as far as anti-dumping duties are concerned, on the Agreement on Implementation of Article VI.[103] A limited number of cps are bound by the provisions on supervision in the multilateral Agreement on Interpretation and Application of Articles VI, XVI and XXIII of the GATT[104] and the revised Anti-Dumping Code,[105] which came into force on January 1, 1980.[106] This will be dealt with in section 4.3.9.

According to Article VII,1, the CP may request from cps reports on the valuation of goods for customs purposes. This is general inquisitive supervision. Review takes place by means of reporting *ad hoc*. Correction in light of such review is possible by means of other mechanisms of supervision. Such correction can take place because of the information made available through these reports. On January 1, 1981, an Agreement on customs valuation came into effect for a limited number of cps.[107]

Upon request by another cp or the CP, a cp must review the operation of its laws and regulations regarding fees and formalities connected with importation and exportation pursuant to Article VIII,2. In case of a request by another cp, there is a special supervision on the basis of a request. In case of a request by the CP there is special supervision by a politically dependent plenary organ. In both instances the functions are review by means of reporting *ad hoc* and correction by means of negotiations and consultations aimed at peaceful settlement, as well as political discussion.

Supervision on import licensing is also provided for in Article VIII. For a limited number of cps, a separate Agreement on Import Licensing has entered into force.[108] Publication of all rules and information concerning import licensing is required. The Agreement provides for the establishment of a Committee on Import Licensing to afford parties the opportunity of consulting. However, consultations and the settlement of disputes remain subject to the procedures of Articles XXII and XXIII of the GATT.[109] The Committee must review at least once every two years the implementation and operation of this Agreement and must inform the CP of developments during the period covered by its review. Provision is made in this Agreement for general as well as specific supervision by the Committee, the CP and the cps. The review function is performed by means of reporting and by means of requests and complaints. The correction function takes place by means of mobilisation of shame, political discussion and, to a lesser extent, consultations and negotiations aimed at peaceful settlement of disputes. However, the last-mentioned mechanism is scarcely used as dispute settlement and remains subject to GATT's central procedure of supervision.

According to Article X,3(b), each cp must maintain or institute judicial, arbitral or administrative tribunals or procedures for the purpose, *inter alia*, of the prompt review and correction of administrative action relating to customs matters. According to Article X,3(c), cps that already possessed such a procedure before GATT became effective to them, need not eliminate or substitute their own version just because it is not an independent process, provided it is objective and impartial. Supervision is provided for as follows: Any cp employing such procedures, must upon request furnish the CP with full information thereon in order that they may determine whether such procedures conform to the requirements of this sub-paragraph. This is a case of specific non-judicial supervision by the politically dependent organ. Its functions are review by means of reporting *ad hoc* and correction by means of political discussion.

The mechanisms of supervision on quantitative restrictions are laid down in Articles XI and XIII. They have been elaborated in several decisions of the CP. They will be discussed in sections 4.3.4. and 4.3.6.

Articles XII, XIV, XV and XVIIIB provide for supervision on import restrictions for balance of payments purposes. This will be dealt with in sections 4.3.5. and 4.3.11.

Supervision on monetary issues is allotted to the IMF pursuant to Article XV. The IMF provides for specific supervision on issues referred to it by the CP. Review by the IMF takes place on the basis of reporting *ad hoc*. Correction might take place by means of other procedures of supervision within IMF or within GATT. The CP take care of the supervision of the monetary policy of any cp, which is not a member of the Fund, in the same way as does the IMF.

The procedures of supervision of the granting of subsidies can be found in Article XVI. They have been elaborated by the CP in several decisions. Also the Agreement on Interpretation and Application of Articles VI, XVI and XXIII deals with subsidies. This will be discussed in section 4.3.7.

Supervision on State Trading Enterprises is regulated in Article XVII as well as in later decisions of the CP. It will be dealt with in section 4.3.8.

Article XVIII provides for supervision of developing countries that are allowed to deviate from GATT. This will come up for discussion in section 4.3.11.

In Article XIX supervision of emergency action on imports of particular products in case of a sudden unexpected increase in imports can be found. This will be dealt with in section 4.3.2.

According to Article XX(h) the CP are to supervise deviations from GATT by national measures undertaken pursuant to obligations under any intergovernmental commodity agreement, which conforms to criteria submitted to the CP and not disapproved by them, or which is itself so submitted and not disapproved. This is specific supervision by the politically dependent organ. Its functions are review by means of reporting *ad hoc* and prevention.

Article XX(i) allows for national measures deviating from the GATT essential for the acquisition or distribution of products in general or local short supply. The CP had to review the need for this provision not later than June 30, 1960. In 1960, 1965 and 1970 this sub-paragraph was continued and review was postponed.[110] Since then this matter has not come up for discussion. This was general supervision and review was its main function.

Article XXIV,7 and 10 provides for supervision of the establishment of Customs Unions and Free-Trade Areas. This will be discussed in section 4.3.12.

Procedures of supervision of waivers are to be found in Article XXV,5. In section 4.3.2. the attention will be focused on these procedures.

Supervision of the observance of the obligation to grant preferences to developing countries is provided for in Article XXXVII,2 and will be discussed in section 4.3.11.

The Agreement on Government Procurement provides for mechanisms of supervision to be dealt with in section 4.3.10. This Agreement took effect on January 1, 1981.[111]

Supervision of the observance of the Arrangement Regarding International Trade in Textiles[112] is provided for in this arrangement itself. This will be discussed in section 4.3.3.

Supervision on Residual Restrictions has been provided for in several decisions of the CP. It will be dealt with in section 4.3.6.

4.1.3. Supervisors within the GATT system

The GATT text attributes supervisory functions to cps as well as to the CP. In practice, other bodies are involved in these functions, too. First of all, the CP may delegate these functions to the Council, according to their decision of June 4, 1960.[113] Also, technical bodies such as WPs, Panels and Committees assist the CP and the Council in performing their supervisory functions. The Secretariat, too, plays its part in the process of supervising, since it receives information, drafts and circulates lists of questions and makes draft reports for the CP and the Council. Finally, in separate Agreements supervision is allotted to other bodies like the Anti-Dumping Committee and the Textiles Surveillance Body.

4.1.4. Interpretation and adjustment

Interpretation and adjustment of the GATT text are necessary prerequisites to supervision in most cases. In international law, interpretation and adjustment is binding only if the organ concerned has been authorised to do so in advance or if the countries involved agree at the time. In GATT, no authority to interpret or to adjust the text has been granted explicitly. Only when a cp brings a complaint that a benefit accruing to it under the GATT has been nullified or impaired or that the attainment of any object of the GATT is being impeded are the CP allowed to give a ruling on the matter pursuant to Article XXIII,2. However, the preparatory work warns that this power cannot be utilised to impose changed obligations.[114]

In practice, the cps have asked the CP to interpret and adjust the GATT also in cases not within the scope of Article XXIII. During the second session of the CP, the Dutch delegation requested a ruling from the Chairman of the CP concerning Article I, because consultations with Cuba on a dispute about discriminatory consular taxes remained unsuccessful. Owing to the Chairman's personal prestige, his interpretation of Article I was accepted without discussion, though the GATT did not authorise him to make it.[115] Later on this procedure was abandoned, since the Chairman's prestige was not strong enough to deal with the disputes that arose.

In 1948 a WP stated that if difficulties in application of the GATT text were to arise, the CP would still have the authority under the terms of Article XXV to settle such cases in the light of the provisions of Article XXV,1.[116] At the third session of the CP in 1949, the Chairman of the CP interpreted the general language of Article XXV,1 as enabling the CP to interpret the Agreement whenever they saw fit.[117] No objections have been raised to these statements. Rulings and recommendations by the CP have been accepted by the cps in most instances. Therefore one can say that the CP are competent to interpret and adjust the GATT on the basis of customary law. In practice the CP have asked Committees, WPs and Panels for proposals concerning interpretation and adjustment, which have always been adopted by the CP as well as accepted by the cps. The Council is also competent to interpret and adjust the GATT upon delegation of this power by the CP. The cps accept its interpretations also.

4.2. Central Procedures: dispute settlement and protection against nullification and impairment

4.2.1. The central dispute settlement procedure

GATT's central dispute procedure is provided for in Articles XXII and XXIII. It has three aims: the realisation of GATT's purposes, the protection of the benefits accruing under the Agreement and dispute settlement. The procedures are not primarily concerned with strict compliance with GATT provisions. Therefore, action can be taken in cases where the purposes of GATT are violated even when no formal GATT provision has been contravened, as for instance when the spirit of the GATT is violated in a way not anticipated at the time of the Agreement.

Also, violations can be legalised if necessary by means of a waiver by the CP, that permits deviation from GATT obligations. Thus, conflicts may be prevented and guarantees may be given so that the benefits accruing to other cps are impaired as little as possible.[118]

From the preparatory work, the impression develops that the draftsmen of GATT Articles XXII and XXIII had various goals in mind. In the first place, these Articles were to be the framework of a dispute settlement procedure. Secondly, they were to compel the cps to comply with the GATT by threatening them with retorsion[119] as a sanction. In the third place, they were to be a means to maintain reciprocity and balance of Concessions in the face of possibly changing circumstances. These goals are not consistent in all circumstances. The issue of whether the authorisation to suspend certain Concessions or obligations referred to in Article XXIII,2 is a sanction, or meant merely to provide for compensation, often gave rise to discussions, because of the discrepancy between the second and third goals.[120]

The procedure must be started by the cps themselves. The General Agreement is not suitable for an enforcement by prosecution. Most disputes are settled by means of consultations. If they do not result in a settlement of the disputes certain GATT organs are competent to make recommendations or to give rulings. These are done by politically dependent organs, not by independent judicial organs.

This procedure has been changed several times. In 1955 the GATT was reviewed. During this review a new paragraph was added to Article XXII concerning joint consultation of cps with the CP.[121] Most changes in the procedures are a consequence of changes of state and GATT practice.

4.2.2. The procedure of Article XXII

Pursuant to Article XXII,1 each cp shall accord sympathetic consideration to, and shall afford adequate opportunity for, consultation regarding such representations as may be made by another cp with respect to any matter affecting the operation of the Agreement. The only precondition for raising representations is that they must affect the operation of the GATT. Pursuant to the second paragraph of this Article, the CP may, at the request of a cp, consult with any cp or cps in respect of any matter for which it has not been possible to find a satisfactory solution through consultation under paragraph 1. So, the failure of the consultations between the cps themselves is a prerequisite for consultations with the CP. The CP are not obliged to consult with the cps pursuant to Article XXII, but they have never refused to consult. Thus, Article XXII provides for consultation in two stages: first between cps themselves and then with the CP.

On November 10, 1958, the CP adopted rules for procedures under Article XXII on questions affecting the interests of a number of contracting parties,[122] according to which every cp seeking consultation under Article XXII shall at the same time inform the Director-General[123] for the information of all cps. Any other cp asserting a substantial trade interest in the matter may, within 45 days of the notification by the Director-General of the request for consultation, advise the consulting countries and the Director-General of its desire to be joined in the consultations. However, the cp or cps to which the request for consultation is addressed must agree that the claim of substantial interest is well founded. If the claim to be joined in the consultation is not accepted, the applicant cp is free to refer its claim to the CP. At the close of the consultation, the cps involved must advise the Director-General of the outcome for the information of all other cps. The Director-General is required to provide such assistance as the parties may request.

The Director-General is not always informed about consultations pursuant to Article XXII,1. The right of States to consult with each other is connected very closely with their sovereignty. Therefore, these rules of procedure should not be interpreted so as to prohibit consultations about which the Director-General has not been informed. Information is only required if a substantial trade interest of a third cp is involved. In case the consulting cps do not meet with this requirement, the cp asserting a substantial trade interest may request the CP to open the consultations.

4.2.3. The procedure of Article XXIII

4.2.3.1. Conditions to submit a complaint

First of all, Article XXIII determines when a cp may start a procedure to protect the benefits accruing to it. Such a procedure is possible 'if the cp considers that any benefit accruing to it directly or indirectly under this

Agreement is being nullified or impaired or that the attainment of any objective of the Agreement is being impeded as the result of:

(a) the failure of another cp to carry out its obligations under the Agreement, or
(b) the application by another cp of any measure whether or not it conflicts with the provisions of this Agreement, or
(c) the existence of any other situation.'

A violation of GATT by another cp is apparently not a necessary condition. This conclusion was confirmed in the case of The Australian Subsidy on Ammonium Sulphate.[124]

For a long period of time the Australian Government had subsidised the domestic production of ammonium sulphate as well as the importation of sodium nitrate, a competing product, because both products were scarce. Chile was one of the countries exporting sodium nitrate to Australia. Later Australia made a Concession not to levy tariffs on the imports of sodium nitrate, against which Chile set another Concession. The benefit of the Australian Concession, however, was impaired since the Australian Government stopped subsidising sodium nitrate, but continued to subsidise ammonium sulphate. The GATT was not violated but the WP dealing with the case considered whether the action of the Australian Government, upsetting the competitive relationship between sodium nitrate and ammonium sulphate, could reasonably have been anticipated by the Chilean Government, taking into consideration all pertinent circumstances and the provisions of the General Agreement at the time it negotiated the duty-free binding on sodium nitrate. The WP concluded that the Chilean Government had reason to assume during these negotiations that the fertiliser subsidy would not be removed from sodium nitrate before it was removed from ammonium sulphate, in particular because:

(a) the two types of fertiliser were closely related;
(b) both had been subsidised and distributed through the same agency and sold at the same price;
(c) the system of subsidisation and distribution had been introduced at the same time; and
(d) the system was still maintained in respect of both fertilisers at the time of the 1947 tariff negotiations.

For these reasons the WP also concluded that the Australian action should be considered as relating to a benefit accruing to Chile under the GATT, and that it was therefore subject to the provisions of Article XXIII.

The involvement of a benefit was apparent in the case of the Uruguayan recourse to Article XXIII, [125] too. Uruguay was of the opinion that the trade policy of 15 developed countries was detrimental to the developing countries. Therefore, it submitted a complaint against them claiming that the maintenance of trade measures by the other cps had nullified or impaired benefits accruing to Uruguay under the General Agreement. In February 1962 the delegation of Uruguay formally submitted to the Council a request that it take action in accordance with the provisions of Article XXIII,2. The Council accordingly appointed a panel of five members which consulted with the 15 'defendant' cps and Uruguay.

Uruguay had provided the panel with a list of all alleged trade barriers, of which some were violations of GATT provisions but others not. The legal basis of the complaint was merely that the maintenance of the trade measures had nullified or impaired benefits accruing to Uruguay under the General Agreement. No further motivation was added. Neither did Uruguay provide supporting data. Uruguay's purpose was to draw attention to the worsening trade position of the developing countries. It wanted the Council to take action to remove the trade barriers and did not ask for an authorisation to suspend its own Concessions or obligations. However, GATT organs cannot dictate certain actions to the cps.[126]

In dealing with this case, the panel thought it essential to have a clear idea as to what would constitute a nullification or impairment, since the existence of one or the other is a condition precedent to the invocation of Article XXIII. In its view, impairment or nullification in the sense of Article XXIII does not arise merely because of the existence of any measures; the nullification or impairment must relate to benefits accruing to the cp under the General Agreement. In cases where there is a clear infringement of the provisions of the General Agreement the action would *prima facie* constitute a case of nullification or impairment and would *ipso facto* require consideration of whether the circumstances are serious enough to justify the authorisation of suspension of Concessions or obligations.[127]

On different occasions, two other cases of *prima facie* nullification or impairment have been mentioned. *Prima facie* nullification or impairment occurs in the first place because of quantitative restriction,[128] and has in the second place been mentioned in relation to subsidies, for a WP stated that a cp which has negotiated a Concession under Article II may be assumed, for the purpose of Article XXIII, to have a reasonable expectation that its value will not be nullified or impaired by the subsequent introduction or increase of a domestic subsidy on the product concerned.[129] This position was reinforced by the report of the panel that reviewed the operation of the provisions of Article XVI in 1961 and by the cases concerning income tax practices maintained by France, Belgium and The Netherlands.[130]

The panel dealing with Uruguay's complaint also stated that it would be incumbent on the country invoking Article XXIII to demonstrate the grounds and reasons for its invocation, if there is no infringement of GATT provisions constituting a *prima facie* nullification or impairment. In a number of cases the defendant cp maintained: (a) that certain measures applied by it were consistent with the provisions of GATT, or (b) that the measures, while not consistent with the provisions of the General Agreement, were permitted under the terms of one of the Protocols dealing with provisional application on account of their being applied pursuant to existing legislation. In cases where the contention was not challenged by Uruguay and was not contradicted by the available records of the CP, the panel thought it beyond its competence to examine whether the contention was or was not justified.

In invoking the provisions of Article XXIII, the Uruguayan delegation repeatedly referred to the general difficulties created for Uruguay by the prevalence of restrictive measures. According to the panel, a general imbalance in benefits under the GATT does not constitute a case of nullification or impairment. The cp invoking Article XXIII has to demonstrate the link between the measures and the benefits accruing to it under the Agreement that have been nullified or impaired.[131] Nevertheless, the panel submitted 15 individual reports on the Uruguayan recourse under Article XXIII with respect to the 15 cps.[132] Since Uruguay had not provided sufficient information, the panel did not find itself in a position to sustain the claim on the basis of Article XXIII in a number of instances.

Uruguay argued that Article XXIII is applicable when a measure limits marketing opportunities. According to the panel, the nullification or impairment must relate to benefits accruing to the cp under the GATT. This decision reduces the difference between the conditions of paragraphs 1(a) and 1(b) of Article XXIII considerably. The panel obviously preferred violation of explicit GATT rules to a nullification or impairment not constituting a breach of GATT as a basis for the procedure of Article XXIII.

There is another case in which a panel has looked for explicit provisions as a basis for an action pursuant to Article XXIII. It concerned the exportation of potatoes to Canada.[133] The panel stated that a benefit accruing to the U.S. had been impaired. An obvious ground for this decision could have been found in Article XXIII,1(b). However, the panel did not invoke this paragraph but rather evaded it by stating that another GATT provision, Article II,1(a) dealing with the Most-Favoured-Nation treatment, had been violated, so that it could use Article XXIII,1(a) as a basis for its decision. Paragraphs 1(b) and 1(c) of Article XXIII provide for a broad jurisdiction for GATT organs. They are allowed to base their decisions not only on specific GATT provisions but also on the general principles of the preamble. Most panels have found the goals mentioned in the preamble unsatisfactory bases for decision.[134]

4.2.3.2. Procedural requirements

The applicant cp may 'with a view to the satisfactory adjustment of the matter, make written representations or proposals to the other cp or cps which it considers to be concerned. Any cp thus approached must give sympathetic consideration to the representations or proposals made to it' pursuant to Article XXIII,1. 'If no satisfactory adjustment is effected between the cps concerned within a reasonable time, or if the difficulty is one of the type described in paragraph 1(c) of Article XXIII, the matter may be referred to the CP' pursuant to paragraph 2 of this Article. So the cps first must consult together before they can refer a case based on Article XXIII,1(a) or (b) to the CP. A consultation held under paragraph 1 of Article XXII would be considered by the CP as fulfilling the conditions of Article XXIII[135] regarding prior consultations. In case a cp wants to refer a matter to the CP concerning the existence of a situation, it does not have to make written representations or proposals to the other cp or cps concerned first.

'The CP shall promptly investigate any matter so referred to them and shall make appropriate recommendations to the cps which they consider to be concerned or give a ruling on the matter as appropriate' pursuant to paragraph 2 of Article XXIII. The CP do not usually investigate the matters themselves. During the second session of the CP their Chairman gave a ruling in the cases of the Cuban consular taxes and the Indian tax rebates.[136] This was possible since the Chairman's personal prestige generated sufficient authority for his rulings to be accepted. During the same session the case of the Cuban Restrictions on Textile Imports phase I[137] was referred to a WP since the CP refused to be stampeded by the United States.[138] WPs consist of an uneven number of government representatives of the competing states and the economic super powers, which were in those days the United States and the United Kingdom. The reason for this composition was to promote the feasibility of the implementation of the final recommendation or ruling. Sometimes neutral cps have had a representative in a WP.[139] The practice was followed up to the seventh session, held in 1952.

The transition from the use of WPs to the use of Panels took place almost underhand. During the seventh session of the CP, their Chairman, Mr. Johan Melander of Norway, suggested all claims be referred to one single WP. The statement implied that the reason for departing from the usual procedure was merely the large volume of complaints business and the change appeared to be hardly a matter of any real consequence. However, five days later the Chairman recalled that it had been agreed to establish a panel. The chairman of the panel was named individually and the other members were named only by country. The panel had to consider, in consultation with the representatives of the countries directly concerned and of other interested countries, complaints referred to the CP and submit findings and recommendations to the CP.[140]

At the time the difference between this procedure and the former one did not seem to be great. Only the composition of the subsidiary organ had been changed. However, in practice the Secretariat and the panel introduced radical changes. The panel took on the role of a decision-making body, independent of the cps, in the West German Duties on Sardines case.[141] This new procedure was launched very quietly, although a large number of the cps must have known what was being done.[142] As the cps that were confronted with the procedure all accepted it, it has become part of the customary law of GATT.[143] Since the Secretariat can express itself more freely within a panel than in a WP, of which the parties involved are members too, its position has been reinforced.

Two cases arose in 1955 during the ninth session which required the establishment of a panel. All the members of this panel were nominated personally. With regard to the cases concerning the U.S. income tax legislation (DISC) and the income tax practices of France, Belgium and The Netherlands[144] a single panel was established on February 17, 1976. It consisted not only of individually nominated representatives that on other occasions were government representatives to the GATT, but also of experts that had no other affiliation with GATT. The proposal to use outsiders came from the United States and then became a joint United States-EEC project. The experts were chosen by the parties themselves because of their expertise in tax matters, since the dispute concerned fiscal issues, not for their experience in GATT affairs. The exact role of the experts, and of their special expertise, was never really determined.[145]

The fourth text relating to the framework for conduct of international trade drafted during the Tokyo Round contains the Understanding Regarding Notification, Consultation, Dispute Settlement and Surveillance and includes an Annex with the Agreed Description of the Customary Practice of the GATT in the Field of Dispute Settlement (Article XXIII,2),[146] hereinafter referred as the 1979 Understanding. According to the Agreed Description, Article XXIII,2 does not indicate whether disputes should be handled by a WP or a Panel. Consequently procedures for both are described, although the Panel procedure is considered usual.[147] In the Understanding, panels are to deliver their findings without undue delay, under normal circumstances within 3 months.[148]

4.2.3.3. Reports, recommendations and rulings

The panel dealing with the Uruguayan recourse to Article XXIII stated once more that the CP are obliged to make appropriate recommendations or give a ruling on the matter in all cases.[149] The Agreed Description of the Customary Practice of the GATT in the Field of Dispute Settlement also contains this obligation.[150] Whilst a ruling is called for only when there is a point of contention on fact or law, recommendations would be appropriate whenever in the view of the CP they would lead to a satisfactory adjustment of the matter, according to the panel. In most cases interpretation of the GATT by the panel is necessary to give a recommendation or a ruling. However, the preparatory work suggests that Article XXIII should not be applied in such a manner as to impose positive obligations on GATT members that are not contained in the Agreement.[151]

In case the CP have to provide for a recommendation or a ruling concerning issues of fact-finding, they are dependent on information provided by the cps. If they provide contrary or inconsistent information, the CP have to make a decision on points of fact.[152] Since decisions on points of fact are always somewhat arbitrary they will only be accepted when both parties really want to reach a solution of the conflict or when the decision is made by a body possessed of sufficient authority and means of power.

GATT organs involved in fact-finding tend to take into account the desires of cps in order that the governments will be more co-operative when decisions have to be implemented.[153] This does not contribute to objectiveness in their reports. The willingness of the governments to co-operate is essential. The strength, or the weakness, of an institution with regard to fact-finding becomes obvious when the willingness to settle disputes is lacking amongst the parties involved.

Panels and WPs are competent to draft reports, rulings and recommendations on the instructions of the CP or the Council. Formally only the CP are competent to give rulings or to make recommendations. In practice, the CP have always adopted the drafts of the WPs and panels, which has strengthened their authority, and reinforced their bargaining powers. The Council is competent to give rulings or to make recommendations too, when the CP delegate this function to it.[154]

4.2.3.4. The sanction of Article XXIII

'If the CP consider that the circumstances are serious enough to justify such action, they may authorise a cp or cps to suspend the application to any other cp or cps of such Concessions or other obligations under the GATT as they determine to be appropriate in the circumstances' pursuant to Article XXIII,2. In 1955 there was a review of the GATT by the CP.[155] The WP which prepared this review considered that the requirement in paragraph 2 of Article XXIII that the circumstances must be 'serious enough' limits the possibility of authorising a cp or cps to take appropriate retaliatory action to cases where endeavours to solve the problem through the withdrawal of the measures causing the damage, the substitution of other Concessions, or some other appropriate action, have not proved to be possible. Moreover, there must be a substantial justification for retaliatory action, as in cases in which such authorisation appears to be the only means either of preventing serious economic consequences to the country for which a benefit has been nullified or impaired, or the only means of restoring the original situation.

In the view of the WP, the first objective, after the CP have decided that a complaint under Article XXIII has been substantiated, should be to ensure the withdrawal of the measures.

The alternative of providing compensation for damage suffered should be resorted to only if the immediate withdrawal of the measures was impracticable and only as a temporary measure pending their withdrawal.[156] The WP has thus established a hierarchy of solutions: the withdrawal of the measure complained about being the primary remedy, followed by the provision of compensation. The Agreed Description of the Customary Practice of the GATT in the Field of Dispute Settlement, Annex to the 1979 Understanding, confirms this hierarchy.[157] Suspension should only be used if no other solution can be found. The CP cannot oblige cps to withdraw any measures or allocate compensation, however.

The panel dealing with the Uruguayan recourse to Article XXIII stated that the requirement that the situation must be serious enough limits the applicability of the provision to cases where there is nullification or impairment.[158] In other words, the complaining cp must have suffered some damage. This indicates that an authorisation to suspend the application of Concessions or other GATT obligations cannot be obtained when the attainment of any objective of the GATT is being impeded.

The authorisation to suspend must be appropriate in the circumstances according to the CP. Only once have the CP given an authorisation to suspend.[159] The CP authorised the Kingdom of The Netherlands to suspend the application *vis-à-vis* the United States of its obligations under the GATT to the extent necessary to allow it to apply a limit of 60,000 metric tons on imports of wheat flour from the United States during the calendar year 1953. The CP thought trade restriction against the U.S. up to 60,000 metric tons appropriate. The authorisation was repeated several times, since it did not result in any change in the American trade policy.[160]

The purpose of the suspension under Article XXIII,2 is to maintain the balance between benefits given to the cps. Suspension is conceived of as an *ultimum remedium*.[161] The minimum period of time that elapses after a recommendation of the CP until an authorisation to suspend is the time span between two sessions of the CP, which is six months. The CP often choose to postpone the authorisation to suspend so as to afford a period in which the disputing cps can cool down. For instance, in the case of French import restrictions,[162] a panel was established in 1962 in connection with the request made by the government of the United States that the CP consider, pursuant to Article XXIII,2, import restrictions applied by the government of France to products on which the EEC had given tariff Concessions to the United States. The panel agreed that the maintenance by a cp of the restrictions constituted nullification or impairment of benefits to which the U.S. was entitled under GATT. Therefore it suggested that the CP could appropriately recommend to the French government the withdrawal of the restrictions, since this was the most satisfactory way of resolving the question, and to the U.S. government that it refrain, for a reasonable period of time, from exercising its right to propose suspension. In 1972 the government of France still applied the import restrictions. Therefore, the government of the U.S. wanted to retaliate, and asked the Council to authorise withdrawal of tariff Concessions on $12.2 million of French trade, to be applied discriminatorily. The Council reaffirmed the earlier panel decision and asked the parties to consult bilaterally on the quantity of retaliation. The parties settled the matter before the Council had to authorise the retaliation. The French government withdrew almost all alleged import restrictions.[163] The delays in the procedure of Article XXIII are thus advantageous to the cp causing nullification or impairment.

The CP have manifested a great reluctance to authorise retaliation. Dam[164] indicates two reasons for this sparing recourse to the principal form of coercion available to the GATT: 'First, the desire to act as conciliators rather than as arbitrators has led the CP to seek to delay as long as possible the imposition of GATT's ultimate sanction. And second, within the context of a concrete dispute it often becomes painfully obvious that no one gains by retaliation. The retaliating party often loses as much as the party retaliated against.' Furthermore, retaliation could induce the latter to withdraw other Concessions, establishing an action-reaction chain that might even lead to the extinction of GATT in the most extreme case. As a result of the operation of the economic law of comparative costs and because of trade diversion,[165] the prosperity of the world would decline, which is the opposite of GATT's purposes. Small countries often have too little to offer to be able to retaliate since their imports are low. The measures that trigger retaliation are often established as a consequence of pressure by domestic producers. The retaliatory measures, however, hurt another group of producers or consumers in many cases, providing no incentive for the first-mentioned domestic producers to reduce their pressure.[166]

'If the application to any cp of any Concession or other obligation is in fact suspended, that cp shall then be free, not later than sixty days after such action is taken, to give written notice to the Director-General[167] of the CP of its intention to withdraw from this Agreement and such withdrawal shall take effect upon the sixtieth day following the day on which such notice is received by him,' states the last clause of Article XXIII,2. This provision has never been applied. Withdrawal from GATT is likely to be too detrimental to the withdrawing cp itself to be feasible in light of the accomplishments within GATT.

4.2.3.5. The Brazilian and Uruguayan proposal for amending Article XXIII

To redress the unequal bargaining position of the developing countries, the Brazilian and Uruguayan delegations introduced a proposal for amending Article XXIII in the early 1960s.[168] It contained four elements:

- (1) an option for developing countries which invoke Article XXIII to employ certain additional measures besides authorised suspension;
- (2) compensation in the form of a financial indemnity where it is established that measures complained of have adversely affected the trade and economic prospects of developing countries and it has not been possible to eliminate the measure or obtain an adequate commercial remedy,
- (3) automatic release for a developing country from its obligations under the GATT towards any developed country against which a complaint has been brought pending examination of the matter in cases where the import capacity of a developing country had been impaired by the maintenance of measures by the developed country contrary to the provisions of GATT, and
- (4) consideration by the CP of what collective action they could have taken to obtain compliance in the event that a developed country did not carry out their recommendation within a given time limit.

This proposal was not adopted.

4.2.3.6. The new procedure for developing countries

On April 5, 1966, the CP adopted new procedures under Article XXIII proposed by the Committee on Trade and Development. They aimed at improving the functioning of the GATT and at maintaining a proper balance between the rights and obligations of all cps taking fully into account the need for safeguarding both the present and potential trade of less-developed parties affected by nullification or impairment.[169] These procedures are far less radical than the proposal made by Brazil and Uruguay.

If consultations between a less-developed cp and a developed cp in regard to any matter falling under paragraph 1 of Article XXIII do not lead to a satisfactory settlement, the less-developed cp complaining of the other's measure may refer the matter to the Director-General so that, acting in an *ex officio* capacity, he may use his good offices with a view to facilitating a solution. In this regard the cps concerned shall, at his request, promptly furnish all relevant information. The Director-General may also consult with cps and inter-governmental organisations as he considers appropriate.

After a period of two months from the commencement of these consultations, if no mutually satisfactory solution has been reached, the Director-General must, at the request of one of the cps concerned, bring the matter to the attention of the CP or the Council, to whom he shall submit a report on the action taken by him, together with all background information. Upon receipt of the report, the CP or the Council shall forthwith appoint a panel, the members of which shall act in their personal capacity and shall be appointed in consultation with, and with the approval of, the cps concerned. In conducting its examination, the panel must take due account of all the circumstances and considerations regarding the application of the measures complained of, and their impact on the trade and economic development of affected cps. The panel must submit its findings and recommendations within 60 days.

Within a period of 90 days from the date of the decision of the CP or the Council, the cp to which a recommendation is directed must report to the CP or the Council on the action taken by it in pursuance of the decision. If it is found that a cp to which a recommendation has been directed has not complied with it in full, the CP may organise suspension of Concessions under the conditions named in Article XXIII. In the event that a recommendation to a developed country by the CP is not applied within the prescribed time limit, they shall consider what measures should be taken besides authorisation to suspend Concessions. If consultations held under paragraph 2 of Article XXXVII[170] relate to trade restrictions for which there is no authority under the GATT, any of the parties to the consultations may, in the absence of a satisfactory solution, request that further consultations be carried out by the CP pursuant to paragraph 2 of Article XXIII, it being understood that a consultation held under paragraph 2 of Article XXXVII will be considered by the CP as fulfilling the conditions of paragraph 1 of Article XXIII if the parties to them so agree.

The three major innovations are that the Director-General now plays an important part, time limits are set, and the panel has to take the economic background into account. Panels usually do not pay much attention to the background and the consequences of their decisions, since they are concerned with conciliation in the first place and lack the authority and means of power to request information that the cps are not willing to give of their own free will. Also they do not have enough manpower to do so. In the fourth text relating to the framework for conduct of international trade, the CP reaffirm that these procedures constitute the agreed customary practice for dispute settlement in GATT.[171]

The special procedure has never been invoked. According to representatives of various developing countries, the reason for not using the procedure is the fear of reprisals by defendants.[172]

4.2.3.7. The 1979 Understanding regarding notification, consultation, dispute settlement and surveillance

The fourth framework agreement reached in the Tokyo Round, the Understanding on notification, consultation, dispute settlement and surveillance in GATT clarified and strengthened existing GATT rules on dispute settlement, especially as regards the use of panels.[173] In this understanding the cps reaffirm their adherence to the basic GATT mechanism for the management of disputes based on Articles XXII and XXIII. In addition, they improved and refined the central mechanism of supervision adopting the following provision: the cps undertake, to the maximum extent possible, to notify the CP of their adoption of trade measures affecting the operation of GATT if possible in advance or otherwise promptly *ex post facto*. Consultations remain the main instrument of dispute settlement. Yet, if a dispute is not resolved through consultations the cps concerned may request an appropriate body or individual to use their *good offices* with a view to conciliation.

A less-developed country bringing a complaint against a developed country may request the good offices of the Director-General,[174] who may consult with the Chairman of the CP and the Chairman of the Council. The Director-General must maintain an informal indicative list of potential panel members. When a panel is set up, the Director-General, after securing the agreement of the cps concerned, should propose the composition of the panel to the CP. The panel members would be preferably governmental but they would serve in their individual capacities and not as representatives of any government or organisation. The parties must respond within seven working days to nominations of panel members. Under normal circumstances the panel must be established within 30 days.

Any cp having a substantial interest in the matter before a panel, and having so notified the Council, should have an opportunity to be heard by the panel. Panels have the right to seek information and technical advice from any source but must inform governments of the states having jurisdiction over such source. Cps must give requested information promptly.

Panels assist the CP by assessing the facts of the case and the applicability of and conformity with the GATT and by making other fundings as requested by the CP. Where the parties have failed to develop a mutually satisfactory solution, the panel should submit its findings in a written form. Panels should aim to deliver their findings without undue delay; in cases of urgency even within three months. The CP should consider WP and panel reports promptly and take appropriate action within a reasonable period of time. If action is required in a case brought by a less-developed country the CP must also take into account the impact of the measures complained of on the economy of less-developed cps concerned.[175]

The CP also agreed to keep under surveillance any matter on which they have made recommendations or given rulings, and to conduct a regular and systematic review of developments in the trading system. The interests of less-developed cps will receive technical assistance from the GATT Secretariat with regard to the matters covered by this Understanding.

4.2.4. The functioning of the central dispute settlement procedure in practice

The central dispute procedure was most used between 1952 and 1958. Forty complaints were submitted to the CP on the basis of Articles XXII and XXIII during this period. It is remarkable that only 20 cps were involved in these actions and six countries account for 75 per cent. of them. Twenty-eight of these complaints were concerned primarily with protecting the trade interest of a particular industry or product. Ten complaints concerned clear violations of GATT, about which there was simply no doubt. Twenty-three appeared to rest on at least *prima facie* nullification or impairment, but in most of these a defence was available to the responding party. Nine of the contested complaints progressed to a ruling on their merits. In seven of these nine the complainant prevailed in at least some part of its legal claim and in one other case a favourable panel decision was returned for further study.

Of the 40 complaints filed during this period, 30 resulted in a settlement satisfactory to the complainant. Of the remaining 10, one ended with a ruling for the defendant, five ended in an impasse and four simply disappeared without a trace. One could draw the conclusion from these data that the dispute settlement procedure was effective. However:

– countries that have lost a dispute may have terminated their offending practices for reasons not related to the GATT complaint;
– the loser may have made the complainant pay for its Concessions with others retaliatory actions;
– a number of complaints were dealt with outside of GATT; and
– there are no data on how many complaints were compromised or dropped, or not even brought, because of anticipated difficulty in securing compliance.[176]

From 1959 to 1961 no use was made of the procedure. In 1962 and 1963 six complaints were submitted. After that a period followed lasting until 1967 in which no complaints were filed. Hudec mentions several reasons for this sudden quiet, which reflected changed attitudes on the part of the governments of the cps. In the first place, the formation of the EEC largely removed the six member countries from their former role as individual litigants. Henceforth they would settle disputes amongst themselves within the EEC. Moreover, the EEC itself was strongly opposed to submitting its early commercial planning to adjudication. Nor did the members of the EEC submit any claims because they did not want to provoke counterclaims, since it was doubtful whether the formation of their common market conformed to the GATT.[177] Secondly, by 1959 many GATT governments were becoming aware of the many major changes on the GATT horizon. They could see that their own response to these changes might require a certain tolerance in GATT law, so that they did not want to take too aggressive a position themselves. The creation of the EEC was not the only doubtful activity. The creation of the EFTA[178] and import restrictions on agricultural products were potential subjects of complaint as well. Thirdly, the Dillon and the Kennedy Rounds were held in this period. The cps were able to discuss their grievances during these negotiations and the unfriendliness of a complaint might have had a negative influence on the negotiations.[179]

Four of the six complaints launched during 1962 and 1963 were consequences of Congressional pressures in the U.S.A. The other two were the Uruguayan recourse to Article XXIII, discussed above[180] and a complaint from Brazil against a preference on bananas proposed by the United Kingdom,[181] which resulted in its withdrawal. One of the American complaints, the so-called chicken war against the EEC,[182] as well as the Uruguayan complaint gave rise to major confrontations that demonstrated GATT's increasing discomfort over legal procedures.[183]

After this, until 1970, the cps hardly dared to face confrontations. In the late 1960s the GATT was violated so often that bringing a claim against one infringer was viewed as an unfriendly act. Moreover, most cps argued that correction of measures and actions violating GATT would only make sense if some overall settlement was reached and measures and actions of other violating cps were corrected, too.[184] Potential plaintiffs that were not blameless themselves were held back because of fear of reciprocity. Two complaints filed in 1966 and 1967 only gave rise to consultations under Article XXII.[185] The cps really did not want to be unfriendly. Two complaints were filed in 1969. One of them was settled before consultations were held with the CP.[186] In the other case the plaintiff, the U.S.A., agreed to wait for the outcome of proposed changes in the respondent's national legislation.[187]

Despite the progressive decline of GATT legal affairs during the early 1960s, the developing countries tried to bring new life into the central dispute settlement procedure. They continued their campaign for third-party decisions against the trade restrictions of developed nations that had started with the Uruguayan recourse to Article XXIII in 1962 and the subsequent proposal of Brazil and Uruguay to amend that article. The developing countries moved the emphasis from the old GATT rules to the implementation of the new commitments based on Part IV. Accordingly they claimed that the developed countries should help developing countries if they could. Between 1967 and 1971 they took the following initiatives:

– First of all they proposed a self-starting panel procedure to examine problems relating to the quantitative restrictions maintained by developed cps on industrial products of particular interest to developing countries.[188] A self-starting panel examines problems of its own initiative and not only after claims have been referred to it. The advantage would be that a solution will arise rapidly. In this case an early removal of the restrictions

was aimed at. The CP adopted this procedure in principle but it has never been used.
- The second proposal to establish an automatic panel procedure to review compliance with the obligations of Part IV was adopted by the CP but has never been used either.[189]
- During negotiations in 1966 it was proposed to grant the Director-General a prosecutorial role. This proposal was not adopted.[190]
- One proposal has been successful. It provided for the establishment of the Group of Three, consisting of the Chairmen of the CP, the Council and the Committee on Trade and Development. As part of its larger mandate, the Group was authorised to consult informally with all cps to seek out specific cases of unjustified trade restriction and to make concrete proposals concerning their removal or amelioration.[191] The Group operated for three years, until the Tokyo Round took over its function.[192]

In 1970 the Nixon administration of the United States filed complaints that were once again animated by criticisms of the Congress that GATT was not effective. These complaints punctured the anti-confrontation balloon. The United States increased diplomatic pressure by submitting these claims and took the risk that it would become evident that nothing could be done about violations of GATT, without risking GATT's collapse. Although most of the decisions were in favour of the United States, the results were often not satisfactory to that country. In the case of the citrus preferences and Association Agreements[193] the U.S. first successfully attacked the EEC preferences for citrus fruit from Mediterranean countries detrimental to U.S. exports. However, these preferences returned in 1970 when the EEC brought into force certain Association Agreements that entered into force in 1970, against which the U.S. has opposed in vain.

The United States submitted three other complaints that did not stir up much dust.[194]

In 1972 the United States filed a complaint against the EEC concerning compensatory taxes by EEC members to correct for the effect of currency fluctuations on the EEC Common Agricultural Policy. Although the EEC Council promised to withdraw the measures up to 95 per cent., the U.S. insisted on examination by a Panel. The EEC kept on resisting this proposal. Finally the U.S. dropped its complaint.[195] A U.S. complaint against French residual restrictions resulted in a satisfactory compromise.[196]

Two other U.S. complaints against the Netherlands[197] and the U.K. were settled before a recommendation or ruling was proposed by a Panel.

An Israeli complaint against the U.K. was settled during the Panel discussions.[198]

In 1973 the EEC brought a complaint against the U.S. concerning U.S. tax legislation, the so-called DISC-case,[199] which led to a counter-claim by the U.S. against Income Tax practices maintained by France, Belgium and the Netherlands.[200] The Panel thought all the tax practices were violations of GATT. This decision came as a shock to many observers, for the features of the three European tax systems were widely practised among GATT members and had been a standard element of tax legislation long before the GATT.[201] These tax measure cases were the most complex ever considered under the GATT Article XXIII procedure. Probably because of their complexity, GATT procedures failed to resolve the issues at hand. The ruling was very theoretical in approach and backed by slim evidence, and the interpretation given of Article XVI,4 was unworkable. Tax practices are very complex and the provisions of the GATT do not provide for sophisticated rules regarding these practices. They will have to be designed by means of thorough negotiations and cannot be determined by means of a Panel ruling.[202] One reason for the unsatisfactory character of the Panel report may have been the participation of two outside experts in tax matters,[203] who must have dealt with the case without taking the special features of the GATT system of balance and compromise into account. Within the Council the adoption of the Panel reports gave rise to heated discussions. These cases have damaged the prestige of the central dispute procedure.

During 1977 and 1978 several claims were dealt with by GATT 'bodies'. Japan submitted a claim regarding suspension of customs liquidation by the U.S.[204] that constituted countervailing duties. The EEC filed a complaint based on Article XXIII,2 against Canada in 1976 about the withdrawal of tariff Concessions. The Panel report on this case was adopted on May 17, 1978.[205] The U.S. brought forward a complaint under Article XXIII,2 about EEC measures on animal feed proteins, consisting of the compulsory purchase of milkpowder. The Panel report about this case was adopted on March 24, 1978.[206] Another U.S. claim based on Article XXIII,2 against the EEC led to the adoption of a Panel report in October 1978. This complaint concerned the EEC programme of minimum import prices, licences and security deposits for certain processed fruits and vegetables.[207]

The U.S. also brought a complaint under Article XXIII,2 against Japan concerning measures on imports of thrown silk.[208] In November 1978 a panel was set up to examine a complaint by Brazil on the EEC sugar export refund system.[209] In 1979 Australia filed a complaint against the EEC regarding export subsidies on sugar.[210] In the same year a Panel was formed to examine Japanese measures on imports of leather, complained about by the U.S.[211]

The results of the Tokyo Round seem to have increased the cps' confidence in the central dispute mechanism. In 1980 a record list of 13 international trade disputes were brought before the GATT Council under the central dispute settlement procedures.

In January the U.S. and Spain requested the Council to set up a panel to examine a U.S. complaint regarding Spanish measures concerning a domestic sale of soybean oil. Canada brought a complaint regarding the U.S. prohibition of tuna imports from Canada.

In February the Council set up a panel to examine the 1979 complaint by the U.S. over Japanese measures affecting imports of manufactured tobacco. In March Canada referred in the Council to a tariff quota established by the EEC for high-quality grain-fed beef. A panel set up in June 1980 is examining this issue. In June 1980 the Council considered a panel report on a complaint by Hong Kong concerning Norwegian restrictions on imports of certain textile products and the Council set up a panel to examine a complaint by Brazil over Spanish tariff treatment of unroasted coffee. In October the U.S. asked for a panel to examine its complaint concerning United Kingdom treatment of poultry imports from the U.S. New Zealand referred in the Council to a reported proposal by Japan to impose quotas on prepared edible fats and sought consultations under Article XXII.

India told the Council that it had requested consultations under Article XXIII with the U.S. concerning U.S. composition of a countervailing duty, without applying the injury criterion, on imports of industrial fasteners from India.

In November 1980, the Council adopted a Panel Report on the Brazilian complaint concerning EEC refunds on sugar imports. The Australian complaint about EEC refunds on sugar was discussed during several Council meetings. The EEC agreed to a request by the cps to discuss possible limitations of its refunds; the discussions about both the Brazilian and Australian cases began in December 1980. Also in November a panel reported to the Council on a complaint by Chile over EEC restrictions on imports of Chilean apples. In the same month a panel reported to the Council that bilateral consultations between Canada and Japan over a Canadian complaint concerning Japanese restrictions on leather imports had been brought to a satisfactory conclusion, and that Canada was consequently withdrawing its complaint.[212]

From 1973 to 1979 most complaints concerned disputes between the U.S., Japan and EEC countries, the three economic superpowers within GATT. After the Tokyo Round more cps initiated proceedings in GATT. The last complaint by a developing country before 1980 was the complaint against the U.S. export subsidy on tobacco filed by Malawi in 1966.[213] The developing countries might have stopped bringing complaints because they did not expect their claims to be successful or, if they should win the case, they doubted whether the recommendation or ruling would be implemented.

Also many developing countries, wanting preferences, have become affiliated with the EEC by means of association agreements; an action against the EEC would not be opportune for a developing country that is trying to build up closer ties with that organisation. In 1980 complaints from Chile and Brazil against the EEC, Brazil against Spain, and India against the U.S. were discussed in the GATT. This might indicate that developing countries have regained confidence in the GATT dispute settlement procedures because of the Tokyo Round changes. However, one should bear in mind that the complaining cps do not belong to the poorest cps and have not invoked the good offices of the Director-General. Also these cps enjoy no special preferences from the developed cps complained about. No complaints were filed lately against developing cps. Probably developed countries are not complaining against developing countries since the latter are incapable of giving them any compensation in case of a 'conviction'.

Neighbouring countries are members of regional organisations in many instances and can therefore settle their problems on a regional scale. The only neighbours whose disputes are dealt with in GATT are Canada and the U.S.

Two of the cps now involved in dispute settlements, Japan and the EEC, were not negotiators of the GATT. Many of the ideas in the General Agreement stem from the U.S., which was economically the most powerful cp in 1947. The two newcomers may feel less impelled to comply with the old GATT norms that they did not draft. Such a tendency could lead to a lower level of consensus and to dispute settlement based on power rather than on rules.

4.2.5. Evaluation

Qualification of the mechanisms of supervision[214]

The modality of supervision based on Articles XXII and XXIII is specific. The criterion applied is whether a violation, measure or situation is detrimental. The GATT text does not constitute the primary touchstone, rather maintaining the balance between mutually granted Concessions is decisive. The procedure is accusatory.

The procedures pursuant to the first and second paragraphs of Articles XXII and XXIII have different forms. The first paragraphs provide for supervision by the cps themselves. In case the results of this supervision are not satisfactory, another form of supervision will follow. Therefore the supervision provided for in the first paragraphs is more than a *'surveillance de façade'*.[215] It is non-judicial supervision. No procedural rules have been established, except for the form of representations under Article XXIII,1.

Article XXII,2 provides for non-judicial supervision, which is pursued by the plenary organ as well as by the cps themselves. No procedures have been laid down within the GATT text itself, but pursuant to the Decision of the CP of November 10, 1958,[216] it is necessary to inform the Director-General in certain circumstances. In that event there is specific and non-judicial supervision according to a fixed procedure.

As far as the review function is concerned, supervision under Article XXIII,1 is objective, whereas the correction function is exercised partly by the cps themselves. Its form is non-judicial and it is exercised, in the last resort, by a politically dependent organ. Usually, a technical phase precedes the political phase. WPs and Panels play an important part in the technical phase, as does the Director-General under the new procedure for developing countries described under 4.2.3.6. These organs of restricted composition gather and evaluate information, sometimes on the basis of questionnaires. They lay down their findings in a report, which may contain draft recommendations or rulings. Since WPs, Panels and the Director-General try to reach a friendly settlement by means of consultations and negotiations, political relations also influence the procedure in the technical phase. The new procedure for developing countries and the 1979 Understanding provide for non-judicial supervision by the Director-General before the CP get involved. Rules of procedure regarding supervision under Article XXIII,2 have not been laid down. However, certain customary rules have developed and have been codified since 1979. The new procedure for developing countries contains procedural requirements. The decisions of the CP are not legally binding.

Supervision under Articles XXII,2 and XXIII,2 has review, correction and creative functions. The instrument of the review function is an inquiry on the basis of a complaint or a request for a recommendation, or a ruling brought forward by one or more cps. The cps themselves are the sources of the information necessary for the review. They provide the information for supervision among themselves by means of exchanges of information and for supervision by GATT bodies using *ad hoc* reports supporting their own position or on the request of the CP or another GATT body. Supervision may also result from unforced notification under the 1979 Understanding. The WPs draft their reports while the cps involved are present and participating. The cps involved do not attend Panel meetings. The reports are discussed in a politically dependent organ. The information obtained is not published. The reports of Panels and WPs are usually published, but their publication is not obligatory. The requirement that the plaintiff must have suffered some detrimental effects excludes the possibility of an *actio popularis*.

The correction function is performed in the first place by friendly settlement. Negotiations, an instrument of correction pertaining to diplomatic supervision, constitute the first phase of the procedure. Independent members of Panels and WPs, and also the Director-General in the event of the new procedure for developing countries, or under the 1979 Understanding, use good offices and mediation. Conciliation is used as well, especially by the Panels. Political discussions are the second instrument used for corrections. These discussions and the possibly subsequent recommendations and rulings give rise to judicial and moral pressure that might lead to correction. This pressure is usually limited since in most cases only the governments concerned know the content of the discussions, recommendations and rulings. Not all proceedings of the CP are published; of those that are, some reports are published only after two years and most issues of international trade policy do not get much publicity. Finally, there is a third possible instrument of correction. As an *ultimum remedium* there is the sanction of authorised self-help coupled with the 'mobilisation of shame'.

Supervision under Articles XXII and XXIII is very creative. The CP, the Council and the subsidiary organs interpret GATT while drafting rulings and recommendations. They take changes in circumstances into account. The procedures are flexible. During GATT's initial period there was more room for creativity than after 1958, because there was then a greater consensus and more confidence in the 'GATT organs'.

Conclusion

The scope of the central dispute settlement procedure is wide. Article XXII concerns every complaint regarding any matter affecting the operation of the GATT and Article XXIII provides protection against nullification or impairment of any benefit under the Agreement. The GATT text does not provide for a sharply defined legal basis for actions (it only mentions nullification or impairment or the attainment of any objective). However, in several reports by WPs and Panels the possible legal grounds for claims have been clarified and the burden of proof has been allocated.[217] In the case of *prima facie* nullification or impairment, the 'defending' cp bears the burden of proof; in other cases the claimant cp has to prove the loss of a benefit. Until 1958 the central dispute settlement procedure was much used. During this period most of the cps were developed countries. With the exception of the United States, all of the cps were individual countries of relatively modest size and power as compared with the whole membership. These cps agreed on the purposes and instruments of GATT. The United States dominated the drafting of the Agreement; the other countries were not powerful enough to deviate from the GATT on their own.[218] Since the cps submitted claims, they demonstrated confidence that the rulings and recommendations of the GATT organs were based on GATT Law and not solely on the relative power of the cps involved. For instance, a small country like the Netherlands was authorised to suspend obligations it owed to the United States.[219] At that time the GATT organs possessed a fair amount of prestige. However, in the U.S. Escape Clause Action on Fur Felt Hat Bodies[220] political motives had a significant influence on the content of rulings and recommendations.

Since 1960 the membership of GATT has changed. The developing-country membership has grown to a numerical majority which has been able to organise itself as a bloc on several occasions. The composition of the developed-country membership was radically altered by the formation and subsequent enlargement of the EEC. With the parallel emergence of Japan as a major economic power, the GATT's developed-country membership has been transformed into a triad of economic superpowers, with only a handful of smaller independents.[221] These changes have led to a decrease in consensus[222] and to a more power-oriented than rule-oriented approach. The cps agree that the world's prosperity should increase but they have different views about the means that should be used to that end. The developing countries see the development of the Third World as the primary objective. The EEC member-states strive for an increase in prosperity by means of regional economic integration and association agreements, establishing preferences that violate the principle of non-discrimination. The developed cps that are not members of the EEC are very dissatisfied with this development. The lack of consensus is shown, too, by the fact that substantive provisions regarding the trade in agricultural products, non-tariff barriers to trade and regional integration are violated.[223]

In the 1960s and 1970s the number of cases declined sharply. Only the United States have put forward a considerable number of complaints. Lack of consensus and confidence was an obvious reason for this decline. Only the three superpowers used the dispute settlement procedure since there is some consensus amongst them as to the means by which prosperity should be increased and since they also command sufficient economic power to make sure that favourable rulings and recommendations are complied with. The prestige of the dispute settlement procedure declined as well. The discussions in the Council about the Panel report on the U.S. DISC legislation and the European income tax practices, followed by a reluctance to comply with the decisions in these cases, are clear examples. The dispute settlement procedure itself became more power-oriented.

The 1980s may be the era of revival for GATT's central dispute procedure. Several developed and three less-developed countries have invoked Articles XXII and XXIII. Possible reasons for this renewed confidence in the GATT may be the many changes in GATT brought about by the Tokyo Round as well as global political and economic developments. It may well be that developing countries who are disappointed by UNCTAD will rely more on the GATT, especially since several new provisions in the GATT are more favourable to developing cps. Moreover, the decline in global economic growth has at the same time increased the temptation of protectionism and the need for the comparative advantage of free trade. Consequently supervision on fair competition is needed more than ever.

The major weakness of the central dispute settlement procedure has always been that it has to be initiated by the cps themselves. In particular, since the beginning of the 1960s, the submission of a claim is perceived as an unfriendly act. The 1979 Understanding tries to mitigate these drawbacks by the undertaking to notify the CP of measures affecting the operation of the GATT and the understanding that requests for the use of Article XXIII should not be considered as a contentious act. Furthermore, cps are likely to file complaints only when they expect that the case will be decided in their favour. Only if the cps expect that a recommendation or ruling will be based on the GATT provisions, will they refer the matter to the CP when consultations among themselves have come to an impasse.[224] The limited number of complaints filed between 1958 and 1979 shows the lack of confidence of the cps in the central disputes procedure in that period. The 1980s may show a different picture.

In many cases a dispute is subject to inordinate delays. A recalcitrant cp has many procedural opportunities to slow down the process. Sometimes disputes have lingered on for more than a decade. During that time violators can enjoy the benefits of their malpractices. If the cps adhere to the time limits set in the Understanding, the procedure will become far more effective.

A solution is sought in the first place by means of negotiations and conciliation, in which the relative economic and political power of the cps plays an important part. Only in the second phase is a ruling or recommendation based on the GATT law given, and then by the same body that acted as a conciliator in the first phase. Because the functions of conciliation and adjudication are mixed, the cps often doubt the objectivity of rulings and recommendations. In addition, the members of the CP and the WPs are government representatives that speak on behalf of the interests of their own country for the most part. The members of the Panels are indeed appointed individually but they are also diplomats, who represent their countries when the Panel meetings are over. Therefore, they are inclined to take the interests of their home country into account as well. The rulings and recommendations are made by politically dependent organs that are sure to be influenced by political and economic power relations. Therefore, recommendations and rulings are often not only technical applications of a previously agreed rule, but are also political or rule-making.[225]

The application of the sanction provided for in Article XXIII,2, that is, the suspension of Concessions or other obligations under the GATT, might lead to a decline in prosperity.[226] Since such a decline is the reverse of the GATT purposes, actual recourse to this sanction is minimal. Since the probability that the sanction will be used is very low, it is not effective. On top of this an economically weak country will not achieve very much by suspending an obligation owed to an economically stronger country because of its lack of power.[227]

Discord regarding GATT's central dispute settlement procedure prevails. The United States has opposed the increasing number of preferences and other malpractices that it thinks to be violations of GATT. The GATT organs have been unable to give rulings or recommendations against these practices because of lack of consensus. In 1974 within the U.S. a Trade Act was adopted.[228] The Congressional hearings on this Act show that the U.S. Government supported the GATT but it also called for legal reform on a number of issues, in particular the general decision-making machinery including the procedure of Articles XXII and XXIII. The Executive Branch also called for expanded authority to retaliate against unfair trade practices of foreign governments independently of GATT in cases where the GATT remedy was deemed unsatisfactory or unavailable.

Even the former Director-General of GATT, Mr. O. Long, in an address delivered in Zurich has directed attention to the perceived growing noncompliance with the GATT rules, and similar implications can be seen in statements made by representatives of cps other than the United States.[230]

To increase the effectiveness of the procedure there has to be consensus concerning the means to realise the purposes of GATT in the first place. The procedure itself should also be modified. The cps could commit themselves to keep the time limits suggested in the 1979 Understanding to reduce the detrimental effects of foot dragging. It should be possible to start the procedure as soon as conflicting measures are announced so they can be judged before they have caused damage. The scope of the procedure should not be reduced, so that a flexible application of the procedure will remain possible, but it is advisable to establish separate bodies for conciliation and adjudication. One of those would try to achieve compromises in the first phase, taking economic and political power relations into account, while the other would give a ruling or recommendation about the 'law' of GATT in the second phase if a compromise had not been reached. To shorten the amount of time involved in dispute settlement permanent bodies could be established thus eliminating delays in searching for members. The adjudicative body should be composed of individuals who do not represent national governments.

Although public discussion of the disputes could contribute to prevention and correction, consideration behind closed doors seems better. First of all, cps are more likely to give concessions in private since they need not be afraid to lose face in public. Secondly, national pressure groups and producers will not know anything about designs for trade liberalising measures to which they might be opposed. The current 'sanction' is not effective. The granting of financial compensation would be more effective than the currently possible authorisation to suspend provided the cps would accept this. At present the GATT has no power to enforce sanctions.

The proposed procedural changes would sharpen supervision within GATT. Whether the cps really want this, remains to be seen. More consensus than is prevalent, is a necessary prerequisite to a strengthening of the central dispute settlement procedure. The Tokyo Round may have been the turning point in the direction of an effective central dispute settlement procedure!

4.3. Specific procedures

4.3.1. Modification and rectification of tariffs

The GATT provides a variety of methods for changing the Concessions and Schedules. There are two ways in which temporary changes can be brought about. The CP can introduce waivers[231] and individual cps can invoke GATT's escape clause.[232] Permanent changes are effected by amendments and through renegotiations of GATT. Article XXX contains the requirements for amending GATT, which are stringent. Changes in Schedules are called renegotiations, or modifications, and are much easier to accomplish principally through Article XXVIII. On top of this, Concessions and Schedules can be changed pursuant to Articles XVIII,7, XXIV,6 and XXVII. In addition, Article II,5 also provides for renegotiations.

In order to induce extensive tariff Concessions in the initial 1947 round of GATT tariff negotiations, the original Article XXVIII established a three-year period of so-called 'firm validity' ending January 1, 1951, during which Concessions could not be withdrawn. The period of firm validity was subsequently extended from January 1, 1954,[233] to July 1955[234] and then to January 1958.[235] On each occasion it was possible for an individual cp to abstain from the declaration of continued firm validity. In that way such a cp remained free to negotiate its Concessions at any time under Article XXVIII. The right to renegotiate was reciprocal with other cps. The WP that prepared the review Session of 1955 drafted a new Article XXVIII, which provided automatic three-year extension periods of 'firm validity'. It also eased the restrictions on renegotiation. This has become the current Article XXVIII. It establishes three kinds of renegotiations. 'Open Season' Negotiations, 'Out-of-Season' Negotiations and Renegotiations where a right to renegotiate is reserved.[236]

4.3.1.1. Open-Season Negotiations

From January 1, 1958, a cp may, every three years, modify or withdraw a Concession according to Article XXVIII, paragraphs 1 to 3. Such a cp is called the applicant cp. The applicant cp must notify the CP of its intention not earlier than six months and not later than three months from the termination date of 'firm validity'.[237] The applicant cp has to negotiate with any other cp with which such Concession was initially negotiated, the so-called 'withwhom', as well as with any other cp determined by the CP to have a 'principal supplying interest'. These two categories of cps, together with the applicant cp, are in Article XXVIII referred to as 'the cps primarily concerned'. Furthermore, any other cp determined by the CP to have a 'substantial interest' has to be consulted.[238]

There can be no doubt as to which cp is the 'withwhom', when the original negotiations establishing the Concessions were conducted on a product-by-product basis. When other negotiating techniques have been used, doubts may arise. The CP have decided that where linear tariff Concessions are made, as there were during the Kennedy Round, the cp with a principal supplying interest in the product concerned shall be deemed to be the 'withwhom'.[239] Sometimes the cp granted 'initial negotiating rights' as an incidental Concession to a cp other than the withwhom. Then, the grantee becomes a 'withwhom' and hence a negotiating partner in the event of modification or withdrawal of the principal Concession involved. Therefore, it is possible that several withwhoms participate in renegotiations regarding one item.[240]

The purpose of enabling a cp with a principal supplying interest to participate in negotiating in addition to the withwhom, is to ensure that a cp with a larger share in the trade affected by the Concession than the grantee shall have an effective opportunity to protect rights which it enjoys under the GATT. The CP are not allowed to determine that more than one cp, or in exceptional instances, two, have a principal supplying interest.[241] In addition, the CP may exceptionally determine that a cp has a principal supplying interest if the Concession in question affects trade which constitutes a major part of the total exports of such cp.[242] Although renegotiations usually take place between two cps, they might be multilateral, since more than one withwhom can be involved, as well as several cps with a principal supplying interest.

The expression 'substantial interest' is not capable of a precise definition. It is, however, intended to be construed to cover only those cps which have, or in the absence of discriminatory quantitative restrictions affecting their exports could reasonably be expected to have, a significant share in the market of the applicant cp.[243] 'Significant share in the market', however, is also an imprecise concept. The cps 'primarily concerned' are entitled to negotiate, the cps with a 'substantial interest' are only entitled to be consulted. In practice, the difference in their positions is rather small since both categories may withdraw equivalent Concessions to compensate or retaliate.

Although Article XXVIII and the Interpretative Note *Ad* Article XXVIII,1(3) state that the CP will determine which cps have a 'principal supplying interest' and 'substantial interest', the CP have decided that this determination is a question in the first instance for the affected cps themselves. Recourse to conventional procedures, including determination by the CP, is required only if a cp claims that it has a principal supplying interest or a substantial interest.[244]

GATT gives guidelines for the outcome of the renegotiations as well. All cps must maintain an equilibrium of tariffs and other barriers: the applicant cp by offering compensation or by allowing the withdrawal of Concessions, the other cps by not requiring too much compensation; as the applicant cp should not have to pay compensation or suffer retaliation greater than the withdrawal or modification sought, judged in the light of the conditions of the trade at the time, making allowance for any discriminatory quantitative restrictions maintained by the applicant cp.[245]

Pursuant to Article XXVIII,2 the cps must endeavour to maintain a general level of reciprocal and mutually advantageous Concessions not less favourable to trade than that provided for in the GATT prior to the renegotiations. Since the general tariff level is not allowed to rise, modifications are limited to structural changes only. Since the introduction of Part IV the requirements contained in the second paragraph of Article XXVIII can be nullified if a developing cp is involved in the renegotiations. It is agreed under Article XXXVI,8 that developed cps do not expect reciprocity from developing cps. Pursuant to Article XXVII,1(a) the developed cps are required to accord high priority to the reduction and elimination of barriers for exports from developing cps. Provisions also apply to renegotiations under Article XXVIII.[246] This might mean, as a consequence, that developed cps would not be allowed to withdraw substantially equivalent Concessions initially negotiated with the applicant cp in case a developing cp withdraws or modifies a Concession without offering compensation.[247] In this way Article XXVIII,3 would be nullified. In addition, the pressure on developing countries not to increase their general tariff level is reduced.

If agreement cannot be reached when 'firm validity' expires, the applicant cp is free to withdraw or modify the Concession.[248] In case the cps 'primarily concerned' have reached agreement but another cp with a 'substantial interest' is not satisfied, the latter is free, within six months, to withdraw upon the expiration of 30 days from the day on which written notice of such withdrawal is received by the CP, substantially equivalent Concessions initially negotiated with the applicant cp.[249] An authorisation from the cp is not required. Consultations and negotiations in advance are the only requirements.

What constitutes a substantially equivalent Concession? The Note ad Article XXVIII,1(6), tells us that it should not be greater than the Concession the applicant cp wants to withdraw or modify, but it does not provide for a technique to determine what constitutes a substantially equivalent Concession. The problem of defining 'substantially equivalent Concessions' arose in the so-called Chicken War Case[250] in which the U.S. sought compensation because the Federal Republic of Germany wanted to withdraw a Concession with respect to poultry. The introduction of the common customs tariff of the EEC led to an increase in the tariff levied on poultry by the Federal Republic of Germany since the German tariff was lower than the new EEC tariff. The central issue was the valuation of the damage to American exports to Germany. The Panel dealing with the case took the actual figures for U.S. exports of poultry to the Federal Republic of Germany during the most recent 12 months for which the figures were available on the chosen base date, adjusting those figures for the discriminatory quantitative restrictions in effect in the Federal Republic of Germany during that period. However, measuring the value of a Concession solely by the quantity of imports entering under the tariff item to which that Concession applies is extremely misleading. It ignores the extent to which the protective effect is increased in raising the tariff by a certain percentage. The protective effect is dependent upon such factors as the *ad valorem*[251] percentage, the relationship between world prices and domestic prices and the price elasticity[252] of the demand for the commodity concerned. It has only a very loose relation to the quantity of trade preceding the increase and the percentage increase. In practice the value of Concessions is estimated by the CP, without using any specified technique.[253] The negotiations and consultations under Article XXVIII are conducted with the greatest possible secrecy in order to avoid premature disclosure of details of prospective tariff changes.[254] The reason for this is not to disturb world trade more than necessary. The CP must be informed immediately of all changes resulting from the renegotiations.[255]

4.3.1.2. Out-of-season negotiations

At any time, in special circumstances, the CP may authorise a cp to negotiate modification or withdrawal of a Concession, pursuant to Article XXVIII,4. The provisions of paragraphs 1 and 2 of this Article apply also to these out-of-season negotiations. If the cps 'primarily concerned' reach agreement in the negotiations, another cp with a substantial interest that is not satisfied may seek compensation. If the cps 'primarily concerned' do not reach agreement within a period of 60 days after negotiations have been authorised or within such longer period as the CP may have prescribed, the applicant cp may refer the matter to the CP. The CP must promptly examine the matter and submit their views to the cps 'primarily concerned' with the aim of achieving a settlement. If no settlement is reached, the applicant cp is free to modify or withdraw the Concession, unless the CP determine that the applicant has unreasonably failed to offer adequate compensation. If such action is taken, the other cps involved have the same rights as in the case of open season negotiations.[256]

In the Interpretative Notes *Ad* Article XXVIII,4, several time limits are laid down for the above described procedures. Moreover, the CP must authorise certain cps, which depend in large measure on a relatively small number of primary commodities and rely on the tariff as an important aid for furthering diversification of their economies or as an important source of revenue, to open out-of-season negotiations unless an undue disturbance of international trade would result. In determining whether an applicant cp has offered adequate compensation, the CP must take due account of the special position of a cp which has bound a high proportion of its tariffs at very low rates of duty and to this extent has less scope than other cps to make compensatory adjustment.

4.3.1.3. Renegotiations under other provisions

Before the 'firm validity' is terminated a cp may reserve the right to modify the appropriate Schedule for the duration of the next period in accordance with the procedures of paragraphs 1 to 3 of Article XXVIII by notifying the CP. The other cps have the right during the same period, to modify or withdraw, in accordance with the same procedures, Concessions initially negotiated with that cp.[257]

Article XXVII authorises any cp to withhold or withdraw Concessions which according to such a cp were negotiated with a government which has not become or has ceased to be a cp. A cp taking such action shall notify the CP and upon request consult with cps which have a substantial interest in the product concerned.

Pursuant to Article XXIV,6, the procedure of Article XXVIII applies if a cp proposes to increase any rate or duty inconsistently with the provisions of Article II as a consequence of the formation of a Customs Union or an interim agreement leading to the formation of such a union.[258] Since at the time Article XXIV was drafted, Article XXVIII only provided for the procedure of paragraphs 1 to 3; this procedure applies to renegotiations triggered by regional integration.

Article XVIII,7 provides for out-of-season negotiations to enable developing countries to modify or withdraw a Concession to promote the establishment of a particular industry.[259]

Finally, if any cp considers that it has not been treated by another cp as the first cp had contemplated by a Concession, it must bring the matter directly to the attention of the other cp. If the latter agrees, but declares a ruling of the court or other proper authority prevents such a treatment, the two cps, together with any other cps substantially interested, must enter promptly into further negotiations with a view to a compensatory adjustment of the matter.[260]

4.3.1.4. Rectification

The GATT does not contain or express a provision dealing with the correction of errors in the text. However, the competence to do so is assumed on the basis of customary rules of the general law of treaties. The CP have adopted procedures for rectifications of a purely formal character. Those changes are made by Certifications. A draft of each Certification must be communicated by the Director-General to all cps and shall become a Certification provided that no objection has been raised by a cp within sixty days.[261]

4.3.1.5. Evaluation

Qualification of the mechanisms of supervision

Supervision on substantial and structural changes is specific. The touchstone for any modification or rectification is the maintenance of the balance among Concessions granted and that of the overall level of tariffs. Violation of the GATT is not mentioned. The form of supervision is non-judicial. Supervision is exercised by the cps themselves in the procedures of Articles II,5, XXIV,6, XXVII and XXVIII,1–3; the CP only have to be informed of the resulting changes. In the procedures of Articles XVIII,7 and XXVIII,4 the CP as well as the cps themselves exercise supervision. The CP check whether there are special circumstances. After that the cps themselves are the supervisors. In case the latter cannot reach agreement, the CP have to submit their views and might prohibit modifications.

The instruments of review are exchanges of information when the cps themselves exercise supervision. In case the CP are involved, the information is provided by *ad hoc* reporting. The information is restricted. The primary instrument of the correction function is friendly settlement by means of negotiations and sometimes by means of conciliation. When the CP are involved, political discussion plays a part as well. This discussion takes place behind closed doors so that internal publicity is the only pressure exerted. The other cps are allowed to withdraw Concessions. This constitutes a sanction that is barely punitive and rather is a means to restore the balance and to prevent unwanted changes. The supervision is highly creative. The creative function is exercised by the cps themselves during consultations and negotiations.

Commentary

The primary goal of adjustment of tariffs is to restore the balance among Concessions. Supervision also aims at the same goal. Renegotiations constitute a flexible instrument that is pre-eminently capable of maintaining the equilibrium. One could get the impression that the GATT system is weak, since its obligations can be changed rather easily. However, one has to bear in mind that the obligations concerned relate to rapidly changing facts. Therefore, the flexibility of the GATT with regard to the contents of its Schedules constitutes a great strength. The supervision is highly creative; it even verges on rule-creation. Since the renegotiations usually take place at the same time as the original negotiations, the distinction between the two is difficult to make.

4.3.2. *Emergency measures, market disruption and arrangements concerning textiles, dairy and bovine meat*

4.3.2.1. GATT's escape-clause: Article XIX

As a consequence of the Concessions made within GATT, domestically produced goods may be priced out of the market. When non-tariff restrictions are reduced an increase in imports may induce a lowering of prices. As a consequence, domestic producers might suffer losses, as a result of which the reallocation of domestic production is necessary. This entails economic and social costs at best. At worst, resources may lie idle.

The GATT does not contain any provisions to regulate the process of adaptation. However, there are provisions which the importing country can use to insulate its domestic producers. Article XIX aims at protecting domestic producers against an unforeseen and sharp rise in imports causing or threatening to cause them serious injury. It allows deviations of GATT in certain circumstances, the so-called escape-clause.[262] Article XIX protects the cps against unforeseen detrimental consequences of the concessions they made. Therefore, the granting of Concessions by the cps is promoted, since Concessions are not immutable.

4.3.2.1.1. Conditions for the application of the escape-clause

If, as a result of unforeseen developments and of the effect of the obligations incurred by a cp under the GATT, including tariff concessions, any product is being imported into the territory of that cp in such increased quantities and under such conditions as to cause or threaten serious injury to domestic producers in that territory of like or directly competitive products, the cp shall be free, in respect of such product, and to the extent and for such time as may be necessary to prevent or remedy such injury, to suspend the obligation in whole or in part or to withdraw or modify the concession, pursuant to Article XIX,1(a). This is called the taking of emergency measures. This can be done as well on request of another cp, in case cp A has made a concession for a certain product to cp B and cp A on a latter date grants a concession to another cp giving rise to an increase in competition on the market for imported products in cp A to the extent that domestic producers in cp B are injured or threatened to be injured. In this case cp A shall be free, if cp B so requests to take emergency measures according to Article XIX,1(b).

The resulting modification is only temporary and concerns only one product or the products of one industry. The cps can invoke Article XIX at any time. The applicant cp need not offer compensation. Nevertheless, compensation is sometimes offered.[263] Article XIX may not be invoked where domestic producers are foreclosed from entering the market in a new type of product because of a sudden and unforeseen increase in imports. This has been determined in the so-called Hatters' Fur Case.[264]

There has to be a causal relation between the Concession or the obligation that the applicant wants to suspend or withdraw and the injurious increase in imports. Moreover, a causal relation must exist between the unforeseen circumstances and the injurious increase in imports. These causal relationships may be hard to prove and judge. On top of this, the term 'unforeseen developments' is nebulous. A cp granting a concession must always take into account some future damage. In the Hatters' Fur Case, the WP has defined unforeseen circumstances as: 'developments occurring after the negotiation

104

of the relevant tariff concession which it would not be reasonable to expect that the negotiators of the country making the concession could and should have foreseen at the time when the concession was negotiated'.[265]

In this case the unforeseen development was a change in fashion. Usually such a change should have been foreseen. Nevertheless, in this particular case the Article XIX prerequisite had been fulfilled since the degree to which the change in fashion affected the competitive situation could not reasonably be expected to have been foreseen by the United States authorities in 1947.[266]

There has to be a causal relation between the increased quantities and the injury as well. An absolute increase is not necessary. Article XIX covers cases where imports may have increased relatively to domestic production.[267] Since a relative increase in imports is a reason to escape, the burden of a decrease in the demand can be passed on to the foreign producers. This would give rise to protectionism. The above-mentioned substantive requirements tend to be relatively unimportant in practice because the burden of proof is borne by the complainant and not by the applicant.[268]

4.3.2.1.2. Mechanisms of supervision

A cp that wants to take emergency action has to give notice in writing to the CP as far in advance as may be practicable and must afford the CP and those cps having a substantial interest as exporters of the product concerned an opportunity to consult with it in respect of the proposed action.[269] If agreement among the interested cps with respect to the action is not reached, the applicant may escape. The affected cps then are free, not later than 90 days after such action is taken, to suspend, upon the expiration of 30 days from the day on which written notice of such suspension is received by the CP, the application to the trade of the applicant of such substantially equivalent concessions on other GATT obligations of which the CP do not disapprove.[270] The original tariff increase, caused by emergency actions, must be applied to all countries equally. The general arguments against discriminatory tariffs apply as fully to Article XIX increases as to any other increases. In the case of retaliatory suspensions against the applicant the most-favoured-nation clause is not applied, for this carries with it the danger of a chain reaction of further tariff increases by third countries. Therefore the suspension only affects the trade of the cp invoking Article XIX in the first place.[271]

In critical circumstances where delay would cause damage which would be difficult to repair, emergency action may be taken without prior consultation on the condition that consultation shall be effected immediately after taking such action.[272] This is called 'emergency escape'. If this action causes or threatens to cause serious injury to the domestic producers in the territory of the affected cps, the latter are free to suspend, upon the taking of the action and throughout the period of consultation, such concessions or other obligations as may be necessary to prevent and remedy the injury.[273] The most-favoured-nation clause applies to this emergency escape.[274]

4.3.2.2. Market disruption

As mentioned under 4.3.2.1., the amount of imports of a certain product may increase because of trade liberalisation which may cause the price of imported commodities to drop. This may lead to market disruption. In 1960 the CP recognised that market disruption occurred or threatened to occur in a number of countries. They mentioned a number of circumstances constituting market disruption. These are:

(1) a sharp and substantial increase or potential increase of imports of particular products from particular sources;
(2) these products are offered at prices which are substantially below those prevailing for similar goods of comparable quality in the market of the importing country;
(3) there is serious damage to domestic producers or threat thereof; and
(4) the price differentials referred to under (2) above do not arise from governmental intervention in the fixing or formation of prices or from dumping practices.

In some situations other elements are also present and the above is not, therefore, intended as an exhaustive definition of market disruption.[275]

There is nothing wrong with market disruption in itself. Trade barriers prevent optimal allocation by creating market failure. In the long run both the importing country and world trade gain from a disturbance of an artificial equilibrium. However, in the short-run the necessary reallocation gives rise to economic and social costs. In the absence of further measures, the domestic producers of the importing country bear these costs. To counteract market disruption the cps have taken measures within the framework of GATT as well as outside this Agreement to stage reallocation or even to prevent it completely. As a result of those measures, consumers in the importing country, as well as the exporting country itself bear the costs of the reallocation or its non-occurrence.

4.3.2.2.1. Measures against market disruption within GATT

Under the GATT a number of measures against market disruption might be taken by the cps:

– Market disruption might be a consequence of Concessions made. Provided such disruption could not have been foreseen at the time the cp made the Concession and the other requirements of Article XIX are fulfilled, the importing country may take emergency action under Article XIX.[276]
– In case a cp is apprehensive of market disruption because of the accession to the GATT of a new cp the former may eliminate the application of the Agreement or of Article II as between that cp and itself. The new cp has the same option.[277]
– An increase in imports might lead to balance-of-payments problems. In that case import restrictions are possible under the conditions of Articles XII or XVIIIB.[278]

106

- If an increase in imports impedes the establishment of a particular industry in a developing country, import restrictions could be allowed under Article XVIIIC and D.[279]
- According to Article XXV,5 the GATT obligations of any cp can be waived.[280]
- Lastly, in Arrangements made within the GATT structure the reallocation of factors of production is regulated, in the textiles sector, the dairy sector and the bovine meat sector.[281]

In all these instances supervision is provided for, the mechanisms of which are described elsewhere.[282] On top of this, during the Kennedy Round agreement was reached to implement the agreed tariff cuts in phases.[283] This gives the importing countries more time to adjust. The costs of reallocation are shared by the producers in the importing country and the consumers in the importing country and the exporting country.

4.3.2.2.2. Measures against market disruption outside GATT

The cps have taken measures against market disruption outside GATT as well. In some cases they took unilateral measures. Agreements concerning 'voluntary' export restrictions have been concluded from the 1930s onwards. Japan, for example, restricted the exports of many products such as textiles, bicycles, radios, canned fish and fruits.[284] The importing country can exert pressure on the exporting country to enter into this kind of 'agreement' by threatening it with even more restrictive unilateral measures or with actions in other fields.[285] With respect to meat, steel wool and synthetic textiles, the United States imposed agreements on exporting countries whereby the U.S. agrees to accept a reasonable and gradually increasing amount of cotton textile imports in exchange for the exporters to observe self-imposed 'voluntary' quotas. Other agreements were aimed at market regulation. Although the importing country does not restrict imports formally, it does so in fact. One of the reasons that such 'agreements' are more advantageous to the importing cps than the application of the GATT provisions is that the former allow for discrimination, which is conflicting with the GATT.

4.3.2.2.3. GATT activities concerning market disruption

The CP discussed the question of the avoidance of market disruption during their sixteenth session in June 1960. The Executive Secretary submitted a report concerning the factual situation for this session, based on consultations with the cps.[286] During this session, a WP was established that reported to the CP during their seventeenth session in late 1960. On the basis of the WP report, the CP recognised the problems of market disruption and its avoidance and established a Committee to study the problem and to make proposals for its solution.[287] This Committee has never met and may be considered to be non-existent at the moment. Nevertheless, the above-mentioned problem still exists. However, within GATT, separate agreements were concluded to regulate markets, which shall be described in the following three sections.

4.3.2.3. Arrangements Regarding International Trade in Textiles[288]

Japan and the Third World countries increased considerably their exports of cheap textiles in the mid-1950s. This gave rise to such serious market disruptions in Western countries that even increased tariff protection was an inadequate answer. Therefore, specific Arrangements were concluded within GATT to regulate the reallocation of production factors, with a view to a gradual process of adaptation.

On February 9, 1962, the participating countries made a Long-Term Arrangement Regarding International Trade in Cotton Textiles, which entered into force on October 1, 1962.[289] Under this Arrangement all the major importers agreed among themselves to accept a reasonable and gradually increasing amount of cotton textiles imports, and the exporters agreed to restrict their exports. The Arrangement provided for supervision,[290] which proved ineffective. The Arrangement was in force until September 30, 1973.[291]

4.3.2.3.1. The 1973 Arrangement

On December 20, 1973, in Geneva an Arrangement Regarding International Trade in Textiles, the Multifibre Arrangement (MFA), was made which came into force for three years on January 1, 1974.[292] The Arrangement was extended in 1977 until December 31, 1981.[293] Its basic objectives are to expand trade by reducing the barriers to trade, while ensuring the orderly and equitable development of trade and avoiding disruptive effects in individual markets. Assistance to the developing countries is a principal aim of the Arrangement.[294] The application of emergency measures is subject to specific conditions mentioned in the Arrangement and is supervised by an international body. By the end of 1980, 42 participants, counting the EEC as a single signatory, had accepted the Protocol extending the MFA.[295]

4.3.2.3.2. Mechanisms of supervision

The Arrangement provides for a Textiles Committee consisting of representatives of the parties to the Arrangement, and is chaired by the Director-General of GATT. It meets at least once a year to prepare such studies as the participating countries may decide, to analyse the current situation on the textiles market and to review the operation of the Arrangement. It reports to the GATT Council.[296] The Textiles Committee has established a Textiles Surveillance Body, further referred to as TSB, to supervise the implementation of the Arrangement. This permanent body consists of a chairman and eight members.[297] The TSB reviews yearly all restrictions introduced or bilateral agreements entered into by participating countries concerning trade in textiles since the coming into force of the Arrangement and reports its findings to the Textiles Committee.[298]

The Arrangement provides for notification and consultation procedures.[299] Participating countries may also refer disputes to the TSB if they cannot solve disagreements amongst themselves.[300] The TSB may make recommendations at the request of a participating country.[301] If, following recommendations by the TSB, problems continue to exist between the parties, these may be brought before the Textiles Committee or before the GATT Council through the normal GATT procedures.[302] In case the matter is referred to the CP or the Council under the central dispute procedure, any recommendations or observations of the TSB are taken into account.[303] Problems of interpretation should be resolved by bilateral consultation in the first instance: any remaining difficulties may be referred to the TSB.[304] The participating countries formally retain their rights under the GATT, including the right to invoke Article XIX. However, all participants have agreed that all possibilities of finding solutions within the framework of the Arrangement should be explored before resorting to Article XIX. Article XIX should not be regarded as a soft option exonerating the importing country from the obligation to justify actions contrary to the text or the spirit of the Textiles Arrangèment.[305]

4.3.2.3.3. The functioning of the 1973 Textiles Arrangement in practice

The TSB has been fairly active. Until October 1976, it had received one notification of existing restrictions, 35 notifications under Article 3, and 62 under Article 4.[306]

From November 1976 to the end of December 1977, 30 Article 3 measures were notified to the TSB as well as 35 bilateral agreements according to Article 4. During the period from January 1 to October 20, 1978, the TSB received three notifications under Article 3 and 43 notifications under Article 4. However, the TSB noted that some importing countries had failed to notify under Article 3,3 and that there had been a considerable delay in notifications under the various provisions of the Arrangement. Moreover, certain notifications contained insufficient detail.[307]

From January 1974 to October 1967 world trade in textiles increased substantially in value terms but was subject to fluctuations. Imports into developing countries increased in 1974 by 18 per cent. and decreased in 1975 by 2 per cent. The share of developing countries in world exports in textiles fell from 31 per cent. in 1973 to 29 per cent. in 1975. Their share of world exports of clothing over this period rose from 51 per cent. to 53 per cent. In 1974 and 1975 there was a downturn in the textile and clothing industries in the developed countries coupled with a continuous increase in the value of clothing imports from developing countries.[308] However, in 1977, trade in textiles and clothing among industrial countries expanded faster than imports from developing countries; imports from Third World countries had been the most rapidly expanding source of supply between 1963 and 1976. Export of textiles and clothing to developing countries increased at a faster pace than trade among industrial countries themselves as well as imports from developing countries. In developing countries growth in the value of exports slowed down considerably for both textiles and clothing in 1977 as compared with 1976. At the same time, their imports of textiles and clothing grew much faster than their exports in 1977.[309] The world production of textiles increased by 2 per cent. in 1978 and by 4 per cent. in 1979; the industrial countries producing 0.5 per cent. more in 1978 and 4 per cent. more in 1979, while the production by developing countries increased with 3.5 per cent. and 4.5 per cent. in those years. The industrial countries had a trade in textiles surplus with the developing countries of $1.5 billion in 1978 and of $1 billion in 1979.[310]

The TSB appears to have worked effectively at a time when other dispute settlement procedures have been in difficulty. In its early stages, the TSB issued rulings on difficult issues such as market distribution and generally commanded respect for those decisions.[311] Yet at the time of the major review of the operation of the Arrangement held in 1976 many representatives of exporting countries were disappointed and concerned about the way the Arrangement has been implemented during the three years of its existence.[312] More recently certain governments have complained that they cannot accept the tight discipline under current conditions in the industry. This view has led to a licence for 'reasonable' deviations in the 1978 extension of the Arrangement.[313]

In 1980, the second major review of the MFA was carried out by the Textiles Committee on the basis of a detailed report by the TSB and a survey by the GATT Secretariat on demand, production and trade in textiles. The developing countries complained jointly about the proliferation of restrictive measures against their imports and erosion of the MFA, especially about the licence for reasonable deviations. A number of countries complained that the MFA had been detrimental to the trade of MFA developing countries. Other countries stated that the MFA had served reasonably well during a period of crisis in maintaining a balance among the interests of importing and exporting countries, given the various objectives of the MFA.[314]

4.3.2.4. The International Dairy Arrangement

The market for many agricultural products is distorted because many governments support their domestic agricultural industry. Although the GATT rules were intended to apply to trade in agricultural and industrial products alike, agriculture has been virtually excluded from trade liberalisation. Government policies of support assuring a high income level for dairy farmers have resulted in important changes in the pattern of world trade and in considerable difficulties in world markets. A significant enlargement of agricultural markets as a result of the Tokyo Round was an essential requirement put forward by agricultural exporters. Therefore, an International Dairy Arrangement was drafted during the Tokyo Round. Some international co-operation already existed in the dairy sector before this Agreement.[315] These arrangements, however, covered only part of the trade in dairy products, and were limited in scope.[316] The International Dairy Arrangement was acknowledged by the CP in 1976 and came into force on January 1, 1980 for those participants who accepted it. It is effective for three years, with provision for further three-year extensions. Members of

110

the UN or of one of its specialised agencies and the EEC can become parties to the Agreement. Provisional application is possible.[317]

The Arrangement aims to expand and liberalise world trade in dairy products while keeping market conditions as stable as possible. Benefits to exporting and importing countries should be mutual and the economic and social development of developing countries should be furthered.[318] The Arrangement covers all dairy products including milk, cream, cheese and butter and casein. The International Dairy Products Council, established under the Dairy Arrangement may decide that the Arrangement is to apply to other products in which dairy products have been incorporated if the Council deems their inclusion necessary.[319] Certain milk powders, milk fat and cheeses are subject to specific protocols, annexed to the Arrangement.[320] Due account must be taken of the special and more favourable treatment on behalf of developing countries.[321]

4.3.2.4.1. Mechanisms of supervision

The Arrangement provided for the establishment of an International Dairy Products Council within the framework of GATT, comprised of representatives of all participants to the Arrangement. It must meet at least twice a year and may establish its own rules of procedure. The chairman may also call special meetings. This Council may invite observers. It is serviced by the GATT Secretariat. It makes decisions by consensus, that is to say that decisions are made if no member formally objects to a proposal. The Council may establish committees to carry out all the functions which are necessary to implement the provisions of the Protocols annexed to the Arrangement. Those committees shall meet at least once each quarter and reach decisions by consensus.[322]

The tasks of the Council are:

– to evaluate the world market situation and outlook;
– to review the functioning of the Arrangement;
– to assist in consultations between participants; and
– to identify possible remedial solutions for consideration by governments, if it finds that a serious market disequilibrium has developed or threatens.[323]

The participants are required to provide regularly and promptly to the Council the information that the latter needs to perform its functions. This includes data on past performance, current situation and outlook, as well as domestic measures and international commitments and any other information deemed necessary by the Council. Developed countries have to assist developing countries in collecting data upon request. The Council instructs the Secretariat to draw up and keep up to date an inventory of all measures affecting trade in dairy products, including commitments from international negotiations.[324]

Any participant may raise before the Council any matter affecting the Arrangement. Each participant shall promptly afford adequate opportunity for consultation regarding any such matter.[325] If the matter affects the application of the specific Protocols annexed to the Arrangement, and the participants are unable to reach a satisfactory solution among themselves, they may bring the matter to the Committee which administers the Protocol concerned. The latter must convene within four days. If a satisfactory solution cannot be reached, the Council is required to meet within a period of not more than 15 days to consider the matter with a view to facilitating a satisfactory solution.[326]

Nothing in this Arrangement shall affect the rights and obligations of participants that are cps to the GATT.[327] This means that if a participant considers that his problem has not been solved to his satisfaction, he can resort to the central dispute settlement procedure of Articles XXII and XXIII of the GATT.[328]

4.3.2.5. The Arrangement regarding Bovine Meat

Bovine meat is another severely distorted market. The trade in bovine meat is extensive and important, since a wide range of countries of all levels of development are large meat producers and exporters. During the Tokyo Round negotiations the Arrangement Regarding Bovine Meat was drafted. After it was acknowledged by the CP in 1979,[329] it came into force on January 1, 1980, for three years for the participants which accepted it. It provides for a possibility for further three-year extensions. The Council may decide that the extensions will cover a different period. It is open for acceptance by the same governments as may accede to the International Dairy Arrangement. Provisional application is possible.[330]

The objectives of the Arrangement are to promote expansion, liberalisation, stabilisation and international co-operation in the international meat and livestock market and trade, as well as to secure additional benefits for the international trade of developing countries.[331] The Arrangement covers bovine meat and any other product that may be added by the International Meat Council. It resembles the International Dairy Arrangement in many ways, though it lacks Protocols.[332]

4.3.2.5.1. Mechanisms of supervision

The Arrangement provides for the establishment of an International Meat Council, within the framework of GATT. The composition and procedures are similar to those of the International Dairy Committee. It is serviced by the GATT Secretariat.[333]

The tasks of the Council are:

– to evaluate the world market situation and outlook;
– to review the functioning of the Arrangement;
– to provide an opportunity for regular consultation on all matters affecting international trade in bovine meat;
– to assist in consultations between participants; and
– to identify remedial solutions for consideration by governments in situations of serious market disequilibrium or threat thereof.[334]

112

The participants are required to provide information in the same way as under the International Dairy Arrangement. The Secretariat must monitor variations in market data and keep the International Meat Council apprised of significant developments. The latter instructs the Secretariat to draw up and keep up to date an inventory of all measures and commitments resulting from international negotiations affecting trade in bovine meat and live animals.[335]

Participants are obliged to enter into discussions on a regular basis with a view to exploring the possibilities of achieving the objectives of the Arrangement, for which the Meat Council shall provide an opportunity.[336]

As in the case of the International Dairy Arrangement, any participant may raise before the Meat Council any matter affecting the Arrangement. Each participant must promptly afford adequate opportunity for consultation regarding such matters.[337] Nothing in the Arrangement affects the GATT rights and obligations of participants that are cps to the GATT, including the possibility of final resort to the central disputes settlement procedure of Articles XXII and XXIII.[338]

4.3.2.6. Evaluation

Qualification of the mechanisms of supervision

Article XIX provides for specific and political supervision of emergency actions. The cps themselves as well as the politically dependent organ exercise supervision. Review takes place primarily by reporting *ad hoc,* which might be followed by review by exchange of information. The correction takes place first through negotiations and sometimes via conciliation aimed at peaceful settlement as well as political discussions in the politically dependent organ. The political phase can be preceded by a technical phase. Correction in the second resort takes place by means of a sanction that is executed by the cps themselves, after authorisation by the politically dependent organ. The creative function is exercised by means of negotiations and political discussions.

Supervision on emergency actions under the Arrangement Regarding International Trade in Textiles is specific; it is performed by the participants themselves as well as by institutional bodies. In the latter case supervision is political, the emphasis falling on the technical phase. Review takes place via reporting *ad hoc,* exchange of information and complaints; correction by means of negotiations, mediation and conciliation aimed at peaceful settlement as well as political discussion. The creative function is performed by means of political discussions and negotiations. This supervision might constitute the basis for supervision under the GATT itself.

The International Dairy Arrangement and the Arrangement Regarding Bovine Meat provide for supervision by the cps themselves as well as by politically dependent organs. With regard to general supervision, the politically dependent organs are assisted by the Secretariat in the technical phase. The function of supervision is mainly review by means of reporting, though correction might be a consequence of the supervision. Specific supervision takes place by means of complaints, consultations and discussions. It is non-judicial and is exercised by the cps themselves as well as the politically dependent organs. The functions are review by means of communication, complaints and reporting *ad hoc*; correction by means of consultation and conciliation aimed at peaceful settlement and political discussion and creation by means of political discussion.

Conclusion

There has been much discussion concerning the multilateral safeguard system[339] lately, and in particular about the way in which Article XIX is applied. Many cps are dissatisfied with Article XIX. First, there is a need for more precise criteria for invocation of the safeguard clause, including the terms 'cause or threaten to cause serious injury' and 'critical circumstances'. Secondly, a time limit to safeguard measures and to ensure that they will decline over a period of time needs to be fixed. Finally, safeguards should be applied on a selective basis. Article XIX does not lay any foundation for socio-economic adjustment, but only allows for *ad hoc* measures. It does not provide the exporting cps with any protection. As a result Article XIX has been evaded many times, to the discontent of the exporting countries, which are mainly developing countries. It seems that in many instances Article XIX has been used not to acquire more time for necessary adjustments but to protect domestic producers.[340]

It often happens that cps, which are faced or threatened with an increase in imports and appear entitled to take emergency action under Article XIX, look for solutions outside of GATT. One of the reasons is that the injured cps are not allowed to discriminate in taking emergency actions under Article XIX. For example, if country A is injured by an increase of imports from country B the former may raise its tariffs. As a consequence, the imports from country B as well as those from third countries are impeded. Imports increase prosperity in the importing country. Therefore, a reduction of imports from third countries is not desired, since such a reduction will make the importing country suffer more than necessary for its domestic producers to be protected. Moreover, third cps might consider compensatory measures since their exports are hampered. To prevent this undesirable situation cps A and B might conclude an agreement regulating B's exports into A.[341] The cps concluding such agreements, which usually restrict the exports from B into A, avoid supervision based on the GATT.

During the Tokyo Round the multilateral safeguard system was discussed extensively. The EEC and Japan only wanted to talk about Article XIX. Other countries wanted to discuss other measures against market disruption that have been taken outside the GATT. Several proposals to amend Article XIX were made. Even a regulation for the adjustment of national economies and an obligation for countries that want to take emergency action to submit an adjustment scheme have been discussed. However, the resistance against commitments regarding domestic economic policy is too strong for the adoption of such a regulation to be feasible within the near future.[342]

During their thirty-fifth annual session, in November 1979, the CP agreed to establish a committee to continue the safeguards negotiations.[343] Although towards the end of the Tokyo Round both developed and developing country participants had accepted selectivity as a working hypothesis, agreement on a new safeguard system has not been reached, as disagreement regarding the implementation of selectivity prevails. Many countries want to apply strict rules, criteria and surveillance arrangements to the use of selective measures and require, *inter alia,* agreement by the affected exporting country in advance and actual material injury to domestic production in the importing country. Also a committee should be established to implement the code. One of its tasks would be to determine in advance whether all conditions for emergency measures have been fulfilled. For certain industrialised countries, some of these conditions were unacceptable, especially the advance determinations by the committee. They favour an approach that allows unilateral, selective action with subsequent review by the committee, especially in critical circumstances where delay would cause damage difficult to repair.[344]

Developing countries additionally attach great importance to reformulation of the existing safeguard rules, and several of them have put forward specific proposals. They would like to receive special and more favourable treatment. Safeguard action should be taken only after consultations, and be subject to authorisation by an appropriate multilateral body. Emergency action should only be allowed in case of actual material injury that is proven, not potential injury and must take into account the injury that might be caused to the export industries in developing countries.[345] These proposals have not resulted in changes in the multilateral safeguard system so far. In November 1979, the CP decided, however, that the Committee on Trade and Development[346] establish a sub-committee to examine any case of future protective action by developed countries against imports from developing countries.[347] This fulfilled a commitment embodied in Resolution 131 of the UNCTAD Conference at Manila in May 1979, inviting GATT to set up such a body.[348] In addition the conditions for safeguard action by developing countries were somewhat relaxed in 1979.[349]

Judgments on the effectiveness of the Arrangement Regarding International Trade in Textiles vary. The sessions of the TSB were not always attended by all its members. Most, though not all, import restricting measures and agreements were notified.[350] Supervision is hampered by lack of statistical material and other information due to late or insufficient notification.[351]

According to many countries the arrangement has been violated by the importing countries.[352] For instance, import restrictions have been introduced without prior consultations. In spite of this Arrangement the export of textiles still is severely restricted. The TSB has given a number of rulings but not all of them are being observed, especially the most recent ones.[353] Yet, in spite of distrust, a breakdown in substantive consensus, and increasing protectionism caused by oversupply, the TSB is said to have influenced governmental decision-making. Certainly, supervision by the TSB could be more effective, but the MFA objectives have been partly reached.[354]

The effectiveness of the International Dairy Arrangement and the Arrangement Regarding Bovine Meat cannot be judged yet, since these are in effect for too short a period of time.

A satisfactory mechanism for supervising emergency action is needed. A mechanism to regulate reallocations on the world market is also desirable. Such a mechanism could be established by amending Article XIX of the GATT or by concluding separate Agreements or Arrangements within GATT to regulate certain markets, as has been done for the textiles, dairy and bovine meat markets. One of the advantages of separate Arrangements is that States might be more willing to accept Arrangements with a limited scope, since the latter impinge less on their sovereign powers than an all-embracing regulation. By the same token, such an all-embracing provision would be more effective since it provides for supervision on emergency action or regulation regarding all commodities. It could be established by amending Article XIX or by adopting an Arrangement regarding all commodities.

4.3.3. Waivers

The drafters of the GATT were aware of the fact that world trade is subject to change and that it is virtually impossible to foresee every change. For example, it could be impossible for a cp that made a concession in 1950 to comply with its commitments. To prevent the situation where such a cp would have no alternative but to violate the GATT, the CP are authorised in Article XXV,5 to waive obligations imposed upon cps under the GATT. This contributes to GATT's flexibility.

Many waivers have been granted,[355] some of which are no longer in force. Waivers have been granted:

- to cps and newly or semi-independent territories to continue special preferential treatment that had been customarily conferred[356];
- to allow a nation to institute a new tariff nomenclature or fiscal reform pending renegotiation of its Schedule to reflect the new system[357];
- for associations of two or more States into preferential regional areas, when such associations do not technically qualify for exception under the criteria of Article XXIV[358];
- to authorise cps that are not parties to the IMF to escape the obligation of entering into a 'special exchange agreement' under Article XV,6[359];
- to allow a member to impose special tariff 'surcharges' because of balance of payment difficulties[360];
- for import quotas on agricultural goods[361];
- to extend time limits[362];
- to grant preferential treatment to developing countries[363]; and
- for other purposes, such as the waiver concerning certain 'hard-core' quantitative restrictions.[364] The latter was granted to cps that were previously allowed to have import restrictions for balance of payments reasons. As their balance of payment problems were solved, their domestic

producers were no longer protected. Since they needed extra protection, waivers have been granted to that end in some cases.[365] The most drastic waiver was the one to the U.S. in connection with import restrictions on behalf of the agricultural sector.[366]

4.3.3.1 Requirements for waivers

4.3.3.1.1 General requirements for waivers

Article XXV,5 contains three conditions for the granting of waivers. The first one is that there have to be 'exceptional circumstances'. These have never been defined. In practice, this requirement has never impeded the granting of waivers.[367]

The second condition is that the GATT does not deal elsewhere with such circumstances. The GATT provides for the competence to grant waivers in Articles XVIIIC and D and XXIV,10.[368] In practice, however, the CP also granted waivers under Article XXV,5 in cases where this could have been done under Article XXIV,10, because they are of the view that the text of Article XXV,5 allows them to waive any GATT obligation and places no limitations on the exercise of that right.[369] As long as the procedural prerequisites are fulfilled, the waiver is valid.[370]

The third requirement is that the decision must be approved by a two-thirds majority of the votes cast that comprises more than half of the cps.[371] The CP are not allowed to delegate their power to grant waivers to the Council.[372] The CP may define certain categories of exceptional circumstances to which other voting requirements apply to the waiver of obligations and may prescribe such criteria as may be necessary for the application of paragraph 5 of Article XXV, but have never done so.[373]

4.3.3.1.2. Requirements for a waiver from Part I

In addition to the requirements stated in Article XXV,5, waivers from Articles I and II are subject to extra requirements under the procedures adopted by the CP on November 1, 1956. Under these procedures:

– Applications for waivers must be submitted with at least 30 days' notice except in exceptional cases calling for urgent action.
– In the interval afforded by such notice the applicant cp must give full consideration to representations made to it by other cps and engage in full consultation with them.
– The CP should not grant a waiver in cases where they are not satisfied that the legitimate interests of other cps are adequately safeguarded.
– Any decision granting a waiver must also provide for an annual report and, where appropriate, for an annual review of the operation of the waiver.[374]

4.3.3.2. Mechanisms of supervision

There is supervision on the granting of waivers since a decision by the CP is required to that extent. However, once a waiver is granted, Article XXV,5 does not provide for supervision on cps that are allowed to deviate from the GATT under a waiver. As far as waivers from Part I are concerned, there is continuing supervision under the procedures adopted on November 19, 1956.[375] Nevertheless, in most decisions to grant a waiver, supervision on the deviations is provided for. Where this is not the case, the waiver has usually been granted for a limited period so that the deviation can be reviewed. When an extension of the waiver is requested,[376] supervision provided for in the decisions can consist of a duty to report,[377] a duty to submit annual reports,[378] consultations with other cps,[379] consultation with the CP, and annual review by the CP.[380] Sometimes a procedure similar to that of Articles XXII and XXIII is provided for.[301] The decision granting the waiver might allow other cps to suspend substantially equivalent concessions that were originally negotiated with the cp to whom the waiver is granted.[382]

The CP are not authorised explicitly to revoke a waiver. In the case where a waiver is granted for a limited period, the CP may refuse a renewal, which is tantamount to a revocation. Some decisions by which a waiver is granted provide for review by the CP. In the process of reviewing a waiver, it could be revoked.

4.3.3.3. Evaluation

Qualification of the mechanisms of supervision

Article XXV,5 provides for specific, non-judicial supervision on the granting of waivers by the politically dependent organ. The function of review is performed by reporting *ad hoc*. Correction and creation are performed by political discussion.

Once the waiver is granted, many kinds of supervision are possible, depending on the decision granting the waiver. It may be performed by the cps themselves as well as by a politically dependent organ and it may be specific as well as general. It is also non-judicial. The review function is performed by means of reporting *ad hoc*, reporting, exchanges of information and complaints; the correction function by means of political discussion, as well as negotiations, mediation and conciliation aimed at peaceful settlement. Very rarely are arbitration and sanctions provided for. The creative function is performed by means of political discussion. Very few decisions do not provide for supervision at all.

Conclusion

According to Jackson, the GATT would be well advised to establish a general set of principles for granting waivers in the future. According to Jackson's suggestions, all waivers would be limited to a period not longer than five years but be renewable. All waivers would require an annual report and, in the event of a request from any cp with a trade interest in the matter, a review or joint consultation. Time limits could be extended up to one year by a majority vote of the CP on the Council, subject to appeal to the CP if any cp wishes. Thirty days' notice would be required for application for almost all waivers. Finally, any waiver could be revoked at any time by a vote of two-thirds of the GATT membership.[383]

Such a change would result in a unification of the mechanisms of supervision on waivers. It would sharpen the supervision without detracting from its flexibility. The cp to whom a waiver is granted, however, would never be certain whether the waiver would remain valid and for how long he can enjoy it. It is not expected that the CP would accept the kind of change Jackson suggests, since the majority of the cps benefits from waivers at the moment.

Jackson also argues in favour of an expansion of the Council's competence. This would reduce the time needed to take decisions.[384] However, the granting of concessions can have drastic consequences. To grant a waiver for an unlimited period of time comes down to amending the GATT. Some have even argued for requiring unanimity for the granting of a waiver from Articles I and II since they amount in effect to an amendment.[385] The CP have rejected this argument, since the opening clause of Article XXX excepts modification under Article XXV from the requirement of unanimity.[386] Because of the drastic consequences waivers may have, one should be careful to delegate the authority to grant them to the Council.[387]

The specific supervision on the granting of waivers is not optimal but it is fairly satisfactory. The CP may provide for supervision on the waivers after they have been granted but are not obliged to do so. At the moment, the cps are not likely to accept supervision on all granted waivers. Therefore the actual provisions seem to give rise to the highest degree of supervision possible.

4.3.4. Quantitative restrictions I: Articles XI and XIII

4.3.4.1. The general prohibition of non-tariff restrictions

Pursuant to Article XI cps are not allowed to institute prohibitions or restrictions on imports and exports other than duties, taxes, or other charges, whether made effective through quotas, import or export licences, or other measures. The most common trade restriction imposed by national governments is the tariff, a 'tax' on imported goods. Tariff rates can be *ad valorem*, specific, or combined. In case of an *ad valorem* rate, a certain percentage of the value of the imported goods has to be paid as a tax; under a specific rate a certain amount of money per imported piece; and under a combined tariff a certain percentage of the value of the imported goods as well as a certain amount of money per piece. All three kinds of tariffs are allowed in principle, provided they are not applied in a discriminatory way and do not exceed the bindings.[388]

Trade restrictions other than tariffs are in principle prohibited under Article XI, which also applies to unbound items. The most common non-tariff restrictions are quantitative restrictions, also called quotas. For this reason Article XI is titled 'General Elimination of Quantitative Restrictions'.

A quota is a certain maximum quantity of a commodity that is allowed to be imported into a country within a certain period of time, usually one year.[389]

There are many kinds of non-tariff restrictions other than quantitative restrictions. Government aid, including subsidies is one of them. Article XVI provides for their application. Another kind is surcharges: tariff increases on top of the permitted rate. These are applied frequently by cps with balance of payments problems. They are not allowed in principle but can be permitted by means of a waiver under Article XXV,5.

Under specific circumstances the GATT allows quantitative restrictions:

- Under Articles XII and XVIII,B quantitative restrictions for balance of payments are permitted under certain conditions.[390]
- Pursuant to Article XVIII developing countries may apply quantitative restrictions under certain conditions.[391]
- Article XI,2, finally, permits the application of such restrictions with regard to agricultural products.[392]

Article XIII provides rules for the application of quantitative restrictions that are allowed. Article XIV allows for an exception to Article XIII in case of balance of payments problems.

Quantitative restrictions may be general; that is to say, that imports from all countries are restricted. Usually the total amount of permitted imports is allocated among the exporting cps according to their former shares in the import of the commodity concerned. Sometimes the first supplying cp is permitted to enter the market of the cp applying the quota although this is in conflict with the most-favoured-nation principle. The quotas may be allocated by means of import licences. Finally, State trading enterprises, possessing a monopoly, might restrict imports quantitatively. This issue is dealt with in Article XVII.[393]

4.3.4.2. The exceptions of Article XI,2

The exceptions provided for in Article XI,2 are related to the position agriculture held in post Second World War trade. Since the demand in this sector fluctuated strongly, programmes to stabilise the agricultural sector were introduced in many countries to guarantee the farmers a minimum income. Such programmes had to provide for a desirable level of sales, prices and incomes. A minimum price for agricultural products would lead to an increase of imports in the absence of trade restrictions. Consequently a large surplus would be created and the farmers' income would drop even more. In times of scarcity, the differences between fixed sale prices and those on the world market would stimulate exports, increasing the scarcities. To prevent such undesirable consequences of free trade the GATT allows the following exceptions to the prohibition of non-tariff barriers in Article XI,2[394]:

(a) export prohibitions or restrictions temporarily applied to prevent or relieve critical shortages of foodstuffs or other products essential to the exporting contracting party;

(b) import and export prohibitions or restrictions necessary to the application of standards or regulations for the classification, grading or marketing of commodities in international trade[395]; and

(c) import restrictions on any agricultural or fisheries product, imported in any form, necessary to the enforcement of governmental measures which operate to restrict the supply of the like product or of a domestic product for which the imported product can be substituted, to remove temporary surpluses and to restrict the supply of an animal product the production of which is dependent on the imported commodity.

It can be concluded from the preparatory works that government programmes that simply take off the domestic market surpluses and dump them abroad are not covered under Article XI,2.[396]

4.3.4.3. The application of quantitative restrictions

Article XIII deals with the application of allowed quantitative restrictions. It is basically an attempt to apply a most-favoured-nations obligation to quotas which are by nature inherently discriminatory.[397] It contains several obligations that apply also to tariff quotas and export restrictions in so far as applicable.[398] First of all, under paragraph 1, no prohibition or restriction shall be applied in a discriminatory way. In the second place, pursuant to paragraph 2, the distribution of trade must approach as closely as possible the shares which the various cps might be expected to obtain in the absence of such restrictions. In paragraph 2, the preferable methods of distribution are also mentioned. Quotas representing the total amount of permitted imports are the most preferred, whether allocated among supplying countries or not.[399] In cases in which quotas are not practicable, import licences or permits without quotas could be applied.[400] Cps are not allowed to require import licences or permits to be utilised for importation from a particular source.[401]

Finally, in cases in which a quota is allocated among supplying countries, the cp applying the restrictions may seek agreement with all other cps having a substantial interest in supplying the product concerned with respect to the allocation of shares. In cases in which this method is not reasonably practicable the shares must be allotted on the basis of the proportions supplied during a previous representative period, due account being taken of any special factors affecting the trade in the product,[402] that are described in an Interpretative Note.[403]

4.3.4.4. Supervision on the application of quantitative restrictions

Supervision on the compliance of the above-mentioned rules is provided for in paragraphs 3 and 4 of Article XIII. Paragraph 3 deals with notification and contains three kinds of obligations:

(1) In cases in which import licences are issued, the cp applying the restrictions must provide upon request of any cp having an interest, all relevant information concerning the administration of the restrictions,

the import licences granted over a recent period, and the distribution of such licences. There is no obligation to supply information as to the names of importing or supplying enterprises.[404]

(2) In the case of import restrictions involving the fixing of quotas, public notice of the total quantity or value of the product or products which will be permitted to be imported during a specified future period as well as of any change in such quantity or value must be provided. Any supplies of the product in question which were en route at the time at which public notice was given shall not be excluded from entry provided that they may be counted against the newly imposed quotas.[405] During the Torquay session in 1950, the CP decided that supplies with a sufficiently confirmed order are to be admitted under the same conditions as supplies en route.[406]

(3) In the case of quotas allocated among supplying countries, the cp applying the restrictions must promptly inform all other cps having an interest in supplying the product concerned of the shares in the quota currently allocated by quantity or value, to the various supplying countries and shall give public notice thereof.[407]

With regard to restrictions applied in accordance with Articles XI,2(c) and XIII,2(d) the selection of a representative period for any product and the appraisal of any special factors affecting the trade in the product must be made initially by the cp applying the restriction, provided that such cp must, upon the request of any other cp having a substantial supplying interest, or upon the request of the CP, consult promptly with the other cp or the CP regarding the need for an adjustment of the proportion determined, or of the base period selected, or for the reappraisal of the special factors involved, or for the elimination of conditions, formalities, or any other provisions established unilaterally relating to the allocation of an adequate quota or its unrestricted utilisation.[408]

Any contracting party applying restrictions on the importation of any product pursuant to Article XI,2(c) must give public notice of the total quantity or value of the product permitted to be imported during a specified future period and of any change in such quantity or value.[409]

4.3.4.5. Evaluation

Qualification of the mechanism of supervision

Supervision on quantitative restrictions under Articles XI and XIII is mostly exercised by the cps themselves and is non-judicial. There is specific supervision only on the selection of a representative period and the valuation of special factors regarding the trade in a certain product. Such supervision is exercised by the politically dependent organ. The review function is performed by reporting *ad hoc*. The correction function is performed by negotiations aimed at peaceful settlement, as well as through the mobilisation of shame. Sometimes the latter function is performed by conciliation aimed at peaceful settlement.

122

Conclusion

The obligations of Article XI never really became effective.[410] Export prohibitions or restrictions under paragraph 2(a) were never needed, since there have been surpluses on the world market for agricultural products since 1947. In the near future the only conceivable export prohibition or restriction would be one for oil, since oil is an essential product.

The import restrictions that are allowed to be introduced under paragraph 2(c) are subject to stringent conditions. The cps found they could not control domestic agricultural support policies sufficiently to permit the kind of import access called for by Article XI.[411] The United States tried to restrict the import of dairy products under Article XI,2, but the CP thought the U.S. failed to comply with the requirements and authorised the Netherlands, who had brought a complaint under Article XXIII to suspend GATT obligations vis-à-vis the U.S.[412] For the rest, Article XI was never invoked. Nevertheless there are numerous import restrictions on agricultural products, many of which are violating the GATT. The U.S. received a complete waiver for its price support programme in 1955,[413] which is still valid. Many countries shelter domestic agriculture behind balance of payments restrictions. Other restrictions are simply in violation of GATT.[414] The European agricultural policy, especially the variable levy, is not in accordance with the spirit of GATT.[415]

When the GATT rules were originally drafted they were intended to apply to trade in agricultural and industrial products alike, though some variation was possible under Articles XI and XIII. In practice, however, trade liberalisation has been far less effective with regard to agricultural products than with regard to industrial products. Trade liberalisation gives rise to more problems in the field of agriculture because of the fundamental political and social factors governing the protection of farmers and the link between production policies and measures and import restrictions. Moreover, the protective measures used in agriculture are varied and complex so that the negotiation of balanced reductions is particularly difficult.

During the Tokyo Round, negotiations on agricultural products have been thwarted by differences in approach between the U.S.A. and the EEC. According to the U.S. the same treatment and solutions should be applied to agricultural products and industrial products alike. For the EEC agriculture has unique characteristics sharply distinguishing it from the industrial sector. The EEC prefers solutions in the form of managed markets and does not want to consider tariffs or other barriers to trade in isolation from other domestic measures. During the Tokyo Round the sub-group 'Agriculture' has dealt with the problems in the agricultural sector. As a result some arrangements regarding certain agricultural products such as grains, bovine meat and dairy products[416] have been made.[417]

The negotiations on agricultural trade restrictions show that the cps admit that Article XI is not effective. Other solutions might be found in the form of separate Agreements and Arrangements or the creation of a general framework for the reduction of trade barriers in the field of agriculture.

4.3.5. Quantitative restrictions II: import restrictions for balance of payments reasons

Under a system of fixed exchange rates, as was agreed upon in 1944 at Bretton Woods, balance of payments surpluses or deficits may arise. These can be absorbed by changes in the monetary reserves in the short run. However, in the long run such an absorption is impossible since the keeping of too many reserves generates domestic inflation and interest costs and since such reserves will eventually be used up in case of continuing deficits. The equilibrium in the balance of payments might be restored in three ways:

(1) the country involved could revaluate or devaluate its currency;
(2) it could take domestic measures to regulate its economy on a macro scale; and
(3) it could restrict or promote imports and exports.

Often a combination of these three methods is applied.

After the Second World War most countries had balance of payments deficits. Because of their obligations under the IMF they were not free to devaluate their currencies. Domestic measures to regulate the economy require a fair amount of internal discipline, which was and still is lacking or insufficient in many countries. Moreover, such measures have tended to be unpopular. Therefore, most countries sought a solution by restricting imports, especially by means of quotas. This is risky since import restrictions by one country will lead to a decrease in exports of other countries that might be faced with deficits in their balance of payments as a consequence. This would be a reason for them to restrict their imports as well. In this way a chain of import restrictions could develop that could even terminate international trade. To prevent this from happening, international regulation is required.

Currently not all States apply a system of fixed exchange rates. From March 1973 onward a large number of western States have operated under a system of floating exchange rates. Theoretically they would not have to intervene in the currency market and would not need monetary reserves for their balance of payments policy, as continuous depreciations and appreciations will maintain an equilibrium in the balance of payments automatically. In practice, however, these countries do intervene in the currency market to promote their exports by means of artificial depreciations or to prevent fluctuations from becoming too wide.

In 1976 Fred Bergsten noted that there were still more than 100 countries maintaining fixed exchange rates in relation to the U.S. dollar, which accounted for 30 per cent. of world trade.[418] Today, this situation has not changed much. Most of these countries are developing countries whose exports are price fixed since such exports consist mainly of primary products. Therefore, their export revenues decrease when they devaluate their currency.[419] Consequently, these countries cannot restore the equilibrium in their balance of payments in case of a deficit by devaluating their currency. Since domestic measures to regulate their economy are not feasible either, the only instrument they have to combat balance of payments deficits is trade restrictions.[420]

A minimum amount of trade restrictions is beneficial to the international community. But so are equilibria in the balances of payments of the various countries and stable exchange rates.[421] Reduction of trade barriers is one of the GATT's intermediate objectives.[422] To that end a number of provisions have been included in the GATT such as Article XI, prohibiting quantitative restrictions. However, a number of exceptions are allowed in certain precisely defined circumstances, such as balance of payments problems, to promote stable balances of payments and exchange rates.

Article XII of the GATT deals with restrictions to safeguard the balance of payments. Article XVIII, B contains almost identical provisions for restrictions to safeguard the balances of payments of developing countries. Several CP decisions have altered and refined the applicable procedures. The second text relating to the framework for conduct of international trade contains a Declaration on Trade Measures for Balance-of-Payments Purposes adopted by the CP in 1979.[423] This text is further referred to as the second framework text.

4.3.5.1. Criteria for exceptions

According to Article XII,1 any cp may restrict the quantity or value of merchandise permitted to be imported, in order to safeguard its external financial position and its balance of payments subject to the provisions of the other paragraphs of Article XII. Under Article XII,2(a) import restrictions instituted, maintained, or intensified by a cp may not exceed those necessary

(1) to forestall the imminent threat of, or to stop a serious decline in its monetary reserves, or
(2) in the case of a cp with very low monetary reserves, to achieve a reasonable rate of increase in its reserves.

Due regard must be paid in either case to special factors which may be affecting the reserves of such cp or its need for reserves, including, where special external credits or other resources are available to it, the need to provide for the appropriate use of such credits or resources.[424] In cases where the CP have to decide whether these criteria have been met, they have to accept the determination of the IMF as to what constitutes a serious decline in the cp's monetary reserves, a very low level of its monetary reserves, or a reasonable rate of increase in its monetary reserves, and as to the financial aspects of other matters covered in consultation in such cases.[425]

4.3.5.2. Rules for application

All cps imposing quantitative restrictions under Article XII are required to adhere to the following rules:

- They must progressively relax quantitative restrictions as conditions improve, maintaining only to the extent that the conditions mentioned above justify them.[426]
- They must avoid unnecessary damage to the commercial or economic interests of other cps.[427]
- They must allow minimum commercial quantities of each description of goods to avoid impairing regular channels of trade.[428]
- They are not allowed to apply restrictions that would prevent the importation of commercial samples or prevent compliance with patent, trademark, copyright or similar procedures.[429]
- In carrying out their domestic policies, cps must pay due regard to the need for maintaining or restoring equilibrium in their balance of payments on a sound and lasting basis and to the desirability of avoiding an uneconomic employment of productive resources.
- They recognise that it is desirable to adopt measures which expand rather than contract international trade.[430]
- However, imports of certain products deemed more essential may be preferred over other imports.[431]

In 1950 the CP elaborated a series of methods that would promote the policies toward which the rules are aimed, that is, minimising the undesirable incidental protective effects of restrictions. These methods include avoiding encouragement of investments in enterprises which could not survive without protection and making domestic producers aware of the fact that foreign competition will return.[432]

Under Article XXXVII,1(b) developed cps are required to refrain from introducing or increasing the incidence of (customs duties or) non-tariff import barriers on products currently or potentially of particular export interest to developing cps. This restricts the possibility to impose quantitative restrictions under Article XII for developed cps.

4.3.5.3. Mechanisms of supervision

4.3.5.3.1. Consultations with a view to introducing or increasing import restrictions

Any cp applying new restrictions or raising the general level of its existing restrictions shall, according to Article XII,4(d), consult with the CP, if possible in advance. In 1966 the CP adopted procedures for dealing with new import restrictions applied for balance of payments reasons. Any cp modifying its import restrictions is required to furnish detailed information promptly to the Director-General[433] for circulation to the cps.[434] In GATT practice it has happened that the Director-General, after learning, through press or other reports, that restrictions were increased, has drawn the attention of the cps to the measure concerned, thus effectively, although not technically, initiating consultations.[435] The cp concerned consequently reported the modification.

126

Should the modification come down to an introduction or increase in a quantitative restriction, consultations are required. The Council, to whom the CP have delegated their competence regarding these matters, should be convened to meet with the shortest possible delay, which should normally not be less than 48 hours and not more than 10 days after the receipt of the notification, to carry out the consultation. In cases where the cp applying the restriction has not asked for a consultation with the CP, the Council may invite that cp to consult in accordance with Article XII,4(a),[436] if the Council considers that there is a *prima facie* case of substantial intensification requiring such a consultation. The Council arranges for the consultations and should invite the IMF to consult as soon as consultations are initiated. The Council reports to the CP.[437] During every consultation the CP must have due regard to any special external factors adversely affecting the export trade of the cp applying restrictions.[438] The CP are required to make provisions for the utmost secrecy in the conduct of the consultations under Article XII.[439]

4.3.5.3.2. Review of existing restrictions

The original GATT required a general review of quantitative restrictions in force on a day not later than January 1, 1951.[440] The CP prepared such a review on the basis of information submitted in response to a questionnaire drafted by the Secretariat and sent to all cps.[441] During the 1955 amendments, Article XII was revised. On that occasion, Article XII,4(b) was drafted saying that on a date to be determined by them, the CP had to review all restrictions still applied under Article XII on that date[442] This review was started in January 1958. The Secretariat drafted another questionnaire to send to all cps and made a draft report, followed by a WP report.[443] The final report was adopted and published in 1959.[444]

4.3.5.3.3. Annual Consultations

Ever since the review of 1958, cps applying import restrictions under Article XII must consult annually with the CP according to Article XII,4(b).[445] The consultations are conducted by the Committee on Balance of Payments Restrictions[446] according to a Plan and Schedule approved by the Council. The Committee formulated a plan of discussion in 1958,[447] that served as a guideline for the consultations. In 1970 new balance of payments import restrictions consultation procedures were adopted.[448] Under these procedures the consultations are based on documents provided by the cp applying the restrictions and the IMF and circulated by the Secretariat. The basic document provided by the cp applying the restrictions must cover eight different points mentioned in Annex II. Annex I provides for the Plan of Discussion for the consultations. At the conclusion of each consultation the Committee on Balance of Payments Restrictions must draw up a report that must be circulated to all cps and must be submitted to the Council for approval and for forwarding to the next session of the CP.[449] The second framework text reaffirms the obligations under the GATT and the procedures for consultations of 1970. In addition, it allows cps which have reason to believe that a restrictive import measure applied by another cp was taken for balance of payments purposes to notify the measure to the GATT. Less-developed cps may at any time request full consultations.[450]

In 1960, 12 cps were required to consult annually.[451] In 1975, five cps were obliged to do so.[452] From November 1977 to November 1978, four unpublished reports came out on annual consultations under Article XII with Finland, Israel, Portugal and Yugoslavia. It has not always been clear whether a cp applying import restrictions is invoking Article XII or Article XVIII,B.[453] Therefore it has not always been clear either, whether the consultations were held under Article XII,4(b) or Article XVIII,12(b). In 1980 the Committee on Balance of Payments Restrictions carried out full consultations with Greece, Israel, South Korea, the Philippines, Portugal and Tunisia. Bangladesh, Egypt, Ghana, India, Indonesia, Pakistan, Peru and Sri Lanka consulted under the simplified procedures scheme.[454]

4.3.5.3.4. Legal remedies for the CP

If in the course of the above-described consultations with a cp the CP find that the restrictions are not consistent with Article XII or XIII, and are not allowed under Article XIV as well, they must indicate the nature of the inconsistency and may advise that the restrictions be suitably modified. However, if they determine that:

(a) the restrictions are being applied in a manner involving an inconsistency of a serious nature with Articles XII and XIII and are not allowed under Article XIV; and
(b) that damage to the trade of any cp is caused or threatened thereby,

they must so inform the cp applying the restrictions and must make appropriate recommendations for securing conformity with such provisions within a specified period of time. If such cp does not comply with these recommendations within the specified period, the CP may release any cp, the trade of which is adversely affected by the restrictions, from such obligations under the GATT toward the former cp as they determine to be appropriate in the circumstances.[455]

4.3.5.3.5. Complaint-initiated consultations

The CP must invite any cp which is applying restrictions under Article XII to enter into consultations with them at the request of any cp provided that:

(a) it can establish a *prima facie* case that the restrictions are inconsistent with Articles XII or XIII and not allowed under Article XIV;
(b) its trade is adversely affected thereby; and
(c) direct discussions between the cps concerned have not been successful.

If as a result of the consultations with the CP no agreement is reached and they determine that the restrictions are being applied inconsistently with the above-mentioned provisions and that damage to the trade of the cp initiating the complaint is caused or threatened thereby, they must recommend the withdrawal or modification of the restrictions. If the restrictions are not withdrawn or modified within such time as the CP may prescribe, they may release the cp initiating the procedure from such obligations under the GATT towards the cp applying the restrictions as they determine to be appropriate in the circumstances.[456]

Article XII,4(d) provides for the same remedies as does Article XXIII, but under the former they are subject to more stringent requirements. The cp initiating the complaint has to establish *prima facie* that the GATT provisions have been violated and that its trade is adversely affected. Violation of the GATT is not a condition to bring a 'claim' under Article XXIII. On the other hand, under Article XII the CP are obliged to recommend the withdrawal or modification whereas Article XXIII requires only rulings and appropriate recommendations, leaving the CP the option not to authorise suspension. A quantitative restriction gives rise to a *prima facie* nullification or impairment even if the former conforms to the GATT.[457] *Prima facie* nullification or impairment requires *ipso facto* consideration by the CP, or a subsidiary organ, to the question whether the circumstances are serious enough to justify the authorisation of suspension of concessions or obligations.[458] In other words, complaints concerning quantitative restrictions require recommendation of their withdrawal unless it is proved that they do not lead to nullification or impairment.[459] This being the case, the difference between remedies under Articles XII and XXIII is negligible. Therefore, Article XII,4(d) has never been invoked in practice. Complaints concerning import restrictions for balance of payments reasons were put forward under Article XXIII.[460]

4.3.5.3.6. Discussions in case of a general disequilibrium

A persistent and widespread application of import restrictions under Article XII indicates a general disequilibrium. In such a situation the CP shall initiate discussions to consider whether other measures might be taken[461] to remove the underlying causes of the disequilibrium. The cps have to participate in these discussions upon the initiation of the CP.[462] This kind of discussion, however, has never taken place.

4.3.5.4. Evaluation

Qualification of the mechanisms of supervision

Within GATT general supervision exists for the introduction or increase of the restrictions for balance of payments reasons. Supervision is exercised by a politically dependent organ, assisted by the Secretariat.

Information necessary for the review function is given by means of reporting *ad hoc*. The correction function is primarily performed by means of political discussion behind closed doors. In case the restrictions are in conflict with GATT and affect or threaten to affect the trade of another cp, correction by means of a sanction is possible. This sanction is to be executed by the injured cp. The creative function is performed by non-public political discussions.

A politically dependent organ exercises general supervision on existing restrictions. The political phase is preceded by a technical one. Information necessary for the review function is gained through reporting. The correction and creative functions are performed in the same way as with supervision on the introduction or increase of restrictions.

Complaint-initiated supervision under paragraph 4(d) is specific, and non-judicial. It is exercised by the cps themselves as well as by a politically dependent organ. Information on behalf of the review function is given by means of complaints and reporting *ad hoc* during the consultations. The correction function is performed by peaceful settlement primarily by means of negotiations and at a later stage via mediation and conciliation by the CP. This function may also be performed by a sanction constituting an *ultimum remedium*. Sanctions are executed by the injured cps themselves after an authorisation by the CP.

The remedies provided in paragraphs 4(c) and 4(d) are not identical. Under the procedure of paragraph 4(c), which is initiated by the CP, the CP may only advise that the restrictions be modified. Only in the case of an inconsistency of a serious nature does the CP have to make recommendations, and the CP may release affected cps from obligations. Under the procedure of paragraph 4(d) the CP may do the latter in case of violations of any nature; they are even obliged to do so if all requirements mentioned in this paragraph are met.

One might question whether the discussions under paragraph 5 can be qualified as supervision. If this is the case, it would be supervision of the maintenance of the equilibrium. It constitutes general supervision by a politically dependent organ. The instrument on behalf of the review function is reporting *ad hoc*. The correction function is performed by political discussions in the first place, but also by negotiations and conciliation aimed at peaceful settlement. The creative function is performed by political discussion. The CP could discuss measures to reduce a general disequilibrium, even if the provision of paragraph 5 did not exist. However, the cps would not be obliged to participate if that were the case.

Commentary

The requirements of paragraph 2(a) under (i) and (ii) are obviously attuned to a system of fixed exchange rates. This is caused by the fact that in 1948 the Bretton Woods system was applied all over the world. Under a system of floating exchange rates, states might want to impose import restrictions to prevent too strong a depreciation. It would be desirable to make such restrictions possible by adding the following as a third criterion to paragraph 2(a): 'to prevent undesirable depreciations'. The same result could be obtained by a very broad interpretation of the term 'monetary reserves', thus making it encompass the value of the currency as well.

Article XII only allows quantitative restrictions when balance of payments problems occur. Some cps, however, want to improve their external position by levying surcharges. Import surcharges are not authorised at all by the

GATT and require a waiver from Article II. In the period from 1970 to 1974 24 cps were applying import surcharges. Only eight of them received a waiver, the other 16 are applied in violation of GATT. Nine of the surcharges applied by cps during this period were not considered in the GATT at all.[463] Other trade measures used to improve balances of payments are export subsidies although they are not generally considered as a balance of payments measure. In Article XVI the GATT rules applicable to those subsidies can be found.[464] Other trade measures applied to combat balance of payments problems are import deposit schemes, that are often violative of Article II, and voluntary export restraints.[465] Japan, for instance, adopted such restraints in 1972 for balance of payments reasons.[466]

Many consultations have been held under paragraphs 4(a) and 4(b) because of introductions or increases of quantitative import restrictions. In 1948 all cps, with the exception of the U.S., applied quantitative restrictions for balance of payments reasons.[467] In 1960 most developed countries had solved their balance of payments problems[468] so they could not invoke Article XII in future. At the moment the wealthiest cps do not apply restrictions that are permitted pursuant to Article XII. Within the OECD, the developed countries have agreed to avoid import restrictions for balance of payments reasons in 1974 for a period of one year.[469] This agreement was extended five times, each time for a period of one year, but it was not extended for 1980. As balance of payment problems increase, it is conceivable that some of them will invoke Article XII in the future. Even the U.S., which has never invoked Article XII, could be forced to do so. Before 1973 the U.S. had never lost its monetary reserves, since everybody accepted the American dollar. Therefore, the U.S. could finance its deficits by issuing its own currency. Now, a strong U.S. dollar is no longer a given fact.

The supervision of import restrictions for balance of payments reasons has functioned reasonably, in spite of the fact that there is less pressure on the cps because of the secrecy of the discussions. Nevertheless, the supervision is not perfect. First of all, not all import restrictions have been reported. Also, surcharges and import deposit schemes have been applied, on which the Committee on Balance of Payments Restrictions, that is actually charged with supervision on import restrictions, cannot exercise supervision. Finally, some import restrictions legitimately introduced under Article XII have not been removed after legitimate reasons for their imposition had lapsed.[470]

The supervision could be improved by providing the Committee on Balance of Payments Restrictions with a broader mandate, comprising supervision on all trade measures for balance of payments reasons and the elimination of residual restrictions.[471] Also the Secretariat could circulate questionnaires, so that more cps would report their restrictions. The complaint-initiated procedure of Article XII,4(d) has never been used since its function has been taken over by the central dispute procedure.[472]

4.3.6. Quantitative restrictions III: residual restrictions

In 1947 all cps, except the U.S., applied quantitative restrictions. Hudec describes the GATT of 1947 as 'the exchange of U.S. tariff reductions for a commitment by the countries of Europe to eliminate their balance of payments restrictions just as soon as conditions permitted'.[473] After 1947 most quantitative restrictions were abolished. In 1960 most developed cps could not invoke Article XII any more since the IMF had certified that their trade and payments situation had improved enough to make restrictions unnecessary.[474] At that time most import restrictions were abolished but not all of them.

During the period in which imports had been restricted, domestic industries were established or maintained that produced at higher costs than their foreign competitors. They could stay in the market because of the protection given by the quotas. If the latter were abolished, however, those industries would be priced out of the market. In some instances governments thought the industries concerned of vital importance since either they did not want to become dependent on the imports of certain goods from abroad, or they wished to prevent unemployment and social unrest. Therefore, they kept on applying quantitative restrictions, although the legal ground to do so had lapsed; these were the so-called residual restrictions.

4.3.6.1. The so-called 'hard core waiver'

The CP recognised that the sudden removal of quantitative restrictions can lead to serious problems for the cp applying those restrictions. Therefore they have taken a decision concerning problems raised for cps in eliminating import restrictions maintained during a period of balance of payments difficulties. According to this decision cps could under certain conditions obtain a waiver to maintain quotas that were allowed under Article XII, after their balance of payments problems had ceased.[475] This constitutes the so-called 'hard core waiver'. The possibility of obtaining such a waiver expired in late 1962.[476] The CP recognised that in certain cases some transitional measure of protection by means of quantitative restrictions may be required for a limited period to enable an industry, having received incidental protection from those restrictions which were maintained during the period of balance of payments difficulties to adjust itself to the situation which would be created by removal of those restrictions. Therefore, the CP decided that, subject to the concurrence of the CP in each case, the obligations of Article XI may be temporarily waived to the extent necessary to allow the maintenance of a restriction applied on imports to meet the exceptional circumstances described above.

The applicant cp had to communicate its request before it ceased to be entitled to maintain the restriction under Article XII and in any case not later than December 31, 1957, or a later date determined by the CP.[477] The applicant had to provide necessary information to support its request. The restriction had to have been continuously in force since January 1, 1955 and its sudden removal had to result in serious injury to a domestic industry. All other solutions consistent with GATT had to be proved not to be practicable and there had to be a reasonable prospect of eliminating the restriction over a comparatively short period of time. Furthermore, the applicant cp had to agree to aim at the elimination of the restriction within a short period of time, to grant other cps a fair and reasonable share of the market for the product concerned. Finally, the total restrictive effect should not exceed the effect of the restriction in force on January 1, 1955. The CP were not allowed to grant waivers for a period exceeding five years from the date it was granted. The restrictions had to be administered in a way consistent with the GATT. The cp concerned had to communicate regularly to the CP the total amount of the product the importation of which would be authorised by it during the following licensing period and to submit an annual report to the CP on the basis of which the CP would review the hard core waivers. Any concurrence given in accordance with this decision did not preclude the right of cps affected to have recourse to Article XXIII.[478]

Belgium was the first cp that, according to the IMF, did not have any balance of payments difficulties. In 1955 that country disinvoked Article XII and received a hard core waiver for a seven-year period.[479] The Federal Republic of Germany was declared 'sound' by the IMF in the summer of 1957. Although it still applied many restrictions it did not request a waiver at first but it issued a statement in June 1957 in which the economic difficulties existing with regard to the further extension of the liberalisation of imports were explained and pointing out that the existing measures were applied in a liberal manner. Late in 1957, it issued a statement announcing the liberalisation it planned between 1958 and 1960, which would only be partial.[480] At first many cps disagreed with this practice but as the debate went on many governments toned down their opposition.[481] In 1959 the Federal Republic of Germany requested and obtained a waiver under Article XXV,5.[482]

4.3.6.2. The reporting procedure for residual restrictions

In 1959 and 1960 the IMF certified that the balances of payments of many developed countries were sound. Nevertheless, these countries maintained import restrictions without even requesting a waiver. However, Australia and the United Kingdom circulated a list of their remaining restrictions together with a statement of proposals to deal with them to all cps, promptly upon disinvocation of Article XII. The United States urged that action should be undertaken against these residual restrictions violating GATT. In 1960 the Council agreed to a procedure along the lines suggested by the U.S.[483] Subsequently the CP approved these procedures for dealing with (new import restrictions applied for balance of payments reasons and) residual restrictions on November 16, 1960.[484]

Under these procedures the cps are invited to communicate to the Director-General[485] lists of imports restrictions which they are applying contrary to the GATT provisions and without having obtained the authorisation of the CP. The cps involved may seek bilateral consultations pursuant to Article XXII,1. The Director-General must be informed of consultations requested so that in cases where the interests of a number of cps are affected, the procedures adopted by the CP on November 10, 1958, apply.[486] If such consultations do not lead to a satisfactory solution any of the parties to the consultations may request that consultations be carried out by the CP pursuant to Article XXII,2. Alternatively a cp whose interests are affected may resort to Article XXIII,2.[487] The invitation to list is not restricted to residual restrictions, but concerns all restrictions that are technically illegal, and, in addition, those protected by the protocol reservation.[488]

A Panel was established to examine the adequacy of the notifications of residual restrictions.[489] Its final report indicates that in 1962, 15 out of 41 cps had notified that they applied residual restrictions, 22 had denied such application and four cps did not respond. The list of residual restrictions applied by France covered only import restrictions against former OEEC countries, Canada and the U.S.[490] Some cps thought that France had maintained too many restrictions. Consultations on this matter took place under Article XXII,2 but produced no satisfactory results.[491]

4.3.6.3. Other attempts to eliminate residual restrictions

The U.S. was dissatisfied since it thought the other cps' attitudes towards France too lenient. After consultations with Italy and France regarding the import restrictions that the two European countries still applied, the U.S. filed a complaint against the two under Article XXIII,2. The complaint against Italy was only a marginal affair from the beginning. When the case came up for plenary discussion, the U.S. withdrew the complaint on the ground that satisfactory progress had been made.[492] A Panel was established to deal with the complaint against France. The Panel ruled that there was nullification of benefits to which the U.S. is entitled under GATT and recommended that the restrictions be removed. It recommended, too, that the U.S. refrain from immediate retaliation.[493] As it became obvious that France had not eliminated its restrictions the U.S. again requested approval of a specific retaliation proposal under Article XXIII,2.[494] The Council reaffirmed the earlier Panel decision ruling that there was nullification and asked the parties to consult bilaterally on the quantity of retaliation. During these consultations the case was settled.[495]

In spite of the reporting procedures of 1960, residual restrictions continued to exist. The Committee on Trade and Development became active on behalf of the elimination of residual restrictions of developed countries against imports from developing countries. In March 1965, it set up a special Group on Residual Restrictions to examine the remaining restrictions on products of export interest to developing countries and to explore the possibility of their early removal. The group held discussions with several developed countries on restrictions applied by the latter to products included in a list of approximately 250 items notified to Committee III.[496] The Committee on Trade and Development suggested that the CP adopt Panel procedures with regard to "hard core" restrictions on industrial products from developing countries.[497] The CP agreed that, *inter alia*, Panels of governmental experts might be established to this end.[498] However, the developed countries did not feel obliged to co-operate. Therefore, the Panels never functioned well.[499]

New Zealand proposed a procedure according to which cps wishing to apply residual restrictions should ask for a waiver to do so. This proposal was not accepted.[500]

In October, the GATT Secretariat proposed the establishment of a Joint Working Group responsible to both the Industrial and Agricultural Committees. It should examine all restrictions regardless of their legal status.[501] The Group met only once and commissioned the preparation of a new inventory.

The Group of Three, established by the Committee on Trade and Development, also concerned itself with residual restrictions.[502] As a consequence, a number of those restrictions have been removed.[503]

4.3.6.4. Evaluation

Qualification of the mechanisms of supervision

The "hard core" waiver provided specific non-judicial supervision of the maintenance of residual restrictions. It also provided general, non-judicial supervision after the waiver was granted. In both instances it was performed by a politically dependent organ. The instruments of the review function were reporting *ad hoc* at the time of the application and reporting afterwards. The correction function was performed through political discussion and the mobilisation of shame. Next to this supervision, supervision under the central dispute settlement procedure remained possible.

The reporting procedure of 1960 provides for general non-judicial supervision by a politically dependent organ. Review takes place on the basis of reporting and correction via the mobilisation of shame. This procedure constitutes the basis for other mechanisms of supervision, especially the central one.

Commentary

The "hard core" waiver has seldom been used. Supervision based on the reporting procedure of 1960 is rather weak. The cps are not obliged to report and, with regard to dispute settlement, the procedure does not add anything to that of Articles XXII and XXIII. Most cps notified their restrictions eventually but they have not always provided sufficient information. The other initiatives of the GATT bodies did not have much success. Only the Group of Three contributed to the elimination of some residual restrictions applied by developed cps against imports from developing countries. However, the number of residual restrictions that remained is much greater than those eliminated.

Hardly any complaints were filed because of the existence of residual restrictions. The Joint Working Group had to explore legal and illegal restrictions alike and to consult on the elimination of both of them. Therefore, one might conclude that the existence of residual restrictions has been accepted as a reality by the cps. However, a number of cps are not prepared to eliminate legal restrictions in exchange for the elimination of illegal restrictions. They are of the opinion that illegal restrictions should be eliminated without any compensation.

The existence of illegal restrictions indicates that there is no complete compliance with GATT. On the other hand, many restrictions were eliminated since the GATT was concluded in 1947. The elimination of the remaining restrictions will involve higher social, economical and political costs in relation to those eliminated earlier. Although those who argue that illegal quantitative restrictions should be eliminated regardless are right from a legal point of view, a sudden elimination can often not be realised in practice. However, an uncontrolled application of quantitative restrictions is far from desirable. Therefore, supervision on such restrictions should be increased, for instance, by establishing a special waiver procedure. As long as the cps do not accept such a procedure, the cps should try to eliminate residual restrictions by means of negotiations.

4.3.7. Subsidies

Governments can influence international trade by granting subsidies or other kinds of aid to producers or consumers. However, international competition will be distorted if domestically produced commodities, as a consequence of subsidies or other kinds of governmental support, are supplied at a lower price than the price of like commodities from abroad. Governments can promote exports, too, by means of subsidies or other kinds of aid. This distorts international trade as well since the price of commodities from such a country will be lowered on the world market. However, world trade will be promoted by such subsidies.

A clear distinction between the different kinds of government aid that are given cannot always be made. Subsidies might constitute a non-tariff barrier. Therefore they are of concern to GATT.

Article XVI deals with subsidies. A precise definition of subsidies is not provided for, either in Article XVI or in the Interpretative Note to this Article. According to the Interpretative Note to Article XVI, the exemption of an exported product from duties or taxes borne by the like product when destined for domestic consumption, or the remission of such duties or taxes in amounts not in excess of those which have accrued, are not deemed to be a subsidy.[504]

A measure can be considered a subsidy within the meaning of Article XVI not only if it causes increased exports or decreased imports but also when exports are at a higher level, or imports at a lower level, than would otherwise exist in the absence of the subsidy. Measures providing an incentive to increased production are considered to be subsidies, too, in the absence of offsetting measures. The concept of 'subsidy' is broadly interpreted. A WP has listed government measures that are considered as forms of export subsidies.[505] This list is not exhaustive.[506]

136

4.3.7.1. Supervision on subsidies in general

4.3.7.1.1. Notifications

Concerning subsidies in general, Article XVI,1 determines that if any cp grants or maintains any subsidy, including any form of income or price support, which operates directly or indirectly to increase exports of any product from or reduce imports of any product into its territory it shall notify the CP in writing of the nature and extent of the subsidisation, of the estimated effect of the subsidisation on the quantity of the affected product or products imported into or exported from its territory and of the circumstances making the subsidisation necessary. On March 2, 1950, the CP decided that all existing subsidies had to be notified to the CP not later than August 1, 1950, and that any new measure of subsidisation or modifications had to be similarly notified after that date as soon as possible after they were instituted. Also, the Secretariat had to transmit to each cp all notifications received.[507] During their ninth Session, the CP adopted a list of standards in connection with notifications under Article XVI.[508] This list was revised during their sixteenth Session.[509] On November 9, 1962, the CP adopted procedures for notifications in which the cps were invited to submit by the end of January 1963 and subsequently every third year, new and full responses to the questionnaires. During 1963 the Council had to examine the adequacy of the notifications received if necessary by re-establishing the Panel or by setting up a WP. The Secretariat has to circulate all notifications to all cps.[510]

4.3.7.1.2. Discussions

In any case in which it is determined that serious prejudice to the interests of any other cp is caused or threatened by a subsidisation the cp granting the subsidy must, upon request, discuss with the other cp or cps concerned, or with the CP, the possibility of limiting the subsidisation.[511] The cp that requests discussions may determine itself whether there is prejudice caused or threatened. The existence of an injury need not be determined first by the CP[512] or another GATT body. Nothing in the terms of Section B of Article XVI[513] limits the scope of consultations envisaged under paragraph 1 of this Article.[514]

Apart from discussions under Article XVI,1 consultations under other GATT provisions are possible especially under Articles XXII and XXIII. For example in the case of the Australian Subsidy on Ammonium Sulphate, consultations were held under Article XXIII and not under Article XVI.[515] There have been few discussions under Article XVI, probably because no cp really wants to open discussions as most of them grant or maintain subsidies themselves.

4.3.7.2. Export subsidies

In 1955 additional provisions on export subsidies were added to Article XVI as Section B.[516] The cps recognise that the granting by a cp of a subsidy on the export of any product may have harmful effects for other cps, both importing and exporting, may cause undue disturbance to their normal commercial interests, and may hinder the achievement of the objectives of the GATT.[517] Accordingly, cps should seek to avoid the use of subsidies on the export of primary products. If, however, a cp grants any form of subsidy, which operates to increase the export of any primary product from its territory, this must not result in the acquisition of more than an equitable share of the world market by that cp.[518] In other words, such subsidies are prohibited. According to Article XVI,4 no cp should extend the scope of any export subsidy on any other product than primary products beyond that existing on January 1, 1955, by the introduction of new, or the extension of existing, subsidies. As from January 1, 1958, or the earliest practicable date thereafter, the cps should cease to grant export subsidies on such products, if this would result in the sale of such products for export at a price lower than the comparable price charged for the like product to buyers in the domestic market. The intention of paragraph 4 is that the cps should seek, before the end of 1957, to reach agreement to abolish all remaining subsidies as from January 1, 1958, or failing this, to reach agreement to extend the application of the standstill until the earliest date thereafter by which they can expect to reach such agreement.[519]

At first, the standstill was extended four times for a period of one year by means of a declaration that the cps were free to accept or not. The cps in the fourth declaration declared that they would communicate to the Executive Secretary a list of export subsidies in force on November 30, 1957, and notify him of any changes in these measures. Also they agreed to an annual review by the CP on the progress made in the abolition or reduction of export subsidies existing on November 30, 1957.[520] This declaration was extended until December 31, 1961.[521] Not until 1964 was a second declaration on the standstill provisions of Article XVI,4 adopted that is similar to the one adopted on November 30, 1957. It was in force until December 31, 1967.[522] No further extensions have been published.

On November 19, 1960, a declaration was adopted that gave effect to Article XVI,4 for cps that sign the declaration.[523] Those cps were not allowed to grant export subsidies on behalf of non-primary products. Seventeen industrialised cps accepted this declaration.

4.3.7.3. Supervision on the operation of Article XVI

According to paragraph 5 of Article XVI, the CP must review the operation of this Article from time to time with a view to examining its effectiveness in the light of actual experience, promoting the objectives of GATT and avoiding subsidisation seriously prejudicial to the trade or interests of cps. To this end, they have established a Panel on Subsidies to undertake preparatory work for the review. This Panel was required to examine the range and extent of subsidies maintained by cps, to discuss with the cps any point requiring clarification and any other comment or suggestion put forward by other cps, to make practical suggestions to the CP and to assemble material for the draft report on the operation of Article XVI.[524] The Panel convened four times in the period from 1959 to 1961.[525]

The Panel could not reach any final conclusions on the effect of subsidies since the latter are hard to distinguish from the effects of quantitative restrictions for balance of payments reasons and tariffs and since the cps themselves had provided too little information on the effects of subsidies, especially regarding non-primary products. Any logical classification of purposes of subsidies as expressed by the notifying countries was impracticable because of the lack of uniformity in the terminology used and differences of emphasis in describing objectives which were essentially the same.[526] This Panel also drafted a revised questionnaire.[527] The notifications proved to be generally inadequate. An invitation by the Panel to provide information on subsidies irrespective of whether in the view of individual cps they were notifiable under Article XVI has been insufficiently followed.[528]

Hardly any requests for discussions under Article XVI,1 were forwarded by the cps. One of the reasons for the reluctance of governments to initiate discussions is that most governments employ subsidies themselves. The Panel considered the number of cases of consultation or complaint of little help in determining the effectiveness of Article XVI. The best test of the effectiveness of the Article is the extent to which it has restrained cps from adopting or increasing subsidies in violation of GATT's objectives. This restraining effect, however, is impossible to measure. The Panel could not agree on an interpretation of what constitutes a subsidy and referred to clarifications of certain aspects of this problem in earlier reports.[529]

4.3.7.4. Supervision on subsidies in practice

The specific supervision on subsidies consists of a notification procedure and consultations. The notifications draw the attention of the cps on the existence of subsidies, which may provoke them to take counter-measures. To this end three GATT procedures could be used:

(1) A cp may levy a countervailing duty, not exceeding an amount equal to the subsidy pursuant to Article VI,3[530];
(2) a cp could invoke the GATT escape clause, provided that all requirements of Article XIX are fulfilled[531]; and
(3) the central dispute settlement procedure is applicable.[532]

The cps may make concessions regarding subsidies such as undertaking to abolish a particular subsidy or not to increase it.[533] Such concessions are included in the Schedules that are an intregral part of GATT. To institute or increase the subsidies concerned would violate GATT and would therefore constitute a *prima facie* nullification or impairment.[534] Moreover, in the case of a subsidy on a product on which the subsidiser has granted a concession, for example, not to levy a tariff exceeding 10 per cent. *ad valorem*, the introduction or increase of a subsidy would be a *prima facie* nullification or impairment for the purposes of Article XXIII.[535]

As was mentioned in paragraph 4.3.7.1.2. the cps used the central procedure to settle their disputes concerning subsidies. A well-known case is that of the Australian Subsidy on Ammonium Sulphate, regarding an import restricting subsidy.[536] There have been more cases regarding export subsidies such as the case of the American export subsidy on raisins in 1953,[537] the Danish complaint about export subsidies on eggs granted by the Government of the United Kingdom in 1957,[538] the Australian complaint against French export subsidies in 1958,[539] the Malawian complaint against an American export subsidy on tobacco in 1966,[540] and the Japanese complaint of 1977 regarding suspension of customs liquidation by the United States.[541] In 1978 Australia and Brazil filed complaints on the EEC sugar export refund system.[542] The number of complaints was rather small, since potential plaintiffs grant subsidies themselves.[543]

In connection with the notifications the CP may institute examinations. They did so, for instance, in pursuance of a notification by some Western cps of the application of export inflation insurance schemes. Under these schemes exporters received refunds for the purpose of inflation correction. At its meeting on July 15, 1976, the Council established a WP on Export Inflation Insurance Schemes to examine, from the point of view of their effects on international commerce and in the light of the GATT provisions, such schemes and any other measures used to attenuate or compensate for the effects of cost inflation. The WP had available an OECD Report, information submitted by cps relating to the schemes and measures concerned, communications from the EEC and Finland and a Statement by France. The WP carried out a detailed examination of the schemes introduced by various cps and discussed them. The WP could not reach any unanimous conclusion as to the compatibility of the export inflation insurance schemes with the GATT provisions. Several members of the WP held the view that such schemes were subsidies in contravention of Article XVI,4 and should be notified under Article XVI,1. They were concerned over the distortive effect of the schemes and over the fact that the programmes encouraged the adoption of similarly distortive measures by other cps. Several other members of the WP, however, held the view that export inflation insurance schemes were only in contravention of the GATT where they could be shown to be subsidies under the terms of Article XVI. Some of them did not consider the schemes in question to be subsidies. In consequence these members did not subscribe to the call for the termination of the existing schemes. Export inflation insurance schemes are not on the list of export subsidies in the WP report of November 19, 1960.[544] However, this list is not exhaustive.[545]

4.3.7.5. The new code on subsidies (and countervailing duties)

During the Tokyo Round an Agreement on Interpretation and Application of Articles VI, XVI and XXIII of the GATT, the so-called Subsidies Code, was drafted, which entered into force on January 1, 1980.[546] This Code does not replace any of the GATT provisions but supplements the GATT. Parts II to VII deal with subsidies.

Under this Code, signatories are obliged to provide information to any other signatory at the request of the latter. Any signatory which considers that such information has not been provided may bring the matter to the attention of the Committee on Subsidies and Countervailing Measures.[547] In case subsidies have not been notified under GATT Article XVI,1, other signatories to the Subsidies Code may do so.[548]

The signatories recognise that subsidies, especially subsidies other than export subsidies, are used by governments to promote import objectives of social and economic policy. The signatories agree that they shall seek to avoid causing, through the use of any subsidy:

(a) injury to the domestic industry of another signatory;
(b) nullification or impairment of the benefits accruing directly or indirectly to another signatory under the GATT; or
(c) serious prejudice to the interests of another signatory.[549]

Export subsidies are prohibited, except export subsidies on certain primary products. An illustrative list of export subsidies is annexed to the Agreement.[550] The provisions of GATT Article XVI,3 apply to export subsidies on certain primary products.[551] For developing countries less stringent rules are applicable.[552]

Article XII provides for consultations. Whenever a signatory has reason to believe that an export subsidy is being granted or maintained by another signatory in a manner inconsistent with the Subsidies Code or that a subsidy in general is being granted or maintained which causes injury to its domestic industry, nullification or impairment of benefits, or serious prejudice to its interests, such signatory may request consultations with such other signatory. If a mutually acceptable solution in the case of export subsidies has not been reached within 30 days of the request for consultations, any signatory party to such consultations may refer the matter to the Committee on Subsidies and Countervailing Measures for conciliation in accordance with the provisions of Part IV of the Code. In cases regarding other subsidies than export subsidies the time period is 60 days. These time periods may be extended by mutual agreement. If the dispute is not resolved as a result of consultations, the Committee must, upon request, review the matter in accordance with the dispute settlement procedure of Part IV. If the Committee concludes that the suspicions of the requesting signatory are true, it must make such recommendations to the parties as may be appropriate to resolve the issue. In the event the recommendations are not followed it may authorise such counter-measures[553] as may be appropriate, taking into account the degree and nature of the adverse effects found to exist.[554]

The Agreement provides for the establishment of a Committee on Subsidies and Countervailing Measures composed of representatives from each of its signatories, which must among other things, afford signatories the opportunity of consulting on any matters relating to the operation of the Agreement on the furtherance of its objectives. The GATT Secretariat acts as the Committee's Secretariat. The Committee may set up subsidiary bodies as appropriate. The Committee and its subsidiary bodies may consult with

141

and seek information from any source they deem appropriate. However, before seeking such information from a source within the jurisdiction of a signatory, it is required to inform the signatory involved.[555] In cases where matters are referred to the Committee for conciliation the Committee is required to immediately review the relevant facts and encourage the signatories involved to develop a mutually acceptable solution. Should the matter remain unresolved any signatory may, 30 days after the request for conciliation, request that a Panel be established by the Committee.[556]

The Committee is obliged to establish such a Panel within 30 days. The latter is required to review the facts of the matter and present its findings concerning the rights and obligations of the signatories party to the dispute. The Panel must deliver its findings within 60 days. It must be composed of three or five members, preferably governmental, who are not citizens of the countries whose governments are parties to the dispute. In order to facilitate the constitution of Panels the Chairman of the Committee should maintain an informal indicative list of qualified persons, who could be available for serving on Panels. Panel members would serve in their individual capacities. The Panel should first submit the descriptive part of its report to the parties concerned and should subsequently submit its conclusions to them. After a reasonable period of time its conclusions are reported to the Committee. Third signatories with an interest in the matter have a right to be informed about the solution. If no satisfactory solution has been reached, the Committee shall present recommendations to the parties within 30 days of the receipt of the Panel report. If those recommendations are not followed within a reasonable period, the Committee may authorise appropriate counter-measures to be undertaken by the complaining party.[557]

No specific action against a subsidy of another signatory can be taken, except in accordance with the provisions of the GATT, as interpreted by the Subsidies Code. Action under other relevant provisions of the GATT is not precluded.[558]

The Committee must review the implementation and operation of the Code annually and it must inform the CP to the GATT of developments during the period covered by such review.[559]

4.3.7.6. Evaluation

Qualification of the mechanisms of supervision

Supervision of subsidies by means of the notification procedure is general, objective and non-judicial. It is performed by a politically dependent organ. Review is performed on the basis of reporting *ad hoc* and correction by the mobilisation of shame. This procedure constitutes the basis for other mechanisms of supervision.

The discussions procedure provides specific, non-judicial supervision by the cps of a politically dependent organ. The review function is performed on the basis of a complaint, the correction function by means of negotiations and conciliation aimed at peaceful settlement and political discussion.

142

There is general, non-judicial supervision on the operation of the provisions of Article XVI by a politically dependent organ assisted by a technical body. The review function is performed on the basis of inquiries and reporting *ad hoc*, the correction function and the creative function are performed by means of political discussions.

The new Code regarding Subsidies (and Countervailing Duties) provides for general as well as specific supervision on subsidies. It is performed by the cps as well as by a politically dependent organ. The latter may be assisted by a subsidiary organ in the technical phase. Reporting *ad hoc* and complaints are the instruments for the review function. The correction function is performed by negotiations and conciliation aimed at peaceful settlement as well as political discussions and recommendations, in which the cps may be authorised to apply sanctions.

Commentary

Subsidies distort international competition. They can have the effects of non-tariff barriers to trade. The effects of subsidies have become more noticeable lately, since tariffs and quantitative restrictions have been reduced under the GATT. This is one of the reasons that subsidies were dealt with not earlier than during the Kennedy and the Tokyo Rounds. Only during the Tokyo Round was a detailed regulation drafted on the subject.

The granting of subsidies need not be detrimental. Subsidies increase the welfare of consumers in the importing country. Furthermore, they constitute an instrument to achieve domestic social and economic goals that might prevail over an optimal international allocation. Governments granting such subsidies, however, should weigh these national interests against those of their trade partners and that of an optimal international allocation. The new Code on Subsidies and Countervailing Duties provides guidelines to this end.

Supervision on the granting and maintaining of subsidies should be stringent, since the latter may have huge impacts on international competition. Supervision by means of the notification procedure of Article XVI,1 is dependent on notifications by the cps. Therefore, cps might withdraw from this kind of supervision. This happened in the early sixties when the Panel, that reviewed the operation of Article XVI in 1961, reported that the information provided by the cps was insufficient and could not be assessed nor qualified.[560] Under the new Code the effectiveness of supervision is increased, since other cps may notify subsidies, too.

The consultation procedure of Article XVI has hardly been used. Nor have there been many complaints about subsidies under the central dispute settlement procedure. One of the reasons that so few proceedings have been initiated is probably that most cps do not wish to raise the issue of subsidies, since they grant or maintain them themselves as well.

Supervision under the new Code is more stringent than under Article XVI. In addition to notification, it provides for dispute settlement. The dispute settlement procedure of the Code strongly resembles that of GATT Articles XXII and XXIII. However, it differs from the latter since it sets

143

limits within which the different phases of the procedure must be dealt with. This could make this procedure more effective than GATT's central dispute settlement procedure. Although GATT's central dispute settlement procedure need not be replaced by the one under the new code, the latter could be used more, since it could be more effective, and since a smaller, more homogeneous group of signatories is involved. Subsidies on production have been considered unfair competition because they lower prices in export markets with which domestic and third-country producers must compete. But production subsidies do not create a divergence between the prices received by a producer for units sold abroad and at home. Export subsidies, however, do distort the international trade in the subsidised commodities directly.[561] They cause buyers in the home market to pay more than those in foreign markets. The GATT sees export subsidies as less desirable, but they are not completely prohibited.

Export subsidies represent a direct attempt by the subsidising government to gain a greater share of foreign markets and help national products to climb foreign tariff walls. An export subsidy is equivalent to a negative tariff.[562] For the parties to the Declaration giving effect to Article XVI,4 export subsidies on non-primary products are not allowed. Developed cps that signed the new Code are likewise restricted. Export subsidies on primary products are subject to stringent conditions.

Supervision on subsidies under the original GATT is insufficient, especially since the number of subsidies granted and maintained increases. The new Code could improve the situation considerably.

4.3.8. State trading enterprises

The GATT system is based on the assumption that private enterprises are importing and exporting commodities on commercial grounds. The GATT seeks to limit the influence of government measures on world trade. The GATT rules cannot easily be applied to State trade since under a State trading system prices do not determine the quantity supplied and the amount of imports and exports are determined on the basis of the central economic plan. Often political considerations underly such an economic plan. To make adherence to the GATT possible for States with a centrally planned economy as well as to control the consequences of the State trading enterprises in States with a free-market economy or with a mixed economy, a number of provisions are included in the GATT. The most important one can be found in Article XVII. Furthermore, Article II,4 deals with State monopolies on behalf of products described in one of the Schedules annexed to the GATT and the cps are obliged to grant no less favourable treatment to imported products than that accorded to like products of national origin according to Article III,4; this also applies if State trading enterprises are in charge of the trade.

Pursuant to the Interpretative Note at Articles XI, XII, XIII, XIV and XVIII, throughout these Articles the terms 'import restrictions' or 'export restrictions' include restrictions made effective through State trading operations. It can be assumed that all GATT provisions apply as far as practicable where State trading enterprises are involved, since there is no indication to the contrary.

4.3.8.1. Rules of conduct for State trading enterprises

Article XVII contains rules of conduct for State enterprises and enterprises to which exclusive or special privileges are granted by a State concerning purchases or sales involving either imports or exports.[563] The Interpretative Note to this Article provides some criteria as to which enterprises are subject to the rules of Article XVII,1.[564] State trading enterprises are required to act in a manner consistent with the general principles of non-discriminatory treatment prescribed in the GATT and shall make any purchases or sales solely in accordance with commercial consideration.[565] These rules do not apply to imports or products for immediate or ultimate consumption in governmental use.[566] In paragraph 3 the cps recognise the importance of negotiations to limit or reduce the obstacles to the expansion of international trade that might be created by State trading enterprises.

4.3.8.2. Mechanisms of supervision

Supervision on State trading enterprises is provided for in paragraphs 4(a), (b) and (d). The cps are obliged to notify the CP of the products which are imported into or exported from their territories by State trading enterprises.[567] The CP may, at the request of a cp which has reason to believe that its interests under the GATT are being adversely affected by the operaion of a State trading enterprise, request that the cp establish, maintain or authorise such enterprise to supply information about its operations related to the carrying out of the GATT provisions.[568] The provisions of paragraph 4 do not require any cp to disclose confidential information.[569]

Supervision on import monopolies is dealt with in paragraph 4(b). A cp establishing, maintaining or authorising such a monopoly of a non-bound item must, on the request of another cp having a substantial trade in the product concerned, inform the CP of the import mark-up of the product during a representative period, or when it is not possible to do so, of the price charged on the resale of the product. In principle, this could apply to private enterprises, but in practice the establishment of an import monopoly is not possible without government support. Supervision on monopolies is more stringent than that on other State trading enterprises, since monopolies are not checked by competitors. Accordingly, an increase of the resale price is not punished by a decrease in sales.

Paragraph 4, which was added to Article XVII when GATT was amended in 1955, did not enter into force until 1957. Before that date few complaints concerning violations of GATT by State trading enterprises were made, probably because little information on their conduct was available. In November 1957 the CP decided to call for notifications under Article XVII,4(a) and specified that each notification should contain certain information.[570] The first set of these notifications was received and published by

GATT in August 1958.[571] A Panel was constituted to review these notifications and concluded that the latter were inadequate. Therefore, it adopted a new questionnaire which was approved by the CP.[572] The new questionnaire contains also a question about the import make-up,[573] so that at present there is no difference between import monopolies and other State trading enterprises as far as supervision is concerned.

Just like the Panel, established at a later point in time for the review of Article XVI, the above-mentioned Panel has interpreted the GATT Article concerned, in this case Article XVII.[574] The Panel invited all cps to furnish the information requested on the questionnaire and to submit statements even when they did not maintain State trading enterprises.[575] The answers to the questionnaire were disappointing, mainly because most responses did not clearly indicate the reasons and purposes which led cps to institute and maintain State trading enterprises, particularly in terms of their effect on trade. As a consequence the CP could not judge the extent to which such enterprises serve as a substitute for other measures covered by the GATT, such as quantitative restrictions, tariffs and subsidies.[576]

On November 9, 1962, the CP adopted procedures for notifications and reviews regarding State trade.[577] The notifications procedure is the same as that for the notification of subsidies.[578] The cps have to respond to a questionnaire every third year starting in January 1963. A subsidiary questionnaire was adopted in 1962 to obtain information relating to the GATT efforts to reduce barriers to the exports of less-developed countries.[579]

4.3.8.3. Evaluation

Qualification of the mechanisms of supervision

Supervision of State trading enterprises is general and non-judicial. Supervision is exercised by the politically dependent organ which might be assisted during the technical phase by subsidiary organs as well as by the cps in some cases. The review function is performed by reporting and reporting *ad hoc*, sometimes on the basis of questionnaires. The correction function is performed by mobilisation of shame and via political discussions. This procedure might underlie other procedures of supervision.

Commentary

Supervision of State trading enterprises is little developed, although general supervision is provided for. The notifications procedure has as a drawback the fact that the supervision depends on the cps which maintain or authorise State trading enterprises. The actual influence of a State trading enterprise on the allocation of commodities is often difficult to assess, especially when such enterprises operate within a centrally directed economy as are prevalent in Eastern Europe. For this reason it is difficult to determine whether cps establishing, maintaining or authorising State trading enterprises comply with GATT.

However, the information provided for in the notifications is useful for the drafting of new GATT provisions and might be of help during negotiations. Moreover, a cp might be restrained from misuse of State trading enterprises because of the obligation to notify. Supervision is weakened by the fact that confidential information need not be provided.

Since 1962, supervision of State trading enterprises has not increased. One of the reasons for this is that there already is supervision on the activities of East-European State trading enterprises, that make the most use of such enterprises, since their Protocols of Provisional Accession are reviewed periodically.

State trading enterprises may restrict imports of export commodities for too low a price. Since the imports of the East-European States exceed their exports, undesirably large import restrictions are not to be expected. However, they would not be able to finance an increase in imports because of their balance of payments deficits.

The EEC and some other Western cps, however, fear low-priced exports from East-European States. Therefore the EEC maintains quantitative restrictions, in violation with GATT, against imports from those States. In 1973, for example, quantitative restrictions inconsistent with Article XIII of the GATT affected 49 per cent. of Hungarian exports to the EEC. As a defence, the representative of the EEC stressed that the quantitative restrictions had been progressively eliminated. Moreover, he argued that the Hungarian system of subsidies constituted a permanent threat which would increase once the Communities had eliminated their quantitative restrictions. The export prices of the products in question were too low, so that there was a *prima facie* case of dumping.[580] Negotiations are being held to eliminate these restrictions.[581]

Stringent supervision on State trading enterprises seems impossible as the impact of their activities on the economy is hard to assess and as Eastern European countries will not allow international supervision on domestic affairs. The same argument applies to State enterprises in other cps, be it to a lesser extent. Therefore perhaps the best way of dealing with this issue would be: annual negotiations between the cps involved about the activities of State trading enterprises. Possibly the management of the enterprises concerned could participate in or attend such negotiations.

4.3.9. Protection against government aid and dumping

4.3.9.1. The reason for compensating duties

If a product is sold on a non-perfect market, or a minimum sales price for such a product is fixed, producers may be saddled with surpluses. To dispose of these surpluses, they might offer the poducts concerned abroad for a lower price than the normal one [582]; in other words, they might dump the products concerned. The difference between the normal value and the export price is called the margin of dumping. Dumping is done by private enterprises and is in principle not forbidden under the GATT, that addresses States. However, the cps must prevent dumping if it causes or threatens material

147

injury to an established industry in the territory of another cp or materially retards the establishment of a domestic industry.

Since products are supplied abroad for a lower price than the normal one, dumping distorts trade abroad. This is likely to injure producers in the importing countries. To prevent injury the importing cps might wish to levy anti-dumping duties.

By the same token the granting or maintaining of subsidies or the actions of State trading enterprises may distort trade. Since in that case barriers to trade are created as a consequence of government interference, there are GATT rules to control these practices.[583] These rules do not eliminate all subsidies and State trading enterprises. Consequently, distortions remain possible, against which cps may want to levy countervailing duties.

A cp which levies compensating duties might overcompensate. This would constitute protection in violation of GATT. In the last decade protection by means of overcompensation has been used as other forms of protection, such as tariffs and quantitative restrictions, lost their strength, because of the GATT.

4.3.9.2. GATT Provisions on Anti-dumping and Countervailing Duties

GATT Article VI mentions the circumstances under which cps may deviate from the GATT to compensate for dumping or government aid. The cps may take compensating measures as long as they do not violate GATT. They are, for example, allowed to increase unbound tariffs, provided they do not violate the Most-Favoured-Nation Clause. Under certain conditions they are even allowed to increase bound tariffs[584] and increase tariffs only with regard to products originating from one country[585] pursuant to Article VI.

Many countries were dissatisfied with the GATT provisions on anti-dumping and countervailing duties and its functioning in practice for three reasons:

(1) the definitions in Article VI are not precise and therefore subject to differing interpretations among the cps;
(2) there is no mention in Article VI of administrative and procedural arrangements for the investigation of alleged dumping and the collection of anti-dumping duties; and
(3) many of the cps were exempt from the obligations of Article VI because of the so-called grandfather clause, which exempts all national legislation predating the signing of or the accession to the GATT.[586]

Since so many cps were discontent, the CP at their thirteenth session established a Group of Experts to exchange information regarding the technical requirements of existing legislation on anti-dumping and counter-vailing duties in their respective countries and to suggest any other technical requirement of such legislation which might be usefully discussed at a later date.[587] This group submitted two reports that were published in 1961.[588] Most attention was given to anti-dumping duties.[589]

In 1967 during the Kennedy Round an Agreement on Implementation of Article VI of the GATT was concluded that came into force in 1968. It has two parts: an Anti-dumping Code and Final Provisions.[590] The Agreement is concluded to interpret the provisions of Article VI of the GATT and to elaborate rules for their application in order to provide greater uniformity and certainty in their implementation.[591] The Agreement only deals with anti-dumping duties. Countervailing duties are not mentioned. Since it is a separate Agreement it applies only as between signatories. However, it might be taken into consideration in disputes involving non-signatories, since the Agreement contains interpretations of Article VI that may be cited as evidence of the *opinio iuris*.

During the Tokyo Round separate Codes on subsidies and countervailing duties as well as on anti-dumping were drafted.[592] These too are separate Agreements that are only binding for signatories. They have been in force since January 1, 1980.[593] Governments that are not cps to the GATT may accede to these Codes on terms to be agreed upon between those governments and the signatories.[594] The acceptance of the 1979 Anti-dumping Code carries denunciation of the 1967 Anti-dumping Code on the date of entry into force of the former for the party concerned.[595]

4.3.9.3. Requirements for Compensating Duties

The first requirement mentioned in Article VI is the existence of dumping or a subsidy or bounty. Dumping occurs when 'products of one country are introduced into the commerce of another country at less than the normal value of the products'.[596] This is so if the price of the exported product:

(a) is less than the comparable price, in the ordinary course of trade, for the like product when destined for consumption in the exporting country, or,
(b) in the absence of such domestic price, is less than either
    (i) the highest comparable price for the like product for export to any third country in the ordinary course of trade, or
    (ii) the cost of production of the product in the country of origin plus a reasonable addition for selling cost and profit.

Due allowance must be made in each case for differences in conditions and terms of sale, for differences in taxation, and for other differences affecting price comparability.[597]

Where the exporting country has a State trading monopoly and fixes all domestic prices itself, importing countries have to take into account that a strict comparison with domestic prices may not be appropriate.[598]

A definition of subsidies is provided neither in Article VI nor elsewhere in the GATT. Multiple currency practices can be considered as constituting a subsidy or dumping in certain circumstances.[599]

A second requirement is that the dumping or the subsidy causes or threatens material injury to an established domestic industry or materially retards the establishment of such an industry. The term industry is intended to include 'such activity as agriculture, forestry and mining as well as manufacturing'.[600] A single firm does not constitute an industry.[601] According to the Anti-dumping Codes, the term domestic industry refers to the domestic producers as a whole of the like product or to those of them whose collective output constitutes a major proportion of the total domestic production.[602]

The importing country determines whether there is injury. There are no requirements as to how this should be done. The 1967 Anti-dumping Code contains more stringent requirements. Investigation and administration procedures are prescribed and rules for the determination of material injury, the threat of such injury and material retardation are laid down. A determination of injury or of threat thereof, shall be based on facts and not merely on allegation or possibility. Positive evidence of injury is required. The authorities are only allowed to determine the injury when the dumped imports are demonstrably the principal cause of material injury or the threat thereof.[603] Provisional measures may be taken only when a preliminary decision has been taken that there is dumping and when there is sufficient evidence of injury.[604]

The CP may waive this second requirement so as to permit one cp to levy an anti-dumping or countervailing duty on the importation of any product for the purpose of offsetting dumping or subsidisation by another cp, which causes or threatens material injury to a domestic industry or a third cp, exporting the product concerned into the first cp. If the CP find that a subsidy is causing or threatening material injury to a domestic industry of the third cp, they are obliged to allow countervailing measures by the first cp on behalf of the third one.[605] In exceptional circumstances, however, where delay might cause damage which would be difficult to repair, a cp may levy a countervailing duty on behalf of another cp without prior approval of the CP. In that case such action must be reported immediately to the CP and the countervailing duty must be withdrawn promptly if the CP disapprove.[606] As a consequence of national programmes for price and income support for primary products, the export price may be lower than the price paid by domestic consumers. If the cps substantially interested in the commodity concerned have determined that the system has also resulted in the sale of the commodity for export at a price higher than the domestic one and the system is so operated as not to stimulate exports unduly and does not otherwise seriously prejudice the interests of other cps, it is presumed that material injury does not result.[607]

The anti-dumping duties should not exceed the margin of dumping. In case of hidden dumping by associated houses, such as multinationals, there is no export price on the basis of which the margin of dumping could be determined. In that case the margin of dumping is calculated on the basis of the price at which the goods are resold by the importer.[608] Countervailing duties should not exceed an amount equal to the estimated bounty or subsidy.[609] Anti-dumping and countervailing duties may not be levied by reason of the exemption of a commodity from taxes on duties borne by the like product when destined for consumption in the country of origin or exportation, or by reason of refund of such duties or taxes.[610] Nor shall any product be subjected to anti-dumping as well as countervailing duties.[611]

150

Pursuant to the Protocols of Provisional Applications these requirements do not apply to anti-dumping and countervailing duties under legislation in force within States before they became a cp to the GATT. However, the 1967 Anti-dumping Code obliges signatories to adjust existing legislation.[612]

4.3.9.4. Mechanisms of supervision

4.3.9.4.1. Supervision under the GATT

Article VI does not provide for specific supervision on all compensating duties. However, should a cp wish to levy compensating duties on behalf of another cp, Article VI,6(b) provides for specific supervision by the CP, or the cps have to request a waiver from the CP. Under Article VI,7 the cps substantially interested exercise supervision amongst themselves on dumping and subsidies on primary products pursuant to systems for the stabilisation of the domestic price or the return to domestic producers. For the rest there is supervision under the central mechanisms of supervision.

4.3.9.4.2. The 1967 Agreement on Implementation of Article VI of the GATT

The 1967 Agreement on Implementation of Article VI of the GATT provides for supervision on anti-dumping duties. First of all, under the first part, the Anti-dumping Code, there is supervision among the signatories themselves. According to Article 5, the authorities must have evidence both of dumping and of injury resulting therefrom.[613] Under Article 6 they have to give foreign suppliers and all other interested parties ample opportunity to present counter-evidence. Throughout the investigation all parties must have a full opportunity for the defence of their interests. To this end the authorities have to provide opportunities for all directly interested parties to meet those parties with adverse interests. Maximum confidentiality is to be granted. The authorities concerned are obliged to notify representatives of the exporting country and the directly interested parties of their decisions regarding imposition or non-imposition of anti-dumping duties, indicating the reasons for such decisions and the criteria applied. They have to make their decisions public, unless there are special reasons against doing so. With regard to provisional measures, the same applies.[614] According to Article 9(b) the authorities concerned must review the need for the continued imposition of the duty, where warranted on their own initiative or if interested suppliers or importers so request and submit information substantiating the need for review. It should be noted that the Code does not address States but State-organs and individuals.

Under Part II, containing final provisions, institutionalised supervision is provided for. Pursuant to Article 15 each party to the 1967 Agreement must inform the CP annually of any changes in its anti-dumping laws and regulations and in the administration of such laws and regulations. According to Article 16, each party must report to the CP annually on the administration of its anti-dumping laws and regulations, giving summaries of the cases in which anti-dumping duties have been assessed definitively.

At their 25th Session held in 1968, the CP established the Committee on Anti-Dumping Practices, in accordance with Article 17 of the 1967 Agreement. It is composed of government representatives of the parties to this Agreement. The Committee normally meets once a year for the purpose of affording parties to the Agreement the opportunity of consulting on matters relating to the administration of anti-dumping systems in any participating country or customs territory as it might affect the operation of the 1967 Anti-Dumping Code or the furtherance of its objectives.[615] This Committee receives the annual reports under Article 16 as well as the notifications under Article 15. It presents an annual report to the CP on its meetings during which information provided by the signatories is discussed. This report has to be adopted by the CP and is published.[616]

The final provisions are addressed to the States. The role played by the CP to the GATT indicates the close connection between the 1967 Agreement and the GATT. Next to specific supervision under this Agreement supervision under Articles XXII and XXIII remains possible according to Article 17 of the 1967 Agreement.

4.3.9.4.3. The 1979 Agreement on Implementation of Article VI of the GATT

The 1979 Agreement on Implementation of Article VI is almost identical to the one of 1967 as far as the requirements for anti-dumping measures are concerned.[617] Yet, it should be noted that there are slight differences in the interpretation of the determination of injury, which might be decisive.[618] In Article 13 of the new Code, it is recognised that special regard must be given by developed countries to the special situation of developing countries when considering the application of anti-dumping measures under the Code, a provision that was lacking in the 1967 Code. A group of developing countries, however, was dissatisfied with the 1979 Code and drafted an alternative text.[619] Under Article 14 a Committee on Anti-Dumping Practices has been established in the same way as the Committee on Subsidies and Countervailing Measures has been established under Article 16 of the Subsidies Code.[620] The former Committee may also set up subsidiary bodies as appropriate.

The Parties to the 1979 Agreement are required to report without delay to the Committee all preliminary or final anti-dumping actions taken and submit, on a semi-annual basis, reports of any anti-dumping actions taken within the preceding six months.[621]

Consultation conciliation and resolution of disputes is provided for in Article 15. If disputes arise between Parties relating to rights and obligations under this Agreement, the Parties should complete the dispute settlement procedures under this Agreement before availing themselves of any rights which they have under GATT.[622] Consultations will be held upon the request of any Party that considers that any benefit accruing to it under the 1979 Agreement is being nullified or impaired or that the achievement of any objective of this Agreement is being impeded by another Party or Parties. If any Party considers that the consultations have failed and anti-dumping duties are actually levied by the administering authorities of the importing country it may refer the matter to the Committee on Anti-Dumping Practices for conciliation. This may also be done when a provisional measure has a significant impact and a Party considers it to be taken contrary to the provisions of this Agreement. The Committee has to meet within 30 days to review the matter and encourage the Parties involved to develop a mutually acceptable solution. If such a solution has not been reached within three months the Committee must at the request of any Party to the dispute establish a Panel, the members of which are to be selected from signatory countries not parties to the dispute, to examine the matter. The resolution of disputes is governed *mutatis mutandis* by the provisions of the understanding regarding Notification, Consultation, Dispute Settlement and Surveillance.

The Committee must review annually the implementation and operation of this Agreement and inform the CP to the GATT of developments during the period covered by such reviews.[623]

4.3.9.4.4. *The code of subsidies and countervailing duties*

The first part of the Agreement on Interpretation and Application of Articles VI, XVI and XXIII of the GATT deals with the requirements for the levying of countervailing duties.[624] First of all, the signatories are required to act in accordance with the provisions of Article VI of the GATT and the terms of the Subsidies Code.[625] Countervailing duties may only be imposed pursuant to investigations to determine the existing degree and effect of the alleged subsidy. The Code prescribes how these investigations should be performed.[626] Public notice must be given of the findings of such investigations[627] and the signatories must report without delay to the Com mittee all preliminary or final actions taken with respect to countervailing duties. Such reports will be available to the GATT Secretariat for inspection by Government representatives. The signatories must also submit, on a semi-annual basis, reports on any countervailing duty actions taken within the preceding six months.[628]

As soon as possible after a request for initiation of an investigation is accepted, and in any event before the initiation of any investigation, consultations should be held with the signatories, the products of which may be subject to such investigation. The consultations should continue during the investigations.[629]

All decisions on the imposition of countervailing duties are taken by the authorities of the importing country. The duty should not exceed the amount of the subsidy found to exist and it is desirable that the duty be less than the total of the subsidy if such lesser duty would be adequate to remove the injury to the domestic industry. Countervailing duties may be replaced by voluntary price undertakings.[630] Under certain conditions provisional measures may be taken.[631] The determination of injury is dealt with in Article 6.

It should be noted that existing national legislation must be brought into conformity with this Agreement. Each signatory has to inform the Committee on Subsidies and Countervailing Duties of any changes in its laws and regulations relevant to this Agreement and in the administration of such laws and regulations.[632] Therefore signatories can no longer invoke the 'grandfather clause' of the Protocols of Provisional Application with regard to the rules of this Code.

Supervision is for the most part dealt with in Parts VI and VII. They are described in Section 4.3.7.5. The mechanisms of supervision differ in some respects from those of the 1979 Agreement on Implementation of Article VI of the GATT. In the first place, there is no list of potential Panel members under the latter. An authorisation regarding appropriate countervailing measures can only be given under the Subsidies Code. Only the Subsidies Code provides for a time limit for recommendations of its Committee. Finally under the Subsidies Code action under the relevant GATT Articles is not precluded, even if the dispute settlement procedures of this Code have not been tried.

4.3.9.5. Evaluation

Qualification of the mechanisms of supervision

Compensating duties as an instrument for correction. Anti-dumping and countervailing duties constitute a sanction against a cp which allows dumping by its producers, or by its State trading enterprises or that grants or maintains subsidies. By allowing compensating duties the GATT opens the possibility for specific supervision by the cps themselves. The review function is performed on the basis of exchange of information and reporting *ad hoc*; the correction function by means of a sanction. Under Article VI,7 the cps are somewhat restricted in the application of this instrument when the export price of primary products is too low as a consequence of national systems for price stabilisation or income support for domestic producers.

Supervision on the levying of compensating duties

Article VI,6b of the GATT provides for specific non-judicial supervision by a politically dependent organ on compensating duties on behalf of another cp. The review function is performed on the basis of reporting *ad hoc*; the correction function by political discussion as well as mediation and conciliation aimed at peaceful settlement.

The 1967 Anti-Dumping Code provides for specific non-judicial supervision by the parties to this Agreement and by individuals and firms within such parties. The review function is performed based on reporting *ad hoc* and petitions by individuals, that the authorities involved have to take into consideration when the need for review is evident from the information provided. The correction function is performed by negotiations aimed at peaceful settlement.

The final provisions of the 1967 Agreement on Implementation of Article VI of the GATT provide for general non-judicial supervision. Supervision in the technical phase by the Committee on Anti-Dumping Practices is more important than that in the political phase by the CP to the GATT. The review function is exercised on the basis of reporting and reporting *ad hoc*; the correction function by means of political discussion.

The 1979 Code provides for general as well as specific non-judicial supervision on compensating measures. It is exercised by a politically dependent organ, the signatories or individuals. The politically dependent organ may be assisted by subsidiary organs in the technical phase. The review function is performed on the basis of reporting and reporting *ad hoc* in the first case and in the second case on the basis of a request or complaint. The correction takes place in the first case by means of the mobilisation of shame and political discussion. In the second case by means of negotiations and conciliation aimed at peaceful settlement and political discussion. When complaints are filed with regard to countervailing duties an authorisation to apply sanctions may be granted. The creative function is performed by political discussion.

Commentary

The specific mechanism of supervision of GATT Article VI,6(b) has never been used.[633] Neither have the central mechanisms of supervision of the GATT been much used with regard to anti-dumping or countervailing duties. Only three such cases have been published.[634]

Many countries have no specific provision for anti-dumping action and have not imposed any anti-dumping duties for years.[635] Others have dead letter provisions which are not used.[636]

The most active countries in this field are the U.S. and Canada. Their legislation prescribes the levying of an anti-dumping duty in all cases where it is established that the imports taxed have been dumped and that injury to the domestic industry is caused or threatened or that the establishment of a domestic industry is retarded. The duties are equal to the margin of dumping in all instances.

The third large anti-dumping duty levying entity is the EEC. However, the authorities might decide not to levy anti-dumping duties even if the conditions are met, since they are obliged to consider the interests of the community before deciding to impose such a duty. The Commission has the discretion to fix the duty, which may be lower than the margin of dumping.[637]

Until recently, although subsidised trade was probably widespread, very few countervailing duties were imposed. With the sole exception of the U.S., the cps have not used countervailing duties commonly. However, since late 1974 the number of countervailing duties imposed by the U.S. increased dramatically, to the discontent of its trading partners.[638]

The impacts of dumping, bounties and subsidies are felt increasingly, since other trade barriers, such as tariffs and quantitative restrictions, have been removed. Government interference increased considerably in Western States after the Second World War, also causing an increase of the number of subsidies. Subsequently the need for countervailing duties became stronger.

Moreover, cps that cannot provide protection for their domestic producers by means of tariffs and quota might want to use anti-dumping or counter-vailing duties to this end, even in violation of the GATT system. To prevent compensating duties from becoming a new substantive non-tariff barrier the GATT should regulate this matter and provide for stringent supervision.

It should be noted that anti-dumping and countervailing duties deprive consumers in the importing countries of an increase in welfare. Therefore the net result of the imposition of such duties for the importing country as a whole may be negative. Moreover, the levying of compensating duties is disadvantageous to the economy of the importing country, compared to the imposition of a tariff.[639]

The 1979 Codes provide for such regulation. Supervision is quite stringent under these Codes, since they provide for a general reporting procedure and a dispute settlement procedure that has to be finished within certain time limits. It should be noted once more that these Codes address individuals.

All developed cps were signatories to the 1967 Anti-dumping Code except for New Zealand, South Africa and Iceland. It would contribute considerably to the objectives of the GATT if many cps would sign the new Codes and apply them.

With regard to anti-dumping and countervailing duties, various régimes apply for the different cps. Because of the 'grandfather' clause in the Protocols of Provisional Application, some cps such as the U.S., are not bound by Article VI of the GATT.[640] The 1967 Anti-Dumping Code and the 1979 Code only apply to their signatories. Therefore there are four régimes regarding anti-dumping duties and three with regard to countervailing duties. However, because of the Most-Favoured-Nation Clause the signatories to the Codes have to give the benefits provided for under these Codes to all cps. Non-signatories cannot be members of the Committees, cannot use the mechanisms of supervision under these Codes, and have no obligations pursuant to the Codes.

4.3.10. Government procurement

Government procurement based on non-market criteria constitutes a barrier to trade. Therefore, the original U.S. draft of the ITO Charter contained provisions requiring national treatment to be extended to imported goods in the case of government purchases and bringing government contracts within the scope of the MFN obligation.[641] However, these clauses were never included in either the ITO Charter or in GATT. The GATT exempts government procurement from national treatment obligations and from State trading obligations.[642] Moreover, Most-Favoured-Nation treatment is not required for government procurement under Article I,1. However, under Article XVII,2 cps must accord fair and equitable treatment to the trade of other cps with respect to imports of products for immediate or ultimate consumption in governmental use and not otherwise for resale or use in the production of goods for sale.

Since 1947, government procurement has increased considerably. In many States purchases of goods by governments presently assume a substantial part of the national economic activity, expressed as a percentage of GNP. Many governments favour domestic suppliers over foreigners, even if this is detrimental to the welfare of the country as a whole. The reasons governments favour domestic suppliers may be that such suppliers are closer and better informed. Moreover, governments often use procurement policies as a conscious means to promote economic development, to attract new industry, to develop and maintain industrial capacity especially in relation to defence, and to increase employment.

With the increase of government procurement and the decrease of man-made barriers, government preferences to domestic producers have become a serious impediment to international trade. In the mid-1960s government procurement as a barrier to trade was discussed within the OECD.[643] Negotiations within the OECD continued for about a decade but reached a stalemate in 1976.[644] Due to this situation, the U.S.A. and a number of developing countries led by India urged successfully that negotiations be transferred to the GATT forum. The subject has been discussed during the Tokyo Round during which an Agreement on Government Procurement was drafted[645] that entered into force on January 1, 1981.[646]

The Agreement on Government Procurement brings a portion of the purchasing of governments into the international trading framework. It creates a set of rules designed to ensure that suppliers from each signatory have an opportunity to bid on certain foreign government contracts. In the Agreement government procurement has been defined as procurement by governmental agencies of products purchased for governmental purposes and not with a view to commercial resale or with a view to use in the production of goods for commercial sale.[647] Governmental agencies include local authorities.[648] The term goods is limited to products as understood in commercial practice and does not include the purchase or sale of services.[649]

4.3.10.1. The 1979 Agreement on Government Procurement

The purchasing to be covered by the 1979 Agreement on Government Procurement is determined primarily by the purchasing entities which each party has identified as being subject to the Agreement.[650] A list of such entities is annexed to the Agreement.[651] The Agreement applies to any law, regulation procedure and practice regarding the procurement by such entities and to products and services identical to the supply of products.[652] The coverage of the Agreement is limited by various provisions and excludes:

(1) purchases below a threshold value of SDR 150,000[653];
(2) products that are excluded on behalf of developing countries as a result of negotiations between developed and developing countries[654]; and
(3) the procurement of arms, ammunition and war materials or procurement indispensable for national security or for national defence purposes.[655]

Single tendering is allowed in a number of instances including purchases for research, parts replacements and urgent purchases.[656]

157

Pursuant to Article IX,4(a) of this Agreement the Parties have to adjust existing legislation.

The basic standards in respect of all laws, regulations, procedures and practices of government procurement covered by the Agreement are those of national treatment and non-discrimination. The Parties are required to immediately and unconditionally provide national as well as Most-Favoured-Nation treatment to the products and suppliers of other Parties and they shall not introduce special rules of origin.[657] Technical specifications may not be prepared, adopted or applied with a view to creating obstacles to international trade nor are they allowed to have the effect of creating unnecessary obstacles to international trade.[658] There shall be no requirement or reference to a particular trademark or the like, unless there is no sufficiently precise or intelligible way of describing the procurement requirements and provided that words such as 'or equivalent' are included in the tenders.[659]

The required tendering procedures are prescribed in Article V. They reflect the basic rules of non-discrimination between foreign suppliers and national treatment and contain the following mechanisms of supervision.

Any conditions for participation in tendering procedures must be published in adequate time to enable interested suppliers to initiate and complete the qualification procedures.[660] Entities are required to publish a notice of each proposed purchase in appropriate publications listed in Annex II to the Agreement.[661] The Agreement prescribes what information each notice of proposed purchase should contain.[662] Moreover, the entities must publish in one of the official languages of the GATT a summary of the notice of proposed purchase containing at least the subject matter of the contract, time limits set for the submission of tenders and addresses from which documents relating to the contracts may be requested.[663]

In the case of selective tendering procedures entities maintaining permanent lists of qualified suppliers must publish annually in one of the publications listed in Annex III a notice of the enumeration of the lists maintained, the conditions to be filled by potential suppliers in view of their inscription on those lists, and the period of validity of the lists and the formalities for their renewal.[664]

At the request of any supplier participating in open procedures, entities must forward the tender documentation. In selective procedures, entities must forward such documentation at the request of any supplier requesting to participate in selective procedures. Entities must reply promptly to reasonable requests for relevant information unless such information would give the requesting supplier an advantage over its competitors.[665]

Entities are required to prepare a report in writing on each contract awarded by means of single tendering. Each report must contain the name of the purchasing entity, the value and kind of goods purchased, the country of origin, and a statement of the conditions justifying the use of single tendering.[666]

Article VI deals with information and review. Any law, regulation, judicial decision, administrative ruling of general application, and any procedure regarding government procurement covered by this Agreement, must be promptly published by the parties in appropriate publications listed in Annex IV. The publication should be done in such a manner as to enable other Parties and suppliers to become acquainted with them. The Parties have to explain their procurement practices and procedures upon request of any supplier.[667] Upon request by any supplier they must promptly provide pertinent information concerning the reasons why that supplier's application was rejected or why he was not invited or admitted to tender.[668] Entities are required to inform the unsuccessful tenderers by written communications or publication[669] and to provide that tenderer upon request with pertinent information concerning the reason why the tender was not selected, both within seven working days.[670] Entities must establish a contact point to provide additional information to unsuccessful tenderers and their procedures for the hearing and reviewing of complaints must be established.[671]

The government of the unsuccessful tenderer may seek additional information on the contract award to ensure that the purchase was made fairly and impartially. To this end, the purchasing government is required to provide information on both the characteristics and relative advantages of the winning tender and the contract price.[672] Available information concerning individual contract awards must be provided upon request to any other party.[673] However, confidential information may not be revealed without formal authorisation from the party providing the information.[674] The Parties are required to collect and provide to the Committee on an annual basis statistics on their purchases.[675]

4.3.10.2. Mechanisms of supervision

In 1981 the Committee on Government Procurement was established, composed of representatives from each of the Parties.[676] The Committee meets as necessary, but not less than once a year.[677] The Committee may establish subsidiary bodies such as *ad hoc* panels and WP's.[678]

In order to facilitate the constitution of panels the Chairman of the Committee must maintain an informal indicative list of governmental officials experienced in the field of trade relations, the list may also include persons other than governmental officials. However government officials are preferred as panel members. When a panel is established the Chairman of the Committee proposes the composition of a panel within seven days. The parties directly concerned must also react in seven days and may only oppose nominations for compelling reasons. Panel members must serve in their individual capacities and may not be citizens of the countries whose governments are parties to the dispute at hand.[679]

The parties are obliged to consult when representations are made.[680] If any party considers that any benefit accruing to it, directly or indirectly, under this Agreement is being nullified or impaired, or that the achievement of any objective of this Agreement is being impeded, by another party or parties, it may, with a view to reaching a mutually satisfactory resolution of the matter, request in writing consultations with the party or parties in question. Each party must afford sympathetic consideration to any request from another party for consultations. The parties concerned must initiate requested consultations promptly.[681] The parties engaged in consultations have to provide information and must attempt to conclude such negotiations within a reasonably short period of time.[682]

If no mutually satisfactory solution has been reached as a result of consultations concerning an alleged nullification or impairment, the Committee must meet at the request of any party to the dispute within 30 days of the receipt of such a request to investigate the matter with a view to facilitating a mutually satisfactory solution.[683] If such a solution is not reached within three months the Committee must at the request of any party to the dispute examine the matter, consult with the parties, make a statement concerning the facts and make such findings as will assist the Committee in making recommendations or giving rulings on the matter.[684] All parties having a substantial interest in the matter and having notified thus to the Committee must have an opportunity to be heard. Confidential information may not be revealed without formal authorisation from the government or person providing the information.[685] Panels should aim to deliver their findings and, where appropriate, recommendations, to the Committee without undue delay.[686] Panels are required to report to the Committee.

Within 30 days of receipt of the panel report the Committee must make a statement concerning the facts, and recommendations to one or more parties. In addition it may make any other ruling which it deems appropriate.[687] If a party to which recommendations are addressed considers itself unable to implement them, it should promptly furnish reasons in writing to the Committee. In that event, the Committee must consider what further action may be appropriate.[688] The Committee must keep under surveillance any matter on which it has made recommendations or has given rulings.[689]

If the Committee's recommendations are not accepted by a party, or parties, to the dispute, and if the Committee considers that the circumstances are serious enough to justify such action, it may authorise a party or parties to suspend in whole or in part, and for such time as may be necessary, the application of this Agreement to any other party or parties, as is determined to be appropriate in the circumstances.[690]

The Agreement provides for annual review by the Committee. The latter has to inform the CP annually of developments during the periods covered by such reviews. Before December 31, 1983, and periodically thereafter the parties are required to undertake further negotiations with a view to broadening and improving this Agreement.[691]

4.3.10.3. Evaluation

Qualification of the mechanisms of supervision

The supervision provided for in the Agreement on Government Procurement takes place on three levels. First of all there is general supervision within the tendering procedures, carried out by the cps themselves. The form of supervision is non-judicial. The review function is performed by reporting.

The correction function by means of mobilisation of shame. Correction takes place also under the subsequent levels of supervision.

On the second level, supervision takes place by means of the provision of information to other parties to the Agreement or to individuals as well as by means of consultations. This is specific non-judicial supervision by the parties themselves. The review function is performed by means of requests and complaints and reporting *ad hoc*. The correction function by means of consultations aimed at friendly settlement.

On the third level there is specific non-judicial supervision by the politically dependent organ. The latter may be assisted in the technical phase by subsidiary bodies. The review function is performed on the basis of requests, complaints and reporting *ad hoc*; the correction function by means of political discussion, conciliation, mediation and consultations aimed at friendly settlement and sanctions. The sanctions that constitute an *ultimum remedium*, are to be executed by the parties to the Agreement themselves. The creative function is performed by political discussion.

In addition to these mechanisms of supervision, general supervision on the operation of the Agreement by the political organ is provided for. It is non-judicial supervision, based on reporting as far as the review function is concerned. The correction and the creative functions are performed by political discussion. Ultimate supervision is performed by the CP to the GATT, a politically dependent body.

Commentary

The Agreement on government procurement contains the most sophisticated mechanisms of supervision that are to be found within the GATT system. In many aspects they resemble the mechanisms of supervision applicable to subsidies. The dispute settlement procedure resembles the central dispute settlement procedure of GATT in many ways.

A commitment by a State with respect to government procurement constitutes a serious commitment with regard to its sovereign rights and was inconceivable in the late 1940s. The fact that a number of States are prepared to make such a commitment on behalf of world trade indicates a willingness of the States to contribute to the objectives of GATT.

About the effectiveness of this Agreement nothing can be said, since it has only recently entered into force. The next few years will tell us to what extent States are in practice prepared to restrict their freedom with regard to government procurement on behalf of the realisation of the objectives of GATT.

4.3.11. GATT and the developing countries

At present two-thirds of the cps are developing countries. There are many internal as well as external causes for their plight including too little revenue from the sale of primary products and a lack of capital to finance industrialisation and other forms of diversification of their economies.

To increase their standard of living, developing countries need industrialisation. The necessary capital means could be obtained by the import of foreign capital or the export of commodities. As the probability of directly transferring real resources from rich to poor nations through concessional aid has diminished, the developing countries now advocate indirect transfers through commercial policies favouring developing countries, such as tariff preferences.[692] Another reason for preferring the increase of export income to the increase of capital import is that capital transfers by means of loans involve interest and have to be paid back. Consequently, capital imports will eventually cause capital exports.

Currently, the exports of developing countries are hampered by tariffs, quantitative restrictions, subsidies, anti-dumping duties, State trading enterprises and other non-tariff barriers created by the developed countries. The introduction of quantitative restrictions outside the scope of GATT such as orderly marketing agreements and voluntary export restraints form an especially serious threat to prospective increases in the developing countries' exports.[693]

Another severe obstacle to the trading strength of developing countries is the escalation in developed country tariffs according to the degree of processing of the imported goods, resulting in different tariff rates on products at different production stages.[694] Consequently, the effective protection on semi-manufactured goods and end products is much stronger than the tariff shows.[695]

Since imports of means of production and durable consumption goods exceeds their exports of primary products and because of their large capital imports, the developing countries continually have to face huge balance of payments deficits.[696] Often these countries can only reduce such deficits by imposing or maintaining quantitative restrictions.

To protect new industries against competition from foreign industries, the developing countries often seek to establish high tariff walls and, more importantly, non-tariff barriers. The administration of tariff barriers is rather complicated. Since the organisational structure of most of these countries is still rather primitive and they do not have a sufficient number of civil servants, Third World countries prefer non-tariff barriers to tariffs since the former are easier to administer.

According to some authors the trade policies of the developed countries and the GATT rules constitute the principal cause of the lagging economic development of Third World countries. They say that the developed countries maintain too many trade restrictions. Within GATT too few and too small concessions have been made with regard to products exported by developing countries, such as primary products. During the rounds of negotiations equivalent concessions are exchanged. For this reason developing countries that can offer hardly any concessions, have received too little concessions. Moreover, the application of non-tariff barriers to trade that developing countries prefer, is prohibited under GATT.

4.3.11.1. Accomplishments within GATT on behalf of developing countries

Nevertheless, some special attention is given within GATT to the problems of 'less-developed countries' as developing countries are called in the text of the GATT and many early decisions. From the first days of GATT onwards developing countries were allowed to deviate from GATT to protect new industries and in case of balance of payments problems.[697] In this way the development of Third World countries was promoted passively.

Such passive promotion, however, proved to be inadequate to the task of narrowing the gap between rich and poor countries. Therefore, more has been and is being done within GATT to improve the position of the developing countries. In 1955 the CP adopted a resolution emphasising the need for an increased capital flow into underdeveloped countries.[698] In 1957 a panel of experts was established to examine the failure of the trade of less-developed countries to develop as rapidly as that of industrialised countries, excessive short-term fluctuations in prices of primary products, and widespread resort to agricultural protection.[699] The panel report was published in 1958 as the Haberler Report entitled: 'Trends in International Trade'.[700] On the basis of this report the CP drafted a programme of action directed towards an expansion of international trade. It 'embraces three principal topics:

(1) the possibilities of further negotiations for the reduction of tariffs;
(2) problems arising out of the widespread use of non-tariff measures for the protection of agriculture, or in support of the maintenance of incomes of agricultural producers; and
(3) other obstacles to the expansion of trade, with particulars reference to the importance of maintaining and expanding the export earnings of the less-developed countries'.

Three committees were established to carry out this programme,[701] all of which reported in May 1959.[702] One of the committees adopted a recommendation that led to the Dillon Round.[703]

Following a Council recommendation to that end, the CP convened a meeting of 44 ministers in 1961 to discuss the three topics mentioned above. The ministers agreed that the CP should take immediate steps to establish specific programmes of action for progressive reduction and elimination of barriers to the exports of less-developed countries and that the CP should be requested to draw up procedures for notifying and reviewing action taken by cps to improve market opportunities for the exports of less-developed countries. The CP formally adopted the conclusions reached by the ministers during their meeting and agreed that immediate steps should be taken to establish specific programmes of action for progressive reduction and elimination of barriers to the exports of less-developed countries and that the procedures requested by the ministers be drawn up. One of the three already established committees, Committee III, was to undertake these tasks and to make recommendations to the CP.[704] The subsequent action programme required annual reports on steps to be taken by developed countries.[705] Yet, since the response of the developed countries to the work of Committee III was disappointing, this action programme was unsuccessful.[706]

In 1963 a ministerial meeting adopted the programme of action, and agreed that the work of Committee III should be extended. They also recognised the need for an adequate legal and institutional framework to enable the CP to discharge their responsibilities in connection with the work of expanding the trade of less-developed countries. According to the ministers of the developing countries and the EEC, the objectives of the GATT should be amplified and its principles revised. Agreement was reached on the establishment of a committee to examine all aspects of the above-mentioned problems. The Council was instructed to take the action necessary to set up such a committee.[707] This committee drafted a 'Chapter on Trade and Development' for inclusion in the GATT.[708]

In 1964 UNCTAD convened for the first time. This increased the pressure on the CP to act in aid of the developing countries. In November 1964 a special session of the CP was called for to complete the drafting of the new chapter on Trade and Development. On February 8, 1965, the amending protocol containing the new chapter as well as a Declaration on De Facto Implementation was opened for signature.[709] The new chapter, Part IV of the present GATT, came into force on June 27, 1966.[710] It contains principles and exhortations to developed cps to promote the economic development of less-developed countries. For the implementation of Part IV and for supervision thereon the CP established the Committee on Trade and Development, hereafter referred to as CTD.[711] The CTD took over the tasks of Committee III and all other subsidiary bodies dealing with problems regarding developing countries.[712]

In addition, several GATT institutions give advice to developing countries concerning development policy, export promotion and the conduct of negotiations. To this end an International Trade Centre was established in 1964 which has been operated jointly by GATT and UNCTAD since 1968.[713] The CTD, the Group of Three,[714] and the Special Assistance Unit within the GATT Secretariat[715] also promote the economic development of the developing countries.

Finally the promotion of the trade interests of developing countries was one of the objectives of the Tokyo Round.[716]

4.3.11.2. Deviations from GATT under Article XVIII

4.3.11.2.1. Classification of the cps

Article XVIII concerns governmental assistance to economic development. Under this Article two groups of cps, described in paragraph 4, may deviate from the GATT. These are:

(a) cps, the economy of which can only support low standards of living and are in their early stages of development, and

(b) cps, the economy of which is in the process of development but which do not come in the category mentioned under (a).[717]

Clear objective criteria are not provided to determine to what category a cp belongs. Primarily, cps determine themselves whether they belong to one of the groups described. To the first group the provisions under Sections A (paragraph 7), B (paragraphs 8–12), and C (paragraphs 13–21) of Article XVIII apply. The second group may submit applications to the CP under Section D (paragraphs 22–23) of this Article.[718]

4.3.11.2.2. Renegotiations on behalf of particular new industries under Section A

If a cp coming within the scope of paragraph 4(a) of Article XVIII considers it desirable in order to promote the establishment of a particular industry with a view to raising the general standard of living of its people, it may modify or withdraw a concession included in the appropriate Schedule annexed to the GATT. It must notify the CP to this effect and enter into negotiations with the withwhom[719] and with any other cp determined by the CP to have a substantial interest therein. If agreement is reached between such cps concerned, they may modify or withdraw concessions under the appropriate Schedules to the GATT in order to give effect to such agreement, including any compensatory adjustments involved.[720]

If agreement is not reached within 60 days after the notification, the cp which proposes to modify or withdraw the concession may refer the matter to the CP, which must promptly examine it. If the CP find that the cp which proposes to modify or withdraw the concession has made every effort to reach an agreement and that the compensatory adjustment offered by it is adequate, that cp may modify or withdraw the concession if at the same time, it gives effect to the compensatory adjustment. If the CP do not find that the compensation offered by a cp proposing to modify or withdraw the concession is adequate, but find that it has made every reasonable effort to offer adequate compensation, that cp may proceed with such modification or withdrawal. If such action is taken, any other cp referred to in sub-paragraph 7(a) may modify or withdraw substantially equivalent concessions initially negotiated with the cp which has taken the action.[721] This procedure strongly resembles that for closed-season negotiations of Article XXVIII,4.[722]

4.3.11.2.3. Quantitative restrictions for balance of payments reasons under Section B

As a result of the large import of commodities and capital and the small export earnings by developing countries, since most of the developing countries maintain fixed exchange rates, and since devaluations (and revaluations) of their currencies have little effect because of the price inelasticity of their imports and exports, Third World countries often are forced to contend with balance of payments deficits. Therefore, the cps recognise that cps coming within the scope of paragraph 4(a) of Article XVIII when they are in rapid process of development, tend to experience balance of payments difficulties. Such difficulties arise mainly from efforts to expand their internal markets and from the instability in their terms of trade.[723]

165

In order to safeguard their external financial position and to ensure a level of reserves adequate for the implementation of programmes of economic development, cps coming within the scope of sub-para. 4(a) of Article XVIII may, under certain conditions, control the general level of their imports by restricting the quantity or value of merchandise permitted to be imported according to paragraph 9 of Article XVIII. This paragraph also mentions criteria for the kind of import restrictions that are allowed. These criteria are practically the same as those of Article XII,2(a).[724] Two differences are that Article XII,2(a) requires an 'imminent threat' and 'very low monetary reserves' whereas Article XVIII,9 speaks of a 'threat' and 'inadequate monetary reserves'.

The CP are bound by findings and determinations by the IMF under Article XV,2. The rules for the application of the restrictions are contained in paragraphs 10 and 11 of Article XVIII and are almost identical to those laid down in Article XII, paragraphs 2 and 3. Only the obligations regarding domestic policy are formulated differently in the two articles and the emphasis is placed on different issues.[725]

Article XVIII,12 provides the same mechanisms of supervision as does Article XII,4,[726] albeit that the periodical review of existing restrictions occurs once a year under Article XII,4(b) and once every two years under Article XVIII,12(b). On December 19, 1972, the Council adopted procedures for regular consultations on balance of payments restrictions with developing countries. Under these procedures developing countries have to transmit to the CP only a concise written statement on the nature of the balance of payments difficulties, the system and modes of restriction, the effects of the restrictions and prospects of liberalisation. The IMF is required to supply balance of payments statistics for each country submitting a statement. The Committee on Balance of Payments Restrictions determines whether a full consultation is desirable. If it decides that such a consultation is not desirable, the Committee will recommend to the Council that the cp be deemed to have consulted with the CP and to have fulfilled its obligations under Article XVIII,12(b) for that year.[727]

Other differences are, that the CP under Article XII,4(e) must have due regard for any special external factors when they exercise supervision and under Article XVIII,12(f) they must have due regard for the necessity to implement the development programme. If a cp against which action has been taken in accordance with the last sentence of sub-paragraph (c)(ii) or (d) of Article XVIII,12, finds that the release of obligations authorised by the CP adversely affects the operation of its programme and policy of economic development, it may withdraw from the GATT. Such a cp must give written notice to the Director-General[728] not later than 60 days after such action is taken. The withdrawal takes effect 60 days after the day on which the notice was received.[729] Article XII does not contain a similar provision.[730]

Quantitative restrictions for balance of payments reasons are sometimes applied to conform to the GATT without it being clear whether this is done under Article XII or Article XVIIIB.[731]

4.3.11.2.4. Deviations from GATT on behalf of a particular industry under Sections C and D

If a cp belonging to a group described in paragraph 4(a) of Article XVIII finds that governmental assistance is required to promote the establishment of a particular industry with a view to raising the general standard of living of its people, but that no measure consistent with the other provisions of this Agreement is practicable to achieve that objective, it may deviate from the GATT, under certain circumstances mentioned in Article XVIII C.[732]

The proposed deviating measure and the special difficulties the measure is supposed to counteract have to be notified to the CP.[733] If, within 30 days of the notification of the measure, the CP do not request the cp concerned to consult with them, that cp shall be free to deviate from the relevant provisions of the other Articles of this Agreement to the extent necessary to apply the proposed measure.[734]

On request of the CP the cp concerned must consult with them as to the purpose of the proposed measure, as to alternative measures which may be available under this Agreement, and as to the possible effect of the measure proposed on the commercial and economic interests of other cps.[735] It is understood that the CP on request shall invite a cp, the trade of which would be appreciably affected by the measure in question, to consult with them.[736]

If, as a result of such consultation, the CP agrees that there is no practicable measure consistent with the other provisions of this Agreement, and concur in the proposed measure, the cp concerned will be released from its obligations under the relevant provisions of the other Articles of this Agreement to the extent necessary to apply that measure. If, within 90 days after the date of the notification of the proposed measure the CP have not concurred in such measure, the cp concerned may introduce the measure proposed after informing the CP.[737]

If the proposed measure affects a bound item the cp concerned must enter into renegotiations with the withwhom and with any other cp determined by the CP to have a substantial interest therein. The CP must concur in the measure if they agree that there is no practicable measure consistent with the other provisions of this Agreement, and if they are satisfied:

(a) that agreement has been reached with such other cps as a result of the consultations referred to above; or

(b) if no such agreement has been reached within 60 days after the notification has been received by the CP, that the cp having recourse to this Section has made all reasonable efforts to reach an agreement and that the interests of other cps are adequately safeguarded. The cp having recourse to Article XVIIIB must thereupon be released from its relevant GATT obligations to the extent necessary.[738]

Provided the CP concur, an industry, the establishment of which has in the initial period been facilitated by incidental protection afforded by restrictions imposed by the cp concerned for balance of payments purposes under the relevant provisions of this Agreement, may be protected by measures of the type described in Article XVIII,13.[739] Such measures would constitute 'legal' residual restrictions.[740]

Deviation from Articles I, II and XIII may not be authorised; in other words,[741] if the CP do not concur with a measure that is being applied, any cp substantially affected by it may suspend the application to the trade of the cp having recourse to this Section of such substantially equivalent concessions or other obligations under this Agreement the suspension of which the CP do not disapprove, provided that 60 days' notice of such suspension is given to the CP not later than six months after the measure has been introduced or changed substantially to the detriment of the cp affected. Any such cp shall afford adequate opportunity for consultation in accordance with the provisions of Article XXII of the GATT.[742]

A cp belonging to the group described in Article XVIII,4(b), may deviate from the GATT under Section D of Article XVIII. Such a cp may apply to the CP for approval to deviate from the GATT under Article XVIII,13 in the interest of the development of its economy and on behalf of the establishment of a particular industry. The CP must promptly consult with such cp. The requirements and procedures applicable to such a request are similar to those applicable to proposed deviations by cps belonging to the group described in Article XVIII,4(a), except for one difference: the CP must concur in measures proposed by cps belonging to the group described in Article XVIII,4(b), for such cps to be allowed to deviate from the GATT.[743]

The measures applied under Sections C and D of Article XVIII are reviewed annually by the CP. In 1958, a questionnaire was drafted to guide the cps in notifying measures under Section C and submitting applications under Section D of Article XVIII.[744]

4.3.11.3. Promotion of trade and development

Part IV of the GATT deals with the promotion of trade and development of less-developed countries. It contains principles, objectives and incitements, but does not provide any enforceable rights. Article XXXVI contains principles and objectives. Pursuant to paragraph 8 the developed cps do not expect reciprocity for commitments made by them in trade negotiations to reduce or remove tariffs and other barriers to the trade of less-developed cps. This means that less-developed cps should not be expected, in the course of trade negotiations, to make contributions which are inconsistent with their individual development, financial and trade needs, taking into consideration past trade developments. This paragraph applies to every procedure under the GATT.[745] It is in conflict with the principle of reciprocity. Under paragraph 9 the cps both individually and jointly must endeavour to adopt measures giving effect to the principles and objectives of Part IV.

Article XXXVII contains 'commitments' of developed cps. But, pursuant to the first paragraph they are only required to give effect to the provisions of Article XXXVII to the fullest extent possible, that is, when no compelling reasons make it impossible. The developed cps must:

- accord high priority to the reduction and elimination of barriers to products currently or potentially of particular export interest to less-developed cps;
- refrain from introducing, or increasing the incidence of, customs duties or non-tariff import barriers on products currently or potentially of particular export interest to less-developed cps;
- (i) refrain from imposing new fiscal measures, and
  (ii) in any adjustments of fiscal policy accord high priority to the reduction and elimination of fiscal measures, which hamper, or which would hamper, significantly the growth of consumption of primary products, or products mainly produced in the territories of less-developed cps[746];
- make every effort, in cases where a government determines the resale price of products produced in the territories of less-developed cps, to maintain trade margins at equitable levels;
- give active consideration to the adoption of measures designed to provide greater scope for the development of imports from less-developed cps and collaborate in appropriate international action to this end; and
- have special regard to the trade interests of less-developed cps when considering the application of measures permitted under this Agreement to meet particular problems and explore all possibilities of constructive remedies before applying such measures where they would affect essential interests of those cps.[747]

Less-developed countries must apply Part IV with regard to the trade of other less-developed countries.[748]

Under Article XXXVIII the cps have to act jointly to promote the objectives of Part IV. In particular the CP must:

- take action to provide improved and acceptable conditions of access to world markets for primary products of particular interest to less-developed cps and to devise measures designed to stabilise and improve conditions of world markets in these products;
- seek appropriate collaboration in matters of trade and development policy with the United Nations and its organs and agencies, including any institutions that may be created on the basis of recommendations by the United National Conference on Trade and Development;
- collaborate with governments and international organisations in analysing the development plans and policies of individual less-developed cps as well as trade and aid relationships;
- keep under continuous review the development of world trade with special reference to the rate of growth of the trade of less-developed cps and make such recommendations to cps as may, in the circumstances, be deemed appropriate;
- seek feasible methods to expand trade for the purpose of economic development; and
- establish such institutional arrangements as may be necessary to further the objectives set forth in Article XXXVI and to give effect to the provisions of this Part.[749]

169

4.3.11.4. Mechanisms of supervision

4.3.11.4.1. Supervision on the implementation of Article XXXVII

Supervision on the 'commitments' of the developed cps under Article XXXVII,1 is provided for in Article XXXVII,2. Any interested cp considering that effect is not being given to any of the provisions of Article XXXVII,1 must report the matter to the CP.[750]

The CP must, on request of any interested contracting party, and without prejudice to any possible bilateral consultations, consult with the cp concerned and all interested cps with respect to the matter with a view to reaching solutions satisfactory to all cps concerned in order to further the objectives set forth in Article XXXVI. In the course of these consultations, the reasons given in cases where effect was not being given to the provisions of paragraph 1 must be examined.[751]

As the implementation of the provisions of paragraph 1 by individual cps may in some cases be more readily achieved where action is taken jointly with other developed cps, such consultation might, where appropriate, be directed towards this end. The consultations by the CP might also, in appropriate cases, be directed towards agreement on joint action designed to further the objectives of this Agreement as envisaged in paragraph 1 of Article XXV.[752]

In addition the cps must afford to any other interested cp or cps full and prompt opportunity for consultations under the normal procedures of the GATT.[753]

4.3.11.4.2. The Committee on Trade and Development

On November 26, 1964, the CP established the Committee on Trade and Development, hereafter referred to as CTD. Its functions are:

(1) To keep under continuous review the application of the provisions of Part IV of the General Agreement.
(2) To carry out, or arrange for, any consultations which may be required in the application of the provisions of Part IV.
(3) To formulate proposals for consideration by the CP in connection with any matter relating to the furtherance of the provisions of Part IV.
(4) To consider any questions which may arise as to the eligibility of a contracting party to be considered as a less-developed cp in the sense of Part IV and to report to the CP.
(5) To consider, on the basis of proposals referred to it by the CP for examination, whether modification of or additions to Part IV are required to further the work of the CP in the field of trade and development and to make appropriate recommendations.
(6) To carry out such additional functions as may be assigned to the Committee by the CP.

The CTD was also given the primary responsibility for supervision of the implementation of points 1 and 4 of the framework texts adopted after the Tokyo Round. This Committee took over the functions of all subsidiary bodies in this field including the review of other GATT provisions than those of Part IV.[754]

The CTD drafted reporting procedures regarding the provisions of Article XXXVII,2, that were adopted by the CP in 1965. Under these procedures the Secretariat must circulate to the CTD all notifications received from the cps. The cps should be requested to notify the Secretariat of any action taken by them in pursuance of the provisions of paragraphs 1,3(a) and (b) and 4 of Article XXXVII. The Secretariat must submit periodic reports summarising the latest position concerning tariffs or quota restrictions affecting items of interest to less-developed countries as well as any action taken in pursuance of the provisions of Article XXXVII. In addition, *ad hoc* reports on matters of interest to the less-developed countries in the trade negotiations may be made available to the CTD. The periodic reports from the Secretariat should include a review of notable developments in GATT and other intergovernmental bodies in matters of interest to the CTD so that the Committee may consider appropriate action. This review may also cover activities under Article XXXVIII,2(e).[755]

In 1971 the CP adopted procedures on consultations concerning the implementation of provisions of Part IV that were drafted by the CTD in 1970 and contain the following provisions. Once a problem of non-compliance is raised in the CTD or brought to the notice of the CTD through a communication addressed to the Secretariat, the Committee may request the Secretariat to prepare the necessary background documentation and to facilitate such consultations between the parties concerned as might be helpful. The CTD must review the matter on the basis of the background information furnished by the Secretariat. If in the meantime no solution has been reached, the CTD must make such arrangements to examine the matter as are acceptable to the parties directly concerned which may include *inter alia* the establishment of a WP or a Panel. Each WP or Panel is free to seek relevant information from the cps directly concerned. It must report to the CTD within six months of its appointment. The CTD must inform the CP of the establishment of any Panel or WP and of the results of the consultations carried out by it.[756]

The CTD reviews the implementation of Part IV on an annual basis. It deals with many issues of concern to less-developed countries. It supervises the implementation of Part IV on the basis of the data submitted to it. It also supervises the implementation of the conclusions of Ministers of the decisions of the CP, of concessions made during negotiations and recommendations done by the Group of Three.[757]

The CTD established several subsidiary bodies to examine issues of interest to developing cps, to do research, and to draft proposals for the CTD. Within the CTD products of export interest to less-developed countries were examined as well as development plans. Special attention was given to stabilisation of and access to the world market in primary products. Other examinations concerned trade and aid and the economy of a single cp: Chad.

In addition, discussions were held about what measures should be taken to adjust the structure and pattern of production and trade. These discussions also concerned the question whether Article XIX should be amended so as to prohibit developed cps to take emergency measures affecting imports of less-developed countries.

Import restrictions affecting less-developed countries were also discussed. Special attention was given in such discussions to residual restrictions, special tariff problems and the trade in tropical and other agricultural products.

Preferences for less-developed countries were also dealt with. A generalised system of preferences was drawn up.[758] Moreover, the promotion of trade amongst less-developed cps was discussed. To this end India, Yugoslavia and the United Arab Republic concluded a Trade Expansion and Economic Co-operation Agreement on December 23, 1967, that is supervised by the CTD.[759] The CTD is not involved in the supervision of the Protocol Relating to Trade Negotiations Among Developing Countries.[760]

Another matter of concern to the CTD is the principle of non-reciprocity on behalf of less-developed countries during negotiations. In consequence of UNCTAD Resolution 82 (III) and General Assembly Resolution 3040 (XXVII) the principles of preferential treatment, non-discrimination and non-reciprocity on behalf of less-developed countries as objectives for negotiations were discussed.

The development of multilateral negotiations was reviewed. In 1967 the developed countries were incited to implement in advance the Kennedy Round reductions on products of interest to developing countries.

The possible amending of Articles XVIII and XXIII were also discussed.

In addition the co-operation between GATT and UNCTAD in the International Trade Centre was dealt with. Finally technical aid to developing countries and export promotion are of concern to the CTD.[761]

4.3.11.4.3. The Group of Three

On January 25, 1971, the CTD established the Group of Three, composed of the Chairmen of the CP, of the Council and of the CTD. The Group had to present proposals to the CTD and the CP with regard to the concrete action that might be taken to deal with the trade problems of developing countries. The Group was authorised to carry out such informal consultations with both developed and developing cps as it might consider necessary, taking into account the work of other GATT committees and bodies.[762]

The Group consulted with individual cps mostly, although it also was authorised to organise multilateral consultations. It recommended specific measures to individual cps.[763]

The CTD also supervised the implementation of the reports and recommendations of the Group of Three by the cps. Since the subjects covered by the Group's mandate became part of the negotiating mandate for the Tokyo Round the work of the Group was suspended for the period of the negotiations.[764] Its mandate was not revived afterwards.

4.3.11.4.4. The Tokyo Round and the developing countries

According to the Tokyo Declaration, the improvement of the trading strength of developing countries was one of the basic goals of the multilateral trade negotiations.[765] The Tokyo Round yielded mixed results for the developing countries. Some benefits may flow from tariff reductions[766] and from some of the new non-tariff barrier codes.[767] The developing countries may also benefit significantly from two framework texts: the Decision on Differential and More Favourable Treatment and Reciprocity and Fuller Participation of Developing Countries and the Decision on Safeguard Action for Development Purposes.[768] The other two framework texts give preferential status to the developing countries.[769]

On November 28 the CP adopted the first framework text in the form of a decision on differential and more favourable treatment, reciprocity and fuller participation of developing countries. Under this decision cps may accord differential and more favourable treatment to developing countries only by means of:

(a) preferential tariff treatment in accordance with the Generalised System of Preferences[770];
(b) differential and more favourable treatment concerning non-tariff measures governed by the provisions of instruments multilaterally negotiated under the GATT;
(c) arrangements amongst less-developed cps in accordance with criteria or conditions set by the CP for the mutual reduction of barriers to trade on products imported from one another; and
(d) special treatment of the least developed countries.[771]

Any cp granting differential or more favourable treatment to a developing country must notify the CP and furnish them with all relevant information and also afford adequate opportunity for prompt consultations at the request of any interested cp. The CP must on request consult with all cps concerned.[772] The decision somewhat reflects the graduation principle[773] in that it expects no concessions or contributions by the least-developed countries that are inconsistent with their development needs and in that it contains the expectation of the less-developed cps that their capacity to contribute to the GATT would improve with the progressive development of their economies and their trade situation.[774]

On the same day, November 28, 1979, the CP decided on Safeguard Action for Development Purposes. This decision relaxes the conditions for governmental assistance to economic development under Article XVIII Sections A and C. Less-developed countries may take emergency actions, if necessary for the application of their development programmes and policies by introducing provisional changes in Schedules and other measures to protect a particular industry. These must be notified to the CP. The CP must review this decision in the light of experience with its operation.[775]

4.3.11.5. Evaluation

Qualification of the mechanisms of supervision

Supervision under Article XVIII. Since the procedure of Article XVIII Section A is similar to that of Article XXVIII,4, dealing with closed-season negotiations, reference is made to the qualification of the former in section 4.3.1. The procedure under Section B is similar to that under Article XII, which is discussed in section 4.3.5.

Sections C and D provide for specific supervision on the imposition of protective measures and general supervision on existing measures. Its form is non-judicial. Supervision is primarily exercised by a politically dependent organ. The review of new measures takes place on the basis of reporting *ad hoc* and exchanges of information; that of existing measures on the basis of reporting. The correction and prevention functions are performed by political discussions and negotiations aimed at peaceful settlement; sometimes conciliation and mediation by the CP are used as well. Where measures are imposed under Section C without the concurrence of the CP, correction by means of a sanction is possible. The sanction is applied by another cp authorised by the politically dependent organ. The creative function is performed by political discussions.

Supervision under Part IV. Supervision under Article XXXVII,2 is specific and it is exercised by the politically dependent organ. No formal procedures are fixed. Reporting *ad hoc* is the instrument used for the review function. Correction takes place by means of political discussion, peaceful settlement by means of negotiations, mediation and conciliation, and by the mobilisation of shame. The creative function is performed by political discussion, and may be public. In most instances, however, the CP meet behind closed doors.

Under Article XXXVII,5 specific supervision of the implementation of Article XXXVII is possible, and may be followed by supervision under the central dispute settlement procedure.

Supervision of the implementation of Part IV as a whole is partly specific and partly general. The form of supervision is non-judicial. Supervision in the technical phase by the CTD is emphasised. In the political phase supervision is exercised by the CP, a politically dependent organ. This phase is in fact only a formality. Review is done on the basis of reporting *ad hoc*, sometimes as a consequence of requests and other times in the form of fact-finding. The correction function is usually performed by non-public political discussions, that may mobilise shame. Sometimes the correction function is performed by peaceful settlement by means of negotiations, conciliation or mediation. Since the norms of Part IV are not precisely determined, there is ample room for creation by means of political discussion.

Supervision by the Group of Three. The Group of Three performed specific supervision. This was supervision in the technical phase, for the reports of the Group had to be adopted by the CP that formally exercised supervision in the political phase. The review function was performed on the basis of information provided under other mechanisms of supervision by means of reporting *ad hoc*, or fact-finding. Correction took place via political discussions, mobilisation of shame, and peaceful settlement by means of conciliation. The creative function was performed by political discussion.

Supervision under the framework texts. Supervision of the granting differential and more favourable treatment to developing countries under the first framework text is specific and non-judicial. It is performed by the CP, a politically dependent body as well as by the cps themselves. Review takes place on the basis of notifications and reporting *ad hoc*. Correction takes place by means of negotiations and consultations aimed at friendly settlement and to a lesser degree by the mobilisation of shame.

Supervision on safeguard actions by the developing countries under the third framework text is specific and non-judicial. It is performed by a politically dependent body. Reporting *ad hoc* forms the basis for review. Consultations could lead to correction. General supervision on the operation of the text by a politically dependent organ is provided for as well. Review will occur on the basis of reporting; correction on the basis of consultations and negotiations aimed at friendly settlement. Creation might take place by means of negotiations.

Commentary

After the GATT was amended in 1955 no cp invoked Section A of Article XVIII to initiate renegotiations. Where developing cps wanted to deviate from the GATT they initiated renegotiations under the procedures of Article XXVIII,4 or they did so illegally.

The opportunity to deviate from the GATT afforded in Article XVIII B was seized many times. Most developing countries have balance of payments problems. In the period from November 1975 to November 1978 consultations were held with six cps under Article XVIII,12(b) and with 14 cps under the procedures for regular consultations adopted in 1972.[776] The Committee on Balance of Payments Restrictions usually judges the reports of developing cps leniently, since it is understood that such cps have no alternative to import restrictions to cure their balance of payments restrictions. Some developing cps apply import restrictions without invoking Article XII or Article XVIII. Others received waivers to impose surcharges or import deposit schemes.

After 1955, Ceylon and Cuba were allowed to deviate under Section C. During the 1960s, however, these releases lapsed.[777] The developing countries scarcely invoked Sections C and D of Article XVIII, since (a) they could take protective measures under Section B, (b) Sections C and D only give an opportunity for limited deviations, and (c) they did not want to be submitted to the general supervision pursuant to paragraph 6.[778] For these reasons, many developing cps deviate from the GATT illegally. Since exports to Third World countries is small, the trade of other cps is little affected, so hardly any action is taken against deviating developing countries.

The CTD has developed into an important active organ. The cps have co-operated by providing some information to the CTD, by participating in consultations and negotiations, and by taking certain measures. On the other hand, they did not always provide sufficient information and the developing countries still face many barriers against their exports.

At first the developed cps were reluctant to participate in the consultations initiated by the Group of Three. At a later stage the situation improved considerably. As a result of the supervision by the Group a number of residual restrictions were removed.[779]

Almost all texts negotiated at the Tokyo Round promise more favourable treatment for developing countries. Whether their situation will improve in reality will depend on the implementation and interpretation of the various Codes and framework texts. The lack of an adequate regulation of safeguard and emergency measures resulting in various illegal protective measures seriously hampers the growth of exports from the Third World. In addition the developed countries are much better represented in the various committees established by the Codes. This may lead to pro-developed-country interpretations of the Codes. Yet, accession to the Codes by developing countries could make those countries more influential. The developing countries certainly did not get all they wanted during the Tokyo Round. However, development issues received considerable attention. Although the Group of 77 expressed dissatisfaction with the results of the Tokyo Round; they may turn out to be the most favourable results for developing countries in this decade.

Despite all endeavours to narrow the gap between rich and poor the position of the developing countries has not improved. Already in 1955, permission to deviate from the GATT was shown to be an inadequate method to promote the development of the poor countries. The principles, objectives and incitements of Part IV did not bring about the desired development either. One of the reasons for this lack of success is that under the GATT the developed cps cannot be forced to act in a certain way. Pursuant to Article XXXVI,8 or point 5 of the first framework text, they are not allowed to require reciprocity from developing countries when they make concessions, but they are not obliged actually to make concessions. Since developed countries will not receive anything in return, they are reluctant to make concessions to developing countries. For this reason the Rounds of trade negotiations are in danger of becoming developed country affairs. Therefore, a way has to be found to induce developed countries to make concessions to developing countries and to lower the barriers imposed by rich countries against the trade from poor countries.

The GATT is not the only forum where the development of the Third World is being discussed. Such development is also of concern to the UN, especially to UNCTAD. Within other organisations promising declarations of principles were adopted, these however, did not provide the developing countries with enforceable rights to a share in the world's prosperity. The developing countries will profit most by the granting of enforceable rights to a share in the world's prosperity. Such rights could take the form of a right of access to certain markets or a right to guaranteed export revenues. They could acquire such rights gradually by means of concessions made on their behalf within GATT. Such an approach might prove more successful in the long run than that of grandiloquent declarations of principles.

176

4.3.12. Regional economic co-operation

States may wish to engage in regional economic co-operation on political as well as economic grounds. More efficient allocation, leading to increased prosperity, may be their economic motive. In addition regional economic co-operation may provide a means to enlarge sales markets. As a consequence of economic co-operation trade barriers within regions are often reduced or eliminated.

Regional economic co-operation may lead to economic integration. Such integration has various stages. The first stage is that of the free-trade area in which trade barriers between the participating States are eliminated so that free movement of goods and services is established. The second stage is that of the customs union. A customs union is a free-trade area with common external customs tariffs. The third stage is the common market which is a customs union in which there is free movement of labour and capital. Finally an economic union could be established, which is a common market in which macro-economic policy is co-ordinated. Within economic unions a common macro-economic policy is also possible.

After the Second World War, many regional agreements were concluded. The Benelux and the BLEU reached the stage of the economic union.[780] The EEC is a common market, in which some aspects of macro-economic policy are co-ordinated. Other regional agreements established free-trade areas or intend to lead to the creation of a free-trade area or a customs union. At the moment about two-thirds of the cps are parties to agreements establishing regional economic co-operation.

The reduction and elimination of trade barriers among a group of States in fact comes down to the granting of preferences to each other which is in conflict with the Most-Favoured-Nation principle of Articles I and XIII. Since regional economic integration might be beneficial to the world's prosperity the draftsmen of GATT did not wish to prohibit regional economic co-operation. On the contrary, the GATT allows for the formation of customs unions and free trade areas and the adoption of interim agreements necessary for the formation of a customs union or a free-trade area under certain conditions. It is even recognised in Article XXIV,4 that increasing freedom of trade by the development through voluntary agreements of closer integration between the economies of the countries to such agreements is desirable. Although more developed stages of economic integration are not addressed by the agreement, it can be assumed that those forms of co-operation are subject to the same rules as apply to customs unions.

The draftsmen of the GATT, however, were also aware of the possible disadvantages of regional economic co-operation. In addition they realised that cps might want to conclude preferential agreements under the guise of agreements aimed at economic integration. To prevent undesirable consequences a number of requirements and conditions for regional economic co-operation are incorporated in Article XXIV.

One of the consequences of regional economic co-operation is a loss of freedom by the participating States to determine their own economic policy.

The extent to which such freedom is restricted depends on the stage of economic integration. A cp may be kept from making concessions because of its regional ties. Since cps have already made concessions within the region it might be impossible, for domestic political reasons, to also make concessions within GATT. Moreover, cps might not need concessions from GATT partners, since they obtained equivalent concessions within the region. For these reasons general liberalisation may be hampered by the formation of regional economic blocs.[781] Regional economic integration has static as well as dynamic effects. Static effects are trade creation and trade diversion. There is trade creation when the elimination of trade barriers gives rise to more trade between the integrating economies. Trade diversion occurs when imports from areas outside of the integrating economies are replaced by imports from participating economies.

The dynamic effects of economic integration are the following. Since trade barriers are eliminated sales markets are enlarged and the competition within the whole area is sharpened. As a consequence inefficient producers are forced to stop production. The remaining producers are incited to large-scale production that might reduce production costs per item. This effect is stronger when small States integrate their economies than when large States do so. For producers from third States, however, the sales market will become smaller. As a consequence they might have to reduce their production scale or even close down. This may lead to an increase in production costs and a loss in efficiency. In addition regional economic integration may stimulate the economies of the States involved. Consequently, the national income will increase, giving rise to more imports that will create trade.[782]

The effects of regional economic integration on the prosperity of the world in general cannot be estimated. The consumers within the integrating region will gain, but the allocation of production factors may become less efficient. In each separate case it has to be judged whether trade creation exceeds trade diversion and whether the costs of production decrease. The government revenues of the integrating States usually decrease since a number of tariffs disappear.

4.3.12.1. GATT's requirements for regional economic integration

4.3.12.1.1. Relationship between paragraphs 4 and 5 to 9 of Article XXIV

The cps recognise that the purpose of a customs union or of a free-trade area should be to facilitate trade between the constituent territories and not to raise barriers to the trade of other cps with such territories.[783] One could deduce from this statement the requirement that a regional arrangement must be trade creating and not trade diverting for it to be lawful under the GATT.[784] The reduction of trade barriers within a limited area always leads to some trade diversion. Therefore such a requirement should be interpreted as demanding more trade creation than trade diversion. Trade creation as a consequence of a rise in national income within the integrating region should be taken into account in balancing the desired and undesirable effects.

Another view as to the meaning of Article XXIV,4 is that in concluding an agreement leading to regional integration the trade effect on each cp outside of the region should be taken into account. In other words, no single trade barrier should be increased as a consequence of the integration.[785] Such an interpretation of paragraph 4 is probably incorrect since the provisions of paragraph 5 concern the trade with other cps on the whole and the general incidence of the duties and regulations and since paragraph 6 provides for a procedure in case bound tariffs are increased as a consequence of regional economic integration.[786]

Paragraphs 5 to 9 contain further provisions on regional economic integration. How paragraphs 4 and 5 to 9 relate to each other is not completely clear. One could perceive of paragraph 4 as containing the substantial requirement for regional economic integration and of the other paragraphs as its technical elaboration. In that case any arrangement for regional economic integration that fulfils the requirement of paragraph 4 would conform to the rules of GATT. Another interpretation is that paragraph 4 only contains an introductory declaration and that the substantive requirements are to be found in the subsequent paragraphs. Finally, one could say that paragraph 4 contains the requirements with regard to the objectives of the regional economic integration whereas paragraphs 5 to 9 contain the requirements for the practical elaboration of such integration. The relation between paragraph 4 and paragraphs 5 to 9 was discussed during the review of the EEC treaty in 1957, but no clear ruling was given on the position of paragraph 4 in relation to the other paragraphs of Article XXIV.[787]

4.3.12.1.2. Requirements regarding the relations between the co-operating cps

Under certain conditions the cps are allowed to deviate from the GATT for the purpose of creating a customs union or a free-trade area. A customs union is defined as the substitution of a single customs territory[788] for two or more customs territories, so that (i) duties and other restrictive regulations of commerce (except, where necessary, those permitted under Articles XI, XII, XIII, XIV, XV and XX) are eliminated with respect to substantially all the trade between the constituent territories of the union or at least with respect to substantially all the trade in products originating in such territories, and (ii) subject to the provisions of paragraph 9 of Article XXIV, substantially the same duties and other regulations of commerce are applied by each of the members of the union to the trade of territories not included in the union.[789] A free-trade area is defined as a group of two or more customs territories in which the duties and other restrictive regulations of commerce (except, where necessary, those permitted under Articles XI, XII, XIII, XIV, XV and XX) are eliminated on substantially all the trade between the constituent territories in products originating in such territories.[790]

A customs union could also be described as a free-trade area with a common external tariff. Consequently the requirements for a free-trade area also apply to a customs union. By the same token the requirements for a customs union apply to common markets and economic unions. Since a

179

customs union, as opposed to a free-trade area, constitutes a customs territory, the GATT can be applied to a customs union.[791] But as long as a customs union does not possess full autonomy in the conduct of its external commercial relations, it cannot become a cp to the GATT.[792]

In the definitions of customs unions and free-trade area, the term 'substantially all the trade' is used, so a part of the duties and other restrictive regulations may be maintained. What duties and regulations may be maintained is not clear, however. The phrase 'substantially all the trade' has a qualitative as well as a quantitative aspect. Therefore only a small percentage of the total trade may be restricted and the exclusion of a major sector of economic activity is not allowed. An exception for most agricultural trade, for example, is not allowed.[793] During the review of the EEC treaty the EEC representative proposed as a quantitative criterion 80 per cent. of the total trade which gave rise to objections.[794] What constitutes a major sector was never determined.

In addition, the GATT text does not state whether under Article XXIV,8(a) a small percentage of the trade between all co-operating cps may remain restricted or that the trade restrictions between all cps individually must be largely eliminated. In the first case it would be possible to establish a customs union or a free-trade area, in which one State keeps on restricting trade with the other participants provided such trade covers less than 20 per cent. of all the trade within the integrating area and the other participants release all trade barriers. This would provide a way for large customs unions of free-trade areas, in which there are no trade restrictions, to conclude preferential agreements with small States by formally incorporating the latter in the union or area without eliminating many restrictions. This issue was discussed during the review of the EEC Treaty in connection with the question whether the association of overseas territories with the EEC was conforming with the GATT. The EEC representative stated that the total trade between all parties should be considered.[795] Such an interpretation must be rejected since the draftsmen of the GATT could never have meant to allow disguised preferential agreements.

Quantitative restrictions against imports from States within the integrating area must be eliminated, too, unless they are necessary restrictions permited under Articles XI, XII, XIII, XIV, XV and XX. So it is possible for a Member State of a regional grouping to apply unnecessary quantitative restrictions only against imports from non-Member States. Such discrimination is permitted provided the regional arrangement is allowed under Article XXIV.[796] Usually such discriminatory quantitative restrictions provide little protection since often most trade takes place within the integrating area. In addition it might be possible for non-members to export commodities to Member States via another Member-State. Such practices are checked by requiring certificates of origin for imported goods.

4.3.12.1.3. Requirements regarding the level of external duties and trade regulations

The duties and other regulations of commerce imposed at the institution of a customs union in respect of trade with cps not parties to such union may not on the whole be higher or more restrictive than the general incidence of the duties and regulations of commerce applicable in the constituent territories prior to the formation of such union.[797] With respect to a free-trade area, the duties and other regulations of commerce maintained in each of the constituent territories and applicable at the formation of such free-trade area to the trade of cps not included in such area or not parties to such agreement may not be higher or more restrictive than the corresponding duties and other regulations of commerce existing in the same constitutent territories prior to the formation of the free-trade area.[798]

These requirements are ambiguous since it is not clear what constitutes applicable duties and regulations of commerce. These could be either the maximum restrictions that the GATT allows for or the restrictions actually applied when the free trade area or customs union was established. The WP reviewing the EEC Treaty discussed this issue without reaching clear understanding.[799] Therefore the CP asked the Executive Secretary of GATT for a legal interpretation of the word 'applicable'. The Executive Secretary 'with consummate diplomacy' stated that:

> When the two interpretations are (re)considered from the point of view of reasonableness and logic the gap between them narrows. On the one hand, if the word were interpreted in the sense of "applied" duties, it would be reasonable, in the computation of a common external tariff, to permit the use of the duties inscribed in the tariff in those cases where duties had been temporarily lowered or suspended to meet particular circumstances of an economic nature or because other types of barriers were being used. On the other hand, if the word were interpreted in the sense of "applicable" duties, it would be reasonable, in the computation of a common external tariff, to disallow the customs duties of a legal tariff if these duties had never actually been applied and there was no reasonable expectation that they ever would be applied.

The issue has never been resolved in GATT.[800] General criteria to determine whether a common external tariff is conformable to Article 5(a) were never developed. Where trade barriers are not increased at all under the common tariff, there is no doubt that the new common tariff is legitimate under the GATT. If all barriers are increased, the common tariff is obviously in conflict with GATT. An evaluation of the common external tariff is difficult when some barriers to trade are increased, while others are lowered. In that case increases and decreases have to be compared to determine whether the new external tariff is acceptable under the GATT.

According to the preparatory works the phrase 'on the whole' does not mean that an average tariff should be laid down in respect of each individual product, but merely that the whole level of tariffs of a customs union should not be higher than the average overall level of the former constituent territories.[801] But what is 'the whole level of tariffs'? And, how should individual tariffs be weighed? One could apply the arithmetical average method as the EEC Member States did when they created the EEC.[802] Such a method is unfair since tariffs levied on scarcely traded products are given the same weight as tariffs on products of which huge amounts are traded. Yet to weigh tariffs by the volume of trade is not fair either, since high tariffs choke off trade, and therefore get a very low weight. A fair method would be to use a weighing factor equal to the quotient of the trade value of unrestricted imports of the commodity and the total unrestricted imports.

181

Since trade is restricted, however, the quantity of unrestricted imports cannot be determined but can only be estimated. The sales price would equal the cost price.[803]

4.3.12.1.4. Preferences under Article I,2

Regional economic co-operation may not affect the preferences under Article I,2. They may, however, be eliminated or adjusted by means of negotiations with cps affected.[804] Some of the integrating cps may levy lower tariffs on certain imported commodities than other integrating cps, because of a preferential arrangement under Article I,2. If the former cps re-export such commodities within the integrating areas the other cps are allowed to collect a duty equal to the difference between the duty already paid and any higher duty that would be payable if the product were being imported directly into its territory.[805]

4.3.12.1.5. Requirements for interim agreements

Because economic integration is time consuming, it usually is impossible to eliminate all interior trade barriers at once when regional agreements are concluded. For this reason the GATT allows for interim agreements leading to the formation of a customs union or a free-trade area, under which the cps may maintain some interior trade barriers. To prevent the use of interim agreements as a cover for illegal preferential agreements any interim agreement must include a plan and schedule for the formation of a customs union or a free-trade area within a reasonable length of time.[806]

When future developments cannot be foreseen, it is impossible to draft a detailed plan or schedule. As a consequence no objections were raised against interim agreements without a detailed plan.[807] What length of time is reasonable was never determined. The Greek Association Agreement with the EEC speaks of 22 years, the Turkish one mentions 23 years.[808] No complaints were made against these association agreements. When developing cps are partners to the regional agreements the integration process can take considerable time, since economic adjustments within Third World countries are time consuming and since their industries and their balances of payments need protection.

Because cps as well as GATT bodies did not force integrating cps to fulfil the requirements regarding plans, schedules, and a reasonable length of time, the attention given to such fulfilment decreased. The NAFTA, for example, does not contain a plan to liberalise the trade in all commodities; only the trade in some commodities is liberalised. In addition there is no schedule. Nevertheless the NAFTA is accepted and tolerated within GATT.[809]

The requirements for duties and other regulations of commerce maintained in each of the parties to an interim agreement are similar to those applicable to the formation of customs unions and free-trade areas.[810]

182

4.3.12.2. Mechanisms of supervision

4.3.12.2.1. Notifications

The integrating cps need not ask permission from the CP to deviate from the GATT when the above-mentioned requirements are fulfilled. However, any cp deciding to enter into a regional agreement must promptly notify the CP. In addition such cp must make available to the CP such information as will enable them to make reports and recommendations.[811] The CP delegated their competence in this area to the Council. The reports are drafted by WPs.

4.3.12.2.2. Renegotiations

As common external tariffs of a customs union are determined, cps may have to increase certain tariffs. If so, they must renegotiate under the procedure of Article XXVIII. In providing compensation, the cps involved must take due account of the compensation already afforded by the reductions brought about in the corresponding duty of the other constituents of the union.[812] In addition, the cps must renegotiate the elimination or adjustment of preferences under Article I,2 with potentially affected cps.[813]

4.3.12.2.3. Supervision on interim agreements

The cps must submit plans and schedules of interim agreements to the CP. The CP must study such plans and schedules in consultation with the integrating cps taking due account of the information made available in accordance with Article XXIV,7(a). If the CP find that an interim agreement is not likely to result in the formation of a customs union or a free-trade area within the period contemplated by the parties to the agreement or that such period is not a reasonable one, the CP must make recommendations to the parties to the agreement. The parties shall not maintain or put into force, as the case may be, such agreement if they are not prepared to modify it in accordance with these recommendations.[814]

Although in principle review by the CP is not required, the CP may recommend appropriate modifications. If the cps involved do not comply with such recommendations they violate the GATT. Consequently, other cps which consider themselves injured by the regional agreement may invoke Article XXIII. If so, the burden of proof rests with the integrating cp addressed.[815]

4.3.12.2.4. The waiver of Article XXIV,10

According to Article XXIV,10, the CP may by a two-thirds majority approve proposals which do not fully comply with the requirements of paragraphs 5 to 9 inclusive, provided that such proposals lead to the formation of a customs union or free-trade area in the sense of Article XXIV. So the cps may deviate from the GATT under agreements that will lead to the creation of a customs union or free-trade area, although barriers to internal/interior trade are not sufficiently eliminated. Also cps may effect preferences under Article I,2 and even increase bound tariffs without entering into renegotiations. Moreover they may increase the overall external tariff or enter into interim agreements without fulfilling the requirements relating to the plan, the schedule or the length of the interim period. But in all these cases the CP must grant a waiver. The procedure of supervision of Article XXIV,10 is almost similar to that of Article XXV,5. Yet the required majority differs. The requirements of Article XXIV,10 are more severe since the agreement must lead to the formation of a customs union or a free-trade agreement. Supervision under paragraph 10 is stricter than that under paragraph 7(a).

4.3.12.3. Regional economic co-operation in practice

As long as the GATT has existed, many regional agreements have been concluded giving preferences to specific cps.[816] In this section, a number of these agreements will be discussed.

In the GATT itself, a number of exceptions are made to allow regional economic co-operation. In this way the Benelux, the Lebano-Syrian customs union, preferential arrangements between Chile and neighbouring countries and special trade arrangements between India and Pakistan could be maintained.[817]

The ECSC could not be established under Article XXIV since this community concerns only the coal and steel sectors. The CP granted a waiver to the cps involved to make the establishment of the ECSC possible.

4.3.12.3.1. The creation of the EEC

The creation of the EEC largely influenced the effectiveness of the procedure of Article XXIV. Although the designs for the EEC included more than the establishment of a customs union, the EEC Treaty had to be reviewed in the light of the requirements of Article XXIV relating to customs unions. This was the test case for the procedure of Article XXIV. A large WP, the 'Committee of the Whole' was appointed, that was comprised of all governments parties to the GATT, to examine the relevant provisions of the EEC Treaty and to recommend appropriate and desirable action for establishing effective and continuing co-operation between the CP and the EEC.[818] During this review four important issues were discussed: the common tariff, quantitative restrictions, trade in agricultural products and association of overseas territories. The Committee appointed four sub-groups to examine each of these issues: the sub-groups A, B, C and D.[819]

Three problems faced sub-group A that examined the common external tariff. The first one concerned the method to be adopted in establishing the common external tariff. The EEC opted for the arithmetic average. The second problem arose because the EEC treaty only provided for a common tariff for a limited number of commodities. The level of the other tariffs was to be determined at a later stage. Therefore the WP could not determine whether the common tariff was 'on the whole higher or more restrictive than the general incidence of the duties and regulations of commerce in existence prior to the formation of the EEC'. This indeterminacy led to postponement of resolution of the legal issues. The third problem related to the necessity of renegotiating with respect to compensation for the bound items that were to be increased in the course of establishing the common external tariff. This matter was subsequently negotiated in the Dillon Round.[820] During the discussions in sub-group A some cps asked for product-by-product and country-by-country studies. The EEC, however, did not want such studies and argued that all that was required was that the common tariff should not be increased on the whole as is stated in Article XIV,5(a).[821]

Sub-group B discussed the difficult problems relating to quantitative restrictions. The first question was whether the customs union could retain import quotas against non-members so long as they did not restrict trade on the whole more than the previously applied barriers. Although the EEC thought it was allowed to retain such quotas, the sub-group held the view that common quantitative restrictions are not allowed under Article XXIV,5(a).[822] Similarly, the sub-group stated that no common import restrictions for balance of payments reasons were permitted. Contrary to the opinion of the EEC, the sub-group held the view that the EEC treaty does not contain an obligation for the Member States to impose common quantitative restrictions on agricultural and fisheries products. The treaty only requires uniformity among the quantitative restrictions imposed by individual States. Nevertheless the sub-group did not reach a final decision.[823]

Sub-group C discussed the long and complicated agriculture provisions. The EEC treaty provides for the establishment of a common market for agricultural products, a common agricultural policy, a common organisation to administer this policy and certain protections for national producers. The other cps were afraid that the EEC would introduce trade restricting measures to implement its common agricultural policy. However, the EEC treaty does not require such measures and the implementation of the agricultural provisions had not yet been undertaken at the time of the review. Therefore incompatibility with the EEC treaty could not be proven. The discussions thus reached a total impasse.[824]

Sub-group D examined the provisions of the EEC treaty relating to the association of overseas territories. The provisions of the EEC treaty allow the overseas territories to share equally the benefits of the Common Market. At the same time, each territory is required to apply to its trade with all the Member States and with the other territories the same treatment as that which it applies to the European State with which it has special relations.[825] Thus the preferences permitted under GATT Article I,2 are extended, which is a violation of GATT. The EEC argued that the whole scheme would be considered as a free-trade area with the EEC on the one hand and each overseas territory on the other hand. Although the overseas territories maintained and even levied new tariffs, the requirement to liberalise substantially all the trade was fulfilled according to the EEC, since the volume of restricted trade was little because the trade into one overseas territory was compared with the trade between the EEC members. Other developing cps expressed sharp criticism against the association of overseas territories.

Consequently the EEC agreed to a commodity study to assess the impact of the associations on third countries.[826]

The review of the EEC treaty did not show that the treaty is compatible with the GATT. A number of questions remained undecided. The CP did not dare to state openly that the EEC treaty conflicts with the GATT. Thirty per cent. of world trade takes place within the EEC. The United States and the United Kingdom supported the EEC on political and economic grounds. A negative judgment on the EEC treaty could have caused the withdrawal of the six EEC Member States. Consequently the GATT would be far less effective.

4.3.12.3.2. Reactions to the EEC treaty

(a) *Reactions in Europe.* To protect themselves against the effects of the EEC treaty, a number of other European countries formed the EFTA in 1960. With regard to industrial commodities, the EFTA conformed to the GATT. Preferential relations were not extended. However, since trade in agricultural products was not liberalised, the GATT was violated. Yet the formation of the EFTA was not hindered by the GATT, one of the reasons being that the CP were equally lenient in reviewing the EEC treaty.[827]

Subsequently, a number of European cps concluded regional agreements with the EEC establishing or preparing a free-trade area. The WPs could not come to a final judgment as to the compatibility of such agreements with the GATT.[828] In 1973 three EFTA Member States acceded to the EEC.

(b) *Reactions of the developing countries.* Since the countries whose exports were affected by the association agreements of the EEC were not compensated during the review of the EEC treaty, they entered into bilateral negotiations with the EEC in Brussels.[829] As a consequence association agreements were concluded with Greece, Turkey, Malta and Cyprus, containing preferences.[830] This conformed to the GATT, according to the EEC, since it concerned interim agreements leading to accession by the associating cps to the customs union. Moreover, so the EEC argued, in this way detrimental effects of association agreements with former territories overseas were prevented. The association agreements with the Mediterranean cps do not fulfil the requirements regarding a plan and schedules. Moreover, the length of the formation period is not reasonable.[831] The WPs reviewing the agreements could not reach agreement as to their compatibility with GATT. Consequently the CP could not make recommendations under Article XXIV,7.

The bilateral negotiations also resulted in other agreements between the EEC and Mediterranean as well as Third World countries, including Algeria, Egypt, Israel, Jordan, Lebanon, Morocco, Spain, Syria, and Tunisia.[832] According to the EEC these are interim agreements leading to the formation of a free-trade area. But, since plans and schedules are lacking, these 'interim agreements' do not conform to the GATT requirements. Yet no agreement was reached as to the compatibility of these agreements with GATT. Consequently no action was taken against them.

After most overseas territories had become independent, the EEC concluded the Yaounde Convention with a number of young African countries to replace the overseas territories system. This Convention established 18 free-trade areas. The WP that reviewed this Convention could not reach a unanimous decision whether this Convention was compatible with GATT.[833] In 1969 the EEC concluded the second Yaounde Convention. A WP, established to review the Convention, could not reach agreement either. For the first time some cps argued that the requirements of Article XXIV are not suitable for the analysis of an integration scheme when there is on the one hand a developed country and on the other a developing country. The developing country should be allowed to restrict part of the imports. In fact this is a recognition that preferential agreements are allowed when a developing country is involved.[834]

In 1975 the EEC concluded the Lomé Convention with 46 developing countries. Under this Convention barriers to trade from the 46 developing countries to the EEC are eliminated while trade from the EEC may be restricted. Many cps welcomed this Convention since it promotes the objectives of Part IV and the establishment of a new international economic order. Others thought the Convention violated GATT. Since the WP could not reach agreement on the compatibility with GATT of this Convention the CP did not take any action against it.[835] The author is not aware of any GATT action with regard to the second Lomé Convention.

(c) *Reactions of the United States.*   According to the United States, the EEC violates the GATT, especially with regard to its agricultural policy and the association agreements. Some say that the United States, because it thought that the EEC violated the GATT, also introduced illegal barriers to trade, especially to protect domestic agriculture.[836] In addition the U.S. proposed changes in GATT to stop the EEC from violating this Agreement.[837]

4.3.12.3.3. *Regional economic co-operation between developing countries*

In 1960 the Latin-American countries established the LAFTA, which was terminated in 1980. Although under this agreement internal barriers were maintained and although it was an obviously protectionist agreement, the CP did not make recommendations under Article XXIV,7(a) and tolerated the LAFTA.[838] The developing countries entered into many protectionist agreements for economic co-operation such as the CARICOM against which the CP undertook no action.[839]

Since the late 1960s preferences to developing cps that deviate from GATT have been allowed. India, the United Arab Republic and Yugoslavia entered into a preferential trade agreement against which no objections arose within GATT.[840] In 1971 the CP granted two general waivers allowing general preferences for Third World countries.[841] In 1976 the Bangkok Agreement was concluded that allows for negotiations to establish preferential agreements among developing cps in Asia and the Pacific. The GATT tolerates the Bangkok Agreement as well.[842] The CP decided on January 29, 1979, that the ASEAN countries may implement the Agreement, under certain conditions. This decision also establishes mechanisms of supervision, including notification, consultations and biannual review.[843]

4.3.12.3.4. Regional economic co-operation with socialist countries

Finland entered into regional agreements with Hungary, Czechoslovakia and the German Democratic Republic.[844] A WP report was published concerning the first two agreements only.[845] In both instances the WPs did not reach agreement. According to some cps an agreement between cps with a free-market economy and cps with a centrally planned economy gives rise to unprecedented problems. Since tariffs are hardly applied by cps with a centrally planned economy it is very difficult to determine the general incidence of trade barriers. Moreover, it is difficult to determine whether the barriers to substantially all the trade within the area are eliminated.

4.3.12.4. Evaluation

Qualification of the mechanisms of supervision

There is general and non-judicial supervision of the formation of customs unions and free-trade areas. It is performed by a politically dependent organ that in the technical phase may be assisted by subsidiary bodies. The review function is performed on the basis of reporting *ad hoc*. The correction and creative functions are usually performed under other, subsequent procedures of supervision.

Supervision of interim agreements is also general and non-judicial, and is performed by a political body, assisted by subsidiary bodies in the technical phase, as well. The review function is performed by reporting *ad hoc*. Correction takes place through political discussion as well as by mediation and conciliation aimed at peaceful settlement. The creative function is performed by political discussions. This procedure may constitute the basis for other mechanisms of supervision.

Supervision on bound tariffs is similar to that under Article XXVIII. Its evaluation can be found in section 4.3.1.

Under Article XXIV,10 there is specific, non-judicial supervision on regional arrangements that do not fulfil all the requirements of paragraphs 5 to 9 of Article XXIV. Such supervision is performed by a politically dependent organ, assisted in the technical phase by subsidiary bodies. The procedures vary according to the kinds of waivers granted. They are similar to the mechanisms of supervision on waivers, discussed in section 4.3.3.

Commentary

GATT's draftsmen obviously wanted to provide a set of regulating norms applicable to regional economic co-operation, to prevent such co-operation from becoming an obstacle to the realisation of GATT's objectives. They did not want to establish an organ competent to give rulings for each individual case but they wanted to establish fixed criteria that would provide security that regional arrangements would not reduce the world's prosperity. Unfortunately these criteria are ambiguous and have proved to be inadequate. For these reasons the cps violated the provisions of Article XXIV repeatedly. Little action was undertaken within GATT against such violations, since there was no agreement within the GATT on the interpretation of Article XXIV. Moreover, the GATT organs doubted their own competence to challenge regional arrangements.

According to the GATT the purpose of regional economic co-operation should be to raise prosperity for the whole world. This would be attained when trade creation because of the co-operation would exceed trade diversion. The draftsmen assumed that this would be so if the co-operating cps would liberalise the trade amongst themselves virtually completely. So discrimination is permitted provided it concerns all trade. This idea constitutes the basis of the requirements of Article XXIV,8. The trade creating effect of proportional tariff reductions is stronger when a high tariff is lowered than when a low tariff is lowered.[846] For this reason preferential agreements under which, for example, 20 per cent. of all tariffs are reduced may contribute considerably to the increase of the world's prosperity. Nevertheless such agreements are not allowed under GATT.

To promote the development of the less-developed countries is the main objective of Part IV of GATT, that entered into force in 1966. Granting preferences is a way to achieve this objective. Preferences may be granted by way of regional agreements, including regional agreements not leading to the formation of a customs union or free-trade area, that are in conflict with GATT. Nevertheless, recently such preferential agreements were concluded as well as tolerated latterly. The CP could grant waivers for such agreements, but no waivers were requested.

Supervision on regional economic co-operation is ineffective. Article XXIV is openly violated for the following reasons. First of all, the conditions for the co-operation are ambiguous. Secondly, the cps do not agree on the issue whether regional co-operation will enhance or harm the world's prosperity. Finally cps violate Article XXIV because other cps do the same thing. There is no consensus as to the validity of the economic theory underlying the conditions of Article XXIV. Moreover, since the objectives of GATT were adjusted in 1966, partial preferences may be desirable.

Supervision on regional economic co-operation could be improved by changing the criteria and strengthening the procedures of supervision. The criteria should relate directly to the objectives of GATT; they should aim at increasing the world's welfare and promoting the economic development of developing countries. This does not require complete trade liberalisation in the short run. The cps should get permission from the CP for each regional agreement. The CP should review such agreements in the light of GATT's objectives. To be able to perform this function the CP would need more discretional power. Yet, whether the cps want to expand the competence of GATT's plenary organ, remains to be seen.

V. EFFECTIVENESS OF GATT SUPERVISION

5.1. Consent and consensus with regard to the objectives of GATT

5.1.1. The level of consensus within GATT

Van Hoof and de Vey Mestdagh discern three basic grades of consensus. The first exists when a problem is identified, and a general feeling exists that it should be solved but the consensus is not strong enough yet to serve as a basis for international legal obligations. A second level of consensus presents itself where States agree on a common purpose to the extent that the elaboration of rules on the subject matter would in principle be possible, but the methods and means to realise this purpose are still lacking. On the third level, there is consensus with regard to both the purpose underlying the rule and the methods and means to realise that purpose.

The cps agree on the objectives mentioned in the preamble. Heretofore the emphasis has been put on expanding the production and exchange of goods, a large and growing volume of real income and effective demand and the raising of standards of living. Although the desirability of developing the full use of the resources of the world is at least doubtful, because of the potential catastrophic consequence for the natural environment, this purpose has never been qualified nor restricted within GATT. Full employment should theoretically flow from the realisation of the other goals. The cps also agree that the economic development of the developing countries should be promoted. In conclusion one can say that consensus exists as to the purposes of GATT.

However, there is no agreement within GATT as to the methods and means by which the GATT purposes should be realised. In the first years of the GATT's existence almost all cps were developed countries with at least reasonable standards of living. They thought the objectives of the GATT would be realised by entering into reciprocal and mutually advantageous arrangements aimed at the reduction of barriers to international trade and the elimination of discriminatory treatment in international commerce. This would lead to an increase in welfare for the whole world while relative differences in welfare between the different States would be maintained. Currently, they still hold the same views, especially where the trade between developed countries is concerned.

The developing countries, a great number of which acceded to the GATT after 1960, disagree with the above-described ideas. According to these countries the actual divergences in the standards of living of the different countries is inequitable. Priority should be given to the development of the economies of the least-developed countries in seeking to raise the standards of living in the whole world. This should be done by entering into preferential agreements, elimination of barriers to trade by developed countries, protection of the industries of developing countries and discrimination in favour of the Third World.

At present the developed countries agree with the developing countries on this issue to a certain extent. The former recognise that it is necessary to lessen the gap between rich and poor for the raising of the standard of living in the world as a whole. The raising of the standard of living in the Third World would increase prosperity in the developed countries, since their consuming market would be argumented. However, most developed cps are not prepared to give up a part of their prosperity on behalf of the Third World countries. Moreover, some developed cps are afraid of becoming dependent on developing countries, for instance, for the supply of essential commodities. The developing countries would like such dependencies to develop.

The cps do not agree on the issue of whether regional economic integration promotes GATT's objectives or not. Integrating cps usually argue that regional co-operation is beneficial to GATT's objectives while the other cps hold opposite views. In summary, one can say that the cps agree on the purpose of GATT but not on the methods and means to realise it. The second level of consensus is reached within GATT.

5.1.2. The adequacy of the GATT rules, consent and consensus

For supervision under GATT to be effective, the GATT provisions must be adequate. In other words: they must have the capacity to achieve GATT's purposes. The primary criterion for the adequacy of the GATT rules is the achievement of GATT's purposes in practice. In addition the level of consent of the cps and consensus among the cps regarding the rules indicate to what extent the rules are deemed to be adequate.

Most-Favoured-Nation treatment and reciprocity undoubtedly contributed to an enormous reduction in trade barriers. During GATT's first decade all cps consented in the application of these two principles. At the moment, however, consent and consensus regarding a strict application of these principles are lacking since developing cps want preferential treatment. Unconditional Most-Favoured-Nation treatment and reciprocity are not adequate to achieve the purposes of Part IV.

The rounds of negotiations were very useful in generating huge amounts of concessions from the cps. Tariff barriers have been reduced considerably, especially on industrial products. In addition, many non-tariff barriers have been eliminated and various agreements and arrangements enhancing GATT's purposes have been made. Although many issues are not yet resolved, and there are still a number of trade restrictions, such as residual restrictions and high duties on primary products, the rounds of negotiations have been very helpful in inducing cps to make concessions and reach agreement on behalf of the world's prosperity. All cps consent in the use of negotiations. Recent complaints from developing cps, that they do not benefit sufficiently from the rounds, do not concern the use of negotiations, but regard the negotiating techniques and the principles applied.

The system of renegotiations promoted the granting of concessions. It provides beneficial flexibility without generating uncertainty. Consent and consensus regarding renegotiations prevail. So, the provisions on renegotiations are adequate to generate reductions in trade barriers and to protect cps from undesirable consequences of the concessions they granted.

The prohibition of quantitative restrictions in GATT is qualified since a number of exceptions are allowed. This prohibition certainly contributed to the reduction of trade barriers and, therefore, to an increase in world prosperity. However, many illegal quantitative restrictions were and are still applied. Moreover, consent and consensus on this rule in general are limited. The cps want the elimination of quantitative restrictions to a certain extent, but they want to maintain some restrictions as well. Therefore, the adequacy of the provisions concerned is meagre.

Some quantitative restrictions are permitted under GATT. The provisions concerned aim at striking a balance between recognised domestic interests of the cps applying the restrictions and the reduction of barriers to trade. First, quantitative restrictions with regard to agricultural products are permitted under Article XI,2, that allows for government interference on behalf of domestic farmers and consumers. Article XI was hardly invoked at all. Consent and consensus are lacking. Trade in primary products is still very restricted. At the moment the interests of domestic producers prevail over the promotion of world prosperity. Therefore, the GATT provisions on agriculture are inadequate.

The second category of quantitative restrictions permitted under the GATT are quantitative restrictions for balance-of-payments reasons. During the first decade of GATT's existence these provisions were adequate. Many war-ravaged European cps had a chance to rebuild their economies under the protection of quantitative restrictions while at the same time gradually eliminating such restrictions. However, after 1960 some illegal residual restrictions remained. In addition, quantitative restrictions are not in all circumstances the most appropriate means to solve balance of payments problems, epecially since not all cps maintain fixed exchange rates. Other instruments, such as surcharges, may be more effective to restore equilibrium and less detrimental to world trade. Currently, a good number of developing cps legally apply quotas under Article XVIII that are unlikely to be eliminated in the short term. There is some discontent among developed countries, because of the continued application of Article XVIII restrictions. There is considerable discontent with residual restrictions applied by the developed cps. Most cps consent to a provision allowing for deviation from GATT because of balance-of-payments problems. There is no consensus, however, as to what means should be applied. The provisions of Articles XII and XVIII were adequate before 1960, but are inadequate now.

Developing countries may apply quantitative restrictions to protect new industries. There are no objections to these provisions. However, they are not adequate to promote the development of the Third World.

The original GATT provisions regarding subsidies are inadequate to deal with the increasing government interference in national economies. For this reason the cps concluded the Agreement on Interpretation and Application of Articles VI, XVI and XXIII of the GATT. In years to come the adequacy of the new provisions will show. There is considerable consent and consensus among developed cps with regard to this new agreement. The developing cps are less involved.

The GATT rules are difficult to apply to State trading enterprises. Although the provisions of Article XVII facilitate such application, the GATT is written in the first place for cps with market economies and is inadequate for the incorporation of cps with centrally planned economies.

The existence of several régimes regarding anti-dumping and countervailing measures indicates a lack of consensus among cps. This reduces the adequacy of the GATT rules concerned. However, almost all developed cps are signatories to the anti-dumping and subsidies codes, that provide adequate rules to deal with anti-dumping and countervailing measures. In practice international trade can be distorted far more by anti-dumping and countervailing measures by the developed cps since the latter have the largest imports. Since most developed cps signed the new codes, the GATT rules concerned are adequate.

The new rules on government procurement are revolutionary. Once they are applied they will open up a large market. They seem adequate to reduce the barriers to trade caused by domestic government procurement policies, but not to completely eliminate such barriers.

One of the weakest provisions of GATT is the rules concerning emergency action, market disruption and market regulation. The rules concerned are ambiguous and consensus is lacking. Since government interference in national economies increases rapidly, market regulation and provisions on socio-economical adjustment on the international level are necessary. The GATT hardly provides for adequate rules. The arrangements regarding dairy products and bovine meat may contain more adequate rules.

The rules regarding dispute settlement are adequate. The procedures for consultations are generally accepted. They obviously enhance the purposes of the GATT. The provisions on protection of benefits are accepted. However, the long periods of time involved reduce their adequacy. The establishment of permanent technical organs or the development of a expeditious procedure to establish such organs would enhance the adequacy of the rules concerned. Implementation of the 1979 Understanding contained in the new framework texts could greatly enhance the adequacy of the central dispute settlement procedure. The existence of central as well as specific procedures augments the adequacy of the procedures concerned.

The rules regarding regional economic integration are inadequate. Consensus is lacking. Strict application of the rules might even impair regional co-operation beneficial to GATT's objectives. In addition the rules are ambiguous. Consequently, Article XXIV was repeatedly violated.

The GATT rules regarding waivers are adequate. They allow a flexible implementation of the GATT rules. As waivers must be granted by a two-thirds majority of the politically dependent organ arbitrary waivers are not granted. Since obligations may be waived by the CP, cps are less reluctant to commit themselves to GATT rules in general. This enhances the achievement of GATT's purposes. No cp opposes the possibility to grant waivers.

The adequacy of Part IV is doubtful. The major drawback of the rules on trade and development is their voluntariness. As long as developed cps are not bound to promote the development of the Third World, such development cannot be guaranteed. In addition, developing cps give more weight to the provisions of Part IV than developed cps do. Although all developed cps pay lip-service to the objectives of Part IV there is some doubt whether they actually want to promote the development of the Third World in practice. As the new framework texts are voluntary as well, their adequacy must be doubted, too.

5.2. Effectiveness of the review function

The effectiveness of the different mechanisms in GATT varies. If an evaluation of review within GATT is to be given, each mechanism of supervision has to be taken into account. A few general remarks about review within GATT can be made however. The diversity of mechanisms of supervision may be confusing for those who want to study supervision within GATT, but because of this diversity the most appropriate instruments and organs can be used in each case.

Many issues that are dealt with are highly political. Therefore, the use of the CP as supervising body is very appropriate. Yet there is room for an indispensable input from experts in the technical phase. Review in GATT is obviously hampered by a lack of manpower in the Secretariat and the cumbersome procedures used to establish WPs and Panels. The reviewing organs are largely dependent on the cps that must provide the necessary information. The co-operation of States in this respect varied until now. An obvious drawback is the lack of financial means to engage in independent research.

5.2.1. The central dispute settlement procedure

The review instruments used under the central dispute settlement procedure are exchanges of information and reporting *ad hoc*. Information is provided by the States themselves. The complaining State is likely to provide adequate information to support its claim. In the last two decades few complaints were brought, which indicated that the cps had little confidence in the central dispute settlement procedure. This lack of confidence reduced the effectiveness of the review function. Lately, more use has been made of the procedures of Articles XXII and XXIII, especially by the developed cps. It may be that these procedures will become more effective in the future.

Review is hampered by the lack of manpower in the Secretariat and the time-consuming procedures to establish Panels and WPs. Until the 1970s the authority of Panels and WPs was remarkably high. Yet since the DISC case their authority has diminished. Maybe the adoption of the new framework will re-establish confidence in and therefore authority for the Panels. Moreover, the competence of the GATT bodies is restricted to make recommendations and give rulings. They cannot award injunctions nor can they prescribe specific actions. The effectiveness of review under the central dispute mechanisms declined during the late 1960s and the 1970s, especially where developing cps were involved. The last years, however, show an increasing recourse to these procedures, mainly be developed cps. There is ground for hope that these procedures will provide effective review in the future.

5.2.2. Specific dispute settlement procedures

Several specific dispute settlement procedures are provided for. First of all, consultations between cps are prescribed when import quotas are introduced under Articles XI, XII, XIII and XVIII, and a cp wishing to invoke the escape clause must afford opportunity to consult. The Subsidy and Anti-dumping Codes also provide for consultations as does the Agreement on Government Procurement. Finally, consultations are part of the mechanisms of supervision on the implementation of Part IV.

The main instrument of review by means of consultations between the cps is exchange of information. Since the availability of information depends on the States' willingness to provide information, the effectiveness of the review function is hampered. On the other hand, the involvement of the States encourages them generally to provide sufficient information.

Where the CP is involved in the consultations reporting *ad hoc* is used as well. The States' willingness to provide information still determines the effectiveness of the review. The data collected under these procedures are hardly processed at all, so there is no review in the strict sense. The informal character of the consultations and the retention of sovereign powers on the one hand hamper effective review, but on the other hand facilitate review with regard to matters the States are reluctant to submit to supervision. Consultations are a flexible mechanism of supervision that are extremely suitable where States are reluctant to relinquish sovereign powers.

The provisions on import restrictions for balance of payments reasons, the Anti-dumping and Subsidy Codes and the Agreement on Government Procurement provide for dispute settlement by a third party. The cps involved give the necessary information with the complaints and by means of reporting *ad hoc*. In so far as the cps concerned are involved in the issue at hand, adequate information will be provided. Some procedures do not provide for effective review since they are not used, such as the procedure under Article XII,4(d), for complaints concerning import quota for balance of payments reasons. The effectiveness of the review under the new Codes and the Agreement on Government Procurement cannot be judged yet, since these instruments only recently came into force.

Under all procedures the third party called upon is a politically dependent organ. Often the proceedings include procedures before technical bodies. Yet, political motives largely influence the composition as well as the recommendations and rulings of the latter. As a result recommendations and rulings often provide practical solutions. In some cases, the cps have doubted the impartiality of the GATT organs, causing GATT organs to lose their credibility as impartial adjudicators and therefore their authority which is detrimental for the effectiveness of the review function.

Until 1980, the cps invoked the central dispute procedure more than specific dispute settlement procedures. The agreements concluded during the Tokyo Round all provide for specific dispute settlement procedures. A strong argument in favour of the use of specific procedures is that experts can judge the often complicated cases. However, the establishment of a large number of WPs or Panels is costly and many developing cps are not able to provide informed representatives. In addition it may be difficult to attract experts to perform a rather limited function. The GATT structure becomes even more complicated as a large number of dispute settlement committees and Panels is introduced. Finally organs with a limited competence may lack authority for effective review and forum shopping may become feasible for the cps. Most specific procedures allow for recourse to GATT's central dispute settlement procedure whether the specific procedure has been used or not. Only the 1979 anti-dumping code requires exhaustion of the specific remedies. Only time will tell whether the new mechanisms of supervision devised during the Tokyo Round will be used and will prove effective.

5.2.3. Renegotiations

Review as a consequence of renegotiations can only be effective when the cps concerned provide sufficient information by means of exchanges of information or reporting *ad hoc*. Mostly, the cps will provide adequate information since they are highly involved. Renegotiations are a typical GATT mechanism, that provides for a flexible instrument. Although the CP or another GATT body may be involved renegotiations are mainly held between the cps themselves. Renegotiations are not primarily aimed at the measurement of certain conduct against the GATT obligations. One could say that desired changes in schedules are reviewed in the light of the maintenance of equilibrium, the creative function being far more important than the review function.

5.2.4. General reporting

Periodic general reporting is required with regard to import quota for balance of payments reasons, residual restrictions, export subsidies, anti-dumping and countervailing measures, the activities of State trading enterprises, government procurement and the promotion of the development of Third World countries. A number of CP decisions, allowing deviations from the GATT require periodic general reporting. Incidental general reporting took place with regard to all subsidies. To a certain extent the cps co-operated by providing the necessary information. However, in most cases no sufficient information was provided or such information was only provided after repeated exhortations from the Secretariat or the WPs or Panels involved.

As a result the first reports were based on incomplete information and the publication of the final reports was often delayed.

Subsequent to general reporting the data collected were processed by the Secretariat or other subsidiary GATT bodies. The Committee on Trade and Development and its subsidiary bodies performed effective review in the strict sense. Only under the mechanisms of supervision based on general reporting is substantive review in the strict sense performed within GATT. The GATT bodies are competent to do so and their reports and statistics are authoritative. They are sometimes hampered because cps do not disclose confidential information. Given the amount of available information, the limited man power of the Secretariat and other GATT bodies, and the lack of financial means, review in the strict sense is remarkably effective. The GATT reports and statistics are widely used.

5.2.5. *Authorisations and approvals*

In some cases the cps may deviate from the GATT with an authorisation of the CP of the so-called waivers under Articles XXV,5 and XXIV,10. Since the applicant cp wants to obtain a waiver, it will provide sufficient information. The GATT bodies providing waivers are politically dependent organs that are capable of judging the actual situation. Political motives are very important. Recently, cps did not apply for waivers to deviate from GATT, but deviated in violation of this agreement, even when they were likely to receive a waiver. This indicates a decrease in authority of the GATT organs. Review under the waiver procedures is effective provided that the procedures are initiated.

Approval of the CP is required for less poor developing countries to protect a domestic industry by means of import restrictions. Such approval was never sought.

In case of emergency, a cp may deviate from the GATT without prior consent or approval. In such cases the CP must be notified as soon as possible and opportunity to consult must be given: review takes place afterwards. The incentive to provide adequate information may be smaller, but a cp that wants to maintain the newly introduced measures must provide adequate information.

5.2.6. *Final remarks*

Review within GATT certainly could be improved. Nevertheless, given the actual willingness of States to submit their economic policy to international supervision review within GATT is effective. The international legal scholar might want to see a more structured international organisation obviously exercising supervision. Yet in practice, a less flexible structure than the actual one would lead to evasion of review and could also be unacceptable for many States.

5.3. Effectiveness of the correction function

5.3.1. Correction by means of consultations and negotiations

Considering GATT's legal status it can only *de facto* be qualified as an international organisation. GATT organs have a very limited capacity to take binding decisions and can only to an extremely limited extent impose adequate sanctions to enforce such decisions. Therefore, the primary instrument for correction within GATT is persuasion, be it by means of discussions or by means of friendly settlement.

Consultations constitute a major mechanism of supervision in GATT. Renegotiations are another important mechanism of supervision. Consultations and negotiations can only be effective to correct or prevent deviations if States can be persuaded. Such persuasion can be promoted by social pressure or the mobilisation of shame. Yet, consultations often take place in secret, making correction less effective. The only sanction available is reciprocity. The other cps, and not the GATT organs, may apply such a sanction.

5.3.2. Correction as a consequence of dispute settlement

Under the various dispute settlement procedures the 'applicant cps' aim at correcting the deviant conduct of the 'defendant cps'. Under such procedures GATT organs may give binding rulings or make recommendations. Yet they lack the competence to give a binding judgment. They cannot apply sanctions themselves. They may only authorise other cps to apply sanctions.

The major instrument used is friendly settlement. Technical and subsidiary GATT organs play an important role in this process. In many instances Panels, WPs and Committees, such as the CTD, played an important role as conciliators. As an *ultimum remedium* reciprocity was used as a sanction, for the applicant cp could be authorised by the CP to suspend obligations or the applicant cp could punish the defendant otherwise outside of GATT. Mediation and good offices were also applied by independent members of Panels and WPs, the chairman of the CP and the Director-General of the GATT.

The success of friendly settlement is largely dependent on the willingness of the cps involved to reach agreement. The effectiveness of the correction function is lessened because the GATT organs cannot apply sanctions themselves, because they cannot give binding judgments and because many procedures are held secretly. In addition, the cps do not always accept rulings by GATT bodies, since the GATT bodies perform an ambiguous function. On the one hand they must provide an impartial ruling concerning the 'GATT law', but on the other hand they act as politically involved conciliators. Moreover, the Panel or WP members usually are government representatives that are used to defend their national interest. For these reasons the rulings of GATT bodies have lost some credibility. Consequently cps are not very much inclined to comply with such ruling which reduces the effectiveness of the correction function. Some deviations that are illegal, such as regional economic integration, import restrictions on agricultural products and residual restrictions, occur openly. Correction of such violations is completely ineffective. Procedures aimed at correction are not even initiated.

Finally the 'sanction' of authorisation to suspend is impracticable. Application may well be detrimental to the 'punishing cp' and is certainly opposed to GATT's objectives. Since the cps are aware of the fact that the application of this sanction usually is prevented, the sanction is an ineffective instrument of correction. Some cps do not correct deviant behaviour, but try to satisfy complaining cps otherwise. Often the dispute settlement procedures are broken off or not even initiated in such cases.

5.3.3. General reporting and correction

Publication of data obtained as a consequence of general reporting sometimes leads to correction. This is especially the case when data are processed and are published in reports that contain recommendations on future policy. Sometimes such reports are used as a basis for further action, for instance by the CTD. However, usually the GATT organs lack the capacity to act on the basis of reports without authorisation by the cps or the CP.

In practice the only instrument of correction of the general reporting procedures is the mobilisation of shame. This is a weak instrument to force States to change international trade policy, especially where important domestic policies are concerned. General reporting in itself is ineffective to correct deviant behaviour.

5.3.4. Authorisations

Authorisations are the pre-eminent mechanism of supervision for effective correction and prevention of undesirable deviant behaviour. The applicant cp is dependent on the GATT organ to obtain permission. Since the GATT organ has the power to grant the authorisation or not, it holds an important sanction to force the cp concerned to behave in the desired way.

5.3.5. Final remarks

Correction takes place within GATT. The willingness of the cps involved to correct their behaviour is indispensable for correction to take place. The cps can be forced by reciprocity and to a lesser extent by the mobilisation of shame. Correction obviously is not the strongest aspect of supervision within GATT.

5.4. Effectiveness of the creative function

5.4.1. Consultations and negotiations

GATT rules can easily be changed and supplemented during consultations aimed at dispute settlement during renegotiations and during other consultations and negotiations. Until 1960, the creative function of such mechanisms was highly effective. Since 1960, the political cohesiveness declined within GATT and consensus regarding a number of vital issues was lacking. Nevertheless, rule creation and rule adaptation still occur during consultations and negotiations. The creative function of such mechanisms of supervision is often more important than the correction function, since consultations and negotiations are not aimed at compliance with the formal GATT rules but at reciprocity and the granting of mutual benefits.

5.4.2. Dispute settlement

The creative function of supervision is also very important in the dispute settlement procedures. GATT bodies may interpret and adjust the GATT rules. Until 1960 the creative function of the central dispute settlement procedure was highly effective. Although the GATT bodies lost some authority, and cohesiveness declined in the GATT, creation by means of rulings is still fairly effective.

In addition, creation occurs during political discussions and conciliations and negotiations aimed at friendly settlement. Creation was extremely effective before 1960. With decreasing cohesiveness in GATT the effectiveness of the creative function of the discussions, conciliations, and negotiations other than the multilateral trade negotiations, declined. Yet, creation is still effective. Often the cps settle their dispute by concluding compromises. In such cases the GATT rules often are not strictly applied, but minor deviations or adaptations are agreed upon.

5.4.3. General reporting

The general reporting procedures do not allow for creation. At the most, the data made available under such procedures may lie at the basis of creation.

5.4.4. Authorisations

The creative function is very important in mechanisms of supervision under which authorisations are granted. Each waiver implies creation. The instrument of creation is political discussion in the politically dependent organ. The creative function is effective, although cohesiveness is declining in GATT. One of the reasons for this effectiveness might be that the CP are forced to deal with the matter, since one of the cps requested them to do so.

5.4.5. Final remarks

The creative function in GATT is the most important function of supervision. Creation takes place by means of consultations, negotiations, adjudication and political discussions. Often the distinction between rule creation and supervision is not clear within GATT because of the predominant role of creation in the various mechanisms of supervision in GATT. One of the reasons for the importance of creation in supervision lies in the fact that the GATT is dynamic and informal. There are no established institutions to enforce a set of rules, but rather a group of government representatives, managing international trade that is constantly changing.

5.5. Conclusion

A well-founded judgment on the effectiveness of mechanisms of supervision requires a profound insight into daily practice and a well-grounded estimate of how daily practice would have been without such mechanisms of supervision. The author does not pretend to be capable to correctly judge daily practice with regard to international trade. In addition, any estimate of daily practice without actual supervision would be highly subjective. Nevertheless, a few remarks about the effectiveness of supervision in GATT, GATT's contribution to the world's prosperity, and GATT's role in the future are in order.

Since 1947, the world's prosperity has increased considerably. The world's prosperity would have undoubtedly increased without GATT's existence, but GATT's contribution cannot be denied. Moreover, many barriers to international trade have been eliminated or lowered. The realisation of these important GATT objectives indicates GATT's effectiveness.

Co-operation within GATT has always been pragmatic and informal. The cps always adapted the rules to the situation at hand. Consequently, a multitude of rules and regulations have been developed each containing their own mechanisms of supervision. In addition, supervision is exercised in a flexible way, leaving plenty of room for creation, often at the cost of correction of deviating behaviour.

The mechanisms of supervision certainly contributed to the achievement of some of GATT's objectives. Because of the existence of such mechanisms States became aware that they must comply with the GATT rules. While exercising supervision GATT bodies found solutions for a number of problems and gave interpretations that otherwise would not have been found. Consequently, disputes were settled and new rules created. Nevertheless, supervision was not perfect, as GATT rules have been violated. There is still a large number of illegal residual restrictions, many regional arrangements are in conflict with GATT, trade in agricultural products is severely restricted and the development of the Third World still lags behind. One of the reasons that the gap between rich and poor has not narrowed at all, is that the developed countries still restrict imports from the Third World by means of residual restrictions and other import restrictions, because of emergency measures and as a consequence of subsidies or other non-tariff barriers. Effective supervision would prevent such violations of GATT.

Yet, strict compliance with the GATT rules might be undesirable. Most trade restrictions are eliminated, especially tariffs. The reduction or elimination of the remaining restrictions might be very expensive; maybe too expensive to be feasible, since a very expensive reduction or elimination would lower the world's prosperity, which is contrary to GATT's objectives. Within GATT the realisation of its objectives always is preferred to strict compliance with its provisions. Yet, cps that want to maintain such restrictions must prove that it would cost more to eliminate or reduce them than it would cost to maintain them; injury to other cps should be prevented and if other cps are injured adequate compensation should be given.

In most cases, however, compliance with GATT will promote GATT's objectives. Improvement of supervision will lead to more compliance. The effectiveness of supervision could be augmented by improving GATT's central mechanisms of supervision or by increasing the various specific mechanisms of supervision.

The central dispute settlement procedure could be improved by shortening the procedure. A permanent judicial organ could be established. However, the cps probably do not want to submit their economic policy to an independent judicial organ. They wish to be able to influence the decisions as they can in the current CP, which is a politically dependent organ. If the CP would have at its disposal more and stronger instruments to induce the cps to comply with GATT, supervision would be more effective, too. The CP could impose fines, for instance. The developed cps, however, are not prepared to extend the competence of the CP since the developing cps have a decisive voice in the CP because 52 out of the 85 cps are developing countries and each cp has one vote. Implementation of the 1979 Understanding is likely to improve the central dispute settlement procedure, but will not make it perfect. In addition, the emphasis within GATT is put increasingly on specific mechanisms of supervision as the textiles arrangements, the 1967 anti-dumping code, and the agreements drafted during the Tokyo Round indicate.

Supervision by means of various specific dispute settlement procedures might be more effective than supervision by means of one central procedure, but this is not necessarily so. Specific organs might be more informed concerning the problems at hand, but small bodies may lack in authority. Moreover, the system might be too complicated and too expensive. Forum shopping is an undesirable possibility, as are overlapping competences. Finally, not all cps may be able to provide capable representatives and the functions might not be interesting enough to attract experts. Only the future can tell whether the establishment of a large number of Committees and Panels will improve supervision. One central body composed of general economic experts should be able to review behaviour with regard to the GATT rules. A certain distribution of tasks is desirable, but it should not lead to dispersion of powers. A real improvement of supervision in GATT will only occur if consensus among the cps increases.

Other changes that might contribute to more effective supervision include the following. More independent research by GATT bodies, such as the Secretariat, the CTD and the Trade Centre would improve effectiveness of supervision. To this end GATT's budget needs to be augmented and more officials need to be hired. Also, a 'public prosecutor' could promote effective supervision. The developing cps would like to establish such an institution to supervise the implementation of Part IV. The Group of Three performed a similar function. As long as cohesiveness and consensus are on the current level the above-mentioned changes are unlikely to occur.

Because of the economic law of decreasing marginal utility the initial reductions of trade barriers contributed more to the promotion of the world's prosperity than the last reductions will contribute. Therefore, elimination and reduction of the remaining tariffs and quantitative restrictions is not the primary task of the GATT in the future. The GATT should aim in the first place at promoting the development of the Third World, regulating markets – especially markets that are of importance to developing cps – and preventing harm to the world's prosperity as a consequence of non-tariff barriers. The development of the Third World is likely to require the elimination or reduction of a number of residual restrictions. Regulation of markets should occur in close co-operation with other competent international institutions. The use of subsidies, State trading enterprises and anti-dumping and countervailing measures should be of growing concern to GATT.

Supervision will not become more effective as long as consensus and consent are lacking. During the 1960s and 1970s consensus was declining. The Tokyo Round could be a turning-point. Several agreements were concluded. However, there are also a few obvious dangers with regard to GATT's cohesiveness. The developed cps tend to make decisions amongst themselves. Co-operation between developed cps within or outside of GATT might lead to express or secret preferential agreements among developed cps. The developed cps might want to do business outside of GATT, because the developing cps have the majority in the CP. Therefore, replacement of the one-State one-vote system in the CP by a system of weighed voting could be necessary. Another reason for this is that the developing countries are also discontented with the GATT because the developed countries cannot be forced to give them preferences or other forms of development aid. If the representation in the CP would reflect better the economic strength of the cps, developed cps might be more inclined to make substantial contributions to the economic development of the Third World and maybe even to commit themselves to do this on a continuing basis.

At present the developing cps are disappointed because of the lack of substantive support by GATT. Therefore, they might hamper the creation of new rules, the establishment of new mechanisms of supervision or the improvement of existing ones unless such changes are obviously in their favour. Disappointment concerning GATT is prevalent as well in the U.S.A.

Consequently, this superpower might introduce barriers to trade to compensate for alleged illegal trade restrictions by other cps, especially the EEC.

Yet, in spite of the violations of GATT, in spite of lack of cohesiveness and consensus, the GATT contributed enormously to the growth of prosperity and trade after the Second World War. Under GATT a sophisticated system of supervision is established which certainly could be improved, but which at the same time might be the best attainable given the current relations between States. The functions performed by the GATT are indispensable for the current international economic system. Any new international economic order would need an institution such as the GATT. The establishment of a new organisation performing these functions would be highly inefficient. Moreover, some of the regulations, made within GATT at a time when there was more consensus and cohesiveness than there is now, might not be adopted again, although they are beneficial to world trade. Therefore, the GATT is an indispensable constituent of any new international order; moreover, such international order would benefit if GATT's competences could be increased and if the GATT could be given the legal status of a true international organisation.

NOTES

1. C. Wilcox, *A Charter for World Trade* (New York, 1972), p. 6.
2. R. E. Hudec, *The GATT Legal System and World Trade Diplomacy* (New York, 1975), pp. 3–8.
3. Economic and Social Council of the UN.
4. 1 UN ECOSOC Res. 13, UN Doc. E/22 (1946).
5. H. Jackson, *World Trade and the Law of GATT* (Indianapolis, 1969), p. 41.
6. C. Wilcox, *op. cit.* (note 1), p. 53.
7. *Idem,* pp. 227–327.
8. U.S. State Department Press Release, December 6, 1950, printed in (1950) 23 Dept. State Bull. 977, cited in Jackson, *op. cit.* (note 5), p. 50; see also *idem,* pp. 42–45, and N. Franken, *De Betekenis van de Algemene Overeenkomst inzake Tarieven en Handel in het Internationale Handelspolitieke Overleg* [The Meaning of the General Agreement on Tariffs and Trade in International Trade Policy Negotiations] (The Hague, 1956), pp. 5–10.
9. During the Havana Conference on Trade and Employment, held from November 1947 to March 1948 only the ILO was discussed.
10. 55 UNTS 308, October 30, 1947; see also D. C. Meerburg, 'De GATT', in: P. VerLoren van Themaat (ed.), *Studies over Internationaal Economisch Recht* [Studies on International Economic Law], vol. I.2 (The Hague, 1977), pp. 10–11.
11. Art. XXXI.
12. On this, see Jackson, *op. cit.* (note 5), pp. 60–63.
13. However, Haiti must be deemed to apply the GATT provisionally through the Annecy Protocol of Terms of Accession to GATT of 1949. 62 UNTS 122, see Jackson, *op. cit.* (note 5), p. 61.
14. D. C. Meerburg, *loc. cit.* (note 10), p. 11.
15. H. G. Schermers, *International Institutional Law* (Leiden, 1972), vol. 1, pp. 5–10.
16. *E.g.* L. J. Brinkhorst, *Grondlijnen van Europees Recht* [Principles of European Law] (Groningen, 1973), p. 1.
17. GATT, Preamble.
18. Reciprocity as a concept is nowhere defined in the GATT text, but is nonetheless a very important concept in GATT practice. See K. W. Dam, *The GATT Law and International Economic Organization* (Chicago, 1970), p. 59.
19. Suppose country A levies a tariff on imports of 20 per cent. and country B one of 10 per cent. and both lower their tariffs by 10 per cent. Then country B loses every protection while country A still has a tariff of 10 per cent. Moreover, B is left with nothing to offer A for a further Concession as far as this item is concerned. Such a system could lead to unfair results. Therefore, the cps have agreed that the binding against increase of low duties or of duty-free treatment shall, in principle, be recognised as a Concession equivalent in value to the reduction of high duties. This rule became part of the GATT text in 1956 and can be found in Article XXVIII *bis,* 2(a). Its application in practice has only been moderately successful. K. W. Dam, *op. cit.* (note 18), p. 60.
20. According to the prevailing macro-economic theories imports are a function of the national income among other things: $M = mY + M$ ant.
21. See also Jackson, *op. cit.* (note 5), pp. 242–245.
22. For example: both country A and country B export sugar. If A negotiates a Concession with C, who imports sugar, C must give the same Concession to B. Consequently, B gets the Concession for free. Therefore, all countries are inclined to wait for other countries to negotiate Concessions.
23. Suppose A is the largest sugar exporter in the world exporting 20 million tons. B exports 10 million tons. If C gives the Concession to B, A gets a bonus of 200 million times the reduction per ton. If A gives the Concession the bonus to B is only 10 million times the reduction per ton. Consequently, the bonus is less if the Concession is given to A, the principal supplier.
24. Meerburg, *loc. cit.* (note 10), p. 28.
25. GATT, Preamble, *Basic Instruments and Selected Documents* (BISD), 16th supplement, p. 203.
26. Art. II,7.
27. GATT Information, GATT/1248 (for the use of news media).
28. See 2.5.2. *infra.*

29. Jackson, *op. cit.* (note 5), pp. 93–95.
30. GATT/1248, *op. cit.* (note 27); see also Jackson, *op. cit.* (note 5), pp. 98–99.
31. For instance, in the Tokyo Round negotiations, Bolivia, Bulgaria, Costa Rica, Ethiopia, Guatamala, Iran, Iraq, Mexico, Panama, Thailand and Vietnam, among other non-cps, participated, without being otherwise related to GATT.
32. See for a definition Art. XXIV,2.
33. Art. XXXIII.
34. Art. XXXV,1.
35. Art. XXX.
36. Protocol of Provisional Application 55 UNTS 308 (1947) ad 1(b). See also Jackson, *op. cit.* (note 5), pp. 108–110.
37. Article I,1. See also Jackson, *op. cit.* (note 5), pp. 255–258.
38. *E.g.* Articles III,7; IV(b); V,2,5 and 6; IX,1; XVII,1; XVIII,20 and XX(j).
39. See Articles II,1 and 4 and VII,5 and 6.
40. *Cf.* the U.S. Schedule 61 UNTS 77 (1950), cited in Jackson, *op. cit.* (note 5), p. 202.
41. Jackson, *op. cit.* (note 5), pp. 202–204.
42. Dumping means to sell surpluses in foreign countries for a price below the normal price, usually below the cost price. See also *infra,* section 4.3.9.
43. See *infra,* section 4.3.7.
44. See *infra,* section 4.3.12.
45. See *infra,* section 4.3.11.
46. See *infra,* section 4.3.3.
47. See *infra,* section 4.2.
48. These will be discussed next in the present chapter; see also Meerburg, *loc. cit.* (note 10), pp. 13–17.
49. Dam, *op. cit.* (note 18), pp. 337–338.
50. To distinguish the CP from the contracting parties acting in their individual capacities capitals are used to indicate this body.
51. See also Jackson, *op. cit.* (note 5), pp. 128–132.
52. The contracting parties to the General Agreement on Tariffs and Trade, BISD, 12th supplement, pp. 10–16.
53. Like in Articles XXIV,10; XXV,5; XXX and XXXIII.
54. Article XXV,4 and Rule 16, BISD, 12th supplement, p. 13.
55. UN Docs. EPCT/209 at i. EPCT/TAC/PV25 at December 11, 1947. Cited in Jackson, *op. cit.* (note 5), p. 123.
56. BISD, 12th supplement, p. 16.
57. BISD, Vol. II, p. 202 and p. 206; 3rd supplement, p. 9 and p. 246.
58. Decision of June 4, 1960, BISD, 9th supplement, pp. 7–9.
59. See *infra,* section 2.6.5.
60. BISD, 9th supplement, pp. 7–8.
61. BISD, 9th supplement, p. 9.
62. BISD, 22nd supplement, p. 15.
63. BISD, 22nd supplement, p. 16.
64. BISD, 22nd supplement, p. 16; 23rd supplement, p. 38; 24th supplement, p. 58; 25th supplement, p. 37.
65. However, Jackson thinks this group has not yet been very influential. J. H. Jackson, 'The Birth of the GATT-MTN System: A Constitutional Approach', in: (1980) 12 *Law & Policy in International Business* 21–58, at p. 49.
66. GATT Activities in 1980, Geneva, April 1981. Sales No.: GATT/1981-1, pp. 15–17.
67. GATT Press Release, GATT/1287, March 27, 1981, p. 1.
68. See also Jackson, *op. cit.* (note 5), pp. 49–50 and 145–147.
69. *Idem,* pp. 148–150.
70. BISD, 12th supplement, pp. 138–139.
71. BISD, 15th supplement, p. 175; see also Jackson, *op. cit.* (note 5), pp. 147–148.
72. See, for example, BISD, 4th supplement, pp. 80–81.
73. BISD, 5th supplement, p. 52.
74. BISD, 13th supplement, p. 76.
75. BISD, 15th supplement, p. 73.
76. BISD, 15th supplement, p. 74.
77. BISD, 21st supplement, p. 13.
78. BISD, 15th supplement, p. 35.
79. Jackson, *op. cit.* (note 5), pp. 150–151.

80. *The Europa Year Book 1978, A World Survey* (London, 1978), vol. 1, p. 33.
81. *Ibidem,* p. 57.
82. *Ibidem,* p. 187.
83. *E.g.* in Article XV,8.
84. *E.g.* in Articles XIX,2 and 3, and XXIV,7. See also Jackson, *op. cit.* (note 5), p. 463.
85. Recommendation of March 20, 1964, BISC, 12th supplement, pp. 49–50.
86. *E.g.* Articles XIII; XVI; XVIIIC,16.
87. *E.g.* Articles XXI; XXIII; XII,4(d); XVIIIB,12(d).
88. *E.g.* Article XIX.
89. Article XXVIII. See also *infra,* section 4.3.1.
90. Article XXIV,6.
91. Article XVIII,7.
92. Article XXVII.
93. See *supra,* section 1.1.
94. Dam, *op. cit.* (note 18), p. 56 and GATT Press Release, GATT/1234, April 12, 1979.
95. BISD, 20th supplement, pp. 19–22 at page 22. Since the Declaration of Ministers was approved at Tokyo, the following round was called the Tokyo Round.
96. Dam, *op. cit.* (note 18), pp. 56–57.
97. *The Tokyo-Round of Multilateral Trade Negotiations* (Geneva, January 1980), Vol. II, pp. 18–19.
98. These were: Canada, Australia, New Zealand and South Africa.
99. Meerburg, *loc. cit.* (note 10), p. 29.
100. See also *supra,* section 2.5.2.
101. See Articles: II,6(a); VI,6; XXV,5; XXIV,7; XVIII,19; XX(h) and XXVIII,4.
102. Not to be confused with the term specific supervision, as used in Part I by Van Hoof and De Vey Mestdagh, *'Mechanisms of International Supervision', supra,* p. 14.
103. BISD, 15th supplement, p. 24.
104. Done at Geneva, April 12, 1979.
105. GATT Doc. MTN/NTM/W/232/Rev. 1, May 11, 1979.
106. GATT Press Release 1254, January 2, 1980.
107. GATT Doc. MTN/NTM/W/222/Rev. 1, March 27, 1979, and GATT Press Release 1254, January 2, 1980, p. 2.
108. Done at Geneva, April 12, 1979. GATT Press Release 1254, January 2, 1980, p. 1.
109. Agreement on Import Licensing Procedures. Articles 1.5, 4 and 5.5.
110. BISD, 9th supplement, p. 17, 13th supplement, p. 18 and GATT Doc. L/3276, December 2, 1969.
111. GATT Press Release 1254, January 2, 1980, p. 2.
112. BISD, 21st supplement, p. 3.
113. BISD, 9th supplement, p. 8.
114. UN Docs. E/Conf.2/C6/W43; W.4g (1948) in Jackson, *op. cit.* (note 5), p. 180.
115. BISD, Vol. II, p. 12. See also Hudec, *op. cit.* (note 2), pp. 66–67 and the Chairman's Ruling, interpreting Article I on request of Pakistan, BISD, Vol. II, p. 12.
116. BISD, Vol. II, p. 40. See also Jackson, *op. cit.* (note 5), p. 136.
117. GATT Doc. CP.3/SR.37, at 5 (1949) in Jackson, *op. cit.* (note 5), p. 135.
118. See *infra,* section 4.3.3.
119. Species of retaliation, which takes place where a government, whose citizens are treated harshly by a foreign government, employs measures of equal severity and harshness upon the subjects of the latter government.
120. Jackson, *op. cit.* (note 5), pp. 169–171.
121. BISD, 3rd supplement, p. 250.
122. BISD, 7th supplement, p. 24.
123. In 1958 this was the Executive Secretary.
124. BISD, Vol. II, pp. 188–196.
125. BISD, 11th supplement, pp. 95–148.
126. Hudec, *op. cit.* (note 2), pp. 152–153 and 220–222; see also section 4.2.3.4.
127. BISD, 11th supplement, pp. 99–100. See also BISD, 26th supplement, p. 216.
128. GATT Doc. L/1222/Add.1 (1960) in Jackson, *op. cit.* (note 5), p. 182.
129. BISD, 3rd supplement, p. 224. Jackson, *op. cit.* (note 5), pp. 182–183.
130. BISD, 10th supplement, pp. 201–210 at p. 209: BISD, 23rd supplement, p. 127, p. 136 and p. 147. See also *infra,* section 4.3.7.
131. BISD, 11th supplement, pp. 100–102.
132. BISD, 11th supplement, pp. 102–148.

133. BISD, 11th supplement, pp. 88–94.
134. Dam, *op. cit.* (note 18), p. 360. See also *supra,* section 2.1.
135. BISD, 9th supplement, p. 20.
136. BISD, Vol. II, p. 12.
137. CP. 2/43 (September 13, 1948), Hudec, *op. cit.* (note 2), p. 278.
138. *Idem,* p. 67.
139. *Idem,* p. 69.
140. *Idem,* pp. 74–75 (SR. 7/7, October 14, 1952).
141. BISD, 1st supplement, p. 48. See also Hudec, *op. cit.* (note 2), pp. 75–76.
142. *Idem,* p. 76.
143. See *infra* about the Agreed Description of the Customary Practice of the GATT in the Field of Dispute Settlement.
144. BISD, 23rd supplement, p. 98, p. 114, p. 127 and p. 137.
145. R. E. Hudec, *Adjudication of International Trade Disputes,* Thames Essay No. 16 (London, 1978), pp. 60–61.
146. Adopted on November 28, 1979, by the CP, BISD, 26th supplement, p. 210. See *infra,* section 4.2.3.7.
147. BISD, 26th supplement, pp. 215–218, especially at 1 and 6(ii).
148. BISD, 26th supplement, p. 214, at 20.
149. BISD, 11th supplement, p. 99.
150. BISD, 26th supplement, p. 215, at 1. See also *infra,* section 4.2.3.7.
151. Jackson, *op. cit.* (note 5), p. 181. See also Chapter IV E and the report by a group of experts on the question of Restrictive Business Practices, BISD, 9th supplement, p. 172.
152. *Cf.* the decision on the Cuban restrictions on Textile Imports phase II, and Hudec, *op. cit.* (note 2), pp. 154–159.
153. *Cf.* the *Treatment by Germany of Imports of Sardines Case,* BISD, 1st supplement, pp. 53–62, and Hudec, *op. cit.* (note 2), pp. 159–164.
154. BISD, 9th supplement, p. 8.
155. See BISD, 3rd supplement, pp. 170–252.
156. BISD, 3rd supplement, pp. 250–251.
157. BISD, 26th supplement, pp. 215–216.
158. BISD, 11th supplement, p. 99.
159. BISD, 1st supplement, p. 32 and p. 61.
160. BISD, 2nd supplement, p. 28; 3rd supplement, p. 46; 4th supplement, p. 31 and p. 99; 5th supplement, p. 28 and p. 142; 6th supplement, p. 121 and p. 157 and 7th supplement, p. 23 and p. 128.
161. *Cf.* the hierarchy of solutions described before.
162. BISD, 11th supplement, p. 94. See also Hudec, *op. cit.* (note 2), pp. 248–250.
163. C/M/80 (September 19, 1972), Hudec, *op. cit.* (note 2), pp. 235–236. The success of the U.S. complaint was surprising since the alleged restrictions were so-called residual restrictions, that had become an accepted fact by this time. (See section 4.3.6.)
164. Dam, *op. cit.* (note 18), p. 364.
165. These concepts are defined and explained in M. Kreunine, *International Economics,* (2nd ed., New York, 1975), p. 218 *et seq.* and pp. 308–311.
166. *Cf.* the consequences of the so-called Chicken War discussed in section 4.3.1. See also Dam, *op. cit.* (note 18), p. 368.
167. At the time this article was drafted this was still the Executive Secretary.
168. BISD, 14th supplement, pp. 139–140.
169. BISD, 14th supplement, pp. 18–20. See also p. 140 at paras. 41–47.
170. Article XXXVII deals with joint action by the CP to further the objectives of Part IV of the GATT.
171. BISD, 26th supplement, p. 211, at 7.
172. Hudec, *op. cit.* (note 145), p. 71, note 128.
173. GATT Activities in 1980 (Geneva, 1981), GATT/1981-1, p. 44.
174. See *supra,* section 4.2.3.6.
175. *Cf.* The Brazilian and Uruguayan Proposal, *supra,* section 4.2.3.5. at (2).
176. Hudec, *op. cit.* (note 2), pp. 90–96.
177. See *infra,* section 4.3.12.
178. European Free Trade Association.
179. Hudec, *op. cit.* (note 2), pp. 216–217.
180. See section 4.2.3.1.

181. Sr. 19/12 (December 19, 1961) and L/1749 (April 11, 1963). Hudec, *op. cit.* (note 2), p. 291.
182. C/M/18 (October 29, 1963) and GATT/819 (November 21, 1963). Hudec, *op. cit.* (note 2), p. 292.
183. *Idem,* pp. 217–218 and 219–223.
184. *Idem,* p. 225.
185. L/2715 (November 6, 1966) and L/2856 (October 23, 1967) Hudec, *op. cit.* (note 2), p. 295. See also p. 223. SR. 24/13 (November 21, 1967). Hudec, *op. cit.* (note 2), p. 292. See also p. 224.
186. C/M/55 (June 30, 1969). Hudec, *op. cit.* (note 2), p. 293.
187. C/M/59 (December 16, 1969). Hudec, *op. cit.* (note 2), p. 293. See also p. 226.
188. BISD, 15th supplement, p. 71.
189. Hudec. *op. cit.* (note 2), pp. 227–228.
190. Hudec, *op. cit.* (note 145), p. 76.
191. BISD, 18th supplement, p. 56 and pp. 70–72.
192. Hudec, *op. cit.* (note 2), p. 228.
193. BISD, 18th supplement, pp. 149, 158 and 166; 19th supplement, p. 97 and 20th supplement, pp. 145–209.
194. L/3406 (June 23, 1970) and C/M/65 Corr. 1 (December 2–3, 1970). Hudec. *op. cit.* (note 2), p. 293; C/M/64 (September 29, 1970). Hudec. *op. cit.* (note 2), p. 294 and BISD, 18th supplement, p. 183.
195. C/M/79 (July 26, 1972) and C/M/186 (September 19, 1972). Hudec, *op. cit.* (note 2), p. 294, also p. 235.
196. L/3726 (July 18, 1972). Hudec, *op. cit.* (note 2), p. 294.
197. BISD, 20th supplement, p. 230 and 236.
198. BISD, 20th supplement, p. 237; see also Hudec, *op. cit.* (note 2), pp. 235–237.
199. BISD, 23rd supplement, p. 98. Case on the tax provisions on Domestic International Sales Corporations.
200. BISD, 23rd supplement, pp. 114, 127 and 137.
201. Hudec, *op. cit.* (note 145), p. 60.
202. J. H. Jackson, 'The Jurisprudence of International Trade: the DISC Case in GATT', in: (1978) *American Journal of International Law* 72, 747–781 at 780–781.
203. Apart from the DISC decision the one other Panel decision that failed to be ratified in GATT was a decision made by a special Panel composed of national experts in the case of Greek duties on LP Phonograph Records, GATT Doc. L/580, 1956. The problem was that the interpretation by the Panel was based on a developed-country theory of tariff schedules unacceptable for developing countries. (Hudec. *op. cit.* (note 145), pp. 66, 67 at note 123.)
204. BISD, 24th supplement, p. 134.
205. BISD, 25th supplement, p. 42.
206. BISD, 25th supplement, p. 49.
207. BISD, 25th supplement, p. 68.
208. BISD, 25th supplement, p. 107.
209. GATT Activities in 1980 (Geneva, 1981), GATT/1981-1, p. 47.
210. GATT Doc. L/4833, October 25, 1979, mentioned by Rodney de C. Grey during the Conference on Non-Tariff Barriers and the Tokyo Round. London (Ontario), May 1980. BISD, 26th supplement, p. 290.
211. BISD, 26th supplement, p. 320.
212. GATT Activities in 1980, *op. cit.* (note 209), pp. 43–60.
213. L/2714 (November 6, 1966) and L/2859 (October 23, 1967). Hudec, *op. cit.* (note 2), p. 292.
214. All paragraphs on qualification of mechanisms of supervision are based on the General Introduction to this project written by Van Hoof and De Vey Mestdagh, *loc. cit.* (note 102).
215. This term has been introduced by M. Kaasik in: *Le contrôle en droit international* (Paris, 1933), p. 347. Cited in Van Hoof and De Vey Mestdagh, *loc. cit.* (note 102), p. 19.
216. BISD, 7th supplement, p. 24. See also section 4.2.2. In 1958 the Director-General was still the Executive Secretary.
217. See section 4.2.3.1.
218. Hudec, *op. cit.* (note 145), p. 21.
219. BISD, 1st supplement, p. 32.
220. Sales No. GATT/1951-3. Hudec. *op. cit.* (note 2), p. 280.
221. Hudec, *op. cit.* (note 145), pp. 21–22.
222. See also section 4.2.4.

223. See sections 4.3.4 to 4.3.6 and 4.3.12, and chapter 5.
224. See also H. H. Jackson, 'Governmental Disputes in International Trade Relations: A Proposal in the Context of GATT', in: (1979) *Journal of World Trade Law* 13, p. 4.
225. See also J. H. Jackson, *MTN and the Legal Institutions of International Trade,* MTN Studies of 96th Congress, 1st session, Committee on Finance U.S. Senate (Washington, 1979).
226. *Idem,* p. 16.
227. See section 4.2.3.4.
228. 19 USC, 2101–2487. Jackson, *loc. cit.* (note 224), p. 2.
229. Hudec, *op. cit.* (note 2), p. 239.
230. Jackson, *loc. cit.* (note 224), p. 2. Notes 8 and 9.
231. See section 4.3.3.
232. See section 4.3.2.
233. BISD, Vol. II, p. 30.
234. BISD, Vol. II, p. 22, p. 61.
235. BISD, 3rd supplement, p. 30.
236. Dam, *op. cit.* (note 18), pp. 81–82.
237. Interpretative Note Ad Article XXVIII, 1(3). (Hereafter cited as: Int. N. Ad XXVIII, 1(3).)
238. Article XXVIII, 1.
239. BISD, 15th supplement, p. 67.
240. Dam, *op. cit.* (note 18), pp. 83–84.
241. Int. N. Ad XXVIII, 1(4).
242. Int. N. Ad XXVIII, 1(5).
243. Int. N. Ad XXVIII, 1(7).
244. GATT Doc. L/5635 (May 31, 1975), p. 2, cited in Dam, *op. cit.* (note 18), p. 85.
245. Int. N. Ad XXVIII, 1(6).
246. Int. N. Ad XXXVI, 8 and Ad XXXVII, 1(a).
247. *Cf.* the Waiver granted to Peru in 1965, BISD, 13th supplement, p. 27.
248. Article XXVIII, 3(a).
249. Article XXVIII, 3(b).
250. GATT Doc. L/2030 (November 21, 1963), cited in Dam, *op. cit.* (note 18), p. 88.
251. *Ad valorem* means: a certain percentage of the value.
252. The price elasticity determines the amount of change in quantity as a consequence of price changes.
253. Dam, *op. cit.* (note 18), pp. 87–91.
254. Int. N. Ad XXVIII.
255. *Ibidem.*
256. Art. XXVIII, 4.
257. Art. XXVIII, 5.
258. See section 4.3.12.
259. See section 4.3.11.
260. Article II, 5.
261. BISD, 16th supplement, p. 16.
262. The United States always incorporated an escape clause in the commercial treaties they concluded during the 1930s and 1940s. The inclusion of the escape clause was a condition for the acceptance of the GATT by the United States.
263. *Cf.* the case of the Increase in the U.S. Duty on Dried Figs. BISD, 1st supplement, p. 38 and 2nd supplement, p. 26.
264. Report on the Withdrawal by the U.S. of a Tariff Concession Under Article XIX of the GATT, Geneva, November 1951 (Sales No. GATT/1951–3), p. 21. Jackson, *op. cit.* (note 5), p. 557. Hereafter cited as *Hatters' Fur Case.* Dam, *op. cit.* (note 18), p. 101.
265. *Hatters' Fur Case,* p. 10.
266. *Hatters' Fur Case,* p. 12.
267. WP report adopted on September 1 and 2, 1948. BISD, Vol. II, pp. 44–45.
268. *Hatters' Fur Case,* p. 23; Dam, *op. cit.* (note 18), pp. 101–103; and Jackson, *op. cit.* (note 5), pp. 556–563.
269. Article XIX,2.
270. Article XIX,3(a).
271. Dam, *op. cit.* (note 18), pp. 104–105.
272. Article XIX,2.
273. Article XIX,3(b).
274. Dam, *op. cit.* (note 18), p. 104.

275. BISD, 9th supplement, p. 26.
276. See section 4.3.2.
277. Article XXV. See also section 2.4.
278. See section 4.3.5.
279. See section 4.3.11.
280. See section 4.3.3.
281. See section 4.3.1.
282. See notes 276 to 281.
283. BISD, 15th supplement, p. 5 and The Geneva Protocol to GATT No. L/2815. Jackson, *op. cit.* (note 5), pp. 570 and 897.
284. J. H. Jackson, *International Economic Relations* (St. Paul, 1977), pp. 668–678.
285. Such as: refusing to give rights to land in national airports.
286. BISD, 8th supplement, pp. 22–23.
287. BISD, 9th supplement, pp. 26–28 and 106–108.
288. See more extensive: G. H. Perlow, 'The Textiles Surveillance Body', *infra,* Part III.
289. BISD, 15th supplement, pp. 25–41.
290. Long-Term Arrangement Regarding International Trade in Cotton Textiles Articles 7 and 8.
291. BISD, 11th supplement, p. 25, 15th supplement, p. 56 and 18th supplement, p. 18; also Perlow, *loc. cit.* (note 288), pp. 4–7.
292. BISD, 21st supplement, pp. 3–19.
293. BISD, 24th supplement, p. 5.
294. Article 1. See also Article 6.
295. GATT Activities in 1980, *op. cit.* (note 209), p. 32.
296. Article 10.
297. According to Article 11.
298. Articles 11, 12.
299. Articles 2 to 5 and 7 to 9.
300. Articles 3.5, 9.5 and 11.
301. Article 11.5.
302. Article 11.9.
303. Article 11.10.
304. Article 12.4 as well as 3 and 11.
305. BISD, 24th supplement, pp. 46–47.
306. Textiles Surveillance Body, *Report of the Textiles Surveillance Body to the Textiles Committee,* October 1976. GATT Doc. COM.TEX./SB/196, November 5, 1976.
307. Textiles Surveillance Body, *Activities of the Textiles Surveillance Body November 1976–20 October 1978,* Report to the Textiles Committee. Attached is the Report by the TSB on its activities during the period from November 1976 to October 1978. GATT Doc. COM. TEX./SB/365, October 23, 1978.
308. COM.TEX./SB/196, *op. cit.* (note 306), Note 45 and BISD, 24th supplement, p. 32.
309. Textiles Committee, *Recent Trends in Production and Trade in Textiles and Clothing,* GATT Doc. COM.TEX./W/55, October 18, 1978.
310. GATT, *International Trade 1979/80* (Geneva, 1980), pp. 79–81.
311. Hudec, *op. cit.* (note 145), p. 65.
312. BISD, 24th supplement, p. 34.
313. Hudec. *op. cit.* (note 145), p. 65, note 120.
314. GATT Activities in 1980, *op. cit.* (note 209), pp. 32–36.
315. Arrangements negotiated in GATT, setting floor prices to international trade in skimmed milk powder and milk fats, and a 'Gentlemen's Agreement' under the auspices of the OECD providing for a minimum price for whole milk powder have been in operation for a number of years.
316. GATT, *The Tokyo-Round of Multilateral Trade Negotiations,* Sales No. GATT/1979-3 (Geneva, April 1979), pp. 18 and 31–33. (Hereafter cited as GATT Tokyo-Round MTN.)
317. International Dairy Arrangement Doc. MTN/DP181 Corr. 1, July 17, 1979 (Restricted) Corrigendum of Annex C of Doc. MTN/DP/8. Article VIII (hereafter cited as Int. Dairy Arr.) and GATT Press Release GATT/1254, January 2, 1980; BISD, 26th supplement, p. 91 and pp. 189–191.
318. Int. Dairy Arr. Art. I.
319. *Idem,* Article II.
320. *Idem,* Article VI.
321. *Idem,* Article IV, 4.

322. *Idem,* Article VII.
323. *Idem,* Article IV.
324. *Idem,* Article III.
325. *Idem,* Article IV, 5.
326. *Idem,* Article IV, 6.
327. *Idem,* Article VIII, 7.
328. See also *GATT Tokyo-Round MTN,* pp. 145–146.
329. BISD, 26th supplement, pp. 189–191 and p. 84 *et seq.*
330. Arrangement Regarding Bovine Meat, GATT Geneva, April 12, 1979, Article VI, 1.2 and 4; BISD, 26th supplement, p. 84. (Hereafter cited as Meat Arr.)
331. Meat Arr. Article I and *GATT Tokyo-Round MTN,* p. 146.
332. Meat Arr. Article II.
333. *Idem,* Article V.
334. *Idem,* Article IV.
335. *Idem,* Article III.
336. *Idem,* Article IV, 5, 101(c).
337. *Idem,* Article IV, 5.
338. *Idem,* Article VI, 6.
339. Multilateral Safeguard System stands for the right to impose or re-impose import controls and other temporary trade restrictions to prevent commercial injury in critical circumstances and the corresponding right of exports not to be lightly deprived of access to markets. GATT Activities in 1977 (Geneva, 1978), p. 31.
340. GATT Activities in 1977, *op. cit.* (note 339), pp. 31–33. Jackson, *op. cit.* (note 5), p. 570. L. Limburg, 'Duivels Reveil' [Develish Revival], *Economisch Statistische Berichten,* 63 (No. 3140), pp. 117–120.
341. See also section 4.3.2.2.2.
342. S. Aranja, 'Non-tariff issues in the MTN', 13 *Finance and Development* 21–24.
343. BISD, 26th supplement, p. 202.
344. GATT Activities in 1980, *op. cit.* (note 209), p. 14.
345. BISD, 24th supplement, p. 37.
346. See section 4.3.11.4.2.
347. BISD, 26th supplement, p. 219.
348. GATT Activities in 1979, *op. cit.* (note 2), p. 34.
349. BISD, 26th supplement, p. 209. See also section 4.3.11.2.
350. See VII.C.4.
351. BISD, 26th supplement, pp. 342–353.
352. BISD, 24th supplement, p. 34.
353. The rulings are recorded in restricted GATT documents. The information concerning the compliance has been given orally by G. H. Perlow, Esq.
354. See for an extensive analysis, G. H. Perlow, *loc. cit.* (note 288).
355. *Cf.* the list in BISD, 25th supplement, pp. 208–214.
356. *E.g.* to the U.S., BISD, Vol. II, p. 9 and to Italy, *ibidem,* p. 10.
357. *E.g.* to the U.S., BISD, 12th supplement, p. 57 and to India, BISD, 20th supplement, p. 26.
358. *E.g.* to the European Coal and Steel Community (ECSC), BISD, 1st supplement, p. 17. See also section 4.3.12.
359. *E.g.* to Czechoslovakia, BISD, 3rd supplement, p. 43.
360. *E.g.* to Peru, BISD, 7th supplement, p. 37, and Uruguay, BISD, 26th supplement, p. 229.
361. *E.g.* to the U.S., BISD, 3rd supplement, p. 32.
362. Jackson, *op. cit.* (note 5), pp. 545–546.
363. *E.g.* to Australia, BISD, 14th supplement, p. 23 and a Generalised System of Preferences, BISD, 18th supplement, p. 24.
364. BISD, 3rd supplement, p. 32.
365. See also section 4.3.6.1.
366. BISD, 3rd supplement, p. 32.
367. Jackson, *op. cit.* (note 5), p. 554.
368. Under Article II, 6 the CP have to approve adjustments of specific duties and charges, included in Schedules. This could be considered to be a waiver of the obligations of Article II.
369. BISD, 1st supplement, p. 86 and Jackson, *op. cit.* (note 5), pp. 543–544.
370. *Idem,* p. 545.
371. Article XXV,5.
372. BISD, 9th supplement, pp. 8–9.

373. Article XXV,5. In the text of the Agreement the term sub-paragraph is used since the fifth paragraph of Article XXV consisted of four sub-paragraphs before 1955. When the GATT was amended they forgot to replace the term 'sub-paragraph' by 'paragraph'. Jackson, *op. cit.* (note 5), p. 543 note 2.
374. BISD, 5th supplement, p. 25.
375. See section 4.3.3.
376. Only waivers to the U.S. granted on August 9, 1948 (BISD, Vol. II, p. 9) and to France granted on November 19, 1960 (BISD, 9th supplement, p. 36), have been granted for an unlimited period, without providing for supervision. These waivers regard preferential treatment on behalf of formerly dependent territories.
377. *E.g.* the waiver to Belgium granted on December 3, 1955 (BISD, 4th supplement, p. 22 and 3rd supplement, p. 41).
378. *E.g.* the waiver to Turkey granted on November 11, 1907 (BISD, 15th supplement, pp. 90–93), and the waiver for Trade Negotiations Among Developing Countries granted on November 26, 1971 (BISD, 18th supplement, pp. 26–28).
379. *E.g.* the waivers to Chile granted on December 30, 1966 (BISD, 15th supplement, pp. 83–85) and to India granted on March 16, 1973 (BISD, 20th supplement, pp. 24–26). Also the waiver for a Generalised System of Preferences (*op. cit.* note 363) and that for Trade Negotiations Among Developing Countries (*op. cit.* note 378).
380. *E.g.* the waiver to Uruguay granted on May 8, 1961 (BISD, 10th supplement, p. 53).
381. *E.g.* the waiver to Uruguay (*op. cit.* note 380).
382. *E.g.* the waiver to India (*op. cit.* note 379).
383. Jackson, *op. cit.* (note 5), p. 548.
384. *Idem,* pp. 545 and 548.
385. GATT Doc. SR. 7/17 (1952): (Jackson, *op. cit.* (note 5), p. 138).
386. GATT Doc. L/403 (1955): (Jackson, *op. cit.* (note 5), p. 138).
387. *Cf.* BISD, 9th supplement, pp. 8–9.
388. See section 2.5.2.
389. The application of quantitative restrictions has a number of disadvantages as compared with that of tariffs. Every restriction of imports increases the price unless there is an oversupply of the commodity involved. Tariffs only raise the price by a few per cent. The increase brought about by quota depends on the scarcity created by the quantitative restrictions. Therefore, the domestic price becomes isolated from the price on the world market. As a result of quotas, domestic producers are able to continue production, even when their costs are extremely high. Under a tariff system, a domestic producer, making goods at a price that exceeds the world price increased with the tariff, will not be able to meet competition and will be forced out of production. Therefore, tariffs are less disruptive for world trade in cases where domestic production is considerably inefficient. Another disadvantage of quotas is that discrimination and corruption in their application are hard to check.
390. See section 4.3.5.
391. See section 4.3.11.
392. See section 4.3.4.2.
393. See section 4.3.8.
394. Franken, *op. cit.* (note 8), pp. 103–104.
395. See also Article XX(d).
396. Dam, *op. cit.* (note 18), p. 259. Referring to Analytical Index, p. 53, dumping is dealt with in section 4.3.9.
397. Jackson, *op. cit.* (note 5), pp. 321–322. Quotas were not brought within the obligations of Article I.
398. Article XIII,5.
399. Article XIII,2(a).
400. Article XIII,2(b).
401. Article XIII,2(c). This is very hard to check.
402. Article XIII,2(a).
403. Interpretative note ad Article XIII,2(d). See also Jackson, *op. cit.* (note 5), pp. 324–325.
404. Article XIII,3(a).
405. Article XIII,3(b).
406. Standard Practices for Import and Export Restrictions and Exchange Controls, December 27, 1950, Franken, *op. cit.* (note 8), p. 114.
407. Article XIII,3(c).
408. Article XIII,4.
409. Article XI,2.

410. Hudec, *op. cit.* (note 145), p. 15.
411. *Idem*, p. 15.
412. BISD, Vol. II, p. 29. See also section 4.2
413. BISD, 3rd supplement, p. 32; 4th supplement, p. 96; 5th supplement, p. 136; 6th supplement, p. 152; 7th supplement, p. 124; 8th supplement, p. 173; 9th supplement, p. 259; 10th supplement, p. 262; 11th supplement, p. 235; 13th supplement, p. 132; 14th supplement, p. 195; 15th supplement, p. 197; 16th supplement, p. 109 and 18th supplement, p. 223.
414. See sections 4.3.6. and 4.3.12.
415. See section 4.3.12; Dam, *op. cit.* (note 18), p. 265; Hudec, *op. cit.* (note 2), p. 203 and Hudec, *op. cit.* (note 145), pp. 15 and 16, note 32.
416. See section 4.3.2., paras. 4 and 5.
417. *The Tokyo-Round of MTN*, pp. 18–34.
418. C. F. Bergsten, 'Reforming the GATT: The Use of Trade Measures for Balance of Payments Purposes' (1977) 7 *Journal of International Economics* 1–18, at p. 5.
419. Revenue = price × quantity. As a consequence of a devaluation the price that foreign consumers pay for a commodity decreases. This gives rise to an increase in quantity demanded. But when the demand is price-inelastic the relative change in quantity demanded is smaller than the relative change in price. Therefore, total revenue will decrease.
420. See also section 4.3.11.
421. When an equilibrium is lacking continually, surplus-countries are forced to finance the deficits of countries with a deficit. If they do not want to do so, they might restrict their trade with deficit-countries.
422. See section 2.1.
423. BISD, 26th supplement, pp. 205–209.
424. Article XII,2(a).
425. Article XV,2.
426. Article XII,2(b).
427. Article XII,2,3(c)(i).
428. Article XII,3(c)(ii).
429. Article XII,3(c)(iii).
430. Article XII,3(a).
431. Article XII,3(b); see also Jackson, *op. cit.* (note 5), p. 685.
432. GATT, *The Use of Quantitative Import Restrictions to Safeguard Balances of Payments,* 29, Sales No. GATT/1951–2 (Geneva, 1951); Jackson, *op. cit.* (note 5), p. 686.
433. In 1960 this was still the Executive Secretary.
434. BISD, 9th supplement, pp. 18–19.
435. Jackson, *op. cit.* (note 5), pp. 700–701.
436. Or Article XVIII,12(a).
437. BISD, 9th supplement, p. 19.
438. Article XII,4(e) + Int. N. Ad Article XII,4(e).
439. Int. N. Ad Article XII.
440. GATT, *Final Act*, Geneva 55 UNTS 194 232 (1947); Jackson, *op. cit.* (note 5), p. 703.
441. GATT, *The Use of Quantitative Import Restrictions to Safeguard Balances of Payments*, 12, Sales No. GATT/1951–2; Jackson, *op. cit.* (note 5), p. 703.
442. See also Article XVIII,12(b).
443. BISD, 7th supplement, pp. 97–98.
444. GATT, *Review of Import Restrictions under Articles XII,4(b) and XVIII,12(b)*. GATT Doc. L/1005 (1959); Jackson, *op. cit.* (note 5), p. 704.
445. See also Article XVIII,12(b).
446. The Committee on Balance of Payments Restrictions is a Permanent Committee, established in 1958 (BISD, 7th supplement, p. 94). It conducts the annual consultations with cps applying import restrictions for balance of payments reasons and consults with the IMF in connection with the consultations under Articles XII and XVIII. It reports to the CP or the Council.
447. BISD, 7th supplement, pp. 97–98.
448. BISD, 18th supplement, pp. 48–54.
449. See also GATT Doc. MTN/S9/W/7, March 15, 1976, pp. 6–8.
450. BISD, 26th supplement, pp. 207–208.
451. BISD, 8th supplement, p. 73.
452. GATT Doc. MTN/S9/W/7, March 15, 1976, p. 8.
453. BISD, 25th supplement, p. 159.
454. GATT Activities in 1980, *op. cit.* (note 173), pp. 42–43.

455. Article XII,4(c). See also Article XVIII,12(c).
456. Article XII,4(d). See also Article XVIII,12(d).
457. GATT Doc. L/1222 Add. 1 (1960); Jackson, *op. cit.* (note 5), p. 182.
458. BISD, 11th supplement, p. 100. (Uruguayan recourse to Article XXIII.)
459. See also Jackson, *op. cit.* (note 5), pp. 706–707.
460. *Idem*, p. 682, footnote 3.
461. The measures might be taken by those cps the balances of payments of which are under pressure or by those cps the balances of payments of which are tending to be exceptionally favourable, or by any appropriate international organisation.
462. Article XII, 5.
463. *Cf.* Bergsten, *loc. cit.* (note 418), p. 2–20.
464. See section 4.3.7.
465. See also section 4.3.2.
466. And not to regulate trade in a specific sector, which is the usual ground for such restrictions. Bergsten, *loc. cit.* (note 418), p. 11.
467. P. Bratschi, 'Allgemeines Zoll und Handelsabkommen (GATT)', *Handbuch für den Praktiker* (Zurich, 1973), pp. 51–52.
468. See section 4.3.5.3.3.
469. Declaration adopted by Governments of OECD Member Countries on May 30, 1974.
470. See section 4.3.6.
471. See also GATT Secretariat, *International Surveillance Systems*, MTN/S9/W/7, March 15, 1976.
472. See section 4.3.5.3.5.
473. Hudec, *op. cit.* (note 2), p. 241.
474. See Article XV,2 and section 4.3.5.1.
475. BISD, 3rd section, pp. 38–41.
476. SR.20/7 (November 1962), Hudec, *op. cit.* (note 2), p. 285, note 15.
477. The hard-core waiver was extended until 1962.
478. BISD, 3rd supplement, pp. 38–41.
479. BISD, 4th supplement, p. 22 and p. 102.
480. BISD, 6th supplement, pp. 63–68.
481. BISD, 7th supplement, pp. 99–107.
482. BISD, 8th supplement, pp. 31–50 and 160–163; Hudec, *op. cit.* (note 2), pp. 242–244.
483. *Idem*, p. 244.
484. BISD, 9th supplement, pp. 18–20.
485. In 1960 still the Executive Secretary.
486. See section 4.2.2.
487. BISD, 9th supplement, pp. 19–20.
488. C/M/4 (February 22–March 2, 1961), Hudec, *op. cit.* (note 2), pp. 245–246.
489. BISD, 11th supplement, p. 206.
490. BISD, 11th supplement, pp. 210–213.
491. Hudec, *op. cit.* (note 2), pp. 248–249.
492. *Idem*, p. 247.
493. BISD, 11th supplement, p. 94; Hudec, *op. cit.* (note 2), p. 218 and pp. 249–250.
494. L/3744 September 12, 1972; Hudec, *op. cit.* (note 2) p. 295; see also section 4.2.
495. Eighteenth Annual Report of the President on the Trade Agreements Program 1973, CSA DC 74–12753; Hudec, *op. cit.* (note 2), p. 236 and p. 293; see also section 4.2.
496. Committee III preceded the Committee on Trade and Development; see section 4.3.11; and BISD, 14th supplement, p. 132.
497. BISD, 15th supplement, pp. 144–145 and p. 155.
498. BISD, 15th supplement, p. 71.
499. Hudec, *op. cit.* (note 2), p. 255.
500. SR.24/10 November 16, 1969; Hudec, *op. cit.* (note 2), p. 255 and p. 386.
501. L/3260 October 17, 1969. Hudec, *op. cit.* (note 2), pp. 256–257 and p. 387.
502. See section 4.3.11.4.3.
503. Hudec, *op. cit.* (note 2), p. 259. See also section 4.2.
504. BISD, 9th supplement, p. 191.
505. BISD, 9th supplement, pp. 185–187.
506. BISD, 24th supplement, pp. 121–122.
507. BISD, Vol. II, p. 19.
508. BISD, 3rd supplement, p. 225.
509. BISD, 9th supplement, p. 193.

510. BISD, 11th supplement, pp. 58–59.
511. Article XVI,2.
512. BISD, 3rd supplement, p. 225; 10th supplement, pp. 206–207.
513. See section 4.3.7.2.
514. BISD, 3rd supplement, p. 226.
515. BISD, Vol. II, p. 199, *seq.* at p. 193. See section 4.2.
516. BISD, 3rd supplement, p. 225.
517. Article XVI,2.
518. Article XVI,3. See for its interpretation BISD, 3rd supplement, p. 226 and Int. N. Ad Article XVI,3.
519. Int. N. Ad Article XVI,4.
520. BISD, 6th supplement, p. 24.
521. BISD, 7th supplement, p. 30; 8th supplement, p. 25 and 9th supplement, p. 33.
522. BISD, 12th supplement, pp. 50–52.
523. GATT — Status of Legal Instruments, p. 73.
524. BISD, 10th supplement, p. 201.
525. BISD, 9th supplement, pp. 184–195; 10th supplement, pp. 201–210.
526. BISD, 10th supplement, pp. 202–205.
527. BISD, 9th supplement, p. 193. See *supra*, note 509.
528. BISD, 10th supplement, p. 206. See also Jackson, *op. cit.* (note 5), p. 389.
529. BISD, 10th supplement, pp. 206–208.
530. See section 4.3.9.
531. See section 4.3.2. This has never happened yet.
532. See section 4.2.
533. Since subsidies or the level of subsidies may be drawn into the negotiations, too. (See WP Report BISD, 3rd supplement, p. 225.) This has been recognised in the rules of procedure for negotiations in 1960 and 1961 (BISD, 8th supplement, p. 116 and for the Kennedy Round (BISD, 12th supplement, p. 36). Jackson, *op. cit.* (note 5), p. 379.
534. BISD, 11th supplement, p. 100 (Uruguay Case). Jackson, *op. cit.* (note 5), p. 182. See also section 4.2.
535. Jackson, *op. cit.* (note 5), p. 387. BISD, 3rd supplement, p. 224.
536. BISD, Vol. II. p. 193.
537. SR.8/12 (October 5, 1953). Hudec, *op. cit.* (note 2), p. 282.
538. BISD, 10th supplement, pp. 207–208.
539. BISD, 7th supplement, p. 22.
540. BISD, 15th supplement, p. 116.
541. BISD, 24th supplement, p. 134. In this case the exporting country complained about countervailing measures of the importing country. See also section 4.3.9.
542. GATT Activities in 1980, *supra* (note 173), pp. 45–49.
543. See also Jackson, *op. cit.* (note 5), pp. 379–382.
544. BISD, 9th supplement, p. 187.
545. BISD, 24th supplement, pp. 116–126.
546. MTN/NTM/W/236 and Corr. 1. Done at Geneva, April 12, 1979. See also BISD, 26th supplement, pp. 189–191 and pp. 56–83; and GATT Press Release, GATT/1254, January 2, 1980.
547. Established by this Agreement. See Article 16.
548. Agreement on Interpretation and Application of Articles VI, XVI and XXIII of the GATT, BISD, 26th supplement, pp. 56–83, Article 7. (Hereafter cited as Subsidies Code.)
549. Subsidies Code, Article 8. See also Article 11.
550. *Idem*, Article 9.
551. *Idem*, Article 10.
552. *Idem*, Article 14.
553. See section 4.3.9.
554. Subsidies Code, Article 13.
555. *Idem*, Article 161.
556. *Idem*, Article 17.
557. *Idem*, Article 18.
558. *Idem*, Article 19,1 and Note 38.
559. *Idem*, Article 19,6.
560. BISD, 10th supplement, pp. 204–205.
561. P. Lloyd, *Anti-dumping Actions and the GATT System*, Thames Essay No. 9 (London, 1977), pp. 47–48.

562. J. J. Barceló, 'Subsidies, Countervailing Duties and Anti-dumping after the Tokyo-Round' (1980) 13 *Cornell International Law Journal* 257–288, at p. 261. According to Barceló:

'One cannot meet the efficiency challenge to export subsidies by arguing that the subsidy advances a collective purpose or non-economic goal. Except for cases of economic or military aid, no country has a plausible good. An export subsidy is also not an efficient corrective policy for a market distortion in the internal economy. If a government seeks corrective action, that action should be tied closely to the original distortion; hence, if a subsidy is entailed, it should be a domestic, not an export subsidy.

Ironically, the inefficiencies stemming from misguided subsidies afflict primarily the subsidising country itself. Thus, GATT rules prohibiting export subsidies benefit the very countries against whom they operate. Such rules, like those limiting import barriers, increase a government's bargaining position with highly organised special interests who may benefit from export subsidies at the expense of the general interest. The inefficiencies of export subsidies, however, also reduce global welfare. How such global inefficiencies affect the interests of non-subsidising countries is analysed below in connection with the trade retaliation and countervailing duty laws.

Domestic subsidies are not as vulnerable to arguments of aggressiveness and inefficiency. Domestic subsidies are the counterpart of domestic taxes, which unlike tariffs, are not closely regulated by GATT. Although domestic subsidies may increase the subsidising country's export flow, they generally carry none of the aggressive overtones of export subsidies. They are normally aimed at legitimate internal socio-economic goals, not at expanding the country's share of foreign markets. In addition, domestic subsidies are not presumptively inefficient or disrtive of "proper" trade flow.'

Idem, pp. 262–263.
563. Paragraph 1(c) deals with any enterprise.
564. See also Jackson, *op. cit.* (note 5), pp. 340–343.
565. Article XVII,1.
566. Article XVII,2 and see also Article III,8 and section 4.3.10.
567. Article XVII,4(a).
568. Article XVII,4(c).
569. Article XVII,4(d).
570. GATT Doc. L/760 (1957), Jackson, *op. cit.* (note 5), p. 351.
571. GATT Doc. L/784 (1958), Jackson, *op. cit.* (note 5), p. 351.
572. BISD, 8th supplement, p. 142 and 9th supplement, pp. 179–185. Jackson, *op. cit.* (note 5), pp. 351–352 (the questionnaire is printed as note 7).
573. BISD, 9th supplement, p. 185 at III.
574. BISD, 8th supplement, p. 142 and 9th supplement, p. 179 and pp. 183–184.
575. BISD, 8th supplement, p. 143.
576. BISD, 9th supplement, p. 183.
577. BISD, 11th supplement, pp. 58–59.
578. See section 4.3.7.
579. BISD, 11th supplement, p. 187. Jackson, *op. cit.* (note 5), p. 353.
580. BISD, 22nd supplement, pp. 55–59. See on dumping, section 4.3.9.
581. *Cf.* BISD, 24th supplement, p. 142.
582. The normal price is the price on a free market with no price control.
583. See sections 4.3.7. and 4.3.8.
584. See also Article II,2(b).
585. When there is dumping to the same degree from more than one source, however, causing or threatening material injury to the same extent, the importing country ought normally to be expected to levy anti-dumping duties equally on all dumped imports. BISD, 9th supplement, p. 189 and Anti-Dumping Code of 1967. Article 8(b) BISD, 15th supplement, p. 81. (This is an exceptional case.)
586. See the Protocols of Provisional Application; Lloyd, *op. cit.* (note 561), p. 4.
587. BISD, 8th supplement, p. 145 and p. 153.
588. GATT Anti-Dumping and Countervailing Rules (1961), Sales No. GATT/1691–2; Jackson, *op. cit.* (note 5), p. 409.
589. *Idem*, pp. 407–409.
590. BISD, 15th supplement, pp. 24–35. Also printed in Jackson, *op. cit.* (note 5), pp. 426–438.
591. Agreement on Implementation of Article VI of the GATT, Preamble.
592. Agreement on Interpretation and Application of Articles VI, XVI and XXIII of the GATT, Geneva, April 12, 1979. MTN/NTM/W/236 and Corr. 1, BISD, 26th supplement, pp. 189–191 and pp. 56–83. (Hereafter cited as Subsidies Code.) Agreement on Implementation of

Article VI of the GATT. MTN/NTM/W/232, Add. 1/Rev.1, Add. 2 and Corr. 1, BISD, 26th supplement, pp. 189–191 and pp. 171–188. (Hereafter cited as 1979 Anti-Dumping Code.)
593. GATT Press Release GATT/1254, January 2, 1980.
594. Subsidies Code Article 19 and 1979 Anti-Dumping Code Article 16.
595. 1979 Anti-Dumping Code Article 16(5).
596. Article VI,1. See also the 1967 Anti-Dumping Code Article 2.
597. Article VI,1.
598. Int. N. Ad Article VI,1(2).
599. Int. N. Ad Article VI,2 and 3(2).
600. Havana Reports, UN Doc. ICITO/1/8, at 74 (1948); Jackson, *op. cit.* (note 5), p. 418.
601. BISD, 8th supplement, p. 150.
602. 1967 Anti-Dumping Code Article 4(a) and 1979 Anti-Dumping Code Article 4(a).
603. 1967 Anti-Dumping Code Articles 5 to 7, and 3; *cf.* 1979 Anti-Dumping Code Articles 5 to 7 and 3.
604. Article 10.
605. Article VI,6(b). See also the 1967 Anti-Dumping Code, Article 12 and the 1979 Anti-Dumping Code, Article 12.
606. Article VI,6(c).
607. Article VI,7.
608. Int. N. Ad Article VI,1(1).
609. Article VI,3.
610. Article VI,4.
611. Article VI,5.
612. 1967 Anti-Dumping Code, Article 14. See also 1979 Anti-Dumping Code, Article 16,6 and Subsidies Code Article 19,5.
613. See section 4.3.9.3.
614. Article 10.
615. BISD, 16th supplement, p. 12.
616. BISD, 17th supplement, p. 43; 18th supplement, pp. 42 and 45; 19th supplement, p. 15; 20th supplement, p. 43; 21st supplement, p. 30; 22nd supplement, p. 21; 23rd supplement, p. 13; 24th supplement, p. 17; and 25th supplement, p. 17.
617. Differences occur in the following Articles of the 1979 Agreement: Articles 1, first phrase; 3; 4(2); 5(1) and (2); 7(4) to (7); 8(5); 10(2) and (3).
618. See Article 3.
619. MTN/NTM/W/232, Add. 1/Rev. 1, Add. 2 and Corr. 1 as amended by MTN/NTM/W/241/Rev. 1.
620. See Chapter XII.
621. Article 14,4.
622. Note 1 to Article 15.
623. Article 16,7.
624. A country confronted with subsidies by another country can countervail under the Trade I provisions of the Subsidies Code (Articles 1–6) or start consultations under the Trade II provisions (Articles 12, 13, 17–19).
625. Subsidies Code, Article 1.
626. *Idem*, Article 2.
627. *Idem*, Article 2(15).
628. *Idem*, Article 2(16).
629. *Idem*, Article 3.
630. *Idem*, Article 4.
631. *Idem*, Article 5.
632. *Idem*, Article 19(5).
633. *The Tokyo-Round of MTN*, p. 130.
634. BISD, 3rd supplement, p. 81; 11th supplement, p. 88; 24th supplement, p. 134.
635. Such as Israel and Switzerland.
636. Such as Japan.
637. Lloyd, *op. cit.* (note 561), p. 17.
638. *Idem*, p. 46. The U.S. considers it exempt from the requirements of Article XVI, because of the 'grandfather clause'. See also India's complaint under Article XXIII about a U.S. Imposition of countervailing duty on industrial fasteners from India. GATT Activities in 1980, *op. cit.* (note 173), p. 60.
639. This will be explained in a publication by the Canada-U.S. Law Institute titled 'Non-Tariff Barriers and the Tokyo-Round' to be published in 1981.

Both tariffs and countervailing duties will lower the total demand for the commodities imported and increase the demand for domestically produced commodities. Both will reduce the consumers surplus and increase the producers surplus within the importing country. However, in the case of a tariff, the Government of the importing country will receive the tax. When it becomes known to exporters that anti-dumping duties are levied they usually increase their prices so as to forgo the duty. Therefore, the economy of the importing country will eventually lose the amount of the imposed duty. The same applies *mutatis mutandis* to countervailing duties. This argument was raised by Prof. Klaus Stegeman during a Conference of Non-Tariff Barriers and the Tokyo-Round Organised by the Canada-U.S. Law Institute, London (Ontario), May 8–10, 1980.

640. However, the signatories of the 1979 Subsidies Code must accommodate their domestic laws under Article 5 of this Code.

641. U.S. Suggested Charter. Dept. of State Publ. No. 2598 at 3 and 4 (1946). Jackson, *op. cit.* (note 5), p. 290.

642. Articles III,8 and XVII,2.

643. OECD, *Government Purchasing in Europe, North America and Japan: Regulations and Procedures* (Paris, 1966).

644. Government procurement was studied by the OECD Trade Committee from 1970 to 1976. See OECD Trade Committee, *Government Purchasing Regulations and Procedures of OECD Member Countries* (Paris, 1976).

645. Done at Geneva, April 12, 1979. MTN/NTM/W/211/Rev. 2 and Add. 1. BISD, 26th supplement, pp. 189–191 and pp. 33–55.

646. GATT Activities in 1980, *op. cit.* (note 173), p. 9.

647. *Cf.* GATT, Article III.

648. UN Doc. EPCT/174 at o (1947). Jackson, *op. cit.* (note 5), p. 292.

649. Int. N. Ad Article XVII, 2; Jackson, *op. cit.* (note 5), p. 292.

650. Agreement on Govn. Proc. Article I,1(c).

651. Annex I.

652. Article I,1(a).

653. Article I,1(b).

654. Article III,4. See also the Note to Article I,1.

655. Article VIII,1.

656. Article V,15.

657. Article II,1 and 3.

658. Article IV,1.

659. Article IV,3.

660. Article V,2(a).

661. Article V,3.

662. Article V,4.

663. Article V,5.

664. Article V,6.

665. Article V,13.

666. Article V,16; The conditions are listed in Article V,15.

667. Article VI,1.

668. Article VI,2.

669. Article VI,3.

670. Article VI,4.

671. Article VI,5.

672. Article VI,6.

673. Article VI,7.

674. Article VI,8. See also Article VI,6.

675. Article VI,9.

676. GATT Activities in 1980, *op. cit.* (note 173), p. 10.

677. Article VII,1.

678. Article VII,2.

679. Article VII,8.

680. Article VII,3, *cf.* GATT Article XXII.

681. Article VII,4, *cf.* GATT Article XXIII.

682. Article VII,5.

683. Article VII,6.

684. Article VII,7.

685. Article VII,9.

686. Article VII,10.
687. Article VII,11.
688. Article VII,12.
689. Article VII,13.
690. Article VII,14.
691. Article IX,6.
692. G. M. Meier, 'The Tokyo-Round of Multilateral Trade Negotiations and the Developing Countries' (1980) 13 *Cornell International Law Journal* 239–256, 243.
693. *Idem*, pp. 241–242.
694. *Idem*, p. 241.
695. See for the calculation of the effective tariff M. E. Kreinin, *International Economics, A Policy Approach*, (2nd ed. New York), p. 294.
696. See sections 4.3.5. and 4.3.11.2.3.
697. BISD, 3rd supplement, pp. 182–189.
698. BISD, 3rd supplement, pp. 49–50.
699. BISD, 6th supplement, p. 18.
700. Sales No. GATT/1958–3.
701. BISD, 7th supplement, pp. 27–29.
702. BISD, 8th supplement, pp. 101, 103, 121, 132 and 135.
703. BISD, 8th supplement, p. 102. See also Jackson, *op. cit.* (note 5), pp. 640–644.
704. BISD, 10th supplement, pp. 25–34.
705. BISD, 12th supplement, p. 36.
706. Dam. *op. cit.* (note 18), pp. 234–235.
707. BISD, 12th supplement, pp. 36–49. The Ministers also agreed to set up an Action Committee to assist them in implementing the action programme and to initiate, process and co-ordinate further measures on behalf of the trade of less-developed countries.
708. BISD, 12th supplement, p. 87. See also Jackson, *op. cit.* (note 5), pp. 644–645.
709. BISD, 13th supplement, p. 2 and p. 10.
710. GATT Press Release 962 (1966). Jackson, *op. cit.* (note 5), p. 646.
711. BISD, 13th supplement, pp. 75–76.
712. See also section 4.3.11.3.
713. BISD, 12th supplement, pp. 148–151; 16th supplement, pp. 98–105.
714. See section 4.3.11.4.3.
715. GATT Activities in 1977, Sales No. GATT/1978–2 (Geneva, 1978), p. 41.
716. BISD, 20th supplement, pp. 20–21.
717. Article XVIII,4.
718. Article XVIII,4.
719. See section 4.3.1.
720. Article XVIII,7(a).
721. Article XVIII,7(b).
722. See section 4.3.1.
723. Article XVIII,8.
724. See section 4.3.5.1.
725. See section 4.3.5.2.
726. See section 4.3.5.3.
727. BISD, 20th supplement, pp. 47–49.
728. When this Article was drafted this was still the Executive Secretary.
729. Article XVIII,12(e).
730. Jackson, *op. cit.* (note 5), pp. 689–690.
731. *Idem*, p. 703.
732. Article XVIII,13.
733. Article XVIII,14.
734. Article XVIII,15.
735. Article XVIII,16.
736. Int. N. Ad Article XVIII,15 and 16.
737. Article XVIII,16 and 17.
738. Article XVIII,18.
739. Article XVIII,19.
740. *Cf.* section 4.3.6.
741. Article XVIII,20.
742. Article XVIII,21.
743. Article XVIII,22 (Section D).

744. BISD, 7th supplement, pp. 85–88.
745. Int. N. Ad Article XXXVI,8.
746. Article XXXVII,1(a), (b) and (c).
747. Article XXXVII,3.
748. Article XXXVII,4.
749. Article XXXVIII,2.
750. Article XXXVII,2(a).
751. Article XXXVII,2(b)(i).
752. Article XXXVII,2(b)(ii) and (iii).
753. Article XXXVII,5.
754. BISD, 13th supplement, pp. 75–76; BISD, 26th supplement, p. 220. See also section 4.3.11.4.4.
755. BISD, 13th supplement, p. 79.
756. BISD, 18th supplement, pp. 61–62.
757. See section 4.3.11.4.3.
758. BISD, 18th supplement, pp. 24–26 and p. 56. See also section 4.3.3.
759. BISD, 16th supplement, p. 17. See also 20th supplement, p. 23 and 25th supplement, p. 8.
760. On November 26, 1971, the CP adopted a decision concerning the implementation of this Protocol (BISD, 18th supplement, p. 26). The CP reviews the operation of the Protocol annually on the basis of a report furnished by the participating countries. The participating countries submitted 6 reports (BISD, 21st supplement, p. 126; 22nd supplement, p. 73; 23rd supplement, p. 147; 24th supplement, p. 154; 25th supplement, p. 163; and 26th supplement, p. 337). The negotiations under the Protocol are aimed at trade and tariff concessions among developing countries.
761. BISD, 13th supplement, p. 77 *et seq.*; 14th supplement, p. 129 *et seq.*; 15th supplement, p. 139 *et seq.*; 16th supplement, p. 89 *et seq.*; 17th supplement, p. 122 *et seq.*; 18th supplement, p. 53 *et seq.* and p. 62 *et seq.*; 19th supplement, p. 19 *et seq.*; 20th supplement, p. 49 *et seq.* and p. 68 *et seq.*; 21st supplement, p. 35 *et seq.*; 22nd supplement, p. 33 *et seq.*; 23rd supplement, p. 32 *et seq.*; 24th supplement, p. 48 *et seq.*; 25th supplement, p. 28 *et seq.*; and 26th supplement, p. 274 *et seq.*
762. BISD, 18th supplement, pp. 70–71.
763. BISD, 19th supplement, p. 40.
764. Hudec, *op. cit.* (note 2), p. 259.
765. BISD, 20th supplement, pp. 19–20. Meier, *loc. cit.* (note 692), pp. 239–240.
766. Tariff reductions granted in the Tokyo Round will result in a general tariff reduction of about one-third. Yet, the most significant reductions will affect traditional industrialised country exports. Moreover, on industrial products of particular interest to the developing countries the weighted average reduction in tariffs is only about one-fourth. Important developing country exports exempt from any tariff reduction include certain textiles, apparel, leather goods, footwear and steel.
   Tariff cuts will erode performance margins under the Generalised System of Preference. The trading position of the developing countries could in fact be worsened more by such erosion than it will improve because of the tariff reductions! But, developing cps will benefit from tariff reductions in the area of finished industrial manufacturers, amounting to 39 per cent. This will reduce tariff escalations. Also tariffs on 2,930 tropical products. Meier, *op. cit.* (note 692), pp. 235–247.
767. Especially, the Subsidies and Anti-Dumping Codes.
768. BISD, 26th supplement, pp. 203–205 and 209–210.
769. BISD, 26th supplement, pp. 205-209 and 210-215.
770. Allowed under a waiver granted in 71. BISD, 18th supplement, p. 24.
771. Point 2. BISD, 26th supplement, p. 203.
772. Point 4. BISD, 26th supplement, p. 204.
773. Under the graduation principle the least developed cps get the most favourable treatment. The further a cp is developed the more it must adhere to the GATT, see also Meier, *op. cit.* (note 692), pp. 247–248.
774. Points 6 and 7. BISD, 26th supplement, pp. 204–205.
775. BISD, 26th supplement, pp. 204–210.
776. BISD, 23rd supplement, p. 169; 24th supplement, p. 159 and 25th supplement, p. 177.
777. Under the original Article XVIII releases were granted to India and Haiti. BISD, Vol. II, pp. 20, 21 and 26. See also Jackson, *op. cit.* (note 5), p. 655.
778. Dam, *op. cit.* (note 18), p. 228.

779. See section 4.3.6.
780. All abbreviations are explained at the beginning of this publication.
781. Franken, *op. cit.* (note 8), pp. 95–96.
782. Kreinin, *op. cit.* (note 695), pp. 308–311.
783. Article XXIV,4.
784. J. Viner, *The Customs Union Issue* (1950), cited in Jackson, *op. cit.* (note 5), p. 601.
785. BISD, 6th supplement, p. 70 and Jackson, *op. cit.* (note 5), p. 601.
786. See *infra*, XVII, B3 and BISD, 6th supplement, p. 70 *et seq.* This is the opinion of the EEC representatives and Jackson, *op. cit.* (note 5), p. 601.
787. BISD, 6th supplement, pp. 70–71. Dam, *op. cit.* (note 18), p. 276.
788. Pursuant to Article XXIV,2a a customs territory is any territory with respect to which separate tariffs or other regulations of commerce are maintained for a substantial part of the trade of such territory with other territories.
789. Article XXIV,8(a).
790. Article XXIV,8(b).
791. Article XXIV,2. Jackson, *op. cit.* (note 5), p. 584.
792. Article XXXIII.
793. *Cf.* the review of the EFTA agreement, BISD, 9th supplement, p. 83 *et seq.*
794. BISD, 6th supplement, p. 99. See also section 4.3.12.3.1.
795. BISD, 6th supplement, pp. 98–99. See also section 4.3.12.3.1.
796. Dam, *op. cit.* (note 18), p. 280.
797. Article XXIV,5(a).
798. Article XXIV,5(b).
799. GATT Doc. L/1479 (1961). Jackson, *op. cit.* (note 5), p. 613.
800. GATT Doc. L/1919 at 2 (1962), *idem*, p. 615.
801. Harry Hawkins in UN Doc. EPCT/C.II/38 at 9 (1946), Jackson, *op. cit.* (note 5), p. 612.
802. GATT Doc. L/1479 (1961), *idem*, p. 613.
803. Trade value equals the product of price and quantity.
804. Article XXIV,9.
805. Int. N. Ad Article XXIV,9.
806. Article XXIV,5(c).
807. See the Association of Turkey with the EEC, BISD, 13th supplement, p. 62 and the Customs Union of South Africa and Rhodesia, BISD, Vol. II, pp. 29 and 176.
808. BISD, 11th supplement, p. 149 and 13th supplement, p. 62.
809. BISD, 14th supplement, p. 115; D. J. Thomas, 'The GATT and the NAFTA Agreement', 15 *Journal of Common Market Studies* 30, September 1976.
810. Article XXIV,5(a) and (b).
811. Article XXIV,7(a).
812. Article XXIV,6.
813. Article XXIV,9.
814. Article XXIV,7(b).
815. Since there is *prima facie* nullification or impairment.
816. See for a list of regional agreements, BISD, 25th supplement, pp. 193–195.
817. See Article I,2, Annex C, E, and F and Article XXIV,10.
818. BISD, 1st supplement, pp. 17 and 85.
819. BISD, 60th supplement, p. 70.
820. P. Lorti, *Economic Integration and the Law of GATT* (New York, 1975), p. 18.
821. BISD, 6th supplement, pp. 70–76; Lorti, *op. cit.* (note 820), pp. 17–18. See also section 4.3.12.1.3.
822. Lorti, *op. cit.* (note 820), pp. 18–19.
823. BISD, 6th supplement, pp. 76–81.
824. BISD, 6th supplement, pp. 81–89; Lorti, *op. cit.* (note 820), pp. 19–20.
825. Article 132, EEC Treaty.
826. BISD, 6th supplement, pp. 89–104; Lorti, *op. cit.* (note 820), pp. 20–21. See also section 4.3.12.1.3.
827. BISD, 9th supplement, p. 70; Hudec, *op. cit.* (note 2), p. 205.
828. BISD, 20th supplement, pp. 145, 158, 171 and 183; 21st supplement, pp. 76 and 83; and 24th supplement, p. 73.
829. GATT negotiations usually take place in Geneva.
830. BISD, 11th supplement, pp. 56 and 149; 13th supplement, p. 59; 19th supplement, p. 90; 21st supplement, p. 94.
831. See section 4.3.12.1.

832. BISD, 18th supplement, pp. 149, 158 and 166; 21st supplement, p. 102; 22nd supplement, p. 43; 23rd supplement, p. 55; 24th supplement, pp. 80 and 88 and 25th supplement, pp. 114, 123, 133 and 142.
833. BISD, 14th supplement, pp. 100–115.
834. BISD, 18th supplement, p. 133; Lorti, *op. cit.* (note 820), p. 23.
835. BISD, 23rd supplement, p. 46.
836. Hudec, *op. cit.* (note 2), pp. 202–203.
837. *Idem*, pp. 239–240.
838. BISD, 9th supplement, p. 87.
839. BISD, 24th supplement, p. 68.
840. BISD, 16th supplement, pp. 17 and 83; 17th supplement, p. 21; 20th supplement, p. 23 and 25th supplement, p. 8.
841. BISD, 18th supplement, pp. 24 and 26.
842. GATT Activities 1976, pp. 60–61; BISD, 25th supplement, pp. 6 and 109.
843. BISD, 26th supplement, pp. 224–226.
844. BISD, 22nd supplement, p. 47; 23rd supplement, p. 67 and 24th supplement, p. 106.
845. BISD, 24th supplement, p. 107; and 26th supplement, p. 327.
846. Dam, *op. cit.* (note 18), p. 289.

PART III

A CASE STUDY: THE TEXTILES
SURVEILLANCE BODY

A CASE STUDY: THE TEXTILES SURVEILLANCE BODY

by G. H. Perlow

CONTENTS

I. INTRODUCTION

The largest industry in the United States, India, Austria, Pakistan, Hong Kong, South Korea and Portugal, among others, is the textile and clothing industry.[1] And in perhaps no other sector of post-war trade, save agriculture, have such persistent cries for protection been raised. Trade in textiles has demanded and received special treatment from national and international authorities since the late 1950s. It is against this backdrop that some of the more important developments in the international regulation of commercial activities have occurred.

One such development – the creation of the Textiles Surveillance Body to supervise the implementation of the current international arrangement governing trade in textiles – forms the focus for this investigation into the effectiveness of multilateral supervision of State behaviour in textile trade. The establishment of this mechanism for multilateral oversight in 1974 was not an inconsequential event. Its quality as a bell-wether was perceived by one observer who recognised the concept of multilateral supervision of textile trade as perhaps one of 'the most important contribution[s] to the development of international economic law'.[2] This paper endeavours to investigate and analyse this specialised case of supervision, and to determine to what extent the 'experiment' has failed or succeeded, and the reasons therefor. The underlying presumption is that the lessons to be learned from the textile experience have applications reaching into other areas of international commercial relations, and perhaps beyond.[3]

II. THE SPECIAL NATURE OF TEXTILE TRADE REGULATION

2.1. The 1950s and 1960s

Textile manufacturing has traditionally been regarded as a 'take-off' industry; that is, a labour-intensive industry common to the first stage of industrialisation.[4] Textiles and clothing have been particularly important in recent decades for labour-abundant less-developed countries (LDCs) seeking to build their export potential and improve their balance of payments position, both crucial for further development. Industrialised countries, though, have found the task of transition to more competitive, capital-intensive activities, in keeping with the shifting of comparative economic advantage, considerably difficult.

With the increasingly rapid industrialisation of Japan and several LDCs in the 1950s and 1960s, resistance grew in industrialised countries counter to the general post-war trend of trade liberalisation, in so far as textiles were concerned. The United States and the United Kingdom, with the most open textile markets in the West, were the first to feel the squeeze from a remarkably resurgent Japanese textile industry.[5] Its powerful U.S. counterpart began applying pressure for protection against Japanese cotton textiles in 1954. The options then open to the U.S. Government, however, were limited. Legal remedies under the General Agreement on Tariffs and Trade[6] (GATT), especially under the waiver clause, Article XXV, and the import safeguard clause, Article XIX, were considered unsatisfactory for political and economic reasons.[7] Import quotas, illegal under the GATT, were ruled out for the adverse effect they would have had on U.S.-Japanese political relations and the U.S. standing within the GATT. The solution eventually sought, and with which the Japanese complied in 1957, was the imposition of export restraints by the Japanese authorities themselves.[8] This resort to a 'voluntary' export restraint (VER) amounted to the reintroduction of a protectionist device, first used in the 1930s, that was to have wide use in the coming decades as a restraint on a variety of products exported from Japan and the developing world.[9]

Trans-shipment and burgeoning cotton textile exports from other developing producers soon defeated the purpose of the U.S.-Japanese VERs.[10] After a similar attempt to restrain Hong Kong's exports failed, the United States initiated the movement to 'multilateralise' and legalise VERs within the framework of an international textiles arrangement. The Europeans, for their part, were interested in finding a legal justification for the continuation of their quantitative restrictions on Japanese textile trade.[11] Meanwhile, Japan foresaw a growing threat to her exports and recognised the need to co-operate with the Europeans and Americans. In fact, Japan apparently preferred negotiating VERs over GATT Article XIX restraints for several reasons, not the least of which was the additional measure of flexibility and control they offered the exporter in determining export ceilings.[12]

This three-way consensus lent impetus to the formation of a GATT working party in 1959 to study the new phenomenon of 'market disruption' in the cotton textiles sector, which was claimed by its alleged victims to be caused by large increases in imports at low prices. The following year the working party recommended to the GATT Contracting Parties that (i) the problem of 'market disruption' be formally recognised, (ii) a multilateral approach to the problem be favoured when bilateral means are unsatisfactory, (iii) 'orderly expansion' of trade rather than trade restriction be the goal of any procedural arrangements, and (iv) existing GATT rights and obligations be left unaffected.[13] The issue of the adequacy of the existing GATT machinery, and particularly Article XIX, to handle market disruption was passed over obliquely; instead, the working party stated that there were 'political and psychological' aspects to the problem that justified the expectation that without more, countries maintaining non-GATT restraints would not be enticed back into the legal fold.[14] Thereupon, the GATT Contracting Parties agreed to recognise the phenomenon and established the working party as a permanent committee to continue to study the problem and 'suggest multilaterally acceptable solutions'.[15]

The framework within which 'constructive solutions' were to be eventually undertaken began to take form at U.S. insistence with its proposal in June of 1961 for an international arrangement that would enable importing countries legally to impose quantitative trade restrictions on cotton textiles to avoid market disruption, while, at the same time, allowing for an 'orderly development' of trade.[16] The ensuing multilateral discussions, primarily in the framework of the GATT, resulted in the drafting and signing of the Short Term Agreement[17] (STA), which ran from October 1, 1961, to September 31, 1962. It was succeeded by the Long-Term Arrangement[18] (LTA), which ran with several extensions up to 1974. The LTA was followed by the Multi-Fibre Arrangement, currently in effect. Thus a system of controlled or managed trade was introduced permitting the 'discriminatory' restriction of trade from particular sources whose exports were causing or threatening disruption. 'Market disruption' as described in the first two agreements mirrored the language used earlier by the GATT Contracting Parties.[19] In return for allowing their disruptive exports limited, exporting countries were entitled not to have import levels cut back below a certain base level determined by a specified reference period, and, should the restraints last more than a year, to a minimum annual growth rate.[20]

For the first time, then, a sector of trade was partially removed from the GATT regulatory structure and placed within its own special framework,[21] albeit clearly intended to be temporary. Though not expressly obligated, importing countries were supposed to have used the period of relief provided by the arrangements to facilitate the adjustment of their inefficient cotton textile industries.[22] If the LTA had worked as optimistically expected, industrial conversion and rationalisation in the developed countries would have been undertaken and completed within the arrangement's initial five-year term. Cotton textile trade restraints would then have been consequently lifted. This, needless to say, was not the case. In 1962, for example, the United States negotiated bilateral restraint agreements under Article 4 with 17 principal suppliers after having unilaterally imposed restraints under Article 3; by 1972 the United States had bilateral agreements with 30 exporting countries. The United Kingdom restricted disruptive imports unilaterally and bilaterally throughout the course of the LTA and did not permit the full annual growth rate therein stipulated.[23] The EEC, which entered the LTA with a more protected market than either the U.S. or the U.K., succeeded in expanding access to its markets, but in conjunction with the negotiation of bilateral restraint agreements that lasted throughout the extended terms of the LTA.

These additional trade restrictions as well as indications of unsatisfactory industrial adjustment in importing countries were the sources of LDC discontent with the LTA. Export potential was restricted in many areas rather than progressively liberalised. Yet LDC exports did increase as a whole from $1,250m. in 1960 to $3,850m. in 1970, although over 70 per cent. of the decade's export expansion was accounted for by developed countries.[24] LDC production increased at a faster clip, but developed countries' increased output was greater in value terms. Developed countries' imports increased by $3,860 million during the 1960s: cotton yarn imports doubled and cotton cloth increased by 50 per cent. Three-quarters of the increased imports, however, originated from other developed countries. It is difficult to conjecture how cotton textile trade might have developed had there been no LTA. It can be surmised that despite the increased numbers of restraints introduced during the currency of the LTA, world trade, including the LDCs' share, would not have expanded as fast as it did without the agreement.[25]

In two important respects the LTA was a failure. First, the elimination of restraints already in force at the inception of the LTA was not entirely accomplished in accordance with Article 2(1)'s call 'to relax those restrictions progressively each year with a view to their elimination as soon as possible'. This failure has been ascribed to loose drafting (*e.g.* no specified time limits) and to the lack of a supervisory mechanism for determining just which pre-existing restrictions had to be eliminated.[26] Secondly, the LTA failed to erect a supervisory structure to regulate the new restraints introduced under Articles 3 and 4 and to ensure that all the rules would be respected. The result was that interpretations of law and fact were unilaterally taken and often suspect. The embryonic form of multilateral control provided in Article 8(b) – '[a]ny case of divergence of view between the participating countries as to the interpretation or application of this Arrangement may be referred to the [Cotton Textiles] Committee for discussion' – was inadequate.[27] Consultations proved a time-consuming and inconclusive way of contesting the unilateral decisions of an import-restricting country; as long as the matter remained in dispute, unilateral restraints were maintained.

With the dramatic advent of new technology in man-made fibre productions in the 1960s, rayon, nylon and polyester became, for the first time, real substitutes for cotton in fabrics and clothing. Far Eastern producers moved aggressively into the new sector, in large measure because their access to cotton textile markets was restricted. LDC sales of man-made yarns and fabrics increased 20-fold between 1967 and 1973 with Taiwan, South Korea and Hong Kong accounting for 40, 23 and 13 per cent., respectively, of LDC exports in 1973.[28] As with cotton textiles a decade earlier, the United States was the first to feel the pinch of the booming exports.[29] Expansion of U.S. imports by 50 per cent. in both 1970 and 1971 triggered a wave of protectionist alarm despite the relatively small share (10 per cent.) man-made textile imports occupied in the U.S. market.[30]

When the United States began negotiating VERs with Japan and other Asian producers in 1971 – recalling the 1957 cotton textile VER that foreran the STA and the LTA – a new, more comprehensive arrangement seemed in the offing. The VERs, meanwhile, succeeded in raising European fears of trade diversion.[31] Concurrently, general dissatisfaction with the inadequacy of the LTA grew to the point where major change became inevitable. The historical pattern had been repeated.

231

2.2. The Multi-Fibre Arrangement

Despite initial opposition among LDCs to a more comprehensive arrangement, intensive preparatory work on a new multilateral agreement began in 1972 under the auspices of the GATT. Three rounds of negotiation in 1973 yielded the Multi-Fibre Arrangement[32] (MFA) covering cotton, man-made textiles and wool[33]; it went into effect on January 1, 1974. The successful outcome of the negotiations has been attributed to several factors. Developing countries came to realise that a new agreement taking better account of their interests would be preferable to the uncertainty and likelihood of uncontrolled protectionism without an agreement. Their dissatisfaction with the LTA along with that of the industrialised importing countries provided the impetus to seek a compromise solution. Negotiating momentum was maintained by (i) limiting the talks to one sector of trade to be subjected to control for a finite period of time, (ii) including only those countries in the talks with an interest in textile trade, and (iii) effective use of the GATT Secretariat as an intermediary body.[34]

The fundamental balance (or conflict, if you will) between importing and exporting countries' interests that had been expressed in the Preamble of the LTA was carried forward into the operative body of the MFA:

> The basic objectives shall be to achieve the expansion of trade, the reduction of barriers to such trade and the progressive liberalisation of world trade in textile products, while at the same time ensuring the orderly and equitable development of this trade and avoidance of disruptive effects in individual markets and on individual lines of production in both importing and exporting countries.[35]

The substantive means to achieve these ends are found for the most part in the central provisions of the MFA – Articles 2, 3 and 4 and Annexes A and B.

Article 2 deals with the elimination or legalisation of all textile trade restraints already in force at the inception of the MFA. Simply put, these pre-existing restrictions, once notified, had to be either justified under the provisions of the GATT or conformed to the MFA within one year of the latter's entry into force.[36] Otherwise, they had to be terminated.[37] Special programmes designed to gradually eliminate pre-existing unilateral quantitative restrictions were also possible.[38] Only the EEC chose to make use of such 'phase-out' programmes.

In keeping with Article 3 an importing country opining that it is suffering market disruption as described in Annex A[39] must first request consultations with the country whose exports are allegedly disruptive. If no mutual understanding or agreement on restraint measures is reached within 60 days from the date consultations were requested, the importing country may impose restraints unilaterally.[40] In 'highly unusual and critical circumstances' when imports, if continued during the 60-day consultation period, would cause serious market disruption resulting in damage difficult to repair, the importing country may restrain trade prior to consultations.[41] Without the exporting country's co-operation, the importing country can act unilaterally after one week's notice, unless such notice would undermine the purpose of the emergency restraint.[42] All Article 3 restraints – whether unilateral, bilateral or 'emergency' – are supposed to be temporary, not exceeding one year; extensions for additional periods are possible, however, and easily obtained.[43]

Annex B sets the minimum standards of liberality with which all new restraints must comply. In a confusing, verbose formulation a 12-month reference period is specified for determining the level of imports below which disruptive imports cannot be restrained.[44] If restraints last longer that one year, the level of imports must be raised 6 per cent. annually.[45] Other flexibility requirements, such as carryover, carryforward and swing, are provided.[46] Through a judicious use of these the volume of imports in any given year can be further increased.

VERs and other types of bilateral agreements are sanctioned under Article 4 provided that 'on overall terms, including base levels and growth rates' they are more liberal than Article 3 restraints.[47] Market disruption, or threat thereof, is not a prerequisite: Article 4(2) permits agreements that merely seek 'to eliminate real risks of market disruption', a virtually undefinable standard. Alastair Sutton has pointed out that since exporting countries are not obliged to conclude Article 4 agreements, questions of a legal and political nature are raised. If an exporting country proved to be a recalcitrant negotiator and if market disruption could not be established, then the importing country would have no recourse to legal protection under the MFA. Sutton maintains that 'in the case of many importing countries it was almost a *sine qua non* of their accepting the MFA at all that exporting countries be willing to negotiate bilateral agreements under this provision'.[48] He argues that the text masksthe real conflicting intentions of the parties, and that any interpretation of Article 4, therefore, cannot be strictly legal, but that also 'the basic yet unwritten conditions of each group must be borne in mind'.[49] David Robertson has agreed that both exporters' and importers' interests must be considered in interpreting the vague terms of the Article, but he views this as a 'substantial restraint' on, rather than a facilitation of the use of trade restrictions.[50] In any event, the weak standards of Article 4 have posed the greatest 'internal' danger to the liberality objectives of the MFA, and for that reason will be discussed later in more detail.

The remaining provisions of the MFA reflect in varying degrees the various interests that went into making the compromise. Article 6, for instance, was intended to secure special and differential treatment for LDCs, new entrants to markets (particularly, Malaysia and the Philippines), small suppliers, and cotton suppliers (India, Pakistan and Egypt); while special treatment for new entrants was not to 'cause undue prejudice to the interests of established suppliers' (Hong Kong). The 'minimum viable production' countries (the Nordics) received recognition of their interests in Article 1(2). All importing countries' interests in avoiding trans-shipment and circumvention are reflected in Article 8; while exporting countries' interest in promoting industrial adjustment in importing countries is explicitly mentioned in Article 1(4).[51] Article 11 represents perhaps the most important collective objective of the exporting countries – the establishment of an impartial body with the authority to supervise the implementation of the agreement. All in all, by tying so many interests together, the MFA began its life with a consensus sufficiently broad to have rendered its implementation satisfactory and most of its goals achievable, but also sufficiently unreliable to have cast doubt on its ability to withstand certain looming difficulties.[52]

III. THE MULTILATERAL SUPERVISION OF THE LAW

3.1. The supervisory organs

The plenary Textiles Committee (TC) and the eight-man Textiles Surveillance Body (TSB) comprise the novel supervisory structure of the MFA. The TSB, in particular, represented at its inception a unique and innovative development in international commercial relations. Unlike GATT panels temporarily created for the specific purpose of dispute resolution, the TSB was designed to be an independent standing body capable of meeting often and regularly with broad and automatic powers of supervision. Though not a judicial body with the authority to promulgate binding opinions, the TSB nevertheless represented a modest, though important, step forward from a purely non-judicial form of supervision of commercial relations. The Textiles Committee, a conventional body consisting of all the signatories of the MFA, traces its origins back to the time of the Short-Term Agreement and the creation of the Provisional Cotton Textile Committee. Then, as now, the Committee was charged with collecting data for studies aiming towards long-term sectoral solutions. Its tasks have since been broadened, although its identification with the GATT structure is retained. The GATT Director-General has always been its appointed chairman.

The MFA allots to the TSB the task of reviewing specific trade restricting measures for their conformity to the rules. The TSB is also made the forum for conciliation and dispute settlement. The Textiles Committee, on the other hand, has the authority to interpret the rules as well as to commission and consider general studies. Both organs are intended to effectuate the pressure necessary to redress rule violations.

The TSB consists of a non-governmental chairman and eight governmental members appointed on a basis 'determined by the Textiles Committee so as to ensure its efficient operations'.[53] An informal basis has developed. The United States, the EEC and Japan have *de facto* permanent seats. It would also appear that there is a cotton exporters' seat (India, Pakistan, Egypt), a Latin American seat, and a Far Eastern seat (Korea, Hong Kong). In practice, selections are made annually by the Textiles Committee following consultations among delegations and the secretariat serving textiles.[54] There have been some grumblings over the years about under-representation,[55] but given the efforts made to balance various interests while maintaining the small size and workability of the body, most MFA members have regarded the annual compositions as satisfactory political compromises. In no case has the TSB's authority or integrity been directly challenged on this basis.[56]

Impartiality of TSB members is a curious thing. With the exception of the independent chairman, TSB members, like GATT panelists, are also their respective country's representatives, who in the Textiles Committee and other fora champion their government's policies and views. Yet within the TSB they must perform duties requiring an objectivity in spirit and fact. To an appreciable degree, the members have done so in a collegiate and fair atmosphere.[57] Experience has revealed an absence of bloc-voting and posturing, few surprises in individual cases, and a natural reluctance to maintain isolated positions.[58] Objectivity apparently suffers only when direct national interests are at stake.

The TSB early decided that in disputes between a party without a representative sitting on the TSB and a party so represented, the latter would delegate the task of argumentation to another in his country's delegation. After presenting their cases and fielding questions, the two advocates were permitted to remain during, and even participate in, the TSB's deliberations including the drafting of recommendations. Consensus necessary to formulate recommendations, however, required neither the assent of the two advocates nor the TSB member from the disputant country. In practice it proved difficult to deliberate in the presence of the advocates; so by subsequent agreement only the continued participation of the advocate whose country was not represented on the TSB was permitted. Neither his assent nor that of the TSB member concerned is necessary to form a consensus.[59]

3.2. The supervisory functions

The supervisory responsibilities of the TSB and the TC are review, correction and 'creation'.[60] The review function entails the collection and processing of factual information for a determination of its conformity to the rules. The correction function has as its goal the correction of wrongful behaviour, both by preventing rule violations before they occur and by redressing them after they are taken. The creative function concerns the interpretation of the rules and their application to fact. It necessarily involves devising new guidelines in response to arising needs and unanticipated developments. All these functions must be effectively exercised for supervision to have maximum impact on State behaviour, on the preservation of the integrity of the legal system, and on the realisation of the Arrangement's ultimate goals.

The TC obtains its factual information from annual reports and *ad hoc* referrals from the TSB. It is also empowered to request data directly from MFA members. In fact, a reporting scheme was agreed upon in 1974, whereby the Secretariat would regularly receive trade and production figures and statistics on the general state of the textile and clothing industry.[61] Information is also collected in the crucial area of industrial adjustment but responses have been spotty due in part to the complexity of the data.[62] The TSB receives much of its information on trade restraints automatically, in accordance with various reporting obligations found in the MFA. Supplementary data may be requested from the MFA members as well as other sources, including technical experts.

Once information has been gathered processing begins. In the TC this task is characterised by general reviews punctuated, however, with consideration of troublesome cases involving particular parties. It discusses the operation of the MFA on an annual basis and submits reports to the GATT Council. It also debates the findings contained in the studies and analyses prepared by sub-groups in such areas as production, trade and adjustment. Published summaries of its meetings reveal the mix of comments, criticism, suggestions and proposals of the national spokesmen and TC chairman spanning the breadth of MFA affairs. On the other hand, TSB reviews are for the most part specific in nature and concern the propriety of the actions and agreements of particular parties. The distinction between the two organs' reviews is not an absolute one. The TC may delegate the authority to conduct a general study to the TSB, and the TSB may refer a specific matter to the TC for its consideration. In connection with its power to interpret the MFA, the TC may also review the actions of specific parties out of necessity.

Dispute settlement, most often in the form of conciliation, contains elements of review and correction. Articles 11(4) and 9 permit the TSB to make recommendations in the usual cases of negotiation or consultation breakdown as well as when a Member State considers measures taken by another detrimental to its interests.[63] In all cases, the facts are collected and reviewed. The parties are invited to present their cases to the TSB and then face questioning. As in GATT proceedings, the primary aim is conciliation rather than legal deliberation.[64] Altogether, the procedure is quite informal although the facts and law involved may be complex.

The correction function is exercised through the force of the discussions and decisions of the two supervisory organs; however, no sanctions as such are available as an instrument of coercion. TSB decisions, in the form of recommendations, observations and findings, are reached by consensus rather than by vote. The legal effects of the latter two are uncertain as are their counterparts in GATT panel proceedings. The MFA does attach clear consequence to TSB recommendations: Member States must 'endeavour to accept [them] in full'.[65] If unable to do so, the country must report the reasons therefor and the extent to which compliance is possible. Any problems that persist may be brought before the TC or the GATT Council. In practice, referral of specific problems to the GATT Council is rare in part because it raises problems of equality since some MFA members have not always been contracting parties to the GATT.[66]

The third task of supervision is one of rule and principle elaboration; in essence, it is a 'creative' function. It is closely related to the other two functions. To the extent that it is exercised by interpreting or applying a legal text in particular situations, it is intertwined with the first function of review. Moreover, the ability to define and declare authoritative norms is necessary for the effective exercise of the second function of correction, particularly in the MFA system relying as it does on the force of normative

236

pressures rather than sanctions. Though often implied or partially concealed by a grant of interpretative authority, the 'creative' function is instrumental in clarifying the purposes of the organisation or arrangement and the principles underlying the legal order.

The MFA places the task of legal interpretation primarily in the hands of the TC,[67] which has the sole legal right to issue opinions in the event of a divergence in view among its members. The TSB, meanwhile, has been granted only a narrow authority to interpret the terms used in Article 12 dealing with the product coverage of the MFA. Before either body actually grapples with an issue, the parties concerned first have to attempt to resolve their differences bilaterally. By permitting 'bilateral interpretations', which may differ from case to case, the higher status accorded to pragmatism and compromise over a more rule-oriented approach becomes apparent. This is also seen at the multilateral level where the importance of consensus as a basis for decision making rivals that of even the GATT. Therein lies the inherent weakness of this type of system: the most sorely needed interpretations are often in those areas touched by controversy where by definition there is no reliable community consensus. Of course, when decisions are based on a reliable consensus they are both credible and effective.

3.3. The flexible exercise of supervisory functions

If the neat division of tasks between the two distinct organs of MFA supervision had been too rigidly regarded, it might have led to a denial of dynamism within the supervisory structure. Without room for change and adaptation it is unlikely that the mechanism could have long been responsive to the demands arising from its objectives and limitations. Fortunately, the spirit of flexibility mentioned in connection with the MFA's rules has also left its imprint on the MFA's supervisory mechanism. This is most clearly seen in the context of interpretative decision making where the TSB has gradually and quietly assumed additional responsibilities in response to unexpressed but felt needs.

The TSB began its life with an express authority to resolve questions of the interpretation of Article 12 and an implied interpretative function based on its authority to review unilateral and bilateral restraint measures for their conformity to the MFA. Nevertheless, the TSB began considering the meaning and application of provisions other than Article 12 quite early in its existence. Thus within the first few months of the operation of the MFA, the TSB determined that Article 2(2)'s requirement that pre-existing restrictions be justified under the GATT did not extend to TSB members that were not GATT contracting parties.[68] In its general report to the Textiles Committee later that year, the TSB referred to its 'discussion' without alluding that it had engaged in any interpretation.[69] The following year, in response to a question raised in the TSB as to the application of the same provision, the TSB 'agreed that [it] should not be construed' as containing a particular obligation.[70]

Gingerly proceeding in this vein,[71] the TSB seemed finally to acknowledge an interpretative function in December of 1975 when by failing to form a consensus on the meaning of Annex B,1(a) it reported that it 'could revert to the question of interpretation of this paragraph should difficulties continue to exist'.[72] The issue had originally been raised after bilateral consultations between negotiating parties revealed differences of opinion on the provision's meaning – precisely the situation in which the TC should have been seised of the matter. Without a protest from anyone, the TSB seemingly overstepped the bounds of its authority and entered a province belonging to the TC.

Yet no conflict has ever arisen between the two organs. Nor has any MFA member charged the TSB with exceeding its interpretative competence. The reason can probably be traced to the observation that there has been no open grab for power; TSB authority has evolved quietly and unawares. There has also been little duplication of effort. Interpretative tasks, which to a large degree amount to consensus-building, have been performed complementarily. As will be shown forthwith, the TSB's assumption of responsibilities was a sharing of responsibilities, which the TC alone could not have effectively undertaken.

3.4. Flexibility in action: the case of the MFA-GATT relationship

The complementary sharing of interpretative authority, and an important limitation on the effective exercise of that authority, can best be seen in the joint handling of one of the major issues of interpretation arising during the MFA's original four-year term: the reconciliation of Article 1(6):

> The provisions of this Arrangement shall not affect the rights and obligations of the participating countries under the GATT,

with Article 9(1):

> In view of the safeguards provided for in this Arrangement the participating countries shall, as far as possible, refrain from taking additional trade measures which may have the effect of nullifying the objectives of this Arrangement.

In essence, the problem concerned the troublesome relationship between GATT rights and MFA rights and obligations in the field of textiles. It was thought that continued recourse to trade restraints permitted under the GATT would undermine the legal safeguards of the MFA and destroy the fragile balance of interests upon which the MFA was built. By invoking, for example, Article XIX of the GATT, permitting unilateral import restraints upon a unilateral finding of serious injury,[73] an import-restricting country could avoid such MFA obligations as mandatory growth rates, base levels and liberality requirements, as well as a showing of market disruption before an impartial multilateral body. GATT Article XIX could also be used to introduce global restraints on a Most-Favoured-Nation basis, regardless of whether injury was attributable to one or all.

238

To be sure, many MFA members continued to maintain GATT restrictions permissibly under MFA Article 2(2) and 3 after they acceded to the textiles arrangement. Developing countries' markets were kept well protected by restrictions under GATT Article XVIII on balance of payments grounds. The EEC and the Nordic countries maintained restrictions on trade with some Eastern European countries that were also justified under the GATT. These, however, must be distinguished from the questionable imposition of GATT restraints on textiles during the currency of the MFA.

The TSB had the first opportunity to consider the issue. Canada, having acceded to the MFA in 1974 with global quotas on men's and boys' shirts imposed in 1971 under GATT Article XIX,[74] chose to reimpose them under Article XIX in November of 1974[75] when they had lapsed rather than replace them with restraints conforming to the MFA. The TSB, having been duly notified of the measure, merely 'expressed the hope that changes in circumstances would make it possible for Canada to bring this measure within the framework of the Arrangement in the near future'.[76] Thus the problem was acknowledged, though no 'unofficial' interpretation was yet attempted.

In early December, the following month, Australia caused a stir by announcing tariff-quotas on a number of textile and clothing goods. The TC, which had its second meeting scheduled for mid-December, took the matter up in the course of its general review. The drift of the discussion turned against Australia's GATT restraints,[77] as they were designed to cut back imports below the minimum permissible levels required by the MFA and had not been officially notified to either the GATT or the MFA members. Though several views on the propriety of the Australian action were aired, no real or conclusive interpretative activity occurred.[78] Meanwhile, the TSB on its own initiative launched a general discussion in February of 1975 on 'the principles implicit in Article 9' particularly with reference to GATT safeguards in the textile field.[79] Thus the TC and the TSB seemingly reversed their roles. By fortuitous timing, the TC conducted a specific review of the Australian conduct, while the TSB undertook a 'creative' discussion that properly fell within the TC's competence.

The TSB's February discussion was resumed in March when it was optimistically reported that conclusions would soon be reached.[80] They were not, and the issue was not seriously taken up again until December of 1976. That year had witnessed six GATT Article XIX restraints on textiles, five by Canada. The last of the Canadian measures, restraining clothing items and unilaterally abrogating bilateral agreements negotiated under the MFA, was more than the supervisory system could tolerate. The timing of the measure was also a bit odd coming as it did one day before the TC's major three-year review of the MFA's operation was scheduled to begin. Again by a fortuitous sequence of events the TC undertook a specific review. This time, moreover, the TC expressly invoked its authority to interpret the MFA; a general discussion on the broader issue ensued. Various views emerged revealing possible areas for agreement and compromise, although none were reached.[81]

At the conclusion of the discussion it was agreed to shelve the matter for 'further thought and reflection'.[82]

Hong Kong quickly got the ball rolling again by complaining to the TSB at its first meeting in 1977 that Canada's abrogation of their two bilateral MFA agreements were 'additional trade measures [having] the effect of nullifying the objectives of the Arrangement' within the meaning of Article 9(1).[83] Canada claimed that by virtue of Article 1(6) the exercise of its GATT rights were not 'additional trade measures'; and hence, the TSB was not empowered to examine Hong Kong's complaint.[84] Nevertheless, the TSB heard statements from both parties, taking the view that the matter fell within its competence. With its authority questioned, however, the TSB refrained from conducting a legal discussion of the merits. Instead, bilateral consultations were recommended with ensuing reports on any progress made in resolving their differences. The subsequent reports[85] revealed that no solutions had been found. They were forwarded to the TC with little further discussion.

Roughly four months thereafter, Mexico complained to the TSB that the Canadian action violated MFA obligations vis-à-vis Member States that were not contracting parties to the GATT.[86] This time a legal discussion took place. The views earlier aired in the TC were recalled with the TSB placing some emphasis on the merit of the 'pragmatic view' that countries imposing GATT restraints should notify the TSB thereof and stand ready to participate in TSB discussions. Most importantly, the TSB 'urged' MFA members not to invoke the GATT 'unless it has been demonstrated that recourse to the procedures of the MFA is not feasible or has proven unsatisfactory'.[87] Thus the TSB planted the signposts pointing the way to an eventual agreement; an 'MFA first' obligation had to be read into the Arrangement. A solution was finally in sight after three years of arduous searching.

The remainder of 1977 was dominated by the question of the renewal of the MFA, due to expire in December, and associated controversial proposals. The issue of the GATT-MFA relationship never received further independent consideration, but was swept into the whirlwind of political discussion and bargaining and settled there. The result was a provision in the Protocol extending the MFA that set forth a variation of the TSB view:

> . . . it was felt that in order to ensure the proper functioning of the MFA, all participants would refrain from taking measures on textiles covered by the MFA outside the provisions therein before exhausting all the relief measures provided in the MFA.[88]

The opposition of several importing countries had apparently been overcome,[89] and a solution at last agreed upon.

The foregoing procedure is not proffered as typical. On the contrary, by revealing the manner, and perhaps the attitude, in which supervisory authority is wielded within the supervisory structure, it would seem to indicate that there is no single approach to interpretative/creative decision-making. In the process outlined, roles are easily reversed and responsibilities shared. The TSB by virtue of its small size, frequent meetings and 'political standing' was able to 'fine-tune' a potential area of agreement revealed by the TC's rough focusing. In other cases involving different interests the approach to consensus-building could well differ.

The foregoing, moreover, reveals an important limitation on the effectiveness of the process no matter how flexibly undertaken: consensus-building takes time. The more controversial the issue, the more time is needed to search for a solution. In the context of the textiles arrangement there is the added complication of the limited tenure and uncertain future of the MFA and, hence, its supervisory organs. The remainder of the paper considers this as well as other factors affecting the effectiveness of supervision.

IV. KEY INFLUENCES ON THE EVOLUTION OF MFA SUPERVISION

Before evaluating the effectiveness of the TC and TSB in supervising the implementation of the MFA, it is helpful to describe several key events that have had an impact on the capabilities of the two organs. The first was the battle between the TSB and the EEC over the latter's compliance with Article 2. The consequent hardening in the EEC's antagonistic attitude towards the TSB in 1977 could not have helped but affect the TSB's effectiveness. Another influential factor was the considerable change wrought in the relationships among MFA members during the hectic months of 1977 when the future of the MFA was being negotiated. The final factor to be discussed will be the shift away from Article 3 restraints in favour of those introduced under Article 4.

4.1. The EEC's phase-out programmes

Article 2 of the MFA required the notification or immediate termination of all textile restraints in force upon accession to the MFA. Those so notified had to be terminated within a one-year period, unless they were (i) justified under the provisions of the GATT, or (ii) modified to conform to MFA Article 3 or 4. In addition, pre-existing unilateral quantitative restrictions, as opposed to pre-existing bilateral agreements, could have been included in special 'phasing-out' programmes adopted and notified to the TSB before March 31, 1975. These programmes were intended to permit the gradual elimination of pre-existing unilateral restrictions in stages within a maximum period of three years ending March 31, 1977.[90] The EEC was the only MFA member to resort to this option; but perhaps for reasons attributable to the lack of effective policy co-ordination, the EEC's programmes were notified well beyond the deadline date and sorely stretched the provisions of Article 2. In some respects they were indubitably violative.[91] The TSB's reactions ranged from expressing regret that some exporting countries were thereby being denied their MFA rights to finding that several of the programmes were simply not in conformity with Article 2.[92] In those cases the TSB recommended that the EEC quickly review the restrictions embodied in the programmes 'with a view to their elimination'. In effect, the TSB 'recommended' a sovereign entity (or, more accurately, an organisation of sovereign entities) abandon a commercial policy instrument because it was being used illegally.

The follow-up EEC report to the TSB could scarcely conceal the displeasure of some of its members; France and the United Kingdom, in particular, had been incensed by the TSB's recommendations. The report began acerbically by drawing 'the TSB's attention . . . to the concern of the Community regarding the manner in which that body . . . discharged its responsibilities in this important matter'[93]; nevertheless, the Community virtuously declared that it 'approached the TSB suggestions conscious that, in the interests of good international practice, the results of its efforts should not be lightly set aside'.[94] The EEC thereupon outlined a course of action that in part lightly set aside the TSB's recommendations. The TSB, in turn, took offence at the EEC's unnecessarily reproachful language[95] and 'regretted' that the EEC had not eliminated all the residual restrictions the TSB had recommended.

Relations soured. In the midst of the complex of negotiations in 1977 and in part, no doubt, for tactical reasons the EEC publicly adopted the views of England and France *vis-à-vis* the TSB. The Community spokesman declared that for the EEC the TSB is:

(a) an organ of conciliation. It is thus to be distinguished from arbitral or judicial bodies;
(b) it therefore goes without saying that, whilst fully accepting the provisions of Article 11(3) [that the TSB take action specifically required of it by the MFA], the Community could not accept that such actions include putting into question the bilateral agreements concluded by any importing participants.[96]

It should be noted that Articles 3 and 4 require the TSB to review agreements and, at least in relation to the former, determine whether they are justified.[97] What triggered this declaration was the inclusion of provisions in the Protocol that extended the MFA '[re]affirming that the terms of the Arrangement regarding the competence of the Textiles Committee and the Textiles Surveillance Body are maintained' and that they 'should continue to function effectively in their respective areas of competence'.[98] As such these reaffirmations were among the few concessions extracted by the developing, exporting countries during the 1977 negotiations.[99] What remained to be seen was whether the EEC would abide by its defiant declaration during the second term of the Arrangement.

The EEC has not yet publicly retracted its 1977 statements; much less officially pronounce on a restored commitment to a vigorous supervisory system. Nor has a confrontation of comparable scale to the phase-out controversy arisen to put EEC intentions to the test. Instead the Community has accepted the Protocol reaffirming TSB authority and been content to let that speak for itself. Its subsequent silence on the issue of multilateral supervisory authority could thus be taken as an acquiescence in the Protocol's reaffirmation and, hence, an implicit reversal of its earlier stance. Two observations buttress this conjecture: first, the Protocol itself and the associated negotiation of many restrictive bilateral agreements, both striking successes for the EEC negotiators, did much to mollify the earlier passion that led to their defiant posturing; secondly, the EEC's post-1978 record is one of greater co-operation with a more cautious TSB. Official reluctance to define or reinforce TSB authority on the EEC political level is no doubt more a function of lingering (and somewhat paradoxical) fears of supranationality than of studied ambivalence.[100]

The impact of the episode on the TSB is similarly difficult to ascertain with precision. One might have expected the TSB to withdraw after the attack by the MFA's largest member and become even less 'legally-oriented'. A quiescent period did indeed follow the hectic negotiations, but this was more attributable to 'shell-shock' and the late notification of agreements than outright resignation.[101] As 1978 progressed, the TSB began assuming a more vocal and critical posture than had hitherto been the case. Since then all bilateral agreements have come under closer scrutiny and questionable elements and practices have been publicly reported. Whether the TSB would go so far as to directly challenge a major importing country as it did in the 'phase-out' controversy is uncertain. On a lesser scale, it probably would issue recommendations that it knew would not be obeyed if it felt, after hard consideration, that action was necessary to prevent further deterioration of the legal spirit and integrity of the MFA.[102]

To characterise the TSB's current working attitude, though, as a direct reaction to the 1977 challenge would be incorrect. The 'psyche' of the TSB is not that of a wounded animal. Yet the threat posed by the EEC has been an element in the set of factors determining the evolution of the nature of textiles supervision. A similar element, challenging the 'legally-oriented' authority of the TSB and, perhaps, fuelling the body's assertiveness, is contained in several ambiguous parts of the Protocol, to be discussed forthwith.

4.2. The 1977 negotiations and the Protocol of extension

On June 21, 1977, the EEC Council of Ministers directed the Commission to commence negotiations on the renewal of the MFA in accordance with negotiating guidelines that left little room for manoeuvre.[103] The thrust of these was to secure maximum protection prior to any extension of the MFA by negotiating bilateral restraint agreements with roughly 30 exporting countries. Global ceilings on 'sensitive products' were to be obtained taking into account their relative 'market penetration', and shares allocated among exporting countries on the basis of their 1976 export performance. In addition, recognition of the justifying concept of 'cumulative market disruption' was to be procured.[104] The negotiating mandate, in other words, sought to legitimise concepts alien to the MFA system and implement restraints in a manner inconsistent with the Arrangement.

In July the debate in the Textiles Committee on the extension and modification of the MFA began to take shape.[105] The tone of the meetings was set by the EEC's announcement of a 'stabilisation plan' designed to forestall further deterioration of European employment.[106] The plan was based on the formula that annual growth rates should vary in inverse proportion to the rate of import penetration from *all* sources. Those 'sensitive products' already having a high rate of penetration would be stabilised (that is, cut back) at the 1976 import levels and have minimal growth rates.[107] Fulfilment of these stabilisation objectives was declared to be an 'absolute prerequisite' to the EEC's continued participation in any multilateral arrangement. Formal changes to the MFA, it was argued, would not be necessary so long as the EEC was permitted to pursue its objectives through a co-ordinated series of bilateral agreements. Failing this, the TC was ominously warned, 'the Community would be obliged to take the appropriate measures to ensure the attainment of its stabilisation objectives'[108] – in other words, exporting countries were told to 'take it, or else . . .'. Needless to say, this prospect aroused little enthusiasm and provoked considerable consternation.[109]

As the July meetings progressed it became apparent that any attempts to modify the text of the Arrangement would result in protracted negotiations running well beyond the expiration date. An attempt to renew the MFA without modifications failed because of the special changes necessitated by the EEC's rigid negotiating mandate. A compromise paper[110] that sought a way out of the dilemma was circulated by the U.S. and received the support of the EEC as well as Hong Kong, South Korea, and the ASEAN countries. The key passage proffered a legal justification for the stabilisation plan: the EEC's bilateral negotiations would be conducted under Article 3 or 4 'which does include the possibility of *jointly agreed reasonable departures* from particular elements in particular cases'.[111] In the U.S. view this merely restated the existing exceptions to the rules already written into the MFA. The majority thought otherwise. Several countries specifically objected to this passage as a highly restrictive amendment introduced 'through the back door'.[112] Nevertheless, the compromise paper was adopted in December[113] and incorporated by reference in the Protocol extending the MFA another four years ending in December 1981. Paragraph 5(3) of the incorporated TC conclusions contained the 'reasonable departures' exception.[114]

Meanwhile, on October 19 the EEC launched a veritable blitzkrieg of bilateral negotiations. In the space of six weeks the Europeans conducted 32 'extremely complex sets of negotiations'.[115] The stabilisation objectives were obtained with what amounted to, for all practical purposes, a system of global and discriminatory quotas. The developing countries, for their part, were left disunited and powerless to stem the onslaught of bilaterals and the potentially disastrous provisions of the Protocol. The EEC's looming threat of more restrictive unilateral restraints proved to be a blow to LDC bargaining power. Time pressure forced a general scramble for a fair share

244

of the EEC pie before the MFA's clock was to cease ticking. The fragmented negotiating structure itself did not contribute to unity. Moreover, the bitterest opponent of the EEC's approach – Hong Kong – was, as a colony, politically weak. The four major cotton suppliers – India, Pakistan, Egypt and Brazil – did manage to settle with the EEC on terms better than specified in the negotiating mandate, after they refused to accept the EEC's original terms. All told, however, the EEC's 'take it, or else' approach combined with a 'divide and conquer' negotiating strategy was a masterful success.[116]

When the smoke cleared, the terrain of the MFA was in a bruised and confused state. The fundamental equilibrium between exporters' and importers' interests had been disturbed in the latter's favour. The basic concepts of 'market disruption' and 'selective application of restraints' were impaired by the new bilateral agreements. And, not the least important, the Protocol with its many 'deliciously vague' phrases, including the 'reasonable departures' clause, threatened to finish the job of tearing the legal fabric of the MFA that had begun with the earlier GATT Article XIX actions.

At first, belated notifications of bilateral agreements as well as confusion occasioned by the reasonable departures clause led to a period of ostensible calm. The EEC, for whom the clause was written, promised to observe great restraint in its application, while the U.S. and Nordic countries, for whom the clause was debatably available, initially decided to forego its use. As 1978 wore on, however, many agreements were notified containing numerous deviations from the rules, although the reasonable departures clause was rarely expressly invoked. Even if it had been, though, no one could claim with certainty that the new restrictive agreements were free of 'unreasonable' departures.[117]

The TSB was plainly faced with a new situation bound to affect the nature of its job.[118] As mentioned earlier, it became more vocal and rigorous in its review of agreements. 'Departures' were noted in two EEC, one Finnish and four Swedish[119] bilateral agreements. Yet the TSB refrained from passing on the 'reasonableness' of departures and declined to declare any agreements 'non-conforming'. Although the TSB debated at length on the question of departures in each agreement, it was thought best to refrain from issuing any objective rules on reasonableness[120] and to leave its determination to the negotiating parties themselves. The *de facto* result thus became that if a departure is 'jointly agreed', which by presumption includes everything in an agreement, then it is presumed 'reasonable' even though it may be clearly inordinate. As of 1980, no exporting country had taken the rare and extreme course of complaining to the TSB about the contents of one of its agreements, which probably would have forced the TSB into making a 'reasonableness' finding. To be sure, the TSB has been making masked findings of 'unreasonableness' by means of recommendations typically requesting the parties to correct departures and other questionable practices in the event that the reviewed agreement is to be modified, renewed or renegotiated; but one suspects the TSB has been going about as far as it can given the political climate created by the EEC's ringing denial in 1977 of a TSB role in challenging the validity of bilateral agreements.

The uncertainties created by the Protocol have also wrought psychological changes indirectly affecting MFA supervision. The emphasis in importing countries' priorities has shifted away from importer-exporter affairs to other increasingly important areas of concern such as new tensions between importers. This tension stems from the increased fear of trade diversion now that fellow-importers can go far in escaping their obligations, thereby making things tougher for those with less restrictive trade restraints that conform to the letter of the MFA.[121] With the notable exception of the 'special permission' that the Europeans acknowledge they received for the negotiation of the bilaterals, all importing countries want to maintain an equilibrium in their relative import 'burdens'. To that end there has been greater pressure applied by and amongst importing countries' officials to exercise self-restraint. The TSB's task then has become a shade less herculean.

4.3. The decline of unilateral restraints and the further rise of bilateral restraint agreements

The bulk of textile trade restraints introduced under the LTA and the MFA have been in the form of bilateral negotiated agreements. Under the LTA, many, if not most, of the bilateral agreements were preceded by unilateral restraints.[122] This pattern has not held up under the MFA. In recent years the use of bilateral agreements has increasingly overshadowed resort to unilateral measures to the point where they have become the overwhelming, if not the sole, means of controlling textile trade. This has been particularly true since the MFA renegotiations.[123]

The predominance of bilateral agreements reflects the importance importing and exporting countries' governments attach to planning in the textiles sector. Moreover, importing countries fully realise that disputes and dispute proceedings are more likely to arise when unilateral measures are taken. Should the TSB question the presence or absence of provisions in a bilateral agreement, the importing country's authorities can always retort that all has been agreed upon by the exporting country.

Two types of bilateral restraint agreement are possible under the MFA. Article 3, which along with Annex B was meant to be the 'core' of the MFA, permits restraint agreements when specific products from specific countries are causing market disruption. On the other hand, Article 4 agreements need only be designed 'to eliminate real risks of market disruption'. Although Article 4 received wide support during the 1973 negotiations, it was primarily intended for the benefit of the United States, which had initiated bilateral negotiations on a broad scale. The EEC was slow in resorting to Article 4 because of the need to first work out internal burden-sharing arrangements and the resistance of liberal elements within the Community, who saw in its vague terms the potential for undue restriction. Yet with the ascendancy of the views of Britain, France and Ireland in late 1977, EEC policy, like that of other importers, became more protectionist.

The result is that nowadays the preponderance of MFA restraint measures find their justification under Article 4.[124]

This development has had an impact on the outlook and nature of TSB supervision. Article 4 agreements are simply less amenable to multilateral supervision than are Article 3 restraints. The latter are negotiated on the basis of a showing of market disruption, which can be tested against the criteria in Annex A of the MFA: whereas Article 4 agreements are based on 'real risks of market disruption' – a virtually unprovable and unproved standard. Not sufficiently linked to the market disruption concept nor to any requirement of proof, Article 4 agreements may well be comprehensive in coverage rather than limited to a particular disruptive product or product group as are Article 3 agreements.[125] They must also 'on overall terms, including base levels and growth rates, be more liberal' than Article 3 agreements.[126] This has meant in practice that all Article 3 and Annex B requirements do not have to be met in an Article 4 agreement as long as it is on 'overall' terms more liberal. 'Overall liberality' like 'real risks' is poor stuff for supervision.

The TSB also receives less information under Article 4 than Article 3. Under the latter, an importing country's request for bilateral consultations must be 'accompanied by a detailed factual statement of the reasons and justification for the request, including the latest data concerning elements of market disruption',[127] which are also forwarded to the TSB along with the text of the Article 3 agreement for review. There is no similar requirement under Article 4; by virtue of a TSB decision, the concerned parties must merely submit along with the text of the agreement 'a short, reasoned statement' indicating that the agreement complies with Article 4.[128] In addition, there is no equivalent in Article 4 of the Article 3(9) obligation to report annually to the TSB 'on the progress made in the elimination of such measures'.

Not only is the TSB hard pressed to work effectively with the more amorphous standards of Article 4, but its competence is narrower as well. With relation to Article 3 agreements, the TSB has the surprising power to 'determine whether the agreement is justified in accordance with the provisions of this Arrangement'.[129] To date, the TSB has never declared an agreement unjustified, much less invalidated it. Though legally feasible,[130] the political environment would simply not support too judicial an approach. Instead, the TSB has limited itself to calling into question the conformity of agreements to the rules of the MFA.[131]

On the other hand, when Article 4 agreements are notified, the TSB merely 'may make such recommendations as it deems appropriate to the parties concerned'.[132] The TSB wasted little time in deciding that it was empowered 'to satisfy itself that bilateral agreements concluded under Article 4 are in conformity with the provisions thereof . . .'.[133] But as Article 3 agreements are tested against the entire MFA, Article 4 agreements need only comply with the shadowy criteria of that provision. No Article 4 agreement has ever been found to be non-conforming in its entirety.

The movement to control and manage textile trade by means of Article 4 bilateral agreements has thus affected the course of multilateral supervision of the MFA. The weaknesses of that provision have assumed greater importance and have underlined the shortcomings in the TSB's powers. It is true that the TSB has continued to embarrass and pressure countries and perhaps constructively influence national decision-making with its more assertive and critical stance, but the overall legal impact of TSB decision and recommendations has been deflated. Without the underlying support from all its members needed to venture findings that Article 4 agreements are non-conforming, much less unjustified, there is little the TSB can hope to do to correct violative agreements negotiated to last the lifetime of the MFA.

The TSB's response has been to encourage and seize opportunities to re-review Article 4 agreements. It has extended its general competence to review all modifications of agreements to include instances where the invocation of a 'consultation clause' results in the establishment of new quantitative restraints.[134] The TSB has also pointedly declared that the validity of its reviews do not outlast the life-span of the MFA[135] – the implication being that agreements running the term of the MFA will be reviewed in light of previous recommendations should the MFA again be extended with the TSB intact. The body has also gone to the unusual length of reminding countries of their rights; particularly, the right to invoke Article 4 and draw the TSB into a disagreement over the implementation of an Article 4 agreement.[136]

V. THE EFFECTIVENESS OF MFA SUPERVISION

5.1. Preliminary remarks

A determination of the effectiveness of the TC and the TSB in quantitative, objective terms is not easy, and is not attempted herein. Nor is the point of this inquiry to delve into an analysis of their performance compared with that of other multilateral bodies. The tack taken here is simply to review the extent to which the MFA's supervisory mechanism has contributed to the proper implementation of the Arrangement in light of its ultimate goals.

As contained in Article 1(2), the core of these arguably contrary goals encompasses, on the one hand, the expansion of trade, the reduction of trade barriers and the progressive liberalisation of world trade, and on the other hand, the development of trade in an orderly and equitable manner and the avoidance of market disruption. As part of the means towards these ends, the right to impose selective quantitative restrictions on imports was granted provided that the substantive conditions specified in the two Annexes and other provisions were met. Exporting countries targeted for a restraint were guaranteed a minimum level below which their exports could not be cut,[137] a 6 per cent annual growth rate and the possibility to exceed limits by switching exports from one product under restraint to another to compensate for changing conditions of supply and demand.[138] A special mindfulness and furtherance of developing countries' interests were also woven into the legal fabric of the MFA.[139] And finally, a hortatory call was made in Article 1(4) to couple MFA restraint measures with domestic industrial adjustment processes 'required by changes in the pattern of trade in textiles and in the comparative advantage of participating countries'.

With the exception of the 'orderly development' of trade and the avoidance of market disruption, no one would doubt that the MFA has fallen short of achieving its objectives, especially those of concern to developing countries.[140] The issue then becomes a determination whether and to what extent the supervisory mechanism is to share the blame by virtue of an ineffective exercise of its functions, or whether it is entitled to credit for preventing the objectives from slipping further away. This in turn requires an awareness of the presence of certain factors beyond the control of the supervisory mechanism that operate to limit the effectiveness of supervision.

Individual consent and collective consensus are two such factors having a considerable impact on effectiveness; this has already been noted respectively in relation to the EEC phase-out programme controversy and the interpretative problem concerning the MFA-GATT relationship. It has also been mentioned that, although motives for negotiating the MFA in 1973 differed in the relative importance assigned to the various objectives, there was an original consensus sufficient for workable supervision. Industrialised countries had wanted a comprehensive arrangement. Developing exporting countries sought to avoid the chaotic, restrictive environment that an absence of a special regulation would presumably have led to; they wished to be able to invest and employ the new technology for synthetics, increase overall textile exports and plan for the future in a stable environment.

The dominant factor affecting the original consensus supporting these goals was the recession of 1974. Demand for textiles and clothing slackened and stagnated as the MFA was just getting under way. Protectionist elements began to grow in strength and effectiveness; they feared that the MFA, negotiated on the unstated presumption of continued growth in production and consumption, would wreak havoc with its automatic growth rates and other guarantees. Although the objectives of the Arrangement continued to receive broad support during its first four-year term, perceptions as to the means necessary to achieve those objectives underwent change. The original consensus underlying central MFA provisions began to crumble. This then is to be viewed as a factor external to the MFA system circumscribing the ability of the supervisory mechanism to contribute to the realisation of the MFA's goals. The TC and TSB are incapable of countering machinations within Member States leading to alterations of fundamental perceptions and realignments of basic interests and policies.

The second factor, internal in nature, limiting the effectiveness of the supervisory bodies is the adequacy (or rather, inadequacy) of the rules themselves for achieving the purposes for which they were enacted. The weaknesses of Article 4 have been mentioned in this regard. These and the shortcomings of other provisions will shortly be touched upon in the review of the effectiveness of the exercise of the creative function.

The following discussion alternately considers and subjectively evaluates the performance of the MFA's supervisory bodies in exercising their three supervisory tasks – review, correction and creation – in light of the afore-mentioned limiting factors.

5.2. The review function

Review entails the collection and processing of facts for a determination of the conformity of State behaviour to law. Effectiveness here means the capabilities of the supervisory bodies to exercise properly these tasks. Capabilities are revealed by the degree to which the observance and non-observance of MFA obligations can be established by the reviewing bodies.

In specific instances the absence or defectiveness of consensus or consent may surface as a reluctance to co-operate with the supervisory body. Since Member States are usually the sole suppliers of relevant data, lack of co-operation can kill or hamper a review. Though TC and TSB competence in particular cases has at times been challenged, no government has ever flatly refused to submit information or face questioning. Experience has shown that most countries fulfil their reporting obligations most of the time. Yet efficient multilateral review has often been defeated by responses that are inadequate or arrive beyond fixed deadlines. Delay is an especially acute problem because textile restraints are normally of short duration and the reviewing bodies themselves must operate within the limited life-span of the MFA.

Effective review simply demands that the process be compressed into as short a period as possible. To the extent that this is defeated by a reluctance to co-operate, the MFA organs cannot be faulted for ineffectiveness, unless they themselves have engendered the reluctance through blameworthy conduct. They can be judged, however, on the degree of guidance, encouragement and discouragement they have provided when they have had the capacity to exert influence. Experience with multilateral surveillance in other contexts has revealed that without any guidance or encouragement, reporting by countries will not yield a sufficient factual basis for efficient review.[141]

Inadequate information has been most common in connection with reports on unilateral and bilateral restraints taken under Article 3.[142] That provision together with the ancillary Annex A (market disruption) and Annex B (flexibility requirements) contain the bulk of the MFA's detailed substantive requirements. It soon became apparent that the TSB was faced with a dilemma when notifications fell short of providing the thorough evidence needed to test the restraint against these provisions. If further information was to be requested, certain risks would be run. A determination of conformity could well be prolonged beyond the point when it still could have a real impact. A request for information could also divert attention and energy away from an amicable settlement of any differences between the concerned parties. And it could have imbued the body in specific cases with an undesired judicial air. On the other hand, to neglect or decline to request supplementary and necessary information would mean that an effective exercise of the review function was being sacrificed to other interests and, hence, not being properly fulfilled.

The TSB's initial response was an attempt to avoid the dilemma by encouraging sufficient supplies of information in the first instance. It required 'a detailed factual statement of the reasons and justifications for the request [for an Article 3 restraint], including the latest data concerning elements of market disruption' to accompany notifications of the details of the restraint itself.[143] The following year this was supplemented with an indicative check-list of relevant information[144] for the stated purposes (i) to avoid delays, (ii) to assist Member Countries in the presentation of information, and (iii) to assist the TSB itself in reviewing measures.[145] Data was to be supplied in relation to price, volume, injury, products, due consideration of exporting countries' interests, and compliance with Annex B. A similar though far less demanding list was prepared for Article 4 notifications[146]; and the Textile Committee at its first meeting had suggested a list of minimum documentation requirements with respect to notifications under Article 2.[147]

The TSB soon found to its chagrin that some notifications continued to arrive with insufficient supporting information. Outside of holding Austrian notifications up as exemplary models[148] and formally urging all countries to supply the information on the check-list 'except where genuine technical difficulties prevent',[149] the TSB's response was not one of vigorous and sustained counteraction. In the case of defectively notified unilateral restraints, the TSB was more apt to favour renewed bilateral consultations among the parties than to pursue further supplementary information. Several Article 3 bilateral agreements were also never conclusively reviewed for lack of information.[150] Practice has shown that whenever the parties concerned with a unilateral restraint have demonstrated any willingness to resume or continue bilateral discussions, or even when the TSB itself thought there was a further possibility for negotiations, that course was recommended in place of continued legal scrutiny.[151] Reviews have also been 'deferred' when the restraints in question were of a particularly short duration and intended to be replaced with Article 4 agreements.[152]

A clue to the TSB's attitude towards Article 3 reviews can be gathered from those instances where it has had sufficient information to deny the validity of a claim of market disruption. In so doing, the TSB would invariably recommend new bilateral consultations based on the possibility that there could be a *real risk* of market disruption.[153] That is to say, the TSB practically invited the parties to conclude an Article 4 agreement when the alternative would have been simply to deny an importing country the right to protection under Article 3. The difference is slight but important. It removed an element of antagonism from Article 3 reviews, and obviated the need to confront importing countries – something the TSB is naturally reluctant to do. The TSB also demonstrated its awareness that the rationale for a dogged pursuit of complete information for review purpose was weakened by the growing preference for Article 4 agreements.

251

Reviews of Article 4 agreements have not suffered for lack of sufficient information because little aside from the agreement itself has to be notified. Rather, lateness has been the chief villain, and to a lesser extent it has hindered Article 2 and 3 reviews as well. Belated Article 2(4) status reports on compliance with that article, for instance, had clearly undercut the effectiveness of the TSB's review of the timely elimination and conformation of pre-existing restraints.[154] Under Article 3, notifications have not only arrived past deadlines, but in a few cases they were 'regretfully' not given.[155] Lateness has also hampered *ad hoc* reviews.[156]

The widespread breach of Article 4(4)'s 30-day deadline for notifying Article 4 agreements has had the most adverse impact on the effectiveness of TSB review. Often these agreements are in *de facto* operation long before they are notified to the TSB. The door is thereby shut on any 'corrective' impact a TSB review might have had on what has become a *fait accompli*. Equally important, the influence the review might have had on parallel, ongoing bilateral negotiations is reduced to naught.

Delay is usually attributed to either internal legal procedures necessary to make an agreement official or to procrastination of a negotiating party seeking further concessions. Both played a part in the EEC's notifications in late 1978 of bilateral agreements that had already been in *de facto* operation since January. The TSB reacted by convincing the Europeans to notify henceforth Article 4 agreements when initialled; subsequent modifications would then be brought to the TSB's attention.

If the plan works and shortens the time between *de facto* operation and notification then the effectiveness of the TSB's review will have been modestly increased. Results will not be dramatic because (i) most trade has already been covered by the barrage of new agreements of early 1978, (ii) modifications and renewals of those agreements, which are likely to be more frequent than the negotiation of new agreements, do not demand as much time in formalising, and (iii) the time between the *de facto* operation and initialling of new arrangements still might exceed 30 days. With regard to the last point, past experience has shown that with new agreements a post-negotiation phase of continued dickering can last two or three months before all the 't's have been crossed. If this is more the rule than the exception, then Article 4(4)'s 30-day notification deadline is unreasonable. A solution may lie along the lines of the EEC-TSB understanding: that is, an understanding with all importing-restricting countries to notify agreements, however informal, within a specified period running from the date they are put into *de facto* effect. From the standpoint of the effectiveness of review and correction, it would be highly desirable to obtain notifications of Article 4 agreements, on a regular basis, whose terms have not yet ossified.

In general, the TSB's usual response to late reports has been to issue formal reminders to comply with the reporting obligation in question.[157] Failing this and individually addressed reminders to elicit a timely response, the TSB has occasionally publicly mentioned the names of transgressors in its reports.[158] This sort of prodding, however, does not have much effect when delay is caused by technical reasons or, for that matter, *raisons d'état*.

The appointment of a Technical Consultant may be a step in the right direction with respect to the former; but even so, the sheer complexity of data on production, trade and industrial adjustment make it unlikely that many MFA members will ever be able completely to fulfil their general reporting obligations, especially *vis-à-vis* the TC's collection of data for its broad studies and analyses. When delay results from internal formalities, the EEC-TSB notification understanding offers a model for similar information supply problems.

The supervisory organs of the MFA are thus seen to be only moderately effective in properly exercising their function of review. The TSB, which is charged with specific review, has not uncovered and labelled all instances of non-observance of the MFA. To an appreciable degree this is due to an intended or unintended lack of co-operation as manifested by late, inadequate or 'forgotten' responses. The reaction of the organs to the information-supply problem in the way of guidance and encouragement has been appropriate. But the TSB's hesitancy to follow through in collecting information for processing does reveal that occasionally effective review is sacrificed to other interests. This is rooted in the dual nature of the supervisory mechanism. The TC and TSB sit as both legal and political bodies, though the relative emphasis within each differs. Internal conflicts inevitably arise from the fusion of these two discordant roles. In the TSB especially, a fine balance must be maintained to prevent a loss of either legal or political credibility. At times, then, thorough information-processing falls victim to political circumstances. The major obstacle to effective review has become the late notifications of Article 4 agreements. It is a relatively non-political problem as compared, for instance, to the thorough processing of Article 4 agreements for all non-conforming provisions. The TSB's ability to overcome it is thus greater. Should the Body fail to resolve the problem of lateness, the conclusion will become inescapable that its capacity to determine MFA violations in a timely manner, and hence its effectiveness at review, will have become unsatisfactory.

5.3. The correction function

The effectiveness of the exercise of the correction function is indicated by the extent to which the supervisory mechanism is able to promote compliance with the rules of law by preventing transgressions before they occur and redressing them after they are taken.[159] To a certain degree, a satisfactory record with respect to redress has a beneficial effect on preventive ability.

Prevention of non-conforming behaviour is impossible to gauge quantitatively. What is important in the MFA context is the influence the views of the supervisory bodies enjoy in the national decision-making process. Within each national policy-making apparatus there may be a range of opinions expressed as to how restrictive a trade restraint should be. In the U.S. government, for example, decision-making in the area of trade can involve the participation of four to five agencies. TC and TSB views are drawn into the process not as a determinative statement of the law but as another opinion of variable influence. Knowledge of a potentially critical TSB review does tend to have a moderating effect on the eventual national decision taken.[160] The desire to stay within the bounds of the rules, based on the recognition of the inviolability of legal obligations, and to maintain an image as a law-abider should not be undervalued as an influence on national policy formation; one need only look to see how national spokesmen will sometimes go to tortuous lengths to present dubious decisions as within the terms of the MFA. This may have accounted in part for the greater reluctance to introduce restraints under Article 3, where it is easier to determine with certainty whether a restraint is non-conforming.

Once a questionable course of action has been decided upon by national authorities, the TSB and the TC must rely on deliberation and persuasion techniques for correction. There are no sanctions, however ineffective, available to coerce compliance. Rather, formal and informal political discussion with its concomitant legal and moral pressures form the backbone of the exercise of the correction function. Conciliation is an additional instrument for correction available to the TSB.

Experience has revealed no surprises. Little can be done to overcome the inertia following a major governmental decision. Minor administrative matters and negotiating demands can and have been 'corrected' at TSB insistence. Yet even with the more important policy decisions, sharp multilateral criticisms in the present combined with recommendations to conform behaviour in the future have a preventive effect when a similar policy must again be formulated.

Despite the moderating influence of the TSB and the TC grounded on notions of the inviolability of the law, an effective exercise of the corrective function is still hampered by the unstated view that the MFA system remains a tentative experiment in multilateralism; there has been no determined commitment or whole-hearted endorsement of the concept to lend the supervisory mechanism a full air of legitimacy. Not surprisingly, the effectiveness of TSB and TC decisions depends disproportionately on their acceptability to the governments in question. A reasoned and persuasive argument may not be sufficient if a party is disinclined to change its course or to resolve a disputed matter. This has triggered some disillusionment, perhaps not fully warranted, with the supervisory system.[161]

The tentativeness of the experiment was underlined in 1977 with the European protestations that despite Article 11(8)'s requirement to endeavour to accept TSB recommendations in full they would no longer accept TSB decisions. With that the MFA ended its first four-year term with a sharp decline in the ability of the TSB to exercise effectively the correction function. Since then, the TSB's corrective ability has made a modest comeback and has been sufficient to 'correct' highly questionable elements in Sweden's bilateral agreements, though unofficial diplomatic pressuring was no doubt helpful. As mentioned before,[162] the increased post-1978 willingness of importing countries to accept and co-operate with TSB authority stems from several factors, including the achievement of satisfaction in protectionist quarters, the diversion of attention to other pressing textile problems and the increased wariness among importers of each other's use and abuse of the rules.

Nevertheless, the effectiveness of the exercise of the correction function has never been up to original expectations because the use of its ticklish instruments has been disappointing. Conciliation is the case in point. There the opportunity arises to exert a corrective influence, tempered, of course, by the political aspect of the task. But despite the oft-stated primacy of conciliation, the TSB's exercise of correction by that means has been minimal. Time and again the TSB has passed over an active, more legally-oriented role in favour of a role as a passive mediator. Whenever there has been the slightest indication of a possibility for renewed bilateral consultations, the TSB has recommended that they be resumed and its conciliation suspended.[163] Only rarely has the TSB explicitly called the parties' attention to specific MFA provisions in its directions for renewed consultations. By repeatedly cutting short an effective multilateral conciliatory approach, the TSB has left itself open to the charge of failing to use fully a major instrument for effectuating correction. To be sure, the TSB has been flexible in its approach to friendly settlement, and the chairman of the TSB has used his good offices in an unofficial capacity to help bridge differences; but this has not compensated for the TSB's passivity.

Political discussion, involving persuasion and deliberation, is the main instrument for effectuating social constraint. In the TSB, all discussion occurs in closed meetings. Questioning can be pointed and harsh. Answers are devoid of the posturing familiar in public forums. Textile Committee meetings, on the other hand, are public. They are preceded, however, by informal meetings that are closed and unofficial. Pressure brought to bear in both types of meetings has had a moderating effect on behaviour, but its limits were exposed during the 1977 negotiations, when even the sharpest and most bitter outcry ever levelled at a single MFA member did not cause the EEC to waver in its determination to implement all aspects of its stabilisation objectives.

The general records of TC and TSB meetings, including conclusions, recommendations and observations are published. This in itself exerts a corrective pressure on transgressors through the quasi-sanction of publicity. There is always the danger, though, that too much publicly expressed criticism can have an effect contrary to that intended, and result in the hardening of the position of an offended party. This might have been the case during 1977 when the EEC was facing mounting impugnation in the TC and an episode of confutation in the TSB. The EEC was known to have been upset with the public documentation of the criticism albeit diplomatically expressed. No direct relation between the publicity and subsequent conduct is supposed, but the attitudes of the Europeans towards the TSB, the MFA and its renewal may have been shaped more by their irritation than by their 'shame' occasioned by the legal and moral pressures brought to bear during the discussions. It may also be true that publicity is less effective in influencing a collective entity such as the EEC. MFA members are more likely to be more concerned with their own 'international reputation' than that of the collective to which they may belong; thus the collective shields its members' reputations by removing the cutting edge of adverse publicity.

Experience has shown that the supervisory mechanism can promote compliance with the MFA. But it has also shown that its moderating influence on national decision-making stops well short of preventing violative policies when they are considered important by the government in question. Even less effective is the mechanism's ability to redress transgressions once taken. The key to a more effective exercise of the correction function is not the introduction of sanctions. Besides being politically unfeasible, they would not be economically effective in the MFA setting. The key lies rather in a re-evaluation and a 'revaluation' of the legitimacy of the TSB. Without that, the correction function will continue to be exercised in a pale and hesitant manner, with the TSB caught in a bind between the need to support the remnants and integrity of the decaying MFA legal system and the need to avoid jeopardising its political credibility.

5.4. The creative function

The ability of the MFA's supervisory organs effectively to interpret rules and apply them to fact is even more a function of political cohesiveness and substantive consensus within the textiles régime than are the review and correction abilities. That a recalcitrant State finds it easier to disagree with the majority over an interpretation than it does over a request for information or a recommendation to act, renders the effective exercise of the creative function more sensitive to discord beyond the control of the supervisory organ. Throughout the first four-year term of the MFA culminating in the restrictive Protocol, the 1974 global recession was the corrosive element most to blame for the weakening of cohesiveness and consensus.

Yet the TSB managed to begin its life auspiciously by preparing for its future supervisory tasks, principally by articulating its own duties and procedures. Though the MFA provided an array of tasks for the TSB and the TC, it left the TSB with the job of developing its own working rules. The TSB quickly decided that efficiency, equity and impartiality were to be its 'guiding principles'. In conformity therewith the TSB devised procedures for dispute settlement, decision-making, and the review of notifications under Articles 3 and 4.[164] Efficiency was seen to be the beneficiary of the TSB's flexible approach to its tasks and its assumption of interpretative chores.[165] Equity later surfaced as a guideline for interpretation itself.

Nevertheless, it proved difficult to obtain greater precision of key provisions and terms. The immediate cause lay in shifting perceptions as to the means necessary to achieve the Arrangement's 'collective purpose', which had been sewn together in 1973 with painfully imprecise terminology in order to secure the broadest consensus possible.[166] For importing countries, the orderly and non-disruptive development of trade assumed even greater importance over time, and eventually was to lead to import stagnation and even contraction in a few cases. Demands were raised for lower growth rates linked to domestic consumption, cut-backs in the import penetration of 'sensitive products' defined so as to cover the most successful imports, recognition of *cumulative* market disruption, and the transformation of the 'minimum viable production' exception to the 6 per cent. growth rate into a special all-purpose escape-clause. Exporting countries had no alternative but to defend their side of the MFA equation with equal fervour. Among the most dissatisfied customers, however, were several smaller importing countries which complained that the vagueness of certain rules aggravated a problem of unequal burden-sharing caused by large differences in the liberality of commercial policies existing at the commencement of the MFA. Creeping polarisation, or rather, fragmentation, demanded the adoption of clear interpretations on specific points but also made it more difficult to develop effective interpretative procedures.

The effective exercise of the creative function has also been hampered by rules that are inadequate for achieving the purposes for which they were enacted. Notable among these is the industrial adjustment clause, Article 1(4), which recommends that MFA restraint measures 'should be accompanied by the pursuit of [adjustment] policies . . . required by changes in the pattern of trade in textiles and in the comparative advantage of participating countries . . .'. This provision is arguably the most important in the MFA. Its purpose is to conduce the provisionality of trade restrictions by encouraging import-restricting countries to use the 'breathing-space' afforded by a restraint to facilitate the rationalisation of the domestic industry.[167] That it 'exhorts' rather than 'requires' is a direct reflection of the weakness of its original underlying consensus: industrialised countries stiffly resisted the imposition of any binding legal obligation to pursue domestic social and economic policies.[168] Thus neither the TC nor the TSB has been able to effectively link Articles 3 and 4 with appropriate adjustment policies. Instead the TC has collected information, not without difficulty, on efforts undertaken,[169] and has attempted to monitor their progress. Creative activity has been nil.

Creative supervision, then, has been encumbered by defects in original consensus as well as subsequent substantive fragmentation. Sometimes both came into play in certain rules, particularly in the vaguely worded guarantees of Annex B. Thus a creative approach to the amorphous exceptions to the 6 per cent. growth rate was undercut by importing countries' uncompromising shift in attitude viewing the prescribed rate as more the exception than the rule. This approach was later legitimised by means of the Protocol's reasonable departure clause, itself fertile ground for creative supervision.

The TSB has made efforts to cope with the weaknesses of Annex B. The necessity to base decisions on consensus, though, often weakened their impact. For instance, the TSB has ruled several times that "swing" provisions[170] should be included in all Article 3 and 4 agreements, that they should apply to all the products covered by an agreement, and that the flexibility margins specified in Annex B,5 were the minimum permissible.[171]

However, because of the large number of agreements that continued to contain no provision for swing, the TSB felt compelled to adopt the debilitating qualification that in those instances it would be presumed that the exporting country had waived its right.

The TSB has also been trying to delimit the gaping holes wrenched open by the Protocol. It has been labelling the more flagrant violations of Annex B as 'departures' and publicly criticising others.[172] This has indirectly helped to define the scope of the reasonable departures clause; but it has been too cautious an exercise of the creative function *vis-à-vis* Annex B and Article 4 to have repaired the legal fabric and increased legal certainty. The TSB has been more confident in applying the Protocol to Sweden's glaringly restrictive agreements. There the TSB ruled that the 'minimum viable production' clause[173] of the Protocol could not be used as a general escape-clause,[174] thereby removing Sweden's legal justification for its departures. The possibility remains, however, for Sweden to seek cover under the reasonable departures clause, despite some opinion holding that that is the exclusive preserve of the EEC.

Article 6 of the MFA, a special prize for LDC's, has fallen into disuse. Article 6(1), providing for special and differential treatment for developing countries, is an example of a rule that is simply not amenable to creative supervision. As it turns out, not unexpectedly, with the exception of Japan and perhaps some State-trading countries, only the exports of 'developing' countries are restrained under the MFA system.[175] It is true that agreements with some of the East Asian newly industrialising countries (NICs) have tended to be more restrictive than others, but this has not evolved into a basis for purposes of comparison among LDCs. Article 6(3), which seeks to avoid having the trade of small volume exporters restrained, is a rule where a complete breakdown in supporting consensus has defeated creative supervision. With the *de facto* advent of the cumulative market disruption concept, all exporters regardless of size tend to be covered by agreements. In its only attempts at creative definition, the TSB found in two instances of dispute that Article 6(3) 'had not been taken fully into account'.[176] Both involved Article 3 restraints. The TSB has yet to mention the provision in connection with Article 4.[177] Difficulty naturally arises in determining whether equitable considerations have been taken into account from an inspection of the face of an agreement.

The 'principle of equity' has assumed particular importance as the basis for deriving rules in areas that the MFA did not foresee. The first application of the principle resulted in the determination that non-participants in the MFA should not be treated more favourably than participants. This required that the supervisory mechanism be kept informed of the treatment accorded to non-participants. The result was the creation of an obligation, not found in the MFA, to notify the TSB of all measures taken *vis-à-vis* non-participants.[178] Equity has also been important in minimising inequalities that arose between MFA members that were GATT contracting parties and those that were not,[179] and between those that had seats on the TSB and those that did not.[180]

The overall record in applying the MFA to new developments in world textile trade has been mixed. The EEC, for example, has argued that disruption can be caused by low prices alone even if the volume of a product is already regulated by a quota. Thus in its agreements with Hungary, Poland and Romania, the EEC included 'price clauses' covering allegedly disruptive situations caused by abnormally low, artificial prices. The MFA is silent on this exact point. The TSB would have preferred to have found such clauses inconsistent with the MFA, but the opposition of the EEC resulted in a 'softer' ruling that price clauses *could* be in conflict with the Article 9(1) obligation to refrain from taking additional trade measures having the effect of nullifying the MFA's objectives.[181] The TSB's approach to another new clause – the 'consultation clause' – has been mentioned earlier.[182] The TSB has been less effective in dealing with problems of product categorisation, including changes in definitions that tend to make the categorisation system itself an instrument of protection. This stems from the failure of the MFA to deal adequately with the issues,[183] the complexity of the data that would have to be studied to determine the effect of, say, a re-classification upon trade, and the limited size and resources of the secretariat serving the TSB.

If there is one area that reveals the failings of the supervisory mechanism in the performance of the creative function, it is in the application of Annex A and its fundamental criteria of 'serious damage', 'actual threat' of serious damage, and 'market disruption'. As in comparable U.S. law,[184] these terms are not defined, even though their application to fact is intended to be central to the process of determining the justifiability of trade restraints. Instead, guidelines in the form of economic factors – such as turnover, profits and employment – are set forth that are meant to indicate the existence of damage.[185] The damage itself must be caused by a sharp and substantial, or imminent, increase in low-priced imports. Once this type of damage is established, a situation of market disruption can be said to exist.

At its most rigorous, market disruption evokes images of cut-throat, but fair, competition; at its worst, the concept serves as a justification for the avoidance of any discomfort caused by overseas competition. The goal of creative supervision, then, should have been to refine the notion of market disruption by clear applications of the terms of Annex A to facts, while keeping the terms tight in meaning and central to the process of imposing restraints.[186]

The TSB and the TC have failed to accomplish this goal. The TC has neglected to interpret the provision. And the TSB has not clearly and systematically applied the terms of Annex A to fact. To a large degree, their failure at creative supervision can be attributed to the unwieldy defects of the Annex itself. Aside from the half-formed terminology, the central conception of causality was not fully developed:

> Such damage must demonstrably be caused by
> [(i) a sharp and substantial increase of imports of particular products from particular
> sources and

259

(ii) prices which are substantially below those prevailing for similar goods of comparable quality in the market of the importing country] *and not by* factors such as technological changes or changes in consumer preference . . . or similar factors.[187]

If this means that technological change, for instance, must in no way play a part in causing market disruption, then market disruption could never be established. After all, the MFA was extended to include man-made fibres as a direct consequence of the technological revolution in the industry during the 1960s. What Annex A glosses over is that any increase in imports is caused by a variety of factors, including technological change and change in tastes. To isolate each cause of an increase and rank them in order of significance is almost impossible.[188] The one causal link that is of most importance in determining the justifiability of a restraint is only partially addressed: it is that between the damage and the allegedly disruptive imports. One suspects that though damage must be demonstrably caused by imports it does not necessarily follow that they be the sole cause, or even the primary cause. This language has unfortunately invited loose unilateral interpretations.

There are other textual weaknesses in the Annex. Definitions of the economic factors are not supplied, nor are there indications as to how they should be used. These problems, however, do not involve the complexities of causality, and the argument can be made that the TC and the TSB are more to blame for a failure to resolve ambiguities and enhance legal certainty.

A general discussion on the concept of market disruption was initiated in the TSB in 1974,[189] though no conclusions in the form of legal findings of general applicability were ever reached. Nor have any emanated from the TC. Admittedly, any sort of broad quantitative formulation of the concept in terms of the various economic factors was beyond their capabilities as it would be for a court of law or even a committee of experts. What has been disappointing is the TSB's reluctance to address the issues and to reviewthe relevant statistics in its public reports. Without the 'airing' of issues and the accrual of knowledge through persistent efforts to apply law to fact, the creative supervision of Annex A was unduly impaired. In the handful of instances where the TSB found that claims of market disruption were notsustained, it did not even mention the reasons therefor in its reports. Nor has it clarified the meaning and application of the economic factors themselves by asking such questions as what constitutes a significant idling of production facilities in the textiles industry (or subdivision thereof). The end result of this effectuality is that the meaning of market disruption and serious damage and their relation to the economic factors are no better understood today than they were in 1974.[190]

The opportunity to exert and establish 'creative authority' over the MFA's central legal and economic concepts has now passed with the accelerated shift to Article 4 agreements over their counterparts in Article 3. The 'requirement' that an Article 4 agreement must be based on a 'real risk of market disruption' amounts to saying that there should be a risk of a threat of serious damage. This standard simply defies credibility. No proof of a 'real risk' is required, nor could it be, given the impracticality of establishing it with legal certainty. In practice, the requirement has come to mean that importing countries should not pursue sweeping programmes of trade control, but should exercise a modicum of sobriety in deciding when to negotiate a restraint.

This exercise in effectiveness has been the most serious one during the half dozen years of the MFA's operation. The effort that went into improving the LTA's conception of market disruption has been rendered nugatory. Under the LTA, developing countries had complained that unilateral interpretations of market disruption resulted in a situation where almost any increase in imports was viewed as justifying its affirmative finding. The same criticism applies to the MFA, despite the introduction of multilateral supervision. In fact, with the preponderance of activity now occurring under Article 4, the MFA, since its renegotiation, has degenerated into a potentially more restrictive agreement than its predecessor.

V. CONCLUSION

The multilateral supervision of the MFA has not lived up to original expectations. The Textiles Committee never evolved beyond a 'review and report' type of body. Its large size inhibits effective decision-making; its interpretative authority could not be properly exercised. The TSB never succeeded in building up its independent authority and influence to the point where its 'political standing' would have been secure enough to hold the erosion of the MFA's legal system in check.

For the supervisory mechanism to have been effective in the exercise of its functions, several onerous obstacles would have had to have been overcome. The first was the fear of a multilateral body asserting its independence – to some the concept of multilateralism embodied in the TSB smacked of an undesired supranationalism. This sensitivity to the potential for an 'autonomous supervisor' obstructed the consolidation of the TSB's statutory powers. Distrust was a manifestation of a related problem: many importing countries did not resolutely commit themselves to a rule-oriented approach to resolving textiles trade problems, even though they desired a framework of rules lending an air of legitimacy to their commercial relations with their weaker trading partners. The MFA reflected this ambivalence: the TSB was granted a respectable foundation of powers to supervise the implementation of the arrangement, but was not assured that it would be able to make full and effective use of them. It was left to devise its own working rules. Thus the collection and processing of complex factual data was entirely dependent on the co-operation of those whose actions were being reviewed. Those countries imposing the most restraints could in effect delimit the bounds of review authority well within the perimeter set by the MFA. Co-operation was also the key ingredient in a rigorous application and interpretation of the rules.

261

Experience has shown that all too often the degree of co-operation was a function of the potent mix of distrust of supranationalism and the pursuit of parochial interests. These interests assumed greater importance, as protectionist forces gathered strength during the first term of the MFA, and more than compensated for the waning of initial distrust as a shackle on the TSB.

Mounting protectionism thus led to the second obstacle in the way of effective supervision: the breakdown of substantive consensus. The combined effect of overseas competition and the 1974 recession led to commercial policy shifts in the importing countries. In Europe, policy dissension was overcome as views cohered around the need to stabilise imports of the most competitive, 'sensitive' products. The widening gap between the MFA's rules and the commercial policy objectives of its most powerful members rendered the tasks of correction and interpretation formidable.

The legal system began contemporaneously to break down. Rules were resisted and became inoperative. When Annex B and especially its notion of an automatic annual growth rate were challenged, the MFA lost any semblance of providing an overall and fair balance of rights and obligations. Normative decay itself was 'legitimised' in turn by the Protocol's reasonable departures clause. As legal dead spots accumulated, 'pragmatism' rather than 'law' became the way to justify behaviour. The 'live and let live' attitude among importing countries affected the TSB. It tilted heavily towards a pragmatic approach; or rather, was pushed, by virtue of the EEC's direct challenge to its legal authority. As a result, the TSB has demonstrated a reluctance, or inability, to come down hard and clearly on all rule infractions for fear of damaging its political credibility.

It is difficult to decide whether the overall performance of the TSB has or has not been satisfactory in the light of these obstacles and others, including a poorly-drafted MFA. Like a faint glow in the darkness, the TSB vanishes when directly scrutinised, but if viewed askance, it reappears. Its 'voice' does affect governmental decision-making, but does not necessarily prevent violative decisions. Through adroitness and flexibility the TSB has contributed to problem-solving and has encouraged a respect for the rules, but it has forgone opportunities to establish itself as a conciliating body and has not done all within its power to promote the rule of law. It has not publicised and explained the reasons underlying its decisions, or absence thereof, and has not taken firm decisions in all instances of violation. It has broadened its review and interpretative competences, but it has not consolidated its authority. It should also be remembered, though, that the TSB has had to operate effectively with less than a wholehearted commitment from MFA participants whose spokesmen sit as its members. One must conclude that the TSB has made a tangible and positive impact on the course of events, and despite instances of ineffectiveness in the performance of its supervisory functions, its efforts have forestalled the total collapse of the rule of law and encouraged parties to keep talking with each other.

The MFA, in one form or another, will probably be continued after the current term expires in 1981. Prediction is a risky business, but here extrapolation would seem possible: after 20 years, a special framework for the conduct of textile trade and diplomacy has become more the rule than the temporary exception. In keeping with the interests of a liberal world economy, the debasement of the textiles regulation into an instrument of protection must be arrested and reversed. This demands the improvement of the mechanism for multilateral supervision. To do that would first require a new compromise, that is, a bridging of substantive differences, and a restoration of a sense of legal reciprocity – by no means an easy feat. Central provisions would then have to be tightened, not just for substantive changes, but with an eye on their amenability to supervision. And the authority of the multilateral mechanism would have to be secured before it could be broadened.

Supporting these reforms would have to be a commitment among the MFA's most powerful members to a rule-oriented approach as the only equitable guarantee of order in the dynamic setting of textile trade. Only then could a common sense of purpose, which has always eluded the textile arrangements because of wide differences in expectations, become realisable. Experience has shown, however, that countries will accept legal rules when the future is predictable, or at least manageable. In situations marked by relatively rapid changes in economic relationships and shifts in patterns of trade, governments are least willing to assume binding obligations on a long-term, medium-term, or even, as in the case of the MFA, on a four-year basis. *Ad hoc* solutions are favoured instead, often to the disadvantage of the weaker trading partner. Since the current 'stability' in textiles trade is a product of an *ad hoc* approach to policy, taken for a large part in defiance of the rules, it does not seem likely that the importing countries will soon revert back to a strictly legal *modus operandi* based on a rejuvenated legal system. Indeed, the EEC is on record as favouring the future discontinuance of the reasonable departures clause; but this does not mean that they would wish to risk repeating their performance as 'legal spoilers' by returning to a set of vigorous and liberal rules.

The subject of trade control along the lines of the MFA has occasionally surfaced in relation to other sectors of trade, but for various reasons has not been ventured. Now, with the MFA model discredited, it is more unlikely than ever to find application in other sectors. It would be unfortunate, though, if the MFA's concept of multilateral supervision were to become tainted with the failure of the MFA and overlooked as a model for application in other settings, such as the proposed import-safeguards code, currently being negotiated under the aegis of the GATT. Though the TSB experiment has not been a striking success, it has still been a step in the right direction. Had those circumstances beyond its control been more favourable, its value as a precedent would undoubtedly be more manifest. Nevertheless, six years of experience have uncovered lessons that cannot be glossed over by the future builders of supervisory structures. The novel form of multilateral supervision fashioned by the MFA will not be drastically changed for the better in the textiles setting. It must, however, be revived and improved elsewhere in the cause of an open system of world trade.

NOTES

1. A. Sarna, 'Safeguards Against Market Disruption—The Canadian View' (1976) 10 JWTL 355, 366. Before embarking on a discussion of textiles, it is helpful to bear in mind that it is a complex sector of trade and production. There are many constantly changing production processes and stages of production, such as fibres, yarns, fabrics, finishing and knitting. Henceforth, the term 'textiles' will encompass the great variety of end-products, including clothing, unless the context indicates otherwise.
2. A. Sutton, 'Equality And Discrimination In International Economic Law (VI): Trends In The Regulation Of International Trade In Textiles.' (1977) 31 *Year Book of World Affairs* 190, 209.
3. On the precedential value of aspects of the international regulation of textiles trade see G. Curzon, *Multilateral Commercial Diplomacy: the General Agreement on Tariffs and Trade and its Impact on National Commercial Policies and Techniques* (1965) 258; K. Dam, *The GATT Law and International Economic Organisation* (1970) 313–14; G. Patterson, *Discrimination in International Trade: the Policy Issues 1945–1965* (1966) 320–321; *cf.* A. Schonfield, G. Curzon, V. Curzon, T. Warley, G. Ray, *International Economic Relations of the Western World 1959–1971,* Vol. 1: *Politics and Trade* (1976) 274–78; B. Balassa, 'The "New Protectionism" and the International Economy' (1978) 12 JWTL 409, 421–422, 426; B. Bardan, 'The Cotton Textile Agreement 1962–1972' (1973) 7 JWTL 8, 34–35; H.-H. Taake and D. Weiss, 'The World Textile Arrangement: The Exporter's Viewpoint' (1974) 8 JWTL 624, 651; J. Tumlir, 'A Revised Safeguard Clause For GATT?' (1973) 7 JWTL 404, 408. Although there has been occasional talk of a world steel agreement, a multilateral and separate approach to trade control in individual sectors of industrial products has not spread beyond textiles.
4. See M. Smith, 'Voluntary Export Quotas And U.S. Trade Policy – A New Nontariff Barrier' (1973) 5 *Law & Pol'y Int'l Bus* 10, 12 n.8; see generally, W. Rostow, *Politics and the Stages of Growth* (1971) pp. 98–100.
5. Textiles were in the forefront of a broad expansion of Japanese exports in the 1950s that caused concern in Western and developing countries alike. Japan's industrial exports grew 600 per cent. between 1949 and 1959 – from U.S.$533m to U.S.$3,413m to K. Dam, *supra*, note 3, at 297. The U.S. industry was also troubled by changing patterns of consumption, development of the textiles industry in Latin America – long a market for U.S. exports, and imports of increasingly competitive man-made fibres, such as rayon. U.S. Int'l Trade Comm'n, USITC Pub. No. 850, 'The History and Current Status of the Multifibre Arrangement 1' (1978) [hereinafter cited as USITC Report].
6. General Agreement on Tariffs and Trade, *signed* October 30, 1947, *entered into force* January 1, 1948, 55 U.N.T.S. 194 [hereinafter cited as the GATT]. Complete text in force as of March 1, 1969, *is reprinted in* (1969) 4 *General Agreement on Tariffs and Trade, Basic Instruments and Selected Documents* 1–76 [hereinafter cited as GATT, BISD]. The GATT, which is the principal international legal instrument governing international trade, is comprehensively examined in J. Jackson, *World Trade and the Law of GATT* (1969).
7. The U.S. had recently resorted to a GATT Article XXV waiver with respect to agricultural products and did not regard it as an opportune time to approach the GATT Contracting Parties with a request for another (protectionist) waiver. Article XIX, permitting global non-discriminatory trade restraints when domestic import-competing industries are seriously injured by import competition, was deemed too blunt an instrument involving potentially costly repercussions. A. Schonfield, *et al.*, *supra*, note 3, at 258. For an analysis of GATT Article XIX and its problems see Tumlir, *supra*, note 3.
8. Japan agreed to limit its exports to the U.S. of cotton textiles and manufacturers to 235 million square yards per year for the five-year period 1957–61. This ceiling was adjusted during the period due to changed conditions with the result that the ceiling in 1961 was 5 per cent. higher than in 1957. USITC Report, *supra*, note 5, at 2, 2n.2.
9. The four U.S.-Japanese voluntary restraint agreements of the 1930s set the pattern of strong import-competing industries pressuring their governments to take action, which, in turn, pressure the exporting countries' governments (or even industries) into 'voluntarily' restraining imports. The term is something of a misnomer as the thinly-veiled threat of harsher, unilateral action underlies most negotiations for such restraints.
10. The following chart reveals that other exporting countries were able to profit in the U.S. market at Japan's expense with the result of a major redistribution of U.S. suppliers:

U.S. Imports of Cotton Textiles, 1958–60
(in millions of equivalent square yards)

Source	1958	1959	1960
Japan	309·2	301·5	273·3
Hong Kong	67·9	206·3	289·7
South Korea	4·8	8·3	13·9
India	3·2	28·1	52·7
France	3·1	14·7	38·0
Spain	1·2	10·1	61·2
Portugal	1·1	4·2	65·6
Egypt	0·9	2·0	54·9
Pakistan	0·4	8·6	16·1
Taiwan	0·2	11·1	23·0

Source: USITC Report, *supra*, note 5, at 4.

The value of Hong Kong's exports to the U.S. had increased from U.S.$5.8m. in 1956 to U.S.$17.4m. in 1957 and U.S.$54.m. in 1958. A. Schonfield, *et al.*, *supra*, note 3, at 259. This period marked the beginning of a remarkable growth in LDC textile exports, particularly from Far Eastern producers, that was to continue throughout the 1960s. Taiwan, for instance, saw the value of its textile exports rise from U.S.$21.3m. in 1960 to U.S.$203.5m. in 1968 and U.S.$479m. in 1970. M. Smith, *supra*, note 4, at 24n.60.

11. The Europeans, like the Americans, had been worried by the threat posed by the Japanese, but unlike the Americans they at first justified trade restrictions under the 'escape-clauses' of the GATT. Article XXXV, which permits non-application of the GATT rules to new members, was invoked by Britain, France and a host of LDCs when Japan acceded to the GATT in 1955. Almost all of those European countries not relying on Article XXXV applied discriminatory quotas on the basis of the Article XII escape-clause concerning balance of payments difficulties. The U.S. thus remained the most open market before and after Japanese accession. By 1958 with the lifting of exchange control in Europe, Japanese exports to those countries relinquishing use of Article XII increased. By 1964 most developed countries' invocations of Article XXXV had come to and end. It is against this liberalising trend that the Europeans sought to exempt textiles.

12. The Japanese government and textile industry did not always willingly accept VERs. Considerable resistance was encountered when the U.S. attempted to cover Japanese exports of synthetic fibres, wool, and blends with VERs in the late 1960s. Prodded by their domestic industry, the Japanese government expressed, for the first time, a preference for import restraints under GATT Article XIX. Negotiations proceeded throughout 1969 and 1970. VERs were finally accepted in late 1971. This episode did not, however, represent a reversal of Japanese policy.

13. GATT, BISD, *supra*, note 6; 9th supplement, p. 107 (1961).

14. *Idem*, 106. In so doing, the working party lent credence to the psycho-political considerations preferred as particular to cotton textiles:

> . . . the psychological impact of imports, though intangible, must be given due recognition. In any given market, a relatively small percentage of an imported item priced well below the domestic price has a major effect in upsetting the price structure and the normal competitive relationships. Moreover, the amount of imports at any specified time is less important psychologically than the potential amount of imports at some later time. Unless later possibilities can be defined, decisions with regard to investment or plant expansion are made more difficult.

U.S. Dep't of Commerce, Business and Defense Services Adm'n, 'Textile Outlook for the Sixties 50 (1969), *as quoted in* B. Bardan, *supra*, note 3, at 28.

15. GATT, BISD, *supra*, note 6, 9th supplement, pp. 26–28 (1961). The Contracting Parties agreed that a situation of 'market disruption' generally contained the following elements:

(i) a sharp and substantial increase or potential increase of imports of particular products from particular sources;

(ii) these products are offered at prices which are substantially below those prevailing for similar goods of comparable quality in the market of the importing country;

(iii) there is serious damage to domestic producers or threat thereof;

(iv) the price differentials referred to in paragraph (ii) above do not arise from government intervention in the fixing or formation of prices or from dumping practices.

In some situations other elements are also present and the enumeration above is not, therefore, intended as an exhaustive definition of market disruption.

Idem, p. 26. In other words, as Kenneth Dam has observed, this meant that there was not a difference in substance, but a difference in degree 'between the conditions that [give] rise to an ordinary increase in international trade and those that [give] rise to the economic impact associated with the concept of market disruption'. K.Dam, *supra*, note 3, at 299. The principle of comparative advantage was thus being challenged.

16. See generally USITC Report, *supra*, note 5, at 6–8. Dam notes that the adjective 'orderly' was becoming as important in the lexicon of importing countries as 'disruptive'. K. Dam, *supra*, note 3, at 300.

17. General Agreement on Tariffs and Trade, Arrangements Regarding International Trade in Cotton Textiles, July 21, 1961 [1961] 12 U.S.T. 1675, T.I.A.S. No. 4884 [hereinafter cited as the STA].

18. Long Term Arrangements Regarding International Trade in Cotton Textiles, February 9, 1962 [1962] 13 U.S.T. 2673, T.I.A.S. No. 5240, *extended* by Protocols of May 1, 1967 [1967] 18 U.S.T. 1337, T.I.A.S. No. 6289; June 15, 1970 [1970] 21 U.S.T. 1971, T.I.A.S. No. 6940, reprinted in GATT, BISD, *supra*, note 6, 11th Supplement, p. 25 (1962) [hereinafter cited as the LTA]. The membership consisted of Group I (net importing) countries: Australia, Austria, Belgium, Canada, Denmark, Finland, France, West Germany, Italy, Luxembourg, the Netherlands, Norway, Sweden, the U.K. and the U.S., and Group II (net exporting) countries: Columbia, Greece, Hong Kong, India, Israel, Jamaica, Mexico, Pakistan, Portugal, Rep. of China, Rep. of Korea, Spain, Turkey and the U.A.R. Poland and Japan, also members, were not categorised.

19. See *supra*, note 15.

20. See LTA Articles 3 and 4 and Annex B. The minimum annual growth rate for products under restriction was 5 per cent. *idem,* Annex B, 2.

21. To be sure, Article 1 of the LTA stated that the measures to be taken under the LTA would not affect the participating countries' rights and obligations under the GATT. However, the LTA conflicted to such a degree with the GATT that it amounted to a special exception and derogation, rather than a complementary adjunct. Consider the obvious example that an exporting country faced with a selective restraint could no longer avail itself of the GATT's most basic principle of non-discrimination. The LTA was not an 'autonomous' system of regulation, though; there were many substantive and institutional connections with the GATT organisation.

22. LTA Article 1 stated in part:

> . . . the participating countries are of the opinion that it may be desirable to apply, *during the next few years*, special practical measures of international cooperation which will assist in *any adjustment that may be required* by changes in the pattern of world trade in cotton textiles . . . [emphasis added].

This led one writer to hail the LTA as 'a revolutionary step, for never before had . . . the attempt . . . been made to deal by an agreed overall plan with the expansion of new industries in one part of the world and the contraction of the same industries in another part . . . [it] is implicitly agreed that factors of production have to be withdrawn from industries which have lost their absolute or comparative advantage and that a reallocation of resources has to take place the world over for a better exploitation of world resources. This is almost an economist's dream.' G. Curzon, *supra*, note 3, at 256–257.

23. See GATT, BISD, *supra*, note 6, 11th supplement, p. 40 (1963).

24. See generally D. Robertson, 'Fail Safe Systems for Trade Liberalisation' 32–33 (Trade Policy Research Centre, Thames Essay No. 12, 1977).

25. See B. Bardan, *supra*, note 3, at 25–26.

26. See A. Sutton, *supra*, note 2, at 194.

27. To be sure, interpretative activity under the LTA was not wholly unilateral in character. The Cotton Textiles Committee did engage in direct interpretation of LTA standards and procedures by means of its formal conclusions. See, *e.g.,* GATT, BISD, *supra,* note 6, 12th supplement, pp. 66, 70–72 (1964).

28. Even so, LDCs accounted for only 6 per cent. of world trade in man-made yarns and fabrics. 'Overseas Development Institute, the Textile Trade, Developing Countries and the Multi-Fibre Agreement 2' (1976).

29. U.S. imports of man-made textiles increased from 31 million lbs. in 1960 to 329 million lbs. in 1970. USITC Report, *supra*, note 5, at 12.

30. D. Robertson, *supra*, note 24, at 36.

266

31. See *idem*, p. 37.
32. Arrangement Regarding International Trade in Textiles, done December 20, 1973 [1974] 25 U.S.T. 1001, T.I.A.S. No. 7840, extended by Protocol of February 1, 1978, reprinted in GATT, BISD, *supra,* note 6, 21st supplement p. 3 (1975) [hereinafter cited as the MFA].
33. Wool was included because the U.S. Government wished to preserve what was left of a weak and small domestic industry.
34. H. H. Taake and D. Weiss, *supra*, note 3, at pp. 650–652.
35. MFA, Article 1(2).
36. MFA, Article 2(2) and (3).
37. *Idem.*
38. MFA, Article 2(2)(i).
39. The MFA refined and elaborated the LTA's description of 'market disruption'. Nevertheless it remained an undefined concept:

> The determination of a situation of 'market disruption' . . . shall be based on the existence of a serious damage to domestic producers or actual threat thereof. Such damage must demonstrably be caused by [the following two factors, which generally appear in combination: a sharp and substantial rise in volume from particular sources, and prices, which are substantially below prevailing market prices] . . . The existence of damage shall be determined on the basis of an examination of the appropriate factors having a bearing on the evolution of the stage of the industry in question such as: turnover, market share, profits, export performance, employment, volume of disruptive and other imports, production, utilisation of capacity, productivity and investments. No one or several of these factors can necessarily give decisive guidance.

MFA, Annex A.
40. MFA, Article 3(5)(i). During the first four-year term of the MFA 21 unilateral restraints were notified under this provision. In addition, Article 3(3) consultations yielded 35 Article 3(4) bilateral agreements, thus avoiding unilateral measures. COM.TEX/SB/196, para. 63 (1976); COM.TEX/SB/365, para. 7 (1978). During the first 23 months of the renewed MFA in 1978 and 1979 only four Article 3(4) agreements and four unilateral restraints were notified. COM. TEX/SB/365, para. 51 (1978); COM.TEX/SB/519, para. 8 (1979).
41. MFA, Article 3(6). Nine restraints had been taken under this 'emergency' provision during the first four years of the MFA. COM.TEX/SB/196, para. 63 (1976); COM.TEX/SB/365, para. 7 (1978). The subsequent 23 months have seen but one such 'emergency' restraint. COM.TEX/SB/519, para. 8 (1979).
42. *Idem.*
43. MFA, Article 3(8).
44. MFA, Annex B, para. 1, obtusely explains that:

> The level below which imports or exports of textile products may not be restrained . . . shall be the level of actual imports or exports of such products during the 12-month period terminating two months or, where data are not available, three months preceding the month in which the request for consultation is made, or, where applicable, the date of institution of such domestic procedure relating to market disruption in textiles as may be required by national legislation, or two months or, where data are not available, three months prior to the month in which the request for consultation is made as a result of such domestic procedure, whichever is the later.

45. Two exceptions to the 6 per cent growth rate are recognised. A lower positive growth rate is permitted if (i) the 6 per cent growth rate would cause a recurrence of market disruption, or if (ii) the 6 per cent. growth rate would damage the 'minimum viable production' of those countries having 'small markets, and exceptionally high level of imports and a correspondingly low level of domestic production'. MFA, Annex B, para. 2. The latter 'MVP' exception has been claimed by some countries to be a principle of general application by virtue of the Protocol's call to take into account the avoidance of damage to minimum viable production. See generally *infra*, notes 119 and 173.
46. 'Carryover' entails allocating an unused portion of the previous year's quota to the present year, and 'carryforward' a portion of next year's quota to the present year with, of course, an equivalent decrease in next year's quota. 'Swing', on the other hand, does not operate to increase the current year's aggregate quota. It allows the exporting country to reallocate a portion of the quota from one product group under restraint to another, whether or not there are two or more agreements covering multiple products. For the relevant minimum limits see MFA, Annex B, para. 5.

47. MFA, Article 4(3). To date, Article 4 agreements have proven more popular than restrictions imposed under Article 3. See *infra*, notes 123, 124 and accompanying text. Seventy-one new agreements were notified during the first four years of the MFA, and 79 during the first 23 months of the MFA's extension. COM.TEX/SB/196, para. 88 (1976); COM.TEX/SB/365, paras. 29, 58 (1978); COM.TEX/SB/519, para. 26 (1979).

48. A. Sutton, *supra*, note 2, at 206.

49. *Idem*, p. 207. The problem that Sutton was worrying about has since been solved by means of 'consultation' clauses. See *infra*, note 134 and accompanying text.

50. D. Robertson, *supra*, note 24, at 39.

51. Adjustment was not made obligatory, however:

> . . . actions taken under this Arrangement should be accompanied by the pursuit of economic and social policies . . . required by changes in the pattern of trade in textiles and in the comparative advantage of participating countries. . . .

MFA, Article 1(4).

52. Some observers were able to predict future problem areas on the basis of shortcomings in consensus: 'it is relatively easy to foresee that the establishment of the Textiles Surveillance Body will lead to considerable difficulties because during the negotiations only an accord on partial aspects but not, for instance, on the budget or personnel policy was achieved'. H.-H. Taake and D. Weiss, *supra*, note 3, at 653. Neither of these unsettled issues led to problems in and of themselves, but as things have developed they were good indicators of the bumpy road ahead for the TSB.

53. MFA, Article 11(1).

54. Letter from Ambassador P. Wurth, Chairman of the TSB, August 3, 1979. The TSB is served by a small staff linked with the GATT Secretariat. In fact, the TSB is financed from the GATT's resources and is housed on GATT premises.

55. See, *e.g.* COM.TEX/2, paras. 29, 30 and Annex (1974); COM.TEX/5, para. 53 (1975); COM.TEX/8, paras. 44, 57, 58 (1977). Some delegations have expressed regret at the permanency of some seats and the inadequacy of rotation but nothing has ever come of suggestions for TSB enlargement. The small size lends itself to frequent meetings and close working relationships. *Cf.* H.-H. Taake and D. Weiss, *supra*, note 3, at 652. The permanency of the three seats does, however, carry advantages not enjoyed by delegations sharing rotating seats. The accumulation of expertise is one such advantage.

56. It has been threatened, as when the Polish representative remarked 'that it would be understandable if his Government was to look at some of the TSB's recommendations with hesistance due to the absence of representation thereon by a Socialist country'. COM.TEX/5, para. 53 (1975). The EEC, initially suspicious and fearful of the authority it believed the MFA conferred on the TSB, sought to 'stack' TSB meetings with its people. See COM.TEX/SB/1, para. 5, n. 1 (1974). The attempt to have all EEC Member States attend meetings as 'experts' when so warranted met with unanimous opposition. Instead, it was agreed that the EEC representative could be assisted by observers from its Member States affected by a matter, who would not be official participants and thus not take part in TSB discussions. In time, as EEC apprehension waned, observers were no longer used.

It should be noted that TSB members are backed up by alternates, often from another country, who attend meetings with all the obligations and rights of participation in the event a TSB member is absent. See COM.TEX/SB/196, para. 11 (1976).

57. But *cf.* J. Jackson, 'Governmental Disputes in International Trade Relations: A Proposal In The Context Of Gatt' (1979) 13 JWTL 1, where the author argues that the similar dual role of GATT panelists 'makes it difficult if not impossible for him to view his actions in such a panel as insulated from the influences of his government's foreign economic policy, and consequently the relationship of that government to other countries in the world, including the disputing parties'. *Idem*, p. 6. To the extent that GATT panelists are hand-picked for each dispute, while TSB members consider all matters raised during the course of their term, one could argue that GATT panelists are more likely to be less affected and hence more impartial. This does not necessarily make them more effective.

58. Interview with Mr. Robert Shephard, U.S. Member of the TSB, in Geneva, January 22, 1980.

59. COM.TEX/SB/30, Annex I (1974), modified by COM.TEX/SB/319, paras. 3, 4 (1978).

60. This classification of supervisory functions is drawn from G. van Hoof and K. de Vey Mestdagh, "Mechanisms of International Supervision," *supra*, pp. 11–14.

. 61. See COM.TEX/3, paras. 14, 15 (1974). A major report on production and trade in textiles and clothing from 1974 to 1976 has been compiled. See COM.TEX/W/35 plus addenda (1976).

62. Thus far two reports have been prepared. See, *e.g.* COM.TEX/W/36 and Add. 1 (1976). The Information-supply problem is discussed in general *infra*, pp. 37–43.

63. See also MFA, Article 9.

64. COM.TEX/SB/44, para. 6 (1974). Jackson has criticised the GATT system for assigning both conciliation and legal deliberation to a single body: '[in] so doing, the panel often is assisting the negotiation with reference to the power positions of the respective parties, and not only with reference to whether an agreed rule favours one or the other party'. These tasks, he adds, are 'probably mutually conflicting'. J. Jackson, *supra*, note 57, at 6.

65. MFA, Article 11,8. This does not mean that recommendations are binding with immediate effect as some would prefer. See, *e.g.* COM.TEX/10, para. 64 (1978).

66. At the time of their provisional accession in 1974 to the MFA neither Bulgaria, Colombia, El Salvador, Guatemala, Mexico nor Paraguay were contracting parties to the GATT. Neither Thailand nor Bolivia were GATT members as of 1978 when they acceded to the Protocol extending the MFA.

67. MFA, Article 10(3).

68. COM.TEX/SB/27, Annex (1974). The TSB then devised a substitute procedure for justification. *Idem*, para. 6.

69. COM.TEX/SB/44, paras. 10, 11 (1974).

70. COM.TEX/SB/83, para. 7 (1975).

71. See, for example, the discussion concerning the 'right to swing' provided in Annex B, para. 5, COM.TEX/SB/89, para. 4 (1975), which was later elaborated in discussions of its relationship with other MFA provisions in COM.TEX/SB/196, para. 97 (1976) and COM.TEX/SB/365, para. 74 (1978).

72. COM.TEX/SB/144, para. 7 (1976). In its report to the TC, the TSB clearly stated that it sought to resolve an issue of interpretation. COM/TEX/SB/196, para, 85 (1976). In the TC's report in late 1976 the existence of the particular issue mentioned without further discussion or comment on the TSB's handling of it. COM.TEX/8, para. 31 (1977).

73. GATT, Article XIX provides in part:

> If, as a result of unforeseen developments and of the effect of the obligations incurred by a contracting party under this Agreement . . . any product is being imported . . . in such increased quantities and under such conditions as to cause or threaten serious injury to domestic producers . . . the contracting party shall be free . . . to suspend the [GATT] obligation . . . or withdraw or modify the [tariff] concession.

GATT, Article XIX,1(a).

74. GATT, L/3613 (1971).

75. GATT, L/4143 (1974).

76. COM.TEX/SB/115, at 8 (1975).

77. COM.TEX/5, paras. 42–47 (1975).

78. Further consideration of this matter along with a subsequent Australian invocation of GATT Article XIX in March of 1975 covering textiles was taken up by the GATT Council without any conclusive results.

79. COM.TEX/SB/56, para. 8 (1975).

80. COM.TEX/SB/64, para. 7 (1975).

81. Most TC members regarded Canada's Article XIX measure a violation of the letter and spirit of the MFA. COM.TEX/8, para. 61 (1977). A narrow consensus emerged, however, that MFA members also party to the GATT retained the option to resort to their GATT rights in the textiles field. Disagreement prevailed as to the conditions under which those rights could be exercised. Many, who saw the MFA as a special derogation of the GATT, thought that the MFA must first prove to be inadequate or impracticable. A few, who viewed the MFA and GATT as parallel agreements, contended that there was no 'MFA first' obligation. Several pragmatists argued that the legal discussion was off-target: the MFA-GATT relationship was not central; what was important was the notification and justification of all measures to the TSB whether taken under the GATT or MFA. See *idem*, paras. 65–69.

82. *Idem*, para. 70.

83. COM.TEX/SB/210, para. 6 (1977).

84. Letter from W. F. Stone, Canadian Deputy Permanent Representative and Minister toP. Wurth, TSB Chairman, January 24, 1977, reprinted in COM.TEX/SB/225, at p. 3 (1977).

85. In keeping with its view that the matter was not within the TSB's competence, the Canadian delegation did not submit a 'report' but a letter, which carefully noted that the consultations

with Hong Kong were informal and outside the framework of the MFA. COM.TEX/SB/222, at 3 (1977).

86. COM.TEX/SB/255, para. 7 (1977).

87. *Idem*, para. 10.

88. Protocol Extending the Arrangement Regarding International Trade in Textiles, para. 9 of the appended Conclusions of the Textiles Committee adopted on December 14, 1977 (1978) reprinted in COM.TEX/10, at pp. 48–50 (1978) [hereinafter cited as the Protocol].

89. Australia and Canada had gone on record as opposing such a provision. COM.TEX/10, para. 106 (1978). No doubt the compromise played some part in Australia's decision not to continue membership in the renewed MFA, and may have been a factor in Canada's late acceptance of the Protocol. France, too, had not been keen on a limitation on her GATT rights. As recently as mid-1977 France announced that she would implement GATT Article XIX restraints on cotton textiles and a range of clothing items, only to be told four days later by the EEC Commission that such authority was vested only in the Community; whereupon, the French measures were indefinitely postponed. EC Bulletin No. 6, 2.2.24 (1977).

90. MFA, Article 2(2)(i).

91. For the rather technical facts and legal arguments see COM/TEX/SB/214, paras. 5, 7 (1977).

92. COM.TEX/SB/196, para. 61 (1976) (programme *re* Pakistan); *idem,* para. 62 (Hong Kong, India); COM.TEX/SB/196/Add. 1, para. 2 (1976) (Brazil, Colombia, Korea, Macao, Malaysia, Mexico, Singapore, Thailand).

93. COM.TEX/SB/212, para. 2 (1977).

94. *Idem*, para. 3.

95. The TSB regretted that the EEC 'could not accept without comments' the implication in its assertion concerning the TSB's approach to its responsibilities. COM.TEX/SB/214, para. 6 (1977).

96. Communautés Européennes, Lettre d'Information du Bureau de Genève, No. 53, at 1 (1977) quoted in UNCTAD, Report, UN Doc. TD/B/C.2/192, at 23 (1978) [hereinafter cited as UNCTAD Report]; see also COM.TEX/10, para. 112 (1978).

97. See *infra*, notes 129–133 and accompanying text.

98. Protocol, *supra*, note 88. Preamble and para. 7 of the appended TC Conclusions.

99. The powers of the TSB were an important issue for the exporting countries during the 1977 negotiations. India had called for a strengthening of the supervisory structure to guarantee that all bilateral agreements would be subject to scrutiny as to their conformity to the MFA. COM.TEX/10, para. 48 (1978). Egypt directly countered the EEC position by claiming that the TSB was primarily an arbitral rather than conciliatory body. *Idem,* para. 64. Many called for a more active TSB role. Macao complained that TSB ex *post facto* reviews of agreements were insufficient; instead, requests for bilateral consultations should first be channeled through the TSB for a determination whether market disruption claims are justifiable. *Idem*, para. 68. The Israeli spokesman was more circumspect when he stated that conciliation was not the singular task of the TSB. He wished that it would be maintained as a 'quasi-legal body'. *Idem*, para. 80.

100. The EEC would prefer a TSB that is an objective, dispassionate 'conscience' of the MFA. Interview with Mr. Tran Van Thinh, Delegate of the EEC to the International Organisations in Geneva, in Geneva, January 21, 1980. An EEC spokesman has stated in the TC that the EEC regards the TSB as having the dual functions of conciliation and surveillance, which includes the examination of restraints and the determination of 'departures' from the rules. COM.TEX/13, para. 29 (1978).

101. Interview with Mr. R. Davies, GATT Secretariat, in Geneva, January 22, 1980.

102. Interview with Mr. J. Beck, EEC Member of the TSB, in Brussels, March 27, 1980.

103. See EC Bulletin, No. 6, 2.2.30 (1977).

104. As claimed by the proponents of the concept of 'cumulative market disruption', the large and growing number of relatively small-volume suppliers seeking liberal access made it necessary to account for the cumulative impact of their imports. According to the concept, restrictions could be placed on trade with new or small exporting countries that were not individually causing market disruption but contributing to such a situation by their mere participation in the market. As such the concept was not only incompatible with Article 6(3)'s protection of small-volume suppliers, but contravened the MFA's basic notion of selectivity and stretched the concept of market disruption beyond recognition.

105. An earlier TC meeting had revealed broad support for the MFA's objectives and a desire to maintain a multilateral framework in one form or another after the MFA's expiry in December of 1977. See COM.TEX/8, para. 52 (1978).

106. The European negotiator pointed out that EEC textile imports had increased by 80 per cent. in volume from 1973 to 1976. Roughly 3,500 textile factories had closed and 500,000 jobs had been lost during the period. It was claimed that if the MFA was renewed as is, a further 1.6 million people, comprising half the 1977 workforce, would lose their jobs by 1982. Developing countries argued that aside from their exports, other factors were causing European unemployment. These included changing patterns and levels of demand, imports from other developed countries and technological change. UNCTAD Report, *supra,* note 96, at paras. 41, 42.

107. The products subject to restraint were divided into five categories according to their import 'sensitivity'. The most sensitive grouping included T-shirts, knitted shirts, knitted jerseys, men's and women's woven trousers, women's blouses and men's shirts. Growth rates were low: imports of cotton yarn, for instance, were negotiated to increase at an annual rate of 0.3 per cent. See UNCTAD Report, *supra,* note 96, at para. 45.

As explained by the EEC spokesman, the stabilisation plan meant that for a 'limited number of these products' growth would not exceed the growth rae of consumption for each of the products concerned; whereas for other products, a growth rate higher than that of consumption would be permitted. The growth rate of less sensitive products could reach or even exceed the 6 per cent. rate stipulated in MFA Annex B. COM.TEX/10, para. 15 (1978).

108. COM.TEX/10, para. 16 (1978).

109. See, *e.g. idem,* paras. 22 (Hong Kong's reaction), 27 (Japan), 46 (India) and 66 (South Korea) (1978).

110. COM.TEX/W/44 (1977).

111. *Idem* (emphasis added).

112. Pakistan, Egypt, India and Brazil (the main cotton exporters) were among the objectors. The latter two submitted a paper based on the U.S. proposal, but without a 'reasonable departure' clause. It received scant support.

113. COM.TEX/W/47 (1977).

114. Protocol, *supra,* note 88, at para. 5.3:

> The Committee agreed that, within the framework of the MFA, [bilateral] consultations and negotiations should be conducted in a spirit of equity and flexibility with a view to reaching a mutually acceptable solution . . . which does include the possibility of jointly agreed reasonable departures from particular elements in particular cases.

115. EC Bulletin, No. 1, at 2.2.28 (1978).

116. Despite their anger at the Commission's overstepping its mandate *vis-à-vis* the cotton exporters, France and Britain in particular were pleased with the results of the bilateral and MFA negotiations. The U.K. Secretary of State for Trade concluded '[we] have obtained very tight restrictions on more than twenty sensitive products, representing about seventy-five per cent. of the United Kingdom imports, and satisfactory restraints on effectively all other products'. *The Times* (London), December 21, 1977, at 15. One commentator called the negotiations 'one of the most successful lobbying actions ever carried out by the protectionest lobby as a whole and the textile industry in particular'. *The Guardian,* February 6, 1978, at 14.

117. *Cf.* Subcomm. on Trade of the H. R. Comm. on Ways and Means, 95th Cong., 2nd Sess., 'Background Material on the Multifibre Arrangement' 3 (Comm. Print 1978) [hereinafter cited as Trade Subcommittee Report]: '[i]n short, the EC was demanding terms which neither the exporting countries nor the United States would consider "jointly agreed reasonable departures".'

118. *Cf.* UNCTAD Report, *supra,* note 96, at para. 51c ('[t]he introduction of the concept of "reasonable departures" has largely changed the function of the Arrangement . . .').

119. The TSB came down hard on the highly restrictive and violative Swedish agreements. The Swedes had not invoked the reasonable departure clause, but relied on paragraph 6 of the TC Conclusions appended to the Protocol, which recognised that the problems of 'minimum viable production' countries should be 'resolved in a spirit of equity and flexibility'. See *infra* note 173.The TSB specifically ruled that that could not function as an escape clause. COM. TEX/SB/519, para. 58 (1979). Since the agreements were short-term in the order of a year or two, the TSB refrained from passing on their conformity. Instead, pointed comments and recommendations were made with an eye on future agreements and extensions of existing ones.

120. It has been said that there cannot be any absolute determinations of 'unreasonableness' for what may be unreasonable in one situation may be reasonable in another: interview with Mr. J. Beck, EEC Member of the TSB, in Brussels, March 27, 1980. On the other hand, any absolute determinations of 'reasonableness' run the risk of turning into an open invitation to violate express MFA rules. Nevertheless, one could argue that several types of MFA violations

have become *de facto* 'reasonable departures' by virtue of the frequency with which they have appeared with impunity.

In an analogous instance, the TSB came to regret its decision that the absence of swing provisions in agreements could be excused, although required by MFA Annex B, if a 'reflection of a mutual recognition of the minimum viable production principle . . .'. COM.TEX/SB/365, para. 74 (1978). This was thereafter seized upon by Sweden to justify the total absence of swing provisions in its bilateral agreements.

121. See, *e.g.* Trade Subcommittee Report, *supra,* note 117, at 3: '[w]e do not know . . . whether the Europeans obtained more restrictive bilaterals than did the United States. If they did, there will be calls by the U.S. industry and labour for a renegotiation of our bilaterals to make them more restrictive and to ensure that textiles are not diverted from the European market to ours'.

122. A. Sutton, *supra,* note 2, at 196. The U.S., for instance, had introduced some 30-odd unilateral restraints under LTA Article 3 that were later superseded by bilateral restraints agreements under Article 4. *Idem,* at 196 n.13. Nevertheless, the shift towards bilateral restraint agreements began under the LTA. See B. Bardan, *supra,* note 3, at 17.

123. The following chart breaks down the types of restraints notified to the TSB over time:

Notification Of Actions To The TSB[a]

	Art. 3(5) unilateral action	Art. 3(6) unilateral action	Art. 3(4) bilateral action	Art. 4 bilateral action
Jan. 1974– Sept. 30, 1976	8	2a 4b	18(N) 3(E)	54(N)[b] 8(E or M)
Nov. 1976– Dec. 1977	13	2a 1b	10(N) 4(E)	17(N)[b] 17(E or M)
—— MFA extended				
Jan. 1978– Oct. 20, 1978[c]	0	0	1(N) 1(E)	19(N) 23(E or M)
Oct. 21, 1978– Nov. 30, 1979	4	1a	2(N)	60(N) 45(E or M)

[a] Notifications of termination of restraints are not included. The symbols 'N', 'E' and 'M' represent notifications of restraints that are new, extended or modified, respectively. With regard to unilateral action under Art. 3(6), the symbol 'a' represents an emergency action taken unilaterally, and 'b' in connection with an understanding. The latter is still essentially unilateral in character. It should be noted that bilateral agreements under Article 4 are often notified to the TSB many months after they are in *de facto* operation, despite the 30-day notification limit of Art. 4(4).

[b] Some of these new agreements represent restrictions pre-existing the MFA that have been converted to Art. 4 agreements as permitted by Art. 2. The U.S., for instance, converted pre-existing restrictions into 18 Art. 4 agreements between Jan. 1974 and Sept. 1976.

[c] During this period Austria instituted a bilateral surveillance system superseding an Art. 3(4) agreement with Hong Kong.

Sources: COM.TEX/SB/196, COM.TEX/SB/365 and COM.TEX/SB/519.

124. The following table shows the ratio of all Article 3 measures (bilateral, unilateral and 'emergency' restraints) to Article 4 measures (bilateral restraints) taken by the major industrialised importing countries:

Ratio of Art. 3/Art. 4 Restraints
Notified to the TSB[a]

	1/74–9/76	11/76–12/77	1/78–20/10/78	21/10/78– 30/11/79
Australia	8/1	0/0	—	—
Austria	3/10	0/3	1/3	2/2
Canada	6/4	2/1	1/0	3/6
EEC	8/11	9/6	6/6	0/23
Finland	0/1	2/1	0/0	0/5
Norway	3/3	0/8	—	—
Sweden	6/7	7/3	0/4	0/10
U.S.	1/21	1/12	0/15	1/18

[a] Often agreements are notified to the TSB after they are put in *de facto* operation.
Sources: COM.TEX/SB/196, COM.TEX/SB/365 and COM.TEX/SB/519.

Sources: COM.TEX/SB/196, COM.TEX/SB/365 and COM.TEX/SB/519.

125. A TSB discussion on the degree of selectivity required by Article 4 with respect to product coverage in agreements revealed 'differences of approach that were difficult to reconcile'. COM.TEX/SB/196, para. 91 (1976). the U.S., in particular, has been negotiating comprehensive agreements.

126. MFA, Article 4(3).

127. MFA, Article 3(3).

128. COM.TEX/SB/35, Annex B, para. 2(b) (1974). The TSB may always request additional information and consult concerned parties.

129. MFA, Article 3(4).

130. But cf. A Sutton, supra, note 2, at p. 208.

131. The TSB has ordinarily accompanied its findings of non-conformity with the observation that the Article 3(4) agreement would be in conformity with the MFA if considered as an Article 4 agreement. In this way, Article 4 has been used as a safety valve when the TSB felt itself pressed into too judicial a role, involving a direct confrontation with an importing country. Thus, for instance, when the TSB found that the EEC had not sustained a claim of market disruption in an EEC-India dispute under Article 3, it noted that 'there might be a real risk of market disruption [as required by Article 4]'. COM.TEX/SB/365, para. 18 (1978). See also COM.TEX/SB/51, para. 51 (1974) (a Canada/Singapore agreement); COM.TEX/8, para. 35 (1977) (Australia/Korea).

132. MFA, Article 4(4).

133. COM.TEX/SB/19, para. 8 (1974); COM.TEX/SB/44, para. 26 (1974).

134. COM.TEX/SB/519, para. 61 (1979). 'Consultation clauses' amount to automatic trigger mechanisms to bring unrestrained products under restraint. In the EEC bilaterals, for example, the clauses enable the EEC to request immediate consultations to agree upon quantitative limits when the imports of an unrestrained product exceed a certain specified percentage of total imports. During the consultation, the EEC can require the exporting country to suspend the issuance of export certificates.

135. COM.TEX/SB/322, para. 5 (1978); COM.TEX/SB/365, para. 70 (1978).

136. COM.TEX/SB/380, para. 4 (1979). Not only may the TSB play an active role in the implementation of an agreement, but it can play a role in its negotiation as well. With respect to Article 3(4) agreements, Article 3(5)(ii) confers authority to review matters raised by either party engaged in bilateral negotiations. Article 11(4), which confers a similar but general competence, could be invoked in relation to Article 4 negotiations, but has not been so invoked.

137. See supra, note 44.

138. See supra, notes 45, 46 and the accompanying text.

139. See, e.g. Article 1(3) ('[a] principal aim . . . shall be to further the economic and social development of developing countries and secure a substantial increase in their export earnings . . . and to provide scope for a greater share for them in world [textile] trade'); Article 6(1) (special and differential treatment for LDCs); and Annex A,III (in considering questions of market disruption account must be taken of LDC interests).

140. But see COM.TEX/10, para. 14 (1978) (assertion made during the 1977 negotiations by the EEC spokesman that the expansion and progressive liberalisation of trade had been substantially achieved vis-à-vis the Community). In fact, the TSB found that overall there had been 'some liberalisation' of world textile trade during the first 2½ years of the MFA's operation; although it is impossible to guage the influence the MFA has had thereon. COM.TEX/SB/196, para. 144 (1976). Trade in 'textiles' (textile yarns, fabrics, made-up articles and related products) declined. Idem, at para. 113. Between 1973 and 1975 the share of developing countries in textile trade declined from 31 per cent to 29 per cent and in clothing trade increased from 51 per cent to 53 per cent; idem para. 115. During the same period, imports of clothing and textiles into developed countries from developing countries increased 29 per cent.: clothing increased 48 per cent. and textiles declined slightly. Their relative share of the markets, though, has not changed greatly.

India, Pakistan and Egypt were the big losers during the 1973–75 period because of their dependence on textile exports as opposed to clothing. Korea was the big winner. Hong Kong remained the world's largest exporter of clothing and became the third largest importer of textiles in 1975. Idem, para. 127.

141. G. van Hoof and K. de Vey Mestdagh, supra, note 60 at 36.

142. See COM.TEX/SB/83, para. 9 (1975); COM.TEX/SB/196, para. 80 (1976).

143. COM.TEX/SB/35, Annex A (1974).

144. COM.TEX/SB/83, Annex (1975).

145. COM.TEX/SB/196, para. 80 (1976).

146. COM.TEX/SB/35, Annex B (1974).
147. COM.TEX/2, para. 11 (1974).
148. COM.TEX/SB/273, para. 6 (1977).
149. COM.TEX/SB/365, para. 71 (1978).
150. See, e.g. COM.TEX/SB/251, para. 2 (1977); COM.TEX/SB/365, paras. 12, 22 (1978).
151. See, e.g. COM.TEX/SB/245, paras. 6–10 (1977); COM.TEX/SB/365, paras. 24–26, 56 (1978) (an Indian-Swedish dispute over the latter's imposition of unilateral restraints; the matter rebounded between the TSB and bilateral discussion without conclusion when the restraints finally expired).
152. See e.g. COM.TEX/SB/196, paras. 71, 72 and 79 (1976).
153. See, e.g. COM.TEX/SB/196, para. 78 (1976).
154. The majority of MFA members had not submitted their reports within the one-year deadline. COM.TEX/SB/83, para. 8 (1975).
155. COM.TEX/SB/364, para. 7 (1978).
156. See, e.g. COM.TEX/SB/144, para. 9 (1976) (TSB chairman criticises the slow response to his request for the submission of information on national import surveillance systems).
157. See, e.g. idem; COM.TEX/SB/364, paras. 7 (1978) (notifications to TSB chairman of requests for Article 3 consultations); COM.TEX/SB/365, paras. 72, 75 (1978); COM.TEX/SB/ 519, para. 53 (1979) (notifications of Article 4 agreements).
158. See, e.g. COM.TEX/SB/83, para. 8 (1975); COM.TEX/SB/115, para. 4 (1975); COM.TEX/SB/519, para. 50 (1979).
159. F. van Hoof and K. de Vey Mestdagh, supra, note 60, at p. 37.
160. Interview with Mr. Robert Shepherd U.S. Member of the TSB, in Geneva, January 22, 1980.
161. Following the EEC's failure to adopt the TSB's recommendations in the phase-out programmes controversy, the Pakistani spokesman remarked that 'even verdicts from this Body [the TSB] in favour of exporting countries did not solve their problems, because decisions of the TSB were acceptable to the importing countries only if they were in their favour'. COM.TEX/10, para. 50 (1977).
162. See supra, pp. 235 and 236–237.
163. See supra, note 151.
164. See COM.TEX/SB/196, paras. 5–9 (1976).
165. See generally supra, pp. 237–238.
166. See comment of the Australian delegate to the TC. COM.TEX/10, para. 73 (1977).
167. Cf. United States Senate Rep. No. 93–1298, 93d Cong., 2nd Sess. 119 (1974), where it was stated in relation to the GATT 'escape-clause', Article XIX:

the rationale for the 'escape clause' has been and remains, that as barriers to international trade are lowered, some industries and workers inevitably face serious injury, dislocation and perhaps economic extinction. the 'escape-clause' is aimed at providing temporary relief for an industry suffering serious injury, or the threat thereof, so that the industry will have sufficient time to adjust to the freer international competition.

Exporting countries tend to emphasise conversion and importing countries modernisation and specialisation among the goals of adjustment.
168. To create obligations on the international level to implement adjustment policies is unacceptable to many countries at this point in time. International adjustment assistance codes have been proposed, but have come to naught for lack of political and economic resolve among countries with large, ailing industries. See, e.g. G. Curzon and V. Curzon, Global Assault on Non-Tariff Trade Barriers 32 (1972). Developed countries have demonstrated their willingness to undertake slow and gradual structural changes by virtue of their liberalisation of trade within the GATT system.
169. See COM.TEX/W/36 (1976).
170. On 'swing' see supra, note 46.
171. See, e.g., COM.TEX/SB/196, para. 97 (1976).
172. See supra pp. 242–243, 245–246.
173. Protocoal, supra, note 88, para. 6 of the appended TC Conclusions:

The Committee recognised that countries having small markets, an exceptionally high level of imports and a correspondingly low level of domestic production are particularly exposed to the trade problems mentioned in the preceding paragraphs, and that the problems should be resolved in a spirit of equity and flexibility . . .

174. See COM.TEX/SB/519, para. 58 (1979).

175. See COM.TEX/SB/196, para. 135 (1976). Industrial countries have declined to tamper with their mutual trade under the MFA presumably because the exports from their mature, less dynamic industries do not cause market disruption. *Cf.* A. Shonfield, *et al., supra,* note 3, at 275. But note the rumblings in the EEC in late 1979 and early 1980 for protection against U.S. synthetics: the British Trade Minister reiterating the EEC position stated in late 1979 that the U.S. double-tier pricing system for oil and natural gas gave U.S. producers an unfair advantage that was 'disrupting the market'. *International Herald Tribune,* November 21, 1979, p. 7, col. 2. There are, of course, important political considerations involved in any restriction of U.S.-EEC trade.

176. COM.TEX/SB/196, para. 136(c) (1976).

177. See COM.TEX/10, para. 74 (1978).

178. COM.TEX/SB/296, para. 9 (1976).

179. COM.TEX/SB/27, Annex (1974).

180. See *supra,* note 58 and accompanying text.

181. See COM.TEX/SB/519, para. 67 (1979). Thus far the EEC had not invoked a 'price clause'.

182. See *supra,* note 134 and accompanying text.

183. See MFA, Article 5.

184. United States: Trade Act of 1974, P.L. 93–618, 19 U.S.C. §§ 2101–2487, 88 Stat. 1978 (1975) [hereinafter cited as Trade Act of 1974].

185. See *supra,* note 39.

186. Dam points to the intrinsic weakness of the 'market disruption' concept when he questions whether it is an objectively verifiable phenomenon with different and distinct consequences from ordinary competition. He recognised that 'if the competitive threat of less-developed countries becomes severe enough, developed countries may not hesitate to mould the notion of "market disruption" to their desire to impose import controls'. K. Dam, *supra,* note 3, at 314. Thus, one goal of multilateral creative supervision should have been to prevent the concept from becoming an excuse for protectionism – indeed a difficult task for an entity commanding insufficient authority.

187. MFA, Annex A, para. 1.

188. *Cf.* T. Enger, 'U.S. Tariff Adjustment and Adjustment Assistance' (1972) 6 JWTL 518, 522.

189. COM.TEX/SB/51, para. 9 (1974).

190. This does not mean that the terms cannot be better understood and their relationships clarified. The U.S. International Trade Commission, charged with the task of determining serious injury to domestic producers who seek import relief under §201 of the Trade Act of 1974, resorted to a dictionary during one proceeding to supply definitions to comparable terms. Stainless Steel and Alloy Tool Steel, U.S. Int'l Trade Comm'n, Investigation No. TA-201-5, USITC Pub. 756 (1976), reprinted in J. Jackson, *Legal Problems of International Economic Relations* (1977) 652–653. The ITC routinely issues public reports discussing the application of economic factors in specific cases, the question of serious injury, the relationship between increased imports and serious injury, and other related matters not broached by Annex A. See generally J. Jackson, *idem* , pp. 649–663. The economic factors have been broken down into three categories by §201(2) of the Trade Act depending upon their relevance to a showing of serious injury, a threat of serious injury, or 'substantial causality' of the injury.

PART IV

SUPERVISION WITHIN THE UN CONFERENCE FOR TRADE AND DEVELOPMENT

SUPERVISION WITHIN THE UN CONFERENCE FOR TRADE AND DEVELOPMENT

by K. de Vey Mestdagh

CONTENTS

I. INTRODUCTION

Ever since the collective awakening of the developing countries during and after the Afro-Asian Conference, held at Bandung (Indonesia) in 1955 – with the aim of stressing the solidarity of the participating countries, and of discussing ways and means to reach the greatest possible economic, cultural and political co-operation among themselves – these countries have been in a continuous offensive in order to establish some sort of an international institution, in which their specific problems related to development and trade would have a central place. This resulted, eventually, in the convening of the United Nations Conference on Trade and Development (UNCTAD), in 1964, at Geneva.

Although, at the beginning of the Geneva session, most developed countries had only one meeting in mind, the developing countries were, after protracted negotiations, successful in obtaining a regular and even permanent

280

character for the Conference. The General Assembly of the United Nations adopted, on December 30, 1964, resolution 1995 (XIX) embodying the recommendations of the Geneva Conference. Thus, UNCTAD – equipped with a standing Board and a Secretariat – came into being as a permanent organ of the United Nations.[1]

Initially, the developed countries wanted to confine UNCTAD's scope of activities to the field of international commodity trade, but at the instance of the developing countries and under the inspiring guidance of the UNCTAD Secretariat, the number of agenda-items steadily increased.

UNCTAD came to play increasingly its own role in the economic relations between North and South. That this role was (and often still is!) not self-evident is demonstrated by the opposition of the industrialised countries to too wide a range of functions. A certain degree of task expansion, however, was even acceptable to the West, as long as UNCTAD was only a platform for the exchange of ideas; as soon as decision making came into the picture, most developed countries were inclined to use any form of safety-brake, arguing that GATT or ECOSOC was the only competent body. The Third World, on the contrary, aimed (and still aims) at a compulsory decision-making function for UNCTAD, and the largest possible mandate to that end.

Apart from the difference of opinion which existed for a long time about the question if UNCTAD is a competent institution for the negotiation of binding decisions, there also exists a firm difference between the developing countries and the developed countries in the demand for effective supervisory mechanisms. In particular, there is an incipient awareness, in the ranks of the developing countries, of the vital importance of supervision regarding the implementation of decisions. As a result, UNCTAD, alongside its function as a forum for debate and negotiation, has gradually been allotted a number of specific supervisory tasks.

General Assembly resolution 1995 (XIX), embodying UNCTAD's 'constitution' and the supervisory mechanism elaborated on the basis of that resolution are most essential in respect of UNCTAD supervision. In addition the documents regarding the restructuring of the international economic relations, drawn up particularly in the 1970s, have provided supervisory functions for UNCTAD. At the same time the more specific fields of commodities, manufacturers, shipping, preferences and technology comprise interesting examples of UNCTAD supervision. The present study does not pretend to give a complete insight into all UNCTAD activities; problems such as debt servicing or economic co-operation among developing countries, although important in the North-South debate, are not extensively dealt with. Emphasis, in the first place, has been laid on those issues which entail any form of a more or less elaborated and/or institutionalised follow-up mechanism.

Within the UN family UNCTAD may be considered as one of the major bodies – if not the most important – dealing with issues of trade and development. This means that UNCTAD is in the middle of a dynamic process of ongoing negotiations, the supervision of which may be somewhat different from supervision of implementation in the strict sense of the word.[2] Initiating negotiations or preventing a dialogue from losing momentum often requires an even more subtle approach by the supervisory organs towards recalcitrant States, than is already the case with supervision *stricto sensu*. UNCTAD exercises both types of supervision. In this study, surveillance of ongoing negotiations will be referred to as supervision of policy development.

II. SCOPE, STRUCTURE AND BUDGET OF UNCTAD

The United Nations Conference on Trade and Development (hereafter referred to as the Geneva Conference) was held in Geneva from March 23 to June 16, 1964. In accordance with the agenda drafted by the Preparatory Committee, five sessional committees comprising all the 120 participating States were set up: the First Committee, on international commodity problems; the Second Committee, on trade in manufactures and semi-manufactures; the Third Committee, on the improvement of invisible trade of developing countries, on financing for an expansion of international trade and on some aspects of international compensatory financing; the Fourth Committee, on institutional arrangements, methods and machinery to implement measures relating to the expansion of international trade; and the Fifth Committee, on expansion of international trade and its significance for economic development and on the implications of regional economic groups.[3]

Although during the initial stages of the Geneva Conference, the institutional question was generally in the background, the Fourth Committee (on institutional arrangements) played a central role. Any recommendation on substantive issues meant very little, as long as the institutional questions on the establishment of a permanent organisation, or any other form of institutional follow-up, were not tackled. The agreement eventually reached in the Fourth Committee involved the redrafting of many provisions of earlier texts tabled in the course of the Conference, particularly those regarding the functions of the Conference, its relation with ECOSOC, the name and size of the standing committee, the number and fields of activity of subsidiary bodies, and the crucial issue of the voting procedures.[4]

The text of the draft recommendation was adopted unanimously on June 15, 1964, and incorporated as Annex A.V.I in the Final Act of the Conference.[5] Regarding the issue of decision making, a Special Committee on conciliation procedures met in New York in the autumn of 1964 and submitted a unanimous report, containing the terms of earlier proposed conciliation procedures. The General Assembly of the UN, without voting, adopted on December 30, 1964, resolution 1995 (XIX) embodying the text of the recommendations of the Conference and of the conciliation procedure proposed by the Special Committee. UNCTAD thus came into being as a permanent organ of the United Nations.[6]

Resolution 1995 (XIX) does not specify the Article of the Charter under which UNCTAD was created. It is, however, generally accepted that the establishment of UNCTAD falls under Article XXII, which provides that the General Assembly 'may establish such subsidiary organs as it deems necessary for the performance of its functions'.[7] Since UNCTAD, although being an organ of the UN and not being based on a treaty, functions as a budgetary semi-autonomous framework within the UN family for the co-operation between States, with a view to promoting common public interests, by means of a permanent institutional set-up (*i.e.* organs with well-defined tasks), it will hereinafter be referred to as an international organisation. The mere fact that UNCTAD was established by a resolution instead of a treaty does not prevent it from functioning as, or even being, an international organisation. The first requirement for the establishment of such an organisation is an international agreement between States. But States may decide to establish an international organisation without using the form of a treaty and without the usual proviso for subsequent ratification by each of the States.[8]

Nevertheless, UNCTAD is not an *independent*, separately established, international entity. Although it functions as an international organisation, being an organ of the General Assembly, it is subordinated to decisions and recommendations stemming from the latter.[9] Yet the General Assembly has not engaged in any detailed supervision of UNCTAD's activities. As parent body, the former has restricted itself to giving guidelines of a general nature.[10]

To get an insight into the supervisory functions exercised by UNCTAD organs and its subsidiary bodies, it is first necessary to examine the purpose of the organisation. This purpose or scope of activities gives the functional delimitations within which UNCTAD is entitled to act. In particular, in the case of UNCTAD – an organisation in which different factions constantly disagree on what powers belong in the realm of its scope of activities – some clarification of its purpose is indispensable. It turns out, however, that it is difficult, if not impossible, to find a satisfactory and comprehensive definition of UNCTAD's role.

Alongside the scope of UNCTAD activities, this chapter will also deal with the institutional aspects of the organisation. General Assembly resolution 1995 (XIX) provides for a Conference, a standing Trade and Development Board (including subsidiary committees), and a permanent Secretariat. Each of these organs and committees fulfils its own task within the UNCTAD supervisory procedures, so that a description of their structure, responsibilities and mutual relationship is of relevance.

Finally, some attention will be paid to the budgetary questions in UNCTAD. With regard to UNCTAD supervision this question plays a role as far as the organisation is involved in technical assistance activities.

2.1. Scope of activities

According to General Assembly resolution 1995 (XIX), which in fact forms the constitution of UNCTAD, the organisation is vested, within the United Nations system, with a central role in the field of international trade and development. With regard to the functions of UNCTAD the resolution reflects the strain between the developed countries, which insisted on maintaining GATT's jurisdiction intact and preserving ECOSOC's primacy in the economic and social field in the UN, and the developing and socialist countries, which saw UNCTAD as the central UN organ for trade and development, and as a transitional machinery leading towards a fully fledged International Trade Organisation.[11]

Hence, in rather ambiguous terms, the first principal function of the Conference is 'to promote international trade, especially with a view to accelerating economic development, particularly trade between countries at different stages of development, between developing countries and between countries with different systems of economic and social organisation, taking into account the functions performed by existing international organisations'.[12]

Other functions of the Conference are the formulation of principles and policies on international trade and related problems of economic development,[13] and the making of proposals and the taking of other steps for putting the said principles and policies into effect.[14] In addition, the Conference may initiate action for the negotiation and adoption of multilateral legal instruments in the field of trade, with due regard to the adequacy of existing organs of negotiation.[15]

In respect of the co-ordinating functions, the text as finally adopted is somewhat vague, if not downright confusing. On the one hand, UNCTAD is to review and facilitate 'generally' the co-ordination of activities of the institutions within the UN system in the field of international trade and related problems of economic development and, on the other hand, it is required to co-operate with the General Assembly and the ECOSOC with respect to the performance of the responsibilities for co-ordination under the UN Charter.[16]

Finally, the Conference is requested to be available as a centre for harmonising the trade and related development policies of Governments and regional economic groupings in pursuance of Article I of the UN Charter[17]; and to deal with any other matters within the scope of its competence.[18]

In drawing up this list of functions, the Geneva Conference tried to demonstrate its awareness of the dangers inherent in the creation of a new institution in the field of economic development. Since duplication and overlapping had long been a concern of international administrations, an additional organisation within the UN system might easily bring more problems than relief, unless special precautionary measures were taken. These measures were suggested, although sometimes ambiguously, in the sections (a), (d) and (e) of the above summary.

In addition to UNCTAD's initial task, in the field of commodity trade, trade in (semi-)manufactures, and financing related to trade, the organisation gradually acquired new assignments. While the developed countries tried to keep the mandate of UNCTAD as limited as possible, fearing that otherwise the work of other organisations would be duplicated, the developing countries constantly pressed for task expansion. They asked for a co-ordinated approach through a single organisation, which would take an over-all view including all aspects of their economic situation. In order to affect the attitude of the developed countries, the developing countries adopted a tactic of step-by-step negotiation.

The Geneva Conference had already agreed on a draft text containing a common measure of understanding on shipping questions.[19] It also had considered and recommended measures on insurance, tourism, technical assistance and transfer of technology, taking into account the need to improve the invisible trade of developing countries.[20]

Task expansion as such, may be found, for instance, in the field of shipping. At the first meeting of the Trade and Development Board, in 1965, the developing countries proposed the establishment of a separate committee on shipping,[21] while the developed countries argued that shipping matters should be included on the agenda of the Committee on Invisibles and Financing, because any proliferation of committees and subsidiary bodies of the Board would decrease its effectiveness and dilute the resources of the Secretariat.[22] Yet the developing countries succeeded in obtaining a committee on shipping, equal in status and terms of reference to the other standing committees in UNCTAD. International shipping legislation, as a highly sensitive matter to the developed countries, was not covered by the adopted programme of work. It took three years for that subject to earn its place on UNCTAD's agenda; more than four years passed before the substance of the issue was really tackled in depth.[23]

The field of technical assistance offers another example of the considerable task expansion in UNCTAD. General Assembly resolution 1995 (XIX), which established UNCTAD, did not contain any reference to technical assistance activities. It was only in 1968 that it was decided to add to UNCTAD's mandate the responsibility of a participating and executing agency of the United Nations Development Programme[24] and, consequently, the supplementary task for its secretariat to support technical co-operation activities. By then, it was considered that UNCTAD had considerably developed its major research and analyses functions and that the UNCTAD Secretariat had become a depository of information and knowledge of development issues which could be put at the disposal of developing countries in the form of substantive or technical support to specific development projects if UNCTAD could have direct access to extra-budgetary resources to make this contribution possible. Particularly since 1969 technical assistance projects for the promotion of the export trade of developing countries, carried out by UNCTAD, have mushroomed and diversified, which meant an important change in view of the previously limited number of UN projects in the field of trade and invisibles.[25]

Since the developing countries considered UNCTAD as the central UN organ for all matters relating to economic development, they emphasised that the organisation also has a role to play in the transfer of technology. It was felt that the Board should consider establishing a committee on science and technology. The general response of the developed countries to this was that the subject should be dealt with through the existing organisations.

Eventually, a 45-member Inter-governmental Group on the Transfer of Technology was instituted. This institutional solution was meant to be temporary. Yet, UNCTAD's role has been placed on a 'continuing basis': in 1974 the Trade and Development Board established the Committee on Transfer of Technology as one of its main Committees.[26]

In recent years, UNCTAD has expanded its agenda to include the problem of trade expansion, economic co-operation and regional integration among developing countries. This issue, which is now known as ECDC (economic co-operation among developing countries) has been, and is, mainly a favourite subject of the UNCTAD Secretariat, because the developing countries, as long as they are not able to set up their own Third World Secretariat, are in great need of any form of service device. As for the developed countries, in addition to their standing objection to new bodies and functions, a majority clearly fears that ECDC would lead to a body specially committed to the Third World (even in terms of membership), in defiance of the fact that at least UNCTAD's work – since it is carried out in the framework of the UN – must be necessarily of a universal character.

Finally, UNCTAD has become increasingly active in the process of restructuring the international economy. During a protracted quarrel, at the end of the first UN development decade, over the question of whether UNCTAD or ECOSOC should prepare the second UN development decade (1970–80), the latter was eventually entrusted with this task. Nonetheless, the debates held in the Trade and Development Board of UNCTAD (eighth/ninth session) and the proposals made, had a decisive influence on ECOSOC's Preparatory Committee and the General Assembly. In fact, the essence of the most important provisions of the international strategy for the second UN development decade, adopted by the General Assembly at its 25th session[27] was negotiated in UNCTAD's Trade and Development Board.[28]

In the 1970s UNCTAD played an important role in the formulation of the Charter of Economic Rights and Duties of States.[29] A proposal made by the Mexican president during the third UNCTAD Conference held in Santiago (1972), to draft such a document, resulted in a resolution adopted by the Conference to establish generally accepted norms to govern international economic relations systematically. A Working Group, under the aegis of UNCTAD, was to draw up the text of a draft charter.[30]

If it were at all possible to give a comprehensive survey of present functions exercised by UNCTAD, it would resemble in the following summary. Quoting once again General Assembly resolution 1995 (XIX), the principal but at the same time very general purpose of UNCTAD is to promote international trade especially with a view to accelerating economic development [. . .] taking into account the functions performed by existing organisations.[31] The generality and also ambiguity of this provision were, from the moment of its formulation, a source of controversy. Not only is it difficult to state what belongs in the field of international trade (or rather what does not belong in the field of international trade) related to economic development; it is more difficult to agree on functions already performed (satisfactorily?) by existing organisations, if the opposing parties are not in agreement on the competences of those organisations, or if the opposing parties are not both members of the same organisations (especially because some do not believe in the efficacy of certain organisations).

In the midst of this functional uncertainty, agreement on some issues and to a certain extent organisational practice – as we have seen in this paragraph – have gradually determined the scope of UNCTAD activities. At present, the following might be considered as regular agenda items:

- Developments in international trade: restructuring the international economy; planning and review of development decades; etc.
- Commodities: commodity agreements: the Integrated Programme for Commodities; The Common Fund; compensatory financing; marketing; distribution and processing of primary commodities; etc.
- Manufactures and semi-manufactures; the Generalised System of Preferences; protectionism; structural adjustments of national economies; restrictive business practices.
- Monetary and financial issues; international financial co-operation for development; transfer of real resources to developing countries.
- Transfer of technology: the Code of Conduct for the Transfer of Technology; strengthening the technological capacity of developing countries.
- Shipping: participation of developing countries in world shipping and the development of their merchant marines; the Code of Conduct for Liner Conferences; cargo sharing in bulk-carrier trade.
- Least developed among developing countries, and landlocked and island developing countries: special programmes of action, etc.
- Trade relations among countries having different economic and social systems.
- Economic co-operation among developing countries (ECDC): appropriate support and assistance to the process and activities of ECDC.
- Institutional questions.

2.2. Structure of the machinery

A number of institutional aspects has been touched upon in the preceding paragraph. Here, we will examine in more detail UNCTAD as an international institution, originally created as an organ of the UN General Assembly.[32] The most important result of the Geneva Conference was the establishment of UNCTAD as a permanent institution.[33] Yet, this achievement was reached only after a sharp confrontation over the nature of the institution to be created. The permanency of the organisation almost foundered, in particular, on the question of voting.[34] The eventual institutional outcome of the Geneva Conference was an unprecedented victory for the less-developed countries. Not only had they been able to call a conference which had been initially resisted by the developed countries, they had been able, for the first time in history, to create a major new international agency which the Western countries had not wanted at all.

The Conference is the highest body of the organisation. In addition to making a provision for the setting up of the Conference, resolution 1995 (XIX) provided for the establishment, at inter-governmental level, of the Trade and Development Board, the Committees of the Board and their subsidiary and advisory bodies. Also an adequate, permanent and full-time Secretariat within the United Nations Secretariat for the proper servicing of the Conference, the Board and its subsidiary bodies, was to be established immediately.

As the plenary organ of UNCTAD, the Conference was to be convened at intervals of not more than three years. The first four sessions of the Conference, however, were held at intervals of four years.[35] UNCTAD V, held in Manila in 1979, was the first Conference convened within the original timelap of three years. The members of the Conference are those States which are members of the UN or members of the specialised agencies or of the International Atomic Energy Agency.[36]

To ensure continuity, the Trade and Development Board (hereinafter referred to as the Board) was established as the more regular meeting organ of the Conference.[37] It meets twice a year. Until 1976, the Board consisted initially of 55 and later of 68 members which were elected at each Conference, on the basis of equitable geographical distribution, ensuring a continuing representation for the principal trading States.[38] However, pursuing a recommendation of the Nairobi Conference (1976),[39] the General Assembly decided that the membership of the Board should be open to all members of the Conference.[40] At present, 122 States[41] are participating in the work of the Board which, of course, severely reduces the advantages of an executive body in a more restricted set-up.

Apart from carrying out the functions of the Conference when the latter is not in session, the Board has four main functions: (i) it keeps under review and takes appropriate action for the implementation of decisions of the Conference; (ii) it initiates its own research and study projects; (iii) it acts as a preparatory committee for future Conferences; and (iv) it submits an annual report to the General Assembly of the UN. The Board (and occasionally the Conference) has established a number of committees, whose function is to work out the details of all proposals in specific fields. These, in turn, have set up sub-committees and specialist groups. Membership of the committees which normally meet once a year, is not limited to Board members.[42]

The Secretariat of UNCTAD is a separate part of the UN Secretariat. The head of the Secretariat is the Secretary-General of the Conference who holds the rank of Under-Secretary-General of the United Nations.[43] His appointment, which is made by the Secretary-General of the UN, must be confirmed by the General Assembly. The staff of the Secretariat is part of the UN Secretariat and is subject of the UN staff regulations and rules.

UNCTAD's place in the UN system was the subject of controversy throughout the Geneva Conference. While the developing countries upheld the view that UNCTAD should be linked directly to the General Assembly, the developed countries maintained that some sort of organic relationship should be established with ECOSOC. The compromise solution was the inclusion of a provision whereby the Board reports to the General Assembly *through* ECOSOC.[44] While this provision obviously means that the Board should not report *to* ECOSOC, it does not indicate the precise function of the Council in receiving and transmitting the annual reports of the Board, other than that of transmitting to the General Assembly 'such comments on the reports as it may deem necessary'. For the developed countries the meaning of the provision was that ECOSOC was to supervise UNCTAD, while for the developing countries it meant that ECOSOC should act only as a 'post office' to transmit the Board's reports to the General Assembly without making any recommendations as to their contents. The latter viewpoint generally appears to have prevailed so far and ECOSOC in fact has performed only a perfunctory function.[45]

2.3. Budgetary questions

During the Geneva Conference, it was decided that a separate budgetary provision should be opened for UNCTAD expenditures, within the regular budget of the UN. In accordance with the practice followed by the UN in similar cases – the same method was already being applied to the International Court of Justice – arrangements were to be made for assessments on States not members of the UN which would participate in the Conference.[46]

The UN General Assembly and the Secretariat firmly control UNCTAD expenditures, according to strict UN budgetary procedures. Yet, the 'budget within a budget' has proved of considerable practical value to UNCTAD, in addition to the symbolic element of singling it out as a distinct entity within the UN institutional hierarchy.[47] Power over the programme through control of the budget is held particularly by the UNCTAD Secretary-General who formulates the budget on the basis of estimates from his division, by officials at the UN headquarters and the Advisory Committee on Administrative and Budgetary Questions (ACABQ), but also by Western countries, who provide more than two-thirds of the funds for the UN budget. Early in the process of preparing the budget the informal Geneva Group of large donors indicates what it considers to be a tolerable budget level; but the large contributors have more influence on total sums than on allocations between fields, and despite their complaints the budget has grown rapidly.[48]

Delegates of the larger Western countries frequently stress the financial implications of various actions, and this emphasis has some effect as a signal to the representatives from less-developed countries. But since the developed countries have no 'item veto', representatives of the less-developed countries who feel intensely about a point can pass it over Western opposition.[49]

As has been already indicated, the budget of UNCTAD is drafted by the UNCTAD Secretariat. This draft budget must be approved by the Fifth Committee of the General Assembly, when it considers the UN budget as a whole. Once the approval has been acquired, the UN Controller allots the

UNCTAD share directly to UNCTAD's Secretary-General to be administered in accordance with the normal UN practices. Although the UNCTAD Secretary-General does not have the freedom to use the appropriations at his discretion – he is formally supervised by the UN Controller and is supposed to use the moneys within the approved allocations under each item – he enjoys autonomy within these broad limits. The fact that the UNCTAD Secretary-General has the available funds at his disposal means a great deal in terms of more efficient daily administration, greater flexibility and enhanced autonomy.[50]

2.3.1. Administrative expenditures

Until 1969, when it began to move into the field of providing services for States through participation in the International Trade Centre and the United Nations Development Programme, UNCTAD was an organisation for meetings and studies. Increasingly, however, UNCTAD's budget exceeded its primary devotion to these activities.

The administrative budget of UNCTAD – administered directly by its Secretariat – is about $25 million per year (figures for 1980). This amount, however, covers only a portion of UNCTAD activities, because in this budget are not included the Conference activities and a certain number of ancillary services, such as purchase accounting, building management, etc. These activities are estimated in the budget to amount to approximately another $24 million per year. The total of roughly $50 million is the regular budget of UNCTAD.[51]

2.3.2. Operational expenditures

Apart from an important proportion of administrative expenditures, which UNCTAD necessarily makes as a forum organisation, a share of the budget is reserved for operational cost. The latter as the result of UNCTAD performing alongside its forum function – as a deliberative organisation and research institution – also a service function in carrying out technical assistance projects for the promotion of the export trade of developing countries.

As regards these technical assistance operations, which are financed through extra-budgetary resources, the budget is estimated to be approximately $12 million. This sum does not include the so-called overhead budget to run these technical assistance operations, which accounts for 14 per cent. of any operation. Consequently, the total of the budget for technical assistance amounts to $13.5 million per year.

From this total of expenditures on technical assistance the United Nations Development Programme (UNDP) accounts for $10.3 million. Donations, in the form of trust funds, of approximately $1.9 million, are given to UNCTAD directly as contributions by individual governments for specific purposes.[52]

III. LEGAL INSTRUMENTS

This chapter deals with the legal instruments at UNCTAD's disposal to promote international trade. 'Legal instruments' must be understood as the legal acts by which UNCTAD exercises its functions in order to effect its purposes.[53] These acts take the form of decisions, such as resolutions, recommendations or declarations.[54] Also, however, UNCTAD fulfils a function of a quasi-legislative character, since one of its tasks is to initiate action for the negotiation and adoption of multilateral legal instruments, such as codes of conduct.[55] Special attention will be paid to the legal character of UNCTAD decisions, as well as of the multilateral legal instruments negotiated under the auspices of UNCTAD. Before doing so, however, the process of decision making will be explored first. In the framework of the subject of UNCTAD supervision, it is important to consider this process in more detail, so as to understand how decisions are wrought. Particularly in respect of the effectiveness of supervision, preparatory decision-making may provide invaluable information.[56]

3.1. Decision making

3.1.1. Voting

During the Geneva Conference the most deeply seated differences of opinion concerned the voting issue. The Conference opened with no thought – neither on the side of the developed countries, nor on the side of the developing countries – of any voting system, other than the generally accepted system of one State one vote. But when the Conference was about two-thirds of the way through, the developed countries increasingly realised that the developing countries were voting 'en groupe', thereby using their built-in majority. Yet they only accounted for a minority share (about one-fifth) of total world trade. Consequently, the developed countries (consisting of the major trading nations) wanted a special form of weighted voting to be incorporated into the institution which they felt now tended to take on a more permanent character. On their part, the developing countries were not prepared to deviate from the principle of one State one vote.

The Geneva Conference nearly foundered on this fundamental question. In an attempt to break the deadlock the Secretary-General, Raul Prebisch, proposed the adoption of a conciliation procedure instead of special voting procedures. Eventually, the voting issue was resolved. The developed countries came to accept the provisions regarding the required voting majorities proposed by the developing countries. The developing countries, on their turn, accepted Prebisch's proposal of a conciliation procedure which in certain cases would have to be followed before voting 'to provide an adequate basis for the adoption of recommendations on proposals of a specific nature for action substantially affecting the economic and financial interests of particular countries'. Because of the lack of time to work out the details of such a procedure, the Conference recommended that a Special Committee be set up to establish a process of conciliation. This Committee met in New York in October 1964 and its recommendations were incorporated into General Assembly resolution 1995 (XIX).[57]

According to paragraph 24 of resolution 1995 (XIX), each State represented at the Conference has one vote. Decisions of the Conference on matters of substance must be taken by a two-thirds majority of the representatives present and voting, while decisions on matters of procedure shall be taken by simple majority. Further, decisions of the Board must be taken by a simple majority of the representatives present and voting.

3.1.2. Conciliation

Alongside the maintenance of equality of voting and a two-thirds majority rule on matters of substance, resolution 1995 (XIX) also established an elaborate system of conciliation which can be requested by a group of at least 10 Conference members, five Board members, or three Committee members, before any vote on a substantive matter occurs.[58] The procedure set forth is designed to provide an adequate basis for the adoption of proposals of a specific nature for action substantially affecting the economic or financial interests of particular countries, which have a realistic chance of meaningful acceptance by the Conference or the Board.[59]

Three main considerations underlie the conciliation procedure as shaped by the Special Committee. First, no informal discussion and conciliation is to be excluded; secondly, formal conciliation is to be initiated only in relation to certain types of proposals; and finally, special conciliation should be essentially flexible.

The conciliation procedure of resolution 1995 (XIX) is fairly simple. Following a request for conciliation, a conciliation group is established. This group is composed of countries especially interested in the matter under discussion. Selection is made on an equitable geographical basis. If the group reaches agreement at the same session of the Conference or the Board, the agreed resolution is voted upon. If an agreement is not reached, the group continues its discussion and reports to the next session of either the Conference or the Board, depending upon which convenes first. If an agreement is still not reached, the Conference or the Board can vote to continue conciliation or vote on the original resolution. If the latter course is taken, the majority and minority views of the conciliation group are expressed in the resolution.[60]

So far, the formal conciliation procedure has never been used. Informal conciliation, however, has become a quite common negotiating method aimed at reaching agreement on draft texts. Probably the mere existence of the formal procedure induces members to compromise rather than to vote on controversial proposals.[61] Another explanation may be found in the fact that the formal conciliation procedure, since it is restricted to proposals 'substantially affecting the economic or financial interests of particular countries', was meant to be initiated by the developed countries. There exists obviously hesitation on the side of those countries to formally invoke conciliation which, if it is successfully concluded, leads to more authoritative resolutions than in the case of adoption under the regular voting procedure.

In spite of the atmosphere of confrontation, which always seems to characterise the North-South encounters, the UNCTAD 'trademark' through the years has been a quest for 'consensus and conciliation'. This is understandable if one realises that the majority of proposals offered in UNCTAD are not based on the principle of *quid pro quo,* but on the principle of equitable distribution of wealth, or redistribution of income, and the restructuring of the world economy. To demand something in return for nothing, even when justified by the most noble considerations of equity, is not a familiar starting-point in international negotiations. Hence, the need for positive and, above all, effective results (that is real redistribution and restructuring) forces the opposing parties to reach a common position. Consequently, during the first 15 years of UNCTAD's existence, whenever a deadlock situation threatened to disrupt meetings, a small group of key members have met with the Secretary-General or a Committee's chairman, in order to work toward some form of consensus.

3.1.3. The group system

Reference has thus far been made to *the* developing countries and *the* developed countries. It has also been mentioned that the developing countries were inclined to vote *'en groupe'.*[62] Apart from the establishment of the permanent machinery of UNCTAD, as the most important institutional result, the main political outcome of the Geneva Conference was the shift in the traditional relationship between developed and developing countries. Previously, the developed countries, individually or collectively, were in a strong position *vis-à-vis* the politically fragmented developing countries. At the Geneva Conference, for the first time, the developing countries acted and manoeuvred together and pressed their demands as a united group.[63] The merging 'group system' became manifest in the resolutions of the developing countries which were tabled as drafts of the 'Group of 77'.[64]

The group of developed countries is classified in UNCTAD as the so-called 'B-group', while the socialist States of Eastern-Europe are called the 'D-group' countries. Although resolution 1995 (XIX) contains four lists of States, classified for election purposes, which closely correspond to the just-mentioned group divisions in UNCTAD,[65] the group system in UNCTAD is informal and has no official standing.[66]

Most major UNCTAD meetings proceed on three levels: (i) the plenary meetings of the formal body (Conference, Board or Committees), where statements are made by representatives of the different countries, and the public debate takes place; (ii) group and sub-group sessions, which are often separate and complicated conferences, trying to attain a common intra-group position with which to confront the other side and (iii) inter-group negotiations in so-called negotiation groups, or in small contact groups, where compromises are wrought. Only then is the final decision approved by the plenary organ.

In this study, the merits of the group system are not considered. Yet, several of its features are relevant here. The group system is a good method of collective negotiation, particularly for the formulation of principles and general trade policies. A meaningful exchange of views is eventually provided for by the fact that every issue is filtered through layers of deliberations. The group system effectuates interest aggregation by combining demands of more countries, harmonising these demands to reduce interstate inconsistencies, and collectively advocating these demands as a simple package. Interest aggregation by means of the group system contributes to the strength and clarity of political communication between the developing countries.[67]

Group B has acquired a considerable degree of organisation and unity, with the assistance of the OECD's work in co-ordinating the positions of the group. The 'Group of 77', which lacks an institutionalised basis like the OECD, moulds collective positions during *ad hoc* conferences convened for this purpose. The group system can be of special importance to the least developed and most powerless of the developing countries, as it may consolidate their positions *vis-à-vis* the developed countries. The group system could also be effective in prompting an alteration in foreign economic policy when a State finds itself isolated as a member of the group clearly preventing progress in a positive response to a demand raised by another group. This situation, however, has not occurred very frequently, but it did, for instance, constitute a factor in the U.S. alteration of position on preferences. The group structure of UNCTAD can amplify and focus the pressure of group demands on isolated States.[68]

Nonetheless, the group system also inhibits the capability of UNCTAD to forge concrete agreements. The inter-group negotiations usually do not begin until group positions are formed which might take considerable time, since group divisions, increasingly, do not conform to important international economic cleavages.[69] By the time negotiations reach the inter-group level, it becomes more difficult to compromise and explore possible solutions, as laboriously constructed group compromises are often considered as 'the last word'. The main difficulty then is the extreme rigidity of negotiating positions in which maximum common denominator demands of the Group of 77 face minimum common denominator concessions offered by the B-group. The distance between these positions on most issues is great and the need to maintain the group position tends to prevent compromise initiatives from individual States that have not secured the unanimous support of their own group.[70]

3.2. The legal character of UNCTAD decisions

General Assembly resolution 1995 (XIX) describes the principal functions of UNCTAD.[71] With regard to the task of the Conference to design new trade relations, these functions are:

- to formulate principles and policies on international trade and problems of economic development;
- to make proposals for putting the said principles and policies into effect and to take such other steps within its competence as may be relevant to this end, having regard to differences in economic systems and stages of development;
- to initiate action, where appropriate, in co-operation with the competent organs of the United nations for the negotiation and adoption of multilateral legal instruments in the field of trade with due regard to the adequacy of existing organs of negotiation and without duplication of their activities.[72]

In respect of the legal character attached to the different instruments which are placed at the Conference's disposal, the terms 'principles and policies', 'proposals' and 'steps', and 'multilateral legal instruments' merit closer consideration.

3.2.1. Principles and policies

The 15 'General Principles' adopted at the first session of the Conference[73] can be looked upon as an – albeit somewhat premature – elaboration of the 'principles and policies' mentioned in General Assembly Resolution 1995 (XIX). These 'General Principles' were incorporated in the Final Act of the Conference explicitly in the form of recommendations. Although the Final Act was signed by all the participant countries, the 'General Principles', being recommendations, cannot be considered as legally binding per se.

Moreover – although not decisive in relation to their legal character – only one (procedural) Principle was generally accepted without abstentions.[74] With regard to the others, one or more of the major industrialised countries voted against or abstained. In the observations, which form part of the Final Act, many developed countries stressed that they regarded the document itself to be only a record of the proceedings of the Conference and of the conclusions, recommendations and other texts adopted by it.[75]

Having decided that one of the functions of UNCTAD should be to formulate principles and policies on international trade and related problems of development, the Conference recommended explicitly that UNCTAD should continued the efforts initiated at the Conference with a view to achieving the broadest possible agreement at the earliest possible moment on a set of principles.[76] The legal character of these principles will depend for a large part on the contents and the form thereof. If they contain conventional or customary international law which is reaffirmed in the form of a declaration, they can be construed as legally binding on that ground. Others, which do not possess this binding character, may have, in spite of that, strong normative implications when they entail already widely accepted rules of State behaviour.

295

3.2.2. Proposals and steps

In connection with the implementation of the principles, the Conference may make 'proposals' and take such other 'steps' as may be relevant.[77] Notwithstanding the rather equivocal wording of this provision, the meaning thereof cannot be interpreted other than that the Conference may adopt resolutions, recommendations and declarations to effectuate the 'General Principles'. As 'proposals' these resolutions, recommendations and declarations cannot be considered as binding upon Member States.

3.2.3. Multilateral legal instruments and the notion of negotiation

The heart of UNCTAD is the process of ongoing negotiation. Between any two general UNCTAD Conferences, frequent negotiations take place on specific topics within the UNCTAD framework. The negotiations are occasionally concluded before a general Conference begins, during a Conference, or quite often, never. Considering the negotiating process, it should be stressed that the general Conference is sometimes used as a policymaking organ, while actual negotiations occur in the Board and its subsidiary bodies.[77]

Though UNCTAD's original mandate covers both the deliberative and negotiation functions, the emphasis until the beginning of the 1970s was largely on general debate of broad policy issues and on resolutions of an essentially recommendatory character. Until then, UNCTAD's negotiating role was limited. It essentially provided a venue for negotiations only in the commodity area. These negotiations and renegotiations, but also more recent conferences, were held under the auspices of UNCTAD. The organisation itself did not participate to any significant degree.

With the sixth and seventh special sessions of the UN General Assembly (respectively held in 1974 and 1975), UNCTAD entered a more operational phase of activity. The negotiating role of UNCTAD, which appeared as a result of UNCTAD IV, held in Nairobi in 1976, was a definite major development and one of the major successes of that Conference. It was decided that negotiations should be held in three areas, *i.e.* the Common Fund (as part of the integrated programme for commodities), transfer of technology and restrictive business practices. More recently the problem of multi-modal transports has been added. Although negotiations in these areas also take place *under the auspices* of UNCTAD, the organisation is directly involved, because it is the substantive organ within the UN family to deal with these questions.

Thus, since the Nairobi Conference the negotiating role of UNCTAD has been clarified. Conference resolution 90 (IV), on institutional issues, states that UNCTAD has performed the task, among others, of providing a major forum within the UN for negotiation in respect of specific agreements and commitments on international trade and related issues of international economic co-operation. The Conference invited the General Assembly to

296

reaffirm and to be guided by this consideration. The resolution in question was adopted without dissent.[78] The extensive range of negotiations on specific issues that have been undertaken within the framework of UNCTAD have led to its becoming a *de facto* major instrument of the General Assembly for negotiations in the field of trade and development, particularly with regard to negotiations on the establishment of a new international economic order.[79] This was also recognised at the fifth Conference held in Manila in 1979.[80]

Agreements reached in or under the auspices of UNCTAD, such as those in respect of several commodities,[81] the Common Fund and the Code of Conduct for Liner conferences[82] are multilateral legal instruments which become binding upon the contracting parties after having been ratified. The Generalised System of Preferences[83] was explicitly meant to be a multilateral legally non-binding instrument. The same holds true for the Set of Principles and Rules for the Control of Restrictive Business Practices,[84] whereas as regards the Code of Conduct for the Transfer of Technology[85] no decision has been taken, as of yet, on its legal character.

IV SUPERVISION IN UNCTAD

As has been made clear in the foregoing, UNCTAD is one of the major fora within the UN system for the adoption of rules in the field of trade and development. The organisation gradually has become a body which itself adopts recommendations, or under auspices of which multilateral legal instruments are developed.[86] This, in the first place, highly political function needs, in order to be exercised effectively, constant supervision. Thus, alongside supervision as regards the implementation *stricto sensu* by individual States of norm-creating instruments adopted by the organisation, UNCTAD also has an important monitoring task in respect of policy development, *i.e.* the creation and adoption of the legal instruments themselves.

By far the major part of UNCTAD's work takes place in the so-called 'gestation period' of rule making.[87] This does not mean that supervision of policy development has no legal basis. With regard to almost each and every example of rule creation in the field of trade and development the long negotiating process is based on obligations or intentions to co-operate, adopted by States in resolutions or declarations. In this respect also the normative framework provided for by the United Nations has to be taken into consideration. In the first place, because UNCTAD has been established as an organ of the General Assembly, much of UNCTAD supervision is indirectly based on resolutions adopted by the latter. Secondly, because resolution 1995 (XIX) requires UNCTAD 'to be available as a centre for harmonising the trade and related development policies of Governments and regional groupings in pursuance of Article I of the Charter'.[88] This reference to Article I of the Charter involves the responsibility, by delegation of the General Assembly, for the achievement of the purposes and objectives of

the United Nations within the scope of UNCTAD's functions and activities[89.]
Consequently, States have accepted, also in the framework of UNCTAD,
the obligation, *inter alia,* to achieve international co-operation in solving
international problems of an economic character.[90] Therefore, the UN
Charter must be considered as a strong normative background for UNCTAD
action, as well as for the co-operation of its Member States.

A clear-cut example of supervision of policy development can be found in
UNCTAD's task in the field of developments in international trade with
regard to the development decades, the New International Economic Order
and the Charter of Economic Rights and Duties of States.[91] The supervisory
functions, *i.e.* the review function, the correction function and the creative
function[92] do apply as much to supervision of policy development as to
supervision of implementation in the strict sense. As regards policy development UNCTAD reviews the positions and behaviour of States, tries to
correct or rather to stimulate States to adopt a positive attitude toward the
instrument to be created, and drafts and redrafts the particular instrument
so that the best result may be achieved.

The Conference, as the plenary organ of UNCTAD, is first of all
responsible for the supervision of policy development, although much of this
task is delegated to the Board and the Committees. These latter two also
exercise supervision on implementation *stricto sensu.*

Thus, within UNCTAD supervision, three highly interrelated levels of
surveillance can be distinguished, *i.e.* the Conference level, the Board level
and the Committee level. Since the work of the Board is a continuation of
the Conference's work, and the Committee work follows naturally from that
of the Board, no major differences can be discerned between the three
levels. Nevertheless, a certain natural allocation of tasks has taken place, in
which one might recognise a graduation from highly to less political; within
this graduation the Committees have the most specialist type of approach.

This means that many issues on which no agreement whatsoever can be
reached remain on the agenda of the Conference, while those items in
respect of which exists a minimum degree of consensus may be passed from
the 'top to the bottom' as well as the other way around. Highly complicated
issues, or items in a dead-lock position, sometimes keep going around in
circles from the Conference to the Board, from the Board to a Committee
(and even sub-committee) and from the Committee up again, via the Board,
to the Conference, etc.[93]

4.1. Supervision by the Board (resolution 19 (II))

General Assembly resolution 1995 (XIX) establishing UNCTAD, provides
in paragraph 15 that the Trade and Development Board 'shall keep under
review and take appropriate action within its competence for the implementation of the recommendations, declarations, resolutions and other decisions
of the Conference and for ensuring the continuity of its work'.

Soon after the Board started functioning, a controversy arose between the developed and the developing countries about the scope of implementation of the Final Act of the first UNCTAD, in pursuance of the above-said provisions. The less-developed countries pressed for detailed investigation of how the developed countries carried out the resolutions adopted by the first Conference. The latter, however, opposed this and argued that the Board should not be converted into an inquisitorial body to carry out a detailed country-by-country examination.[94] To them, GATT alone represented the right forum to review the implementation of trade measures; the function devolving on UNCTAD was to provide a forum for the 'identification and discussion' of relevant matters. According to the developing countries, UNCTAD had to be geared towards operational effectiveness. It was argued that proper importance should be given to the assessment of 'implementation of policies' in order to ensure progress in the adaptation of instruments and measures to the new conditions of world trade and development.[95]

A compromise in this so-called 'implementation crisis' was reached at the second session of the Trade and Development Board in September 1965. A resolution was adopted – resolution 19 (II) – in which the Secretary-General of UNCTAD was requested to prepare annually a report on trade and economic development, in order to enable the Board to fulfil its supervisory functions.[96] Though this resolution concerns, strictly speaking, supervision of the decisions of the first Conference only, it has been interpreted to cover decisions of subsequent sessions of the Conference as well. It also applies to the decisions of the Board itself which carries out the functions of the Conference when the latter is not in session.[97]

4.1.1. Modality and form of 19 (II) supervision

Resolution 19 (II) of the Board comprises general supervision, since it deals with a periodical review and assessment of the progress of the implementation of UNCTAD decisions. The Secretary-General must prepare an annual report, in which task the members of the Conference are requested to assist by providing information. One element of the modality of general supervision is its inquisitorial character, which contributes to its effectiveness in that surveillance can be exercised independent from a suspicion or accusation.[98] What the developing countries had in mind, was the creation of an effective supervisory mechanism, by establishing procedures for clearly determining government action or inaction with regard to implementation.

However, as it became clear that the developed countries would regard such an 'inquisition' as intolerable (the more effective, the less attractive), the eventual wording of the resolution was watered down. The information, upon which the UNCTAD Secretariat would be mainly dependent, *i.e.* the information from the States themselves, has to be provided by the members 'in a form which they will find appropriate'.[99]

The Board is required to make arrangements to obtain reports from and establish links with inter-governmental bodies whose activities are related to its functions. In order to avoid duplication it avails itself, whenever possible, of the relevant reports made to the Economic and Social Council and other United Nations bodies.[100] The Board must also establish close and continuous links with the regional economic commissions of the United Nations and with other appropriate regional bodies.[101] Since the regional commissions are subsidiary organs of ECOSOC, it might appear rather strange that the Board should establish direct links with them. The explanation is that, although the developing countries expressed at the Geneva Conference considerable disappointment with ECOSOC, they have always been satisfied with the performance of its commissions in their respective regions. In the opinion of the developing countries, each regional commission was to become a sort of regional arm of UNCTAD, responsible for the implementation, within its area, of the decisions of UNCTAD.[102] To effectuate co-operation of the inter-governmental bodies, the regional economic commissions and the specialised agencies of the United Nations, they were invited by resolution 19 (II) to supply the Secretary-General of UNCTAD with information relevant to the preparation of the annual Secretariat report.[103]

Given the procedure of resolution 19 (II), the task of data-processing must be fulfilled by the Secretary-General of UNCTAD. On the basis of the report prepared, during this technical phase, by the Secretariat, the Trade and Development Board has to discharge its function of keeping under review and taking appropriate action for the implementation of the recommendations of the Conference. Since surveillance is exercised, in the last resort, by a politically dependent organ[104] it is evident that UNCTAD supervision based on Board resolution 19 (II) is non-judicial in form. Also of interest in this context is the fact that there are no pre-fixed rules of procedure and that the assessment by the Board – apart from any social constraint, or the normative effect resolutions may have – is of a non-binding character.

4.1.2. Instruments of 19 (II) supervision

As will be remembered, the instruments of supervision are the ways and means used to effectuate the three main functions of international supervision, *i.e.* the review function, the correction function and the creative function. In respect of the review function no effective instrument is provided for in resolution 19 (II). States are requested to provide information, but in a form which they will find appropriate. Thus, the UNCTAD Secretariat depends mainly on the willingness of governments to supply information. According to the developed countries, reporting is not an obligation but an enlightened practice and governments individually have the latitude to decide on the nature, form and definition of information that they will offer.[105] Directly in relation to resolution 19 (II) the Secretary-General used to send out questionnaires to all governments in order to prepare an annual implementation report. As will be shown hereafter the average response was so minimal that the practice of these implementation reports was not continued.[106]

The correction function of UNCTAD supervision is instrumentalised in the debate held by the Trade and Development Board. The political discussion following upon the technical phase of fact-finding by the Secretary-General and his staff, may function as the censor of State behaviour. Yet, traditionally the implementation debate by the Board is inconclusive – as we shall see in more detail hereafter – in the sense that hardly any agreed conclusion is adopted.[107] The political constraint emanating from the discussion held by the Board, can be increased if a standpoint regarding a given subject is prepared by one or more of the groups in UNCTAD, in particular if a country finds itself isolated as the member of the group clearly preventing progress in a positive response to a demand raised by an opposing group, or in the implementation of decisions already agreed upon. Moreover, policy is also made when representatives of a State must find something to say at a publicised meeting on a prearranged subject.[108] As regards policy development the correction function of UNCTAD supervision is even more subtly exercised than in the case of supervision of implementation *stricto sensu*. Stimulating or convincing a State, or group of States, to adopt a favourable approach toward the creation of a certain instrument requires a different attitude from the supervisory organ than pressing a State to live up to what it has agreed upon.

The instrument of the creative function may be also recognised in the political discussion. As a corollary of keeping under review the decisions of the Conference, the Board equally may take *appropriate* action for the implementation of such decisions.[109] Since the Board, as will be remembered, carries out the functions of the Conference when the latter is not in session,[110] taking 'appropriate action' can mean that it may adopt resolutions, recommendations, etc.[111] and that it may initiate action for the negotiation and adoption of multilateral legal instruments.[112] By discerning as supervisory organ the causes of and the reasons for deviation and the difficulties met by a particular State fulfilling obligations laid down in a given legal instrument, the Board may modify or interpret more liberally the rules concerned. In respect of policy development it may happen that an issue, as to which enough agreement exists, is passed on to the Committee or sub-committee level for further elaborations or drafting. If an item is, politically speaking, in a dead-lock position so that no development can be effectuated, it is often handed over to the Conference to be decided upon.

4.2. Developments in international trade

As has been expounded at some length, UNCTAD gradually acquired, alongside its primary responsibility in the field of commodities, manufacturers and financing, new assignments.[113] An important item which appeared regularly on the agenda of the Conference and the Board since the beginning of the 1970s concerned the restructuring of the international economy. In the framework of, for instance, the Second United Nations Development

Decade and the negotiations on the New International Economic Order, the review of developments in international trade became increasingly important.

4.2.1. UNCTAD's supervisory role in the Second United Nations Development Decade

According to General Assembly resolution 2626 (XXV), establishing the International Development Strategy for the Second United Nations Development Decade, an overall appraisal of the progress in implementing the Strategy must be made by the General Assembly, through the Economic and Social Council (ECOSOC).[114] At the Twenty-fifth Session of the General Assembly the role of ECOSOC, as co-ordinating and supervisory body, was still highly disputed. At the outset, most developing countries preferred UNCTAD, as the organisation pre-eminently fitted to review the implementation of the Strategy. Nonetheless, the Council successfully reaffirmed its central place, mainly as a result of a substantial enlargement, in 1973, of its membership.[115] Already in 1971 ECOSOC instituted the Committee on Review and Appraisal, which had to prepare the discussions in the Council, on the basis of the expert advice of the Committee for Development Planning (CDP).

A difficulty – which was mainly a problem of co-ordination – was that the overall appraisal had also to be based (apart from the comments and recommendations of the CDP) on evaluation at the national and regional level[116] and on the review exercised by UNCTAD, UNIDO and the specialised agencies of the United Nations.[117] In particular, regarding UNCTAD's role in this respect, many questions remained. For instance, a majority of developed countries feared that the UNCTAD Secretariat would use its sectoral contribution, which it had to make to the overall review and appraisal, to exceed its competence, and to bypass ECOSOC in reviewing trade and development problems.[118]

4.2.1.1. Adaptation of procedures (Conference resolution 79 (III))

Conference resolution 79 (III) – adopted at the third UNCTAD Conference, held in Santiago in 1972 – provides for a mechanism necessary for the review and appraisal of the objectives and measures on the International Development Strategy, falling within the competence of UNCTAD,[119] in the discharge of its responsibility in the context of the Strategy.[120] To that end the Board meets in a special session once every two years, to formulate recommendations on the basis of a report to be prepared by the Secretary-General of UNCTAD. This session should be held at a time suitable to the overall review and appraisal procedure envisaged in General Assembly resolution 2801 (XXVI) of December 14, 1971. Also on the basis of this latter Assembly resolution,[121] the Trade and Development Board was invited by the Conference[122] to adapt the review procedures already established, within UNCTAD, to the preparatory work for the overall review and appraisal[123] so as to avoid unnecessary duplication in that field. Hence, a

302

certain integration was to take place between UNCTAD's own procedures for reviewing and assessing implementation of recommendations, resolutions and other decisions, on the basis of Conference resolution 19 (II)[124] and UNCTAD's review in the field of the Strategy for the Second Development Decade.

During its thirteenth session, in 1973, the Trade and Development Board decided in accordance with the time schedule envisaged in Conference resolution 79 (III), to undertake the second review[125] of the International Development Strategy for the Second UN Development Decade at a special session in April – May 1975.[126] This special session, the sixth of the Board to which we return later, was meant to be at the same time the so-called mid-term review and appraisal of the Strategy.

4.2.2. UNCTAD's role in the NIEO resolutions

Meanwhile, the General Assembly adopted, in May 1974, the Declaration and Programme of Action on the Establishment of a New International Economic Order (NIEO).[127] According to section IX, paragraph 8, of the Programme of Action, the implementation of the Programme should be taken into account at the time of the mid-term review and appraisal of the International Development Strategy. Considering also paragraph 7 of the same section, which states that the Programme of Action complements and strengthens the goals and objectives embodied in the Strategy, it becomes clear that the review procedures of both the Strategy and the Programme were meant to coincide.

4.2.2.1. Further integration (Board resolution 122 (XIV))

The Programme of Action stressed that the General Assembly shall conduct an overall review of the implementation of the Programme as a priority item.[128] ECOSOC must define the policy framework and co-ordinate the activities of all organisations, institutions and subsidiary bodies within the UN system which shall be entrusted with the task of implementing the Programme of Action. All organisations concerned are requested to submit progress reports to ECOSOC on implementation.[129] ECOSOC requested in a resolution all organisations, institutions, subsidiary bodies and conferences of the UN system to take immediate measures to implement the provisions of the Declaration and the Programme of Action within their respective fields of competence and to make them fully conducive to the accomplishment of this task.[130] On the basis of these ECOSOC provisions the Trade and Development Board of UNCTAD requested, in its resolution 122 (XIV), the Secretary-General of the Conference to include in his report on the mid-term review and appraisal of the Strategy appropriate information and suggestions in order to enable the Board to undertake a comprehensive review, in the fields of competence of UNCTAD, of the implementation of the Declaration and the Programme of Action.[131] As a result, at the sixth special session of the Trade and Development Board, held in March 1975, the International Development Strategy was considered in the light of the Declaration and the Programme of Action on the Establishment of a New International Economic Order.[132]

4.2.3. The Charter of Economic Rights and Duties of States and General Assembly resolution 3362 (S–VII)

However, all this did not mean that UNCTAD had completed its task in the field of supervising developments in international trade. Some further action, undertaken by the General Assembly, required co-operation by UNCTAD, in respect of surveillance. In December 1974 the General Assembly adopted the Charter of Economic Rights and Duties of States.[133] Article 34 requires that an item on the Charter shall be included in the agenda of the General Assembly at its thirtieth session (1975) and thereafter on the agenda of every fifth session. In order to give effect to this provision the General Assembly adopted, a year later, a resolution on the implementation of the Charter.[134] This resolution requests UNCTAD, among other organisations, to study the progress achieved in the implementation of the Charter and to report to the General Assembly through the Economic and Social Council.[135]

In the same year, 1975, the General Assembly adopted, during its seventh special session, resolution 3362 (S–VII) on Development and International Economic Co-operation. As this resolution did not provide for any specific review procedure, another resolution was adopted by the General Assembly in December 1975, regarding the implementation of the decisions adopted at its seventh special session. In particular all organisations, institutions and subsidiary organs of the UN system were requested, herein, to assign the highest priority to the implementation of the measures set out in resolution 3362 (S–VII) and to submit progress reports to the Assembly, through the Economic and Social Council, within their respective fields of competence.[136]

4.2.3.1. Biannual review and appraisal (Board decision 146 (XVI))

On the baasis of the above-mentioned resolutions of the General Assembly, UNCTAD was obliged to integrate these new supervisory tasks with the already existing review procedures of Conference resolution 79 (III)[137] and Board resolution 122 (XIV).[138] Hence, during its fourth session held in Nairobi (1976) the Conference requested the Trade and Development Board to establish an appropriate review mechanism.[139] This Conference resolution resulted in a decision of the Board, 146 (XVI), in which the mechanisms for carrying out the implementation and review functions relating to General Assembly resolutions 2626 (XXV), 3202 (S–VI), 3281 (XXIX) and 3362 (S–VII) were combined. It was decided that at the special sessions of the Board foreseen in Conference resolution 79 (III) – which took place every two years for the review and appraisal of the implementation of the International Development Strategy for the Second UN Development Decade – the progress achieved should be reviewed. At the same time further improvement of the role of UNCTAD in the implementation of the

Programme of Action on the Establishment of a New International Economic Order, the Charter of Economic Rights and Duties of States and the General Assembly resolution on Development and International Economic Co-operation should be assessed.[140]

4.2.4. Towards the Third United Nations Development Decade

As a consequence of the above-mentioned resolutions and decisions, the UNCTAD Board discussed the different matters under consideration in a number of special and regular sessions.[141] These discussions were, because of the broad nature of the subject matters, necessarily of a highly general character. Extensive deliberations – during which the Board was not able to reach agreement on the many and complex issues involved – could not result in much more than meagre conclusions noting the shortfalls in the implementation of the Strategy for the Second UN Development Decade and other documents. Consequently one cannot speak of any form of strategic implementation debates; as the summary records show, discussions were characterised by long political statements, giving ample room to hobby-horse riding by the different country groups and individual States. Nevertheless, the documentation prepared by the UNCTAD Secretariat for these sessions of the Board, was always highly appreciated because of its thorough and specified character. Especially, UNCTAD Secretariat reports have been considered a valuable contribution to the debates of the General Assembly and the Economic and Social Council.[142]

Since 1977, the formulation of the Strategy for the Third UN Development Decade has been a regular issue in the discussions of the Board. In 1980, a High-Level Intergovernmental Group on the contribution of UNCTAD to the decade was convened, while in the same year a special session of the Board was dedicated to UNCTAD's contribution.[143] The High-Level Intergovernmental Group was unable to enter into meaningful negotiations and was therefore not in a position to submit to the Board a document embodying a consensus. Neither was the Board able to come to agreement. Consequently, it was decided to transmit only the reports of the different sessions of the Group and the Board to the General Assembly.[144] Thus, also UNCTAD – in its own field of reviewing developments in international trade – entered a new decade in an atmosphere of general disarray.

4.3. Committee supervision

In conformity with General Assembly resolution 1995 (XIX) the Board has established a number of subsidiary organs which it deemed necessary to the effective discharge of its functions.[145] At present there exist six so-called Main Committees[146] and one Special Committee.[147] Under the terms of reference, as adopted by the Board,[148] the Committees exercise within their specific competence the basic functions that devolve upon the Conference and the Board. The Committees are thus entrusted with the task of giving effect to decisions of the Conference and the Board, ensuring the continuity of work. The membership of all the Main Committees of the Board was made open-ended. Any state member of UNCTAD can join a Committee by notifying its intention to the Secretary-General of UNCTAD.[149]

As for the specific supervisory functions of the Committees, they are asked to assist the Board in its task of keeping under review and taking appropriate action, within the Board's competence, on the recommendations, resolutions and other decisions of the Conference and the Board in their respective fields of interest.[150] As a general basis for supervision in UNCTAD, Board resolution 19 (II)[151] also plays an essential role in respect of Committee supervision. This resolution contains, among other provisions, the request to the Secretary-General of UNCTAD to supply Committees with such information and analysis as the Board may deem necessary for them to assist in its supervisory task.[152] All Committees have periodic review sessions in which a debate takes place on the basis of the documentation provided by the Secretariat of UNCTAD.[153] Thus, a technical phase of factfinding by the Secretariat precedes the political phase of the implementation debate. As will be shown hereafter, the most crucial phase of the gathering of information by the Secretariat often is also the most troublesome. The review function of Committee supervision cannot be exercised, ultimately, on a basis other than the highly loose provision in resolution 19 (II) which requests States to provide information in a form which they themselves will find appropriate.[154] As has been submitted above, this request does not supply the UNCTAD Secretariat with an effective instrument to collect the necessary information.[155]

In the following pages we will treat in greater detail the supervisory functions exercised by the Committee on Commodities; the Committee on Manufactures (especially with regard to UNCTAD's supervisory function as provided for in the Set of Principles and Rules for the Control of Restrictive Business Practices); the Committee on Shipping (also as a possible reviewing body for the Code of Conduct for Liner Conferences); the Special Committee on Preferences reviewing the implementation of the Generalised System of Preferences; and the Committee on Transfer of Technology (which has been proposed to play a role in the follow-up mechanism provided for in the draft Code of Conduct on the Transfer of Technology).

4.3.1. Commodities

The Geneva Conference gave general approval to the establishment of a committee on commodity arrangements and policies within the framework of the continuing institutional machinery of UNCTAD. The Conference, also generally, formulated terms of reference for the new committee and requested that they be given prompt and favourable consideration.[156] Pursuant to these considerations, the Trade and Development Board established in 1965 the Committee on Commodities.[157]

306

The Committee on Commodities exercises functions to promote general and integrated policies in the commodity field. It has the task of improving the terms of trade of developing countries and negotiating international commodity arrangements to stabilise the prices of primary products. The Committee is also requested to consider and recommend general measures to be taken parallel with international commodity arrangements regarding specific commodities or groups of commodities.[158]

As regards supervision, the Committee on Commodities studies and makes recommendations with a view to taking appropriate action within its competence for the implementation of the recommendations made by the Conference, the Board or the Committee itself.[159] As to the correction function of supervision, it is interesting to note that the Committee may undertake and publish studies and statistical reports on trade in commodities, and prepare reviews of the market situation of various primary commodities.[160] A major purpose of these activities, according to another paragraph of the terms of reference, is to enable the Committee to bring to the attention of the Board and through appropriate channels to the governments participating in the Conference, its views and recommendations as to the need for governmental or intergovernmental action and to deal with problems or emerging problems which its studies may disclose.[161] The Committee on Commodities should meet twice between Conferences and submits periodic reports to the Board on its work.[162]

To assist in its work, the Committee established during its first session a Permanent Sub-Committee on Commodities which, with the assistance of the Secretary-General of the Conference, carries out in intersessional periods the functions which the Committee on Commodities may assign to it.[163] The Permanent Sub-Committee met only once, in 1966. According to Secretariat personnel it was an absolutely disastrous meeting, mainly because the Sub-Committee was supposed to exercise supervision of implementation *stricto sensu*. Since that supervision was country orientated, every word of criticism or appraisal was weighted thoroughly. Word by word and line by line was spelled out, without having operational significance. No country was bound by the eventual result.[164]

In accordance with the recommendations of the Geneva Conference the Committee on Commodities also set up a Permanent Group on Synthetics and Substitutes.[165] This group deals with problems arising from competition between natural products and synthetic substitutes and other substitute products. It recommends governmental and inter-governmental measures.[166] The Group was regularly convened until 1974. It has not met since then, as the problems of competition between natural products and synthetics and substitutes have been dealt with in preparatory meetings and negotiations on individual commodities as a result of the adoption of the Integrated Programme for Commodities.

4.3.1.1. The Integrated Programme for Commodities

The restructuring of international trade in commodities was the major issue at UNCTAD IV, held in Nairobi (1976). The main result of that session of the Conference was the adoption of a comprehensive and far-reaching decision which endorsed the concept of an Integrated Programme for Commodities (IPC).[167] The central theme of the IPC was the need to treat the problems of individual commodities within a common framework of principles and mechanisms. The Programme consists in establishing producer-consumer schemes for ten 'core' commodities and eight 'other' primary products of importance to the developing countries in international trade, linked together by a common institution for the financing, *inter alia*, of stocking operations.[168]

In conformity with Conference resolution 93 (IV) on the IPC, the Board established, in 1976, an *ad hoc* Inter-Governmental Committee on the Integrated Programme for Commodities.[169] Its task is to co-ordinate the preparatory work and the negotiations, to deal with major policy issues that may arise, including commodity coverage and to co-ordinate the implementation of the measures under the IPC.[170] It thus should exercise supervision of policy development as well as of implementation in the strict sense.

Because of the adoption of the IPC and the creation by the Conference of the *ad hoc* Inter-Governmental Committee, there was no need for the Committee on Commodities to meet in the foreseeable future. The reasoning behind this was that the *ad hoc* Inter-Governmental Committee had to exercise the supervisory functions over the IPC, as an overview committee. It was felt by the Conference that there would be overlapping responsibilities, if both committees were to meet in parallel. Thus, since 1975, the Committee on Commodities has not been convened in spite of a resolution adopted at UNCTAD III, that recommends that the main Committees should meet twice between two sessions of the Conference.[171]

The *ad hoc* Committee has met periodically to review the progress under the Integrated Programme and has adopted a number of decisions dealing with major policy issues which were aimed at achieving better progress.[172] Comprehensive reports on progress made under the IPC were presented to the Trade and Development Board at its eighteenth session.[173]

During the debate at the eighteenth session of the Board, the Chairman of the *ad hoc* Inter-Governmental Committee stated that the question of how far the Committee should be involved in the substantive work on each commodity had not been resolved. Indeed, two extreme views had emerged in respect of the nature and scope of the Committee's functions. There were, on the one hand, those who took the position that the Committee's functions should be limited to the preparation and review of schedules of meetings and that it should not get involved in the substantive work on products for which appropriate preparatory bodies existed. On the other hand, there were those who believed that the Committee had a negotiating function. The main task performed by the Committee had been to facilitate and indeed to give impetus to the work under resolution 93 (IV).[174]

Since the *ad hoc* Inter-Governmental Committee was meant to co-ordinate the individual commodity negotiations as well as the Common Fund negotiations, the developing countries hoped that the Committee should monitor what happened especially in the individual commodity negotiations. The

308

market-orientated developed countries, however, have never accepted that any negotiations as regards producer-consumer problems would take place anywhere else than within the scope of the individual commodity negotiations. In their view, producers and consumers should negotiate commodity by commodity, without any interference by third parties. One of the results of this attitude is that the *ad hoc* Inter-Governmental Committee, thus far, has been playing only a marginal role.

Finally, the Trade and Development Board adopted a resolution which emphasised that the *ad hoc* Inter-Governmental Committee, in conformity with its mandate, must play a positive and active role in monitoring and assisting governments to evaluate the preparatory work and negotiations. Particularly so in making recommendations on major policy issues, so as to facilitate the implementation of the IPC.[175]

4.3.1.2. Developmental aspects and overall policy guidance

The suggestion has been put forward that international action with regard to certain developmental aspects of commodity policy and the stabilisation of export earnings, which in some cases might involve work of a somewhat longer duration than the negotiations on individual commodities, might be considered within the Committee on Commodities. However, it was recalled, these aspects of commodity policy also come within the purview of Conference resolution 93 (IV) on the IPC and any future work thereon would be closely related to the negotiations on individual commodities.[176] This raised the question of the relationship between the Committee on Commodities and the *ad hoc* Inter-Governmental Committee.

At the fifth Conference of UNCTAD, held in Manila (1979), a resolution was adopted, which entrusted the Committee on Commodities with the task of dealing with the above said questions. The Committee was requested to give particular attention to processing and product development, marketing and distribution, and research and development, market promotion and horizontal diversification and to take into account the on-going work on individual commodities with a view to providing over-all policy guidance as necessary.[177] As regards these developmental aspects of commodity policies, the Secretariat was asked to submit systematic and thorough studies to the Committee on Commodities.[178]

In accordance with decision 200 (XIX) of the Board, the *ad hoc* Inter-Governmental Committee for the IPC was continued until the end of 1980. Responsibility for further work on the IPC beyond that date was entrusted to the Committee on Commodities. The last session of the *ad hoc* Committee and the first session, since 1975, of the Committee on Commodities were jointly held in September 1980.[179] To be able to discharge effectively the functions envisaged in Conference resolution 93 (IV) on the IPC, the Committee on Commodities will have to play an active role in giving impetus to negotiations on individual commodities. As in the case of the *ad hoc* Committee, this will involve the consideration of the main difficulties encountered in the preparatory meetings and negotiations on individual commodities with a view to providing guidelines and recommendations for overcoming these difficulties. The Committee on Commodities will also have to supervise the work on individual commodities outside the framework of the IPC. The transition from what was essentially a deliberative role in the past to an increasingly active negotiating role in the future will call for flexibility in its methods of work.[180]

4.3.1.3. Strengthening the activities of UNCTAD in the field of commodity supervision

Until 1974 not much attention had been paid, by the UNCTAD Secretariat or the Committee on Commodities, to the collection of information in the field of commodities. As is suggested by the discussions held in the annual sessions of the Committee on Commodities, this question did not seem to be too problematic.[181] The systematic collection of basic statistical data on commodities (as distinct from the interpretation and analysis of such data) was not a major function of the UNCTAD Secretariat. Within the United Nations system, this activity was carried out by the United Nations Statistical Office, FAO, IMF and GATT. Other inter-governmental bodies such as OECD, the Commonwealth Secretariat and the various specialised commodity bodies, as well as a number of private and governmental research and information agencies, also collected information. In order to avoid duplication of work the UNCTAD Secretariat generally relied on basic commodity statistics collected and published by the bodies mentioned, although the statistics often became available too late for up-to-date monitoring of developments.[182]

Nevertheless, there were two exceptions to the general rule that UNCTAD was a user rather than a collector of statistics. Firstly, to enable it to follow closely the evolution of the market situation for principal primary commodities, the UNCTAD Secretariat had to collect price information, as far as possible from original sources,[183] or from the commercial press and periodicals which published market quotations promptly. Since this information was needed in any case for other work of the UNCTAD Secretariat, and since it could be disseminated at little extra costs, the Secretariat had for some years been making it available to other international organisations and to interested government departments through its Monthly Commodity Price Bulletin.[184] The second exception is related to the quarterly bulletin Tungsten Statistics, which was issued by the Secretariat for the Committee on Tungsten (of the Committee on Commodities).[185] In publishing this bulletin, containing basic statistics of production, consumption, trade, stocks and prices collected directly from governments, the Secretariat was carrying out a necessary task which no other organisation had undertaken.[186]

In 1974, the UNCTAD Secretariat issued a report on the 'Strengthening of the activities of UNCTAD in the context of the Programme of Action on the Establishment of a New International Economic Order, adopted by the General Assembly'.[187] The report was restricted to activities in connection with aspects of the development of trade in raw materials. It concentrated

310

on those activities which were related to the monitoring of developments and the collection of statistical and other information, the analysis and interpretation of such information and its dissemination. The report was to be discussed at the fourteenth session of the Trade and Development Board (1974–1975).

The Secretariat suggested a strengthening of activities in the fields of: (i) terms of trade of developing countries, (ii) pricing policy, (iii) improvement of existing marketing and distribution arrangements, (iv) improvement of the competitive position of natural vis-à-vis synthetic materials, and (v) expansion of export earnings of developing countries dependent on commodity trade. Implementation of the proposals, subsequently made by the Secretariat for strengthening UNCTAD's monitoring and analytical activities would be possible only with a considerable improvement in the quantity, quality and timeliness of the statistical data and market information reaching the Secretariat. It was also necessary to strengthen the manner or form in which that information was made available to governments.

The sources used thus far were various secondary ones, governmental and private, which gave a rather up-to-date statistical picture of events.[188] However, these statistics often conflicted with each other and with data published by governments. The data from these secondary sources, moreover, inevitably included a large number of estimates arrived at by procedures which were not made clear and the reliability of which therefore could not be assessed. In any case the information was not sufficiently up-to-date, or sufficiently detailed, for analytical and monitoring purposes.[189]

According to the Secretariat, the problem could be solved if the UNCTAD Secretariat obtained the necessary statistical information in the same way as it already did for Tungsten, i.e. by means of a questionnaire to governments. This would permit the collection of information which is not only more up-to-date, but also better standardised and hence more comparable. Where estimates had to be made, moreover, the Secretariat could ensure that they were based on consistent assumptions and procedures. Alternatively, such information might be collected centrally, provided the specific requirements of UNCTAD were met.[190]

A further factor, stated by the Secretariat, which hampered following developments in world commodity trade was the delay with which detailed data on the quantities and values of the imports and exports of individual commodities of individual countries, especially developing countries, became available. The Secretariat suggested that, by agreement between the United Nations Statistical Office and the UNCTAD Secretariat, governments could be asked to complete and to send simultaneously to both bodies, with special urgency, a questionnaire seeking a very limited amount of up-to-date trade information, namely quantities and values of imports and exports of the principal primary commodities imported and exported by each country.[191]

During the discussion held at the fourteenth session of the Board, the developing countries as well as the developed market economy countries endorsed the report of the Secretary-General. Yet, according to representatives of some developed countries, the matter should be considered further by the Committee on Commodities at the eighth session (to be held in 1975), in the light of more complete documentation.[192] To that end, a resolution was adopted by the Board in which furthermore the Secretary-General of UNCTAD was requested to arrange for the regular distribution of the UNCTAD Monthly Commodity Price Bulletin. Governments were requested to co-operate with the Secretariat in the collection and the provision of statistical and other information and in the monitoring of developments in the field of commodities and competing synthetic substitutes.[193]

The Commodity Price Bulletin was being distributed, by that time, regularly to all governments of State members of UNCTAD. On the question, however, of the improvement of the quantity, quality and timeliness of statistical data reaching the UNCTAD Secretariat, and of how UNCTAD's work in surveying world commodity developments might be strengthened, only exchanges of views had taken place with respectively the United Nations Statistical Office and the Secretariat of FAO.[194] It might be interesting to note, that neither in the report of the Secretariat, nor in the discussion held in the Committee on Commodities, was mention made of any co-operation by governments in collecting information. Reference was only made to agencies within the United Nations system and private sources.[195]

At present the general feeling among the Secretariat members of the commodity division is that UNCTAD first of all should try to stimulate policy development in the field of commodities.[196] Although not sufficiently provided for, the Secretariat does rely on published sources as regards individual commodities.[197] UNCTAD analysis should be much more of a 'cross commodity' approach in the sense that the over-all effect of the commodity sector on developing countries' economies (price levels, balance of payments, etc.) is taken into consideration. Thus, supervision should be not so much a question of collecting information in order to serve or facilitate supervision *stricto sensu*, but more a catalistic process based on already collected data which focuses on policy aspects. The review of progress in negotiations, *i.e.* policy development, in the field of the IPC and the Common Fund are primary responsibilities of UNCTAD.

If, at all, UNCTAD does overcome from time to time the problems of an autonomous task of data collection in the field of commodities, it will encounter even more difficulties in the future. As there is a tendency in UNCTAD to broach the institutional and structural aspects of commodity trade and especially the problems of processing, marketing and distribution,[198] the Secretariat will meet with a wall of reluctance from the side of governments (particularly those from developed market economy countries) to provide information thereon. Who owns what, who sells to whom, who undertakes the transportation, etc., are all aspects of commodity trade which mostly belong in the realm of private enterprise, in which many governments pretend to have no say or competence as to the provision of information.[199]

4.3.2. Manufactures

Pursuant to General Assembly resolution 1995 (XIX) and the Final Act of the Geneva Conference, a Committee on Manufactures was established by the Board in 1965.[200] One of the main functions of this Committee is to assist the Board in its task of keeping under review and taking appropriate action within its competence for the implementation of the decisions of the Conference, as they bear on the exports of manufactured and semi-manufactured articles from developing countries.[201] Such action by the Board may include, in particular, bringing to the attention of governments recommendations of the Conference in respect of a variety of subjects in the field of trade in manufactures and semi-manufactures. The Committee may undertake studies and carry out other functions within the competence of the Board as it may consider necessary to promote exports from developing countries.[202] The Committee may also make recommendations to the Board on matters within its terms of reference; such recommendations may include proposals for the preparation of draft agreements, or other measures to promote understanding and co-operation, concerning trade in manufactures and semi-manufactures.[203] The Committee shall report periodically to the Board on its work.[204]

In order to facilitate the supervisory functions of the Committee on Manufactures, the Secretariat prepares an annual review of recent trends and developments in trade in manufactures and semi-manufactures. Alongside special tabulations prepared by the UNCTAD Secretariat, mostly based upon national export and import statistics, data for the annual review are derived from collections such as the UN Monthly Bulletin of Statistics, the UN Statistical Yearbook, the UN Commodity Trade Statistics (Statistical Papers), the UN Yearbook of Industrial Statistics and many other published sources.

As is shown by the discussions held in the Committee on Manufactures, the Secretariat reviews are considered by all groups of countries as fairly correct. Yet, the sensitivity with regard to the exactness of data is high. Thus, especially, developed market-economy countries note every year certain errors and omissions in the Secretariat's inventory for inclusion in a further corrigendum. Although the collection of information in the field of manufactures and semi-manufactures does not seem to be problematic, it has been regretted during more recent Committee sessions, that the trade statistics of a number of countries are not more complete and detailed. This meant, *inter alia*, that it was not possible to compare the market access for the goods of developing countries imported into the socialist countries of Eastern Europe with those imported into the developed market-economy countries.[205]

The Committee on manufactures focuses regularly on such matters as the liberalisation of non-tariff barriers, the participation of the developing countries in the multilateral trade negotiations (held under the auspices of GATT), international trade in textiles, and adjustment assistance measures.

Through the years, special attention has been paid to the problem of restrictive business practices.

Restrictive business practices – such as price-fixing arrangements, resale price-maintenance, exclusive dealing, tied sales and also acquisitions, mergers and takeovers of enterprises holding dominant positions of market power – play a determinant role in international trade and in particular in exports to and from developing countries. Since 1968, governments have been searching for an appropriate instrument at international level to eliminate or effectively control these practices.[206]

4.3.2.1. Principles and rules for the control of restrictive business practices

The question of restrictive business practices (RBP's) has figured as an important item of discussion at four of the five Conference sessions of UNCTAD. At UNCTAD II, in 1968, a tentative start was made on work in this area.[207] The Conference called for a study of RBP's adopted by private enterprises of developed countries, with special reference to the effects of such practices on the export interests of the developing countries. This was followed, in 1970, by the call in the International Development Strategy for the Second United Nations Development Decade for the identification of RBP's particularly affecting the trade and development of developing countries.[208]

UNCTAD III, in 1972, set the direction for the present work on RBP's, when it recommended that attention should be paid to the possibility of drawing up guide-lines for the consideration by governments of developed and developing countries regarding RBP's. In contrast to the resolution at UNCTAD II, which was voted, this was an unanimous decision of the Conference. Subsequently, the Committee on Manufacturers decided, following the work of the First *ad hoc* Group of Experts (which consisted of experts acting in their individual capacity), to institute an inter-governmental group of experts.[209] This group should examine *inter alia* the possibility of formulating multi-laterally acceptable principles on RBP's which would aim at remedying those practices adversely affecting the trade and development of developing countries. UNCTAD IV (1976) having before it the work of the two expert groups, accordingly agreed that negotiations should be held with the objective of formulating a set of multilaterally agreed equitable principles and rules for the control of such RBP's. To facilitate the achievement of this and other agreed action, the Conference established the Third *ad hoc* Group of Experts on RBP's and called upon it to prepare detailed proposals and recommendations.

It was because of the progress made by this Expert Group in the formulation of the set of principles and rules that the Board, in September 1978, recommended to the General Assembly that a UN Conference on RBP's be convened to negotiate such a set of principles and rules. In turn, the General Assembly decided to convene the Conference and authorised UNCTAD V to establish the dates for the Conference and to take other appropriate actions. UNCTAD V fulfilled this mandate in setting the dates of 19 November to 7 December 1979 for the Conference and in providing for prior consultations in September on procedural and related matters.[210]

4.3.2.2. UNCTAD supervision on RBP's

At the first session of the UN Conference on RBP's a proposal of the chairman of the negotiating group which dealt essentially with institutional matters, as distinct from the body of principles and rules, was adopted by the negotiating group and accordingly transmitted to the president of the Conference. The text of this proposal was – by and large – an 'agreed text' (with footnotes dealing with reservations on particular words or concepts).[211] During the second session of the Conference, held in the Spring of 1980, the final text was unanimously adopted.[212]

Under section F, called 'International measures', three paragraphs concern the supervisory role of UNCTAD. Paragraph 2 stipulates that States and regional groupings communicate annually to UNCTAD information on steps taken by them to meet their commitment to the set of principles and rules. Also, information should be provided on the adoption, development and application of legislation, regulations and policies concerning RBP's.

Alongside this review function of supervision which, as a matter of fact, does not provide UNCTAD with an effective instrument to collect information other than that it implies requests to member States, some form of the correction function is instrumentalised in paragraph 3. The latter asks UNCTAD for a continued annual publication of a report on developments in RBP's legislation and on RBP's affecting international trade. As formulated in that paragraph, the report should be based upon publicly available information and as far as possible other information, particularly on the basis of requests addressed to all Member States or provided at their own initiative and, where appropriate, to the UN Centre on Transnational Corporations and other competent international organisations.

Paragraph 4, on consultations, involves certain innovatory ideas concerning the supervisory role of UNCTAD in a complaint type of procedure. The text says that where a State, particularly a developing country, believes that a consultation with another State or States is appropriate in regard to an issue concerning control of RBP's, it may request a consultation with those States with a view to finding a mutually acceptable solution. When such a consultation is to be held, the States involved may request the Secretary-General of UNCTAD to provide mutually agreed conference facilities. Although a certain role is envisaged for UNCTAD, the notion of 'conference facilities' leaves the question open whether UNCTAD should provide the physical facilities only, or something more substantial.

Under sub-paragraph (d) it is said that where a satisfactory conclusion is reached as a result of consultations, and if states involved so agree, a joint report on the matter should be prepared by those States. If they so wish this may be done with the assistance of the UNCTAD Secretariat. The report should be made available to UNCTAD for inclusion in its annual report on RBP's.

Paragraphs 5 and 6 deal with UNCTAD assistance to the developing countries in devising appropriate legislation and, in more general terms, in coping with the problems related to RBP's. In providing technical assistance (experts, seminars, courses, a handbook on RBP's etc.) UNCTAD could possibly also enhance the effectiveness of the review function of its supervision on RBP's as regards the provision of information by the developing countries on the adoption, development and application of legislation, regulations and policies.[213]

Section G, on the international institutional machinery, provides for the terms of reference of an Inter-governmental Group of Experts on Restrictive Business Practices.[214] According to its different functions this Group of Experts is clearly envisaged to be *the* supervisory body, within UNCTAD, in the field of RBP's. One of its functions will be to make appropriate reports and recommendations to States on matters within its competence.[215] At the first Conference, the Group of 77 – striving after effective supervision *stricto sensu* – proposed a specification or clarification of this function by adding to the terms of reference an examination and review of the progress made by States to meet their commitment to the set of principles and rules and to make recommendations thereon to States with a view to ensuring its effective application and implementation.[216] Since this form of strict supervision of implementation was not acceptable to Group B, a watered-down version was added, in the final text, to the terms of reference. Paragraph 2 (a) under (vi) reads, vaguely worded, as follows: 'To make appropriate reports and recommendations to States on matters within its competence, including the applications and implementation of the Set of Multilaterally Agreed Equitable Principles and Rules.' Reports on the work, of the Inter-governmental Group, shall be submitted (to the Board?) at least once a year.[217]

To exclude any doubt as regards the limitations of the functions of the Inter-governmental Group, it is provided for that it shall not act like a tribunal or otherwise pass judgment on the activities or conduct of individual governments or of individual enterprises. It should avoid becoming involved when enterprises to a specific business transaction are in dispute.[218]

Finally, paragraph 3, of section G, stipulates that – subject to the approval of the General Assembly, five years after the adoption of the Set of Principles and Rules, a United Nations Conference shall be convened under the auspices of UNCTAD for the purpose of reviewing all relevant aspects. As an effectuation of the creative function of UNCTAD supervision in the field of RBP's, the Inter-governmental Group shall make proposals to the Conference for the improvement and further development of the Set of Principles and Rules.

At the time of writing the Set of Principles and Rules has only just been adopted, so that not much can be said about the working in practice of the supervisory follow-up. Nonetheless, this working in practice will be crucial as to the implementation of the agreement. The latter in particular since the instrument will not be legally binding, but takes the form of recommendations.[219]

316

Independent from the progress made as to the coming into operation of the 'Set of Principles and Rules', the UNCTAD Secretariat reviews annually the main legislative and other developments, in industrialised and developing countries, in the control of restrictive business practices. At UNCTAD V (Manila 1979) it was decided, in this respect, that continued action should be taken, within the framework of UNCTAD, to collect *inter alia* publicly available information and as far as possible other information, particularly on the basis of requests addressed to all Member States, or provided at their own initiative; and to disseminate such information.[220] The annual report is the principal instrument used for the dissemination of the information collected.

By the material gathered in the different reports it is suggested that a large number of governments, from developed as well as developing countries, is quite willing to provide data, even automatically. One of the reasons therefore will probably be the fact that many governments try to regulate or prohibit restrictive business practices themselves, in particular by cartel and competition legislation. Consequently, governments seem less afraid (on the contrary, they seem to be proud) to lift a corner of their veil of sovereignty.[221]

4.3.3. Shipping

The Committee on Shipping was established and its terms of reference were adopted by the Trade and Development Board on April 29, 1965.[222] The general task of the Committee is to study and make recommendations on how international shipping, the improvement of port operations, the enhancement of participation of shipping lines of developing countries in shipping conferences, multimodal transport containerisation, and the development of merchant marines can most effectively contribute to the expansion of world trade, in particular of the trade of developing countries. Also it is charged to promote the systematic compilation and publication of statistics on matters pertaining to its field of competence. The Committee shall submit periodic reports on its work to the Board.

Unlike the case of the other committees of the Board, the terms of reference of the Committee on Shipping are not unequivocal as to its supervisory functions. The programme of work adopted by the Committee is more explicit in that it deals, *inter alia*, with review of current and long-term aspects of maritime transport. The Secretariat of UNCTAD should make such reviews (related to the programme of work of the Committee) which should take the form of reports to be published annually. These reports should include review of legislation and regulations of an economic nature. They should further include information regarding the evolution of freight markets on the basis of available data for liner, tramp, bulk carrier and tanker freight rates, changes in the demand for and supply of vessels, as well as other aspects of shipping services and their costs.[223] The Secretariat reports are considered at the regular sessions of the Committee on Shipping.

4.3.3.1. Working Group on International Shipping Legislation

During the New Delhi Conference of UNCTAD in 1968, the Committee on Shipping was instructed to create a Working Group on International Shipping Legislation.[224] A majority of the Conference observed that the existing international legislation on shipping did not cover many important economic and commercial aspects of maritime activity. It was recognised that the law must take note of the changing needs of society.[225] The Working Group was established by the Committee on Shipping during its third annual session in 1969.[226] In the field of international shipping legislation the Working Group has its own supervisory tasks, specifically related to the review function and the creative function. Surveillance by the Working Group is restricted to supervision of policy development.

The Working Group has the following terms of reference:

(a) to review economic and commercial aspects of international legislation and practices in the field of shipping from the standpoint of their conformity with the needs of economic development, in particular of the developing countries in order to identify areas where modifications are needed;

(b) in the light of this review, to make recommendations and prepare the necessary documentation relating thereto to serve as a basis for further work in this field, to be submitted to the United Nations Commission on International Trade Law for the drafting of new legislation or other appropriate action and, when necessary, to consider other measures to implement fully the provisions of paragraph 1 of resolution 14 (II);

(c) to report its findings and recommendations to the Committee on Shipping.[227]

4.3.3.2. Commercial information

The main problem UNCTAD is confronted with in its work in shipping, preponderantly showing up in the field of freight rates, is the question of interference with activities of private firms (shipowners). The B Group has always been arguing that studies by the UNCTAD Secretariat would involve a disclosure of confidential information to which governments have neither access nor the legal powers to force shipowners to divulge. After protracted negotiations a resolution was adopted at the New Delhi Conference of UNCTAD (1968) which directed the UNCTAD Secretariat to pursue its programme of work relating to level and structure of freight rates, conference practices and adequacy of shipping services. Governments were invited to co-operate with the Secretariat in this endeavour, and to stimulate – within their 'legal limitations' – shipowners, conferences and shippers to provide the relevant information.[228] To obtain the needed information for its studies, the Secretariat distributed questionnaires which governments were to pass to interests concerned.[229] However, the conferences and the maritime powers were unwilling to co-operate. Only one-half of the questionnaires were returned, and the answers that were received suggested an 'organised boycott of the UNCTAD probe by conference lines'.[230]

318

In the 1974 debate held in the Committee on Shipping, representatives of countries from all groups made various comments on the manner of preparing the review by the secretariat and the sources of information used, in particular stressing the danger of relying for information on press reports. The representatives of some developed market-economy countries suggested that the Secretariat should attempt to obtain from the governments concerned confirmation of information regarding their shipping policies that was derived from press reports.[231] In his response, the representative of the Secretary-General of UNCTAD underlined the lack of information. He noted that the press was often the only source of data available to the Secretariat and that attempts to obtain more reliable information from governmental and other sources in sufficient time for the preparation of the review had not always been successful.[232]

During the 1975 debate held in the Committee on Shipping, the spokesman for the B Group stated that his group recognised the difficulties involved in securing the commercial information necessary for the review. The group was ready to participate in an examination of how delegations could assist the Secretariat in obtaining and verifying data.[233] As to the collection of information on freight rates, the representative of a developed market-economy country, speaking on behalf of the National Shippers' Councils of Europe, noted the lack of detail. The difficulties experienced by the Secretariat of UNCTAD in obtaining sufficient reliable data had been similar to those experienced by the National Shippers' Councils of Europe in their own investigation. To obtain meaningful results from studies, such as the Secretariat reports, it was, in the Council's view, imperative that accurate data should be available in a form acceptable to both conferences and shippers' organisations.[234] Not only, however, with regard to the general review of the Secretariat, did the availability of data come up for discussion. Also, there appeared to be a need for more specific information on, for instance, technical and economic assistance to shipping and ports from bilateral and other sources outside the United Nations systems.[235]

The attitude of the Secretariat is to publish whatever information is available, and to distribute it in mimeographed form. Corrections are made afterwards if there are any comments from governments. Usually there are, since governments are highly sensitive with regard to data, concerning their own country, which they consider incorrect. At its 1977 session, the Committee on Shipping decided to allow governments six months after issuance of the mimeographed Review of Maritime Transport to submit comments prior to printing of the Review.[236]

4.3.3.3. A Code of Conduct for Liner Conferences

UNCTAD's work in shipping has been identified as being of high technical quality.[237] Yet UNCTAD also moves beyond the technical aspects of shipping and addresses the broader economic, political and legal implications of shipping services. Throughout its existence, the Committee on Shipping has been concerned with the liner conference system. A liner conference is

319

composed of individual shipping lines which operate in the same trade. There is not more than one conference in each trade. It is, however, usual for outbound and inbound voyages on the same route to be covered by two different conferences – often with identical membership. The individual lines, members of a conference, enter into a conference agreement with each other. Conference agreements regulate the prices – *i.e.* freight charges – charged by the individual member lines for their services. It is evident that the conferences reach decisions and take action on many matters which are of vital interest to the shippers.[238]

At its fourth session in 1970, the Committee on Shipping considered the question of the liner conference system.[239] Subsequently, during the second session of the Working Group on International Shipping Legislation, in March 1971,[240] the initiative for a code of conduct for liner conferences emerged. This question of a code of conduct was discussed in various fora and finally led to the United Nations Conference of Plenipotentiaries on a Code of Conduct for Liner Conferences, which was held in Geneva, at the end of 1973 and in the Spring of 1974.[241] The Conference adopted at its last meeting a Convention on a Code of Conduct for Liner Conferences providing rules for membership of conferences, relations among member lines, freight rates, settlement of disputes and other matters.

Apart from detailed provisions for the settlement of disputes between shippers and shipowners (including international mandatory conciliation procedures), which fall outside the scope of this study,[242] two Articles of the Code of Conduct are of importance as to supervision by UNCTAD. In the first place, Article 47 provides that each Contracting Party shall take such legislative or other measures as may be necessary to implement the convention. Equally, each Contracting Party shall communicate to the Secretary-General of the United Nations (who shall be the depository) the text of the legislative or other measures which it has taken in respect of the implementation. Although not provided for (as such), the Secretary-General of the United Nations, for reasons of effectiveness, will most probably delegate certain powers to the Secretary-General of UNCTAD. In its turn, UNCTAD's Secretariat might supply the Committee on Shipping and the Working Group on International Shipping Legislation with the necessary information.

Secondly, Article 52 concerns Review Conferences in respect of the Code of Conduct. A Review Conference shall be convened five years from the date on which the Convention comes into force. The aim of the Conference is to review the working of the Convention, with particular reference to its implementation, and to consider and adopt appropriate amendments. The convener of the Review Conference is the Secretary-General of the United Nations, as the depository, which does not preclude UNCTAD from serving the actual conference.

In its 1975 session, the Committee on Shipping had, for the first time, the Code of Conduct for Liner Conferences, as a review item, on its agenda.[243] During the fifth Conference of UNCTAD, held in Manila (1979), the Secretary-General of UNCTAD was requested to analyse the experience in the implementation of the Convention in conference trades to which the Code applies and to report periodically on progress thereon to the Committee on Shipping. For that purpose the Contracting Parties concerned were requested to facilitate the prompt supply of relevant information.[244]

Thus, as well as an annual review within the Committee on Shipping and the Working Group on International Shipping Legislation, the Review Conference (which has to be convened every five years) will be brought automatically within the framework of UNCTAD. UNCTAD will assume the task of servicing the supervisory follow-up of the Code of Conduct for Liner Conferences, because there is no other substantive body in the field of shipping.

Notwithstanding many resolutions and declarations stating the positive attitude of the major trading nations towards the Code, it has not yet entered into force, six years after it has been adopted. In this respect UNCTAD still has a supervisory task in the field of policy development. Conference resolution 106 (V) requests the Secretary-General of UNCTAD to give guidance and assistance, on request, to the governments of developing countries in putting the Code into effect. The Secretariat has responded to several such requests which it had received from both developed and developing countries. In a *note verbale* the Secretary-General has reiterated the readiness of the UNCTAD Secretariat to assist governments in the process of ratifying or acceding to the Convention and implementing its provisions.[245]

4.3.4. Preferences

On October 13, 1970, the Trade and Development Board approved the establishment of a Generalised System of Preferences, as adopted earlier by the Special Committee on Preferences.[246] Originally in GATT and since 1964 in UNCTAD, the developing countries pressed for a system whereby the developed countries would lower their tariff barriers for products originating from developing countries. For products from developed countries tariffs were to remain unchanged. The purpose was to promote the export and economic development of developing countries. In 1968, during the New Delhi Conference of UNCTAD, unanimous agreement was reached in favour of the establishment of a Generalised System of Preferences.[247] The objectives of such a system, of preferential or free entry of exports of manufactures and semi-manufactures of developing countries to the developed countries, which had to be generalised non-reciprocal and non-discriminatory, should be to increase the export earnings of the developing countries, to promote their industrialisation, and to accelerate their rates of economic growth.

The agreement reached provided that a Special Committee on Preferences be established to continue consultations on the matter. The general aim thereof was to settle the details of the arguments to be set up by the various preference-giving countries, with a view to seeking legislative authority and the required waiver in GATT. By July 1969 all developed countries intending to grant preferences had submitted negative lists of products on which they were not prepared to grant preferences, and positive lists giving those items on which they were willing to grant preferential treatment. The submissions were provisional, and were intended to serve as the basis for consultations with the developing countries in the Special Committee on Preferences. At the session of the Special Committee held in the Autumn of 1970, agreement was reached on mutually acceptable arrangements for a generalised system of preferences (GSP) to be introduced in 1971.[248]

Section VIII of the so-called 'Agreed conclusions' – the document which contained the final agreement on the GSP[249] – stated that for the review and implementation mechanism, an appropriate UNCTAD body should be established.[250] The third UNCTAD Conference, held in Santiago in 1972, decided to establish the Special Committee on Preferences as a permanent machinery within UNCTAD, with terms of reference as described in section VIII of the agreed conclusions. Thus, the Special Committee became the 'appropriate UNCTAD body' which had to supervise the implementation of the GSP.

According to its terms of reference, the Special Committee would review the effect of preferences on exports and export earnings, industrialisation and rates of growth of the beneficiary countries. It would also consider the effects on the export earnings of developing countries from the sharing of their existing tariff advantages with the rest of the developing countries as a result of the GSP, the complementary efforts made by developing countries to utilise as fully as possible the benefits from the grant of preferences, and the measures taken by the socialist countries of Eastern Europe.

An annual review to assess and analyse the functioning of the system was provided for. A triennial review was to assess the benefits of the system, and to consider the possibilities for its improvement and modification. A comprehensive review near the end of the ten-year period (the period for which the GSP was established) would consider whether the system was to be extended. *Ad hoc* consultations on matters which would require urgent consideration were envisaged; they may take place with the assistance of the UNCTAD Secretary-General.

4.3.4.1. Collection of information

As has been already advanced, the main problem, common to the majority of Committee supervision, is the lack of information; or rather the difficulty of gathering the necessary facts and figures.[251] Ever since the first review session, held in April 1973, the Special Committee on Preferences, but also the Secretariat – which prepares studies to assist the Special Committee in its periodic review – have pressed the preference-giving countries to provide data on the implementation of their various schemes. During the first review session of the Special Committee, the preferences-giving countries (the market-economy countries, as well as the socialist countries of Eastern Europe) were requested to make appropriate administrative arrangements for the prompt dissemination of information.[252] The analysis prepared by the

Secretariat was perforce limited because published sources contained little or no information on imports which actually received preferential treatment. To overcome this difficulty the Secretariat of UNCTAD addressed to Member States *notes verbales* requesting detailed information on such imports and urged both preference-giving and preference-receiving countries to supply information on a regular basis on the operation and the trade effects of the GSP.[253]

The information received for the first session varied from country to country as to the details and arrangements, and did not permit either a comprehensive or a comparative analysis of the experience and trade effects of the granting of generalised preferences.[254] With regard to form or contents, however, no firm guidelines were given, apart from a question to use magnetic computer tapes and the request to provide data on total, dutiable, covered and preferential imports from each beneficiary,[255] and data on covered and preferential imports of products defined at the tariff line level from the world as well as from each beneficiary.[256]

In spite of the encouragements from UNCTAD's side, repeated almost annually, the Secretariat, in its preparatory report to the fourth review session of the Special Committee (1976), still had to state that the information supplied by the preference-giving countries varied with respect to the extent of detail on individual products and individual beneficiaries, as well as with respect to the period covered. The data often did not separately distinguish imports of dutiable products and imports which actually received preferential treatment.[257] As a result of these data limitations – in some cases it was necessary for the Secretariat to estimate import value – a precise over-all assessment of the trade effects of the GSP was precluded.

In the comprehensive review, as asked for in Section VIII of the agreed conclusion on the GSP,[258] prepared by the Secretariat (for the fifth session of the Conference), the lack of detailed trade and other relevant data is emphasised once more. In order to arrive at comparable trade figures, estimates had to be made for certain preference-giving countries which supplied only partial information. Moreover, the available information varied from scheme to scheme with respect to detail. The latest information provided to the Secretariat by preference-giving socialist countries of Eastern Europe was even one year behind and only for two countries.[259]

Although the reports on the implementation of the GSP, prepared by the UNCTAD Secretariat, try to give as much factual information as possible, no case-by-case evaluation is provided. The report is hardly more than a compilation of data supplied by the governments. The conclusion and recommendations are of a highly general nature. Although, in exceptional cases specific countries are named,[260] generally there is only talk of preference-giving and preference-receiving countries.

On the basis of the documentation provided by the Secretariat of UNCTAD, an annual implementation debate takes place in the Special Committee on Preferences. Within the purvue of this study, the two most interesting parts of that debate are the review of the schemes of generalised preferences of developed market-economy countries, and the review of measures by the socialist countries of Eastern Europe. These two reviews are composed of statements made by the various preference-giving countries (sometimes interrupted or followed by comments of beneficiaries), and a general debate during which most preference-receiving countries have a chance to utter appreciation and/or criticism in respect of the operation of specific schemes.

As in the case of many other UNCTAD meetings, the implementation debate held in the Special Committee consists of a series of monologues rather than genuine discussions. Yet, as is shown in the reports of the Special Committee[261] the preference-giving countries are often inclined to react upon comments of beneficiaries or the representative of the Secretary-General of UNCTAD. Sometimes, even promises are made to (re)consider or adapt certain policies.[262] Generally, however, there are no detailed and intensive consultations between the groups of countries on the individual schemes. The implementation debate is not mandatory of nature. Nonetheless, it seems to have, because of its more or less individual approach, normative implications. In this light the implementation debate seems to be, at least potentially, a workable instrument of the correction function of supervision by the Special Committee on Preferences.

However, the implementation debate is not only an instrument of the correction function; it may also play a role as review instrument, by providing additional information. Especially, since the information supplied, in first instance, is often insufficient, this role may be essential. Hence, in the 1976 implementation debate, the representatives of several developing countries expressed appreciation for the additional information provided by the delegations of preference-giving market-economy countries in their statements, which had enabled them to have a better and clearer appreciation of the various schemes. They suggested, however, that further efforts should be made to provide in advance to the UNCTAD Secretariat relevant and up-to-date information on the operation of their respective schemes, so as to enable the special Committee to carry out its evaluations on the basis of adequate and comparable data.[263]

Not only additional information from the market-economy countries is required. During the same review session, the representative of the Secretary-General of UNCTAD indicated that only partial information had been received by the Secretariat on the effects of tariff preferences and other preferential measures introduced by the socialist countries of Eastern Europe under the GSP. He invited the representatives of the countries concerned to provide or supplement that information at the current session of the Special Committee, so as to enable the Committee to review the operation and effects of their schemes. Such information would also be of special importance to beneficiaries and enable them to improve their understanding and make better use of the trade opportunities offered.[264]

The periodic reviews do provide a forum in which developing countries, individually or collectively, can make specific requests for improvements. However, several years after implementation of the system, and despite significant improvements, the GSP still falls far short of the expectations and trade needs of developing countries. An indication of this can be seen in the fact that the product coverage amounts to only about 30 per cent. of dutiable imports by preference-giving countries from beneficiaries, while the trade which actually receives preference is less.[265] This suggests, *inter alia*, that the framework of periodic reviews might not have been adequate to ensure a more substantial improvement of the system.[266]

At its 1977 review session, the Special Committee on Preferences adopted resolution 5 (VIII) by which it agreed 'to the desirability of receiving procedures for consultations on individual schemes of preference-giving countries, including the improvement of existing procedures and the establishment, as appropriate, of additional procedures, with a view to the continued improvement of the various aspects of the generalised system of preferences'. In the same resolution, the Special Committee requested the Secretary-General of UNCTAD 'to make proposals in this respect'.[267]

The consultations referred to in resolution 5 (VIII) are the consultations provided for in section VIII of the Agreed Conclusions on the GSP which contain the terms of reference of the Special Committee.[268] These Agreed Conclusions embrace the possibility of holding *ad hoc* consultations on specific aspects of the system that require urgent consideration.[269] So far, however, these *ad hoc* consultations have not been utilised, largely because institutional arrangements did not make clear when such consultations are to take place and on whose initiative. Furthermore, the Secretary-General of UNCTAD was to be involved in such consultations only if his assistance was desired by Member States. Neither was the mandate clear from the substantive point of view, since it is not always possible to establish which aspects of the GSP do require 'urgent consideration'.[270]

The proposal made by the Secretariat, according to resolution 5 (VIII), contains an innovation in the existing procedures, in that it divides the task of the Special Committee into two parts. In the first place, plenary meetings of a public character would be devoted to GSP issues of general importance such as the duration of the GSP, its legal status, the principle of non-discrimination, etc. Secondly, in addition to the plenary meetings, plurilateral consultations between developing countries on the one hand and individual preference-giving countries on the other would be organised to allow for intensive and private discussions of the individual schemes. According to the Secretariat, from the point of view of substance, these meetings would be more effective because of the possibility of concentrating efforts on one scheme at a time and they would allow government representatives to engage in a full exchange of views on problems encountered, in particular with regard to products of special export interest to beneficiary countries.[271]

At its eighteenth session, the Board endorsed the proposal made by the Secretariat. It was decided, *inter alia*, that during the sessions of the Special Committee on Preferences, informal plurilateral consultations should be held on individual schemes, if so requested (between preference-receiving countries on the one hand, and the preference-giving country concerned on the other). The plurilateral consultations would be private and confidential in character.[272] To assist the UNCTAD Secretariat in preparing the necessary background material for the plenary meetings, as well as for the private plurilateral consultations, both preference-giving and preference-receiving countries are requested to provide, well in advance of the sessions of the Special Committee, such detailed and comprehensive information as may be required.[273]

In concluding it might be stated, that the annual implementation debate, held in the Special Committee, is potentially a feasible instrument of the correction function of preference supervision. In principle, effectiveness can be enhanced if, according to Board decision 179(XVIII), a division will be made between a general and a more specific debate. However, since the effectiveness of the debate largely depends on the information disseminated by the various governments, attention in the first place should be focused on the instruments of the review function. As long as the main instrument available is only based upon the loose obligation of a *note verbale* by the Secretary-General of UNCTAD, resolution 1 (V) of the Special Committee, or, eventually, upon Board resolution 19 (II), States will consider it their own competence to decide what information will be provided. To a certain extent the implementation debate can be instrumental *vis-à-vis* the review function in supplying additional information. To have a meaningful debate, however, countries must provide the Secretariat with the necessary information well in advance of the sessions of the Special Committee in order to allow the Secretariat to prepare adequately and in good time the relevant documentation.

Also, if the innovation proposals, in respect of the procedures for consultation, as adopted by the Board, will be effectuated, the question of collecting information remains crucial. The Secretariat leaves no doubt about it: 'the existing notification and reporting procedures should also be improved. Both preference-giving and preference-receiving countries should supply well in advance of the proposed consultations detailed information on the operation, trade effects and utilisation of advantages provided under the individual schemes. Although these countries have supplied information in the past, there is need for making such reporting more systematic, detailed and timely.'[274]

4.3.5. Technology

One of the areas of task expansion within UNCTAD has been the strengthening of the technological capacity of the developing countries, in particular through the transfer of technology.[275] To deal with this area effectively, the Board established in 1974, the Committee on Transfer of Technology as one of its Main Committees.[276] The main supervisory task of this Committee is to assist the Board in keeping under review and in taking appropriate action within the Board's competence for the implementation of the recommendations, declarations and other decisions made by the Conference and the Board in the field of transfer of technology. To that end the Committee undertakes studies, gathers statistical data, informs governments as to the need for the possibility of governmental and inter-governmental action, provides general guidance regarding technical assistance to developing countries, and submits periodic reports to the Board on its work.[277]

So far, the Committee has met in session three times.[278] In the report on the third session mention was made of the review of progress in implementing Conference resolutions 87 (IV) and 112 (V).[279] In these resolutions regarding the strengthening of the technological capacity of developing countries, the Secretary-General of UNCTAD was requested to invite governments to submit information concerning the subject-matter.[280] During the third session of the Committee, the representative of the Secretary-General noted that the number of replies received was too few to permit a comprehensive analysis to be made.[281] By resolution the Committee appealed to the defective governments to submit the information required and decided to postpone the review to its next session.[282]

Except for this more general review, the Committee also deals with specific items such as the economic, commercial and development aspects of the industrial property system, technical and operational assistance, and the Code of Conduct on the Transfer of Technology. In the field of industrial property the work of the Committee is primarily related to UNCTAD's contribution to and imprint on the process of revision of the Paris Convention for the Protection of Industrial Property. The revision of this Convention is negotiated in a Diplomatic Conference convened under the auspices of the World Intellectual Property Organisation (WIPO). A number of governmental expert groups have been set up in UNCTAD, the reports and results of the sessions of which were transmitted to the Director-General of WIPO and to national governments to be taken into consideration.[283]

With the aim of making technical and operational assistance in the field of transfer of technology more effective, the fourth UNCTAD Conference (Nairobi 1976) decided to establish an Advisory Service.[284] Progress reports on the work of the Advisory Service, drawn up by the UNCTAD Secretariat are discussed in the Committee on Transfer of Technology. The Advisory Service's technical and operational activities comprise to date four main areas: (i) technology planning and policy at the national level; (ii) regional and subregional centres dealing with the transfer and development of technology; (iii) activities in sectors of critical importance to developing countries (mainly the pharmaceutical sector, but also, *e.g.*, food processing and capital goods and machinery); and (iv) programmes aimed at the training of personnel and exchange of experience among developing countries.[285]

4.3.5.1. Code of Conduct on the Transfer of Technology

The negotiation of an international code of conduct on the transfer of technology has been one of the major negotiating exercises under the auspices of UNCTAD in the late 1970s. During its Nairobi Conference (1976), UNCTAD decided to establish an inter-governmental group of experts in order to prepare a draft code of conduct.[286] In 1978 the inter-governmental group finished a draft text to be submitted to the United

Nations Conference on an Internatinal Code of Conduct on the Transfer of Technology which was held in the same year.[287]

The substantive provisions of the draft code fall into two broad categories: provisions concerning the regulation of transfer of technology transactions and of the conduct of parties (private as well as public) who enter into such transactions, and provisions relating to measures by governments concerning transfer of technology. Provisions under the first category embody mutually agreed standards applicable to all transfer of technology transactions. Those under the second category deal with desirable or permissible action which countries may wish to take, either on account of their national policies relating to the acquisition of technology or because they deem such action appropriate in order to assist developing countries.

The fourth session of the Conference on an International Code of Conduct was held in the Spring of 1981. During that session no agreement was reached on the remaining issues and it was decided to refer the whole matter to the UN General Assembly. If the General Assembly would recommend to reconvene the Conference, the next session thereof would certainly not be held earlier than Spring 1982.

According to the latest draft text, resulting from the previous Conference sessions, implementation will be based mainly on voluntary international collaboration. Such collaboration 'may' include, inter alia, exchange of available information on the transfer of technology and on development of national legislation in this respect; promotion of objectives and principles of the Code; and consultations which may lead to greater harmonisation of national legislation and policies. The text clearly refrains from any binding formulation.[288]

A number of proposed provisions contain supervisory functions for UNCTAD. According to the draft text the international institutional machinery for the monitoring of the Code is to be provided within UNCTAD, either in the form of a new Special Committee (as proposed by the Group of 77) or by the existing Committee on the Transfer of Technology (as proposed by Groups B and D). The Committee should meet as often as necessary, but at least once a year; it may create appropriate subsidiary bodies to assist in its work.[289] The functions of the Committee shall be, inter alia, to provide a forum and modalities for consultations, discussions and exchange of views between States; to undertake and disseminate periodically studies and research; to collect and disseminate information; to make reports and recommendations to states; to organise symposia and workshops concerning the application of the provisions of the Code; and to submit annual reports to the Trade and Development Board.[290]

As in the case of restrictive business practices,[291] here too, it is stipulated that in the performance of its functions, neither the Committee nor its subsidiary organs may act like a tribunal or otherwise pass judgments on the activities or conduct of individual governments or of individual parties in connection with a specific transfer of technology transaction. The Committee should also avoid involvement when parties to such a transaction are in dispute.[292]

The Secretariat for the Committee shall be the UNCTAD Secretariat. At the request of the Committee it shall submit relevant studies, documentation and other information to the Committee. It shall consult with and render assistance to States, particularly the developing countries, at their request, in the application of the Code at the national level. Subject to approval of the UN General Assembly, four or six years after the adoption of the Code, a United Nations Conference must be convened under the auspices of UNCTAD for the purpose of reviewing all aspects of the Code.[293]

4.4. Technical assistance

Technical assistance, although important, is only a marginal activity of UNCTAD which complements the main role of policy development. Hence, in this field, the organisation has not developed a capacity to undertake substantive evaluation. The review of the technical assistance funds[294] is so far being practically only exercised by UNDP. UNCTAD follows the established procedures as executing agency of UNDP. *e.g.* participation in the tripartite reviews organised by UNDP at the project level.[295] When UNDP is embarking on sectoral evaluation which is of interest to UNCTAD, then UNCTAD may also participate.

As a result of a resolution adopted at UNCTAD V, held in Manila in 1979,[296] the Secretariat is requested – for the first time, again, after a period of five years – to prepare an annual report summarising all UNCTAD's technical assistance activities and their financing for submission to the Board.[297] Apart from a general discussion, however, the Board has no authority to add to deduct any funds. Yet, the Board can exert positive influence on the funds coming from UNDP, by considering that they are, for instance, insufficient or that UNCTAD is not the appropriate institution and that they should be given to other agencies.

In allotting funds, UNCTAD does not choose the technical assistance projects. It tries to respond to requests from governments. Especially on the country level UNCTAD cannot impose any project. On the inter-country level, in a subtle way, more initiative as regards project ideas may be unfolded by UNCTAD (in co-operation with UNDP). Of course, it is checked in advance whether project ideas from the UNCTAD Secretariat will get the support of a sufficient number of governments. This possible initiative may permit the Secretariat to orient a project or programme towards more support for the negotiation role of UNCTAD. The review, nonetheless, exclusively takes place in the framework of UNDP.

More than two-thirds of the budget dedicated to technical assistance is spent on the inter-regional, regional and sub-regional level. UNCTAD is only to a limited extent active on the country level. A sizeable part of the programme consists of direct support to the negotiation function of UNCTAD. The aim thereof is to help governments of developing countries in being better equipped to participate in negotiating conferences.[298] In this latter activity of UNCTAD one might discern the possibility of a financial incentive as regards supervision. This in the sense that such financial/technical assistance can contribute to policy development, supervision of which is an essential UNCTAD activity.

Moreover, technical assistance may play a role in supervision *stricto sensu* particularly with regard to the review function. Especially, many developing countries encounter insurmountable difficulties in answering highly technical questionnaires on a multitude of specialised subjects. Often, these countries simply lack sufficient adequate personnel to do the job. Therefore, response might be enhanced by, for instance, organising seminars, by publishing manuals and by providing advisory services to governments. Examples of this kind of assistance can be found, *inter alia*, in the field of shipping, in connection with the Generalised System of Preferences and in the sector of transfer of technology.[299]

V. EFFECTIVENESS OF UNCTAD SUPERVISION

In the preceding chapter a rather complex picture has been drawn as far as the number of supervisory organs and procedures, within the UNCTAD framework, are concerned. Also, in that context, the interrelation of the different levels of supervision, *i.e.* the Conference level, the Board level and the Committee level has been mentioned. Issues submitted to supervision are passed on from one level to the other, mainly depending upon the level of consensus, while the Secretariat is the nucleus as to the provision of documentation.

Although most Committees base their supervisory activities on provisions in their terms of reference or programme of work, the spine of UNCTAD supervision is constituted by General Assembly resolution 1995 (XIX), paragraph 15, and as a corollary Board resolution 19 (II).[300] The latter, being the central point to focus on, provides however, as a typical compromise between developed and developing countries, only for a very moderate supervisory mechanism.[301] As might be recalled, the principal actors in trade and development, *i.e.* the States, are requested to supply information in a form which they will find appropriate. It is upon this loose obligation that the Secretary-General of UNCTAD must rely in preparing its annual report which serves as documentation for the implementation debate in the Board, and in supplying the different Committees with information and analyses necessary for their supervisory task.

In terms of the distinctions made in Part I of this book,[302] the greater part of UNCTAD supervision is of a general modality. As has been shown, in most cases supervision is exercised on a periodic basis and independent of particular circumstances. An exception to this can be found in the adopted innovation proposals as regards the Generalised System of Preferences. On the basis of those proposals consultations on individual schemes can be held, if so requested.[303] Although this possibility is clearly created in view of a more effective implementation of the system, as yet no conclusions can be drawn. Another exception of this kind is to be found in the field of restrictive business practices, for which the Set of Principles and Rules for the control of these practices provides a complaint type of procedure.[304]

The question is to what extent the supervisory mechanism, essentially based on Board resolution 19 (II), contributes to the realisation of the norms which UNCTAD sets out to establish in the economic relations between developing countries on the one hand and the developed market-economy countries and socialist countries on the other. In the following we will try to analyse the effectiveness of UNCTAD supervision by considering the three functions of the supervisory mechanism, *i.e.* the review function, the correction function and the creative function.

In assessing the effectiveness of UNCTAD supervision it is important to bear in mind a number of considerations. First, the tremendous complexity of the issues faced by UNCTAD. UNCTAD is not an operational organisation which could be judged by the number of projects carried out in the field. As has been put forward above, UNCTAD's role as regards technical assistance has substantially grown since 1969, but the organisation has not acquired any supervisory functions, whatsoever, in this field.[305] UNCTAD's primary aim is to change the trade and aid policies of the developed countries so as to take account of the development needs of developing countries. In view of this purpose, the political significance of the organisation as articulator, aggregator and communicator of interests should be kept in mind.[306] As a corollary, an important part of UNCTAD surveillance is supervision of policy development which consists mainly of reviews of State behaviour, stimulating States to adopt a favourable attitude towards progressive norms in the field of trade and development and the drafting and redrafting of proposals. This supervision of policy development must be evaluated, as has been noted, slightly differently from supervision of implementation *stricto sensu*.[307] In addition it must be stated that even with documentation of a policy shift it may not be clear to what extent it is a direct consequence of UNCTAD supervision (or a response to the more general pressures which produced UNCTAD in the first place). It is much easier to assert that UNCTAD supervision accelerates the pace of certain reforms favourable to the developing countries, than it is to suggest that it produces these reforms.[308]

Secondly, the principle of non-reciprocity underlies the greater part of the recommendations and resolutions of UNCTAD. Developed countries are asked to do something in favour of developing countries without any immediate equivalent consideration. This is, of course, a different proposition from dealings on the basis of reciprocity where the *quid pro quo* operates as a powerful incentive for action. What the principle of non-reciprocity means, essentially, is that developing countries have no bargaining power except that of persuasion and the enlightened interpretation of the self-interest of developed countries. Nonetheless, the growing awareness of mutual interests and global interdependencies did introduce new elements in the North-South dialogue – tending to result in more genuine bargaining instead of unilateral demands and unilateral concessions – and enhanced the negotiating position of the developing countries.

Thirdly, the decision-making process and the results thereof, mostly in the form of non-binding legal instruments, should be taken into consideration. UNCTAD is placed in the midst of a highly dynamic process aimed at restructuring the international economic relations. Its function therein, of keeping up the pace of change, implicates a number of restrictions. Thus, for instance, much of UNCTAD's work results in so-called 'soft law' which has certainly normative effects, but cannot be considered as legally binding. Keeping in mind decision-making in UNCTAD,[309] this creation of non-binding rules is for the moment the most effective way to fulfil the functions of the organisation. The highly developed mechanism of conciliation, developed in General Assembly resolution 1995 (XIX), shows the delicacy of the material to be dealt with in UNCTAD. That these formal conciliation procedures have never been used, detracts nothing from the fact that in practice consensus and informal conciliation have prevailed in decision-making. The fact that most results are of a non-binding character, makes any form of supervision even more pertinent.

5.1. The review function

As might be recalled the review function of international supervision is realised in the phase in which State behaviour is placed against the background of a given legal norm. To that end the ways and means to collect the necessary information in respect of such State behaviour are highly essential. In fact, the availability of information is a *conditio sine qua non* to every exercise of supervision.[310]

The central instrument of the review function of UNCTAD supervision is to be found in Board resolution 19 (II). This resolution requires that the annual report of the Secretary-General of UNCTAD shall be based, *inter alia*, on the information furnished by Member States. To effectuate this provision, the Secretariat used to send requests for information, in the form of so-called *notes verbales*, to the governments, together with a schedule regarding the way to answer. This schedule equated with the division of UNCTAD activities, *i.e.* a general part, commodities, manufactures, financing, etc. The so-called implementation reports, directly based on the information collected, were drawn up only until 1974.[311] The response was to such an extent insufficient – in 1974, only 24 answers out of 146 States – that it was decided not to continue this practice.

As was mentioned earlier, the developed countries took the stand that individual governments had the latitude to decide on the nature, form and definition of information that they would offer. They, accordingly, proceeded to supply data of a general nature which could only be used by the UNCTAD Secretariat to produce an over-all survey of trends and patterns of international trade and development, instead of an evaluation report, which could indict individual governments for their lapses in implementation.[312] Normally, most developed countries did not follow the schedule suggested by the Secretariat. They only made up a very general overview in which one, or maybe two, paragraphs were to the point.[313] The fragmentary answers consisted only of favourable figures and mixed up, without distinction, measures effectively implemented and measures foreseen to be taken. Moreover, the answers were not restricted to activities undertaken in the field of UNCTAD; there was also talk of measures taken in the framework of other organisations.[314]

Hardly any answer was received by the Secretariat from the developing countries. From the 88 members of that group in 1970, 10 to 15 answered, of which only two wrote in time so that the answers could be used for the preparation of the implementation report. Some of this inertia can be explained by the lack of practice and of qualified personnel to collect adequate information and to answer the questions posed.[315]

Although the implementation reports were not much of a success, the Secretariat continued, also beyond 1974, to send out requests for information and questionnaires, in the form of *notes verbales*, on a variety of subjects. Annually, approximately 20 of such *notes verbales* (often necessarily followed by reminders) on issues like shipping legislation, technology, restricted business practices and commodities (*e.g.* tropical timber, iron ore, cotton, tungsten, etc.) are sent out. Except for tungsten, on which a quarterly questionnaire is distributed, the average response by States is low. Although the number of replies differs slightly from subject to subject, this average, in the years from 1974 to 1979, was only 23 per cent. Depending on the subject, other international organisations and UN bodies and organs receive questionnaires as well. Normally they give comprehensive replies because the questions posed are within their particular mandate too.

As we have seen, *e.g.* with regard to the requests for information on the Generalised System of Preferences, there is a trend to ask for data in the form of computer tapes. Governments are obviously not willing to go too often through the laborious work of filling in questionnaires. Working with computer tapes which can be used for other purposes as well, means less additional constraint for government employees. There is among Secretariat staff members a strong feeling that too many questionnaires would work counter-productively. What is needed is more consistent and comparable information. To this end computer tapes can have a positive effect.[316]

In order to enhance the response of the developing countries there is a need to maintain and intensify technical assistance, in particular supplied to the less advanced ones. With regard to the same example of the Generalised System of Preferences, a project financed by UNDP is carried out by the UNCTAD Secretariat to promote full awareness of the advantages and implications of the system. In addition to a series of regional seminars, the project provides advisory services to governments at their request. These services are supplied through short-term visits and/or through correspondence and are intended to help preference-receiving countries to solve specific problems encountered in the operation of the GSP.[317] An important ingredient of technical assistance in connection with the GSP would be the prompt dissemination of detailed information on individual schemes to both exporters in preference-receiving and importers in preference-giving countries and their education, especially with regard to the application of the rules of origin.[318] Also in the field of shipping[319] and transfer of technology[320] training programmes are launched with the help of UNDP. Technical assistance not only enables developing countries to implement decisions, there often is a feedback effect allowing the UNCTAD Secretariat to keep abreast of developments. Thus, education at least in the form of, for instance, manuals and digests on the different issues subject to questionnaires could contribute to a more consistent and comparable response.

As regards the review function of UNCTAD supervision the Secretariat plays a technical but nonetheless important role. It may be on the basis of a request by the Conference, the Board or a Committee that the Secretariat prepares reports (or so-called 'progress reports' in the case of supervision of policy development) on the implementation of decisions. In that case the Secretariat possesses specific 'legislative' authority. Sometimes the Secretariat does not act upon such a specific decision, but nevertheless, in view of preparing documentation for the agenda of a particular meeting, circularises governments asking them to provide information.[321] The UNCTAD Secretariat analyses, or reproduces, the responses it gets, and draws whatever conclusions it may be able to. In the introductory material to most reports the questionnaires are mentioned on which these reports are based as well as the governments circularised, while reference is made to the number of replies received. Sometimes countries are individualised.

Except for some casual high responses and the practically full reply to the quarterly questionnaire on tungsten, governmental information, both of developed as well as of developing countries, plays necessarily a minor role in the preparation of the documentation by the Secretariat. The latter is mostly contingent on public sources like issues of the UN Statistical Office, Congressional Records, financial and economic journals, etc. Of course, this system implies serious limitations; since it is impossible to examine all material, the Secretariat has to be selective. On the other hand, as easy as it might be to collect information on all sorts of aspects of, for instance, the EEC, it can be impossible to find adequate information with regard to developments within and among developing countries and their relations with the developed world.[322]

In collecting information, the UNCTAD Secretariat encounters even more problems when it concerns private or semi-private trade data. As we have seen in the case of the Committee on Shipping, the effective collection of information on freight rates breaks down on the argument of most developed market-economy countries that studies by the UNCTAD Secretariat would involve a disclosure of confidential information.[323] The same problem occurs, in respect of, for instance, the ownership of flags of convenience and the Committee of Manufacturers' assessment of restrictive business practices, and will arise if the Committee on Commodities is going to deal with the more structural and institutional aspects of commodity trade. In the latter case, the commodity division of the UNCTAD Secretariat has to collect information on producing, marketing and distribution issues, like who owns what, who sells to whom, who undertakes the transport, etc. These are all issues on which governments are reluctant to provide data, even if they could get information for internal use.

5.2. The correction function

It has been explained in Part I of this book that the correction function of international supervision comprises prevention and redress of deviant State behaviour.[324] In purview of UNCTAD supervision of policy development stimulation has been added in the present study. The correction function of UNCTAD supervision is for the most part instrumentalised in the various debates held in the Conference, the Board, the Committees and the Sub-Committees and Groups.

Being for an important part a forum for ongoing negotiations UNCTAD supervision consists primarily of surveillance of policy development, of which stimulation is a major function. As has been advanced, prevention and redress are based on a somewhat different approach from stimulation. Stimulating governments to adopt the most favourable attitude towards progressive trade and development norms, implies even more subtle pressure and manipulation than is already required in the case of prevention or redress. With regard to policy development it is not yet the implementation of the eventual norm, but the creation of that norm which is at stake.

In the case of prevention or redress, as well as stimulation, it must, of course, be kept in mind that there are numerous other factors than UNCTAD supervision which affect State behaviour. The international economic and political situation, as well as domestic circumstances (*e.g.* a change of government in a particular country) are often most decisive as to changes in government policy.[325]

The question of policy development and of implementation *stricto sensu* of UNCTAD decisions is, in the first place, discussed in the annual sessions of the Board, which meets at the end of August every year. The term 'debate' must not be interpreted in the strict sense of the word, *i.e.* an adversarial examination of a question. In reality these sessions of the Board rather consist of series of monologues without their being any real confrontation in the discussion. Except, maybe, for some more technical matters, like shipping and to a certain extent preferences, debates held in other UNCTAD bodies proceed along the same lines.

As will be remembered, most developed countries interpret Board resolution 19 (II) to mean that there can only be general debates and not case-by-case examinations of the policy measures taken by individual countries. The developed countries readily criticise the statistical imperfections of Secretariat documentation and, mostly, consider conclusions too pessimistic. Statements of the delegates of these countries consist, like the larger part of the information provided by them, of favourable figures, while no distinction is made between measures that are taken and that still have to be taken. Moreover, as in the written information provided by the industrialised countries, the delegates of these countries do not restrict their arguments to the implementation of UNCTAD decisions, but mention equally measures taken under the auspices of other organisations.[326]

The developing countries, on the other hand, use to propose a reinforcement and an amelioration of the supervisory mechanism based on Board resolution 19 (II). They blame the developed countries for not being more co-operative. However, although sometimes violent, reproaches are usually of a general character. Only in exceptional cases are attacks directly made against a specific country or a group of countries.[327]

As a result, debates are general and vague, as is customary in a situation where supervision is not focused on the performance of individual countries. Moreover, the implementation debate in the Board, as well as most other debates, is traditionally inconclusive in the sense that hardly any agreed conclusions are adopted, although the organ in question is supposed to assess the implementation or progress in implementation. The debates resemble many other general debates in the United Nations, where developing countries attack over-all performance and trends, while developed nations protest their good will, sincere efforts and positive actions.[328]

Nonetheless, there are exceptions. In respect of the implementation of the Generalised System of Preferences, for instance, the preference-giving countries are often inclined to react upon comments of beneficiaries.[329] According to staff members of the UNCTAD Secretariat, the implementation debate as regards preference has – if the correction function is not instrumentalised in prevention, or redress – at least a 'containing effect'. In other words, the debate limits the damage by, in this case, pressing for the restriction of protectionist measures.[330]

In particular, as far as supervision of policy development is concerned, country groups may exert some pressure upon their individual members, either as a result of political constraint, by virtue of the mere fact that the individual member stands alone, or in actually pressing the individual member to adopt a given policy. As has been noted, the group system urges for group positions which have to be decided prior to the inter-group negotiations.[331]

Of course, a major requirement for restructuring international economic relations, to which UNCTAD fulfils a sort of hinge-function, is the so-called 'political will' to adopt new policies. Stimulation may be aimed at changing the political will in general (the general atmosphere) or the will of a particular country. It may also be used, however, to compensate technical or political inabilities and shortcomings in the case the political will is present.

Thus, a sizeable part of UNCTAD's technical assistance programme may be considered as technical-financial incentives in the framework of the correction function, *i.e.* stimulation as regards supervision of policy development. UNCTAD assists developing countries to prepare themselves for negotiating conferences, either within UNCTAD[332] or outside the organisation[333] in order to enhance effective participation of those countries.

If the UNCTAD Secretariat fulfils an important role as regards the review function in collecting, combining and analysing information, it equally has a task in respect of the correction function of supervision. In the foregoing, we have already touched upon the possibilities of technical assistance as stimulation in purview of policy development. Technical assistance programmes are mainly a Secretariat matter.

Also, the publication of data in the implementation reports and progress reports, drawn up by the Secretariat, introduces a corrective element or *stimulus* in UNCTAD supervision. This may not lead to the conclusion, however, the States are easily inclined to change attitude as a result of the publication of facts and figures concerning their behaviour. Nevertheless, there are areas in which governments are sensitive as to the impression their performance makes in general and the reflection of that performance in the documentation provided by the Secretariat in particular. With regard to the issue of shipping, for instance, we have seen that the developed market-economy countries pressed for a possibility to submit comments, in order to confirm data collected by the Secretariat, prior to the printing thereof.[334]

Another possibility of, especially, stimulation which is used by UNCTAD to put pressure on governments (and which is mainly a Secretariat instrument), is the publication of background studies. Thus, through requesting studies in other international organisations, contracting studies by outside experts, or conducting studies within UNCTAD, the organisation attempts to create new policy alternatives and keep those alternatives alive in the hope that even if they are not adopted now, decision makers will be well aware of them if conditions are more conducive to reform in the future. At least, UNCTAD plays an important role in getting governments and other international organisations to evidence more awareness of the implications of their policies for the trade and development prospects of the developing countries.[335]

5.3. The creative function

The creative function is, in the case of UNCTAD supervision of implementation *stricto sensu*, carried out through the elaboration or interpretation of already existing norms, which are not specific or effective enough to be applied in practice. As regards supervision of policy development the creative function is fulfilled by the drafting process aimed at the creation of new norms. Both manifestations of the creative function are difficult to separate since interpretation and drafting are often one phenomenon in the same dynamic context of UNCTAD's work.

The question whether the creative function is effectively exercised within the framework of UNCTAD supervision leads us back to the issue of the political cohesion of the organisation and more in particular to the process of decision-making.[336] It may be recalled that UNCTAD supervision is dealt with on three possible levels, *i.e.* the Conference level, the Board level and the Committee level. These levels are closely related to the level of consensus among the participating countries regarding a specific subject. Thus, most items on which no agreement can be reached remain in the highest political realm of the periodic Conferences, while supervision of issues as to which some sort of consensus has been formed may be exercised by the Board, a Committee or subsidiary group.

It goes without saying that – even if during the review phase deviant State behaviour can be established and even if as a result of the corrective element of UNCTAD supervision recalcitrant States are placed under constraint – the adaptation of existing rules or the drafting of new ones draws most heavily on the existing measure of agreement. Consequently, the level of UNCTAD supervision indicates, to a certain extent, the possibilities of an effective realisation of the creative function.

As has been submitted in the foregoing, UNCTAD's supervision of implementation *stricto sensu*, in particular regarding the implementation reports on the basis of Board resolution 19 (II), has not been developed into an effective mechanism. What counts for the review and correction function, subsequently holds also true for the creative function. More is achieved, in this respect, with regard to different codes of conduct and other multilateral legal instruments, adopted under the auspices of UNCTAD, with a specific role for the latter in the follow-up mechanisms.[337] With the exception of the Generalised System of Preferences, however, supervision provided for in these instruments is still too young – or not yet operative – to be evaluated meaningfully.

Generally effectively has UNCTAD supervision, and in particular the creative function thereof, been exercised in the field of policy development. As a major forum for negotiation in the dialogue between developed and developing countries, supervision in this field not only entails the review of State behaviour and the stimulation of a positive attitude towards norms to be created, but also the drafting and redrafting of those norms.

Thus, UNCTAD has been active, in a more general framework, by effectively participating in the preparation of the Second United National Development Decade and the Charter of Economic Rights and Duties of States,[338] the assessment of which clearly falls within the category of supervision of policy development. Equally UNCTAD has been active by keeping under almost constant review developments in international trade which involves creative elements in the laborious reports and innovatory studies by the Secretariat and the draft proposals for structural change from the side of Member States. But also in respect of more specific issues, the creative function of supervision of policy development has been continuously exercised. Mention can be made of the regular sessions of the main Committees and particularly the work of the *ad hoc* Inter-Governmental Committee on the Integrated Programme for Commodities and the Working Group on International Shipping Legislation,[339] and the negotiating processes preceding the Generalised System of Preferences, the Code of Conduct for Liner Conferences, the Set of Principles and Rules for the control of Restrictive

338

Business Practices, the ongoing negotiations on a Code of Conduct for the Transfer of Technology, and recently the adoption of the Common Fund.

The UNCTAD Secretariat has always played a crucial role in emphasising current problems in the field of trade and development and in generating new ideas in that respect. Mention has been made already, as regards the correction *c.q.* stimulation function, of the reports and studies drawn up by the different Secretariat divisions. Alongside the function of placing governments under a certain degree of contraint, these reports and studies create at the same time major possibilities to ventilate ideas and to make proposals. Since most Secretariat publications are directly related to sessions of the Conference, the Board, the Committees or any other subsidiary UNCTAD organ, proposals made therein do effectively influence the drafting process. In particular the Group of 77 makes frequent use of Secretariat proposals; also the developed market-economy countries, gathered in the B Group, may draw their conclusions, as far as it concerns their draft proposals in the negotiating process *vis-à-vis* the Group of 77.

In fact, as regards the creative function of supervision of policy development, staff leverage is closely related to the style of group bargaining; the influence of the UNCTAD Secretariat is especially critical in the early and middle stages of the bargaining process. Indeed, many of the Group of 77 positions are merely restatements of UNCTAD proposals, or, within the purview of negotiating tactics, sometimes even more radical demands than those of the Secretariat.[340]

5.4. Conclusions

Drawing conclusions from what has been said about UNCTAD supervision is a hazardous undertaking for someone who followed a mainly legal and theoretical approach. Nevertheless, from all the paperwork in the form of texts of resolutions, codes, sets of rules, reports of discussions in UNCTAD organs and Secretariat studies, some impressions force themselves on the reader.

UNCTAD seems to be effective as supervisor of policy developments – *i.e.* of ongoing negotiations as regards the creation of new rules in the field of trade and development – as far as it reviews and stimulates Member States and contributes to the drafting process. If this result – in the field of norm creation, rather than norm implementation – seems, at first sight, insufficient in the framework of the present study on international supervisory mechanisms, it must be emphasised that UNCTAD had fulfilled its functions ever since its establishment in 1964, and even more so since the so-called world economic stagnation of the 1970s, in a hostile environment. The external economic situation, which involves the measure of inclination to integrate and thus to redistribute, has always been decisive for success or failure within UNCTAD.

Even after 15 years of practice, the antagonist factions, divided into the Group of 77 and the B Group, cannot agree upon the precise scope of activities and the competences of UNCTAD. Thus, in an atmosphere of constant disagreement – not only on substantive matters to be dealt with by the organisation, but also on the tasks of the organisation itself – UNCTAD has to cope with problems of trade and development. Subsequently, but also because these problems are of an essentially redistributive character, most developed countries are not inclined – if it is at all possible to agree upon a norm – to place themselves under effective supervision of implementation. At best, the hard core of powerful B Group countries considers any form of co-operation as benign resignation to non-binding rules. Particularly pervasive becomes this attitude as soon as a request is tabled for a country-by-country approach in which deviant State behaviour must be established. Effective instruments of review with a view to collecting the necessary information on such State behaviour have never been provided for, whereas the means available, such as requests for information and questionnaires in the form of *notes verbales*, with some minor exceptions, never brought about any significant response. However, since it cannot be expected, realistically, that UNCTAD's external political environment will change in the near future, technical solutions have to be sought so as to diminish deficiencies.

Although the UNCTAD Secretariat can rely to a certain extent on publicly available information, the foregoing must necessarily lead to the conclusion that effective instruments of the review function, to collect data, must be established in order to come to meaningful supervision of implementation *stricto sensu*. This conclusion becomes even more pertinent now that UNCTAD increasingly broaches questions which are closely related to private enterprise – an area in which governments, especially those of developed market-economy countries, are unwilling to intermingle. Effective data collection can be reached not by increasing the number of questionnaires which would result in overburdening government officials, but rather by trying to enhance the response to the already existing ones. If possible, the character of questionnaires should be changed, for instance, from a list of open-ended questions to questions which can be answered by a simple yes or no. In this respect special attention should be paid, by means of increased technical assistance, to the developing countries. In particular to the less-developed ones, which often lack the technical and administrative abilities to implement UNCTAD decisions, or to answer questionnaires sufficiently. Also, consideration should be given to other instruments of the review function such as missions to collect information which have been suggested (and incidentally used) by the shipping division of the UNCTAD Secretariat.

In spite of all this – and it has been noted before – UNCTAD is relatively effective as an organisation in the field of policy development. This particular area of ongoing negotiations between North and South does not provide for immediate successes, but UNCTAD has proved to be an aggressive intruder into the development debate. By persistently paying attention to Third World problems, by constantly reviewing State behaviour in the ongoing negotiating process, by stimulating States in its triple function of *de facto* agent of one of the parties, 'honest broker' between the parties and at the same time 'watchdog' over the parties, and by trying to contribute to the drafting and redrafting of proposals, UNCTAD plays within the limits of the given political-economic setting an important role in the restructuring of the international economic relations.

In reviewing State behaviour, supervision of policy development is less dependent upon national data, than in the case of supervision of implementation in the strict sense; as supervisor of the negotiating process UNCTAD can rely more on the 'international' behaviour of States and information provided by other international organisations. In correcting or stimulating States, UNCTAD, potentially, can mobilise as much international pressure and political constraint as is available at a certain moment; and in the creative process of drafting and redrafting norms UNCTAD can use its technical abilities to the maximum.

Even if UNCTAD, as an international organisation, is not yet fitted to supervise effectively the implementation of adopted norms – and to this there are hopeful exceptions in some more technical areas and with regard to the follow-up mechanisms created in a number of multilateral legal instruments – it fulfils a specific normative function in the restructuring towards a new international economic order. It seems that, in the field of trade and development, this function can hardly be fulfilled by any other member of the United Nations family, because none of those has the institutional structure nor the decision-making process, in the form of group bargaining, of which UNCTAD has become, after 15 years of protracted political struggle, the embodiment *par excellence*.

The group system entails a number of obvious disadvantages; nevertheless, its main implication of political pressure is most significant in the North-South dialogue. As a consequence of inter-group bargaining, the UNCTAD negotiating process is essentially based on a model of conflict. Results have to be attained by conciliation and thus by compromise which in its turn is an inherent feature of consensus building. The latter should be considered as the first task of UNCTAD which does not stand in the way of elaborating consensus into multilateral legal instruments like codes of conduct or treaties.

It goes without saying that expectations regarding consensus building may not be put too high. If it counts for other organisations, it certainly counts for UNCTAD, that its success is commensurate with the political will of its Member States to co-operate; and especially the will of the rich countries to establish a more equitable international economic order. UNCTAD's role as a 'consensus builder', in this respect, could be considerably enhanced if distrust fostered by most developed countries *vis-à-vis* the work of its Secretariat could be obviated. This, however, seems only attainable if UNCTAD no longer functions as *de facto* Secretariat on behalf of the Group of 77. To that end the developing countries should finally come to agreement on some sort of a Third World Secretariat.

NOTES

1. A/Res/1995 (XIX), section 1, D. J. Djonovich, Vol. X (New York, 1974), p. 71.
2. See G. J. H. van Hoof and K. de Vey Mestdagh, 'Mechanisms of International Supervision', *supra*, p. 7.
3. D. Cordovez, 'The Making of UNCTAD, Institutional background and legislatiive history', (1967) JWTL 281; *Report of the Conference, Proceedings*, Vol. I, pp. 101–368.
4. Cordovez, *loc. cit.*, p. 305.
5. The Final Act of the Geneva Conference consists of a Preamble which contains the background, constitution and proceedings, findings, reasons and considerations of the Conference; a consolidation of the Recommendations of the Conference and the texts of all recommendations, the observations of delegations and other documents.
6. Cordovez, *loc. cit.*, p. 306–307.
7. *Idem*, p. 309; Also B. Gosovic, *UNCTAD, Conflict and Compromise (The Third World's Quest for an Equitable World Economic Order through the United Nations)* (Leiden, 1972), note 45, p. 44.
8. H. G. Schermers, *International Institutional Law*, Vol. I (Leiden, 1972), p. 7 (the author cites many examples). See also A. J. Peasly, *International Governmental Organizations*, (revised 3rd edition, 1974), Vol. I, p. vii; organisations are included governed by documents with less than the status of treaties which have become effective through the enactment of the governing body of the organisation itself or through some similar procedure, *e.g.* the United Nations Industrial Development Organisation (at p. 1333). The latter organisation has, like UNCTAD, been established as an organ of the General Assembly, but as to UNIDO it was explicitly stated that it should function as an autonomous organisation within the UN; see A/Res/2152 (XXI), November 17, 1966, Section I.
9. Schermers, *op. cit.*, Vol. I, p. 9.
10. Gosovic, *op. cit.*, p. 177.
11. B. Gosovic, *op. cit.*, p. 44.
12. A/Res/1995 (XIX), Art. 3(a).
13. *Idem*, Art. 3(b).
14. *Idem*, Art. 3(c).
15. *Idem*, Art. 3(c); the Articles 3(b), (c) and (e) will be dealt with, in more detail, in Chapter 3 of this study.
16. *Idem*, art. 3(d); also Cordovez, *loc. cit.*, p. 310.
17. A/Res/1995 (XIX), art. 3(f).
18. *Idem*, art. 3(g).
19. I. Haji, 'UNCTAD and shipping', (1972) 6 *JWTL* 62.
20. See the Final Act of the Geneva Conference, Annex A.IV.21, 22, 23, 24, 25 and 26.
21. TD/B/SR.10, p. 62.
22. TD/B/L.23, p. 9.
23. J. S. Smid, 'International Legislation on Shipping', (1969), 3 *JWTL* 318.
24. A/Res: 2401 (XXIII), December 13, 1968.
25. TD/B/WP/2, p. 3.
26. Board decision 117 (XIV), September 13, 1974, TD/B/639.
27. A/Res/2626 (XXV), October 24, 1970.
28. Also Gosovic, *op. cit.*, pp. 189–197.
29. A/Res/3281 (XXIX), December 12, 1974.
30. Conference Resolution 45 (III), *Report and Annexes*, Vol. I, p. 58; adopted by roll-call vote, with abstentions of nearly all the developed countries.
31. A/Res/1995 (XIX), art. 3(a).
32. *Idem*, Section I.
33. Also Gosovic, *op. cit.*, p. 29.
34. *Infra*, p. 291.
35. New Delhi, 1968; Santiago, 1972; and Nairobi, 1976; see A/Res/2904 (XXVII), September 26, 1972, which amended resolution 1995 (XIX) in the sense that the Conference should be convened at least every four years.
36. A/Res/1995 (XIX), Art. 1; the Conference comprises 163 Member States, see *UNCTAD Monthly Bulletin*, no. 166, October 1980.
37. In resolution 1995 (XIX), Art. 4, the Board is called 'a permanent organ of the Conference'.
38. See resolution 1995 (XIX), para. 5, and A/Res/2904 (XXVIII), para. 6.
39. Resolution 90 (IV), Section I, para. 5.

40. A/Res/31/2, September 29, 1976.
41. *UNCTAD Monthly Bulletin,* no. 166, October 1980.
42. A/Res/1995 (XIX), arts. 14–23.
43. As proposed by the developing countries which intended to enhance the political standing of the person who is in charge of the Secretariat of UNCTAD.
44. A/Res/1995 (XIX), Art. 22; and Cordovez, *loc. cit.,* p. 312.
45. Gosovic, *op. cit.,* p. 179.
46. A/Res/1995 (XIX), Art. 29.
47. Gosovic, *op. cit.,* pp. 183–184.
48. J. S. Nye, in: 'UNCTAD: Poor Nations' Pressure Group', in Cox and Jacobson, eds., *The Anatomy of Influence,* 1973, p. 345.
49. Nye, *ibidem,* p. 351.
50. Cosovic, *op. cit.,* pp. 184–185.
51. See for more exact figures: *Proposed Programme Budget for the Biennium 1980–1981,* A/C.5/34/27.
52. TD/B/WP/2, Annex, p. 1.
53. See the discussion on the varying kinds of decisions in: S. M. Schwebel, ed., *The Effectiveness of International Decisions,* (Leyden, 1971), at p. 379 *et seq.*
54. A/Res/1995 (XIX), art. 3, paras. b. and c.
55. *Idem,* art. 3, para. e.
56. It may be noted that, as regards terminology, the UNCTAD Secretariat works on a technical distinction between resolutions and decisions.

Resolutions are, with a very few exceptions, composed of a preambular part and an operative part. Decisions, on the contrary, consist of straightforward paragraphs which are not preceded by recalls, reflexions or agreements. There are certain issues that lend themselves to decisions rather than resolutions (such as house-keeping affairs). This distinction between resolutions and decisions, however, is not always strictly applied.
57. Cordovez, *loc. cit.,* pp. 300–307; and R. N. Gardner, 'The United Nations Conference on Trade and Development', in R. N. Gardner and M. F. Millikan, eds., *The Global Partnership, International agencies and economic development* (New York, 1968), pp. 114–120.
58. A/Res/1995 (XIX), Art. 25.
59. 'Meaningful acceptance' points to the support of members having the capacity to give effect to the proposals, *i.e.* the major trading States. It thereby cannot cover proposals which, whilst capable of securing the two-thirds majority, could never find such an acceptance; see also D. W. Bowett, *The Law of International Institutions,* (London, 1975), pp. 359–360.
60. R. Krishnamurti and D. Cordovez, 'Conciliation Procedures in UNCTAD, An Explanatory Note,' (1968) 2 *JWTL* 445.
61. Gardner, *loc. cit.,* n. 57, p. 119.
62. *Supra,* p. 291.
63. Gosovic, *op. cit.,* p. 291.
64. Initially, the group was called the 'Group of 75' according to the first 75 developing countries taking part in the Geneva Conference. Nowadays the 'Group of 77' numbers in fact 119 developing countries.
65. Roughly, Group A consists of the African and Asian countries; Group B consists of the developed countries with a market economy; Group C consists of the Latin-American countries; and Group D includes the socialist countries of Eastern Europe.
66. Gosovic, *op. cit.,* pp. 269 *et seq.*; within the informal group system China is not a member of one of the groups and, consequently, acts on its own.
67. R. S. Walters, 'International organization and political communication: the use of UNCTAD by less developed countries', (1971) 25 *IO* 824–825.
68. R. S. Walters, 'UNCTAD: Intervener between Poor and Rich States', (1973) 7 *JWTL* 542.
69. In particular the 'Group of 77' consists of countries at different stages of economic development, *e.g.* least-developed countries, less-developed countries, newly-industrialised countries, oil-exporting countries, oil-importing countries, etc., all with greatly differing economic interests and a disparity of basic economic resources.
70. See Gosovic, *op. cit.,* pp. 276–279 and 324–328; also R. S. Walters, *loc. cit.,* n. 68, pp. 541, *et. seq.*; in this respect the energy issue might be mentioned which caused much confusion and delay at the fifth Conference held in Manila, 1979; and R. L. Rothstein, *Global Bargaining: UNCTAD and the quest for a new international economic order* (Princeton, 1979), pp. 192 *et seq.*
71. *Supra,* pp. 283–284.
72. See Article 3, paras. b, c and e.
73. *Proceedings of the first session,* Vol. I, pp. 18–22.

74. General Principle 13.
75. E/Conf.46/139, Annex B.
76. Recommendation A.I.3, *Proceedings,* Vol. I, p. 26; also Cordovez, *loc. cit.,* p. 307.
77. See also the three major negotiation stages distinguished by Raul Prebisch, referred to by J. S. Nye, *loc. cit.,* n. 48, p. 368.
78. *Proceedings of UNCTAD IV,* Vol. 1, p. 38.
79. *Measures to enable UNCTAD to carry out its role more effectively,* Report by the UNCTAD Secretariat, TD/245, April 20, 1979, p. 3.
80. Conference resolution 114 (V).
81. Coffee, olive oil, sugar, tin and cocoa.
82. TD/CODE/13, 1974.
83. TD/332, 1970.
84. TD/RBP/CONF/8, 1979.
85. TD/CODE/TOT/25, draft 1980.
86. Supra, p. 296 *et seq.*
87. G. J. H. van Hoof and K. de Vey Mestdagh, *supra,* p. 28.
88. A/Res/1995 (XIX), Art. 3(f).
89. See also Cordovez, *loc. cit.,* p. 310.
90. UN Charter, Art. 1(3), *j°.* Arts. 55 and 56.
91. *Infra,* p. 301 *et seq.*
92. G. J. H. van Hoof and K. de Vey Mestdagh, *supra,* p. 11 *et seq.*
93. *E.g.* the ticklish affair of the flags of convenience.
94. TD/B/L.63, Add. 4, October 11, 1965; also P. P. Kanthan, 'The legal limitations of GATT and UNCTAD towards mutual cooperation' (1975) 15 *IJIL* 73.
95. K. Ahooja-Patel, 'Meeting of the UNCTAD Board' (1968) 2 *JWTL* 714.
96. TD/B/71.
97. E. M. Chossudovsky, 'Some reflections in the light of UNCTAD's experience', in: 'Etudes et Travaux de l'Institut Universitaire de Hautes Etudes Internationales', no. 13: *Les Résolutions dans la Formation du Droit du Développement* (Colloque, 1970), (Geneva, 1971), pp. 181–182.
98. G. J. H. van Hoof and K. de Vey Mestdagh, *supra,* p. 14.
99. Board resolution 19 (II), para. 2.
100. A/Res/1995 (XIX), para. 18.
101. *Idem,* para. 19.
102. Cordovez, *loc. cit.,* p. 316.
103. Board resolution 19 (II), para. 3.
104. In the so-called political phase; G. J. H. van Hoof and K. de Vey Mestdagh, *supra,* pp.19–20.
105. Gosovic, *op. cit.,* p. 222.
106. *Infra,* p. 332.
107. Chossudovsky, *loc. cit.,* n. 97, p. 181; the political discussion may be referred to as 'parliamentary diplomacy' as defined by the former US Secretary of State, Dean Rusk, which resembles – in most cases not *vis-à-vis* individual States, but with regard to any of the three groups of States functioning in UNCTAD – so-called 'collective legitimisation', see I. Claude, *The changing United Nations,* (Random House), 1967, p. 73 *et seq.*
108. See for a more elaborate study on the composing and maintaining of group positions: Gosovic, *op. cit.,* p. 271 *et seq.*
109. A/Res/1995 (XIX), Art. 15.
110. *Idem,* Art. 14.
111. *Idem,* Art. 3, para. b.
112. *Idem,* para. e.
113. *Supra,* p. 284 *et seq.*
114. A/Res/2626 (XXV), 24 October, 1970, para. 83.
115. This enlargement (from 27 to 54) was originally (in 1971) a US proposal to reassert its "Leadership and authority' and to make it into an 'effective force for leadership in the second Development Decade', see Gosovic, *op. cit.,* p. 197.
116. A/Res/2626 (XXV), 24 October, 1970, paras. 80 and 81.
117. *Idem,* para. 82.
118. For the discussions in the Board, see: A/7214, p. 53; A/7616, p. 9 and A/8015/Rev. 1, p. 6.
119. *Supra,* p. 284.
120. Also Board resolution 81 (XI), September 17, 1971.
121. A/Res/2801 (XXVI), para. 8.
122. Conference resolution 79 (III), para. 5.
123. A/Res/2626 (XXV), October 24, 1970, para. 82.

124. *Supra,* p. 298.
125. The first biennial review was carried out at the fifth special session of the Board, in April–May 1973 (see TD/B/429/rev. 1, p. 1).
126. Board resolution 102 (XIII), para. 4; the meeting was eventually convened in March 1975.
127. Respectively A/Res/3201 (S–VI) and A/Res/3202 (S–VI), May 1, 1974.
128. A/Res/3202 (S–VI), Section IX, para. 2.
129. *Idem,* paras. 3 and 4.
130. ECOSOC resolution 1911 (LVIII), August 2, 1974.
131. Board resolution 122 (XIV), para. 2 (d) and para. 4, September 13, 1974.
132. Agreed conclusion 129 (S–VII) of the Board, March 21, 1975.
133. A/Res/3281 (XXIX), December 12, 1974.
134. A/Res/3486 (XXX), December 12, 1975.
135. *Idem,* para. 6.
136. A/Res/3506 (XXX), para. 2, December 15, 1975.
137. *Supra,* p. 302.
138. *Supra,* p. 303.
139. Conference resolution 90 (IV), para. 3 (a), May 30, 1976.
140. Board decision 146 (XVI), October 23, 1976; also Agreed conclusion 152 (S–VIII) of the Board, May 4, 1977.
141. E.g., TD/B/SR.413–425; TD/B/SR.428–443; and TD/B/SR.457–461 and 464.
142. E.g., TD/B/530; TD/B/642; and TD/B/757.
143. TD/B/785; TD/B/791; TD/B/797; and TD/B/SR.527 and 532.
144. TD/B/798, para. 65.
145. A/Res/1995 (XIX), Art. 23.
146. Committee on Commodities; Committee on Manufactures; Committee on Invisibles and Financing related to Trade; Committee on Shipping; Committee on Transfer of Technology; and Committee on Economic Cooperation among Developing Countries.
147. Special Committee on Preferences.
148. See: TD/B/740 in respect of the Main Committees, and TD/B/332 regarding the Special Committee on Preferences.
149. Conference resolution 80 (III), Section C.
150. TD/B/740, Annex II.
151. See *supra,* p. 298.
152. Board resolution 19 (II), para. 6.
153. The frequency of the meetings of the Main Committees is governed by Conference resolution 80 (III), para. 11(a), which states that normally the Main Committees should meet twice between two sessions of the Conference. See also board decision 45 (VII), para. 14 and Ahooja Patel, *loc. cit.,* n. 95, p. 715.
154. Board resolution 19 (II), para. 2.
155. *Supra,* p. 300.
156. Final Act, Annex A, II, 1.
157. Board decision 7(I), April 29, 1965, TD/B/740, Annex II.
158. *Idem,* paras. 1, 5 and 12.
159. *Idem,* para. 12.
160. *Idem,* para. 3.
161. *Idem,* para. 10.
162. Conference resolution 80 (III), para. 11(a); and Board decision 7(I), para. 14.
163. *Idem,* para. 11; also TD/B/C.1/16, paras. 101–109; the Permanent Sub-Committee should hold at least two sessions a year, one of which should immediately precede the session of the Committee on Commodities. The second session of the Permanent Sub-Committee should be held in the same place as the Committee. At that particular session the Permanent Sub-Committee would prepare a summary of the current market situation in selected commodities for consideration by the Committee, *vide* para. 107.
164. Personal interviews, held in February 1980.
165. Final Act, Annex A, II, 7.
166. TD/B/740, Annex II, Board decision 7(I), para. 13; also TD/B/C.1/16, paras. 96–100.
167. Conference resolution 93 (IV), *Proceedings,* Vol. I, p. 6.
168. The 'core' commodities are: coffee, cocoa, tea, sugar, hard fibres, jute, rubber, copper and tin. At UNCTAD IV, in Nairobi, it was agreed that meat, bananas, vegetable oils, tropical timber, phosphate, iron ore, manganese and bauxite should also be included in the arrangement at a later stage.
169. Board resolution 140 (XVI), October 23, 1976, TD/B/638.
170. Conference resolution 93 (IV), Section IV, Art. 8, *Proceedings,* Vol. I, p. 6.

171. Conference resolution 80 (III).
172. See resolution 1 (III) of July 15, 1977, and resolution 3 (VI) of July 15, 1978; also TD/228, para. 28.
173. TD/B/IPC/AC/21 and A/33/15, p. 49; TD/228, para. 28; and TD/B/IPC/AC/34.
174. A/33/15, para. 207, p. 50.
175. Board resolution 173 (XVIII), September 17, 1978, TD/B/729.
176. *Review of implementation and follow-up action,* Report by the UNCTAD Secretariat, TD/228, para. 29.
177. Conference resolution 124 (V), Section D, Art. 1.
178. *Idem,* Section C.
179. See TD/B/IPC/AC/L.22.
180. See TD/B/C1/212: Future role and work programme of the Committee on Commodities.
181. See the reports of the Committee on Commodities from 1965–1974.
182. TD/B/497, para. 7.
183. *E.g.,* commodity exchanges, such as the New York Cocoa Exchange and the Liverpool Cotton Exchange.
184. TD/B/497, para. 8.
185. This committee stems from the UN *ad hoc* Committee on Tungsten (1963) which in 1965 had become the present Committee on Tungsten.
186. TD/B/497, para. 10.
187. TD/B/497; also A/Res/3202 (S–VI), Section IX, para. 4.
188. Examples of these secondary sources are: the Institute of Geological Sciences, London; Metallgesellschaft A.G., Frankfurt am Main; World Bureau of Metal Statistics, London and Birmingham.
189. TD/B/497, para. 21.
190. *Idem,* para. 23.
191. *Idem,* para. 23.
192. See *Report of the Board to the UN General Assembly,* A/9615/Rev. 1, paras. 124–130.
193. Board resolution 123 (XIV), TD/B/532.
194. TD/B/C.1/167, paras. 3–5.
195. TD/B/C.1/167, para. 8; and TD/B/C.1/182, paras. 214 *et seq.*
196. Personal interviews, held in February 1980.
197. Some questionnaires on individual commodities, such as tropical timber, cotton and iron ore, are still sent to governments, but a response average of approximately 10 to 15 per cent. does not improve market transparencies and does certainly not allow any decisive conclusions.
198. *Supra,* pp. 309–310 (note 177).
199. See comparable difficulties encountered by the Committee on Shipping, *infra,* p. 318.
200. Board decision 9 (I), TD/B/L.31; see also TD/B/740, p. 31.
201. See the Terms of Reference of the Committee on Manufactures, para. 4, TD/B/740.
202. *Idem,* para. 9.
203. *Idem,* para. 10.
204. *Idem,* para. 13.
205. See the statement by a representative of a developed market-economy country, at the 1977 review session, TD/B/663, para. 9.
206. R. Krishnamurti, 'UNCTAD Group of Experts on Restrictive Business Practices', (1973) 7 *JWTL* 711; and C. R. Greenhill, 'UNCTAD, Control of Restrictive Business Practices', (1978) 12 *JWTL* 67.
207. Conference resolution 25 (II), *Proceedings,* p. 38.
208. A/Res/2626 (XXV), Art. 37.
209. Resolution 9 (VII) of the Committee on Manufactures, TD/B/576, Annex I.
210. A compendious survey of RBP's developments in the framework of UNCTAD can be found in TD/RBP/CONF/8, pp. 1–3; also Conference resolution 103 (V).
211. *Idem,* p. 14.
212. TD/RBP/CONF/L.11 and Corr. 1, April 21, 1980.
213. Section F, para. 2.
214. Instead of a new Group of Experts, Group B proposed an existing Committee within the framework of UNCTAD to provide the institutional machinery: see TD/RBP/CONF/8, p. 18, note 16.
215. TD/RBP/CONF/L.11, Section G, para. 2, a (vi).
216. TD/RBP/CONF/8, p. 19, footnote 18.
217. TD/RBP/CONF/L. 11, Section G, para. 2, a (vii).
218. *Idem,* para. 2, b.

219. TD/RBP/CONF/L.11/Add. 2.
220. Conference resolution 103 (V), para. 4(a).
221. TD/B/750; and TD/B/831.
222. See Board resolution 11 (I) and decision 12 (II), TD/B/L.31, Annex A. 1; also TD/B/740; and *supra*, p. 284.
223. Item VI of the programme of work, TD/B/240, Annex II (since 1969 it is wrongly stated in the Introduction to the Reviews of Maritime Transport that these reviews are prepared in accordance with item V of the programme of work).
224. Conference resolution 14 (II), *Proceedings*, Vol. II, p. 50.
225. *Idem*, see Preamble.
226. Resolution 7 (III), TD/B/240, Annex I.
227. *Idem*, para. 2.
228. Conference resolution 3 (II), *Proceedings*, Vol. I, p. 46.
229. TD/B/C.4/43; TD/B/C.4/45; and TD/B/C.4/47.
230. Gosovic, *op. cit.*, p. 145.
231. TD/B/521, para. 39.
232. *Idem*, para. 40.
233. TD/B/591, para. 7.
234. *Idem*, para. 125.
235. *Idem*, para. 88.
236. TD/B/648, p. 63.
237. R. S. Walters, 'UNCTAD: Intervener between Poor and Rich States' (1973) 7 *JWTL* 532.
238. TD/B/C.4/20 and Add. 1–5, Vols. I and II.
239. Resolution 5 (III), TD/B/240, Annex I; also the Committee Report on the fourth session, TD/B/301.
240. See for the establishment of the Working Group, Conference resolution 14 (II), *Proceedings*, Vol. I, p. 50; and Committee on Shipping Resolution 7 (III), TD/B/240, Annex I; for the report of the Working Group on its second session, see TD/B/C. 86.
241. TD/CODE/13; and TD/CODE/13/Add. 1.
242. *Idem*, see Arts. 23–46.
243. TD/B/591, paras. 55–66; and also Official Records of the Trade and Development Board, eighth session, 1977, TD/B/648, paras. 32–53.
244. Conference resolution 106 (V), para. 8, June 1, 1979, TD/L.163. As regards information for the purpose of preparation of material for the Review Conference, see also Code, Art. 46(e).
245. TD/B/C.4/L.137, p. 27.
246. TD/B/300/Rev.1; TD/B/329/Rev.1; and TD/B/332, the latter containing Board decision 75 (S–IV): Generalised system of Preferences.
247. Conference resolution 21 (II), *Proceedings*, Vol. I, p. 38.
248. TD/B/329; and TD/B/300.
249. See foregoing note; also TD/B/332; and J. D. Greenwald, 'Generalised tariff preferences of developing countries: the UNCTAD agreed conclusions' (1971), 10 *CJTL* 111–132.
250. Originally there was no consensus regarding the machinery to fulfil this supervisory role. The B Group favoured the Committee on Manufactures, while the Group of 77 and the D Group asked that the mandate of the Special Committee on preferences be extended. In essence the developed countries were against a committee on preferences because it would have offered a convenient institutional focus for a full-fledged critical and probably acrimonious examination of the general preferences. They shunned any sort of 'implementation' procedure precisely because preferences are granted voluntarily, as a unilateral concession. Since, in their opinion, there are no mutual rights and obligations, the donors should be free to do as they please. See Gosovic, *op. cit.*, p. 233.
251. *Supra*, p. 306.
252. Resolution 1 (V), April 13, 1973, TD/B/442, p. 39.
253. *E.g.* TD/B/C.5/30, p. 2.
254. *Ibidem*; also TD/B/489, p. 2.
255. As governed by CCCN chapters 1–24 (agricultural products) and 25–99 (industrial products and raw materials).
256. TD/B/C.5/53, Annex III, p. 1.
257. TD/B/C.5/61, p. 5.
258. *Supra*, p. 322.
259. TD/B/C.5/63, p. 25/26.
260. TD/B/C.5/58, p. 14.
261. TD/B/442 (1973); TD/B/489 (1974); TD/B/598 (1976); TD/B/653 (1977).

262. TD/B/442, paras. 81 and 89–91; TD/B/489, paras. 153 and 177; TD/B/598, para. 58; and TD/B/653, para. 68.
263. TD/B/598, para. 94.
264. *Idem*, para. 115.
265. TD/B/C.5/63, p. 25.
266. TD/B/713, para. 14.
267. TD/B/653, p. 33.
268. TD/B/329/Rev. 1; also *supra*, p. 322.
269. Section VIII, para. 3.
270. TD/B/713, para. 6.
271. *Idem*, paras. 17 and 18.
272. Board decision 179 (XVIII), para. 2, TD/B/729, p. 6.
273. *Idem*, p. 5.
274. TD/B/713, para. 18.
275. See *supra*, p. 284.
276. Board decision 117 (XIV), September 13, 1974, TD/B/639.
277. See the Terms of Reference of the Committee on Transfer of Technology, paras. 3–8, TD/B/639.
278. TD/B/539; TD/B/736; and TD/B/C.6.(III)/Misc.4.
279. TD/B/C.6(III)/Misc.4, paras. 52–56.
280. See Conference resolution 112 (V), para. 28.
281. TD/B/C.6(III)/Misc. 4, para. 52; also TD/B/C.6/53.
282. *Idem*, Annex I, Resolution 11 (III).
283. See TD/237, paras. 51–78; and TD/B/C.6(III)/Misc.4, para. 81–89.
284. See Conference resolution 87 (IV), para. 13, *Proceedings of UNCTAD IV*, p. 17.
285. TD/B/C.6(III)/Misc.4, paras. 57–62.
286. Conference resolution 89 (IV).
287. See TD/CODE TOT/1.
288. Draft International Code of Conduct on the Transfer of Technology, as of April 10, 1981, TD/CODE TOT/33, paras. 7.1 and 7.2.
289. *Idem*, para. 8.1; also TD/CODE TOT/27, paras. 76 and 77.
290. *Idem*, para. 8.2.1.
291. *Supra*, p. 316.
292. TD/CODE TOT/33, para. 8.2.2.
293. *Idem*, paras. 8.3. and 8.4.
294. See *supra*, p. 290.
295. Tripartite reviews are exercised by the assistance-receiving country, UNDP and the executing agency concerned. UNCTAD became an executing agency of UNDP in 1968, see *supra*, p. 285.
296. Conference resolution 114 (V), para. 11(a), UNCTAD/CA/1350.
297. TD/B/WF/2.
298. *E.g.* the assistance given to the developing countries in preparing the multilateral trade negotiations under the GATT, and the negotiations held within the framework of the IPC; see TD/B/WP/2.
299. See for more detailed information TD/B/WP/2.
300. TD/B/71.
301. *Supra*, p. 298 *et seq.*
302. See G. J. H. van Hoof and K. de Vey Mestdagh, *supra*, p. 11.
303. *Supra*, p. 325.
304. *Supra*, p. 315.
305. *Supra*, p. 326.
306. See Walters, *loc. cit.*, n. 67, p. 819.
307. *Supra*, p. 297.
308. Also Walters, *loc. cit.*, n. 68, p. 550.
309. *Supra*, p. 291.
310. See G. J. H. van Hoof and K. de Vey Mestdagh, *supra*, p. 21.
311. See TDO.321, 74/595, of April 19, 1974.
312. P. P. Kanthan, 'The legal limitations of GATT and UNCTAD: towards mutual cooperation' (1975) 15 *IJIL* 73.
313. See 'Etudes et Travaux de l'Institut Universitaire de Hautes Etudes Internationales', (Colloque des 20 et 21 Novembre, 1970) no. 13: *Les Résolutions dans la Formation du Droit International du Développement* (Geneva, 1971), p. 35.

314. See M. Meyer and J. Rose, *Le contrôle de l'application des recommendations de la CNUCED, ibidem*, p. 143.

315. S. El-Naggar, *ibidem*, pp. 35–36.

316. Personal interviews, held in February 1980.

317. TD/B/442, p. 31, and TD/B/C.5/68. Main areas of difficulty are: lack of understanding by exporters, manufacturers and, in some cases, officials of the legal language used by the preference-giving countries in the documents relating to their schemes; the classification of goods; the differing tariff cuts; the rules of origin; and the yearly changes in GSP limitations in some major schemes.

318. TD/B/C.5/63, p. 43.

319. TD/B/C.4/L.137.

320. TD/B/C.6/53.

321. *E.g.* in the cases of restrictive business practices and transfer of technology.

322. S. El-Naggar, *loc. cit.*, note 313, *f°* 315, pp. 35–36.

323. *Supra*, p. 318.

324. See G. J. H. van Hoof and K. de Vey Mestdagh, *supra*, p. 11.

325. See for an elaborate study on policy development in the field of the Integrated Programme for Commodities, and *inter alia* the internal factors that have conditioned the behaviour of the United States in this respect, R. L. Rothstein, *Global Bargaining: UNCTAD and the Quest for a New International Economic Order* (Princeton, 1979).

326. M. Meyer and J. Rose, *loc. cit.*, n. 313, *f°* 314, p. 141.

327. *Idem*, p. 144.

328. Gosovic, *op. cit.*, p. 223; and E. M. Chossudovsky, *Some Reflections in the Light of UNCTAD'S Experience, loc. cit.*, n. 313, p. 181.

329. *Supra*, pp. 322 *et seq.*

330. Personal interview, held in February 1980.

331. *Supra*, p. 293; see *inter alia* the change of attitude of the U.S. government towards the Generalised System of Preferences, A. K. Bhattacharya, 'The influence of the international secretariat: UNCTAD and generalized tariff preferences', (1976) 30 Int.Org. 75.

332. *E.g.* restrictive business practices, the Integrated Programme for Commodities, Codes of Conduct, etc.

333. *E.g.* the assistance given to the developing countries in preparing the multinational trade negotiations under the GATT.

334. *Supra*, p. 318.

335. See R. S. Walters, *loc. cit.*, n. 68, pp. 527 *et seq.*

336. *Supra*, p. 291.

337. See the Set of Principles and Rules for the Control of Restrictive Business Practices, the Code of conduct for Liner Conferences, and the Generalised system of Preferences.

338. *Supra*, p. 303.

339. Respectively, *supra*, p. 308 and p. 318.

340. The central element of the power of UNCTAD and in particular its Secretariat rests on the need of the developing countries to create and control a forum to initiate, co-ordinate and negotiate Group of 77 policy packages. Only UNCTAD is in a position to respond, for no other institution provides the necessary kind of staff and resources. See on this subject A. K. Bhattacharya, 'The influence of the international secretariat: UNCTAD and generalized tariff preferences' (1976) 30 Int.Org. *et seq.*; and R. L. Rothstein, *Global Bargaining, UNCTAD and the Quest for a New International Economic Order* (Princeton, 1979).

PART V

SUPERVISION WITHIN THE INTERNATIONAL MONETARY FUND

SUPERVISION WITHIN THE
INTERNATIONAL MONETARY FUND

*by R. Barents**

'Without effective surveillance, there is no system.'
G. William Miller, Governor of the Fund and the Bank for the
United States. Summary Proceedings Annual Meeting IMF 1979,
116.

'It is the supervision and management of the interdependence
which gave the fund its fundamental and unique role.'
R. A. Mundell in *The New International Monetary System*, ed. by
R. A. Mundell and J. J. Polak (New York, 1977), 244.

CONTENTS

I. INTRODUCTION

In this Part some remarks will be made on the supervisory mechanisms of the International Monetary Fund. As the supervisory mechanisms project as a whole has been expounded in the introductory chapter,[1] only the method of examination used here necessitates a justification.

This part consists of two sections. In the first of these (Section II) the phenomenon of supervisory mechanisms will be approached deductively. In this part, some remarks will be made on the possible significance for the supervisory mechanisms of the fact that the universal international economic organisations came into being during the same period (at the end of the Second World War) and had the same background (the restructuring of international trade). The point of departure will be the theory of international economic law as it has been developed elsewhere in legal literature.[2] In the second part (sections III to VI) the supervisory mechanisms of the IMF itself will be dealt with. This will be done by means of a method of inductive comparison. The supervisory mechanisms underlying the original Articles of Agreement of the IMF will be compared with the procedures which have been developed in the course of time, and which are applied under present IMF law and practice.

Attention will be paid only to the supervisory mechanisms, and no extensive treatment will be given of IMF law.[3] Only in section III will some elements of the substantive law of the IMF be described, this being necessary to the following sections.

II. SUPERVISORY MECHANISMS IN INTERNATIONAL ECONOMIC LAW

2.1. Introductory remarks

The literature on international economic law, which is relatively scarce, points out that this particular field of law has developed around a core of principles, applied more or less unchanged throughout the centuries.[4] These principles include the phenomenon of the minimum standard, this being an elementary code of behaviour concerning a specific subject, as well as a principle of freedom and a principle of equality with a certain number of variants. These principles are not of a normative or legal nature. On the contrary, they only embody the minimum conditions which have to be complied with by States in the exercise of their economic sovereignty, in order to achieve an orderly and functional State interaction. The fundamental nature of these principles is reflected, as stated above, by their having remained relatively unchanged throughout the centuries. Since these principles can be qualified as basic conditions for transnational State economic behaviour, their fulfilment – whether factual or within a normative framework – tends to unify, to a certain extent, the national and international legal rules with respect to economic interaction between States.

The problem arises with respect to the maintenance of these principles when governmental intervention in economic life reaches such a degree as to produce transnational effects, or even when a regulation of transnational economic interaction is implied (*'Aussenwirtschaftsrecht'*). The maintenance of these principles is then placed in a field of latent tension between an internal and external economic equilibrium, with a necessary adjustment process on the balance of payments in case of a disequilibrium. Expressed in legal terms, this implies a continuous interaction between national and international economic law. The maintenance of these principles and the subsequent elementary regulation of economic interaction between States, more or less necessitates a subordination of national to international economic law. An illustrative example of this process can be seen in the four freedoms of the EEC. These four freedoms (free movement of goods, persons, services and capital) illustrate how such a derogation can reach an ultimate degree by qualifying them as self-executing, as the Court of Justice of the European Communities has done.[5]

In the nineteenth century, the necessary framework for the implementation of these principles was only partially constituted by international legal rules and was mainly concerned with the many bilateral treaties with respect to commerce and shipping. For the rest, this order was a *de facto* order, the result of the social and economic patterns in force at that time. The role of governments as 'night watchmen,' the reigning doctrine of liberalism, the general outlook on mankind and the world, as well as the absence of modern economic concepts and management, resulted in a more or less automatic functioning of the adjustment process on the balance of payments through the action of the gold standard.[6] In combination with the dominating position of the British pound, and a multilateral and liberalised international trade, regulation of international economic relations was achieved, without there being a legal basis in the form of an international organisation or other facility which would guarantee the fulfilment of the above-mentioned principles. Thus, around the second half of the last century, international economic law was hardly developed, simply because there was no need for it.[7] However, the inter-war period, during which governments began to intervene in the economic process on a large scale, proved that a fulfilment of those principles could not be achieved without a specific international legal structure. The rapid growth of the '*Aussenwirtschaftsrecht*,' the legal expression of 'beggar my neighbour' policies, produced a rapid erosion of the previously mentioned principles. Stödter thus reluctantly admits 'that international law is utterly silent and non-existent in controlling those forces which today lie at the foundations of international relations.'[8]

The question with regard to supervisory mechanisms in the field of international economic relations could thus only obtain legal relevance through the establishment of a normative framework in which the fulfilment of the several principles was made subject to international economic law. Chronologically, the subject of supervision in international economic law can be placed during and shortly after the Second World War, the period in which the foundations of the present international economic order were laid down. Since then the functioning of international economic organisations has constituted a main feature of this international economic order and, at the same time, it constitutes the hardcore of international economic law. It is within the framework of these organisations that the continuous and latent conflict between the internal and external equilibrium on the balance of payments was made subject to legal rules. The nature and structure of the legal framework of international economic relations is, therefore, of great importance for the object and shape of supervisory mechanisms. Some elements of this problem will be dealt with below.

2.2. The post-war international economic order

The shaping of the post-war international economic order was mainly an Anglo-American matter, in which the United States had the dominant position. Having emerged from the war as the great victor and, economically and militarily, the strongest State, a leading role in the reorganisation of international economic relations was inevitable for the United States. The fundamental change in the international balance of power and a certain measure of idealism created a better climate for such action than in the pre-war period, in which all efforts to achieve a legal framework for international economic relations had been unsuccessful.

The pillars of this order: the United Nations, as the co-ordinating organisation and embodiment of an embryonic universal legal order between States; the Bretton Woods system, covering the international exchange of payments and capital; and the International Trade Organisation (planned but never realised) to deal with international trade—to a large extent reflect the American view of the world. Further, it must be stressed that at the root of the post-war international economic order, there lay no dogmatic conceptions. What the framers had in mind was primarily an elimination of the 'beggar my neighbour' policies of the 1930s, resulting in a steady contraction of international trade.[9] In first instance, it was the use of certain instruments of national economic policy, aimed at the adjustments of transnational trade and payments, that needed regulation: the manipulations of exchange rates, restrictions on trade and payments, export subsidies, all sorts of monopolistic action by raw materials suppliers and, last but not least, the phenomenon of bilateralism. It was the unco-ordinated use of these protectionist instruments that destroyed the old liberal order. A liberalised and multilateral exchange of goods and payments would promote an expansion of international trade, which would result in an efficient international division of labour. The consequent, rising standard of living would create a fertile breeding ground for democratic principles. Economic nationalism and political extremism would be banished. The final purpose of post-war international economic co-operation therefore was a political one. In order to achieve lasting world peace, not only a regulation of the physical actions of States was necessary, but also the establishment of a specific legal infrastructure with respect to international economic relations. These ideals of freedom and equality, the latter above all in the sense of non-discrimination – deeply rooted in the pattern of the Western and, especially, American culture – were embodied in the well-known Article IV of the Atlantic Charter,[10] the first concrete result in the legal sphere of Anglo-American co-operation during the Second World War. Bearing in mind the scarce attention paid to the issue of economic relations in the Treaty of the League of Nations,[11] the United Nations Charter unsurprisingly contained a clear statement on the relationship between these political and economic aspects. The purpose, under Article III,7 of the Charter, is to attain international economic co-operation, which is further elaborated under Articles LV and LVI. The former provision declared the promotion of a higher standard of living as a task of the United Nations. The latter declared it a duty of Member States to promote this task collectively, as well as individually. From this legal construction, it can be deduced that each State has a duty to promote an economic policy, aimed at the pursuit of a higher standard of living and of full employment.

Yet, according to the principle of sovereign equality, States should retain complete sovereignty in the economic sphere.[12]

The American drafters in particular considered a strategy in three different fields necessary, in order to realise the concept of the Atlantic Charter and the legal purposes of the United Nations Charter. In the monetary field, this was to be a régime for the use of exchange rates and foreign currency restrictions, together with a credit mechanism for the maintenance of the degree of liberalisation achieved, in case of balance of payments difficulties. In the trade sector, a régime was necessary on the use of customs tariffs and quotas, as well as all other kinds of trade-restricting measures, such as subsidies, State aids, regulation of raw materials markets and restrictions on competition. These régimes were to be made subject to strict multilateral supervision. Finally, in the field of capital exchange, a mechanism was necessary through which private capital would flow to favourable investment possibilities, initially in order to facilitate recovery from war damage and, subsequently, in order to be used for development programmes. Indirectly, there was also some consideration paid to co-operation in the agricultural sector.

2.3. The universal economic organisations

A clear discrepancy exists between the Atlantic Charter's initial idealism and the legal reality of the post-war international economic order. In order to realise the philosophy of expansion and liberalisation, the deviating points of view of the two protagonists, the United States and the United Kingdom, had to be reconciled. Both countries adhered to the philosophy of the market economy as the foundation of the international economic order, but disagreed on the degree of planning by which this order was to be attained. Because of their importance for world trade, and their dominating economic position, the Americans, in particular, advocated universal application of the principle of non-discrimination. The British, on the contrary, were in favour of provisions for preferential treatment, a point of view which was related, of course, to the Commonwealth System, as established in the 1930s. Also, the United Kingdom favoured a policy providing for full employment, even though this could be detrimental to a full liberalisation of international trade. As a result of the war efforts – the Allied armies had not yet set foot in Normandy – the contrasts in the monetary and financial field were less sharp during the negotiations on the Bretton Woods institutions, which negotiations were given priority. The different points of view first appeared in the British plan of Lord Keynes, and the American plan of White. The former was of a more visionary nature and provided for the establishment of an International Clearing Union, vested with many powers in the field of trade policy, development aid, the creation of international liquidities and the regulation of the raw materials market, by which a real universal economic policy would be feasible. The Americans' dominance, due to their position as the greatest money supplier, however, resulted in the establishment of the much more modest International Monetary Fund and the International Bank of Reconstruction and Development, in 1944, in accordance with White's more modest plan.

According to their Charters, both organisations aimed at the promotion of international trade, the IMF through a regulation of the instruments of monetary policy, the Bank through the mobilisation of private capital flows for productive purposes. With regard to the IMF, a system of fixed exchange rates, based on gold, was established, together with a prohibition on currency restrictions. In practice, however, this gold standard was reformed into a gold-dollar standard, by linking all the other currencies to the almighty dollar, the convertibility of which was guaranteed. Exceptions to these obligations were possible with respect to the exchange rate system, in cases of a 'fundamental disequilibrium' and at a State's own initiative, but only with the consent of the Fund. In order to maintain the achieved degree of liberalisation in case of balance of payments difficulties, a pool of gold and currencies was provided for, contributed by Member States according to a quota system based on their economic strength. The Bank was established in a similar way. According to its quota system, a Member State paid an initial sum and guaranteed the rest. Because of this, the Bank would primarily be able to promote the flow of capital to favourable investment possibilities by the provision of guarantees. Both organisations had an identical institutional structure, on a quasi-corporate law basis, illustrated *inter alia* by the system of weighted voting.

The international legal regulation of international trade relations appeared to be more difficult, because of the contrasts already mentioned. The 'Proposals for the Expansion of World Trade and Employment' – published for discussion by the United States in 1945 – evolved only after various preparatory conferences into a definite draft, which was signed by most States at the establishing conference in Havana in 1948. In the Havana Charter, an integral institutional and substantive legal system for international trade was laid down in 106 articles. The main points of this Charter[13] concerned international investments, customs tariffs, internal taxes, quotas and other trade restrictions, subsidies, State aids, conduct of enterprises and a system with regard to international commodity agreements, all to be supervised by an International Trade Organisation. This 'Magna Charta of Free Trade' provided – to a greater extent than the Articles of Agreement of the IMF – some possibilities for exceptions to the obligations of liberalisation, in favour of domestic political economic purposes, especially concerning employment and economic development. This different orientation was one of the causes of the Truman administration deciding at the end of 1950 not to present the Charter to Congress for approval. In this way, one of the important pillars of the post-war international economic order was swept away. The General Agreement on Tariffs and Trade (GATT), only meant as a transitional measure, has been able to fill the gap only partially. While the GATT principally presented a system for the reduction of customs tariffs, the elimination of quotas and related subjects, having as its leading principles non-discrimination, the Most-Favoured-Nation Clause and reciprocity, only the more liberally oriented provisions of the Havana Charter remained.

2.4. Some legal features of the post-war international economic order[14]

In a legal sense, the post-war international economic order is characterised by the normative nature given to the principle of comparative advantage in international trade. This principle is founded on the traditional free trade theories of the nineteenth century. Having an optimum efficiency as its logical justification, with a maximising of world income, this principle implied an international circulation of factors of production, impeded as little as possible, together with the market mechanism as the co-ordinating element. In a legal sense, this implied a revival of the principle of freedom, expressed in the pursuance of a liberalisation of trade and a stable monetary system with convertible currencies, both to be maintained by multilateral supervision through the international economic organisations. On the other hand, the sovereignty to States implied an explicit establishment of the competence of States with regard to their economic policy. As stated before, this left its traces in the Charter of the United Nations, while the Articles of Agreement of the IMF also give evidence of this in many places.

Another result of the sovereignty of States in economic affairs concerned the equal treatment of States, which implied that in the legal regulation of post-war international economic relations, no distinction could be made according to economic status or circumstances. Thus, a material equality of the treatment of States through a differentiation of rights and duties in the economic field, was excluded.

By the application of these two starting points, the characteristics of the nineteenth-century international economic order were continued. The essential difference, however, was that the increasing economic role of the government needed an international legal framework in order to co-ordinate the transnational effects of national economic policy. To provide for such a framework, a construction was chosen to provide for a solution to the latent conflict between the maintenance of an internal and an external economic equilibrium. Whereas, on the one hand, States retained their full sovereignty with respect to their internal economic policy, the principle of freedom demanded that maintenance of external equilibrium prevailed over maintenance of internal equilibrium as much as possible. A solution for this problem was found in a system of general rules, binding on each participating State, having a strong prohibitory nature, and completed by a transitional period and escape clauses which were to be supervised multilaterally. These basic rules were also characterised by their uniform character. As already stated, formal sovereignty of States impeded a differentiated legal treatment in international economic relations and, therefore, hardly any attention was paid to differences in standards of living. As in the economic theory of those days, orientated towards the classical free trade concept, hardly any attention was paid to the problem of underdeveloped countries, it is not surprising that in international economic law, dominated by the principle of formal sovereignty, such different treatment was also missing. A different legal orientation was also prevented by the colonial status of most non-industrialised countries. However, the above-mentioned legal concept did not imply that the question of economic underdevelopment was not recognised. In each of the several treaties, the word 'development' is found, but not used as a concept which could lead to the formulation of legal principles, that could result in specific treatment. Parallel to the recovery from war damage, the problem of economic underdevelopment was seen as a question which had to be solved primarily through the principle of freedom, *i.e.*, the flow of capital to favourable investment opportunities and industrialisation. The third chapter of the Havana Charter gives evidence of this. As mentioned above, the participating States had a uniform position with regard to the basic rules of the system, all of them were equally subject to the rules of the Bretton Woods system, and the planned ITO. Wherever economic differences in the financial field impeded strict equality, an adjustment to economic reality took place by means of the quota system, so that a reciprocity between the rights and duties of States remained, and legal homogeneity was preserved.

Thus, the old principles of international economic law, the minimum standard, the principle of freedom and the various modalities of the principle of equality were revived, this time within a rigid legal framework.

2.5. The legal evolution of the international economic order

From a legal point of view, the main feature of the post-war order was the functioning of international economic organisations. As mentioned above, these organisations provided for the necessary institutional and substantive legal framework for the canalisation of the latent tension between national and international economic law. They confirmed that in a world of national States, the economic policies of which present increasing transnational effects, a legal framework is necessary to guarantee an orderly international economic interaction, through a fulfilment of the old principles.

Initially, international economic law, as embodied in the constituent treaties of the international economic organisations, was characterised by a classical structure, strongly influenced by concepts of private law, parallel to classical national economic law. Being based on the principles of liberty and equality, this law was mainly used as an instrument to establish a certain order. Based on the Ricardian principles of an optimal division of labour through market forces, these treaties were restricted to regulating entry to markets on the basis of the freedom and equality of all the participants in international economic interaction, by which international trade would achieve an optimum degree of specialisation. The legal regulation of both pillars of this order, the IMF and GATT, therefore, was achieved through binding rules, equally valid for all participants, through exemptions from these obligations and through sanctions in the case of non-observance thereof. Thus, the main task of the international economic organisations was to control the established order of basic conditions with regard to the transnational economic behaviour of States.

The dominating role of the market mechanism in this order, not only has a function in co-ordinating the market process – the allocation of the factors of production – but also has an integrating function. Integration of the economies of the participating Western States was not so much an objective of these organisations, but more a result of the liberalised exchange of goods and payments achieved. As an objective, and thereby as a justification for further-reaching measures, economic integration on a sub-regional level plays a role in the European Communities. In practice, it is often hard to distinguish objectives and results in an integrated economic sphere: the so-called 'Zijlstra' principle applies.[45] Economic integration reduces the effect of national policy instruments to such an extent that a need for policy co-ordination increases, as can be clearly seen in the case of the EEC. Therefore, negative integration through liberalisation necessitates, sooner or later, positive integration: the co-ordination or even unification of economic policies. In classical international economic law, the process of negative integration is achieved mainly in a non-political manner: through market forces, this being illustrated by the technical and functional structure of the organisations. A process of positive integration is only to be achieved through active government involvement and, thus, implies an increase in the political aspects. It is, therefore, not surprising that the original instruments of the international economic organisations, mainly directed at a process of negative integration through liberalisation of international trade, were hardly appropriate for shaping a process of positive integration. Nevertheless, co-ordinating activities by these organisations became necessary even in the early stages of their existence. The transformation of the OEEC into the OECD, as an embryonic centre of policy co-ordination for the Atlantic world, illustrates this development. In a more limited economic sphere, as in the EEC, the tardy progress towards economic and monetary union illustrates the difficulties of the transition from negative to positive integration. This 'management of interdependence' has important consequences for the classical structure of international economic law, as indicated above. Since the Second World War, it has been possible to see that international economic order gradually evolves into a mixed international economy, in which the international economic organisations try to influence the outcome of the market process through the use of various policy instruments that have been developed in the course of time, such as the instruments of information, consultation and conditional financial incentives.

2.6. Supervision in international economic relations

From the developments indicated in the previous section, it can be deduced that the original supervisory mechanisms of post-war international economic organisations were shaped primarily in what can be qualified as the 'neo-classical' stage of international economic law. In this stage, the economic behaviour of States was regulated through a system of basic rules with respect to national policy instruments (currency measures, trade restrictions), the use of which could threaten the maintenance of liberalised and multilateral international trade. A strong similarity with private law concepts such as the binding force of contracts and good faith is evident, as is the semi-corporate law structure of these organisations. These basic rules can be qualified as positive obligations: only the result, this being the maintenance of these rules, has a legal relevance. The economic policy necessary to fulfil these obligations remained within the exclusive competence of the participating States, to be conducted according to their economic, social and political systems.

Within this structure it was understandable that the supervision which the international economic organisations had to exercise primarily concerned the maintenance of these basic rules. Thus, supervision became real through the power to grant exceptions to the basic rules and to identify potential or existing infringements. Accordingly, supervision had a functional nature and, in principle, only involved an examination of the consistency of State behaviour and the basic rules. It must be emphasised that the supervision did not concern the economic policy of the participating States that was necessary to implement or maintain these positive obligations. By choosing this structure, the need for the supervisory institutions to render a formal judgment on the economic policy of States was avoided, this being a field, as indicated above, in which the sovereignty of States had to be preserved. The various treaties give evidence of this. By confining supervision to the observance of the general and lasting basic norms, it was, in fact, reduced to the principally technical question of norm testing. Supervision, therefore, was of an objective nature, in the sense that the supervisory authority could refer directly and concretely to the wording of the various agreements, in order to justify the use of the measures to enforce the maintenance of the basic prohibitions. Finally, the outlined features of the supervisory mechanisms also had important institutional implications. In principle, no forum for high level political consultations was required, as is shown by the semi-corporate law structure of these organisations already mentioned.

A characteristic feature of this neo-classical stage, was that international economic law was mainly concerned with the regulation of market entry and market behaviour, in such a way that undistorted competition could be achieved, and with it an optimal international division of labour. With respect to the outcome of the international market process, a neutral attitude was taken, in principle. As explained before, this concept proves to be inadequate when the continuous liberalisation of trade results in an increasing economic interdependence, which makes close co-ordination of economic policy by States necessary. The gradual evolution from a system of basic rules to a system of management and co-ordination of economic policy inevitably results in consequences for the nature, form and content of the supervisory mechanisms. Generally speaking, supervision in a situation of strong economic interdependence can no longer primarily be concerned with the maintenance of the basis norms, but, on the contrary, must concern itself with the co-ordination and guidance of the economic process, in order to guarantee the achieved degree of liberalisation. With regard to the supervisory institutions, this development no longer presumes a more or less non-active 'prosecution policy' but, instead, active intervention in and guidance of domestic and international economic affairs. Supervision orientated towards guidance of economic policy differs in several respects from supervision aimed at the implementation of the basic prohibitions. Supervision in the sense of guidance is implemented by its own policy instruments, such as information, several types of consultations and various conditional financial incentives. Another important consequence of this development is the fading away of the distinction between the three functions of supervision in the sense of norm control. The guidance of policy is dependent on the instruments that are used for it, just as, on the national level, the outcome of the market process is continuously influenced by governments. Further, from an institutional point of view, guidance of economic policy implies an explicit political role for the guiding authority. As a process of negative integration is mainly reached through the market, positive integration can only be realised by a process of active political decision-making.

III. SOME ELEMENTS OF THE LAW OF THE IMF

3.1. Some historical aspects

As mentioned above, the Mutual Aid Agreement of 1942 between the United States and the United Kingdom created a favourable climate for the drafting of various plans for post-war co-operation in the international monetary field. Against the background of the 1930s, characterised by a wide-spread application of restrictive trade measures and exchange rate manipulations, H. D. White, Assistant Secretary, United States Treasury and G. M. Keynes, Honorary Advisor to the British Treasury, drafted their plans, which were revealed in 1942.[16] From a theoretical point of view, Keynes's plan was to be preferred. His draft provided for the establishment of a supranational body, the Clearing Union, which would act as the Bank of Central Banks. The accounts of the Union were to be expressed in an international currency, named the 'Bancor,' related to gold. His draft further provided for a supplement for international reserves through allowing Member States to draw on the Union, as a result of which debit balances in 'Bancor' could occur. Each State would have a quota on which its drawing rights would be based. The sum of these quotas, around 35 billion dollars, would constitute the amount by which international liquidity could be increased. The problem concerning the adjustment process with respect to the balance of payments would also be the subject of regulation. The Union would be able to force deficit and surplus States to apply corrective measures. However, the advantage of White's plans was its higher degree of realism, which made it politically superior. His draft was also more orientated towards the American need for free and multilateral world trade, without an excessive violation of the economic sovereignty of States. White's plan provided for the establishment of an international stability fund, the members of which, when coping with temporary maladjustments in their balance of payments, would be able to purchase foreign currency from the 'pool' to be contributed by all members. Further, the freedom of States, with regard to changes in exchange rates would be restricted, and provisions would be laid down for the application of restrictive measures. In this plan, the basis of the present IMF could already be recognised.

In 1943, the plans became a topic of negotiation between the United States and the United Kingdom, together with other related topics within the framework of post-war economic co-operation, as foreseen by the Atlantic Charter and the Mutual Aid Agreement. As far as plans in the monetary field were concerned, these negotiations led to the Joint Statement by Experts on the Establishment of an International Monetary Fund, in which the balance was favourable to White's plan. The United Nations Monetary and Financial Conference was held at Bretton Woods from July 1–22. This Conference, in which 44 States participated, resulted in the signature of the Articles of Agreement of the International Monetary Fund and of the Articles of Agreement of the International Bank for Reconstruction and Development. The former agreement came into force on December 27, 1945. During the first meeting of the Board of Governors, in March 1946, a decision was taken to establish the Fund in Washington. About one year thereafter the Fund opened its doors.

3.2. Purposes of the IMF

The purposes of the Fund are laid down in Article I of the Articles of Agreement in the following words:

'(i) To promote international monetary co-operation through a permanent institution which provides the machinery for consultations and collaboration on international monetary problems.

(ii) To facilitate the expansion and balanced growth of international trade, and to contribute thereby to the promotion and maintenance of high levels of employment and real income and the development of the productive resources of all members as primary objectives of economic policy.

(iii) To promote exchange stability, to maintain orderly exchange arrangements among members, and to avoid competitive exchange depreciation.

(iv) To assist in the establishment of a multilateral system of payments in respect of current transactions between members and in the elimination of foreign exchange restrictions which hamper the growth of world trade.

(v) To give confidence to members by making the Fund's resources temporarily available to them under adequate safeguards, thus providing them with opportunity to correct maladjustments in their balance of payments without resorting to measures destructive of national or international property.

(vi) In accordance with the above, to shorten the duration and lessen the degree of disequilibrium in the international balance of payments of members.

The Fund shall be guided in all its policies and decisions by the purposes set forth in this Article.'

In the six purposes of the Fund, a distinction can be made between a final purpose and some intermediate ones. The first paragraph starts by institutionalising international collaboration between members of the Fund in the monetary field. As a result of this collaboration, the attainment of the final purposes of the Fund, outlined in the second paragraph, should be facilitated. Subsequently, this international co-operation is dealt with under three headings:

1. The promotion of exchange stability as expressed in the third paragraph, which is to be realised by a system of exchange rates.

2. The establishment of a multilateral system of payments, expressed in the fourth paragraph, to be realised by rules of conduct concerning the use of exchange restrictions.
3. The granting of financial aid to members in their effort to control temporary maladjustments on the balance of payments, expressed in the fifth paragraph, to be realised by providing the Fund with financial resources.

In the sixth paragraph of Article I, these three intermediate purposes are summarised once again. Together, they must create a situation in which the final purpose of the Fund can be attained. Thus, monetary co-operation between member countries, which is to be concentrated on these three subjects, is not a purpose in itself. It constitutes one of the methods for attaining partial economic integration between member countries and, once achieved, protecting the system from alterations which could eventually occur in the international monetary field. It is this system, established by the three above-mentioned functions, that is or was called the 'Bretton Woods' system.

It must be stressed that this catalogue of functions has never been amended, although from a substantive point of view, the creation of the special drawing rights, by an amendment of the Articles of Agreement in 1969, implied the inclusion of a fourth intermediate purpose. Besides the adjustment problem, the liquidity problem too became an object of regulation. For the avoidance of inflationary and deflationary impulses on the world economy, the Fund was to provide for the necessary supply of international liquidity by the allocation or cancellation of special drawing rights. Performance of this task would also contribute to the attainment of the Fund's final purpose.

As to the Fund's final purpose, some important changes have gradually occurred.[17] The events of 1971, when the convertibility into gold of the United States dollar was suspended, reflected the necessity for fundamental changes in the interests of an appropriate functioning of the international monetary system.

The dominating relation between the Fund's existence and free international trade constitutes a characteristic of the final purpose of the Articles of Agreement. Promotion of international trade by stable exchange rates would be the Fund's major contribution to the furtherance of a better international economic order. At the time of Bretton Woods, this concept was understandable. One has to realise that the framers of the Fund had in view primarily the situation of the 1930s, and that in their opinion the restructuring of international trade had the greatest priority. Further, at that time the international economic order was, particularly, an order for the Western world. The participation of the Socialist States in this order was very limited, while most of the underdeveloped countries still had colonial status. The final purpose of the Fund was deduced from this 'one-world' conception, and the three original functions, worked out in greater detail in the substantive law of the Articles of Agreement, were the results of this background. These underlying factors have now fundamentally changed. A contribution to a more just and relevant international economic order is not exclusively a matter of promoting international trade. As a result of the increase in and diversity of the members of the Fund, who have tripled in number since 1953, the problem of economic underdevelopment in the international monetary system has been more and more emphasised. In order to contribute to a better and more relevant international economic order, the Fund will have to pay attention to the problem of rich and poor[18] in its policies. The shift in the final purpose of the Fund is worded as follows in the Outline of Reform of the Committee on Reform of the International Monetary System and Related Issues (Committee of Twenty): 'It is agreed that there is need for a reformed world monetary order based on co-operation and consultation within the framework of a strengthened IMF that will encourage the growth of world trade and employment, promote economic developments and that will help to avoid both inflation and deflation.'[19]

3.3. The substantive law of the IMF

In this sub-paragraph, an outline will be given of how the functions of the IMF described above are worked out in greater detail in the Articles of Agreement. As indicated, this elaboration mainly concerns four subjects, which constitute the core of the substantive law of the IMF. The system of exchange arrangements (Article IV) and the provisions on exchange restrictions (Article VIII) together constitute what is called the 'Bretton Woods Code of Conduct'. The régime concerning the financial resources of the Fund is laid down in Articles V, VI and VII. A fourth subject concerns the special drawing rights, which will be touched only upon marginally in this study.

The system for exchange rates under the original Articles of Agreement was founded on the par-value system, and the obligations of member countries to maintain this system. Alongside this, a general obligation to collaborate with the Fund was imposed on all members, in order to promote a stable system of exchange rates, to maintain orderly exchange arrangements with other members and to avoid competitive manipulations of exchange rates.

In the par-value system, the value of every currency of each member country of the Fund, was expressed either in gold, or in United States dollars, having the weight and content as at July 1, 1944. Because the United States dollar was closely linked to gold, according to national legislation, in both cases there was a stable relation between the currencies of the members of the Fund, and each currency was linked directly or indirectly to gold. Gold, therefore, constituted the core of the par-value system. As, in practice, almost all members linked their currencies to the dollar, a system developed which was described as the gold-dollar or the gold-standard. This special position of the dollar in the international monetary system was founded on the important economic position of the United States at the time of the

Second World War. The Articles of Agreement can be seen as a recognition of this special position.

The Articles of Agreement provided for both procedural and substantive provisions, according to which a change in the par-value of a currency could take place. The substantive rules laid down two criteria: a change in the par-value could take place only in cases of a 'fundamental disequilibrium;' and a change could not have a 'competitive' nature. The procedural provisions gave the Fund a somewhat passive role. The most important of them was that only the member concerned, and not the Fund, was entitled to propose a change in the par-value of a currency. The Articles of Agreement also took care of the consequences of a change in par-value inconsistent with the provisions: one consequence of this could be automatic ineligibility to make use of the Fund's financial resources.

The way in which members fulfilled the obligation to uphold the value of their currency could be determined by themselves. The only obligation they had was to maintain an exchange rate which could only deviate from the par-value of their currencies within a certain margin. In practice, this obligation mostly implied that a central bank or comparable institution would conduct an intervention policy. Because of the linkage to the dollar, intervention was usually accomplished by means of dollars. The United States fulfilled its obligation by guaranteeing the convertibility of the dollar into gold.

The system of stable exchange rates as laid down in the Articles of Agreement functioned, at least from a formal point of view, until August 15, 1971. On this date, there was a *de facto* termination of the system, when the United States suspended the convertibility of the dollar into gold. Member countries, which had linked their currencies to the dollar, no longer conducted an intervention policy to maintain the margins within which their currencies could fluctuate with respect to their par-values. The system of stable exchange rates was then transformed into a system of more or less fleeting exchange rates. In December 1971, a conference of the so-called Group of Ten, took place in Washington. This conference led to the Smithsonian Agreement, according to which new values (central rates) with respect to the dollar were established for the various currencies. This led to a temporary reconstruction of the system of stable exchange rates, though the margins of fluctuation were larger than before. Consequently, a devaluation of the United States dollar took place on May 18, 1972. In its decision 'Central Rates and Wider Margins', the Fund then accepted the system of central rates. Formally, the system was inconsistent with the Articles of Agreement. However, a certain degree of legitimisation could be obtained through the declaration in the preamble to the decision that a member who operated in accordance with its provisions, gave evidence of fulfilment of the obligation to collaborate with the Fund laid down in Article IV, Section 4 (a). In this decision, the system based on the Smithsonian Agreement functioned, more or less, until March 1973. The second devaluation of the dollar then led to a definite surrender of the system of stable exchange rates. The situation following this date was of a pluriform nature. Fund members accepted a diversity of exchange rate systems, dependent on their specific circumstances and needs; needless to say, all the systems were also inconsistent with the Articles of Agreement, until the second amendment, which took effect in 1978. Nevertheless, the Fund tried to 'legalise' the situation by its decision 'Guidelines for the Management of Floating Exchange Rates' of January 1974.

The second amendment of the Articles of Agreement mentioned above, led to the insertion of a complete new text of Article IV. As the contents of this new article will be dealt with in Section VI of this study, it is sufficient to mention here that under this provision no choice is made between several possible systems of exchange rates. In the first Section of this Article, some weak obligations concerning economic and monetary policies are imposed on member countries, reflected by the wording: 'each member undertakes to . . .'. Given the obligation of a proper notification to the Fund, each member is free to choose the system of exchange rates it desires to pursue. Section 3 of the provision charges the Fund with the obligation to oversee the international monetary system in order to ensure its effective operation, and the compliance of each member with its obligations. The Fund has to adopt specific principles for the guidance of members with respect to their exchange rate policies. Under Section 4 of the Article, the Fund is entitled to determine, through an 85 per cent. majority of the total voting power, that the international economic situation is such as to permit the introduction of a wide-spread system of stable, but adjustable par-values. Actually, this provision seems to imply that the old Bretton Woods system of fixed exchange rates could be re-introduced, even if the adjustment possibilities of the par-values are greater. This Section is worked out in greater detail in Schedule C of the Articles of Agreement.

The provision in which the prohibition of exchange restrictions is mentioned (Article VIII) carries the title 'General obligations of members.' This Article also contained provisions with respect to the obligation of member countries to inform the Fund on several subjects. The basis of the restriction régime is constituted by provisions with respect to a minimum convertibility of currencies. Member countries have to comply with three specific obligations. First, they may not impose restrictions with respect to payments and transfers for current international transactions. Second, they may not engage in discriminatory currency practices and multiple exchange rates. Third, assets in national currency, which have been obtained by other members, shall be repurchased from these members in exchange for gold, or currency of those members. The first and last obligations only concern current transactions; they are not valid for capital transactions. Members are more or less autonomous in the way in which they handle the international exchange of capital. That is why one can speak – by virtue of the Articles of Agreement – of a minimum convertibility of the currencies of member countries of the Fund. With respect to the prohibition of exchange restrictions a deviation from this obligation can only take place with the consent of the Fund.

The Articles of Agreement provide for two exceptions to this restriction régime. In the first place, member countries can be authorised by the Fund to take discriminatory measures against any member whose currency has become scarce because of its persistent balance of payment surplus. This so-called scarce currency clause includes a procedure which should be followed where a currency is declared scarce. Second, a transitional period is provided for. This provision was originally meant to enable member countries to transform their war economies to take account of conditions of peace. Under this provision, they could deviate from the prohibition on exchange restrictions.

In the late 1940s, the exchange restriction régime and convertibility obligations had significance only for the United States and some Latin-American countries. The Western-European countries being characterised by non-convertible currencies. The aim of having convertible currencies and multilateral exchange in these countries was attained through co-operation within the framework of the OEEC. At the end of 1958, most Western-European countries declared their currencies convertible, and subscribed *de facto* to the obligations of Article VIII; informal acceptance of this system followed in 1961.

As regards the transitional provision, this has become an almost permanent escape clause for most underdeveloped countries which have adhered to the Fund, but which were not able to fulfil the obligations of the restriction régime completely, particularly the substantive law of the IMF between developed and underdeveloped countries. In 1975, 42 out of 126 member countries of the Fund had accepted the system under Article VIII. Almost all developed States belonged to this group, as well as a number of oil-producing States in the Middle East and South America. Under the second amendment of the Articles of Agreement, Article VIII was maintained, but Article XIV was reformulated on the basis of its practical application.

IV. SUPERVISORY MECHANISMS IN THE IMF: THEIR ORIGINAL FORM AND NATURE

Sections IV to VI will examine the extent to which the general conclusions with regard to supervisory mechanisms in international economic organisations, which were included in a previous section, can be affirmed or refuted by the law and practice of the IMF. For that purpose, the supervisory mechanisms as laid down in the Articles of Agreement will be compared, in their original form and content, with those mechanisms which have become operational in the course of time. To some extent, this evolution has left its mark in the second amendment of the Articles of Agreement, some aspects of which will be discussed in Section 6.

4.1. The control aspect of supervisory mechanisms

It is self-evident that the supervision to be exercised by the IMF is concerned with the implementation and maintenance of the rules laid down in the

Articles of Agreement. However, in this Section the control aspects will be emphasised, in order to stress the difference with the guidance aspect discussed later.

Where the transnational economic behaviour of States has been regulated by the Articles of Agreement and by the GATT, this has been done through a system of basic conditions. In the first instance, this structure can be explained historically. Looking back at the system based on the gold standard, it is easily understood that in Bretton Woods the drafters primarily had in mind regulation of the policy of States with respect to exchange rates and currency restrictions. In the inter-war period, both instruments pre-eminently constituted a method of adjusting the balance of payments to the disadvantage of other States. This, in an address to the United States Monetary and Financial Conference in Bretton Woods, in 1944, President Roosevelt stated:' Commerce is the lifeblood of a free society. We must see to it that the arteries which carry that blood stream are not clogged again, as they have been in the past, by artificial barriers created through senseless economic rivalries.'[20]

From this point of view, a prohibition of such 'beggar my neighbour' policies in the monetary field became obvious. To the extent that exemption from these prohibitions was necessary or inevitable – but only if non-discriminatory – the use of these monetary instruments was made subject to strong multilateral supervision, by way of prior consent from the Fund. This method of regulation must be stressed, since it shows that neither was the Fund constructed for a transfer to it of powers from Member States in the field of economic and monetary policy, nor was this organisation equipped with powers aimed at a co-ordination of, or guidance on, economic policy. Also, the Articles of Agreement did not provide for clear guidelines for the economic policies to be pursued by member countries in case of balance of payments difficulties.

Apart from the background of the 1930s, proposals that would go further than mere prohibitions, had to fail inevitably because of too great an infringement of the sovereignty of States. Even the finally drafted 'code of conduct' included a considerable transfer of sovereignty, given the almost non-existent rules of international monetary law. Illustrative of the stage of development of international law in this respect is the statement of the Permanent Court of International Justice in 1929, in its judgment of the Serbian Loans, that 'it is indeed a generally accepted principle that a State is entitled to regulate its own currency.'[21]

With this background, the brilliant draft of Lord Keynes for an International Clearing Union was doomed to fail because of the deep infringement of monetary sovereignty it implied. A comparison with White's draft shows that the Union would have been vested with many strong directive powers and, in fact, would have meant an embryonic internationalisation of conjunctural (short-term economic) policy. More specifically, this draft not only included determination by the Union of the extent of international liquidity, and thus a take-over by the 'Bancor' of the position of the United States dollar as the reserve currency, but it also implied an enormous grant of credit by the United States to the European countries, through the possibility of 'overdrafts'. In the United States, there was strong protest against both these factors. During the negotiations, White could state that this draft 'could be regarded as involving a surrender of sovereignty' and 'would require special legislation in the United States which would be presented as tying up the dollar to a phony international unit.' Concerning the organisation to be established, White 'was open-minded about the name, but the work "Union" in the title would be politically impossible'.[22]

With respect to the exercise of supervision as laid down in the Articles of Agreement, the approach implied that control of State behaviour in the monetary field constituted the essential feature. The existence of general basic norms with regard to monetary behaviour – the code of conduct – required facilities for the gathering of information by the Fund, necessary to show the existence of a real or potential infringement. Conduct in accordance with the Articles of Agreement could then be brought about by the application of the methods of enforcement already mentioned. Thus, in the agreements, the review and correction function of supervision can be clearly distinguished.[23]

Review of member countries' policies was given shape by a general obligation on the Member States to furnish the Fund with such information 'as it deems necessary for its operations.' An outline of this obligation was indicated under 12 headings. A closer look at this list shows that the information was mainly concerned with the balance of payments, in order to enable the Fund to control the implementation of obligations with respect to exchange rates and restrictions. None of these 12 items, however, directly concerned the internal economic policy of Member States; for instance – purposes and instruments of economic policy, government income and expenditure, taxes, prices and incomes policy. A supplement to this obligation was constituted by the provision on consultation for those States which, according to Article XIV, had not yet accepted the régime of restrictions as laid down in Article VIII.

If, as a result of this control, indicated, of course, by its formal features, a potential or actual infringement of the code of conduct became apparent, the Agreement provided for various methods of enforcement. As Gold has pointed out on several occasions, the use of the word 'sanctions' is not correct in describing these means, not only because of the negative nature of this concept, but also because some of these measures are not meant to be applied in a punitive manner.[24] In ascending order, four groups of these enforcement methods, or 'remedies' as they are called by Gold, may be distinguished. Together they constitute the correction function of IMF supervisory mechanisms. In the first place, the Articles of Agreement provide for 'a judgment of peers.' This includes an informal and confidential statement of opinion by the Fund to the member country concerned, and also another method, vaguely formulated as making 'representations.' Secondly, publication of reports with respect to monetary and economic developments in a Member State are provided for. Thirdly, there may be an increase in charges where a member has used Fund resources for too long a period and, fourthly, there is the withholding of advantages. This list includes a statement by the Fund that a member is no longer eligible to use its financial resources, and that the Articles of Agreement themselves provide for such ineligibility, which is concerned with a non-authorised change in the par-value of a currency. Furthermore, the Agreement opens a possibility for the application of discriminatory measures against the Member State where a currency is declared to be 'scarce.'[25] Finally, an *ultimum remedium* is provided for: the possibility of forced withdrawal from the Fund.

As the obligations of the code of conduct were of a permanent nature, to be complied with by every member country regardless of its political and economic system or stage of development, IMF supervision as foreseen by the Articles of Agreement had a primarily static nature. The creative aspect of supervision, therefore, could be limited to an amendment of the Articles of Agreement, or the interpretation of them.[26]

4.2. The functional nature of the supervisory mechanisms

A second feature of the supervisory mechanisms as laid down in the original Articles of Agreement was their preponderantly functional nature.

As explained above, the establishment of the Fund could not bring about direct influence by the organisation on the internal economic policy of Member States. The Fund was only able to supervise the observance of the code of conduct, and enforce it through the various methods of enforcement with which it was endowed. It was the task of the Member States to pursue the policies of the objectives of the code of conduct. In this field they kept their sovereignty, and there was no possibility of the Fund – at lease formally – becoming involved. Only the financial resources of the Fund could provide for some breathing space, to facilitate an adjustment process by internal measures. Thus, from a legal point of view, the code of conduct could be defined as a system of negative obligations, to be implemented according to the principle of good faith. In other words, underlying the code of conduct was a hypothesis with respect to the economic policies of Member States, *i.e.*, to give priority to the maintenance of an external equilibrium and, linked to that, a choice between the various objectives of economic policy. This hypothesis, which, in an earlier Dutch publication, the present author defined as the 'principle of good economic conduct,'[27] appears in several places in the Articles of Agreement, but without their being – and this should be emphasised – a general positive rule with regard to the economic policy to be pursued. The existence of this principle, and the implied specific responsibility of member countries for economic policies, is illustrated primarily by the wording of the purposes of the IMF, especially as expressed in Article I,2: 'to contribute thereby to the protection and maintenance of high levels of employment and real income and to the development of the productive resources of all members as primary objectives of economic policy.' Also in Article I,5: 'and thus providing them with opportunity to correct maladjustment in their balance of payments.' Although both Articles indicate the sovereignty of Member States in respect of their economic policy, in the absence of any direct Fund influence thereon, they nevertheless presuppose that such a policy should be pursued.

Another indication of the existence of this principle is found in the general obligation to co-operate, laid down in Article IV, section 4(a):

> 'Each member undertakes to collaborate with the Fund to promote exchange stability, to maintain orderly arrangements with other members, and to avoid competitive exchange alterations.'

Again this wording presumes a corresponding economic policy on the part of the Member States. The way the Articles of Agreement regulate the use of the Fund's financial resources is another pointer. The possibility of using these resources was not meant to be a method of enforcement by the Fund *vis-à-vis* member countries. The Agreement only provided for safeguards for the appropriate use of the financial resources:

> 'No safeguard provided for the Fund is more important than the provision that the countries request for foreign currencies indicates the uses to which those currencies will be put are consistent with the purposes of the Fund. This means that countries which conduct their affairs in good faith in accordance with the undertaking to act in conformity with the purposes of the Fund, will not in any circumstances divert the resources of the Fund to undesirable uses. In international agreements between sovereign States, no method of enforcement can be as important as reliance on the good faith of the participants.'[28]

Thus, the achievement and maintenance of a multilateral and liberalised system of payments, emanates from a specific division of tasks between the Fund and member countries, underlying the Articles of Agreement. This division of tasks can be sketched as follows. Those aspects of economic policy with a more or less static nature, such as maintaining equilibrium in the balance of payments, stability of price levels, full employment and a stable currency, remain under the sovereignty of member countries. The more dynamic aspects, such as the expansion of international trade through the elimination of restrictions and detrimental currency practices, fall within the competence of the Fund. Through a realisation of the above-mentioned objectives of economic policy (the principle of good economic conduct), member countries would create the necessary 'infrastructure' to permit the implementation of the code of conduct and, thus, contribute to the liberalisation and expansion of international trade.

As indicated before the IMF was not equipped with powers to influence the economic policy of member countries directly, as this was not considered as a real alternative. The only way to regulate State behaviour in the monetary field was by imposing general and binding obligations. Thus, an abstraction of the internal economic policies of member countries took place, by making States themselves responsible for the implementation of the code of conduct, through a 'good' economic policy. In this respect, the IMF's code of conduct resembles the four freedoms of the EEC (free flow of goods, persons, services and capital). Both codes of behaviour are instrumental in the liberalisation and expansion of international trade. Like the Articles of Agreement, the EEC Treaty, in Article 2, sums up a number of the objectives which this organisation should attain: harmonious development of

374

economic activities, continuous and balanced expansion of trade and raising the standard of living. Under Article 104, the static aspects of economic policy remain within the competence of Member States. However, by expressly mentioning the domestic economic policy objectives, the EEC Treaty obliges Member States to conduct a 'good' economic policy as a necessary condition for the realisation and maintenance of the Common Market as a supreme form of liberalisation. The EEC Treaty goes even further, by providing for the coordination of economic policy, although the provisions concerned are of a primarily procedural nature.

With regard to the IMF's supervisory mechanisms, the above-outlined division of the tasks underlying the code of conduct, implied that these mechanisms were not and could not be directly concerned with the domestic economic policy of member countries. This conclusion is supported by the supervision exercised by the IMF with respect to the exchange rate policy of its members. The initial determination of a par-value for a currency, fell within the exclusive competence of the member country concerned. The Fund was only entitled to object to the correctness of the value established, but if it did not agree to a different par-value, the country concerned was deemed to have withdrawn from the Fund *ipso iure*. The imposition of a par-value by the Fund and, thus, the exercise of direct influence in the internal economic spheres, was excluded. Such a construction was applied to an even greater extent in the case of a change in a country's par-value. Only member countries had a right to propose such a change, and the Fund could only withhold its consent to the proposed change if it was of the opinion that the requirement of a 'functional disequilibrium' had not been fulfilled.

> 'These provisions are not a substantive limitation of what the Fund is expected to do, but merely a reassurance to the countries that their vital matters were kept in mind by the framers of the proposal, and the member countries' inherent autonomy in domestic affairs is not threatened.'[29]

This view is supported by the fact that, under the original Articles of Agreement, an unauthorised change in the par-value did not mean invalidity of the new par-value, or that the Fund could establish a proper one, but only that the member concerned automatically became ineligible to use the Fund's resources. The careful wording of the various provisions reflects the fact that the determination of the value of its currency is a State's major instrument for the regulation of its economic relations with other States. As such, the establishment and change of the par-value of a currency can only be marginally separated from sovereignty in the economic field, which, in turn, has consequences for the supervision which the Fund could exercise.

4.3. The technical nature of supervision

Another characteristic feature of the original supervision to be exercised by the IMF was its techical nature. The word 'technical' is chosen to stress the fact that the original supervision related to the fulfilment of the code of conduct, and not to the management of economic policy as such. Three examples taken from the substantive law of the IMF may clarify this aspect.

The first example is constituted by the consultations under Article XIV mentioned above. Their main purpose was to identify the extent to which member countries were able to apply an Article VIII régime, the prohibition of exchange restrictions. The wording of these provisions and the practical use made of it, indicated the fact that the Fund was not expected – at least expressly – to give a clear judgment on the internal economic policy of a member country which had invoked this Article.

The second example is furnished, once again, by the rules concerning the use of the Fund's resources. As mentioned above, the Articles of Agreement provided exclusively for a number of safeguards to protect the resources against an exceedingly long use, or a use inconsistent with the Fund's purposes. However, they did not provide for the use of financial resources as a policy instrument by the Fund, in the sense that the resources could be made conditional upon a certain economic policy being conducted by the member country that had applied for them. Under Article V, Section 3 ('Conditions governing the use of the Fund's resources'), it is asserted that:

> 'a member shall be entitled to buy currency of another member from the Fund . . . subject to the following conditions.'

Hereafter, four conditions are mentioned which do not relate to the economic policy of the member country requesting the use of those resources. They concern only the amount, and the period during which the resources could be used.

A third example is provided by the wording of the scarce currency clause. The Articles of Agreement declare:

> 'if the Fund finds that a general scarcity of a particular currency is developing . . .'

They do not provide for the possibility of relating such a declaration – and thereby the authorisation of discrimination against the country whose currency is concerned – to conditions regarding economic policy, such as a change in par-value (revaluation) or import-increasing measures.

> '. . . that the demand for a member's currency seriously threatens the Fund's ability to supply that currency . . . the Fund . . . shall formally declare such currency scarce.'

In each of the above-mentioned examples, the Articles of Agreement carefully avoid the passing of a judgment by the Fund on the past or future economic policy of the member country concerned. What is demanded from the Fund, however, is an examination of whether or not the various specific obligations or conditions for receiving advantages have or have not been fulfilled, and, if they have, the use of its methods of enforcement, or a refusal to fulfil a request.

An important presupposition for such a system as outlined before, by which the economic policy of a State was framed in a system of basic conditions, constitutes either the presence of a sufficiently homogeneous economic substructure, or the presence of a dominating position of one of the participating States. It must be doubted whether the first one applied to the 44 States gathered in Bretton Woods, not at least regarding the non-industrialised countries. The second hypothesis had more relevance: 'The dollar is the one great currency in whose strength there is universal confidence. It will probably become the cornerstone of the post-war structure of stable currencies.'[30]

4.4. Institutional aspects

The form and nature of the IMF's original supervisory mechanisms, described in previous Sections, inevitably exercised an influence on the institutional structure of the organisation. As indicated, the economic policy of member countries was regulated by the Articles of Agreement through a code of conduct in the monetary field. By this method, a direct influence on the economic policy of States could be avoided, while, on the other hand, regulation did nevertheless take place, through the implementation of the general rules on which the supervisory mechanisms were concentrated. Thus, international co-operation was conducted primarily in the monetary field, against which background it was understandable that the relation between the IMF and its member countries was channelled through central banks and/or treasury departments instead of Ministries of Foreign Affairs.[31] Having a long history, monetary co-operation between States was mostly the concern of central banks, which operated more or less independently of the political decision-making institutions. Illustrative in this respect is the way in which the gold standard operated according to the unwritten 'rules of the game', with the British pound as a pivot.

Thus, the supervision to be exercised by the IMF was not considered as being of a primarily political nature, but rather technical and non-political. Gardner cites a striking statement of Morgenthau, Minister of Finance, at the time the Bretton Woods Agreement Act was being defended in Congress: 'The thought was that those countries could come to a World Bank or a World Fund and get their financial needs taken care of without having to sell their political souls.[32] . . . These are to be financial institutions run by financial people, financial experts and the needs of a country are to be taken care of wholly independent of the political connections.' The statements of Senator Wagner during the debates on this Act are also well known. On behalf of the Senators belonging to the Bretton Woods delegations he declared: 'I have just checked with Senator Tobey, and neither of us heard any politics at all in Bretton Woods.'[33]

Against this background, the semi-corporate of the IMF's institutional structure, with participating States as 'shareholders,' having an annual 'shareholders' meeting, with the Board of Governors and with management by the Executive Board and Managing Director, is not particularly surprising.

However, the background sketched above did not deter either the United States or the United Kingdom from trying to adapt this structure to their specific needs. The differences were caused by the fact that the United States, being a surplus country and the Fund's greatest money supplier, had an interest in close control by the Fund on the use of its money. The United

Kingdom, on the other hand, being a deficit country, had a great interest in access to the financial resources of the Fund with as few inpediments as possible. This distinction between the two countries had great significance for the supervisory tasks of the Fund where they concerned the financial resources and – implicitly – the powers to exercise guidance towards deficit countries. Within the institutional structure of the Fund, the main relevance of this question was for the role of the Executive Board.

Because of its position as a deficit country, the United Kingdom wished to avoid a strict examination of requests for credit from the Fund. It, therefore, proposed that the members of the Executive Board should be nominated from high-ranking officials holding important posts at home. The Board would have to meet only periodically, and the Directors could influence national policies in their home countries. These thoughts coincided with the vision of Lord Keynes. Keynes was strongly in favour of establishing the organisation of international economic relations on a strictly scientific and technical basis. These thoughts had already been laid down in his 'A Treatise on Money' (1931), and were also reflected in the proposed institutional structure of his International Clearing Union. Through this set-up, far-reaching transfers of sovereignty would be possible on the one hand, while, on the other, political questions could be avoided. 'I dare to speak for the much so-called experts. I even venture sometimes to prefer them, without intending any disrespect for politicians. The common love of truth, bred of scientific habit of mind, is the closest of bonds between the representatives of nations.'[34] It needs no explanation that the United States held a totally opposite view.

These differences resulted in the ambiguous formulation of Rule 15 in the By-laws of the Fund: 'that the Executive Directors shall function in continuous session at the principal office of the Fund and shall meet as often as the business of the Fund may require,' in which, nevertheless, the American point of view can be recognised.

This result had important consequences for the IMF's supervisory function. The requirement of permanent presence significantly reduces the possible influence of Executive Directors on national policy. With the Board of Governors meeting only once a year, the Fund's supervision was inevitably reduced to the control of compliance with the code of conduct, with hardly any possibility of exercising a positive influence on the political element of the economic policy of member countries.[35]

This political vacuum was filled by the United States, however, with the inevitable consequence that, especially during the first decade of its existence, the Fund was regarded as being an extension of the American Treasury:

'There was also a tendency for member governments, before submitting a formal proposal or request to the Fund to ask their Executive Director to discuss it with other Directors first. Quite frequently the Executive Director for the member concerned went to the Director of the United States. . . . If the United States' Director concurred, the member would then continue with the procedures of the Fund.'[36]

When, at the end of the 1950s, after most Western-European currencies had become convertible and the question of international liquidity had gained importance, the guiding task of the Fund acquired a greater significance, this political vacuum became more serious. In the course of the 1960s this lacuna constituted one of the causes for the political supervision necessary for an adequate adjustment process on the balance of payments shipping outside the Fund to the various institutions of the so-called Group of Ten.

The General Arrangements to Borrow, signed in 1961 between the Fund and the Western countries, which together had a main share in international trade, were one of the first signs of the shift. In this Group of Ten, frequent discussions on the various levels took place between representative countries, *inter alia*, in Working Group 3 of the OECD and the Bank of International Settlements.

Seen from this perspective, the post-war period of the Pax Americana may be compared with the Pax Britannica of the nineteenth century: the free-trade period with the absolute domination of the pound sterling.[37]

V. DEVELOPMENTS IN THE PERIOD 1945–1971[38]

Soon after the Fund became operational, the rather static nature of its supervisory mechanisms made an adaptation of these mechanisms necessary in order that guidance with respect to the economic policy of the members could be exercised. The Fund had to take this course because of the American policy of strengthening the safeguards of the organisation to guarantee a strict use of its financial resources. The way in which these resources could be made available – conditionally or unconditionally - to members was not unambiguously laid down in the Articles of Agreement. As has been mentioned, essentially only formal conditions had too be fulfilled, and the serious economic difficulties of the Western-European members made the Americans worry about the policy of the Fund. In 1948, therefore, the IMF decided to make access to its financial resources conditional.

As indicated above, the Articles of Agreement formulated four conditions which a member had to fulfil when making a request to buy currencies from the Fund. Two of them are of a formal nature: the member must not be declared ineligible to use the Fund's resources, and the currency concerned must not have been declared 'scarce.' The two substantive conditions concern the amount of currency that could be purchased from the Fund and the period for which these currencies could be used. The question remained, however, as to whether, then these conditions were fulfilled, a member was automatically entitled to purchase the currencies, or whether the Fund could exercise a discretionary power in accepting the request, refusing it or making it subject to certain conditions. Under strong American pressure, the Fund adopted the latter interpretation as the basis of its future policy, by entitling itself to challenge the legality of a request to purchase currencies. Under the first amendment of the Articles of Agreement, in 1969, this interpretation acquired a stronger basis by the inclusion of Article V, Section 3(D), which provision under the second amendment became Article V, Section 3(C).

Thus, the correct and, in particular, temporary use of its financial resources, made it inevitable for the Fund to formulate conditions concerning the way in which the country making a request was forced to conduct its economic policy. The negative way in which the fulfilment of the 'principle of good economic behaviour,' described in the previous Section, was supervised by the Fund was thus transformed into positive supervision through active guidance of the economic policy of the members. In 1952, this conditionality was institutionalised in the stand-by arrangements, which in later years were refined in many ways, and which became the main instrument of the Fund, making its financial resources available with a linkage to internal economic policy. Alongside the European Payments Union, established in 1950 as a part of co-operation within the OEEC, the IMF constituted one of the elements for implementing the policy of liberalisation in the monetary field, by achieving a multilateral system of payments. When the currencies of most Western-European countries were declared convertible in 1958, at least on the Atlantic level, the ideal of a 'one convertible currency world' was achieved.

At the beginning of the 1960s, the result of the policy of liberalisation, conducted for more than a decade within the framework of GATT, the IMF and the OEEC plus the strong economic interdependence of the Atlantic States, became more apparent. The efficient concept of an international division of labour through market forces, was expressed in strongly expanding international trade, rising faster than the already impressive growth rate of the GNP. Alongside the need to further liberalised trade – acknowledged by the Kennedy Round – the need for a close co-ordination of economic policies also became apparent, in order to maintain the degree of liberalisation already achieved. In a legal sense, this development was recognised by the transformation of the OEEC in 1961, which organisation, according to its objectives, was established in particular to co-ordinate the economic policy of the industrialised States. After Japan and later, Australia and New Zealand acceded, this 'rich men's club,' accounted for more than two-thirds of total world trade. This bloc, with its strong interdependence and fast expanding economies, created a completely different climate for the IMF than that foreseen by its framers, the Bretton Woods system of fixed exchange rates was based on the hypothesis that, on the one hand, the external equilibrium of the balance of payments would be maintained by the necessary internal adjustment measures – once again reference is made to the principle of good economic behaviour – and, on the other hand, that changes of a more fundamental nature would be translated through adjustments of the par-value. However, this concept proved to be highly fictitious as far as the speed and extent of the internal adjustment process were concerned, and also the use of the exchange rate instrument. This resulted, *inter alia*, in chronic deficit and surplus situations, undermining confidence in several currencies and leading to large capital movements. Consequently, the concept of a more or less tacit and spontaneous co-ordination of

380

economic policies by compliance with the basic conditions of the Articles of Agreement faded away. Instead, within the framework of the OECD and co-operation between central banks, several instruments and institutions were created through which a more positive co-ordination of economic policies could be pursued, such as a 'multilateral surveillance system' within the Group of Ten, close consultations on various levels, and all sorts of additional credit mechanisms.

Further, international monetary relations were still relying to a great extent on the American dollar as a reserve currency. The founding fathers had neglected Keynes' suggestion for a machinery for the creation of international liquidity, with the result that in the post-war period this task was fulfilled by the continuous expansion of a dollar surplus, resulting from the chronic United States' balance of payments deficits. Only in 1968, after more than 10 years of discussion, was a marginal solution for this dilemma achieved, through the creation of the SDR mechanism by an amendment of the Articles of Agreement. However, both strategies, with respect to the adjustment and liquidity problem, could not prevent an increase in economic disparities between the industrialised countries, with varying inflation figures and great disturbances of exchange markets as external symptoms, which resulted in increasing difficulties with respect to compliance with the code of conduct. With the suspension of the convertibility into gold of the dollar in 1971, the post-war par-value system was terminated *de facto*. After a temporary and only partial restoration within the framework of the Smithsonian Agreement, allowing greater margins, the system of fixed exchange rates ended definitely in 1973, succeeded by floating exchange rates. The régime of the Articles of Agreement with respect to exchange rates and through this, indirectly, the economic policy of member countries, was therefore factually terminated, which was recognised from a legal point of view by the second amendment of the Articles of Agreement, resulting from the Jamaica Agreement of 1976.

VI. THE EVOLUTION OF SUPERVISORY MECHANISMS: INSTRUMENTS OF GUIDANCE

The developments outlined earlier lead to two conclusions with respect to the IMF's supervisory mechanisms. In the first place, the original supervisory mechanisms – concentrated on the methods of enforcement – were hardly operational. Secondly, this led to the coming into existence of other supervisory mechanisms, which will be dealt with below. Both conclusions reflect the gradually increasing inadequacy of the original framework of the IMF to regulate the economic policy of member countries through a monetary code of conduct, and the increasing need for supervision in a positive sense, *i.e.*, in the form of guidance of economic policy.

6.1. The inadequacy of the original supervisory mechanisms

As stated above, the various methods of enforcement were hardly operational, as a result of which the original supervisory mechanisms were to a great extent deprived of their effectiveness. The few cases in which they were applied, seem to underline their ineffectiveness.

The fund has never exercised its powers of informal consultation, or to make 'representations,' or to present or to publish a report. Only in a few cases has an overdue payment resulted in increased financial charges, while in one case, of France, an unauthorised change of the par-value automatically resulted in the ineligibility of this country to use the Fund's resources. In the beginning of the 1950s Poland withdrew from the Fund after the organisation initiated proceedings to declare this member country ineligible. With regard to Czechoslovakia, expulsion followed after such a declaration had taken place. Although both cases indeed concerned a failure to fulfil obligations under the Articles of Agreement, the background of the sharpening Cold War should be taken into account. The French case not only reflected the inadequacy of the legalistic approach – for nearly eight years this country applied exchange rates inconsistent with the Articles of Agreement – but also resulted in diminishing the authority of the Fund, already reduced by the devaluations in 1949, in which it hardly played a role. The scarce currency clause has never been applied, although there have been cases in which the conditions to apply this clause were certainly fulfilled.

However from this, at a first glance very satisfactory record, it may not be deduced that the fulfilment of obligations was optimal. The annual reports of the Fund and its official history clearly show that a considerable number of members failed to establish a par-value for their currency or applied multiple exchange rates. It has already been mentioned that adjustments of the par-value in cases of a fundamental disequilibrium were scarce, and only took place after considerable delay. The way members consulted with the Fund before changing their par-value is also symptomatic. After the French incident, the Fund was forced to assume a very accommodating attitude towards such behaviour, which according to the Articles of Agreement should undoubtedly be qualified as violation. The Fund's inability to apply its methods of enforcement can thus be traced to an early stage of its existence.

A definitive judgment on the causes of this development can, of course, only be rendered by the Fund itself. Nevertheless, some observations can be made on this matter. In the first place, the rather superfluous remark must be made that the IMF developed in quite a different way than could be foreseen by the Bretton Woods framers. The general orientation of the Articles of Agreement regarding deflationary developments and exchange rate manipulation during the interwar period did not suit the post-war developments in which, in particular, inflationary tendencies were present. Also, as a consequence of the flourishing exchange restrictions, the exchange rate instrument had only a secondary importance. Of further importance was the dominating position of the United States, as a result of which – later

– one could doubt if the Fund really functioned as an international organisation determining its own policy within the margins left by the member countries. The Fund's inactive first decade, caused by exclusion from the European Recovery Programme, Marshall Aid, monetary co-operation within the framework of the OEEC and EPU, and difficult access to its financial resources due to American pressure, forced the organisation to the periphery of international monetary relations, of which it should have been the centre.

On second thoughts, however, these developments do not seem to have determined the fate of the supervisory mechanisms laid down in the Articles of Agreement. Rather, they seem to have increased some inherent legal shortcomings. *First,* the supervisory mechanisms were centred around the methods of enforcement discussed in the previous paragraph. This raised the problem of the general ineffectiveness of the use of sanctions by international organisations against sovereign states. Even the original form of supervisory mechanisms reflected this, since, according to the Articles of Agreement, the application of some methods of enforcement was not made conditional upon the violation of an obligation. However, the consciousness of the inadequacy of a mere transposition of national law concepts to the international level could not prevent the rather legalistic structure of the supervisory mechanisms, which, even indirectly, were connected with non-compliance with obligations. Indeed, the hypothesis underlying this structure was that the various factors causing an infringement of the code of conduct could be controlled satisfactorily. It is a paradox that the legalistic character, and supervision to protect the financial resources of the Fund from improper use, presented far too few safeguards, and resulted in a greater discretionary freedom for the Fund to challenge requests for drawings and make them subject to economic policy conditions. *Secondly,* as already indicated, underlying the contractual nature of the Fund's monetary code of conduct was the hypothesis of good economic behaviour by the member countries. In theory, this construction left intact the sovereignty of member countries in internal economic affairs. However, increasing economic interdependence, on the one hand, and gradually increasing economic interventions of governments, on the other, more and more complicated the adjustment process with respect to the balance of payments. To co-ordinate the economic policy of member countries in this area necessitates supervision in the positive sense, with the provision of specific instruments and facilities.

The inadequacy of this legal structure is illustrated by the EEC Treaty. This Treaty clearly shows that the regulation of the economic policy of Member States through a system of basic conditions must be supplemented by an active co-ordination of economic policy. Thus, the first main instrument of the Treaty, a large scale liberalisation, instituting the Common Market, is accompanied by a second main instrument; co-ordination of economic policy and, in some cases, even (for instance, agriculture) a common policy, although, as indicated above, the EEC provisions for co-ordination are mainly of a procedural nature. While the IMF provided for regulation of the economic policy of States through a system of a negative integration, it lacked a framework and supervisory instruments for positive integration through active guidance and co-ordination of economic policies.

6.2. The development of alternative supervisory mechanisms: instruments of guidance

The increasing need for active co-ordination of economic policy implied a gradual shift for the Fund from the technical/monetary aspects of the code of conduct or the more dynamic field of macro-economic policy. Nevertheless, the development of alternative mechanisms of supervision to contribute to this need – as mentioned before, the Fund is not alone in this – had to take place within the original structure of the Articles of Agreement. From an early stage the Fund developed some specific instruments for this purpose: the use of information, consultation and, as already indicated, the use of its financial resources. Although each of these instruments was mentioned in the Articles of Agreement, none of them had the nature of a supervisory mechanism or instrument or, to be more specific, of a method of enforcement.

With regard to the instrument of information, this appeared from the above-mentioned provisions of Article VIII, Section 5(c): 'it shall act as a centre for the collection and exchange of information on monetary and financial problems, thus facilitating the preparation of studies to assist members in developing policies which further the purposes of the Fund,' from which the passive and static role of the organisation appears. Concerning consultations, it should be noted that a special obligation thereto does not exist in the Articles of Agreement, whereas the most important case in which this instrument has been used, concerned the restrictions during the transitional period (Article XIV). The financial resources themselves did not constitute a method of enforcement, but the ineligibility to make use of them did have this character.

However, to avoid any misunderstanding, it must be stressed that it is no way suggested that there exists an absolute distinction between supervision in the old sense (norm control) and the new sense (guidance of economic policy). Rather, one is dealing with two aspects of the phenomenon of supervision which are not exclusive, but on the contrary, flow into each other.

The provisions inserted in the Articles of Agreement by the first amendment in 1968, with regard to the special drawing rights, offer a practical and illustrative example of the supplementary and overlapping nature of both aspects of supervision. On a microlevel, the technical and very complicated aspects of the functioning of the system of special drawing rights necessitate close supervision, in order to guarantee the basic requirement of confidence by the participating States in this artificial reserve asset. With regard to two important aspects of the use of special drawing rights, the criterion of need and the obligation to accept, methods of enforcement are provided for cases of non-compliance with these rules. The old construction of a non-authorised change in a par-value has stood as a model for this. Also, the Fund has the power to designate participating States which have to accept special drawing rights in exchange for actual convertible currencies. In this respect, the supervision has the character of a close norm control. On the macrolevel, however, the Fund was charged with partial supervision of both quantity and quality of international liquidity. This supervision by the Fund mainly concerns developments in international liquidity, and, in connection with this, the calling of attention to inflationary or deflationary tendencies in the world economy. The guiding function is expressed in the competence of the Fund to create international liquidity by the allocation of special drawing rights, thus potentially influencing the course of the world economic situation, and, in so doing, indirectly guiding the behaviour of States in the desired direction. In particular, if the long-expected substitution account, about which no agreement could be reached in the course of 1979–80, is realised, then the aspect of guidance would become important.

The course of this gradual shift can be found in the evolution of the law of international economic organisations already discussed. According to neo-liberal conceptions, the drafters at Bretton Woods looked upon the IMF as one of the supervisory institutions for the prevention of disturbances of the international market by States. By regulating State behaviour through a framework of basic conditions, equal access to the market was ensured, and a continuous process of integration by market forces could take place. However, the fundamental outcome of the market process itself was left unaffected. It was for this very reason that the draft of Lord Keynes was thought unacceptable, because of the power to influence the market process generally through control of international liquidity and, specifically, through the possibility of 'overdrafts'. Nevertheless, the growing interdependence of, in particular, the Western economies, and the difficulties in the adjustment process of the balance of payments, made it inevitable for the Fund to become active in the field of policy co-ordination, and to influence the outcome of the market process. As indicated, alternative instruments were needed for this task, which for legal purposes implies a different interpretation or application of existing rules. In the present practice of the Fund, the above-mentioned instruments have enormous significance. As far as the instrument of information is concerned, the Articles of Agreement only refer to information with respect to the balance of payments. The instrument of consultation is hardly mentioned at all, and the financial resources of the Fund were not meant to be an instrument to influence the economic policy of member countries directly. At least, in the original Articles of Agreement, their use as an instrument of supervision is unclear and limited. This last aspect was also one of the causes of the various instruments of policy co-ordination on an international level being framed outside the IMF framework, especially within the OECD and Group of Ten.

An interesting comparison can be drawn between the way supervision is treated in international economic law and the supervisory role of governments in economic affairs on a national level. The rules of economic law which concern entrance to the market (establishment of enterprises, provision of services, quality rules for products, etc.) and market behaviour (competition law) are characterised by their more or less static and permanent nature, to be applied through licences or exemptions, by administrative or criminal sanctions. However, when governments wish to influence the outcome of the market process itself, this is done, *inter alia,* by instruments which do not always have a clear legal nature, for instance, budgetary policy, State aids, regional policy, income policy, etc.

6.3. Consultations as an instrument for the co-ordination of economic policy

The modifications in form and content of the supervisory mechanisms and related legal problems are clearly illustrated by the evolution of consultations within the IMF.[39] As mentioned before, the use of this instrument under the Articles of Agreement is only expressly provided for within the framework of the interim period of Article XIV.

The purpose of the interim period was to provide for the transition from a war to a peace economy, and to recover from war damage. During this period, the maintenance of exchange restrictions was permitted (Article XIV, Section 2). According to Section 4 of this Article, the Fund was to start with annual reports on these exchange restrictions three years after the beginning of its operations and, after five years, was to start consultations. With regard to these consultations, the Fund could 'if it deems such action necessary in exceptional circumstances make representations . . .' One could even doubt if Article XIV really concerned the use of consultations as an instrument of the Fund, as the wording of this provision states '. . . any member still retaining . . . *shall* consult with the Fund . . .'.

In the course of time, this technique has become a major instrument through which the Fund's surveillance of members' economic policy is made effective in accordance with their obligations in the Articles of Agreement. In this phase (1950–56) was a reflection of the fact that development by the Fund of conditional policies with regard to its financial resources, made it necessary to raise consultations above the level of an ordinary fact-finding procedure with regard to compliance with obligations arising from the exchange rate and exchange restrictions régime. The problem was raised that the legal basis of Article XIV, Section 4, was deemed to be limited in this respect, but it was also feared that the Fund would extend its supervisory activities to the field of international trade. In this phase, consultations still took place mainly in Washington, while the Executive Directors also played a role in missions to member countries. During the second phase (1957–60), a regular pattern of periodic consultations developed, mainly with Western-European countries. This pattern continued during the third phase (1960–71), but with the difference that these consultations lacked a sound legal basis, as the acceptance of the system under Article VIII implied the end of the transitional period, and thus the end of consultations under this provision. The solution to this legal problem was found in the continuation of these consultations on an informal basis, the so-called 'consultations under Article VIII'. At the same time, the number of consultations increased, as a result of the growing number of countries that acceded to the Fund. The consultations themselves take shape through regular missions to member countries. Before a mission departs, the Fund's staff prepares the necessary documentation for discussions. Then, a mission consisting of four or five staff members visits the country and discussions take place with the central Bank and/or the Treasury Department for a period ranging from two days to two weeks. After its return, the mission makes a report to the Executive Board, in which report, when it concerns a country which has invoked Article XIV, a decision of the Executive Board containing a view and opinion of the Fund on the use of this escape clause is laid down. 'In these years an ever-widening range of financial and economic topics became primary'. With the end of the Bretton Woods system, a fourth phase began (1971–76). From a legal point of view, the termination of the system of par-values implied a serious weakening of the normative framework for the economic and monetary policy of States. For obvious reasons, this lacuna produced a strengthening of the guiding elements of the supervisory procedures. On the one hand, this was achieved by using Article IV, Section 4, containing a general obligation to co-operate, as a legal base, to strengthen the obligatory nature of the consultations. On the other hand, the practical organisation of these consultations was changed in such a way '. . . as to put less emphasis on the reporting of factual information and more on the assessment of both the member's current economic situation and the policies it was pursuing or formulating'. A series of special consultations during this interim period with countries 'whose external policies were regarded as of major importance to the world economy' (the Group of Ten) fits into this policy.[40] The following schedule can serve as an illustration of these activities:

Years	Consultations under Art. XIV	Consultations under Art. VIII	Total
71/72	53	24	77
72/73	59	26	85
73/74	61	28 (9)*	89
74/75	53	36 (22)*	89
75/76	61	33 (18)*	94
76/77	59	34	93
77/78	59	35	94

* special consultations   Source: Annual Reports

A fifth phase began in 1978, when the second amendment of the Articles of Agreement came into force. The new Article IV provides for obligatory consultations for all members of the Fund, as part of the task of the organisation to exercise surveillance of the exchange rate policy of the participating States. The use of consultations for supervisory purposes has thus been recognised by the Articles of Agreement. The supervisory aspect of the consultations is reflected not only in their use as a means of clarifying the economic and financial policy of a member country, but also because they 'provide an opportunity for the detailed review by the Fund of the economic and financial policies of individual members'. Alongside this analysis there is the repeatedly emphasised 'benefit of an independent appraisal' of economic policy, in which respect it seems obvious to presume that a certain criticism by the Fund is not excluded. This analysis and criticism may result in a request for advice. 'The authorities of the member can raise with the Fund any special difficulties stemming from the actions on policies of members.' However, advice is not conditional upon a request: 'consultations give members an opportunity to discuss their financial and economic problems with international officials familiar with the problem of many other countries and who can give information helpful for assessing alternative policies.' With regard to developing countries, a transition from advice to technical assistance can be seen. This activity of the Fund has attained enormous proportions, in particular during the last decade. By its very nature, technical assistance has a considerable policy-guiding aspect.

6.4. The conditionality of financial resources as an instrument for policy co-ordination

The various legal aspects of the way the Fund uses its financial resources have received considerable attention from writers[41] and only the techniques of the stand-by arrangement will be discussed here, this being the most important way the Fund exercises supervision in the form of guidance of economic policy.

In the early days of the Fund's Activities, member countries appeared to be not so much in need of direct drawings, but of the assurance that drawings could be made for a certain period and up to a certain amount. Having these possibilities 'in stock', the country concerned could conduct a policy to improve its balance of payments position. These drawings – one could define them as 'deferred' drawings – were not explicitly provided for in the Articles of Agreement, which only mentioned 'making . . . payments'. Nevertheless, the Fund deemed such drawings possible, and provided for the basis for the stand-by arrangement in a decision in 1952. The rules and customs that developed in practice with regard to this facility were laid down in subsequent decisions. The stand-by arrangement was also recognised legally by the second amendment of the Articles of Agreement, and this technique has long constituted the most important way in which the Fund provides its resources. Under Article XXX (B), the stand-by arrangement is described as 'a decision of the Fund by which a member is assured that it will be able to make purchases from the general resources account in accordance with the terms of the decision during a specified period up to a specified amount'. This definition seems to imply that, at least according to the Articles of Agreement, the stand-by arrangement does not constitute an international agreement between a member country and the Fund, but only a decision of the organisation. This is of great importance for the guidance function of the stand-by arrangement.

The stand-by arrangement is laid down in two documents, a so-called 'letter of intent', and a document containing the decision of the Fund to provide for this arrangement. This letter of intent, usually signed by the Minister of Finance or the Governor of the Central Bank, explains the economic and monetary policy the member country concerned will pursue, or that it is to conduct a policy which, generally, has been agreed upon in informal discussions with the Fund's staff. In order to support this policy, the member country requests to make drawings from the Fund for a certain period and up to a certain amount. Normally, the programme outlined in this letter of intent indicates certain goals in relation to the current or expected position of the balance of payments. The presentation of these goals is expressed in qualitative or quantitative terms, in such a way that it can be determined without problems whether the goals have been realised or not. These 'performance criteria' concern, for instance, the maximum increase of public expenditure, credit expansion, budgetary deficits, the obligation not to introduce multiple exchange rates, restrictions on currencies and products, and so on. In the letter of intent, the member generally declares that in case of non-compliance with these criteria, it will not make further drawings from the Fund under the stand-by arrangement. In the decision of the Fund, a reference is usually made to the letter of intent and the support of this policy by the granting of a stand-by arrangement. Other objects concern regular consultations and information on current developments, the duration and the extent of drawings, repurchased obligations, etc. In the course of time, the stand-by arrangement has developed into a technique by which strict and severe conditions with regard to economic policy may be imposed on a member country. The sometimes severe criticism by developing countries of this 'stranglehold' is especially directed against this technique.

For a long time, the Fund has held the opinion that a stand-by arrangement does not constitute an international agreement. This opinion was expressed and reaffirmed in decisions of the organisation in 1968 and 1979, in which a codification was laid down of policy with regard to stand-by arrangements. In the scarce literature on this subject, this view seems to be implicitly denied. With regard to the problem of supervision, this approach is understandable, since it provides for a possibility to distinguish clearly the three functions of supervision. The obligations with respect to information and consultation in these decisions reflect the review function, and enable the organisation to control whether or not the obligations the member concerned has undertaken have been violated when the performance criteria have not been realised. If one considers the agreement thus concluded as an application of the obligations of the Articles of Agreement, then one can also speak of a violation of the Treaty. The ineligibility to make further drawings can then be seen as a method of enforcement, and further consultations and adjustments of the stand-by arrangement as an exercise of the creative function.

Not only does this approach deny the true nature of the stand-by arrangement, but it also neglects the function of this technique as an instrument for guidance of economic policy. Besides the fact that the qualification of a stand-by arrangement as an international agreement from the point of view of international law is incorrect, external features of this phenomenon could also lead to no other conclusion. Only the decision of the Fund itself may be viewed as an elaboration of the obligations of the Articles of Agreement. Non-compliance with this decision constitutes a violation of these obligations, which, however, exclusively concern matters like the repurchase of currencies, regular information, charges, etc., but are definitely not concerned with the economic policy of the member concerned. Such intentions are laid down in the letter of intent, which constitutes only a unilateral policy declaration by the member. It is important that a decision of the Fund should expressly avoid various subjects of the letter of intent, but should, in general, only refer to its existence in its first paragraph. It must be taken into account that when the Fund decides to approve a stand-by arrangement, it is exercising its power to establish terms for the use of its resources, in order to guarantee the use of its resources in conformity with the Articles of Agreement.

The mere fact that under positive law, one cannot speak of an agreement between parties, since the construction of the stand-by arrangement has expressly been chosen to prevent the existence of such an agreement, has fundamental consequences. In the first place, non-fulfilment of the conditions of performance laid down in the letter of intent does not constitute a violation of contractual or treaty obligations. Thus, constitutional procedures for the approval of such an agreement are avoided, and the formal trans-formation of the standy-by arrangements into municipal law, and the notification of them to the United Nations, are not necessary. The practical aspect that a State may hesitate to deal with the Fund on a contractual basis is also removed. Thus, co-operation with the Fund is made possible, not only because of the fact that sovereignty is not affected, but because access to Washington is already at a very early phase. Thirdly, a member is not in default if non-compliance with the performance criteria is caused by external factors, for instance, reduced expert earnings resulting from a decline in the prices of raw materials. The last-mentioned example shows that it is unreal-istic to speak about the violation of obligations. For the practice of the Fund, it is of fundamental importance that, from a legal point of view, a stand-by arrangement in no way implies an interference in the domestic economic policies of member countries. In this respect, it must be noted that under the original Articles of Agreement, the Fund had no power to exercise such influence. Both the member country and the Fund can maintain their own responsibilities under a stand-by arrangement: the member country with regard to the exercise of its economic sovereignty, the Fund with regard to the protection of its financial resources. When a member country has not fulfilled the performance criteria, it will not make further drawings on the Fund. Thus, the situation is avoided in which the Fund is obliged to give an opinion on compliance with these obligations and, subsequently, to declare ineligibility as a sanction. Both the Fund and the member country maintain their own responsibility and freedom of action. From a legal point of view, a stand-by arrangement does not imply supervision in the form of an examination of obligations. Yet, there is a guidance of economic policy, as a stand-by arrangement may imply considerable supervision on the domestic economic policies of a member country; one has only to refer in this connection to the various objections by developing countries to this technique.

6.5. The new Article IV

The factual termination of the par-value system in 1971, by the suspension of the convertibility into gold of the American dollar, resulted in a new series of negotiations within the framework of the Committee of Twenty. The economic recession, the financial consequences of the oil crisis and the various aspects of the North-South relationship, made it possible to reach only a partial agreement with respect to a new legal framework for international monetary relations in 1976. This so-called Jamaica Agreement led to the second amendment of the Articles of Agreement, which came into force in 1978. The new Article IV in fact legalised the existing situation of floating exchange rates in various forms.

In this provision, the basic elements of supervision in the sense of guidance of economic policy are laid down. An important element of this supervision is that the maintenance of orderly exchange rate conditions is dependent upon the underlying economic and social conditions, which implies that supervision inevitably has to concern itself with these aspects. As indicated in the original conception of the Articles of Agreement, this sub-structure was expressly excluded from the supervision to be exercised by the Fund. The stand-by arrangement constituted an important breach in this conception, which is now recognised by Article IV through its so-called 'layered' structure.

This provision starts by stating that 'the provisions on exchange arrangements are based on the recognition that an essential purpose of the international monetary system is to provide for a framework that both facilitates the exchange of goods, services and capital among countries and sustains sound economic growth and that a principal objective of the system is the continuing development of the orderly underlying conditions that are necessary for financial and economic stability'. The general obligations of members to collaborate with the Fund and with other members in order to assure orderly and stable exchange rates are founded on this wording. Then, four specific obligations are summed up, according to which each member shall be bound:

'1. To endeavour to direct its economic and financial policies towards the objective of fostering orderly economic growth with reasonable price stability, with due regard to its circumstances.
2. To seek to promote stability by fostering orderly underlying financial and economic relations.
3. To avoid the manipulating of exchange rates in order to prevent effective balance of payments adjustment or to gain an unfair competitive advantage over other members.
4. To conduct an exchange rate policy in accordance with the above-mentioned obligations.'

391

For the supervisory role of the Fund, the major significance of the new Article IV concerns the abandonment of the old functional system, by which the economic policy of member countries was regulated through the monetary code of conduct without, however, attributing to the organisation a power to exercise direct influence. The obligation of member countries to conduct a sound economic policy is expressed in a positive sense, which, although the content of this provision is of an indicative nature, nevertheless constitutes a legally binding obligation to be enforced by the Fund through a 'firm surveillance over its exchange rates policies'.

It is, in particular, on the basis of this new Article IV that the instrument of consultations is strengthened. From the wording of this Article 'to adopt specific principles for the guidance of all members . . .', and from the fact that consultations with the Fund are now of an obligatory nature, it appears that this instrument can now be qualified as a general mechanism of supervision. The elimination of the distinction between obligatory and non-obligatory consultations has been accomplished by the Executive Board by means of its decision: 'Surveillance over Exchange Rate Policies'.[42] Accordingly, each round of consultations is now to be completed by a decision of the Executive Board. Although the contents and procedure of the consultations have remained more or less the same, their normative character has been strengthened, and the Fund is now in possession of an instrument to give a clear judgment on a member's economic policy. In the above-mentioned decision, the Executive Board has formulated a number of principles which it will take into account in the exercise of its 'firm surveillance'. If there are 'developments . . . which might indicate the need for a discussion with a member', the Managing Director has to inform the member concerned confidentially 'and shall conclude promptly whether there is a question of the observance of the principles'. In the case of non-observance, the Managing Director has to consult informally and confidentially, and to report to the Executive Board within a period of four months. In a second decision[43] of the Executive Board, these last-mentioned consultations have been supplemented so that the Managing Director can also initiate consultations without the existence of the developments mentioned above, 'if he feels that changes in the member's exchange arrangements or exchange rate policies, is sufficiently important for the member or for other members to warrant a special discussion'. Although the 'prosecution' character of the first-mentioned decision has been lessened, the Managing Director nevertheless keeps his strategic position because he still has the possibility of initiating consultations on the basis of the first-mentioned decision.

The above-mentioned special consultations with member countries which have a special responsibility for international trade 'to obtain a comprehensive picture of the economic circumstances and policies of the member countries taken as a whole', now have a stronger legal basis. The economic recession emphasised the need to strengthen the co-ordinating task of the Fund with a 'desirable economic strategy' directed at non-inflationary economic growth and an effecively functioning adjustment process in the balance of payments. Annually, the Executive Board composes the so-called 'World Economic Outlook', to supply the annual meetings of the Board of Governors and the periodical meetings of the Interim-Committee with a framework for their discussions. 'These understandings now form part of the framework within which the policies of individual countries are appraised and they are therefore a part of the process of surveillance.' This combination of the use of information and consultation confirms the aspect of guidance of economic policy of the supervision exercised by the Fund.

VII.   SOME CONCLUDING REMARKS

This brief treatment of both instruments of supervision reflects the fact that the supervisory role of the Fund is mainly concerned with the guidance of economic policy, or, to express it in more general terms, to influence the outcome of the international market process. As under the original Articles of Agreement no clear legal basis existed for this task, the evolution indicated could take place only by a wide – mainly factual – interpretation of these provisions. The development of new supervisory instruments was marginally confirmed by the first amendment in 1968. A clear recognition only occurred under the second amendment in 1978, through the new Article IV. Sections IV and VI of this study seem to confirm the remarks made about supervision in international economic organisations in Section II. That supervision with regard to the regulation of the economic policy of States is mainly concerned with guidance, confirms the character of the international economic order as a mixed economy, in which international economic organisations influence the outcome of the international market process.

For the phenomenon of supervision itself, this evolution from norm control to guidance of policy implies that the traditional framework of analysis of the three functions of supervision is no longer tenable. As the development of the IMF shows, supervision in the meaning of, or guidance of, economic policy can no longer be analysed by distinguishing between the review, correction and creative functions, but, on the contrary, by distinguishing between the instruments of supervision. Each instrument discussed includes aspects of these three functions of supervision, but – and this is a characteristic of guidance – a clear distinction is no longer possible.

NOTES

* This report, concluded in August, 1980, only reflects the personal opinion of the author.
1. *Supra*, chapter 1.
2. See P. VerLoren van Themaat, *The Changing Structure of International Economic Law* (Leyden, 1981); English translation of his *Rechtsgrondslagen van een nieuwe internationale economische orde* (Alphen a.d. Rijn, 1979).
3. An extensive treatment of the IMF-law is given in my contribution 'Organisaties op het gebied van het internationale monetaire stelsel en de ontwikkelingsfinanciering' (Organisations in the field of the International Monetary System), in *Studies over Internationaal Economisch Recht* (*Studies on International Economic Law*), Vol. I, 3, a (Alphen a.d. Rijn, 1977), p. 31 *et. seq.* See also M. R. Shuster, *The Public International Law of Money* (Oxford, 1972); D. Carreau, *Le Fonds Monétaire International* (Paris, 1970) and both books of H. Aufricht, *The Fund Agreement: Living Law and Emerging Practice* (Princeton, 1969) and *The International Monetary Fund, Legal Bases, Structure, Functions* (London, 1964). The best source, however, are the numerous books on the IMF law by its former legal counsellor, Joseph Gold.
4. See P. VerLoren van Themaat, *op. cit., supra*, note 2, p. 114 *et seq.*
5. To be more specific, the Court attributed direct effect to *inter alia* the articles 12 and 16 (customs duties and charges having equivalent effect), 30 and 34 (quantitative restrictions and measures having equivalent effect), 36 (escape clause), 37 (state monopolies), 48 (free movement of labour), 52 (freedom of establishment) and 59 and 60 (freedom to provide services).
6. See especially R. Triffin, *The Future of the European Payments System*, Wicksell lectures 1958 (Stockholm, 1958), p. 17 *et seq.* Also, L. B. Jeager, *International Monetary Relations*, (Chicago, 1965), p. 251 *et seq.* For a more general explanation, see W. Röpke, 'Economic Order and International Law' (1954–II) 86 *Recueil des Cours de l'Académie de Droit International* 224 *et seq.*
7. Barents, *loc. cit., supra*, note 3, p. 9 *et seq.*
8. R. Stödter, 'Völkerrecht und Weltwirtschaft' (1950) 13 *Zeitschrift für ausländisches und öffentliches Recht und Völkerrecht* 74.
9. Especially R. A. Gardner, *Sterling-Dollar Diplomacy; The History and Origins of Our International Economic Order*, (rev. and exp. ed., London, 1969) and A. L. K. Acheson *et al., Bretton-Woods Revisited* (Toronto, 1972).
10. According to this article, the heads of State of both countries declared that their countries '. . . endeavour with due respect for their existing obligations to further enjoyment by all States, great or small, victors or vanquished, of access on equal terms, to the trade and raw materials of the world, which are needed for economic prosperity.'
11. See Article 23(e).
12. See P. J. G. Kapteyn, 'De Verenigde Naties en de internationale economische orde' (The United Nations and the International Economic Order), in *Studies over Internationaal Economisch Recht* (*Studies on International Economic Law*) Vol. I. 1 (Alphen a.d. Rijn, 1977), p. 4 *et seq.*
13. See C. Wilcox, *A Charter for World Trade* (New York, 1949) and W. A. Brown, *The United States and the Restoration of World Trade* (Washington D.C., 1950).
14. The subject in paragraphs 2.4 and 2.5 was treated more extensively in my article "De internationale economische orde in rechtschistorisch perspectief' (The international economic order in an historical legal perspective) [1980] *Nederlands Juristenblad* 309–322.
15. J. Zijlstra and B. Goudzwaard, *Economische politiek en concurrentieproblematiek in de EEG en de Lid-Staten* (*Economic Policy and Problems of Competition in the EEC and the Member-States*) EEC, Series Concurrentie No. 2 (Brussels, 1966), especially, pp. 39–44. With regard to EEC matters, see P. J. G. Kapteyn and P. VerLoren van Themaat, *Introduction to the Law of the European Communities* (London etc., 1973), p. 52.
16. The full title of the Keynes Plan: 'Proposal for an International Clearing Union,' and White: 'Preliminary Draft Proposals for a United Nations Stabilisation Fund and a Bank for Reconstruction and Development of the United and Associated Nations.' Both drafts have been published in J. K. Horsefield, ed., *The International Monetary Fund, 1945–1965* (Washington D.C., 1969), Vol. III, p. 3 *et seq.*
17. For a complete picture see S. Strange, *International Monetary Relations*, Vol. 2 of *International Economic Relations of the Western World (1957–71)*, ed. by A. Shorfield (Oxford, 1976).
18. See also U. Petersmann, 'Völkerrechtliche Fragen den Weltwährungsreform' (1974) 34 *Zeitschrift für ausländisches und öffentliches Recht und Völkerrecht*, 497 *et seq.*

19. See *International Monetary Reform*, Documents of the Committee of Twenty (IMF, Wash. D.C., 1974), p. 7.

20. Message by F. D. Roosevelt, Document no. 40, *Proceedings and Documents of the United Nations Monetary and Financial Conference held at Bretton-Woods* Vol. I, p. 71, Department of State Publication, no. 2866 (New Hampshire, July 1–22, 1944).

21. Case concerning the Payments of Various Serbian Loans issued in France. (P.C.I.J., series A, Nos. 20–21 (1929), p. 44.)

22. Citations from A. van Dormael, *Bretton-Woods, Birth of a Monetary System* (London, 1978), p. 110 *et seq.*

23. For a further elaboration, see G. Stratman, *Das Internationale Währungsfonds* (Göttingen, 1972), *passim.*

24. J. Gold, 'The "Sanctions" of the International Monetary Fund,' 66 A.J.L.L. (1972), pp. 737–762, and his *Legal and Institutional Aspects of the International Monetary System: Selected Essays* (Washington D.C., 1979), p. 148 *et seq.* for further details.

25. Extensively, see Stratmann, *op. cit., supra,* note 23, p. 170 *et seq.*

26. See E. Hexner, 'Interpretation by Public International Organizations of their Basic Instruments,' 53 A.J.J.L. (1959), pp. 341–370; F. A. Mann, 'The Interpretation of the Constitutions of International Financial Institutions' (1968–69) 43 B.Y.I.L. pp. 1–12 and J. Gold, *Interpretation by the Fund,* IMF-Pamphlet Series, No. 11 (Washington D.C., 1968).

27. Barents, *loc. cit., supra,* note 3, p. 95 *et seq.*

28. Bretton-Woods, *Proceedings,* pp. 638–639.

29. Bretton-Woods, *Proceedings,* pp. 638–639.

30. Van Dormael, *op. cit., supra,* note 22, p. 72.

31. See, *inter alia,* R. W. Russel, 'Transgovernmental Interaction in the International Monetary System, 1960–72', *International Organization* (1973), pp. 454–455; illustrative is also P. P. Schweitzer, 'Political Aspects of Managing the International Monetary System', (1976) *International Affairs* 212.

32. Gardner, *op. cit., supra,* note 9, p. 22.

33. *Ibidem.*

34. Horsefield, *op. cit., supra,* note 16, p. 121.

35. See S. Strange, 'IMF: Monetary Managers', in: R. W. Cox and H. K. Jacobson, eds., *The Anatomy of Influence; Decision Making in International Organization* (New Haven, 1973), pp. 263–297.

36. See Horsefield, *op. cit., supra,* note 16, Vol. II, p. 11.

37. See, *inter alia,* H. van B. Cleveland, 'Reflections on International Monetary Order', 11 *Columbia Journal of International Law* (1972) 403 *et seq.*

38. See, *inter alia,* S. Strange, *op. cit., supra,* note 17.

39. See Barents, *loc. cit., supra,* note 3, p. 76 *et seq.*

40. *Annual Report* 1974, p. 64.

41. See especially J. Gold, *The Stand-By Arrangements of the International Monetary Fund; A Commentary on their Formal, Legal and Financial Aspects* (Washington D.C., 1970).

42. Decision No. 6392 (77/63) of April 29, 1977, A.R. 1977, pp. 107–109.

43. Decision No. 6206 (79/13) of January 22, 1979, p. 136.

PART VI

SUPERVISION WITHIN THE WORLD BANK

SUPERVISION WITHIN THE WORLD BANK

by G. J. H. van Hoof

CONTENTS

I. SOME GENERAL CHARACTERISTICS OF THE WORLD BANK

1.1. Introduction

In law the World Bank consists of three separate international financial organisations; the International Bank for Reconstruction and Development (IBRD), the International Development Association (IDA), and the International Finance Corporation (IFC). In fact, however, they should be considered as one financial institution.[1]

The Bank was established in 1945, the IFC and the IDA in 1956 and 1960 respectively. In general, the common objective of these institutions can be described as an attempt to help raise standards of living in developing countries by channelling financial resources from developed countries to the developing world. Each of the three organisations undertakes to realise this common objective in its own specific way, which differs from that of the other two. The major differences resulting from certain basic rules formulated in their respective constitutions are as follows: as the Bank finances its lending operations primarily from its own borrowings in the world's capital markets, it has to charge an interest rate at approximately conventional/commercial levels. Funds for IDA credits, on the other hand, come mostly in the form of subscriptions, general replenishments from its more industrialised and developed members, special contributions by its richer members, and transfers from the net earnings of the Bank. This enables the IDA to provide the poorer developing countries with credits free of interest, although it charges an annual service fee of 0.75 per cent. on the disbursed portion of each credit. The main distinctive feature of the IFC operations as compared to those of the Bank and the IDA lies in the fact that its Articles of Agreement do not require it to obtain a guarantee from the country in which it makes an investment. The omission of this requirement is specifically designed to facilitate IFC's function of assisting the economic development of less-developed countries by promoting growth in the private sector of their economies and helping to mobilise domestic and foreign capital for this purpose.

The interest in and the attention paid to the World Bank has been steadily increasing during recent years, particularly from a political point of view. This can be traced back to two factors, which are closely interconnected. First of all, there have been sweeping developments with regard to what is interchangeably described as the question of underdevelopment, as North-South relations, or simply as the problem of poverty in certain areas of the world. The inequitable economic situation in the Third World has now made itself felt as one of the foremost, if not the most urgent, problems of the international community, particularly as a result of the process of decolonisation. In consequence, opinions concerning the causes and possible solutions of this problem have undergone considerable changes, or have at least become much more differentiated.

Secondly, the World Bank itself has shown a remarkable transformation of character. From being essentially a typical investment bank during the first part of its existence it has gradually evolved in the direction of what could be called a development agency. In quantitative terms this evolution is reflected in the multiplication of the volume of lending by the World Bank. In qualitative terms, it is exemplified by such major shifts in policy as, for instance, the establishment in 1960 of a soft loan window in the form of the IDA and, more recently, its attack on absolute poverty by placing a greatly increased emphasis on investments that directly affect the well-being of the masses of poor people in developing countries. These and other developments have contributed to making the World Bank one of the most important exponents of institutionalised efforts to solve the problem of poverty in the world.

1.2. History of the World Bank

1.2.1. The Bank

During the Second World War plans were already being advanced aimed at preventing a recurrence of the economic crisis of the 1930s and at rebuilding the severely damaged economies of most European and some Asian countries. In these plans a number of international organisations were proposed to be closely connected with the projected United Nations Organisation. These organisations were to deal with the three most important fields of the international economic relations: international trade, international monetary questions and international investment.

With regard to the first-mentioned field, efforts to bring about an international organisation in the strict sense of that term have failed, and a more limited set-up has been chosen in the form of the General Agreement on Tariffs and Trade (GATT) of 1947.[2] With regard to the second and the third field, two international organisations have been established: the International Monetary Fund (IMF) and the International Bank for Reconstruction and Development (the Bank) respectively.

As far as the Bank is concerned,[3] two factors in particular have determined the character of the organisation as eventually embodied in its Articles of Agreement. First, planning with regard to the Bank has been almost exclusively in Western – or rather Anglo-American – hands. As a result the provision of the Articles of Agreement are all but completely based on the prevailing Western ideas at that time. Secondly, the deplorable situation regarding international loans during the period preceding the Second World War certainly made an impact. The fact is that with regard to a very considerable percentage of the loans made during the 1920s, debtors did not meet their obligations.[4] Both factors mentioned affected the early plans for the Bank's establishment.

Undoubtedly the most important of these plans has been the one published on November 20, 1943 by the U.S. Treasury entitled: 'Preliminary Draft

Outline of a Proposal for a Bank for Reconstruction and Development of the United and Associated Nations'.[5]

Broadly outlined, the main characteristics of the proposed organisation as envisaged in the 'Preliminary Draft Outline' can be described as follows: The starting point was the primary role accorded to private capital. The Bank would not be empowered to lend or invest in cases where private funds could be obtained on reasonable terms. Therefore, the Bank was not to supply short term capital, because private investors were considered to be able to meet this kind of demand. As far as long term financing was concerned, the Bank was expected to play a more substantial role, but here too, the primacy of private capital was upheld. The Bank's main objective was to encourage and promote an adequate international flow of private funds. Consequently, its first and foremost task was to be the guaranteeing of private investments abroad. It was considered that direct financing by the Bank itself would become only a marginal activity as compared to its other contemplated functions.

Proposals regarding the capital structure of the Bank were also geared to this 'secondary' role. The 'Preliminary Draft Outline' provided for a capital of 10bn U.S. dollars, 20 per cent. of which would be paid either in gold or in currency. The remaining 80 per cent. would have to be callable capital and, therefore, serve as a guarantee fund.

Similarly, proposals in the 'Preliminary Draft Outline' with respect to the Bank's operations reflected the fact that they originated in the West, primarily in the United States, and also the negative experiences in the field of international lending before the Second World War. It was proposed, for instance, that the government of the country of the borrower should guarantee the interest and the repayment of the principal, that loans should be untied and that the bank should not be guided by political considerations when deciding on requests for loans. Most provisions contained in these proposals were eventually incorporated in the Articles of Agreement and will be mentioned below.[6]

In 1944 there were European reactions to the American proposals. In that year a preparatory meeting to the Bretton Woods Conference took place in Atlantic City. At that meeting proposals were tabled in the form of a document, that became known as the 'boat draft,' because it was drawn up by the delegations of a number of European states during their joint boat trip to the United States.[7] The 'boat draft' did not substantially deviate from the 'Outline'. On most issues differences were only marginal. Even more than the Americans, the Europeans wanted to put the emphasis on the Bank's guarantee function.

The 'Preliminary Draft Outline' and the 'boat draft' formed the basis for the negotiations at the Bretton Woods Conference held from July 1–22, 1944 in the United States with the participation of 44 states.[8]

Commission II of the Conference dealt with the Bank. It met for the first time on July 3 and as early as July 6 a 'Preliminary Draft Outline of a Proposal for a Bank for Reconstruction and Development' was tabled. Although it was made clear that this draft was not to be considered a proposal of any delegation,[9] it was in fact a combination of the U.S. 'Preliminary Draft Outline' and the 'boat draft'. As stated before, these two documents were very similar and it is probably for this reason that the negotiations at Bretton Woods were successfully concluded in a rather short period of time. Agreement on the final text was reached on July 21.

The Articles of Agreement of the Bank entered into force on December 27, 1945.[10] The Bank opened for business on June 25, 1946.

1.2.2. The International Finance Corporation

As noted in the preceding paragraphs, the founding fathers of the Bank regarded it as a major task of the proposed organisation to encourage and promote private investment and the private entrepreneur in developing countries. However, at a very early stage of its existence it became evident that the Bank was handicapped in this respect by the provision in its Articles of Agreement which stipulated that: 'When the member in whose territories the project is located is not itself the borrower, the member or the central bank or some comparable agency of the member which is acceptable to the Bank, fully guarantees the repayment of the principal and the payment of interest and other charges on the loan' (Art. III (4)(1)).

This requirement severely limited the activities of the Bank in the industrial sector for a number of reasons. Private entrepreneurs are often not in favour of government guaranteed loans, because this would entail the risk of becoming more dependent upon that government.

Governments themselves are not always prepared to provide such guarantees because they might be accused of favouring certain industries. The Bank has tried to evade this kind of problem by making loans to national 'Development Finance Companies', which in their turn have re-lent the money in the industrial sector of the country concerned.[11] This, however, was not considered to be an entirely satisfactory approach.

After a rather extensive period of preparation it was therefore decided to establish the IFC in order to supplement the Bank in this respect.[12] The Articles of Agreement of the IFC entered into force on July 20, 1956.[13]

1.2.3. The International Development Association

The campaign for the establishment of an international institution with the capacity to aid developing countries at more favourable conditions than the Bank, started as early as 1949.[14] The developing countries made increasing efforts towards this end during a period of about ten years, particularly within the framework of the United Nations. Undoubtedly, the tenacity on the part of the developing countries contributed considerably to the eventual establishment of the IDA.

The need for an institution like the IDA arose as a consequence of the continuously growing external debt of the developing countries. This steadily increasing indebtedness gradually eroded their creditworthiness and made them, at a certain point, almost ineligible for Bank loans on commercial terms, the so-called 'hard loans.' In other words, a gap was appearing between what the Bank had to offer and what (a number of) its less-developed clients needed. Closing this gap would require broadening or supplementing the Bank's instruments by creating the possibility of making loans on less stringent terms than the conventional terms, the so-called 'soft loans.'[15] Initially, the developed countries (and, as a consequence, also the Bank itself) opposed the creation of an institution empowered to lend at more lenient terms than the Bank itself. As conditions attached to Bank loans already rested on a non-profit basis, softening them would amount to partial grants, which in their view was undesirable. Nevertheless, during the 1950s it became increasingly clear that underdevelopment was inevitable if loans could only be obtained by the developing countries at conventional hard terms. This led to the developed countries becoming increasingly prepared to effect changes in the direction adopted by the developing countries. The 1958 Monroney Proposal in the U.S. Senate for the establishment of the IDA was instrumental in that respect. The proposal was launched at a very appropriate time. Since 1954 the Agriculture Trade Development and Assistance Act (Public Law 480) had empowered the U.S. government to accept inconvertible currencies as payment for the sale of food surpluses. As a result of such so-called 'P.L. 480 sales' the United States had obtained large quantities of inconvertible currencies. Via the proposed IDA these funds could be used for development finance.[16] The Monroney Proposal was accepted by the U.S. Senate and subsequently adopted by the Board of Governors of the Bank in the form of a resolution which instructed the Executive Directors to draft a treaty establishing the IDA. After agreement on the final text was reached among the States concerned, the Articles of Agreement of the IDA entered into force on September 15, 1960.[17]

1.3. Purposes

1.3.1. The Bank

As noted in the introductory paragraph, the ultimate common objective of the World Bank can be described in very general terms as the raising of the standard of living in its member countries. Article I(iii) of the Articles of Agreement of the Bank expresses this idea a little more broadly in stating as the main purpose of the Bank '. . . raising productivity, the standard of living and conditions of labour . . .'. In the view of the founding fathers, all this would be achieved by a long-range balanced growth of international trade and the maintenance of equilibrium in balances of payments. Article I(i) is only slightly more specific; it requires the Bank 'To assist in the reconstruction and development of territories of members . . .'.

During the Bretton Woods Conference controversy arose regarding the question of which purpose should be given priority: reconstruction or development.[18] The Articles of Agreement do not provide a clear-cut answer to this question.[19] The dilemma has, however, been resolved in practice. At a very early stage in its existence it became the Bank's established practice to lend only for developmental purposes. The constitutions of the IFC and the IDA no longer even mention 'reconstruction.'

The remaining paragraphs of Article I do not really formulate purposes, but rather describe the means and guidelines for the realisation of the very general purposes mentioned above. The Bank is empowered to guarantee or participate in loans and if necessary to supplement these activities by financing loans directly (Article I(ii)). Loans must be arranged so that the more useful and urgent projects will be dealt with first (Article I(iv)), while operations in general are subject to the proviso that due regard must be paid to the effect of international investment on business conditions in the territories of members (Article I(v)).

1.3.2. IDA

The close relationship of the IDA with the Bank is reflected in Article I which contains the IDA's purposes. According to this article, the IDA has to further the developmental objectives of the Bank and to supplement its activities. This is subordinated to its main objective, of promoting economic development, increasing productivity and raising standards of living in the less-developed areas of the world included within the Association's membership. The IDA's most distinctive feature, as compared with the Bank, is that it is authorised to realise these objectives 'in particular by providing finance . . . on terms which are flexible and bear less heavily on the balance of payments than those of conventional loans . . .'.

1.3.3. IFC

Although the IFC shares the World Bank's general objective of promoting economic development, it is expressly instructed in Article I of its Articles of Agreement to concentrate on 'encouraging the growth of productive private enterprise in member countries'. It supplements the Bank in that it is authorised to do what the former cannot do, *viz*. '. . . assist in financing . . . without guarantee of repayment by the member government concerned' (Article I(i)). Furthermore, the IFC must bring together investment opportunities, domestic and foreign private capital and experienced management (Article I(ii)) and seek to stimulate the flow of private capital into productive investment (Article 1(iii)).

1.4. Membership

Provisions regarding membership are very similar in the constitutions of all three organisations. The treaties lay down only one precondition for membership: in the case of the Bank, membership of the International Monetary Fund is required (Article II(1)(a) and (b))[20] while membership of the Bank is required in the case of the IFC and the IDA (Article II(1)(a) and (b) IFC and IDA).

A distinction is made between original and other members of the three organisations. Original members are those listed in Schedule A annexed to all three treaties (Article II(1)(a) Bank, IDA and IFC). Other states may join at such times and in accordance with the terms determined by the respective organisations (Article II(1)(b) Bank, IDA and IFC). Admission is decided on by a resolution of the Board of Governors (Article V(2)(b)(i) Bank, Article VI(2)(c)(i) IDA and Article IV(2)(c)(i) IFC), the most important elements of which are provisions concerning the size of the contribution, the way in which the contribution has to be paid and the required membership of the IMF, c.q. the Bank.[21]

Members have a right to withdraw from the organisations (Article VI(1) Bank, Article VII(1) IDA and Article V(1) IFC). This right was exercised with regard to the Bank by Poland in 1950,[22] by Cuba and the Dominican Republic in 1960[23] and by Indonesia in 1965.[24] The two last named countries later rejoined the Bank.[25]

Finally, in the event of a member's failure to fulfil any of its obligations, it can be suspended and eventually even expelled (Article VI(2) Bank, Article VII(2) IDA and Article V(2) IFC). Up to now this has happened only once, in 1953 in the case of Czechoslovakia.[26]

Since the establishment of the Bank its membership has steadily increased. The Bank began with 45 States. On June 30, 1980 its membership included 135 countries, while action was pending on membership for Djibouti, Dominica, St. Vincent and the Grenadines, Seychelles and Zimbabwe.[27] Switzerland is not a formal member as a result of its policy of neutrality.[28] In addition, the countries of Eastern Europe are notable by their absence. With the exception of Roumania, none of them is a member of the Bank anymore.[29] A number of East European states, and in particular the Soviet Union, actively participated in the Bretton Woods Conference. At one stage everything seemed to indicate that the Soviet Union would indeed become a member of the Bank, but at the end of 1946 it became clear that this was not going to be the case. Apart from the fact that the first signs of a worsening political climate between the Soviet Union and the other allies were already becoming apparent at that time, the following reasons are believed to underlie the decision not to adhere to the Bretton Woods system: (a) the procedure adopted for allocating votes among members in accordance with their subscriptions; (b) the requirement to report their national gold and foreign exchange holdings and to transfer part of them to the U.S. where the IMF and the World Bank have their headquarters; (c) the terms on which they were allowed credits to correct their balance of payments.[30]

The People's Republic of China, on the other hand, very recently joined the ranks of the World Bank. On May 15, 1980 the Executive Directors decided that the Government of the People's Republic of China represented China in the Bank and its affiliates.[31]

407

On June 30, 1980, the IDA had 121 members and action was pending on membership for Djibouti, Dominica, the Solomon Islands, the United Arab Emirates and Zimbabwe,[32] while IFC membership comprised 113 countries.[33]

1.5. The funds of the World Bank

1.5.1. The Bank

1.5.1.1. Introduction

The funds available to the Bank for the financing of its loan operations stem from different sources. The most important of these are the Bank's capital, its reserves and its borrowings on the capital markets. These will be discussed in some detail below. In addition to the three sources mentioned, Article IV(8)(i) authorises the Bank to sell securities which it has either issued, or guaranteed, or in which it has invested, provided it obtains the approval of the member in whose territories the securities are to be sold. At the end of fiscal year 1979 the cumulative total of such sales of participations in new loans and of maturities of the Bank's loan portfolio was $2,976m equivalent.[34]

The Bank's most recent asset for financing its lending to developing countries is the 'Interest Subsidy Fund' belonging to the so-called 'Intermediate Financing Facility' created by the Executive Directors on July 29, 1975 and effective from December 23 of the same year. It is usually termed 'Third Window,' because it enables the Bank to make loans at an interest rate which is 'harder' than those of the IDA but 'softer' than those charged on normal Bank loans. Of the interest due on 'Third Window' loans, 4 per cent. is financed out of the 'Interest Subsidy Fund', which consists of voluntary contributions of a number of Member States and Switzerland. At the end of fiscal 1976 loans up to $600m could be financed in this way.[35]

1.5.1.2. The capital of the Bank

Generally, the term 'capital' denotes the subscriptions the Member States have to contribute to the Bank on the basis of its Articles of Agreement. However, a distinction has to be made between different types of capital. A central place has to be accorded to the authorised capital, because the other types of capital are ultimately derived from it. The 'authorised capital' is the maximum amount to which the Bank may issue shares. It can be divided into subscribed and unsubscribed capital. The 'subscribed capital' consists of the total value of the Bank's shares actually bought by the Member States. Theoretically, authorised and subscribed capital could be equal. In fact, however, the latter has always been smaller. In that way the unsubscribed portion of the authorised capital can be used in the case of admission of new members or of an increase of the subscription of individual Member States. Each Member State has the obligation to subscribe to a minimum number of shares of the Bank. For original members this number is laid down in Schedule A annexed to the Articles of Agreement (Article II(3)(a)). For

408

other members, it is fixed in the resolution by which a State is admitted to the Bank.[36]

The subscribed capital is made up of two parts: the paid-in and the callable capital. The paid-in capital constitutes 20 per cent. of the subscribed capital and can as a rule be used by the Bank for its operations (Article II(5)(i)). The remaining 80 per cent. is the callable capital, which Member States have to pay only when they are required to meet the Bank's obligations incurred by making or guaranteeing loans or participating in them (Article II(5)(ii)).

A further distinction has to be made between usable and non-usable capital. According to Article II(7)(i) $^1/_{10}$ of the paid-in capital (2 per cent. of the subscribed capital) is payable in gold or U.S. dollars and $^9/_{10}$ (18 per cent. of the subscribed capital) in the currency of the member concerned. These currencies, however, can be loaned by the bank only with the approval in each case of the member whose currency is involved (Article IV(2)(a)). Therefore, the usable capital consists of the part of the paid-in capital payable in gold and that portion of the part payable in currencies with regard to which the approval of Article IV(2)(a) has been obtained, as well as the net profits of the Bank.[37] It is clear that the smaller the usable capital, the more the Bank becomes dependent upon the capital market to borrow the funds needed to finance its loan operations.[38] Its capacity to attract money from the capital market in its turn is to a large extent determined by the level of its callable capital. The callable capital constitutes a fund which serves as a guarantee to those from whom it borrows that the Bank will be able to meet its obligations. Consequently, the larger the volume of the callable capital, the better the opportunities to raise money in the capital market.

Raising the level of the callable capital has been the main motive for the first increases in the authorised capital, which have been taking place since 1959.[39] The Bank started with an authorised capital stock of $10,000m (in terms of U.S. dollars of the weight and fineness in effect on July 1, 1944) divided into 100,000 shares having a par value of $100,000 each. After the Selective Capital Increase of May 1977[40] the authorised capital is now $41,015m. The subscribed capital totals $30,869m, 90 per cent. of which is callable ($27,782m), and 10 per cent. paid-in ($3,087m), while $2,270m of the paid-in part is usable capital.

At the moment, the authorised capital of the Bank is again about to be increased. In 1979 the Executive Directors recommended a General Capital Increase of $40,000m. Just as in 1977, the purpose of this most recent increase is to keep the subscribed capital at a sufficiently high level in relation to the total volume of the Bank's lending; this is because Article II(3) stipulates that the amount outstanding of guarantees, participations in loans and direct loans is not to exceed the sum of the unimpaired capital, reserves and surplus of the Bank. Of the recommended $40,000m increase, 7.5 per cent. will have to be paid in, while 92.5 per cent. will represent callable capital.[41]

1.5.1.3. The reserves of the Bank

Since 1948, the Bank has made profits every single year.[42] They result from the retained earnings on its loan operations. In 1964 the Bank changed its policy with regard to its reserves. Since that time, both the earnings from lending activities and the resulting 1 per cent. fee which is charged annually on the disbursed portion of each loan are deposited in the 'General Reserve'.[43] Before that date this 1 per cent. charge was added to the 'Special Reserve'. Furthermore, it was decided in 1964 that in the future part of the net earnings would be transferred to the IDA in the form of grants.[44] On June 30, 1979, the Bank had contributed a total amount of $1,425m to the resources of the IDA.[45] As a result on June 30, 1980, the 'Special Reserve' was $0,293m, while the 'General Reserve' amounted to $2,600m.[46]

1.5.1.4. The Bank's borrowing

Article IV(8)(iii) authorises the Bank to borrow the currency of any member with the approval of that member. Initially, the Bank has been heavily dependent for its borrowing on the American capital market. This situation has gradually changed and estimates indicate that at present 27.7 per cent. of the Bank's obligations are held by investors in Germany, 19.7 per cent. in the United States, 15.9 per cent. in Switzerland, 14.1 per cent. in Japan and 14.2 per cent. in OPEC countries, while the remaining 8.4 per cent. of outstanding borrowings are held by institutions in more than 90 countries.[47]

The Bank has an excellent standing on the capital market, primarily because of the comparably favourable ratio between the total of its outstanding obligations and the level of its callable capital. On June 30, 1979, the Bank's callable capital amounted to $35,936m.[48] Compared to the amount of its outstanding obligations, which totalled $29,667m on the same date,[49] this provides a rather safe guarantee for the Bank's bond holders. The Bank expects to increase its gross borrowing by about $1,000m equivalent a year into the mid 1980s, when the 1979 General Capital Increase will have taken effect.[50]

1.5.2. The IDA

The bulk of the funds which the IDA has at its disposal to finance its lending operations consists of contributions made available by its Member States. Formally, it is authorised to borrow on the capital market, like the Bank and the IFC, but it is clear that this is not really possible for the IDA; it would be impossible to continue to provide the so-called soft loans (in the case of the IDA usually called 'credits') and at the same time obtain the necessary funds on the conventional (hard) conditions prevailing on the capital market.

The Articles of Agreement of the IDA contain a number of complicated provisions regarding the system of subscriptions (Articles II and III). Broadly outlined they amount to the following. The Articles of Agreement provide for two categories of membership: Part I, which comprises the rich countries and Part II, which is composed of developing Member States. On June 30, 1980, the Part I category included 21 members, the remaining members being Part II countries.[51] Part I members have to pay their full subscription in gold or convertible currency, all of which can be used by the IDA for lending. Part II members, on the other hand, pay only 10 per cent. of their subscription in gold or convertible currency. The remaining 90 per cent. is paid in the member's own currency and cannot be used for lending without the approval of the member concerned.

The initial capital of the IDA was $1,000m, which is small considering the task with which it had been charged. Furthermore, it takes a long time before IDA money is repaid by borrowers, because of the long grace and amortisation periods attached to IDA credits. From the outset, therefore, it was clear that IDA members would be asked to contribute money, on a periodic basis, to finance its activities. Thus, in 1964, agreement was reached on the first replenishment of IDA resources. Meanwhile, five replenishments have taken place. After the first four replenishments the total sum made available by the Member States amounted to $10,730m, 95.56 per cent. of which came from Part I countries and 3.44 per cent. from Part II members.[52] The most recent replenishment amounted to $7,638m.[53] On June 30, 1980, $8,093m of this sum had been subscribed.[54] Finally, as noted above, the IDA has received grants from the bank on a regular basis since 1964. On June 30, 1979 these grants totalled $1,425m.[55]

1.5.3. The IFC

The provisions regarding the capital in the Articles of Agreement of the IFC are very similar to those of the Bank. In the case of the IFC, however, the distinction between paid-in and callable capital does not exist, because Member States have to pay their full subscription in gold or United States dollars (Article II(3)(c)). The IFC also had to start with a relatively small authorised capital of $100m (Article II(2)). In 1965 an attempt was made to remedy this handicap by empowering the IFC to borrow from the Bank. For this purpose both the Articles of Agreement of the IFC[56] as well as those of the Bank[57] were amended. In practice, loans from the bank constitute a major source of income for the IFC. On June 30, 1979 they totalled $483m.[58] In November 1977, however, the capital of the IFC was considerably increased to $650m. Of the 480 offered for subscription $306m had been subscribed by the end of the fiscal year 1979.[59]

1.6. Provisions concerning operations

Apart from those already mentioned above, the most important provisions setting the limits for the World Bank's loan and guarantee operations are the following: the Bank has to be able to rely on the fact that borrower will be in the position to meet its obligations under the loan and may only lend or guarantee for the purpose of a specific project, except in special circumstances. Bank loans are to be untied, *i.e.* no conditions can be imposed that the proceeds of a loan shall be spent in the territories of any particular member or members (Article III). Finally, Articles IV(3)(b) and IV(3)(c) incorporate the idea that the bank normally finances the foreign exchange costs of a project and expects the borrower or the government to meet the local costs. Only in exceptional circumstances may the Bank, either directly or indirectly, finance the local foreign costs involved in a project.

As far as the IDA is concerned, the provisions regarding its operations are very similar to those of the Bank. There is, of course, the notable exception that the IDA is empowered to provide money for developmental purposes on so-called soft terms. The hard or soft character of a loan (or credit) is largely determined by three factors: the rate of interest, the length of the amortisation, and the grace period. The amortisation period is the time in which the total loan matures, while the grace period is the time which elapses between the disbursement of the loan and the moment at which the first repayment of principal is due. Therefore, the lower the interest rate and the longer both periods mentioned, the softer the character of the loan or credit. IDA credits do not carry any interest, but an annual service fee of 0.75 per cent. is charged, which is intended to cover administration costs.[60] In the fiscal year 1980, the lending rate of the bank ranged from a low of 7.9 per cent. to a high of 8.25 per cent.[61] IDA credits take fifty years to mature and have a grace period of ten years. Bank loans generally have a grace period of five years and are repayable over twenty years or a shorter period.[62]

In most respects IFC provisions regarding operations are also very similar to those of the Bank. However, the Articles of Agreement of the IFC do contain a number of specific provisions resulting from the fact that the IFC is operating as a public organisation in the private sector. They purport to prevent a high level of involvement by the IFC in the enterprises in which it has made investments. Article III(3)(iv) prohibits the IFC from assuming the responsibility for managing any enterprise in which it has invested and from exercising voting rights for this purpose or for any other purpose which, in its opinion, is properly within the scope of managerial control. Similarly, the IFC must seek to revolve its funds by selling its investments to private investors whenever it can appropriately do so on satisfactory terms (Article III(3)(vi)).

1.7. Institutional structure

The structure of the organisation and management of the Bank and of the IDA are completely identical; that of the Bank and of the IFC are very similar. In addition, the Board of Governors, the Board of Directors and the President of the Bank perform these functions with regard to the IDA (Article VI(2)(b), VI(4)(b), VI(5) IDA). Moreover, the IDA is administered by the same staff as the Bank.[63] On June 30, 1979 it was composed of 2,382 non-secretarial members.[64] The IFC's Board of Governors and Board of Directors are also the same as those of the Bank (Article IV(2)(b) and

IV(4)(b) IFC). In addition, the President of the Bank is *ex officio* Chairman of the Board of Directors of the Corporation (Article IV(5)(a)). Furthermore, the Corporation has a President (appointed by the Directors on the recommendation of the Chairman), who is the chief of its operating staff (Article IV(5)(b)). The IFC has its own staff which comprised 183 professionals on June 30, 1979.[65]

Because of these common features with respect to the institutional structure of the three organisations, the brief survey below will concentrate on the Bank.

1.7.1. The Board of Governors

The Bank's Board of Governors consists of one governor and one alternate appointed by each Member State. All powers of the Bank are vested in the Board (Article V(2)(a)). Apart from a number of specifically enumerated powers, the Board may delegate authority to the Executive Directors (Article V(2)(b)). Except where otherwise provided, the Board decides by a simple majority of the votes cast. The Bank has a system of weighted votes. Each Member State is given 250 votes plus an additional vote for each share of stock held. As a consequence of this system the number of votes in the Board of Governors differs greatly from one Member State to the other. At present, for instance, the United States holds 21.49 per cent., the United Kingdom 7.37 per cent., the Federal Republic of Germany 6.62 per cent., Japan 5.63 per cent., France 3.88 per cent. and the Netherlands 1.96 per cent. of the votes. On the other hand, countries like India, Indonesia and Mexico have only 3.34 per cent., 1.07 per cent. and 0.26 per cent. respectively.[66] If no further steps were taken, this rather big gap between developed and developing countries would be even greater as a result of the General Capital Increase recently agreed upon. However, the Executive Directors have recommended measures to overcome this undesirable effect.[67]

The system of weighted voting in the IDA is similar to that of the Bank. Each member has 500 votes plus one additional vote for each $5,000 of its initial subscription (Article VI(3)). The distribution of votes would also have sharply deteriorated in the IDA to the disadvantage of the developing countries if no steps had been taken, because the bulk of funds available through the subsequent replenishments have been furnished by the developed countries. The Articles of Agreement of the IDA, however, make a distinction between additional subscriptions (Article III(1)) and supplementary resources (Article III(2)), the main difference being that the former carry a proportional increase in voting rights, while the latter do not. To prevent a further imbalance in voting-power only a small part of the subsequent contributions of Part I members have been considered as additional subscriptions and the remainder as supplementary resources, while Part II country contributions have been fully regarded as additional subscriptions. As a result the Part I members at this moment have 63.6 per cent. of the votes, while the total voting power of Part II members is 36.64 per cent.[68]

413

1.7.2. The Board of Directors

The Board of Directors is composed of twenty members. Five of them are appointed, one by each of the five members having the largest number of shares (Article V(4)(b)(i)). At this moment the United States, the United Kingdom, the Federal Republic of Germany, Japan and France have the right to appoint a Director.[69] The remaining fifteen Directors are elected by the Governors of the other Member States according to a complicated procedure as laid down in Schedule B annexed to the Articles of Agreement (Article V(4)(b)(ii)). As a result of this procedure each elected Director represents a number of countries (from three to over twenty) on the Board; in some cases these countries can be extremely heterogeneous.

The Articles of Agreement make the Directors responsible for the conduct of the general operations of the Bank (Article V(4)(a)). In addition, the Directors are granted a number of specific powers, such as the right to choose the President of the Bank and the right to decide on questions of interpretation arising with regard to provisions of the Articles of Agreement (Article IV). However, in practice the most important powers exercised by the Directors are those delegated by the Board of Governors.

The Directors constitute the permanent organ of the Bank and meet as often as business requires (Article V(4)(e)). They take their decisions by a majority of votes cast, except where other provisions are made (Article V(4)(b)). Each appointed Director is entitled to cast the same number of votes as are allotted to the member appointing him. Elected Directors cast the number of votes, which counted towards their election according to the procedure contained in Schedule B (Article V(4)(g)).

1.7.3. The President and the staff

The President of the Bank is appointed by the Directors. He is Chairman of the Board of Directors, but has no vote except a casting vote in case of an equal division of votes. He may participate in meetings of the Board of Governors, but has no vote at these meetings (Article V(5)(a)). He is the chief of the operating staff, the members of which he appoints and dismisses, and he is responsible for the conduct of the Bank's ordinary business (Article V(5)(b)). Up to now the President of the World Bank has always been a U.S. citizen. From 1968 until 1981 the office was held by R. S. McNamara. His successor is the present head of the World Bank, A. W. Claussen.

The Board of Governors, the Executive Directors and the President and the staff are the Bank's main decision-making organs, although there are some others.[70] The decision-making process of the World Bank is rather complex. The body in which all powers are formally vested, the Board of Governors, plays only a more or less symbolic part. Its role is limited to supervising the general features of World Bank policy. A more active involvement is hardly conceivable for an organ which generally meets only once a year and is composed of over 130 members. The regular major decisions on policies, budgets and lending and borrowing commitments are made by the Executive Directors. Recommendations on other matters and major administrative decisions are within the province of the President, while day-to-day operational and administrative decisions are delegated through the whole structure of management.

The World Bank is often considered to be a 'staff or management dominated' organisation. Obviously, the staff of an organisation dealing with the often highly technical matters involved in development financing is bound to have a substantial influence on its policies and operations. At any rate, such influence is likely to be greater than in the case of an international organisation of a more general political character. However, political considerations are far from absent in the field of development co-operation. Indeed, as is usually the case in economic matters, they sometimes even play a decisive role. This also applies to the World Bank. It therefore appears that the staff is autonomous only to the extent that its decisions are confined to what, in the final analysis, is regarded as being desirable or acceptable by the Executive Directors and, ultimately, the Board of Governors, which both reflect the political constellation of the World Bank's membership. This point will be elaborated below.[71]

1.8. Activities of the World Bank

The character of the World Bank has changed rather dramatically since the Bank was founded in 1945. Generally speaking, the image of the organisation has evolved from that of a commercial investment bank in the strict sense of the term towards what could be called a development agency. Changes have taken place of both a quantitative and qualitative nature. First of all, the annual amount of the Bank's lending has grown substantially. After almost ten years of being in business this amount was $300 to $400m a year. In 1958 it had already doubled to between $700 and $800m annually.[72] The biggest increase in annual lending has occurred in the 1970s. From 1973 to 1977 it almost tripled from $2,000 to $5,800m.[73] During the fiscal year 1980 it reached a level of $7,644m.[74]

Even more important than these increases in the volume of the Bank's lending have been the quantitative changes which have taken place with regard to its policy. Completely in line with the ideas of its founding fathers, the Bank, in the early years of its existence, operated on the basis of so-called 'sound banking principles.' This policy, strongly favoured by the then President Black, caused the activities of the Bank in that period to be largely confined to projects of basic infrastructure (roads, railways and power) and the industrial sector.[75] In this respect, the establishment of the IFC in 1956 was no more than a minor adjustment to the vested policy of the Bank at that time. The coming into being of the IDA, on the other hand, in fact was the beginning of a major shift in the World Bank's policy. Obviously, the creation of a soft loan window was a deviation from the so-called sound banking principles. The IDA has heavily influenced the Bank and indeed determined a good deal of the World Bank's image as a whole. Like the

Bank, it has experienced considerable growth. During the fiscal years 1964–68 it provides credits to a total of $1,300m, for the period 1969–73 its volume of lending was $3,900m, while new commitments during the fiscal years 1974–78 amounted to $7,900m.[76] During the fiscal year 1980 IDA commitments totalled $3,838m.[77]

From a qualitative point of view some changes were already visible during the 1960s, but a breakthrough came only in the early 1970s after McNamara had become President of the World Bank. At that time the World Bank launched what has become known as its attack on the absolute poverty, meaning the situation in which the poorest 40 per cent. of the population in the developing countries finds itself.[78] Since then this has consistently been a main theme in the policy of the World Bank.

It was summarised by McNamara in his 1979 address to the Board of Governors: 'If we focus on the ultimate objectives of development, it is obvious that an essential one must be the liberation of the 800 million individuals in the developing world who are trapped in absolute poverty – a condition of life so limited by malnutrition, illiteracy, disease, high infant-mortality and low life-expectancy as to be below any rational definition of human decency.'[79] This shift in policy has made itself felt in several respects. First of all, the World Bank's economic philosophy has changed. Up to the 1970s the Bank had laid almost total emphasis on economic growth as a vehicle for economic development. Its operations began with the premise that eventually the benefits of economic growth would 'trickle down' auto-matically and therefore benefit all sectors of the population. During the 1970s doubts increased about the soundness of this premise.[80] It has now been replaced by an approach in which the promotion of accelerated growth is combined with attempts to raise the productivity and the living standards of the absolute poor.[81]

As a result such new problems as unemployment, income distribution, land reform, institution building and environmental aspects have come within the scope of the World Bank's dealings with the developing countries. Lending has been increasingly directed towards the poor and less-developed countries in Asia, Africa and Latin America. In terms of sectors of lending, emphasis has shifted from transport and industry to sectors which reflect the new orientation of the World Bank, such as agriculture and rural develop-ment, urban development, water supply and sewerage population, nutrition and education.[82] Finally, over the years activities other than financing have evolved within the framework of the World Bank and have become increas-ingly important. Today such activities as technical assistance, co-ordination of development assistance and research are standard features of the World Bank's operations.[83]

All this certainly does not imply that the problem of absolute poverty in the world has now been solved. On the contrary, one gets the impression that absolute poverty is increasing rather than decreasing.[84] Obviously, it would be too simple an excuse to blame the World Bank for this state of affairs, although critics maintain that the World Bank is also guilty of not having really reached the poor.[85] It should be kept in mind that the organisation provides barely 1 per cent. of the total investment in the developing countries. On the other hand, the World Bank is the main multilateral development finance institution and its role, therefore, is that of a catalyst. It has made the fight against absolute poverty the nucleus of its policy. However, the quantitative and qualitative changes mentioned above, as the World Bank has itself conceded, have not yet gone far enough to affect significantly the well-being of the poor. Some aspects of the development process – for example the development of human resources and the meeting of the basic needs of the poor – have seen only limited success.[86] It is therefore fair to evaluate the various aspects of the World Bank's functioning in the light of their impact on the problem of absolute poverty.

II. SUPERVISION WITHIN THE WORLD BANK

2.1. Introduction

As was pointed out in Part I of this book, one of the main aspects, and indeed the most characteristic aspect of international supervision, is its review function. We noted that this function is exercised whenever the behaviour of States is judged for its conformity with international law by a supervisory body with an international status.[87] Obviously, this implies the existence of obligations on the part of the States. Within the framework of most international organisations the obligations of each of the Member States will be more or less similar, although not necessarily identical. With regard to international organisations operating in the field of development co-operation, the situation is fundamentally different. Within those organisations two categories of Member States have to be discerned, both having different kinds of obligations.

On the one hand, there is the category of donor countries, which is composed of those Member States providing in one way or another the funds which enable the organisation to fulfil its functions. The group of recipient countries, on the other hand, includes those Member States to which the funds concerned are made available by the organisation in the pursuit of its objectives and purposes. As far as the World Bank is concerned, the distinction mentioned is clear cut and to a large extent even formalised. The donor countries are the Part I members of the IDA, while the recipient countries make up the Part II membership.[88] The World Bank no longer makes loans to its developed Part I members; while funds are almost entirely furnished by Part I members, the contributions of the developing Part II members are obviously only marginal.

As far as obligations are concerned, donor and recipient countries have one aspect in common; the Articles of Agreement of the Bank, the IDA and the IFC do not contain very concrete obligations with respect to either category, at least as far as their main activities, obtaining and lending funds, are concerned. The Articles of Agreement constitute a very broad framework, the core of which consists of directives and guidelines for the conduct of operations by the three organisations. Recipient countries cannot derive a right to a loan from the treaties and consequently the latter embody no obligations with regard to the use of such loans. Similarly, apart from provisions dealing with initial subscriptions, the Articles of Agreement do not contain obligations in respect of additional contributions. In both cases, therefore, such obligations have to be created by additional legal instruments. The Articles of Agreement undoubtedly constitute the general legal framework within which these obligations are created; the direct basis, however, is to be found elsewhere. In the case of recipient countries this legal basis is constituted by the so-called Loan Documents that the World Bank concludes with countries to which it makes a loan. In the case of donor countries the agreements between the States concerned form the legal basis; these are negotiated before every additional contribution, whether it is an increase of the capital of the Bank or the IFC, or a replenishment of IDA funds.

This, however, is the extent of the similarity between obligations of recipient and those of donor countries. The situation with regard to the obligations of both categories is almost the complete opposite particularly in the case of supervision. The World Bank's system of supervising the obligations of recipient States is elaborated and well developed. As will become clear from subsequent paragraphs, the World Bank has made great efforts to improve this type of supervision. In comparison, supervision of obligations of donor countries is non-existent. Consequently, there will be no detailed account below of the World Bank's supervisory activities with respect to donor countries. Nevertheless, it seems appropriate to look briefly at some of the questions raised by donor supervision.

2.2. Supervision with regard to obligations of donor Member States

Within the framework of the World Bank by far the most important contribution of the rich countries to the realisation of the organisation's purposes lies in the fact that they provide the funds for its operations. The World Bank does not make demands, for instance, regarding particular aspects of their economic policy. Therefore, obligations for donor countries within the framework of the World Bank are only to be found in the field of development financing, if they are to be found at all. The observations below, therefore focus on this point.

At first sight, the lack of donor supervision in the World Bank seems only natural. It can be fairly easily explained on the basis of a narrow definition of supervision on the one hand, and a traditional concept of norms of international law, on the other. From such a point of view the explanation would run as follows: supervision can only be exercised with respect to existing norms of international law; there are no such norms of international law prescribing for the rich countries' clearly defined behaviour in the field of international development financing: *ergo*, because of the lack of a norm to that effect, there is nothing to supervise. We noted above that apart from provisions dealing with initial subscriptions, the Articles of Agreement of the Bank and the IDA do not contain hard and fast obligations with respect to additional contributions. Such obligations arise only after an agreement is reached between the States concerned to increase the capital of the Bank or the funds of the IDA.

Nevertheless, the line of reasoning just described seems too easy a way out of the problem. Its point of departure is too rigid. As is explained in Part I of this book, the creative function of supervision is especially designed to cope with the situation which has arisen in quite a few fields of international law, where a number of broad norms have been created which are indeterminate and, in some respects, uncertain.[89] Obviously, further elaboration of such norms, which would render them more determinate and less uncertain, would greatly enhance their ordering role in international relations and should therefore also be pursued through supervision. However, their present broad character does not mean that such norms do not entail any obligations at all for States. Even if such norms do not lay down in every detail a prescribed behaviour for States to follow, they at least prohibit certain types of behaviour, leaving States only a limited number of options. Consequently, these norms contain binding elements, despite the fact that concretisation in some respects is desirable or even necessary.

Similarly, in the case of the World Bank, the donor States have subscribed to the purposes of the organisation mentioned above,[90] and it is clear that these purposes can only be achieved if the rich countries continue to provide funds.

A general obligation to continue financial support to the organisation – *i.e.* to co-operate in increases in the capital of the Bank and replenishments of IDA funds – can therefore be assumed to exist. This is particularly true of the IDA; because of the capital structure of the organisation it was clear from the very beginning that its members would have to contribute on a regular basis to keep the IDA in existence.[91] Practice would seem to confirm the existence of such a general obligation. The donor countries have in the past agreed to several increases of the Bank's capital, *e.g.* replenishment of the IDA's funds.[92] However, the question of the more specific obligations, *i.e.* the size and the time of the increase or replenishment, is much more difficult to answer. The increases in the case of the Bank would seem to have presented less problems than the replenishments in the case of the IDA. The former were mainly designed to keep the subscribed capital at a sufficiently high level in relation to the total volume of the Bank's lending. While only a small percentage of the total increase has to be paid in, the Bank's capacity to borrow can be expanded considerably.[93]

The history of the efforts to refund the IDA is not entirely felicitous. In fact, the process has become extremely cumbersome. The fact that the replenishments are now made every three years instead of every five years as contemplated on the one hand, and the protracted character of the negotiations on the other, have made the process of refunding almost continuous. In such a state of affairs relatively minor setbacks or delays in the negotiations may result in the organisation coming to a complete standstill. In particular, the lack of prompt ratification of replenishment by the United States has greatly hampered the IDA's functioning and could only be (provisionally) remedied by the willingness of other donors to fill the vacuum.[94]

Most important for our purpose here is that the donor States' general attitude does not seem to allow the conclusion that the donors feel bound to contribute a fixed amount or a certain percentage as their share of an agreed total. The element of certainty has even decreased in this respect. While percentage shares of contributions were relatively stable and unchallenged at the time of the first three replenishments, subsequent negotiations have raised the question of how to share the burden, and this has consequently become a major problem.[95] Similarly, the total amount of the individual replenishments does not present a very reliable pattern. Up to now each replenishment has exceeded the previous ones in nominal amounts, but the most recent replenishments show hardly any or no increase at all in terms of real value.[96] The predictability of the size of future replenishments is therefore very low and the possibility cannot even be excluded that the amount might decrease in real terms.

This bleak outlook is reflected in the recent move of the United States administration which announced a reduction of 26 per cent. in development aid. The U.S. undertook to meet its obligations with respect to the IDA, but this could probably be understood to apply only to those obligations resulting from the agreement which was recently concluded on the Sixth Replenishment.[97] It is abundantly clear that this U.S. change of policy must necessarily affect the size of its contribution to future replenishments. The U.S. Congress had previously stated its preference for a considerable reduction of the U.S. share in IDA funding.[98] If IDA funds are to remain at the same level, the burden will have to be taken over by other donors. It is doubtful whether these would be able or willing to bridge the gap. The concept of reciprocity is present even in the field of development assistance in the sense that each donor has to contribute what the others consider to be its fair share, and therefore it is not inconceivable that a refusal to contribute by one of the major donors will trigger off similar reactions in others.

The above observations make it clear that certainty and predictability concerning the future flow of funds cannot be secured within the framework of the World Bank itself. The World Bank has to compete for a share of the total amount of funds which the rich countries make available for development financing. It is perfectly obvious that, even supposing the World Bank did well in this competition, the amount of the funds it would be able to acquire would be closely related to the total available funds. In the final analysis, the World Bank is also dependent upon the overall performance of the donor countries in the field of what is usually called Official Development Assistance (ODA). On the other hand, the latter issue falls outside the scope of the organisation's operations as such and has to be dealt with by a forum like the United Nations, which has a more general function. Thus, the conclusion that can be drawn concerning the above, is not that donor supervision is inconceivable – one could even argue that the present state of affairs requires supervisory measures with respect to donor countries – it merely seems that the World Bank is not the most obvious framework for setting up such a supervisory system.

2.3. Supervision with regard to obligations of recipient Member States

2.3.1. General

Before embarking upon a more detailed analysis of the surveillance exercised by the World Bank over the activities of those to whom it makes a loan or a credit, some general observations have to be made.

2.3.1.1. Supervision within the Bank, the IDA and the IFC

The supervisory methods used by the Bank and the IDA are identical. Both organisations, moreover, have the same project cycle in which supervision has a place.[99] Like the supervisory systems of the Bank and the IDA, the IFC's system is mainly based on periodic reporting by borrowers, visiting missions by members of its staff and regular internal management reviews. Moreover, the IFC's supervisory system now also requires a project completion report and a project evaluation programme has been introduced to study the experiences with mature projects on a selective basis.[100] However, because its specific task is to further economic development by encouraging the growth of productive private enterprise in developing countries, the IFC's project cycle is different from that of the Bank and the IDA. The IFC's project cycle, and therefore its supervisory system, will not be dealt with separately here. Consequently, references made below to project cycle and supervision are to be understood as referring to the project cycle and the supervision of the Bank and the IDA. Apart from the desirability of avoiding the repetition which would result from the consecutive description of two supervisory systems with a considerable number of common features, there is the following reason for excluding the IFC. The purpose of the present study is to analyse the supervisory process of the World Bank and the contribution it could make to the solution of the problem of underdevelopment. As the preceding paragraphs have shown, the IFC is by far the least influential of the three organisations which constitute the World Bank. Compared to those of the Bank and the IDA, the funds invested by the IFC in developing countries are very small indeed. The IFC's impact on the image of the World Bank as an institution for development finance bears no comparison to that of the Bank or the IDA, in qualitative terms either. Finally, as IFC is operating in the private sector, its investments do not give rise to obligations on the part of Member States. Consequently, those States are not involved in the supervisory process as is the case within the framework of the Bank and the IDA. Bearing in mind what has been said above, it seems justified to focus attention on the latter two organisations.

2.3.1.2. Supervision with regard to project and programme lending

The major part of this study will be confined to the World Bank's supervisory functions in connection with lending for projects.[101] As noted above, the World Bank has started to undertake new types of activities such as technical assistance, co-ordination of development assistance and research.[102] These, however, are largely ancillary to its main task of making loans and credits. Technical assistance, for instance, often takes the form of services supplied by the World Bank in addition to and in connection with the providing of funds in the form of a loan or credit.[103] Moreover, these other activities, unless they are connected to a certain project, usually do not give rise to direct obligations for Member States and, consequently, do not generate supervisory activities on the part of the World Bank.

The Articles of Agreement of both the Bank and IDA require that loans be made for *specific* projects, except in special circumstances.[104] Until 1978, of all the loans and credits made by the Bank and the IDA over 90 per cent. had been for specific projects.[105] In recent years the percentage of non-project loans in the total sum of lending actually decreased.[106] All this would seem to indicate that the World Bank has retained the 'exceptional cases' philosophy of the founding fathers.[107] During the 1970s, however, arguments have been forwarded that the World Bank's new orientation towards absolute poverty would justify an expansion of lending in the non-project sector.[108] This kind of outside pressure has probably contributed to the major policy shift with regard to non-project lending which the World Bank has announced in its most recent Annual Report. The direct impetus for this change originated in the Development Committee[109] which requested the Executive Directors 'to explore the criteria that could govern programme and sector loans in situations where external disequilibria had not yet become severe.'[110] As a realisation to this the World Bank introduced its so-called 'structural adjustment lending.' It is seen as one response in an effort to help supplement, with longer term finance, the relatively short term finance available to prevent the current account deficits of many developing countries from becoming so large that they seriously jeopardise the implementation of current investment programmes and foreign exchange-producing activities. Structural adjustment lending is a new form of assistance, but it is said to be a natural evolution in the traditional programme lending of the World Bank. While programme lending is concentrated on measures dealing with immediate difficulties, structural adjustment lending envisages the probability of multi-year programmes being developed and supported by a succession of loans.[111]

Lending for structural adjustment is expected to amount to between $600m and $800m in fiscal year 1981.[112] It will therefore absorb a considerable part of the World Bank's funds. As a result, supervision with regard to non-project lending will become increasingly important in the future. At the time of writing, it is difficult to get a clear picture of the character of supervision in non-project lending. Publications of the World Bank refer to this type of supervision only in passing. It was stated, for instance, that non-project

422

lending warrants a strong supervisory effort, albeit somewhat different from the one with regard to project loans.[113] Generally speaking it can be expected that the increase of non-project lending will make World Bank supervision more difficult. As a result of their more general character, the new type of structural adjustment loans will probably lack the advantages which, from the point of view of supervision, are connected with project lending, *viz.* the specific and detailed description of the object of financing.[114] On the other hand, the differences in this respect between these two kinds of lending should not be overestimated. According to the World Bank, structural adjustment lending 'has the specific objective of helping countries reduce their current account deficit to more manageable proportions over the medium term by supporting programmes of adjustment that encompass *specific policy, industrial and other changes* designed to strengthen their balance of payments, while maintaining their growth and developmental momentum.'[115] Furthermore, the examples of structural adjustment loans given by the World Bank do not necessarily point to very general pro-grammes, but also include more specific arrangements.[116] Structural adjust-ment loans, therefore, are not in all respects the opposite of loans for specific projects. At any rate, supervision with regard to non-project lending encom-passes a (large) number of features which are also characteristic of super-vision of specific projects. Consequently, analysis of the latter will shed light on the former.

2.2.3.3. Foundations and character of World Bank supervision

The considerations which for a long time have prompted the World Bank to persevere with its exceptional cases philosophy with respect to non-project lending are more or less the same as those underlying its 'approach' or 'attitude' towards the supervision of projects it finances. This supervision is mainly based upon two considerations: (i) the need to make sure that the borrower[117] will be in a position to repay its debt; (ii) ensuring that the developmental objectives of the project are realised. The Bank is both a developmental and a financial institution and each project for which it lends must satisfy both features of the institution.[118]

In the view of the World Bank there is no conflict between, on the one hand, its development efforts, and on the other hand, its financial interests: 'The fact is that creditors and stockholders insist on prudent financial policies as a condition for the development efforts of the Bank. So do our borrowers. Viable projects, attention to creditworthiness, assessment of risk, adequate liquidity and reserves are required by the management of the Bank and by its creditors and stockholders. There is nothing in this list which is inconsist-ent with our development efforts, or with the needs or aspirations of the developing world.'[119] This close link, which the World Bank considers to exist between financial and developmental considerations, may also explain why the World Bank applies the same standards of appraisal to both projects supported by IDA credits and projects financed by Bank loans.[120] The fact that the IDA, like the Bank, obtains its funds from governments of Member

States and is therefore not dependent upon the capital market, does not influence the way in which its projects are appraised. In addition to softer terms with regard to the funds provided, the IDA also seems to be able to apply softer standards for the appraisal of projects. However, as noted above, the World Bank does not see any discrepancy between its development objectives and financial requirements, but actually considers the latter to be a necessary condition of the former, or at least a strong support for it. Moreover, the IDA estimated that its ability to continue to attract funds from governments depends, no less than does the Bank, on its ability to prove that projects which are financed are productive enough to yield an economic return of at least ten per cent. or more.[121]

The considerations described above as underlying the World Bank's *approach* to supervision are reflected in the provisions of the Articles of Agreement which constitute the legal basis for its supervisory activities. Article III(5)(b) of the Bank requires it to ensure that the proceeds of any loan are used only for the purposes for which the loan was granted, paying attention to considerations of economy and efficiency and without regard to political or non-economic influences or considerations. According to Article III(5)(c) the Bank may only permit a borrower to draw on the account to which the amount of the loan is credited to meet the expenses of the project as they are actually incurred.[122] These provisions create an obligation for the World Bank to exercise supervision, an obligation held *vis-à-vis* its membership as a whole. They do not, however, actually provide an adequate legal basis for the World Bank's right to conduct its supervisory functions *vis-à-vis* a particular Member State to which it has made a loan. That basis is to be found in the loan agreements concluded between the World Bank and a borrower at the time a loan or a credit was made. In these documents the general provisions of the Articles of Agreement are often elaborated into very detailed obligations for the borrower, reflecting the far-reaching supervisory powers of the World Bank.

The term 'loan documents' is a very general one, which in fact denotes different types of legal instruments pertaining to a particular loan or credit. First of all, there are the *loan* or *credit agreements* between the Bank or the IDA and the Member State to which the loan or credit is made. As noted above, however, Bank loans do not necessarily have to be made to Member States, but can also be granted to private or public organisations.[123] If a Bank loan is made to an entity which is not a Member State, the Member State concerned has to guarantee the loan. In such a case there will be two separate legal documents, *viz.*, a *loan agreement* between the Bank and the borrower and a *guarantee agreement* between the Bank and the Member State concerned. Moreover, if the loan or credit is made to a Member State but another entity is charged with the execution of the project, a so-called *project agreement* is concluded between the latter and the Bank or the IDA. Finally, with borrowers other than Member States the Bank engages in still other kinds of contracts under different names, such as, for instance, a *shareholders' agreement,* the purpose of which is to create an additional guarantee and to lay down modalities for the financing of the project.[124]

424

Even though the loan documents form the legal framework within which World Bank supervision takes place, they provide only a partial picture. The loan documents by themselves would give a limited impression of the scope of World Bank supervision with regard to its activities in that field.

In fact these activities far exceed the formal limit set by these legal documents.[125] Similarly, it is misleading to judge the real impact of the World Bank's supervision by the place it formally occupies in the project cycle as a whole. This project cycle, which represents the different stages of a project financed by the World Bank, consists of six phases: identification, preparation, appraisal, negotiations, implementation and supervision, and evaluation. Formally, these different phases take place in a more or less chronological order; this therefore suggests that supervision is exercised at a relatively late stage in the project cycle. As the following discussion of the World Bank's supervisory activities will clearly show these are in practice neither confined to those powers formally conferred in the loan documents nor limited in time to the supervision phase *per se*. The advice and suggestions given, and the pressure which is sometimes exerted by the World Bank during identification, preparation, appraisal and negotiation are obviously not based on the loan documents. These kinds of activities very often contain elements of supervision, whether they are elements of the review, the correction or the creative function of supervision;[126] from this it follows that the World Bank's supervision with regard to a project is exercised on a permanent basis. During these earlier stages of the project cycle, *i.e.* before the conclusion of the loan documents, the Member State concerned does not yet have any obligations, at least not from a strictly legal point of view. However it is important to remember that recipient Member States will generally be very eager to have their projects approved and will therefore as a rule be in no position to resist the requirements and demands made by the World Bank. Therefore, the existence of a formal relationship (or the lack of it) does not substantially affect the actual relationship between the World Bank and recipient Member States as far as supervision is concerned. Moreover, just as the World Bank's supervision is an ongoing process, so is its relationship with recipient Member States in general. In other words, a loan to a particular country is usually not an isolated affair. More often than not it is only one element in the total of the World Bank's assistance to that State; this assistance often comprises a number of projects. After a project has been identified it is incorporated into a multi-year lending programme for the country concerned and this forms the basis for the World Bank's future work in that country.[127] Thus, supervision may spill over, as it were, from one project to another. It goes without saying that this even enhances the World Bank's possibility of exercising effective surveillance of the performance of the recipient state in question.

A key instrument in this continuously exercised supervision is the so-called country economic reporting. In simple terms this is the screening by the World Bank of the economy of client States to which it makes loans or credits. As the scope and character of the World Bank's supervision cannot be properly understood without taking into account its country economic reporting, some attention has to be paid to the latter before embarking upon an analysis of the specific phases of the project cycle.

2.3.2. Country economic reporting

Country economic reporting is a very important form of technical assistance, which was mentioned as one of the activities the World Bank developed as a result of its evolution towards becoming a development agency.[128] Country economic reporting started at a relatively early stage of the Bank's existence, although it was then known by a different name. Technical assistance is not mentioned in the Articles of Agreement of the Bank. Article V(5)(v) of the IDA, however, explicitly empowers the organisation 'to provide technical assistance and advisory services at the request of a member.' Long before the establishment of the IDA it had already become clear that the Bank could not limit itself to simply accepting or rejecting proposed projects. The developing countries found it increasingly difficult to submit suitable projects which would meet the high standards set by the Bank. The Bank therefore realised that it should make suggestions or recommendations with regard to certain aspects of a particular project. Originally, this kind of assistance in identifying suitable projects was mainly made available in response to proposals by governments and borrowers.

The initial steps in this direction were taken as a result of the first so-called 'general survey mission' to Colombia in 1947. The purpose of such general survey missions was to try to formulate a national development programme in co-operation with the authorities of the country concerned. To that end these missions visited the country and subsequently drew up a report concerning certain aspects of its economic situation. Up to 1965 the Bank sent twenty-five general survey missions to as many different countries.[129] Since then, 'general survey missions' have been replaced by the system of country economic reporting.

The purpose of the latter is essentially the same as that of the survey missions. However, while a 'survey mission' to a country only took place once, country economic reporting was from the beginning intended to be an ongoing process. This has in fact happened. Once a basic analysis of a country's economy has been made, it is updated at regular intervals, usually every six months, in order to obtain a more profound understanding of a country's affairs. Country economic reporting became particularly important after McNamara became President of the World Bank. This is the result of the emphasis placed since that time on the problem of absolute poverty. Dealing with this problem obviously requires that close attention be paid to the development strategy of developing countries and that a framework be set up for evaluating its national and sectoral policies and problems.

The World Bank itself seems to regard its country economic reports as no more than a guideline and not as an absolute yardstick for judging a country's performance. The quality of the World Bank's economic analysis is clearly dependent upon the situation in a given country. The World Bank cannot give a complete picture if the country concerned has done no groundwork at all and where statistical data, for instance, are lacking. Nevertheless, in many instances the World Bank's analysis is probably one of the most reliable bases on which to build a country's economic programme, and in countries that have not made a strong effort themselves it is probably even the most important basis.[130] The World Bank's economic reports are very comprehensive and encompass a great number of aspects of a State's economic situation.[131] The system of country economic reporting has enabled the World Bank to help developing countries to plan their development programme in a more systematic way. Furthermore, general economic analyses are often supplemented by sectoral studies, in which policy and institutional problems are pinpointed and desirable changes are indicated. Such sectoral studies are carried out by the World Bank or through one of the co-operative programmes together with a UN specialised agency, or they may be financed by the United Nations Development Program (UNDP), by bilateral aid programmes or by a specific provision for studies in a Bank or IDA loan made previously. In other cases sectoral analyses are conducted by the countries themselves. On the basis of these sectoral reports projects may be generated which can be submitted to the World Bank for financing. Thus, the system of country economic reporting is an important tool to assist recipient countries in identifying suitable projects.

It may be true that developing countries have become less interested in advice on overall policies and planning and that a number of them are perfectly capable of producing their own surveys. However, this does not justify the conclusion that country economic reporting amounts to no more than 'creating of additional work to enable the various layers of the supervisory hierarchy to function[132]. First, a considerable number of countries still need assistance because they are not capable of adequately conducting their own planning. Secondly, country economic reporting serves more purposes than the one mentioned above. If the World Bank is to perform its functions in a responsible manner it cannot rely solely on its clients' own surveys when it has to judge the soundness of proposed projects. Answering the question whether or not a certain project is likely to contribute significantly to the economic development of a country requires insight into the economy of that country by the World Bank itself. Finally, country economic reporting is also an instrument through which the World Bank can increase its own knowledge of the development process. It is vital for the World Bank to keep up to date in this respect, particularly now that this process has turned out to be far more complex than it seemed when the World Bank redirected its policies towards combatting absolute poverty.

At any rate the above shows that the World Bank starts monitoring the activities of recipients long before the actual phase of supervision begins. As far as the phase of identification and preparation are concerned, this supervision can generally be described as taking a creative form in that suggestions and recommendations are made to improve a country's economic situation in general and to enhance its possibilities of project generation in particular. As will be seen below, supervision at this stage can at the same time be considered to perform a review – or correction – function, as country economic reporting is also the basis upon which the World Bank judges the credit-worthiness required by a country to be eligible for a loan or a credit.[133]

Finally, it should be pointed out that it is not absolutely correct to refer to the activities of the World Bank in this phase as a review, correction or creative function of supervision. At this stage (*i.e.* before the loan documents enter into force) there are no formal legal obligations and strictly speaking, therefore, there can be no supervision either. However, due to the special character of the relationship between the World Bank and many of its recipient countries, which is not confined to one single project, but usually has a more ongoing nature comprising a series of successive projects, these activities do in fact resemble supervision in the strict sense of the term.[134] As a result, the supervisory activities of the World Bank with respect to a project or projects previously agreed upon will exert a strong preventative effect on the project or projects in preparation.

2.3.3. The project cycle

2.2.3.1. Introduction

As noted above, the World Bank's project cycle comprises several phases. It is not always possible to make a clear distinction between each individual phase. In general, however, they are distinctive enough to warrant separate discussion.[135] The phases are as follows:

(1) identification
(2) preparation
(3) appraisal
(4) negotiation
(5) implementation and supervision, and
(6) evaluation.

2.3.3.2. Identification

In view of what has already been said about country economic reporting, this phase can be dealt with briefly. Most projects are brought forward by those countries which are candidates for borrowing, often in close co-operation with the World Bank. Sometimes, projects are proposed by private sponsors. All projects must satisfy a standard of prima facie feasibility which amounts to the requirement that technical and institutional solutions are likely to be found at costs commensurate with the expected benefits. If a project meets this standard it is 'identified' by the World Bank and subsequently incorporated into a multi-year lending programme for the country concerned. Lending programmes are designed to facilitate the planning and budgeting of the World Bank's operations and to ensure the availability of the resources required to take each project through the successive phases of its cycle.

2.3.3.3. Preparation

Responsibility for the preparation of a project formally rests with the borrower. However, as with identification, the World Bank has over the years become increasingly involved in preparation. Originally the World Bank was reluctant to engage in project preparation, fearing that this might interfere with its project appraisal by prejudicing its objectivity. As noted above, sound banking principles were gradually less strictly applied and, moreover, experience indicated that a more active role on the part of the World Bank was necessary to ensure a sufficient number of properly prepared projects.[136] Nowadays, there are even cases in which the World Bank does the preparatory work itself. This is admittedly exceptional, the rule being that the borrower conducts the preparation with some kind of assistance from the World Bank.

Such assistance may take several forms. The most remarkable at the moment is the so-called 'Project Preparation Facility'. It was created in 1975 to overcome shortcomings in the ability of borrowers to complete project preparation and to support the entities responsible for preparing or carrying out the projects. Under this facility, the Bank advances funds to meet gaps in project preparation and for institution building. These advances are repaid from the loan for the project concerned as soon as the loan becomes effective.[137] Other possible forms are special loans for technical assistance, reimbursing the borrower under the loan for preparatory work done earlier, or including funds for this purpose in a loan for another project in the sector. Finally, co-operative programmes between the World Bank and other specialised agencies, as well as bilateral aid programmes, can be important sources of support.

The preparation of a project generally takes two years. Criticism of the length of this period has been countered by the World Bank with the argument that such a considerable investment in time usually pays for itself several times over because it allows for working out the best arrangements regarding the different aspects of the project concerned.[138]

The actual preparation itself starts out with a so-called project brief which describes the objectives of the project, identifying principal issues, and establishing the schedule for its further processing. With the project brief as a basis the remainder of the preparatory work essentially consists of working out those aspects of the project which will later come up for appraisal by the World Bank. These aspects include economic, technical, commercial, financial, organisational and managerial questions. These will be discussed in the next paragraph.

It is particularly crucial during the preparation phase to single out those technical and institutional alternatives which are likely to produce the best results with regard to the project's objectives. To that end, feasibility studies are conducted to identify and prepare preliminary designs of technical and institutional alternatives and to compare their respective costs and benefits; they then proceed to a more detailed investigation of the more promising alternatives until the most satisfactory solution is finally found.[139] Sometimes a so-called 'pilot' project is initiated, which is basically an experimental preliminary plan for a project, in order to determine whether the larger investment is worthwhile.

When the preparation has been completed the project is scheduled for appraisal.

2.3.3.4. Appraisal

Appraisal is undoubtedly a very crucial phase of the project cycle. It is at the same time the culmination of the preceding phases and the foundation for the implementation of the project. It is also intimately linked to supervision, which is the logical extension of appraisal. In the process of appraisal, the targets are set which will serve as the standards used in supervising the project.

Unlike preparation and implementation, but like supervision, appraisal is the sole responsibility of the World Bank. It is conducted by the World Bank staff, sometimes supplemented for this purpose by individual consultants. A wide range of specialists is involved, particularly engineers, economists and financial analysts, but also, wherever necessary, agronomists, architects and educationalists. Appraisal usually includes a three to four week period *in situ* and possibly, depending on the quality of the preparatory work, a subsequent mission or missions to the country concerned. The World Bank's general approach with regard to appraisal is one of healthy scepticism; in other words, nothing is taken for granted.[140] Its review comprises not only a comprehensive and systematic screening of the project's intrinsic aspects, but also of the whole economic complex of which the programme will form a part. The aspects covered may be broken down into six general categories: economic, financial, commercial, technical, managerial and institutional aspects.

2.3.3.4.1. Economic aspects

In the evaluation of the economic aspects of a proposed project, the two factors which were said to underly the World Bank's supervisory 'attitude'[141] and consequently also its appraisal, become particularly apparent. On the one hand the World Bank has to make sure that the loan or credit will be repaid (financial factor); on the other, it has to ensure that the project in question contributes significantly to the development of the country's economy as a whole (developmental factor). In the pursuit of these general objectives the economic appraisal is essentially conducted at three different levels, although these might not always be easily distinguishable. These are the national level, the sectoral level and the level of the project itself.

At the level of the national economy, the economic appraisal takes the form of the criteria applied by the World Bank to determine what countries are eligible for Bank loans and/or IDA credits. To a certain extent the criteria applied by the Bank and the IDA are the same. In some respects, however, they differ. Obviously, in both cases the prospective borrower has to be a member of the organisation. Furthermore, eligibility for both Bank

loans and IDA credits requires creditworthiness and good economic performance. It is not easy to keep these two criteria completely separate. As far as
the Bank is concerned, the emphasis is laid on the former, while within the
framework of the IDA the latter plays a more important role. According to
its Articles of Agreement, the IDA has to direct its lending particularly
towards countries which cannot afford to service Bank loans on conventional
terms (Article I). Thus, its standard of creditworthiness necessarily differs
from that of the Bank.[142] In general, therefore, this criterion does not greatly
affect the IDA's decision-making with regard to the allocation of its funds.
Questions concerning creditworthiness may arise in the case of countries
which cannot clearly be considered as belonging either to the category of
countries eligible for Bank loans or to the category eligible for IDA credits;
for instance, countries which are poor in terms of *per capita* income but do
not suffer a shortage of foreign exchange (*e.g.* major oil exporting countries
like Nigeria and Indonesia) or, conversely, countries which do suffer from
such a shortage, but do not meet the IDA's poverty criterion.[143] The IDA
relies more on the criterion of economic performance, although it is very
difficult to apply in practice. Very generally speaking, the World Bank
considers a sound economic performance to be a policy that, in time, will
reduce the borrowing country's dependence on foreign grants and concessional loans and will enable it, instead, to finance investments increasingly
from its own resources and established capital markets.[144] In more concrete
terms, the economic philosophy of the World Bank has for a long time been
the 'Western blueprint' for economic development with a strong emphasis
on financial and monetary stability, and economic growth. This philosophy
has not been entirely abandoned,[145] but the World Bank's new poverty
oriented policies have prompted a more balanced approach in which the
so-called distributional effects of development are taken into account.[146]
Like other standards of appraisal, economic criteria are more or less
continuously subject to change, at least in some respects. The changes occur
as a result of new experience or new knowledge which were formerly not
available.[147] This shows that to a certain extent standards for appraisal are
dependent upon subjectivity on the part of the appraiser.

As noted above, creditworthiness probably has a bigger impact than
economic performance within the framework of the Bank. Unlike the IDA,
the Bank draws its funds mainly from the capital markets, and is in principle
capable of obtaining all the funds needed to finance viable projects in
member countries. The Bank, in other words, has no allocation problem.
While economic performance is certainly not neglected as a criterion, this
results in a somewhat stronger focus on creditworthiness. In the Bank's own
words the evaluation of a potential borrower's creditworthiness is undertaken
as follows: 'The Bank's staff examines the country's *per capita* income, and
its potential for the future. It looks at the country's population growth, its
savings rate, and the vehicles through which savings occur. It examines the
country's foreign exchange position, its sources of borrowing, its tax base,
its terms of trade, and prospects for the future. In this connection, the Bank
closely monitors the potential borrower's external debt, its interest and

principal requirements for the immediate and foreseeable future. It studies the country's reliance on commodities, whether one or several. It prepares the economic analyses required to show how the country's exports could be affected by declines in international commodity prices. It examines the country's imports, and whether imports could be curtailed in order to conserve the necessary foreign exchange to meet debt obligations. It examines the country's tariff structure, its reliance on food and energy imports, its overall economic health, and the relative commitment of resources to productive and unproductive projects.'[148] Bearing all this in mind it is certainly not difficult to agree with the statement 'that few commercial institutions or governments are equipped to make this kind of study before making a loan.'[149]

Finally, in addition to the criteria listed above, the IDA has developed another criterion, which does not apply in the case of the Bank. This is the so-called 'poverty criterion', consisting of a *per capita* income level in member countries beyond which IDA credits are severely rationed. No absolute upper limit is set which cannot be deviated from under any circumstances, but it definitely indicates a strong prejudice against lending to members in which the average annual *per capita* income is above this level. Similarly, a lower level does not create an automatic preference in favour of lending.[150] Currently, the IDA's poverty level is set at $520 *per capita* in 1975 U.S. dollars.[151]

As remarked above, the World Bank's system of country economic reporting is a major instrument for conducting the economic evaluation at the national level.[152]

Economic appraisal at the sectoral level runs, *mutatis mutandis,* along the same lines. Here too, sectoral studies are used to answer the key question of whether the project is in a sector of the economy whose development is likely to contribute significantly to the development of the whole economy. In other words, does the sector concerned deserve priority? For this purpose the investment programme for the sector, the strengths and weaknesses of sectoral institutions and key government policies are all examined.

Finally, the World Bank tries to calculate the economic justification of the project itself by making a cost/benefit analysis of the project to the country as a whole, the result of which is usually expressed as an economic rate of return. In making such an analysis major difficulties are often encountered. The actual price of production factors, for instance, does not always reflect their real economic value. This is because of various distortions such as protection tariffs and quantitative restrictions on imports and exports, unrealistic rates of exchange, government control of interest rates, prices, production and sales, or private monopolistic controls of production and prices. To overcome this difficulty the World Bank uses the device of 'shadow' prices.[153] Furthermore, some aspects of a project, particularly the indirect costs, which may significantly affect the costs and benefits of a certain project, are extremely difficult or even impossible to calculate. This is particularly true of the World Bank's 'new' style of projects which are aimed at combating absolute poverty and therefore usually contain more distributional elements. The benefits of projects in such sectors as education, water supply and sewerage do not always lend themselves to very accurate calculation. Here again a certain amount of subjectivity is involved in appraisal: 'It is for this reason, in turn, that no amount of formal analysis can substitute for experience with actual projects in many places and under many different conditions, the kind of experience that enables an appraiser to "see" the unquantifiable benefits of a project clearly enough to have confidence in his judgement about its worths.'[154] Despite the unknown factors involved, the World Bank maintains its standard that every project, whether 'old' style or 'new,' must have a satisfactory economic return.[155]

2.3.3.4.2. Technical aspects

Basically, technical appraisal deals with the question whether the project is sound from a technical and engineering point of view, which is obviously crucial to its success. The World Bank does not undertake any engineering for its projects itself; its role is limited to judging the capacity of those who actually do the engineering. Although the World Bank (and its borrowers) make use of consultants in virtually all phases of the project cycle, for instance to conduct pre-investment studies or with regard to the implementation of a project, consultants' advice is particularly sought for detailed engineering and design. Generally speaking, this comprises the technical, economic and architectural work required to define a project in detail. In more concrete terms, it may consist of a wide variety of assignments and cover all the aspects involved in the technical appraisal of a project.[156]

Technical appraisal concerns questions regarding the physical scale of the project, the appropriateness of the technology used and the location and lay-out of its facilities. The scheduling of the implementation is extremely critical and has to be realistically planned. It includes the scheduling of all the activities necessary for the successful completion of the project as well as the arrangement of these activities in a coherent order to arrive at the completion of the project as a whole on the most economic basis. This schedule of implementation constitutes the direct foundation on which the supervision, *stricto sensu,* will be exercised at a later stage.

Closely related to the scheduling of implementation is the analysis of the estimated costs of the project's execution. The budget in which the estimated costs are calculated should be itemised in relation to contracts for estimated construction and equipment, in order to enable a comparison of the actual costs when they occur with the estimates made.

2.3.3.4.3. Managerial and organisational aspects

Management and organisation are two sides of the same coin; the former is concerned with the manpower qualified to manage a project successfully, the latter deals with the organisational infrastructure which the management needs as a support to function properly. These days they are usually described together as 'institution-building.' Recently, institution-building has become one of the most important objectives of World Bank lending.[157]

433

According to the World Bank 'the transfer of financial resources and the construction of physical facilities, however valuable in their own right, are less important in the long run than the creation of a sound and viable local institution, interpreted in its broadest sense to cover not only the borrowing entity itself, its organisation, management, staffing, policies and procedures, but also the whole array of government policies that condition the environment in which the institution operates.'[158]

With regard to both the managerial and organisational aspects the most difficult problem encountered is the lack of experience and ability in the developing countries. Very often it is impossible to avoid bringing in outside assistance, however reluctant developing countries may be to employ foreigners in responsible positions. At any rate it is an established policy of the World Bank that local personnel should be used as effectively as possible and that, wherever possible, foreigners should train local personnel to replace them as soon as is practicable.

During the operational phase of a project and after its construction or setting up has been completed, questions arise about the optimal degree of centralisation or delegation of responsibility. There are no readily available general answers to such questions, because everything depends on the scale of operations, their geographical distribution, the degree of specialisation of personnel, and the number of persons to whom responsibility can be delegated. These factors vary greatly from one project to another. It is because of these problems involved in the managerial and organisational aspects of projects, that appraisal has been described as 'an art and not a science'.[159] These difficulties of appraisal are worsened by the nature of the World Bank's new style projects. For, in recent projects the general socio-cultural situation in a given country has a much greater impact than in the more traditional ones, for instance those projects belonging to the transportation and power sectors. While institution-building, therefore, has become an overriding issue, it is at the same time the most difficult one in that its success depends so much on understanding the socio-cultural environment. The Bank has come to recognise the need for a continuous re-examination of institutional arrangements, an open-mindedness to new ideas, and a willingness to adopt a long-term approach that may extend over several projects.[160]

2.3.3.4.5. Commercial aspects

Commercial aspects can be considered to be a sub-class of the technical aspects.[161] Appraisal from a commercial point of view deals with a specific kind of technical question, i.e. whether adequate arrangements have been made for obtaining the materials and services needed for the construction and the operation of the project. As far as the construction phase is concerned, the problems involved are quite similar for all projects. Appraisal in this respect amounts to reviewing the proposed arrangements for procuring materials and services. These arrangements are generally required to satisfy three conditions. They have to guarantee that the goods and works involved

434

are obtained in an economic and efficient way, they have to offer the World Bank's Member States and Switzerland an opportunity to compete in providing goods and works financed by the World Bank, and they must encourage the development of local contractors and manufacturers in the borrowing country. The World Bank considers that these conditions can best be met through international competitive bidding making suitable allowances for preferences for local or regional manufacturers and, where appropriate, for local contractors.[162] For the evaluation of bids regarding the quality, experience and reliability of the supplier, the term of delivery and payment et cetera, the advice of consultants is often indispensable.

With regard to the operating phase, arrangements have to be made to obtain the necessary power, labour and raw materials. Obviously, requirements in this respect differ widely depending upon the sector to which the project belongs.[163]

2.3.3.4.6. Financial aspects

Financial appraisal basically has two closely related purposes. First, it is necessary to establish how much money is required to make the project operational and secondly, from what sources that money is to be obtained. As noted above, the World Bank usually finances only the foreign exchange costs of projects and expects the borrower or the government to meet some or all of the local costs.[164] An increasing number of projects for which the Bank or IDA provide funds is therefore financed jointly or on a parallel basis by other national and multilateral organisations.[165] Such projects are in many instances appraised and also supervised by the World Bank. The latter draws up a financial plan that will make funds available at such a time that the project can be implemented on schedule. As regards projects which include revenue-producing facilities, the appraisal is also concerned with their financial viability. The purpose is to ensure that the project will be in a position to meet its financial obligations and to enable it to generate funds from internal resources to earn a reasonable rate of return and to make a satisfactory contribution to its future capital requirements. In that respect the prices charged for basic services, like electric power, which are incurred by a project are often a point of controversy between the World Bank and the borrowing country. The government often wishes to subsidise such services to the consuming public for a number of reasons and will therefore be reluctant to increase such rates. The World Bank, on the other hand, insists that adequate prices are a *sine qua non* for lending to revenue-producing projects.[166]

Finally, the World Bank often imposes conditions which are aimed at ensuring that the expected financial arrangements for the project will not be subsequently jeopardised. These may include restrictions on the borrower's freedom to incur additional long-term debts, or limitations on the distribution of earnings, or the requirement of tariff increases if the rate of return falls below a certain level.[167]

The findings and recommendations resulting from the appraisal are laid down in a report. The approval of this report by the management of the World Bank for negotiation with the borrower marks the end of the appraisal phase.

2.3.3.5. Negotiation and the conclusion of the loan documents

The negotiation phase is actually an extension, and in many instances a repetition, of what has taken place in the preceding stages. On the basis of the appraisal report the informal understanding gained during the preceding period is formalized through negotiations into fully-fledged arrangements. For the most part the negotiations can be a formality, because there has usually been such a close relationship between the World Bank and the prospective borrower during the identification, preparation and appraisal, that differences of opinion between them are most likely to have been worked out before negotiations as such are undertaken. Nevertheless, a number of issues may remain open, particularly because initially there will be a tendency to focus on the broad objectives of the project, leaving matters of detail temporarily unresolved. However, there also has to be agreement on details, and the actual negotiations constitute the mechanism through which complete agreement on all aspects of the project can be reached.

The next step is the drafting of the so-called loan documents, which convert these agreements into legal obligations once they enter into force. Before they enter into force however, the loan documents, together with the appraisal report as amended according to the agreements reached, and a report of the President of the World Bank, are presented to the Executive Directors. If the Directors approve the loan or credit, the loan documents are ready to be signed. On behalf of the World Bank this is usually undertaken by the President or one of the Vice-Presidents with the authorisation of the Directors.

The loan documents, which the World Bank concludes with its borrowers contain a number of interesting aspects from a legal point of view. These cannot all be dealt with within the framework of the present study.[168] In this section the discussion will be limited to a number of general characteristics of these loan documents. In the following section the provisions which have a direct bearing on the supervision of the World Bank will be examined in more detail.

The document or documents concerned with all loans and credits obviously contain a number of provisions which are the same in every case. For practical purposes, the World Bank has laid down these standard clauses in a separate document, which makes it possible to incorporate these clauses into the Loan Documents by a single reference. At the moment these standard clauses are contained in the General Conditions Applicable to Loan and Guarantee Agreements of 15 March, 1974 for the Bank (hereafter referred to as 'General Conditions Bank') and the General Conditions Applicable to Development Credit Agreements of the same date for the IDA (hereafter referred to as 'General Conditions IDA'). The General

Conditions of the Bank and the IDA are very similar. Therefore, reference will only be made below to those of the Bank, unless a provision in the IDA's General Conditions deviates substantially from the corresponding provision of the Bank.

Obviously, the General Conditions as such do not have a binding character. The Bank and the IDA are in principle bound only by their respective Articles of Agreement. Borrowers, guarantors and other parties to the loan documents derive their obligations only from the latter. The General Conditions themselves stipulate that their terms and conditions apply only to the extent that there are provisions in the loan documents concerning them and subject to any modifications contained in the loan documents (Article 1.01). Furthermore, if any inconsistencies arise between a provision of the General Conditions and a provision of the loan documents, the latter prevail (Article 1.02 General Conditions). Usually, the first article of all loan documents provides that the General Conditions shall be an integral part of the loan document concerned. Sometimes, minor modifications are made in view of the particular circumstances of the loan or credit in question, but these do not alter the substance of the General Conditions.

The bulk of the General Conditions consists of material provisions, but they also contain stipulations regarding the entry into force of the loan documents. The latter provisions, as will become apparent, already imply a certain degree of surveillance on the part of the World Bank. In putting conditions on the entry into force of the loan documents, the World Bank starts its supervision *stricto sensu* at the moment when legal obligations do not yet exist. Generally, the loan documents do not become effective until evidence has been furnished to the satisfaction of the World Bank that the execution and delivery of the loan or credit and – in the case of the Bank – the Guarantee Agreement, have been duly authorised or ratified by all necessary governmental and corporate action[169] and that the condition of the borrower not being a Member State (which only applies in the case of the Bank) has undergone no material adverse change since the date of the Loan Agreement (Article 12.01(a) and (b) General Conditions Bank).

Moreover, Article 12.01(c) of the Bank's General Conditions provides that the Loan Agreement cannot take effect until all other events specified in it as conditions for effectiveness have taken place. These specified events can be manifold. When other agreements have to be concluded in connection with a loan or a credit, such as a project agreement or another type of agreement, entry into force of the Loan Agreement will be made dependent on them.[170] Conversely, the project agreements stipulate that they enter into force simultaneously with the Loan or Credit Agreement to which they pertain.[171] Furthermore, stipulations are often added dealing with, *inter alia,* the following issues: internal measures which the Member State has to take to enable the project to be executed, the requirement to re-lend the funds of the loan or credit to entities in charge of the execution of the project, the establishment of an organisation responsible for the execution of the project, the appointment of key personnel in certain positions and the hiring of experts and consultants. Even at this stage, before the loan documents have entered into force, the World Bank sends missions to supervise the implementation of these *a priori* conditions. The main task of these missions is to speed up the entry into force of the loan documents by helping the borrower to fulfil the conditions in question.[172]

The time which the borrower has to meet this type of obligation is rather short, generally no more than a couple of months. If the Loan Agreement has not taken effect by the date specified in it, the obligations of the parties under the loan documents are terminated. The World Bank may, however, establish a later date for the entry into force after considering the reasons for the delay (Article 12.04 General Conditions).

Finally, the General Conditions give the loan documents absolute protection against deviating provisions of national law or even the Articles of Agreement of the World Bank. Article 10.01 states that the rights and duties of the Bank or the IDA, the borrower and the guarantor under the Loan or Credit Agreement and the Guarantee Agreement shall be valid and enforceable in accordance with their terms, despite the law of any state or political subdivision of a state to the contrary. In addition the Article provides that neither the Bank nor the IDA, nor the borrower, nor the guarantor shall be entitled in any proceeding under this Article to assert any claim that any provision of the General Conditions or of the Loan, Credit or Guarantee is invalid or unenforceable because of any provision of the Articles of Agreement of the Bank. Thus the loan documents constitute the supreme law between the parties. A controversy arising between two parties to the loan documents that cannot be settled by agreement between the parties has to be submitted to arbitration by the Arbitral Tribunal provided for by Article 10.04 of the General Conditions.[173]

2.3.3.6. Supervision of the implementation

2.3.3.6.1. General

The actual implementation of the project, *i.e.* its construction or setting up, and the subsequent operation, on the one hand, and its supervision on the other, take place simultaneously, though they can be clearly distinguished. Implementation is ultimately the responsibility of the borrower; supervision is solely the task of the World Bank. Because of the fact that the World Bank assists in the implementation, for instance in the form of organisational studies and the training of staff and management or consultants to help supervise the project, the two activities sometimes overlap in practice. The World Bank itself considers supervision to be primarily 'an exercise in collective problem solving, and as such [is] one of the most effective ways in which the Bank provides technical assistance to its member countries'.[174] It is true that 'co-operative' elements play an important part in the World Bank's supervision, but the 'coercive' elements cannot be overlooked. Indeed, it seems to be a mixture of the two, and the loan documents, which are mainly aimed at serving as a basis for the World Bank's supervision, contain provisions of both a 'co-operative' and 'coercive' character. Admittedly, in practice the distinction is often blurred, because it is difficult to tell whether a certain action by the borrower resulted mainly from World Bank pressure or was brought about by its advice and suggestions.

One aspect of the relations of the World Bank with its clients, in which both the co-operative and the coercive elements of supervision can be seen is the use of consultants. As noted above, both the World Bank and its borrowers seek the assistance of outside consultants at practically all the different stages of the project cycle.[175] As regards consultants retained by borrowers,[176] the World Bank claims to hold the point of view that the selecting and hiring of consultants is the responsibility of the borrowers. Sometimes an obligation to hire consultants is incorporated in the loan documents. An example of this is the provision which requires the other party to a Project Agreement to 'employ a financial advisor *whose qualifications, experience and terms and conditions of employment shall be satisfactory to the Bank*' (italics added).[177] The World Bank claims that its general policy is to leave the responsibility for selection, administration and supervision of the consultants they employ to the borrowers.[178] However, the italicized words in the phrase quoted above are the rule rather than the exception and this seems to indicate that the responsibility the borrower is alleged to have is to some extent misleading. This seems to be confirmed by the further elaboration of the World Bank's policy in this respect. Apart from exceptional cases in which the Bank takes over the selection process,[179] this policy is described by the World Bank itself as follows: . . . the Bank's responsibility is only to provide guidance . . . to *determine* whether the proposed consultants are qualified for the job and to *ensure* that the consultant's conditions of employment are satisfactory. The Bank's involvement in these cases is normally limited to:

(a) review and *approval* of terms of reference and budget for services, prior to the invitation of consultants;
(b) review and *approval* of the firm or list of firms proposed to be invited by the borrower; and
(c) review and *approval* of the contract resulting from negotiations between the borrower and the selected firm, prior to the signature of the contract.' (Italics added.)[180]

Furthermore, although the World Bank considers that the supervision of the consultants is the full responsibility of the borrowers, its staff may visit the project area, as part of their normal project preparation or supervision activities, for the purpose of exchanging view on the progress of the work, and at the same time they may review the consultants' interim findings.[181]

The picture emerging from all this can hardly be said to be one of autonomy or even final responsibility for the borrower. It is probably closer to the truth to suppose that in the event of a conflict of opinions the real decision-making power in this respect rests with the World Bank. Obviously this rarely happens, but does not detract from the fact that the World Bank's supervision and control over the use of consultants is in fact very rigorous.

In fact, it seems that this rigorous attitude is fairly characteristic of provisions in the loan documents which concern supervision. The loan documents consisting of the Loan and Credit Agreements and the provisions incorporated from the General Conditions, and sometimes supplemented by Project and Guarantee Agreements, in most cases have a similar structure. Obviously, the basis of a Guarantee Agreement is the creation of the guarantee obligation for the Member State concerned. The standard clause in this respect reads that 'the Guarantor unconditionally guarantees, as primary obligor and not as surety merely, the due and punctual payment of the principal of, and interest and other charges on, the Loan, and the premium, if any, on the prepayment of the Loan and the punctual performance of all the other obligations of the borrower, all as set forth in the Loan Agreement'.[182] In addition, it usually contains a general clause which is very important from the point of view of supervision, according to which the Guarantor shall take all actions necessary or advisable on its part, as promptly as is required, to enable the Borrower to comply with its obligations under the Loan Agreement punctually.[183] Such action includes granting access to a member of the World Bank's staff to the territory of the Member State concerned for the purpose of conducting supervisory activities.

The provisions of Project Agreements are confined to the execution and the operation of the project. Moreover, these provisions are to a large extent also laid down in the Loan or Credit Agreement concerned. Combining them, the loan documents generally incorporate provisions dealing with the following subjects which have a direct bearing on the supervision of the World Bank: provisions concerning the Loan or the Credit itself, the execution of the project, management and operations, financial and other covenants and remedies.

The more specific provisions contained in the loan documents are virtually all an elaboration of one broad provision in the General Conditions, which, by virtue of its incorporation in the loan documents, constitutes the basis for the World Bank's supervisory activities which are not specifically provided for in the loan documents. This general provision will be discussed first.

2.3.3.6.2. Co-operation and information; financial and economic data

Article IX of the General Conditions of both the Bank and the IDA forms the basis for the World Bank's supervisory powers in general. The Article is entitled: 'Co-operation and Information; Financial and Economic Data,' and is for all practical purposes the same for the Bank and the IDA. In the case of the Bank it reads:

> Section 9.01. *Co-operation and Information.* (a) The Bank, the Borrower and the Guarantor shall co-operate fully to assure that the purpose of the Loan will be accomplished. To that end, the Bank, the Borrower and the Guarantor shall from time to time, at the request of anyone of them:
> (i) exchange views through their representatives with regard to the progress of the Project, the benefits derived therefrom and the performance of their respective obligations under the Loan Agreement and Guarantee Agreement and other matters relative to the purpose of the Loan; and (ii) furnish to the other party all such information as it shall reasonably request with regard to the progress of the Project, the benefits derived therefrom and the general status of the Loan.
> (b) The Bank, the Borrower and the Guarantor shall promptly inform each other of any condition which interferes with or threatens to interfere with, the progress of the

Project, the accomplishment of the purposes of the Loan, the maintenance of the service thereof or the performance by anyone of them of its obligations under the Loan Agreement and the Guarantee Agreement.

(c) The member of the Bank which is the Borrower or the Guarantor shall afford all reasonable opportunity for accredited representatives of the Bank to visit any part of its territory for purposes related to the Loan.

Section 9.02. *Financial and Economic Data.* The member of the Bank which is the Borrower or the Guarantor shall furnish to the Bank all such information as the Bank shall reasonably request with respect to financial and economic conditions in its territory, including its balance of payments and its external debt as well as that of its political or administrative subdivisions and of any entity owned or controlled by any such subdivision, and of any institution performing the functions of a central bank or exchange stabilisation fund, or similar functions, for such member.

The very general wording of this Article speaks for itself. It is clear that all the basic instruments of supervision, *i.e.* the instruments of the review function,[184] can be based on it. In fact, the Article contains very broadly formulated obligations on the part of the borrower and the guarantor to furnish information with regard to all aspects of the project as well as about the Member State's financial and economic situation in general on request of the World Bank, to provide unrequested information if events occur that might interfere in any way with the project or any of their obligations, and to furnish facilities necessary for inspection by the World Bank for purposes related to the loan. It is true that these provisions are couched in 'co-operative' terms in the sense that some obligations are mutual. However, there can be little doubt that in practice the borrower and the guarantor will be the obliged party most of the time, the World Bank being the beneficiary. After all, the World Bank is supervising the borrower and the guarantor, not vice-versa. Despite its comprehensive nature, Article IX of the General Conditions is always, to a greater or lesser extent, elaborated and supplemented by provisions in the loan documents.

2.3.3.6.3. Provisions on the loan or credit

The loan documents incorporate the General Conditions and set out the definitions pertaining to the project in question in Article I. Article II contains a number of provisions concerning the loan or credit itself stating the amount of the funds made available, determining the rate of the service charge (in the case of a credit) and the interest and the commitment charge (in the case of a loan) as well as the way in which these have to be paid, and also setting out the amortisation schedule usually annexed to the Agreement. From the point of view of supervision two sets of provisions concerning the loan or credit are particularly important.

The first is the regulation concerning the withdrawal of the proceeds from the loan or the credit. The proceeds resulting from a loan or a credit are not made available to the borrower all at once, but he can obtain them according to a schedule drawn up at the time the loan or credit is negotiated. As a result the Loan and Credit Agreements contain a standard clause stipulating the amount of the loan or credit that may be withdrawn from the Loan or Credit Account in accordance with a schedule annexed to the Agreement. The schedule may be amended from time to time by agreement between the borrower and the Bank or the IDA, for expenditures made (or, if the Bank or the IDA shall so agree, for proposed expenditure) in respect of the reasonable cost of goods and services required for the project and to be financed out of the proceeds of the loan or credit.[185] Obviously, disbursement of every loan or credit must conform with the provisions of the Loan or Credit Agreement concerned. The great majority of loans and credits, however, follow the same disbursement procedures and these standardised rules are laid down in 'Guidelines for Withdrawal of Proceeds of World Bank Loans and IDA Credits'.[186]

There are different methods of withdrawal, but some general rules contained in the General Conditions apply to all of them. The borrower has to deliver a written application of the form and content in accordance with the World Bank's reasonable request (Article 5.03). He has to furnish evidence of the authority of the person or persons authorised to sign applications for withdrawal and the authenticated specimen signature of any such person (Article 5.04), as well as such supporting evidence as the World Bank shall reasonably request (Article 5.05). Finally, each application and the accompanying documents and other evidence must be sufficient in form and substance to satisfy the World Bank that the borrower is entitled to withdraw from the Loan or Credit Account the amount applied for, and that the amount to be withdrawn is to be used only for the purposes specified in the Loan or Credit Agreement (Article 5.06).

The first method of withdrawal is an application for reimbursement after the borrower has made a payment, which is eligible for financing under the loan or the credit. Such a payment may be for a completed transaction or a down or progress payment on a contract. The application in each case is the same: a separate application for each currency involved (although this may cover a number of purchase transactions), and each item for which reimbursement is requested should be related to the appropriate category in the Schedule of Withdrawal of Proceeds in the Loan or Credit Agreement. The documentation required will differ. In the case of a completed transaction the borrower is required to submit an invoice from the supplier and specified evidence of payment to the supplier as well as of the shipment. In the case of a progress payment shipping evidence will not be available, but has to be furnished as soon as possible after shipment has taken place.[187]

A borrower may also request that the Bank or the IDA will make a payment directly to a supplier on behalf of the borrower. Evidence supporting the application should consist of a copy of the contract of purchase order and, if possible, a copy of the supplier's invoice, while shipment evidence has to be furnished immediately after the shipping.[188]

Two additional, largely similar, methods of withdrawal are based on Article 5.02 of the General Conditions. According to that Article the Bank (and the IDA) may, upon request of the borrower and upon such terms and conditions as shall be agreed upon, enter into special commitments in writing to pay amounts to the borrower or others in respect of expenditures to be financed under the Loan or Credit Agreement. The provision is used in practice when a borrower wants to open a letter of credit, while the commercial bank in the supplier's country is unwilling to do so without some guarantee or security. Two forms have been developed, *viz.* an irrevocable agreement to reimburse and a qualified agreement to reimburse. In both cases, if the borrower's request is approved, the Bank or the IDA issue to the commercial bank concerned an agreement to reimburse the commercial bank for payments under the letter of credit. In the case of an irrevocable agreement the World Bank's special commitments are not affected by any subsequent suspension or cancellation of the Bank's loan or the IDA credit. In the case of a qualified agreement, on the other hand, suspension or cancellation would cause the World Bank's obligations to the commercial bank to cease. Which of the two procedures is to be used will depend primarily on the borrower's relations with the commercial bank in the supplier's country.[189]

The second set of provisions referred to above, which are particularly relevant in the context of supervision, concern the procurement of goods and works. When there is only a Loan or Credit Agreement, the rules concerning procurement are contained in the provisions on the loan or the credit; when there is also a Project Agreement it is usually found among the provisions on the execution of the project. As in the case of withdrawal, the World Bank has established 'Guidelines for Procurement under World Bank and IDA Credits'.[190] Like the 'Guidelines for Withdrawal' these 'Guidelines for Procurement' are not binding as such. The rights and obligations of the borrower derive only from the Loan Documents. The procurement of goods and works to be financed out of the proceeds of the loan or credit are governed by the provisions of a Procurement Schedule usually annexed to the Loan, Credit or Project Agreement. The first provision of that schedule normally stipulates that, except where otherwise provided for in the schedule, goods and works are to be procured under contracts awarded in accordance with procedures consistent with those set forth in the World Bank's Guidelines for Procurement.[191]

It was already pointed out that the World Bank attaches great value to goods and works being procured on the basis of international competitive bidding in order that procurement takes place in accordance with its views.[192] For this reason the Guidelines describe procedures which help to ensure satisfactory international competitive bidding. International competitive bidding has the purpose of providing prospective bidders from all member countries and Switzerland with adequate notification of a borrower's requirements and of offering all bidders an equal opportunity of bidding on the necessary goods. Generally speaking the World Bank requires the bidding documents to be clear as to the type and the size of the contracts that will be awarded, and it prescribes the way in which the invitation to bid should be advertised in order to notify the international community in reasonable time for it to have the opportunity to bid.[193] More specifically, the Guidelines for Procurement contain a great number of frequently very detailed directives with regard to both form and content of the bidding documents as well as procedures for the opening of bidding and the evaluation and award of the contract.[194] All these directives constitute many requirements over which the

World Bank exercises supervision in one way or another. The loan documents specify whether the borrower should submit bidding documents to the World Bank for review before issuance to tenderers, and whether the report evaluating the bids is subject to the World Bank's review prior or subsequent to a final decision on the award being made.[195]

The consequences of not complying with the World Bank's requirements are the same in both cases. If the Bank determines that the intended award (in the case of prior review) or the actual award (in the case of subsequent review) was not consistent with the terms of the Loan or Credit Agreement with the borrower, it will promptly inform the borrower of its findings and state the reasons for them and, without inhibiting any remedy of the World Bank under its agreement with the borrower, the contract will not be eligible for financing by the World Bank.[196]

These are the general rules concerning the World Bank's supervision of procurement by the borrower. In addition, the more detailed requirements clearly show that the World Bank's surveillance in this respect is very stringent. This is true, for instance, with respect to the prequalification of firms which is sometimes considered advisable. Unless the Loan or Credit Agreement provides otherwise, the borrower has to inform the World Bank in detail of the procedure to be followed before applications to qualify are invited, and should introduce such modifications in the procedure as the World Bank shall request. The list of prequalified firms, together with a statement of their qualifications and the reasons for the exclusions of any applicant for prequalification, should be furnished by the borrower to the World Bank for its review and comments before the applicants are notified.[197] Finally, the preferences sometimes accepted for domestic or regional manufacturers in order to foster the development of local potential, are subject to conditions which are agreed upon by the World Bank.[198]

The above leaves no doubt that the World Bank takes procurement very seriously. In certain types of projects it might indeed be the crucial factor. At the same time, the World Bank's far reaching involvement in procurement sheds a somewhat different light on its insistence that procurement is the complete responsibility of the borrower.

2.3.3.6.4. Provisions on the execution of the project

Under this heading a number of provisions are usually incorporated in the loan documents which are obviously an elaboration of the general rules concerning supervision in the General Conditions. If the borrower has to re-lend the funds to the entity executing the project, the Loan or Credit Agreement stipulates that a subsidiary loan agreement shall be entered into between the borrower and executive agency concerned. It also stipulates that the terms and conditions must be approved by the World Bank. It is not unusual for such terms and conditions to be already mentioned in the Loan or Credit Agreement itself.[199] Apart from these, the Agreements in such cases set forth a number of more general obligations for the borrower which amount to the duty to take all action necessary and to prevent anything interfering with the fulfilment of its obligations by the executive agency.[200]

The article on the execution of the project in the Agreements with the executive agency – be it the borrower or a distinct entity – usually starts out with a provision requiring the project to be carried out with due diligence and efficiency in conformity with appropriate administrative, financial and – depending on the nature of the project – other practices, as well as dealing with services, the provision, as promptly as required, of the funds, facilities and other resources required for the purpose.[201] Furthermore, the Agreements make provision for adequate insurance in respect of the imported goods to be financed out of the proceeds of the loan or credit, and the executive agency undertakes to have all goods and services financed out of the loan or credit which is to be used exclusively for the project.[202]

The Agreements with the executive agency lay down a number of requirements specifically for the purpose of supervision, which together seem to have become a standard clause. This clause creates a set of obligations on the part of the executing agency which is clearly aimed at facilitating the World Bank's supervisory activities. The Project Agreement between the Bank and the Kenya Posts and Telecommunications Corporation can be taken as an example.[203] Its Article 2.05(a) provides that 'KPTC shall furnish to the Bank, promptly upon their preparation, the plans, specifications, reports, contract documents and work and procurement schedules for the Project, and any material modifications thereof or additions thereto, in such detail as the Bank shall reasonably request'. Paragraph (b) lays down the following obligations for KPTC: (i) to maintain records and procedures adequate to record and monitor the progress of the Project (including its capital costs), to identify the goods and services financed out of the proceeds of the loan, and to disclose their use in the Project; (ii) to enable the Bank's accredited representatives to visit the facilities and construction sites included in the Project and to examine the goods financed out of the proceeds of the loan and any relevant records and documents; and (iii) to furnish to the Bank at regular intervals all such information as the Bank shall reasonably request concerning the Project, its cost, the expenditure of the proceeds of the loan and the goods and services financed out of such proceeds. Additional provisions give the Bank's representatives the right to examine plants, installations, sites, works buildings, property and equipment of KPTC and any relevant records and documents as the Bank may reasonably request (Article 2.05(d)). Furthermore, the KPTC is required to exchange views with the Bank at the latter's request, regarding the Project's progress, the performance of its obligations and other matters relating to the purposes of the loan (Article 2.07(a)). Apart from the rules just mentioned, which are common to Loan/Credit and Project Agreements, individual Agreements – depending on the nature of the Project – not infrequently embody even more specific duties to be performed by the executing agency.[204]

Finally, it should be noted that the World Bank now includes in the loan documents the obligation for the executing agency to prepare and furnish the Bank or the IDA with a so-called Project Completion Report, of such scope and in such detail as the Bank or the IDA shall reasonably request. The Project Completion Report has to deal with the execution and initial operation of the Project, its cost and the benefits estimated to be derived from it, the performance by the executive agency and the Bank or the IDA of their respective obligations and the achievement of the purposes of the loan or the credit. This Project Completion Report, which has to be submitted not later than six months after the completion of the project, constitutes an important element of the World Bank's evaluation, to which reference will be made later.[205] At the same time, however, the knowledge that a report will have to be drawn up at the end, will certainly be an incentive for the executive agency to record the progress of the project from the start in a systematic way, which in its turn will facilitate the supervision by the World Bank.

2.3.3.6.5. Provisions on management and operations, on financial covenants and on other covenants

The loan documents sometimes include certain provisions under these different headings which form yet another elaboration of those provisions on the execution of the project. Generally speaking, they purport to ensure that the executive agency conducts its affairs in accordance with appropriate business practices and to make sure that the agency follows sound financial policies, for instance, by having its account and financial statements audited by independent auditors acceptable to the World Bank. Provisions on other covenants may deal with a variety of subjects depending on the nature of the project and the executing agency. They may assign the Loan or Credit the highest priority in relation to other external debts of the country concerned.[206]

2.3.3.6.6. Remedies and arbitration

A. *Remedies* Finally, the loan documents, in combination with the General Conditions, deal with a number of issues which taken together constitute the remedies available to the parties to the loan documents. They include remedies for the borrower and/or the executive agency *vis-à-vis* the World Bank. However, the bulk of these provisions create sanctions with which the World Bank can support its supervisory activities. In the following sections the focus will be on the latter type of provisions, which are most relevant from the point of view of supervision. The World Bank has three types of sanctions at its disposal. These are suspension, cancellation, and acceleration of maturity.

Suspension Article 6.02 of the General Conditions empowers the World Bank to suspend in whole or in part the right of the borrower to make withdrawals from the Loan or Credit Account in the case of a number of exhaustively enumerated events. Suspension may result from the failure on the part of the borrower or the guarantor to make any payment to which he was obliged under the Loan or Credit Agreement (Article 6.02(a) and (b)), and in general from the failure to perform any other obligation under the loan documents. This obviously includes any specific duty to be performed by the borrower related to the supervision of the World Bank. Moreover, the broadly worded powers of the World Bank to suspend the right of withdrawal of proceeds are not confined to events which are connected with one particular loan or credit. The suspension of any loan or credit is a justifiable cause for the suspension of all other loans or credits.

One might expect that this enumeration would cover the whole range of possible violations by the borrower or the guarantor of their obligations. Nevertheless, the General Conditions add as a separate ground for suspension, the event that information furnished by the borrower or the guarantor and which the World Bank relies on in making the loan or the credit, has been incorrect in any material respect (Article 6.02(i)). The reasons for suspension mentioned above are related to the conduct of the borrower or guarantor. Suspension of the right of withdrawal can also occur without there being any blame on the part of the borrower or the guarantor. Article 6.02(e) enables the World Bank to suspend the right of withdrawal when an extraordinary situation arises after the date of the Loan or Credit Agreement, which makes it improbable that the project can be carried out or that the borrower or the guarantor will be able to perform their obligations.

The criteria justifying suspension apply equally during the period after the Loan or Credit Agreement has been signed but before it has entered into force (Article 6.02(g) and (l)). Finally, the Loan or Credit Agreement often specifies additional events, which in the particular circumstances of the loan or credit concerned may lead to its suspension (Article 6.02(k)).

Cancellation Loan or Credit Agreements can be cancelled by the World Bank if they have been suspended for a continuous period of 30 days.[207] Not complying with obligations concerned with supervision may therefore eventually lead to the termination of the right of withdrawal on the part of the borrower. Suspension or cancellation of a loan or a credit does not lift any of the obligations of the borrower or the guarantor; all the provisions of the Loan Agreement and the Guarantee Agreement continue in full force (Article 6.06). Obviously, the borrower remains bound to repay his debt to the World Bank.

Acceleration of maturity Part of the sanctions applied by the World Bank against a defaulting borrower may consist of an acceleration of the maturity of the loan or the credit. Article VII of the General Conditions empowers the World Bank to declare the principal of the Loan or the Credit outstanding to be due and payable immediately, together with the interest and other charges thereon. The events which give rise to the World Bank's right to accelerate the maturity are more or less the same as those which are a ground for suspension.[208]

B. Arbitration In addition to the provisions on remedies, the General Conditions contain an elaborate article (10.04) on arbitration. Obviously, arbitration as such does not constitute a remedy in the sense of a sanction.

Nevertheless, it is clear that arbitration and remedies are closely connected. Arbitration is therefore dealt with here. The scope of arbitration within the framework of the World Bank is very wide. Any controversy between the parties to a Loan or Credit Agreement or to a Guarantee Agreement, as well as any claim by any such party against any other such party arising under those Agreements, shall be submitted to arbitration, if it cannot be settled by agreement (Article 10.04(a)). It is clear that arbitration can be resorted to both before and after the use of the remedies mentioned above whenever negotiations have not provided a solution.

Article 10.04(c) lays down the composition of the Arbitral Tribunal. Each side shall appoint one arbitrator. The third arbitrator (the Umpire) shall be appointed with the agreement of both parties. If agreement fails, any party may request the appointment of the Umpire by the President of the International Court of Justice within 60 days after notice has been given of the institution of the arbitration proceedings (Article 10.04(e)), or, failing appointment by him, by the Secretary-General of the United Nations.

The General Conditions leave the procedure largely to the discretion of the parties or the arbitrators respectively (Article 10.04(f) and (g)). They stipulate only that proceedings are to be instituted in the form of a notice from one party to the other. Such a notice has to contain a statement setting forth the nature of the controversy or claim to be submitted to arbitration and the nature of the relief sought, as well as the name of the arbitrator appointed by the party instituting such proceedings (Article 10.04(d)). Furthermore, the Arbitral Tribunal has to afford all parties a fair hearing (Article 10.04(h)). The Arbitral Tribunal, which takes decisions by majority vote, gives its decision in writing. It is final and binding upon the parties, who have to abide by and comply with it (Article 10.04(h)).

Finally, the settlement of controversies between the parties (Article 10.04(j)) must take place through the arbitration arranged, which cannot be substituted by any other procedure.

2.3.3.6.7. Supervision in practice

After the above analysis of the provisions in the loan documents which are relevant from the perspective of supervision, the actual functioning of the World Bank's supervisory activities can be dealt with briefly.

The World Bank's project supervision system covers all World Bank assisted projects under execution. Supervision takes place in a variety of ways.

The World Bank considers its supervision to be of the utmost importance. As Baum observes, 'Supervision is the least glamorous part of project work, but it is in several respects the most important.'[209]

There is evidence that there is a direct relationship between the quality of World Bank supervision and the results achieved in many projects.[210] For this reason it is not surprising that the resources allocated to supervision have recently increased substantially, both in absolute terms and relative to other project tasks.[211] Staff time spent on supervision is already considerable.

For instance, the time devoted to field supervision alone averaged 27 manweeks for the agricultural projects reviewed in 1979.[212] Even so, the World Bank recently indicated that further steps are being taken to strengthen its supervisory effort.[213]

A. Periodic reports An important element is the duty of borrower to report regularly on the physical execution of the project, its costs, the financial status of revenue earning projects, and on the evolution of project benefits. These progress reports have to be submitted according to a schedule agreed upon during the negotiations.[214]

B. Project Completion Report As noted above,[215] the more recent Loan and Credit Agreements now also require borrowers to prepare a Project Completion Report when project implementation nears completion. Normally it is due within six months of the completion of the Bank loan or IDA credit disbursement. The Project Completion Report represents the culmination of the preceding progress reports. The Project Completion Report should be a comprehensive review of the extent to which the objectives and expectations, on the basis of which the Bank loan or the IDA credit was approved, have been achieved or show promise of success. '. . . Its purpose is not to record a comprehensive history of the project, but to consider candidly, in the light of what actually happened up to that time, whether in retrospect the project was worth doing and what lessons are to be learned from this experience.'[216] For this purpose the report usually deals with the following aspects: the objectives of the project, its economic and social impact, its contribution to institution-building, the financial performance of the project, the implementation of the project and the compliance with the loan documents by the borrower and finally, the role of the World Bank in the entire project.[217]

C. Field missions In addition, the World Bank regularly sends field missions to projects under execution. The frequency of such missions is closely related to the complexity of the project, the progress in its implementation and the number and complexity of the problems encountered. As a rule a project is visited every six months. However, projects classified in the special so-called 'problem category,' which usually constitute less than 10 per cent. of the total, may be called on by a World Bank mission as often as three of four times a year.[218]

D. Other activities Finally, the supervisory system of the World Bank includes a number of activities which are not only designed to promote the adequate implementation of a specific project as such, but also serve the more general purpose of improving the World Bank's policies and procedures for future projects. It is not always easy to decide whether these activities should be categorised under supervision or evaluation, which will be dealt with in the next paragraph; they consist of a regular review of the progress in solving implementation problems on the middle management level, a semi-annual review of the status of the more serious problem projects by senior management and an annual general discussion of problem projects. Over the years all this has resulted in a substantial increase in the resources to supervision, both in an absolute sense and in relation to other project tasks.[219]

2.3.3.7. Evaluation

Evaluation is the final stage of the World Bank's project cycle. At the same time evaluation is the link between past and future projects of the World Bank. The basic purpose of evaluation is to assess to what degree and how efficiently operational projects are producing the anticipated results in order to profit from the experience with regard to new projects. In other words, evaluation is intended to gather information from past projects and to feed this back into new projects.

As noted above, supervision and evaluation sometimes overlap and a number of World Bank activities serve both the purposes of supervision and evaluation.[220] The same is true with regard to the monitoring and evaluation activities which the World Bank now regularly incorporates in projects, in particular the new style projects. On the one hand they provide the borrowers with a more effective mechanism for modifying projects in the light of experience, while on the other hand, they gain information from the project which can be used in the preparation and implementation of future projects.[221]

Thus, the beginning of the evaluation phase cannot always be established precisely. Evaluation has certainly begun as soon as the World Bank's *Operations Evaluation Department* (OED) becomes engaged in the project cycle. The origins of this Department date back to 1970. In that year the President of the World Bank established a separate operations evaluation unit as an experiment. Since that time the functioning of this unit has been regularly reviewed by the President and the Executive Directors and in 1974 it was decided to create a new post of Director-General, Operations Evaluation.[222] Both the post of this Director-General and the Department are organised in such a way as to satisfy to the largest possible extent the requirements of sound evaluation: on the one hand, independence from the management for the greatest credibility; on the other hand, integration into the management for the quickest assimilation of useful lessons. The OED is entirely separate from the operating staff of the World Bank and reports directly to the Executive Directors and the President. Its Director-General, who is appointed by the Directors for a renewable period of five years and can be removed only by them, has a rank equivalent to that of a Vice-President. He is ineligible for subsequent appointment or reappointment to the staff of the World Bank except in unusual circumstances. He appoints the staff members of the OED. Most of them are drawn from assignments elsewhere in the World Bank, although recruitment from outside is possible. Those who come from the ranks of the World Bank are normally fairly senior officers and are transferred to the OED for a period of about three to four years.[223] This arrangement is intended to ensure both independence from and familiarity with the functioning of the World Bank.

The World Bank considers that its evaluation system has been designed as a two-tier system. On the one hand, it consists of self-evaluation by the relevant operational units; on the other hand, reviews of these self-evaluations, and of the operational experience that they cover, are conducted by the OED.[224] As was explained above,[225] the loan documents now regularly require the borrower or the executive agency to submit to the Bank or the IDA a Project Completion Report. At the same time, a Project Completion Report is prepared by the World Bank's staff involved in the project concerned. Before the end of the project, when it is nearing completion, consultations take place between the OED and the relevant World Bank staff and the staff of the borrower assigned to complete the project; these consultations are concerned with issues on which the Project Completion Report should focus. The purpose of this early contact is to enhance the efficiency of the work regarding the Project Completion Reports. The Project Completion Reports constitute the basic element in the OED's Project Performance Auditing, which consists of a limited review of all completed projects and a thorough review of a selected few.[226]

While the Project Performance Audit begins with reviewing the Project Completion Report(s) in all cases, about half of the projects are subsequently evaluated along the lines of an abbreviated procedure. This procedure results in a brief Project Performance Audit Memorandum which is usually limited to general conclusions on the project's achievements and to experience of wider relevance. Projects eligible for this abbreviated audit are those which have a satisfactory economic return, do not exceed the estimated time or costs or exceed them only to a limited extent, and projects which produce a Project Completion Report which deals adequately with the experience of the project and the ensuing lessons for the future.

Not more than 25 per cent. and not less than 15 per cent. of all projects are selected by the OED for a more exhaustive treatment, which includes a visiting mission for discussions with borrower governments and their implementing agencies. The decision to conduct such a detailed review can be based on the intrinsic importance of the project experience and its relevance for World Bank practice, or the nature of issues raised by the project or by commentators on the World Bank's role in it. The reason might also be an inadequate Project Completion Report or simply to take examples at random.

Finally, the remaining projects are subjected to a review at a level somewhere between that of the abbreviated process and the thorough treatment.

The Project Performance Audit results in a Project Performance Audit Report. The draft of this report is sent to various persons and entities for comment. These include the borrower and the Executive Director of the country concerned, co-lenders, implementing agencies and consultant firms, and the department and other staff of the World Bank responsible for the project, who were primarily involved. When these comments have been given due consideration the report is drawn up in its final version and is submitted to the Executive Directors and the President via the Director-General.

Obviously, the ultimate goal of evaluation is for the findings resulting from it to be reflected in the World Bank's policy. To achieve this, the OED publishes a review of all Project Performance Audit Reports every year for the purpose of disseminating these findings among the World Bank's own ranks as well as its members. Moreover, the implications of the reports are reviewed annually by the Central Projects Staff with the appropriate OED staff and the Regional Offices in meetings specially arranged for this purpose. The Executive Directors and the President are kept informed of progress in this respect through the Annual Review of Project Performance Audit Results, which summarises the major findings of all Project Performance Audit Reports issued in the preceding calendar year and the World Bank's response to them.[227]

2.4. Effectiveness of World Bank supervision

2.4.1. Introduction

Generally speaking the above survey of the World Bank's supervision gives the impression that it is a very elaborate and smoothly functioning system which provides the organisation with a strong influence over those to whom it lends money. The results of the World Bank's supervisory efforts are likely to compare favourably with those of other international organisations. The most striking reason for this relative success is the fact that the World Bank offers something its recipient Member States badly want or even need, *viz.* funds for financing economic development. Developing countries as a rule have a hard time obtaining these funds elsewhere on the same conditions and they can therefore be expected to be prepared to conform with the requirements of the World Bank's supervisory system to a considerable extent. A less obvious, but probably also very important factor is the relatively long and undisturbed evolution of the World Bank. The organisation is one of the oldest specialised agencies of the UN family and has, during a large part of its existence, taken a back seat in international relations. For the first 20 years at least, the World Bank followed fairly conservative policies, which were more or less generally acceptable, and the subject matter it had to deal with – development financing – was considered a highly technical affair without any major political implications. This relatively quiet period provided the World Bank with ample opportunity for gathering experience in the sometimes highly technical aspects of its task, for building a strong and coherent institutional structure and for equipping itself with a highly qualified staff whose expertise is undoubtedly one of the elements responsible for the World Bank's strong supervisory system.

All this should not obscure the fact that World Bank supervision also has shortcomings, which are revealed when one takes a closer look. In order to get a more comprehensive picture of its results, the supervisory system of the World Bank will be evaluated below in terms of its effectiveness. For, as noted in Part I of this book,[228] the question of effectiveness is the most important consideration in international supervision. It was also pointed out that two factors largely determine the effectiveness of international supervision, *viz.* the consent or consensus of the State or the States in question to the rules concerned, and the adequacy of those rules, *i.e.* their capacity to achieve the purpose for which they were enacted.[229] Both factors are closely interrelated particularly in the sense that consent determines the adequacy of the rules to a large extent. Adequacy as such primarily reflects the procedural supervisory rules in the strict sense of the term and is therefore concerned with the technical and juridical adaptation of those rules to the environment in which they have to function. The adequacy of the World Bank's supervisory rules will be evaluated below in terms of their modality, form and instruments.

Consent primarily determines the contents of the substantive rules, as well as the degree to which the object and purpose of the substantive rules can be achieved.[230] At the project level the object and purpose can be easily ascertained, because they are set forth, often in considerable detail, in the loan documents. Moreover, they usually have a rather concrete nature and can therefore be measured, if not always quantified. Obviously, the projects financed by the World Bank are intended to contribute to its more general goals such as promoting the economic development of Member States, raising the standards of living and more recently, obtaining a more equitable distribution of the fruits of economic development among various sectors of the population. Whether the projects actually serve these general goals in every respect is a difficult question to answer because of the imprecise nature of the goals and the subjective approaches which arise when they are given a specific content. The question concerns aspects of the policy of the World Bank. This study concentrates on the supervision within the framework of the World Bank and policy questions in principle fall outside its scope. As will be seen, however, it is not possible to keep the creative aspects of supervision and policy completely separate. Thus, problems relating to policy making within the World Bank will inevitably be discussed in the following sections.

2.4.2. *The modality of the World Bank supervisory system*

The modality of the World Bank's supervision is clearly general rather than specific, because it is of a permanent nature and is initiated in terms of the international obligation itself, *i.e.* the loan documents. The exercise of supervision by the World Bank does not necessarily depend on the (alleged) existence of a set of circumstances inconsistent with the borrower's obligations under the loan documents, nor does it have to be triggered off by a suspicion or even accusation by the supervisory body or a third party.[231] The World Bank's supervision is permanent in the sense of being constant rather than periodic or regular. The word 'constant' in this respect does not imply that all projects are monitored on a daily basis, though some projects are, at least during certain periods of the project cycle. The World Bank, moreover, seems to be in a position where information on the state of affairs concerning a particular project is always available, enabling it to take action if and when the need to do so arises.

The World Bank's system of surveillance over the activities of recipient States shares the advantages from the point of view of effectiveness which usually go with general supervision. It is exercised in a benevolent atmosphere, often with strong co-operative elements, rather than in an antagonistic manner. Coercive action can in many instances be forestalled, not only because potential violations of the borrower's obligations are deterred by the preventative effects of permanent supervision in the strict sense, but also as a consequence of the anticipatory effects resulting from its supervision in the broader sense of that term, i.e. its creative aspects. It should be remembered that the World Bank is involved in a project from its very inception, i.e. from the first stage of the project cycle. Moreover, the World Bank's relationship with most of its client States is not confined to one single project. For instance, of all the projects reviewed in 1979, over 80 per cent. were one of a series in the country or project concerned.[232] In these cases, therefore, the World Bank can build on experience gathered on previous occasions. Taken together, these circumstances produce a situation in which the World Bank is usually well informed about the recipient country while the latter is likely to have a pretty good idea of what to expect from the World Bank. Thus, it is possible for each side to have a clear understanding of the other's views and intentions, which obviously reduces the chances of there being problems somewhere along the line of the project cycle. It goes without saying that an open and trusting relationship is crucial to the successful completion of any project and it seems that the World Bank's record in this respect can be rated fairly highly. Nevertheless, it could certainly be improved, as the occasional 'communication breakdowns' between the World Bank and its borrowers show.[233]

Furthermore, the World Bank's supervision is exercised in an egalitarian manner. Apart from deviations caused by the peculiarities of certain projects or special circumstances prevalent in a particular country, supervision is approximately the same with regard to all projects. Supervisory provisions are to a large extent standardised in the General Conditions, which are made applicable to all projects usually with only minor changes. In addition, a number of specific elements pertaining to the project, such as the procedures for procurement and the hiring of consultants, are largely standardised too. These egalitarian aspects of supervision avoid any State from feeling that it has been singled out for particularly harsh treatment. This makes the supervision more easily acceptable to them and, consequently, more effective.

Finally, the disadvantages sometimes attached to general rather than specific supervision, are to a large extent alleviated in the case of the World Bank. Specific supervision was considered to result in a more detailed investigation of the performance of the States concerned than general supervision.[234] Because of the involvement of a third party with an interest in having the case investigated as thoroughly as possible, specific supervision is likely to come up with more detailed information about the behaviour of the State in question. General supervision runs the risk of remaining superficial if the supervisory body has to rely solely on information supplied by the 'defendant' without being able to play a more active role in gathering the necessary data. The discussion of the review function of supervision which follows will show in greater detail that the World Bank is in no way forced to adopt this passive role, but can in fact actively collect information in a very thorough fashion.[235] The World Bank has a very strong incentive to play an active role with regard to supervision because it is an 'interested party' itself. In order to be able to attract the funds required for continuing its work, it is crucial to the World Bank that borrowers repay their debts and that projects achieve their developmental objectives.

2.4.3. The form of World Bank supervision

As it has a general character, the form of the World Bank's supervision is necessarily non-judicial as opposed to judicial or quasi-judicial.[236] Much of what has been observed with regard to the modality therefore applies equally to the form. In addition, the following observations can be made. In Part I of this book supervision was said to be non-judicial if it is exercised, in the last resort, by a politically dependent organ of an international organisation and leads, by way of a procedure which is generally not very well defined, to a binding decision or a non-binding recommendation, depending on the constitutional powers of the organ.[237]

The World Bank's supervision fits this description. It is, in the last resort, exercised by the Executive Directors.[238] In view of the structure of World Bank supervision, the Executive Directors undoubtedly constitute a politically dependent organ.[239] However, a major part in the supervisory process is played by the staff of the World Bank. It therefore resembles the two-tiered structure which is typical of non-judicial supervision; it consists of a technical phase and a political phase. In the model as outlined in Part I of this book,[240] the function of the expert organ in the technical phase is limited to data processing which is sometimes accompanied by a tentative opinion. The role of the World Bank's staff, however, goes beyond this. As noted above,[241] decision-making power within the World Bank ultimately rests with the Executive Directors c.q. the Board of Governors. However, these powers are to a large extent delegated to the President and the staff, or have to be left to them because of the complicated and highly technical aspects of the World Bank's work. The World Bank is a staff dominated organisation in the sense that within the often broad margins set by the policy of the management, the staff has ample room for manoeuvre. Identification, preparation and appraisal of projects are conducted by the staff. The Directors only become involved in the process shortly before the loan documents are concluded. Afterwards, their link with the project is even more indirect and distant.

On the other hand, the procedure of World Bank supervision, though largely standardised, is characterised by flexibility. While rigidity of procedural provisions in judicial forms of supervision serves to benefit and protect the State which is the object of the scrutiny, in non-judicial supervision the same rigidity would produce the opposite effect. The majority of problems encountered by the World Bank in its relations with developing countries are not legal problems but rather economic, financial, social, cultural or political problems. Consequently, the World Bank has to be able to take into account the particular circumstances of each project and each country. The loan documents facilitate carrying out supervision in a flexible manner. In these documents the uniform provisions of the General Conditions can be shaped and adapted in such a way as to be appropriate for the particular situation in each individual case.

Finally, the decisions of the World Bank in the course of the project cycle have a binding character, whether formally or in reality. First, the World Bank has the power of deciding whether or not to make a loan or a credit. In reaching a decision in this respect the World Bank should be guided only by the directives contained in its Articles of Agreement and the prospective borrower has no influence on the decision whatsoever. This enables the World Bank to lay down in the loan documents all the provisions which it deems necessary or desirable. At the other end of the scale there is the World Bank's right to suspend or cancel a loan or credit on the conditions specified in the loan documents. These conditions are formulated in such broad terms that this right can in fact be exercised in the case of any non-observance on the part of the borrower of any provision in the loan documents. Problems are usually resolved through co-operation between the parties. Certainly a co-operative attitude on the part of the borrower is in many instances indispensable; sheer coercion cannot always produce acceptable results. But this does not detract from the World Bank's predominant position. The *ultimum remedium* of coercion will be present in the background when a borrower tries to settle its controversies with the World Bank. Equally important in this respect is the fact that the World Bank has widely recognised expertise in the field of development financing. As such, the World Bank's view in controversial matters carries great authority, which is likely to carry a good deal of weight even as far as the other party in the dispute is concerned.

2.4.4. The instruments of review of the World Bank supervision

In Part I it is repeatedly emphasised that the supervisory organ's knowledge of the facts on which its work is based should be as detailed as possible[242]; this knowledge is a *sine qua non* for effective supervision. The higher the quality of the information available, the more effective the supervision. One of the main reasons for the World Bank's relative success in the field of supervision is its skill in efficiently gathering the necessary information.

The World Bank seems extremely well equipped to obtain the data needed. The tools it has at its disposal for this purpose were discussed in detail in the preceding survey of the provisions concerning supervision contained in the General Conditions and the loan documents.[243] This survey shows that the World Bank is entitled not only to all information regarding the project, but also more generally to information concerning the other party's financial and economic situation in the broadest sense. Borrowers and guarantors (and also implementing agencies when they are different entities) have a more 'passive' obligation to furnish the information requested by the World Bank as well as an 'active' duty to report; the latter not only systematically at specified times during the implementation of the project but also *ad hoc* when conditions arise which, in one way or another, interfere or threaten to interfere with completion of the project. The World Bank can always follow up information received by asking more detailed questions or by discussing in greater depth certain aspects connected with the project. Last but not least, it can 'check' all data provided through inspection on the spot in the form of its visiting missions to recipient countries. The loan documents provide for a right of the World Bank to send such missions virtually when and as often as it deems expedient. The borrower or guarantor country grants permission to World Bank representatives for entry into its territory for the full duration of the project's implementation and sometimes even longer, *i.e.* during the time the project has come into operation. The World Bank, in other words, is not dependent upon *ad hoc* consent in each case. The requirement of *ad hoc* consent constitutes a major impediment to the effectiveness of the instrument of inspection in general.[244]

Finally, for the effective exercise of the review function it is not only instrumental to have the powers to gather information which is as exact as possible, it is equally important for it to be able to distinguish between pertinent and less relevant information. The World Bank's long experience and consequent expertise in project matters has been repeatedly emphasised above. In addition, it should be remembered that the World Bank's system of Country Economic Reporting[245] enables it to view individual projects in the broader perspective of the sector or national economy and consequently enhances its capacity to detect the causes of setbacks in a project's progress by soliciting the right information and, as a result, to arrive at possible remedies.

In conclusion it is probably safe to say that international organisations with more far-reaching review powers *vis-à-vis* Member States than the World Bank are hard to find. Indeed, given the degree of organisation prevalent in present day international society a more comprehensive system of review is actually difficult to imagine. Nevertheless, having optimal tools in theory is one thing, making optimal use of them in practice is quite another. The World Bank's review does not perform optimally in practice. That is, of course, hardly surprising in view of the extreme complexity of the tasks the World Bank faces. Within the context of development co-operation the word 'optimal' to a large extent even defies definition. All that can be strived for is the possible results.

A very important aid in this respect was the World Bank's setting up, some 10 years ago, of an institutionalised process for the evaluation of the overall results of its work.

The evaluation has already proved to be a powerful vehicle for detecting inadequacies in the World Bank's project orientated activities.[246] In particular, the variation in the quality of supervision in the most recent evaluation cycle has been highlighted. With regard to agricultural projects, for instance, previously indicated deficiencies seemed to have persisted: 'there was lack of staff continuity and balance in the expertise represented on supervision missions, the timing of the missions has not been optimal in relation to the emergence of problems, the focus of mission's concern in some cases appears to have been misplaced, and there has been insufficient follow up on certain project components . . . some cases of failure to achieve major project objectives in the present group could not have been rescued by improved supervision; there are, however, other projects where problems could have been mitigated and project results improved by a strong supervision effort.'[247] Similarly, after noting the great value of supervision with regard to educational projects, it was concluded that 'some of the supervision problems noted in the previous Reviews did recur in this group, including (a) insufficient use of educators on supervision, (b) lack of continuity, (c) absence of country visits during crucial phases of implementation, and (d) insufficient assistance during early stages of implementation.'[248]

Discoveries of defects like these and other shortcomings in the way instruments of review are employed in practice enable the World Bank to eliminate bottlenecks in the supervisory process and thus increase the chance of the successful completion of projects.

2.4.5. Instruments of correction of World Bank supervision

The instruments of correction of World Bank supervision are as follows: In addition to the *ultima remedia* of suspension of membership or even expulsion from the organisation, which are provided for in the Articles of Agreement,[249] the loan documents give the World Bank the right to suspend or cancel the loan or the credit if the borrower does not meet his obligations.[250] All these are measures taken as a last resort and are not usually employed in practice,[251] but they can have a strong deterrent effect.

Less coercive and more co-operative elements undoubtedly also play a role. Correction does not depend completely on measures with the character of sanctions. The numerous contacts the World Bank maintains with borrowers offer ample opportunity to exercise the correction function. Strictly speaking, an exchange of views between the World Bank and one of its clients is not as instrument of correction, but obviously it may very well result in corrective behaviour deemed necessary because of violation of the loan documents or to prevent such behaviour. Actually, it is impossible to classify the various instruments of World Bank supervision neatly into the categories of review, correction or creation. Most of them have aspects of all three functions. A visiting mission, for instance, is likely to serve the review, the correction as well as the creative function. Consequently a good deal of the World Bank's corrective action does not take the form of sanctions but is more or less part of – and one might add, concealed in – its review and creative activities.

As noted above, the World Bank's supervision is basically intended to serve two goals: first, to have the borrower pay back the funds made available by the World Bank, and secondly, to realise the developmental objectives of the project.[252] As far as the first goal is concerned, it is important that the obligations regarding the repayment of the loan or credit are concrete and very clear. The way in which the debt has to be repaid is set out in the loan documents, usually in an amortisation schedule annexed to them. The provisions of such a schedule are generally very simple. Whether or not these provisions have been violated can be readily determined; there is very little scope for differing interpretations. This clarity of the obligations regarding repayment forces the borrower to meet them scrupulously and therefore has a strong deterrent effect on potential violations. It adds to the effectiveness of the World Bank's supervision, and is one of the reasons for the World Bank not having to write off a single loan during more than 30 years of lending.

Other major incentives for developing countries to maintain impeccable financial relationships with the World Bank are summarised in a statement of its Vice-President and Treasurer: 'In the event of a default, no further disbursement would be made on that loan or any other loan we had outstanding in the country. And, no new loans would be committed until the default had been cured. Borrowers know our policies in this regard, and given the substantial amount of our undisbursed loans, I suggest they would be extremely reluctant to take steps to jeopardise the transfer of future resources. A default to the Bank also carries serious consequences that would affect the credit of the country involved, both with other countries and with commercial suppliers of resources. If, for example, principal or interest payments on loans are even thirty days late, the Executive Directors representing all 131 member governments are formally notified of the delinquency.'[253]

Obviously, this goes far beyond the mere 'mobilisation of shame' which forms the basis of their supervision's effectiveness for most international organisations. The World Bank can mobilise instruments which have an effect not only on a country's honour or prestige, but directly affecting its international economic relations. The fact that the World Bank can offer or withhold funds and services which the developing countries are usually eager to get, permeates the whole character of its supervision. It also influences the second objective of World Bank supervision, the realisation of developmental goals.

In this respect the obligations on the part of the borrower will sometimes present more difficulties in that their content is open to varying interpretations. Certainly the provisions of the loan documents are usually fairly concrete and clear. Moreover, after the conclusion of the loan documents the World Bank has at its disposal the specific instruments of correction provided for by those documents. It is in particular during the period preceding the conclusion of the loan documents that its generally strong position, derived from the fact that it is a lending institution, seems most relevant.

In this connection reference is usually made to the 'leverage' of the World Bank. Generally, leverage denotes the exercise of influence by the lender to persuade or induce the borrower to do something he would not otherwise have done as a condition of receiving a loan or a credit.[254] World Bank leverage usually takes the form of conditions posed by the organisation which the borrower has to satisfy in order to obtain the loan or the credit. Such conditions may concern the project itself or, more generally, the sector in which the project is situated or even the national economy.[255]

It is hardly possible to generalise about the effectiveness of the World Bank's leverage. A great deal depends on the particular circumstances of each case. Broadly speaking, three factors determine the degree of effectiveness: the nature of what the Bank has to offer, the eagerness on the part of the borrower to obtain that offer and the 'price' that has to be paid for it. It was noted above that the first two factors permeate the supervision of the World Bank, and their importance needs no further explanation. The third factor is the degree to which a country has to adapt its economic policy in order to satisfy the World Bank or, in more neutral terms, the gap between what the World Bank, on the one hand, and the prospective borrower on the other, considers to be a desirable economic policy. It is clear that the smaller the gap, the more effective the leverage of the World Bank will be or rather, the less the leverage that needs to be exercised. It is therefore very important that the World Bank tries to come to terms with prospective borrowers on these matters as early as possible in the project cycle. The evaluation of the World Bank has proved that particularly in this respect supervision has a number of defects. These are concerned mainly with the creative function of supervision, which will be dealt with below.

2.4.6 Instruments of creation of World Bank supervision

2.4.6.1. Delimitation of the creative function of World Bank supervision

The dividing line between the review and correction function on the one hand, and the creative function on the other, is rather thin. All three involve interpretation, but the creative function may go beyond mere interpretation and take on law-making characteristics with varying degrees of strength. It is usually a reliable indication that the line between review/correction and creation is being crossed when the consent or consensus with regard to substantive rules becomes more relevant for the effectiveness of supervision, than the adequacy of procedural rules.[256]

In other words, the adequacy of the rules concerned is of particular importance with regard to the effectiveness of review and, to a lesser extent, of correction, while consent or consensus plays a larger role with respect to the effectiveness of creation. It is even harder to distinguish clearly between the creative function and law-making or policy-making in the proper sense of that term. The effective exercise of both types of activity is to a large extent dependent upon the consensus factor, *i.e.* the political cohesion of the organisation concerned. Similarly, the main instrument of the creative function, *i.e.* the political discussion in the policy-making organ,[257] is also very important with regard to law-making or policy-making. In the case of the World Bank the general policy is outlined by the Board of Governors *c.q.* the Executive Directors. It is in these organs that the broad political discussion between the Member States takes place. Clearly, some of this discussion cannot be considered to belong to the supervisory activities of the World Bank. At a certain point the bounds of the creative function are overstepped and the discussion assumes the character of law making, or rather policy making, in the proper sense of that term.

As noted above, however, it is far from easy to know exactly where to draw the line. In addition, a good deal of the more concrete aspects of the World Bank's policy is being formulated at the project level via the contacts between individual borrowers and the staff. The creative function of supervision at this level can be said to intervene at both ends of the project cycle, *i.e.* in the very beginning during the identification and preparation phase and at the very end during the stage of evaluation. The information gathered through evaluation is fed back into the identification and preparation of following projects. If the preceding and the follow-up project (or projects) concern the same country, and if the information gathered from the former is used directly for the latter, this can be considered to be the exercise of the creative function. For, although such successive projects are based upon separate legal obligations in a formal sense, they are closely connected from a functional point of view. Once again it should be emphasised that this results from the fact that the World Bank's relationship with its client States usually takes the form of a longer term lending programme consisting of several loans.[258] On the other hand, the experience resulting from evaluation is also channelled to the Executive Directors,[259] and is consequently also used as an instrument in support of law making or policy making in general. This complicates the problem of drawing a line between creating and policy making to an even greater extent because this line is often blurred, particularly at the level of the Directors.

It seems that it is the consensus factor rather than the adequacy of World Bank supervision which can be most easily improved. The impact of insufficient consent or consensus will be discussed in the following section in relation to a number of important issues of the World Bank's work. As the consensus factor influences both creation and law making or policy making, it is therefore necessary within the framework of the present study to attempt to distinguish between those activities. For the purpose of this study the distinction will be made along the following lines: policy can be said to be involved when the economic philosophy underlying the World Bank's activities comes into play, *i.e.* when that philosophy is discussed, tested, reconsidered and eventually changed. Exercise of the creative function will be used to mean the adaptation of the World Bank's activities in a certain

461

direction within the framework of the existing policy or philosophy, *i.e.* when changes or proposed changes are concerned with the manner in which the policy is conducted. In addition, it is sometimes helpful to ask the question whether the change or adaptation affects all the World Bank's recipient States in general or is applicable only to one particular country. Law making or policy making concerns all Member States, while the exercise of the creative function of supervision is usually directed to a single State. Once again it is important to avoid too rigid an application of this distinction. If, as a result of evaluation of an older project, certain defects can be remedied in a newer project in the same country, this experience is likely to be used for the benefit of other countries as well. Nevertheless, the above would seem to be a sufficient reason to keep apart the creative function and law making or policy making in the following discussion of the consensus factor.

2.4.6.2. The consensus factor

It has been repeatedly emphasised above that the consensus factor plays a crucial role with respect to the creative function of World Bank supervision. The World Bank's most recent evaluation cycle reveals a number of aspects of that work which had unsatisfactory results because of consensus related problems. This is particularly evident with regard to two very important aspects of the World Bank's work, *viz.* institution-building and sector environment. The evaluation of the World Bank does not recognise insufficient consensus or a total lack of consensus as the root of these problems in all cases. Nevertheless, there seems to be a definite link between the poor results in these areas and the degree of consensus with respect to them. Consequently, as we will attempt to demonstrate below, improvements could result from efforts to strengthen consensus in these fields.

A. Institution-building. The World Bank considers institution-building to be one of its predominant objectives.[260] The work involved in institution-building can be classified in four categories: (i) establishment of new institutions; (ii) new project units in existing departments; (iii) reorganisation of existing institutions; and (iv) strengthening the organisational, managerial, financial and training capabilities of existing institutions.[261]

The success of institution-building has been mixed over the past few years. According to the 1979 Review some 44 per cent. of the efforts achieved substantial success in reaching agreed objectives, around 33 per cent. were partially successful, and in 22 per cent. of the cases the results were judged to have been negligible.[262] The reasons given for failure are 'lack of commitment and support on the part of the borrowers, and persistent differences between the Bank, the borrowers and expatriate consultants on institutional objectives and the means of reaching them'. In a few cases borrower support declined during the course of project implementation for reasons beyond the control of the World Bank. In the majority of cases, however, 'borrower commitment to proposed institutional design was uncertain from the very beginning, and there were reservations about the association and role of expatriate experts'.[263]

In order to remedy this kind of defect the World Bank has proposed developing an institutional profile of the sector and a time-phased programme for action in co-operation with the borrower. In broad terms this profile should define existing capabilities in a given sector and identify its needs. The interim requirements of expatriate consultants could be determined on this basis, as well as the need for change and improvements that would have to be implemented in the course of time in a training programme. In this way the profile could serve as a frame of reference for strengthening domestic capabilities in a given sector over a period of time. In addition, the World Bank hopes to overcome political resistance to expatriate experts and to enlist the borrower's commitment to an agreed institutional effort[264] making the development of this profile a joint exercise. In proposing to draw up a profile jointly with the borrower, the World Bank has not yet made it clear what the precise character of this co-operation will be. What is clear from the outset, however, is that the success or failure of the approach depends on whether it is really going to be a joint undertaking. The best way to make sure that the borrower continues to support the institutional goals of a project is genuinely to take his views into consideration when these goals are being formulated. Therefore, the development of institutional profiles should be entrusted to some kind of joint commission consisting of representatives of the World Bank and the borrower with a process of decision-making which ensures full borrower participation.

B. *Sector environment* With regard to sector environment similar problems were encountered to those facing institution-building. Here too, the major defect consisted of the policy environment created by the borrowing country conflicting with project objectives. In this case an effort to relate sector and project objectives more closely was recently initiated by an increased use of so-called country sector memoranda. These are intended to provide a brief synthesis of sector knowledge and to summarise the World Bank's strategy in the sector in terms of policies and projects.[265] Some success might be expected from this, as sector analysis does seem to have been neglected to some extent in the past. Apparently, this lack of sector emphasis was partly due to the organisational structure of the World Bank, in which area departments concentrated on macro-economic aspects, while the project departments focused on problems at the project level.[266]

It seems doubtful, however, whether increased attention on sector environment as proposed by the World Bank, will suffice. Relying on these country sector memoranda does not necessarily guarantee that the root of the problems concerning sector environment is really tackled. The country sector memoranda which are drawn up by the World Bank on its own are only the first step. They summarise sector knowledge and World Bank sector strategy. On that basis bottlenecks can be detected. In order to remedy inadequate sector environment, however, this has to be followed up by some kind of action which is aimed at ensuring that the country concerned recognises the defects and undertakes to redirect its sector policies along the lines agreed upon by the World Bank and the country concerned. As in the case of institution-building, this could be achieved through the establishment of a commission consisting of representatives of the World Bank and the particular borrowing country.

2.4.6.3. The growing importance of consensus

The above demonstrates that consensus plays a crucial role, particularly where the creative function of supervision is concerned. Moreover, it is likely that this will be even more the case in the future. This conclusion is prompted by two more or less contradictory tendencies which are now apparent.

On the one hand, there is a tendency for the World Bank to become more deeply involved even in those phases of the project cycle which it considers to be the responsibility of the borrower. This tendency is particularly apparent with respect to project preparation and design. At the moment a very high proportion of projects are changed during implementation. According to the 1979 Annual Review of the projects with a clearly defined physical content, 61 per cent. had to be changed during implementation.[267] The cost and time overruns were equally considerable. Of those projects for which costs estimates had been made about 33 per cent. showed cost overruns of 25 per cent. or more.[268] Similarly, 60 per cent. of the projects for which physical completion could be easily estimated, required over 25 per cent. more time than estimated.[269] While it is acknowledged that such project modifications and related costs and time overruns in certain cases represent flexibility in response to changing circumstances, a recurring element in evaluation is that some of them must be attributed to insufficient preparation and design.[270]

In the description of the preparation phase of the project cycle it was pointed out that over the years the World Bank has increasingly become involved in the preparation of projects as a result of the inability of developing countries to suggest a sufficient number of suitable projects themselves.[271] The recently detected deficiencies in the preparation of projects seems to increase the likelihood of even stronger World Bank participation in the early stages of the project cycle. At the moment the World Bank adopts a more limited role in this respect; changes in projects should be remedied by a more rigorous review of proposed changes and a study to identify their causes.[272] This reluctance can be explained by the emphasis which the World Bank also places on appropriate role assignment between itself, the borrower and consultants throughout the project cycle so as to improve the local ability to prepare and manage projects.[273] If the World Bank played a dominant role in the preparation of projects, this would certainly have negative effects on institution building.

Nevertheless, for yet another reason it seems inevitable that the World Bank will become more deeply involved. During the early 1970s the World Bank initiated a new policy aimed at combating absolute poverty in developing countries. By now this new policy is firmly established and its consequences are already clearly apparent.[274] It will have an even more dramatic impact at the project level in years to come. It is to be expected that an increasing percentage of projects will consist of 'new style' projects in which the so-called distributional effects play a major role. These 'new style' projects in several respects present difficulties which are not found in the more traditional ones. Obviously the reason for this is that the former projects are much more ambitious in that they are designed to benefit the very poor sections of the population. In short, the success of such projects depends to a greater extent on the environment in which the project is located.

The various aspects of this project environment are very difficult to grasp. It usually requires sophisticated analysis to understand them and thorough scientific research to determine their impact on projects, and to devise remedies to neutralise their potential negative consequences. For many developing countries this is too difficult simply because they lack the resources to perform the task. Thus, as a result, there will be a growing need for World Bank assistance in this respect.

At the same time the policy shift of the World Bank has encouraged the second of the two tendencies mentioned above. The fact that the success of the new type of projects depends more on sector environment will place a heavier emphasis on borrower policies in the future. If these are not fully compatible with the objectives of the project, it stands little chance of successful completion. In order to prevent borrowing countries from conducting policies which conflict with project objectives it is necessary to acquire the wholehearted consent of the borrower with respect to the project objectives. In other words, deeper involvement on the part of the World Bank in these aspects of the project work has to be matched by increased participation in the whole process on the part of the borrowing country concerned. The new type of projects require that full borrower support with regard to the whole process is enlisted to an even greater extent than the traditional projects did. If this support is absent, deeper involvement on the part of the World Bank can at best result in a kind of 'take-over' by the latter which would in any case be doomed to failure.

In terms of the instruments of the creative function of World Bank supervision employed in the present study, this creative function can only be exercised effectively through a process of decision-making in which all relevant parties can fully participate. With respect to the World Bank's project work the borrowing countries are obviously parties.

The above presupposes that borrowing countries are at least prepared to conduct policies directed at combating absolute poverty even though they may not be able to implement them. There is also a category of countries, however, which simply refuse to conduct these policies because they attach no great value to combating poverty. Obviously, it is important to distinguish between these two categories. In the case of disinterested countries the achievement of World Bank objectives stands little chance of success or rather depends on the leverage which the World Bank is able to exercise with regard to them.[275] The suggestions for improving the effectiveness of the World Bank's creative function which will be discussed in the following sections are, therefore, mainly relevant to the first-mentioned category of countries because they are actually aimed at generating a sufficient degree of consensus. Obviously it is hardly possible to arrive at such a consensus if there is disagreement about the basic question of what the ultimate goal of a policy should be and not merely about the way of how to realise the agreed upon goal. Nevertheless, the suggestions referred to might have an impact even on the second category of cases. These suggestions are all aimed at building consensus between the World Bank and its borrowers by a deeper involvement of the latter in the work of the former. This deeper involvement could also have an effect in cases where a country is unwilling to accept the goals of the World Bank and where these goals could therefore only be attained through leverage if they could be attained at all. First, genuine participation of the developing countries would make the leverage of the World Bank more justifiable. If developing countries are allowed to contribute more to the formulation of World Bank policies, they have less reason to consider pressure from the organisation to conform with such policies as outside interference. Secondly, the very fact that developing countries could genuinely participate in the work of the World Bank implies that their policies will come closer to those desired by the World Bank. As a result the leverage of the latter can be more effective, or rather, is less necessary because the gap between what the World Bank wants and what the borrower is prepared to do becomes smaller.[276]

In this light the suggestions which will be discussed below might produce some positive results even with respect to cases of Bank/borrower relationships which are the least promising.

2.4.6.4. The effectiveness of the creative function; some suggestions for improvement

A. Introduction

There are three basic areas in which steps could be taken to further consensus building in Bank/borrower relationship and thus enhance the effectiveness of the creative function of World Bank supervision. First, changes could be brought about in the World Bank's policy making or decision making structure as such; *i.e.* in the composition and/or voting procedure of the Board of Governors and the Executive Directors. Secondly, changes in the composition and the organisation of the World Bank staff could have a beneficial effect in this respect as the staff, apart from its comparatively large influence on the formulation of World Bank general policy, obviously plays a decisive role with regard to the day-to-day application of general policy lines. Thirdly, the World Bank's 'bilateral' relations with its individual borrowers seems ripe for improvement, particularly at the level of the various stages of the project cycle.

The three areas mentioned above will be discussed in some detail below. To some extent they overlap, particularly the second and the third areas. On the other hand, there are some differences. Changes with regard to the decision/policy making structure of the World Bank would obviously be more far-reaching than those in the other two areas. The first mentioned changes would not be confined to the creative function of supervision but their effects would also extend to the more legislative aspects of the World Bank's work, *i.e.* policy making *per se*. Changes in the policy making structure would also be more effective with respect to consensus building than those in the other two areas. At the same time, however, the first mentioned changes would require the amendment of the Articles of Agreement and their political realisation is considerably less easily accomplished than in the case of the others.

B. Changes in the decision making structure of the World Bank

The simplest way to achieve improved consensus within the framework of the World Bank would be to allow the developing countries greater participation in the World Bank's policy making process, *i.e.* to give them a larger number of votes in the Board of Governors and the Executive Directors. Obviously the policy making organs offer the best opportunities for achieving a real consensus. Changes in that area would not only have a material effect in that developing countries would be allowed to have a greater influence on the World Bank's policy, but there would probably also be a psychological effect in that they would feel more like real participants in the whole process. At present, policy is to a large extent 'imposed' on them. As a result of the provisions concerning the voting procedure within the framework of the World Bank,[277] the policy making organs are dominated by the developed countries. At this moment the rich Member States of the Bank[278] possess 63.82 per cent. of the votes while the poor countries have 36.18 per cent. In the case of the IDA the total voting power of the rich and the poor countries is 63.36 per cent. and 36.64 per cent. respectively.[279]

The results of this policy making process which is dominated by the rich countries, are injected into the project cycle by means of the criteria which the World Bank uses to appraise proposed projects.[280] In this sense this appraisal could also be said to have 'executive' aspects.[281] It was also noted that appraisal is best conducted by an independent organ; *i.e.* an organ in which the borrower's interests are not directly represented; this, however, is on the condition that the situation is balanced by genuine borrower participation at the 'legislative' level, *i.e.* within the policy making organs. Within the framework of the World Bank this is not the case.

In response to the situation described above, several proposals have been advanced in recent years to give the developing countries more votes in the World Bank's policy making organs.[282] Although some slight improvement in favour of the developing countries has become apparent during recent years, the ratio in voting power between rich and poor countries has not basically changed since the founding of the Bank and the IDA, despite the fact that the number of developing members has increased dramatically. As far as the Bank is concerned the *status quo* has been more or less maintained because the growing number of developing members has been balanced by an increase in the number of votes for the developed Member States resulting from their additional contributions to the capital of the Bank. As the process of decolonisation can be considered to be over, there is a danger that this ratio will grow more disproportionate to the detriment of the developing countries, because in the future additional contributions are still likely to come mainly from the developed countries.[283] Within the framework of the IDA the situation has remained largely unchanged, because the link between the amount of the contribution to the IDA and the number of votes has actually been abandoned at least to some extent, as a result of the above mentioned distinction between additional subscriptions and supplementary resources.[284] The present distribution of votes between rich and poor countries within the framework of the World Bank obviously results frrom the fact that the weighting of votes is based almost entirely on the contributions of the Member States to the capital of the organisations. Only a very small proportion is awarded on the basis of the principle of equality, in the case of the Bank 10.00 per cent.[285] (250 votes for each State), in the case of the IDA 1.72 per cent.[286] (599 votes for each State).

A proposal has been put forward to increase dramatically the percentage of these initial votes (the number of which is equal for every Member State).[287] The higher the percentage of these votes, the more the voting procedure within the World Bank would resemble a one state/one vote system. This would certainly be one way to remedy the present unequal division of power in the World Bank. On the other hand, developments in this direction seem undesirable because they would not result in a fair representation of the various interests involved. While in the present situation differences in interests between Member States are overemphasised, a distribution of a large number of votes on the basis of equality would ignore these differences, which are actually very relevant for the functioning of the World Bank. The World Bank is an institution for development finance and as such there are two major distinct types of interests concerning its Member States. On the one hand, there are obviously the donor countries which provide the funds for the organisation's operations and which will naturally want to exercise control over the way these funds are used. However, the amount of a state's financial contribution is not the only interest at stake. Equally important within the framework of a development finance institution is the fact that the recipient countries are in need of World Bank assistance. This need of assistance should therefore be given adequate weight in the distribution of votes.

Consequently, it would not seem at all unreasonable to split the votes between donor and recipient countries on a 50:50 basis.[288] This system would acknowledge the fact that both interests mentioned are of equal importance within the framework of the World Bank. Within each group votes should be awarded on the basis of criteria which are an elaboration of the interest constitutive of the group; *i.e.* in the case of the donor countries the financial contribution, and in the case of the recipient countries, mainly the degree to which they need assistance.

As far as the donor countries are concerned, the present situation in which the number of votes depends on the amount of a State's financial contribution, could be maintained.[289] The amount of each State's financial contribution has to be calculated on the basis of its 'capacity to pay' which in its turn is to be determined on the basis of a number of criteria indicating a donor country's economic strength. It is common knowledge that the total amount of development assistance as well as the amount of the contribution of each individual donor country, the so-called burden sharing, have become very controversial issues over the past decade.

The distribution of votes within the group of recipient countries is probably more problematic because of the difficulty in defining sufficiently clear criteria which adequately express the degree to which the various developing countries are in need of World Bank assistance. If the decision was made to enlarge the developing countries' share in the total voting power, these countries should obviously be allowed to decide how they want to distribute amongst' themselves the votes assigned to them. A number of criteria immediately spring to mind in this respect.

First of all, the degree to which a country needs World Bank assistance is obviously reflected in its poverty level. This is probably best expressed in a country's Gross National Product *per capita* (*per capita* income). The World Bank distinguishes between so-called middle income countries (*per capita* income between \$500 and \$1,999), poor countries (*per capita* income between \$200 and \$499) and very poor countries (*per capita* income less than \$200).[290] Some of the votes allocated to the developing countries could be divided on the basis of this distinction according to the following ratio: 3 for the group of very poor countries, 2 for the group of poor countries, and 1 for the middle income countries. This ratio would reflect the idea that Member States are entitled to more votes as they are poorer. Within each group votes could be distributed on the basis of the size of the population.

The size of the population should also be used to determine the allocation of another portion of the votes among developing countries in order to rectify imbalances which would result from distributing all the votes on the basis of *per capita* income in the way described above. Furthermore, this would express the idea of the equality of the world's people. Finally, even the criterion of the amount of the financial contribution could be considered to play a role in this respect, although at first sight this might not seem a very suitable basis for the distribution of votes between developing countries. It should be remembered, however, that developing countries cannot all be considered in the same light. On the contrary, there are far-reaching differences between them, and the 'richer' developing countries not infrequently have more in common with the developed countries than with the poorest countries. It is therefore reasonable that such countries should provide a proportional financial contribution in accordance with their capacity to pay. In this respect it would probably be an additional incentive if a part of the votes for the developing countries were awarded on the basis of the amount of their financial contributions.

The above observations are only a few examples of the way in which a

469

more equitable distribution of power, and consequently a more genuine partnership, could be realised within the framework of the World Bank. These and other such formulae all have one thing in common: their realisation is in fact dependent upon the political will of the rich developed countries which are members of the World Bank. Changes such as those advocated above would require the amendment of the Articles of Agreement. For proposed amendments to become effective, acceptance by three-fifths of the members, having four-fifths of the total voting power is required (Article VIII(a) Bank, Article IX(a) IDA). As a result of the present distribution of votes, the United States alone or the United Kingdom, the Federal Republic of Germany and Japan together are in the position to block proposed amendments.[291]

The chances of realising proposals such as those mentioned above seem very slim at the moment. In the present situation, characterised by economic recession, it is difficult even to maintain the flow of development assistance from the developed countries at a sufficient level to sustain the lending programme envisaged by the World Bank.[292] It is therefore very unlikely that in the near future the developed countries would be prepared to renounce part of their control over the policies of the World Bank in favour of the developing countries, and at the same time provide funds at a level equivalent or superior to the present one.

C. Changes in the composition and organisation of the World Bank staff

(a) Composition The World Bank has always been dominated by the West.[293] This not only applies to the voting power within the organisation as described in the preceding paragraph, but also with respect to the recruiting policy for staff members. Traditionally the geographical distribution of the World Bank staff favoured the developed countries.[294] In 1971, for instance, more than 75 per cent. was recruited from the so-called Part I countries and Switzerland.[295] In 1975 developing country nationals constituted 29.2 per cent. of the total, while in 1980 this figure rose to 33 per cent.[296] Compared to the situation ten years ago this is still only a very marginal improvement. As far as the high level positions are concerned the situation is even worse. During the early 1970s 85 per cent. of them were occupied by nationals of rich Member States.[297] In 1978, only eleven of the sixty-five principal officers of the World Bank were nationals of developing countries.[298]

Even if, for one reason or another, this imbalance in representation of the World Bank staff could be justified in the past, this is no longer the case. The World Bank's original point of view used to be that the Western blueprint for economic development was applicable to all situations and all countries. As a result it was thought that in all cases problems could be solved by employing classical methods. The World Bank simply knew better and the best people to put this philosophy into practice were obviously the experts from the rich countries.

However, the nature of the World Bank's work has changed dramatically since it has become oriented towards combating absolute poverty in the developing world. This policy shift and the ensuing new style projects have

470

confronted the World Bank with new kinds of problems which very often require unorthodox solutions. These changes should be reflected in the recruitment of staff members. It is very likely that alternative solutions to cope with the new problems might come from people from the developing countries themselves, as they are probably most familiar with the local circumstances which have an increasing impact on World Bank financed projects. A more diversified recruitment policy becomes even more important when it is realised that, 'development knowledge is not simply a stock with transferable properties'[229] and that, 'innovation and learning should be the main characteristics of a development agency'.[300]

In addition to considerations of expertise, political/psychological arguments also lend support to the practice of including a larger percentage of people from developing countries in the World Bank staff. The contacts between the World Bank and the borrowing countries, particularly in the case of negotiations concerning a loan, can be expected to be more harmonious when the World Bank's team includes people who generate trust with the other side because they are considered to be in touch with the particular situation in the country concerned, than when the World Bank is represented by people who are regarded as 'outsiders', at least by the negotiation partner. This area of the Bank/borrower relationship, which is often referred to as development diplomacy, is very sensitive. According to Mason and Asher: 'To the less developed world, the Bank often seems arrogant, remote and demanding. Some of its own staff as well as outsiders believe that more training in the diplomacy of development would be helpful.'[301] Although by itself it is not sufficient, the participation of a larger number of people from developing countries in the activities of the World Bank is likely to enhance the effectiveness of its development diplomacy.

The above does not imply that for positions on the World Bank staff, every non-Westerner is preferable to every Westerner. Obviously, persons from the Third World can be insensitive to the social and political problems of developing countries and therefore be less inclined to support or even accept the necessary changes.[302] It is clear that the World Bank should try to recruit those who have a different attitude with regard to these problems. This is admittedly not an easy task, given the political situation in many developing countries.

Finally, it should be borne in mind that the representation of people from the Third World on a larger scale can also have its negative side. People from developing countries qualified to serve on the World Bank staff are undoubtedly also needed very badly in their own countries. It would, therefore, not be in the interest of those countries, nor would it serve the purpose of the World Bank in the long run, if its recruiting activities in the developing countries were to result in a brain drain. The best solution would probably be to set up a kind of 'exchange programme' in which a position with the World Bank would be somehow integrated with a career in the employee's country of origin. This arrangement could be beneficial to both the World Bank and the developing countries. For the World Bank primarily because this integration would probably result in more qualified persons being prepared to join the World Bank for a certain period of time. Secondly, because the World Bank would always have a number of people on its staff who were very close to the local situation. As far as the developing countries are concerned, the idea could be attractive because it would provide a number of their own people with important international experience in a field connected with their vital interests.[303]

(b) Organisation Organisational issues connected with the activities of the World Bank staff are manifold.[304] They cannot all be dealt with in the present study. One, however, should be singled out here because it is particularly relevant to the Bank/borrower relationship. This is the question of the decentralisation of the activities of the World Bank, because it would literally bring the World Bank closer to the borrowing countries and its project work there. The World Bank has always been and still is a highly centralised institution. The Articles of Agreement clearly anticipated decentralisation of the World Bank's activities,[305] but this has never materialised. At present the World Bank's professional staff comprises about 2,400 persons, of whom over 95 per cent. are employed at the Washington headquarters.[306] It has established three regional missions and twenty-seven resident missions.[307] Most of these, however, are very small and consequently their functions and powers are limited.[308]

It is high time for the World Bank to decentralise its activities further. This would mean a larger number of resident missions which would have to be better equipped, both with respect to the number of their staff, as well as from the point of view of the functions and powers delegated, than they usually are now. Both the organisation itself and the borrowing countries would benefit greatly if the decentralisation were conducted in the proper manner. Generally speaking, the advantage for the World Bank would be a greater physical proximity to and a better knowledge of those factors which primarily determine the success or failure of its projects.

It seems important for the World Bank to reduce the distance between itself and the location of projects, particularly as the new style projects resulting from its anti-poverty policy require even more data on local circumstances.[309] Well-equipped resident missions could play a valuable role in supervision in general.[310] More specifically they could see to the quality of the creative function of World Bank supervision, for instance by serving as a source of information for the purpose of project identification and pre-paration.[311] Obviously all this cannot be achieved even by frequently sending visiting missions to borrowing countries. It goes without saying that the picture obtained in that way is not nearly as complete as when information is gathered through permanently stationed representatives.

Any major reorganisation as envisaged above automatically entails a number of difficulties,[312] but those involved in decentralisation of World Bank activities are not insuperable. The success or failure of a resident mission mainly depends upon two factors which are closely interrelated: its effectiveness within the World Bank system and its acceptability for the host country.

To be effective a mission should have sufficient strength *vis-à-vis* the World Bank. The size of its staff should not be too small. As far as possible functions and real powers should be granted to the mission. Far-reaching decision making powers could be delegated to a mission, particularly with respect to supervision and project identification and preparation. The delegation should be genuine. Decisions falling within the scope of a mission should be left to that mission and not be reversed at higher levels of the hierarchy. This would not only demotivate the mission itself but would also breed mistrust on the part of the host country. For the host country too, can have a stake in the resident mission's effectiveness. This brings us to the question of acceptability.

Some developing countries might not want to host a resident mission at all. In general, however, a great deal will depend on the character of the mission. Developing countries are not likely to be prepared to tolerate missions which they consider to be no more than intruders and watchdogs in their internal affairs. The skills of the mission's staff in what is called development diplomacy are decisive in this respect. If the staff is able to have to a real dialogue with the host country, the acceptability of its activities will increase. If the host country is kept fully informed about the mission's activities and is even invited to somehow participate in its work, the contracts between the Bank and its borrowers are obviously facilitated. At any rate the borrower is given a channel through which he can inform the World Bank about his own points of view. Similarly, it might provide opportunities for borrowers to influence certain aspects of the World Bank's policy indirectly. All this could create not only acceptability, but even an interest on the part of the host country for the mission to have a strong position *vis-à-vis* the World Bank itself. In short, one of the most important advantages of resident missions could be to serve as a tool to build consensus in Bank/borrower relationships.

D. 'Bilateral' aspects of Bank/borrower relations

It was more or less assumed above that an eventual decentralisation of the World Bank's activities would take the shape of a larger number of resident missions. A resident mission is a bilateral affair between the World Bank and a particular borrowing country, which could in principle handle all business of mutual interest. However, in addition to resident missions there seems to be room for improving bilateral relations, certainly with regard to some countries.[313] As noted above, the World Bank's relationship with many of its client States is a continuous one in the sense that a loan is usually part of a lending programme for a particular country covering a longer period of time.[314] In such cases there seems to be an excellent basis on which to build a further-reaching integration between the efforts concerning projects on the part of the World Bank and those of the borrowing country.

It has already been said that institutional profiles as proposed by the World Bank could best be drawn up by a joint commission consisting of members of the World Bank staff and representatives of the borrowing country concerned.[315] The role of such commissions could be broadened to encompass those aspects of the project work which require close co-operation between the parties in order to reach a genuine consensus. The analysis of the World Bank's project cycle showed that almost all of its phases are eligible for this close co-operation. Commissions like these could very well function alongside and interacting with eventual 'new style' resident missions such as those described above. While the latter could be particularly helpful with respect to identification, preparation, and the review and correction function of supervision, the former's role should concentrate on the creative function of supervision and project evaluation.

Joint commissions should be based in Washington. Their membership should be as permanent as possible in order to enhance the building of genuine consensus between the two sides.[316] At least as far as the borrowers are concerned membership will necessarily have to vary, depending upon the expertise necessary for the kind of project or subject matter under consideration. The element of continuity could be maintained by enabling borrowing countries to accredit a permanent representative at the World Bank headquarters. This representative could co-ordinate the activities of the various experts of his country. The importance of the physical proximity of borrowers to the World Bank's decision making process should not be underestimated. Due to the very strong position of the World Bank *vis-à-vis* its borrowers,[317] there is a permanent danger that it might misjudge the degree to which a borrower is genuinely consenting to the various aspects of a project. In a manner of speaking, many developing countries have their backs against the wall, as regards the World Bank. They badly need the funds the World Bank has to offer and can therefore be supposed to make concessions too easily in some cases, in the sense that they are not able or prepared to live up to them afterwards. As a result the World Bank's effectiveness might paradoxically turn out to be counter-productive in that there is the risk of being deceived by borrower's formal position. In such cases the formal consent of the borrower may later prove non-existent or at least not genuine enough. More or less permanent involvement of the borrower, particularly in those aspects of the project work which can be said to have a 'legislative' character, *viz.* the creative function of supervision, could possibly prevent such situations from arising.

Finally, the World Bank's system of evaluation potentially provides opportunities for consensus building. Essentially, evaluation is a learning process for the World Bank itself, in fact a very important one, because the lessons learned from it are fed back into the project cycle and into new projects, as well as being channelled into the policy making process in general.[318] For this learning process to be as effective as possible, it is very important that the project work is evaluated from the point of view of all sides participating in it. In this respect it is encouraging that Loan and Credit Agreements now reflect the agreement with borrowers that they prepare a project completion report when project implementation nears completion and that such reports are duly taken into account in the evaluation. Similarly, the incorporation of a monitoring and evaluation capacity in projects themselves has to be considered a step forward.[319]

However, the involvement of borrowing countries in the evaluation process seems ripe for improvement. According to the World Bank itself, evaluation requires both full independence from the management for greater credibility, and full integration into management for the most rapid assimilation of useful lessons.[320] For this reason most staff members of the Operations Evaluation Department are normally transferred from positions elsewhere in the World Bank and are usually fairly senior officials.[321] One very important aspect of the World Bank's project work is formed by the results as perceived by the borrowing countries themselves. This aspect should be adequately represented in the activities of the Operations Evaluation Department. As far as can be judged from the outside, the participation of borrowing countries in the evaluation seems to be limited to the Operations Evaluation Department, which welcomes a limited number of appropriate officials to work with it for defined periods of time.[322] This is not in proportion to the borrowing countries' influence on projects. Their participation should therefore be institutionalised in order to give full weight to this important dimension of the project work and thus to strengthen the World Bank's evaluation.

This institutionalisation could be linked to setting up the above-mentioned joint commissions. The accredited representative, which borrowing countries should be enabled to appoint in Washington,[323] could participate in the evaluation of his country's projects. Apart from the beneficial influence on the World Bank's evaluation itself, this could at the same time have advantages for the borrowing country. As the accredited representative is intended to act as a permanent liaison between the World Bank and his country, he can function as a channel through which the experiences gathered from the evaluation can be fed back effectively to the borrowing country concerned.

NOTES

1. The relationship between the three organisations has been very aptly described by E. Reid, *Strengthening the World Bank* (Chicago, 1973), p. 12: 'When it lends money at more or less conventional rates of interest on loans guaranteed by the government concerned, it calls itself the International Bank for Reconstruction and Development or World Bank, and lends from its World Bank account; when it lends interest-free money on loans guaranteed by the government, it calls itself the International Development Association and lends from its IDA account; when it invests money in private enterprises without government guarantee, it calls itself the International Finance Corporation and invests from its IFC account.'
2. In practice, however, the GATT has evolved into an international organisation. On the GATT, see Part II of this book.
3. For a detailed description of the history of the Bank, see R. Oliver, *International Economic Co-operation and the World Bank* (London, 1975). See also E. Mason and L. Asher, *The World Bank since Bretton Woods* (Washington D.C., 1973) Chapter 2. The negotiations concerning the provisions of the Articles of Agreement are analysed by H. Bitterman, 'Negotiations of the Articles of Agreement of the International Bank for Reconstruction and Development' (1971) 5 *The International Lawyer*, 59 *et seq.*
4. See R. Oliver, *op. cit.* (note 3), Chapter 3.
5. See H. Bitterman, *loc. cit.* (note 3), 63 *et seq.*
6. See *infra* pp. 411–412.
7. See R. Oliver, *op. cit.* (note 3), p. 174 *et seq.* This so-called 'boat draft' was based on a British plan of 1941 entitled 'Proposals for an International Clearing Union,' of which Keynes had been the *auctor intellectualis.*
8. The participating states were: Australia, Belgium, Bolivia, Brazil, Canada, Chile, China, Columbia, Costa Rica, Cuba, Czechoslovakia, Dominican Republic, Ecuador, Egypt, El Salvador, Ethiopia, France, Greece, Guatemala, Haïti, Honduras, Iceland, India, Iran, Iraq, Liberia, Luxembourg, Mexico, Netherlands, New Zealand, Nicaragua, Norway, Panama, Paraguay, Peru, Philippines, Poland, South Africa, the Soviet Union, the United Kingdom, the United States, Uruguay, Venezuela and Yugoslavia.
9. See R. Oliver, *op. cit.* (note 3), p. 183.
10. UNTS, p. 134 *et seq.* The Articles of Agreement of the International Monetary Fund entered into force at the same date; see 2 UNTS, p. 48 *et seq.*
11. For more details on these Development Finance Companies, which served and still serve more purposes than merely the evasion of government guarantees, see R. Diamond and W. Gulhati, 'Some Reflections on the World Bank's Experience with Development Finance Companies', *Economic and Political Weekly*, Vol. VIII, No. 23, (June 1973) pp. 47–56; see also the World Bank's publication: *Development Finance Companies, Sector Policy Paper* (Washington D.C., April 1976).
12. See for the history of the IFC, E. Mason and R. Asher, *op. cit.* (note 3), p. 345 *et seq.*
13. 264 UNTS, p. 117 *et seq.*
14. See for the history of the IDA, E. Mason and R. Asher, *op. cit.* (note 3), p. 380 *et seq.*
15. See for the specific differences between hard and soft loans within the framework of the World Bank, *infra*, p. 412.
16. However, the large US holdings of inconvertible local currencies which had such an important impact on the establishment of the IDA never played a role in its operations. The provision in the Articles of Agreement enabling the IDA to be a recipient of inconvertible currencies (Article III(2)(a)) has remained a dead letter. (See E. Mason and R. Asher, *op. cit.* (note 3), pp. 392–393.)
17. 439 UNTS, p. 249.
18. See H. Bitterman, *loc. cit.* (note 3), p. 70 *et seq.* and R. Oliver, *op. cit.* (note 3) p. 184 *et seq.*
19. See also Article III(1)(a) and (b).
20. On the reasons for the establishment of this link with the IMF, see R. Oliver, *op. cit.* (note 3), pp. 174–175 and 185.
21. See, for instance, Resolution No. 304 (September 16, 1976), *Summary Proceedings 1976*, p. 218 *et seq.* on the admission of the Comoros.
22. World Bank, *1949–1950 Annual Report*, p. 43.
23. World Bank, *1960–1961 Annual Report*, p. 9.
24. World Bank, *1965–1966 Annual Report*, p. 24.

25. World Bank, *1961–1962 Annual Report,* p. 8 and *1966–1967 Annual Report,* p. 20.
26. World Bank, *Summary proceedings 1953,* pp. 24–25.
27. World Bank, *1980 Annual Report,* p. 11.
28. See E. Mason and R. Asher, *op. cit.* (note 3), p. 138 *et seq.*
29. Non-aligned Yugoslavia is a member of the Bank and the IDA as well as the IFC.
30. See the Report of the Independent Commission on International Development Issues (hereinafter the Brandt Report) *North-South: A programme for survival* (MIT Press, 1980), p. 202.
31. World Bank, *1980 Annual Report,* p. 96.
32. *Ibidem,* p. 11.
33. *Ibidem,* p. 14.
34. World Bank, *1979 Annual Report,* p. 117.
35. World Bank, *1976 Annual Report,* pp. 7–8; subsequent Annual Reports, however, no longer mention the Third Window, which leads A. van de Laar, *The World Bank and the Poor* (1979), p. 30, to the conclusion that it 'appears to be closed'.
36. See *supra,* p. 407.
37. See *infra,* p. 410.
38. See *infra,* p. 410.
39. According to Article II(2)(6) the authorised capital may be increased by a three-fourths majority of the total voting power.
40. World Bank, *1977 Annual Report,* pp. 6–8.
41. World Bank, *1979 Annual Report,* pp. 10–11.
42. See E. Rotberg, *The World Bank: A Financial Appraisal* (World Bank, Washington D.C., 1978), p. 16.
43. Until 1976 this fund was called the 'Supplemental Reserve'; see World Bank, *1976 Annual Report,* Appendix G, Note B, p. 127.
44. World Bank, *1963–1964 Annual Report,* pp. 15–16.
45. World Bank, *1980 Annual Report,* Appendix G, Note E, p. 162.
46. *Ibidem,* Appendix A, p. 151.
47. *Ibidem,* pp. 85–86.
48. *Ibidem,* p. 151.
49. *Idem.*
50. E. Rotberg, *The World Bank's Borrowing Program: Some Questions and Answers* (Washington D.C., 1979), p. 1.
51. World Bank, *1980 Annual Report,* pp. 172–174.
52. World Bank, *1977 Annual Report,* p. 150 *et seq.*
53. *Ibidem,* p. 6 J° p. 155.
54. World Bank, *1979 Annual Report,* p. 119 and World Bank, *1980 Annual Report,* p. 88.
55. See *supra,* p. 410.
56. See the present Article III(b)(i).
57. see the present Article III(b).
58. International Finance Corporation, *1979 Annual Report,* p. 45.
59. *Ibidem,* p. 45.
60. See the publication of the World Bank: *International Development Association* (World Bank, Washington D.C., April 1978), p. 5.
61. The Bank's lending rate formula requires a positive spread of 0.5 per cent. between the cost of funds borrowed by the Bank, which is estimated for a 12 month period, using the actual cost of borrowing for the past six months and the estimated costs for the succeeding six months, and the interest rate charged on Bank loans to member countries; see World Bank, *1980 Annual Report,* p. 84.
62. *Ibidem,* p. 3.
63. World Bank, *1980 Annual Report,* p. 3.
64. World Bank, *1979 Annual Report,* p. 112.
65. International Finance Corporation, *1979 Annual Report,* p. 26.
66. World Bank, *1980 Annual Report,* pp. 172–174.
67. World Bank, *1979 Annual Report,* pp. 10–11.
68. World Bank, *1980 Annual Report,* pp. 172–174.
69. *Ibidem,* p. 197.
70. The Articles of Agreement mention the Advisory Council (Article V(6)) and the Loan Committees (Article V(7)). The Council was abolished in 1949 (see J. Morris, *The Road to Huddors-field, the story of the World Bank* (1963) p. 225). The Loan Committees' task consists of studying the merits of a proposed project and on that basis submitting a report containing a

recommendation regarding whether or not the Bank should guarantee, participate in or make a loan with regard to the project concerned (Article III(4)(iii)). Finally, in October 1974 the Bank and the IMF jointly created the so-called 'Development Committee' (see World Bank, *1977 Annual Report*, p. 14), whose task is to maintain a survey of the development process and to advise and report to the Board of Governors of the Bank and the Fund on all aspects of the broad questions of the transfer of real resources to the developing countries and to make suggestions for considerations by those concerned regarding the implementation of its conclusions (see Resolution no. 297, *Summary Proceedings 1974*, p. 179 *et seq.*

71. See *infra*, pp. 467–470.
72. See E. Mason and R. Asher, *op. cit.* (note 3), p. 192.
73. World Bank, *1977 Annual Report*, p. 4.
74. World Bank, *1980 Annual Report*, p. 8.
75. See Schonfield, 'The World Bank' in Luard (ed.), *The Evolution of International Organizations* (London, 1967), p. 234.
76. See R. S. McNamara, Address to the Board of Governors (Belgrade, Yugoslavia, October 2, 1979), p. 32.
77. World Bank, *1980 Annual Report*, p. 8.
78. World Bank, *Summary Proceedings 1972*, pp. 21–30.
79. See R. S. McNamara, *op. cit.* (note 76), p. 19.
80. See, for instance, World Bank, *Summary Proceedings 1972*, p. 34 and even more clearly World Bank, *1977 Annual Report*, p. 8, which reads: '. . . the Bank has found that the benefits of growth cannot be assumed to "trickle down" automatically . . .'; see also the World Bank, *World Development Report, 1980* (Oxford University Press, 1980), pp. 35–36.
81. See R. S. McNamara, *op. cit.* (note 76), pp. 19–20.
82. For trends in lending by sector see: World Bank, *1977 Annual Report*, p. 17 and World Bank, *1980 Annual Report*, p. 66.
83. See World Bank, *1980 Annual Report*, pp. 75–77 and 80–81.
84. The *World Development Report* 1981 estimates that in 1980 about 750 million people lived in absolute poverty in the developing world (excluding China), which amounts to about 33 per cent. of its population. Moreover, the projections for the year 2000 are not very favourable either. (See the World Bank, *World Development Report, 1981* (Washington D.C., 1981), pp. 16–18.)
85. See in particular: A. van de Laar, *The World Bank and the Poor* (1979).
86. World Bank, *1980 Annual Report*, p. 24.
87. See Part I of this book, p. 11.
88. See *supra*, pp. 406–407.
89. See Part I of this book, p. 11–14.
90. See *supra*, pp. 405–406.
91. See *supra*, p. 411.
92. See *supra*, pp. 409 and 411.
93. Whenever the Bank approaches its statutory lending limit, the expansion of the total volume of lending requires a capital increase. In the *Brandt Report* (note 28), p. 249, an alternative has been suggested: the ratio of 1:1 between the Bank's lending and its total capitalisation could be altered into a 2:1 ratio. There are no signs yet that this suggestion is going to be followed.
94. For a detailed account of the problems involved in replenishments of IDA funds see A. van de Laar, *op. cit.* (note 35), pp. 61–67.
95. On principles of burden-sharing, see *ibidem*, pp. 72–76.
96. *Ibidem*, p. 67.
97. World Bank, *1980 Annual Report*, p. 9.
98. A. van de Laar, *op. cit.* (note 35), p. 73.
99. See *infra*, pp. 428 *et seq.*
100. See the publication of the World Bank, *Operations Evaluation, World Bank Standards and Procedures* (2nd ed., Washington D.C., August 1979), p. 14.
101. The Articles of Agreement do not define the term "project." Projects financed by the World Bank vary greatly in size, character and complexity and it can safely be concluded that in practice no two projects are exactly the same. The World Bank, therefore, has taken the term very broadly as to mean (a proposal for) a capital investment to develop facilities to provide goods and services, See J. King, *Economic Development Projects and Their Appraisal* (Baltimore, 1967), p. 3.
102. See *supra*, pp. 415–417.
103. See on technical assistance and the different ways in which it is provided by the World Bank, E. Mason and R. Asher, *op. cit.* (note 3), Chapter 10.
104. See *supra*, p. 411.

105. See W. Baum, 'The World Bank project cycle', *Finance and Development* (Dec. 1978), pp. 2 *et seq.*
106. World Bank, *1977 Annual Report,* p. 10 juncto p. 17 and World Bank, *1980 Annual Report,* p. 66.
107. In this connection, see the narrow interpretation by the Executive Directors of this 'special circumstances-requirement,' World Bank, *1977 Annual Report,* p. 10.
108. See in particular, the *Brandt Report, op. cit.* (note 30), pp. 232-234 juncto pp. 274–275; see also E. Reid, *Strengthening the World Bank* (Chicago, 1973) p. 225; E. Mason and R. Asher, *op. cit.* (note 3), Chapter 9; and A. van de Laar, *op. cit.* (note 35), pp. 47–48.
109. See *supra,* note 70.
110. World Bank, *1980 Annual Report,* p. 67.
111. *Ibidem,* pp. 67–68.
112. *Ibidem,* p. 68.
113. See publication of the World Bank, *International Development Association* (Washington D.C., April 1978), pp. 16–18.
114. See *infra,* pp. 441–444.
115. World Bank, *1980 Annual Report,* p. 68 (emphasis added).
116. *Idem.*
117. 'Borrower' in the case of the Bank means a member government itself, a public agency or corporation, or a private body or corporation with the guarantee of the government. IDA credits are made to governments only, but the funds can be passed on to another entity responsible for carrying out the project (see World Bank, *1980 Annual Report,* p. 3).
118. See W. Baum, *loc. cit.* (note 105), p. 2.
119. Thus, Vice President and Treasurer of the World Bank E. Rotberg, *The World Bank: A Financial Appraisal* (World Bank, Washington D.C., March 1978), p. 5, see also pp. 10–11.
120. *Ibidem,* p. 25.
121. See publication of the World Bank, *International Development Association* (Washington D.C., April 1978), p. 22.
122. The IDA's Articles of Agreement contain similar provisions in Article V(1)(g) and V(1)(l).
123. See *supra,* note 117; eligibility for IDA credits on the other hand is limited to Member States.
124. See, for instance, the Shareholders' Agreement of November 30, 1979 between the Bank and the shareholders of a Colombian joint venture 'Interionession Electrica S.A.' pertaining to loan number 1725 CO. See for further examples R. Lavalle, *Le Banque Mondiale et ses Filiales: Aspects Juridiques et Fonctionnements* (Paris, 1972), p. 194.
125. See also A. Sureda and C. Vuylsteke, 'La surveillance exercée par la Banque Mondial' in: G. Fischer and D. Vignes, ed., *L'Inspection international* (Brussels, 1976) pp. 299–314 (esp. 301).
126. See Part I of this book, pp. 11–14.
127. See W. Baum, *loc. cit.* (note 105), p. 5.
128. See *supra,* pp. 415–417.
129. See E. Mason and R. Asher, *op. cit.* (note 3), p. 295 *et seq.*
130. A. van de Laar, *op. cit.* (note 35), p. 223 observes that a World Bank report often 'represents the first attempt in a country to make a systematic analysis of the economy as a whole to project the development process over a number of years'.
131. See, for instance, the recent report on Ecuador: *Ecuador; Development Problems and Prospects* (Washington D.C., July 1979) which is a study of more than 600 pages, reviewing in great detail many aspects of Ecuador's economy.
132. This is suggested by A. van de Laar, *op. cit.* (note 35), p. 240.
133. See *infra,* p. 430–431.
134. See also *infra,* pp. 438–452.
135. The following discussion of these phases is mainly based upon the above-mentioned article in *Finance and Development* by W. Baum, the World Bank's Vice President of the Project Staff, who in that capacity is responsible for the overall policies, standards and procedures of its project work.
136. According to W. Baum, *loc. cit.* (note 105), p. 6: 'Experience has demonstrated that we do not get enough projects to appraise unless we are involved intimately in their identification and preparation'.
137. See World Bank, *1980 Annual Report,* p. 76; Advances from the Facility amounted to $20·4m in the fiscal year 1980, while its commitment authority was increased to $57·5m.
138. See W. Baum, *loc. cit.* (note 105), p. 6.
139. *Ibidem,* p. 5; see also E. Mason and R. Asher, *op. cit.* (note 3), p. 307 *et seq.*

140. See J. King, *op. cit.* (note 101), p. 5.
141. See *supra*, p. 423.
142. See also Article V(1)(c) IDA according to which 'The Association shall not provide financing if in its opinion such financing is available from private sources on terms which are reasonable for the recipient *or could be provided by a loan of the type made by the Bank*' (emphasis added).
143. See in this respect the publication of the World Bank, *International Development Association* (Washington D.C., April 1978), p. 11.
144. *Ibidem*, pp. 11–12.
145. See E. Mason and R. Asher, *op. cit.* (note 3), p. 479 *et seq.*
146. See *supra* pp. 415–417.
147. In this respect see A. van de Laar, *op. cit.* (note 35), p. 1, who refers to the 'confusion' surrounding international development efforts, such as, for instance, the fact that 'we find a flow of sometimes contradictory recommendations that seem to succeed each other at two year intervals'.
148. See the World Bank's Vice President and Treasurer, E. Rotberg, *op. cit.* (note 119), p. 00.
149. *Idem.*
150. As a matter of fact, some countries, due to their specific economic situation, are granted Bank loans and IDA credits at the same time, the so-called 'blending'.
151. See the publication of the World Bank, *International Development Association* (Washington D.C., April 1978), p. 11.
152. See *supra* pp. 426–428.
153. See W. Baum, *loc. cit.* (note 105), p. 7.
154. J. King, *op. cit.* (note 101), p. 8.
155. See W. Baum, *loc. cit.* (note 105), p. 7; see, however, A. van de Laar, *op. cit.* (note 35), p. 221, who maintains that rates of return 'do not play much of a role in the selection from a range of fully worked-up alternative project proposals'.
156. See the publication of the World Bank, *Uses of Consultants by the World Bank and Its Borrowers* (Washington D.C., April 1974), pp. 2–3.
157. See also A. van de Laar, *op. cit.* (note 35), pp. 199–202.
158. See W. Baum, *loc. cit.* (note 105), p. 6.
159. See J. King, *op. cit.* (note 101), p. 11.
160. W. Baum, *loc. cit.* (note 105), p. 6.
161. *Idem.*
162. See the publication of the World Bank, *Guidelines for Procurement and World Bank loans and IDA credits* (Washington D.C., March 1977), pp. 1–2.
163. See J. King, *op. cit.* (note 101), p. 12.
164. See *supra*, p. 412.
165. World Bank, *1980 Annual Report*, pp. 77–80.
166. W, Baum, *loc. cit.* (note 105), p. 7.
167. See J. King, *op. cit.* (note 101), p. 14.
168. For a detailed analysis of the various legal aspects of the loan documents, see in particular: A. Broches, 'International legal aspects of the operations of the World Bank' (98 RDCAI (1959–III), 300–309), and R. Lavalle, *La Banque Mondiale et ses Filiales: Aspects Juridiques et Fonctionnement* (Paris, 1972), Chapter IX.
169. The procedure to be followed for the conclusion of loan documents on the part of the Member States is obviously determined by the relevant provisions of the national legal system of the Member State concerned; see R. Lavalle, *op. cit.* (note 168), pp. 200–201.
170. See, for instance, Article 6.02(a) of the Loan Agreement between the Republic of Kenya and the IBRD of April 11, 1979, Loan number 1680 KE, and Article 6.01(a) of the Credit Agreement between the Arab Republic of Egypt and the IDA of March 21, 1978, credit number 774 EGT.
171. See Article 5.01 of the Project Agreements between the IBRD and the Kenya Posts and Telecommunications Corporation of April 11, 1979, loan number 1680 KE and of the Project Agreement between the IDA and the Arab Republic of Egypt Telecommunication Organisation of March 21, 1978, credit number 774 EGT.
172. See A. Rigo Sureda and C. Vuylsteke, *loc. cit.* (note 125), pp. 306–307.
173. See *infra*, p. 448.
174. See W. Baum, *loc. cit.* (note 105), p. 8.
175. See *supra* p. 433.

480

176. The use of consultants retained by the World Bank itself has been left out of consideration, because this obviously does not involve any supervision by the World Bank over activities of the borrower.

177. Article 2.02 of the Project Agreement between the IBRD and the Kenya Posts and Telecommunications corporation of April 11, 1979 pertaining to loan number 1680 KE.

178. See publication of the World Bank, *Uses of Consultants by the World Bank and its Borrowers* (Washington D.C., April 1974), p. 8.

179. *Ibidem*, p. 10.

180. *Ibidem*, p. 8.

181. *Ibidem*, pp. 10–11.

182. See, for instance, Article 2.01 of the Guarantee Agreement between the Republic of Colombia and the IBRD of November 30, 1979, pertaining to loan number 1725 C.

183. See *ibidem*, Articles 3.02(a) and 3.03.

184. See Part I of this book, pp. 20–23.

185. See, for instance, Article 2.02 of the Loan Agreement between the Republic of Korea and the IBRD of September 27, 1979, loan number 1758 KO; and Article 2.02 of the Development Credit Agreement between the Republic of Indonesia and the IDA of August 13, 1979, credit number 946 IMD; a provision of the same tenor, but in more general wording, is embodied in Article 5.01 of the General Conditions of both the Bank and the IDA.

186. Publication of the World Bank, Washington D.C., October 1974.

187. See publication of the World Bank, *Guidelines for Withdrawal of Proceeds of World Bank Loans and IDA Credits* (Washington D.C., October 1974), pp. 2–4.

188. *Ibidem*, p. 4.

189. *Ibidem*, pp. 4–7.

190. Publication of the World Bank, Washington D.C., March 1977.

191. See, for instance, schedule 4 annexed to the Loan Agreement between the Republic of Korea and the IBRD, loan number 1758 KO.

192. See *supra*, p. 435.

193. See *Guidelines*, pp. 3–5.

194. *Ibidem*, pp. 6–17.

195. *Ibidem*, pp. 6 and 15; see also pp. 22–23.

196. *Ibidem*, p. 23.

197. *Ibidem*, pp. 5–6 juncto p. 20.

198. *Ibidem*, pp. 15–16.

199. See, for instance, Article 3.01(b) of the Loan Agreement between the Republic of Kenya and the IBRD of April 11, 1979, loan number 1680 KE and Article 3.01(b) of the Development Credit Agreement between the Arab Republic of Egypt and the IDA of March 21, 1978, credit number 774 EGT.

200. See Article 3.01(a) and (e) of the Agreements mentioned in the preceding note.

201. See, for instance, Article 3.01(a) of the Loan Agreement between the IBRD and Interconexion Electrica S.A. of November 30, 1979, loan number 1725 CO and the Development Credit Agreement between the Republic of Indonesia and the IDA of August 13, 1979, credit number 946 IMD.

202. See, for instance, Article 2.04(a) and (b) of the Project Agreement between the IBRD and the Kenya Posts and Telecommunication Corporation of April 11, 1979, pertaining to loan number 1680 KE, and of the Project Agreement between the IDA and the Arab Republic of Egypt Telecommunication Organisation of March 21, 1978, pertaining to credit number 774 EGT.

203. See note 202 above.

204. See, for instance, Project Agreement between IDA and ARETO, March 21, 1980, pertaining to credit number 774 EGT.

205. See *infra*, pp. 450–452.

206. For examples of these types of provisions in Loan Documents, see the Loan Agreement between the IBRD and Interconexion Electrica S.A. of November 30, 1979, loan number 1725 CO and the Project Agreement between the IDA and the Arab Republic of Egypt Telecommunication Organisation of March 21, 1978, pertaining to credit number 774 EGT.

207. See Article 6.03 of the General Conditions, which enumerates three more grounds for cancellation.

208. See Article 7.01(a)–(b).

209. See W. Baum, *loc. cit.* (note 105), p. 9.

210. See the publication of the World Bank, *Annual Review of Project Performance Audit Results* (Washington D.C., November 1979), p. 84.

211. See W. Baum, *loc. cit.* (note 105), p. 9.
212. See *Annual Review of Project Performance Audit Results* (Washington D.C., November 1979), p. 23.
213. *Ibidem,* p. 84.
214. See W. Baum, *loc. cit.* (note 105), p. 8.
215. See *supra,* p. 446.
216. See the publication of the World Bank, *Operations Evaluation: World Bank Standards and Procedures* (Washington D.C., August 1979), p. 11.
217. *Ibidem,* pp. 11–12.
218. See W. Baum, *loc. cit.* (note 105), p. 9.
219. See *Annual Review of Project Performance Audit Results* (Washington D.C., November 1979), p. 8.
220. See *supra,* p. 425.
221. See the publication of the World Bank, *Operations Evaluation: World Bank Standards and Procedures* (Washington D.C., August 1979), p. 13.
222. *Ibidem,* p. 8.
223. *Ibidem,* pp. 8 juncto 23.
224. *Ibidem,* p. 10.
225. See *supra,* p. 449.
226. Besides this Project Performance Auditing the OED carries out Evaluation Studies and Operational Policy Review. The former normally examine the impact of sets of projects in a country, or countries, or in a sector, or sectors, and their implications for the World Bank's policies, practices, and procedures; the latter examine the actual application of specific policies and procedures governing the management and administration of the World Bank's lending and technical assistance programmes. (See *Operations, Evaluation: World Bank Standards and Procedures* (Washington D.C., August 1979), pp. 18–19.)
227. See for more details on the World Bank's evaluation system the publication of the World Bank: *Operations Evaluation; World Bank Standards and Procedures* (Washington D.C., August 1979), pp. 15–21.
228. See Part I of this book, p. 27.
229. *Ibidem,* pp. 40–45.
230. As explained in the introductory report, one has to know the object and purpose of the rules which have to be supervised in order to be able to assess the degree of effectiveness of international supervision in each case, because the effectiveness of a supervisory system is determined by the extent to which it contributes to the achievement of the object and purpose of the rules concerned. (*Ibidem,* p. 39.)
231. Except for the outside consultants who are sometimes hired, third parties do not play a role in the World Bank's supervision.
232. See the publication of the World Bank; *Annual Review of Project Performance Audit Results* (Washington D.C., November 1979), p. 85.
233. See *infra,* pp. 466–475.
234. See Part I of this book, *supra,* p. 14.
235. See *infra,* pp. 456–458.
236. See Part I of this book, *supra,* pp. 18–20.
237. *Ibidem,* p. 26.
238. On the division of labour in practice between the Executive Directors and the Board of Governors, see *supra,* pp. 414–415.
239. See *supra,* p. 414.
240. See p. 18.
241. See *supra,* pp. 413–415.
242. See for instance pp. 21 and 35.
243. See *supra,* pp. 438–448.
244. See Part I of this book, *supra,* p. 23.
245. See *supra,* pp. 426–428.
246. See in this respect C. Willoughby, 'Ex post Project Evaluation – the Bank's Experience' (1977), *Finance and Development,* Vol. 14, No. 1, pp. 29–31.
247. *Annual Review of Project Performance Audit Results* (Washington D.C., November 1979), pp. 22–23.
248. *Ibidem,* p. 70.
249. See *supra,* p. 407.
250. See *supra,* p. 447.

251. Nevertheless, it happens that loans or credits are indeed cancelled; see, *Annual Review of Project Performance Audit Results* (Washington D.C., November 1979), p. 9.

252. See *supra*, p. 423.

253. E. Rotberg, *The World Bank: A Financial Appraisal* (Washington D.C., March 1978), p. 12.

254. Leverage is a complex phenomenon and it is impossible to discuss all the various aspects here. For a detailed discussion of leverage refer to E. Mason and R. Asher, *op. cit.* (note 3) chapter 13; and E. Reid, *Strengthening the World Bank* (Chicago, 1974), Chapter 11; for a case study see: Cargill, 'Efforts to Influence Recipient Performance: Case Study of India', in: J. Lewis and I. Kapur (eds.), *The World Bank, Multilateral Aid and the 1970's* (Lexington, 1973), p. 89 *et seq.*

255. See *supra*, pp. 430–433.

256. See *supra*, p. 453.

257. See Part I of this book, p. 24.

258. See *infra*, pp. 473–474.

259. See: *Operations Evaluation World Bank Standards and Procedures* (August 1979), pp. 23–24.

260. See *supra*, p. 434.

261. *Annual Review of Project Performance Audit Results* (Washington D.C., November 1979), p. 11.

262. *Idem.*

263. *Ibidem*, p. 12.

264. *Ibidem*, p. 230.

265. *Ibidem*, p. 86.

266. E. Mason and R. Asher, *op. cit.* (note 3), p. 70.

267. *Annual Review of Project Performance Audit Results* (Washington D.C., November 1979), pp. 5 juncto 84.

268. *Ibidem*, p. 6.

269. *Ibidem*, p. 7.

270. *Ibidem*, pp. 5, 6, 7, 83, 84.

271. See *supra*, p. 429.

272. *Ibidem*, (as note 270), p. 84.

273. *Ibidem*, p. 11.

274. In this respect see the two annual addresses by the President of the Bank to the Board of Governors on September 25, 1978 at Washington D.C., in particular pp. 20–31, and on October 4, 1979 at Belgrade, in particular pp. 21–41.

275. See *supra*, p. 460.

276. *Idem.*

277. See *supra*, pp. 412–415.

278. For our purposes the group of rich countries of the (World) Bank can be considered to comprise the so-called Part I members of the IDA. The poor countries are those which in the IDA constitute the group of Part II members; see World Bank, *1980 Annual Report,* pp. 172–174.

279. World Bank, *1980 Annual Report,* pp. 158–159 and 172–174.

280. See *supra*, pp. 430–436.

281. See *supra*, pp. 430.

282. See, for instance, *A New United Nations Structure for Global Economic Co-operation, Report of the Group of Experts on the Structure of the United Nations System* (United Nations, New York, 1975), pp. 85 *et seq.*; Ohman, 'Comment: A Social Radicalism', in: J. Lewis and L. Kapur (eds.), *op. cit.* (note 254), pp. 27–28; E. Mason and R. Asher, *op. cit.* (note 3), pp. 737 *et seq.*; and E. Reid, *op. cit.* (note 1), pp. 204 *et seq.* See in this respect also the *Brandt Report* (note 30), pp. 250–251, which states: 'A genuine, as distinct from an illusory, consensus calls for more equal representation. In this situation, what is essentially needed is a move towards greater equality and partnership, which should be reflected in revisions in the voting pattern no less than in the structure of the top management. This will in time break down mistrust and build confidence'.

283. It is true that with regard to the recently agreed upon General Capital Increase the Executive Directors have recommended measures to prevent such a development (see *supra*, p. 413 but it is not clear yet what the exact nature of these measures will be.

284. see *supra*, pp. 413–414.

285. 33,750 out of 335,468 votes.

286. 60,500 out of 3,509,383 votes.

287. See *A New United Nations Structure for Global Economic Co-operation, Report of the Group of Experts on the Structure of the United Nations System* (United Nations, New York, 1975), p. 86.

288. See in this respect Ohman, *loc. cit.* (note 282), pp. 27–28.

289. See *supra*, pp. 413–414.

290. For the countries belonging to these respective categories see 1979 *World Bank Atlas*, pp. 4–5; see also the World Bank, *World Development Report 1981* (Washington D.C., August 1981), pp. 134–135.

291. See *supra*, p. 413.

292. In this respect see the speeches by the President of the Bank, McNamara: Address to the Board of Governors, Washington D.C., September 25, 1978, pp. 24–27; Address to the Board of Governors, Belgrade, October 2, 1979, pp. 27–28.

293. See also *supra*, p. 402.

294. For a detailed analysis of the development concerning World Bank staff see A. van de Laar, *op. cit.* (note 35), pp. 92–107.

295. See E. Mason and R. Asher, *op. cit.* (note 3), pp. 879–880.

296. World Bank, *1980 Annual Report*, p. 10.

297. See E. Reid, *op. cit.* (note 1), p. 186.

298. See the *Brandt Report*, (note 30), p. 248; according to the World Bank itself, representation of staff from developing countries among senior ranks, *i.e.* those at the managerial level and above, in 1980 amounted to 27.5 per cent. of the total, as opposed to 22 per cent. at the end of fiscal 1975 (*1980 Annual Report*, pp. 10—11).

299. See A. van de Laar, *op. cit.* (note 35), p. 214.

300. *Ibidem*, p. 215.

301. E. Mason and R. Asher, *op. cit.* (note 3), pp. 71–72; see also E. Reid, *op. cit.* (note 1), pp. 92–93.

302. See also E. Reid, *op. cit.* (note 1), p. 186.

303. See also *A New United Nations Structure for Global Economic Co-operation, Report of the Group of Experts on the Structure of the United Nations System* (United Nations, New York, 1975), p. 87 *et seq.*; and E. Reid, *op. cit.* (note 1), p. 187.

304. See A. van de Laar, *op. cit.* (note 35), pp. 209–248 and the studies cited there.

305. Article V(10) provides that: (a) The Bank may establish regional offices and determine the location of, and the areas to be covered by, each regional office; (b) Each regional office shall be advised by a regional council representative of the entire area and selected in such manner as the Bank may decide.

306. See the *Brandt Report* (note 30), p. 248.

307. World Bank, *1980 Annual Report*, pp. 199–200.

308. See A. van der Laar, *op. cit.* (note 35), p. 244; see also E. Mason and R. Asher, *op. cit.* (note 3), p. 742.

309. In this respect see A. van der Laar, who, in discussing the alleged lack of real understanding of the local conditions on the part of the Central Project Staff, submits that this 'is a grave structural problem inherent in the distance between supervisory levels and the reality of conditions in LDCS' (*op. cit.* (note 35), p. 239).

310. In *Annual Review of Project Performance Audit Results* (Washington D.C., November 1979), p. 23, it was said, at least with regard to one project, that 'Bank staff stationed in the country played an important part in supervision. . . .'

311. In the same sense see E. Mason and R. Asher, *op. cit.* (note 3), p. 742.

312. The nature of these difficulties obviously depends upon the exact scale of the reorganisation. The ideas in this respect would seem to differ considerably. E. Mason and R. Asher, for instance, consider that resident missions should be fairly small, a maximum of about 10 to 12 members (*op. cit.* (note 3), p. 742). E. Reid, on the other hand, suggests a reorganisation on a much larger scale when he proposes transferring regional offices from Washington to regional headquarters thereby reducing the Washington staff by more than half (*op. cit.* (note 1), pp. 183–184).

313. This would apply to an even greater extent if it were decided to decentralise World Bank activities by expanding the number and the role of regional missions. Obviously, in such a case the ties with particular borrowing countries would be weaker.

314. See *supra*, p. 461.

315. See *supra*, p. 463.

316. It should be remembered that one of the defects of supervision pointed out by the World Bank itself is the lack of staff continuity; *i.e.* the non-fulfilment of the requirement that effective supervision has to be based on adequate knowledge of the project from its inception on the part

of the supervisory organ. Staff continuity was therefore emphasised as an important factor in the success of a project. See *Annual Review of Project Performance Audit Results* (Washington D.C., November 1979), p. 22.

317. See *supra*, p. 467.
318. See *supra*, pp. 450–452.
319. See *supra*, p. 451.
320. See *Operations Evaluation; World Bank Standards and Procedures* (Washington D.C., August 1979), p. 7.
321. *Ibidem*, p. 21.
322. *Ibidem*, p. 22.
323. See *supra*, p. 474.

PART VII

SUPERVISION WITHIN THE INTER-NATIONAL ATOMIC ENERGY AGENCY

SUPERVISION WITHIN THE
INTERNATIONAL ATOMIC ENERGY AGENCY

by C. Grossman

CONTENTS

I. INTRODUCTION

It appears from international efforts undertaken so far, that a major issue in the acquisition and development of peaceful nuclear energy is the danger of proliferation: the possibility that the acquisition of nuclear knowledge, facilities and materials for peaceful purposes could lead to an enlargement of the (select) club of Nuclear Weapon States (NWS) (horizontal proliferation[1]).

It is hardly surprising that the peaceful use of nuclear energy should be intimately connected with the danger of proliferation. The military danger comes with access to peaceful technology; difficulties, if any, are minimal in developing nuclear weapon technology from scientific knowledge developed from the operation of peaceful nuclear reactors. If the nuclear materials are present, the ability to 'make the bomb' is there as well.[2]

Accordingly, supervision problems concerned with the peaceful uses of atomic energy have mainly dealt with the proliferation issue: how to allow the 'good' (peaceful use) while avoiding the 'bad'. The magnitude of the dilemma posed is further enhanced by the scientific change constantly introduced into the cycle of production and commercialisation of peaceful nuclear energy. New technology e.g. in the field of uranium enrichment, continually increases the risk of proliferation by, inter alia, enlarging the number of routes by which nuclear material might be obtained that could be used to produce nuclear explosives. While the light water reactor of the fifties used nuclear fuel that could not be used directly to make nuclear weapons, thus limiting the risks of proliferation, the spread of enrichment plants and reprocessing plants in the early seventies has created a new situation. Enrichment plants and reprocessing plants that isolate the plutonium and uranium remaining from spent fuel rods can lead to the production of bomb material. The fastbreeder reactor, using plutonium instead of enriched uranium as fuel, and turning out more plutonium than is put into the system, also would enlarge the proliferation risk due to the large amount of plutonium involved.[3]

The purpose of this study is to analyse the main international effort to supervise the peaceful use of nuclear energy, viz., the safeguard system administered by the International Atomic Energy Agency (IAEA) under agreements concluded in virtue of the Treaty on the Non-Proliferation of Nuclear Weapons (NPT).[4] IAEA safeguards are also applied in cases other than those contained in the agreements under the NPT, but the safeguards administered by the Agency under the Treaty constitute the main safeguard activity of the Agency.[5]

At the end of 1980, 69 Non-Nuclear Weapon States (NNWS) had agreements in force with the Agency under the NPT. Of the remaining NNWS that have ratified the NPT – 41 in number – only three had significant nuclear activities (Turkey, Venezuela, Republic of China), and the first two of these had begun procedures for bringing their agreements with the Agency into force.[6]

Safeguards applied under arrangements other than the NPT covered only 11 NNWS (Argentina, Brazil, Chile, Colombia, Cuba, the Democratic People's Republic of Korea, India, Israel, Pakistan, South Africa and Spain). However, six of these States did not have all their nuclear activities under safeguards.[7]

The NPT did not set up a permanent organ entrusted with the supervision of the non-proliferation obligations laid down in the Treaty. The non-proliferation obligations were to be supervised by means of safeguards negotiated with 'an outside organisation', viz., the IAEA. Accordingly, this study will analyse the purposes, modalities, functions, mechanisms and effectiveness of the safeguards of the IAEA in the light of the non-proliferation issue. In addition it will describe, to the extent that they are relevant for the analysis, the adoption of the IAEA Statute; its purposes and functions; the Agency's organs and their decision making power; and the adoption of the NPT.

Because of the subject-matter of safeguards, *i.e.*, non-proliferation, the problem of supervision, relevant in general in international law, acquires an extra dimension here. Its analysis permits one to shed light on the way in which supervision in respect of a vital issue has kept pace with both the needs posed by a field constantly affected by technological change, and a framework of different political realities.

II. THE ESTABLISHMENT OF THE IAEA

The earliest attempt to establish an international authority concerned with atomic energy took place almost immediately after the Second World War, in 1946. The U.S. proposed, through what has come to be known as the 'Baruch-plan' (taking its name from Mr. B. M. Baruch, U.S. representative to the United Nations Atomic Energy Commission), that an international authority should be created that would both be in charge of *all* nuclear development and monopolise *all* nuclear materials.[8] This authority was to have powers to undertake inspections in all countries. There were to be sanctions for violations on the basis of mechanisms that excluded the U.N. veto system. The U.S., the only country having atomic weapons at the time, was to dispose of its atomic weapons after realisation of the plan.

Disagreement between the U.S. and the U.S.S.R. accounted for the failure to arrive at a consensus in favour of this far-reaching proposal. The main problems concerned the question of whether the new Agency should provide for a veto power; whether it was necessary to prohibit all nuclear weapons first, before regulating their control; and lastly, the extent of the supervision the Agency would be allowed to exercise.[9]

As a result of this failure, the U.S. developed a policy of strict secrecy concerning atomic energy, while the U.S.S.R. continued, and other countries embarked upon, programmes designed to achieve atomic capabilities.[10]

A new political, technological and economic climate was created by the attainment of atomic weaponry by the U.S.S.R. in 1949, and the U.K. in 1952 and by the further discovery of the possibility of applying nuclear technology for peaceful purposes. In 1953, President Eisenhower gave expression to this new situation by means of his 'Atoms for Peace' speech before the UN.[11]

As a result of a three-year negotiating process, in 1956 agreement was finally achieved on the creation of an international framework that would allow transfer of nuclear material and devices to other countries for peaceful ends, under a system of international supervision (safeguards) to be administered by an international agency.[12] The Statute of the International Atomic Energy Agency was adopted at a special conference which met from September 20 to October 26, 1956, at the headquarters of the UN in New York. All Member States of the UN and Member States of the Specialised Agencies had been invited to the conference. The Statute entered into force on July 29, 1957, the date on which the ratification conditions prescribed in Article XXI,E of the Statute had been complied with.[13]

The agreement expressed in the Statute was less far-reaching than the goals of the Baruch plan. While the latter had aimed at establishing an international nuclear cartel, the former did not expressly prohibit independent national development of atomic energy, including that of atomic weapons. Similarly, the countries were not obliged to place their nuclear materials or facilities under Agency supervision. However, though no explicit independent non-proliferation obligation was set up in the Statute, it was hoped that by giving the NNWS access to the benefits of atomic energy, and requiring safeguards, these States would be deterred from developing independent atomic capabilities leading to the production of atomic weapons. At the same time, by means of giving institutional privileges to the nuclear States, it was hoped that they would submit their atomic co-operation schemes with third States to Agency supervision, and hence to a non-proliferation régime.[14]

2.1. Objectives and functions of the Agency

In accordance with Article II of the Statute the objective of the Agency is to 'seek to accelerate and enlarge the contribution of atomic energy to peace, health and prosperity throughout the world' and to 'ensure so far it is able, that assistance provided by it or at its request or under its supervision or control is not used in such a way as to further any military purpose'.

The objectives of the IAEA are to be realised through functions laid down in the Statute in Article III,A(1–6). Four types of functions are set forth for the IAEA:

(a) to receive, take custody and provide nuclear material, services, equipment and facilities;
(b) to encourage, assist and carry out research, to foster the exchange of scientists and scientific and technical information;
(c) to establish and administer safeguards to prevent diversion to military uses;
(d) to establish, adopt and apply health and safety measures.

The first-mentioned function was intended by the drafters of the Statute to be the Agency's most important one.[15] They thought that States would offer to place nuclear materials under the Agency's supervision, these materials then being lent to other States by the Agency. However fulfilment of this function required that suppliers and receiver States acted through the Agency in their nuclear dealings by their own free political choice. No obligation was laid down in the Statute.[16] A complex of circumstances accounts for the absence of the necessary political will: (i) a trend toward bilateral and regional dealings; (ii) resistance to safeguards administered by the Agency; (iii) less interest in the introduction of nuclear power than was originally expected; and (iv) more interest on the part of most developing

492

States in receiving technical assistance than nuclear fuel.[17] As a result of these factors, the Agency's role turned out to be more that of a broker – arranging and supervising bilateral transactions among interested States – than that of a custodian or merchant of nuclear items.[18] However, an institutional framework was provided for in the Statute should it be required by new political conditions.[19]

As a result of the processes involving the first function, promotional and technical assistance turned out to be the most important Agency function during the first decade of its operation. This assistance concentrated upon the transfer of knowledge which was given either free or at a minimum cost to the under-developed States.[20]

The Statute lays down in Article III,A(5) the scope of the situations requiring Agency safeguards: (i) Agency projects – the only case under the Statute in which they are obligatory; (ii) at the request of parties in bilateral and multilateral agreements; and (iii) at the request of an individual State in any of its activities in the field of atomic energy. The purpose of safeguards is to ensure that assistance provided by the Agency, either at its request or under its supervision or control, is not used in such a way as to further any military purpose. Considering that the Statute gave only a framework for the safeguards system, and also that safeguards must be incorporated in an agreement between the Agency and State(s), in order to be valid, the Agency developed a general safeguards document. This document also' aimed at achieving homogeneity in the different agreements. The practical need for this creative exercise which the Governing Board of the IAEA embarked upon, was stressed even more by the difficulties encountered in the negotiation of the first agreement for the application of safeguards.[21] A first general document was approved in 1961; after being modified later, it achieved its final form in 1965.[22]

The experience in supervision acquired by the Agency under this document was essential for the development of a new safeguard document to be applied under the NPT, which will be analysed later. After the entry into force of this treaty the Agency's main supervision effort focused on the safeguards administered under the NPT.

Under Article III,A(6), the Statute lists as the last function of the IAEA the development and application of health and safety standards. The Agency's activities under this function have been mainly promotional.

During the first years of operation, the Agency's work in this field of standards development was mainly limited to a case-by-case approach, instead of the formulation of general recommendations. This approach was no longer appropriate in the context of rapid expansion in the construction of nuclear power plants, which accentuated the need for formalised safety criteria.[23] In September 1974, the IAEA's Governing Board set up a Senior Advisory Group in charge of implementing a Nuclear Safety Standards (NUSS) Programme, which was designed to prepare internationally agreed recommendations on thermal neutron nuclear plants. This group selected topics to be included in Codes of Practice and a list of subjects for Safety Guides.

The Codes of Practice 'set out the objectives and minimum requirements which must be fulfilled to provide adequate safety for these plants (thermal neutron nuclear power plants), their system and components'.[24] The Safety Guides 'recommend a procedure or procedures that might be followed to implement the codes of practice'.[25] Five codes of practice, concerning (i) governmental organisation; (ii) siting; (iii) design; (iv) operation; and (v) quality assurance for safety; and the first 24 safety guides had been published by the end of 1980. A further 27 safety guides are under preparation.[26]

To assist the Member States in following the codes and guides the Agency undertakes various promotional activities. It has held scientific seminars; it sends missions to various countries; it evaluates safety conditions in certain plants; and it holds international and regional training courses.[27]

The Senior Advisory Group for NUSS was also entrusted with the study of the future of the Programme in the light of the 'Three Mile Island accident' that took place in the United States in 1979. A report has been prepared.[28] A manual concerning emergency procedures in case of radiation accidents was issued by the Agency in 1980.[29] Other activities, such as research seminars and training, are also undertaken by the Agency to keep pace with scientific development in the area of safety and review its standards accordingly, and to promote the interchange of experience and train qualified personnel.[30]

According to its Statute, the IAEA's safety standards are to be applied to the Agency's own operations making use of materials and equipment provided by the Agency (Agency Projects). In other cases, unless a voluntary submission takes place, the safety standards have only a recommendatory value.[31] There have, thus far, been no voluntary submissions.

Even in the cases where safety standards should be applied and the Agency is entrusted with their supervision, the supervision has been softened.[32] A Health and Safety Document, mainly for Agency Projects, approved by the Agency on March 31, 1960, established that safety is largely a matter of national concern and left great latitude to the States to apply their own safety measures if the Agency considered the safety system adequate. This document is a model that – as in the case of safeguards – develops the statutory provisions and, in the last resort, derives its legal value from its incorporation into agreements with States.[33]

In any case, the Agency's competence to assess the adequacy of the system has been established. Before transfers of IAEA materials and equipment take place, the concerned Member State should submit a safety report to the Agency.[34] Safety reviews by the IAEA can take place during the construction of a plant, once during the first year of operation, and then once a year. However, mainly due to the fact that inspections take place only when accidents are reported, or on the Board's instructions – and that has not yet occurred – no safety inspections are in fact carried out. This situation is mainly due to policy considerations on the part of IAEA. According to Szacs it is felt by the Agency that health and safety threats are inherently local and only remotely international.[35] Consequently, while the Agency's safeguards function is focused on supervision, the health and safety function consists

494

primarily of the establishment of standards and emergency procedures. Being the central point for promotional activities, the Agency, while keeping its right of supervision, has not come to feel that it should force its control on unwilling States.[36]

2.2. Relationship with the UN and membership

The IAEA is an international governmental organisation which – in accordance with its Relationship Agreement with the UN which entered into force on November 14, 1957 – enjoys the status of an autonomous international organisation within the UN system.[37] The IAEA did not become a Specialised Agency of the UN because it was considered that its responsibilities deriving from the subject matter with which it is concerned, required a direct relationship with both the UN Security Council and the General Assembly.[38]

While specialised agencies communicate with the UN through ECOSOC, the IAEA, by virtue of its Relationship Agreement, submits reports to:

- the General Assembly of the UN (annually);
- the Security Council (when appropriate); and
- other UN Organs (on matters within their competence).

Initial members of the Agency were those Member States of the UN or of any of its Specialised Agencies, which signed the Statute within the ninety-day period that it was open for signature, starting October 26, 1956, and which subsequently deposited their instruments of ratification.

Other States – whether or not members of the UN or of its Specialised Agencies – can become members of the Agency if their membership, recommended by the Board of Governors, is approved by the General Conference (in both cases only a simple majority being required), and if they proceed to deposit an instrument of ratification of the Statute.

2.3. The Organs of the IAEA

The organs of the Agency laid down in the Statute are: the General Conference, the Board of Governors and the Director General with the Secretariat.

The General Conference consists of representatives of all Member States. It meets in regular session once a year (usually in September, at the Head-quarters of the Agency in Vienna, but sometimes in the capital of a Member State).

The General Conference has the power to discuss any question or matter within the scope of the Statute, to make recommendations to the membership and to the Board, to request reports from the Board and to take decisions on any matter referred to it for this purpose by the Board.

The specific powers granted to the General Conference should usually be exercised following recommendations from the Board.[39] Only in the following cases are such recommendations not necessary: election of Board members; consideration of the annual report of that body; approval of amendments of the Statute; requests for advisory opinions made to the ICJ; fixing of the scale of contributions; restoration of a member's right to vote; carrying out the general reviews of the Statute; and organisation of the Conference itself.

Decisions of the Conference are taken by a majority of the members present and voting, except when the Statute provides that a two-thirds majority is required (financial questions, amendments to the Statute, suspension of a member) or when the Conference decides by majority that a question should be decided by a two-thirds majority. This last point has arisen in the case of some procedural issues mentioned in the Rules of Procedure.[40]

A majority of the Agency Members constitutes a quorum.

The Board of Governors consists of 34 government representatives, 12 designated by the Board and 22 by the General Conference in accordance with Article VI,A(1) and (2).

The Board selects: (a) the nine members most advanced in the technology of atomic energy, including the production of source material; and (b) the member most advanced in the technology of atomic energy, including the production of source material, in each of the eight areas mentioned in the Statute in which none of the nine members' States already mentioned are located.[41] The General Conference, in accordance with Article VI,A(2), selects 20 members, having as a criterion due regard to equitable representation on the Board of the members in the eight areas mentioned in the Statute. Thus the Board will always include in this category (a) five representatives from Latin America, four from Western Europe, four from Africa, two from the Middle East and South Asia, one from South East Asia and the Pacific and one from the Far East; (b) one further member from among the members from the Middle East and South Asia, South East Asia and the Pacific, and the Far East; and (c) one further member from among the members from Africa, the Middle East and South Asia, South East Asia and the Pacific.

The actual composition of the Board and its form of selection is a result of a modification of the Statute initiated by the NNWS. At the General Conference of 1968 these States strongly expressed their dissatisfaction with what they considered an unrepresentative Board, the Board being the central organ of the Agency. Originally, the Board had consisted mainly of the more advanced States in the field of nuclear energy and the suppliers of source material, elected through co-option.[42]

The Board of Governors, which meets at such times as it may determine (usually four or five times a year at Headquarters), is the executive organ of the Agency. The Board has general authority to carry out the Agency's functions in accordance with the Statute and subject to its responsibility to the General Conference, as provided for in the Statute. The approval of the

General Conference is required for the adoption of the Budget, the appointment of the Director General, the conclusion of agreements with other organisations, the submission of reports to the UN, the approval of States for membership, the suspension of members, and the formulation of general rules for the staff. The following matters are subject to rules approved by the General Conference: the exercise of the borrowing powers of the Agency, the acceptance of voluntary contributions, the use of the General Fund and the formulation of the staff regulations.

The Governing Board takes decisions by a normal or by a two-thirds majority of its members present and voting. A two-thirds majority is required with respect to the fixing of the extent of the Agency's budget.[43] The Governing Board can determine other questions which are to be decided by a two-thirds majority.[44]

The Director General is the chief administrative officer of the Agency. As such, he is responsible for the appointment, organisation and functioning of the Agency's Secretariat, under the authority and subject to the control of the Board of Governors.[45] The Secretariat consists of 577 professional staff and 865 general service staff. The Director General is appointed by the Board of Governors with the approval of the General Conference for a period of four years (Article VII). The Secretariat is divided into four departments, each headed by a Deputy Director General.[46] Neither the Director General nor the Secretariat may seek or receive instructions from any source external to the Agency. They are under an obligation not to disclose the Agency's confidential information, and to refrain from actions which might unfavourably reflect on their positions as Agency officials. Member States should refrain from attempting to influence them.[47]

III. THE NON-PROLIFERATION TREATY (NPT)

3.1. Adoption

The IAEA Statute has only limited non-proliferation value; it does not expressly forbid either giving assistance in the development of nuclear weapons nor the independent development of those weapons by NNWS.

The U.S. and U.S.S.R., which were the most concerned with these non-proliferation issues, embarked upon private negotiations from 1962 onwards to create a framework dealing with them.[48] The main obstacle was that while the U.S.S.R. wanted to exclude any possibility of a Multilateral Nuclear Force (MLF) being created by Nato in Europe (because they were afraid that this would directly or indirectly involve West-Germany with Nato Nuclear Weapons), the U.S. wanted to leave open that possibility. By 1965, support for the MLF idea was fading away both in the United States and Europe, a fact that, *inter alia*, moved President Johnson to give it up.[49]

However, the basic consent achieved between the U.S. and the U.S.S.R. did not automatically lead to the approval of a Non-Proliferation Treaty.

Different issues arose involving other interests and the expectations of different international actions; the NNWS raised security and economic issues which they wanted to see reflected in the NPT. They considered a unilateral non-proliferation obligation on their side as basically discriminatory, unless it was related to the issue of nuclear disarmament by the NWS. At the same time, they looked for pledges from nuclear States on the transfer of peaceful nuclear technology and access to the benefits of Peaceful Nuclear Explosions (PNE).[50]

Another issue was raised in relation to Euratom safeguards. In order to protect its integration scheme, the partners in Euratom, the nuclear agency of the European Communities, wanted the safeguards under a non-proliferation treaty to be those administered by their own organisation, while non-European countries considered this discriminatory, and a form of self-inspection.[51]

After a process of negotiations that took place in different fora, agreement was eventually reached in the form of a Non-Proliferation Treaty adopted by the General Assembly of the UN on June 12, 1968. The structure and supervisory mechanisms prescribed in the Treaty reflect the different concerns that arose during the negotiations that led to its adoption.

3.2. Structure

The NNWS accept the obligation neither to manufacture nor otherwise acquire nuclear weapons or other nuclear explosive devices; they further undertake not to accept their transfer or control directly or indirectly, nor to seek or receive any assistance in their manufacture (Article II).

The NWS undertake not to transfer to any recipient State nuclear weapons or other nuclear explosive devices or control over them, directly or indirectly, and not to assist, encourage or induce their manufacture or acquisition or control over them (Article I).

To compensate the NNWS for their commitment 'not to go nuclear', the following provisions were included. In the first place an obligation was laid upon all States to pursue in good faith at an early date negotiations on effective measures relating to the cessation of the nuclear arms race and to nuclear disarmament, as well as negotiations for a non-proliferation treaty on general and complete disarmament under strict and effective international control (Article VI). This nuclear disarmament aspect is what has come to be known as 'vertical' non-proliferation in comparison with the 'horizontal' non-proliferation of the NNWS[52] In the Preamble to the Treaty the disarmament aspect is also stressed.[53]

Secondly, the NNWS obtained the inclusion of a provision relating to their right of access to the benefits of peaceful atomic energy without discrimination (Article IV,1). All States would co-operate in the further development of the application of nuclear energy for peaceful purposes, 'with due consideration for the needs of the developing areas of the world' (Article IV,2). In addition, NWS will assist NNWS in carrying out nuclear explosions for peaceful purposes under international supervision (e.g., engineering projects) (Article V).[54]

3.3. Supervisory mechanisms under the NPT

The NPT lays down certain specific supervisory mechanisms, *viz.*, (a) safeguards, (b) Review Conferences, (c) the right of parties to withdraw from the Treaty and (d) a Conference that is to be convened to decide upon the continuance of the Treaty after 25 years. In addition, elements of supervision are also to be found in Article X of the Treaty.

Under the NPT safeguards are to be applied in two cases.

First, with respect to all source or special fissionable material in all the peaceful nuclear activities of the NNWS parties to the Treaty (Article III,1).

Secondly, each Member State undertakes not to provide to NNWS, for peaceful purposes, source or special fissionable material or equipment, or material designed or prepared for the processing, use or production of special fissionable material, unless under safeguards (Article III,2).

Consequently, safeguards under the NPT do not cover:

(a) the nuclear activities of the NWS;
(b) non-peaceful activities other than the manufacture of nuclear weapons or other nuclear explosive devices in the NNWS which are parties to the Treaty (for example, atomic fuel of submarines);
(c) peaceful nuclear activities in non-parties which do not fall within the scope of Article III,2[55];
(d) mining and extraction of uranium and thorium.

Safeguards are to be laid down in agreements negotiated with the IAEA by States, either individually or collectively, within the time fixed by Article III,4.

The (exclusive) purpose of the safeguards laid down in the Treaty is to verify the fulfilment by the States of the non-proliferation obligations assumed by them under the Treaty, with a view to preventing diversion of nuclear materials from peaceful uses to nuclear weapons or other nuclear explosive devices (Article III,1).[56]

In addition to safeguards, a mechanism to review the operation of the Treaty as a whole is foreseen, in the form of periodical Conferences of Parties to the Treaty. The first Conference was to be convened five years after the entry into force of the Treaty and thereafter conferences will take place at intervals of five years if a majority of the Parties of the Treaty submit a proposal to this effect to the Depositary Governments (Article VIII,3).

The Treaty also lays down a right to withdraw from it; notice of withdrawal must be given three months in advance to the other parties and to the UN Security Council. This right may be exercised if a Party decides that exceptional events – to be described in the above-mentioned notice – related to the subject matter of the Treaty, have jeopardised its most fundamental interests. A supervision rationale is present here in a double sense; first, the fact that the other Parties, and especially the Security Council, must be informed of the withdrawal means that measures could be taken by the UN if peace were endangered; secondly, the existence of the right to withdraw is, of itself, a supervision rationale, since a supervisory function could be present if, for example, a State felt encouraged to comply with the obligations of the Treaty because of the threat that another State, or other States, could withdraw.

Supervisory functions can also be found in the Conference that, in accordance with Article X,2, will be convened to decide on the continuation of the Treaty 25 years after its entry into force. Decisions on the issue of continuation are to be taken by a majority of the Parties.

IV. IAEA SAFEGUARDS AGREEMENTS UNDER THE NPT; THE BLUE BOOK

Following a pattern similar to that of agreements made under the IAEA Statute, in 1971 the Board of Governors of the Agency adopted a model based on a proposal of the Special Safeguards Committee that was created in 1970, to be used as the basis for negotiating safeguards agreements between the Agency and the parties to the NPT. This model, the title of which is 'The Structure and Content of Agreements Between the Agency and States Required in Connection with the Treaty on the Non-Proliferation of Nuclear Weapons' is known as the 'Blue Book'.[57]

The Blue Book's function is to be a model agreement and, as such, it plays a role in achieving homogeneity in the agreements between the IAEA and NPT parties. At the same time, by interpreting and concretising the way in which the IAEA sees the safeguards under the NPT, it constitutes a creative exercise based on the safeguards experience of the Agency under its Statute. However, in the last resort the full legal value of the Blue Book stems from the fact that its provisions are incorporated in a safeguards agreement with the Agency. Nevertheless, considering that the Parties are obliged to negotiate safeguards agreements with the IAEA in accordance with the safeguards system of the Agency, and that the Blue Book is the expression of that system with reference to the NPT, the Blue Book cannot be considered merely as a guide for negotiations.[58]

The Blue Book consists of a Part I and a Part II, plus certain definitions. Part I gives the general framework of the safeguards obligations of the State under the NPT, the purpose and scope of safeguards, and their mechanisms. It also includes other issues, such as the measures relating to verification of non-diversion, provisions on interpretation and application of the agreement, settlement of disputes, provisions on international responsibility, and provisions concerning amendments of the agreement, its entry into force and duration. Part II specifies the procedures to be applied in implementing the safeguards provisions of Part I. Finally, the Blue Book provides definitions of the key technical terms used in it.

4.1. Purpose of safeguards and their function

The purpose of the safeguards as conceptualised in paragraph 28 of the Blue Book, is 'the timely detection of the diversion of significant quantities of nuclear material from peaceful nuclear activities to the manufacture of nuclear weapons or of other nuclear explosive devices or for purposes unknown, and deterrence of such diversion by the risk of early detection'.[59]

The Agency has developed criteria in order to establish what is meant by 'significant quantity' and by 'timely detection'. A significant quantity of nuclear material is the amount needed for a fission explosive (8 kg. of plutonium, 8 kg. of U.233, 25 kg. of U.235 contained in highly enriched uranium, or 75 kg. of U.235 contained in low enriched or natural uranium). Timely detection refers to the time that it may take, after diversion has taken place, for a State to convert the diverted material into a form suitable for the manufacture of a nuclear explosive device (for a significant quantity of plutonium or highly enriched uranium days or weeks, for plutonium in highly radioactive spent fuel, in a period from weeks to months; for 75 kg. of U.235 in natural or low enriched uranium, a period of a year or less).[60] These values are used by the IAEA guidelines, which could be changed on the basis of additional practical experience and scientific advice.[61] In addition, considering that the IAEA must strive for a safeguard system which has the probability of meeting the criteria developed for significant quantities and timely detection, the degree of probability of meeting these goals must be defined.

The Blue Book does not explicitly mention the concept of degree or certitude of detection. The IAEA, interpreting the model as implicitly embodying this concept, seeks an *a priori* probability of detection which is usually 90 per cent. or higher (most often 95 per cent.).[62]

The accent lies on the *preventive corrective function* of timely detection.[63] The risk, and near certainty, of early detection, and consequent exposure by the Agency, has a deterrent impact on potential violators. In addition, exposure would allow the Agency and the UN (if the World Organisation so decides) to take the coercive measures prescribed in the Statute and in the UN Charter, with the purpose of avoiding the manufacture of a nuclear explosive.

Prevention – which should, in fact, be the *leitmotiv* of all effective supervisory mechanisms – takes on an extra dimension here, because of the subject matter of safeguards: if the accent lay on detection rather than prevention, it would simply be too late.

In accordance with what has been mentioned above, it is not necessary to prove what (subjective) purpose a State might have in diverting significant quantities of nuclear material. That would introduce an unnecessary *onus probandi* on the part of the IAEA, which would be all the more difficult considering the secret character which an illegal nuclear weapon facility would have. Paragraph 28 talks of the detection of diversion of 'significant quantities.' This requirement calls for objectivity: by establishing in advance the amount of nuclear material which is considered to be a significant quantity, possible subjective interpretations are excluded.[64]

The corrective preventive function of safeguards does not mean that the review, the (other than preventive) correction, or the creative function identified in the introductory paper of the research project of which this study forms part, are absent in IAEA supervision. The instruments of safeguards fulfil a review function. Material accountability generates data, containment measures protect data, and surveillance verifies it. Corrective functions other than preventive correction will be present when measures taken by the Agency or the UN have not avoided diversion; if continued, their purpose will no longer be preventive.

The creative function has been apparent in the Board's development of a model agreement on the basis of the Agency's safeguard experience, the provisions of which are designed to be incorporated in agreements with State(s), and in different Agency activities undertaken with the purpose of improving the safeguards system.[65]

4.2. Instruments of safeguards

The three basic mechanisms of safeguards are (i) material accountancy, (ii) containment, and (iii) surveillance. In addition, (iv) design information and control should also be mentioned.

Material accountancy is made up of a collection of measurements and other determinants which enable the IAEA and the State to know of the location and movement of nuclear material.[66]

Material accountancy is realised by means of a system, administered by the State(s), of accounting for and controlling all nuclear material. It is based on an initial physical inventory of the nuclear material, and should include the measurements mentioned in the Blue Book, according to the agreements with the IAEA. Regular reports on the movement of nuclear materials are sent to the IAEA by Member States.[67] This accounting system forms the backbone of the safeguards administered by the Agency; it generates an important part of the data which is supervised by the Agency. And, 'if data is not generated, it cannot be transmitted, if it is not transmitted, it cannot be verified, and if it is not verified, there are no international safeguards'.[68]

The accounting system registers the flow of nuclear material through all the peaceful nuclear activities of a State. The system registers the flow not only within one plant, but from plant to plant, either within or outside the country concerned. The plants are subdivided into Material Balance Areas[69] and at Strategic Points[70] safeguards are applied. In addition to the records, which must be open to inspection, there is also a duty to report to the IAEA.[71]

The national accounting system is complemented by containment and surveillance.

Containment covers measures taken to prevent the undetected movement of nuclear materials or equipment.[72] Containment is realised by resorting to special seals. Its purpose is to make sure that no nuclear material leaves a certain location in an illegitimate way, by indicating if the integrity of the containment measure has been maintained or if it has been breached. Facility operators should immediately notify the IAEA if it is necessary to break a seal, or if a seal has been broken. The sealing facilitates inspections since, as long as a seal is unbroken, it is certain that no material has been removed. It also serves the purpose of identifying items of nuclear material.[73]

Surveillance consists of instrumental or human observation with the purpose of indicating movements of nuclear material.

Instrumental surveillance is realised by means of cameras or other technical devices placed at strategic points.[74]

Human observation is realised through Agency inspectors. The inspectors control the accounting system, make independent measurements, control the instruments, the containment and the surveillance mechanisms.

The Agreements provide for *ad hoc,* routine, and special inspections. *Ad hoc* inspections take place to verify the information contained in the initial report on the nuclear material, to identify and verify changes in the situation since the date of the initial report, and to identify and verify the quantity and composition of nuclear material before its export from or its import into the State.[75]

Routine inspections – which constitute the major part of the Agency's inspection effort – are made to verify that reports are consistent with records, to verify the location, identity, quantity and composition of all safeguarded nuclear material, to verify information on possible causes of material being unaccounted for on shipper/receiver differences and uncertainties in book inventories.[76]

Special inspections are made to verify the information in special reports and also if the Agency considers that information obtained in other ways is not adequate to fulfil its responsibilities under the Agreement.[77]

The Agreement further regulates, in accordance with the Blue Book, access for the purpose of inspections, the frequency and intensity of routine inspections, the notice given for inspections, the designation of inspectors and the conduct of inspectors.[78] The IAEA's Director General must submit the names, qualifications and nationalities of proposed inspectors to the concerned State. The State has the right to refuse an inspector, in which case such inspector is removed from the list of inspectors finally nominated. The number of inspections conducted will depend on the extent of the nuclear activities of a given country. A large reactor has given rise to an inspection quota of 50 man-days a year. A man-day is a day on which a single inspector has access to a plant at any time, for a total of not more than eight hours. A man-year is defined as 300 man-days.[79] A processing plant such as Windscale in the United Kingdom gives inspection quotas of six man-years. The IAEA has the right to distribute the inspection quotas with respect to the facilities in a given country.

The most atypical feature of IAEA inspections is that authorisation by the State(s) is not required for each *ad hoc* and routine inspection; there need only be a notice in advance, as prescribed in the agreements. In addition, a proportion of routine inspections may be carried out without advance notification. Special inspections require consultations between the Agency and the State, but disagreements may be submitted to an arbitral tribunal competent to take binding decisions.[80] The conclusion of the technical phase consists of an Agency statement of the amount of Material Unaccounted For (MUF) over a specific period within each Material Balance Area.[81]

The statement of the MUF shows the difference between the book inventory and the physical inventory at the end of a period. Due to the technical complexities involved in correct measurements of the materials under safeguards, it becomes extremely important to establish whether MUF is due to diversion, or is attributable to measurement inaccuracy. The IAEA has developed inaccuracy percentages, which, if they are not exceeded, do not imply diversion; *e.g.,* for an isotope enrichment plant, no greater inaccuracy than ± 0.2 per cent., for plutonium and reprocessing plants for irradiated uranium, no more than ±1 per cent.[82] These percentages are variable in so far that improvement in techniques could lead to their change.

The Agency, as agreed with the State, should give information on the results of the inspections, and the conclusion it has drawn from its verification activities in respect of each Material Balance Area.[83]

The IAEA must carry out its inspections in such a way that States' peaceful nuclear activities are disturbed to the smallest possible extent. States have a right to nominate representatives to be present at inspections though they must in no way interfere with them. IAEA inspectors cannot operate nor direct the operation of any equipment. In addition, the agreements provide for the protection of production secrets. The IAEA may request only the minimum of information needed to carry out its supervisory activities.[84] The Agency is obliged to report the results of the inspection and, in general, any remark concerning safeguards *only* to the concerned State. Information on the supervisory activities is given to the Board in summary form, except in the case of suspected diversion.[85]

Supervisory costs are divided up so that the IAEA pays for its own expenses, as does the country being checked. However, exceptional costs incurred by States as a result of Agency requests are to be borne by the Agency.[86] In order to specify in detail how the procedures laid down in the Agreement are to be applied in each specific case, the Blue Book provides for Subsidiary Arrangements between the Agency and the State concerned.[87]

The State provides the Agency with design information on each facility. This includes identification and description of the facility, description of features of the facility relating to material accountancy containment and surveillance, and description of the existing and proposed procedures for nuclear material accountancy and control.

This information is used to prepare the technical document that is to lay down how safeguards are to be applied: the Facility Attachment, which is part of the Subsidiary Arrangements.[88] The Agreement provides norms concerning the verification by Agency inspectors of the design information.[89] This design information permits a degree of flexibility in the supervisory activities that can be included in the arrangement. Factors such as the

504

technical process involved, the quality of the operator's methods, the level of control of the national system and its capacity to act independently of the operator, will influence the choice of procedures to be applied.[90] Specifically, it will bear upon the extent to which independent verification by the Agency will take place.

4.3. Safeguards and the form of IAEA supervision

The instruments of safeguards constitute the technical phase of the super-vision of the non-proliferation obligation laid down in the NPT.

In cases where there has been a *finding of diversion* by the IAEA Board the form of the supervision that follows is non-judicial: the technical supervisory phase is followed by one in which political considerations could play a rôle.

If a dispute arises out of the interpretation or application of the Agreement between a State and the Agency, *not involving a finding of diversion,* the dispute is to be submitted to an arbitral tribunal at the request of either party. The decision of this tribunal – comprising of one arbiter designated by each Party, and a third designated by the two arbiters – is binding.[91] Although this procedure does not apply to cases involving a finding of diversion, it has direct relevance for IAEA supervision, as the following example will show. When the Agency and the State disagree on the need for additional access to information and locations by other (special) inspections than those specified in the Agreement, this issue is to be resolved by means of resort to the arbitral tribunal.

4.4. The political phase of I.A.E.A. supervision

The corrective purpose of the political phase takes place within the Board of the IAEA.

Various mechanisms have been established in the Blue Book for corrective purposes in the political phase. First, there is the transmission of the inspectors non-compliance report by the Director General to the Governing Board. This report, which contains Agency verifications of diversion, forms the basis for deliberations in the Board. Secondly, there are the actual deliberations of the Board. Since no case of this kind has yet occurred under the NPT the impact of the Director General's report in relation to other (political) considerations (fortunately) cannot be assessed. Thirdly, there are the opportunities (in the language of the Blue Book) that are afforded to the State to give the Board any necessary reassurance.[92]

In addition to this, the Agreements include provisions that give the State(s) the right to request that any question ·arising out of the interpretation or application of the Agreement be considered by the Board, as well as the right to participate in the discussions of that organ about any such questions.[93]

Other mechanisms, such as negotiations and other procedures agreed by the parties, are possible if the Board decides that the Agency has not been able to verify that there was no diversion.[94]

Direct coercive measures may be applicable as well, if the State concerned is an IAEA member: direct curtailment or suspension of assistance furnished by the Agency; call for the return of materials; suspension from membership.[95]

The Agency may also make reports to the Security Council and the General Assembly of the UN, and to all IAEA members.

Another mechanism in the political phase is the competence of the Board to call upon a State to take immediate action when, on the basis of a report from the Director General; this action is considered essential and urgent in order to ensure verification that nuclear material is not being diverted, irrespective of whether procedures for the settlement of a dispute have been invoked. A final finding of diversion being not explicitly necessary, makes this mechanism a sort of provisional measure.

4.5. Modality and safeguards

The safeguards system (i) applies only to specific well-defined circumstances, (ii) concerns only situations of importance, and (iii) deals with individual cases which are judged on their own merits. At the same time it is a permanent system including accounting, containment and surveillance that take place continuously or at regular intervals, without any need for accusation or suspicion. Consequently, it seems justified to suggest that safeguards constitute a complex system in which general and specific features are combined.

V. EFFECTIVENESS OF SAFEGUARDS

The effectiveness of the safeguards system administrated by the IAEA should be assessed, in the first place, in the light of its general preventive (corrective) function, namely, the timely detection of diversion and deterrence based on the risk of early detection. According to the IAEA Annual Report for 1980, the Secretariat, as in previous years, 'did not detect any anomaly which would indicate the diversion of a significant amount of safeguarded nuclear material . . . for the manufacture of any nuclear weapon, or to further any other military purpose, or for the manufacture of any other nuclear device'.[96]

This conclusion was achieved on the basis of inspection and evaluation (review) activities undertaken by the Agency. In 1980, more than 1,100 inspections in more than 500 nuclear power plants in the NNWS were carried out; six million surveillance pictures were taken; 3,000 seals were applied; reports concerning 700 installations were received and 400,000 data entries were stored in the Agency computer.[97] A comparison with the data for 1979

506

shows an increase in the above-mentioned activities of the Agency.[98] In addition, the keenness of the safeguards system was shown by the fact that more than 200 anomalies were detected and, upon Agency investigation, satisfactorily explained.

Highly important in the assessment of safeguard effectivity are the creative functions performed by the Agency. The identification of the concrete purpose of safeguards under the NPT and its instruments on the basis of the previous safeguard experience of the Agency, and the development by a Special Committee on Safeguards of the Blue Book, as a 'model' agreement are the first creative actions to be named. In addition the constant Agency assessment of the safeguard system should also be considered.

In 1975 a Standing Advisory Group on Safeguard Implementation was established to provide the Agency with recommendations on basic safeguard criteria (for example, timely detection and significant quantities) in order to permanently scrutinise the effectiveness of safeguards.[99] From 1976 Safeguards Implementation Reports (SIRs) have been presented annually to the Board of Governors by the Director General. The SIRs convey to Member States the assurance, obtained by the supervisory activities, that no proliferation has taken place; they are intended as an instrument of systematic and critical scrutiny of safeguard implementation; they recommend steps that should be taken by the Agency, the States and the facility operators to improve the efficiency of safeguards.[100] The transmittal to the States of Agency assurances that no proliferation has taken place has the function of promoting confidence, by invalidating any suspicion that a State could have that a 'malevolent neighbour' is striving for something one is oneself prepared to forgo.[101]

The SIRs also show the annual degree of progress obtained through Agency activities in the field, at headquarters and by co-operation with the States, in solving the problems identified. Problems and recommendations related to Agency and States activities are also formulated.

The 1980 SIR (as in previous years) testifies to an increase in safeguard effectivity, due mainly to an increase in Agency personnel,[102] improvement in the application of safeguards, better co-ordination of Agency activities and better co-ordination with the States.[103] This improvement is partly attributable to Agency activities in the field of research, and improvements in technology and organisation, e.g., improvement in the co-ordination and quality of the inspectors' activities; creation of a working group in charge of the elaboration and normalisation of the activities of inspectors, and of improving the internal procedures for presenting reports; the examination by two consultative groups and by an international working group of problems concerning containment and surveillance; automatisation of non-destructive essay techniques and application of safeguards to enrichment plants; application of a new system of computerised information on safeguards; consultations with States and creation of 'comités de liaison' to improve the national account systems.

Problems and recommendations identified in the SIR include the increase in the average time required to secure the consent of States to the designation

507

of new inspectors; the need for all States to apply the recommendations concerning the State systems of accounting for and controlling nuclear material; the deterioration in the promptness of the reporting by NPT States[104]; the need to improve procedures of notification of international transfers of safeguarded items; the need to improve co-ordination between Agency programmes to support safeguards; the need to elaborate methods of application of safeguards for certain types of facilities (for example heavy water reactors); and the need to apply safeguards to other facilities (for example, enrichment plants).

The creative functions performed by the IAEA, as well as the fact that no proliferation has taken place in the case of NPT States, have strengthened the (generally) accepted perception of the value of safeguards procedures. During the Second Review Conference of the NPT, held in Geneva from August 11 to September 7, 1980, the participants expressed their satisfaction with the safeguards procedures for existing facilities.[105]

However, it remains difficult to sustain the submission that supervision could prevent proliferation completely if a State decided to 'make the bomb.' The following aspects should be taken into account in this connection:

1. Diversion of quantities of fissionable material could take place unnoticed by ascribing them to the accepted margin of error in material accountancy. This would have the most significance in large scale civilian nuclear programmes.[106] In addition, it has already been mentioned that the probability of detection of diversion amounts to 90 per cent., and, hence, safeguards are not completely fool-proof.

2. It is possible to obtain fissionable material under the pretext that it is for non-proscribed military purposes.[107]

3. The above-mentioned possibilities are more dangerous considering that the possibility of 'making the bomb' can come about in a very short time. This is, *inter alia,* a result of the spread of nuclear knowledge.[108] A country could design and develop all the non-nuclear components of a nuclear explosive, which is not prohibited by the NPT. If the diversion in question was of plutonium or highly enriched uranium, to turn them into an explosive could be a question of days.[109]

4. The deterrent effect of the discussions in the Governing Board, and of the possible sanctions could be too late and too little. This is important considering that the technical instruments of safeguards can detect diversion (in order to allow international action), but cannot avoid that diversion (physically) taking place.[110] Even assuming that enough evidence could be presented to the Board (and hence, also, that inspection is not suffering errors, *force majeure,* or undue influences), the discussion of such a delicate political issue could take more time than is needed to make the bomb. In addition, the sanctions available to the IAEA, do not appear adequate in relation to the gravity of the violation. Besides, it remains to be seen whether the adoption of effective and immediate sanctions by the UN Security Council will ever become operative. The Security Council has seldom used its coercive powers under Chapter VII of the UN Charter.[111]

Other factors could also have an impact upon control being undertaken by the IAEA, affecting the whole purpose of the NPT, and its supervisory system:

1. The lack of universality of the NPT. The States that have not ratified the NPT – among them States that can make a bomb if they have not yet done so[112] – could provoke a snowball effect on neighbouring States. This possibility is the more serious considering that the NPT is abrogable, and its duration is 25 years. In addition to the above-mentioned problem, the lack of universality of the NPT leads to discrimination *vis à vis* the NNWS that have ratified the Treaty. While such States must submit *all* their nuclear activities to safeguards (full scope safeguards), exports by NWS to NNWS do not require this kind of safeguards. Under Article III,2 of the NPT, only the specific nuclear material or facility imported should be subjected to safeguards.

2. The NNWS opinion that NWS have not complied with the disarmament provisions of the NPT. NNWS have repeatedly criticised the lack of advance on this issue, as shown during the First and Second Review Conferences of the NPT members. The lack of progress in disarmament could emphasise the discriminatory application of the NPT, and consequently weaken its legitimacy.[113] (If having, developing and increasing atomic arsenals is defended as a factor of power, NNWS could be tempted to acquire these power factors.)

3. The proliferation danger stemming from the development and possible commercialisation of enrichment and reprocessing plants and fast breeder reactors. These new technologies increase the risk of proliferation. In addition, IAEA safeguards have been applied mainly to the relatively easy parts of the fuel cycle (light water reactors).[114] In spite of the fact that the IAEA is currently undertaking intensive research, experience in safeguarding new sorts of facilities is nevertheless scanty and tremendous technical problems are involved.[115]

The above-mentioned developments have led some NWS and some States which export nuclear items[116] to feel that the NPT approach is insufficient, and to take measures directed at restricting the export of sensitive technology, to tie exports to the acceptance of full-scope safeguards, to reserve a right of consent for the enrichment or reprocessing of nuclear materials exported and to propose schemes for the internationalisation or regionalisation of enrichment and processing.[117]

However, these developments have met with resistance from States that consider them ruled out by the NPT[118]; as yet, no consent has been achieved on those measures.

The Third World countries that have ratified the NPT (and have accepted both discrimination in favour of NWS in atomic weapons, and full-scope safeguards) do not accept that, in the light of Article IV of the NPT their right of access to peaceful nuclear technology and items could be restricted. This would create an additional 'have'–'have not' category of States in the field of the peaceful use of nuclear energy.

As in the case of the lack of advance on the disarmament issue, restrictive technological policies and measures – if not based on consensus in the international community – could endanger the fabric of the NPT by accentuating the discriminatory character of the Treaty for Third World countries. This is all the more dangerous as the danger of proliferation is, in the first place, a political problem, and unilateral acts can lead to an erosion of the political will not to embark upon policies of proliferation.

In conclusion, it could be said that the safeguards system administered by the IAEA has till now provided a creative means for the supervision of the non-proliferation obligation of the NNWS under the NPT.

By showing that supervision in this field is possible, safeguards have not provided any additional arguments in favour of proliferation, that could have stemmed from the control so far undertaken. However, whether the degree of legitimacy of this supervision will be an asset in maintaining and even upgrading it in order to meet the new challenges coming, *inter alia,* from technological changes, will depend in the last resort on the political and strategic issues relevant to non-proliferation.

NOTES

1. Horizontal proliferation means the acquisition by NNWS of atomic weapons. Vertical proliferation means an increase in the arsenals of the NWS: both the number of weapons and their explosive power and accuracy of delivery. See *infra*, pp. 497–498, 509–510.
2. Stockholm International Peace Research Institute (SIPRI), *The NPT; The main Political Barrier to Nuclear Weapon Proliferation,* (London: Taylor & Francis Ltd. 1980), p. 1; W. A. Smit and P. Boskma 'Laser Fusion'; *Bulletin of the Atomic Scientists,* December 1980, p. 37.
3. J. van Ginkel, H. J. Neuman, C. J. Visser, *Kernenergie en Kernwapens; Nederland en het non-proliferatiebeleid* (Nederlands Instituut voor Vredesvraagstukken, Staatsuitgeverij, 's-Gravenhage, 1977), p.p. 77-82.
4. See text in UN Doc. A/Res/2373 (xxii), Annex INFCIRC/140.
5. Other forms of safeguards are possible under the Statute of the Agency. See *infra*, p. 493.
6. IAEA, *The Annual Report for 1980*, p. 40. Three NWS the U.K., the U.S.A. and France, have concluded agreements with the IAEA on their nuclear activities not having national security significance. The agreements with the U.K. and the U.S.A. entered into force on August 14, 1978 and December 9, 1980 respectively. The agreement with France is still awaiting ratification. These agreements are based on voluntary offers. Under the NPT only NNWS are obliged to conclude safeguards agreements with IAEA. France is not a party to the NPT.
7. The six states were India, Israel, Pakistan, South Africa, Spain and Egypt; *ibidem*, p. 40.
8. U.S. State Department Publication, 1976, Appendixes 13–16.
9. P. Szasz, *The Law and Practices of the International Atomic Energy Agency,* (Vienna: IAEA, 1970), p. 17.
10. J. S. Nye, 'Non-Proliferation: A Long-Term Strategy', April 1978, *Foreign Affairs*, pp. 604–605.
11. UNGA, Official Records, 8th Session, 470th meeting, paragraphs 79–126.
12. P. Szasz, *op. cit. supra*, note 9, pp. 23–41.
13. See text in 276 UNTS 4.
14. P. Szasz, *op. cit. supra*, note 9, p. 550.
15. *Ibidem*, pp. 381–382.
16. See Article IX, A.
17. P. Szasz, *op. cit. supra*, note 9, p. 360.
18. *Ibidem*, p. 381.
19. See *infra*, pp. 509–510.
20. P. Szasz, *op. cit. supra*, note 9, p. 453.
21. *Ibidem*, p. 551.
22. IAEA Doc. INFCIRC 66/Rev. 22.
23. 21 *IAEA Bulletin*, (1979), Nos 2/3, p.13.
24. *Ibidem*, p. 14.
25. *Ibidem*. For a list of issues covered by safety guides, see *ibidem*, pp. 15–16.
26. IAEA, *The Annual Report for 1980*, p. 27.
27. *Ibidem*.
28. *Ibidem*.
29. *Ibidem*, p. 26.
30. *Ibidem*.
31. See Statute, Article III,A(6).
32. P. Szasz, *op. cit. supra*, note 9, pp. 659–660.
33. Doc. INFCIRC/18.
34. See Statute, Articles XI,E(3); XI,F(2); XI,F(4); XII,A, B, C.
35. P. Szasz, *op. cit. supra*, note 9, p. 660.
36. *Ibidem*, p. 696.
37. INFCIRC/11, Part I.
38. F. L. Kirgis Jr., *International Organizations in their Legal Setting, Documents Comments and Questions* (St. Paul, Minn., 1977), pp. 13–15.
39. See *infra*, pp. 496–497.
40. See Rules 15, 19, 66, 69 (d, e), 105.
41. North America, Latin America, Western Europe, Eastern Europe, Africa and the Middle East, South Asia, South East Asia and the Pacific, the Far East.
42. P. Szasz, *op. cit. supra*, note 9, p. 137.

43. The IAEA is financed by both regular and voluntary contributions from the Member States. The regular budget for 1980 was U.S. $75,656,000. The voluntary contributions amounted to U.S. $10.5m.

44. Such is the case with the election of the Director General and a number of procedural issues; Rules of Procedure, 33, 36 (c,f), 59, 60.

45. See Article VII,D and B of the Statute. For activities concerning supervision see *infra*, pp. 503, 505–508.

46. Technical Assistance and Publications, Technical Operations, Research and Isotopes, Safeguards and Inspection, Administration.

47. See Statute, Article VII,F.

48. Stanford Arms Control Group, *International Arms Control; Issues and Arrangements* (Stanford, 1974), pp. 297–298.

49. *Ibidem*, pp. 295–297.

50. *Ibidem*, pp. 299–301.

51. W. Häfele, 'NPT Safeguards', in: *Nuclear Proliferation Problems* (SIPRI, 1974), pp. 147–148.

52. J. C. Woodliffe, 'The Non-Proliferation Treaty Revisited', *NILR* XXVII, 1980/1, pp. 51, 53, note 93.

53. See Preamble, paragraphs 9, 10, 11, 12, 13.

54. IAEA, *20 Years International Atomic Agency* (1977), p. 86.

55. J. Prawitz, 'Arguments for extended NPT Safeguards', in: *Nuclear Proliferation Problems* (SIPRA, 1974), pp. 159–160.

56. See *Infra*, pp. 23–20.

57. IAEA Doc. INFCIRC/153.

58. Compare with INFCIRC/66 P. Szasz, *op. cit. supra*, note 9, pp. 558–560.

59. Safeguards are directed against proliferation through states. The term 'physical protection' refers to proliferation through 'subnational' activities (for example: terrorism, sabotage).; H. Grümm, 'IAEA Safeguards: Where Do We Stand Today?' (1979) 21 *IAEA Bulletin*, No. 4, p. 35.

60. W. H. Higinbotham 'Safeguards techniques' in *Nuclear Energy and Nuclear Weapon Proliferation*, (SIPRI, 1979), p. 191.

61. IAEA, 'The Present Status of IAEA Safeguards on Nuclear Fuel Cycle Facilities' (1980), 22 *IAEA Bulletin*, Nos. 3/4, p. 5.

62. *Ibidem*.

63. W. Häfele, *op. cit. supra*, note 51, p. 153.

64. *Ibidem*; see *infra*, p.504.

65. See *infra*, pp. 507–508.

66. IAEA, *Non-Proliferation and International Safeguards* (Vienna, 1978), pp. 18–19.

67. See paragraphs 51–58 of the Blue Book.

68. IAEA, *Non-Proliferation and International Safeguards*, p. 18.

69. 'Material Balance Area' means an area in or outside a facility; see paragraph 110 of the Blue Book.

70. 'Strategic Point' means a location selected during examination of design information. Under normal conditions, the information from all 'strategic points' taken together, can be combined so that the information necessary and sufficient for the implementation of safeguard measures is obtained and verified. See paragraph 116 of the Blue Book.

71. In accordance with the Blue Book the State is required to (a) provide the IAEA with information concerning facility design features and all other information relevant to safeguards; (b) maintain records for each facility or material balance area; and (c) provide the IAEA with reports in respect of nuclear materials based on the records kept. The IAEA also collects information of its own through inspection, and it evaluates all the information received and collected to determine its completeness, accuracy and validity. See IAEA, 'The Present Status of IAEA Safeguards on Nuclear Fuel Cycle Facilities' (1980), 22 *IAEA Bulletin*, Nos. 3/4, pp. 6–7.

72. IAEA, *loc. cit.* (note 66), p. 20.

73. *Ibidem*.

74. *Ibidem*, pp. 21–26.

75. See paragraph 71a, b and c of the Blue Book.

76. See paragraph 72a, b and c of the Blue Book.

77. See paragraph 73a and b of the Blue Book.

78. See paragraphs 74–89 of the Blue Book.

79. See paragraph 109 of the Blue Book.

80. See *infra*. p. 505.
81. See paragraph 90 of the Blue Book.
82. Norges Offentlige Utredninger, *Nuclear Power and Safety* (Norway, 1978), p. 225.
83. See paragraph 90 of the Blue Book.
84. Norges Offentlige Utredningen, *op. cit., supra*, note 82, p. 223.
85. H. Grümm, *loc, cit., supra*, note 59.
86. Norges Offentlige Utredningen, *op. cit., supra*, note 82, p. 227. M. I. Shaker *The Nuclear Non-Proliferation Treaty, Origin and Implementation 1959-1979*, (Oceana Publications, 1980) Vol. I–II, p. 764.
87. See paragraphs 39–40 of the Blue Book.
88. *Ibidem*.
89. See paragraphs 42–48 of the Blue Book.
90. R. Rainer and B. Sanders, 'The IAEA's NPT safeguards; national control and International Safeguards', in *Nuclear Proliferation Problems* (SIPRI, 1974), pp. 135–137.
91. See paragraphs 20–22 of the Blue Book.
92. See paragraph 19 of the Blue Book.
93. See paragraph 22 of the Blue Book.
94. See paragraph 19 of the Blue Book.
95. See paragraph 18 of the Blue Book.
96. IAEA, *The Annual Report for 1980*, p. 40.
97. IAEA, *The Safeguards Implementation Report for 1980*, Doc GOV/2028, p. 4.
98. IAEA, *The Safeguards Implementation Report for 1979*, Doc GOV/1982, p. 4.
99. See *supra*., pp. 501–502.
100. See IAEA, *The Special Safeguards Implementation Report for 1976*, Doc GOV/1842; *The Safeguard Implementation Report for 1977*, Doc GOV/1911; *The Safeguards Implementation Report for 1978*, Doc GOV/1939.
101. H. Grümm, *loc. cit., supra*, note 59.
102. The Budget allocated to safeguards by the IAEA after the entry into force of the NPT more than doubled in proportion to the years before. See J. Rotblat, 'Nuclear Proliferation: Arrangements for International Control', in: *Nuclear Energy and Nuclear Weapon Proliferation* (SIPRI, 1979), p. 274. The staff of the Department of Safeguards rose from 79 to 213 between 1970 and 1979, the number of facilities inspected from 90 to 500, the number of annual inspections from 172 to 1100.
103. IAEA, *The Safeguards Implementation Report for 1980*, Doc GOV/2028, p. 7.
104. The (average) promptness of reporting by states deteriorated from 36 days in 1979 to 65 days in 1980.
105. See SIPRI, 'The Second NPT Review Conference,' in: *Yearbook for 1981*, p. 306.
106. SIPRI, *The NPT: The Main Political Barrier to Nuclear Weapon Proliferation* (1980), pp. 20–21.
107. See *supra*, p. 499.
108. J. Nye 'Maintaining a non-proliferation régime,' (1981), 35 *International Organization*, pp. 18–20. A proliferation process concerns motives as well as the possibilities of gaining access to nuclear weapons. The motives should be sought in both the national security policy of a state and in the pursuit of prestige. Possibilities have to do with access to technology, installations and nuclear materials. See W. A. Smit 'Over Kernwapens: Het Nonproliferatiestreven door de jaren heen' (On Nuclear Arms: The Non-proliferation Endeavour through the years), (1981) *Transaktie*, pp. 5–6.
109. SIPRI, 'The Non-proliferation Treaty,' in *Yearbook for 1980*, p. 320.
110. W. A. Smit, *loc. cit., supra*, note 108, p. 13.
111. K. Skubiszewski 'Use of Force by States; Collective Security: Law of War and Neutrality', in: M. Sørensen, ed. *Manual of Public International Law* (1978), pp. 789–795.
112. Especially Argentina, Brazil, India, Pakistan, Israel and South Africa.
113. W. Epstein, *Retrospective in the NPT Review Conference; Proposals for the future* (The Stanley Foundation, 1975), pp. 7–12. Ph. Towle, 'Nuclear Non-proliferation: Deadlock at Geneva, *The World Today*, (October 1980), pp. 371–374.
114. J. Rotblat, 'Nuclear Energy and Nuclear Weapon Proliferation,' in *Nuclear Energy and Nuclear Weapon Proliferation* (SIPRI, 1979), p. 418.
115. W. A. Higinbotham, 'Safeguards Techniques' in *Nuclear Energy and Nuclear Weapon Proliferation* (SIPRI, 1979), pp. 190–196.
116. B. Z. Cowan, 'A Look at US Nuclear Non-Proliferation Policy,' (PASIL, April 26–28, 1979), pp. 161-166, 177–181.

117. On the Agreement adopted in 1976 in London by fifteen states suppliers of nuclear materials and equipment (Belgium, Canada, Czechoslovakia, France, F. R. Germany, German D. R., Italy, Japan, the Netherlands, Poland, the Soviet Union, Sweden, Switzerland, the U.K., the U.S.A.) known as the 'London club' see SIPRI, *loc. cit.* (Note 106), *pp. 7–9; A. Kapur, International Nuclear Proliferation*: Multilateral Diplomacy and Regional Aspects, (1979), pp. 77–80; W. A. Smit, *loc. cit., supra*, note 108, pp. 25–31. On unilateral states exporting policies see A. Kapur, *op. cit.*, pp. 92–119; B. Sanders, 'Nuclear Exporting Policies,' in *Nuclear Energy and Nuclear Weapon Proliferation* (SIPRI, 1979) pp. 241–248. On proposals to create a new international agency (INFA: International Fuel Agency) in charge of enrichment, fuel fabrication, reprocessing and waste disposal plants, see J. Rotblat, 'Nuclear Proliferation Arrangements for International Control' in *Nuclear Energy and Nuclear Weapon Proliferation* (SIPRI, 1979), pp. 283–284. This proposal considers, *inter alia*, that since the IAEA both promotes the use of nuclear energy and deals with its misuse, a certain conflict of interests is present: safeguards imply an element of suspicion which does not go together with promotion. On the INFCE (The International Fuel Cycle Evaluation Programme), see U. Farinelly, 'A Preliminary Evaluation of the Technical Aspects of INFCE', in *Nuclear Energy and Nuclear Weapon Proliferation* (SIPRI, 1979), pp. 261–269.

118. SIPRI, 'The Second NPT Review Conference', in *Yearbook for 1981*, pp. 317–318.

514

PART VIII

SUPERVISION WITHIN THE ORGANISATION FOR ECONOMIC CO-OPERATION AND DEVELOPMENT

SUPERVISION WITHIN THE ORGANISATION FOR ECONOMIC CO-OPERATION AND DEVELOPMENT

by H. A. H. Audretsch

CONTENTS

I. GENERAL ASPECTS OF THE OECD

1.1. The origin of the OECD

The OECD is an organisation for inter-governmental economic co-operation among 24 Member States, spread over four continents. All countries, except one, Yugoslavia, have the status of full member.[1] When the OECD Convention entered into force, September 30, 1961, the Organisation consisted of 20 Member Countries; only two more than its predecessor, the Organisation for European Economic Co-operation (OEEC).[2] Nevertheless, the enlargement may be considered as fundamental; two mighty States, the U.S.A. and Canada joined as full members.[3] Europe had by then reached such a high degree of prosperity that it could match itself with the economically strongest countries in the world.[4] Thus, new perspectives for strengthening the co-operation, taking up new tasks and setting broader objectives had been opened. Especially it was believed to be necessary that the economically more advanced nations should assist the countries in process of economic development. In short, the European partners – now belonging to the first group of nations – should share the burden of development assistance to the Third World countries, together with primarily the U.S.A. and Canada.[5]

Moreover, experience from the 1950s showed that the OEEC was not capable of meeting and solving major problems occurring at that time. Absence of co-ordinated internal and external policies proved to be more and more frustrating. Differences in approach between the partners, differing views on the further development of Europe, especially in politics, made a reconsideration of the original co-operation necessary. No *communis opinio* about a United States of Europe proved to exist. When, in 1957, six out of the 20 OEEC Member States created the European Economic Community and Euratom, a fundamental revision of the OEEC became inevitable. The pan-European free Trade Area idea had suffered defeat. In order to prevent Europe from falling into more regional groupings without any institutionalised links with the U.S.A. and Canada, a reconstitution of the OEEC was strongly stressed by the two latter countries. Actually, the U.S.A. succeeded in safeguarding the links with Europe. A basis for co-ordination of policies and a fairer burden-share in development assistance was established. Formally, the new tasks and objectives were laid down in a new convention. *De facto,* the convention appears to contain a continuation of the former co-operation, taking into account the above-mentioned economic and political changes. so it may be rightly said that the OECD forms a reconstituted OEEC.[6] Even the legal capacity of the OEEC is to be continued by its successor,[7] the OECD. Various acts (decisions) of the OEEC could remain effective after the coming into force of the OECD, when approved by the OECD Council.[8]

1.2. Aims and Tasks

1.2.1. Aims

The aims of the OECD are laid down in Article 1 of the Convention. Next, a series of undertakings for the Member States is summed up in Article 2. In

Article 3 some means are mentioned by way of which the aims might be achieved and the undertakings fulfilled. The decision-making process is laid down in Articles 5 and 6.

Article 1 OECD reads:

'The aims of the Organization for Economic Co-operation and Development (hereinafter called the Organization) shall be to promote policies designed:

(a) to achieve the highest sustainable economic growth and employment and a rising standard of living in Member Countries, while maintaining financial stability, and thus to contribute to the development of the world economy;

(b) to contribute to sound economic expansion in Member as well as non-Member Countries in the process of economic development; and

(c) to contribute to the expansion of world trade on a multilateral, non-discriminatory basis in accordance with international obligations.'[9]

It appears that in the OEEC the aims were formulated in a more concrete way than in the OECD. This can be easily explained by reference to the moment when and the circumstances under which the co-operation was started. Once the economic recovery of Western Europe was accomplished, it became more difficult to formulate concrete objectives. In fact, the number of future candidates of the OECD was too big and their political ideas too diverse. So, the formulation of the aims remained rather vague and less strict. The main objective of the Organisation refers to the promotion of the economic and development policies of the co-operating Member States. Primarily, emphasis is laid on quantitative aspects, such as: growth, a rising standard of living and economic expansion. In achieving these objectives the world economy would be served too. The OECD had to be the framework within which a co-ordination of policies could take place.

The main objects under Article 1 are supplemented by a series of sub-aims, laid down in Article 2 OECD. Thus, the members agree that they will both individually and jointly:

'(a) promote the efficient use of their economic resources;

(b) in the scientific and technological field, promote the development of their resources, encourage research and promote vocational training;

(c) pursue policies designed to achieve economic growth and internal and external financial stability and to avoid developments which might endanger their economies or those of other countries;

(d) pursue their effort to reduce or abolish obstacles to the exchange of goods and services and current payments and maintain and extend the liberalization of capital movements; and

(e) contribute to the economic development of both Member and non-Member Countries in the process of economic development by appropriate means and, in particular, by the flow of capital to those countries, having regard to the importance to their economies of receiving technical assistance and of securing expanding export markets.'

The co-operation is essentially based on the recognition by the members of the increasing interdependence of their economies. This clearly appears from the preamble. Problems like inflation, balance of payments difficulties, monetary instability, unemployment etc. can hardly be solved by the states, independently from each other. All states have to take into account the interests of others, with whom they have economic relations. For this purpose, the OECD functions as a permanent forum for information, consultation, political guidance and organisational support. Consequently, the following obligation is laid down in Article 3 OECD:

> 'With a view to achieving the aims set out in Article 1 and to fulfilling the undertakings contained in Article 2, the members agree that they will:
> (a) keep each other informed and furnish the Organization with the information necessary for the accomplishment of its tasks;
> (b) consult together on a continuing basis, carry out studies and participate in agreed projects; and
> (c) cooperate closely and where appropriate take coordinated action.'[10]

The field covered by the Organisation is wide. In principle the multilateral co-operation relates to all international economic and financial problems that may arise. All States may participate in all activities of the OECD, and so they do, in practice. Only in a few rare instances do some countries stay aside, either because they have no interest, or they disagree.[11]

1.2.2. Tasks

Information, political direction and co-ordination

How wide ranged and how far reaching the aims of the OECD are, may be proved by its tasks and activities and the field the Organisation takes into consideration. As may be deduced from the above-cited Articles 1, 2 and 3 OECD, it is clear that the main tasks consist of informing and consulting each other on policies and the promoting of co-ordinated actions. The fields covered are economics, trade, financial and fiscal affairs, agriculture and fisheries, social affairs, development assistance, technical co-operation, environment, science and technology, energy (including nuclear energy).[12] Moreover, liberalisation is (and has been) a major activity. It is closely linked with the sub-aim of Article 2(d) OECD, cited above. Abolishment of barriers to trade, services, payments, capital movements – in short a freer and larger circulation of goods and invisibles – should improve the general economic development of all countries concerned.[13] Actually, when the reconstitution of OEEC took place about 95 per cent of all intra-European exchanges of goods were liberalised. So, in the OECD the emphasis is laid on liberalisation of invisibles and capital movements. The elimination of tariff-barriers has never been a target of the OECD. It has always been regarded as the task of GATT to solve this problem.[14]

Review

In view of the said aims and tasks a major activity of the OECD consists of reviewing the policies of the Member States. These reviews may range from drawing up surveys, exchanging information, to confrontation and real examination of policies. The surveys may be accompanied by serious comments, conclusions, prognoses and recommendations. Moreover, the results of a review are, as a rule, made public either in short communiqués or *in extenso,* in reports. To mention three important yearly review publications:

(1) the so-called *OECD Economic Survey* (country by country);

(2) *Development Co-operation, Efforts and Policies of the Development Assistance Committee. Report by the Chairman of the DAC.* The latter report contains a survey of current development issues and a comprehensive review of the development assistance policies of the DAC-members[15] and other donor-countries[16];

(3) *Energy Policies and Programmes of IEA Countries. Review.* These reports, as of 1977, present the results of the review of the performance of national programmes and policies in the field of energy.

In the course of its existence the OECD has widened and deepened its activities. It has tried to bring the reviews more and more to perfection. Policy analyses are, if possible, combined with a review of policy issues or with an attempt to formulate issues and the necessary recommendations in this respect.[17]

Shift from quantitative aspects to qualitative aspects

Moreover, a change of approach in reaching the aims is to be noted. In the sixties much emphasis was laid on the quantitative aspects: growth, rise, expansion of the economy. At the end of that decade a shift took place. Qualitative aspects began to play an increasingly major role. General well-being of man, adequate standards of living, environmental conditions, natural resources, social climate came into consideration.[18] Growing attention was paid to research, innovation and last, but not least, to (conservation of) energy. In view of the latter problem new activities were undertaken within a new autonomous subsidiary body, the International Energy Agency.[19] Nuclear energy matters were dealt with by another (semi-autonomous) body, the Nuclear Energy Agency.[20] Contacts with developing countries were established within the Development Centre.[21] As such, this Centre now functions as the OECD's 'window' to the Third World and as a point of impact to co-operate with other organisations in the said field, *e.g.* the UNCTAD and FAO.

1.3. Institutional framework

From an institutional point of view the OECD, like the OEEC, belongs to the traditional, inter-governmental type of international organisations. OECD has two permanent bodies, *viz.* (i) the Council and (ii) the Executive Committee, assisted by (iii) a Secretariat and (iv) a number of subsidiary bodies.

(1) The Council

The decision-making power lays within the hands of the Council, composed of representatives of all Member States, at present 24.[22] As a rule the Council meets once a year in a session of Ministers. For the rest the meetings are in sessions of Permanent Representatives. The Council can take decisions

521

on both the level of Ministers and the level of Permanent Representatives. The Council designates its Chairman and two Vice-Chairmen. The Council meeting at sessions of Permanent Representatives is presided by the Secretary-General.[23] The Council may establish subsidiary bodies.[24]

(2) The Executive Committee

The Executive Committee, to be appointed by the Council, consists of 14 members. The Council yearly decides which countries will be represented in the Executive Committee. In practice, the seven big Member States have a permanent representative in the Committee, whereas the smaller countries in rotation take part in the Executive Committee. The Executive Committee functions as a screen for the Council. It examines whether an act is suitable to be dealt with by the Council. Thus, all reports, proposals, documents submitted by a Committee to the Council are subject to the prior consideration of the Executive Committee.[25] Next, it functions as a stimulator in the decision-making process. The Executive Committee can give instructions to the various subsidiary bodies to study certain questions.[26] Its task is a highly political one.

The Executive Committee in Special Session

As from 1972 the Council decided to establish an Executive Committee in Special Session. It is charged with analysing of and consulting on international monetary, trade, investment and related economic issues having regard to the intention of Member Governments to work for reform of the international monetary system and, at the same time, to achieve further progress towards trade liberalisation. Thus, it should stimulate co-operation between the members in the above-mentioned areas.

(iii) The Secretary-General

The Secretariat is headed by the Secretary-General of the Organisation appointed by the Council for a period of five years.[27] The office of the Secretary-General is of an independent and impartial character. Consequently, the Secretary-General, his two Deputies (Secretaries-General) and Special Counsellors shall neither seek, nor receive instructions from, any authority within or without the Organisation.[28] The same applies to the staff serving the Secretariat. As indicated above, the Secretary-General has obtained a stronger position in the OECD than in the OEEC.[29] He has the following four major tasks:

(a) Co-ordination of all information to the Member States and the various OECD bodies.

(b) Initiation and stimulation of the decision making process within the Council and the Executive Committee. The Secretary-General can apply his formal right of initiative in his capacity of Chairman of the Council meetings on the Permanent Representatives' level. Moreover, he is entitled to submit

522

proposals to the Council at ministerial level. He can fulfil the same initiative and stimulating role in the various subsidiary bodies, either by being present himself or by being represented in the subsidiary body. In drawing up the agenda[30] and in convening the meetings of the Council and its subsidiary bodies, the Secretary-General can exercise considerable influence. The minutes of the meetings are, as a rule, taken by the Secretariat and circulated to the members and bodies concerned.

(c) Execution of the Council decisions, in conformity with the Council's instructions and directives. Supervision over the execution by the Member States of their obligations *vis-à-vis* the Organisation. For this purpose the Secretary-General is entitled to ask the Member States for the necessary information. The Secretary-General is responsible to the Council.

(d) Establishment and maintenance of the external relations between OECD, other international organisations or States.

In order to serve the Council in an effective and efficient way the Secretariat is divided into a number of departments.[31] The general direction and co-ordination rests upon the Secretary-General, his two Deputies and Special Counsellors. They cover all major activities of OECD in the macro-economic field, employment, energy, North-South relations, external relations and Positive Adjustment Policies (PAP). The staff support comes from the various units, according to their special expertise (legal service, North-South relations, planning). The planning unit is especially charged to support the Special Group on Positive Adjustment Policies.[32]

In total, the Secretariat consists of about 1,500 persons.

(4) Subsidiary bodies

As circumstances require, the Council may establish subsidiary bodies[33] either on an *ad hoc* basis or permanently. As a rule these bodies are not autonomous. However, autonomous and semi-autonomous bodies may also be set up, *viz.* the IEA, NEA, Development Centre, OECD-Fund.[34] Overall the OECD has in its principal fields about 30 main committees. Most of them have sub-committees, working-parties and/or working-groups. In total the number of subsidiary bodies lies between 150 and 200. Subsidiary bodies have no decision-making power, except in the case of being autonomous or semi-autonomous. Nevertheless, their role in the decision-making process is essential. They prepare studies, they submit proposals for decision to the Executive Committee or the Council.[35] The subsidiary bodies have to report to the Council about their activities. The liaison between the Committees, the communications *inter se,* between them on the one hand, with non-Member Governments and international organisations on the other hand, is served by the Secretary-General.

The number of delegates to each Committee is rather small. Having regard to the great number of committees and other subsidiary bodies, and taking into account that usually all Member Countries can and mostly do participate in the work of the Organisation, the total number of meetings must be fairly high. One could even draw the conclusion that apart from holidays, OECD delegates are permanently in session. Of course, delegates participate according to their knowledge and interest. Often, however, the same persons are engaged in a great number of committees. This is due to the fact that the Member Countries usually try to keep the number of delegates they send to ordinary commission meetings (in Paris) restricted.

A great deal of preparatory work has to be done by the Secretariat. It forms the centre of gravity of the Organisation. The Secretary-General has to ensure the continuity and the progress of the work. Within his hands lies the responsibility for the co-ordination between the various subsidiary bodies and the departments of the OECD Secretariat.

It is to be noted that in the OECD a parliamentary body is absent. However, with the social partners (both trade unions and management unions), working contracts have been established.[36] Labour and management meetings occur at regular intervals.[37]

1.4. Legal instruments

OECD has the following legal instruments at its disposal[38]:
– decisions;
– recommendations;
– agreements;
– declarations, and
– resolutions.

Decisions are legally binding upon the Member States, who have voted in favour. Recommendations, declarations and resolutions are not formally binding legal acts.[39]

The number of decisions[40] with a material content is small. From practice it appears that decisions mostly deal with:

(a) institutional and/or procedural aspects;
(b) technical and/or administrative problems;
(c) liberalisation of trade and payments.

From a political and economic point of view, the subjects under (a) and (b) are not the most important. The liberalisations are a different matter. In the OEEC the liberalisation of trade and of payments was one of the main aims. It is due to the Code of Liberalisation of Trade, that the freeing of trade was almost realised under the OEEC. This Code has been replaced by the Code of Liberalisation. Under the OECD two problems remained urgent: the freeing of invisible operations and capital movements. For this purpose the OECD has set up the Code of Liberalisation of Current Invisible Operations and it has taken over the OEEC Code of Liberalisation of Capital Movements. Services, however, are still not sufficiently covered in the OECD.

The various other decisions are more numerous. Although legally non-binding they deal with important matters: the further execution, implementation and/or definition of often rather vaguely formulated principles to co-operate and to co-ordinate policies. The legal form appears to be not so relevant. What is of most concern, is whether the partners have reached – unanimously – consensus on a certain concrete matter. If this is laid down in a recommendation, all the members who have subscribed to this act, feel morally bound to comply with it. Moreover, all decisions imply review by the OECD. Generally, the members are requested to inform the OECD in which manner they have adhered to a decision. The right to review all decisions is derived from the basic obligation in that respect laid down in the OECD-Convention.[41] The Member States have expressly agreed that they will inform the Organisation with all information necessary for the accomplishment of its tasks. Of course, review may occur in different forms and modalities. Moreover, the ways and means to effectuate review (supervision) may also differ.[42] They may vary from a mere exchange of information to inspection and examination by means of confrontation.[43] It should be mentioned that there are no provisions dealing with sanctions.[44]

1.5. Means to achieve the aims

Substantially the Convention enumerates the following means to achieve the aims:
(a) exchange of information;
(b) consultation;
(c) co-operation and co-ordination.[45]

Keeping each other informed and furnishing the Organisation with the necessary information is the most general way of co-operating. The Organisation then can fulfil a clearing-house function, drawing up (statistical) surveys and distributing them to the Member States. Moreover, receiving information may form the starting point for review, consultation, examination, future forecasts, policy making and decision making.

Consultation can take place in various forms and for various reasons: review of policies; explanation of behaviour; reaching consensus in the decision-making process; creating closer co-operation and co-ordination of policies.

Co-operation, leading to co-ordinated action is the most far-reaching instrument for achieving the basic aims. Such a co-operation is *inter alia* aimed at in the Programme on Positive Adjustment Policies.[46] Co-operation may also result in concrete participation in joint-projects.[47]

Financial stimuli,[48] as a means to achieve the aims, are not mentioned. However, they do play a role. Reference should be made to the Financial Support Fund, established in 1975, but not yet brought into force.

The necessity to reach co-ordination of policies, or to undertake co-ordinated action, became apparent directly after the reconstruction of Western Europe started. First, co-ordination was pursued sector by sector. Little by little it became clear that co-ordinated action should take place in an overall way. The OEEC, however, was not instituted and not equipped to cope with this problem. This was one of the reasons for reshaping the OEEC into the OECD.

Nevertheless, the first impetus in the right direction was given under the OEEC, after the Suez crisis in 1956. At that time it was decided to set up an Economic Policy Committee (EPC). The EPC was charged with the task of following closely, by way of country examination and confrontation[49] of policies, the general economic trends and developments of the Member States. Thus, the stage was set for the by now well-known annual economic country reviews, reporting on the economic situation and the future prospects. With the reconstitution of OEEC the task of the yearly economic reviews has been assigned to the Economic Development Review Committee (EDRC).[50] The task of formulating general economic policy options has remained the work of the EPC.[51] In doing so, it has to rely, to a considerable degree, on the above-mentioned economic country reviews.[52]

1.6 Decision-making

'A Council composed of all the Members shall be the body from which all acts of the Organisation derive.'[53] These 'acts' – decisions[54] – are, as a rule, to be taken by mutual agreement of all the Member States.[55] Each member has one vote. Abstention does not invalidate the decision-making. So, the decisions will be applicable to those who voted in favour but not to the abstaining Member.[56] The decisions are internationally binding upon the States. So, in order to have effect within the national legal order they usually have to be transformed or taken over. The Convention provides that 'no decision shall be binding on any Member until it has complied with the requirements of its own constitutional procedures. The other Members may agree that such a decision shall apply provisionally to them'.[57] This explains why the OECD-decisions may be qualified as quasi-treaties.[58] Every Member can judge for itself whether a parliamentary approval for a decision is required.[59] The OECD may, by decision of the Council, approve of Agreements with its Members, non-Member States and international organisations. By accepting such a decision of the Council the OECD makes it clear that the Organisation as such wants to become a party to an agreement. Consequently the Council usually makes a recommendation to 'press' the Members to ratify an agreement.[60]

Unanimity, reached by consensus, certainly is the rule within OECD. In some rare occasions, *inter alia* within the IEA, other voting procedures are provided.[61] It has already been noted above[62] that the subsidiary bodies have, as a rule, no decision-making power. The Council has to give its fiat. Very often the 'legislatisation' of a decision is but a formality. However, it cannot be left out. Semi-autonomous bodies formally rest under instruction and supervision of the Council. Autonomous bodies have a decision-making power on their own. The Council is not entitled to give instructions, nor can the Council call autonomous bodies to account. The rules concerning decision-making, the meetings, the agenda, the representatives etc. are laid down in the *Rules of Procedure of the Organisation.* In principle they apply to all bodies and all decisions.[63]

The legal instruments have already been indicated.[64] It has also been noted that substantially the decisions deal with exchange of information, consultation, co-operation and co-ordination.[65] Financial stimuli as such are not mentioned.[66]

Proposals for decisions are usually based on and backed by statistical surveys, reports and studies,[67] prepared within the Secretariat of the OECD. This may be called the technical phase. Next, discussions and consultations take place on various political levels, especially within the subsidiary bodies. So, a certain growing understanding for each other's problems develops and consensus may be reached. Thus, an integrational effect may result from this kind of co-operation. Moreover, this effect may be stimulated by the system of reviewing and evaluating the national policies on a regular basis and taking the consequences thereof.[68]

1.7 Budget

The OECD is financed by its Members apportioned in accordance with a scale to be decided upon by the Council.[69] As a measuring-stick the gross national product is taken.[70] The Secretary-General is responsible for the draft budget. He has to present it to the Council in accordance with the Financial Regulations adopted by the Council.

Apart from the 'regular' annual budget, there are the subsidiary budgets for the (semi-)autonomous bodies and special programmes.[71] Here, different scales are applied because, as a rule, not all Members participate in such bodies and/or activities. As soon as the budget is approved, the Secretary-General is entitled to cash the contributions and to make the necessary expenditures. The financial account stays in the hands of the Board of Auditors, consisting of four independent financial experts.[72]

1.8. Concluding Remarks

Both the OECD and the OEEC are marked by a pragmatic way of handling. Moreover, the latter paved the way for its successor, the OECD. Scarcity of means of production and finances forced the OEEC partners to weigh the needs carefully, before dividing and spending the Marshall Aid. Within a rather simple institutional framework a decision-making process, based on consensus, evolved, combined with a process of supervision, *a priori* and *a posteriori*. The OEEC system is generally regarded as having been quite successful and basically the system was to be continued when the reconstitution of OEEC took place. Although solidarity may have slackened off from the sixties, the framework for permanent discussion and consultation remained alive. The decision-making process, together with various supervisory mechanisms, has continued to be a general feature of the Organisation.

Co-operation has gradually been pushed on, sometimes in new fields, *viz.* energy policy, and sometimes in new directions, *viz.* positive adjustment policies. Co-ordination of policies is still a major item, although the degree of its binding effect and the degree of providing details may not be of the highest standard required for co-ordination. But this is quite understandable, having regard to the number of participants, their rather broad and vaguely formulated objectives, and their wish to remain their own masters. However, the fact remains that there exists a permanent organisation in which the partners inform and consult each other regularly on programmes, targets, studies and policies in all areas of economic life. First they do so on the level of experts, next on the various political levels. A certain integrational effect, a growing understanding of each other's problems results from this kind of co-operation. Personal contacts between the administrative authorities ensures that this co-operation forms part of their daily work. Also, the actual and frequent exchange of information, constitutes a positive aspect, the more so where these data are gathered and worked out on a comparable basis. Studies, economic reviews and outlooks, and statistical surveys form an important part of the OECD co-operation. In practice, this material is often used as (the) reference, because of its high standard. So the OECD data are used both in the policy-making process by national authorities and by trade and industry. A certain influence and consciousness of the interdependency of the various economies surely results from the OECD. This influence may be stimulated by the system of reviewing and evaluating both the general economic policies of the partners and parts and sectors of national policies, in the light of the aims and undertakings as set out in the OECD Convention. As to the latter – review in specific sectors like industry and management – mention should be made of the actual endeavours to reach co-operation and co-ordination with regard to Positive Adjustment Policies. The co-operation includes:

(1) examination of specific policies in the light of the orientations for positive adjustment policies;
(2) exchange of views on national experience in dealing with PAP;
(3) periodic examination of the progress made in resolving the difficulties;
(4) examination of the information available and the methods used in Member Countries to analyse and publicise the costs and benefits of the specific policies to consumers, producers and tax payers.

The results to be expected from PAP co-operation are threefold:

(1) a continuous dialogue on structural adjustment strategies of individual Member Countries and a better understanding of these policies;
(2) a number of general policy conclusions by the Special Group of the Economic Policy Committee (EPC) on Positive Adjustment Policies which may further clarify the orientations for PAP;
(3) a report on the methodological aspects of information systems and techniques for policy evaluation, with a view to identifying the best options available to the Member Countries.[73]

Having regard to these evaluation- and consultation-systems aiming at policy direction and policy guidance, having recourse to the organisational support of a qualified Secretariat, there is justification for looking a little closer into these review procedures. First, this will be done from a general point of view. Next, the subject will be dealt with sector by sector.

II. SUPERVISION IN THE OECD

2.1. General

2.1.1. Some characteristics of OECD supervision

As a general statement one can say that supervision mechanisms are marked by the organisation for which and in which they are meant to work. Both the founders' philosophy and the actual functioning of an organisation play a major role for unfolding the mechanisms. Moreover, an interplay may be reached, which may influence the organisation as a whole and supervision in particular.

As for the OECD one can speak of a 'new born' OEEC. It still bears the marks of the 'OEEC birth' and its previous 13 years of experience: its members are all more or less equally orientated and have the same backgrounds, culturally, economically and politically. They are all Western, or Western-orientated countries belonging to the developed part of the world (with the possible exceptions of Portugal, Spain, Turkey and Yugoslavia). When the OEEC was reconstituted into the OECD, the latter had firm links with the U.S.A. and Canada. It could rely on a typical pragmatic way of handling problems. OEEC started as a dynamic and a most practical organisation, be it of a traditional, inter-governmental type; it opted for a non-formalistic approach of tackling problems in an open, prompt and fair manner. This 'philosophy' has been continued under the OECD. Efforts and achievements are reviewed, needs are identified and, according to the circumstances, the necessary decisions are taken. In principle, every State remains free to choose its own policies, but it should also take into consideration what has been decided within the OECD.[74] As has previously been indicated,[75] co-ordination has become a must, *nolens volens*, and so has supervision. According to the general inter-governmental tendencies – also typical for the OECD – supervision is, in principle, exercised by inter-governmental bodies. There is no judicial body for reviewing either the behaviour (and decisions) of the OECD bodies or the behaviour of the Member States. So, the bodies charged with a supervisory task are primarily manned with persons designated by the governments of the participating States.

Three main organs play a role in the OECD in this respect: the Council; the Executive Committee and the various subsidiary bodies.[76] To remove any appearance of partiality, independent experts are usually engaged to assist the said bodies. Moreover, much of the preparatory work is done by

529

the Secretary-General,[77] his counsellors and staff. The Secretary-General may also engage independent experts-consultants *ad hoc*.

The general statements and the specific distinctions made with respect to international supervision by Van Hoof and De Vey Mestdagh in Part I of this book, also apply *grosso modo* to OECD.[78] Experts can be said to tackle the subject more from a technical point of view, in principle they are free from political considerations. But, as the OECD deals with economic relations and economic law, political aspects do play a major role. The political stage cannot be omitted. Indeed, technical review is, as a rule, combined with, or finalised by, political review. There is a constant participation of all parties concerned, especially the governments.[79]

The litigious issue forms the object of deliberations between the supervisory agency and the State concerned, by means of conciliatory procedures and through mutual concessions, having recourse in most cases to compromise solutions. This political review-stage is essentially flexible and contingent. Indeed, it reflects much of the actual practice of inter-governmental international co-operation. The political aspects not only relate to the procedures as such. They also indicate that in the last instance the responsibility lies in the hands of politicians; in the case of OECD in the hands of the Council. The Council takes decisions with political implications. The preliminary work – the investigations into the matter from a technical point of view – is done by the various subsidiary bodies.[80] They usually report on their findings in a provisional way, a draft report with draft recommendations. It is up to the Council to decide upon such drafts. It may approve of the draft, and it may then decide for its publication. If the Council disapproves of a draft, for political reasons, it may ask for another report or investigation. The subsidiary body concerned will then take into account the political considerations that played a role in the Council's discussion and decision. The Council might also, on the basis of the findings, conclude during the (political) debates that an 'obligation' under discussion should be more specified or adjusted or amended. The Council acts in a creative manner, either exercising supervision in its creative function or deciding as a law or policy maker.[81]

Supervision can be exercised either occasionally or permanently. In OECD both modalities occur.[82] As to the functions of supervision, the review, correction and creative functions are to be found.[83] The supervisory method usually applied in the fields of economic development policy, development assistance policy and energy policy is the overall test. For the rest random tests are, as a rule, applied.[84] Moreover, if a review takes place it is intended to be substantial, not merely formal.[85]

The matter under review is mainly of an economical and political character. This clearly follows from the aims and tasks of the OECD.[86] Supervision is thus directed on the one hand to a review of structures and orientations of national policies and on the other hand to the effect given to recommendations, guidelines and rules set for a closer co-operation, co-ordination and/or positive adjustment. These 'rules' are mostly not of a strictly juridical kind. They deal with a behaviour to be aimed at in the economic and/or political sphere, such as improvement of the economic situation; positive adjustment policies[87]; freedom of trade; relations with developing countries. The objectives should be achieved by exchange of information, consultation and co-ordinated actions. The 'obligations' appear to be mostly rules of 'soft' law, moral engagements to do one's best promoting and steering policies in certain ways and directions. The steering activities form the core of the co-operation.

The review function is, as pointed out in the introductory study of Van Hoof and De Vey Mestdagh,[88] one of the most characteristic functions of supervision. It is exercised to assess the facts, the situation, aims, issues and policies. In short, the reviews aim at a clear statement of affairs.

Next, a critical follow-up may take place. The outcomes of the assessment are examined and compared with the objectives, rules, targets, guidelines and programmes set within the Organisation. This comparison may take place in the form of an open discussion, consultations, or a real examination or confrontation session. The latter form is to be found when *inter alia* the economic development policies, trade policies and development assistance policies are reviewed. Political aspects then play an important role: they are usually brought forward to 'soften' a prior statement, to make a state's behaviour more understandable for the partners and to formulate a review-statement in a diplomatic way. It is said that firm criticism may be heard 'indoors', within a committee charged with review.[89] But such criticism is covered, as a rule, in public reportings. From the wording, however, it may be deduced that a behaviour, a situation, or a fact has given rise to rather critical observations.

If a behaviour is found to be not in conformity with objectives and rules, a discussion usually takes place either to obtain correction or to 'adjust' the rule in the specific case. In the latter case the creative function of supervision is exercised.[90]

It should be noted that although supervision may be distinguished according to its various functions, a clear-cut division in stages cannot be made. In practice the exercise of supervision very often implies the fulfilment of the said functions simultaneously. And so, a certain appraisal of national policies, situations and acts is established. Mutual understanding develops, paving the way to map out issues and principles in common and to continue the application of the system's regular review. Thus, a process of information, discussion, consultation, confrontation and examination is kept activated. This process is not an end in itself, but is followed with a view to achieving the aims and fulfilling the undertakings set in the Convention.[91]

Basically, the review procedures are started within the various subsidiary bodies. They do the preparatory work in close co-operation with the Secretary-General and his departments.[92] The members of the various bodies, where possible, do their supervisory work at home. They only meet incidentally and for short periods in Paris.[93] The regular contacts are maintained via the Secretary-General and the national Permanent Representatives at the OECD. The latter should maintain the political relations with all partners. This occurs *quasi* permanently via the traditional diplomatic channels, on all levels.[94]

In conclusion, it appears that there is a great deconcentration of tasks within the OECD.[95] Final decisions, however, are taken – whether they deal with law-making, policy-making or a mere fiat for publication of a report[96] – as a rule at top-level, by the Council. Below, a more detailed survey, sector by sector, will be given.[97]

2.1.2. Collection of information

The right to collect the relevant information forms one of the essential requirements for the well-running of any organisation. It applies especially where observance of international obligations is at stake. As to the right to collect information and the obligation to supply it, the Convention is short, but clear. Article 3 OECD provides that the members 'keep each other informed and furnish the Organisation with the information necessary for the accomplishment of its tasks.' Thus, the duty to supply information is made dependent on the question as to whether it is necessary for fulfilment of the tasks of the OECD. When this is the case, the obligation applies both to the members mutually and in relation to the Organisation.

Information as such may give rise to questions, uncertainties, even misunderstanding. In such cases a clarification by way of consultation can be useful. It may solve problems at an early stage. Actually, consultation is provided for,[98] and regularly applied in practice.

The obligation to supply each other with the necessary information should be completed with the right to ask each other for information. For the OECD this is the case. In particular, committees are entitled, with the agreement of the Secretary-General, to ask the Member States for further information *inter alia* by means of questionnaires.[99] The Council, who establishes the committees, has the same right. In drafting and dispatching such questionnaires the Secretary-General plays an important role.[100] Moreover, one finds provisions on the obligation to supply information in various decisions setting up committees and working out the Convention. It may be said that in OECD there is a general right to ask for information and a general obligation to give it, when such is requested. There is no general obligation to supply it 'automatically.' But, in the terms of reference of a given committee, this may be laid down differently, *e.g.* by way of prior notification.[101] Sometimes information is supplied at regular intervals, according to a certain model or scheme. This is formally called reporting or the bringing out of reports (*e.g.* annual report, quarterly report).[102] It is a special instrument like inquiry and inspection. Consultation, in consequence of supplying information, has already been mentioned.[103]

A special kind of consultation developed in the OEEC and the OECD is the confrontation or the examination. Originally, the examination procedure has been set up to reach a fair division of the Marshall Aid. Because this aid was limited, it had to be allocated to those who needed it most.[104] Afterwards, as of 1956, the confrontation method has been taken over by the Economic

Policy Committee for reviewing the general economic policies of the members. Little by little, the method has spread to most of the other sectors of the OECD.

Confrontation

In its most perfect form – as applied by the Economic Development Review Committee[105] – the confrontation procedure consists of five stages:

1. The procedure is initiated by the drawing up of a memorandum by each of the Member States.
2. Thereupon the Secretariat prepares a paper for internal discussion, the memorandum serving as the basis for the paper.
3. Moreover, the Secretariat, together with the representatives of two countries functioning as examiners, issues a questionnaire which has to be answered by the third Member Country under examination.
4. The discussion paper, the memorandum and the questionnaires are then discussed within the specialised committee, first in restricted sessions, ultimately *in pleno*.[106]
5. Publication of the facts, the findings and possible recommendations for the future,[107] as agreed upon in the plenary session.

Particularly in the economic development country review and the development assistance review the confrontation method is applied in the above-mentioned form.[108] The confrontation method does not only function as a means to obtain information. It also functions as a means to obtain compliance with the treaty obligations, and to reach consensus on certain lines of conduct and issues for the future (recommendations). In other words, confrontation fulfils various functions of supervision.[109]

Closely related to the problem of the instruments of information[110] is the question of the sources of information. From what material can the information be drawn? Another question of course is: how reliable is the material (source)?

Important sources to be used in supervision practice are official publications by national (semi-)authorities. To enumerate some: statistic figures; budgetary debates; minutes of Parliamentary discussions; reports; opinions; socio-economic programmes and prognoses; laws and statutes; judicial judgments.[111] Moreover, the social partners and pressure groups make their opinion known in publications. Next, 'non-official' information can be obtained from the mass-media, newspapers, scientific studies etc.

2.1.3. Instruments of supervision

The instruments of supervision may be devised according to the functions which supervision fulfils. Thus, communications, reports, inspection, notification can all be said to be instruments of the review function. Friendly settlement and sanctions are instruments of the corrective function. Consultations and political discussions do fulfil a role for all three functions of supervision, whereas confrontation is primarily used in relation to the review and correction function.[112] All these instruments are used within the OECD, except pure sanctions, such as suspension of membership, expulsion, fines. Sanctions in the broad sense, including all kinds of pressure to raise public opinion and to 'mobilise shame' are applied.

Because of the importance of the consultation in almost all sectors of the OECD, a few comments must be added. First, it should be noted that working sessions and discussion meetings, all sectors taken together, occur *quasi* permanently.[113] The consultations are informal and flexible in method, channelled by the Secretary-General to the relevant Committee. The real confrontation method is, as sketched above,[114] more formalised. It is characterised by a face-to-face discussion, well prepared by experts from the Secretariat and the examiners from the Member Countries. The specialists are on the one hand country experts and on the other hand subject experts. So, both aspects are taken into account. Moreover, the national examiners come from two other countries than the country under examination. Thus, questions and comments are raised from different national backgrounds. This may pressure the State under examination to explain in detail its policies and the motives behind them. Because of the confidential character of the discussions the atmosphere is one of frankness and constructive criticism. Real difficulties, differences of views and approach are usually ironed out before the Council stage is reached. In this final stage, when a decision has to be made on the publication of the results, a more diplomatic approach is the norm.[115] Although the results may not always seem to be very dramatic, a number of achievements are obtained. First, such confrontation may prevent States from resorting to isolated national measures to cope with internal difficulties. Secondly, confrontation sessions are liable to bring to light essential problems and the need to choose priorities in policy making. Last, but not least, intensive consultations have made the various States 'more courageous in embarking together upon difficult policies than they would have been acting separately and at different times.'[116]

2.2. Supervision in various sectors of the OECD

From a structural point of view the OECD's activities are assigned to specific sectors. For each sector one or two main committees have been set up. They do the preparatory work for the Council. If necessary, the main committees have recourse to other subsidiary bodies, which they may set up.[117] The Secretariat has been subdivided along the same lines, according to the main sectors the OECD is dealing with. The main subjects or sectors are:

1. Economic affairs and statistics
2. Trade policy
3. Financial and fiscal affairs
4. Agriculture and fisheries, food
5. Social affairs, manpower and education

534

6. Development co-operation
7. Technical co-operation
8. Environment
9. Science, technology and industry
10. Energy.

Sector by sector a brief sketch will be given of the main activities in the field concerned and the methods applied for supervising the Member States. Consequently, the main committees will be dealt with and their mandate will be looked at below.[118]

2.2.1. *Economic affairs and statistics*

(a) Bodies and tasks

With regard to the objectives of the OECD it is clear that economic affairs and statistics play a major role. Two main committees deal with the subject matter:

(1) the Economic Policy Committee (EPC)
(2) the Economic and Development Review Committee (EDRC).[119]

Both Committees are backed by the Economics and Statistics Department of the Secretariat, having two main branches:

(1) the General Economic, Monetary and Growth Studies Branch (with four divisions);
(2) the Country Studies and Economic Prospects Branch (with five divisions).

(1) The Economic Policy Committee

The Economic Policy Committee (EPC) was established under the OEEC, during, and as a consequence of, the Suez crisis in 1956. According to its mandate the EPC has to keep under review the economic and financial situation and policies of the Member States. In doing this, the EPC will pay special attention 'to the internal effects of national policies in the light of the increasing independence of their economies and of the recognition that efforts of individual countries will be influenced by the actions of others, with a view to establishing a climate of mutual understanding conducive to the harmonious adjustment of policies'.[120] After the 1973 energy crisis the Council requested the EPC to examine also all economic and financial problems that may arise in relations between the OECD members and oil-producing countries.[121] Thus, the EPC functions as a major forum for reviewing short-term and medium-term general economic policies of the countries in order to achieve, via international co-ordination, the objectives set in the Convention. Several times a year top-level officials directly concerned with economic and financial policy making meet to discuss their policies in closed-door confrontation sessions. In view of the variety of the work and the complexity of activities a number of subsidiary bodies have been set up:

1. Working Party No. 1 on Macro-Economic and Structural Policy Analysis.[122]
2. Temporary *ad hoc* Groups of Working Party No. 1.
3. Working Party No. 3 on Policies for the Promotion of Better Payments Equilibrium.[123]
4. Working Party on Short-term Economic Prospects.
5. Temporary Working Party.

As the names of the above-mentioned bodies indicate they are all concerned with current analyses, short-term forecastings and medium-term orientations in the fields of general economic policies and balance of payments policies. The major policy items currently being restoring price stability; promoting investment-conditions and employment; defraying inflation[124] and preparing positive adjustment policies.[125] Moreover, attention has to be paid to the close links between energy policies and general economic policies. Short-term macro-economic analysis and forecasting have to pay due attention to developments on the energy side, especially in the oil markets. This implies a close co-operation between the Secretary-General and the Combined Energy Staff (OECD-IEA) preparing the work to be done within the EPC. Increased attention will be paid to the external repercussion of national policy measures. It is quite clear that co-ordination of general economic policies has to be based on detailed data from each country separately. In part, the data processing work is done by the Working Party on Short-term Economic Prospects, for the balance the Economic and Development Review Committee provides the EPC with the necessary data. The latter is backed by the Country Studies and Economic Prospects Branch of the Economics and Statistics Department of the Secretariat. Another important unit of this Department is the Economic Statistics and National Accounts Division. It files questionnaires on public expenditure, financial data and (un-) employment in order to obtain economic indicators, to process them and to distribute them to the Member States. The economic development of the various members is reviewed by the Economic and Development Review Committee. Its findings and recommendations are laid down in the annual *Economic Country Surveys*.

Summarising, the work of the EPC consists of examining the general economic policies, analysing economic data for short- and medium-term forecastings, exchanging views on the conclusions to be drawn from the findings and proposing recommendations for closer co-operation and positive adjustments.

(2) The Economic and Development Review Committee

The mandate of the EDRC is to be found in the Report of the Preparatory Committee.[126] The EDRC is, with others, responsible for the annual examination of the economic situation of Member Countries. It has to study, make comments and recommend to the Council on the development programmes. The review is exercised in the light of the policy issues and criteria set by the Council at its various meetings in the context of co-ordinated actions.[127] The method used by the EDRC is the confrontation or examination method, described above.[128] Every country has tor provide the EDRC with data on its economic situation and economic policies (*inter alia* statistics). These data are examined by an examination committee, consisting of both country specialists and subject specialists, who may request the country under examination to give the necessary explanations. Thus, it may be asked why a country has changed its policy, what it has done to live up to the OECD policy issues, what the authorities intend to do to cope with structural problems etc. The examination takes place in close co-operation with the Country Studies and Economic Prospects Branch of the Economics and Statistics Department of the Secretariat. Detailed inquiries are filed by the Secretariat. As a rule a visit is also paid to the country under review, by the examination committee. Thus, the matter can be discussed on the spot with top-level officials responsible in the field under examination. The discussions both within the examination committee and the examination meeting of the EDRC, *in pleno*, are confidential. The atmosphere is frank and open. Criticism may be uttered freely, and noteworthy achievements may be singled out for comment. Finally, the report has to be altered in a manner agreed in the plenary final session so that it can be published under the title *OECD Economic Survey*.

The material obtained during the review procedure is used for various purposes. Thus, it also serves to draw up the half-yearly *OECD Economic Outlook*.[129] This is done by the Secretariat. The *Outlooks* deal with short-term economic prognoses and development cycles. They should assist the Member Countries orientating and adjusting their economic policies, along the lines indicated by the OECD and agreed upon within the Organisation. Although the conclusions of the EDRC and the Secretariat cannot be enforced as such, their influence and impact on both policy makers, business and public opinion seems to increase more and more.

(3) The Committee for Monetary and Foreign Exchange Matters

This Committee dates from 1973. It has only met in session during the first years. After 1975 it was only to meet at the request of three or more countries.[130] In general, however, the financial questions are dealt with by the Committees on Financial Affairs.[131]

(b) Evaluation

The supervisory procedure in the field of economic affairs appears to be non-judicial, partly technical, partly political. Supervision is initiated on the basis and as a consequence of the general obligation to co-operate and to co-ordinate where appropriate.[132] Economic policy is reviewed quasi-permanently. It may be qualified as a 'general supervision,'[133] fulfilling review, correction, and creative functions. The various functions may be exercised, simultaneously but varying in degree, according to the stage of supervision.

In the technical stage of the confrontation procedure the fact-finding and the review function will be stressed. In this phase primarily, experts specialised in the matter and/or the country do the preparatory work. When the restricted confidential discussions with representatives of the Country under examination are held, the corrective function may play a major part. That is especially the case when problems have been noted relating to complying with the criteria and issues agreed upon in common. Finally, in the political stage the creative function may be fully employed to reach agreement: for instance, the interpretation and/or adaptation of an issue (*i.e.* a guideline) concerning a country having difficulty in adhering to the Convention. The general instruments for reaching correction or creative action are confidential consultations and political discussions. The latter occur primarily in restricted sessions of the examination commission and, last but not least, *in pleno*. Then, all members of the EDRC and the EPC are entitled to raise questions and to discuss the (final) draft report. Here all the Member Countries can exercise, according to the circumstances, their political powers. One does not encounter the word 'sanction' for various reasons:

(1) Legal sanctions are not foreseen in the Convention.

(2) The economic review procedure as such embodies a silent power[134] for ultimate effort to comply with the issues of the Convention. Within the restricted and confidential sessions a good deal of pressure may be exercised by way of discussion and consultation.

(3) The co-operation rests on a voluntary basis. In principle all members are free to abstain from a (political) decision. They should do so if they feel that they cannot fulfil an obligation.[135] Moreover, it is possible to accept an obligation under the condition that certain escape clauses are added. In OECD practice it appears that differences of opinion may give rise to consultation and discussion, but rarely create deadlocks. It is generally regarded as the task of the reviewing committee to reach a solution before the final stage is reached.

(4) Co-ordination in the OECD is usually exercised by way of such weak instruments that it makes little or no sense having sanctions and using them. Every real problem, well explained in a confrontation session, will lead to a sort of common understanding leaving room for adjustment either in the specific case or as a more general guideline.

From an examination of the supervisory procedures and practices in the field of economic policy one gets the impression that the statements and recommendations are seriously taken into account. The confrontation sessions are generally felt as useful.[136] The members under examination all appear to be co-operative in informing, confidentially, the examination committees. An important feature to note is that this mechanism has worked right from the beginning for over 30 years without any interruption. It has improved and is adjusted according to the needs, *quasi* permanently. It is generally agreed that the publications and forecastings are of a high standard.[137] One of the main results may be that the members have learned that they should take into account the international effects of their doings *vis-à-*

vis other countries. Moreover, it has become clear that a reappraisal of national economies is necessary in the light of fundamental changes in world economy: this was emphasised after the severe oil crisis of 1973. It gave rise to the need to reassess aims and techniques of economic policies. Within the OECD it also gave rise to study on the linkage of various problems (*e.g.* energy supply, prices and employment, wages, social standards) and macro-economic performance. Thus, for example, the relations with oil producing countries as such have become an issue of discussion. Moreover, a reconsideration of the problems of the poorer countries has become urgent (North-South relations).[138] Still another feature of the continuing development within the field of economic policy is the establishment of the Financial Support Fund of the OECD, since 1975.[139] Last but not least, more emphasis is to be given to short-term policies together with prognoses on medium-term orientation and their inter-linkage.[140] Thus, it appears that a continuing review has not only an assessing effect but also a dynamic effect, providing new political directions and stimulating action therein and pushing forward the OECD's activities, especially in economic affairs.

2.2.2. Trade policy

(a) General

The actual trade activities are to a large extent summarised in the so-called Trade Pledge or Declaration on Trade Policy of June 4, 1980.[141] This Declaration embodies efforts to maintain and to improve an open multilateral trading system, making use of the mechanisms of the Trade Committee for information and consultation with a view to both a periodic (annual) general review of developments and issues in trade policies and specific cases (*ad hoc* trade problems). This Trade Pledge is quite in line with the preamble of the OECD Convention where trade is regarded as one of the most important factors favouring economic development and the improvement of international economic relations. One of the aims of the OECD remains the reduction and abolition of all obstacles to the free movement of goods, services and payments combined with a total liberalisation of capital movements. Under the OEEC a high degree of quota-free trade has been reached. Payment facilities were obtained through the European Payments Agreements and the European Payment Union. The break-down of tariff-barriers was taken over by GATT in the early sixties. The elimination of the remaining import restrictions remained a target to be reached under the OECD. It has succeeded in this respect.[142] Elimination of non-tariff-barriers, such as administrative and technical obstacles, is still activated. Many of the obstacles are not directly related to trade. Indirectly, however, they may have an impact on trade. In this respect one has to think of various regulations on public health and security, safety, quality control, statistics, prevention of fraud etc. Another category of measures that may hinder fair free trade relate to dumping, government purchasings, export credits,[143] import and export licences, classification rules, voluntary auto-limitation of exports[144] etc.

An important aspect of trade relates to the commerce with less-developed countries. Free entry on the OECD markets and a reasonable income is of high concern to these countries. The major objectives within the OECD are now to avoid restrictive measures *vis-à-vis* those countries which are dependent on the export markets in the industrialised world and to promote conditions for mutual trade in manufactures and commodities between the developed and the developing countries. Thus, the North-South dialogue forms an important issue for consultation and discussion between the members. However, a real OECD line of conduct in developing a policy for the Group as a whole *vis-à-vis* the Third World is still awaited.[145] Nevertheless, discussion on an operationalising of a Common Fund for Primary Commodities goes on.[146]

Also, review on developments and prospects in trade with East European Countries is to be continued.

Another aspect relates to tax obstacles and double taxation. As to the latter subject a draft convention for the avoidance of double taxation on income and capital has been set up.[147] Thus, a kind of harmonisation of bilateral conventions on double taxation should be established.

Restrictive business practices also have an impact on trade. Along the lines of the OECD scheme it will be dealt with under the heading Financial and Fiscal Affairs.[148]

(b) Bodies, tasks and activities

The main body engaged with trade policy matters is (1) the Trade Committee. It is assisted by (2) a High Level Group (on Commodities, including Sub-Groups); (3) a Working Party of the Trade Committee; two Groups of experts [(4) on Export Credits and Credit Guarantees and (5) on Preferences]; and (6) a Joint Working Party of the Trade Committee and the Committee for Agriculture.[149] The Trade Committee is backed by the Trade Directorate of the OECD Secretariat. This Directorate is of a limited size.[150]

(1) The Trade Committee

As to the structure of the Trade Committee, it consists of senior officials responsible for the execution of trade policy in their country. They usually meet three or four times a year. The continuity in the work is guaranteed by the deputies who represent the senior officials and the delegates to the subsidiary bodies. From the beginning a liaison with the EEC, EFTA and GATT was arranged, ensuring representation in the meetings of the Trade Committee. The Trade Committee has the following functions:[151]

1. Confrontation of the general trade policies and practices at regular intervals or whenever requested by a member, having in mind the need for maintaining a system of multilateral trade which would enable members to exchange goods and services freely with each other and with other countries

540

under conditions of reasonable overall equilibrium in international balance of payments.

2. Examination of specific trade problems (primarily of interest to members and their overseas territories).

3. Consideration of any short- and long-term problems falling within the terms of reference of the Trade Committee.

One of the purposes of the establishment of the Trade Committee and its review/examination function is to enable any member to obtain prompt consideration and discussion by the Committee of trade measures taken by another member 'which would adversely affect its interest, with a view to removing or minimising such effects'.[152] Another purpose, especially of the regular annual examinations is to identify the main problems and tendencies emerging in international trade relations and to agree on trade policy orientations in line with the objectives of the Convention and the successive decisions (*e.g.* Trade Pledge). Especially macro-economic considerations have to be taken into account with a view to positive adjustment policy problems.[153] This implies close co-operation with other bodies, concerned with the same problems.

Information. The essential task, which underlies all activities of the Trade Committee, is to make sure that the members provide all necessary information. Next, the Trade Committee has to keep the members informed with up-to-date information. The information duty is laid down in the Convention itself.[154] In this specific case the information should be procured by way of notifications to the Organisation. *De facto* the Secretary-General takes care of the exchange of the information between the members.

Confrontation. From the quoted passage[155] on the functions of the Trade Committee it clearly appears that confrontation is an essential feature of its activities. First, as to its existence, the confrontations are to be held at regular intervals (annual reviews). They relate to both the general trade policy of each member and its trade practices, and to specific problems of topical and practical importance. In the latter case, if circumstances so require, *ad hoc* confrontation sessions can be arranged. To give an example, this can be the case in the event of a major change in the trade policy of a member since the last regular confrontation or if, following a substantial change in the situation in a Member State, the country concerned does not take the appropriate measures with regard to its trade policy.[156] The regular confrontations are meant to obtain an overall insight into the various trade policies of the members and to procure the necessary background information for subsequent sessions. Thus, an evaluation of trade policies may be possible. Having noted problems, an effort can be made to solve them. So, the confrontations are to be combined with consultations and recommendations from the OECD. Because of the interdependence between trade policy, financial, fiscal, and general economic policy there has to be a close co-ordination between the various bodies.

Consultation. Confrontation may be followed by consultation. Moreover, consultations can take place prior to confrontation. Every Member State is entitled to request for consultations. In practice this does occur rather often. It is interesting to note also that the EEC, who participates in the work of the OECD, makes requests for (prior) consultations.[157]

Examination. The Trade Committee is called upon to examine automatically all specific measures taken by the Member States.[158] If necessary, the examinations will be followed by consultations. The examinations should enable the OECD to keep developments in policies and trade practices under day-to-day review. A *conditio sine qua non* is of course that the members give full and prompt notification of all the measures they take.[159] Efforts are made to make the examinations more effective. *e.g.* by taking adjustment problems and policies into account. Moreover, examination may also relate to problems arising out of a periodical confrontation of the trade policies.[160]

In conclusion it can be said that the activities designed to promote an open multilateral trade system are primarily based on (i) a regular, annual review of, and consultations on, the general trade policies of the members and (ii) an *ad hoc* review of, and consultations on particular cases and issues. The method used has much in common with the procedure practiced by the EPC and EDRC.[161] To summarise:

(1) information (mostly by notification);
(2) fact-finding, examination, confrontation;
(3) consultation and
(4) recommendation (either in a corrective or in a creative direction).

In line with the general tendency within OECD there is little formalism. Any member may raise a problem and ask for examination, consultation and discussion.

(2) High Level Group on Commodities

Commodities play an important role in trade policies. Thus, a High Level Group on Commodities has been established, as from May 1975, under the aegis of the Executive Committee in Special Session.[162] The High Level Group, consisting of directors-general or experts responsible in the area, should continue discussions on commodity problems with a view to better defining national policies in a more co-ordinated way. This should facilitate a group-like approach at global (UNCTAD) conferences dealing with commodities.[163]

(3) Working Party of the Trade Committee

The W.P. of the Trade Committee is composed of Members of the Permanent Delegations to the OECD, charged with the carrying forward of the work of

542

the Trade Committee, between the latter's sessions. As guidance it takes the discussions and conclusions of the Trade Committee.

(4) Group on Export Credits and Credit Guarantees

According to the terms of reference the above group – made up of senior government officials and senior officials of export credit and credit insurance institutions – is responsible for holding regular confrontations on the national policies pursued in the field concerned. Such confrontations should lead to an assessment of the problems, an evaluation of the policies and discussions to solve or to mitigate problems. Moreover, the Group should work out common guiding principles – Guidelines for Officially Supported Export Credits.[164] It also has to review and to monitor the application of the latter guidelines. In doing so, it should consider all the possibilities for improving co-operation in this field by means such as prior consultation, prior notification, inquiries or other suitable methods. With regard to the confrontations held by DAC and the field covered in that area, a liaison is established to consult on the co-ordination of actions.

(5) Group on Preferences

This Group is convened when needs arise. The Group should hold multilateral consultations on the operation of the system of generalised preferences (G.P.S.) in favour of developing countries. It reports on this subject to the Trade Committee, making an evaluation of the system as a whole and proposing possible modifications or improvements. The Group should also prepare the annual examination of the operation of the G.P.S. within the framework of UNCTAD and if possible with consultations within GATT.[165]

(6) Joint Working Party of the Trade Committee and the Committee for Agriculture

With regard to the improvement of international trade, especially in agricultural products, it was thought useful to organise good co-ordination between trade and agriculture. Thus, a Joint Working Party of the Trade Committee and the Committee for Agriculture was set up. This Working Party is of a restricted composition, its members being chosen from both Committees. Primarily the Working Party is entrusted with the examination of questions of interest to both the Trade Committee and the Agricultural Committee. Like the Trade Committee itself, the Working Party is entrusted with:

(1) annual examinations;
(2) organising consultations;
(3) the preparation of adequate information procedures.

Here too, the Preparatory Committee suggested the introduction of a system of notification. Moreover, the Working Party was given a creative task. It had to formulate criteria for measures of aids to export during consultations on import restrictions or aids to exports of agricultural products.

543

Evaluation. From the practice described above it clearly appears that review (via information, notification, examination) and consultation are normal operations in matters of trade. The incidental and permanent review procedures are regarded as useful and helpful to get an insight into the various policies and to orientate and stimulate the policies in a more co-ordinated manner.[166]

2.2.3. Financial and fiscal affairs

General

Financial and fiscal affairs embrace a large field ranging from international investment, multinational enterprises, international financial markets, fiscal affairs, competition policies (restrictive business practices, consumer policies), and international tourism to maritime transport matters. Actually, 10 main committees, all having their various working groups of working parties, are active in this field. Dealing with each of these subsidiary bodies would exceed the limits of this study. Only the broad outlines will be traced with emphasis on the review aspects.

Financial and fiscal affairs both deal with invisibles, such as services, facilities, business behaviour, payments, flow of capital, investment and taxes (*e.g.* evasion). For various subjects the OECD has elaborated guidelines and codes, *e.g. OECD Guidelines for Multinational Enterprises* (M.E.), the *Code of Liberalisation of Capital Movements* and the *Code of Liberalisation of Current Invisible Operations*. The Guidelines on M.E. relate to review over various issues such as restrictive business practices, technology transfer, capital control, employee relations, disclosure of information, accounting standards. The two Codes of Liberalisation deal with the freeing of international capital movements and current invisible transactions. Currently, in a period of economic recession, the Codes are active as they include a mechanism to review the behaviour of the members with respect to restrictions of capital investments and international transactions of services. So these two aspects will be dealt with first. They fall largely under the responsibility of the Committee on International Investment and Multinational Enterprise (IME), and the Committee on Capital Movements and Invisible Transactions (CMIT).

The Liberalisation Codes on (1) Capital Movements and (2) Current Invisible Operations

From the Codes[167] it appears that the Committee on Capital Movements and Invisible Transactions (CMIT)[168] has 'to consider all questions concerning the interpretation or implementation of the provisions of this Code or other acts of the Council relating to the liberalisation' of either capital movements or invisible transactions.[169] It has to report its conclusion to the Council. The supervisory task of the Committee on CMIT is twofold:

1. It has to examine at regular intervals the measures that have been taken to liberalise capital movements and invisible operations (elimination of existing reservations).

2. It has to review the reservations lodged by a Member State, either on an item mentioned in the Annex to the Code or under Article 7 of the Code. That provision relates to various clauses of derogation which may be invoked for reasons of serious economic or financial disturbance in the Member State concerned.

Both the measures of implementation and derogation have to be notified in due time to the Committee on CMIT.[170] First of all the Committee has to investigate whether the lodging of a reservation is justified. If a reservation is not disapproved, it is re-examined every six months.[171] The examination is moreover directed to making suitable proposals for helping the member concerned to withdraw its reservations.

The Committee has to investigate complaints about frustrating the Code or non-fulfilment of the obligations arising from the Codes. If the Committee finds that a reservation has not justifiably been invoked, it remains in consultation with that State, with a view of restoring compliance with the Code. If, after a reasonable period of time the non-compliance continues, the situation has to be examined by a special Ministerial Group, unless the Organisation decides on some other exceptional procedure.[172] The same applies to the case in which a State has invoked derogations for reasons of balance of payments difficulties based on arguments which cannot be approved by the Committee on CMIT. Whenever necessary the Committee consults other OECD committees on any question relating to the liberalisation of current invisible operations.[173]

In short, it appears that on the basis of the Codes a system of notification and reporting has been set up with a view to examining and re-examining (a) existing reservations and (b) new reservations (derogations from the Code) in order to keep any reservations under control and to stimulate further liberalisation. The latter is *inter alia* reached by a critical review, questioning whether a reservation or derogation is still really needed. Here a horizontal approach of analysing the experience across all Member Countries is applied. Thus, reservations and derogations from the Code are to be compared with each other. The factors have to be found which block a (further) liberalisation.[174] Next, proposals can be made for deblocking liberalisation.[175]

Closely connected with the above-mentioned problems are the freeing of payments and insurances. For this purpose two committees have been set up: Payments Committee and the Insurance Committee. Both have to study the possibilities of freeing the said field and make the necessary proposals to the Council. Moreover, the Payments Committee is charged with reviewing and commenting on reports of the CMIT to the Council with respect to payments and capital movements.

International Investment and Multinational Enterprise

Closely related to the above-mentioned issues of the Codes of Liberalisation are the subjects of international investment and multinational enterprise.

The object is the functioning of enterprises in the international context. With respect to this issue the OECD has set up guidelines, containing codes of conduct of enterprises, rules for international investment (national treatment rule), transfer pricing and restrictive business practices. Member States are advised to adhere to the Declaration on the Guidelines[176] in order to have them applied by the relevant enterprises falling within their authority. It is up to the Committee for International Investment and Multinational Enterprise (IME) to develop and strengthen co-operation among the Member Countries in the field of international investment and multinational enterprises. As a matter of fact its task is very much fixed by the 1976 Guidelines and the related decisions.[177] First of all, it has to review the guidelines experience over a period of three years. The first review took place in 1979. Now, the Committee is preparing its second review, especially concerned with the implementing of the conclusions of the 1979 Review. The Member States have to report on their experience to the Committee. The Committee, moreover, consults with the Business and Industry Advisory Committee (BIAC) and the Trade Unions Advisory Committee on the promoting of reference to, and the use of, the OECD Guidelines for M.E. The Committee should also endeavour to clarify the meaning and scope of the Guidelines. Out of this examination proposals for political actions should be made *e.g.* with respect to positive adjustments and regional developments.

The Committee on IME is backed by a Working Group on the Guidelines, a Working Group on International Investments Policies and a Working Group on Accounting Standards. BIAC and TUAC, and representatives of the accounting profession participate in the work through regular consultations. The Working Group, particularly, is charged with the problem of disclosure of information by multinational enterprises.

In conclusion it can be said that the Committee on IME is a forum for information and consultation in this specific field. As to the consultation function the Committee also tries to assist the Member States to prepare discussions on the relevant issues in other international organisations.[178]

Domestic and Financial Markets

The financial markets, trends and prospects in this area are reviewed by the Committee on Financial Markets and its Working Groups.[179] It reports to the Council and proposes the recommendations it deems necessary. The Financial Committee is composed of governmental experts chosen by reason of their knowledge and reputation. Observers from the IMF and the World Bank may attend the meetings. The Committee operates in close co-operation with all the main banking institutions. Thus, regular consultations take place with representatives of the major banks engaged in international lending. An actual problem is the proper functioning of the recycling process of funds from surplus to deficit countries.[180] Other issues of review are the national regulations affecting international banking operations. The various policies are examined in order to reach conclusions for a more co-ordinated

546

approach, shaping regulatory frameworks safeguarding efficient and safe banking in the Member Countries.[181]

Fiscal Affairs

In the field of fiscal affairs the Committee on Fiscal Affairs together with its Working Groups[182] play a major role. The Committee has clearly a supervisory task. It has to investigate and report on the information which the Member States have to notify to the Committee on the implementation of the Draft Conventions on Avoidance of Double Taxation[183] between the Member States. The States have to inform the Committee on any new or revised bilateral Tax Convention. They have to indicate, if they have not followed the provisions of the Draft convention, the reasons for this. The Committee is also engaged in advising the Council on the feasibility of concluding fiscal conventions. Thus, two Model Conventions on Mutual Assistance in the assessment and collection of taxes are to be completed, together with guidelines for a better co-operation of exchanges of information between national tax administrations.[184] The Committee thus functions as a forum for exchange of information and experience, proposing guidelines for closer co-operation in the field of taxes. A still topical issue is concerned with fiscal aspects relating to energy, *e.g.* tax provisions to stimulate domestic energy sources, tax aids to certain industries, etc.[185] Various studies are undertaken to make the national fiscal policies more clear-cut in order to reach a co-ordination of policies.

The OECD is very active in fiscal affairs and its Model Conventions have a great impact.[186] There is much consultation between the members. The flow of information is safeguarded by a system of regular notification with regard to the (non-)adoption of the Model Conventions.

The Functioning of the Markets

Competition – and consumer policy – are of ever increasing importance, having a direct impact on the implementation of positive adjustment policies, being part of the general economic policy options of OECD.

With the beginning of the OECD a Committee of Experts on Restrictive Business Practices has been created. A first task of this Committee is to examine and to compare legislation on restricted business practices.[187] This is in fact a continuous undertaking, reviewing the developments in competition law. The review also embraces mergers and concentrations, and the actions taken by States to have such operations notified. The Committee has a reporting and monitoring function concerning the implementation of the Council Recommendation on Co-operation between the Member Countries on Restrictive Business Practices Affecting International Trade.[188] The said Recommendation contains co-operation guidelines with regard to notification – and consultation – procedures. Moreover, it provides for an informal and formal conciliation procedure, first to be applied on a bilateral basis.[189] In the long run an open-ended agreement on mutual assistance in the application of national laws is the target.[190] Having regard to the large field which is

547

covered, various specific problems are dealt with in special working parties.[191] They all study the problems falling within their particular area, reporting to the main Committee (and the Council) and proposing adequate recommendations.

Consumer Policy

Consumer policy is the responsibility of the Committee on Consumer Policy. It is charged with problems of informing and protecting the consumer in an effective way. In order to reach a certain co-ordination of policies its primary function is to collect information on the various national policies, exchange experience, discuss and consult with the partners. The Committee submits its findings in annual reports. It monitors an informal notification procedure concerning safety regulations for consumer products, unsuspected hazards, and new consumer products.

It is interesting to note that the WP[192] asked for proposals about the necessity for formal procedures concerning information of, and consultation on, safety regulations, and recommended the postponement of specific procedures of implementation of the Council's recommendation until it had gained sufficient practical experience. The States should take advantage of the notification and consultation procedure without resorting to formal arrangements.[193] So, once again it becomes clear that in the OECD a practical, non-formal approach is to be preferred. Moreover, the Consumer Policy Committee has to study the relationship between consumer policy and other aspects of economic policy. The Committee does not restrict itself to the Member States, it also co-operates with other international organisations, aiming *inter alia* at a broader exchange of information.[194]

Tourism

The co-operation in the field of tourism is reviewed by the Tourism Committee. It publishes annually a report on 'International Tourism and Tourism Policy in OECD Member Countries.' First the Committee collects material and prepares it for statistics and analysis of the various prospects of international tourism. Next, it has to deal with specific problems like the staggering of holidays, environmental aspects, protection and safety of the tourist as a consumer. The statistical work is done by a Working Party on Statistics. As in other fields the review of the policies should enable the governments and the tourist industry branches to adjust their policies, plans and programmes and to reach a certain degree of co-ordination.

Maritime Transport

In the field of maritime transport the Committee for Maritime Transport is responsible for consultations concerning the policies of the members. It has to keep the OECD informed on significant developments in the field of maritime transport. The Committee may submit recommendations to the Council. In doing so, it must consult other bodies within and without the

548

Organisation. In the latter case it keeps in close contacts with the International Maritime Consultative Organisation (IMCO), the ILO and UNCTAD. The Committee is assisted by a Working Group which has taken over the tasks of the former Working Group on Flags of Convenience.[195] The Group has *inter alia* to establish links with other countries and organisations on questions not dealt with by the Special Group on International Organisations. Moreover, the Working Group of the Maritime Transport Committee has to analyse a variety of problems connected with maritime transport. It tries to cover gaps in the work done by IMCO and ILO, thus complementing their activities. An urgent problem studied by the Working Group relates to the costs of energy. Another problem dealt with is that of oil carriers, the increasing difficulties caused by competition from the shipping lines of State trading countries. Statistics on seaborne trade are a regular feature. Another Group is the Special Group on International Organisations. It is charged with reviewing the shipping aspects, particularly of a political and an economic nature, of the work undertaken by UNCTAD and other organisations that the Maritime Committee may designate. The key task now is to co-ordinate the shipping interests of the OECD Member Countries in advance of the meetings in the UNCTAD area and to prepare these various meetings. It should try to reach agreement upon common lines for policies and action. Moreover, it has to take into account decisions reached within other organisations.[196] The Maritime Committee lays down its findings in an Annual Report, which moreover summarises the principal matters of concern in world shipping as a whole and in the OECD countries in particular. Problems the Member States have *inter se* regarding the liberalisation of services are still to be solved. A solution is worked at in close co-operation with the Committee on Capital Movements and Invisible Transactions, which is engaged with the revision and updating of the Code of Liberalisation of Current Invisible Operations.[197] Here too, consultations are undertaken with both TUAC and BIAC. Naturally, it also keeps in contact with the Manpower and Social Affairs Committee and the Insurance Committee.

2.2.4. *Agriculture and fisheries, food*

Two main Committees were created in September 1961: the Committee for Agriculture and the Fisheries Committee. The first is assisted by a number of Working Parties and Working Groups.[198] The setting-up and the mandate of both Committees is similar. In general terms both are responsible to the Council to consider, advise and recommend to the OECD on agricultural and fishery problems, and policy options. They review the decisions taken in their specific fields.

More specifically the Committees have to examine the policies by way of country-by-country confrontation and consultation with a view to promoting the harmonious development of these policies among the Member Countries. An examination of the overall situation of agriculture and fisheries in the Member Countries and prospects for the future has to be included. As for agriculture a Working Party on Commodity Analysis and Market Outlook has been set up,[199] to analyse the policy developments. Its findings as to the future prospects are to be included in the Committee's *Annual Review.* The Committees have to study the possibilities for improving the marketing and distribution of the agricultural, fishery and food products. The market situation has to be examined in close co-operation with the Trade Committee. The examination is entrusted to a Joint Working Party. It has *inter alia* to examine, annually, all import restrictions and aids to exports. Next, it has to consider all administrative and technical obstacles to trade in agricultural products. The Joint Working Party has to organise consultations on the above-mentioned problems and must make proposals for a notification procedure regarding restrictions to trade, including a procedure for reference of cases in practice. The cases should be examined by the Joint Working Party. Technical assistance in agricultural research is another item of study. Having regard to the food difficulties in developing countries and in other parts in the world a close co-operation is needed with the Development Assistance Committee (DAC). Moreover, consultations and exchange of views have to take place in other fora as in the World Food Council, FAO and other organisations. Mid-term and longer-term prospects get more and more important.[200] Thus, the Agricultural Committee should try, on the basis of its reviews, to map out a strategy for the future (the 1980s) making the necessary adjustments or indicating policy options for adjustment to changing and changed situations, such as the increasing price of energy, the need for a better environment, and various structural changes. Apart from a sectoral approach which is inherent to an agricultural policies review the link with the general economic policies is not to be forgotten. The interlinkage and interplay between policies is dealt with by the Working Party on Commodity Analysis and Market Outlook. Here too, the task is an analysing one, including some monitoring of review aspects, but the work is primarily meant to facilitate and to stimulate policy options.

It should be mentioned that consultations between the OECD and non-governmental international agricultural organisations also take place. There is a liaison with the International Federation of Agricultural Producers (IFAP) and the European Confederation of Agriculture (ECA). Representatives of these organisations participate in technical OECD meetings. The outcome of the consultations is taken into account within the Committee for Agriculture.

Fisheries

The Annual Review of Developments in Fisheries include a survey of financial aid systems provided by governments and the necessary recommendations for reduction or abolition. As in the Agricultural Committee the method followed is the country-by-country confrontation. Thus, a forum for discussion is created for examining the actual policies and proposing future policy lines, aiming at co-ordination and co-operation. The Fisheries Committee also reviews the measures taken regarding jurisdiction in fishing zones

550

and management of the corresponding fish resources by countries which have not so far concluded their policies in this respect. Other features of regular examination are the problems connected with international trade in fisheries. Parallel with the above-mentioned policy confrontations various studies are undertaken with respect to fishery problems.

2.2.5. Social affairs, manpower and education

(a) General remarks

Social affairs, manpower and educational questions have become increasingly important. Under the OEEC emphasis was laid on the liberalisation of manpower movements. Social questions, closely linked with manpower problems, were to be dealt with by the Manpower Committee. Under the OECD, however, social affairs as such were given more weight, as may already become clear from the creation of a Manpower and Social Affairs Committee.[201] Education, up to 1970 falling within the scope of 'Scientific and Technical Personnel', also became a separate item. This is quite in line with the general tendency and must, after the 1970s, meet with the qualitative aspects and aspects of life. Thus, manpower policy had not only to be regarded as a means for the promotion of economic growth as such: it had also to be directed towards the more qualitative aspects of the growth process. Moreover, in the 1970s a decline of growth had to be faced, unemployment and increasing social burdens due to further unemployment. Youth unemployment has become a serious problem. The social aspects are clear. Income transfers as such do not solve the problems. The same applies to education. Transfer of knowledge is not *per se* a guarantee for employment and economic expansion. Here planning and adjustment of social and educational policies to the actual trends[202] and changing public attitudes – a policy-making – are needed. Problems prove to be very interlinked. Moreover, they become ever increasing. To mention some: the need for recurrent education for both youth and adults, the role of women in the economy, the migration of workers and the quest for social security. To discuss all these problems in the OECD arena a number of committees have been set up.

(b) Bodies and tasks

The main body active in the field of social affairs and manpower is the committee bearing the name Manpower and Social Affairs Committee, assisted by various working parties.[203] Its principal task is to analyse the general situation and policies in the field of manpower and social affairs, undertaking specific studies and reviewing the individual countries' policies separately, on a regular basis. The latter implies that yearly one (or two) countries are subjected to a close examination of their manpower and social policies, whereas the reports on other countries are merely updated. The countries to undergo an examination are selected as presenting special aspects from which useful lessons can be drawn. The examination takes place in the form of a confrontation, rather similar to the model described for the general economic reviews.[204] One major distinction is to be marked: the country under review is selected, but its actual participation rests on a voluntary basis. As for the economic policy reviews all countries are subjected to a review they have agreed upon when setting up the competent review bodies.

The Social Policy Review is based on a background report drawn up by the national authorities concerned. A team of independent examiners is appointed who visit the country under examination, prepare their report and questions. The latter form the basis for the plenary review meeting of the Committee. The planning and administrative co-ordination is served by the relevant Directorate of the Secretariat.

Mention should also be made that the social partners, organized in TUAC and BIAC, are regularly consulted on all review and study activities dealing with social, manpower, and educational matters.

What has been said for the Manpower and Social Affairs Committee applies *grosso modo* also to the Education Committee. It tries (i) to analyse the various educational problems and policies via the examination of overall national policies in education under a country review procedure. Next, (ii) it prepares policy options for discussion and recommendation. Last but not least, (iii) the Education Committee is responsible for exchanging information and promoting co-operation. This is *inter alia* done by drawing up comparable cross-country statistics.[205]

Centre for Educational Research and Innovation (CERI)

In 1967 CERI was created with a view to meeting, by means of joint action by the Member States, certain needs for educational research and innovation. The Centre works within the framework of the OECD. Its main task is to draw up and carry out a Programme on Educational Research and Innovation. The main objectives of this Programme are:

- to promote and support the development of research activities in education and undertake proper research activities;
- to promote and support pilot experiments with a view to introducing and testing innovations in the educational system;
- to promote the development of co-operation between the Member Countries in the field of research and innovation of education.

The Centre has its own Secretariat and Governing Board, composed of national experts of the participating countries. The Board is assisted by an Executive Group in preparing and supervising the Programme. This Group is responsible for the liaison with the Education Committee and other Committees concerned in the matter. The Programme and other activities (*e.g.* research projects) are in principle financed by the Centre.[206] The staff of the Centre forms part of the Secretariat of the OECD. As its mandate ended at the end of 1981 evaluation discussions will have to make clear whether and how programmes will be continued. Meanwhile a programme on the interaction of the educational system with other social sectors will go

552

on. Various operational activities[207] are undertaken. Although being *in se* very interesting, they do not fall within the scope of the present study.

2.2.6. Development co-operation

Development co-operation and development assistance is a matter of continuing concern to OECD, partly in the form of financial resource flows,[208] partly in the form of technical assistance[209] and partly in the form of intellectual assistance[210] (research, training, documentation and studies). The majority of the OECD Member Countries[211] joined the Ministerial Resolution of July 23, 1960[212] to constitute a Development Assistance Committee, having *inter alia* the following mandate:

> '. . . to consult on the methods for making national resources available for assisting countries and areas in the process of economic development and for expanding and improving the flow of long-term funds and other development assistance to them.
> . . . to make periodic reports to the Council.
> . . . to make recommendations.
> . . . to invite representatives of other countries and international organisations to take part in particular discussions as necessary.'

Thus, the mandate covers several items which have been elaborated over the years, partly becoming traditional activities, partly asking for a continuous evolution according to the needs and developing concepts about the economic relations between the rich and the poor countries.[213]

Confrontation

A major regular task consists of reviewing aid policies and aid programmes. These reviews take the form of mutual confrontations by the members, following more or less the procedural lines already sketched for the economic policies and economic development policies review.[214] First, the country under review presents a memorandum to the competent Directorate of the Secretariat. Next, a list of questions is drawn up in close co-operation with two other, examining, countries. In the course of the preparations for the review consultations take place. Sometimes visits are paid to examine a financial aid project on the spot (in a developing country). The examination *in pleno* is led by the two examining countries (examination committee), every member is entitled to join the discussion. The results of the confrontation session are summarised in a communiqué being published in the DAC Chairman's *Report on Development Co-operation*. This overall review of each member's efforts and policies may be said to be unique. Whereas donor countries usually review the recipient countries as to whether they come under the terms (donor countries make) for receiving assistance and whether they are fulfilling the stipulated conditions, here the donor countries are critically reviewing each other. Not only the volume of assistance is subject to review but also the distribution of it and the effectiveness of aid allocations. The implementation of two Guidelines, one on the Local and Recurrent Cost Financing, the other For Improving Aid Implementation, are reviewed as part of the DAC Aid Reviews.[215] Thus, the Aid Review provides an opportunity to (i) assess progress both towards the quantity[216] and quality of aid and (ii) exchange experience. Since 1980 DAC has extended its review task by instituting a joint review, dealing with the major aspects of the programmes of all DAC members together. Whether this joint review will be continued, is not yet known.[217]

Having regard to the fact that trade, scientific and technological aspects, agriculture and food, social aspects, current global (North-South) discussions are closely linked with development assistance as such, DAC co-operates with many other main Committees in the OECD.[218] Moreover, it meets from time to time on a high level basis, to discuss and decide on important issues.[219] Another feature of the DAC review deals with the trends in volume and structure of development assistance by non-DAC members[220] (e.g. OPEC countries), trends in non-concessional financial flows, IMF facilities and external indebtedness.

As the programming and implementation is part of the review,[224] the outcome of the analyses should enable DAC members to improve their methods and procedures; to respond in a flexible way to changing require-ments; to simplify aid procedures and to strengthen the administrative capacity in developing countries. The Guidelines for improving aid imple-mentation constitute to some extent, as they say themselves, a list of 'best practices.' In other words, they are a kind of standard to measure national practice.[222] An interesting aspect of the aid management review is the concern DAC members have expressed to indicate to the public that the aid is spent in an efficient and successful manner.[223] DAC functions as a review centre for aid policies. But it does more. DAC is an important forum for discussion and consultation on policy issues. It tries to decide on priorities and to prepare some common approach for inter alia Global Negotiations.[224] It co-ordinates the different viewpoints and activities. In doing this it also keeps in contact with non-governmental organisations, which seek to collab-orate increasingly with official agencies. Other subjects which invite attention from DAC members are human rights, the role of women, population (planning), food aid, energy and industrialisation, environmental protection. Partly, however, these subjects are still in the stage of study, falling rather within the scope of the Development Centre than DAC.

The Development Centre

The Centre has been set up as an autonomous subsidiary body for helping to solve development problems by (i) research on urgent economic policy questions; (ii) advanced training of officials; exchange of experience; and (iii) by provision of documentary information; making knowledge available for the developing nations, especially to increase the intellectual resources. Last, but not least (iv) the Centre serves as a liaison between the developed and the less-developed world. For that reason it may be said to be the OECD 'window' to the Third World. The Centre tries to plan and to extend its research – and training activities with all kinds of institutes and institutions, national or international, public or private – being active in the same field with the aim of promoting contracts and co-operation. As part of the exchange function on development experience the Centre pursues a continuous dialogue between researchers, practitioners and specialists from North and South, inviting them to participate in the work of the Centre for a period of time.[225] As to the publication, documentation and dissemination tasks, the Centre has laid a basis for a system of voluntary exchanges of documents by specialised institutions both in Member and non-Member States to be at the disposal of policy-makers in the underdeveloped countries. How useful the Centre may be, especially as a discussion and consultation place as a preparatory stage for policy-making in the OECD, it can hardly be dealt with from a viewpoint of supervision and supervision mechanisms. For that reason it will not be dealt with in further detail.

The Sahel Club

Mention must also be made of the Sahel Club. The Club was set up in 1976 with the help of the OECD, groups of African States and those countries and international organisations which take part in the aid project to cope with the drought problems in the Sahel. It is an unofficial body founded as a consequence of concerted action and highly sponsored by the OECD.

2.2.7. Technical co-operation

Closely connected with the problem of development assistance is the problem of technical co-operation with the developing countries. From the above it appears that within DAC efforts are undertaken to improve and to co-ordinate technical assistance given by DAC members to the poorer countries. OECD itself, however, does not give such assistance from its own resources. It only has a monitoring function. But, for some poorer European countries an exception is made. Greece, Iceland, Portugal, Spain, Turkey and Yugoslavia can benefit from a technical assistance programme guided by the OECD, in particular by the Technical Co-operation Committee. This Committee will now be dealt with:

In considering the choice of activities the Committee shall focus its work on improving the responsiveness and effectiveness of public management generally, and shall have particular regard to the need to effect improvements in public administration, the economy of rural areas and industrial policy implementation.

In carrying out its mandate, the Technical Co-operation Committee shall maintain close working relationships with other Committees concerned, as appropriate, and take into account the work of national and international agencies having relevant interests, in order to avoid duplication.

The Technical Co-operation Committee shall report annually to the Council on its activities.

The activities of the Technical Co-operation Committee are, as may be concluded from the mandate, technical, aiming at an efficient public management and adapting government administration in such a way that it can cope with the actual economic and social problems. Having to deal with not only administration problems but also with economic development problems like changes from agriculture patterns to industrialised life, social and environmental aspects, the Committee has to keep in contact with the bodies dealing with those problems in general: the Committees for Agriculture, Environment, Social Affairs, Manpower and Education, Technology and Industry. Moreover, professional organisations have to be consulted. The details of the activities are worked out in a Co-operative Action Programme[226] (which cannot be dealt with here, having regard to the scope of this study). But in general, it appears that the Committee has a guiding task, operating as a place for consultation and a forum for exchange of experience in technical co-operation. In doing this, it plays a supervisory role over the programmes of technical assistance arranged for those countries that are the recipients of the aid.[227] The results are reported, annually, to the Council.

2.2.8. Environment

Since the late sixties environment has come within the scope of OECD as a separate item of concern. In 1970 the Environment Committee was established to be responsible for:

'examining on a co-operative basis common problems . . . with a view to proposing effective means of preventing, minimising or solving them . . . ;
encouraging wherever appropriate the harmonisation of environmental policies among the Member Counties;
providing Member Governments with policy options or guidelines to prevent or minimise conflicts that could arise between Member Countries in the use of shared environmental resources or as the result of national environmental policies;
the Committee may organise, as appropriate and with the agreement of the countries concerned, consultations to that effect;
reviewing and consulting on actions taken or proposed by Member Countries in the environmental field and assessing the results of those actions;
assisting the Member Countries to develop improved means of assessing trends in environmental quality and, on an internationally comparable basis, to improve the information base for decisions pertaining to environmental policy.'

The Environment Committee is backed by a Group of Economic Experts, which has to carry out or to supervise the implementation of projects and tasks assigned to the Environment Committee and its subsidiary groups on the economic aspects of major environmental problems and issues. Another group is the Group on the State of Environment, which has to report on that state in the OECD Member Countries, in accordance with a Recommendation calling for systematic monitoring and reporting on the evolution of the state of environment.[228] In doing so, the Group has to advise on and review the work of the Secretariat on environmental information and reporting. Other bodies in this field are the Chemicals Group, the Management Committee for the Special Programme on the Control of Chemicals, the Group on Energy and Environment, the Waste Management Policy Group and the *Ad Hoc* Group on Urban Problems. Thus, it appears that the general subject of environment is split up into a number of specific areas: environmental economics, resources, energy, chemicals, urban problems and the state of the environment. As for environment and economy, it is clear that both subjects raise problems which have to be reconciled.

In a period of recession such a task is not an easy one. However, the Member Countries have obliged themselves to take into account the 'Guiding Principles Concerning International Economic Aspects of Environmental Policies' and the 'Implementation of the Polluter-Pays Principle'.[229] For this purpose a questionnaire has been sent to the Member States to collect information as a basis for reviewing the usefulness of the latter Principle. As for the Chemicals Programme a procedure for information exchange has been set up in order to circulate information and to promote harmonisation of legislation and administrative regulations. Moreover, the data should enable the competent bodies to propose guidelines and concerted approaches to the problems. The 'state of the environment' is a recent activity – with links to natural resources, economics, energy, quality of life – and is aiming at an assessment of the economic policy situation in the various Member Countries.[230] Part of the programme consists of reviewing the policies in the Member States. First of all, such a review, by the Environment Committee in close co-operation with the Group on the State of the Environment, contains an inventory of the national policy. Next, it contains an evaluation with certain conclusions for improvement. The country reviews should enable all countries to learn from the experience of the country that has been examined. As is the case with other policy examinations the preparatory stage may give rise to consultations and discussion between the examiners and the country under review. After the final discussion *in pleno* and having obtained the approval of the Environment Committee the review document is to be published by the Secretariat.[231] The creative political aspects are in evidence. The review should enable the Committee to propose actions and policy options for improving the environmental policies in specific countries. Moreover, conclusions may be submitted to the Council to be adopted as general guiding principles.

2.2.9. Science, technology and industry

The three areas, science, technology and industry, *in se* much interrelated, have become more and more important. Already under OEEC the problems of industry and economic growth were linked with the problems of scientific and technical personnel and the need for scientific research. The OEEC[232] refers to 'progressive modernisation of equipment and techniques.' The OECD[233] is more explicit: '. . . the members agree that they will . . .: (a) promote the efficient use of their economic resources; (b) in the scientific and technological field, promote the development of their resources, encourage research and promote educational training . . ..' Early in 1970 a reshuffling of Committees took place, with a view to tackling the interrelated problems more efficiently. It reflects the clear intention of the partners to co-operate more closely in three main directions: (i) expansion of research, development and innovation activities; (ii) technological innovation; (iii) effective management and control of technology. Emphasis is now laid on positive structural adjustment and stimulation of economic growth. The reorganisation on the Council level found its counterpart in the Secretariat. In 1974 the Secretary-General established a new Directorate for Science, Technology and Industry, facilitating a more integrated approach of the activities carried out by the Committee for Scientific and Technological Policy and the Industry Committee.[234]

From a point of review both Committees appear to be important. For this reason the mandate will be looked at, more closely.[235]

Committee for Scientific and Technological Policy (CSTP)

The Committee is responsible for encouraging co-operation among the Member States in the field of scientific and technological policies, 'with a view to contributing to the achievement of their economic and social aims.' Thus, it should play an active role in:

'(a) promoting the exchange among Member Countries of experience and information concerning policies for science and technology, and facilitating the definition of such policies;

(b) proposing means for the more effective co-ordination of national and international efforts in scientific and technical research and development including, where appropriate, facilitating the implementation of joint research programmes;

(c) calling the attention of Member Governments to the areas in which efforts for innovation of special importance, particularly with a view to meeting new needs in the public sector, and in the light of the appropriate contribution of the social sciences;

(d) calling also the attention of Member Governments to the foreseeable developments of technology and their economic, social and cultural consequences;

(e) examining the implications of new developments in the fields of scientific and technical information and documentation and of the computer sciences, in the light of the increasing interaction of computer, communication and information systems.'

To summarise the above: as in other fields the first task is to collect information and to exchange it. For this purpose the Member Countries report to the Committee on their national policies in the field of science and technology. The most important issues are examined by the Committee in the light of the objectives set by the OECD (confrontation method). The results are laid down in country studies, drawn up by Working Groups consisting of governmental and non-governmental experts. As in the field of economic development policy such reports ask for a close consultation between the examining group and the country under review. Here too, findings as such are accompanied with suggestions for the future. As formulated in the mandate, the Committee shall propose means for co-ordination of policies. The reports should especially enable the Committee for Scientific and Technological Policy[236] to map out long-term planning and priorities in the said field. Apart from this review of policies, there is the promotion of research in both state and private areas, by setting up research programmes and joint projects.

Industry Committee

Since the establishment of the OECD the Organisation has at its disposal an Industry Committee. In general, the Industry Committee reviews the industry

558

policies of the Members and the major problems of positive adjustment to changing economic conditions. The Committee obtains its information by sending questionnaires to the Member Countries and by confronting their policies with the aims set out within the OECD (country studies). Apart from examination of the industry policies in general, specific problems are investigated such as the trends in industrial investments, labour skill, depressed industrial sectors (like shipbuilding and textile industry), pulp and paper, energy.

The results of the findings in the Industry Committee (I.C.) as well as those obtained from other bodies are discussed within the Committee. Whenever appropriate the I.C. may make proposals to the Council. Moreover, it may set up working parties to prepare its work on specific industrial problems. Regularly, the findings are published in reports.

A very important item is regional policy. Regional development policies are closely linked with industrial policies. Thus, Working Party No. 6 on Regional Development Policies was set up to examine the nature and scale of regional problems. It provides the Member Countries with information, reports and advice on the most appropriate policies for dealing with the regional problems. Up to now a series of country reviews has been carried out with the purpose of elaborating certain development strategies and achievable goals. Short-term indicators and statistical data are gathered by Working Party No. 9 on Industrial Statistics. It is not possible, within the scope of this study to deal with all the working parties. One, however, should be mentioned. With a view to the 'Special Programme of Work for the Organisation on Positive Adjustment Policies' and *Ad Hoc* Working Party on Industrial Adjustment Questions has been created, for a limited period.[237]

Steel

As problems in the steel industry were increasing the Council decided (1978) to create a Steel Committee. It is one of the objectives of the Committee to follow the national and international evolutions and to draw up common outlooks. Moreover, it must review at regular intervals the policies and governmental actions in the steel sector. It must also determine the shortcomings in the existing data in order to ameliorate the data and their comparability between the Member States. In order to prepare the basic data and the economic analyses for the discussion in the Steel Committee, a Working Party was set up.

Shipbuilding

Another matter of concern is shipbuilding. Here too, the national policies are permanently reviewed, principally by the Council's Working Party No. 6 on Shipbuilding. The application of the General Guidelines for Government Policy in Shipbuilding is to be supervised by a special working party on that matter. It also supervises the Understanding on Export Credits for Ships and the General Arrangement for the Progressive Removal of Obstacles to Normal Conditions of Competition in the Shipbuilding Industry.

Road Transport

The subject of industry is not complete without mentioning road transport. As of the end of the sixties the Member Countries have expressed their willingness to participate in an international programme of co-operation in the field of road research. As becomes clear from the terms of reference of the Steering Committee it is the task of the Committee to draw up and to continue a Programme of Co-operation in the Field of Road Research. It studies *inter alia* on research needs, recommends on projects and co-ordinated research activities. In sub-programmes several specific problems are dealt with like Pedestrian Safety; Urban Transportation; Road Traffic and Safety; Road Construction and Maintenance; International Road Research Documentation. In all cases emphasis is laid on the studying of the various problems, exchanging information in order to improve knowledge on road transport and related problems. It has become clear that transport policies as such are not reviewed. The problems are only tackled in relation to the liberalisation of goods, services and persons. More generally the subject of transport falls within the scope of CEMT (Conférence Européenne des Ministres de Transport). This subject, in the margin of OECD activities, will not be dealt with.

2.2.10 Energy

(a) General remarks

Throughout the history of the OEEC and the OECD energy has been an important subject for consultation and co-operation. First, after World War Two (shortage of) coal brought about major problems. Later, the role of coal was taken over by oil and natural gas. The problems, however, were solved but for only a short period. The Suez crisis of 1956–57 showed the danger of an energy gap. It clearly indicated the need to cope with such a gap on the international level. Once again this came apparent in the 1973 oil-crisis, which heavily shocked the (Western) world economy. Particularly, this crisis – which is still felt – gave the impetus to a series of energy co-operation activities within the OECD. The initiative for establishing the International Energy Agency (IEA) and the setting up of a long-term programme of energy co-operation date from that 1973 crisis. The Programme includes a system of information on the international oil and energy markets. Various programmes are carried out within the OECD by the IEA in which first 18, and now 21 Member Countries co-operate.[238] The IEA as such is an autonomous body, having its own rules. Notably, the IEA does not have an exclusively unanimous voting system; in certain cases it also has a majority voting. The details will be mentioned below.

The importance of the IEA group of countries in the world energy consumption may be shown by the fact that they, together, account for more than 50 per cent. of world total energy requirements and almost 93 per cent. of the total energy requirements of the industrialised countries that are members of the OECD. Apart from bringing about a better structure of supply and demand, a major problem to be faced is the need for reducing excessive dependence on oil in meeting energy needs. New and other energy sources have to be developed in the near future.

Thus, summarised, the main aims are:

(1) co-operation within the IEA group for reducing excessive dependence on oil by
    – energy conservation and
    – energy research and development for alternative energy sources;
(2) information system on the oil markets;
(3) consultation with oil companies;
(4) co-operation with oil-producing and oil-consuming countries, with a view to stabilising international trade in oil and rationalising the management and use of world energy resources;
(5) emergency preparation to cope with the risks of disruption of oil supplies and to share, in an equitable way, the available oil stocks (set up for emergency cases).

Nuclear energy will be dealt with separately. In that field a separate Agency, the Nuclear Energy Agency, has been set up.[239]

(b) Various bodies in the field of energy

The OECD Committee for Energy Policy

Before dealing with the IEA and the International Energy Programme, it should be indicated that within the OECD, more or less parallel to the IEA, a Committee for Energy Policy was set up (April 29, 1975). The reason for this lies in the fact that not all the OECD members were willing to join the IEA (France, especially, was opposed to the establishment of the IEA). In order not to create a gap on such an important item as energy (oil), the Council established the said Committee. Its mandate is quite broad. The Committee's competence extends to 'all energy resources.' It must promote co-operation between the members in the field of energy policy. For this purpose, it will undertake studies, and exchange views. In line with the IEA model it undertakes regular reviews of the longer-term prospects of the energy markets, particularly on the basis of the updating of the Long-Term Energy Assessment. The Energy Policy Committee also reviews the energy situation (markets) in its national and international aspects. Emergency and supply questions are also dealt with: the Energy Policy Committee has taken over the responsibilities of the former Oil Committee. That Committee was set up for reviewing oil stockpiling and working out emergency plans and procedures for apportionment of oil supplies.

It is interesting to note that the former Oil Committee was entitled, for the implementation of the procedure for apportionment among Member States of the supplies subject to special allocation, to decide by a two-thirds majority vote. The Member who had not agreed, had the right to request the Council to review the decision. Pending the decision of the Council, the majority decision could be executed, as provided for in the 'Apportionment Principles and Criteria.' In fact, the same rule is applied in the IEA, as we will see later on. It clearly shows that in cases of emergency a veto is not acceptable. Indeed, a veto would make the whole system senseless and inoperable. In mid-1980 a High Level Group for Energy Technology Commercialisation was created for a duration of one year.[240]

Although the Energy Policy Committee activities are formally executed under the aegis of the OECD, independently and separately from the activities of IEA, a close link between the two exists. Thus, a combined Energy Staff has been set up, which serves both the IEA Secretariat and the OECD Secretariat. All data from the IEA and Energy Policy Committee are mutually exchanged, so giving effect to the wish of the Energy Policy Committee to establish a close liaison with the IEA. Moreover, a liaison with the NEA and other bodies and committees within the OECD is foreseen, for the purpose of 'taking into account as fully as possible the economic and environmental aspects of energy policies.'[241] Contacts with (oil) industry are institutionalised. The latter are grouped together in the International Industry Advisory Board. This Board advises on matters of availability of oil and the implementation of apportionment measures (recommendations). The Energy Policy Committee has in fact but little importance and influence, because the bulk of the work has been taken over by the IEA. The IEA has the manpower and experience, whereas the 'pure' OECD possibilities are rather marginal.

The International Energy Agency

The legal basis of the International Energy Agency (IEA) lies in a Council Decision and in the Agreement on an International Energy Programme (IEP).[242] The IEP immediately became provisionally applicable for all the signatories. The implementation of the IEP is in the hands of the IEA. First, a sketch of the structure of IEA will be given. Next, the International Energy Programme will be discussed.

1. INSTITUTIONAL STRUCTURE OF THE IEA

The IEA has the following organs[243]:

- a Governing Board;
- a Management Committee, and four permanent Standing Groups on:
- Emergency Questions (SEQ);
- The Oil Market (SOM);
- Long-Term Co-operation (SLT);
- Relations with Producer and other Consumer Countries.

Moreover, a Committee on Energy Research and Development has been established.[244] The Governing Board is composed of Ministers or their delegates from each of the participating countries (now 21 members). The

562

Management Committee is composed of senior representatives of each participating country. The Standing Groups are also composed of one or more government representatives of each participating country. The IEA has a Secretariat at its disposal, headed by the Executive Director, who is appointed by the Governing Board. The staff serves as the combined Energy Staff to both the IEA and the OECD (especially the Energy Policy Committee).

The functions of the Governing Board are to:

- adopt decisions and make recommendations which are necessary for the proper functioning of the IEP[245];
- review periodically and take appropriate action concerning developments in the international energy situation, including problems relating to the oil supplies and the economic and monetary implications of these developments.

The Governing Board may delegate any of its functions to any other organ of the Agency. As indicated above, the Board appoints the Executive Director of the IEA, who is also the head of the Secretariat. Upon the proposal of the Governing Board of the IEA the OECD Council may confer additional responsibilities upon the Agency. Annually, the Governing Board has to report to the OECD Council on the activities of the Agency.[246]

The Managing Committee carries out those functions assigned to it in the IEP Agreement and any other function delegated to it by the Governing Board. It may examine energy questions and make proposals to the Governing Board, especially on the basis of reports of the various Standing Groups. It may be compared with the Executive Committee of the OECD. The functions of the Standing Groups are (partly) laid down in the IEP Agreement. Moreover, functions may be delegated to it by the Governing Board. Essentially, their task is to review and report to the Managing Committee on the matters falling within their various spheres *i.e.* emergency matters, long-term co-operation, oil market situation, relations with producer countries and other countries. The three first-mentioned Standing Groups may consult with oil companies on any matter falling within their competence. These various high-level groups have formed sub-groups and working parties to assist them in specific tasks. From the above it appears that the decision-making power lies within the Governing Board. Decisions are binding upon the Participating Parties, recommendations are not legally binding.

As for the voting procedure, matters of a procedural kind are decided by a majority vote. The same applies to decisions on the management of the Programme, including decisions applying provisions of the IEP agreement which already impose specific obligations on the Participants.[247] Unanimity is required for all other decisions, including in particular decisions imposing new obligations on the participating countries. When a majority is required, three types of weighting may be applicable: a general voting weight, every country having the same number of votes; a special weight based on the oil consumption; and thirdly a combined voting weight of the two first-mentioned weights. Majority requires 60 per cent. of the total combined voting weights and 50 per cent. of the general voting weights cast. Moreover, in certain cases special majorities have been provided for.[248] From the voting schemes it appears that no country has the absolute power to block a majority vote. Thus, for adopting emergency measures a decision requires only half of the countries voting and 60 per cent. of the combined voting weights. However, for a decision not to activate emergency measures a higher majority is required.

The Governing Board may decide, acting by unanimity, to alter the voting weights e.g. in view of accession of new members or due to withdrawal. The weight may also be changed, on the basis of the annual review, when a country's share in the total oil consumption has changed or for any other reason.[249]

Another special feature concerning the decisions taken by unanimity should be mentioned. They may provide that they will not be binding on one or more participating countries or that they will only be binding under certain conditions.[250]

VOTING SCHEME (as from January 1, 1980)[251]

	General voting weights	Oil consumption voting weights	Combined voting weights
Australia	3	1	4
Austria	3	1	4
Belgium	3	2	5
Canada	3	5	8
Denmark	3	1	4
Germany	3	8	11
Greece	3	1	4
Ireland	3	0	3
Italy	3	5	8
Japan	3	15	18
Luxembourg	3	0	3
The Netherlands	3	2	5
New Zealand	3	0	3
Norway	3	0	3
Spain	3	2	5
Sweden	3	2	5
Switzerland	3	1	4
Turkey	3	1	4
United Kingdom	3	6	9
United States	3	47	50
Total	60	100	160

A majority requires 60 per cent. of the combined voting weights and 50 per cent. of the general voting weights cast.
For specific types of decisions there are special majorities. Norway has a special relationship with the Agency.

A. Short-term: emergency preparation. From the above it already follows that the programme relates to *inter alia* establishing an emergency self-sufficiency plan. This part is primarily meant to cope with (rather) short-term problems in oil supplies.

First, all members have confirmed that they will maintain sufficient reserves for consumption.[252] It is up to the Standing Group on Emergency Questions (SEQ) to review, on a continuing basis, the effectiveness of the measures taken by the members to meet their reserve commitment.[253]

Secondly, every country has to maintain an effective programme of contingent oil-restraint measures enabling it to reduce the rate of consumption according to sustained reduction in oil supply (or according to the reduction in supply that can reasonably be expected). The restraint should be 7 per cent. if the supplies are cut by at least 7 per cent.; and 10 per cent. if the supplies' cut is higher than 12 per cent.

The programme of demand-restraint is reviewed and assessed by the SEQ. Moreover, the SEQ reviews the measures actually taken by each participating country.

Finally, if supplies are cut down for more than 7 per cent. of the normal level of supply every participating country has to take the necessary measures in order to make the activation of the oil-sharing system possible. This system should ensure that a fair and equitable allocation of the available oil supplies is obtained. As a basic principle it is agreed that (when allocation is carried out pursuant to the IEP agreement) each country has a supply right equal to its permissible consumption, less its emergency reserve draw-down obligation.[254] The modalities and definitions of various terms are worked out in the Agreement and the Annexes to it.

In order to have the oil-sharing system executed, each country has to maintain an effective national emergency oil-sharing organisation. Usually this is a joint government-industry body.[255]

It is clear that the regular review and the assessment of the oil-sharing system falls within the competence of the Standing Group on Emergency Questions (SEQ).

It is essential for the whole operation of the emergency system that the IEA receives all the necessary information. From the IEP agreement it appears that the activation of the system depends on criteria laid down in the Agreement.[256] Thus, it becomes operative whenever a certain situation occurs or is expected (without reasonable doubt) to occur. In that case it is up to the Secretariat to make a finding and to establish the amount of reduction.[257] The Secretariat promptly informs the Management Committee, which has to review the accuracy of the data compiled and the information provided. This has to be done within 48 hours. Then the report is sent to the Governing Board, which has to meet, also within 48 hours, to review the findings of the Secretariat, in the light of the report of the Management Committee. In making its findings, the Secretariat consults with oil companies (institutionalised in the Industry Advisory Board) to obtain their views regarding the situation and the appropriateness of the measures.[258] The activation of emergency measures is considered to be confirmed, after the review by the Management Committee and the Governing Board, unless the Governing Board decides not to activate the measures, or to activate them only in part or to fix another time limit for their implementation.[259] For such a decision a special majority is required.

So, in principle a decision may be altered by the Board, but the initiative and decisive power to conclude that an emergency situation exists lies, *de facto*, in the hands of the Executive Director of the IEA Secretariat. To reverse such a decision is not easy. As soon as an emergency situation, pursuant the Agreement, is confirmed to exist the Participating Countries have to implement, within 15 days, the emergency measures.[260]

The deactivation of the emergency measures lies also in the hands of the Executive Director. The procedure is similar to the activation procedure.[261] In actual practice the Secretariat has set up, with a view to checking the preparedness and the effectiveness of the whole emergency system, periodic tests. Scenarios of oil cuts and possible crises are drawn up, which have to be coped with, as they would be if they actually happened. Such tests may bring to light a variety of problems in management, co-ordination and information. In particular, the emergency data system has to prove to be accurate and prompt. It appeared to be necessary[262] to examine, especially, the emergency data system more closely. For that purpose a special Working Party has been set up.

Evaluating the emergency allocation system, it appears that an IEA crisis programme can come into force *quasi* automatically, under supervision of the Executive Director and the Standing Group on Emergency Questions. The latter check whether the States have fulfilled their obligations and whether they have actually taken sufficient and effective measures. The findings of the SEQ are reported to the Governing Board, which assesses the facts and decides on the necessary steps to be taken. In some respects the automatic system of the coming into force of the oil-sharing system bears in itself an element of supervision. The Member States should behave according to the agreed system. Alternative behaviour is in principle not allowed and falls automatically under the review-activities of SEQ. The periodical checking of the emergency system by putting crises to a test appears to be an appropriate system to keep it updated with the ever changing practices and situations.

B. Long-term co-operation in the field of energy. *(1) Energy policy planning and co-operation.* Another major area where the IEA is active, concerns energy policy planning in the long run. For that purpose a Standing Group on Long-Term Co-operation (SLT) has been provided for in the IEP agreement.[263] Various objectives have been set, which should be reached by the Member States through close co-operation. Thus, conservation objectives for the group have been set for 1985. The SLT has to report regularly to the Governing Board on the progress towards the achievement of these objectives of the group.

The participating countries have agreed to have their programmes and policies relating to this matter, systematically reviewed each year. Actually, these reviews have taken place every year, since 1977. From the Long-Term Co-operation programme[264] it appears that the reviews are designed:

'– to provide a thorough and systematic assessment of evolving programmes and policies on the basis of common criteria;
– to identify areas in which programmes might be improved;
– to promote co-operation in the area of conservation, including a detailed exchange of information, experience and expertise in the area of conservation.'

The reviews are conducted by the SLT. The results, conclusions and recommendations relating to each of the reviewed countries are reported to the Governing Board. The latter decides upon its publication.

The actual process of reviewing the programmes and policies of the participating countries takes place in the form of confrontations. Thus, it has features in common with the earlier mentioned economic reviews in the OECD.[265] The review process is described in the first annual report (1977) which was drawn up under the responsibility of the SLT.

The review procedure. The review consists of two parts: an overall report and a series of country reports. In both cases a series of aspects is taken into consideration: progress in attaining oil import objectives; energy conservation; energy supply; adequacy of the efforts; the progress on the principles on energy policy. In the overall review attention is also paid to the long-term oil market projections in general, *i.e.* the outlooks for the future. The overall report is drawn up on the basis of both the material gained about each country separately, and general data derived from answers to questionnaires and findings of those in charge of the review. The material is not restricted to the year under consideration. It may extend to previous years and previous reviews. Whereas in the economic development review procedure two Member Countries take the lead over a third country in the examination, here only one country takes the lead. Each review is led by a *rapporteur*, who undertakes intensive study of the material available about the country under review. Such a study is not restricted to desk-research. Review teams pay visits to the countries concerned to discuss the matter on the spot with both governmental officials and non-governmental bodies.[266]

Although the examination is formally led by the *rapporteur*, all members of the SLT are entitled to put questions and to take part in the examination. Thereupon, a draft report is drawn up, which is first examined by the Chairman of the SLT and its Sub-Groups and the Secretariat. Notably, the Executive Director plays an important role. They all may make suggestions about the draft report but it is up to the *rapporteur* to decide on their acceptance or rejection. Next, the *rapporteur* discusses the report with the country reviewed to ensure factual accuracy. Finally, each report is submitted to the SLT for consideration as to whether it is a fair report. The *rapporteur* and the country concerned are invited to comment on the final version and to participate in the plenary discussion. Here adjustments may still be added and criticism raised. Although, up to now, the SLT has always endorsed the reports, they rest under the final responsibility of the *rapporteur*. The overall report, together with the country reports are submitted to the Governing

Board. It discusses the report and decides on its publication together with the conclusions and recommendation relating to each of the countries reviewed.

In October 1977 the Governing Board adopted the so-called Twelve Principles for Energy Policy.[267] They provide a framework for national policies and programmes. Moreover, the Governing Board accepted an Oil Import Group Objective for 1985. Thus, the criteria against which the national policies and programmes are reviewed are not static and irrevocably fixed. Of course, the basis is still to be found in the IEP, but at any other meeting of the Board, new principles and targets may be set. Thus, the Agreement of Principles for IEA Action on Coal and expectations regarding evolution of the world oil market over the medium to long term have also to be taken into account.[268]

From the above it may be concluded that the review process is quite elaborate. The examinations go into deep detail and cover a wide range of energy aspects.

Another objective the members have agreed upon is the establishment of medium-and long-term plans for the IEA Group as a whole for the accel-erated production of alternative sources of energy, taking into account the national programmes and policies of the participating countries. It is up to the SLT to review and revise these medium-term objectives as such, and make the necessary recommendations for adjustment to the Governing Board. Moreover, the SLT reviews the progress made by its members towards the achievement of the objectives. These reviews take place on a periodic basis. The results are also laid down in the above mentioned *Energy Review Report* to the Governing Board. The review process has already been described. From the Long-Term Co-operation Programme adopted by the Governing Board on January 29 and 30, 1976, it clearly appears that the review is meant to promote interaction. A passage is quoted, which proved to be identical with the passage on oil conservation, mentioned before:

'The Participating Countries agree to conduct periodic reviews within the Agency of their national programmes and policies relating to accelerated production of alternative sources of energy. These reviews shall be designed:
(a) to provide a thorough and systematic assessment of evolving national programmes and policies, on the basis of common criteria;
(b) to identify areas in which programmes might be improved;
(c) to promote cooperation in the area of accelerated production, including a detailed exchange of information, experience and expertise in the production of alternative sources of energy.'

The review is not restricted to a mere check of the situations and behaviours as such. The review is meant to be 'creative' both for the IEA itself and its members. From the experience gained with the objectives, the SLT may propose adjustments of the objectives (policies/programmes). But, it also follows from the above-mentioned (b) and (c) that the international review by high-level experts aims at assisting the IEA members in making political decisions, in line with the Group objectives. Such decisions often require changes in national patterns of energy utilisation. Mostly, they have both great economic and great financial impacts, which have to be faced and

568

solved. Next, the effects on the policies of the other members have to be taken into consideration.

From the yearly reviews one can learn that rather severe criticism has been voiced regarding the results obtained by the Member States. For both conservation and accelerated developments it is stated in the 1978 Overall Review[269] that the efforts in the said field must be judged inadequate! For the countries individually, the judgments are in similar vein! From the 1979 Review[270] which gives also an overview over the past five years, the conclusions remain pessimistic. The SLT therein concludes *inter alia* that: 'Even though much has been accomplished since 1974, it is not enough. Overall, the urgency of the response does not match the gravity of the situation or the dimension of the challenge. There is no country that cannot and should not do more.' As a consequence of this and other statements the SLT has enumerated a series of courses of action which should be given urgent and serious consideration by all IEA members.[271]

It has already been pointed out that the Governing Board is well aware of these difficulties and needs. Thus, it adopted the Principles for IEA action on Coal as part of the IEA's efforts to reduce, in the long run, the dependence of oil through steam coal utilisation.[272] At the same time[273] the Ministers decided upon procedures for review of the IEA countries' coal policies. These should include regular consultation in the said field. Moreover, the Ministers agreed to meet more frequently in order to keep the energy situation under review. Thereupon[274] the Governing Board decided to hold, from 1980, quarterly reviews on all aspects concerning energy. It will notably examine 'whether specific measures in place of each country are adequate and are being effectively implemented, and whether additional measures are necessary; . . . Ministers will meet promptly to consider what corrective action is necessary if the performance of countries in keeping within their import limitations is not satisfactory, or if there is a major change in the supply situation.'[275]

As a general measure of co-operation the members have agreed that 'in order to encourage and safeguard new investment in the bulk of conventional alternative sources of energy' they shall ensure that imported oil is not sold in their domestic markets below a certain fixed price, a 'minimum safeguard price' (MSP). This is the first time that IEA members have accepted such an obligation for protecting their own investments in indigenous energy resources. The implementation of this commitment is reviewed by the SLT, which also reviews periodically the national efforts in making real progress in identifying and commercialising new energy sources. To undertake studies, to prepare and to conduct national reviews under the Long-Term Co-operation Programme, a series of Sub-Groups have been set up.[276]

(2) Energy research, development and demonstration. What has been said above about the long-term energy policy planning applies *mutatis mutandis* also to energy research, development and demonstration in the IEA countries. The key decisions on a strong energy policy, combined with an oil import reduction target (of 26 million barrels per day (mbd) by 1985) – and

an intensified review system date from the 1977 Paris Meeting[277] of the Governing Board. There a series of Group objectives were formulated and the Twelve Principles for Energy Policy endorsed.

For practical reasons the implementation in the research and development field is reviewed under the responsibility of the Committee on Energy Research and Development (CRD). The CRD is assisted by a number of subsidiary bodies. They report to the CRD on a wide range of energy research and development topics both in government and private sectors. These bodies identify activities amenable to joint action. Moreover, they prepare proposals for specific joint projects and experimental programmes. There are now about 50 projects, undertaken by or in several countries through the so-called 'implementing agreements'. To enumerate some sectors: coal technology; solar energy; fusion power; geothermal energy; wind power; ocean energy.

It should be emphasised that the Research and Development Review by the Committee on Energy, just like the review exercised by the SLT, is part of the overall IEA process of reviewing the efforts of the IEA members. At the basis lies the IEP Agreement. Review is not the only task of the CRD. It is also part of a more general setting.

(1) The CRD should develop and expand a strategy for energy research, development and demonstration (RDD). It should, moreover, oversee the implementation.

(2) The CRD functions as a forum for consultation, collaboration and co-ordination in the field of RDD (collaborative projects).

(3) In the light of its work in preparing a strategy, it has to review the national RDD programmes. Thus, it should become apparent where opportunities for collaboration lie, where these should be promoted and in what manner. It is up to the Governing Board to take, on the proposal of the CRD (together with the SLT), the necessary decisions and recommendations.

The review procedure. As in the energy policies and programmes of the IEA Countries Review, the RDD Review consists of two parts: an overall review and a series of country reviews. The first part consists of a general assessment, with summary conclusions and recommendations with respect to individual countries. This part is prepared and conducted under the responsibility of the CRD. The second part falls under the responsibility of the *rapporteurs* who have examined, by way of confrontation, the individual countries. Actually, the *rapporteur* is assisted by a co-*rapporteur*, both having a nationality other than the country under examination. Both parts are published together, after having been discussed by the Governing Board. In 1980 the third report, the *1979 Review of National RDD Programmes*, was made public. Like the SLT review it is not restricted to the year 1979. The Review starts with a summary assessment of the past five years, thus going back to the starting point of the IEA. So, material from the previous years may be supplemented in the course of the annual reviews. Moreover, they can be adjusted and completed.

The overall report is drawn up both on the basis of the findings in the individual country reviews and on the basis of other material gained within the IEA. The review process has much in common with the review process within SLT outlined above.[278] A draft report is drawn up on the basis of studies, discussions and visits to the country under examination. After the draft report has been examined by the Chairman of the CRD and the Secretariat, it is once more checked with the country under review. Thereafter, it is brought in for a general discussion within the CRD. In order to provide a basis for a uniform approach to each country review, the CRD has formulated basic issues and a number of questions related to these issues. They are quoted here[279]:

NATIONAL ENERGY RD & D PROGRAMME REVIEWS

BASIC ISSUES

I. Energy RD & D Policy and Objectives
   (a) Are energy RD & D policy and its objectives clearly defined?
   (b) Are they consistent with and derived from the overall national energy policy and the IEP?

II. Government Energy RD & D Programmes and Budgets
   (a) Are the scope, size, internal distribution, and future prospects of government energy RD & D programmes and budgets consistent and well-balanced with the policy and objectives above, and with resources available to the country?
   (b) Is the priority given to energy RD & D programmes and budgets consistent with the severity of the energy situation?

III. Organisation for Establishing and Implementing Energy RD & D Policy
   (a) Are the governmental structures for establishing and implementing energy RD & D policy and programmes effective and well co-ordinated?

IV. Measures to Facilitate Development of New Technologies and their Application by Industry
   (a) Are there adequate incentives by the government to encourage private energy RD & D investments?
   (b) Are there adequate mechanisms and processes to facilitate the transfer of government's and industry's RD & D results to commercial use?
   (c) Are there adequate programmes to treat institutional and regulatory impediments to the development and application of new technologies?

V. Support for the IEA RD & D Co-operative Programmes
   (a) Is the participation in IEA co-operative RD & D activities commensurate with the size and scope of resources available to the country?

As the CRD itself states,[280] it is clear that the resulting judgments have to be made in the light of the particular circumstances of the country concerned. Moreover, the historical experience and performance in the realm of technology development and exploitation has to be taken into account too. The RD reviews actually started in 1977, with an initial coverage by correspondence. This method, however, proved to be insufficient. Thus, a visit on the spot was added. In 1978, three countries were examined in more detail and actually visited by a review team. During the 1979 review nine countries were subjected to similar 'in depth' examinations and examiners' visits. Nine countries were reviewed in a more limited way. Two countries, Luxembourg and Turkey, have not yet been reviewed.[281]

Of course, it has to be kept in mind that the RD & D programme review is but one element in the overall effort to promote the development and use of new technologies in order to make the IEA members less dependent upon oil as their major energy source. The other elements are the elaboration of the programme of collaborative projects and the working out of a RD & D strategy.

It should be noted that the IEA does not itself undertake research projects. It co-ordinates, monitors and stimulates. Moreover, it facilitates exchange of information. It should also be noted that non-IEA members may participate in joint-projects: Brazil and Mexico do so.

Short evaluation of the '1979 Review on Research, Development and Demonstration'. When the first five years are examined, it appears that most of the IEA countries have made a start with energy RD & D policies and programmes. The CRD states that the governments show an increasing awareness of their obligations to institute effective measures to facilitate the development and application of new technologies by industry. However, the CRD cannot yet judge the measures of their effectiveness.

The programme of collaborative projects has continuously expanded, with 'encouraging results'. However, this is only a small portion of the total energy RD & D effort of the IEA members. The CRD notes that an important step in the review process consists of determining the relationship between a national energy policy in general and a RD & D policy in particular: it has made a series of recommendations concerning the linkage of both policies and their implementation consequences. The adequacy of the responses has not yet been evaluated.[282] Special attention has been paid to the problem of informing the public. It is clear that the public must be aware of the problems. It must be co-operative in solving them. This implies *inter alia* also making new technologies (*e.g.* in the field of nuclear energy) known to the public, which has to decide whether these technologies are acceptable and necessary.

Along the lines of the basic issues the CRD has examined the national RD & D budgets, both as to their size, scope and priorities.

As for the structures for establishing and implementing RD & D policies and programmes the review clearly shows that there seems to be little system in this area. The CRD has made some recommendations, but their effectiveness has to be tested in the coming years. The CRD notes that the information on industrially financed RD & D is still insufficient. Half of the total IEA members (including the U.S.A.) have no data on the scale, distribution and nature of industrial effort in RD & D. Partly, the lack of information is due to the reluctance of industry to divulge information. The review contains a systematic catalogue of governmental measures, mostly being financial incentives, for facilitating new developments. There is little comment on these measures.

In the summary conclusions[283] the CRD states that certain improvements have been achieved:

> '(i) progress in defining policies and in setting priorities in RD & D, but further progress is still called for in assessing the benefits and costs of various lines of technology development (the availability of the IEA Strategy Development Project results should now provide some assistance in the future);

(ii) with two exceptions, all countries have increased their RD & D funding over the last year in real terms, but it is still questioned as to whether the increases are an adequate recognition of the contribution technology development can make to reduced dependence upon oil;

(iii) recognising that the development of conservation technology is not as expensive as some supply technologies, its important potential contribution still does not appear to be reflected in the level of its funding, even though this area does gain some support from incentives which are applied through other channels than RD & D;

(iv) nearly three-quarters of the total RD & D effort is being devoted to technologies predominantly concerned with electricity generation, virtually all of which produce heat. More attention to those technologies may be necessary in order to use the heat thus produced as a substitute for liquid fuels;

(v) the lack of scope and detail reported on industrial energy RD & D effort is a severely limiting factor in forming overall judgments on national programmes. This deficiency should be addressed urgently;

(vi) in spite of the number and scale of projects planned by government and industry and the increased activity reported on government measures to commercialise fossil fuel technologies, there appears to be scope for much more progress;

(vii) participation in IEA collaborative projects, although increasing still represents a significant untapped potential for achieving economies and risk-sharing through co-operative action, while recognising that the number of such projects is of less significance than their importance to national programmes and the scale of effort involved.'

These conclusions appear slightly more positive than those of the previous years. However, a series of shortcomings in effort is indicated. Of course, this is partly due to the fact that policies and programmes in a RD & D area were more or less totally absent before the IEA started. Thus, many countries are still facing the problems of the preliminary stage.

Firm criticism, as to the general energy policies, is to be found in the first Review (1977). The Governing Board concluded *inter alia* that various efforts were insufficient (conservation; alternative energy) and even inadequate to achieve the Group objectives.[284] Little progress was made in setting up policies corresponding to the seriousness of the problems. The commitments laid down in the 'Twelve Principles' of October 1977 were still to be fulfilled. Little or no attention was given to them, was the serious statement.[285] The Governing Board then stressed that the recommendations contained in the country reports should be taken into account by each of the members, carrying out its national energy policies. It ended by saying: 'The response of the governments concerned to these recommendations should be specifically examined during the course of the next reviews.'[286]

Has the situation by now changed? Rather more than a year later[287] the Governing Board examined the energy prospects and reviewed the progress made by the IEA countries in implementing the Twelve Principles[288] for Energy Policy. Indeed, the Group Objective of limiting oil imports[289] by 1985 seemed to be capable for realisation. However, this 'success' resulted more from the lower level of growth of the economies than from extra efforts by the members, was the conclusion reached by the Ministers. As for the medium- and long-term prospects the Ministers remained pessimistic. In order to assist increased coal use, the Ministers agreed on Principles for IEA Action on Coal and they decided upon procedures for reviewing the coal policies of the IEA members.[290] Although less firm criticism was uttered, at least in the communiqué, the Governing Board expressed its will to meet more frequently in order to keep the situation under review.

At the end of the year 1979 the Governing Board met again, at ministerial level.[291] The most important decision taken here was to review quarterly the results achieved by each country in meeting the oil import ceiling set for 1980 and 1985. The same applies for the oil supply developments. The Ministers will meet promptly 'to consider what corrective action is necessary if the performance of countries in keeping within their import limitations is not satisfactory, or if there is a major change in the supply situation'. In order to get more insight into the market conditions the Ministers agreed to improve the information system on stock movements, including information on stocks at sea, in bonded areas and consumer stocks. Moreover, they agreed to seek to develop a system of consultation on stock policies, among governments and between governments and oil companies. Additional measures should be considered regarding a more co-ordinated approach to spot market activities. Here, a system of registration of all entities trading oil into and from the IEA is receiving consideration. A Code of Conduct should be developed for all oil-market participants. From all this, it clearly appears that the IEA wants particularly to get a better grip on the spot market operations. Of course, this is only possible if all the IEA members have the necessary data collected and handed over to the IEA.

All in all, it may be concluded that via exchange of information, experience from research, review of policies and programmes, adjustment of objectives, positive efforts are made to reach a long-term energy policy. Within the IEA, the members try to co-ordinate their policies in an effective manner. However, as may be deducted from the review-reports and the criticism in the various communiqués the fulfilment of the objectives (principles/targets) has, until now, left much to be desired.

C. Information system on the international oil market. In order to make both the emergency programme and the energy policy co-operation workable in the long term, the participating countries have accepted that they must take all the appropriate measures[292] to ensure that all oil companies within their jurisdiction, make such information available to the governments, that they can provide the Secretariat with the necessary data.[293] According to the IEP agreement[294] the information system consists of two sections: (i) a General Section on the situation on the international oil market and activities of oil companies; (ii) a Special Section designed to ensure the efficient operation of an emergency measures system.[295]

The Secretariat is responsible for the operation of the system. It compiles the information in monthly and quarterly oil statistics and makes it available to the participating countries. Moreover, it draws up short- and medium-term outlooks for world oil supply and demand. The system is operated on a permanent basis, both under normal conditions and during emergencies, and in a manner which ensures the necessary confidentiality of the information made available. The data which have to be supplied to the Secretariat, under the General Section, are summed up in the Agreement.[296] They cover information on *inter alia* corporate and financial structure of oil companies; investments; their terms of arrangement for access to major sources; production etc.

Under the Special Section[297] the countries have to supply a series of specified data on: consumption and supply; demand restraint measures; levels of emergency reserves; transportation facilities; current and projected levels of international supply and demand and all other data, as decided by the Governing Board, necessary to ensure the efficient operation of an emergency oil-sharing plan. More details and precise procedures for obtaining the data on a regular basis, including accelerated procedures in times of emergency are (to be) worked out by the Standing Groups concerned.

For the General Section this task is carried out by the Standing Group on the Oil Market (SOM), for the Special Section by the Standing Group on Emergency Questions (SEQ). In both cases the procedures take place in close consultation with the oil companies. This is rather evident since the oil companies have actually to provide the said information, which is, however, mostly supplied to the Secretariat via the national governments. In view of these consultations a permanent framework has been established under the auspices of SOM.[298]

Whereas the SEQ is charged with the review and the reporting to the Management Committee on any matter falling within the scope of the emergency programme,[299] the SOM has an identical task with regard to the information and consultation system.[300] So, it reviews permanently the operation of the General Section. If necessary, it can make appropriate proposals for changes, to the Governing Board, having the decision-making power. The Special Section is subject to review by the SEQ.[301]

The SOM has also to evaluate the results of the consultations with, and the information from, oil companies. The findings are laid down in reports to the Management Committee, which reviews these reports and makes appropriate proposals to the Governing Board.

When dealing with the review task of SEQ, it has previously been mentioned that the Secretariat had noted some difficulties in the emergency data system.[302] A Working Group had to examine the problems in detail and recommend solutions to the SEQ. From this example it clearly appears that the review of the information operation makes sense. Its effectiveness should be, and actually is, regularly tested. If necessary it is adjusted and improved. Not only SOM and SEQ can identify deficiencies in the information chain, the Secretariat itself can also do so, being the first utiliser of the data.

It should be noted that the Governing Board decided,[303] to improve the information system *inter alia* on stock movements. Moreover, the list of oil companies which report oil flows directly to the IEA should be extended. Next, more information was said to be necessary regarding state-to-state transactions. Thus, the information procedures still prove to be in a developing process.

D. Relations with producer countries and with other consumer countries. It should also be mentioned that the Participating Countries will endeavour[304] to promote co-operative relations with oil-producing and oil-consuming countries, including developing countries. The aim is to set up a dialogue. This task is to be carried out by a Standing Group bearing the name 'On relations with Producer and other Consumer Countries'. It may review and report to the Management Committee on any matter falling within the scope of the 'relationship'.[305] Moreover, it may consult with oil companies on the same subject. Although it is clear that both the IEA and the other countries concerned can take advantage of good relations, the starting up was difficult. However, little by little an exchange of information becomes more intensive. The contacts with developing countries have particularly become more important. The IEA partners have also agreed to exchange, *inter se,* views on their relations with oil-producing countries and their co-operative action which might be relevant for the IEP.[306] Thus, a certain co-ordination via the IEA may be reached. The IEP Agreement enumerates a number of items to be considered, studied and reviewed, when deciding on the relations with third countries. However, from the point of view of surveillance the provisions still seem to be of little interest. The declarations of intent to strengthen the ties have to be worked out in explicit principles. Of course, there is also the need of an adequate response from outside, expressing the will to 'collaborate'.

But, having regard to the fact that rising oil prices have an overall impact on world economy and are especially harmful for the developing countries, the need for response seems to be apparent. The OECD/IEA Members have expressed their will to co-operate closely in the forthcoming international negotiations with the aim of restructuring international economic relations.[307] There again the need for co-operation with interested developing countries was underlined. They should be helped to identify and develop indigenous energy resources. The OECD Countries announced that they were also ready to strengthen industrial and technological co-operation with oil-exporting countries.

Energy co-operation had previously been discussed, at the Conference on International Economic Co-operation.[308] The results are, however, generally regarded as rather poor.[309] Nevertheless, the OECD and in particular the IEA, proves to be a forum for consultation between the partners, creating a common understanding *vis-à-vis* the developing countries. The relations with OPEC countries have improved. Although, formally, certain barriers are not yet removed there exists *de facto* an intensive exchange of information.

Concluding comments concerning the IEA. From the above it appears that the review process plays a vital role in the striving of the IEA Members to co-operate closely and effectively in the field of energy. The review relates to the readiness to cope with emergency situations, conservation activities, energy policy planning in general, and research, development and demonstration policies in particular, national coal policies, relationship with third countries, especially oil-producing and other consumer countries.

First object of the review consists of making a statement of affairs, if possible on the basis of common criteria, questionnaires and visits on the spot. Each country is subject to review. The details have been set out above. Such assessments may bring to light deficiencies and shortcomings. Thus, it appeared that when the IEA partners were subjected to review of their national energy programmes and policies, some of them had neither programmes nor policies with regard to energy.

Having made an inventory a review in the sense of a testing of the results to the basic agreement (IEP), the various energy principles, agreed upon by the Governing Board on its successive meetings, can take place. From such a check it may become clear if a member has maintained objectives and principles, and to what extent and in which manner. The efforts may be compared to the outcome of previous reviews. Here it may be questioned whether improvements have been made and whether certain recommendations, either general or specifically addressed to the country under review, have been fully taken into account. Has the conduct to be corrected, or have the objectives, or principles and/or recommendations to be adjusted or revised? Thus, the so-called creative part of the review may be applied.

The review is certainly meant to be an instrument of detailed exchange of information between the members. But, insight into each other's programmes and policies is not the only object. Good knowledge of each other's policies and plans, combined with an *exposé* on the experience and expertise gained within the IEA Member Countries serves to facilitate the realisation of national policies and programmes. The review should make the national policies more positive towards national decision-making. An independent appraisal of both the individual and the overall situation should make the choice of needs and priorities less difficult. Moreover, the national policies can be set out more in line with the 'common' options. Thus, the review, being an instrument for exchange of information is at the same time a means for closer co-operation and finally co-ordination of national policies. In other words, the review has a steering effect on the national policy-making and decision-making.[310]

Conclusion

If one examines the review process on energy matters one gets the impression that it is intensive, far-reaching and of a high standing. This provisional conclusion may be due to the solid assessments of the facts, the expertise and accuracy on the matter under review. Although shortcomings have been noted, the review systems appear to work rather effectively. Both the governments and the oil companies appear to be convinced of the need of such reviews.

2.2.11. Nuclear energy

For more than 20 years the OECD has been active in the field of nuclear energy. In 1961 the OECD Council approved the former OEEC decision[311] to establish a European Nuclear Energy Agency (ENEA). The ENEA has been changed into OECD Nuclear Energy Agency (NEA), with effect from 1972, this being the consequence of the participation of Japan in the work of the previous Agency. Some years later Canada and the United States of America joined.[312] The primary purpose of the Agency is to promote co-operation and the sharing of information among its Member Countries and to encourage common approaches in policies and practices in the nuclear energy field. Thus, a harmonisation of measures taken at the national level, is aimed at.[313] The tasks assigned to the Agency are carried out, under the authority of the Council, by a Steering Committee and those bodies which the latter deems necessary to set up.[314] The Agency has its own Secretariat which forms part of the OECD Secretariat.[315]

More specifically the Agency is concerned with providing the governments and industry with the necessary technological bases for further development of nuclear energy and related issues. Thus, it promotes studies and undertakes consultations on programmes and projects.[316] It also promotes the formation of joint undertakings for production and uses of nuclear energy for peaceful purposes. Additionally, it can conclude agreements for the creation of joint undertakings with the participating countries.[317] Given the need to prevent the proliferation of nuclear explosive devices, a security control is provided for, worked out in a special Convention.[318] A Control Bureau is charged with the supervision of the (due) implementation of agreements for co-operation and/or joint undertakings between the NEA and the governments concerned. In this respect the Control Bureau examines the reports relating to the exercise of control. In cases where it considers that infringements have been committed it should take the necessary steps to remedy the infringement. Where appropriate the Control Bureau has to recommend to the Steering Committee the measures to be taken. Moreover, the Control Bureau has to notify any (probable) infringement to the Steering Committee and report, periodically, on all its activities.[319]

From the report *NEA Activities in 1980*[320] it appears that the items actually dealt with relate to (i) radiological and environmental impacts of nuclear fuel cycle activities; (ii) nuclear safety research and licensing; (iii) nuclear law; (iv) nuclear development and fuel cycle studies; (v) technical co-operation and (vi) nuclear science.[321]

(i) In this area progress has been made in developing revised international safety standards, providing an up-to-date basis for legislation and regulation at the national level for the protection of both workers and population.[322] Moreover, two studies, one on fundamental concepts to radioactive waste disposal and the other on legal, administrative and financial questions of long-term management of radioactive waste, have been undertaken. Both studies are intended to assist national authorities when taking the necessary decisions.

An interesting feature in the field of waste management and disposal is the dumping of radioactive waste into the deep ocean, which is, as of 1975,[323] subject to international regulation and supervision by national authorities. Moreover, the OECD countries have agreed, since 1977, to submit their

578

proposed arrangements to international scrutiny, and surveillance within the framework of a 'Multilateral Consultation and Surveillance Mechanism for Sea Dumping of Radioactive Waste', established by the NEA.[324] This Mechanism was set up to further the purposes of the international London Convention[325] and as a practical means of providing increased assurance that the dumping in the ocean is carried out in conformity with its terms and those of the IAEA recommendations and relevant guidelines. Close contacts are maintained between the NEA group of experts charged with the assessment of dumping practices and the OECD Environment Committee, regarding the co-ordination of environmental policies. Moreover, a collaboration with the IAEA and IMCO[326] is established. In 1980 two sea-dumping operations were carried out, supervised by two examining countries neither of which were the dumping countries.[327] All the operations took place in conformity with the internationally established rules and procedures.[328]

Disposal of high level waste in suitable geological emplacements is still under study, as part of a co-operative project. Two workshops were held for exchanging information on the results obtained by the said studies.

(ii) Exchange of nuclear safety information is still a priority task. The co-operation is directed by the Committee on the Safety of Nuclear Installations (CSNI). It constitutes a forum of exchange of information between licensing authorities and research groups. Thus, it keeps up-to-date a *Nuclear Safety Research Index*. The information task includes an Incident Reporting System (IRS), which was officially launched in January 1980 for a trial period of two years. During 1980 about 40 incidents were reported. The reports are exchanged in order to alert reactor operators and to enable the responsible authorities to take appropriate measures against similar incidents. Moreover, much emphasis is given to the need for pooling knowledge, research and development programmes and a continued exchange of practical experience. The technical details are left aside, being not relevant for the purpose of this study.

(iii) It is one of the Agency's statutory tasks to encourage the harmonisation of national laws and regulations in the field of nuclear energy.[329] Achievements have been reached in the sphere of nuclear third party liability and in the area of radioactive waste disposal.[330] Dissemination of information should help to promote the same objective.[331]

(iv) The NEA assists its members, in evaluating the technical and broad economic conditions underlying national decisions on nuclear energy development. Thus, the Agency assesses how much uranium is available and under which conditions. Moreover, an inventory has been made upon which the world's undiscovered resources can be based. For this purpose the NEA sends experts to the countries concerned to investigate the areas having good potential for further uranium resources and to discuss the information with local specialists. The NEA also co-ordinates, jointy with the IAEA, the exploration techniques, in order to improve them and to make the knowledge quickly known among the interested parties.

(v) Since 1971 a co-ordinating Group on Gas-Cooled Fast Reactor Development has endeavoured to establish a co-ordinated programme for work.

Eleven countries and two international bodies are represented in the Group.[332] One of the characteristics of technical co-operation is reflected in the establishment of joint undertakings, such as Eurochemic in Belgium and the Halden project in Norway. In the project various institutes and companies from different Member Countries participate. One of the main areas of the project relates to the monitoring and controlling of a reactor *inter alia* in abnormal situations. The outcome of the research should provide the basis for establishing design and operational guidelines. Another project is the International Food Irradiation Project, guided in its work by the recommendations of Joint FAO/IAEA/WHO Experts Committees on the Wholesomeness of Irradiated Food. From the research it was apparent that a recommendation on the general acceptability of irradiation treatment of foods could be drawn up. This has to be prepared by the Joint Expert Committee, then approved and recommended to the governments under the Codex Alimentarius Commission's procedures.

(vi) The nuclear science programmes of the NEA concentrate on long-term applied physics research to resolving technological problems of nuclear power. They group together the activities of two specialised committees and are supported by the NEA Data Bank at Saclay (France). The Data Bank is a specialised information centre, which assists the Member Countries in making effective use of the substantial output of research in nuclear science. It has a computer facility over a wide range of nuclear energy applications with access to the largest computer park in Europe. Thus, data can be transmitted to other computers. The 'packaging' of programmes ensures that the transmission to the user is safe and that it will be used for the purpose intended.

The general organisation and administration has already been dealt with.[333] A problem to be faced is the co-ordination between the various committees, all having a highly specialised character. It is up to the Steering Committee to assure a solid co-ordination. It does so by examining regularly the programmes of the various standing committees of the NEA.

Summary

The NEA has functioned for more than 20 years as a forum for exchange of information both for technical and research purposes. Within the NEA efforts are undertaken to realise harmonisation of legislation on, *e.g.*, nuclear safety, and nuclear third liability. Together with other international organisations, like the IAEA and the WHO, norms and standards for radiation protection and public health are worked out. A system for multilateral consultation and surveillance mechanism for sea dumping of radioactive waste has been adopted and carried out. Nuclear safety aspects are continuously subject to research and review. Consultations on nuclear development and co-operation, mostly exercised in joint projects and programmes, take place within the NEA. Nuclear science is backed, by *inter alia*, the establishment of a NEA Data Bank (at Saclay), assisting the Member Countries in making effective use of the information, gathered in a common effort. All in all, it appears that the NEA certainly plays an important supervisory role, be it in a technical and not so common field for the average jurist.

III. CONCLUSION: 'IN SEARCH OF EFFECTIVENESS'

Judging the effectiveness of supervision or supervisory mechanisms is a precarious and difficult undertaking. Effectiveness can be looked at both on the short-term and in the long(er) run. It can be affected by the review procedure, which may differ from organisation to organisation. Moreover effectiveness is affected by those who are in charge of the review task and those who are subjected to the review. Are the first-mentioned capable persons? Are the latter inclined to supply the necessary information and to co-operate? Are they averse to criticism? Effectiveness is also influenced by the possibility of ensuring compliance or the facility to adjust the rules in general or in a specific case (creative function of supervision). On the one hand, this will depend on the authority the supervisory body has. On the other hand it will depend on the instruments at hand. Moreover, is the 'rule' as such (irrespective of its legal status) fit for reaching the intended aim? Such should be supposed. But, society is ever changing and so, rules have also to be adjusted. There often arise differences of opinion in interpreting and working out the rules. In principle there should be a *communis opinio* as to the means of achieving the aims. It can be stated that the effectiveness is also influenced by the degree of agreement (consensus) among the partners that have created a rule. Consensus may favour the effectiveness of a review of a Member Country's behaviour. From practice it appears that consensus is often difficult to reach, even for fixing vague rules, guidelines or recommendations. Moreover, such rules are usually accompanied by a series of escape clauses. Nevertheless, it may be seen as a positive element if the members of an organisation agree to have their behaviour, as to their compliance with treaty obligations, reviewed. It should be regarded as a first step in the direction of effective review. This accounts also for review of moral obligations (guidelines). Of course, the effectiveness may vary, according to the functions of supervision. For the mere review function, information is of vital importance. For the corrective function much depends on the actual degree of solidarity which is present amongst the Member Countries. The same applies more or less for the creative function. Much depends on the question whether the members are inclined to discuss problems sincerely and to assist each other to overcome real problems. From the introductory part[334] it may be deduced that there exists a kind of common co-operative spirit to tackle problems in a non-formalistic, open, prompt and fair manner. In principle all members agree that their policies should be subjected to a kind of examination, which eases open the way to adjustment and co-ordination. Confrontations may sometimes be hard to undergo, but may, like a thunder-shower, clear the sky. Examinations may underline the need for further co-operation and co-ordinated actions. As may have become clear from the foregoing chapter, the co-operation is more and more forced by the growing interdependence, the interlinkage of problems and the policies for coping with those problems. The means for reaching the objectives of the Convention are limited to exchange of information, consultation, discussion and co-ordinated actions. The formal acts are usually not legally binding decisions, recommendations and guidelines. The institutional framework is of a classical character. The daily management is ensured by the Secretary-General, his counsellors and staff. He is responsible for assisting the various Council Committees and Working Groups (etc.) which prepare the bulk of the work of the Council. Part of their work is, as appears from the description of the various aspects above (Chapter II), assessing various national policies and issues, judging them and making proposals for adjustment. Awareness of the need to cope with problems in common and in an effective way, stimulates the means to map out common principles, issues and options. A regular evaluation and a continuing system of monitoring national policies give a dynamic character to the work of the Organisation. In general, the final responsibility for the whole functioning of the OECD rests in the hands of the Council, whatever role the various subsidiary bodies and the departments of the Secretariat may play. The Council decides on the priorities and the working programmes. The Council fixes the mandates of the bodies which it may create. The Council has a decisive role upon the effectiveness of supervision. It is up to the Council to decide what should be made public (be it favourable or otherwise for a Member Country). In its *tour d'horizon* – either on the ministerial level or at level of permanent representatives – the Council draws (some) conclusions as to the effectiveness of actions taken within the OECD. The Council investigates, in a general way, whether the states have done their best to contribute to the pursuance of the basic purposes of the Convention. In other words the Council examines the adequacy of a State's attitude, together with the adequacy of a rule to achieve the purpose. It is clear that from soft-law rules the expectations cannot be too high. However, review, discussion and consultation may raise the level and push forward co-operation. In communiqués pledges may be recalled, as moral incentives to live up to the pledge.

When one tries to draw some conclusions on the effectiveness of these review and evaluations systems, one has to keep in mind what in reality can be expected from a legally non-binding rule established within a certain international organisation. What can be expected from the organisation itself? Did the founding fathers intend to have the partners subjected to an international forum, having the authority to force observance of international guidelines? From an international inter-governmental organisation, such as the OECD, this can not be expected. The international climate is surely still vitiated considerably by suspicion and national susceptibilities. Every international co-operation implies some kind of infringement upon the national sovereignty.[335] This applies especially to supervision, which is *in se* exercised by a third party. The mere notion of supervision is surrounded by taboos, which are difficult to overcome! In order to make this exercise as painless as possible, the review should be exercised according to well-fixed procedures and by impartial bodies. If possible, the bodies should be independent from the States. However, as practice shows, such a step is not easily made. States prefer to keep a finger in the pie, by being represented in a supervisory body, and having, themselves, the last word.

Finally, effectiveness of supervision is not only defined by the safeguard of the rules, the procedures and the bodies applying them, but also by the way the results are received and regarded. Here one should look both to the parties concerned and the third parties. As for the OECD reviews, they are certainly regarded as authoritative. Such a good image can be considered as favourable for continuing and improving the existing review procedures.

3.1. Effectiveness of the review function

Supervision can be divided according to its various functions into review, correction and creative action.[336] The effectiveness can be looked at according to the same subdivisions. In Part I of this book the following questions, in this respect, are put forward:[337]

(1) are the supervisory bodies adequate;
(2) are the supervisory procedures adequate;
(3) is there a possibility to check and verify the findings with the obligations;
(4) what instruments are available for exercising the review function; how effective are they in practice?

Adequacy of the supervisory bodies

From the foregoing it appears that in the various areas where the OECD is active, the review system at top level is uniform. Ultimately, it is up to the Council to examine, consult and discuss what has been found in specific review undertakings by specific bodies. These bodies originate partly, directly or indirectly, from the Council, partly from the Secretariat. The first category is engaged from the national administrations, sometimes assisted by independent experts. The levels may vary, from ministers, directors-general, senior officials to juniors. The Council itself meets either on ministerial level or at level of permanent representatives.

As to the adequacy of the governmental bodies, much depends on the interest the States have to charge competent persons with working for a subsidiary body or a working party. Moreover, a difference of approach is to be expected, dependent on the question whether a committee-member operates as a representative of his country, or in his own capacity. Moreover, it depends whether or not the member is a politically responsible person (minister). In the first case less independence is usually to be expected. National, governmental influence is more likely to be exercised than in the latter case where independence should not be questioned. The same applies to the expertise of the supervisor. This raises the question as to whether pure political organs are really adequate to review the implementation of, and the compliance with, the Convention. A definite answer is difficult to give.

As a favourable and positive answer one can put forward the following. First, the political expertise of the political organ combines well with the political character of the subject under review. It seems to be indispensable that policy options, and their implementation in the national States are not only dealt with on a technical and/or lower political level, but also on a higher level. Such occurs in practice (a) by sessions of Ministers, responsible in the field concerned, (b) by a general Ministerial Meeting once a year and (c) by meetings of Directors-General, so-called High Level Group meetings. The Ministers bear political responsibility and have to oversee the political implications. However, they tend to refrain from details. That might be seen as a negative point. A meeting once or twice a year on top level has a rather general character. And this is also characteristic of the conclusions. In many respects the only way out is to subscribe in resolutions or recommendations to what has been assessed or recommended before by those who do and did the preparatory work: the various subsidiary bodies together with the Secretary-General, his counsellors and staff.

Thus, it should also be questioned whether the Secretary-General is well-equipped to keep the behaviour of the OECD members well under review (and perhaps even under control!). The answer to this question depends on various factors, *inter alia* on the aspect of personnel. The Secretary-General, his two deputy Secretaries-General and four special counsellors call on the services of six main units.[338] The total permanent staff, the six units, consists of 66 persons.[339] In total the Secretariat counts about 1000 members, assisted by nearly 600 persons falling under the heading Administration (Executive Directorate). In general, one can conclude that the Secretariat is of an adequate size to exercise its various functions.

It is clear that the emphasis is laid on economic affairs and statistics. The annual review exercise – country by country – remains the basic element of the Economic and Statistics Department, being of vital importance as a major source of information for all the other parts of the Secretariat. The data collected here serves to set up the half-yearly Economic Outlooks. For the year 1980 the number of half-day sessions to be held in connection with economic affairs and statistics was estimated at 125. An important number (48) was reserved for the Economic and Development Review Committee (EDRC). From this number it may be concluded that a great deal of the time has to be spent on the review aspect. But also from a budgetary point of view it is evident that the economic review sector is the heaviest. The appropriations are more than twice as high as in any other area. The costs for the administration are not taken into consideration here. Although the number of (planned) half-day sessions of the Committees on Economic Affairs is considerably high, it appears that in other areas the number is sometimes ever higher.[340] However, the fact remains that, particularly for the subject of review, the number of sessions for the EDRC is by far the highest. In other areas the number of Committees and/or groups is much bigger, thus reducing the average number for each committee.[341] In total, the number approaches 1500 half-day sessions. These sessions have to be prepared and attended by members of the Secretariat. A high proportion of those sessions will relate to the review of the national policies and the observance of the Convention by the Member States. One has only to recall the OECD's activities in the field of economic policies, fiscal and financial affairs; energy policies; trade and multinational enterprises; development aid co-operation. Review and co-ordination from the core of the work in these fields. Next, a series of studies will have to be dealt with. They serve as a basis for discussion, information and setting up 'strategies' or guidelines, within the Council.

In conclusion, the Secretariat appears to be an adequate body for preparing, helping and backing the Council in exercising its various functions.[342]

From a qualitative point of view the Secretariat can guarantee independence and expertise, in all the fields in which the OECD is involved. The organisational structure is flexible. It can be adjusted and actually is adjusted according to the needs for sound management. Efficiency is also secured by taking into account the horizontal links between the Directorates. Policies get more and more interlinked. So, their mutual impact has to be watched. At the same time double work has to be avoided too. Although financial restraint appears to be evident in the OECD Secretariat, it still appears to be able to respond to the needs for information, consultation and co-ordination. From a quantitative point of view it appears that the Secretariat is of a manageable size, having both a considerable number of experts and administrative personnel to do the necessary preparatory work. Studies, draft reports, draft acts still come in a regular flow, being regarded as of a high standard. One has to bear in mind future economic prospects.

Whether the various subsidiary bodies as such are adequate, cannot be answered definitely. One can only suppose that the countries which have an interest in the matter do check and do send qualified persons to participate in work of those bodies. For the rest much depends on the chairman of a committee or a group. The chairman has to organise the meetings in close co-operation with the Directorate of the Secretary-General, ultimately responsible in the matter under consideration.

Adequacy of the supervisory procedures

In fact, the question of the adequacy of the supervisory procedures is closely linked with the two other questions raised above. Is there a possible means to verify the data and what instruments of review are available? To put it in other words and in a logical sequence: can information be obtained, checked and processed in an adequate manner?

From the foregoing survey it can be stated that in the OECD there is a right for the supervisors to obtain information and an obligation to supply it. The basic provision is laid down in Article 3 OECD. Usually, the States are obliged to inform and consult the OECD on request. Sometimes, there is an obligation to inform the organisation automatically. Such obligations may be laid down in the terms of reference of specific subsidiary bodies or in a specific act (whatever form it may have).

As instruments for obtaining information a great variety occurs: the communication; the notification; the reporting; the inspection or visit on the spot; the examination and confrontation; the inquiry or questionnaire; the consultation.

Another feature when dealing with the problem of effectiveness concerns the 'completeness' of the information and the promptness of the supplying of information. Much depends on the organisational approach of those in charge of the review. Clearly marked questionnaires with fixed timetables for response usually appear to be effective, combined with the sending of reminders in due time. If the review takes place regularly, *e.g.* quarterly or annually, the partners get accustomed to a rhythm. In economics, development aid co-operation, and energy, the policies are annually reviewed. The first two have a tradition of twenty years – and even thirty years if we take the OEEC examinations into account – the latter, energy, of a few years. In other areas the annual review is also a common occurrence: competition and consumer policy; competition policies; agriculture policies. Moreover, in almost every sector, reviews at regular intervals take place. The information is usually procured on schedule.[343] Sometimes, lateness will frustrate part of the review system. This is *e.g.* the case where statistical data have to be procured directly. However, statistical reviews covering daily, weekly and/or monthly data, *e.g.* on the oil supply situation, can easily be adjusted. As for the oil market situation both the oil companies and the Member States are requested to supply to the IEA monthly, definite data over the past month, current data over the month concerned and provisional data for the next month. It is clear that in such a situation, with the modern techniques of data processing, the situation can be fairly well assessed, even day by day. Apart from energy matters which are nowadays regarded as of vital importance to our economies, quick information is also required in the field of environment, nuclear energy, especially with a view to take safety measures against *e.g.* pollution or radiation. 'Early warnings' should prevent deterioration of dangerous or harmful situations, enabling the parties concerned to take the immediate necessary measures. The same applies to trade. Apart from regular information on trade practices, important changes have to be notified immediately. And so derogations from the codes of liberalisation (of respectively invisible operations and of capital movements) have to be notified forthwith to the OECD.[344]

In practice it appears that prior information is difficult to obtain, for political reasons. Much of the effect of an act is feared to be lost, if it is made public (even in restricted circles), before it is applied.

Prompt and correct information is not only important for the effectiveness of the review function of supervision, but also for its corrective and creative functions. Moreover, it is important for the laying down of the data in (draft) reports or other kind of papers (reviews/surveys, etc.). Publication should not be hindered by slowness in providing the requested information. Thus, the annual Economic Country Reviews by the EDRC are due to be published during the year following the year under review. The same applies to the DAC publications, reviewing the efforts and policies of the members of the

Development Assistance Committee. Here the members are requested to deliver their memoranda before mid-June. As a rule, the greater number have fulfilled this obligation before autumn. It is said[345] that before the end of the year all requested data is received. The quality of the data is said to be usually of a high standard.[346]

Concerning the procedures for getting information one can be brief. The use of questionnaires, *i.e.* formulas with a set of fixed questions and memoranda, is practised satisfactorily.[347] Over the years, they have been more elaborated, improved and adjusted to the needs. Via methodical work and improvements, important results have been obtained for the preparation of forecasting trends in economies, trade and finances. To quote a passage, relating to the subject of economic country review and economic prospects: 'The same methods can be used to check the compatability of national objectives and projections and to undertake simulations on the basis of alternative sets of policy assumptions. This analytical framework (for the preparation of a consistent set of forecasts) should prove of continuing value in the design of realistic concerted strategies.'[348]

From the above it appears that the procedure of systematic requests is not only meant for obtaining information, but also to check it. One of the objectives of uniform formulas is to make the outcomes comparable. First, this should be done for the OECD as such. If possible, comparability should exist with data other organisations obtain, process and procure. Here efforts are undertaken with the economic and statistical services of the EEC. But also world-wide close co-operation with the UN is needed. 'Another line of development will be the redrafting and extension of the questionnaire on national accounts, an enterprise undertaken jointly with the UN Statistical Office and which will be considered in depth in 1980 . . . (within the Data Processing and Statistical Services Directorate of the OECD Secretariat).'[349]

One of the most elaborate methods for verifying the data, are the often cited examination or confrontation sessions held in connection with economic country reviews by the EDRC. Similar procedures take place in almost all fields of the OECD: trade and trade practices, invisibles, development, assistance, environment, energy policies. In all cases experts from the Secretariat may visit the country concerned and discuss the matter with competent officials: and, too, additional information and explanation may be requested. The countries concerned are usually given the opportunity to comment on and dispute the data which, in their opinion, is not correct. Finally, all findings can usually be discussed in the plenary session of the subsidiary body concerned and, as the case may be, in the Council. Only after these procedures have been fulfilled will a report or a communiqué on a country's behaviour be made public.[350]

3.2. Effectiveness of the corrective and the creative function

Finally, the effectiveness as to the follow-up of the review function should be looked at. From the above it may have become clear that correction and creative action, guidance of national tendencies in policies, making guidelines for national behaviour are integral parts of the review process. The OECD creates the facilities for assessing facts and behaviour, but it also forms the forum for political discussion, consultation and political understanding. Consensus is the catchword. Firm disapproval of conduct, if discovered, will not be made public. That is regarded as unhelpful to the atmosphere aimed at. Good intentions are presupposed. As stated above, it should be a State's own responsibility to direct its policies, having regard also to what has been 'agreed' upon within the international context. So, the OECD's guiding principles and recommendations are said to be taken into sincere consideration. A State should be free, if necessary, to defend its own policies. On the other hand, criticism uttered within the OECD circles, may be welcomed by a government to defend a certain view at home, e.g. vis-à-vis the parliament. So, it may subscribe to a common conduct, pleading that such is in the country's interest from a point of view of international solidarity. Only in cases of emergency, especially with regard to the oil market, have the countries agreed to subject themselves to decisions taken by majority voting. Here, effects may be expected ipso iure. The same applies to creative actions. Effectiveness is not primarily due to the available instruments, but to the knowledge that co-operation is a must for survival. If that is the case, any instrument will be likely to be effective.

Effectiveness of the corrective function should not be overestimated. Of course, consultation, political discussion and the mobilisation of shame – if not overdone – do their work. They create a psychological climate to align with the partners and to reconsider policies, facts, and behaviour if these do not meet with general approval. Such a disapproval is usually quietly uttered. Public confrontations would be regarded as unfriendly acts rather strange to these equal-minded circles. Moreover, it may be questioned whether firm criticism would not be misinterpreted. Stimulating governments to adopt certain policies, in line with each other, implies even more subtle pressure and manipulation than is already required in the case of prevention or redress.[351] The latter being the main function of correction. Nevertheless, the debates in the plenary sessions of the Council cannot be said to consist of monologues without any real effect.[352] Confrontation effects, however, should not be expected here. The very examinations take place in camera, in the smaller subsidiary bodies. Corrective effects should be obtained, in principle, in the same way. In globo, a general re-examination may take place in the Council, re-affirming conclusions already reached in a previous stage, i.e. within a special committee or group, in collaboration with the relevant division of the OECD Secretariat.

Publication of the reviews and, as the case may be, communiqués relating to the matter under review, may be expected to have some corrective effects or at any rate 'directive' effects. Thus, ever since the oil crises the OECD has stressed certain economic policy priorities, and positive adjustment policies, which should be taken into consideration by the partners.[353]

Directive effects of the Secretary-General are found in the half-yearly Economic Outlook.[354] The prospects should be looked at against the background of the priorities set in the Programme of Work. Thus, in itself the *Outlook* contains a kind of review, combined with statements and conclusions by the independent body of the OECD – the Secretary-General – which does not necessarily coincide with the views of the Member Countries. However, it is generally known that the view of the Secretary-General is highly esteemed. His views are broadly discussed in political and business circles, and in the world press. So, some effectiveness should be attributed to his 'corrective' statements. Another means for possibly influencing behaviour and policies is formed by studies. Within the OECD a great number of occasional studies are undertaken and published. These studies may back-up certain views already laid down in reviews and/or recommendations. The OECD studies undertaken by Secretariat experts or *ad hoc* consultants from outside, are regarded as being of a high standard and worthy to be taken into consideration as a reference facility. And so, the various corrective influences mentioned above, may work perhaps only slowly, but they keep the members moving in the direction aimed at. Moreover, those influences may contribute to the taking of creative actions. These may lie in the further development of existing 'rules' and their interpretation. Next, new decisions may result as a consequence of reviews, provided that consensus is reached. As may be deducted from the foregoing chapter, both the Council, the Executive Committee and the Secretary-General play an active role in fulfilling a creative function.

3.3. Summary and concluding remarks

In effect review, correction and creative actions are much interlinked and likely to influence each other. They form no closed circles, but they spiral forward, as mutual understanding ripens and the interest for co-operation is more deeply felt and trusted. Within the scope of the OECD this system works fairly well. If it does so, this is but partly due to the supervisory procedures. Capable personnel are vital for success. In the last resort, however, all depends on the willingness of the Member Countries to commit themselves to certain common approaches and reviews of their respective policies. In the main areas where the OECD is operative – economics, financial and fiscal policies, trade, development assistance, energy – such willingness appears to be present. The States concerned have committed themselves to provide the Organisation with the necessary information, to consult each other and to discuss policy options. They have agreed to subject their policies to confrontation by other members, thus reaching a fair examination and assessment of a situation. In most cases one can speak of a rendering to account of a country: an evaluation of policies, issues and options via consultation and discussion. In general, various possibilities exist to check data.

The various methods of examination have been practised for years (*e.g.* economies; development assistance; trade; finances; nuclear energy). They are continuously open to improvement and often backed by individual studies. No doubt they have been of great use for promoting the basic objectives of the OECD Convention. Regular reviews have created an atmosphere of understanding being the starting-point for possible mutual influencing of policies. The working sphere within the OECD is generally qualified as good, efficient and informal. This encourages effectiveness!

This conclusion, partly drawn from impressions gathered from OECD circles, is also backed by opinions about the OECD from outside the organisation. Especially, the results of the various reviews, as laid down in the publications, are highly esteemed. In the economic country reviews, the outlooks are regarded as being solid, objective assessments. They are internationally used with trust. Another facet influencing effectiveness is perhaps the fact that the OECD as such, has not created high hopes as to far-reaching forms of integration. Common policies, as in the European Communities, with involved legal obligations and far-reaching impacts on the national level, are not aimed at. On the contrary, no infringement on national sovereignty by supranational powers seems to be the leading principle. The OECD only creates a consultation and discussion forum enabling its members to get into 'gentlemen's agreements', *i.e.* decisions based on consensus. No member is forced or should be felt to be forced to give its consent to a decision which it does not favour. However, all the members being aware of the practical necessity to co-operate, seem to take into serious consideration all political issues discussed in the OECD. So they do take into consideration the findings of review processes, even when these may lead to recommendations not in line with their own national interest. This way of approach (consensus) if for a good number of Member States more appealing than the (legal) course to be taken in *e.g.* the European Communities. Moreover, no European Commission for the OECD has been created, having or claiming political powers. OECD has only a Secretariat, *de jure* not pretending to be more than that.[355]

All in all, it clearly appears that the OECD partners favour a flexible recycling process of assessment, evaluation and adjustment. Thus, they exert themselves to co-operate and to take advantage of their membership of the Organisation. Whether this is the way to promote a new international economic order can not be answered. At any rate the system appears, within the OECD, on one hand by its diversity and flexibility, and on the other hand by its unity, to be rather effective and attractive for a large organisation having a relatively great number of participants.

NOTES

1. Full members of the OECD are at present the following 24 countries: Australia, Austria, Belgium, Canada, Denmark, Finland, France, the Federal Republic of Germany, Greece, Iceland, Ireland, Italy, Japan, Luxembourg, the Netherlands, New Zealand, Norway, Portugal, Spain, Sweden, Switzerland, Turkey, the United Kingdom and the United States. Yugoslavia participates in the work of the Organisation with a special status.

2. The OEEC Treaty was signed on April 16, 1948 by 16 countries. The Federal Republic of Germany became a full member on October 25, 1949. The United States of America and Canada became associated members, as of June 1950. Spain and Yugoslavia participated in some of the activities, as of 1955. In 1959 Spain became a full member. Eastern Europe, though in need of help, did not participate in the work of the OEEC. This was due to pressure from the U.S.S.R. withholding the Eastern European countries from joining a multilateral programme which was so infringing on the sovereignty of the States (!).

3. See note 2. A close co-operation between the U.S.A., Canada and Western Europe existed as of the establishment of the OEEC, but not on an equal footing. The U.S.A. primarily served as a 'nurse,' giving Marshall Aid for four years (1948–52). For more details see *inter alia* J. Gimbel, *The Origins of the Marshall Plan* (Stanford, California, 1976).

4. The immediate task of the OEEC (Article 1,2) 'to undertake the elaboration and execution of a joint recovery programme,' was accomplished. *Cf.* note 3 and the *Report of the Preparatory Committee on the OECD* (the so-called 'Blue Book'), published by the OECD (Paris, 1960).

5. Compare the preamble of the OECD Convention. It may be stated that the need for a burden sharing was the strongest reason to remodel the OEEC.

6. In the preamble of the OECD Convention it is expressly stated that the parties to the Convention agreed 'on the following provisions for the *reconstitution*' of the OEEC as the OECD.

7. Article 15 OECD.

8. Article 15 OECD; see also *Report of the Preparatory Committee, op.cit, supra*, note 4, Part II.

9. For comparison Article 11 OEEC is cited: 'The aim of the Organisation shall be the achievement of a sound European economy through the economic co-operation of its Members. An immediate task of the Organisation will be to ensure the success of the European recovery programme in accordance with the undertakings contained in Part I of the present Convention.'

10. The same obligation was found in Article 9 OEEC Convention, which reads: 'The Contracting Parties will furnish the Organisation with all the information it may request in order to facilitate the accomplishment of its tasks.'

11. Thus, because of political disagreement France has not joined the International Energy Agency (IEA), see *infra*, p. 562.

12. See *infra*, pp. 535–536.

13. See in this respect also Article 4 and 11 OEEC. *Cf.* A. H. Robertson, *European Institutions* (London, 1959), p. 38 *et seq.*

14. On a regional scale the subject of tariffs is dealt with *e.g.* by the EEC, EFTA and Benelux. As for liberalisation of visible transactions the International Monetary Fund (IMF) plays an important role. On the European level this objective was first pursued by the European Payment Union (EPU, 1950–55), next the European Monetary Agreement (1955–72) and last, but not least, the EEC.

15. DAC – Development Assistance Committee – comprising all major developed countries of OECD, to be dealt with, *infra*, p. 553 *et seq.*

16. Reference is made to OPEC donors, centrally planned economy countries, some developing countries. It should be noted that here difficulties arise because of the lack of systematic official reporting by non-DAC donors.

17. In this respect it should be noted that the OECD has intensified its meetings at top-level. Thus, apart from the general annual Council Meeting at Ministerial Level, sectoral committees may meet and actually do so, at Ministerial Level. Moreover, the heads of delegations meet regularly, the Executive Committee also meets in Special Session and last, but not least, Directors-General of the various national competent Departments meet in High-Level Groups. See also notes 25 and 64. This implies, that political discussions are not reserved for the Council meetings alone, but that much intensive work is done beforehand, in the preparatory stage as well.

18. Actually, since 1970, environmental policies are taken into consideration in relation to the general economic policies.

19. See for more details, *infra*, p. 556 *et seq.*

20. Originally European Nuclear Energy Agency (ENEA); after the accession of Japan changed into Nuclear Energy Agency (NEA).

21. See M. J. Hahn and A. Weber, *Die OECD, Organisation für Wirtschaftliche Zusammenarbeit und Entwicklung* (Baden-Baden, 1976), pp. 306–307.

22, See *supra*, note 1.

23. Article 10, 2 OECD, *cf.* Article 17 OEEC. Under the OEEC the Secretary-General was only entitled to prepare the Council meetings but not to preside those meetings.

24. Moreover, the Council is entitled to set up its own Working Parties. To enumerate the most important: Special Group on Positive Adjustment Policies (P.A.P.); Liaison Committee with International Non-Governmental Organisations; Liaison Committee with the Council of Europe; the High-Level Group on Commodities; the Budget Committee and the Group on North-South Economic Issues. As to the Special Group on P.A.P., see at p. 528.

A High-Level Group consists of Directors-General of national departments (see note 17).

25. Rule 25a, *Rules of Procedure OECD.*

26. Rule 22a, *Rules of Procedure OECD.*

27. Normally five years, but not necessarily. The structure of the Secretariat is as follows (1980): Secretary-General; two Deputy Secretaries-General; Executive Director for the IEA and Co-ordinator for Energy Policies; Special Counsellor on Economic Matters; two Special Counsellors; six divisions. Total permanent staff: 66 persons.

28. Article 11, 2 OECD, *cf.* Article 18 OEEC.

29. *Cf.* note 23.

30. Rule 12, *Rules of Procedure OECD.*

31. Departments of the Secretariat: General Direction and Co-ordination; Economic Affairs and Statistics; Environment; Development Co-operation; Technical Co-operation; Trade; Financial and Fiscal Affairs; Science; Technology and Industry; Social Affairs, Manpower and Education; Food, Agriculture and Fisheries; Energy; Administration; Information; Data Processing and Statistical Services; Part II section: *inter alia* IEA; Development Centre; NEA; CERI; special programmes.

32. See *supra*, p. 522.

33. Article 9 OECD, *cf.* Article 15 OEEC. See also the *Rules of Procedure OECD*, Rules 21–26.

34. See notes 11 and 20. As for the Development Centre see *infra*, p. 554. Up to now the Fund is not yet operative.

35. It has to be noted that the subsidiary bodies usually meet at the level of experts. However, if necessary (highly political issues are at stake) the sectoral bodies may also meet at various political levels (Directors-General, Ministers of the sector concerned). *Cf. supra*, note 17.

36. See *Report of the Preparatory Committee, op.cit., supra,* note 4, p. 70 (point 132); Liaison. Committee with International Non-Governmental Organisations, created in 1962. It is primarily the Secretary-General's responsibility for maintaining liaison with the most representative organisations of the different sectors of economic life.

37. For 1981, 20 meetings were planned.

38. Article 5 OECD, *cf.* Article 13 OEEC.

39. Unanimous vote is the rule. However, abstention does not invalidate the decision-making. Decisions (acts) are not applicable to those who have abstained from voting. See Article 6 OECD. Hereinafter the wording decision will be used for all acts. When, however, a legal binding decision is at stake, decision will be written in capital.

40. See note 39.

41. Article 3 OECD, *cf.* Article 9 OEEC.

42. See *supra*, pp. 520–521.

43. The examination procedure is *inter alia* applied for reviewing the general economic policies, development assistance policies, and trade policies. These procedures will be dealt with later on. See *infra*, sections 2.2.1., 2.2.2. and 2.2.6. respectively.

44. Under the OEEC there was a possibility of being able to exclude a Member State in case of non-fulfilment of an obligation. The members could decide, by mutual agreement, 'to continue their co-operation within the Organisation, without that member' which failed to fulfil its duties. Prior to such a decision, the State concerned had to be invited to conform with the Convention, within a given period. This provision has, as far as is known, never been applied.

45. Article 3 OECD, *cf.* Article 9 OEEC.

46. See for more details on Positive Adjustment Policies (P.A.P.), *infra*, p. 528.

47. Both Member States and private legal persons (companies) can do so. Usually the State acts as an intermediary. Joint projects are *inter alia* executed by the Nuclear Energy Centre Halden and the Nuclear Energy Centre Nederland (Petten); Eurochemic (Belgium).

48. First, in the OEEC financial support to give guidance to policies for reconstruction of Europe played the most important role; later the European Payments Union was established; then the European Monetary Agreement; moreover, after the oil crisis (1973) an OECD Financial Support Fund was set up. See for the Fund *e.g.*, Hahn and Weber, *op.cit. supra*, note 21, p. 376 *et seq.*

49. *Cf.* note 43.

50. See *Report of the Preparatory Committee, op.cit, supra,* note 4, p. 30.

51. See also its role for Positive Adjustment Policies, *infra*, p. 528.

52. Economic Country Reviews to be established by the EDRC. For more details, *infra*, pp. 536–537.

53. Article 7 OECD.

54. See note 39.

55. Article 6, 1 OECD.

56. Article 6, 2 OECD.

57. Article 6, 3 OECD.

58. See Hahn and Weber, *op.cit., supra,* note 21, p. 76.

59. Rule 20, *Rules of Procedure OECD,* provides that 'If a member is absent or reserves its position but does not accede with a period determined by the Council, the Council shall decide whether the decision shall remain binding as between the members which have acceded.'

60. See Rule 18, *Rules of Procedure OECD.*

61. Other examples are to be found in the voting rules of the Committee for Invisible Transactions, the Steering Board of NEA and DAC.

62. See *supra*, pp. 523–524.

63. Rule 29, *Rules of Procedure OECD.*

64. See *supra*, pp. 524–525.

65. See *supra*, p. 525.

66. See *supra*, p. 525.

67. See *inter alia* the series of studies on tax systems. They lead to the setting up of an OECD model convention for avoidance of double taxation on income and capital. In practice this model convention is followed in almost every country.

68. These consequences may result in: correction of behaviour; creative action by the Organisation; political decisions by the Organisation. See for the functional division of supervision, *supra*, pp. 11–14.

69. See Article 20 OECD.

70. A maximum contribution is fixed on 25 per cent of the budget. Originally this was done in order not to overburden the U.S.A. However, nowadays it may be questioned whether this is still correct, regarding the GNP of *e.g.* Japan.

71. The so-called Part II of the Budget.

72. There is a tendency to cut down expenses, or at any rate to keep them under control. As of December 1979 a Working Party to the Council on Budgetary Procedures was created to examine the modification to be made to the budgetary procedures. Various reductions have been made, for freeing resources for increased work in higher priority areas. Thus reductions in the 1981 budget have been proposed *inter alia* in the field of Environment, Development Co-operation, Science, Technology and Industry and for the Development Centre (Part II). See Chapter 1.9 of the *OECD 1981 Programme of Work and Budget* (C(80), 181 – restricted).

73. See *Ibidem,* paras. 2.14. and 2.15.

74. Indeed, as far as it has adhered to such a decision.

75. See *supra*, p. 525.

76. See *supra*, p. 522 *et seq.*

77. The Secretary-General is supposed to do his work fully independently of the Governments. This applies also to the supervisory task. See *supra*, under point (iii), at p. 522.

78. See *supra*, p. 18 *et seq.*

79. See the interesting analysis of P. Berthoud, *Le contrôle international* (Geneva, 1946), pp. 284–285.

80. As indicated above (see *supra*, p. 523), the subsidiary bodies may also be composed of highly political bodies, *e.g.* when meetings occur by high-level groups (Directors-General) or on Ministerial Level.

81. This distinction is based on the range of the effects of the creative acts. If a 'rule' is assessed or interpreted in a specific case or for a specific state as a result of a review, one can speak of

the exercise of the creative function of supervision. See *supra*, Part I, pp. 11–14 and Part VI, pp. 460–461. To a certain extent the creative function may be compared to the judicial function of the judge – assessment of law in specific cases brought before the judge – in national law. The law-making function is exercised when the general economic philosophy underlying the OECD comes at stake and is assessed *in general*. It applies, as a rule, to *all* Member States, while the supervision is exercised with respect to a specific case. But as Van Hoof, *supra*, p. 462, correctly states: 'Once again it is important to avoid too rigid an application of this distinction.'

82. See *supra*, p. 524.

83. See *supra*, pp. 11–14.

84. Of course, the random tests have to be carried out with discretion and according to a plan, in order to be of a representative character. See also my study on *Supervision in European Community Law* (Amsterdam, New York, Oxford, 1978), pp. 4, 176 and 181 *et seq*. Experience shows that with a reasonable number of random tests on the totality of a matter, a fairly correct impression on the whole can be obtained.

85. Formal check: test of compliance with the rules, objectives etc. from a merely formal point of view. Substantial review: actual practice is reviewed as well. Desk-research is then often supplemented by inquiries, interviews, inspection on the spot.

86. See *supra*, p. 519.

87. See *supra*, p. 528.

88. See *supra*, p. 10.

89. Information gained by personal interviews.

90. *Cf. supra*, note 81.

91. See Article 3 OECD Convention. The objectives set out in the Convention should be interpreted *lato sensu*: the basic Convention and all the rules based on or derived from the Convention.

92. See *supra*, pp. 522–523. The co-ordination between the various subsidiary bodies is ensured by the Secretary-General. The co-ordination within the Council falls primarily under the responsibility of the Executive Committee. Sometimes mixed bodies or liaison committees are established to consult and inform each other on aspects of mutual concern.

93. See *supra*, pp. 523–524.

94. Council; Executive Committee (in Special Session); High-Level Group; Working Groups, Committees.

95. However, all subsidiary bodies are supposed to report from time to time about their activities. This may be done either to the Council, the Executive Committee or the Committee under which responsibility a sub-committee has been set up. See Rule 23, *Rules of Procedure OECD*.

96. When the Council has approved of the publication of a report (*e.g.* Economic Development Review) the publication itself takes place under the responsibility of the Secretary-General.

97. See *infra*, p. 534 *et seq*.

98. Article 3(b) OECD reads: '[the members agree that they will] . . . consult together on a continuing basis . . .'.

99. See Rule 26, *Rules of Procedure OECD*.

100. This task of drafting inquiries is a clear consequence of his co-ordinating function. See Rule 26, *Rules of Procedure OECD*.

101. Notification procedure is to be found *inter alia* in the field of: trade (prior notification on export credits and credit guarantees); invisibles; restrictive business practices; environment; fiscal affairs; agriculture.

102. A reporting procedure is applied *inter alia* in the field of economic development policy (resulting in the *Economic Country Surveys*); energy; development assistance policy; environment.

103. See note 98.

104. Moreover, it had to be confirmed whether a country stuck to a plan for which it had obtained aid. In the OEEC the examination was in the hands of four wise men. Out of the discussions between this Group of Four, the representatives of the Member States and experts, the so-called confrontation procedure developed into its actual form.

105. See *infra*, p. 536.

106. The discussions within the Committee concerned are of a confidential nature.

107. Sometimes the review is published *in extenso, e.g.* the *Economic Survey(s)* by the Economic Development Review Committee; sometimes the data are published concisely, *e.g.* the results of the development assistance reviews: short communiqués and the yearly *Development Co-operation Report* by the Chairman of the Development Assistance Committee.

108. The confrontation procedure will be dealt with further on, when attention is paid to the EDCR and DAC separately, *infra*, p. 536 and p. 553 *et seq*, respectively.
109. See *supra*, p. 24.
110. *Ibidem.*
111. It should be noted that law and statutes as sources of information play a less important role in the OECD than *e.g.* in relation to the European Communities. That clearly follows from the differences of approach and scope between the OECD on the one hand and the EC on the other hand. OECD recommendations usually relate to political intentions and economic planning without being legally binding. Their impact has to be sought in the domain of general economic policy-making.
112. In practice, the permanent review procedure has created a new economic diplomacy characterised by, consultation, co-operation and mutual criticism.' See *The OECD at work* (OECD, Paris 1964).
113. *Ibidem*, p. 6, they have been qualified 'as an international conference in permanent session.' See also note 112.
114. See *supra*, p. 533.
115. See *supra*, pp. 520–521.
116. *The OECD at work, op. cit., supra,* note 112, p. 9. As a general remark also stated by Merle, 'Le contrôle exercé par les organisations internationales sur les activités des Etats membres,' *AFDI*, 1959, p. 431.
117. See Rules 21–26, *Rules of Procedure OECD*.
118. Special programmes, the Centre for Educational Research and Innovation (CERI), the Development Centre belonging to Part II Section of the OECD are left aside. The IEA and the NEA, however, will be dealt with under the heading "Energy", para. 2.2.10.
119. Formally a third committee falls within the field of Economic Affairs: the Committee for Monetary and Foreign Exchange Matters. Actually, it is not active. See note 130.
120. See *Report by the Preparatory Committee, op. cit., supra,* note 4, paras. 12(a) and (b).
121. For that purpose a Temporary Working Party of the EPC has been set up, open to all members. The Working Party reports to the EPC, whereas the Secretary-General informs the Council. The Working Party does the fact-finding, collects the data and prepares the substance of the deliberations and explores 'new constructive approaches for improving world economic relations, and especially North-South relations,' See: *Minutes of the 383rd Meeting of the Council.*
122. Working Party 1 has taken over the tasks of the former Working Parties Nos. 2 and 4, on 'Problems concerning economic growth and allocation of national resources' and on 'Costs of production and prices,' respectively. The merging took place in 1980, by the EPC. Thus, a single'policy analytical Working Party, with a medium-term emphasis has included the following in its Work Programme: a medium-term scenario exercise; inter-relationship between energy supply and prices and macro-economic performance and policy; structural changes in wages and price formation; determinants of public sector expenditure and revenue and the role of the government budget in a medium-term context; selective labour market strategies; the impact of inflation on profits and profitability. It is clear that the analytical work will relate to the concern for positive adjustment, so that a close link is to be envisaged between Working Party 1 and the P.A.P. Committee; see notes 73 and 123.
123. Improvement of the policy analysis in two particular areas is aimed at: (a) relationship between domestic policies, macro-economic performance and exchange rates; (b) domestic and external compatibility of monetary and fiscal policies.
124. The most deep-seated problem is still inflation. Thus, policies against inflation have to be studied, in close co-operation with the Special Group on Positive Adjustment Policies (see *supra*, p. 528) and the Manpower and Social Affairs Committees. Another important item forms the effects of inflation profits and profitability; and the allocation of resources.
125. See *supra*, p. 528. The creation of the Special Group on P.A.P. underlines the emphasis which is laid on medium-term orientation.
126. Para. 13 of the said Report. It may be recalled that the Preparatory Committee was requested to recommend on the effects to be given to OEEC decisions when remodelling the OEEC into OECD.
127. These issues are usually laid down in a recommendation or a declaration ('Soft law decision'). See Hahn and Weber, *op. cit., supra,* note 21, pp. 281–282.
128. See *supra*, p. 523.
129. This does not, however, mean that the *Outlooks* are some kind of summaries of the Economic Surveys. The *Outlooks* give a prognosis for the future, whereas the *Surveys* give an assessment of the past.

130. See *supra*, p. 534, note 115.

131. The reason for suspending the meetings after 1975 lies *inter alia* in the fact that the European Monetary Agreement had by then been terminated.

132. Article 2 j°, Article 3(c) OECD.

133. See *supra*, p. 14.

134. Thus, Hahn and Weber, *op. cit., supra,* note 21, p. 282.

135. See Article 6 OECD. Abstention does not veto a decision. Unanimity is the rule. Moreover, it is generally also reached whenever important decisions are to be formulated. However, it may be questioned whether the unanimity rule should always be applied. This is particularly so in the instance of supervision. When a State fails to fulfil an obligation, it might veto the publication of a report as long as the criticism is not covered in a diplomatic way. However, deadlocks rarely seem to occur.

136. Information gained from personal interviews.

137. Governments, Parliaments, business and press make references to these publications as being particularly authoritative.

138. In particular, the Temporary Working Party of the EPC serves as a forum to discuss North-South questions.

139. The decision for a Fund directly originates from the oil crisis. The Fund should work as a safety-net for its members. However, the practical importance of the Fund has been removed by developments within the IMF and the EEC (establishment of the European Monetary System).

140. As to the working activities of the various bodies, practical data is to be found in the *Annual Report* by the Secretary-General on the *Activities of OECD*.

141. Published in: *Activities of OECD in 1980*, Reported by the Secretary-General (Paris, 1981), pp. 93–94. The Declaration refers to the basic objectives of the Convention and the 1974 Trade Declaration.

142. Much of the success is due to confrontation sessions as may be concluded from *The OECD at work, op. cit., supra,* note 112, p. 43.

143. The 'Arrangement on Guidelines for Officially Supported Export Credits' is to be revised. See also *infra*, p. 543.

144. *E.g.* with respect to textiles. Compare the Textile Trade Regulations (multi-fibre arrangements), dealt with in Part III. Another example: the pressure on Japan to limit *inter alia* car exports to the U.S.A. and Europe.

145. See *e.g.* the Tokyo Round conferences and the problems mentioned in note 144. In such cases the OECD as such does not operate as an organisation. Perhaps this has to be ascribed to the fact that the conflicts, partly, arise between the partners of the OECD. Another reason may lie in the fact that multilateral trade negotiations primarily fall within the scope of GATT.

146. A few more details about the *Common Fund* in *Activities of OECD in 1980, op. cit., supra*, note 141, p. 22.

147. Renewed in 1979.

148. See *infra*, pp. 544 *et seq.*

149. Specification of the bodies with their probable number of half day meetings in 1981: High-Level Group on Commodities (with sub-groups) (18); Group on Export Credits and Credit Guarantees (18); Group on Preferences (4); Working Party of the T.C. Trade Committee (30); Joint Working Party of T.C. Trade Committee and Committee for Agriculture (12); Trade Committee (12).

150. The Trade Directorate (1981) consists of the Office of the Director, three divisions (General Questions and Trade Relations among Member Countries; Commodities; Trade Relations with Non-Member Countries) and a Central Unit and Secretariat, the total number being 21 persons.

151. *Report by the Preparatory Committee, op. cit., supra,* note 1, p. 32.

152. See note 154. The details had to be worked out by the Preparatory Committee. However, it limited itself to the broad lines. Thus, the Trade Committee should be able to respond in a flexible way.

153. In relation to the Special Programme of Work of the OECD on Positive Adjustment Policies, see *supra*, p. 523.

154. Article 3a OECD; see *supra*, pp. 531 *et seq.*

155. See *supra*, pp. 540–541.

156. *Report of the Preparatory Committee, op. cit., supra,* note 4, p. 42.

157. See *Activities of OECD in 1975*; Report by the Secretary-General (Paris, 1976), p. 23.

158. See Article 2e OECD.

159. *E.g.* bi- or multilateral forms of protection.

160. See heading *Confrontation* at p. 533.
161. See *supra*, pp. 535–536 and 536–537, respectively.
162. See *supra*, p. 522. Executive Committee in Special Session dates from 1972 and is *inter alia* concerned with trade.
163. See also *supra*, p. 540.
164. See *supra*, p. 539.
165. It is not quite clear how important the Group actually is.
166. *Supra*, pp. 540–541.
167. Article 19 Code of Liberalisation of Current Invisible Operations and Article 18 Code of Liberalisation of Capital Movements respectively.
168. The Committee on CMIT consists of 12 members chosen by reason of their knowledge in the field concerned and of the personal standing which they enjoy in the Organisation or in their respective countries. They are appointed by the Council from persons nominated by the Member States.
169. It should be kept in mind that in practice the Codes primarily relate to invisible transactions and capital movements between on the one hand EEC and on the other hand Japan and the U.S.A. Within the EEC itself the relevance of the Codes has become of little importance, because of the freedom reached in this area by all EEC Member States.
170. The CMIT Committee determines the periods within which the information has to be provided.'
171. Article 13 Code of Liberalisation of Current Invisible Operations.
172. In case a derogation is invoked by a member in the process of economic development, the OECD may grant a special dispensation (Article 2(a) Code).
173. There already exists a close co-operation with the Committee on Financial Markets and the Committee on International Investment and Multinational Enterprise (IME).
174. Thus, for example the CMIT has examined existing reservations in the field of films. The CMIT recommended to consultations with experts on the possibilities of removing the (more) onerous restrictions. These consultations resulted in setting up a Group of Film Experts. This Group should recommend more liberal laws and regulations.
175. The Code of Liberalisation of Current Invisible Operations is to be revised and updated, especially with a view to liberalise services. This will be done in close co-operation with the Trade Committee and the Insurance Committee.
176. Declaration by the Governments of the OECD Member Countries on International Investment and Multinational Enterprises of June 21, 1976, and related Decisions on National Treatment and on Incentives and Disincentives for International Direct Investment, especially the revised Decision of the Council of June 13, 1979.
177. See note 176.
178. *E.g.* in the UN a Commission on Transnational Corporations is preparing a Code of Conduct for TNC's. The problem is also tackled with the IMF and the World Bank.
179. Group of Financial Statisticians; *Ad hoc* Group of Experts on Debt Management; *Ad hoc* Group on Banking.
180. An import surplus bloc is formed by the OPEC countries. Deficit countries consist of both developed and underdeveloped countries. The latter explains why these financial problems have also to be studied in close co-operation with the DAC (Development Assistance Committee).
181. It goes without saying that in a field so closely related to economic affairs close contacts are established with the EPC (Economic Policy Committee) and Working Party No. 3 on Policies for the Promotion of Better Payments Equilibrium.
182. Working Party on Tax Avoidance and Evasion; Working Party on Multinational Enterprises, Working Party on Tax Analysis and Statistics; Working Party on Double Taxation.
183. Draft Convention with respect to taxes on estates and inheritances (1966); Draft Convention with respect to income and capital (1963), both revised: the 1977 Model Convention on Estates and Inheritances and the 1977 Model Convention on Income and Capital. The Draft Convention on Mutual Assistance had to be submitted before the end of 1973. It was completed during 1981.
184. One Model Convention is a bilateral instrument, the other a multilateral instrument.
185. The analyses to be made in this field take place in close contact with the IEA.
186. Impression gained from personal interviews.
187. This examination has resulted in the 'Guide to legislation on Restrictive Business Practices', which is updated regularly. It contains a review of new legislation and enforcement of existing legislation both by the administrative authorities and the judiciary.
188. Recommendation dating from 1967 and renewed in 1973 and 1979.
189. Decision C(71), p. 49, para. 11.

190. Decision C(71), p. 49, para. 13.
191. Working Party No. 3 on Co-operation between Member Countries on Restrictive Business Practices affecting International Trade; Working Party No. 9 on Mergers, Concentration and Competition Policy; Working Party No. 10 on Competition Policy in Member Countries; Working Party No. 11 on Restrictive Business Practices of Multinational Enterprises; Working Party No. 13 on Buying Power.
192. Working Party No. 3 on the Safety of Consumer Products.
193. Decision C(71), p. 73.
194. With *e.g.* UNIDO and the EEC. To complete the listing it must be mentioned that the Consumer Policy Committee is backed by a Working Party No. 5 on Consumer Marketing Practices and a Working Party No. 6 on Consumer Information Systems.
195. The Working Group of the Maritime Transport Committee started on January 1, 1971.
196. Thus, it has to take into consideration the implications of the entry into force – probably in 1981 – of the UN Convention on a Code of Conduct for Liner Conferences.
197. See *supra*, pp. 544–545.
198. To mention three: Working Party No. 1 on Agricultural Policies, Working Party No. 2 on Commodity Analysis and Market Outlook and the Joint Working Party of the Trade Committee and the Committee for Agriculture.
199. As from May 1980.
200. Actually, the country reviews have been scaled down, in order to put the emphasis on more general, longer term problems as future prospects and positive adjustment policy options.
201. From 1961.
202. To enumerate some aspects: moderate economic growth, inflation, structural unemployment, budget constraints, critical position of youth and women in the labour market, the sharing of working time.
203. *E.g.,* on employment, social indicators and migration.
204. See *supra*, p. 541.
205. To be published in the *Education Statistics Yearbook*. Future versions will be based on common questionnaires agreed upon between the OECD and the UNESCO Secretariat.
206. The expenditures fall under the separate Part II of the Budget.
207. To mention some: Educational Responses to Changing Needs of Youth, concerning the effectiveness of dissemination of certain information; Educational Responses to Changing Needs of Adults; the Education Role of the Family; Innovation in Education etc. Within the field of education there has been a Programme on Educational Building. For reasons of budgetary limitations it is cut off from the Budget. The work, however, is to be continued and financed by the interested countries directly, having no reflection any more on the OECD budget.
208. This aspect is primarily dealt with by the Development Assistance Committee (DAC)
209. This aspect falls primarily within the scope of the Technical Co-operation Committee.
210. This aspect is to be dealt with in particular by the Development Centre, an autonomous body of the OECD, established in 1963.
211. Since January 1, 1981 only Iceland, Ireland, Greece, Turkey, Spain, Portugal and Luxembourg are not members of DAC. However, the Commission of the EC as such is a member, thus bringing the total number of DAC members to 18.
212. *OECD, Acts of the Organisation 1960* (Paris, 1961), p. 13.
213. Terms are varying in the course of the years. Actually there is a trend to speak of North-South relations and more generally of the New International Economic Order (NIEO) problems and issues. Formerly, the term Third World-Developed (Western) World was used.
214. See *supra*, pp. 532–533 and 535–536 respectively.
215. The first-mentioned guideline was accepted on May 3, 1979, the second was adopted by the DAC High-Level Meeting, held on November 19 and 20, 1979, both are published in the *1979 DAC Review on Development Co-operation* (Paris, 1979), pp. 175 and 187 *et seq* respectively.
216. The quantitative efforts are guided by the standards set in the *1972 Recommendation on Terms and Conditions of Aid,* published in: *Activities of OECD in 1972,* Report by the Secretary-General (Paris, 1973), pp. 103–107.
217. Since 1982.
218. *E.g.* co-operation with Trade Committee, and Committees on: Financial and Fiscal Affairs; Social Affairs, Industry, Science and Technology; Economic and Statistics Department of the Secretariat; Development Centre; High-Level Group on Commodities.
219. See the *Guidelines, supra,* p. 553.

220. A difficulty in reviewing such aids is the absence of systematic official reporting, such as that established within DAC circles itself. Informal consultations take place with non-DAC aid agencies.
221. See *supra*, p. 553, at note 216.
222. Practice embraces factual practice, legislation and administrative regulation.
223. The tax-payer should know that the money is not thrown away or used for purposes for which it is not meant (*e.g.* buying arms instead of food).
224. Global Negotiations on International Economic Co-operation for Development; UN Conference on new and renewable sources of energy; UN Conference on problems of the least-developed countries; the preparation of the International Development Strategy (IDS) for the Third United Nations Development Decade.
225. Usually two or three months. The exchange may take the form of a short study visit or participating in a seminar.
226. References to the programme are to be found in the annual *OECD Programme of Work and Budget*.
227. The recipients are: Turkey, Greece, Portugal and Yugoslavia.
228. Recommendation C(79), p. 114.
229. See *e.g.* the recommendations of the Environment Committee at Ministerial Level in May 1979, partly cited in the Annex 5, *Activities of OECD in 1979*, Report by the Secretary-General (Paris, 1980), p. 121 *et seq.*
230. See note 288.
231. Up to now Japan and Canada have been reviewed; New Zealand was subjected to review in 1980 and Greece was examined in 1981.
232. Article 2 OEEC.
233. Article 2 OECD.
234. See the 1981 *Programme of Work and Budget,* pp. 117 *et seq.*
235. There is an increasing interaction with committees operating in other fields like Development Co-operation, Trade, Manpower and Social Affairs, the North-South Group and the Special Group on Positive Adjustment Policies.
236. This will specifically be done when the Committee meets at High Level or at Ministerial Level.
237. Date of creation: March 20, 1980 – duration up to the end of June 1982.
238. Finland, France and Iceland do not participate in the IEA. Norway participates under an agreement with the Agency.
239. The NEA started in late 1957 as ENEA (European Nuclear Energy Agency). On May 17, 1972 it was replaced by the NEA, an agency open for all members of the OECD, and not exclusively for European countries as had been the case with the ENEA. Actually (1981), all OECD members, except New Zealand, participated in the NEA.
240. After the submission of a two-phased programme for the commercialisation of new energy technology a decision will be taken as to the follow-up"
241. Resolution C(76), p. 91, Part I, point 6.
242. Decision of November 15, 1974 [C(74), p. 203]. The Agreement was signed on November 18, 1974 and it entered definitely into force on January 1, 1976.
243. Article 49 IEP.
244. Article 49, para. 2 IEP.
245. Article 6 of the Council Decision of November 15, 1974 (see note 213).
246. Article 7, Council Decision 74/203.
247. Article 61 IEP.
248. Article 62 IEP.
249. Article 62, para. 5 IEP.
250. Article 61, para. 2a and b IEP.
251. In April 1980 Portugal joined the IEA. Thus, the voting scheme had to be adjusted.
252. Article 2 IEP. Since 1980 the reserve for consumption is fixed on 90 days.
253. Article 4 IEP.
254. Article 7 IEP.
255. Article 6, para. 1 j° para. 4 IEP.
256. Article 12 *et seq* IEP.
257. Article 19 *et seq* IEP.
258. Article 55, para. 3 IEP.
259. Article 19, para. 3 IEP.
260. Article 19, para. 3 IEP.
261. Articles 23 and 24 IEP.

262. During the 1979 review, see *Activities of OECD in 1979, op. cit., supra,* note 229, Chapter 4. Conclusions from the Tokyo Summit, June 28–29, 1979.
263. Article 57 jointly with Article 41 *et seq* IEP.
264. As adopted by the Governing Board at its 18th meeting on January 29–30, 1976. See: *Energy Policies and Programmes of IEA countries, 1977 Review* (Paris, 1978), Chapter VIII.
265. See *supra,* p. 533 and pp. 535–537.
266. It may be recalled that visits on the spot are a common feature in the OECD review procedures, *cf.* EPC, EDRC and DAC reviews.
267. See *Energy policies and programmes of IEA countries, 1977 Review,* pp. 14–15.
268. See *Energy Policies and Programmes of IEA countries, 1979 Review* (Paris, 1980), p. 229 and *Activities of OECD in 1979, op. cit., supra,* note 229, pp. 109–110.
269. *Energy Policies and Programmes of IEA countries, 1978 Review* (Paris, 1979), pp. 32–33.
270. *Energy Policies and Programmes, op. cit., supra,* note 268, p.16.
271. *Ibidem,* p. 17.
272. See note 268.
273. May 21 and 22, 1979, see *Activities of OECD in 1979, op. cit., supra,* note 229, pp. 109–110.
274. December 1979, see *ibidem,* p. 114, point 5. See also IEA document GB(80), p. 21.
275. See the Communiqué of December 12, 1979, *ibidem,* p. 113 *et seq.*
276. Sub-Group on Accelerated Development of Alternative Energy Sources; Sub-Group on Conservation; Expert Groups on Energy Conservation in Industry; Expert Groups on Conservation in Buildings; Expert Group on Public Motivation, Education and Information; Nuclear Sub-Group.
277. Paris meeting October 5, 1977; see *supra,* p. 568, note 267.
278. See *supra,* pp. 567 *et seq.*
279. See '*Energy Research, Development and Demonstration*' in the *IEA Countries, 1979 Review of National Programmes* (Paris, 1980), p. 33.
280. See *ibidem,* p. 9.
281. From the latest report, *Activities of OECD in 1980, op. cit., supra,* note 146, it appears that Australia, Austria, Belgium, Canada, Denmark, Germany, Greece, Ireland, Italy, Japan, The Netherlands, New Zealand, Norway, Spain, Sweden, Switzerland, United Kingdom and United States have been reviewed.
282. '*Energy Reserach, Development and Demonstration,*' *op. cit., supra,* note 279, p. 11.
283. *Ibidem,* pp. 31–32.
284. Conclusions from the 35th Meeting held in Tokyo on April 12 and 13, 1978; see *Activities of OECD in 1978,* Report by the Secretary-General (Paris, 1979) pp. 115–116.
285. Point 8 of the conclusions, mentioned in note 254.
286. Point 10(a) of the same conclusions, see note 254.
287. May 21 and 22, 1979.
288. Official Text of the Principles, adopted during the October 1977 Paris meeting of IEA ministers.
289. To 26 million barrels a day (26mbd).
290. Results are at this moment not yet available.
291. October 10, 1979, Paris.
292. Legislative, administrative and practical measures.
293. Data on *inter alia* production, consumption, stockpiling. See Article 27 IEP.
294. Article 25 *et seq.* IEP.
295. System described in Chapters I to IV IEP.
296. Article 27 IEP.
297. Article 32 *et seq.* IEP.
298. Article 37 IEP.
299. Chapters I to V IEP.
300. Chapters V and VI IEP, Article 56 IEP.
301. Article 36 IEP.
302. *Supra,* p. 569, note 269.
303. December 12, 1979.
304. Article 44 IEP.
305. Article 58, para. 2 IEP.
306. Article 46 IEP.
307. See Communiqué of the Meeting of the Council at Ministerial Level in June 1980, published in: *Activities of OECD in 1980, op. cit., supra,* note 141, pp. 87–91.
308. The CIEC, held in Paris, during 1975–1977.

309. So, scepticism as to the success of the UN Conference on a New International Development Strategy, is understandable.
310. Barents has come to similar conclusions in his study on the IMF, *supra*, p. 393.
311. Council Decision of December 20, 1957.
312. Council Decisions of, respectively, May 9, 1975 (for Canada) and October 12, 1976 (for U.S.A.), C(77), p. 183 (Final). Moreover, Australia is a member of the NEA. Actually all members of OECD, except New Zealand have joined the NEA. The Commission of the European Communities participates in the work under the NEA statute, whereas the IAEA (International Atomic Energy Agency) participates by a special agreement.
313. Statute (of the OECD) NEA, Article 1(b). It should be noted that the co-operation relates only to the development of nuclear energy for peaceful purposes.
314. Article 2, Statute NEA.
315. See *1981 Programme of Work and Budget*, pp. 286–287.
316. Article 4, Statute NEA.
317. Article 5, Statute NEA. Such agreements should contain provisions under which countries not taking part in a joint undertaking may accede or benefit from the result (Article 5, c(IV)).
318. Convention on Security Control, July 22, 1959. The controlling task is assigned to the Control Bureau, which has to work out:
  (i) security regulations establishing the technical procedures of control for the different types of undertaking;
  (ii) clauses concerning the application of security regulations to be included in agreements;
  (iii) the observation of the obligations arising out of the control convention and agreements;
319. See: Article 8 of the Convention on Security Control. From the Minutes of the 53rd Session of the Steering Committee for Nuclear Energy it appears that the said committee authorised the Director of Control to suspend, until further notice, the application of the NEA Security Control Regulations and to initiate reconsideration of this matter in the event of a significant change in the circumstances under which this suspension of the application of the NEA Security Control Regulations had been decided. (NECM (76), p. 2. item 6).
320. Ninth Activity Report of the OECD NEA, *NEA Activities in 1980*, (Paris, 1981).
321. The budget of the NEA is covered by Part II of the Budget. It includes appropriations for the Secretariat and the NEA Data Bank at Saclay.
322. The international basis for radiation protection concepts is the work of the International Commission on Radiological Protection (ICRP). In 1977 it recommended a revision of basic standards. Consequently, the NEA, IAEA, WHO and ILO jointly considered the recommendations and worked out the proposed revisions.
323. Convention on the Prevention of Marine Pollution by Dumping of Wastes and other Matter, the so-called London Convention, entered into force in 1975.
324. See note 323.
325. See note 323.
326. The IMCO is charged with the Secretariat functions of the London Convention, see *supra*, note 323.
327. See the *NEA Activities in 1980, supra*, p. 22, note 320.
328. According to the *NEA Activities in 1980*, p. 22; see note 320.
329. See Article 8 NEA Statute.
330. See *Study on Legal, Administrative and Financial Aspects of Long-Term Management of Radioactive Waste*, p. 15. Third Party Liability is based on the Paris Convention of July 29, 1960 and a Supplementary Convention of Brussels of January 31, 1963. Both Conventions have been revised and updated. The amendments have still to be endorsed by the Council (*NEA Activities, in 1980, op. cit., supra,* note 320. p. 34).
331. Article 8, a(VI) NEA Statute. In practice information is given by publications in *inter alia* the NEA *Nuclear Law Bulletin*. In the field of computerised information legal data are processed from the Member Countries for insertion in the IAEA's International Nuclear Information System.
332. See *NEA Activities in 1980, op. cit., supra,* note 320, p. 41.
333. The total staff consists of 85 persons, of whom 58 are in the Secretariat and 27 in the Data Bank.
334. See *supra*, p. 518 and p. 529.
335. Compare Valticos, 'Aperçu de certains grands problèmes du contrôle international,' in *Mélanges Maridakis* (Athènes, 1964), vol III, p. 509.
336. See *supra*, pp. 529–532.
337. See *supra*, p. 35 *et seq.*
338. See pp. 522–523.

339. Private Office 21 members; External Relations 11; Legal Service 10; Council and Executive Committee Secretariat Division 12; Planning & Evaluation Unit 9; Liaison and Co-ordination Unit 3. The most important Directorate, the Economics and Statistics Department has over 150 staff members.

340. To quote the estimated numbers for 1980. Between parentheses the number of sessions in 1979 is marked: Sessions of the Council, the Executive Committee and other bodies 149 (133); Environment Committee and sub-groups 110 (194); Development Assistance Committee and other working parties 103 (112) – DAC: 56, of which 24 on aid review; Technical Co-operation Committee 8 (8); Trade Committee 108 (124); Committees in the sector of Financial and Fiscal Affairs 271 (331); Committees in the field of Science, Technology and Industry 226 (274); Committee on Manpower and Social Affairs 92 (98); Committee on Agriculture and for Fisheries 159 (159). From this survey a slight reduction of sessions can be noted. Probably this is the consequence of the financial restraint and the need for sound management, which the OECD has to take into account, as mentioned in the Introduction (p. 1) of the OECD *1980 Programme of Work and Budget*.

341. About 10 to 12 halfway sessions, as a rule.

342. Evaluation, review, policy-making.

343. Learned from personal interviews.

344. See *supra*, pp. 541–542.

345. Learned from personal interviews.

346. Learned from personal interviews.

347. *E.g.* within DAC.

348. *OECD 1980 Programme of Work and Budget* (C(79), 180 (restricted).

349. *Ibidem* note 348, p. 22.

350. The publications appear as the responsibility of the Secretary-General. Assessments given with respect to a country's prospects do not necessarily correspond with those of the national authorities concerned.

351. Compare pp. 581–583.

352. *Ibidem.*

353. Summarised the States should aim at:

–sustainable, non-inflationary growth and high employment in relation to not only macro-economic policies, but also the energy problem and positive adjustment strategies;

–maintenance of an open trading system symbolised by the OECD Trade Pledge and the work done on multinational enterprises.

Moreover, the North-South relations should be intensified and international co-operation in a longer-term perspective, should be promoted.

354. See note 350.

355. *De facto* it may perhaps sometimes do more.

PART IX

SUPERVISION WITHIN THE COUNCIL FOR MUTUAL ECONOMIC ASSISTANCE

SUPERVISION WITHIN THE COUNCIL FOR MUTUAL ECONOMIC ASSISTANCE

by A. Bloed

CONTENTS

I. INTRODUCTION

An analysis of the supervisory mechanisms operating within the Council for Mutual Economic Assistance (CMEA) – better known in the Western world as COMECON – and of their effectiveness might seem to require some justification, since little or no attention is usually paid to socialist international organisations in studies dealing with the functioning of the major international economic organisations in the world of today.[1] This meagre interest in the CMEA, which could be considered to be the main socialist international economic organisation, would not appear to reflect the reality of the situation for several reasons.

First, approximately one-third of total world industrial output is attributable to the 10 Member States of the CMEA – the U.S.S.R., Poland, the G.D.R., Czechoslovakia, Hungary, Romania, Bulgaria, Mongolia, Cuba and Vietnam.[2] This fact indicates that it is important to assign to the CMEA Member States a place which corresponds to their economic position, especially within the framework of the negotiations for the establishment of a New International Economic Order (NIEO). In the seventies, therefore, there was a growing interest in the (potential) role of the CMEA States – especially, of course, of the European CMEA States – in the area of a NIEO, from both Western and developing countries. As far as the latter are concerned, it should be noted that, after the wave of decolonisation in the fifties and sixties, the (in Soviet eyes) 'natural alliance' between Third World countries and the socialist camp has gradually been eroded. This tendency was clearly expressed in the increasingly explicit demands which the developing countries have addressed to the East European States. These demands concern, in particular, the accomplishment of structural improvements in mutual economic relations and have been embodied, especially, in resolutions adopted at UNCTAD IV (Nairobi, 1976) and UNCTAD V (Manilla, 1979). One may also refer to the growing irritation in the Western world

606

about the lack of a substantive contribution by the CMEA States towards a restructuring of the international economic order, especially in the North-South context.[3]

Besides the above-mentioned justification for paying due attention to the CMEA, the supervisory mechanism also proves to be a valuable point of entry for a study of the CMEA. This can partly be explained by the very different ways in which economic co-operation and 'integration' between the CMEA countries have been and are being developed, in comparison with the Western system of economic relations. In spite of, or rather, precisely because of this contrast, the practical experiences of the CMEA and its Member States in the field of supervision might also be important for other countries and economic organisations.

Because of the many unknown and unusual characteristics of the functioning of the CMEA, and the project of economic co-operation and integration which it is intended to promote, it might be useful to start with a short survey of the main features of the CMEA system (in a broad sense), as far as this is necessary for a better understanding of the CMEA supervision dealt with in this study.

A first, preliminary remark, which is often made in studies on the socialist international organisations, and which should certainly be repeated here, concerns the problem of the sources for the present study: the lack of (reliable) data and background information has been a major problem. Supervision within the framework of the CMEA is one of the least discussed aspects of the functioning of the organisation in the available literature: this unsatisfactory state of affairs can undoubtedly be explained partly by the delicacy of the subject, *inter alia*, in view of the strict conceptions of State sovereignty, adhered to by most CMEA States. An explanation for this dearth of attention could certainly *not* be found in the practical insignificance of the issue. On the contrary, the practice of the CMEA shows the great importance of the supervisory mechanisms for the effective functioning of the organisation. These mechanisms have been studied for many years within the CMEA with the object of introducing improvements in their functioning, which has sometimes been considered to be not (fully) satisfactory.[4] One of the best indications of this is offered by the adoption of several amendments to the CMEA Charter in June 1979, most of which concerned the functioning of the supervisory process of the CMEA, the scope of which has (officially) been enlarged considerably. This question will be dealt with at greater length below.

A second preliminary remark concerns the scope of this study. It will analyse the supervisory mechanisms of the CMEA and their effectiveness as far as the fulfilment by the *Member States* of their obligations under the CMEA Charter is concerned. Private law problems, however important they may be for the functioning of the CMEA, will be dealt with only marginally. Several other specialised socialist international economic organisations which, formally, have a high degree of independence, whether they are international legal subjects or not, will not be discussed at length. However, attention will be devoted to the functioning of the bilateral inter-governmental committees which operate between all CMEA States. Although these committees do not possess legal personality, their analysis is of great importance to the present subject.

II. PURPOSES AND PRINCIPLES OF CMEA INTEGRATION

2.1. Purposes of CMEA co-operation

The CMEA, officially founded in 1949 as a reaction to the Marshall Plan, aims at the promotion of 'the further deepening and improvement of co-operation and the development of socialist economic integration, the planned development of the national economies, the acceleration of economic and technical progress in these countries, the raising of the level of industrialisation of the countries with a less-developed industry, a continuous growth of the labour productivity, the gradual approximation and equalisation of economic development levels and the steady increase in the well-being of the peoples of the Member Countries of the Council' (Article I(1) of the Charter of the CMEA).[5] Among these general purposes the raising of the level of industrialisation of the less-developed Member States and the approximation and equalisation of their economic development levels has a special place: in this field very great differences exist among the CMEA States, especially since the admission of Mongolia (1962), Cuba (1972) and Vietnam (1978) to membership of the organisation. The CMEA, transforming these general purposes into concrete norms, has favoured the latter three countries with preferential treatment, based upon the (socialist) principle of comradely mutual assistance.[6]

In 1971, the purposes of the CMEA laid down in Article I(1) of the Charter were confirmed and supplemented by the Comprehensive Programme. This Programme formulates *inter alia* the following new purposes:
> 'the strengthening of the positions of the CMEA Member Countries in the world economy and the securing of the ultimate victory in the economic competition with capitalism';
> 'the strengthening of the defensive capacity of the CMEA Member Countries'.[7]

The last-mentioned purpose indicates the important supporting role of the CMEA with respect to the military defence of the Eastern European countries. In fact, a close link exists between the CMEA and the Warsaw Treaty Organisation (WTO).[8]

All the purposes of the CMEA, as laid down by the Member Countries mainly in the Charter and the Comprehensive Programme, purport to promote 'the interests of the building of socialism and communism in their countries and ensuring a stable peace throughout the world'.[9] This indicates the highly political character of the ultimate purpose of the organisation.

This description of the purposes of the organisation indicates the very broad scope of the CMEA which, in practice, encompasses co-ordination of economic planning and joint planning in specific lines of production, scientific and technical co-operation, specialisation and co-operation in production, communication, trade, and financial and monetary relations.

At first, the activities of the CMEA were mainly directed towards the promotion of the traditional international trade-turnover.[10] After 1962, attention was turned to the development of an 'international socialist division of labour' on the basis of co-operation and specialisation agreements. Lack of success, together with the growing economic recession in the second half of the sixties, appears to have been decisive in heralding a new phase of CMEA co-operation: the development of 'socialist economic integration' on the basis of the voluminous 'Comprehensive Programme for the Further Extension and Improvement of Co-operation and the Development of Socialist Economic Integration by the CMEA Member Countries', adopted by the 25th Session of the CMEA in 1971.[11] This Programme has been drawn up for 15 to 20 years, and enumerates essential economic and organisational measures which are to be carried out by stages at dates laid down in the Comprehensive Programme.[12] The Programme constitutes the basis for a number of institutional and economic reforms or innovations, such as, *inter alia*: the setting up of joint ventures, the facilitation of the establishment of direct links between enterprises in different CMEA States, joint planning of individual branches of industry and lines of production, and a strengthening of the role of the CMEA within the (developing) system of international economic organisations among the socialist countries.

At the same time, one has to realise that the phase of 'socialist economic integration' will not be accompanied by the establishment of supranational organs, nor by the liquidation of the national economic frontiers of the Member States. A particular feature of CMEA integration is that up till now it has developed in the form of an intensification and enrichment of economic co-operation.[13] Nevertheless, continuously developing economic co-operation within the CMEA leads to increasingly firm interweaving of the economies of the CMEA Member States, with strong effects upon other spheres of life. Especially in the Soviet Union, writers have emphasised that this development of 'rapprochement' will finally result in a 'coalescence' of the socialist countries.[14] This ideologically inspired ideal, however, is certainly not (wholeheartedly) supported by all CMEA countries.[15]

2.2. Principles of CMEA co-operation

According to the CMEA Charter – which was supplemented on this point in 1974 – co-operation between the Member States takes place 'in accordance with the principles of socialist internationalism on the basis of respect for State sovereignty, independence and national interests, non-interference in the internal affairs of the countries, complete equality of rights, mutual advantage and comradely mutual assistance.'[16] This description of the principles shows the central place of the concept of socialist internationalism in the framework of the CMEA. In fact, socialist internationalism is very often considered to be the main principle which governs *all* relations between

609

socialist States. However, there is much obscurity about the exact content and the legal character of the principle. Although all these aspects of the concept need not to be analysed for the purpose of the present study,[17] some remarks would seem useful.

As far as the content of socialist internationalism is concerned, the concept is usually considered to be both a separate principle and a kind of 'guiding principle' which encompasses and combines several others,[18] derived both from the principles of general public international law (*inter alia*, the principles of sovereignty and non-interference in internal affairs) and from the principles which are exclusively applied in relations between socialist States. These 'socialist' principles are, in particular: friendship, co-operation, comradely mutual assistance and the obligation of each socialist State to harmonise its own national interests and the interests of the socialist international community as a whole.[19] These principles play an important role in the relations between the socialist States, also within the CMEA. Among them, the principle of mutual assistance occupies a central place, and has several times even been identified with socialist internationalism as such. The following quotation from the Czechoslovak lawyer M. Potocný is illustrative in this respect: '. . . the principle of comradely assistance (. . .) is the most proper expression of socialist internationalism and uses therefore to be considered in the socialist doctrine to be an independent principle and described as the principle of socialist internationalism in the own sense of the word. This is the guiding principle in the system of the principles of socialist internationalism and affects also the contents and ways of the application of the other principles of socialist internationalism which the socialist community has taken over from the contemporary common international law as principles of generally democratic character that are universally recognised and valid.'[20]

One may therefore state that the principle of mutual assistance constitutes the core of socialist internationalism. The Soviet lawyer Tunkin describes the principle as follows: 'The principle of comradely mutual assistance includes the right of each State of the socialist world system to receive assistance from the other socialist States, and the obligation of each socialist State to render assistance to the other socialist States. This obligation concerns equally the political, economic, military and other relations.'[21] CMEA Secretary N. W. Faddeev sketches the importance of the principle for CMEA co-operation in the following way: 'The mutual assistance (. . .) is the principal characteristic of the economic relations of a new type. The unconditional observance of this principle is the basis for the solution of all questions, arising in the co-operation of the fraternal countries.'[22] As has been noted before,[23] this principle constituted the basis, *inter alia*, for the granting of preferential treatment to the less-developed CMEA Member States Mongolia, Cuba and Vietnam.[24]

As far as the legal nature of socialist internationalism is concerned, great differences of opinion exist between the individual Member States. Some countries, guided by the Soviet Union, defend the view that it has been transformed into a principle of (socialist) international law and that, as such, it is binding upon all socialist States.[25] The opinions of other countries, however, are much less uniform in this respect.[26] Generally speaking, one could say that socialist internationalism has been accepted by all socialist States as a political and ideological principle, whilst its legal character is contested.[27]

This short and necessarily rough sketch of the intricate problem of the principle of socialist internationalism seemed to be justified for the purposes of the present study because of its effects upon co-operation between CMEA Member States, including CMEA supervisory processes.

2.3. Some features of 'socialist economic integration'[28]

The structure of the economies of the Eastern European countries and of their co-operation is quite different from the structures existing in the Western world. For this reason, it might be useful to sketch briefly some of the main features of economic co-operation within the CMEA framework, to the extent that this is necessary for a better understanding of the present study.

2.3.1. Role of the CMEA Member States; public law – private law

In general, the role of States in the legal regulation of international economic relations has been – and largely still is – limited to the creation of a legal framework through national and international legal instruments. Within the limits of this framework, concrete economic relations are developed not by the States, but by private parties (be they individual persons or enterprises) as subjects of private law: of their own free will they make use of the possibilities offered by the legal frameworks created by the States.

The way in which the CMEA Member States develop their economic relations shows remarkable differences from this general picture. This is mainly a consequence of the fact that the CMEA States operate in two capacities in this field: on the one hand as sovereign States and, as such, as (traditional) subjects of international law; on the other hand as the owners of the national means of production.[29] The second capacity of the socialist State finds expression mainly in its function as the authoritative planner of economic life on its territory, and in the State monopoly of foreign trade. This indicates that the CMEA States are not only engaged in the creation of a legal framework for the development of their economic relations, but themselves conduct the concrete economic relations within that framework too. In other words, the 'international legal regulation affects not only the traditional sphere of co-ordination of the *economic policy* instruments, but also the establishment of trends and volume of *material links*'.[30] As a matter of fact this situation also has an influence upon the functioning of the socialist international economic organisations: besides the traditional functions which they have in common with non-socialist economic organisations, they also

611

fulfil tasks which are characteristic of producers' associations; the planning of the international division of labour in the CMEA region is a clear example.[31] In view of all this, it might be expected that in the socialist countries no distinction is made between the State, as a subject of international public law, and its national economic organisations (enterprises, etc.) in the field of international economic relations: the State encompasses and guides economic life as a whole, and has to be kept responsible and liable in cases of violations of obligations. In principle, this is the generally accepted view in Eastern European legal writing, which does not accept an (artificial) distinction between the State as a subject of public law and as a subject of private law: both elements are considered to be two sides of one and the same coin which cannot be separated.[32] In practice, however, a more differentiated approach has been developed, since the traditional concept created more and more problems, especially in the field of international economic relations: Western enterprises were extremely reluctant to do business with the U.S.S.R. in particular, because of the risk that the latter would invoke State immunity in cases of dispute.[33] As a consequence, the socialist countries have also accepted the concept of international private law in the area of international economic relations. For reasons of convenience, this distinction between international public and private law is also applied in economic relations between CMEA States[34] and plays a cardinal role, especially in the field of supervision.[35]

2.3.2. Co-ordination of planning

Since 1971, the year of the adoption of the Comprehensive Programme, the main instrument for the promotion and achievement of co-operation and 'integration' has remained the same: co-operation in planning activities, especially the co-ordination of national economic planning in all fields of mutual interest.[36] A new element, however, was the provision for joint planning in specific fields. The somewhat ambiguous and voluntary character of the common planning activities is put quite plainly in the Comprehensive Programme, which states that socialist economic integration 'does not affect questions of internal planning'[37] and is founded 'on the basis of complete voluntariness'.[38]

The co-ordination of planning is a very complicated process which passes through several different phases from simple exchanges of information to the adoption of recommendations and the conclusion of formal treaties between States and the signing of agreements between national economic organisations. For the purpose of the present study it is not necessary to describe this process in detail,[39] but some remarks which are important for our study must be made here.

First, co-ordination of planning is mainly a bilateral process. Consultations on co-ordination are conducted on a multilateral basis within the CMEA, but their results are usually neither binding nor intended to be binding. Detailed agreements, concluded mainly on a bilateral level, must follow upon this process. The title of the well-known 'Co-ordinated plan of multilateral integration measures 1976–1980', adopted by the 29th Session of the CMEA in 1975, is very confusing in this respect, because the plan has much less to do with multilateral integration measures than its name suggests. Essentially, the document is only a compilation in an ostensibly multilateral form[40] of mainly bilateral agreements concluded earlier.

The second remark concerns the source of the obligations entered into by the CMEA Member States. Concrete obligations stemming from the process of the co-ordination of planning do not usually result from CMEA resolutions, but from treaties between the Member States, mostly concluded outside the framework of the CMEA. Several of these treaties have been negotiated within the framework of CMEA organs, which recommend the Member States to sign and ratify them. As will be discussed below[41] the implementation of these treaties is supervised by the CMEA. Many other treaties on economic co-operation, however, are the result of negotiations – mainly on a bilateral basis – conducted completely outside the CMEA. The bilateral inter-governmental economic committees[42] in particular play a predominant role in this field. Although there is a strong connection between these committees and the CMEA, the CMEA is not directly concerned with the supervision of the implementation of the agreements concluded within the framework of these committees. In other words, though both these committees and the CMEA function in the same area (economic and scientific/technical co-operation between the CMEA Member States), the concrete nature and scope of their activities is different.[43]

One other characteristic feature connected with the source of the obligations which relate to the co-ordination of planning between the CMEA States should be referred to here, viz., that the socialist States are engaged in the co-ordination process in two capacities: both as (traditional) subjects of international law and as the owners of the national means of production. As has been explained above,[44] this situation has not prevented the socialist countries from making a distinction between international economic relations, governed by international public law and economic relations, governed by international private law.

In practice, this distinction is not very rigid. Nevertheless, it is very important – especially from the point of view of supervision – to take this distinction into consideration when studying the process of planning-co-ordination. Although the CMEA Member States conclude international agreements (governed by international public law) on the co-ordination of planning in all important fields of the economy, concrete obligations concerning trade-turnover, specialisation and co-operation in production, etc., are not entered into on a State-level, but exclusively between the economic organisations (enterprises) of the CMEA countries. In essence, the inter-State agreements only contain obligations for the States to take the necessary steps to have their national enterprises conclude the contracts provided for. As a result, the (private law) contracts concluded between the national enterprises of the CMEA countries – as the principal form for implementing the inter-State agreements – are governed by international private law, and as such are, in principle, excluded from the (inter-State) CMEA régime.[45]

613

Therefore, it is possible to state that co-ordination of planning starts at the inter-State level, but ends at the level of enterprises. Libánský described this process in the following way: 'the results of the co-ordination of the planning and joint planning are not put into practice by the subsequent inter-State agreements; the latter are only one more link in the chain of the international socialist planning process. The results of the common planning-activities are only accomplished through agreements concluded (. . .) between the economic organisations' of the countries.[46]

The co-ordination of planning between the CMEA States covers practically all fields of economic life: trade, production, investments, research, prognosis, etc. Despite all the innovations of the seventies, however, the quantitatively most important field has remained the planning of the foreign trade among the Member States.[47] Some remarks on this subject would thus appear to be justified.

2.3.3. Foreign trade between socialist States[48]

Foreign trade between the CMEA countries has to be planned in the interests of stable national economic planning: on the one hand the State must secure the imports necessary for the development of the national economy, and on the other hand it needs certainty about its export possibilities, because these must furnish the financial means necessary to pay for imports. The normal method for securing these interests consists in the conclusion of long-term foreign trade agreements, in the framework and as a result of the co-ordination of planning. For several economic reasons which need not be explained here,[49] these agreements are bilateral.[50] They contain specific undertakings concerning imports and exports, and both parties also undertake to take all the necessary steps to induce their national enterprises to conclude separate contracts to implement the inter-State treaty. 'Thus the actual deliveries and acceptances of goods are made not by the State parties to the trade agreements, but by juridically independent enterprises, endowed with legal personality. They make civil law contracts and they may sue and be sued at home and abroad. While the inter-State trade treaty may contain the basic elements concerning the quality, quantity, price, etc. of the goods to be mutually delivered, the contracts concluded between the foreign trade corporations transform these international obligations into civil law commitments replacing the general language of the former by a text of precision as is needed in a commercial contract.'[51] Consequently, the contracts, concluded by foreign trade enterprises, are governed by private law.

In order to guarantee a trade co-operation which develops as smoothly as possible, the CMEA States have created a special uniform legal régime in this field, thereby harmonising their national legislation in the area of economic relations. For that purpose, the CMEA adopted the well-known 'General Conditions for the Delivery of Goods between Organisations of the CMEA Member Countries' (GCDG 1968).[52] The GCDG proved to be highly successful in the field of harmonisation and unification of the legal rules governing the sale and purchase of goods in foreign trade.

614

Substantial results have also been achieved in the field of rules for the settlement of disputes which may arise in the course of the implementation of contracts concluded between national enterprises.[53]

This short survey of some aspects of socialist economic integration may suffice as a kind of introduction to the context within which the CMEA supervisory process takes place.

III. STRUCTURE OF THE CMEA

3.1. Institutional aspects

3.1.1. *Institutional system of socialist economic integration*

In order to be able to understand correctly the place and role of the CMEA within the complex institutional system of international economic co-operation and integration between the CMEA Member States, it is necessary to have a brief sketch of the institutional aspects of that system.

Because of the complicated nature of this system, encompassing many institutions with quite different features, some classification is desirable. A first, general classification may be accomplished by making a distinction between the institutional system *stricto sensu* and *largo sensu*[54]:

— the system *stricto sensu* only encompasses inter-governmental institutions, the activities of which are governed by public international law. This system *stricto sensu* can be subdivided (according to the number of Member States) into multilateral and bilateral institutions: the multilateral institutions encompass the inter-governmental organisations,[55] whilst the bilateral institutions consist mainly of the bilateral inter-governmental committees;

— the system *largo sensu* encompasses not only the bilateral and multilateral inter-governmental institutions, but also all the common organisations of an international character such as common institutes, common laboratories, and international economic organisations, *e.g.*, common enterprises, common associations, etc.[56] Here too, a distinction between bilateral and multilateral institutions has to be made. A common problem of these organisations of an international character is their legal personality: if they have personality, they are subjects of private law and not of public international law.[57]

A somewhat closer examination will now be made of the most important institutions of the system *largo sensu*, in the following sequence:

(a) the CMEA;
(b) the specialised inter-governmental organisations of the CMEA;
(c) the bilateral inter-governmental committees;
(d) the international economic organisations.

The *CMEA* is a multilateral inter-governmental organisation with consultative and co-ordinating functions in all the fields where there is economic and scientific/technical co-operation among its Member States. The CMEA, which takes the central place in the institutional system of socialist economic integration as a whole, can act through the adoption of recommendations, decisions and other types of resolutions on questions which fall within its competence, and by concluding international agreements with Member States, third States and international organisations.[58] On the basis of its Charter and Comprehensive Programme, it conducts direct or indirect relations with all institutions operating within the system of economic co-operation, thereby ensuring its position as the principal economic organisation of the socialist countries. The CMEA encompasses a large number of permanent principal and auxiliary organs, of permanent and temporary working organs and of scientific institutes.

Firmly connected with the CMEA are its multilateral *specialised (inter-governmental) organisations*. These are legally independent subjects of international law, but on the basis of, *inter alia*, special agreements, close co-operation with the CMEA has been developed, making these organisations specialised organisations of the CMEA.[59] At the present time, there are the following specialised organisations: two financial organisations (International Bank on Economic Co-operation; International Investment Bank), seven (production-) organisations in the field of industry and agriculture (*e.g.* Intermetall; Interelektro; Interkhim), three organisations in the field of transport (*e.g.* the Organisation of the Common Freight Car Pool), two organisations in the field of communications (*e.g.* Intersputnik), and three organisations engaged in scientific/technical co-operation (*e.g.* the International Centre for Scientific and Technical Information).[60] These organisations are charged with co-ordinating and/or operational tasks in their specific fields of activity.[61]

Multilateral co-operation within the CMEA and its specialised organisations is supplemented and given concrete form by the *bilateral inter-governmental economic and scientific-technical committees*. These international organs were established between all CMEA Member States on the basis of inter-governmental treaties in the fifties and sixties, in order to promote the development of economic relations on a bilateral level. They consist of two national sections, usually headed by vice-Prime Ministers, and they convene at least once a year. In practice, several temporary and permanent sub-commissions and working-organs have been created by each committee.[62] These bilateral committees play a very important role in the field of economic co-operation between the socialist countries, especially with respect to the co-ordination of planning.[63]

Besides these institutions, whose functioning is governed by public international law, the institutional structure of socialist economic integration encompasses several so-called *international economic organisations*.[64] Though some of these organisations have been created on the basis of treaties between States and others on the basis of private law agreements between national organisations, all of these international economic organisations are either subjects of private law or do not have any legal personality at all, and their members are always national economic organisations.[65] These international economic organisations – the so-called 'socialist multinationals' – have been created for the performance of co-ordinating activities, but also to perform joint economic activities and activities in the fields of scientific research and project-building, production, services and foreign trade. Their activities may encompass the whole cyclus of a production process (from research, design and development to production and sale) or parts of it.[66] Besides these multilateral organisations, a number of bilateral economic associations and enterprises have also been established.[67] The existing joint enterprises constitute a part of the international economic organisations.[68] Although these institutions are subjects of private law, too, in practice a close connection exists between all the bilateral and multilateral private law subjects and the inter-governmental institutions.[69]

As has been mentioned above, the CMEA takes the central place in the institutional structure of socialist economic integration.[70] This has been confirmed in the Comprehensive Programme, which places an obligation on the Member States to 'take' the CMEA recommendations 'into account' in the functioning of the bilateral inter-governmental committees, in direct relations between State organs and national organisations of the CMEA countries, as well as in the functioning of the (private law) international economic organisations.[71] The relation between the CMEA and its specialised organisations is especially close. Though preserving their status as formally independent subjects of international law, the latter have accepted the obligation to 'take into account' CMEA resolutions, directed towards them, and to supply the CMEA with information on the results of this consideration. In their turn, the specialised organisations are entitled to refer issues to the CMEA, which is then obliged to deal with them and to inform the specialised organisations about the outcome of the discussions.[72] The basis for these mutual rights and obligations is formed by the agreements and protocols concluded between the CMEA and its specialised organisations.

This brief and incomplete survey of the institutional structure of socialist economic integration may suffice to illustrate the position of the CMEA as a kind of king-spider in a large and complicated web.

3.1.2. Institutional structure of the CMEA

The institutional structure of the CMEA is also rather complex, encompassing several principal and auxiliary organs.

The CMEA has five principal organs:

(a) the Session of the Council;
(b) the Executive Committee;
(c) the Committees;
(d) the Standing Commissions and
(e) the Secretariat.

The *Session* of the Council is the supreme organ in which all Member States are represented. Nowadays, the national delegations are normally headed by Prime Ministers[73] and, at important meetings, by the leaders of the communist or workers' parties. The Session of the Council meets 'at least' once a year in the capital of one of the Member States. This supreme organ deals with fundamental questions of economic, scientific and techno-logical co-operation and determines the major policies of the organisation.[74]

The *Executive Committee* (E.C.), directly subordinate to the Session, is the principal executive organ of the CMEA. All Member States are repre-sented in it by their permanent representative (a vice-Prime Minister). It meets, as a rule, once every three months. The E.C. has a key position within the CMEA, being charged with taking decisions on all important questions concerning economic, scientific and technical co-operation among the Member States within the limits of the policy directives of the Session.[75] The E.C. has been specially designed to carry out systematic supervision of the fulfilment by member countries of the Council of the obligations entered into in the process of economic co-operation (Article VII, 4(a) of the CMEA Charter). In addition, the E.C. has been charged with guiding and supervising the activities of the Committees, Standing Commissions and Secretariat of the CMEA and its other organs.

Committees have been established by the Session of the CMEA to ensure the comprehensive consideration and solution, on a multilateral basis, of major problems of co-operation in the fields of the economy, science and technology (Article VIII of the CMEA Charter). This description indicates that the Committees have to deal with comprehensive problems, the solution of which is considered to be of vital importance for the further development of co-operation. At present, three such Committees exist: the Committee for Co-operation in the field of Planning Activity, the Committee for Scientific and Technical Co-operation and the Committee for Co-operation in the field of Material-Technical Supply. In the Committees, the Member States are represented by the heads of the appropriate national organs.

Since 1956 more than 20 *Standing Commissions* have been established; these can be divided into horizontal and vertical commissions or general and branch commissions (*e.g.* commissions for statistics, for standardisation, and commissions for chemical industry, agriculture, and black metallurgy). They consist of national delegations, as a rule headed by the competent branch-ministers. The practical, concrete work in the CMEA takes place mainly within these Standing Commissions.[76] That work encompasses, *inter alia*, the drafting of multilateral agreements between the States.

The *Secretariat* of the CMEA is an executive and administrative organ with its seat in Moscow. It is said to consist of 2,500 staff members.[77] Its major task is to prepare materials and proposals for the meetings of CMEA organs, and to make arrangements for and assist in holding those meetings. It also has special supervisory tasks, for which it has a special department at its disposal.

Within the framework of the CMEA, a number of auxiliary organs have been established. A special group is formed by the so-called Conferences

618

('Beratungen' or 'soveshchaniia') of the heads of ministries and departments of the CMEA Member States, which have been created by the Executive Committee; their aim is the promotion of co-operation in matters relating to water management, inventions, internal trade, legal questions and labour and price policies in the member countries. In contrast to the principal CMEA organs, the Conferences are not empowered to make recommendations to the CMEA States. They may prepare proposals for consideration by other CMEA organs, and adopt so-called co-ordinated proposals on questions within their competence.[78]

Finally, the CMEA structure encompasses two institutes: the CMEA Institute on Standardisation and the International Institute on Economic Problems of the World Socialist System, both established by the Session of the CMEA.[79]

3.2. Decision-making

3.2.1. Principles

The decision-making process within the CMEA is governed by two important principles:

(a) the unanimity principle and
(b) the interest principle (Article IV, 3 of the Charter).

Both principles, which are closely interrelated, are only vaguely defined in the Charter, and their interpretation has changed rather drastically during the years of the existence of the CMEA, this resulting in amendments to the CMEA Charter in 1979.

In principle, unanimity is always required in CMEA decision-making, even in the case of decisions on procedural matters. This means that the principle is applicable without exceptions *ratione materiae*, and constitutes a rather exceptional situation in comparison with other international organisations, its consequence being that each Member State would in practice have a right of veto. This was probably the case for the first two decades of the CMEA's existence, but in practice the possibility of vetoing a draft resolution has been restricted to a large degree by the interpretation of the interest principle as laid down in the Comprehensive Programme in 1971, and the CMEA Charter, which was amended to this effect in 1979.

The CMEA Charter originally described the interest principle only in very general terms:

> 'All recommendations and decisions in the Council shall be adopted only with the consent of the interested Member Countries of the Council, each country being entitled to declare its interest in any matter being considered in the Council.
>
> Recommendations and decisions shall not apply to the countries which declared themselves as having no interest in a given question. Each of these countries, however, may subsequently join the recommendations and decisions adopted by the remaining Member Countries of the Council'.[80]

This provision defines the interest principle not only as a general principle in the decision-making process, but also as a right of each Member State to declare its interest or absence of interest in any question under consideration by the CMEA. Though this might lead to the idea that in all questions a formal declaration of interest or lack of interest by all Member States is required, the practice is less formal: an interest on the part of the States is always (tacitly) presumed, unless a State declares the opposite. So, only a lack of interest has to be announced explicitly. A declaration to that effect, which must be placed on record, may be made at any stage in the discussion of a question.[81]

From these general remarks concerning the interest principle, the question arises as to which criteria – if any – should be applied in judging the validity of declarations of (a lack of) interest. The answer to this question is very important, in particular in those instances when a State declares its interest in order to prevent the taking of some action – with which it disagrees – by other States. Though an unequivocal answer to this question in all its aspects is not possible, the following remarks can be made.

In the sixties it was suggested that the right to declare an interest in any question, whatever it might be, combined with the unanimity principle, constituted a practical right of veto for each Member State.[82] This view implied that both the declaration of a positive and of a negative interest were considered to be legally admissible; in other words, according to this interpretation the principle did not only apply to those instances when a State desired positively to participate in certain projects under consideration, but also to those cases when a State wanted to declare its interest in a certain project only in order to block the taking of decisions in that matter, even though these decisions would not affect its real interests in any way. The interpretation of the interest principle would thus be: 'Interested is that country which considers itself to be interested.'[83]

This construction, however, was increasingly conceived as an unwarranted obstacle to the promotion of economic co-operation, especially in view of the fact that the CMEA Charter opens wide possibilities for limited groups of States to undertake projects within the CMEA framework, without affecting the interests of non-interested Member States (CMEA resolutions 'shall not apply' to non-interested countries, as is stated in Article IV, 3 of the Charter). Gradually, the interpretation of 'positive interest' was accepted: it was more or less agreed, in practice, that a Member State only had a right to declare its interest in a given question and, consequently, to block the passing of a pertinent resolution, if the adoption of that resolution might directly affect the interests of that State.[84] It is submitted here that this interpretation corresponds with the general obligations arising from membership of the CMEA, *viz.*, the obligation to contribute to the achievement of the CMEA's purposes, to respect the CMEA's principles (of socialist internationalism) and to give all necessary assistance to the CMEA in the performance of its duties.[85] In this context there is no place for anything like a 'negative interest principle'.

To a certain extent the new interpretation was officially recognised in the Comprehensive Programme of 1971, which contains several important provisions concerning the application of the interest principle. First of all, the Programme outlined the general framework, stressing the obligation

> 'to investigate the forms, means and methods of economic and scientific-technical co-operation which will make it possible for all CMEA Member Countries to participate in it, (which) will stimulate the interest of each country in the broadest participation possible in this co-operation'.[86]

This provision is generally interpreted as being aimed at the promotion of economic co-operation in an ever-increasing number of areas between as many CMEA States as possible, by using all the possibilities offered by the interest principle.[87] The 'positive' interpretation of the interest principle has been expressed still more strongly in the subsequent paragraphs of the Comprehensive Programme, which read as follows:

> 'Any CMEA Member Country shall be entitled to declare at any moment its interest in participating in a measure of the Comprehensive Programme in which, for one reason or another, it did not desire to participate before, on terms to be agreed upon between the interested countries and the country in question.
> The non-participation of one or several CMEA Member Countries in individual measures of the Comprehensive Programme *shall not hinder* the interested countries in realising the joint co-operation. The non-participation of some countries in certain measures shall not influence co-operation and collaboration in other fields of activity'.[88]

Finally, in 1979, the CMEA Charter was brought into line with this development. A newly-added provision runs as follows:

> 'Non-participation by one or several Member Countries of the Council in individual measures which are of interest to other Member Countries of the Council shall not hinder realisation by the interested countries of co-operation on such measures in the Council.'[89]

Although these provisions of the Comprehensive Programme and the CMEA Charter constitute an important codification of the 'positive' interpretation of the interest principle, they certainly do not suffice to answer all questions which may (and do) arise in the practical functioning of the CMEA. One such question is whether a right of veto still exists and, if so, under what conditions it may be exercised. Though it is sometimes contended, without reservation, that a right of veto no longer exists,[90] this does not seem to conform to the situation in practice. In the legal doctrine of CMEA States, several criteria have been developed for the application of the interest principle,[91] and they undoubtedly reflect practice to a great extent. These criteria, aiming at a decrease in the exercise of a right of veto do not, however, eliminate this right completely. In situations in which a declaration of interest by a Member State is contested by others, no legal solution – *inter alia*, in the form of outvoting – against the will of the said State is available. In practice, this amounts to the existence of a right of veto for such a State.[92] If this State exercises the right, the other interested States have no other choice than to realise the co-operation in question formally outside the CMEA.[93] On the other hand, this possibility also constitutes the best guarantee for preventing a Member State from obstructive activity, and the best stimulant for positive participation, since a State has a chance of exerting influence on co-operation taking place within the CMEA, which possibility does not exist when the same co-operation develops outside the CMEA.

Therefore, the exercise of a right of veto has largely been eliminated within the CMEA both in theory and in practice. Consequently, it might be better not to speak of a 'unanimity rule' in the CMEA, but of a principle of 'relative unanimity'.[94]

The interest principle is usually said to guarantee the principle of State sovereignty, and at the same time to stimulate economic co-operation by harmonising the interests of the different Member States as far as possible. It is a well-known fact that great differences exist among the CMEA Member States with respect to, *e.g.*, population, level of economic development and national resources. All this can make it quite difficult to reach unanimous agreement among all CMEA States,[95] and even for countries with the same level of economic development it can be difficult to reach agreement, *inter alia*, because of 'production patriotism' in the national enterprises.[96] On the other hand, the substance of the questions under debate often makes unanimity unnecessary.[97]

Though the interest principle makes it relatively easy for States to withdraw from (draft-)projects with which they partly or completely disagree, this possibility is not always present. In a number of instances the passing of resolutions presupposes the consent of all the Member States. Among these are questions of a fundamental character concerning the functioning of the CMEA and concerning fundamental aspects of economic co-operation.[98] First, resolutions which contain, in Sandorski's terminology, 'decisions of a general character'[99] require the consent of all CMEA Member States. Such resolutions create general rules concerning the procedure, structure and proper functioning of the organs of the CMEA, which are adopted by way of decisions,[100] and it is quite understandable that the interest principle cannot be applied in these cases: it is inconceivable that a State could declare that it has no interest in, *e.g.*, the admission of new Member States, questions of the CMEA budget, the approval of amendments to the Charter, the appointment of the main CMEA officials by Session and Executive Committee or the conclusion of treaties between the CMEA and other international organisations or third States.[101] This standpoint was officially recognised at the highest level of the CMEA in the mid-seventies.[102]

Second, the consent of all Member States is also required for recommendations on fundamental aspects of economic co-operation; these aspects relate mainly to the framework within which economic co-operation takes place. The drafting and adoption of the Comprehensive Programme might serve as an illustrative example. Another example is the adoption of the long term target-programmes[103] in important economic branches. It is generally accepted that the application of the interest principle is diminishing in practice,[104] but it is unknown whether precise criteria exist on the basis of which the principle may be considered inapplicable in certain cases.

The possibility of decision-making by majority forms a highly sensitive topic within the CMEA framework. Romania has always been, and still is, a notably severe opponent of the idea as a consequence of its strict concept of sovereignty.[105] Nevertheless, there seem to be a growing number of Eastern

European scholars who are openly in favour of the idea.[106] However, such a drastic change in the CMEA's functioning is not to be expected in the near future.[107] Though not within the CMEA itself, the majority rule has gained ground in some of the specialised organisations of the CMEA (*e.g.* Intersputnik and the International Investment Bank), albeit within strict limits.[108]

3.2.2. *Reservations*

The problem of the admissibility of reservations in relation to recommendations and, in general, to resolutions of the CMEA has only recently arisen in practice.[109] That is the main reason why a clear and uniform approach to this problem cannot yet be detected in East European legal literature.

The problem is said to have been raised in the middle of the seventies by Romania, in the context of preparations for several amendments to the CMEA Charter about which that country had great doubts.[110] The problem of reservations thus seems to have been introduced as a kind of additional obstacle to hamper negotiations, as it is said to have had only very limited practical significance. As a consequence of a Romanian proposal, a special CMEA working-group was established, charged with working out a common standpoint on the subject. This background may help in understanding the phenomenon of reservations, which at first sight seems to be rather a curiosity within the decision-making system of the CMEA. A curiosity because the principle of (relative) unanimity, together with the interest principle, would appear to offer a wide range of possibilities for all Member States to co-operate within the CMEA without being obliged to resort to reservations to prevent certain legal effects which are deemed undesirable.

A first problem posed by the question of the admissibility of reservations to CMEA resolutions and, in particular, recommendations, is closely connected with ideas on the legal nature of CMEA recommendations which have been nationally confirmed (accepted).[111] Those authors who adhere to the view that accepted CMEA recommendations have the character of an international treaty, tend to defend the admissibility of reservations within the limits of international law (especially those embodied in Part I, Section 2 of the Vienna Convention on the Law of Treaties).[112] Others, who adhere to the view of a *sui generis* character of accepted recommendations, often deny the admissibility of reservations.[113] A compromise has been defended, *inter alia*, by the East German lawyer, Rüster, who had earlier taken the view that reservations were inadmissible,[114] but who afterwards changed his mind, and tried to combine elements of both approaches.[115] He correctly submits that a right to make reservations undoubtedly affects the principle of unanimity of the interested Member States of the CMEA. On the other hand, he takes into account that reservations facilitate the greatest possible participation by States in international agreements – despite differing views on less important questions. In the CMEA this aim is, in principle, served by the principles of unanimity and interest. He concludes from this that reservations should only be admissible in the CMEA under stricter conditions than have been provided for in the Vienna Convention on the Law of

Treaties. In this context, Rüster specifically argues, *inter alia*, that an objection by a Member State to a reservation made by another Member State during a session of a CMEA organ, must lead to the non-adoption of that recommendation or, at least, of the provisions to which the reservation and objection relate.[116]

In general, the ideas formulated by Rüster and others seem to have been accepted by the CMEA Member States. After protracted negotiations in the above-mentioned CMEA working-group, the final result was an agreement between all the Member States.[117] The agreement – laid down in a document which was approved by the Executive Committee in 1980 – provides for the admissibility of reservations, but under rather strict conditions. Since the document has not been published, it is not possible to discuss its contents in detail here.[118] It is said, however, that the document[119] contains criteria such as the following: the reservation must be compatible with the object and purposes of the resolution and with the purposes and principles of the CMEA Charter; the application of the recommendation as a whole must not have been a precondition for the consent of the Member States.[120]

Though reservations may now be made in relation to recommendations and other types of resolutions, this does not hold true for Standards, concerning which it has been expressly agreed that reservations are not allowed.[121]

IV. LEGAL CHARACTER OF CMEA RESOLUTIONS

According to the Charter the principal organs (other than the Secretariat) of the CMEA are competent to adopt two main types of resolutions ('postanovleniia'):

(a) Recommendations ('rekomendatsii'), and
(b) Decisions ('resheniia').[122]

In practice, however, several additional types of resolutions have gradually been developed:

(c) Agreements[123]
(d) Co-ordinated proposals[124]
(e) Finally co-ordinated agreements[125]
(f) CMEA Standards.

These different types of resolutions are strongly interrelated in practice: one and the same project (for instance, specialisation in the production of a certain type of motor car) will be the subject of several types of resolutions according to the phase of preparation of that project. So, one can discern complicated 'chains' of resolutions within the CMEA.[126]

It is not necessary for our purpose to analyse all the legal aspects of the various types of resolutions thoroughly, and the following survey of their main characteristics should suffice.

4.1. Recommendations

Recommendations are by far the most important type of resolution on economic and scientific-technical co-operation, not only within the CMEA, but in the system of socialist international economic organisations as a whole.[127] Within the CMEA, recommendations may be addressed only to Member States, and only the principal organs of the CMEA (other than the Secretariat) are empowered to adopt them. They are adopted on questions of economic and scientific-technical co-operation (Article IV, 1 of the Charter). In practice, they cover the whole field of material economic co-operation between the Member States, and are of the highest importance in the work of the CMEA.

After recommendations have been adopted by CMEA organs, they are officially communicated to the Member States 'for consideration'.[128] For the implementation of recommendations by the interested Member States decisions will have to be taken by the governments or other competent State organs; this means incorporation into the national law of the interested Member States (see Article IV, 1 of the CMEA Charter).[129]

As for the legal effects of the recommendations, the generally accepted view is that CMEA recommendations are 'qualified' recommendations,[130] which indicates that their adoption by CMEA organs creates certain rights and obligations.

Although in the first years of the existence of the CMEA the opinion was sometimes expressed that recommendations created only moral or political obligations for the Member States,[131] nowadays it is generally accepted that the adoption of a recommendation by a CMEA organ creates the following legal obligations for the interested Member States[132]:

(1) an obligation to communicate the adopted recommendation to their governments or other competent organs for consideration[133];
(2) an obligation to notify the Secretary of the CMEA of the results of that consideration by the State organs within 60 days of the day on which the protocol of the CMEA organ concerned was signed.[134]

In other words: there is the obligation to inform the CMEA about the decision taken at the national level.[135] If the State organs decide not to accept a recommendation, the question arises whether the State is obliged to justify its decision.[136] Such a situation, however, seems to occur only very rarely.[137]

After the acceptance of the substance of the recommendation by the national authorities, the interested Member States are obliged to guarantee the implementation of the accepted recommendation (Article II, 4(a) of the Charter) and to inform the CMEA about this implementation (Article II, 4(d) of the Charter).

The acceptance of recommendations by the Member States creates an obligation on the CMEA in its turn to co-operate in their implementation. The main form which this co-operation takes is the examination of the information supplied by the Member States concerning the implementation of the recommendations.[138]

Writers have paid much attention to the nature of recommendations after their acceptance by State organs: does acceptance of a recommendation imply its transformation into an international treaty, or is the legal nature of an accepted recommendation *sui generis*?[139] Whatever the answers to this question may be, it is an undisputed fact that the Member States have a legal obligation to implement the substance of recommendations accepted by them, and that the CMEA is empowered to supervise this implementation.[140]

In view of the varying content of recommendations, however, one has to take a more differentiated approach towards their binding force. In the first place, this is a consequence of the fact that 'recommendations' is used generically in the CMEA, encompassing different kinds of resolutions. As a result, the legal effects of the adoption and acceptance of a recommendation are not identical in all cases.[141] It might be useful to illustrate this fact with two examples. The General Conditions for the Delivery of Goods of the CMEA (GCDG) were adopted with a recommendation to the Member States to apply these conditions to all mutual deliveries of goods. After acceptance by all the Member States the GCDG gained binding force, creating mutual rights and obligations for the Member States. On the other hand, several recommendations have only a persuasive or optional character, such as model conditions or standard treaties. In 1976, for instance, the Executive Committee approved the Uniform Provisions on the Founding and Activity of International Economic Organisations, with a simultaneous recommendation to the Member States to use these Uniform Provisions as guidelines.[142] Other recommendations are even more weakly formulated, only calling upon the Member States to take the provisions concerned into account when they should deem this suitable. It is clear from their wording that such recommendations are not apt for binding force. In general, one may say that recommendations which do not contain the essential elements for the creation of clear mutual rights and obligations, *i.e.* an unambiguous definition of the subjects and objects of the rights and obligations,[143] create only a duty on the Member States accepting such recommendations to examine the possible application of the general guidelines or proposals contained in the recommendations concerned in each concrete case.[144] Nevertheless, it has to be borne in mind that such recommendations indirectly acquire a certain binding force because of the fact they are usually accompanied by an order to (lower-ranking) CMEA organs to take the recommendations concerned into account when working out connected questions. Such orders constitute decisions on organisational questions, and are binding.[145]

When discussing the binding force of accepted recommendations one also has to take into account that the substance of the great majority of recommendations has been formulated in such general wording that concrete rights and obligations for the Member States are not created. Usually, recommendations constitute a precondition for the subsequent conclusion of

626

international treaties between the Member States in which their mutual rights and obligations are given more concrete form.[146]

In East European writings the question of the desirability of a transition to adopting directly binding decisions in the field of economic co-operation (in contrast to the present-day situation of only qualified recommendations) has sometimes been discussed. Though such a development is generally deemed not to be desirable at the present time, it is considered to be a possible innovation for the future, especially in view of the final Marxist-Leninist ideological goal of a 'merger of nations' into a socialist world-community.[147]

Because of the fact that the term 'recommendation' covers resolutions whose content varies widely, recommendations are sometimes classified into two groups:

— recommendations on concrete economic questions (*e.g.* the delivery of a quantity of goods);
— recommendations on economic questions of a fundamental character (concerning the framework, bases and general directions of economic co-operation, or areas of it, in the longer term, *e.g.*, the principles and methods of pricing policy in the field of foreign trade and the GCDG).[148]

In practice, a great deal of interpretation has often been needed to decide whether a certain resolution was a recommendation or not, a consequence of the, frequently, rather loose wording of resolutions.[149] In order to limit these and other problems, in 1976 the Executive Committee adopted an extensive 'Report on the raising of the effectiveness of the recommendations of the CMEA'.[150] From that time, the only resolutions having the effect of recommendations are those which clearly contain the formula: 'The Member States of the CMEA are recommended. . . .'[151] The 'Effectiveness Report' also contained provisions concerning the drafting of recommendations; they should be formulated as concretely, completely and precisely as possible.[152] Moreover, it was stipulated that recommendations should contain an exact enumeration of the addressees, who may only be the Member States of the CMEA.[153]

Because of the fact that the resolutions adopted by CMEA organs are usually not published, it is difficult to get a clear insight into the number of recommendations adopted.[154] Another complication was and is the fact that many resolutions contain not only recommendations, but also other types of decisions, which are not always easily distinguishable.[155] Judging from the literature, however, the number of recommendations adopted is quite considerable. Ustor wrote that in the year 1970, for example, 590 recommendations were adopted by the Standing Commission for Standardisation.[156] A more recent source states that in 1977 the Secretariat drafted more than 100 documents containing recommendations; the total number of recommendations, however, is much higher, because of the 'complex character' of many of these documents.[157]

Finally, mention should be made of a special group of 'recommendations', *viz.* the recommendations of the CMEA to its specialised organisations and to international economic organisations. Only their name is the same as the CMEA's 'normal' recommendations; their legal character is quite different.[158] In view of the fact that they are outside the scope of this study, they will not be discussed here.

4.2. Decisions

Decisions are adopted on organisational and procedural questions (Article IV, 2 of the Charter). They may be addressed to both Member States and CMEA organs. All CMEA organs are empowered to take decisions.[159]

Decisions have binding force from the date on which the protocol of the CMEA organ concerned is signed, unless they expressly provide otherwise or unless the character of the decision implies otherwise; entry into force might be dependent upon the fulfilment of certain conditions, or might be postponed to a later date. Decisions on procedural questions usually come into force at the moment the decision is taken.

As a consequence of all this, national 'consideration' of a decision is unnecessary, nor does a decision give rise to an obligation for the Member States to supply the CMEA with information about its fulfilment. All such obligations provided for in the Charter concern only recommendations and agreements.

Some examples of decisions on procedural questions are the convocation of sessions of CMEA organs, the confirmation of agendas, and the election of chairmen, while examples of decisions on organisational questions would be the creation of (working-)organs, the confirmation of rules of procedure, the approval of the budget of the CMEA and the admission of new Member States.[160]

4.3. Agreements

'Agreements' (in Russian: 'dogovor'ennosti') constitute a type of CMEA resolution developed only recently.[161] Until 1979 specific rules on agreements had been provided for only in the statutes of the newest CMEA organs.[162] In 1978, however, the 32nd Session of the CMEA declared 'the direct agreement' (as one of the 'operational forms of the final co-ordination of questions of co-operation') to be suitable for all the political organs of the CMEA.[163] This was officially confirmed in 1979 through the adoption of certain amendments to the CMEA Charter. In this respect the most important provision is the newly-added paragraph 4 of Article IV of the CMEA Charter, which reads as follows:

> 'The consideration in Council organs of questions of economic and scientific/technical co-operation may be concluded by agreements between the Member Countries of the Council on the implementation of measures agreed upon by them. Agreements shall come into force following the procedures established by the legislation of the countries participating in the agreements, and shall be implemented in accordance with the procedures established in these countries.'

At the same time, the scope of the supervision exercised by the CMEA was enlarged and now also relates to agreements.[164]

In practice, agreements are especially and increasingly[165] entered into as a kind of interim stage in a longer process of negotiation on a certain issue. The purpose of such agreements is to reach a binding interim result, on the basis of which the negotiations can continue towards a more firmly established final result[166] (e.g. in the form of a treaty). Agreements are, above all, used as instruments in the many phases of the complicated and lengthy process of co-ordination of national planning.[167] They serve as alternatives to recommendations. There are, however, some important differences between agreements and recommendations. As far as their scope is concerned, agreements deal with individual, concrete questions of co-operation[168] during a process of negotiation, whereas recommendations are adopted with respect to more stabilised and more comprehensive matters.[169] However, there are no legal criteria for this distinction, which has developed in practice. Indeed, it has correctly been argued that, in principle, agreements may be entered into in all matters which belong to the competence of the CMEA, except for those questions for which a specific decision-making procedure has been provided for in the Charter or in other normative documents of the CMEA.[170] The 1979 amendments to the Charter do not limit further the functional scope of agreements.

A far more important difference between agreements and recommendations concerns their legal nature. Agreements cannot be characterised as CMEA resolutions. In fact, agreements are not expressions of the will of the CMEA as such, nor are they adopted in the form of CMEA resolutions. In the above-mentioned Session Report 'Basic directions . . .',[171] agreements were defined as 'direct agreement(s) between the representatives of the countries in the organ concerned'.[172] Though the newly-added paragraph 4 of Article IV of the CMEA Charter is more vague in its definition of agreements (see above), the Charter also describes agreements as 'agreements, reached in the framework (of the organs) of the Council' in other articles, as amended in 1979.[173] These descriptions of agreements clearly call to mind the 'framework decisions' which are found in European Communities' practice: decisions of the representatives of the Member States in the framework of the E.C. Council.[174] Although a thoroughgoing comparative analysis of these legal instruments is not necessary here, it should be said that the parallels mentioned should not be extended too far. Both CMEA agreements and E.C. framework decisions are 'framework agreements' in the sense that both are reached by State representatives within the framework of the organisation in question, without being embodied in resolutions of the organisation. Similarly, the legal effects ensuing from the decisions might be comparable. In contrast to E.C. framework decisions, however, CMEA agreements are quite firmly embedded within the legal régime of the CMEA. This implies that the CMEA not only offers convenient 'accidental' opportunities to a number of States to reach international agreements on the fringes of official meetings of CMEA organs, but that the CMEA itself also has a substantial role to play in this field. Before substantiating this statement, it appears desirable to make some general remarks about agreements.

Limiting this analysis to CMEA agreements, it is important to note that it has been generally recognised that agreements need no ratification or national acceptance (confirmation) unless this is explicitly provided for in the agreement itself, or prescribed in the national legislation of the State(s) concerned.[175] This fact has been complemented by the rule that the representatives of the CMEA States in the organs concerned are assumed to have full powers to enter into agreements about questions which are within the competence of these organs. So, they are not obliged to produce specific full powers in written form.[176]

As has been stated above, a close connection exists between agreements and the legal régime of the CMEA. Though agreements are not expressions of the will *of* the CMEA,[177] they are reached *within the framework* of CMEA organs. Consequently, agreements have a number of organisational and procedural effects, which have been developed in practice, and officially confirmed by the introduction of appropriate amendments to the CMEA Charter in 1979: agreements have to be inserted in the protocols of the sessions of the organs in the same way as recommendations (usually with a marginal note in the protocol that the CMEA organ 'takes note' of them); they have to be registered by the Secretariat; the States concerned are obliged to supply the CMEA with information about their implementation after they have come into force and the relevant CMEA organs have to supervise that implementation.[178] This indicates that, despite several differences between recommendations and agreements,[179] they are treated identically in the field of registration, information and supervision.

The binding force of agreements appears to be somewhat problematic, especially since the adoption of the 1979 amendments to the CMEA Charter. In contrast to the situation with recommendations, the States concerned do not explicitly 'guarantee' the implementation of agreements. In the statutes of several CMEA organs, however, they do undertake to *implement* the agreements 'in accordance with the procedures established in these countries'.[180] Together with the above-mentioned obligation to give information about implementation, which the CMEA is empowered to supervise, this could lead to the conclusion that agreements are legally binding upon the States concerned.[181]

Undoubtedly this conclusion reflects the opinion of all CMEA States with the exception of Romania. This State took the view that agreements should not create legal obligations for the Member States; in the view of Romania legal obligations could only arise from the traditional CMEA recommendations and decisions, and from international treaties. For this and other reasons, Romania appeared to be a firm opponent of the inclusion of any general reference to agreements in the CMEA Charter.[182] It has correctly been argued that the Romanian standpoint was in contravention of the statutes of several CMEA organs, in which agreements had been provided for *with* Romanian consent; in these provisions the entry into force of agreements is not made dependent upon national acceptance.[183] In 1979 this

630

evidently rather vehement conflict between Romania and the other CMEA States was solved, *inter alia*, by the inclusion of a new paragraph 4, which clearly has the character of a compromise, in Article IV of the CMEA Charter. In comparison with the existing rules in the statutes of CMEA organs, this new paragraph (quoted above[184]) introduced an important new element into the legal regulation of agreements: the obligation to implement agreements – in accordance with national procedures – is now preceded by the condition that the entry into force of the agreements is dependent on 'the procedures established by the legislation of the countries participating in the agreements'. Not much imagination is needed to suspect that Romanian legislation probably makes the entry into force of agreements dependent upon their explicit national acceptance by the competent State organs, as in the case of CMEA recommendations. Another striking feature of the 1979 amendments to the Charter concerns the fact that, although agreements have been introduced into the Charter, the scope of Article II, 4(a) – which contains the obligation to guarantee the implementation of accepted recommendations – has *not* been extended to agreements. This is the more remarkable since such an amendment would have been almost self-evident for agreements (which have entered into force) in view of the other amendments.

In the light of the binding force of agreements, this new provision in relation to agreements constitutes a backward move in comparison with the earlier provisions. In fact, resemblance to traditional CMEA recommendations has been increased, and the situation is most probably that nowadays only Romania requires national confirmation of agreements, while the other CMEA States recognise agreements to be binding from the moment that they have been reached in the framework of CMEA organs, unless the text of the agreement has expressly provided otherwise, or the nature of the agreement implies otherwise.

4.4. Co-ordinated proposals

'Co-ordinated proposals' (in Russian: 'soglasovannye predlozheniia') are resolutions adopted by the Conferences[185] of the CMEA on questions within their competence. The Conferences, not being principal CMEA organs, are not empowered to adopt recommendations. They can take the initiative to have recommendations adopted by the appropriate CMEA organs by putting forward proposals to that end. Within the limits of their own competence they may adopt only co-ordinated proposals on questions of economic and scientific-technical co-operation.[186] It is generally agreed that such proposals may only be adopted on those issues which may be nationally implemented by the State organs represented on their own authority.[187] All the provisions of the Statutes of the Conferences relating to this matter are, in essence, identically formulated. The Statute of the Conference on Legal Questions – which might serve as an example – states that the Conference may 'achieve the co-ordination of questions within its competence. In doing so, it should be borne in mind that the proposals, co-ordinated by the Conference, on the questions concerned shall be implemented in the Member Countries of the Council in conformity with the established procedure in these countries'.[188] The method of adopting co-ordinated proposals is similar to that for recommendations (*e.g.,* the interest principle applies). After the proposals have been adopted, however, fundamental differences exist: proposals are not submitted to the States for national consideration, nor is there an obligation to 'guarantee' their implementation or to supply the CMEA with regular information about that implementation, as is the case with recommendations.[189] The Statutes of the Conferences contain only the provision that the Conferences 'shall regularly consider information' from the national delegations 'on the implementation' of the co-ordinated proposals.[190]

From all this it has been concluded by some authors that co-ordinated proposals are not legally binding upon the Member States[191], though this conclusion has been contested by others. East German legal experts in particular defend the binding force of co-ordinated proposals, basing themselves, *inter alia* on the above-mentioned implementation and information clauses.[192] Some of them even put the binding force of co-ordinated proposals on a par with that of agreements.[193] It is assumed by the present author that this forms the prevailing view in the CMEA States. It has to be noted, however, that the provisions concerning the implementation of co-ordinated proposals seem to be more weakly formulated than the corresponding clauses concerning agreements. With respect to agreements which have come into force, the States promise that they 'shall be implemented', whereas for co-ordinated proposals the States have undertaken that '*it should be borne in mind*' that they 'shall be implemented'. The Romanian point of view regarding the binding force of co-ordinated proposals is identical to its (initial) standpoint concerning agreements[194]; it deems co-ordinated proposals to be non-binding, unless they are treated in the same way as recommendations (with national acceptance or confirmation as the main feature). Romania has made several official declarations to this effect.[195]

4.5. Finally co-ordinated agreements

Under the CMEA Charter[196] Committees and Standing Commissions are empowered to create working organs to deal with the preparation of some matters for the principal organ, and also to co-ordinate certain matters themselves.[197] The latter function is accomplished by way of 'finally co-ordinated agreements' (in Russian: 'okonchatel'nye soglasovaniia'): the Member States have agreed that 'all questions for which the adoption of recommendations by the countries or a decision by . . . [the Committee or Commission] are not required, shall be finally co-ordinated and decided by the working organs. . . .'[198]

For which questions recommendations are required may be decided by the working organ itself, unless it has been ordered by the principal organ to prepare proposals or material for consideration by the latter body. In practice, however, explicit orders by the principal organ to its working organs to finally co-ordinate and decide upon certain questions are often a precondition for the actual use of this form of CMEA decision-making.[199] This fits into the overall picture of the decision-making process within the CMEA, in the sense that CMEA organs[200] are usually very reluctant to make use of powers granted to them which do not require official confirmation by higher-ranking organs or by Member States.

The scope of finally co-ordinated agreements encompasses questions of economic and scientific-technical co-operation (within the limits of the competence of the relevant principal organ) and organisational and procedural questions.[201] The Statutes or Rules of Procedure of the organs concerned do not contain provisions on the legal effects of finally co-ordinated agreements nor is the literature very clear on this subject. It has been said that the finally co-ordinated results are usually implemented by the members of the working organs, who take the necessary decisions to implement the results of the co-ordination within their own States.[202] That does not say anything, however, about the legal effects of the agreements in question. In the present author's view, the formulation of the pertinent clauses favours binding force for these agreements, as it is explicitly stated that the questions concerned 'shall be finally co-ordinated *and decided. . . .*'[203] Within the CMEA the terms 'decision' ('reshenie') and 'decide' ('reshat'') are always used to indicate the binding force of CMEA resolutions. One has to note, however, the lack of implementation and information clauses, which might lead to an opposite conclusion.

What has been stated about the Romanian point of view in the preceding section, applies equally to finally co-ordinated agreements.

This short survey of the main characteristics of finally co-ordinated agreements, co-ordinated proposals, and agreements may make clear why these types of decisions have been characterised as the *'soft law'* of the CMEA by some authors.[204]

4.6. Standards

A last, and very special, type of CMEA resolution is formed by CMEA Standards. They are based, *inter alia*, on the Convention on the Application of the Standards of the CMEA, which entered into force in 1975.[205] CMEA Standards, which are an instrument of common technical policy, are considered as one of the forms of CMEA decision-making, governed by a specific legal régime.[206]

CMEA Standards form the main instrument of co-operation between the Member States in the field of standardisation.[207] Though quite a lot of organs are engaged in their elaboration, they are adopted only by the Standing Commission on Standardisation.[208] Their purpose is to promote the extension of mutual foreign trade, and of specialisation and co-operation in production;

in view of these aims, gradual unification of national standards was deemed to be desirable.

The way in which CMEA Standards are created by way of a long and complicated process is very interesting, but needs no detailed discussion here.[209] It is sufficient to note that the road towards the creation of a Standard is marked by several kinds of resolution, decisions, agreements and finally co-ordinated agreements being the most significant.

The legal character of CMEA Standards has been clearly worked out, in contrast to several other types of CMEA resolution. All Standards are adopted by the above-mentioned Standing Commission, and are directly binding upon the Member States: Standards need no national acceptance to obtain binding force (Article I of the Convention). However, the Convention does contain a provision according to which Member States have the right to set aside the obligation in individual cases, by means of an express declaration that they will not apply the Standard in question (Article I, 8 of the Convention).

As far as the implementation of Standards is concerned, the Convention states that the Member States shall apply them (a) in international treaty relations between the Member States and their economic organisations, and (b) within the national economy of the Member States.

The supervisory task of the CMEA in relation to Standards is, to a high degree, identical to its competence regarding recommendations.

V. SUPERVISION IN THE CMEA

5.1. Supervisory organs

One of the striking features of the CMEA supervisory mechanism is the involvement of a multitude of organs. The centre of this complicated structure, however, is undoubtedly the Executive Committee, supported by the Secretariat. All the CMEA organs involved in supervision will be dealt with briefly hereafter.

5.1.1. Session of the CMEA

Though the Executive Committee occupies the central place in the supervisory mechanism of the CMEA, the role of the Session is certainly not negligible. The functions of the Session as laid down in the CMEA Charter do not contain an explicit reference to supervisory tasks. Indirectly, however, the supervisory function of the Session may be inferred from its competence to 'discuss all questions within the competence of the Council'[210] and from its obligation to 'consider (. . .) the report of the Executive Committee on the activities of the Council'.[211] Indeed, the annual reports of the Executive Committee form the main instrument for the supervision exercised by the Session.[212] These reports contain a general evaluation of co-operation within the framework of the CMEA, including possible shortcomings in the implementation of the major CMEA recommendations and agreements. This reference to 'major' instruments indicates the fact that supervision by the Session concerns only the most important problems.[213]

The Session is also involved in organising supervision of the implementation of CMEA recommendations, both in respect of CMEA organs and in the Member States. The Session and the Executive Committee have 'frequently considered' questions on the organisation of supervisory activities.[214]

Thus, the Session is engaged in the supervisory machinery of the CMEA through both organisation and exercise of supervision. The 35th Session meeting, which took place in Sophia in July 1981, furnishes an example. During this meeting the Hungarian Prime Minister, Geörgy Lazar, delivered a speech which was rather critical of the functioning of the CMEA in general, and of the effectiveness of the supervisory procedures in particular.[215] In his speech, the Prime Minister was reacting to the annual report of the Executive Committee on the activities of the CMEA.

5.1.2. Executive Committee

In accordance with Article VII, 4(a) of the CMEA Charter, as amended in 1979, the Executive Committee has been charged with 'organising and carrying out systematic supervision of the fulfilment by the Member Countries of the Council of the obligations arising from the recommendations of Council organs accepted by them, and from the agreements, reached in the framework of those organs, which have entered into force, as well as of progress in co-operation in the framework of multilateral agreements concluded on the basis of such recommendations and agreements'.

This is the main provision concerning supervision within the CMEA as a whole. The text has been drastically changed by the amendments of 1979,[216] resulting in a considerable extension of the scope of the supervisory function of the Executive Committee. Until 1979, the Charter only empowered this organ to supervise the implementation of recommendations. Now, the Executive Committee also has the task of supervising the implementation of agreements and of multilateral treaties concluded on the basis of CMEA recommendations and agreements. As will be seen hereafter,[217] this extension of the scope of the supervision to be exercised by the Executive Committee may be considered to be a mere codification of developments in practice.

Attention has to be drawn to another innovation introduced by the 1979 amendments: since 1979, the Executive Committee is not only obliged to 'carry out', but also to 'organise' supervision. Without doubt this points to a strengthening of its supervisory function, especially by enhancing its leading role in this field in relation to the lower-ranking organs of the CMEA. In essence, however, this also forms a codification of developments in practice.

Apart from Article VII, 4(a) of the CMEA Charter, there are no other provisions on the supervisory task of the Executive Committee, neither in the Charter nor in the Rules of Procedure. The article quoted, however, justifies an important conclusion: the Executive Committee is charged with supervising the implementation of *all* CMEA recommendations and agreements, irrespective of the organs which adopted them or in the framework of which they have been reached.

It may be assumed, however, that in practice the Executive Committee only supervises the implementation of recommendations and agreements originating from itself or from the Session, plus those recommendations and agreements of lower-ranking organs the implementation of which has met with problems. These cases may come to the attention of the Executive Committee through the annual reports on the activities of the .relevant CMEA organs and/or through reports from the Secretariat. As far as all other cases are concerned, one may consider the supervisory task of the Executive Committee as only a formal one, and the supervision exercised by the lower-ranking organs as being final for practical purposes.

From the absence of other provisions it has to be concluded that the Executive Committee has not been granted specific powers to exercise its supervisory function. Moreover, the normal principles of the decision-making process also have to be applied to the supervisory procedure. This implies that each Member State may act as *iudex in sua causa*, and has the power to block resolutions which are – in its eyes – negative about its national policy.

Because of its composition – each Member State being represented in the Executive Committee by a vice-Prime Minister – the Executive Committee evidently does not exercise judicial or quasi-judicial supervision of the fulfilment by Member States of their international obligations. As a political organ it undoubtedly exercises political supervision.[218]

5.1.3. Secretariat

Within the supervisory mechanism of the CMEA the Secretariat plays a cardinal role in laying the foundations for (political) supervision by other CMEA organs. Its competence and task in this field are based, *inter alia*, upon Article X, 2(e) of the CMEA Charter, in which it is stipulated that the Secretariat shall 'organise and keep a record of the implementation of the recommendations and decisions of the organs of the Council as well as of the agreements, reached within the framework of these organs, and prepare appropriate proposals for their consideration'.[219] The aim of these 'proposals' is to 'ensure the implementation of the recommendations and decisions of the organs of the Council'.[220] In order to carry out these (and other) functions the Secretariat has been granted the right to request and receive 'the necessary materials and information' from the Member States.[221] It is the task of the Secretariat, then, to 'summarise' the information received on progress in implementing CMEA recommendations.[222] It has to be stressed, however, that the Secretariat has no power to address its proposals directly to the Member States. It may only submit them to the other CMEA organs for consideration.[223]

The Secretariat seems to be well equipped for its supervisory tasks, given that a special 'office for the registration of the implementation of recommendations', directly subordinate to the Secretary, exists within the structure of the Secretariat.[224] Little is known, however, about how it works in practice.

From the foregoing, one may conclude that the supervisory functions of the Secretariat are twofold: firstly, it has a highly technical task as a clearing-house for recording the implementation of recommendations; secondly, it has (or *may* have) quasi-political functions in preparing the political supervision debates of the other CMEA organs by proposing, for example, solutions in cases of non-implementation or inadequate implementation of CMEA recommendations.

5.1.4. *Other CMEA organs*

Most other CMEA organs have also been endowed with supervisory tasks, limited, however, to the area of their activities.

Within these functional limits the tasks of the three *Committees* of the CMEA are similar to those of the Executive Committee. Just like the Executive Committee, the Committees have to 'exercise systematic supervision' of the fulfilment by the Member States of their obligations arising from Committee recommendations. The Committees, however, do not only supervise the implementation of the recommendations adopted by themselves, but also of those recommendations of the Session and Executive Committee which have been adopted after proposal by the Committees.[225]

The Planning Committee may delegate much of its supervisory task to its Bureau. As is stated in its Statute, the Bureau 'supervises by order of the Committee (. . .) the fulfilment by the Member Countries (. . .) of obligations arising from Committee recommendations accepted by them; considers at its sessions information from the representatives of the countries in the Bureau on progress in the implementation of those recommendations and, if necessary, makes proposals to the Committee promoting their implementation'.[226] It may be inferred from the passage quoted that the supervisory task of the Bureau depends upon explicit orders from the Planning Committee, and is limited to Committee recommendations.

The Committees also have supervisory tasks concerning agreements, though these functions have apparently been developed in practice, without having a well-defined basis in the Statutes or Rules of Procedure.[227] Since the 1979 amendment of the CMEA Charter, Article II, 4(d) – which contains an obligation on Member States to inform the CMEA about the implementation of recommendations and agreements – might be considered to serve as an indirect legal basis for these functions.

It may be derived from the Rules of Procedure that the Secretariat plays an important preparatory role in relation to the Committees' supervisory tasks: it registers adopted recommendations, summarises the information about their implementation and, if necessary, prepares proposals to promote their implementation.[228]

The supervisory functions of the *Standing Commissions*, as defined in their Statutes, are very similar to those discussed above[229]: *systematic* supervision, *regular consideration* of information to be supplied by the Member States and the making of *proposals*, if necessary. Here, however, the recommendations to be supervised are limited only functionally (and not *qua* organ). A new, additional provision concerns the fixing of time-limits and procedures by the Commissions for the submission of information by the delegations of the Member States. Without doubt the same procedure is also applied by the higher-ranking CMEA organs, although this has not been expressly set out in their Statutes or Rules of Procedure.

It should be recalled that until 1979 the supervisory powers under the CMEA Charter of the Executive Committee, the Committees and the Permanent Commissions had formally – though not in practice – been limited to recommendations. Moreover, the general obligations arising from Article II, 4(a) and (d) of the CMEA Charter were characterised by the same limitation.

Only in 1979 was the scope of the relevant provisions (except for Article II, 4(a) of the Charter) extended to agreements. This formed a codification of developments in practice. Practice appears to be rather flexible in the sense that when a (formal) limitation is considered to be too strict, the Member States try to find alternative solutions either by extending the scope of the provisions in practice,[230] or by the creation of new supervisory procedures.

The latter was the case, *inter alia*, with the Conferences; since they are empowered to adopt only co-ordinated proposals,[231] a special supervisory régime has been agreed upon. This procedure seems to be weaker than some others as it provides only for 'regular consideration' by the Conferences of 'information' from the national delegations 'on the implementation' of the co-ordinated proposals[232] without there being an express obligation on the Member States to supply the CMEA with such information. Nevertheless, such an obligation might be inferred from the provision just quoted.[233]

The exact method of meeting this obligation by (the delegations of) the Member States has been variously arranged, but also here the intermediary role of the Secretariat forms a common feature: this organ keeps a record of the resolutions adopted, and summarises the information coming from the delegations on the implementation of the co-ordinated proposals. All the Rules of Procedure of the Conferences provide for this function of the Secretariat.[234] The Rules of Procedure of one Conference also stipulate that the Secretariat is to send its summary to the heads of the delegations.[235] Still more detailed are the Rules of Procedure of two other Conferences: the Rules of the Conference of the Heads of Water Management Organs add the following provision to the general registration and summarising function of the Secretariat: 'Thereby it should be borne in mind that the said information shall be communicated to the Secretariat of the Council by the Heads of the Water Management Organs in December of each year.'[236] The very careful formulation of this obligation is striking. Finally, in the Rules of Procedure of the Conference on Legal Questions still another procedure has been chosen: the period for the submission of the necessary information by the Member States is determined by the working-plans of the Conference.[237] It may undoubtedly be assumed, however, that the supervisory work of all

Conferences is included in their working-plans, in which the periods for the submission of materials necessary for the fulfilment of the working-plans, are determined.[238] Similarly, it may be assumed that the results of the regular supervision debates form part of the annual reports to the Executive Committee on the work done and on other activities.[239] In this way, non-implementation or inadequate implementation of co-ordinated proposals might be brought to the attention of the CMEA's central supervisory organ.

One may conclude from this survey that though the general supervisory régime of the CMEA formally only applies to recommendations and agreements,[240] almost identical procedures have been established for other types of resolutions.

Though the advantages and disadvantages of the establishment of a special CMEA Court of Justice or Court of Arbitration have been under discussion for a considerable time among the Member States, nothing has come out of these discussions up till now.[241]

5.1.5. Excursus: bilateral inter-governmental Committees

The more than twenty bilateral inter-governmental Committees (or economic commissions) on economic, scientific and technological co-operation[242] are not CMEA organs, and no official relations have been established between these Committees (which lack legal personality) and the CMEA.[243] Nevertheless, there exists a strong interconnection, based on the Comprehensive Programme (1971): 'The CMEA Member Countries shall take steps to ensure that CMEA recommendations on questions of co-operation in the fields concerned are taken into account in the activities of bilateral inter-governmental commissions on economic and scientific-technical co-operation. . . .'[244] Moreover, the legal instruments which govern the activities of the bilateral Committees also establish a firm connection with CMEA activities as a rule.[245]

These bilateral Committees are of the greatest importance for economic relations between CMEA Member States.[246] This is one of the consequences of the fact that mutual economic relations are still mainly conducted at a bilateral level (for several reasons which need not be described here).[247] As a result, the bilateral Committees are at the core of economic co-operation in Eastern Europe: they not only give concrete form to agreements arrived at multilaterally within the CMEA, but also take measures going beyond this.[248] These activities result, inter alia, in a large number of treaties in all the fields of economic and scientific-technical co-operation.[249] The implementation of all these treaties is supervised by the bilateral Committees, which are empowered to take measures to remove possible impediments to successful implementation.[250] Moreover, the Committees are also said to supervise many other agreements on economic co-operation to which both the States concerned are parties.[251] From the available literature it might be inferred that this supervision is prepared by the Committees' sub-commissions, which have to submit annual reports on the results of their activities to the Committees.[252] In some Committees the secretaries of both sections have been explicitly charged with supervisory functions, though this is probably the general case anyway.

The functions referred to here are mainly a technical matter (the collection of information).[253] In the past, the bilateral Committees have actually been charged with the obligatory settlement of some specific disputes between enterprises arising in the course of the implementation of bilateral (private law) contracts on specialisation and co-operation in production.[254] This is important not only with respect to supervision by the Committees in general, but also to the fact that *private law* disputes were being settled by *intergovernmental* organs. By virtue of the Moscow Convention on Arbitration, concluded later, such disputes are nowadays subject to arbitration.[255] The supervisory activities of the bilateral Committees are said to be detailed and very effective, and this in turn is said to be a consequence of, *inter alia*, the constructive, business-like co-operation within the Committees, the careful balancing of mutual benefits, and the issues to be supervised, being clearly elaborated mutual rights and obligations.[256] It is said that there is no question of conflict between the supervisory activities of the bilateral Committees and of the CMEA organs: in practice their activities should be seen to be complementary to rather than incompatible with each other, because the CMEA organs mainly pay attention to (sometimes rather vaguely worded) obligations concerning multilateral projects, whereas the Committees are first and foremost engaged in the supervision of detailed bilateral questions (*inter alia*, bilateral trade agreements and the functioning of bilateral common economic associations and enterprises).[257] This was confirmed in 1979 by the amendment of Article VII, 4(a) of the CMEA Charter, which clearly limits CMEA supervision to the implementation of CMEA recommendations and agreements and to those *multilateral* agreements which have been concluded on the basis of CMEA recommendations and agreements. (This might create the impression that *bilateral* treaties, even if concluded in virtue of CMEA resolutions, are beyond the scope of CMEA supervision.[258]) Nevertheless, the implementation of the multilaterial treaties referred to may be supervised both by the CMEA and by the bilateral Committees of the participating countries. Though this could be a source of conflict, it is said that, in practice, the above-mentioned observation concerning the complementary character of the supervision is incontestably valid. Moreover, it is said that one may discern a preference by the States to have resort to the bilateral Committees for supervisory activities, in order to prevent possibly embarrassing discussions in much larger fora.

In view of all this, further justification for having touched upon the bilateral Committees – though they are not CMEA organs – would appear to be unnecessary.

5.2. Scope of the supervision

Economic co-operation between CMEA Member States takes place in several forms, within the framework of several international institutions, and on different levels.[259] Because of this rather complicated situation, a question arises as to the exact scope of the supervision exercised or to be exercised by the CMEA. It is beyond any doubt that the supervisory mechanism of the CMEA applies to the implementation of the resolutions adopted by its organs and accepted by its Member States. The seventies, however – after the adoption of the Comprehensive Programme – saw the adoption of an increasing number of resolutions (primarily recommendations) which were to be implemented by the conclusion of bilateral or multilateral treaties between the interested States outside the framework of the CMEA.[260] The text of a draft treaty often formed the content of a recommendation[261] and there is then a question whether the CMEA is empowered to supervise not only the implementation of the resolution, *i.e.* whether the treaties provided for have been concluded, but also the implementation of the treaties themselves. The practice of the organisation and the text of the CMEA Charter (as amended in 1979) indicate that this question has been answered in the affirmative.

This constitutes a remarkable development from a formal point of view. It could be argued that after the ratification of a treaty – the conclusion of which has been recommended to the States concerned by a CMEA organ – the task of the CMEA has been fulfilled: the object of the recommendation – *i.e.* the conclusion of a treaty – has been realised and the concluded treaty, not being a legal act of the CMEA, has to be implemented by the contracting States without any further involvement of the CMEA.[262] If one or more States should not implement the treaty, or not implement it effectively, the other parties could have recourse to the traditional diplomatic means, and the bilateral inter-governmental Committees. Practice, however, is different. The CMEA has an important task with respect to the supervision of the implementation of such treaties. In fact, they are subject to the same supervisory régime as recommendations and agreements.[263] This practical development was officially confirmed by an amendment to the CMEA Charter in 1979. The Member States agreed that the Executive Committee should supervise 'progress in co-operation in the framework of multilateral agreements concluded on the basis of (. . .) recommendations and agreements', [264] which have been adopted by or reached within CMEA organs. Some observations concerning this new provision should be made here.

Firstly, in contrast to the established procedure relating to CMEA recommendations and agreements, an explicit obligation on the Member States to supply the CMEA with information about the implementation of the treaties concerned has not been provided for.[265] An obligation of that kind might, however, be inferred from the general obligation of the Member States 'to make available to the Council the materials and information necessary for the carrying out of the tasks entrusted to it'[266]; the supervision of the implementation of the treaties in question being one of these tasks.

Secondly, not all treaties on economic co-operation between the Member States are covered by the new provision in the CMEA Charter. It applies only to (a) *multilateral* agreements, (b) concluded on the basis of CMEA recommendations and agreements. Though this might point to the fact that the implementation of bilateral treaties is not covered by CMEA supervision, this impression does not completely correspond with the CMEA Charter or with CMEA practice: together with the new provision on the supervision of treaties, another provision was added to the Charter which provides for 'the fullest possible exchange of information on the most important measures worked out and elaborated by the countries on a bilateral basis in order to carry out the measures of the long-term programmes of multilateral co-operation.'[267] In the context of the CMEA Charter, this last provision may serve as a legal basis for CMEA supervision of the implementation of bilateral treaties, limited, however, to the 'most important' treaties which are a result of the long term programmes of co-operation of the CMEA. [268] This conclusion corresponds with the practice within the CMEA.[269]

All this indicates that the scope of CMEA supervision is, indeed, far-reaching, the more so if one takes into account that the CMEA is not only involved in the supervision of the fulfilment by the Member States of obligations arising from CMEA resolutions (including the subsequent multi-lateral treaties) but also, indirectly, supervises the activities of all other institutions in the field of socialist economic integration,[270] regardless of whether these concern public law or private law subjects.[271] In general, co-operation between the CMEA and all other international institutions – the specialised organisations, international economic organisations, etc. – is based on agreements and protocols; it consists mainly of mutual exchange of information on working-plans, permanent working contacts during the pre-paration of materials, mutual exchange of information on the results of meetings of organs of the organisations concerned, and the making of proposals.[272] The last-mentioned form of co-operation in particular may serve as the main instrument for the supervisory function of the CMEA in relation to the other institutions, these being obliged to take such CMEA proposals into account. The supervisory function of the CMEA in this field has been laid down explicitly in the Session report 'Basic directions . . .' (1978) which states that 'the Executive Committee and/or the corresponding branch organ (. . .) shall exercise supervision over the activities of the [international economic] organisations and shall periodically receive reports on their activities and the direction of their further work.'[273] The effectiveness of this supervision seems, however, to be rather doubtful, taking into account the complaints about the unsatisfactory state of affairs in the co-ordination of the activities of the CMEA and the (other) international economic organisations. However, since this form of supervision is not covered by the present study – which is directed towards the supervision by the CMEA of the fulfilment by the Member States of their obligations – it will not be analysed in greater detail here.

Finally, as far as the territorial scope of CMEA supervision is concerned, it should be noted that Yugoslavia, which State participates in the work of a number of organs of the CMEA as a non-Member, would seem to be under the same legal régime concerning supervision as are CMEA Member States.[274]

5.3. Obligations of the Member States regarding supervision

Which obligations rest upon the Member States in relation to supervision by the CMEA? The main obligation derives from the Charter, in which it is stated that '[t]he Member Countries of the Council agree (. . .) to inform the Council about progress in the implementation of the recommendations of the Council accepted by them and of the agreements reached by them in the framework of the Council'.[275]

This very generally worded obligation is indirectly supplemented by two other general obligations: 'to render the necessary assistance to the Council and its officials in the performance of the functions provided for in the present Charter' and 'to make available to the Council the materials and information necessary for the carrying out of the tasks entrusted to it'.[276]

Two remarks should be made in connection with these obligations. First, as far as agreements are concerned, the obligation to supply the CMEA with information on the basis of the quoted Article II, 4(d) of the Charter has, curiously enough, not been made dependent upon their entering into force. It is submitted that such a requirement has to be implied, especially in view of Article VII, 4(a) of the Charter, which limits the supervisory tasks of the Executive Committee concerning agreements to those 'which have entered into force'. Moreover, it is simply not likely that the States would be obliged to supply the CMEA with information on the *implementation* of agreements which have *not* (yet) entered into force: as a rule, implementation is still out of the question in this phase.

Secondly, it has to be noted that, as far as recommendations are concerned, the obligation to supply the CMEA with information refers only to the implementation of recommendations *after* their acceptance by the interested Member States. This obligation is preceded by the undertaking to notify the Secretary (or the respective section of the Secretariat) of the CMEA of the results of the consideration of recommendations by the national authorities within 60 days from the day on which the protocol of the CMEA organs which adopted the recommendations was signed.[277] Thereupon, the Secretariat has to notify the other Member States[278] of the results without delay.[279]

These provisions indicate that the supervisory mechanism of the CMEA functions even before the recommendations obtain binding force. This 'preliminary' supervision[280] seems to be of some importance in the rare cases in which the interested Member States refuse to accept a recommendation. For a better understanding of this issue, it is necessary first to have a closer look at the exact scope of the obligations of the Member States in this phase of preliminary supervision. Only two obligations can be derived from the Charter and the Rules of Procedure: the interested States are obliged (a) to consider the recommendations with a view to their possible acceptance and (b) to inform the Secretariat about that consideration within 60 days.[281] The law of the CMEA does not contain specific conditions which the Member States must respect in fulfilling these obligations. This should not, however, lead to the conclusion that the Member States are completely free in deciding how to fulfil these obligations: in this field too they are bound by the generally recognised principles of international law and, in the present context, especially by the principle that States should fulfil their obligations in good faith.[282] Applied to CMEA recommendations, this means that the consideration of recommendations by the national authorities of the interested Member States should be performed in good faith.[283] *In concreto*, it means that a Member State which voted in favour of the adoption of a recommendation by a CMEA organ should make serious efforts to accomplish national acceptance of that recommendation. This conclusion is justified not only from the point of view of general international law, but also in the light of the principles of the CMEA itself; the principles of socialist internationalism, with 'fraternal mutual assistance' as its central principle,[284] are particularly important in this respect.[285] Moreover, this conclusion is, in general, undoubtedly endorsed by the CMEA Member States in practice.

This being so, the next question is this: if a State, after the national consideration of CMEA recommendations, decides in good faith *not* to accept them, is that State legally obliged to inform the CMEA of the reasons for its decision? The existence of such an obligation has been defended, *inter alia*, by the Polish lawyer Skubiszewski.[286] Though refusals to accept recommendations seem to occur only very rarely, an answer to the question posed is not without practical value, for the recommendations concerned might contain agreements the realisation of which is vital for some or all of the Member States. In general, it has to be observed that an obligation to give reasons for a refusal might well be defended as a logical consequence of the above-mentioned obligation on the Member States to consider the possible acceptance of a recommendation in good faith. However this may be, it is very doubtful whether this view finds support in the *opinio iuris* of the CMEA States: the generally accepted view is that a vote in favour of the adoption of a recommendation by the representative of a Member State does not legally bind that State, which is legally entitled to refuse national acceptance of a recommendation.[287] The alleged legal obligation to give reasons for such a refusal appears to be considered by the States as exceeding the limits of the purely procedural obligations resulting from the adoption of a recommendation by a CMEA organ.[288] In other words, accepting an obligation to give reasons would, in their opinion, imply raising the obligations resulting from CMEA recommendations above strictly procedural limits. The conclusion that there is no obligation to give reasons is indirectly supported by the Executive Committee's 'Report on the raising of the effectiveness of CMEA recommendations'[289] which does not contain any reference to such an obligation, although several paragraphs were devoted to the reporting procedure in question and some proposals (of a mainly administrative character) to improve its functioning were made.[290]

Assuming the formal correctness of this conclusion, one nevertheless has to take into account that there are great differences between CMEA recommendations, *inter alia*, in the sense that non-participation by one State in the execution of certain recommendations might make it impossible for the remaining States to implement them.[291] In such cases it is hard to see that a State might be allowed to impair even the vital interests of other

Member States while at the same time the competence of the latter to call that State to account for its attitude is denied. This holds more true if seen in the context of the principle of 'comradely mutual assistance' which plays such a vital role in relations between CMEA States.[292] It is, therefore, quite imaginable that a practice has developed according to which a Member State in such a vital position may be asked to explain its decision to refuse to accept a certain recommendation. The 'defending' State, then, seems to be not legally, but morally/politically obliged to respond, just as the contents of a recommendation have no legal, but only a moral/political character in the 60-day period.[293] Seen in the light of CMEA practice,[294] it might be presumed that the refusing State will take the initiative in starting such a debate. However that may be, nothing can be said with certainty about the real practice during this phase of CMEA's supervision because of the lack of published material.

Usually, however, recommendations of the CMEA are accepted by the interested Member States. This acceptance creates an obligation to guarantee the implementation of the contents of the recommendation and, at the same time, an obligation to supply the CMEA with information about progress in its implementation.[295] This means that the second phase in the supervisory mechanism of the CMEA relating to the *implementation* of recommendations (material supervision) is completely dependent upon national legal acts, a consequence of the system of the 'quasi-normative'[296] activities of the CMEA.

An additional obligation has recently come about for CMEA States: when it is impossible for a Member State to implement an accepted recommendation for whatever reason, it is obliged to inform the other interested Member States and the CMEA organ concerned of this.[297] This obligation was created by the above-mentioned Executive Committee 'Report on the raising of the effectiveness of the recommendations of the CMEA' of 1976.[298]

It has to be stressed that in the past the above-mentioned obligations had related only to recommendations. After the adoption of the amendments to the CMEA Charter in 1979, the situation has changed slightly: since then, the obligation to supply the CMEA with information on the implementation of nationally accepted recommendations has been extended so as to include agreements.[299] The other obligations dealt with above still apply only to recommendations.

There are no provisions concerning supervision of the implementation by Member States of *decisions*, which might be explained by their small functional scope, which is limited to the internal functioning of the CMEA (organisational and procedural questions).[300]

As a rule, supervision of other types of CMEA resolutions has been provided for in the Statutes or Rules of Procedure of the relevant organs. A brief survey of these provisions – as far as the obligations of the Member States are concerned – must suffice here.

With regard to *co-ordinated proposals*, there is no express obligation to supply the CMEA with information about their implementation. The Statutes of the Conferences allow only for the provision that the Conferences shall 'regularly consider information from the delegations of the Member Countries of the Council in the Conference on the implementation of proposals co-ordinated by the Conference relating to questions within its competence'.[301] An obligation on the Member States to supply the CMEA with information might be inferred from this clause. It has been argued, however, that this obligation is not incumbent on the Member States, but directly on their representatives (*i.e.* the heads of the national organs concerned) in the Conferences.[302] This argument is not convincing: the representatives are representing their States, and are acting on behalf of their States.[303] Thus, the States themselves are obliged to supply the CMEA with the necessary information.[304]

There are no provisions concerning the supervision of *finally co-ordinated agreements* or, at any rate, none have been published. The supervisory régime of recommendations, however, would also seem to be applied to *Standards*.

As has been noted above, the CMEA also has supervisory functions in relation to the implementation of multilateral treaties which have been concluded by the Member States on the basis of CMEA recommendations and agreements.[305] In this field, however, no explicit obligations on the Member States regarding the CMEA supervisory process have been provided for, neither in the Charter nor in the Statutes or Rules of Procedure of the individual organs. It is submitted that an obligation to keep the CMEA informed on the implementation of the treaties in question might be advanced on the basis of an extensive interpretation of Article II, 4(d) together with Article VII, 4(a) of the CMEA Charter: the obligation to inform the CMEA on the implementation of recommendations and agreements necessarily includes the implementation of the multilateral treaties which have been concluded in the implementation of these recommendations and agreements. Moreover, such an obligation appears to be essential for the proper functioning of CMEA supervision of the implementation of the treaties in question: without such an obligation on the Member States, and a corresponding right for the organisation, the CMEA would be powerless in cases of absent or inadequate information. This conclusion seems to be supported by the Session report 'Basic directions . . .'[306] which provides for a strengthening of CMEA supervision of the implementation of, *inter alia*, multilateral treaties, which has to take place 'on the basis of information from the countries'. With respect to this information the report states that the CMEA organs concerned shall 'agree upon the range of problems to be reflected in the information from the countries, and the frequency of its submission to the Secretariat of the Council'.[307]

Finally, an obligation on the Member States which is only indirectly connected with the supervisory process of the CMEA should be mentioned here. This obligation concerns the information which CMEA States are bound to provide to one another through the CMEA on all bilateral and multilateral agreements concluded by them on economic and scientific-technical co-operation. This obligation is based on two 'Procedures' of the Executive Committee: 'Procedure for the exchange of information between CMEA Member Countries on bilateral and multilateral agreements concluded by them on economic and scientific-technical co-operation',[308] and the 'Procedure for the mutual transfer through the CMEA Secretariat by the Member Countries of agreements on economic and scientific-technical co-operation, concluded between CMEA Member Countries'.[309] In this field, however, the functions of the CMEA are, in essence, limited to registration and transfer. The obligations of the Member States under these Procedures are also rather limited: they are obliged only to give information about the *conclusion* of agreements and possible subsequent changes in them, not about the *implementation* of these agreements. Although these information procedures have only limited direct significance for the supervisory function of the CMEA, they are of importance in those instances where the treaties in question are the result of CMEA recommendations and/or agreements: in this way the CMEA Secretariat and the Member States are kept well informed about the implementation of these recommendations and agreements (within approximately two to three months after the date on which the treaties have come into force).[310] The implementation of the 1969 Procedure was the object of supervision by the CMEA Conference on Legal Questions in 1981. Although it is said that proposals for the improvement of its functioning have been provided for,[311] nothing is known to the present author about the results.

5.4. Modalities and forms of CMEA supervision

5.4.1. *General and systematic supervision*

From all the foregoing it follows that the 'traditional' supervision exercised within the framework of the CMEA must be seen as 'general' supervision.[312] Apart from the recently established specific consultation procedure which will be dealt with below,[313] CMEA supervision does not appear to be limited to specific cases under specific conditions. On the contrary, all the pertinent provisions in the Charter, Statutes and Rules of Procedure show a supervisory mechanism which functions *systematically* and *periodically*, independent of the existence of certain circumstances.

Another common feature of CMEA supervision is its two-phase nature: a technical phase and a political phase. In the technical phase the work is done by the Secretariat, mainly by collecting information about the implementation by the Member States of CMEA resolutions, by analysing the data and drawing up reports on behalf of the political CMEA organs. In exercising this function the Secretariat is dependent upon the information supplied by the Member States. It has to be repeated, however, that the task of the Secretariat is not purely technical, since it has also been given competence to make proposals to the political CMEA organs on measures to be taken by them in order to ensure a better implementation of recommendations and agreements which have not or have not effectively been executed by one or more Member States, or whose effectiveness might be enhanced (without having been violated).[314] It is said that this competence does not exist on paper only, but is actually exercised by the Secretariat when this is deemed to be necessary and desirable.

In the second phase, supervision is exercised by the political CMEA organs in which all the Member States are represented. The reports drawn up by the Secretariat serve as the basis for these political debates, during which the delegations may ask for additional (oral) information from one another or may give additional information of their own volition. These supervision debates have a non-judicial character[315] which implies that political expediency may sometimes outweigh strict observance of the fulfilment of legal obligations.[316] Usually, the supervisory debates in the lower-ranking political CMEA organs are final, and in such cases the central supervisory tasks of the Executive Committee have only formal significance in relation to these organs. Only in exceptional cases – when the committees, permanent commissions or conferences are not able to reach an agreement on all the issues under supervision – are the disputed questions brought to the attention of the Executive Committee through the annual reports, or otherwise, for a final solution. Theoretically, the Executive Committee is competent to refer such questions to the Session of the Council through its own annual reports on CMEA activities.[317] In practice, this seems to occur only very rarely, if at all.

5.4.2. Specific supervision: consultation procedures

In 1976 the Executive Committee introduced reforms into the CMEA supervisory mechanism through the adoption of the 'Report on the raising of the effectiveness of the recommendations of the CMEA'.[318] These reforms marked a deviation from the traditional structure of CMEA supervision, for they established two specific supervisory procedures. As the term 'specific'[319] indicates, the commencement of these procedures is dependent upon certain circumstances arising. In the Report these have been defined as circumstances which 'hinder (. . .) timely or complete implementation' of the obligations of a country arising from a recommendation of the CMEA which it has accepted.[320] In such a situation, the State concerned 'must inform' the other interested States and the CMEA organ which adopted that recommendation about its difficulties.[321] This procedure, however, leads neither to a right to denounce the recommendation unilaterally, nor to a release of the State from its obligations ensuing therefrom. The obligation to inform aims only at opening a consultation procedure. As was stated in the Report, the information has to be supplied 'in order that the questions which have arisen may be considered and settled by the representatives of the interested countries on terms agreed upon between them'.[322] It has to be observed that the circumstances which give rise to the obligation to inform have been defined rather broadly: they amount to a situation whereby a State which finds itself unable to fulfil its obligations partly or wholly, or only with delay, because of apparently unforeseen circumstances, is obliged to inform the other interested States and the CMEA organ concerned about this. The subsequent consultation or renegotiation procedure may result in the adoption of a new recommendation on the same subject (reframing) or in a modification of the existing recommendation (revision). It may also lead to a direct agreement between interested States, especially when the implementation of the recommendation has been realised through the conclusion of agreements or treaties.[323] Due attention has to be paid to this last possibility because it implies that the problem may be solved through direct negotiations between the interested States. In accordance with the text of the Report quoted above,[324] this means that the obligation on a State which is in breach to inform the CMEA organ concerned as well, would not necessarily lead to consideration and settlement of the question by that organ. This is only obligatory when such negotiations are aimed at a reframing, revision, reconfirmation or withdrawal of a recommendation for which only the (principal political) CMEA organs are empowered.

The consultation procedure is apparently relevant to cases in which the difficulties in the fulfilment of obligations ensuing from a recommendation have arisen as a result of developments against the will, or out of the control, of a State, or as the result of contemplated developments with unintentional negative effects upon the proper implementation of the recommendation concerned. It is possible, however, that a State might deliberately violate its obligations, in which case the 'Report on the raising of the effectiveness . . .' provides for another specific consultation procedure. In contrast to the first one, it is obligatory for this procedure to take place *within* the CMEA framework. The relevant passage of the Report is directed at cases 'where a recommendation which concerns certain countries is not applied by one or several of these countries as a consequence of which the obligations on the other countries which accepted the recommendation lose their original significance or obtain a unilateral character'. This being the case, 'that recommendation must be reconsidered or withdrawn by the CMEA organ which adopted it'.[325] This procedure, as described in the Effectiveness Report, shows some serious imperfections, obviously reflecting disagreement among the Member States about its exact scope. These imperfections include: uncertainty as to who has to take the initiative in starting the procedure; the absence of an express obligation on the State in breach to supply information; the period within which CMEA organs have to consider the problem has not been determined.

Though these consultation procedures have to be seen as a valuable elaboration of the CMEA supervisory system, it should also be observed that the competence of the CMEA in this field has not been enhanced: the initiative in starting the consultation procedure either rests with the State which is in breach (not with the CMEA or with other Member States) or has not been determined at all. Nor has anything been changed as regards the complete lack of enforcement powers of the CMEA against Member States which are in breach or are unwilling to fulfil their obligation to start the consultation procedure. In this last situation, however, the State concerned may undoubtedly be called to account for its attitude during the traditional periodical supervision debates during which the non-fulfilment of its obligations may come up automatically.

5.4.3. Excursus: arbitration

As has been observed above,[326] there is no international judicial or arbitral organ within the framework of the CMEA with optional or obligatory jurisdiction in disputes between the Member States concerning their mutual rights and obligations, though the establishment of such an organ has long been under study by experts in the CMEA countries.[327] It has also been provided for in the Comprehensive Programme: 'Proceeding from the necessity for consistent observance by the CMEA Member Countries of the principle of State responsibility for obligations arising from agreements concluded among them on economic and scientific-technical co-operation, the countries shall work out and implement the necessary measures, in particular methods and procedure for the settlement of controversial issues which may arise between them with respect to such responsibility. In doing so, the results of a study of the proposal to establish an international CMEA arbitration organ should be taken into account.'[328]

Up to now, however, efforts to establish a CMEA Court of Justice or Court of Arbitration have been unsuccessful,[329] due to numerous obstacles such as the composition of the court, its competence, etc.[330] These problems will have been compounded by the admission of Cuba and Vietnam, raising additional questions such as the law to be applied by a CMEA court.[331]

These and other reasons have led a special working group of the CMEA Conference on Legal Questions to conclude that the establishment of a CMEA Court is not yet justified by practical requirements, especially in view of the level of development of questions connected with the material responsibility of CMEA States.[332] This last argument is by no means illusory: Usenko has correctly observed that in this field the solution of substantive problems (*i.e.*, State responsibility) has to precede the solving of procedural questions.[333]

All this does not mean, however, that the idea of establishing a CMEA Court has been abandoned completely. The issue is still being discussed by several Eastern European, especially Polish, authors.[334] Moreover, a related problem was discussed within the CMEA in 1981: the setting up of an *ad hoc* international arbitration organ for the consideration of disputes which might arise from the application of the Convention on the responsibility for damage caused by nuclear radiation casualties during the international transport of processed atomic fuel from the nuclear power stations of CMEA States. This convention concerns mainly the G.D.R., Poland and the Soviet Union in relation to the atomic fuel transports between the U.S.S.R. and the G.D.R. across Polish territory.[335] Whether such an *ad hoc* court of arbitration with optional jurisdiction will actually be created, remains to be seen. If so, it might afford the CMEA States a good opportunity to obtain valuable practical experience.

In general, it may be observed that the CMEA States, with the notable exception of Poland, are not very eager to establish a CMEA Court of Arbitration. This is not only the case with respect to disputes between the States, but also those between the economic organisations (enterprises, etc.)

650

of the CMEA member countries. The setting up of an international organ for the settlement of that kind of private law dispute has been rejected so far for financial and practical reasons,[336] but undoubtedly also for reasons of principle. A system of arbitration[337] for this kind of dispute[338] already exists, and operates through national arbitration tribunals, which are organised by and attached to the Chambers of Commerce of the CMEA countries.[339] In practice, most CMEA States would prefer the improvement and strengthening of this nationally organised system instead of the creation of one CMEA organ. This is quite apparent from the Comprehensive Programme, which deals more extensively with this system than with a future CMEA arbitration organ. In this Programme the Member States agreed upon the following:

> 'The countries shall carry out co-ordinated measures for further improvement of the functioning of the existing foreign trade arbitration organs of the CMEA Member Countries, and of the procedure for examining disputes between the economic organisations of these countries which may arise from agreements and treaties (contracts) on questions of economic and scientific-technical co-operation, having in view, in particular:
> – the extension of the competence of national foreign trade arbitration organs, by placing under their jurisdiction private law disputes between economic organisations, arising from relations in any field of economic and scientific-technical co-operation between CMEA Member Countries;
> – the expansion of the exchange of information (including the exchange of arbitration awards) between the arbitration organs of CMEA Member Countries, in order to promote the uniform application by the countries' arbitration organs of the provisions of the "General Conditions for the Delivery of Goods between Organisations of the CMEA Member Countries" (GCDG/CMEA 1968), and of other documents regulating individual fields of economic and scientific-technical co-operation;
> – the approximation and unification of the rules of procedure of the national arbitration organs attached to the chambers of commerce of the CMEA Member Countries.'[340]

These provisions of the Comprehensive Programme served as the basis for some very important documents drafted by the CMEA Conference on Legal Questions in subsequent years. The main document is the 'Convention on the Settlement by Arbitration of Private Law Disputes resulting from Relations of Economic and Scientific-Technical Co-operation' of 1972.[341] On the basis of this Convention – usually called the Moscow Convention or the Convention on Competences – the competences of the national arbitration organs have been considerably enlarged. Until 1973 these organs had exclusive jurisdiction only in private law disputes arising from international trade transactions.[342] Since the entry into force of the Moscow Convention, national arbitration boards have exclusive jurisdiction in 'all disputes between economic organisations, arising from contractual and other private law relations which originated between them as part of economic and scientific-technical co-operation among countries participating in the present Convention'.[343] These 'relations' have been defined as relations which have been established 'by contracts for the purchase and sale of goods, for specialisation and co-operation in production, for the fulfilment of sub-contractual, construction, assembly, design, prospecting, scientific research, design and development and experimental work, and for transport and other services, as well as other private law relations arising in the process of economic and scientific-technical co-operation among countries participating in the present

Convention'.[344] The economic organisations which may be the litigants in national arbitration organs under the Moscow Convention encompass a whole range of private law subjects, which have been enumerated in the Convention as 'enterprises, trusts, associations, combines, main administrations ([or] administrations) operating on the basis of economic accountability, as well as scientific research institutes, design and development bureaus and other similar organisations which are subjects of private law and are located in different countries participating in the present Convention'.[345]

Though the national arbitration organs have exclusive jurisdiction in all the above-mentioned private law disputes, some specific disputes have expressly been excluded from the scope of the Moscow Convention. The main exception concerns 'claims concerning the obligation to conclude a contract or to accept particular contractual conditions'.[346] This provision is to the effect that national arbitration boards have no compulsory jurisdiction in disputes which may arise *before* the conclusion of private law contracts. In other words, if the parties (enterprises, etc.) are not ready or able to reach agreement on the conclusion of a private law contract – which has to be concluded as a result of obligations entered into on the inter-governmental level – neither party may have resort to arbitration without the consent of the other party. This is the result of the still-prevailing view that the conclusion of contracts between economic organisations may not be enforced through arbitration, first and foremost because of the fact that the contents of both long-term and annual inter-governmental agreements, providing for the conclusion of such contracts, belong to the sphere of public international law. Consequently, the CMEA States are of the opinion that these agreements do not directly create a private law obligation to conclude such contracts, which could be enforced through (obligatory) arbitration.[347]

In the Moscow Convention it has been stipulated that the awards of national arbitration tribunals are final and binding. They have to be executed in the same way as the decisions of the State courts of the country concerned.[348]

Following the conclusion of the Moscow Convention[349] another agreement, laid down in the Comprehensive Programme and providing for the unification of the rules of procedure of the arbitration boards,[350] was implemented by the CMEA States, through the adoption of the 'Uniform Regulation . . . for arbitration tribunals attached to the chambers of commerce of the CMEA Member Countries', with its annexed 'Statute on arbitration fees, expenses and costs of the parties'.[351] The Uniform Regulation contains provisions on a whole range of questions connected with the work of the national arbitration boards, *inter alia*, concerning the structure of these boards, the law to be applied and the procedure to be followed. This Regulation was deemed to be necessary in view of the different national provisions on many of these questions, which sometimes had a negative influence on the interests of the economic organisations concerned.[352]

Through the creation and implementation of the Moscow Convention and the Uniform Regulation, the CMEA has made a considerable contribution to a fruitful harmonisation and unification of the procedures of national arbitration. Nevertheless, this does not guarantee uniform application by the national arbitration boards of all the applicable rules. This is caused, *inter alia*, by the fact that legal conceptions may have a different meaning in the legal orders of the different CMEA States. This is, for instance, the case with certain conceptions used in the CMEA General Conditions for the Delivery of Goods (*e.g.* 'price discount').[353] In order to promote the uniform application of the rules, the Comprehensive Programme also provided for an expansion of the exchange of information (including arbitration awards) between the arbitration boards.[354] This is effectuated in particular by means of conferences of the presidents of the national arbitration tribunals, held every two years, to exchange information and to discuss problems of common concern. Though these conferences undoubtedly have a positive influence in terms of unifying the application of the rules by the different arbitration tribunals, they are often considered to be insufficient to achieve a desirable unification.[355] In this context, the idea of a common court of appeal has been put forward,[356] but it has been rejected up till now, on the ground that the periodical conferences of the presidents of the arbitration tribunals provide a sufficient instrument for achieving uniform practice.[357] In this way a remarkable contradiction continues to exist: commercial disputes of an international character, arising from or in connection with international economic agreements and subject to an international (procedural) régime, are settled by national organs.[358]

In the meantime, efforts to improve the existing arbitration system are continuing. These efforts are said to concern questions such as the suspension of arbitral awards and the joining of third parties to a case,[359] questions which are considered to require uniform regulation. The CMEA Conference on Legal Questions decided at its 19th meeting in December 1980 to study the experience so far with the Moscow Convention and the Uniform Regulation, and to elaborate additional proposals if necessary. It is said that this examination has been effectuated in the course of 1982.[360]

Although the existing arbitration system only applies to private law subjects and is, therefore, outside the *direct* scope of the present study, ignoring this system would not have been justified, because of the actual nature of economic co-operation between the CMEA States.[361] It might suffice to recall that concrete obligations concerning economic co-operation entered into by the CMEA States are usually implemented through the conclusion of private law contracts by their enterprises. In other words, the obligations of the CMEA *States* in this field have to be fulfilled by means of *private law* acts. Hence, there is good reason to discuss the arbitration system – which is engaged in the settlement of disputes which may arise from the implementation of these acts concluded pursuant to State obligations – in the present study. This indicates once more that, although a clear distinction has to be made between the public law and private law levels formally, a very close connection exists in practice.

Finally, it should be stressed expressly that the arbitration system applies only to private law subjects and *not* to States. The CMEA Member States are not subject to any (quasi-)judicial régime for the settlement of their mutual disputes. This does not detract from the fact that the States do have a substantial influence upon the chances of their economic organisations fulfilling obligations arising from the contracts which they conclude and, as practice has shown, this may also affect the responsibility of those economic organisations. A well-known example of this is an award of the Arbitration Court of the Polish Chamber of Foreign Trade in a conflict between a Polish and an East German enterprise, in which it was found that an enterprise is not liable for the non-fulfilment of a contract if the circumstances leading to the non-fulfilment are directly brought about by the State, *e.g.*, by diminishing the allocation of necessary resources.[362] This example, however, is not illustrative of the present-day situation; the original, unsatisfactory results (as exemplified above) were generally considered to be detrimental to the smooth development of economic co-operation, and measures have been taken by several States to improve the situation, so that acts by planning or other executive State authorities can no longer be invoked by enterprises to relieve them of responsibility under a contract. This change has been accomplished by national legislation and/or the insertion of corresponding provisions in treaties. As far as national legislation is concerned, the Czechoslovak law on international trade of December 1963 rules out the possibility of enterprises invoking *force majeure* in the case of State intervention. The law states that circumstances which hinder the fulfilment of an obligation and which could have been prevented by the enterprise concerned, 'such as the lack of an official authorisation necessary for it to perform (its) duty', will not relieve that enterprise of its responsibility.[363] This means that in the case of a contract of sale, the seller has a duty to obtain all the necessary documents and authorisations from the State authorities before the final conclusion of the contract.[364] If he fails to do this, and the authorities refuse the necessary documents subsequent to the conclusion of the contract, the seller may be held responsible.

As indicated above, similar results may be achieved by the insertion of provisions in treaties. An example is offered by the protocol concluded between Poland and the G.D.R. on December 19, 1968, which supplemented the CMEA GCDG of 1968 with additional provisions applying to the bilateral relations between the States. In paragraph 2 of this protocol, the States agreed that acts of national planning authorities (*i.e.* State organs) which resulted in it becoming impossible for an enterprise to fulfil its obligations, would not relieve that enterprise of its responsibility.[365] It has to be noted, however, that not all State interventions are covered by this provision, it concerns only acts of national planning authorities.

In this way some of the severest imperfections affecting the responsibility of private law economic organisations have to some extent been righted. Although this is undoubtedly an important contribution to the further development of international economic relations, the greatest problem continues to exist, that problem being the responsibility of the CMEA States themselves.[366] Adequate legal regulation of this problem is of the greatest importance in view of the extensive involvement of the socialist State in economic life; as the owner of the national means of production, the State

654

determines and organises the economy as a whole, as well as external economic relations, mainly through its planning mechanism. Despite all this, the CMEA States are fiercely opposed to being subjected to any system for obligatory third party settlement of disputes involving State responsibility. Indeed, in all fields of international relations they are against any system which goes beyond the traditional instruments for the peaceful settlement of disputes based on completely voluntary submission by the States concerned; (compulsory) arbitration and judicial settlement are out of the question, since these instruments are held to be incompatible with State sovereignty.

All this implies that, despite the incontestable improvements which have been introduced into the arbitration system[367] of the CMEA countries, some fundamental shortcomings remain unsolved.

5.5. Functions and instruments of CMEA supervision

As in other international economic organisations and arrangements, the supervision exercised by the CMEA may have three functions: a review function, a correction function and a 'creative' function.[368] In general, the review function consists of considering the behaviour of States and judging whether it is in conformity with international rules. The correction function aims at redressing the wrongful actions of States, while the 'creative' function is concerned with the interpretation, elaboration and individualisation of (general and often vague) rules according to practical needs. In order to prevent the danger of labelling as 'supervision' anything that an organisation does in interpreting and elaborating its norms, the 'creative' function should be strictly connected to the supervisory process. This means that the interpretation and elaboration of existing rules, and the establishment of new guidelines by an organisation may only be seen as an expression of the 'creative' function of supervision if they are a direct result of or are directly connected with the supervisory process.

Starting with the review function, it should be noted that the principal instruments are the reports drawn up by the Secretariat on the implementation of CMEA resolutions by the Member States. In this task, the Secretariat is highly dependent on the information which has to be submitted periodically by the CMEA States. As it has been stated earlier,[369] the States are obliged to make available to the Council 'the materials and information, *necessary* for carrying out the tasks entrusted to it'.[370] It is very obvious that the crucial term 'necessary' may be interpreted by the Member States in quite divergent ways. To a certain degree this situation may be counterbalanced by the fact that the Secretariat has been granted the right not only to 'receive', but also to 'request' materials and information from the Member States.[371] The information has usually to be supplied by the Member States on the basis of questionnaires drawn up by the CMEA organs concerned. From the limited data available on this subject it may be inferred that these questionnaires are drafted by one or more delegations, and are subsequently approved by the organ concerned after being discussed and, if need be,

655

amended. The questionnaires are apparently used with respect to the implementation of only the most important CMEA resolutions. The CMEA organs do not only draw up questionnaires, they also fix exact time-limits within which the information asked for has to be supplied.[372] This process of approving questionnaires and fixing time-limits is achieved by means of decisions which are directly binding upon the Member States.[373] In the process of drawing up questionnaires, the role of the Secretariat seems to be a supporting and administrative rather than an initiating one. Nevertheless, it may reasonably be assumed that the Secretariat also makes use of questionnaires on a wide variety of subjects in order to be able to prepare economic and statistical surveys and studies.[374] It goes without saying that these activities of the Secretariat are highly important for the effectiveness of the review function of CMEA supervision in general. Nevertheless, the impression remains that the exact modalities of meeting the obligation to supply information still fall within the discretion of the CMEA States to a high degree. This is one of the grounds for the complaints about insufficient supply of information by the Member States.[375]

The exact time-limits for the submission of information by the Member States is, as a rule, determined from case to case by the CMEA organs concerned. Exceptionally, this has been fixed by the Statutes or Rules of Procedure of the organs.[376] In practice, for a long time the CMEA States were obliged to supply the CMEA with information on the fulfilment of their obligations arising from recommendations of the Session and the Executive Committee every six months. This procedure, which was applied in the sixties, was changed following the adoption of the Comprehensive Programme. Nowadays, the States have to inform the Executive Committee once a year (in the first quarter) about their implementation of the Comprehensive Programme and about all organisational, legal and other measures taken by them to implement that Programme. The scope of this new information procedure, introduced by the Executive Committee, seems to have been enlarged, in the sense that it is no longer limited to recommendations of the two highest CMEA organs.

A second instrument of the review function of CMEA supervision, closely connected to the first one, is the oral supply of information by the Member States during sessions of CMEA organs. Here, a distinction has to be made between general and specific supervision modalities. In the general supervision process this information is additional to the reports of the Secretariat, and may be given on the request of other delegations or of a delegation's own accord. In the specific supervisory process (the consultation procedure), this information may be the sole instrument of the review function, though in these cases too the possibility of the drawing up of specific reports by the Secretariat may not be excluded.

It has to be noted that to a large extent the above observations are generalisations. Due to a lack of information, it is very difficult to make a thoroughgoing, fruitful analysis of the exact situation concerning the supervision of the implementation of the different kinds of CMEA resolutions. For instance, one has to be aware of the fact that the precise manner of meeting the obligation to supply information is not and cannot be uniform in all cases because of the very divergent contents of CMEA resolutions. In this context one may refer to the Polish lawyer Skubiszewski, who has stated that the nature of certain recommendations limits the obligation to supply the CMEA with information on their implementation in practice.[377]

The afore-mentioned reports of the Secretariat (including possible proposals by the Secretariat) and information from the national delegations constitute the basis for the political supervisory debates in the CMEA organs, and these debates form the principal instrument of the correction function of CMEA supervision. In other words, political discussion is the only means available within the CMEA to try to 'correct' wrongful behaviour by Member States. These discussions are subject to the ordinary principles and rules of the CMEA decision-making régime, which implies, in particular, the application of the principles of unanimity and of interest, and competence to adopt only (non-binding) recommendations. Since all interested Member States are represented in all CMEA organs, not much imagination is needed to see that the possibilities of the CMEA proceeding against deviant States are very limited (or even lacking altogether). In fact, it amounts to a situation in which each State may act as *iudex in sua causa* by blocking draft resolutions it finds unpalatable. Nevertheless, the periodical or specific supervisory debates might exert, and do exert, a certain influence upon the behaviour of States with respect to the fulfilment of their obligations, both preventively and correctively.[378]

Within the CMEA framework the political supervisory debates are not only the main instrument for the correction, but also for the 'creative' function. It is extremely difficult, however, to separate these functions clearly. As has been noted before, the supervisory debates may result in the adoption of recommendations. These recommendations may once more confirm the obligation to implement the contents of recommendations adopted and accepted previously, which are now being supervised. It is also possible, however, that in view of newly-arisen circumstances the contents of recommendations are modified or even withdrawn and, if need be, superseded by a new recommendation.[379] The last possibilities are directly connected with the specific consultation procedures, but undoubtedly have general relevance in the CMEA supervisory process.[380] If the CMEA organs apply these revision and reframing competences during the supervisory debates, one might argue that they serve both the correction and the creative functions.

VI. EFFECTIVENESS OF CMEA SUPERVISION

6.1. Preliminary remarks

To give a well-balanced evaluation of the effectiveness of the supervision which is exercised by the CMEA forms the most difficult part of the present study. Serious obstacles have already been encountered repeatedly, due to a lack of necessary data, and this lack is even more apparent in this chapter, since in many instances only scattered and sometimes contradictory information is available. Nevertheless, a discussion of the effectiveness of CMEA supervision has its value as an attempt to get a somewhat better insight into the functioning of this supervisory mechanism and the role it plays in economic co-operation in Eastern Europe. In view of the above-mentioned problems, however, the next pages sometimes merely hint at some important aspects, and must therefore be treated with some caution.

For a more effective survey it might be useful, first, to consider the effectiveness of supervision within the CMEA, and, next, that of supervision exercised outside the CMEA framework.

6.2. CMEA supervision

The foregoing chapters have shown that the powers of the CMEA to take measures to induce the Member States to fulfil their obligations are very limited. It may adopt recommendations to that end, but it has not been granted any power to enforce them.[381] Likewise, it has supervisory powers, but no legal power to proceed against Member States which obstruct the supervisory process. Though this situation is not necessarily detrimental to the effectiveness of the CMEA supervisory process, some Eastern European scholars presumably have this in mind when they press for an increase in the powers of the CMEA to supervise the implementation of recommendations accepted by the States, including the power to settle disputes.[382] This indicates some dissatisfaction with the current situation, and this discontent has also been clearly reflected in the activities of the CMEA in the course of the years. In the seventies much attention was paid to the improvement of the supervisory mechanism, which was evidently considered an essential precondition for the further improvement of economic and scientific-technical co-operation among the CMEA Member States. This found clear expression, *inter alia*, in the Executive Committee's 'Report on the raising of the effectiveness of the recommendations of the CMEA' of 1976,[383] in the Session report 'Basic directions for the further improvement of the organisation of multilateral co-operation among CMEA member countries, and of the activity of the Council' of 1978,[384] and in the several amendments to the CMEA Charter (1979) which have been analysed in the preceding chapters. The Effectiveness Report was particularly concerned with a quite thorough evaluation of the supervisory process in the CMEA. Moreover, the issue remains under consideration: the Conference on Legal Questions is said to have supervised the implementation of, *inter alia*, the Effectiveness Report in a meeting in 1982, during which supervisory problems undoubtedly came up again. This should have resulted in another report, to be approved by the Executive Committee.[385]

Some imperfections in the present functioning of the CMEA supervisory mechanism, and possible methods of improvement as developed within the CMEA, will now be discussed. The information about the supervisory process put forward here is mainly based on the situation as it was until roughly the mid-seventies. The positive, practical effects of CMEA supervision will also be evaluated, as will some general obstacles which hamper (or might hamper) the smooth development of economic co-operation in general, and the effectiveness of CMEA supervision in particular.

Mention was made above[386] of the distinction between 'preliminary' supervision of the results of national consideration of CMEA recommendations within 60 days after their adoption by CMEA organs, and the subsequent supervision of the implementation of these recommendations (if accepted). The effectiveness of 'preliminary' supervision will be discussed first.

This preliminary supervision aims at a clear survey of the mutual rights and obligations of the Member States, through registration and subsequent distribution by the CMEA Secretariat of the results of the consideration of CMEA recommendations by the competent national authorities. In practice, these 'results' may amount to the full or partial acceptance of a recommendation or to refusal to accept it. Whatever the results may be, the interested Member States are obliged to inform the Secretariat within 60 days of the date of signature of the protocol of the meeting of the organ concerned, unless explicitly provided for otherwise. Practice, however, has shown some deviations from this rule, both concerning the 60-day period and the content of the national information.

The 60-day period does not always appear to be respected.[387] One CMEA State did not supply the required information concerning a recommendation of the Executive Committee for more than a year after the expiry of the said period. In addition, in several Standing Commissions delegations of certain countries have failed to inform the Secretariat entirely about the results of the national consideration of recommendations. In other instances, the Secretariat was informed that the State would decide upon the acceptance of a recommendation at a later stage (for instance, at the signature of a treaty which constituted the contents of the recommendation). Although one might argue about the lawfulness of this latter phenomenon,[388] in practice it has caused considerable delay in the conclusion of some agreements on specialisation and co-operation in production. This delay resulted from the fact that there was uncertainty as to relations between the interested States, some of which had already accepted the recommendation while others had not.

Another problem is concerned with the content of the national information: although national acceptance is required only for recommendations, States have sometimes informed the Secretariat about their approval of the *resolutions* ('postanovleniia') or *protocols* of meetings of CMEA organs. In other instances, States have informed on their acceptance of recommendations concerning questions which were of interest to them, without indicating exactly which questions they had in mind. It goes without saying, that because of the absence or inadequacy of national information, the CMEA Secretariat has not been able to keep an exact record of all the recommendations accepted by CMEA States or to supervise their implementation properly. In 1976, in order to improve this situation, the Executive Committee laid down some procedural requirements to which the national information had to conform, *viz.* an exact indication of precisely which recommendations had been accepted, by means of a reference to the relevant paragraph of the protocol of the meeting of the CMEA organ. Moreover, the Executive Committee considered it necessary for the Secretariat to strengthen its supervision of the prompt submission of the required information by the States, and of compliance with the said requirements. It did not indicate, however, how the strengthening of the role of the Secretariat should take place, but it was hoped that preliminary CMEA supervision might be improved in this way.

After the national acceptance of recommendations, the Member States are obliged to guarantee their implementation. Consequently, preliminary CMEA supervision is followed by supervision of the implementation of accepted recommendations in practice. In order to enable the CMEA to exercise this important task, the Member States are obliged to supply the CMEA periodically with information on implementation, and for this purpose questionnaires are used.[389] The information thus obtained is summarised by the Secretariat and subsequently distributed among all Member States. This is the formal procedure, but how does it function in practice? The practice appears to be not very different from that obtaining in other international economic organisations or organs,[390] in the sense that the quality and quantity of the information supplied by the Member States leaves much to be desired, with all the negative consequences of this. Within the CMEA, this has been clearly expressed by the Executive Committee, which has stated that, as a rule, the information from the countries differed so much that the summarised version of the Secretariat did not give a complete presentation of the situation concerning implementation of the recommendations of the Session of the Council, and of the Executive Committee. Although this evaluation concerned practice in the sixties and is limited to the Session and the Executive Committee, it apparently still held true in the seventies. Moreover, it appeared to be a general phenomenon with respect to all CMEA organs. In relation to the Standing Commissions, for instance, it has been expressly stated that in a series of cases the information from the national delegations was insufficient. All this led to the survey of the state of affairs concerning the implementation of CMEA recommendations being limited, which was, of course, detrimental to an effective functioning of the CMEA supervisory mechanism. It is somewhat surprising, therefore, that the Executive Committee seems not to have introduced measures aimed at an improvement of the information procedure (other than the recommendation to hold regular supervisory debates; see below), which may only be explained by the unwillingness of one or more CMEA States to accept a stricter regulation. This implies, as stated above,[391] that the exact modality of supplying the CMEA with information still seems to fall largely within the discretion of the Member States.

The suggestion from this material is that the principal instrument for the regular supervisory debates in the CMEA organs – the reports of the Secretariat – did not constitute a perfect basis. Another factor hampering

660

the effectiveness of CMEA supervision was the nature of these debates and, moreover, their absence on some occasions. This observation may be illustrated by some examples. As noted above, in the sixties the Member States informed the CMEA about their implementation of Session and Executive Committee recommendations twice a year, the information being summarised by the Secretariat. Strikingly, neither the information from the States nor the reports of the Secretariat were discussed at meetings of the Session and the Executive Committee. This situation has changed following the adoption of the Comprehensive Programme. Nowadays, the supervisory debates are organised regularly, the desirability and necessity of this having been emphasised by both organs several times. The supervisory activity of the Session is mainly based upon the annual reports of the Executive Committee on the activities of the CMEA, while the Executive Committee mainly uses the Secretariat reports for its supervision. The Executive Committee also has supervisory tasks in relation to the lower-ranking organs, these being practised mainly by discussion of the reports which these organs have to submit to the Executive Committee. In view of the effectiveness of this type of supervision, it is significant that these reports were until recently *not* discussed by the Executive Committee. This might be inferred from the decision that the Session took in 1978 'to *restore* the practice of the periodical discussion by the Executive Committee of the reports of CMEA organs on their activity and execution of the orders of Session and Executive Committee'.[392] Since then, the Executive Committee has reportedly again exercised its supervisory competence in relation to the lower-ranking organs.

As far as the holding of supervisory debates in lower-ranking organs themselves is concerned, the present author has only had information about the Standing Commissions at his disposal. Regular supervisory debates do take place in these Commissions, but here too there were some less-favourable factors, the main one being that in some Commissions supervisory activity was not carried out systematically, while the information from the States was not always discussed at meetings of the Commissions.

What has been described above may explain why in 1976 the Executive Committee recommended the regular organisation of supervisory debates in the CMEA organs. It concluded that practice had shown that the factual situation concerning the implementation of CMEA recommendations could best be determined by the consideration of the question at meetings of the organs concerned. That is why it appeared 'suitable' to the Executive Committee to hold, 'by agreement between the representatives (delegations) of the countries in the CMEA organs', a periodic discussion at meetings of those organs of the information from the States about the measures adopted by them to implement 'individual, highly important recommendations of CMEA organs', and to describe the situation concerning the implementation of these recommendations in the annual reports on activities.[393] Similarly, in 1978, the Session called for a strengthening of the 'regular supervision' of the fulfilment of obligations by the Member States, 'on the basis of the information from the countries and *its periodic discussion*'[394] by the political CMEA organs.

It may be assumed that such political supervisory debates are now regularly held by all political CMEA organs. The nature of these debates is highly dependent upon the level of the organs concerned. In general, it may be stated that the higher the level of the organs, the more 'diplomatic' the supervisory debates are. This means that in the highest-ranking organs the delegations usually criticise one another in highly diplomatic terms – which is certainly not unusual in international practice – whereas in the working groups and the groups of experts established by the lower-ranking organs, there are not infrequently pointed discussions with sharp criticism of, *inter alia*, the record of fulfilment of obligations by the States.

The next question which has to be answered concerns the effectiveness of these supervisory debates. Although only a tentative answer to this question may be given, some general observations can be made, mainly concerning the supervision which is exercised by the Executive Committee.

As has been stated several times above, there is no doubt that the Executive Committee plays a central role within the CMEA supervisory process. Despite the several shortcomings described above, the Committee is said to exert great influence towards proper fulfilment of their obligations by the Member States. Moreover, this influence is not limited to CMEA matters, but extends to the totality of economic co-operation between the CMEA Member States. The Committee owes this authoritative position first and foremost to its high-level composition, since all States are represented in it by vice-Prime Ministers. It exercises its supervisory tasks 'in a general sense', *i.e.* it supervises, above all, the main trends in economic co-operation among the CMEA States, leaving the supervision of the more detailed questions to the lower-ranking CMEA organs, to the specialised organisations of the CMEA and to the bilateral economic committees. Thanks to the authority of the Executive Committee, its supervision is said to have strong preventive effects; though it has no legal power to enforce fulfilment of obligations, the States are rather wary of the possibility of being recorded as 'non-fulfillers', and do their best to comply with their obligations before the supervisory debates. All this points to the fact that the very existence of a supervisory mechanism, together with the high authority of the Executive Committee, has a positive influence upon the effectiveness of the activities of the organisation in general, and of its supervisory process in particular, an influence which is reportedly felt far outside the (formal) organisation. This might seem rather striking, especially in view of the usually rather vague and general wording of the obligations of the Member States with respect to CMEA supervision, as pointed out above. However, these commitments, together with the high level of the Executive Committee, do not adequately explain the effectiveness of CMEA supervision. Some other factors contributing to the precise and prompt fulfilment of their obligations by the Member States have to be taken into account; three will be mentioned here.

A first factor to which attention should be paid in this context concerns the nature of the co-operation within the CMEA. Although the CMEA offers the best possibilities for multilateral economic co-operation among the Member States, the organisation does not have exclusive competence in this field. In practice, this can have several consequences. In the analysis of the decision-making process, it was observed that a State which tries to obstruct the adoption of a recommendation on a certain project might be confronted with the unpleasant fact that the other interested States still go ahead and realise the pursued project, outside the CMEA framework and without the participation of the obstructing State.[395] Similar consequences are possible in the field of supervision: if a State violates its obligations and is reluctant to solve the question in agreement with the other interested States, thus obstructing the CMEA supervisory process, it runs the risk of being excluded from the 'game', since the other interested States might choose to take up the same project outside the CMEA, without the participation of the unco-operative State. Such a solution, however, is only feasible in projects for which the participation of the defecting State is not indispensable. In general, therefore, the Soviet Union, with its huge economic potential, is not likely to experience such a fate. Moreover, because of its political implications, this solution will be resorted to only very rarely, if at all. Its main significance rests in its preventive effects. All this boils down to the conclusion that although the CMEA has no enforcement competences in terms of legal sanctions, in practice such competences do exist. This may also be concluded from the second factor.

This second factor, which also contributes to the effective functioning of CMEA supervision, concerns the structure of the group of CMEA States. Because of its enormous economic potential, and because of its strong position as the main supplier of energy and raw materials, the Soviet Union is sometimes able to exert decisive influence upon the behaviour of the other CMEA States, and thus upon the effectiveness of the CMEA supervisory process as well. This phenomenon, however, has hardly anything to do with the (effectiveness of) supervision *by the CMEA*, being limited, moreover, to the non-Soviet CMEA States. Because of its practical importance for the functioning of the CMEA it has to be mentioned here, but its actual influence upon the effectiveness of CMEA supervision is hard to assess.

A third factor is inherent to the system of economic co-operation among the CMEA States. This co-operation takes place on the basis of more-or-less detailed planning, and is strongly interconnected in all fields. The conse-quence of this is that disturbances in one field – for instance, caused by the non-implementation of CMEA recommendations – might create disturbances in other fields. This implies that a State's violations of its obligations might create quite unpleasant boomerang-effects for that State. Consequently, States will think twice before deciding to act contrary to their commitments.

These and other factors of an organisational, economic and political character undoubtedly exert a positive influence upon the effectiveness of CMEA supervision. On the other hand, however, there are several obstacles which hamper (or might hamper) this effectiveness. These obstacles are painfully apparent, especially when one or more CMEA States have violated their obligations. Although it has just been observed that the structure of economic co-operation discourages this, States may nevertheless decide not to comply with their obligations, for instance, because they expect this to produce more advantages than disadvantages for them. This is certainly not a hypothetical situation, and though one has to guard against exaggerations, it should be noted that such violations are not exceptional. This may be illustrated, *inter alia*, by the practice of Eastern European countries which sell as many goods as possible to hard currency countries, even when they have entered into agreements to deliver such goods to CMEA States. When this occurs, the latter have no legal instruments to obtain redress from the State in breach[396] (apart from the traditional means available under international law). Another illustration is offered by the many references to, and calls for, the urgent necessity of strict compliance with all obligations entered into by the States.[397] This points – to put it mildly – to a not wholly satisfactory situation in this field.

While describing the above phenomenon, we are touching upon one of the weakest points in the legal system of economic co-operation among the socialist States as a whole, *viz. the responsibility of the CMEA States* resulting from infringements of their obligations. Though a thoroughgoing analysis of this complicated question is not necessary for the purpose of the present study, some general observations may be made.

The (material) responsibility of States[398] is a problem of much greater practical importance in the system of socialist economic integration than in the economic relations between Western countries. This results from the fact that the CMEA States act not only as (traditional) subjects of public international law, but also as the owners of the national means of production.[399] Consequently, the CMEA States themselves conclude material agreements concerning trade and co-operation, as well as specialisation in production, the infringement of which may involve material losses for the other State(s) concerned. The international law principle that the State which violates its obligations is responsible for all the consequences of this is generally recognised by the CMEA States.[400] In CMEA practice, however, the only means to obtain redress open to the CMEA State which has suffered detriment is the traditional procedure of diplomatic negotiations. If no agreement can be reached by the States concerned in this way, there are no possibilities for settling the question without the consent of the other State(s).[401] This could have a destabilising effect upon economic co-operation among the socialist countries, the more so since the CMEA States are involved in this process to an ever-increasing degree. This development makes the elaboration of practical methods and procedures for the application of the principle of State responsibility all the more necessary.

Hence, it is certainly not surprising that the CMEA Member States have been studying this problem for a number of years. The necessity of finding adequate solutions has also been stressed in a carefully formulated passage in the Comprehensive Programme:

> 'Proceeding from the necessity for consistent observance by the CMEA Member Countries of the principle of State responsibility for obligations arising from agreements concluded among them on economic and scientific-technical co-operation, the countries shall work out and implement the necessary measures, in particular methods and procedure for the settlement of controversial issues which may arise between them with respect to such responsibility'.[402]

Consultations on these questions take place mainly in the framework of the CMEA Conference on Legal Questions which, however, has still not succeeded in finding final solutions for all the problems in a way which is acceptable for all Member States.

Several approaches to the solution of the State responsibility question can be discerned among Eastern European scholars. Some of them favour solutions which put the main accent on *State* responsibility,[403] a solution which would turn the existing practice in which the main emphasis rests upon the (private law) responsibility of national economic organisations. Others are of the opinion that the most proper solutions can be found in an increase in the (private law) responsibility of enterprises, as expressed, for instance, in the 1968 protocol on the conditions for the delivery of goods between Poland and the G.D.R.,[404] a solution which would lead to a strengthening of the existing practice. (Still others are of the opinion that the existing practice does not require any essential changes, a rather conservative view which is certainly not the prevailing one in the CMEA countries.)

Up to now, no final agreement on this question has been achieved. Nevertheless, some first steps have been taken, however limited their practical significance may still be. A first and important result is the elaboration by (a working group of) the CMEA Conference on Legal Questions of the 'Conditions on the Material Responsibility of States concerning agreements on economic and scientific-technical co-operation', adopted at the 29th meeting of the Session of the CMEA in 1975.[405] Despite the formal entry into force of these Conditions, they are still not applied in practice (except for some instances of a bilateral and very limited nature). This is said to be a consequence of the surviving disagreement among the Member States on the question of the kinds of inter-State agreements to which the Conditions have to be applied.[406] This question is said to be down for further negotiations by the Conference on Legal Questions in the beginning of the eighties.

Another, though much less significant step, was taken by, *inter alia*, the Polish-Soviet Commission on economic and scientific-technical co-operation at its 12th Session in 1972. It approved the 'Model inter-departmental Polish-Soviet agreement on specialisation and co-operation in production'. This model treaty is of some importance, *inter alia*, because (in Article VI) it expressly provides for the material responsibility of the parties (*i.e.* States). This provision, however, has only a more-or-less symbolic function, once more confirming the *principle* of responsibility while at the same time explicitly indicating that its application is dependent upon the further elaboration of the principle and its scope and contents.[407]

The limited progress achieved so far in this field is without any doubt connected with its huge complexity, and its sensibility: the strict adherence to the principle of State sovereignty by (some) Eastern European States is a well-known fact which makes the finding of solutions for the transformation of the principle of State responsibility into practical methods and procedures a very laborious affair.

This is the main, but certainly not the only, explanation for the difficulties in finding adequate solutions for the problem of the (material) responsibility of the States. Some other factors also play a part, though not all of them need to be analysed here. Among those which do require mention[408] there is, in the first place, the rather revealing fact that many very important inter-State commitments are rather ill-defined: agreements are often vaguely worded, which results in obscurity as to the exact mutual rights and obligations. This, in its turn, may result in problems concerning supervision and State responsibility. Similar obscurities exist in relation to the questions whether and in which cases international legal obligations arise. The discussion of the legal effects of the different types of CMEA resolutions in a preceding chapter offers quite a few examples of these problems. In the seventies, the CMEA tried to introduce improvements in this field, *inter alia*, by drafting recommendations only after thorough preparation and with exact wording.[409] The Effectiveness Report certainly aimed at decreasing these obscurities.

A second factor concerns the difficulty in devising methods of calculating the damage directly and/or indirectly resulting from violations of obligations by the States.

A third factor concerns the question of whether, in a regulation on State responsibility, one has only to take into account objective aspects (*inter alia*, the non-fulfilment of an obligation as such), or also subjective aspects (*inter alia*, guilt, *vis maior* etc.).[410]

A fourth factor concerns the responsibility of States after the conclusion of private law contracts. Writers disagree on the question of whether the non-fulfilment of such private law contractual obligations by enterprises might entail State responsibility. Some authors deny this, arguing that once a contract between enterprises has been concluded the State has fulfilled its obligations (*i.e.* the obligations of a State to take the necessary measures to have its enterprises conclude the contracts provided for); in the case of an infringement of a private law contract, the enterprises concerned may have resort to the existing sanction and arbitration system. Others, however, defend the view that the obligations of a State also take in the implementation of the contracts concluded by enterprises and that, consequently, under certain conditions infringements of such contracts may entail State responsibility.[411]

A last factor to be mentioned here concerns the settlement of disputes which may arise during the negotiations connected with the material responsibility of States in concrete cases. The CMEA Conditions of 1975 are said to contain only rather weak provisions in this field.[412]

These factors may give some insight into the background of the year-long, rather fruitless negotiations aimed at solving the complicated problems resulting from State responsibility within the CMEA framework (and also outside it).

It is important to note, however, that the difficulties concerning State responsibility should not be exaggerated. Though in principle a (usually) clear legal distinction exists between the public law and the private law levels of international economic relations (roughly corresponding to the State and the enterprise levels), the practice of the CMEA States is much less formal. Indeed, this formal distinction is often not discernible in practice. For instance, there is a widespread practice in the CMEA countries that when a private law contract is violated during its implementation by enterprises, the resulting conflict is solved by government departments of the States concerned. This means that the private law and public law levels are strongly interwoven in practice.[413] Because of this smooth practice several Eastern European experts consider the forcing of the issue of State responsibility to be of little practical significance, and even potentially harmful. Although there is certainly some truth in this last view, the absence of possibilities for redress when political negotiations between the States prove to be fruitless, may have considerable negative effects upon the development of socialist economic integration.

All this may serve to show the serious limitations to which CMEA supervision is subject. Although the supervision exercised by the Executive Committee is reportedly effective – mainly in its preventive effects – the shortcomings of the supervisory mechanism of the CMEA sketched above undoubtedly compromise its general effectiveness. An unconditional judgment on the effectiveness of CMEA supervision would thus be of doubtful value. It is submitted that the actual effectiveness of its review, correction and creative functions should be queried. This 'conclusion' appears to be supported by the repeated calls by CMEA organs for a 'strengthening' of CMEA supervision, and also by the discussions at the 35th meeting of the CMEA Session in Sophia in July 1981. Here the Hungarian Prime Minister Geörgy Lazar criticised the functioning of the CMEA rather sharply. He reportedly stated: 'We have to pay more attention to the speeding-up of decision-making and to the solving of problems connected with the implementation of questions on which we have reached agreement.' Moreover, he reportedly called for a 'more critical analysis' of the question why the CMEA was failing on some points in the implementation of its plans for international co-ordination in the fields of energy, industry and agriculture.[414] In this, the Prime Minister was undoubtedly also alluding to the CMEA supervisory process.

It would, however, not be correct to draw the 'conclusion' arrived at about the effectiveness of CMEA supervision without bearing in mind that the CMEA has several 'rivals' in the field of supervision which will be discussed briefly below.

6.3. Supervision outside the CMEA

The 'rivals' (or rather 'supporters') of the CMEA in the field of supervision are mainly the bilateral economic committees and the specialised international economic organisations. Whereas the latter exercise supervision in their own specific fields of activity (for instance, the chemical industry), the bilateral committees are deeply involved in the arrangement of economic relations between the two countries concerned, and the supervision of the commitments entered into by them. This supervision, exercised by the committees, is said to be very effective. This is due partly to the fact that the commitments to be supervised are usually well-defined, partly to a business-like atmosphere and partly to the eagerly guarded balance of mutual advantages.[415] In this context, an important factor contributing to effective supervision is that concrete business between the two States is done in these committees, and no time is 'wasted' dealing with abstract ideas, principles or policies. Thus, sensitive questions of State prestige do not suddenly emerge, and all this appears to have a positive influence on the effectiveness of the very detailed supervision which is exercised by the committees. It is hard, however, to prove this observation empirically, because of a lack of data.

Supervision is also exercised in a quite different framework, *viz.* in the form of negotiations between the leaderships of the communist or workers' parties. This method, however, seems to be used only in highly complicated and controversial issues[416] and on an *ad hoc* basis. Such negotiations may be conducted, for instance, in the framework of the famous annual 'holiday trips' which the Eastern European party chiefs spend with their Soviet colleague in the Crimea. One can only guess, however, about the effectiveness of this type of political 'supervision'.

NOTES

1. One of the exceptions to this 'rule' is the study by P. VerLoren van Themaat, *The Changing Structure of International Economic Law* (The Hague etc., 1981).
2. See, *inter alia*, M. Kudriashov, 'SEV-mezhdunarodnaia ekonomicheskaia organizatsiia novogo tipa' [The CMEA – an international economic organisation of a new type], *Ekonomicheskoe Sotrudnichestvo Stran-Chlenov SEV*, 1975, no. 1, p. 106; *Mir sotsializma v tsifrakh i faktakh 1979; Spravochnik* [The world of socialism in figures and facts 1979; A handbook] (Moscow, 1980), p. 13.
3. The Eastern European States do not feel obliged to render economic assistance to the developing countries, basing this negative attitude, *inter alia*, on the argument that they never possessed and thus never exploited colonies, and are also not to be blamed for the energy, monetary and other crises in the world. See P. Knirsch, 'Comecon and the Developing Nations', in *Comecon: Progress and Prospects; Colloquium 1977* (Brussels, 1977), pp. 221–236; see also E. Laszlo & J. Kurtzman, eds., *Eastern Europe and the New International Economic Order; Representative Samples of Socialist Perspectives* (UNITAR, New York etc., 1980); S. Polaczek, 'The New International Economic Order and the CMEA Countries', *Studies on International Relations*, no. 13 (Warsaw, 1979), pp. 57–71.
4. See section 6.2., *infra*, p. 658.
5. In this study the English quotations from official CMEA documents are translations by the author, based on the original texts in Russian. The latter have for the most part been published by the CMEA Secretariat in: *Osnovnye Dokumenty Soveta Ekonomicheskoi Vzaimopomoshchi* [Basic Documents of the CMEA], 2 Volumes (Moscow, 1976–77/Buffalo, N.Y., 1979). Another main source of documents is P. A. Tokareva, ed., *Mnogostoronnee ekonomicheskoe sotrudnichestvo sotsialisticheskikh gosudarstv* (*Dokumenty za 1972–1975 gg.*) [Multilateral economic co-operation of the socialist States (Documents 1972–1975)] (Moscow, 1976). The text of the CMEA Statute with the 1979 amendments has up till now (Spring 1981) been published only in English – a rather poor translation – by the CMEA Secretariat (Moscow, 1980). A Russian text in stencilled form was, however, available to the author. [After the present study was completed, the following important collection of recent documents was published: P. A. Tokareva, ed., *Mnogostoronnee ekonomicheskoe sotrudnichestvo sotsialisticheskikh gosudarstv* (*Dokumenty 1975–1980 gg.*) (Moscow, 1981). In this collection the Russian text of the CMEA Statute in the 1979 version is also included, as well as the rules of procedure of Session and Executive Committee and the Statute of the CMEA Secretariat as amended in 1979.]
    Some valuable collections of CMEA documents in other languages are W. E. Butler, ed., *A Source Book on Socialist International Organizations* (Alphen aan den Rijn, 1978); *Grund-dokumente des RGW* (Berlin, G.D.R., 1978); *Wirtschaftliche und wissenschaftlich-technische Zusammenarbeit der RGW-Länder – Dokumente* (Berlin, G.D.R., 1981); *The multilateral economic co-operation of socialist States; A collection of documents* (Moscow, 1977).
6. This principle is described in section 2.2. of the present study, see *infra*, p. 609.
7. Section 1, §5 of the Comprehensive Programme (see also note 11).
8. Thus, the permanent representative of the Soviet Union at the CMEA, K. Katushev, stated that the supply of the materials needed for the armaments industry is a 'fundamental goal' of the CMEA long-term target-programme for machine building; see his article 'Sovet Ekonomicheskoi Vzaimopomoshchi: 30 let' [The Council for Mutual Economic Assistance: 30 years], *Planovoe Khoziaistvo*, 1979, no. 1, p. 15. See also D. Hillebrenner, ed., *Warschauer Vertrag; Schutz des Sozialismus – Sicherung des Friedens* (Berlin, G.D.R., 1980), pp. 72–75. According to this last source (p. 71), the United Secretariat of the WTO has a 'permanent connection' with the CMEA. See also V. G. Kulikov, ed., *Varshavskii Dogovor – Soiuz vo imia mira i sotsializma* [The Warsaw Treaty – Alliance for the sake of peace and socialism] (Moscow, 1980) pp. 109–110.
9. 3rd subsection of the preamble of the CMEA Charter.
10. For a short historical survey of the activities of the CMEA, see G. Schiavone, *The Institutions of Comecon* (London and Basingstoke, 1981), pp. 17 *et seq.* See also M. Hegemann, *Kurze Geschichte des RGW* (Berlin, G.D.R., 1980).
11. An English translation of the Comprehensive Programme has been published by the CMEA Secretariat (Moscow, 1971). In other languages in *Grunddokumente des RGW, op. cit., supra,* note 5, pp. 47–141; R. Bystricky, *Le droit de l'intégration économique socialiste* (Geneva, 1979), pp. 355–456; *Osnovnye Dokumenty SEV, Tom I, op. cit., supra,* note 5, pp. 33–160 (hereafter referred to as: Compr. Progr.).

12. Section 1, §7 of the Compr. Progr.

13. The Polish lawyer Wasilkowski described it as follows: 'Le trait particulier de l'intégration économique socialiste consiste en ce que jusqu'à présent elle s'effectue surtout par l'intensification et l'enrichissement des liaisons économiques internationales et non pas par la suppression des frontières économiques dans le cadre de la communauté'. See A. Wasilkowski, 'Aspects juridiques de l'intégration économique socialiste's in: *Académie de Droit International, Colloquium 1971* (Leyden, 1972), p. 287; *cf.* L. Bauman & B. Grebennikov, 'Towards Extending CMEA Co-operation', *International Affairs* (Moscow), 1981, nr. 6, p. 25.

14. See, *inter alia*, Iu. F. Kormnov, L. I. Lukin & Iu. A. Pekshev, *Sozialistische ökonomische Integration – Ergebnisse und Perspektiven* (Berlin, G.D.R., 1975), pp. 3–10; B. I. Ladygin, V. I. Sedov & R. R. Ultanbaev, *Istoricheskii opyt sotrudnichestva stran SEV* [The historical experience of the co-operation of the CMEA countries] (Moscow, 1980), pp. 87 *et seq.*: J. Krüger & S. Quilitzsch, *Sozialistische Gemeinschaft; Entwicklungstendenzen in den 70er Jahren* (Berlin, G.D.R. 1978), p. 92; J. Krüger & S. Quilitzsch, eds., *Zusammenarbeit und Annäherung in der sozialistischen Gemeinschaft* (Berlin, G.D.R., 1977); Bauman & Grebennikov, *loc. cit.*, *supra*, note 13, pp. 25–26; *Völkerrecht-Lehrbuch*, Teil I (Berlin, G.D.R., 1973), p. 49.

15. Some countries consider the process of socialist economic integration mainly as a technical process which is necessary as a consequence of purely economic reasons. *Cf.* my summary of the comment of the Polish lawyer Wasilkowski at a colloquium at Leyden in 1979, in T. M. C. Asser Institute, *EEC-COMECON Relations; Colloquium IX-1979* (The Hague, 1980), pp. 31–32.

16. Article I,2 of the CMEA Charter; identical in section 1, §2 of the Compr. Progr.

17. See for a thoroughgoing analysis Th. Schweisfurth, *Sozialistisches Völkerrecht?* (West-Berlin/Heidelberg/New York, 1979); see also B. A. Ramundo, *The Soviet Socialist Theory of International Law* (Washington, 1964).

18. See, *e.g.*, P. A. Tokareva, *Mezhdunarodnyi organizatsionno-pravovoi mekhanizm sotsialis-ticheskoi ekonomicheskoi integratsii* [The international organisational-legal mechanism of social-ist economic integration] (Moscow, 1980), p. 96; see also G. I. Tunkin, *Völkerrechtstheorie* (West-Berlin, 1972), p. 481.

19. J. Mrázek, 'Mezinárodněprávní zásady vztahů mezi socialistickými státy' [The international legal principles of relations between socialist countries], *Studie z mezinárodního práva* (Prague), vol. 14, 1979, pp. 17–45 (44); Tunkin, *op. cit.*, *supra*, note 18, p. 479; H. Kröger, ed., *Sozialistische Staatengemeinschaft und Völkerrecht* (Berlin, G.D.R., 1979), pp. 47–59.

20. M. Potočný, 'On the Question of the International Legal Character of the Principles of Socialist Internationalism', in *International Relations* (Czechoslovak Review for foreign politics), Selection of studies from Volume 1972 (Prague, 1973), p. 44.

21. Tunkin, *op. cit.*, *supra*, note 18, p. 477; see also Kröger, *op. cit.*, *supra*, note 19, p. 96.

22. N. W. Faddejew, *Der Rat für Gegenseitige Wirtschaftshilfe* (Berlin, G.D.R., 1975), pp. 52–53.

23. Section 2.1., see *supra*, p. 608.

24. See section 2, §4 of the Compr. Progr.; see also Bystricky, *op. cit.*, *supra*, note 11, pp. 22–23, 73; S. Kupper, 'Alte Programme für schwierige Aufgaben; Zur 33. Tagung des RGW', *Deutschland-Archiv*, 1979, nr. 8, p. 795; Kröger, *op. cit.*, *supra*, note 19, p. 95.

25. See, *e.g.*, Tokareva, *op. cit.*, *supra*; note 18, pp. 95–97; Potočný, *loc. cit.*, *supra*, note 20, pp. 40–50 at p. 47; Kröger, *op. cit.*, *supra*, note 19, p. 46.

26. Especially Romania seems to deny the legal character of the principle, see D. Frenzke, 'Das Prinzip des Internationalismus aus der Sicht der rumänischen Völkerrechtsdoktrin', *Recht in Ost und West*, 1974, nr. 4, pp. 145–159 at pp. 148–152. The Romanian position is inspired in particular by the military and political consequences of the postulate (Brezhnev-doctrine!).

27. *Cf.* R. Bierzanek, J. Jakubowski & J. Symonides, *Prawo międzynarodowe i stosunki międzynarodowe* [International law and international relations] (Warsaw, 1980), pp. 21–23; Potočný, *loc. cit.*, *supra*, note 20, p. 42.

28. The Soviet lawyer Usenko has defined the process of socialist economic integration as follows: 'Socialist economic integration is the objective process of rapprochement and interna-tionalisation of the economic life of the peoples of sovereign and independent socialist countries, which process is being developed as a result of the socialist international division of labour; the accelerated development of this [process] in the present phase is secured by a system of measures which are systematically realised by the CMEA Member States on the basis of agreements between them, directly aimed at the solution – through the uniting of the efforts of these countries – of the acute (matured) problems of their economic and scientific-technical progress in the interest of an increase of the well-being of their peoples and the approach of the victory in the competition with capitalism', see E. T. Usenko, 'Mezhdunarodnopravovye

problemy sotsialisticheskoi ekonomicheskoi integratsii' [International legal problems of socialist economic integration], *Sovetskii Ezhegodnik Mezhdunarodnogo Prava*, 1970, p. 19.

29. L. Ficzere, 'Mezhdunarodnaia institutionnaia sistema integratsii SEV' [The international institutional system of CMEA integration], in *Soveshchaniiu predstavitelei stran-chlenov SEV po pravovym voprosam 10 let* [Ten years Conference of representatives of the CMEA member countries on legal questions] (Budapest, 1980), p. 24; *Sozialistische ökonomische Integration; Fragen der Theorie und Praxis* (Berlin, G.D.R., 1979), p. 9.

30. 'A. Wasilkowski, 'Legal Regulation of Economic Relations Within the Council for Mutual Economic Assistance. Trends of Development', *Polish Yearbook of International Law*, vol. V, 1972–73, p. 8 (italics in the original text).

31. *Idem*; see also section 1, §2 of the Compr. Progr.

32. W. Seiffert, ed., *Sozialistische ökonomische Integration – Rechtsfragen* (Berlin, G.D.R., 1974), p. 175 and the Soviet lawyer M. M. Boguslavski quoted there.

33. K. Grzybowski, *Soviet Private International Law* (Leyden, 1965), pp. 159–163, 36–37.

34. Bystricky, *op. cit.*, *supra*, note 11, p. 293; Grzybowski, *op. cit.*, *supra*, note 33, p. 161.

35. See, *inter alia*, section 5.4.3., *infra* p. 649 *et seq.*

36. See the preamble of section 4 of the Compr. Progr.

37. Compr. Progr., section 1, §2.

38. Compr. Progr., section 17, §2.

39. Publications on the subject include the following: M. Kemper, ed., *Zusammenarbeit der RGW-Länder in der Planung – Rechtsfragen* (Berlin, G.D.R., 1977); G. Proft, ed., *Planung im RGW* (Berlin, G.D.R., 1980); O. K. Rybakov, *Planovye osnovy ekonomicheskoi integratsii stran-chlenov SEV* [The planned bases of the economic integration of the CMEA member countries] (Moscow, 1979); Iu. A. Pekshev, *Dolgosrochnye tselevye programmy sotrudnichestva stran-chlenov SEV* [The long-term target-programmes of co-operation of the CMEA member countries] (Moscow, 1980).

40. R. Damus, *RGW – Wirtschaftliche Zusammenarbeit in Osteuropa* (Opladen, 1979), pp. 135–137; V. Libánský, 'Der internationale sozialistische Planungsprozess und der rechtliche Mechanismus der sozialistischen ökonomischen Integration', in: Kemper, *op. cit.*, *supra*, note 39, p. 98. See also I. Ikonnikov, 'Osnovnye printsipy i zadachi Soglasovannogo plana mnogostoronnikh integratsionnykh meropriiatii stran-chlenov SEV na 1981–1985 gg' [Fundamental principles and functions of the Co-ordinated Plan of mulitateral integration measures of the CMEA member countries for 1981–1985], *Ekonomicheskoe Sotrudnichestvo stran-chlenov SEV*, 1980, nr. 5, pp. 96–98.

41. See section 5.2., *infra*, p. 640.

42. See section 3.1.1., *infra*, p. 615 and section 5.1.5., *infra*, p. 639.

43. See further, section 5.1.5., *infra*, p. 639.

44. See section 2.3.1., *supra*, p. 611.

45. Practice is in this respect less rigid, see section 5.2., *infra*, p. 640.

46. Libánský, *loc. cit.*, *supra*, note 40, p. 99.

47. See *inter alia* Damus, *op. cit.*, *supra*, note 40, pp. 138–139.

48. For a short survey of the main legal aspects, see also Bystricky, *op. cit.*, *supra*, note 11, pp. 203–217.

49. See for that, *inter alia*, Damus, *op. cit.*, *supra*, note 40, pp. 153–185; J. M. P. van Brabant, *Bilateralism and structural bilateralism in intra-CMEA trade* (Rotterdam, 1973).

50. H. de Fiumel, 'Die Bedeutung der internationalen Abkommen im Prozess der sozialistischen ökonomischen Integration', in O. Wolff von Amerongen, ed., *Rechtsfragen der Integration und Kooperation in Ost und West* (West-Berlin, 1976), pp. 103–119 at p. 117; Wasilkowski, *loc. cit.*, *supra*, note 13, p. 297.

51. E. Ustor, 'Decision-making in the Council for Mutual Economic Assistance', 134 *Recueil des Cours de l'Académie de Droit International* (1971–III), p. 263.

52. I. Szász, *A uniform law on international sales of goods; the CMEA General Conditions* (Budapest, 1976). The GCDG system started as early as 1951 with the General Uniform Conditions of Commerce of the CMEA, and has been radically changed several times, lastly in 1979.

53. See section 5.4.3., *infra*, p. 649.

54. Ficzere, *loc. cit.*, *supra*, note 29, p. 30.

55. These multilateral inter-governmental organisations can be divided in their turn into the CMEA, as the organisation with functions in the field of economic co-operation as a whole, and a number of specialised organisations, functioning in the areas of credit and finance, specific branches of production, transport, communications and scientific-technical co-operation, Tokareva, *op. cit.*, *supra*, note 18, pp. 72–73.

671

56. Ficzere, *loc. cit.*, *supra*, note 29, p. 31.

57. For more information about these institutions, see Tokareva, *op. cit.*, *supra*, note 18, pp. 159–199; V. I. Menzhinskii, ed., *Mezhdunarodnye organizatsii sotsialisticheskikh gosudarstv – Spravochnik* [The international organisations of the socialist states – A handbook] (Moscow, 1980), pp. 212–250; V. V. Vorotnikov & D. A. Lebin, eds., *Mezhdunarodnye ekonomicheskie i nauchno-tekhnicheskie organizatsii stran-chlenov SEV: Spravochnik* [The international economic and scientific-technical organisations of the CMEA member countries: A handbook] (Moscow, 1980); A. I. Zubkov, ed., *Mezhdunarodnye khoziaistvennye organizatsii sotsialisticheskikh stran: problemy upravleniia* [The international economic organisations of the socialist countries: problems of management] (Moscow, 1981); H. Bruder, W. Kunz & S. Leidreiter, *Internationale ökonomische Organisationen der RGW-Länder* (Berlin, G.D.R., 1980).

58. Article III, 2 of the CMEA Charter.

59. Ficzere, *loc. cit.*, *supra*, note 29, pp. 33–40; V. V. Fomin, *Otnosheniia SEV s mezhdunarodnymi ekonomicheskimi organizatsiiami sotsialisticheskikh gosudarstv* [The relations of the CMEA with the international economic organisations of the socialist states], in E. T. Usenko, ed., *Sovet Ekonomicheskoi Vzaimopomoshchi; Osnovnye pravovye problemy* [The Council for Mutual Economic Assistance; Fundamental legal problems] (Moscow, 1975), pp. 286–310.

60. Menzhinskii, *op. cit.*, *supra*, note 57, p. 56.

61. *Idem*, pp. 57–201; Tokareva, *op. cit.*, *supra*, note 18, pp. 59–139. See also the publications quoted in note 57.

62. Tokareva, *op. cit.*, *supra*, note 18, pp. 140–152 (144–146).

63. M. Kemper, ed., *30 Jahre RGW; Rechtsfragen seiner Tätigkeit* (Berlin, G.D.R., 1979), p. 24.

64. The term 'international economic organisations' is very confusing because it (wrongly) calls to mind inter-governmental organisations. It is, however, generally used in the practice of the socialist countries.

65. Menzhinskii, *op. cit.*, *supra*, note 57, p. 212; Ficzere, *loc. cit.*, *supra*, note 29, p. 28; Tokareva, *op. cit.*, *supra*, note 18, pp. 190, 193; Kemper, *op. cit.*, *supra*, note 63, pp. 29, 64–66.

66. Menzhinskii, *op. cit.*, *supra*, note 57, p. 213.

67. Tokareva, *op. cit.*, *supra*, note 18, pp. 188–189; Menzhinskii, *op. cit.*, *supra*, note 57, pp. 243–250.

68. *Idem*; see also: P. Lorenz, *Multinationale Unternehmen sozialistischer Länder* (West-Berlin, 1978) and L. Zurawicki, *Multinational Enterprises in the West and East* (Alphen aan den Rijn/Germantown, 1979), pp. 97–122.

69. Kemper, *op. cit.*, *supra*, note 63, pp. 66–67; see also section 5.2., *infra*, p. 640.

70. Besides those mentioned above, still more institutions exist which, however, need not be described for the purpose of the present study; see Kemper, *op. cit.*, *supra*, note 63, pp. 29–30, 46.

71. Section 16, §4 of the Compr. Progr.; in practice the relations of the CMEA with its specialised organisations and the relations of the CMEA with the (private law) international economic organisations are almost identical, Kemper, *op. cit.*, *supra*, note 63, pp. 66–67.

72. Kemper, *op. cit.*, *supra*, note 63, pp. 62–63; Ficzere, *loc. cit.*, *supra*, note 29, pp. 34–37.

73. Formerly by the permanent representatives of the Member States, who are, at the same time, vice-Prime Ministers of their governments.

74. One must bear in mind, however, that high-level meetings, formally outside the CMEA framework, exert a decisive influence upon the policy of the CMEA. The well-known 'holiday trips' by communist party leaders to their Soviet colleague, Brezhnev, in the Crimea, where highly important questions are discussed each year, are of crucial interest in this context. Katushev, *loc. cit.*, *supra*, note 8, p. 8; Hillebrenner, *op. cit.*, *supra*, note 8, p. 70; Kemper, *op. cit.*, *supra*, note 63, p. 49.

75. W. Seiffert, ed., *Das System rechtlicher Regelung der sozialistischen ökonomischen Integration – Grundriss* (Berlin, G.D.R., 1976), pp. 80–81.

76. Damus, *op. cit.*, *supra*, note 40, p. 114.

77. *Informatie-bulletin van de Ambassade van de U.S.S.R. in Nederland* [Information-bulletin of the Embassy of the U.S.S.R. in the Netherlands], no. 28, July 22, 1978, p. 5.

78. Menzhinskii, *op. cit.*, *supra*, note 57, p. 82. See also section 4.4., *infra*, p. 631.

79. Menshinskii, *op. cit.*, *supra*, note 57, pp. 86–88.

80. Article IV, 3 of the CMEA Charter in the 1974 version. In 1979 some important new provisions were added to it, see *infra*, p. 621.

81. Ustor, *loc. cit.*, *supra*, note 51, p. 210; Ficzere, *loc. cit.*, *supra*, note 29, p. 46; L. Rüster, *Die internationalen ökonomischen Organisationen der RGW-Länder – Rechtsfragen* (Berlin,

G.D.R. 1980), pp. 33–34, ('Als Faustregel kann gelten, dass jedes Mitgliedsland so lange an einer bestimmten Frage interessiert ist, wie es nicht ausdrücklich seine Nichtinteressiertheit erklärt oder diese durch Nichtteilnahme zum Ausdruck gebracht hat'). The lack of an interest may also cover all questions belonging to the competence of specific standing commissions. This is expressed, in particular, by the absence of representatives of the country concerned in those commissions, see Menzhinskii, *op. cit.*, *supra*, note 57, p. 65.

82. J. Caillot, *Le C.A.E.M.; Aspects juridiques et formes de coopération économique entre les pays socialistes* (Paris, 1971), p.83; J. Sandorski, 'The legislative competence of the Council of Mutual Economic Assistance', *Polish Yearbook of International Law*, vol. I, 1966–67, p. 410; H. de Fiumel, *Rada Wzajemnej Pomocy Gospodarczej; Studium prawnomiędzynarodowe* [The Council for Mutual Economic Assistance; An international law study] (Warsaw, 1967), pp. 41 *et seq.*

83. Usenko, *op. cit.*, *supra*, note 59, p. 212.

84. A. Wasilkowski, *Zalecenia Rady Wzajemnej Pomocy Gospodarczej* [The recommendations of the Council for Mutual Economic Assistance] (Warsaw, 1969), pp. 234–250, 350–351; Usenko, *op. cit.*, *supra*, note 59, p. 213. See also Rüster, *op. cit.*, *supra*, note 81, pp. 35–36.

85. *Cf.* Usenko, *op. cit.*, *supra*, note 59, p. 210, who refers to the general obligation for the Member States 'to continue the development of all-round economic co-operation (. . .) in the interests of the building of socialism and communism in their countries and ensuring a stable peace throughout the world', as laid down in the preamble of the CMEA Charter.

86. Section 17, §2 of the Compr. Progr.

87. See, *inter alia*, Kröger, *op. cit.*, *supra*, note 19, p. 169.

88. Section 17, §§3 and 4 of the Compr. Progr. (italics added).

89. Article IV, 3 of the CMEA Charter as amended in 1979. This provision has been interpolated between the original two sub-paragraphs quoted above (*supra*, p. 619). The last sub-paragraph has also been amended and now reads as follows: 'Recommendations and decisions shall not apply to the countries which declared not to *participate in their adoption or to have no interest in a given question*' (italics added). The newly-added part (in italics) seems to indicate a distinction between non-participation in the adoption of resolutions by countries which do have an interest, and the status of not being interested. *Cf.* N. Mironov, *CMEA and Third Countries; Legal Aspects of Cooperation* (Moscow, 1981), pp. 65–66.

90. CMEA Secretariat, *Collected Reports on various Activities of Bodies of the CMEA in 1978* (Moscow, 1979), p. 180; *cf.* Kudriashov, *loc. cit.*, *supra*, note 2, p. 107.

91. Illustrative in this respect are the views expressed by E. T. Usenko, the principal Soviet expert on CMEA law, in Usenko, *op. cit.*, *supra*, note 59, pp. 209 *et seq.* He defends, *inter alia*, the views that the right to declare an interest must be interpreted in the context of the purposes and principles of the CMEA (p. 210), that a formal declaration of interest preconditions an objective, real interest which consequently has to be reasoned (p. 215), that the interest in accordance with the CMEA Charter has to be a positive interest (pp. 217 *et seq.*) and that the interest must be 'obvious and direct' (p. 217).

92. Explicitly so: Usenko, *op. cit.*, *supra*, note 59, p. 216. His ideas, however, are contested in this respect by L. Rüster and W. Seiffert in their review of the book edited by their Soviet colleague Usenko, see *Staat und Recht*, 1977, no. 4, pp. 429–433 at p. 431. On the other hand, the Polish lawyer J. Sandorski advocates the *future* introduction of a possibility for majority votes on resolutions which recognise a State as 'negatively interested' in order to curb its possible 'obstructive activity', see his *RWPG – Forma prawna integracji gospodarczej państw socjalistycznych* [The CMEA: Legal form of the economic integration of socialist states] (Poznań, 1977), p. 153.

93. Usenko, *op. cit.*, *supra*, note 59, p. 217.

94. Wasilkowski, *op. cit.*, *supra*, note 84, p. 350; Ustor, *loc. cit.*, *supra*, note 51, p. 209.

95. Ustor, *loc. cit.*, *supra*, note 51, p. 210; A. Wasilkowski, 'Die Bedeutung der Beschlüsse internationaler Organisationen im Prozess der sozialistischen ökonomischen Integration', in Wolff von Amerongen, *op. cit.*, *supra*, note 50, p. 132; Usenko, *op. cit.*, *supra*, note 59, p. 210; D. Graichen a.o., *Sozialistische ökonomische Integration; Aufgaben der Industriebetriebe und Kombinate* (Berlin, G.D.R., 1979), p. 19.

96. M. Nikl, 'International Aspects of a New Stage in the Development of the Council of Mutual Economic Assistance', in *International Relations* (Czechoslovak Review for Foreign Politics), Selection of Studies from volume 1972 (Prague, 1973), p. 28.

97. L. Valki, 'Beschlussfassung und Mechanismus der Zusammenarbeit im RGW', in Wolff von Amerongen, *op. cit.*, *supra*, note 50, p. 87.

98. See also Kröger, *op. cit.*, *supra*, note 19, p. 169.

99. Sandorski, *op. cit.*, *supra*, note 92, p. 152.

100. *Ibidem*. See also R. Szawlowski, 'Die Resolutionen der internationalen Wirtschaftsorgani-
sationen der sozialistischen Länder als Quelle des Rechts der Integration', in Wolff von
Amerongen, *op. cit.*, *supra*, note 50, pp. 150–151. For more data about CMEA decisions, see
section 4.2., *infra*, p. 628.
101. Ustor, *loc. cit.*, *supra*, note 51, p. 244; Collected Reports, *op. cit.*, *supra*, note 90, p. 180;
Menzhinskii, *op. cit.*, *supra*, note 57, p. 66.
102. Verbal information from Eastern European experts.
103. For these programmes, see Pekshev, *op. cit.*, *supra*, note 39.
104. The Czechoslovak lawyer Keselý explicitly points to this development, see V. Keselý,
'Razvitie printsipa zainteressovannosti v usloviiakh sotsialisticheskoi ekonomicheskoi integratsii'
[The development of the principle of interest under the conditions of socialist economic
integration], in *Pravovye voprosy deiatel'nosti SEV* [Legal questions of the activity of the
CMEA] (Moscow, 1977), pp. 94–100 at p. 97.
105. See, for an expression of this view in diplomatic terms, *Lumea* (Bucharest), nr. 24, June
15–21, 1979, p. 14.
106. See, *e.g.*, the frank ideas and proposals of Sandorski, *op. cit.*, *supra*, note 92, pp. 151–154.
In contrast hereto, Valki, *loc. cit.*, *supra*, note 97, pp. 84 *et seq.*; O. Bogomolov, 'Fruitful
Cooperation', *International Affairs* (Moscow), 1980, no. 7, p. 67; Kröger, *op. cit.*, *supra*, note
19, pp. 170–171.
107. *Cf.* Kupper, *loc. cit.*, *supra*, note 24, p. 796. However, the Soviet lawyer Usenko
considered the adoption of resolutions by majority vote already possible, under present-day
conditions; when some of the Member States expressed their opposition without, however,
declaring that they were interested. Such a case may arise if a State desires to express its stand
towards a resolution, but does not wish to block its adoption. 'Under this variant [of voting] a
resolution may be adopted by a majority of votes and applies to all member countries of the
Council.' Usenko observes that this possibility is rather theoretical, because in the practical
functioning of the CMEA organs, the Member States join the majority in such cases. (Usenko,
op. cit., *supra*, note 59, pp. 214–215.) It has to be noted, however, that the 1979 amendment
introduced into the last sub-paragraph of paragraph 3 of Article IV of the CMEA Charter, may
be interpreted as an official removal of this 'theoretical' possibility, since this amendment seems
to prescribe an explicit vote in favour of the adoption of a resolution in order to create legal
effects for the Member States concerned; see *supra*, note 89.
108. Seiffert, *Grundriss, op. cit.*, *supra*, note 75, p. 107; Szawlowski, *loc. cit.*, *supra*, note 100,
p. 151; Kröger, *op. cit.*, *supra*, note 19, p. 170; Tokareva, *op. cit.*, *supra*, note 18, p. 117.
109. For approximately two decades the CMEA has known the practice of so-called 'protocol
notices' ['*Protokollnotizen*' or '*Protokollvermerke*'], which seem to have much in common with
reservations, without, however, the traditional legal effects of reservations; 'protocol notices'
are not legally binding, and do not affect the contents and legal effects of resolutions. The
States have used them, *inter alia*, to explain their reasons for a certain attitude (for instance, no
interest), or to explain their intentions. See A. Kohout, 'K povaze a režimu nejdůležitějších
právních aktů přijímaných v rámci Rady vzájemné hospodářské pomoci' [On the character and
régime of the main legal acts adopted in the framework of the Council for Mutual Economic
Assistance], *Studie z mezinárodního práva* (Prague), 1980, vol. 15, pp. 59, 78; Rüster, *op. cit.*,
supra, note 81. pp. 37–38.
110. This could be explained by the alleged Soviet proposal to replace the unanimity principle
by a majority principle in the CMEA decision-making process; see W. Seiffert, 'Die Rechtsent
wicklung im RGW; 30 Jahre Comecon', *Deutschland-Archiv*, 1979, no. 2, p. 155; Kupper, *loc.
cit.*, *supra*, note 24, p. 796; D. Ghermani, 'Rumanien und der RGW', *Wissenschaftlicher Dienst
Südosteuropa*, 1978, no. 7, p. 190 (see also, Jens Reuter's article in the same journal at p. 192).
111. See also section 4.1., *infra*, p. 624.
112. See, *inter alia*, Ustor, *loc. cit.*, *supra*, note 51, p. 227; E. T. Usenko in his introduction to:
Pravovye voprosy deiatel'nosti SEV, *op. cit.*, *supra*, note 104, p. 5; *cf.* Szász, *op. cit.*, *supra*,
note 52, p. 84.
113. See, *inter alia*, Seiffert, *Grundriss, op. cit.*, *supra*, note 75, p. 89.
114. L. Rüster, 'O nekotorykh aspektakh rekomendatsii SEV kak pravovogo instituta' [On
some aspects of CMEA recommendations as legal institutions], in *Pravovye voprosy deiatel'nosti
SEV*, *op. cit.*, *supra*, note 104, pp. 100–114 at pp. 104–105.
115. Rüster, *op. cit.*, *supra*, note 81, pp. 37–40. The same author expressed similar views in
Kröger, *op. cit.*, *supra*, note 19, p. 177. *Cf.* Kohout, *loc. cit.*, *supra*, note 109, pp. 59 *et. seq.*,
pp. 78–79.

674

116. Rüster, *op. cit.*, *supra*, note 81, pp. 38–40. *Cf.* his even more strictly formulated suggestions in Kröger, *op. cit.*, *supra*, note 19, p. 177. *Cf.* also Articles 19–23 of the Vienna Convention on the Law of Treaties.

117. This result could be achieved only after the amendments to the CMEA Charter had been agreed upon in 1979, after which time Romania seemed to lose its interest in the problem of the legal regulation of reservations. In order to illustrate this with an example, one may point to the fact that, before 1979, it was reportedly impossible to reach agreement on the question whether a reservation made during the adoption of a recommendation in a CMEA organ should be repeated at the national acceptance of it in order to be valid. Only Romania was firmly against this construction, but abandoned its opposition to it shortly after the approval of the 1979 amendments to the CMEA Charter. This may illustrate at the same time why, during all the negotiations on the problem of reservations, the delegations of several other CMEA countries are said to have had the strong impression that the problem was only used as an instrument, without having a substantial practical content in itself.

118. One piece of information is an official Romanian proposal concerning reservations, made in 1976, which reads as follows: 'In exceptional cases, when the full consent of all interested countries cannot be achieved about individual provisions of a resolution (document) to be adopted by a CMEA organ, the resolution (document) may be adopted with a reservation by one or several countries concerning individual provisions of such a resolution (document). However, such a reservation must not be incompatible with object and purposes of the resolution. The reservation shall be fixed in the text of the resolution of the CMEA organ'.

119. The document is said to have been drafted as a (non-binding) guideline. In the context of the system of CMEA resolutions, however, it more probably has the character of a (binding) decision.

120. *Cf.* also Rüster, *op. cit.*, *supra*, note 81, pp. 39–40.

121. Section II, 10 of the Statute on the CMEA Standard. See on Standards in general, section 4.6., *infra*, p. 633.

122. Article III, 2(a) of the CMEA Charter; 'Recommendations and decisions are adopted by way of *postanovlenii*', as has been stated by Usenko; see Usenko, *op. cit.*, *supra*, note 59, p. 208.

123. In German, 'Übereinkunft'; in Russian, 'dogovor'ennost'.

124. In German, 'Abgestimmter Vorschlag'; in Russian, 'soglasovannoe predlozhenie'.

125. In German, 'Endgültige Abstimmung'; in Russian, 'okonchatel'noe soglasovanie'.

126. See, for an example, Kemper, *op. cit.*, *supra*, note 63, pp. 107–108. See also L. Rüster, 'Zur Entwicklung der Rechtsformen der Tätigkeit des RGW', *Staat und Recht*, 1977, no. 1, pp. 37–38.

127. Tokareva, *op. cit.*, *supra*, note 18, p. 70.

128. The Secretariat has been charged with sending certified copies of the protocols of the sessions of CMEA organs to *all* Member States, and not only to the countries to which the recommendations have been addressed. This is connected with the right of non-interested Member States to join the recommendations adopted by the other Member States at a later phase (Article IV, 3 of the CMEA Charter); Usenko, *op. cit.*, *supra*, note 59, p. 221.

129. In this study, the term 'adoption' is used to indicate the adoption of resolutions by CMEA organs and the term 'acceptance' to indicate the acceptance of recommendations by the interested Member States through national incorporation.

130. Wasilkowski, *loc. cit.*, *supra*, note 95, pp. 133–134.

131. Rüster, *loc. cit.*, *supra*, note 114, pp. 101–102.

132. Usenko, *op. cit.*, *supra*, note 59, p. 221.

133. This obligation is based on the generally accepted interpretation of Article IV, 1 of the CMEA Charter which, since 1979, reads as follows: 'Recommendations shall be adopted on questions of economic and scientific-technical co-operation. Recommendations shall be communicated to the Member Countries of the Council for consideration.

The implementation by the Member Countries of the Council of the recommendations accepted by them shall be carried out by decisions of the governments or of other competent organs of these countries in conformity with their legislation.' In 1979 this provision was amended by adding the word 'other' to its last sentence, a mere grammatical adaptation.

134. See, *e.g.*, rule 25 of the Rules of Procedure for the Session of the CMEA. Practice, however, shows examples of deviation from this 60 days' term, see Szász, *op. cit.*, *supra*, note 52, at p. 82, note 7 together with p. 85. The recommendation itself may also provide for a prolongation of this term, for instance in cases where the contents of the recommendation concerned require action by the national legislative organs, see Usenko, *op. cit.*, *supra*, note 59, pp. 221–222.

135. Some writers have defended more far-reaching obligations. The Czechoslovak lawyer Kohout, for instance, is of the opinion that the adoption of a recommendation by a CMEA organ not only creates the above-mentioned procedural obligations for the Member States, but also the obligation to refrain from all actions which might 'deprive the recommendation of its object and purpose'. This obligation should also apply to the non-interested Member States, which did not participate in the adoption of the recommendation. Kohout justifies his opinion with a reference to the elaboration of the interest principle as laid down in §4 of section 17 of the Comprehensive Programme, Kohout, *loc. cit.*, *supra*, note 109, pp. 28, 74.

136. See section 5.3., *infra*, p. 642.

137. Rüster, *op. cit.*, *supra*, note 81, p. 55.

138. Wasilkowski, *Zalecenia*, *op. cit.*, *supra*, note 84, p. 352; *cf.* Usenko, *op. cit.*, *supra*, note 59, p. 233.

139. See *inter alia*, Seiffert, *Grundriss*, *op. cit.*, *supra*, note 75, pp. 89–90; Usenko, *op. cit.*, *supra*, note 59, pp. 223 *et seq.*; Caillot, *op. cit.*, *supra*, note 82, pp. 94–99; Ustor, *loc. cit.*, *supra*, note 51, pp. 220 *et seq.*; Ficzere, *loc. cit.*, *supra*, note 29, p. 48; Rüster, *op. cit.*, *supra*, note 81, pp. 46–57. A decisive influence on this discussion has been exercised by the Soviet jurist E. T. Usenko, *inter alia*, in his 'O iuridicheskoi prirode rekomendatsii Soveta Ekonomicheskoi Vzaimopomoshchi' [On the legal nature of the recommendations of the Council for Mutual Economic Assistance], *Sovetskoe Gosudarstvo i Pravo*, 1963, no. 12, pp. 86–94.

140. However, that does not take away the fact that different notions about the legal nature of accepted recommendations might have substantive consequences, especially in the fields of the admissibility of reservations to and the denunciation of recommendations. See section 3.2.2., *supra*, p. 623 and: Rüster, *op. cit.*, *supra*, note 81, pp. 37–40, 70–73; Ustor, *loc. cit.*, *supra*, note 51, p. 227; Seiffert, *Grundriss*, *op. cit.*, *supra*, note 75, p. 89.

141. Rüster, *loc. cit.*, *supra*, note 126, pp. 39–40; Kröger, *op. cit.*, *supra*, note 19, p. 176.

142. *Osnovnye Dokumenty SEV*, Tom II, *op. cit.*, *supra*, note 5, p. 184; *Wirtschaftliche und wissenschaftlich-technische Zusammenarbeit*, *op. cit.*, *supra*, note 5, p. 154.

143. Usenko, *op. cit.*, *supra*, note 59, pp. 235–236.

144. Kröger, *op. cit.*, *supra*, note 19, p. 176. In this same publication it is also argued that deviating individual arrangements are only warranted when necessitated by the concrete conditions of specific cases, see p. 176; see also Rüster, *op. cit.*, *supra*, note 81, p. 66.

145. Rüster, *op. cit.*, *supra*, note 81, p. 67.

146. De Fiumel, *loc. cit.*, *supra*, note 50, p. 107.

147. Usenko, *op. cit.*, *supra*, note 59, pp. 227 *et seq.*; Usenko, *loc. cit.*, *supra*, note 139, pp. 92 *et seq.*; *cf.* Sandorski, *op. cit.*, *supra*, note 92, p. 154.

148. W. Spröte & H. Wünsche, *Sozialistische ökonomische Organisationen* (Berlin, G.D.R., 1972), p. 56; Wasilkowski distinguishes five types of recommendations: recommendations on purposes and principles of co-operation, on the conditions of co-operation, on the co-ordination of national economic plans, on the specialisation of production and on the conclusion of international agreements, see Wasilkowski, *loc. cit.*, *supra*, note 13, pp. 307–310.

149. Besides 'to recommend . . .' CMEA organs also used wording such as 'it is considered to be appropriate . . .', 'it is deemed to be necessary' or 'the member countries of the CMEA are requested . . .', see Rüster, *op. cit.*, *supra*, note 81, p. 61.

150. The original Russian title is: 'Doklad o povyshenii effektivnosti rekomendatsii Soveta Ekonomicheskoi Vzaimopomoshchi'. Unfortunately, this important report has not been published. Nevertheless, several parts of it are known from other sources, *inter alia*, from Rüster, *op. cit.*, *supra*, note 81. The Report was added as the 5th annex to the protocol of the 78th session of the Executive Committee (November 1976).

151. Kemper, *op. cit.*, *supra*, note 63, p. 76. A problem which still has to be solved concerns the character of those resolutions on economic and scientific-technical co-operation which do not contain such a formula.

152. Rüster, *op. cit.*, *supra*, note 81, p. 60.

153. This stipulation ended the practice, developed in the CMEA, of addressing recommendations not only to the Member States, but also to organs, delegations or representatives of the countries, see Rüster, *op. cit.*, *supra*, note 81, p. 58.

154. Szawlowski, *loc. cit.*, *supra*, note 100, p. 153.

155. The Comprehensive Programme is an example of it. See also Rüster, *op. cit.*, *supra*, note 81, p. 57.

156. Ustor, *loc. cit.*, *supra*, note 51, p. 241. In December 1980 the same Commission adopted 300 Standards, see *Neues Deutschland*, December 13–14, 1980 p. 2. See also note 208.

157. Kemper, *op. cit.*, *supra*, note 63, p. 76, note 7. Another source reveals that between 1956 and 1973 the standing commissions of the CMEA adopted 5,300 'decisions'; in view of the

context, the reference is undoubtedly to recommendations, see I. Vörös, 'Pravovye problemy spetsializatsii i kooperirovaniia proizvodstva v ekonomicheskoi integratsii stran-chlenov SEV' [Legal problems of specialisation and co-operation in production in the economic integration of the CMEA member countries], in *Soveshchaniiu, op. cit., supra*, note 29, p. 165. See also *Sodruzhestvo stran-chlenov SEV; Politiko-ekonomicheskii slovar'-spravochnik* [The community of CMEA member countries; a political-economical dictionary-handbook] (Moscow, 1980), pp. 173, 174. The quantity of resolutions does not of course say anything about the quality of the co-operation, but it might nevertheless give an idea of CMEA activities.

158. Kemper, *op. cit., supra*, note 63, pp. 81–82; Usenko, *op. cit., supra*, note 59, pp. 245–246.
159. Usenko, *op. cit., supra*, note 59, p. 208.
160. *Ibidem*, pp. 239–243; Rüster, *op. cit., supra*, note 81, pp. 73–75; Kemper, *op. cit., supra*, note 63, pp. 91–94.
161. One has to bear in mind, however, that the characterisation of agreements as CMEA resolutions is not an absolute one, as will be seen in this section.
162. See, *inter alia*, Article II, 4 of the statute of the Committee for Co-operation in the Field of Planning Activity and section I, 5(b) of the statute of the Bureau of this Committee.
163. Section II, 7 of the Session report 'Basic directions for the further improvement of the organisation of multilateral co-operation among CMEA member countries, and of the activity of the Council', added as the 7th annex to the protocol of the 32nd Session of the CMEA. The complete text has not (yet) been published, but several parts can be found in East European literature (*cf.* the remark in note 150). See Rüster, *op. cit., supra*, note 81, p. 87.
164. Especially, Article II, 4(d), Article VII, 4(a) and Article X, 2(d) and (e) of the CMEA Charter.
165. Seiffert, *loc. cit., supra*, note 110, p. 154.
166. L. Franz & M. Kemper, 'Übereinkunft und endgültige Abstimmung – Entscheidungs-formen in den Organen des RGW', *Staat und Recht*, 1979, no. 8, p. 715.
167. H. Bär & M. Kemper, 'Die rechtliche Regelung der Planungszusammenarbeit der Mitgliedsländer des RGW im Überblick', in: Kemper, *op. cit., supra*, note 39, pp. 44–47.
168. Rüster, *op. cit., supra*, note 81, p. 88; O. Kampa a.o., 'Sozialistische ökonomische Integration und Rechtsentwicklung', *Staat und Recht*, 1978, no. 10, p. 940; Kohout, *loc. cit., supra*, note 109, pp. 58, 78.
169. Kemper, *op. cit., supra*, note 63, p. 79.
170. Menzhinskii, *op. cit., supra*, note 57, p. 68. One example of such a specific procedure is the admission of a State to membership of the CMEA, which is only possible by a *decision* of the Session (Article II, 2 of the CMEA Charter).
171. See note 163, quoted in Rüster, *op. cit., supra*, note 81, p. 89.
172. Section II, 7 of the said Report.
173. Article II, 4(d), Article VII, 4(a) and Article X, 2(d) and (e).
174. See, *inter alia*, P. J. G. Kapteyn & P. VerLoren van Themaat, *Introduction to the Law of the European Communities after the accession of new Member States* (London etc., 1973), pp. 119–123.
175. Rüster, *op. cit., supra*, note 81, p. 89; Ficzere, *loc. cit., supra*, note 29, p. 49; Menzhinskii, *op. cit., supra*, note 57, p. 67; Franz & Kemper, *loc. cit., supra*, note 166, p. 717.
176. Rüster, *op. cit., supra*, note 81, p. 89; Kohout, *loc. cit., supra*, note 109, pp. 57–58, 78.
177. Vorotnikov & Lebin, *op. cit., supra*, note 57, p. 37: 'When recommendations and decisions are legal acts of the CMEA, agreements are the acts of the countries participating in the agreement'.
178. Article II, 4(d), Article VII, 4(a) and Art. X, 2(e) of the CMEA Charter in the 1979 version. See also Rüster, *op. cit., supra*, note 81, p. 90.
179. One more difference, in addition to those already mentioned, ensues from the fact that agreements do not constitute legal acts of the CMEA. Consequently, the procedural rules of the CMEA concerning the decision-making process, including the interest principle, are not applied to agreements; Rüster, *op. cit., supra*, note 81, p. 90 and Article IV, 4 of the CMEA Charter. Though the legal basis of it is unknown, it is contended sometimes that non-participating States may join agreements at a later phase on terms to be agreed upon; Menzhinskii, *op. cit., supra*, note 57, p. 67.
180. Article II, 4 of the Statute of the Planning Committee might serve as an example: 'Agreement reached within the framework of the Committee on questions within its competence for which recommendations have not been adopted shall be implemented in the Member Countries of the Council in accordance with the procedures established in these countries.'
181. See, *inter alia*, Tokareva, *op. cit., supra*, note 18, p. 116.
182. Seiffert, *loc. cit., supra*, note 110, p. 155.

183. *Ibidem*; see for instance the provision quoted in note 180 which was adopted in 1972 with the approval of Romania.

184. *Supra*, p. 628.

185. See, on the Conferences, section 3.1.2., *supra*, p. 617.

186. Some authors assume that all the principal CMEA organs (except the Secretariat) are empowered to adopt co-ordinated proposals; see, *inter alia*, Kohout, *loc. cit.*, *supra*, note 109, pp. 50–51, 76.

187. Kemper, *op. cit.*, *supra*, note 63, pp. 85–86.

188. Article III, b of the Statute of the Conference on Legal Questions. The official German text is: The Conference 'kann (. . .) die Abstimmung von Fragen vornehmen, die in ihre Zuständigkeit fallen. Dabei ist davon auszugehen, dass die von der Beratung abgestimmten Vorschläge zu den betreffenden Fragen in den Mitgliedsländern des Rates in Übereinstimmung mit der in diesen Ländern festgelegten Ordnung verwirklicht werden', see *Grunddokumente des RGW*, *op. cit.*, *supra*, note 5, p. 205.

189. Rüster, *op. cit.*, *supra*, note 81, p. 77.

190. See, *inter alia*, Article II, H of the Statute of the Conference on Legal Questions.

191. Usenko, *op. cit.*, *supra*, note 59, p. 245; Ficzere, *loc. cit.*, *supra*, note 29, pp. 48–49 who submits that the implementation of co-ordinated proposals falls within the discretion of the States concerned; Kohout, *loc. cit.*, *supra*, note 109, pp. 50–52, 76.

192. See Rüster, *op. cit.*, *supra*, note 81, pp. 77–78; Kemper, *op. cit.*, *supra*, note 63, pp. 85–87.

193. Kemper, *op. cit.*, *supra*, note 63, p. 87.

194. See section 4.3., *supra*, p. 628.

195. *Inter alia* laid down in the 'Report on the raising of the effectiveness of CMEA recommendations', see *supra*, note 150.

196. Article VIII, 3(c) and Article IX, 3(c).

197. See, *inter alia*, rule 39 of the Model Rules of Procedure of the Standing Commissions and rule 30 of the Rules of Procedure of the Committee on Material-Technical Supply.

198. See, *inter alia*, rule 35 of the Rules of Procedure of the Committee on Material-Technical Supply.

199. Rüster, *op. cit.*, *supra*, note 81, p. 86.

200. The same applies to organs of other socialist international organisations with similar powers.

201. Franz & Kamper, *loc. cit.*, *supra*, note 166, p. 719.

202. Rüster, *op. cit.*, *supra*, note 81, p. 86; Kemper, *op. cit.*, *supra*, note 63, p. 88; Franz & Kemper, *loc. cit.*, *supra*, note 166, p. 719.

203. See, *inter alia*, rule 44 of the Model Rules of Procedure of the Standing Commissions.

204. Seiffert, *loc. cit.*, *supra*, note 110, p. 154.

205. Romania is not a party to this Convention and has made a special declaration about its attitude towards CMEA Standards, see *Osnovnye Dokumenty SEV*, Tom II, *op. cit.*, *supra*, note 5, p. 277.

206. Rüster, *op. cit.*, *supra*, note 81, p. 80. Though it is sometimes contended that Standards form the contents of CMEA recommendations (see H. Echter, 'Standardisierung von Erzeugnissen im Prozess gemeinsamer Planungstätigkeit – Rechtsfragen', in Kemper, *op. cit.*, *supra*, note 39, pp. 207, 209), this is not confirmed by the rules governing the adoption of Standards. Section II, 10 of the Statute on the CMEA Standard states that the 'confirmation' of Standards is achieved by the 'adoption of a corresponding decision' ('reshenie'). Köhler characterises Standards as 'a new type of recommendations (. . .), the legal effects of which have been determined in a special international treaty', see A. Köhler, 'Weiterentwicklung von Rechtsformen der Tätigkeit des RGW bei der Organisierung der Spezialisierung und Kooperation', *Staat und Recht*, 1977, no. 8, p. 837. See also W. Claus, 'Zur Bedeutung der Standards als Rechtsakte im RGW für die Ost-West-Kooperation', *Osteuropa-Wirtschaft*, 1980, no. 4, pp. 287–291.

207. On the process of standardisation in the CMEA, see P. Joseph, 'COMECON Integration: the Place of Standardization', in *Comecon: Progress and Prospects*, *op. cit.*, *supra*, note 3, pp. 59–74; S. I. Stepanenko, *Mezhdunarodnye Standarty* [International Standards] (Moscow, 1979), pp. 10–71.

208. Rüster, *op. cit.*, *supra*, note 81, p. 79; see, however, section II, 10 of the Statute on the CMEA Standard. From 1975 to December 1980, 2,700 Standards were adopted, see *Neues Deutschland*, December 13–14, 1980, p. 2.

209. See Echter, *loc. cit.*, *supra*, note 206, pp. 201–211; Stepanenko, *op. cit.*, *supra*, note 207, pp. 34–55.

210. Article VI, 1 of the CMEA Charter.

211. Article VI, 5(a) of the CMEA Charter.

212. Reports of other organs – for instance the Planning Committee – also play a role in this field, see, *inter alia*, the communiqué of the 33rd meeting of the Session (June 1979), in *Neues Deutschland*, June 30–July 1, 1979, p. 6.

213. For instance, the fulfilment of obligations entered into in the framework of the co-ordination of national economic plans, see Rybakov, *op. cit.*, *supra*, note 39, p. 136, and, *inter alia*, the communiqué of the 31st meeting of the Session (June 1977), in: *Vneshniaia politika Sovetskogo Soiuza i mezhdunarodnye otnosheniia – 1977 god; Sbornik dokumentov* [The foreign policy of the Soviet Union and international relations – 1977; Collection of documents] (Moscow, 1978), pp. 123–127 at p. 126. Several examples of such broad supervision are offered by the communiqués of the Session meetings. For instance, at the 33rd meeting of the Session 'the implementation of the five long-term target-programmes of co-operation' was considered.

214. Section IV, 28 of the 'Report on the raising of the effectiveness . . .', see, *supra*, note 150.

215. This is discussed in greater detail in section 6.2., *infra*, p. 658.

216. Before the adoption of the 1979 amendments, the passage of Article VII, 4(a) of the CMEA Charter only contained an obligation for the Executive Committee to 'carry out systematic supervision of the fulfilment by the Member Countries of the Council of the obligations arising from the recommendations of organs of the Council accepted by them'.

217. See section 5.2., *infra*, p. 640.

218. Thus the opinion of the Polish lawyer H. de Fiumel, in *L'intégration en Europe: la CEE et le COMECON* (Brussels/Louvain, 1976), pp. 142–143.

219. The passage on agreements was added in 1979. It must be assumed that the corresponding provisions in the Statute on the CMEA Secretariat have also been amended in this sense; such amendments have not yet been published, and the old text of this Statute has been used here. (After the present study was concluded, the text of the Statute on the CMEA Secretariat as amended in 1979 was published by Tokareva in the 1981 collection of documents quoted in note 5 (pp. 74–77). The text of Article I, 1(g) has now been adapted to the new situation following the 1979 amendments of the CMEA Charter, in that it now includes agreements and multilateral treaties.)

220. Article I, 2(c) of the Statute on the CMEA Secretariat.

221. Article I, 2(a) of the Statute on the CMEA Secretariat.

222. Article I, 1(g) of the Statute on the CMEA Secretariat.

223. Article X, 2(c) of the Charter together with Article I, 2(c) of the Statute on the CMEA Secretariat.

224. See the structure scheme in the book published by the CMEA Secretary, Faddejew, *op. cit.*, *supra*, note 22, pp. 82–83.

225. Article I, 4 of the Statute on the Committee for Co-operation in the field of Planning Activity; Article II, 9 of the Statute on the Committee for Scientific and Technical Co-operation; Article I, 10 of the Statute on the Committee for Co-operation in the field of Material-Technical Supply. As an example, reference may be made to the co-ordination of planning: the Planning Committee regularly prepares a programme for co-ordination activities which has to be approved by the Executive Committee (or the Session). After that approval, the Committee supervises the bilateral co-ordination of economic plans in order to assure the latter's compatibility with the multilateral programme adopted by the Executive Committee (or Session), see M. Engert & M. Reich, *Concentration, specialization and cooperation in the CMEA-region* (discussion paper submitted to the Third Session of the Workshop on East-West European Economic Interaction held in Vienna, April 1977); see also Rybakov, *op. cit.*, *supra*, note 39, pp. 132 *et seq.*

226. Article I, 3 of the Statute on the Bureau of the Committee of the CMEA for Co-operation in the field of Planning Activity. (By amendment of March 1981 the scope of this provision has been enlarged considerably. The amendment was published after the present study was completed.)

227. See also section 4.3., *supra*, p. 628.

228. Rule 22, 4 of the Rules of Procedure of the Planning Committee; rule 16, 4 of the Rules of Procedure of the Committee for Scientific-Technical Co-operation; rule 15, e of the Rules of Procedure of the Committee for Co-operation in the field of Material-Technical Supply.

229. Article I, 4 of the Statute on the Standing Commission on Electric Energy might serve as an example: the Commission shall 'exercise systematic supervision of the fulfilment by the Member Countries of the Council of the obligations arising out of recommendations of Council organs on energetics accepted by them; it shall regularly consider at its sessions the information of the delegations of the countries in the Commission on the course of the implementation of

those recommendations and, if necessary, work out measures making for their implementation; it shall determine the procedure and terms (periods) for the submission of the said information by the delegations of the countries in the Commission'. All the Statutes on the other standing commissions contain similar provisions, limited to their fields of activity.

230. Until 1979 this was the case with agreements which were subjected to the same supervisory régime as recommendations. In 1979 this resulted in corresponding amendments to the CMEA Charter.

231. See section 4.4., *supra*, p. 631.

232. See, *inter alia*, Article II, h of the Statute on the CMEA Conference on Legal Questions.

233. See also section 5.3., *infra*, p. 642.

234. See, *inter alia*, rule 22, e of the Rules of Procedure of the Conference of the Heads of Price Agencies of the CMEA Member Countries.

235. Rule 22, e of the Rules of Procedure of the Conference of the Heads of Labour Organs of the CMEA Member Countries.

236. Rule 22, e.

237. *Idem*.

238. See, *inter alia*, Article IV, 5 of the Statute on the Conference on Legal Questions.

239. See, *inter alia*, Article IV, 6 of the Statute on the Conference on Legal Questions.

240. See also section 5.3., *infra*, p. 642.

241. See also section 5.4.3., *infra*, p. 649.

242. Usenko characterises these committees as 'collective organs of the socialist States concerned', see Usenko, *op. cit.*, *supra*, note 59, p. 56.

243. H. Winter, *Institutionalisierung, Methoden und Umfang der Integration im RGW* (Stuttgart, 1976), p. 36; Seiffert, *Grundriss, op. cit.*, *supra*, note 75, pp. 93–97.

244. Section 16, 4 of the Compr. Progr. Although not directly referring to the bilateral economic committees, a new function of the CMEA, as laid down in the CMEA Charter in 1979, is also of relevance: the CMEA 'shall assist the Member Countries of the Council in the co-ordination of their multilateral co-operation in the framework of the Council and the bilateral co-operation of these countries, by ensuring the fullest possible exchange of information on the most important measures worked out and elaborated by them on a bilateral basis in order to carry out the measures of the long term programmes of multilateral co-operation' (Article III, 1(e) of the CMEA Charter). Undoubtedly this new provision originated from dissatisfaction with the co-ordination of multilateral CMEA co-operation and economic co-operation on a bilateral level between the Member States. This dissatisfaction was expressed, *inter alia*, by the Session in its report 'Basic Directions' in 1978 (see note 163).

245. See, *inter alia*, Tokareva, *op. cit.*, *supra*, note 18, pp. 142–143; an example is Article 2 of the agreement between the U.S.S.R. and the G.D.R. (1966) which states: 'The Government Commission of Equal Representation shall be guided in its activity by the principles of the CMEA Charter as well as by the principles of the present agreement and shall take into account the recommendations and decisions of the CMEA in its work.' The text of this agreement and of the commission statute attached to it has been published by A. Uschakow as an annex to his article 'Institutionelle Formen der Wirtschaftsbeziehungen zwischen der DDR und der UdSSR', *Deutschland-Archiv*, 1980, no. 5, pp. 523–527.

246. Tokareva, *op. cit.*, *supra*, note 18, p. 149: 'The significance of the inter-governmental commissions within the system of the other organisational-legal instruments of integration is *extremely large . . .*' (italics added).

247. See for that, *inter alia*, the literature mentioned in note 49.

248. E. Faude, ed., *Sozialistische ökonomische Integration* (Berlin, G.D.R., 1977), p. 87.

249. See, *inter alia*, the extensive press release on the 28th session of the commission of the U.S.S.R. and the G.D.R., *Neues Deutschland*, July 1, 1981, p. 6.

250. Tokareva, *op. cit.*, *supra*, note 18, p. 147; Faude, *op. cit.*, *supra*, note 248, p. 87; Seiffert, *Grundriss, op. cit.*, *supra*, note 75, p. 96.

251. Information based on interviews with Eastern European experts. As far as the commission U.S.S.R.-G.D.R. is concerned, this competence might be based on Article 3, 9 of the above-mentioned agreement (see note 245), which states that the commission 'shall supervise the implementation of the agreements concluded between the contracting parties on economic and scientific technical co-operation and of its own decisions, and shall take the measures which are necessary for their implementation'.

252. Tokareva, *op. cit.*, *supra*, note 18, p. 146.

253. See, *inter alia*, Article 8 of the agreement, establishing the committee Poland-G.D.R. in *Dokumente zur Aussenpolitik der Regierung der Deutschen Demokratischen Republik*, Band VIII (Berlin, G.D.R., 1961), pp. 423–428.

254. H. de Fiumel, 'Les accords de spécialisation et de coopération dans la production conclus entre les entreprises des pays membres du CAEM', *Polish Yearbook of International Law*, vol. V, 1972–1973, pp. 37–38, 40.

255. Article VI, 1 of the Moscow Convention, see section 5.4.3., *infra*, p. 649.

256. Verbal information from East European experts.

257. Tokareva, *op. cit.*, *supra*, note 18, p. 189.

258. See, however, section 5.2., *infra*, p. 640.

259. See, *inter alia*, section 2.3. and 3.1.1., *supra*, p. 611, resp. p. 615.

260. P. M. Alampiev, O. T. Bogomolov & Y. S. Shiryaev, *A New Approach to Economic Integration* (Moscow, 1974), pp. 76–77; H. Hutschenreuter, 'Regierungsabkommen und Ministervereinbarungen im System vertraglicher Rechtsformen der internationalen Spezialisierung und Kooperation der Produktion im Bereich des RGW', *Staat und Recht*, 1979, no. 6, pp. 512–531 at pp. 514–515; Rüster, *loc. cit.*, *supra*, note 126, p. 41; De Fiumel, *loc. cit.*, *supra*, note 50, pp. 109, 117. See also N. V. Mironov, *Pravovye formy sotsialisticheskoi integratsii; Mezhdunarodnye mezhvedomstvennye soglasheniia* [Legal forms of socialist integration; The international inter-departmental agreements] (Moscow, 1977), pp. 21–59; V. Keselý, 'Politickoprávne aspekty medzinárodnej zmluvy, základnej formy vzťahov členských krajín RVHP' [Political and legal aspects of international treaties; the basic form of the relations of the CMEA member countries], *Studie z mezinárodního práva* (Prague), vol. 15, 1980, pp. 81–113.

261. Kampa a.o., *loc. cit.*, *supra*, note 168, p. 939; Usenko, *op. cit.*, *supra*, note 59, p. 233.

262. Usenko correctly states that these treaties lose their connection with the organisation in the framework of which they have been drafted after their signature by the States, see Usenko, *op. cit.*, *supra*, note 59, p. 233.

263. Rüster, *op. cit.*, *supra*, note 81, p. 90.

264. Article VII, 4(a) of the CMEA Charter as amended in 1979.

265. The corresponding Article II, 4(d) of the Charter was not amended in this sense in 1979. Similarly, the scope of Article X, 2(e) – providing for the supervisory functions of the Secretariat – was not extended to the treaties in question either.

266. Article II, 4(c) of the CMEA Charter.

267. Article III, 1(e) of the CMEA Charter as amended in 1979. See also note 244.

268. See on these programmes, *inter alia*, Pekshev, *op. cit.*, *supra*, note 39.

269. See also section 5.1.5., *supra*, p. 639.

270. See for these institutions, section 3.1.1., *supra*, p. 615.

271. Kemper, *op. cit.*, *supra*, note 63, p. 66.

272. *Ibidem*; Rüster, *op. cit.*, *supra*, note 81, pp. 107–111; see also section IV of the Session report 'Basic directions . . .', see *supra*, note 163.

273. Section IV, 1(a) of the report 'Basic directions . . .', see *supra*, note 163.

274. Ustor, *loc. cit.*, *supra*, note 51, pp. 247–248; Articles III and IV of the Agreement between the CMEA and Yugoslavia (September 17, 1964).

275. Article II, 4(d) of the Charter as amended in 1979.

276. Article II, 4(b) and (c) of the Charter.

277. See, *inter alia*, Rule 25 of the Rules of Procedure of the Session, Rule 23 of the Rules of Procedure of the Executive Committee and Rule 33 of the Model Rules of Procedure of the Standing Commissions. This undertaking only concerns the interested Member States, see Usenko, *op. cit.*, *supra*, note 59, p. 222.

278. Relating to Standing Commissions: 'the delegations of the other countries in the Commission'.

279. See the Rules quoted in note 277. Rule 23 of the Rules of Procedure of the Executive Committee might serve as an example; the relevant part of it reads as follows:

> 'Recommendations shall be communicated to the Member Countries of the Council for consideration. The implementation by the countries of the Executive Committee's recommendations accepted by them shall be carried out by decisions of the governments or other competent organs of these countries in conformity with their legislation. Within 60 days from the day of signing the protocol of the session of the Executive Committee, a Member Country of the Council shall inform the Secretary of the Council on the results of the consideration by the government or other competent organs of the country of the recommendations of the Executive Committee. The Secretary of the Council shall notify the other Member Countries of the Council thereof without delay.'

280. The term 'preliminary supervision' is used to indicate that this phase of supervision does not include the implementation of the resolutions themselves.

281. Article IV, 1 of the Charter and the Rules quoted in note 277.

681

282. See, *inter alia*, the 'Declaration on Principles of International Law concerning friendly relations and co-operation among States in accordance with the Charter of the United Nations' (Resolution 2625 (XXV) of the UN General Assembly). The text of this declaration has been published, *inter alia*, in: I. Brownlie, ed., *Basic Documents in International Law*, 2nd ed. (Oxford, 1978), pp. 32–40 at p. 40.

283. See also Lauterpacht's separate opinion, appended to the 1955 Advisory Opinion on 'South-West Africa – Voting Procedure', *International Court of Justice Reports*, 1955, p. 120 ('Although there is no automatic obligation to accept fully a particular recommendation or series of recommendations, there is a legal obligation to act in good faith . . .').

284. See section 2.2., *supra*, p. 609.

285. Besides, reference should be made to the implied obligations for a State emanating from its mere membership of the CMEA: this requires behaviour in accordance with the realisation of the purposes of the CMEA.

286. K. Skubiszewski, 'Le Conseil d'Entraide Economique et ses Actes', *Annuaire Français de Droit International*, 1966, vol. XII, p. 566, relying upon Lauterpacht's separate opinion quoted in note 283. See also: K. Skubiszewski, 'Die Empfehlungen des RGW und ihre Auswirkungen', in: Wolff von Amerongen, *op. cit.*, *supra*, note 50, pp. 144, 145.

287. See, *inter alia*, Usenko, *op. cit.*, *supra*, note 59, p. 222: 'Voting by the representative of a State in the Council for the adoption of a recommendation does not bind the State, and it may reject it [the recommendation] after consideration within the country'. See also E. T. Usenko, '25 let mezhdunarodnoi organizatsii novogo tipa' [25 years of an international organisation of a new type], *Sovetskii Ezhegodnik Mezhdunarodnogo Prava*, 1974 (Moscow, 1976), p. 27. See also Article II, 4(d) of the Charter, which limits the obligation to supply information about the implementation of recommendations to nationally *accepted* recommendations; this is the interpretation generally adhered to, see, *inter alia*, Rüster, *op. cit.*, *supra*, note 81, p. 55.

288. See section 4.1., *supra*, p. 624; see also Szász, *op. cit.*, *supra*, note 52, p. 82.

289. See note 150.

290. See section 6.2., *infra*, p. 658. The conclusion arrived at does not deprive the reporting procedure in the 60 days' period of any real sense: The reporting procedure is intended, *inter alia*, (a) to inform the CMEA and its Member States in a quick and well-organised way about which international rights and obligations resulting from nationally accepted recommendations have been entered into by which Member States, and in relation to which other Member States, and (b) to enable the CMEA to exercise its registration and supervisory functions concerning the implementation of these recommendations.

291. For example, a recommendation concerning the delivery of crude oil by one Member State to other Member States becomes illusory if the selling State refuses to accept the recommendation.

292. See section 2.2., *supra*, p. 609.

293. Usenko, *op. cit.*, *supra*, note 59, p. 222. The same conclusion imposes itself in view of CMEA's principles of socialist internationalism, see section 2.2., *supra*, p. 609.

294. See, *inter alia*, the consultation and renegotiation procedure in section 5.4.2., *infra*, p. 648.

295. See Article II, 4 of the CMEA Charter.

296. This term indicates that the normative contents of non-binding recommendations can gain binding force only through national acts, see Skubiszewski, 'Die Empfehlungen', *loc. cit.*, *supra*, note 286, p. 144.

297. For a further analysis, see section 5.4.2., *infra*, p. 648.

298. See note 150.

299. Article II, 4(d) of the CMEA Charter as amended in 1979.

300. See section 4.2., *supra*, p. 628.

301. Article II, h of the Statute on the Conference on Legal Questions. The Statutes of the other Conferences contain similar clauses.

302. See Rüster, *op. cit.*, *supra*, note 81, p. 78.

303. Kemper, *op. cit.*, *supra*, note 63, p. 85.

304. See also section 5.1.4., *supra*, p. 637.

305. Article VII, 4(a) of the CMEA Charter as amended in 1979; see section 5.2., *supra*, p. 640.

306. See note 163.

307. Section III, 1 of the Report.

308. Approved in 1965; since 1969 this Procedure applies only to agreements concluded by CMEA States with third countries, see *Osnovnye Dokumenty SEV*, Tom II, *op. cit.*, *supra*, note 5, p. 412.

309. Approved in 1969.

310. See para. 2 together with para. 3 of the Procedure of 1963 and para. 1 together with para. 8 of the Procedure of 1969.

311. Verbal information from East European experts.

312. See on this terminology, *supra*, p. 14.

313. Section 5.4.2., *infra*, p. 648.

314. See also section 5.1.3., *supra*, p. 636.

315. See, *inter alia*, *L'intégration en Europe*, *op. cit.*, *supra*, note 218, pp. 142–143.

316. Verbal information from East European experts.

317. See section 5.1.1., *supra*, p. 634.

318. See note 150.

319. See *supra*, p. 14.

320. Section 4, 27 of the Report, see *supra*, note 150; see also Rüster, *op. cit.*, *supra*, note 81, p. 72.

321. *Idem.*

322. *Idem.*

323. Rüster, *op. cit.*, *supra*, note 81, pp. 72–73.

324. It only states that the question has to be dealt with by 'the representatives of the interested countries', without prescribing which framework has to be chosen. Usually, however, the CMEA organs will provide the best forum.

325. Section 4, 27 of the Report.

326. See section 5.1.4., *supra*, p. 637.

327. See, *inter alia*, Usenko, *loc. cit.*, *supra*, note 28, p. 24.

328. Compr. Progr., section 15, 3.

329. See also H. de Fiumel's and E. T. Usenko's comments in: *L'intégration en Europe*, *op. cit.*, *supra*, note 218, pp. 142–143.

330. See Caillot, *op. cit.*, *supra*, note 82, pp. 99–100.

331. Verbal information from East European experts.

332. J. Szilbereky, 'Desiat' let raboty pravovogo soveshchaniia SEV' [Ten years work of the CMEA legal conference], in *Soveshchaniiu*, *op. cit.*, *supra*, note 29, p. 9. About 'material responsibility' see section 6.2., *infra*, p. 658 and note 398.

333. *L'intégration en Europe*, *op. cit.*, *supra*, note 218, p. 143.

334. See, *inter alia*, B. W. Reutt, 'Rozstrzyganie sporów wynikających z odpowiedzialności majątkowej państw RWPG' [The settlement of disputes arising from the material responsibility of the CMEA States], in: H. de Fiumel, ed., *Problemy odpowiedzialności majątkowej państw RWPG* [Problems of the material responsibility of the CMEA States] (Wrocław/Warsaw etc. 1975), pp. 99–111 at pp. 103–111; H. de Fiumel, *Prawnomiędzynarodowa odpowiedzialność majątkowa państw* [The material responsibility of States under international law] (Wrocław/Warsaw etc. 1979), pp. 105–111, 132.

335. Verbal information from East European experts.

336. Ustor, *loc. cit.*, *supra*, note 51, p. 272.

337. A somewhat confusing term since this arbitration system has much in common with ordinary courts of law. *Cf.* H. Strohbach, 'Wesenszüge und Besonderheiten der Schiedsgerichtsbarkeit in den Mitgliedsländern des RGW' in Seiffert, *op. cit.*, *supra*, note 32, p. 188.

338. These disputes usually concern matters which are quite traditional in international practice, such as 'the determination of the nature of the contractual relations of the parties, the interpretation of the conditions of a contract concerning prices, quantity, quality of the goods, period of performance and other conditions, the contents of the trade terms concerned (f.o.b., c.i.f., c.a.f.), the meaning of the expressions, order of words, conceptions and terms used in a contract', see M. Rozenberg, 'Tolkovanie dogovora v praktike Vneshnetorgovoi arbitrazhnoi komissii pri TPP SSSR' [The interpretation of contracts in the practice of the Foreign trade arbitration commission attached to the Chamber of Commerce and Industry of the U.S.S.R.], *Vneshniaia Torgovlia*, 1981, no. 2, p. 40.

339. These arbitration boards are not State organs, but social institutions; they do not represent State authority nor do they have State competences. See H. Fellhauer & H. Strohbach, *Handbuch der internationalen Schiedsgerichtsbarkeit* (Berlin, G.D.R., 1969), p. 32.

340. Section 15, 9 of the Compr. Progr.

341. The Convention was approved by the Executive Committee in 1972 and entered into force in August 1973.

342. This jurisdiction ensued from Article 90 of the GCDG 1968.
343. Article I, 1 of the Moscow Convention.
344. Article I, 2 of the Moscow Convention.
345. Article I, 3 of the Moscow Convention.
346. Article III, 1 of the Moscow Convention. For other exceptions, see Article VI.
347. J. Juhász, 'Arbitrazh v SEV' [Arbitration in the CMEA], in: *Soveshchaniiu* . . ., *op. cit.*, *supra*, note 29, p. 109.
348. Article IV, 1 and 2 of the Moscow Convention. See also I. O. Khlestova, 'Unifikatsiia pravil ispolneniia inostrannykh arbitrazhnykh reshenii v stranakh-chlenakh SEV' [The unification of rules concerning the execution of foreign arbitral decisions in the CMEA member countries], *Sovetskoe Gosudarstvo i Pravo*, 1981, no. 1, pp. 110–114.
349. For a more detailed study of this Convention, see I. O. Khlestova, *Arbitrazh vo vneshneekonomicheskikh otnosheniiakh stran-chlenov SEV* [Arbitration in the external economic relations of the CMEA member countries] (Moscow, 1980), pp. 70 *et seq.*; Juhász, *loc. cit.*, *supra*, note 347, pp. 106 *et seq.*
350. Section 15, 9 of the Compr. Progr.; see the quotation on p. 651 *supra*.
351. Approved by the Executive Committee in February 1974, and subsequently implemented by all Member States through the introduction of new national statutes on arbitration tribunals which entered into force on different dates in 1975 (except for Cuba: May 1976).
352. Khlestova, *op. cit.*, *supra*, note 349, pp. 53–54.
353. Juhász, *loc. cit.*, *supra*, note 347, p. 115.
354. Section 15, 9 of the Compr. Progr.; see the quotation on p. 651 *supra*.
355. The Polish scholar Reutt plainly considers 'the impossibility of a uniform interpretation of the norms (. . .), binding upon the Socialist Community as a whole' precisely as the 'fundamental shortcoming' of the existing system of arbitration, Reutt, *loc. cit.*, *supra*, note 334, p. 111. See also Strohbach, *loc. cit.*, *supra*, note 337, p. 185; Juhász, *loc. cit.*, *supra*, note 347, p. 117.
356. See, *inter alia*, Reutt, *loc. cit.*, *supra*, note 334, p. 111; Strohbach, *loc. cit.*, *supra*, note 337, p. 185.
357. Ustor, *loc. cit.*, *supra*, note 51, p. 272.
358. In this sense, Strohbach, *loc. cit.*, *supra*, note 337, p. 185; see also Seiffert, *Grundriss*, *op. cit.*, *supra*, note 75, p. 331.
359. Juhász, *loc. cit.*, *supra*, note 347, p. 118.
360. Verbal information from East European experts.
361. This has been expounded at greater length in section 2.3., *supra*, p. 611.
362. The enterprise was considered to be entitled to invoke *force majeure*: Award of February 11, 1958 (Case No. 17/57). See A. W. Wiśniewski, 'Awards of the Court of Arbitration at the Polish Chamber of Foreign Trade in Warsaw', *Polish Yearbook of International Law*, vol. IX, 1977–78, pp. 267–269.
363. Article 252, 2 of the Czechoslovak law on international trade (no. 101 of December 4, 1963), quoted in Bystricky, *op. cit.*, *supra*, note 11, pp. 290–291 note 32. However, a provision to that effect markedly fails in, *inter alia*, the G.D.R. 'Law on international economic treaties' of February 5, 1976; text of this law in *Gesetzblatt der DDR*, I, no. 5, and in *Gesetz über internationale Wirtschaftsverträge, Textausgabe Deutsch-Russisch* (Berlin, G.D.R., 1978).
364. Bystricky, *op. cit.*, *supra*, note 11, pp. 290–291 note 32.
365. De Fiumel, *Prawnomiędzynarodowa odpowiedzialności* . . ., *op. cit.*, *supra*, note 334, p. 80; J. Jakubowski, 'Odpowiedzialność majątkowa państw RWPG a odpowiedzialność majątkowa jednostek gospodarczych' [The material responsibility of the CMEA States and the material responsibility of the economic organisations], in De Fiumel, *Problemy* . . ., *op. cit.*, *supra*, note 334, p. 68.
366. See further section 6.2., *infra*, p. 658.
367. The arbitration system has been the subject of abundant study. Besides the literature quoted above, reference is made to: M. Kemper, H. Strohbach & H. Wagner, *Die Allgemeinen Lieferbedingungen des RGW 1968 in der Spruchpraxis sozialistischer Aussenhandelsschiedsgerichte – Kommentar* (Berlin, G.D.R., 1975), especially pp. 386–425; Bystricky, *op. cit.*, *supra*, note 11, pp. 279–293 and the literature quoted by him at p. 285, note 18.
368. This distinction has been taken from Part I, *supra*, p. 11.
369. Section 5.3., *supra*, p. 642.
370. Article II, 4(b) of the CMEA Charter (italics added).
371. Article I, 2(a) of the Statute on the CMEA Secretariat.
372. See section III, 1 of the Session report 'Basic directions . . .', quoted in section 5.3., *supra*, p. 642.
373. *Cf.* Köhler, *loc. cit.*, *supra*, note 206, p. 836.

374. One example is the compilation of the CMEA Statistical Yearbook by the Secretariat ('Statisticheskii Ezhegodnik Stran-Chlenov SEV'). *Cf.* the practice in the field of co-ordination of planning: E. Siljanow, 'Der Rechtscharakter der Plankenziffern in der Planungszusammen-arbeit der RGW-Mitgliedsländer', in: Kemper, *op. cit., supra,* note 39, p. 160.

375. See further section 6.2., *infra,* p. 658.

376. This is only the case in the Rules of Procedure of the Conference of the Heads of Water Management Organs which mentioned 'December of each year' as the time in which the States should submit their information (rule 22, e). See also section 5.1.4., *supra,* p. 637.

377. He specifically mentions recommendations on the purposes and principles of the CMEA, Skubiszewski, 'Die Empfehlungen . . .', *loc. cit., supra,* note 286, p. 145; *cf.* his colleague De Fiumel, who stresses the very general wording of the contents of most CMEA recommendations, *loc. cit., supra,* note 50, p. 107.

378. See chapter 6, *infra,* p. 657.

379. See section 5.4.2., *supra,* p. 648. These competences have been laid down explicitly in the 'Report on the raising of the effectiveness of the recommendations of the CMEA', see *supra,* note 150.

380. See, *inter alia,* Spröte & Wünsche, *op. cit., supra,* note 148, p. 63; Rüster, *op. cit., supra,* note 81, p. 70.

381. Wasilkowski, *loc. cit., supra,* note 13, p. 337.

382. Wasilkowski, *op. cit., supra,* note 84, pp. 301–307; K. Pécsi, *Economic questions of production integration within the CMEA* (Budapest, 1978), p. 12; I. I. Lukashuk, 'Normotvor-cheskaia deiatel'nost' SEV' [The norm-creating activity of the CMEA], *Sovetskii Ezhegodnik Mezhdunarodnogo Prava,* 1980 (Moscow, 1981), p. 49.

383. See note 150.

384. See note 163.

385. Verbal information from East European scholars.

386. Section 5.3., *supra,* p. 642.

387. An example is the recommendation on the GCDG 1968, which was accepted by Czecho-slovakia with a delay of 15 days, see Szász, *op. cit., supra,* note 52, p. 85.

388. On the one hand the competence to postpone the taking of a standpoint by the State has nowhere been provided for, and might thus be considered to be unlawful, on the other hand, a national decision about such a postponement might be construed as the 'result' of the national consideration of recommendations.

389. See section 5.5., *supra,* p. 655.

390. *Cf., inter alia,* the practice in UNCTAD, *supra,* pp. 332, 333.

391. Section 5.5., *supra,* p. 655.

392. Section III, 3 of the Session Report 'Basic directions . . .', see *supra,* note 163 (italics added).

393. Section IV, 30 of the 'Report on the raising of the effectiveness . . .', see *supra,* note 150. It should be stressed that according to this report, the supervisory debates should be limited to the *most important* recommendations.

394. Section III, 1 of the Session report 'Basic directions . . .' see *supra,* note 163 (italics added).

395. See section 3.2.1., *supra,* p. 619.

396. One must keep in mind the fact that a complex – though not adequate – sanction system exists in relation to (private law) national economic organisations, see, *inter alia,* Seiffert, *Grundriss, op. cit., supra,* note 75, pp. 52–57, 230–234, 309–313; Szász, *op. cit., supra,* note 52, pp. 135–182. These possibilities for redress, however, do not exist in relation to the *States,* which is very important in those instances where (private law) contracts have not (yet) been concluded.

397. See, *inter alia,* the remarks of the G.D.R. Prime Minister Stoph, quoted in Kupper, *loc. cit., supra,* note 24, p. 797. See also W. Vogt, *Integration – Politik und Ökonomie* (Berlin, G.D.R., 1978), pp. 122–123. Usenko mentions 'the strict fulfilment of the obligations mutually entered into in the (. . .) relations of the socialist countries' as 'one of the requirements of socialist internationalism', see Usenko, *op. cit., supra,* note 59, p. 239.

398. The CMEA term 'material responsibility' roughly corresponds with 'contractual responsi-bility' in Western terminology. Within the CMEA, the concept of material responsibility is generally used in relation to contractual obligations of an economic character, the violation of which may involve certain (material) damage. As far as the CMEA States are concerned, this responsibility may arise only from the non-fulfilment of mutual obligations which are connected with the exchange or production of goods of a certain pecuniary value. Hence, the concept is

also sometimes described as 'pecuniary responsibility'. See De Fiumel, *Prawnomiędzynarodowa odpowiedzialność. . . .*, *op. cit.*, *supra*, note 334, pp. 46–58 (52), 129–130.
399. See also section 2.3.1., *supra*, p. 611.
400. From the manifold literature the work of V. A. Mazov might be singled out: *Otvetstvennost' v mezhdunarodnom prave* [Responsibility in international law] (Moscow, 1979).
401. The possibility of retorsion or reprisal may be feasible in individual instances, but is mainly of theoretical significance, and is therefore not discussed here.
402. Section 15, 3 of the Compr. Progr. (see also section 1, 6 and section 4, 15). Usually, the term '*material* responsibility' for the non-fulfilment or inadequate fulfilment of commitments is used in the CMEA framework. In the passage referred to, dealing with *State* responsibility, only the phrase '. . . the principle of State responsibility' has been used, obviously to leave open the question what that responsibility will amount to.
403. Among others, the Polish lawyer H. de Fiumel and his Soviet colleague E. T. Usenko are in favour of this approach; see, *inter alia*, De Fiumel's publications quoted in note 334.
404. This protocol was mentioned in section 5.4.3., *supra*, p. 649 (see also note 365). Among others, the Polish lawyer Jakubowski and his G.D.R.-colleague L. Rüster are in favour of this approach, see, *inter alia*, Jakubowski, *loc. cit.*, *supra*, note 365, pp. 68–70.
405. Die Fiumel, *Prawnomiędzynarodowa odpowiedzialność . . .*, *op. cit.*, *supra*, note 334, p. 57.
406. Szilbereky, *loc. cit.*, *supra*, note 332, pp. 8–9. At the time of the adoption of the Conditions by the Session, this question was reportedly left open for further negotiations. Unfortunately, the text of the conditions has not been published.
407. K. Równy, 'Treść zobowiązań umownych a zagadnienie odpowiedzialności majątkowej państw RWPG' [The contents of treaty obligations and the question of the material responsibility of the CMEA States], in: De Fiumel, *Problemy . . .*, *op. cit.*, *supra*, note 334, pp. 56–57, 60–61.
408. Mainly based on: M. Kemper, 'Die Erhöhung der ökonomischen Verantwortlichkeit der RGW-Staaten für die Erhaltung ihrer wechselseitigen wirtschaftlichen Verpflichtungen durch das sozialistische Recht', in: W. Seiffert, *op. cit.*, *supra*, note 32, pp. 164–180. See also V. A. Wasilenko, 'Voprosy material'noi otvetstvennosti stran-chlenov SEV po ekonomicheskim i nauchno-tekhnicheskim dogovoram mezhdu nimi' [Questions of material responsibility of the CMEA member countries under economic and scientific-technical treaties between them], *Sovetskii Ezhegodnik Mezhdunarodnogo Prava*, 1974, pp. 180–197.
409. *Cf.* H. de Fiumel, 'Znaczenie odpowiedzialności majątkowej państwa we wzajemnej współpracy gospodarczej krajów członkowskich RWPG' [The significance of the material responsibility of the State in the mutual economic co-operation of the CMEA member countries], in De Fiumel, *Problemy . . .*, *op. cit.*, *supra*, note 334, p. 24; *cf.* concerning inter-departmental agreements on specialisation and co-operation in production: Hutschenreuter, *loc. cit.*, *supra*, note 260, p. 519.
410. Kemper, *loc. cit.*, *supra*, note 408, pp. 167–169.
411. The Polish lawyer De Fiumel is strongly in favour of this last conception, see his *Prawnomiędzynarodowa odpowiedzialność . . .*, *op. cit.*, *supra*, note 334, pp. 76–90, 130. *Cf.* also Jakubowski, *loc. cit.*, *supra*, note 365, pp. 64 *et seq.*; M. Frankowska, 'Okoliczności wyłączające odpowiedzialność majątkowa państwa a współpraca gospodarcza państw RWPG' [Conditions excluding material State responsibility and the economic co-operation of CMEA States], in De Fiumel, *Problemy . . .*, *op. cit.*, *supra*, note 334, pp. 77–98.
412. Verbal information from East European experts.
413. See, *inter alia*, Kemper, *loc. cit.*, *supra*, note 408, pp. 163–164.
414. See the Dutch daily 'NRC/Handelsblad' of July 3, 1981, p. 11; text of Lazar's speech in: *Ekonomicheskoe Sotrudnichestvo Stran-Chlenov SEV*, 1981, no. 4, pp. 8–11(11). See also, the rather critical speech of the Romanian Prime Minister, *Lumea*, 1981, no. 28, pp. 6 and 22.
415. See for an analysis of the concept of 'mutual advantages' in the economic reality, *inter alia*, L. Csaba, 'Some problems of the international socialist monetary system', *Acta Oeconomica* (Budapest), vol. 23, 1979, no. 1/2, pp. 17–37 at pp. 22 *et seq.* As far as the political views upon the application of the concept of mutual benefit and assistance is concerned, see especially: S. Polaczek, *Międzynarodowy rynek socjalistyczny – nowy typ współpracy* [The international socialist market; New type of co-operation] (Warsaw, 1978), p. 82.
416. Seiffert, *Grundriss . . .*, *op. cit.*, *supra*, note 75, p. 54.

PART X

A COMPARATIVE ANALYSIS IN THE PERSPECTIVE OF CHANGING STRUCTURES OF THE INTERNATIONAL ECONOMIC ORDER

A TOPICAL COMPARATIVE ANALYSIS IN THE PERSPECTIVE OF CHANGING STRUCTURES OF THE INTERNATIONAL ECONOMIC ORDER

by P. van Dijk
with the assistance of K. de Vey Mestdagh

CONTENTS

I. INTRODUCTION

The present Part, in giving a comparative analysis of the supervisory mechanisms dealt with in the preceding Parts, does not purport to cover everything that has been said by the other participants on the individual organisations and with respect to each particular item of the uniform scheme of analysis. Since all separate reports have been included in full, this would lead to a considerable repetition of information. Moreover, that information should be provided and read firstly in its own context, since lifting the data on the individual organisations out of their proper context and only discussing them together with similar data on the other organisations bears the risk of creating too easily the impression that these data are all, indeed, comparable. In fact, however, the degree of comparability can be assessed only if the norms and procedures which form the object of comparison are studied – not only with a view to their formal features but equally from the perspective of their substantive character and actual functioning.[1] It was, therefore, considered important that the reader would be offered the opportunity to carry out this research himself, on the basis of the separate reports, and to draw his or her own conclusions as to the comparability. This having been said, it is equally necessary for a comparatist to make an effort to go beyond the particular features of the individual objects to be compared, and to discern common patterns which by definition must present a certain degree of abstraction with respect to these individual objects.

As is stated in the General Introduction, it has been the aim of our research to have legal theory make its contribution to the discussion of the required structural changes of the international economic order and of the role which supervisory mechanisms can play in bringing about these structural changes. Consequently, the topical comparative analysis is confined to those institutional and procedural issues of the supervisory mechanisms in international economic organisations which are deemed to be the most relevant issues in that perspective. To place that perspective in a somewhat broader context it seems indispensable to give a short survey of the history, contents, legal character and supervisory devices of the NIEO concept as the concept which has played such a dominant role in the discussions on the structure of the international economic order during recent years.

II. THE EMERGENCE, ELABORATION AND OBJECTIVES OF THE NIEO CONCEPT

2.1. A brief historical survey

The call of the developing States for a New International Economic Order finds its most important historical explanation in the fundamental change of the international social and political climate after the Second World War. Just as after the First World War, but on a much larger scale, the discussions held among the allied powers about new structures for the international organisation of States set the stage for the liquidation of the remaining colonies. The development of friendly relations among nations, based upon respect for the principle of equal rights and self-determination of peoples, was listed among the aims of the United Nations in Article 1 of its Charter, while under Article 73 the States that administered non-self-governing territories accepted the obligation to promote self-government. In particular, the Declaration on the Granting of Independence to Colonial Countries and Peoples, which was adopted by the General Assembly of the United Nations on December 14, 1960, and which declared, *inter alia,* that all peoples have the right to self-determination and, by virtue of that right, may freely determine their political status and freely pursue their economic, social and cultural development, gave a strong political impetus to the birth of a great number of new States. After their admittance to the United Nations, these newly independent States, by virtue of the principle of sovereign equality laid down in Article 2, paragraph 1 of the UN Charter, took part in this organisation on the same footing and with the same rights as any other Member State. Most of these new States were aligned with neither the Western group nor the socialist countries, but formed an independent third group, later on to be called 'the Group of the Non-Aligned Countries'. As a result, the structure and functioning of the United Nations changed dramatically. Moreover, most of the newcomers had an under-developed economy, and therefore found themselves in a position which was far from equal to that of their former colonial rulers. In that situation, it was logical that they used their newly gained political and juridical status in the United Nations and other organisations to initiate and lend force to a programme aimed at greater economic equality between the States and more equitable international economic relations.[2] As Ervin Laszlo has put it: 'The majority felt that their *de iure* political colonisation ended only to be replaced by a *de facto* economic colonisation.'[3]

The increasing number of developing countries within the United Nations' membership, coupled with the growing awareness on the part of these members of the strength of the voting power that they could bring about by their co-operation, has led to a number of resolutions, adopted by the General Assembly, that formulated the main principles and targets of a programme towards greater economic equality and equity. This movement has become known as the 'revolution of rising expectations'. The First United Nations Development Decade, proclaimed for the 1960s and adopted by Resolution 1710 (XVI) of December 19, 1961, was only a very modest start of this movement and was not even based upon an initiative of the developing countries, but on that of the United States.[4] Nevertheless, it could be considered 'a symbol of the collective responsibility of the international community for the development of the Third World'.[5] It aimed, *inter alia,* at attaining an 'annual rate of growth of aggregate national income of 5 per cent. at the end of the Decade', and at an increase of the flow of financial resources to the developing countries of 1 per cent. of the combined national income of the developed countries.

A first real break-through, both in an institutional and in a norm-setting sense, was presented by the first United Nations Conference on Trade and Development (UNCTAD I) in Geneva in 1964. As is set out in Part IV, the developing countries managed, in spite of the opposition of most developed countries, to make the UNCTAD into a permanent institution of the United Nations, with regular conferences where problems relating to development and trade would have a central place on the agenda. In the norm-setting field, the adoption by UNCTAD I of 15 General and 13 Special Principles 'to govern international trade relations and trade policies conducive to development'[6] provided the developing countries with a pioneering document that was to play an important role in all future discussions of development strategies and the restructuring of the international economic order; a NIEO document *avant la lettre*.

In the 1960s, other institutional and norm-setting developments occurred, which directed more attention to the special situation of the developing countries, such as the inclusion of a Chapter IV 'On trade and Development' in the General Agreement of Tariffs and Trade (GATT), modifying the principle of reciprocity in favour of the developing countries (1965)[7]; the establishment of the United Nations Development Programme (UNDP) to organise international technical co-operation and to support and supplement the national efforts of developing countries in solving the problem of their economic development (1965)[8]; the establishment of the United Nations Industrial Development Organisation (UNIDO) to promote industrial development and to assist in, promote and accelerate the industrialisation of the developing countries (1966)[9]; and the adoption by the General Assembly of the 'Declaration on Social Progress and Development', which laid down the principles on which social progress and development had to be founded, the objectives of social progress and development, and the means and methods to achieve these objectives, stressing the responsibilities of both the developing and the developed countries (1969).[10]

The goals and targets of the First Development Decade, although modestly and vaguely formulated, were not achieved during the 1960s. In 1970, the General Assembly proclaimed the International Development Strategy for the Second United Nations Development Decade.[11] The goals and objectives were formulated in clear, quantitative terms: the annual rate of growth of the gross product of the developing countries was to be raised at least 6 per cent. as a whole, and 3.5 per cent. per head. The target of the transfer of financial resources to developing countries was set again at 1 per cent. but here this percentage applied to the gross national product of each individual developed country, with the additional provision that 0.7 per cent. had to be provided in the form of official development assistance.[12] The Strategy included a number of detailed policy measures to achieve its goals and objectives, as well as special measures in the interest of the least-developed and the land-locked developing countries. Finally, it included arrangements 'to keep under systematic scrutiny the progress towards achieving the goals and objectives of the Decade, to identify shortfalls in their achievement and the factors which account for them and to recommend positive measures, including new goals and policies as needed',[13] and called for measures to mobilise public opinion in support of the objectives and policies of the Decade.

In spite of this clear drafting and of the positive intentions which motivated it, it became clear very soon that the Strategy would not survive the economically turbulent beginning of the decade without serious harm. Within a timespan of only three years the international economic community was faced with an emergency in world food supplies, an almost total collapse of the international monetary system and an energy crisis. These events did not only hamper an effective implementation of the Strategy, but they also made it obsolete. Moreover, they prompted the awareness on the part of the developing countries that the shortcomings of the international economic and financial mechanisms, which maintained and aggravated their economic vulnerability, could not be redressed by incidental measures, but were of a structural character, and could therefore be obviated only by a restructuring of the international economic system. However, the energy crisis, in particular, evoked by the concerted action of the OPEC countries in the field of oil-pricing and oil-distribution, clearly indicated that the developed economies were vulnerable as well, and that the developing countries collectively, as in the case of the OPEC countries, might constitute an economic force as the suppliers of commodities. This turned the developing countries into more assertive negotiating partners. However, the developed countries, confronted with their own economic problem, caused – or at least accelerated – partly by the energy crisis, became less inclined to increase their economic assistance to the Third World, and to consent to a restructuring of the economic system which would aggravate their financial problems, raise their unemployment rate and increase the amount of unused industrial capacities.[14]

On behalf of the Non-Aligned Countries, and in response to the Washington Energy Conference of February 1974, the President in Office, President Boumédienne of Algeria, took the initiative for a Special Session of the UN General Assembly, to be held in 1974 and to be dedicated, for the first time, not to peace and security problems but to 'all questions relating to all types of raw materials'.[15] The request was the result of the Fourth Conference of Heads of State or Government of the Non-Aligned Countries in Algiers in September 1973, and reflected the concern expressed at this Conference about the failure of the Second Development Decade and about the policies of a number of developed countries that were held to be responsible for it.[16] In fact, the Sixth Special Session dealt with a much broader spectrum of development problems and issued the Declaration on the Establishment of a New International Economic Order and the Programme of Action on the Establishment of a New International Economic Order.[17] Both documents were adopted by consensus. However, during the last meetings most industrial States made so many reservations, and gave so many different individual interpretations of essential paragraphs, that hardly any trace of a real consensus was left.[18] The main objections of the Western countries were directed against the emphasis the Declaration placed on the necessity of a *new* international economic order, and against a number of principles and implementation measures such as: (1) the principle of the permanent sovereignty of every State over its natural resources and all economic activities, and the right to nationalisation (Declaration, item 4(e); Programme, items I.1.(a) and (b), VII.1(b) and VIII (a)); (2) the foundation of producers' associations (Declaration, item 4(t); Programme, item I.1.(c)); (3) the linking of the export prices of raw materials, commodities, semi-manufactured and manufactured goods to the prices of these goods and capital equipment imported by them from developed countries through indexation, for the sake of the developing countries (Declaration, item 4(j);

696

Programme, item I.1.(d)); and (4) the code of conduct for liner conferences (Programme, item I.4.(iv)).[19]

In the meantime, the UNCTAD had become the forum for the drafting of a Charter of Economic Rights and Duties of States. A proposal to this end was made by the Mexican President, Luis Echeverría Alvarez, at UNCTAD III in Santiago on April 19, 1972. In Resolution 45 (III) the plenary session decided to set up a Working Group for the drafting of the Charter on the basis of (1) the general and specific principles approved by UNCTAD I; (2) further proposals made at UNCTAD III; (3) the relevant resolutions adopted within the United Nations framework; (4) the principles laid down in the Charter of Algiers of 1967 (prepared by the Group of 77, prior to UNCTAD II); and (5) the Declaration and Principles of the Action Programme of Lima of 1971 (adopted at the Group's preparatory meeting for UNCTAD III). The Charter was to provide a legal basis for a new economic order 'to protect duly the rights of all countries and in particular the developing States'.[20] President Echeverría had stated the following when making the proposal: 'A just order and a stable world will not be possible until we create obligations and rights which protect the weaker States. Let us take the economic co-operation out of the realm of goodwill and put it into the realm of law.'[21]

After the Working Group had come to a deadlock with respect to issues such as nationalisation, producers' associations, international regulation of the activities of transnational corporations, the duty of general disarmament and re-allocation of funds to development aid, the general application of the Most-Favoured-Nation Clause, and the indexation of import and export prices,[22] the UNCTAD Trade and Development Board decided to refer the matter to the 29th Session of the UN General Assembly. There, the discussions in Committee II showed that the Western countries were not prepared to adopt the Charter by consensus. The plenary meeting adopted it by Resolution 3218 (XXIX) with a vote of 120 in favour, 6 against (Belgium, Denmark, the Federal Republic of Germany, Luxembourg, the United Kingdom and the United States), and 10 abstentions (Austria, Canada, France, Ireland, Israel, Italy, Japan, the Netherlands, Norway and Spain). The main objections of the Western States concerned the regulation of the permanent sovereignty over natural resources and of the right of nationalisation in Article 2.

The Summit of Non-Aligned Countries in Algiers in 1973, which had induced President Boumédienne to take the initiative for the Sixth Special Session of the General Assembly on commodity problems, had called for a special session to be devoted to problems of development and international co-operation. In the General Assembly, a proposal to that effect, made by Morocco, was adopted by Resolution 3172 (XXVIII) of December 17, 1973. This resulted in the Seventh Special Session, held in September 1975. It was characterised by a positive and constructive atmosphere and a conciliatory and moderate tone, which was due especially to (1) a certain change in attitude on the part of the industrialised countries, in particular the United States; (2) the willingness of the developing countries to leave the most controversial issues out of the discussion; and (3) the fact that the agenda was a more pragmatic one, compared to all preceding discussions of principles and abstract programmes.[23] As representatives attending the Session commented, in comparison to the Sixth Special Session this one was marked by a shift from 'confrontation' to 'conciliation'.[24] Discussions focused mainly on the drawing-up of guidelines for negotiations in other fora (a 'commitment to negotiate'). In order to avoid a display of any remaining dissension it was agreed that reservations with respect to the final resolutions would be included in the records of the Session but not aired in a public meeting. Resolution 3362 (S–VII) was adopted by consensus on September 16, 1975. However, a lengthy list of reservations issued by the United States clearly indicated that a considerable gap still existed between the various positions both during and after the Session, in spite of the positive atmosphere of the negotiations and the moderate formulation of the resolution.[25] The United States even indicated at this stage 'that it cannot and does not accept any implication that the world is now embarked on the establishment of something called the New International Economic Order'.[26]

Next, an event in the North-South dialogue which took place outside the framework of the UN but appeared to have certain repercussions on further UN activities in the field, should be mentioned. At the end of 1974, after the first oil crisis and during the same period in which the US convocated the Washington Energy Conference, the French President took the initiative for a conference on energy problems and related issues. The developing countries invited made their participation conditional upon the inclusion of issues relating to commodities in general and development issues in the agenda of the conference. This resulted in the Conference on International Economic Co-operation (CIEC), held in Paris from December 1975 to June 1977. Virtually all participants and observers, however, concede that the CIEC ended as a failure, mainly because of miscalculations on each side with respect to the other's power, over-estimation of its own negotiating power and of the other side's capability for making concessions, conflicts within the blocks, irreconcilable bargaining strategies, and mutual distrust.[27]

As it is stated by one writer: 'The guarded optimism which has been generated by the Seventh Special Session was dissipated by the altogether unremarkable results of the CIEC Conference . . . But none was prepared to concede that the new international economic order was dead, so soon after its launching.'[28]

The lack of a formal connection between the CIEC and the UN had greatly dissatisfied the developing countries, especially because of the restricted set-up of the Conference and the limited representation of countries. These countries, therefore, made the General Assembly adopt a resolution during its 32nd Session, in 1977, to the effect that all negotiations of a global character relating to the establishment of the New International Economic Order should take place within the framework of the UN system.[29] Since the Third World resented the fact that ECOSOC, whose mandate seemed to predestine it to play a central role in the NIEO negotiations, was composed of one-third of the UN members only, and in order to give the negotiating framework a more permanent structure, the General Assembly decided to establish a Committee of the Whole to assist it by acting as a focal point in:

(a) Overseeing and monitoring the implementation of decisions and agreements reached in the negotiations on the establishment of the New International Economic Order in the appropriate bodies of the United Nations system;

(b) Providing impetus for resolving difficulties in negotiations and for encouraging the continuing work in these bodies;

(c) Serving, where appropriate, as a forum for facilitating and expediting agreement on the resolution of outstanding issues; and

(d) Exploring and exchanging views on global economic problems and priorities.[30]

From the very first moment, there has been lack of agreement on the precise mandate of the Committee of the Whole. Consequently, instead of getting down to business, the members of the Committee indulged in fruitless discussions which, in fact, turned it into just another forum for general debate. While the developing countries stressed the point that the Committee should be endowed with negotiating authority, most industrialised countries took the stand that it should not pre-empt the functions and powers of other UN bodies, but that it could play a constructive role through informal contacts and discussions.[31] The Secretariat of the UNCTAD also contested the Committee's competence, afraid as it was that the Committee would usurp UNCTAD's function in the restructuring process. As a consequence, the Committee has accomplished very little. It has ultimately assumed the role of a preparatory committee for the so-called New Round of Global Negotiations (NRGN).[32]

The launching of this New Round, proposed by Algeria during UNCTAD V as a new CIEC and supported by the Non-Aligned Countries at their 1979 meeting in Cuba, was to take place during the Eleventh Special Session of the General Assembly, in 1980.[33] However, during that session a strong controversy arose between the Group of 77 and the Western countries on where the negotiations would have to take place. The G-77 countries wished to concentrate the negotiations in the General Assembly which then could decide to refer certain technical issues to the Specialised Agency concerned. The Western countries took the position that concrete results were to be expected only if the negotiations took place in the competent Specialised Agencies, in particular as far as the financial, monetary and trade issues were concerned, which in their opinion should be dealt with by the IMF, the World Bank and the GATT respectively. Finally, a compromise was adopted, but with the negative vote of the Federal Republic of Germany, the United Kingdom and the United States. Since without the participation of these three States negotiations would be meaningless, the decision was taken to postpone the launching of the NRGN.[34] During the subsequent consecutive ordinary sessions of the General Assembly, several efforts have been made by the acting Presidents of the General Assembly to find a way out of the impasse through formal and informal consultations, but without any concrete result.[35] The International Development Strategy for the Third United

Nations Development Decade provides that the review and appraisal of the implementation of the Strategy will take into account the results of, *inter alia*, the global negotiations relating to international economic co-operation for development.[36] It is very unlikely, however, that there will be any such results in 1984, when the General Assembly has to carry out the first review and appraisal.[37]

2.2. The NIEO documents; principles and objectives of the NIEO

The Declaration and the Programme of Action on the Establishment of a New International Economic Order, together with the Charter of Economic Rights and Duties of States and the Resolution on Development and International Economic Co-operation, constitute the basic NIEO documents. Together, they contain a comprehensive, albeit not very systematic set of negotiated principles and policies underlying and guiding the endeavours towards changing the structure of the international economic order.

2.2.1. Fundamental NIEO principles

The fundamental principles underlying the NIEO-concept are, in our view, the following:[38]

2.2.1.1. The principle of freedom or sovereignty of States

This principle includes the right of every nation to adopt the political, economic and social system it deems most appropriate (self-determination); the right of permanent sovereignty of a State over its natural resources; the right of territorial integrity; and the right to deal with its internal affairs without intervention by other States. This principle of freedom has been laid down in Article 1(2) and Article 2(4) and (7) of the UN Charter and has been elaborated upon in the Declaration of Principles of International Law Concerning Friendly Relations and Co-operation among States in Accordance with the Charter of the United Nations (hereafter: Declaration of Principles).[39] Therefore, it was an obvious starting-point for the NIEO documents.

The principle of self-determination is referred to in the NIEO Declaration in section 1 (independence) and section 4(a)(d)(h) and (i); in the Programme of Action in chapter I.1(a); and in the Charter in the preamble, in chapter I(a) and (g), and in Articles 1, 7, 16 and 26.

The right of permanent sovereignty over natural resources is mentioned in the NIEO Declaration in section 4(e) to (i); in the Programme of Action in chapters I.1(a), VII.1(b) and VIII(a); and in the Charter in Articles 2 and 16.

The right of territorial integrity is referred to in the NIEO Declaration in section 4(a), and in the Charter in chapter I(a) and (c) and in Article 16.

700

The prohibition of intervention is laid down in the NIEO Declaration in section 4(a) and (e); in the Programme of Action in chapter V(a) with respect to transnational corporations; and in the Charter in chapter I(d) and in Articles 17 and 32, and with respect of transnational corporations in Article 2(2)(b).

2.2.1.2. The principle of equality.

This principle has two aspects, a formal and a substantive one. The formal aspect is mainly relied upon in the NIEO context to stress the equal right of all States fully and effectively to participate in the decision-making concerning the international economic relations. This is the institutional aspect of the equality principle, usually referred to as 'sovereign equality'.[40]

The substantive aspect could be summarised as 'equal treatment'. As is generally recognised nowadays, substantive equality is only achieved if equal situations are treated equally, while at the same time unequal situations are treated unequally to the extent that this is appropriate and necessary to remove or neutralise the inequality.[41]

With respect to international economic relations this implies that equal treatment is not accomplished by the mere application of the principle of reciprocity, the Most-Favoured-Nation-Clause and the abrogation of discriminatory regulations and measures. It also requires preferential treatment of developing countries in proportion to the degree of their underdevelopment.[42] As has been stated by R. Prebisch, the first Secretary-General of UNCTAD: 'no matter how valid the principle of the most-favoured-nation may be in trade relations among equals, it is not an acceptable and adequate concept for trade among countries with highly unequal economic power'.[43] And, as is rightly observed by VerLoren van Themaat: 'without any principles of substantive equality rooted in positive law, the principle of freedom is of little value either to states or their nationals when there is considerable economic underdevelopment, partly resulting from economic dependence on other states'.[44] Reference to the principle of equality in a general sense is made in the NIEO Declaration in the preamble and in the sections 1, 3, 4(a) and 6; in the Programme of Action in its preamble and in chapter VI; in the Charter in its preamble (several references), in chapter I(b) and (g) and in Articles 2.2(c), 10 and 17; and in the Resolution in the preamble.

The principle of equal participation is referred to in the Declaration in sections 2 and 4(c); in the Programme of Action in chapter II, section 1(d) and (g) and section 2(c), in chapter IX.5 and in chapter X.6(a)(i); in the Charter in Article 10; and in the Resolution in chapter II, section 16.

The Declaration mentions the prohibition of discrimination in its section 4(d). The Programme of Action refers to non-discrimination in chapter II.2(b) and stipulates equal treatment of developing countries by developed countries in chapter VII(e). The Charter refers in its preamble to co-operation among all States, irrespective of their economic and social systems, and elaborates on this in Article 4. It mentions the principle of equal treatment by developing countries with respect to socialist countries in Article 20, and refers to the Most-Favoured-Nation treatment in Article 26. Finally, there are numerous references to substantive equality in the sense of preferential treatment of the developing and the least developed countries: in the Declaration in section 4(n) and (s); in the Programme of Action in its preamble and in chapter I, sections 2(f), 3(a)(ii) and (x) and (b) and 4(v), in chapter II, section 1(e) and section 2(d), (h) and (i), in chapter IV, last sentence, in chapter VII(e) and (f), in chapter X(b) and sections 3 and 8; in the Charter in the preamble (at various places), in chapter I(e)(i) and (m), and in Articles 18, 19, 21, 24, 25 and 29; and in the Resolution in chapter I, sections 1, 2 and 7–12.

2.2.1.3. The principle of equity and (social) justice

The principles of equality and equity hold a lot in common. In general, one could say that an economic order in which substantive equality between the members of a society has been achieved, will necessarily also display equity and social justice: 'equality is equity'.[45]

However, the contrary is not necessarily true: 'equity does not necessarily imply equality'.[46] 'Equity' is a broader and more complex concept than 'equality' and does not refer primarily to a comparison between the situation of one member of a society and that of other members, but to the broader question whether that situation, or a certain solution reached, is fair in itself taking into account all the circumstances of the case.[47] This becomes clear if one substitutes the word 'equity' in the NIEO resolutions by 'equality'. Thus, *e.g.* in Article 26 of the Charter, which reads: '. . . International trade should be conducted without prejudice to generalised non-discriminatory and non-reciprocal preferences in favour of developing countries, on the basis of mutual advance, *equitable* benefits and the exchange of most-favoured-nation treatment'. Application of the principle of *equality* to international trade relations would make these relations very rigid since an equal balance of benefits, also in a substantive sense, can only be guaranteed through bilateral trade agreements. The same holds good for 'just and *equitable* terms of trade' in Article 28 of the Charter. Another example is offered by Chapter I, section 1(d) of the Programme: 'Just and *equitable* relationship between parties'; equality could be guaranteed, if at all, only through a complete price-indexation.

These few instances indicate that the principle of equity is referred to especially in relation to issues which because of their complex or precarious character are not appropriate for a full-fledged application of the equality principle, but for which nevertheless a fair result is claimed through the development and, where necessary, the restructuring of the international economic order. It can be concluded at the same time that the concept of 'equity' is not only broader but also vaguer than the concept of 'equality' and that, therefore, its achievement is more difficult to be measured. Sometimes one cannot escape the impression that the concept serves as a compromise in cases where an agreement on equality could not be reached, the compromise implying that existing norms and acquired rights must not be abolished but they must be applied or exercised in a more fair way.

A distinction could further be made between equity as a procedural and as a substantive principle. As a procedural principle, equity delineates a method by which an 'equitable solution' may be found in matters of distribution or apportionment. As a substantive principle, equity serves to support a claim to alter existing legal relationships, or the application of existing rules, or to create new rules and procedures, in order to redress existing injustice or disparity and thus to reach an 'equitable solution'.[48]

Since the whole NIEO discussion is aimed at the establishment of more equitable economic relations, it is not surprising that the NIEO documents are impregnated with the idea of equity and justice. Explicit reference can be found in the NIEO Declaration in the preamble and in sections 1, 4(b) and (j), and 5; in the Programme of Action in chapter I, sections 1(d), 2(h), 3(a)(vii) and 4(i) and (vi), in chapter II, sections 1(d) and 2(c), in chapter VI and in chapter X, section 6(a)(ii); in the Charter in the preamble, in chapter I(e) and in Articles 6, 8, 10, 14, 26, 27(2), 28 and 29; and in the Resolution in its preamble and in chapter I sections 3(a) and 10, and chapter II section 15.

2.2.1.4. The principle of solidarity
The realisation of both the principles of (substantive) equality and of equity and justice in international economic relations can be brought about only if these relations can be based upon the principle of solidarity between States, not merely as a moral principle, but as a principle incorporated and developed in international law.[49]

Apart from ethical considerations, which are often emphasised in the NIEO discussion, but only play a restricted role in the actual regulation of economic relations, as governments are not guided primarily by ethics in conducting their foreign affairs,[50] the main rationale of the principle of solidarity lies in the increasing interdependence of States. Consequently, the contents of the principle of solidarity, as elaborated in the law of international economic organisations have been determined by this rationale. On the basis of a comparative study of these international economic organisations, Ver-Loren van Themaat distinguishes the following three legal manifestations of the principle of solidarity:
(1) the obligation of individual States to take the interests of other States, their subjects, or the common interest into consideration in their policy;
(2) mutual (bilateral or multilateral) financial or any other form of aid in combating economic problems, including technical aid to developing countries and trade preferences to compensate for their disadvantages;
(3) harmonisation of economic policies in a co-ordinated manner, by means of other steering instruments.[51]

Leaving apart the aspect of preferential treatment, which has here been dealt with as an aspect of the principle of substantive equality rather than the principle of solidarity, there are several references to aspects of the principle of solidarity in the NIEO documents.

The duty of States to prevent or restrict negative effects of their economic policies or of specific measures on the economies of other States is mentioned in the Declaration in section 4(q); in the Programme of Action in chapter I section 2(d), and in chapter II section 1(a),(b) and (c); and in the Charter in Articles 3, 18, 24 and 30.

The necessity to give mutual assistance and financial aid (and to renegotiate the debts of developing countries) is referred to in the NIEO Declaration in section 4(i), (k), (l), (o) and (p); in the Programme of Action in chapter I section 2(c), chapter II section 1(e), (f) and (h) and section 2(a), (f) and (g), III(a), (c) and (d), chapter IV(c), chapter V(c), chapter VII section 2, chapter IX section 6, chapter X(e) and (f) and sections 2–4; in the Charter in Articles 16 and 22; and in the Resolution in chapters II, III, IV section 8 and V sections 2 and 5–12.

The growing interdependence and the necessity of international co-operation, including the right to international co-operation of, for example, producers of commodities, is recognised by the NIEO Declaration in its preamble and in sections 3, 4(b), (s) and (t), 5 and 6; in the Programme of Action in its preamble and in chapter I.1(b) and in chapter VII (co-operation among developing countries); and in the Charter in the preamble, in chapter I(n) and in Articles 3, 4, 5, 6–9, 11–14, 17, 23 and 27–31; and in the Resolution in the preamble and in chapter I, sections 1, 2 and 3, chapter IV, sections 6 and 7, chapter V section 3 and chapter VI (co-operation among developing countries). Finally, there are references to other aspects of the principle of solidarity in the Programme of Action in chapter I sections 1(d), (e) and (f), 2(a), (b), (e), (f) and (g), 3 and 4, all implying the duty of developed States to take the interests and needs of the developing countries into account.

2.2.1.5. The principle of respect for human rights

Since the establishment of the United Nations after the Second World War, the principle of respect for human rights and fundamental freedoms has been recognised as one of the leading principles in achieving international co-operation and as one of the main purposes of that co-operation. This is expressed in Article 1, paragraph 3, of the UN Charter and is repeated in the Friendly Relations Declaration of 1970 in the section on 'The duty of States to co-operate with one another in accordance with the Charter'. Consequently, it would seem to be a matter of course that general respect for human rights is included in the fundamental principles underlying the NIEO concept.

However, the NIEO documents but rarely refer to it. It is included in the 'Fundamentals of international economic relations' in chapter I of the Charter of Economic Rights and Duties of States under (k), while the 'promotion of international social justice' under (m) could also be related to human rights. But the principle has not been further elaborated in any of the provisions dealing with the economic rights and duties of States, apart from some references to the prohibition of discrimination and *apartheid*

(NIEO Declaration, sections 1 and 4(i); Programme of Action, chapter I, section 1(a); and Charter, Article 16). The emphasis is on the rights of States and peoples rather than on those of individuals and groups of individuals. Understandable as this may be in view of the policy priorities of the developing States – and the socialist States – it is one of the indications of the somewhat unbalanced character of the NIEO documents.

In 1977, partly as a result of a debate initiated in UNESCO, the UN Commission on Human Rights asked the Secretary-General of the UN to study the international dimensions of 'the right of development as a human right'.[52] Thus, the discussion of the notion of the 'right to development' and the confusion surrounding it, received governmental support and was introduced into the NIEO discussion. In 1979, both the UN Commission on Human Rights and the General Assembly adopted a resolution stating that the right to development is a human right and that development should be enjoyed by States and individuals.[53] Thus far, this development has contributed very little to putting more emphasis on the principle of respect for human rights in the NIEO discussion, because the character and contents of the right to development and its relation to the said principle are still unclear, and because the developing countries have relied on the concept mainly to strengthen their claim to new structures of the economic relations *between* *States*. This would not seem to do justice to the classification of the right to development *as a human right*. To quote a recent study on the right to development carried out by a Committee of the Dutch branch of the International Law Association:

> A right to development as a legal phenomenon of current international law draws its meaning and content from the interplay and close coherence between the well-being of individuals and their community as a whole. In any state it can happen that individuals do live in a situation of absolute poverty. It needs no argument that the human rights of those very persons are not being implemented by the state concerned. When such a state is in a position to improve this wrongful situation with its own resources, a right to development makes no sense, for it does not add anything new to the whole system of human rights. However, when a state, according to objective standards, is not in a position to do so, due to its socio-economic under-development, then it does make sense to introduce a right to development, if it is interpreted and applied as the right of everybody to live in a state which is able to eliminate absolute poverty, and the right of a state to be in a position to do this. Such a right to development, in other words, provides for a link between the right of self-determination of peoples and nations and everyone's right to a social and international order in which the rights and freedoms set forth in the Universal Declaration of Human Rights can be fully realised; the right to development can be considered as the rim of the coin, the two sides of which are formed by the right to self-determinaton and the right to a social and international order as described above.[54]

In our view, the internationally accepted principles and rules concerning respect for human rights must be considered to be an integral and fundamental part of international economic law in general and of international development law.[55]

2.2.2. *Main NIEO objectives*

The scope of the present study does not require a comprehensive description of the institutional, procedural and substantive objectives in the area of international economic development such as have been proposed, specified and developed in the discussions and decisions on a new international economic order. As a matter of fact, there is no reason why we should give such a description, since an excellent one has been provided by the United Nations Institute for Training and Research in collaboration with the Centre for the Economic and Social Study of the Third World.[56] It lists 25 key issues of the world economy relevant to the NIEO, subdivided in six categories, while for each separate issue the individual objectives are described with reference to the documents in which they were articulated and the fora in which this took place.[57] The categories and issues listed there are the following:

(a) Aid and assistance issues
 1. Attaining United Nations official development assistance targets;
 2. providing technical assistance for development and eliminating the brain drain;
 3. renegotiating the debts of developing countries;
 4. undertaking special measures to assist land-locked, least-developed and island developing countries;
 5. using funds from disarmament for development.

(b) International trade issues
 6. Improving the terms and conditions of trade of developing countries: tariff and non-tariff barriers, GSP, duties and taxes on imports, invisible trade;
 7. adopting an integrated approach to commodities: the integrated programme, buffer stocks, producers' associations, indexation;
 8. developing an international food programme;
 9. adjusting the economic policies of developed countries to facilitate the expansion and diversification of the exports of developing countries;
 10. improving and intensifying trade relations between countries having different social and economic systems;
 11. strengthening economic and technical co-operation among developing countries.

(c) International financial issues
 12. Reforming the international monetary system: using special drawing rights for development assistance and as the central reserve asset of the international monetary system, promoting stable rates of exchange and protection from the effects of inflation;
 13. assuring adequate participation by developing countries in World Bank and IMF decision making;
 14. increasing the transfer of resources through the World Bank and IMF.

(d) Issues of industrialisation, technology transfer and business practices
 15. Negotiating the redeployment of industrial productive capacities to developing countries;
 16. establishing mechanisms for the transfer of technology to developing countries;

17. regulating and supervising the activities of transnational enterprises and eliminating restrictive business practices;
18. improving the competitiveness of natural resources and ending their waste;
19. providing equitable access to the resources of the sea-bed and the ocean floor.

(e) Social issues
20. Achieving a more equitable distribution of income and raising the level of employment;
21. providing health services, education, higher cultural standards and qualification for the work force, and assuring the well-being of children and the integration of women in development.

(f) Political and institutional issues
22. Assuring the economic sovereignty of States: natural resources, foreign property, choice of economic system;
23. compensating for adverse effects on the resources of States, territories and people of foreign occupation, alien and colonial domination or apartheid;
24. establishing a system of consultations at global, regional and sectoral levels with the aim of promoting industrial development;
25. restructuring the economic and social sections of the United Nations.

III. THE LEGAL CHARACTER OF THE NIEO DOCUMENTS

3.1. Introduction

Before making a few remarks about the legal character of the NIEO documents, it should be stressed that their formal legal character is not necessarily decisive, and is not even necessarily one of the most important factors, in determining the 'compulsory value' of these documents and of the individual provisions they embody.[58]

> In the international process, the forces that converge to impinge upon and constrain states to behave one way or another, are broader than the narrow considerations of legality, and include the moral, the political, the social and the economic aspects. Thus, that a norm is or is not strictly juridical is not a conclusive criterion for its propensity to affect state practice. Indeed, strictly juridical norms may and often do yield to these other ingredients of the international legal process.[59]

However, this does not detract from the fact that for many different reasons, such as procedures of implementation, supervision and enforcement, it is of great relevance that the legal character of the principles and rules laid down in the NIEO documents be determined as precisely as possible.

As all four NIEO documents discussed here have been adopted by General Assembly resolutions, the starting point of any examination of their legal character must be the well-known fact that, with certain exceptions that have no relevance in this context, these resolutions – and the documents thereby adopted – cannot have the force of law *proprio vigore*.[60] Consequently, if such force is to be attributed to them, it has to be by virtue of a source other than the decision of the General Assembly.

3.2. The NIEO documents and existing international law

First, the NIEO documents, or the individual principles and rules embodied therein, can be legally binding because they are a codification, a repetition or an authoritative interpretation of existing legally binding principles and rules. In this case, the legal force of the documents or provisions is identical to the legal force of the principles and rules the contents of which it restates.

Thus, legal force can be derived from *a treaty or other agreement governed by international law*. Although such an agreement does not require a special form[61] and can also be presented as, for example, a 'Declaration', a 'Charter', a 'Final Act' or a 'Programme of Action', it is obvious that none of the four NIEO documents can be qualified as an agreement governed by international law in a strict sense. The 'intent to be bound', which is a *conditio sine qua non* for such an agreement, was and still is lacking, at least on the part of the developed States. It is equally obvious that several important provisions in the documents do already form part of treaties. Thus, the principles of sovereign equality, territorial integrity, non-use of force, non-intervention and good faith have been incorporated in Article 2 of the UN Charter, while the principles of self-determination and of respect for human rights are expressly mentioned in Article 1 of the UN Charter and have found further regulation in the UN Covenants on Human Rights. Preferential treatment as one of the aspects of the principle of (substantive) equality has been worked out in Article XVIII and in Part Four of the General Agreement for Tariffs and Trade, in the Lomé Convention between the European Economic Community and the developing countries belonging to the ACP group, and in a large number of other preferential trade agreements.

Legal force can also be derived from the fact that certain principles and rules are part of *customary international law*. The very complex and much disputed issue of the constitutive elements of customary law[62] implies that it is often hard to assess the existence and exact contents of the rules of customary international law in a certain field. So much is certain, that one would claim too much when stating that the NIEO documents as such, collectively or individually, constitute customary law, no matter whether one adopts the position that customary law requires only *opinio iuris*, or only *usus*, or both.[63] For it is subject to doubt that the adoption of these documents fulfils either of these requirements, particularly in relation to the Western States, given the sharp difference of opinion that accompanied this adoption. One could, however, regard certain principles, such as the principle of State sovereignty over its natural resources, as instances of customary law, leaving apart the question to what extent this is also true of all the

708

consequences connected with these principles in the documents. The procedural principle of equity would be another such instance.

A third source of international law from which certain NIEO principles and rules can derive legal force are the *general principles of law*. This source is also of a complex and much debated character.[64] Its existence as a separate source of international law has even been disputed.[65] To the extent that the general principles as listed among the sources in Article 38 of the Statute of the International Court of Justice have to be understood as general principles of national law which can be transplanted into the international sphere, this 'source' cannot be of much help here. The application of national legal principles to international relations can only be an application *per analogiam*; national law cannot grant legal force to international law. The adoption of the NIEO documents cannot be considered to have effectuated such a 'transplantation' itself because, as has been stated above, the resolutions adopting them cannot create law *proprio vigore*. But if one interprets general principles of law as those principles and rules that are of such a fundamental character under the prevailing concept of law that they are legally binding, irrespective of whether they have been laid down in legislation, and if one takes into account those principles that are part of every legal system, both national and international, as well as the fundamental principles that are specific to international law, characterisation as a separate source seems justified and of great value. Compared with the other sources, this source has the distinctive feature that the binding force of its principles and rules is not dependent on acceptance by individual States. One could mention the following examples of such fundamental general principles of international law, which are also mentioned in the NIEO documents: the principle of sovereignty, the principle of non-use of force, the principle of good faith, the substantive principle of equity, and fundamental human rights and freedoms such as the prohibition of torture and the prohibition of racial discrimination.

Another source of international law, although it is not mentioned in Article 38 of the Statute of the International Court of Justice, is those decisions of international organisations which are directed to the member States and are binding with respect to their conduct.[66] Organisations that have the power to make such decisions are rare. Even more so are decisions that embody the principles and rules as are discussed here. More likely is the situation in which States are legally bound to implement certain principles and rules in a specific way on the basis of a decision taken by an organisation of which they are members. Regulations and directives of the European Economic Community relating to the principle of non-discrimination, and decisions taken within the framework of the EEC or of other organisations concerning themselves with preferential treatment, could be mentioned as examples.

Finally, the NIEO documents or provisions therefrom can derive their legal force from a unilateral act of one or more States. No matter whether one calls these unilateral acts sources of international law or sources of obligations.[67] As it was stated by the International Court of Justice:

It is well recognised that declarations made by way of unilateral acts, concerning legal or factual situations, may have the effect of creating legal obligations. When it is the intention of the State making the declaration that it should become bound according to its terms, that intention confers on the declaration the character of a legal undertaking, the State being thenceforth legally required to follow a course of conduct consistent with the declaration.[68]

Although the unilateral act the above passage refers to does not require a specific form, it is obvious that the words used and the legal and factual context in which the act is performed have to be such as clearly to indicate the intention of the State in question legally to bind itself.[69] Thus, if a government announces in the national parliament that it will meet the target set by the International Development Strategy concerning financial resource transfer to developing countries during the period in which it is in power, the State concerned does not place itself under an international obligation. If the same government would make this announcement in the General Assembly of the United Nations, without any reservations and mentioning a fixed period of time, the situation may well be different. Other examples of unilateral acts that might create legal obligations connected with the NIEO documents could relate to, *e.g.*, the non-use of force principle (for example, a no-first-use declaration), to the principle of substantive equality (for example, a declaration to grant preferential treatment to imports from developing countries, or to grant a neighbouring land-locked State free access to the sea), or to any of the other principles and rules discussed so far.

3.3. The NIEO documents and the 'intent to be bound'

Secondly, principles and rules embodied in the NIEO documents can be legally binding on the ground that the States or some States have manifested their will to accept them as binding by including them in these documents, and by adopting these documents through resolutions of the General Assembly.

The mere fact that a majority of the Member States has voted in favour of a resolution adopting one of these documents, does not constitute such a manifestation of will, not even on the part of those States which have voted in favour. Indeed, they may vote in favour precisely because of the fact that it concerns a legally not binding instrument. Unless a State expressly accepts a resolution or parts of it as binding upon it, through a unilateral or collective statement, the 'intent to be bound' has to be construed from a number of data connected with the contents and context of the resolution in questions such as:[70]

(1) The positions adopted by individual States through their representatives during the preparatory stage of the resolution as appearing from, *inter alia*, the *travaux préparatoires*;
(2) The voting patterns followed by the individual States at the moment of the adoption of a resolution, as well as reservations made and interpretative declarations formulated;[71]

710

(3) The content and phrasing of the resolution, *i.e.* its law-creating character; its compulsory phraseology ('shall' rather than 'should' or 'will', 'accept' or 'recognise' rather than 'intend'); its connection to other principles and rules of international law; the inclusion of rights and obligations and their character (in general, a prohibition is more difficult to evade than a duty, and an obligation to negotiate is less compelling than an obligation to a specific performance); the degree of precision in which the rights and obligations have been formulated;[72] the insertion of escape-clauses and of provisions regulating the opportunity to formulate reservations; and finally the name that has been given to the resolution such as: 'Declaration', 'Charter', 'Principles', 'Programme of Action', etc.;

(4) The supervisory mechanism provided for, indicating the readiness of the States to subject themselves to procedures for the assessment of the implementation of the resolution;

(5) The subsequent practice with respect to the resolution indicating the attitude which the States adopt in practice towards the commitment laid down in the resolution.

What is the 'source' or 'manifestation' of the legally binding norm in these cases? If one starts from the assumption that the sources listed in Article 38(1) of the Statute of the International Court of Justice are the only sources of their kind, it is necessary to subsume the provision concerned under this list. Thus, the manifestation of the intent to be bound can either be a concurrence of opinions giving birth to an international agreement, or the expression of an *opinio iuris* which together with the preceding *usus* constitutes a norm of customary law, or the recognition of a general principle of law. However, as can already be inferred from the above passage, in which we refer to unilateral declarations as a source of international law in spite of the fact that it has not been included in the list of Article 38(1), we hold the opinion that this list is not a closed one.[73] In our view the States, as the international legislature *in origine*, have the power to create rules that are binding upon them in the form and under the name they wish, without there being any need for these expressions of their intention to create law, and to be bound by it, to be related in any way to the traditional sources of international law.

3.4. The NIEO documents and the development towards customary law

Thirdly, principles and rules embodied in the NIEO documents can be legally binding in virtue of the fact that their inclusion in these documents and the subsequent adoption by the General Assembly marks the decisive stage in their development towards customary international law as the expression of an *opinio iuris* following an *usus* which has preceded the adoption of the resolutions.

As has been said above, the adoption of the NIEO documents cannot be considered as the expression of an *opinio iuris*, at least not on the part of the Western States, given the broad cleavage of opinion it left. This does not foreclose, however, the conclusion that for individual principles and rules on which there was agreement, the adoption did constitute the final stage in the development towards customary law.

3.5. The NIEO documents and 'directive principles of policy'

Finally, there may be principles and rules embodied in the NIEO documents in respect of which it must be concluded that they do not constitute binding law, but are nevertheless of great legal significance as what has been called 'directive principles of policy' which 'operate as signposts to be followed by the making of legislation or the exercise of state power'.[74]

Indeed, the conclusion that a certain provision in a resolution of the General Assembly is not legally binding, does not imply that such a provision is not binding in any respect, nor that it has no legal effect whatsoever. First of all, they may have the considerable normative effect of constituting moral or political obligations.[75] Moreover, they may have a great legal value as part of a GA resolution. As was stated by Judge Lauterpacht in his separate opinion in the *South-West Africa – Voting Procedure* opinion of the International Court of Justice of 1955:

> Whatever may be the content of the recommendation and whatever may be the nature and the circumstances of the majority by which it has been reached, it is nevertheless a legal act of the principal organ of the United Nations which Members of the United Nations are under a duty to treat with a degree of respect appropriate to a Resolution of the General Assembly. Although there is no automatic obligation to accept fully a particular recommendation or series of recommendations, there is a legal obligation to act in good faith in accordance with the principles of the Charter. . .[76]

Viewed from this perspective, it might indeed be upheld that even provisions which are not legally binding, 'may serve as elements of an international *ordre public*'[77] and as such influence the international and national bodies where their interpretation of international and national law is concerned. Here, too, the exact normative value of each individual provision and its legal implications has to be determined, taking into account the *travaux préparatoires* of the resolution concerned, the circumstances of its adoption and the composition of the majority, the contents and wording of the provision, the system of supervision to which the States are subject, and the subsequent practice.

3.6. Some concluding remarks

We must add to this that not only one and the same resolution, but also one and the same provision of a resolution may contain elements of more than one of the categories described above. Moreover, a provision or part of a provision belonging to one category may, under the influence of the so-called 'creative function' of a supervisory procedure provided for,[78] or of the practice of the international organisation or individual States, progressively develop elements of another category, thus re-enforcing its normative value.[79]

It would be impossible to give a detailed analysis of the legal nature of the individual provisions of the NIEO documents.[80] Such an analysis would not seem to be required for the purposes of the present study. The aim of the above observations was merely to stress the point that the issue of the legal character of the NIEO documents and their individual provisions raises very complex questions that have no general answer, because the circumstances determining this legal character may differ from provision to provision. Additionally, they cannot be answered once and for all, since a progressive development of the normative value of a provision may take place under the influence of subsequent legislation and subsequent State practice.

It is obvious that the exact determination of the legal character of a certain provision is of great importance in respect to the supervision of its implementation. It may determine the procedure of supervision to be followed, the instruments of supervision to be used and the measures that can be taken in the case of non-implementation. This is not to say, however, that only the implementation of legally binding principles and rules is subject to supervision, nor that a supervisory mechanism that does not provide for legal sanctions is meaningless. As was observed by Judge Lauterpacht in his individual opinion referred to above: 'A system of supervision devoid of an element of legal obligation and legal sanction can nevertheless provide a powerful degree of supervision because of the moral force inherent in its findings and recommendations.'[81] Indeed, an effective supervisory mechanism may be instrumental, not only in determining and clarifying, but also in re-enforcing the normative value of the norm whose implementation is supervised.

IV. MECHANISMS OF SUPERVISION PROVIDED FOR IN THE NIEO DOCUMENTS

4.1. Introduction

From the outset, *i.e.* since the first UNCTAD conference in 1964, there has been a power struggle between this new body and the principal organ of the UN for economic and social affairs, ECOSOC. This struggle can be regarded as a reflection of the disagreement between the developing (and socialist) States on the one hand and the developed, market economy countries on the other hand on the question which of the two institutions should be the main organ dealing with issues of trade and development. The latter group of States has adopted the position that ECOSOC is obviously the organ that is most suited for this function, because of its mandate as laid down in the UN Charter. The developing countries, conversely, have voiced a steadily increasing number of objections against the attribution of this function to ECOSOC, because of its restricted membership. They have always favoured 'their' UNCTAD as an institution in which the Third World countries are better represented and that therefore is more suited to deal with economic matters in the development context.

4.2. Supervision in the NIEO documents

The disagreement mentioned above became manifest during the discussion on the International Development Strategy for the Second United Nations Development Decade and the issue of supervision. Most developing countries preferred the UNCTAD as the body competent for carrying out the task of an over-all review and assessment of the progress made in the implementation of the Strategy, while the developed countries favoured ECOSOC as the most appropriate body. Eventually, ECOSOC prevailed (due to, *inter alia*, the prospect of an enlargement of membership) and was given a central role in the supervision of the Strategy. According to Part D of Resolution 2626 (XXV) of the General Assembly, the review and assessment were to be carried out at a national, regional and global level, 'keeping in view the need for streamlining the existing machinery and avoiding unnecessary duplication or proliferation of review activities' (para. 79). With regard to the supervision at a global level a distinction was made between sectoral review and over-all appraisal. Sectoral review was to be carried out by UNCTAD, UNIDO and the Specialised Agencies 'according to the procedures already established and to be adapted as necessary' (para. 82), while the over-all appraisal was to be carried out biannually by the General Assembly, through ECOSOC (para. 83). In 1971, ECOSOC instituted the Committee on Review and Appraisal to this end. Its task was to prepare the review and appraisal by ECOSOC on the basis of the (non-governmental) expert advice of ECOSOC's Committee for Development Planning. In 1973, ECOSOC's membership was doubled from 27 to 54.

The General Assembly and ECOSOC have also been entrusted with the supervision of the implementation of the Programme of Action on the Establishment of a New International Economic Order. According to Chapter IX, section 3 of Resolution 3202 (S–VI) of the General Assembly:

(a) All organisations, institutions and subsidiary bodies concerned within the United Nations system shall submit to the Economic and Social Council progress reports on the implementation of this Programme within their respective fields of competence as often as necessary, but not less than once a year.

(b) The Economic and Social Council shall examine the progress reports as a matter of urgency, to which end it may be convened as necessary, in special sessions or, if need be, may function continuously. It shall draw the attention of the General Assembly to the problems and difficulties arising in connection with the implementation of this Programme.

UNCTAD is mentioned in this context only with regard to the development of international trade in raw materials. The implementation of the Programme of Action was to be taken into account during the mid-term review and appraisal of the Strategy by the General Assembly in 1975. This should then lead to new commitments, changes, additions and adaptations concerning the Strategy, taking into account the Programme of Action and the NIEO Declaration (*idem*, section 8). However, this adaptation has not taken place, although it was clear in 1975 that the Strategy had become inadequate if only because of the unexpected and drastic economic and financial changes which had taken place in the early seventies.[82]

The Charter of Economic Rights and Duties of States of 1974 contains the following provision with respect to the review of its implementation in Article 34:

> An item on the Charter of Economic Rights and Duties of States shall be included in the agenda of the General Assembly at its thirtieth session (*i.e.*, in 1975, *vD*) and thereafter on the agenda of every fifth session. In this way a systematic and comprehensive consideration of the implementation of the Charter, covering both progress achieved and any improvements and additions which might become necessary, would be carried out and appropriate measures recommended. Such consideration should take into account the evolution of all the economic, social, legal and other factors related to the principles upon which the present Charter is based and on its purpose.

The General Assembly entrusted ECOSOC with the task of reviewing the implementation of the Charter, with a view to preparing the consideration by the General Assembly.[83] ECOSOC was requested to report on the progress achieved to the General Assembly at its 32nd session in 1977, during which the third biannual review and appraisal of the Strategy was also to take place.

The fourth NIEO document, the Resolution on Development and International Economic Co-operation, adopted by the General Assembly during its Seventh Special Session in 1975, did not contain any specific provisions for review of implementation.[84] For this purpose, a separate resolution was adopted, concerning the implementation of decisions made at the Seventh Special Session.[85] It stated that the assessment of this implementation was to be carried out by the General Assembly during its 31st session in 1976, with a view to facilitating, *inter alia*, the appraisal of the Development Strategy for 1977.[86]

On the basis of the above consideration of the NIEO documents it can be concluded that in the field of supervision:

(1) the General Assembly and ECOSOC are entrusted with a central role in the over-all review and appraisal;
(2) sectoral and regional supervision is requested from subsidiary organs, specialised agencies and regional organisations;
(3) the provision regarding the contribution individual States have to make to the supervision, as this is included in the Strategy, is rather vague, relates to developing countries only and deals with the setting-up and functioning of evaluation machinery and services exclusively.

In the 1970s, the following over-all review- and appraisal-activities have taken place:

1972: first biannual review and appraisal of the Second Development Decade (DD2);
1975: second biannual/mid-term review and appraisal of DD2;
review of the implementation of the Programme of Action;
review of the implementation of the Charter;

1976: review of the Resolution on Development and International Economic Co-operation;

1977: third biannual review and appraisal of DD2;

progress report on the implementation of the Charter.

All these evaluations were of a highly abstract and very general character. The General Assembly 'discussed' the progress made in the implementation of the NIEO documents by 'debating' – which in UN jargon does not mean much more than an exchange of statements by officials and delegates – the issue on the basis of a rather unspecified agenda and of materials which contained insufficient information for a real evaluation.

In 1977 the General Assembly expressed its concern over the fact that the negotiations on the establishment of the NIEO thus far had produced only limited results. In order to give these negotiations a new impetus within the framework of the United Nations, and in consideration of the Third World's resentment of the fact that ECOSOC, which had been attributed a central role in the NIEO documents, was of a restricted representation, the General Assembly decided to establish a Committee of the Whole to assist it in its central role in, *inter alia*: 'Overseeing and monitoring the implementation of decisions and agreements reached in the negotiations on the establishment of the new international economic order in the appropriate bodies of the United Nations system.'[87] However, as stated above,[88] the Committee of the Whole has so far not been a very effective body, trapped as it was from the beginning in discussions on its precise mandate. In fact, it has never performed any real supervisory function. For the review and appraisal of the implementation of the International Development Strategy for the Third UN Development Decade, the General Assembly has established another committee of universal membership, which will report to the General Assembly through ECOSOC in 1984.

4.3. Some concluding remarks

The inadequacy of the supervisory procedures provided for in the NIEO documents, or at least their failure in practice, seems to be due mainly to the following three factors.

The first factor causing their deficiency lies in the NIEO concept itself, as launched and developed within the UN. Its purposes as laid down in the NIEO documents touch upon such a wide field of both institutional and substantive issues of international economic relations, that an over-all appraisal of the progress made in this field leads to too general a discussion for review purposes. Besides, the contents of the NIEO concept vary from conceptual exhortations and social-economic indications to detailed growth and aid targets, all based upon much-disputed and multi-interpretable principles and rules of international law, the normative value of which is difficult to determine. The NIEO documents purport to formulate a conceptual framework of principles and rules that are to restructure international economic relations as well as to lay the basis of a process-political framework of a development plan. In so general a context implementation debates tend to become bogged down in differences of opinion concerning concepts as long as the discussion is not focused upon very concrete issues. It is submitted that the General Assembly and its Sixth Committee should concentrate on the conceptual framework of principles and rules. In this respect, the GA Resolution in which UNITAR was invited to make an inventory of the principles and norms relating to the NIEO,[90] constituted as such a very positive development (leaving apart here the way UNITAR has performed its task[91]). A more detailed formulation of these principles and norms, and more consensus on it, may pave the way for more effective implementation debates in the future. Process-political discussions, on the other hand, could be conducted better in a sectoral way, and in separate fora. Indeed, if all Member States of the UN would agree on a single, comprehensive development plan, it could hardly be sufficiently specific to deal with all development issues and with the restructuring of the international economic relations in an adequate way. Neither the General Assembly nor ECOSOC would seem to be the appropriate forum for the necessary planning and for the supervision of its implementation.[92]

A *second factor* which has had a negative impact on NIEO supervision thus far is the defective evaluation at the national level. As stated above, this evaluation is provided for only in relation to the Development Strategy and even there exclusively for developing countries and merely with respect to matters of machinery and procedure. The readiness on the part of States to assess critically their own domestic and foreign policies, to make the results available and to subject themselves to international supervision is usually very small. This certainly also holds good for developing countries. Not only do they often lack the know-how and facilities to carry out this national evaluation promptly and thoroughly, but they also consider the obligation to give public information about their economic state of affairs to be incompatible with their national prestige and sovereignty. The developed market-economy countries, which are willing to do this in the framework of the OECD and – be it to a lesser extent – of GATT, are much more reluctant to do so in the UN context, where, in their opinion, they are too often subjected to unjustified criticism by States which are themselves to blame in many respects. Consequently, the UN Secretariat lacks the necessary information for an over-all review and appraisal, while critical evaluations of the policies of those States about which there is sufficient information, would clash with claims of sovereignty and reciprocity.[93]

The third factor hampering effective NIEO supervision is that the several review procedures, carried out on different levels and by different bodies, are difficult to harmonise and synchronise. The jurisdictional dispute between ECOSOC and UNCTAD, referred to above, has become even more complicated since the installation of the Committee of the Whole in 1977. Moreover, the lack of cohesion and co-ordination between the other UN organs, subsidiary bodies and specialised agencies in the field of social-economic planning and supervision constitutes a major impediment to the proper functioning of the system. During the last decades, a proliferation of development programmes and agencies has taken place within the UN system as an institutional response to the demands of the new Member States and their dissatisfaction with the functioning of the system. In practice, this has led to an increasing number of overlapping responsibilities, resulting in a complex structure of interlinkages that have not been sufficiently co-ordinated and which could be better described as an organisational network rather than a system.[94] A number of expert reports have been issued on the question of a more effective co-ordination and reorganisation of the UN family in the field of development.[95] However, thus far none of these has led to a significant solution.[96] In the midst of this disarray, the NIEO documents have assigned a role to the various organisations and bodies in the supervisory machinery. To a certain extent, this reflects an awareness of the importance of sectoral and regional supervision. Unfortunately, these have been integrated in a system of such weakness and inefficiency that their impact was doomed to be equally weak and ineffective.

V. SUPERVISORY MECHANISMS OF INTERNATIONAL ECONOMIC ORGANISATIONS; SOME COMPARATIVE OBSERVATIONS

5.1. Introduction

From the foregoing it may be concluded that whatever institutional structure may ultimately be chosen or newly created in order to restructure the international economic order, for a long time to come the existing international economic organisation will continue to play an important role in the formulation of rules governing such an order and in the supervision of their implementation.

This being the case, it seems useful to discuss and compare further the supervisory mechanisms of existing international economic organisations in this' perspective, on the basis of the various individual studies contained in the foregoing Parts. This is intended to serve mainly the following purposes:
(1) to study the main problems brought about by these mechanisms, to examine in what respects these problems are comparable and to consider to what extent solutions worked out in the one organisation could also be applied to others;
(2) to relate the conclusions thus reached to the role which these organisations may play in the restructuring of the international economic order, both individually and collectively, and to develop some provisional thoughts about the main problems for which a solution would have to be devised in order to strengthen their capacity to play that role.

At the beginning of this section, a threefold *caveat* would seem to be appropriate:
(a) As indicated in the General Introduction, the present research project did not intend to cover all the existing international economic organisations

of a global as well as a regional scope. A selection had to be made. This leaves open the possibility that organisations which have not been dealt with in the present study, might present certain features which would also have been relevant to our subject. This should be kept in mind when reading the comparative observations set forth below.

(b) The international economic organisations that have been dealt with in this study differ quite substantially from each other, both as to their structure, purposes and instruments as well as to their economic and political infra-structure.[97] This means that one has to be very careful in drawing general conclusions from a comparison between these organisations. The comparative method requires that only those objects are compared, which are really comparable as to the elements which are included in the comparison. Where the law of international organisations is concerned, this implies that only those organisations should be included in a comparative study, whose structure, functions, instruments and economic and political infrastructure come closest to the existing or yet to be established organisation(s) for the benefit of which the comparative study is carried out.[98] Put in the perspective of a restructuring of the international economic order, this would seem to imply that those organisations are the most relevant whose purposes are of an economic character and whose membership is of a universal composition, since the economic order here alluded to is meant to include all States. However, practice shows that world-wide organisations may greatly benefit from the experiences of regional organisations and other organisations with a limited membership, both during their process of establishment and for their further development. Due to their more homogeneous membership and comparable economic and political structure, the latter organisations have often reached a higher level of integration and, consequently, a more advanced practice of co-ordination and co-operation. Therefore, it would seem wise also to take into account the theory and practice concerning the supervisory mechanisms of certain of these organisations.

(c) It should be constantly kept in mind that not all supervision related to the field of activity of international economic organisations takes place within the framework of these organisations. The traditional supervisory procedures like diplomatic consultations and *démarches* continue to be operative on a bilateral and multilateral basis in the margin of or outside the organisations, with the possible involvement of non-Member States.[99] These aspects cannot be taken into consideration in the present study, although they will undoubtedly also play a part in the future, whatever shape the supervisory system in international economic relations will take.

It is not possible to include in the comparison all those aspects of supervision which have been discussed in the preceding Parts. Those issues had to be selected which emerged from the reports on the individual organisations as common problems with a manifest bearing upon the restructuring of the international economic order and upon the role supervision may play in this process. These issues will be discussed with respect to the three functions of international supervision which have been distinguished in the previous Parts, *viz.* the review function, the correction function and the creative function.[100]

5.2 The review function

The review function of supervision as defined in Part I has been described as the process of judging whether behaviour conforms to a rule of law, and the review function of international supervision *vis-à-vis* States as the process of judging by a supervisory body with an international status whether the behaviour of States conforms to a rule of international law.[101] This definition is oriented exclusively towards the behaviour of States. It is obvious, however, that the conformity of State behaviour to the rules of international law is not the main purpose and not even an independent purpose of international economic organisations, but only one of the aspects of the achievement of its purposes. The review function should be performed, as well as evaluated for its effectiveness, against the following background: review has to be directed and must be proportionate to the achievement of the purposes of the organisation concerned. The achievement depends partly – not exclusively – on the implementation of the rules laid down in the treaty establishing the organisation or enacted in the course of time by the organisation. The implementation of these rules, in its turn, depends partly – not exclusively – on the behaviour of the Member States. Moreover, it has to be kept in mind in this context that State behaviour which formally is not in conformity with a certain rule, may nevertheless contribute to the substantive implementation of that rule, either because the non-conformity is meant to be a reaction to the non-conformity of the behaviour of another State and therefore to exercise pressure upon the latter State to change its behaviour, or because the actual meaning of the rule or of its purpose has changed.

A second comment with respect to the above definition of the review function concerns the words 'rule of law' and 'rule of international law'. These words might seem to imply that review of State behaviour can take place only in relation to rules which are of a legally binding character. If this were to be the case, then the scope of review within most international economic organisations would be a very limited one indeed, since most organisations contain only few legal obligations of a substantive character for their Member States in their founding treaties, and have a highly restricted power, if any at all, to address decisions to the Member States which are legally binding. Therefore, there should be recalled here what has been said before, *i.e.* (1) that supervision of the implementation of rules which are not legally binding is provided for in many cases and may be equally instrumental to the achievement of the purposes of the organisation and at the same time add to the normative value of the rules concerned[102]; (2) that the question of the legal character of a rule is a complex one that cannot be answered on the sole ground of its formal legal basis and form, and of the powers of the institution from which the rule originates[103]; and (3) that it is nevertheless important to know the exact legal nature of the rules involved since that may have consequences for the instruments and functions of the supervisory procedure.[104] These remarks lead us to the first issue of comparison under the heading of the review function: the legal character of the norms to be applied.

5.2.1. The legal character of the principles and rules the implementation of which has to be reviewed

The legal character of the principles and rules, which together constitute the body of norms of an international economic organisation against which the behaviour of the Member States may be reviewed, varies from organisation to organisation. And even within one and the same organisation this legal nature may vary from norm to norm. Moreover, a certain principle or rule which in virtue of the constitution of the organisation is a legally binding one, may be of such a character only as to the result to be achieved by it, while leaving the Member States a broad discretion as to the form and methods of that achievement.[105] This implies that the review of the achieved results can be much stricter than the review of the form and methods chosen by the State to that end.

As has been discussed in detail above in connection with the legal character of the NIEO documents,[106] a principle or rule may derive its legally binding force from a 'source' other than the constitution of the organisation. In other words: even if the instrument in which the principle or rule has been embodied is not of a legally binding character according to the law of the organisation concerned, the principle or rule itself may nevertheless have such a character, because it forms the codification or reiteration of an already existing norm of international law or because it constitutes the finalising stage of the creation of such a norm. Although the reviewing body must judge the behaviour of the Member States for its conformity with the principles and rules of the organisation, it should not consider their legal character exclusively according to the form given to these principles and rules by the organisation concerned, but also take the legal character of their contents into consideration. This should be different only when they derive their legally binding force exclusively from a source of international law which does not form part of the legal order of the organisation. Thus, a rule which has been laid down both in a not legally binding OECD code and in a legally binding EEC regulation cannot on that basis alone be applied as a legally binding rule within the OECD framework, not even to those Member States which also belong to the EEC.

Finally, the reviewing body has to be constantly aware of the fact that the legal character of a principle or rule is a dynamic matter. A norm which at the moment of its adoption was not of a legally binding character may have become binding through the subsequent practice of the organisation or by reason of some specific event which indicates the express or implied recognition of that binding character by the Member States. Whether this development has actually taken place cannot always be determined with certainty except in the rare cases that the States have expressed themselves unequivocally in that respect. This determination may therefore be one of the important creative functions of the reviewing body, and may even constitute the finalising stage in the law-creating process.[107]

This having been said, the following survey must be restricted to the legal character of the norms of the individual organisations *as to their form*. A discussion of the question whether and to what extent the legal character of each of these norms *as to their contents* differs from their formal legal character requires a detailed study which cannot be performed within this context.[108] However, even a description of the formal legal character of the principles and rules of the individual organisations may provide a useful general picture of the legal frame of reference against which the review function has to be performed.

The norms of the GATT are almost exclusively laid down in the General Agreement itself and the Schedules annexed to it. Secondary norms are rare, due to the fact that the GATT was not set up as an international organisation and consequently was not endowed with a norm-creating organ of its own. If the GATT norms have to be changed or supplemented, negotiations start between the contracting parties which may result in an amendment of the Agreement or Schedules or in a separate agreement alongside the GATT like the Multi-Fibre Arrangement.[109] All the norms laid down in the General Agreement are of a legally binding character. The same holds good for the commitments contained in the Schedules. When reviewing State conduct for its conformity with these norms and commitments, however, the general and specific rules allowing for deviating from them under certain conditions have to be taken into account.[110]

Almost the opposite picture is presented by the UNCTAD. While its constitutive document, Resolution 1995 (XIX) of the General Assembly, does not contain any principle or rule of a substantive nature, such principles and rules have been adopted by the (preceding) first as well as by the consecutive Conferences in resolutions, recommendations and declarations. This has been done in the performance of UNCTAD's function, under Article 3(c) of Resolution 1995 (XIX), to formulate principles and policies on international trade and related problems of economic development. In addition, UNCTAD is entrusted with the negotiation and adoption of multilateral legal instruments: Article 3(e) of Resolution 1995 (XIX). Although they have a clearly legislative aim, UNCTAD's resolutions, recommendations and declarations are of a recommendatory nature only. The legal character of the multilateral legal instruments adopted within the framework of UNCTAD depends on the form chosen for and the intention of the States expressed in each individual instrument. Thus, the commodity agreements and the Code of Conduct for Liner Conferences negotiated within the UNCTAD framework have the character of treaties which become legally binding after ratification, whereas the Set of Principles and Rules for the Control of Restrictive Business Practices was meant not to be legally binding.[111]

722

For both the IMF and the Bank the Articles of Agreement contain several legal obligations for the Member States in relation to the financial resources of the distinctive organisations. In addition, in the case of the IMF legal obligations result for the State concerned from the approval by the Fund of the stand-by arrangements and letters of intent after negotiations between the Fund and the Member State which applied for the stand-by arrangement.[112] In the case of the Bank additional financial obligations are undertaken on the basis of specific agreements among those States which are prepared to enlarge their contributions. The exact legal character of these agreements is not very clear yet, but once such an agreement has been concluded, the additional contributions must be deemed not to be of a continuing totally voluntary nature. However, no procedure supervising their implementation has been provided for.[113] With respect to the recipient States specific legal obligations are laid down in each individual case in the Loan Document, which is a legally binding agreement between the Organisation and the State concerned.[114]

The IAEA Statute contains both rules of a not legally binding and rules of a legally binding character, the latter in relation to the delivery of nuclear material which a Member State has made available and in connection with any atomic energy project in which the Agency assists. Additional legal obligations may be created through agreements where the IAEA is requested to apply safeguards concerning the Non-Proliferation Treaty.[115]

The Convention of the OECD contains only broadly formulated aims and policies and general undertakings by the Member States in the pursuit and for the achievement of these aims and policies. Concrete legal obligations are created by the unanimous decisions of the Council and by the agreements between the Organisation and its Member States. However, the decisions become binding only after a kind of quasi-ratification in accordance with the constitutional procedures of each individual State.[116] In addition, the Council may make recommendations to the Member States. Accordingly, the OECD has created both legally binding and not legally binding instruments. Among the first category should be mentioned the Liberalisation Codes on Capital Movements and on Current Invisible Transactions, and the International Energy Programme of the International Energy Agency. The second category consists of several 'guidelines' and other recommendations adopted by subsidiary bodies or special meetings, like the Guideline on Local and Recurrent Cost Financing and the Guideline for Improving Aid Implementation of 1979, adopted by the DAC High Level Meeting, the Guiding Principles Concerning International Economic Aspects of Environment Policies proposed by the Environment Committee and the Guidelines for Multinational Enterprises, issued by the representatives of the governments within the OECD framework.[117]

Unlike the other organisations, in the case of the CMEA the exact legal character of the principles and rules adopted by the Session of the Council is unclear, even in a formal sense. To some extent this is still the case with recommendations, but it applies even more so to the agreements. Other legal obligations are undertaken by the Member States in agreements concluded between themselves within the framework of the CMEA. The exact legal nature of the 'co-ordinated proposals' and of the 'finally co-ordinated agreements' is also rather uncertain, whereas the CMEA Standards are legally binding unless a State has expressly declared that it will not apply the Standard concerned.[118]

The foregoing leads to the following provisional remarks:

(a) The principles and rules that belong to the norms of an international economic organisation are by no means all legally binding by virtue of the constitution of the organisation. Moreover, if the Member States do not want them to be legally binding, they can always opt for instruments which do not belong to the legally binding category under the constitution. When principles and rules are legally binding, they are so because (1) they derive this character from the constitutive treaty of the organisation concerned, or (2) they are a reformulation of existing principles and rules of international law, or (3) the States which have agreed on those principles and rules want them to be legally binding, either because they consider them to be in their best interest or to be at least the best balanced weighing of the interests involved, or because subjection to them constitutes a condition for the benefits which the States wish to obtain through the organisation.

(b) Whereas in the short run the legal character chosen is an expression of the will of the States to observe the principles and rules involved, this is not necessarily the case in the long run, as may be illustrated by the almost systematic deviations from the binding rules in the case of GATT. The procedural, formal and substantive features of legally binding norms tend to make them more static than non-binding norms and therefore increase the risk of a growing divergence between norm and interests.

(c) The legally binding character of principles and rules is often alleviated to a large extent by the devices for escaping their effects on a temporal or structural basis. In particular, if conditions for the use of these devices are broad and/or review of that use is incidental and/or loose, the deviation may in fact become the rule rather than the exception.

(d) Lastly, it is submitted that the legal character of the principles and rules the implementation of which is reviewed, does constitute one of the elements of, but is not necessarily decisive for, the effectiveness of the supervisory mechanism. More important than the formal legal character is the factual consensus between the States concerned with respect to these principles and rules.[119]

5.2.2. Collection of information

For an effective review of State behaviour the collection of information is of primary importance. It is essential to the authority and impartiality of the supervisory body that it can base its findings upon objective and verifiable facts. And not only is review impossible if there is no information available about State behaviour, but it also makes it impossible to determine whether a supervision procedure should be started at all.

Precisely because of the importance of the availability of information to the achievement of the purposes of the organisation, the clearing-house or fact-finding function is usually one of the duties or even the principal duty of its secretariat. However, an organisation also depends on external sources for its information, in addition to the information derived from the fact-finding activities, carried out by its own secretariat. These external sources are mainly, but not exclusively, provided by the Member States themselves. This is why, especially in situations and/or fields in which it is difficult for the organisation to collect all the information needed for an effective review itself, the reporting procedure[120] proves to be such an efficient tool. In general it can be said that the collection of information about State behaviour is not only a very complicated, but also a very delicate matter.

In the case of some of the organisations dealt with in the previous Parts, the collection of information needed for the review of the behaviour of the Member States is somewhat less problematic, due to the fact that they have effective incentives at their disposal to stimulate States to provide them with this information. This particularly holds true for the World Bank and the IMF. Their strong position *vis-à-vis* their Member States as suppliers of capital provides them with a political and financial leverage to put pressure upon countries to supply correct and adequate information in time. Thus, the World Bank may suspend and eventually cancel a loan if the information furnished by the borrowing country proves to be incorrect.[121] The same holds good for the IMF which, precisely in view of effective supervision and the possibility to take action in case of unsatisfactory information, makes most of its facilities available in instalments.[122] Generally, a country has to meet all the conditions set by either the Bank or the IMF, including conditions pertaining to the regular supply of information, before it becomes eligible for financial support.

Another organisation which appears to be fairly successful in data collection is the OECD. This cannot be explained on the basis of financial incentives. Unlike its predecessor, the OEEC, which was set up for the preparation, co-ordination and administration of a recovery programme for which financial aid was granted by the United States in the framework of the 'Marshall Plan', the OECD does not concern itself with the providing of financial aid, except in relation to developing countries, which are not members of the organisation. The explanation cannot be found in the subject matter of the information provided either, since this information relates to the highly delicate field of national economic, social and monetary policy. Nor can the explanation be found wholly in the organisation's homogeneous political and economic infrastructure, although it undoubtedly is an important factor in this respect. Indeed, the CMEA, which is also based on a homogeneous infrastructure, encounters considerable difficulties in the gathering of information.[123] The explanation submitted here is that the success of the OECD in this field depends on its homogeneous infrastructure combined with the open structure of the societies involved and the willingness on the part of the governments to exchange information, the relatively high level of consensus on the goals of the Organisation and, last but not least, its well-developed supervisory technique of examination and confrontation with possible political pressure and the mobilisation of shame involved in it.[124] The open structure of society and the fairly free availability of information makes the collection of data less dependent on the co-operation of the governments and renders the collected data more easily verifiable. The examination technique guarantees that the information supplied by the State concerned will be confronted with and checked against the data collected by the organisation and the other Member States, and that the State will be accountable for discrepancies and blanks. This makes it practically impossible for the countries under surveillance to be negligent in providing the required information.

The IAEA, too, appears to be quite successful in obtaining the data it needs for an effective fulfilment of its supervisory function. The signatories to the Non-Proliferation Treaty, as well as a number of other States, have subjected themselves to an elaborate system of safeguards which is designed to secure the supply of correct, detailed and up-to-date information, which comprises a highly sophisticated system of human and technical inspection on the spot. A clear self-interest for the individual States will undoubtedly be the main incentive behind the system. Nonetheless, it happens more and more often that the States do not report in time.[125]

When discussing the four organisations mentioned above, their active participation in fact-finding should be emphasised. Not only may they use other sources than those provided by the States concerned, but they may also send missions to the country under supervision to collect information and verify implementation.[126]

The other organisations dealt with in the preceding Parts, namely GATT (including the TSB), UNCTAD and CMEA, have less successful experiences with the collection of information. In the case of these organisations, the collection of the information needed for effective supervision shows many serious shortcomings. Although hardly any government has ever flatly refused to submit information, responses and reports appear to be inadequate or inaccurate and/or are submitted with much delay in many cases. And precisely in these very organisations a vaguely defined power to request information that is to provide a basis for consultation between the States concerned, or for political discussion within the organisation, is the only instrument of review in most instances.[127] Several reasons could be given for this unsatisfactory situation.

In GATT the required information directly concerns vital aspects of foreign economic and trade policy which the governments are obviously reluctant to reveal, because such exposure could make them more vulnerable. In comparison with the OECD, here the information asked for is more specific and the group of participating States less homogeneous. Moreover, the moderate and indulgent reaction on the part of the other governments to insufficient or delayed information does not provide a very strong incentive to try and do away with these inadequacies. This attitude can be explained by the fact that the other governments realise that they may well find themselves in a comparable situation at some time.[128]

726

In UNCTAD the developed States are not induced to exert themselves to provide information as long as they do not expect substantial benefits from the review procedure. For the developing countries the principal impediments consist of the lack of a sufficient number of experts to collect the information and the fear that their sovereign rights will be interfered with.[129]

The situation in GATT and UNCTAD suggests that insufficient supply of information occurs only in situations of conflicting interests of a great number of heterogeneous States. The little we know about the practice of the CMEA seems to indicate, however, that even in an organisation of a small number of States with a comparable political and economical system, there is no guarantee for (comradely) co-operation in the field of supervision. Both the quality and the frequency of the information supplied by the CMEA members appears to be unsatisfactory.[130]

To the extent that the responses to questionnaires and other inquiries are inadequate, the independent fact-finding by the secretariats of the organisations becomes more important. Investigations seem to indicate, however, that the data collection by secretariats is most sophisticated and well-developed in precisely those situations in which the supply of information by the governments is fairly satisfactory. This can be explained by the fact that in a situation in which there are incentives for the governments to co-operate with the organisation in the data-gathering the climate is also favourable for the collection of information from other sources, since the secretariat will not be hampered by political objections of governments.[131] In the case of the TSB, for example, the hesitation of the organs to play a more active role in the fact-finding is due mainly to the fear of making the impression of instigating a quasi-judicial, inquisitorial procedure, which could deter the governments from further co-operation. They therefore prefer to encourage the governments to supply the information themselves, by sending them detailed inquiries, while in the case of continuous defective information they favour renewed bilateral negotiations by the parties concerned over the continuation of their own review activities.[132] In the case of the GATT as a whole, the main impediment to independent data collection would seem to be caused by lack of manpower in the secretariat on the one hand and the extremely complex structure of the different mechanisms and procedures on the other, combined with the confidential character of some of the information. GATT's data collecting appears to be most effective where general reporting is concerned. There it results in reports and statistics which are considered authoritative and are widely used.[133] In the case of UNCTAD, the task of the secretariat is not only hampered by the unsatisfactory information from the governments, but also by the fact that the field of economic activities to be covered is too broad and complex when measured against the manpower and other resources available. The secretariat encounters special problems when collecting information from developed countries about private or semi-private trade, and about other more or less confidential matters.[134] The secretariat of the CMEA seems to be well equipped for fact-finding purposes, but little information about its functioning is available.[135]

The foregoing remarks and the reports on which they are based lead to the following observations:

(a) States are more prepared to provide an organisation with the information required for the review of their behaviour, if they expect to profit from it. Their willingness may be enhanced by the fact that the benefits which a State expects from the organisation are made conditional on the State's co-operative attitude with respect to supervision. A compliant attitude of States may also be based upon fear of unfavourable reactions on the part of the organisation or of other Member States to their failure to provide the requested information. All this may be related to features like the purposes, the political power and economic vulnerability of the State concerned in comparison with other States, the political and economic infrastructure of the organisation, and the availability of alternative sources of the profits aimed at.

(b) States are reluctant to reveal information if this might affect or even counteract their national policy. Therefore, guarantees have to be provided that the other States will supply the same kind of information, and that those data, which have been classified by the State to that end, will be treated confidentially.

(c) A State can only provide the information it has at its disposal. In many cases governments do not have direct access to all the data on private economic activities. These data can be essential to effective supervision. That is why certain international instruments oblige or exhort States to supply this kind of information.[136] However, this does not solve the problem of lack of access to that information. Therefore, international codes dealing with these activities should also contain provisions about the supply of information by private companies, as is the case in the draft of a United Nations Code of Conduct on Transnational Corporations.[137]

(d) A State is able to provide the requested information only if it has the expertise and the facilities needed for an adequate response to the request addressed to it. Especially in the case of the smaller and recently independent developing countries, the drawing up of the required reports may constitute a very heavy burden for their small or not yet well-trained governmental apparatus. As a consequence, they may be easily inclined to give priority to other matters, so that their reports are delayed or are submitted in an inadequate presentation. The organisation concerned could help to improve the reporting by providing direct technical assistance, or by organising training seminars, distributing manuals or rendering advisory services. Assistance of this kind has been provided for, *inter alia*, in the 1979 GATT Understanding Regarding Notification, Consultation, Dispute Settlement and Surveillance,[138] and in the International Dairy Arrangement,[139] and within the framework of UNCTAD in the fields of shipping and transfer of technology.[140] Similarly, in relation to the review and appraisal of the implementation of the Third United Nations Development Decade on the national level, it has been stated by the General Assembly that: 'where necessary, the evaluation capacity, comprising also the statistical capability, of the countries concerned, should be strengthened, including through assistance, upon their request, from appropriate multilateral and bilateral sources'.[141] In addition, efforts should be aimed at rendering the reporting no more complicated, comprehensive and elaborate than strictly necessary. Experiments with reporting in the form of computer tapes in the framework of UNCTAD are interesting in this respect, although there is not yet any indication of possible improvements.[142] And one may wonder if this will not entail the same handicaps for developing countries.

(e) If information is to constitute a reliable basis for review, it has to be verifiable. Several devices for furthering verifiability could be taken into consideration. If the information concerns data which can be verified only at the spot, such as data about production methods or about stocks, procedures have to be installed to make such verification possible. The procedures set up in the fields of the production, storage and trade of nuclear materials by IAEA and Euratom are the most sophisticated and advanced ones,[143] but there are other examples.[144] A procedure in which the reports are submitted for comments to those directly concerned with the matters involved can serve as another device for verification. Article 23(2) of the Statute of the International Labour Organisation, stipulating that Member States have to communicate their reports on the implementation of the ILO conventions to the representative employers' organisations and labour unions in their respective countries well illustrates this.[145] The same ILO reporting system contains another well-developed device for verification, *viz.* investigation by an independent body of experts.[146] The expertise and knowledge of such a body enable it to assess the correctness and completeness of the data supplied by the governments. The organisation might also wish to consult one or more experts in the country concerned, in order to obtain information that makes verification possible, as is frequently done by, for instance, the Commission of the European Communities.[147]

(f) Another important factor is the periodicity of the reporting procedure. Not only does its regular recurrence provide the governments with the necessary routine, but it may also induce them to create specific machinery for the periodic supply of information on the same issues. Periodicity also allows a comparison with earlier reports and thus provides a picture of the progress made, thereby making information more verifiable at the same time.[148]

(g) If a situation on which information is required is of an exceptional nature and of limited duration, and if it does not cause any irreparable damage, the supervisory body has to consider carefully in each individual case whether it is desirable to put pressure on the State in question to come up with timely and detailed information, since this obligation might divert the attention of the authorities from the necessity to redress the situation.[149] In this case, such an incentive might turn out to be counterproductive. On the other hand, the preventive effect of the review procedure should also be taken into consideration.

5.2.3. *The role of the secretariats*

The role of the secretariats of international economic organisations in the review procedure emerges from the individual studies as a highly important

729

and very active role, not only with respect to the collection of information, but also in view of its processing. In the organisations dealt with, the technical phase of non-judicial supervision appears to be primarily the domain of the secretariats.

The World Bank offers the best illustration of this fact. With its Secretariat of about 4,500 persons, it might even be characterised as a staff-dominated organisation. The policy of the management set such broad margins in most cases, that the staff is left with ample room for manoeuvre and, consequently, for implementing policy on its own. The identification, preparation and appraisal of projects fall under the responsibility of the staff. The Directors become involved in this process only shortly before the Loan Documents are concluded. After that, their involvement with the individual projects is even more indirect and distant.[150]

The IMF has more or less the same institutional structure as the World Bank, but its Secretariat is much smaller: about 1,400 persons. In the case of this Organisation, the responsibilities of the Directors and those of the staff are more closely interwoven, due to the fact that the Member States, through the Directors, are more actively involved in the allocation of funds. Nevertheless, most of the preparatory work, such as the preparation of studies and collection of documentary materials, and also the missions to the countries concerned are carried out by the staff.[151]

The GATT Secretariat, which numbers about 300 staff-members only, is responsible for the collection of information and the processing of this information into reports on trade data and on the development of trade policy. Although it is not always successful in acquiring all the relevant data from the contracting States, its reports and statistics are widely used as an authoritative source. This enhances to a certain extent the impact of the Secretariat on national policy-making.[152] On the whole, however, GATT is reported by an expert as not having developed a staff 'able to cope with the extraordinary complexity of world trade and to provide substantial leadership for trade policy'.[153]

About the same could be said of the UNCTAD Secretariat, which has a staff of about 265 persons. However, the reports, documents and figures it produces are not of the same informative value as those of the GATT Secretariat. Consequently, they are less influential. This is partly due to the even broader field of trade and development the UNCTAD has to cover, and partly to the fact that the Secretariat, to an even larger extent than its GATT counterpart, depends on secondary sources such as national and international economic and financial reviews and periodicals, while many figures have to be estimates, because the States fail to supply it with adequate information.[154] Moreover, most of the developed States are inclined to consider the UNCTAD studies as being biased in favour of Third World views on issues of trade and development, which also reduces their impact.

The IAEA Secretariat, on the other hand, a body of about 1,400 staff-members, has a good quantity of 'authentic' material at its disposal. This is not only due to the special procedures designed within the IAEA to secure the supply of information, but also to the active role the Secretariat itself is empowered to play and does play in the fact-finding. Thus, in 1980, over 1,100 inspections were carried out in more than 500 nuclear plants, while at the same time millions of surveillance pictures were taken, and thousands of seals were applied. In addition to its permanent professional and general service staff, the IAEA Secretariat employs around 130 inspectors on a contractual basis. The numerous data collected are processed by the Secretariat and – since 1976 – presented to the Board of Governors in the form of an annual Safeguards Implementation Report.[155]

Where the OECD is concerned, daily management falls under the responsibility of the Secretary-General with his counsellors and staff of about 1,500 persons. The Secretariat has the task of assisting the various Council Committees and Working Groups which do most of the preparatory work for the Council's activities. Emphasis is placed on surveying developments in national and international economic and monetary policy, and on statistics. The basic element of preparatory work is the annual country-by-country review prepared by the Economic and Statistics Department of the OECD Secretariat, which is the major source of information for all the other parts of the Secretariat.[156]

An equally important function in the technical phase of international supervision is performed by the CMEA Secretariat, an institution of about 2,500 staff-members. It collects and analyses information on the implementation of resolutions and decisions of the Council. At the same time it functions as the collector of notifications regarding the acceptance of recommendations and in relation to the specific consultation procedure.[157]

From the foregoing brief remarks on the role of the secretariats it may be concluded that the establishment and maintenance of a highly qualified and well-equipped secretariat is of the utmost importance as a first and vital step on the road to an effective supervisory mechanism. No matter what other bodies and procedures are established, they will depend to a large extent on the data-collecting and processing and the administrative support performed by the secretariat staff. And if the Member States are not willing to establish such special bodies and procedures, or prove reluctant to subject their behaviour to the existing ones, it becomes all the more important for the secretariat to have the availability of the manpower and facilities necessary to carry out the technical part of the review function to the fullest possible extent. Even if there is no follow-up in the form of a political phase, the technical phase, if performed in a skilful, detailed and objective way, can still have a corrective as well as preventive effect. In order to achieve these effects, however, it is absolutely necessary that the following conditions are met:

(a) Secretariats must be organised in such a way that they have sufficient manpower, equipment and other material facilities at their disposal to be able satisfactorily to carry out their tasks, and adequately to cover the field of activities of the organisations concerned. The Member States must be aware that money spent on a secretariat is a good investment, provided that the conditions mentioned below are met. They are the first to profit from

731

the reports and statistics which a well-equipped secretariat can provide – and often is in a better position to provide than the national agencies. Moreover, it is in their interest that the secretariats regularly review the implementation of the international obligations by the Member States, a function which the States cannot perform to the same degree as these secretariats, neither technically nor politically. Particularly in a time of financial restraints a well-equipped secretariat might prove to be an effective tool for saving money on the national budgets.

(b) The foregoing holds true only if the secretariats can rely on sufficient economic and technical competence among their personnel. Both the collection and the processing of data in the complex fields of economic policy and international economic relations require a high degree of expertise in economics. This requirement becomes even more urgent when it comes to reviewing the conformity of State behaviour to certain standards and rules in these fields. And, the technique of data collection as such can be mastered only by experts in information systems. This is not to say that a good secretariat should be top-heavy; it should be able to provide the required expertise combined with sufficient support from technical and administrative personnel. This is the more urgently required in cases where the expertise – or the time – is lacking on the part of the governmental representatives participating in the reviewing process.[158] It is evident that a strict application of the requirement of equitable geographical distribution in recruiting staff will not always match the intention to select the best available experts. The same holds true for the repartition of functions among the nationalities of the Member States, which often hampers a sound career-planning and thus can easily demotivate competent persons from applying for a position or, when they have joined the staff, may take away the stimulus for an optimal performance.[159] A hopeful sign in this respect may be the determination, expressed by the UN Secretary-General in his 1982 Report on the work of the Organisation, 'to ensure that performance and merit are the essential criteria for professional advancement'.[160] Another aspect to be mentioned is the balance which has to be found between the necessity of a regular influx of new expertise and experience from the national level on the one hand and the building-up of experience with the functioning of the organisation on the other.[161]

(c) There must be sufficient guarantee that the secretariat staff can function independently from the national authorities. Only if this condition is met, can the results of the secretariat's activities acquire the status of an authoritative source in the eyes of the national authorities on a general and long-term basis. This requires sufficient safeguards against undue influence by the Member States both with respect to the recruitment and during the discharge of its duties by the staff.[162] As representatives of the common interests of the organisation the staff members may find themselves in a rather precarious position in situations where their activities concern issues on which the views of the Member States differ substantially. Every initiative taken or view adopted by the secretariat is bound to disappoint or even upset a group of governments. An active role and outspoken position on the part of the staff may then deepen the disagreement and hence prove to be counterproductive.[163] On the other hand, since only an independent and active secretariat can build up the authority required to contribute to the effective functioning of the organisation, attempts on the part of Member States to exert undue influence may backfire in the long run.[164] All this leads to the conclusion that the independence of the secretariat must be clearly laid down in the constitution of the organisation,[165] and that the organisation concerned must be given the powers and facilities to protect its staff members effectively. As the International Court stated in its advisory opinion in the Bernadotte Case:

> In order that the agent may perform his duties satisfactorily, he must feel that this protection is assured to him by the Organisation, and that he may count on it. To ensure the independence of the agent, and, consequently, the independent action of the Organisation itself, it is essential that in performing his duties he need not have to rely on any other protection than that of the organisation (save of course for the more direct and immediate protection due from the State in whose territory he may be).[166]

(d) The Secretary-General, as head of the secretariat, must not only bring his special expertise into the secretariat but also his political weight. This requires that the position offered must be able to attract first class candidates. The Secretary-General should have sufficient leeway for organising the secretariat in the most efficient way and for recruiting the best possible staff.

(e) A secretariat can function in an optimal way only if its tasks are defined broadly enough, and if it is endowed with the necessary powers, especially regarding its own independent data-collecting and processing. Room must be left for a dynamic interpretation of its functions and power in accordance with the needs of the circumstances.

(f) In view of the fact that many secretariats and other organs and subsidiary bodies see their activities frustrated by a shortage of budgetary funds and the unwillingness of the Member States to allocate additional financial means, it is of the highest importance for an effective and impartial functioning of a secretariat, that its costs be adequately covered by the regular budget – and that charging it with additional tasks is accompanied by a fixed commitment to bear the additional costs.

(g) Since international economic relations are the domain of many international organisations and their secretariats, efficient use of the available manpower and facilities, and a productive exchange of experience and information both call for a close co-ordination and co-operation between those organisations and their secretariats.[167]

5.3. The correction function

In the first Part the correction function has been described as the function designed to ensure the compliance with international legal obligations through persuasion or pressure from outside.[168] However, as has been observed at the beginning of the present chapter, the accomplishment of the aims of an international organisation is not necessarily fostered by a strict implementation of its rules.[169] In some cases deviating State behaviour may function as a corrective incentive *vis-à-vis* the deviating behaviour of another State; in other cases it may initiate or support a dynamic interpretation of the organisation's aims, when the rules have not kept pace with these aims in the light of changed circumstances.

Moreover, in the case of protracted negotiating processes in the field of international economic relations, the correction function is not only, and not even primarily, directed towards correcting State behaviour of the past but also towards directing future State behaviour.

5.3.1. The correction function directed towards policy development

In Part IV it was observed with respect to UNCTAD – and comparable trends can be discerned in the case of GATT and OECD – that there supervision is primarily directed towards policy development, and not so much towards evaluation of implementation in the past. This implies that the correction function as well is first and foremost directed towards stimulating policy-fulfilling State behaviour.[170] A similar picture is offered by the IMF, where supervision appears to be characterised by steering incentives rather than by correction in a strict sense.[171]

In connection with this stimulating function of supervision the secretariats of the organisations again have an important role to play. Their studies and reports will usually form the main documentation on which the discussions about policy development are based. These studies and reports may consist of information and data provided by the governments, or collected from other sources by the secretariats themselves, or they may be prepared by or in co-operation with *ad hoc* consultants. They may contain an assessment of the States' implementation of their obligations, as discussed above with respect to the review function. They may, however, also describe the current state of the national and international economic affairs in a more general way, like the half-yearly 'Economic Outlook' of the OECD Secretariat. Moreover, they may have the character of a report about the progress of on-going negotiations, in order to take stock of the different positions and to evaluate the results achieved so far. Finally, they may be more directly related to policy development, *e.g.* by giving an inventory of the main problems for which a solution has to be found, and even by indicating policy alternatives. An exceptionally progressive example of such policy-oriented activities of a secretariat is presented by the Commission of the European Economic Community. Not only can the Council request the Commission toundertake studies and to submit appropriate proposals (Article 152, EEC Treaty); this 'Secretariat' even has in most cases the exclusive right of initiative for the enactment of regulations, recommendations and decisions steering and implementing the Community policy.[172] On a more moderate scale the role of the secretariats in the policy development is also found in the organisations dealt with in the preceding Parts.[173] This role is not necessarily a spin-off of the supervision activities of the secretariats, but very often this appears to be the case.

The connection between supervision and policy development is coming to the fore even more clearly in the activities of the policy-making organs of the organisations. In fact, these organs also carry the ultimate responsibility for the correction function, in the case of both judicial and non-judicial supervision. Due to this combination of functions, but even more because of their being composed of representatives of the Member States, these organs will prefer to create incentives for steering State behaviour and look for a policy approach which is a reflection of State consensus and State attitudes rather than putting pressure upon governments to change their national policy or executive measures. Clear examples are to be found in the general attitude of the Contracting Parties of GATT towards violations by States of their obligations.[174] The case study on the TSB reveals more or less the same for the Board.[175] More difficult to prove, but not less likely, is the 'adapting' attitude of the Session of the Council in the CMEA *vis-à-vis* a recalcitrant State in certain specific cases.[176]

In the context of a gradual development towards a restructuring of the international economic order the importance of supervisory procedures for policy development is evident. The NIEO postulate in itself originated as a reaction against the behaviour of the developed States and as a claim in support of the attitude of the developing States. Therefore, studies and reports on State practice and on the current national and international economic situation, drawn up in the framework of supervisory procedures of the several international economic organisations, and the discussions and actions based upon them, can be highly instrumental as catalysts of structural changes.

5.3.2. *The political debate*

The correction function of international supervision, in the strict sense of the term, can be effectuated by a multitude of instruments, ranging from subtle socio-political constraint and quiet diplomacy to downright sanctions.

In the World Bank, and to a lesser degree also in the IMF, the Secretariat staff possess autonomous decision-making powers to a large extent, which enables them to take corrective decisions themselves, *e.g.* by not granting or renewing loans.[177] And in the European Communities, too, the Commission (High Authority for the Coal and Steel Community) has the power to make such decisions and even impose financial sanctions in certain cases.[178] Furthermore, in these Communities, it is the Court of Justice which exercises an important corrective function by rendering judgments on State behaviour which due to the Court's authority have a highly corrective effect in almost all cases.[179] The same kind of adjudication has been provided for in the Cartagena Agreement,[180] but its impact in practice still is not clear. In all other international economic organisations the political debate, in the plenary organ of State representatives or in the executive body of a restricted membership, turns out to be the most widely used corrective instrument.

The degree of correction exercised by these debates depends on many factors, such as: (1) the size and composition of the supervisory body; (2) the normative value of and consensus on the obligations which are the subject of supervision; (3) the preparation during the review phase by the secretariat and/or bodies of independent experts; (4) the possibilities of financial or other incentives; (5) the availability and effectiveness of sanctions; (6) the measure of inter-dependence within the group of States concerned; (7) the economic or political vulnerability of the State concerned; (8) the publicity surrounding the debate; (9) the inside or outside pressure from non-governmental circles, *e.g.* labour unions, or from public opinion in general.

Looking at the political debate especially in GATT and UNCTAD – and for that matter also in the plenary sessions of the UN General Assembly – one cannot escape the conclusion that debating in large fora is not very effective as far as correction *stricto sensu* is concerned. The political debate in large fora may be an important instrument of 'parliamentary diplomacy' through which the organisation gives expression to its 'collective legitimisation' and thus may act as 'a dispenser of politically significant approval and disapproval of the claims, policies, and actions of States'.[181] Certainly, some political pressure may emanate from such debate, if only in the form of the so-called 'mobilisation of shame' which, depending on the circumstances of each individual case, can no doubt exert political, social and moral constraint. But those plenary debates, with their own pace and language, producing long statements and interventions, but little real discussion, are not likely to result in strong and unambiguous decisions with a truly corrective effect. That is why, particularly within GATT, the discussions aimed at correction are often held within a more restricted set-up of working parties and panels and/or behind closed doors.[182] Even within the OECD, which is an organisation of limited membership, the focal point of the correction function is not to be found in the debates of the council but rather in the examinations which take place *in camera* in smaller bodies of State representatives.[183]

Some further comments have to be made concerning publicity. The role of publicity in relation to the correction function cannot be described in unequivocal terms. Much depends on the concrete situation and especially on the specific phase of the supervisory procedure. In general, publicity can be said to enhance the pressure exercised *vis-à-vis* a State and thus to be instrumental to the correction pursued. In respect of the so-called 'mobilisation of shame' publicity is even an essential element. But during the discussions and negotiations concerning State behaviour, publicity may very well have a counter-productive effect. Publicly expressed criticism is often considered as an unfriendly act, violating the *comitas gentium*, and may result in a hardening of positions. This may even be the case in situations where a State is economically vulnerable, because in that situation governments will often try to mobilise nationalistic feelings by resisting foreign interference. In closed meetings, on the other hand, discussions may be very pertinent and even harsh, and devoid of all the careful posturing that is

736

familiar to public debate, without having similar negative effects. There the opposition of the State concerned against the 'persuasion of reasonableness' may put its representative in complete isolation and thus maximise the pressure while at the same time this representative is in a better position to make concessions if he can do so with 'face-saving' for his government. This is not to deny, however, that some form of publicity, at a certain moment, is in most cases necessary as a pressure instrument. Much depends here on how the course and the outcome of the debate are formulated for the records and the press-releases and how broad the circle of distribution is. It requires a continuous balancing between, on the one hand, feelings of national self-consciousness and pride, and on the other hand the convincing force of the criticism stemming from a well-respected body of either independent experts or representatives of (preferably like-minded) governments.[184] The foregoing can best be illustrated with reference to the so-called 'confrontation technique' of the OECD. Periodic examinations and confrontations take place in nearly all areas of OECD competence. They are organised as closed sessions of small groups of State representatives, hearing 'both sides" and making a thorough examination including, if necessary, visits on the spot; they allow for very detailed discussions and sometimes severe criticism, motivated also by the common interest the States have in the fulfilment of the obligations by each of them. Only in the final stage of the confrontation are plenary meetings convened which result in the publication of a report or communiqué concerning a country's behaviour. The latter has only a limited corrective effect; the main correction must have been obtained during the examination *in camera*.[185]

The composition of the supervisory body is important for the corrective effect of the debate mainly in the following three respects: (a) the expertise and political experience of the representatives; (b) the level of the representation; and (c) the affiliation of the representatives.

(a) In relation to the review function it has been stressed that the complex and difficult nature of the issues to be reviewed requires sufficient expertise on the part of the reviewing body. The same is true, be it to a less extent, for those who participate in the correction debate. Although they can profit from the reports and studies drawn up by expert committees and/or the secretariats, a thorough discussion on the basis of these reports and studies and the drawing of convincing conclusions from them is possible only if there is enough expertise among the delegates. However, expertise alone is not enough. The specific character of the corrective debate implies that the participants at the same time possess a good feeling of the political climate in general, the political situation in the individual States concerned and the room for manoeuvring possessed by each of the other participants in the debate. Only then is it possible to evaluate which amount of pressure is needed and advisable and which concessions are feasible. That is exactly why the lobbying surrounding the debates is often more important than the debates themselves.

(b) Meetings of governmental representatives can be convened at very different levels, varying from the Heads of State or Heads of Government to low-ranking civil servants. As a rule each government is free to appoint its own representative and consequently also to determine the level at which it will be represented. This is not always the case. For certain organs it is stipulated in the basic treaty that it consists of members of government.[186] In other cases, this is commonly understood to be an implied requirement (at least on certain occasions).[187] It is self-evident that top-level meetings are more likely to bring about break-throughs in a discussion and will get much more publicity and thus generate more political and social pressure. Furthermore, if well-prepared, such meetings probably create the best possible climate for concessions, particularly because all the participants are in a position really to negotiate, including the possibility to threaten with counter-measures or to offer incentives, thus paving the way for compromises. An example of a supervisory mechanism in which the level of representation appears to play an important role is that of the CMEA. Although it may be concluded from the communiqués that the higher the level of the supervisory organ is, the more 'diplomatic' the supervisory debates are, this certainly does not imply a decrease in effectiveness. The Executive Committee, whose meetings play a central role in the supervision process, derives its high authority from the fact that it is composed of the vice prime-ministers. It supervises the main trends of the economic co-operation between the CMEA States leaving the more detailed questions to lower-ranking organs. Supervision by the Executive Council is considered to have strong preventive effects.[188]

(c) From the two foregoing paragraphs it follows that the correction function will be most effective if it is exercised by representatives rather than by independent experts. The latter may, and in certain procedures actually do, already play an important function in reviewing State behaviour for its conformity with the principles and rules of the organisation concerned and in reporting their findings. In general, however, they will not have the required authority to make the States take the measures that are required according to the findings. This is only different for certain international judicial organs and arbitration tribunals, like – in most instances at least – the Court of Justice of the European Communities. If we speak about 'representatives' we do not refer to governmental representatives only, but also to, e.g., the parliamentarians in the European Parliament and the employers' and trade unions' representations in the political organs of the ILO. They too, in virtue of their close links with national interests and their political influence, can be very instrumental in putting pressure upon governments.

5.3.3. Friendly settlement of disputes

The allegation or finding that a State has not fulfilled its obligations as a member of an international organisation, will usually originate a dispute between the State concerned and the organisation and/or one or more of the

738

other Member States. Although in the international society the settlement of disputes is much less regulated and institutionalised than is the case in a national rule-of-law society (the *Rechtsstaat*) and is to a large extent still left in the hands of the States themselves,[189] this does not mean that international law leaves the States complete discretion in that respect. The prohibition of the use of force, laid down in Article 2, para. 4, of the UN Charter, is now recognised as a general principle of international law.[190] This implies that disputes as those referred to above have to be settled in a friendly way. Moreover, States are not free in all cases to select and initiate a procedure for settlement themselves. In many organisations, specific procedures for dispute settlement have been established which have priority over other possible procedures;[191] in certain cases they even have an exclusive character.[192] Besides, in certain instances a specific procedure for friendly settlement is open only if the dispute cannot be settled by means of negotiations[193] or after conciliation has been sought for in vain.[194] If specific procedures for friendly settlement have been provided for, the taking of unilateral measures of reprisal, even of a non-violent character, is as a rule excluded[195] or is allowed only if none of those procedures has proved to be an effective remedy.[196] In some organisations or treaties the collective taking of reprisals against a defaulting State is provided for as a sanction.[197]

Under international law many procedures for the peaceful settlement of disputes have developed which play a part in the efforts to keep or bring State behaviour in conformity with international legal norms. They operate both outside and within the framework of an international organisation and may range from consultation between the States involved in the dispute, via good offices, mediation, inquiry and conciliation – under the direction of one or more other States, one or more persons of great authority, an *ad hoc* commission, or an organ or subsidiary body of an international organisation – to specific judicial and non-judicial procedures agreed upon between the parties or provided for within an international organisation.[198]

As has been indicated in Part I, judicial settlement of disputes still plays a very minor role in the international society.[199] This is also the case for international economic organisations with, as a notable exception, the European Communities. Dispute settlement is usually left to the policy-making organs. Several reasons may be put forward for this:[200]

(a) Policy-making organs are on the whole in a better position than courts to effect a compromise bringing about a solution that is acceptable to all the parties concerned. Although conciliation may match very well the judicial function, the public and adversary character of the proceedings and the duty of the court to apply the law make such a result less likely.[201]

(b) Policy-making organs have more room to solve the dispute by an interpretation of the principles and rules of the organisation which is based more upon the purposes of the organisation and the political and economic circumstances than on the wording of the text and its juridical meaning. They may also create new rules taking into account new developments and thus reduce or eliminate the conflict between the State behaviour and the existing rule. Although a court will also deem itself competent to give a dynamic interpretation to the applicable rules, especially if the *opinio iuris* has changed, it will have to keep in mind that it is entrusted with the application of the law and not with the creation of new law.

(c) Many of the principles and rules which play a part in the dispute may not be legally binding or contain policy goals rather than specific obligations. In such a case adjudication not only is less appropriate but may even be impracticable.

(d) Policy-making organs operate less formally than courts and as a rule allow the States concerned to participate in the deliberations and even in the decision-making. States in general prefer this position which enables them better to explain all the aspects of their case without having to confine themselves to the legal aspects. Indeed, courts are often considered as organs which operate outside the political life of the organisation. Although composed of highly qualified lawyers, they do not necessarily include experts in the issues involved. And although meant to be of a representative composition both as to geographical distribution and concerning the different legal systems, States do not always consider them to be a true reflection of political reality with its diversity of opinions and interests.[202]

This is not to deny, of course, that judicial procedures offer important advantages over non-judicial procedures. The composition and procedure of the courts is designed to guarantee an independent and impartial hearing of the case and a final decision that is based upon the principles and rules which have been agreed upon by Member States or the organisation. The detailed procedure laid down in official rules as well as the public character of the proceedings are an additional guarantee that justice is done. Political influences are shut out as much as possible and the principle *nemo iudex in sua causa* is applied. This might be important, especially for politically weaker or less influential States which are involved in a conflict with a powerful State. It requires, however, that the court entrusted with the dispute settlement has such an authority that its decisions are very likely to be obeyed. As has been said before, this appears to be the rule only in highly integrated organisations or organisations with a rather homogeneous membership like the European Communities and the Council of Europe, and even there the international courts concerned have to manoeuvre very carefully in order not to lose the States' confidence.

In some organisations the non-judicial settlement procedure has to be given priority. If this has not led to a solution of the conflict the case must be referred to an independent arbitrator to be appointed by the President of the International Court of Justice,[203] to its own arbitration organ,[204] to the International Court of Justice,[205] or to either an *ad hoc* arbitration tribunal or the International Court of Justice.[206] Thus the advantages of both procedures may be combined in such a way that the arbitrators or the court get to deal with a dispute after it has been discussed in a political forum and a friendly settlement has first been sought in vain.

Such a staggered procedure with priority for the political phase would seem to be the best solution for most organisations, also for the economic organisations, where most disputes concern highly complex and policy-related issues. The political phase of the correction procedure can be instrumental in reaching compromises and developing greater consensus with respect to the principles and rules and in shaping a complaint attitude on the part of the States, while judicial decisions and advisory opinions may subsequently strengthen the legal authority of those principles and rules.

5.3.3.1. Consultation

By far the most frequently employed instrument of correction by way of a friendly settlement in international economic organisations is that of – more of less – institutionalised consultation between the organisation and a Member State or between two or more States.

Examples of the first form of consultation – between the organisation and a Member State – are to be found in the practice of the IMF. However, a *caveat* seems at place here. The IMF notion of consultation covers both the collection of information by the staff and the assessment and discussion of State behaviour. It therefore, in IMF terms, stands more or less for supervision in general and consequently is as important for the review function as for the correction function. In most cases of IMF practice consultation takes place as part of missions. These missions provide an opportunity for a detailed review of the economic and financial policies of the individual States. At the same time they are directed at influencing State policy and thus are meant to generate corrective or steering elements in order to achieve a friendly solution of any divergence between the IMF rules and State conduct.[207] This is particularly manifest in the case of supervision concerning stand-by arrangements and other conditional facilities where compliance with the performance criteria by the State concerned is a condition for (additional) drawings on the respective funds.[208]

The second, more traditional, form of consultation – between two or more States involved in a dispute – is to be found in most international economic organisations.

Within the purview of GATT various consultation procedures of that kind have been provided for. As a rule an attempt at consultation is required before the States may have recourse to other means of dispute settlement. This is the case, *inter alia*, in the 1979 Understanding Regarding Notification, Consultation, Dispute Settlement and Surveillance, which relates to GATT's central dispute settlement procedure.[209] Consultations can be initiated by special request or at the occasion of a complaint, a notification or a simple exchange of information channelled through the Secretariat.[210]

In 1978, the Trade and Development Board of UNCTAD decided that during the session of the Special Committee on Preferences, a body entrusted with the supervision of the Generalised System of Preferences, informal plurilateral consultations should be held on individual schemes if so requested. These plurilateral consultations are to take place between preference-receiving and preference-giving States. They are private and confidential in character. Similarly, mutually agreed consultations are provided for in the 1980 Set of Multilaterally Agreed Equitable Principles and Rules for the Control of Restrictive Business Practices.[211]

In the OECD the Member States are entitled to request for consultations either prior to or after the confrontation procedure. Consultations take place in almost all fields under OECD competence: economic affairs and statistics, trade policy, international investment and multinational enterprises, restrictive business practices, agriculture, fisheries, environment and scientific and technological policy. Consultations are being held in restricted sessions and are as a rule confidential.[212]

As from 1976, the CMEA members are required to notify the other interested Member States and the Organisation whenever circumstances arise which hinder a timely or complete implementation of their obligations. Such a notification is meant to lead to a consultation procedure. In addition, a special consultation procedure is provided for in case a State deliberately violates its obligations. It has not been determined, however, who has to take the initiative to start the consultation procedure if this is not done by the defecting State itself.[213]

From this brief survey it may be concluded that, especially in the field of international trade, the States rely heavily on consultation as a procedure of dispute settlement. Though many would not even count consultation among the settlement procedures because it would seem to be the logical step to take prior to any such procedure, the Member States of the different organisations dealt with have deemed it appropriate expressly to refer to it and assign to it an important role. This is no cause of surprise if one realises that the advantages of non-judicial dispute settlement set-out above are all very much inherent in the consultation procedure. The procedure is mostly very informal and *ad hoc*, and has as a rule a private character which makes it easier for States to arrive at concessions. Apart from the specific IMF procedure discussed above and, to a less extent, the CMEA procedure, consultation still leaves the dispute settlement totally in the hands of the States concerned. These are usually States which in some way or another are involved in the dispute and therefore have an interest in a solution that is acceptable to all of them and offers sufficient prospect for compliance. For that reason they will be inclined to take a pragmatic approach leading to bilateral and multilateral interpretations of the rules concerned which may differ from case to case according to the circumstances. This approach offers good possibilities for a steering function and furthers the creation of adapted rules. Taking into account these advantages and considering the practice described above the conclusion seems justified that consultation has an important part to play, within the framework of supervision, in paving the way for and also contributing to the establishment of a NIEO.

One should of course not lose sight of the risks which the consultation procedure may entail. Since it is conducted mainly by the States, there may be a tendency to make the procedure even more informal and private by having it take place outside the framework of the organisation. This could harm the authority of the organisation and decrease the confidence in its supervisory function. And even if the procedure formally remains within the structure of the organisation, the flexible approach of varying groups of States towards the interpretation of the rules of the organisation and the differing interests in the outcomes of the consultations might impair the uniform application of these rules and thus negatively affect future policy and norm-creation by the organisation. It would therefore seem of vital importance to long-term international co-operation that the organisation plays a part in the consultation in all cases. This holds good not only for the preparatory stage, but even more so for later phases, where the organisation should be in a position to point at any deviations in the interpretation given by the participating States to the rules and to assess the final solution for its conformity with its purposes and policy. Here too, an important role could be played by the secretariats.

5.3.3.2. Other procedures: mediation and conciliation

Apart from consultation not many other procedures for peaceful settlement of disputes are expressly referred to in the context of the organisations dealt with here. In GATT, several procedures have developed according to which working parties and panels of restricted composition are established to gather and evaluate information on a dispute and to prepare a report for the Contracting Parties. Their performance leaves ample room for good offices, mediation and conciliation and this has been one of the purposes of the panels in order to make a substantive debate by the Contracting Parties superfluous. In actual practice, however, members of working parties and panels are more and more reluctant to perform these – in their opinion adjudicative – functions. After all, the members of the working parties are governmental representatives and the panel members, although appointed in their individual capacity, are in most cases diplomats. Not only are they personally inclined to give much weight to State interests and in particular to the interests of their respective national State; GATT as a whole has shifted towards a more power-oriented approach accompanied by a decline of the prestige of the dispute settlement procedures, especially its rule-oriented elements.[214] The case study on the Textile Surveillance Body reveals the same tendency. Time and again the TSB has passed over an active, rule-oriented, conciliatory role in favour of a more passive role. Whenever there was the slightest indication of a possibility for renewed bilateral consultations, the TSB was rather too eager to recommend that they be resumed and to suspend its conciliation.[215]

In the other organisations conciliation no doubt forms an element of other corrective procedures like the examination and confrontation procedure in the OECD or the political debate in the Executive Committee of the CMEA, but it is not provided for as a separate procedure.

In our opinion this scanty and even declining role of good offices, mediation and conciliation in international economic organisations is much to be regretted. It would seem that especially in a situation where consensus on policies and rules is decreasing among the Member States because of a growing conflict of short-term interests, there is an increasing need for a mediating and conciliatory role by an independent third party or on behalf of the organisation representing the common interest. And this in particular when consultation has led to no result or to a result that conflicts with the rules and policy of the organisation. This role can, however, be exercised in an effective way only if a specific procedure is established for that purpose with certain minimum rules and with a clear provision on who can take the initiative in what circumstances and on the rights and duties of the governments involved. In addition, practice would seem to indicate that this role should be placed in the hands of independent experts, who are not linked with national interests but enjoy authority because of their expertise and practical experience inside and outside the organisation. The conciliatory role of the Commission of the European Communities might serve as an example here, even if one takes into account that conditions are exceptionally favourable there because of the relative homogeneity of the Member States in spite of their many conflicts of interests, and because of the permanent status of the Commission and its large staff.[216] But in quite another field, supervision under the European Convention on Human Rights, an example is to be found of a rather effective conciliatory procedure under the direction of a non-permanent group of independent experts, the European Commission of Human Rights, with a small staff.[217] We will discuss some of the requirements for effective third-party mediation and conciliation later on.[218]

5.3.4. Sanctions

Sanctions in international law usually do not have a punitive element. Apart from some very exceptional cases, international criminal law combined with international enforcement procedures does not exist. The purpose of sanctions against States is to exert such pressure as to induce the State concerned to act in conformity with the law and to redress the consequences of its violations. They are therefore comparable to sanctions under national private or administrative law rather than criminal law.

As has been indicated in Part I[219] sanctions are only rarely provided for in international law and even more rarely applied. The establishment of international organisations has changed that situation only to a limited extent. Although most constitutions provide for some sort of sanction in relation to the membership of the organisation, such as suspension of the right to vote and expulsion, the organisations are in general reluctant to apply these kinds of sanctions because of their counter-productive effect. Indeed, if warning a State that one of these measures could be taken, combined with a mobilisation of shame, does not have a corrective or preventive effect, it is fairly doubtful in most cases that the actual imposition of the sanction will have that effect. Also the power of the Security Council of the United nations to take enforcement measures has hardly become effective[220] dependent as the exercise of this power is on the consensus among the Permanent Members and on the co-operation of the other Member States. The most effective are those sanctions by which the organisation can withhold something of which the State has an urgent

744

need – *e.g.* the cancellation or suspension of a loan – and sanctions which counterbalance the benefits of the rule-violation or turn them into damages – *e.g.* the permission to the other States to take retaliation measures. Even the powers to apply these kinds of sanctions, however, are very rarely used, as is revealed by the studies in the foregoing Parts.

The World Bank suspends or cancels loans or credits only very seldom in cases where a borrowing State does not fulfil the conditions set.[221] The IMF sanctions in the field of exchange rates and currency supervision, such as 'representations', 'publicity' and 'increased burdens', have never developed into a real practice. In those few instances in which they were applied, the cases were too isolated to allow for any general conclusion. In fact a much more important corrective or rather preventive instrument appears to be the 'denial of benefits' from the beginning. It is utilised in case and as long as a Member State, wishing to draw from any of the funds, does not comply with the conditions or performance criteria set by the IMF or the Bank.[222]

Sanctions other than the so-called 'mobilisation of shame' and the possibility of retaliation measures by the other States, are not provided for in the case of OECD. Since co-operation rests in essence on a voluntary basis, the organisation depends on the persuasion ensuing from its own reports and reinforced in the confrontation sessions and during the political debate. In fact, some sort of common understanding may result from this, leaving room for adjustments either of a general nature or in that specific case.[223]

Not much is known about the use of sanctions within the CMEA and its effectiveness. Since the Organisation has no exclusive powers in the field of economic co-operation between the Member States, there is the implied sanction of what can be called 'locking out'. If a State does not comply with its obligations and is not prepared to settle the ensuing dispute, it runs the risk of being partly isolated because the other States might choose to continue the same project outside the CMEA and without the participation of the defecting State.[224] This in fact amounts to a collective retaliatory measure.

GATT sanctions are also mainly retaliation measures by contracting parties which have suffered damage from deviant behaviour of another party. The Contracting Parties, the main GATT organ, may authorise the suspension of the application of concessions or other obligations under the GATT, if there is substantial justification for this. It has, however, manifested great reluctance to do so, aware as it is of the fact that usually no State would really gain from such measures while they might evoke an action-reaction chain which would sharply contravene the principles and purposes of GATT. Moreover, small or economically weak countries are often not in a position to retort since their imports are too low and/or of too vital importance to their own economy. And since the authorisation of retaliation places the enforcement in the hands of a State and makes it subject to the interests of that State, there is the risk, evidenced by practice, that the defecting State will satisfy the injured State in some other way rather than correcting its deviant behaviour. Developing countries have long been very reluctant even to start a procedure which has been especially designed for their benefits, out of fear that the defendant developed State would take retaliatory measures and consequently aggravate the injury suffered. Only recently have they started lodging complaints against industrial States.[225]

Where the IAEA is concerned, the imposition of sanctions in the context of the supervision of the implementation of the Non-Proliferation Treaty would only seem meaningful as a preventive measure. If a violation has occurred, the discussion of such a delicate political issue and the collection of convincing evidence will most probably take more time than is needed for the making of the nuclear arms. The deterrent effect which the debate and the eventual sanctions by the Board could have, would probably be too late and/or too little. And in any case they cannot counter-balance the gravity of the violation. This is why timely inspection and preventive measures are so important here.[226]

The foregoing leads us to the following conclusions with respect to sanctions:

(a) Sanctions in the form of retaliatory measures by States as a rule cause harm rather than contribute to the realisation of the purposes of international economic organisations. Unless they are applied at the instigation and/or under the control of the organisation, they should preferably be replaced by measures taken by the organisation.

(b) Sanctions by an organisation in the economic sphere are likely to be effective only if:

(1) they consist of withholding, suspending or withdrawing rights, privileges or services which are of great interest to the economy of the State concerned and for which there are no alternatives within short-term reach for that State, or

(2) they cause in another way comparable harm to a State's economy in a field where that State is sufficiently vulnerable and where the co-operation by the other States in carrying out the measures of the organisation can be adequately supervised and guaranteed.

(c) Sanctions in the field of the membership of the organisation will as a rule have a corrective effect only if the interdependence in the field of co-operation and/or the prestige of the organisation are of such a level that suspension or (threat of) loss of membership or of the right to vote is likely to do the State concerned serious material or non-material harm.

(d) Less far-reaching measures like the adoption of a resolution condemn-ing a certain State's behaviour, the publication of the report on which such a resolution is based, the mobilisation of shame which may result from such publicity, the decision not to elect a State as a member of a certain organ or commission – all of them measures which according to national legal stan-dards would hardly be considered as 'sanctions' – appear to occupy a very important place among the sanctions in the international relations. Their effectiveness here again depends on several factors such as the measure of interdependence, the vulnerability of the State concerned, the prestige of the organisation and its membership, the freedom of information within the State concerned on which the domestic effect of the publicity and the mobilisation of shame depend, etc. In particular, because of the counter-

746

productive effect that retaliatory measures, economic boycotts and the cutting-off of financial and technical assistance may have on the development of international economic co-operation, this category of sanctions should receive more attention and the possibilities for greater refinement deserve further study.

5.4. The creative function

In Part I the creative function has been described as the function of supervision which consists of the clarification and elaboration of existing rules in order to make them sufficiently specific to be applied in a concrete case. It has also been explained that this function is an important element of international supervision because of:

(1) the scarcity of applicable rules coupled with the incidental character of independent legislative procedures, and

(2) the vagueness and ambiguity of the applicable rules.[227]

From what has been said above, it is clear that 'rules' does not mean here only legally binding rules but also rules which have not (yet) that legal character. In the latter case, the creative function of the supervision procedure may exactly have the effect of a 'progressive' development towards such a character, for instance through the process of registering further recognition by the States involved of such a rule as a binding one.[228] Moreover, the creative function may affect the purposes of the organisation. After all, the continuous review of State behaviour for its conformity with the principles and rules of the organisation, directed towards the implementation of the purposes of the organisation, may not only result in the correction or adaptation of State behaviour and/or in the dynamic interpretation and possible adaptation of the applicable rules, but also in the adaptation of the purposes. The inflexibility which is characteristic of the amendment procedures of the constitutions of international organisation is compensated to a certain extent by the creative elements of the supervision process. That gives the creative function of supervision a special relevance in the perspective of a restructuring of the international economic order. Some of the adaptations of the purposes, principles, procedures and rules of the international economic organisations towards a more just and equitable international economic order may be effectuated outside the formal framework of an amendment procedure through the creative function of supervision. At the same time this process may pave the way for an amendment at a later stage which will then meet with less difficulties because the proposed amendments have already been 'moulded' in the practice of the organisation.

5.4.1. Acceptance and consensus

According to the rules concerning the interpretation of treaties, laid down in Part II, Section 3, of the Vienna Convention of the Law of Treaties, a treaty shall be interpreted in good faith in accordance with the ordinary meaning to be given to the terms of the treaty in their context and in the light of its object and purpose.[229] The same rule has to be followed, by analogy, for the interpretation of rules enacted on the basis of a treaty.

Since the supervisory procedure in an international organisation, like all its activities, is directed towards the implementation of the purposes of the organisation, those purposes are a highly relevant focal point for the interpretation of the principles and rules to be applied; especially so if the wording of the principles and rules is not clear and unambiguous or, taken literally, would lead to a manifestly unreasonable result.[230] This makes it very important to determine what exactly the purposes of the organisation are and how they themselves have to be interpreted. As said above, this may, right from the beginning of the supervisory procedure or at a later stage, lead to a creative approach towards these purposes. It is clear, however, that those who are called to interpret the purposes cannot do so completely at their own discretion. They are bound by the intention of the States which together form the organisation. Their interpretation has therefore to start from the original intention of the founding fathers of the organisation. Next, they have to investigate whether and how this original intention has developed during the practice of the organisation and whether the ensuing interpretation can still be said to be based upon a consensus among the Member States. After all, as is put forward in Part I, the effectiveness of supervision is to a high degree determined by the acceptance of and consensus on the applicable principles and rules. This *a fortiori* holds good for the creative function, especially where this leads to the creation of new rules.[231]

The views of the individual Member States – and consequently the consensus among them – with respect to the purposes of an organisation are constantly influenced by political, economic and social developments. This is also true *a fortiori* in the field of international economic relations. As has been said in the beginning of this Part, the most important developments in this respect have been the decolonisation and the resulting influx of new members into the world-wide organisations combined with the fact that these new members were mainly countries with a developing economy.[232] These developments have had and still have a strong impact on the ideas and expectations among the members in respect of the purposes and the functioning of their organisations.

Was the post-war international economic order, designed at Bretton Woods, assured of the widespread agreement among the market-economy nations as the major participants in the world economy of those days, the subsequent rise of independent States with a developing economy generated a quest for new economic and legal principles and rules which would better reflect their economic situation and the need for more equitable economic relations. The Bretton Woods system came under growing attack, based as it was on the principles of freedom of trade in an open market system, formal equality of the participants in the world economy and Most-Favoured-Nation treatment. The growing assertiveness of the developing countries on the one hand, and the reluctant or declining attitude of the developed countries on the other hand, had a clear impact on the efforts at consensus-building in the international economic community, as is illustrated, *inter alia*, by the history, content and follow-up of the NIEO documents.

A special place in this growing 'dissensus' is taken by the Soviet Union and the East European countries. Through the years they have paid lip-service to the Third World's quest for changes but they seem little inclined to play an active role in the restructuring process. The principal reason advanced by these countries themselves is that they are not to be held responsible for the phenomenon of underdevelopment which in their opinion is the result of past colonialism, present neo-colonialism and exploitation by multinational enterprises. This argument has not prevented the gradual erosion of the – in the eyes of the socialist countries – 'natural alliance' between them and the Third World.[233] This does not concern co-operation among the CMEA countries themselves, although four of them – Cuba, Mongolia, Romania and Vietnam – are considered or consider themselves to belong to the developing countries. It does affect, however, the CMEA relations with the Third World and therefore also international decision-making in relation to the restructuring of the international economic order.

Within the OECD – and the European Communities for that matter – the 'dissensus' described above may also play a role. Although these organisations do not count developing States among their members, it becomes more and more difficult to agree on a common approach towards the Third World, even more so now that the North-South issue is increasingly linked with the present economic crisis. Opinions differ strongly on whether to take a defensive position or to recognise the necessity to adjust and restructure national and international economic policy.

Those in charge of international supervision have to take into consideration this declining consensus with respect to the purposes of the organisation concerned and the principles and rules to be applied and, on the other hand, must particularly try to use the creative function as an instrument of adjustment.

In the case of the World Bank and the IMF the main objection on the part of the developing countries concerns the fact that their voting power is not an equitable reflection of their number and interests and that, as a consequence, they cannot adequately participate in the policy-making and decision-making of these organisations. Since it is mainly these same countries which are the subject of supervision, the supervisory organs should take this lack of equal representation into account when applying the rules of the organisation. Guidance for this could be found in the policy-statements by the President of the Bank and the Managing Director of the IMF, which as a rule are more advanced than the inter-governmental policy-making.[234]

Although in the case of GATT it can be said that there is still a rather broad agreement on its purposes as they have developed more in favour of the developing countries in the sixties and seventies, this is not true of the methods and means to achieve these purposes. Consensus is lacking as to major issues like the scope of the Most-Favoured-Nation treatment and the

749

reciprocity principle, the prohibition of quantitative restrictions, anti-dumping and countervailing measures, emergency action, market regulation and regional economic integration and the like.[235] Here indeed supervision seems to have counterbalanced this lack of agreement, at least to a certain degree, through its creative function. This was possible through a pragmatic rule application and the use of dynamic and informal methods of dispute settlement. The working parties' and panels' primary task is not to enforce a set of rules; they are rather *ad hoc* bodies designed to manage international trade. Where cohesion among the participating States is decreasing, the solution of a dispute will in most cases take the form of a compromise in which the fact of the solution is more important than the strict application of the rule.[236] It is evident that this affects the interpretation and application of the rules and will often lead to their *ad hoc* adaptation.

UNCTAD in a way is the embodiment of the North-South conflict, especially manifested in its 'group system'.[237] This system has had a clarifying but at the same time polarising effect, which as yet has not been channelled into effective decision-making by the Conferences. This situation has not so far led to well-defined rules of economic behaviour. Consequently, the basis for a creative function through a specifying interpretation and further elaboration or adaptation of such rules is also lacking. UNCTAD has proved more effective in the constant initiation, guidance and supervision of negotiation processes; *e.g.* the evaluation of negotiation positions and the reformulation of proposals. This 'supervision of policy development' is of a strongly creative nature but is exercised in the framework of the norm-setting task of UNCTAD rather than as a function of supervision *stricto sensu*.[238] The situation is somewhat different in the case of the conventions and codes of conduct prepared or to be prepared in the framework of UNCTAD. They become formally distinct from the regular policy of UNCTAD and acquire a life of their own. They are like ships which sail away from the yard but return every five years for a major check-up.[239] These periodical reviews may have an important creative element.

In conclusion it can be said that in a situation of a strong and stable consensus among the Member States concerning the purposes, principles, procedures and rules of the organisation there is no need and in fact no room for an extensive creative function of supervision. The supervisory bodies can restrict themselves to an interpretation of the rules in accordance with this consensus and thus to a strict application. If, on the other hand, there is a broad consensus but one that has changed since the purposes, principles, procedures and rules were adopted, the creative function should lead to an extensive interpretation and if needed an adaptation of the rules in accordance with the newly reached consensus. If consensus is lacking, then the creative function has to include a good deal of negotiation in order to produce either agreement among the States concerned on an *ad hoc* interpretation of the rule or an *ad hoc* solution which is not totally in conformity with the applicable rule, or to build consensus among all Member States on a certain interpretation or a new definition of the rule. And if the 'dissensus' is so structural that applicable rules are still lacking, the creative function of supervision has to be combined with policy-making and legislation. It is evident that in the last two situations the way for the creative function can be paved quite substantially by the secretariat or a body of independent persons, but that the outcome needs to be endorsed by a body of inter-governmental composition.

5.4.2. Consultation and renegotiation

In section 5.3. dealing with the correction function, consultation has been discussed as a means of friendly settlement. From what has been said about the creative function in case of a change in, or lack of, consensus, it is clear that consultation may also play a significant role in the creative function of supervision. Indeed, it is mainly through consultations between the organisation and its Member States, and among the States themselves, that (a new) consensus has to be worked out and rules have to be created or adapted in accordance with this consensus.

In some cases the notion of consultation is found alongside the term 'renegotiation'. This is explicitly so in the GATT. Although difficult to distinguish as to their procedure and their final outcome, one could in that case reserve the term 'consultation' in a strict sense for the activities which are primarily aimed at the implementation of existing purposes and norms and thus at the correction of State behaviour, while 'renegotiations' are directed at the modification or adaptation of norms. For example, the periodic changes in concessions and schedules in the GATT framework are effected by amendments or through renegotiations.[240] However, decrease of the political cohesion within the GATT has made this distinction rather theoretical. For both the consultations and the renegotiations it can be said that the creative element tends to be more important than the corrective one, since they both are in fact not primarily aimed at a strict compliance with the rules but at a pragmatic system of reciprocity and the granting of mutual benefits.[241]

In the CMEA specific consultation procedures may easily become renegotiations if they are directed at change rather than application of norms. States have to notify circumstances which hinder a timely and complete implementation of their obligations in order to enable the interested States to 'consider and settle' the problems. The subsequent consultation procedure may result in either the adoption of a new recommendation on the same subject or a modification of the existing one. It has been submitted that consultations may even lead directly to an agreement between the interested States themselves, in particular when the implementation of the recommendation has been effectuated through the conclusion of agreements or treaties.[242]

In the case of renegotiations rules do exist but they are lacking a sufficient consensual basis and/or are no longer adequate in the actual situation. What has been said under 5.4.1. is even more true here: renegotiations can be prepared and supported but not conducted by the secretariats or independent bodies. If rules are lacking, then the consultations do not take the form of renegotiations but of negotiations pure and simple which do not form part of the supervisory process.

5.4.3. *Review sessions/review conferences*

The convening of review sessions or review conferences at regular intervals to assess the progress made in the fulfilment of the purposes of an international organisation or any other legally binding or not legally binding international arrangement, is a modern supervisory device provided for in a growing number of international documents in the field of economic relations as well as in other fields. For some of these documents the review conference even constitutes the main supervisory 'procedure', as in the case of the Final Act of Helsinki concerning security and co-operation in Europe.[243] These review sessions or conferences share as an important feature their creative function. In addition to a review and appraisal of the implementation of the treaty or other arrangement concerned, they are at the same time aimed at considering and negotiating the possibilities of an improvement of the procedures and further development of the rules. For that reason they are sometimes referred to as 'follow-up' sessions or conferences.

This relatively new phenomenon is not yet reflected in the constitutional treaties of the international economic organisations discussed here, leaving apart the general provisions concerning the amendment procedures of these treaties.[244] Review sessions or conferences are provided for, however, in several documents in the supervision of which these organisations play a part. Thus, the Non-Proliferation Treaty, the implementation of which is supervised within the framework of the IAEA, provides in Article VIII(3) for periodical review conferences at intervals of five years, and in Article X(2) for a conference after 25 years to decide on the continuation of the Treaty.[245] Within the framework of UNCTAD, its Trade and Development Board was directed to hold special sessions every two years for an over-all review and appraisal of the implementation of the International Development Strategy for the Second United Nations Development Decade and of the Charter of Economic Rights and Duties of States; this in preparation of the review and appraisal by ECOSOC and the General Assembly.[246] The International Development Strategy for the Third United Nations Development Decade states in this respect, that the General Assembly will carry out the review and appraisal 'with the assistance, as appropriate, of a body of universal membership, which would report through the Economic and Social Council', and invites the Committee for Development Planning to submit its observations and recommendations.[247] Furthermore, under the auspices of UNCTAD, a conference is convened five years after the adoption of the Set of Mutually Agreed Equitable Principles and Rules for the Control of Restrictive Business Practices to review the implementation of the Set and discuss its improvement and further development.[248] Equally, under the auspices of UNCTAD a review conference will be convened as provided for in Article 52 of the Code of Conduct for Liner Conferences, to review the implementation of the Code and to consider and adopt appropriate amendments.[249] The proposed International Code of Conduct on the Transfer of Technology and the proposed Code of Conduct for Transnational Corporations also provide for review conferences.[250] Mention should further be made of the triannual review sessions of UNCTAD's Special Committee on Preferences to assess the implementation of the Generalised System of Preferences and to consider the possibilities of its improvement and modification as well as its extension after 10 years.[251] Finally, within the OECD, the Committee on International Investments and Multinational Enterprises holds periodical sessions to prepare the review by the governments of the Member States of the experience gained in the application of the Guidelines for Multinational Enterprises and to consider the further clarification of the Guidelines.[252]

It goes without saying that in those cases where special review sessions or review conferences are not expressly provided for, in fact every regular session of the organs and subsidiary bodies of the organisations can perform the same function within their respective fields of competence by including a review of the implementation of certain rules and a discussion of their further development in their agendas, and even by singling out one or more of their meetings specifically for this purpose. It is submitted, however, that a practice of special review meetings or review conferences, as the case may require, at regular intervals, may considerably enhance international supervision and more specifically its creative function. The inclusion of express provisions to that effect in the basic treaties of the international economic organisations or in their individual decisions, recommendations and treaties adopted in their framework, is therefore strongly recommended here. It offers a better guarantee for a detailed and comprehensive review and appraisal of the implementation of the procedures and rules concerned, and of the possibilities of their adaptation and further development. After all, it assures that periodically a whole session or conference will be devoted exclusively or mainly to exactly these issues and will therefore have been prepared exactly in that perspective, both by the secretariat or other body of the organisation and by the specialists at the level of the participating governments. It also offers a better guarantee that concrete results will come out of such sessions or conferences for the same reason, since the results aimed at will in all probability have been more thoroughly discussed and scrutinised for their feasibility during the preparatory exchanges of views at the various levels.

5.4.4. The role of the secretariats

Attention has been given above to the technical role of the international secretariats regarding the collection and processing of information. It has been observed there that this role may in some cases receive a more substantial and even quasi-political character in the sense that the staff of the secretariat performs almost the whole review function by itself.[253] In relation to the creative function of supervision, too, the role of the secretariats can be of great importance. In most of the international economic organisations under consideration the secretariats have been entrusted with the task – either through practice or in virtue of the rules of procedure of the separate organs – to make proposals for the interpretation, elaboration or modification of existing rules or the adoption of new rules. These proposals may be made *ad hoc* or on a regular basis, at the request of an organ of the organisation or in preparation of a review session. Frequently, proposals are prepared or studies issued at the initiative of the secretariat itself in order to draw the attention of the Member States to problems of great concern or to give new incentives to a negotiation process. The very special right of initiative of the Commission of the European Communities has already been mentioned.[254] Other international secretariats may also take an active approach in this respect, depending on the authority of the highest officials of the secretariats and their readiness to promote or at least support such an approach. If they manage at the same time to maintain an objective and high standard, and generate confidence among the Member States, the latter may welcome the active role played by the secretariats in doing the conceptual work for which the political bodies and the individual Member States do not have enough time and sometimes lack the expertise.

Thus, within the OECD a large number of occasional studies are prepared and published. Since these are usually regarded as being authoritative and of high standard, they entail both corrective and creative effects. They may serve as a basis for the interpretation and further elaboration of existing norms and for the adoption of new norms.[255]

The CMEA Secretariat, too, sometimes exercises a quasi-political function with creative effect when preparing the political supervision debates of the other CMEA organs and proposing solutions in case the implementation of recommendations is lacking or ineffective. This power does not exist on paper only, but is actually exercised when deemed necessary and desirable.[256]

In the case of the World Bank and the IMF the role of the Secretariats is a very active one, as has been observed above.[257] The staff maintains the regular contacts with the authorities of the beneficiary States and conducts the country missions, and thus becomes familiar with the special situations and specific difficulties. At the same time the staff performs most of the supervision. It therefore causes no surprise that the staff also has an important contribution to make to the creative function, especially at the stage of the conclusion of a new Loan Document or the consideration of new monetary facilities respectively. Moreover, the involvement of the staff gives it considerable influence on the decision-making which results from the consultations between the organisation and its Member States.[258]

In GATT the need for a strong creative element in the supervision process is mainly due to the declining consensus on the way the GATT principles should be implemented and the resulting emphasis on practical *ad hoc* solutions based on a reciprocal weighing of interests. The main preparation rests, however, in the hands of the working groups and panels. The Secretariat seems to play a less active role. Its reviews and studies have a less direct political impact. They are considered as technical reports and are widely used as sources of practical information, which may of course ultimately influence the creative function of supervision in an indirect but not less effective way.[259]

By far the most disputed secretariat of the organisations here under discussion is that of UNCTAD. This is mainly due to the fact that, from its inception onwards, it has developed into an active promotor of the interests of the developing countries instead of acting as a 'neutral' service device. The stage for this type of role was set by the first Secretary-General of UNCTAD, Raúl Prebisch. As a result, most industrialised countries consider the activities and proposals of the Secretariat to be insufficiently representative of the total membership of UNCTAD, while the developing countries maintain that these activities and proposals reflect the purposes for which UNCTAD was established. This problem is mainly created and kept alive because the Third World lacks its own international forum and international secretariat.[260] In that situation, the 'Group of 77' uses the UNCTAD forum and its Secretariat for that purpose. As to the creative function of the supervision of policy development it has been concluded that staff leverage is closely related to the style of group bargaining.[261]

In concluding this sub-section the same observations hold true which were made in sub-section 5.2.2. in relation to the independence, expertise and facilities of the secretariat staff.[262] In relation to the creative function a balance has to be found between on the one hand the necessity that a number of high-level staff members, and in particular the Secretary-General or Director, as the case may be, have broad practical experience in international or national legislation and administration, and on the other hand the requirement that they maintain no special links with, and are not prejudiced in favour of, any national government.

5.4.5. The role of international adjudication

In interpreting, clarifying and specifying the rules to be applied, courts play an important role, not only in the application but also in the further development of these rules. This holds true in particular for common-law systems, where very substantial parts of the law are judge-made. But it is in fact also the practice in those legal systems where the courts' competence is formally restricted to the application of pre-existing law. The international legal system belongs to the latter category. And there, too, the courts have taken a creative approach in many instances, as appears from the case-law of the International Court of Justice,[263] the European Court of Human Rights,[264] and the Court of Justice of the European Communities.[265]

However, courts, and international courts in particular, have to be careful not to jeopardise their authority and even their existence by too active and dynamic an approach in this respect. The same consensus among the States which was said to be indispensable for any international rule to be effective,[266] constitutes also the factual basis of the jurisdiction of the international courts. This is particularly the case for courts like the International Court of Justice and the European Court of Human Rights, whose jurisdiction is of a voluntary character and depends on the consent – *ad hoc* or by previous implication – of the parties involved. In actual fact, however, it is also true, in the long run, for courts with compulsory jurisdiction, such as the Court of Justice of the European Communities. When an international court is called upon to interpret and apply a certain rule with respect to which no clear consensus exists within the international community concerned at that time, or which has a compromisory content because of lack of consensus on a more specific content, the court should take a restrictive rather than a creative approach. If not, it runs the risk that its decision or advisory opinion will not be respected and followed by those States for which it has disadvantageous implications. And this would damage the authority of the interpretation given by the court and the authority of the court itself.

We find ourselves here more or less in a vicious circle: the creative function of supervision is of special importance to the international legal system because of the uncertain and ambiguous nature of many international rules and the absence of an institutionalised international legislature; this creative function could in theory best be exercised by international courts, composed as these are of distinguished international lawyers representing all or the main legal systems of the States concerned, as the case may be; but it is precisely that uncertain and ambiguous character of so many international rules that constitutes the main bar for a more general creative adjudication. To be sure, in most cases the unclear and ambiguous wording is not due to poor legal drafting but reflects the lacking consensus on a more precise and less ambiguous formulation. This lack of consensus would make the outcome of a creative interpretation by a court unpredictable for the parties involved, while predictability and legal certainty constitute the main factors for the willingness of States to accept supervision by international adjudication.[267]

Of course, some clarification and thus creation will be involved in each and every court decision, given the fact that a general rule has to be specified to apply it to a concrete case. But this creation is possible only within certain limits, if the court is to continue enjoying the confidence of the States. As is observed by Bindschedler:

> This is the dilemma in which the permanent courts find themselves. On the one hand, they ought to abide by existing legislation if they are not to lose the confidence of the parties and if the outcome of the proceedings is not to become wholly unpredictable; but on the other hand they are expected to provide solutions appropriate to new requirements. The case law of the International Court of Justice demonstrates this clearly. One of its characteristics is vacillation between strict conservatism and unexpected innovation. This is no doubt one of the principal reasons why governments are reluctant to submit disputes to it.[268]

In conclusion it can be stated that, if consensus is lacking as to the development of the law into a specific direction, international courts are as a rule not in a position to take the lead with sufficient authority. This may be different to a large extent within an international community with a highly integrated infrastructure or with common values in the field in which further development of the rules is required. Both the Court of Justice of the European Communities and the European Court of Human Rights have in several judgments followed a creative interpretation that was unexpected, or at least not undisputed, among the Member States, but was nevertheless accepted as an authoritative statement of the law. But even these Courts have to manoeuvre very carefully and are not in a position to solve disputes among the Member States or between a State and the Organisation concerning the contents and meaning of a rule, if vital interests are considered to be at stake. To put it in general terms: the foundation of any adjudication is the willingness of the parties to accept a common basis of law. If this willingness is lacking, court decisions cannot substitute for it. As long as that situation lasts, any creative function has to remain in the hands of non-judicial bodies, whose competence is not restricted to legally binding rules and whose composition and political backing enables them to work towards political compromises of a not legally binding character in order to bring about the necessary consensus.

Given the present situation in most international economic organisations, where legally binding rules of a substantive character are scarce and consensus with respect to such rules is even scarcer, there would seem to be little perspective for creative adjudication in the foreseeable future. The establishment of new courts would not substantially change this state of affairs, unless such a measure would reflect a determination on the part of the States to make new efforts in the direction of more specific rule-making and to be guided to that end by a creative interpretation and application of the existing rules by these new courts.

5.5. Some concluding remarks: the relation between the character of the norm and the function of supervision

Although in most international supervisory procedures all three functions of supervision – review, correction and creation – play some role, the study of the functioning of supervisory mechanisms in international economic organisations indicates that in some cases emphasis is on the correction function as a follow-up of the review function, but that in most cases the review is followed or accompanied mainly by the creative effects of the supervision. Which of the two is the case in a concrete situation, depends on several aspects of that situation and of the framework within which the supervision takes place. Generally speaking, however, the conclusion can be reached that the two main determining factors in this respect are the contents of the norms involved and the measure of consensus between the States concerned regarding these norms. The question of whether the norm is legally binding is highly relevant for certain modalities of supervision, especially adjudication and arbitration, but less so in connection with the functions of supervision.

In this connection a distinction can be made between 'principles' and 'rules'. These two categories of norms are to be found in the constitutions of all the organisations dealt with and in most of the decisions and resolutions issued by these organisations. The term 'principles' indicates, or is at least used here to indicate, those norms which stipulate a goal to be sought but do not prescribe the instruments to be used and concrete efforts to be taken to reach that goal. By 'rules' are meant those norms which prescribe a specific action, procedure or behaviour on the part of the organisation and/or the Member States in order to reach a certain goal.[269]

In many instances the principles find further specification in rules in the same treaty, decision or resolution. This is the case, for instance, in the Treaty establishing the European Economic Community where the principles of Part One have been elaborated in the other Parts of the Treaty, and in the Convention of the OECD in respect of the principles set out in Article 2 of the Convention.

In other instances, principles set out in the basic instrument of the organisation have been elaborated later on in subsequent instruments. Thus, the principles contained in Article XXXVI of the General Agreement on Tariffs and Trade concerning less-developed countries have been specified to a certain extent in the commitments laid down in Articles XXXVII and XXXVIII, but have been elaborated more fully in new principles and rules in the agreement concluded at the Tokyo Round of 1979 concerning differential and more favourable treatment, reciprocity and fuller participation of developing countries.[270] Another example is offered by the Generalised System of Preferences, adopted by the Trade and Development Board of UNCTAD, which specifies several of the General and Special Principles adopted by the first Conference on Trade and Development.[271]

In a third group of cases, finally, the principles and the specifying rules are incorporated in one and the same provision, *e.g.* the provision concerning the Most-Favoured-Nation treatment in Article I of the General Agreement on Tariffs and Trade.

Both principles and rules can be of a legally binding or of a not legally binding character. Examples of the latter category are to be found, for instance, in the NIEO declarations and in the recommendations of UNCTAD. Principles that are not themselves legally binding can be elaborated in legally binding rules, as is the case with the agreements concluded within the framework of UNCTAD,[272] but it is also possible that a legally binding principle finds specification in not legally binding rules, a step which is then usually meant to be an intermediate one. Thus, several of the rules laid down in the NIEO declarations may be said to further specify, in not legally binding instruments, the principles of development co-operation laid down in Articles 55 and 56 of the UN Charter.

Since principles are aim-norms rather than conduct-norms and as such do not prescribe specific behaviour, they do not usually constitute a sufficient basis for the correction function of supervision. The review function, however, is very important with respect to these norms, especially if it can be combined with the creative function. The fact that a principle has not (yet) been elaborated in specific rules may find its reason in the early stage of development of the norms concerned, in the complexity of the issues to be regulated and/or in the lack of sufficient consensus with respect to the required rules. In all these situations the review procedure may deepen the insight in the issues involved, strengthen the confidence in the way in which the organisation deals or proposes to deal with these issues, and thus produce a growing consensus concerning the action and behaviour required from the organisation and the Member States. It is then the creative function of the supervision which can 'translate' this growing consensus into a further elaboration of the principle and, by doing so, in its turn strengthen the consensus still further. Such a 'translation' can take different forms and may be of a varying intensity, ranging from the norm-creating effect of subsequent practice to the preparation of a treaty.

Rules in the above-mentioned sense of conduct-provisions leave more room for the correction function of supervision, because they prescribe a specific action or behaviour for the States. It is obvious, however, that the norms concerned will hardly ever be so specific and detailed, that the supervisory body can apply them to the specific case or situation without the necessity of at least some elaboration or adaptation. Moreover, as has been stated above several times, in many situations it may be more appropriate and serve better the fulfilment of the purposes of the organisation, when emphasis is not so much put on the correction of past behaviour of States by means of sanctions but rather on the steering of future State conduct by way of incentives, consultation, conviction and/or clarification of the norms. In the latter case there is a shift from the correction function towards the creative function. We will return to this a little later.

As was previously pointed out, the difference in character between principles and rules can in many cases be explained largely on the basis of a difference in consensus among the States as to the measures to be taken. The same holds good for the differences to be found among the rules concerning the obligations to be undertaken and the priorities to be set for reaching the goal agreed upon.[273] This may be reflected in the specificity of the rule and in the State practice with respect to the rule. If a certain rule or set of rules is worded in very general terms, or is precisely formulated but contains qualifications which leave much room for State discretion, for instance by using terms like 'where feasible' or 'to the extent possible', the review of their implementation can be very instrumental to their further specification. For this specification to indeed take place, the review will have to be combined more with the instruments of the creative function than with those of the correction function.

This may be illustrated by reference to Article IV of the Articles of Agreement of the IMF. After the system of fixed exchange rates had ended in 1973 and was succeeded by floating exchange rates, this found expression in an amended text of Article IV, effective as from April 1978. As a consequence the new provision contained less specific obligations as compared to the strict obligations embodied in the old Article IV. This is also reflected in the supervision procedure. Under the old provision the function of supervision was mainly directed towards review and correction. On the basis of the obligation of the Member States to inform the Fund with respect to any intended change in the par value of their currencies and of the obligation to co-operate with the Fund to promote exchange stability, their exchange policy was reviewed for its conformity with the norms set in Article IV and in case of deviations correction was striven after by means of formal or factual sanctions. Under the new provision emphasis is much more on consultation as a means to enable the Fund to 'exercise firm surveillance over the exchange rate policies of members' and to 'adopt specific principles for the guidance of all members with respect to those policies' (Article IV(3)(b)).[274]

An equally illustrative example is to be found in the supervision concerning the International Energy Programme of the OECD. The Programme contains legal norms both with respect to a short-term programme concerning the establishment of an emergency self-sufficiency plan to cope with short-term problems in oil supply, and with respect to a long-term co-operation in the field of energy. The former norms are of a specific character and contain the obligation to maintain sufficient reserves for consumption. This reserve commitment is supervised on a regular basis by the Standing Group on Emergency Questions. It reports to the Governing Board, which makes an assessment and decides on the steps to be taken. Emphasis here is clearly on review and correction. The norms concerning the long-term co-operation have the character of aim-provisions rather than conduct-provisions. Consequently, supervision by the Standing Group on Long Term Co-operation has so far been mainly directed towards the development of more specific rules and has resulted, for instance, in the adoption by the Governing Board of a Long Term Co-operation Programme in 1976 and of the Twelve Principles for Energy Policy in 1977.[275]

As an illustration of the impact of a general decline of consensus with respect to rules which are formulated in specific terms, reference can be made to the experience under the GATT. According to the formal set-up, supervision of the implementation of the basic norms laid down in the GATT is very strict and mainly aimed at the correction of deviations. This holds true particularly for the supervision with respect to the conditions under which these basic norms themselves allow for certain specific deviations and escapes. Previous consultations are prescribed in most cases and sometimes even previous permission is required, which should enable this form of supervision to have a maximum preventive effect. In practice, however, deviations from the basic norms have become a regular pattern rather than an exception, and this not exclusively in the case of a small group of exceptionally vulnerable States. At the same time, the obligation of (previous) consultation is very often violated, and the other conditions under which deviations and escapes are permissible, are also not adhered to. This development has made it clear that the existing norms and procedures are no longer adequate to cope with the present political and economic situation. At least, they are no longer considered to be adequate by the individual contracting parties in relation to their specific situation in a world of growing interdependence, which makes co-ordination of national economic policy the more urgent but at the same time makes national economies more vulnerable, especially in the case of developing countries. This situation has led to a number of formal and factual adaptations of both norms and procedures. An example of the former is the inclusion into the Agreement of Part IV on Trade and Development, which contains norms enabling the contracting parties to deviate from certain basic norms in favour of developing countries. An example of the latter are the procedures on consultation and annual review, adopted by the Contracting Parties in 1971 at the proposal of the Committee on Trade and Development, for the supervision of the implementation of the provisions of Part IV. Given the fact that the provisions of Part IV have the character of principles rather than rules, it gives no cause for surprise that here again emphasis is on consultation and negotiation directed at a friendly solution and/or at the steering of future State conduct, and on a further elaboration of the norms.[276] The same holds true, in a more general way, for the flexibility introduced into the central dispute settlement procedure under the GATT by the adoption, at the Tokyo Round of 1979, of the Understanding on Notification, Consultation, Dispute Settlement and Surveillance.[277] A combination of new norms and adapted procedures, this time in relation to a specific branch, is also to be found in the form of the Multi-Fibre Arrangement, discussed in Part III.

Another development which has to be mentioned here and which to a large extent coincides with the ones described above, is, as the study on the IMF calls it, 'the gradual evolution from a system of basic rules to a system of management and co-ordination of economic policy'.[278] The traditional system of basic rules, which still prevails in the international economic organisations, contains a set of standard norms aimed at the liberalisation of international trade. These rules are based upon the principles of sovereign freedom and (formal or substantive) equality of the States.[279] They contain many implications for the economic policy of the States, but do not directly interfere with the way the States conduct their economic policy in order to implement the basic rules. Within this traditional system supervision is primarily concerned with the implementation of these rules and their objectives, and concentrates on keeping or bringing State behaviour in conformity with these rules. Liberalisation of international trade leads, however, to greater interdependence. As a consequence, States get a greater interest in the economic policy of other States because of the impact it may have on their own economy. This calls for co-ordination of national economic policy and thus for direct interference by the international organisation in this field. For supervision this development, again, has as a consequence a stronger need for the creative function in order that the rules guiding State behaviour can be adapted, and in order that instruments may be used which are directed more towards consultation, negotiation and conciliation, supported if possible by conditional incentives, to steer the process of positive economic integration.[280]

VI. A SPECIAL ISSUE: SUPERVISION OF MULTINATIONAL ENTERPRISES

6.1. Introduction

After the comparative analysis of the preceding chapter and before making some concluding observations, in the context of our subject it would seem useful to discuss an issue that has not been dealt with in the studies of the separate organisations but is nevertheless of practical importance to supervision in the field of international economic relations, particularly in the perspective of restructuring the international economic order. This is the supervision, through the States or directly, of the activities of multinational enterprises.

The multinational enterprises (MNEs) – the United Nations' jargon prefers to call them transnational corporations (TNCs) – are, according to the definition here adapted, those enterprises or clusters of enterprises which extend their business operations under one guiding direction to two or more countries and have influence and power in their own markets.[281] Because of the multinational character of their activities on the one hand, which enables them in certain respects to escape territorially limited national jurisdiction,[282] and their sometimes very influential economic power and vast financial resources on the other hand, MNEs keep free from national supervision of both their home States and their host States in many instances. At the same time, they are as yet subject to almost no international supervision, since existing international supervisory procedures are based upon the concept of State responsibility and only in very exceptional cases on the concept of direct responsibility of private entities. State responsibility for the activities of 'their' MNEs in most cases either does not exist under international law or cannot be put into effect for the above-mentioned reasons. In view of the fact that the MNEs have become important vehicles for international investments and for the production, transport and marketing of goods, technology and services, lack of the possibility of international supervision of their activities means in fact that for that reason alone international supervision in the field of economic relations can be only partially effective at best. But for national economic and social policy, too, the MNEs have become powers which may develop into adversaries of the government and dominate their socio-economic counterweights such as the trade unions.[283] At the same time the home State may use 'its' MNEs as an instrument to influence unduly the economy of one or more of their host States.[284] Therefore, both at the national and at the international level the need has been recognised for more specific and effective regulation of the activities of the MNEs and of the powers and duties of the national and international authorities in relation to them.[285] This is in order to protect the economy of the host States and their workers, consumers, creditors, etc., to control the MNE's influence on the international economic relations but also to protect the MNEs against certain measures by their home or host States, guarantee equal treatment and create the stability and predictability which are indispensable to sound business policy. The international regulations, which sometimes are (also) directly addressed to the MNEs or, in other cases, deal with the powers and duties of the home and host States, have taken different forms but are usually dealt with under the name 'Codes of Conduct'. The legal character and legal effects of these Codes of Conduct, and the supervisory procedures which apply to them, will be the subject of the present chapter.

6.2. Codes of Conduct for multinational enterprises; their legal character

The legal response to the recognised need for some sort of international supervision of the activities of multinational enterprises has mainly taken the form of the drafting of Codes of Conduct for these enterprises. Initiatives into that direction were taken by several international organisations, both governmental and non-governmental, world-wide and regional. These have resulted in the adoption of a number of such Codes while others are still in the process of preparation. Without any pretention of exhaustiveness, the following such Codes could be mentioned here.[286]

(a) *On the world-wide governmental level*:
> 1974: UN/UNCTAD, Code of Conduct for Liner Conferences;[287]
> 1977: ILO, Tripartite Declaration of Principles Concerning Multinational Enterprises and Social Policy;[288]
> 1980: UN/UNCTAD, The Set of Multilaterally Agreed Equitable Principles for the Control of Restrictive Business Practices.[289]
> Still in the process of preparation or adoption:
> UN, International Agreement on Illicit Payments;[290]
> UN/UNCTAD, International Code of Conduct on the Transfer of Technology;[291]
> UN, Code of Conduct of Transnational Corporations.[292]

(b) *On the regional governmental level*:
> 1970: Andes Pact, Andean Investment Code;[293]
> 1976: OECD, Guidelines for Multinational Enterprises (revised and reapproved in 1979);[294]
> 1977: European Communities, Code of Conduct for Companies with Subsidiaries, Branches or Representatives in South Africa.[295]
> Still in the process of preparation:
> European Economic Community, Directive concerning Information and Consultation of Employees in Multinational Enterprises ('Vredeling Proposal').[296]

(c) *On the non-governmental level*:
> 1972: International Chamber of Commerce, Guidelines for International Investments;[297]
> 1973: International Chamber of Commerce, International Codes of Marketing Practice;[298]
> 1975: International Confederation of Free Trade Unions, Charter of Trade Union Demands for the Legislative Control of Multinational Corporations;[299]
> 1977: International Chamber of Commerce, Recommendations to Combat Extortion and Bribery in Business Transactions.[300]

One of the most striking features revealed by a study of the legal character of these Codes is the fact that in most cases the international organisations which adopted them did so in the form of a legal instrument different from their normal regulatory acts.

This is most striking in the case of the International Labour Organisation, which chose the form of a declaration, while the ILO Constitution mentions only conventions and recommendations as the legal acts of the Organisation. The form of a convention, which would become legally binding for the Member States after ratification, was not acceptable for the employers' organisations participating in the negotiations.[301] The form of a recommendation, which is not legally binding, would have had the advantage that the supervisory mechanism provided for in Article 19 of the ILO Constitution concerning recommendations would then have become automatically applicable. However, ILO recommendations are directed to the Member States only, whereas the Tripartite Declaration is addressed jointly to the governments of the Member States and the employers' and workers' organisations as well as to the multinational enterprises which have the Member States as their home or host countries. Moreover, recommendations are in general meant to be implemented by national legislation and/or other national measures, whereas the Tripartite Declaration concerns issues which, at least partly, transcend the national framework. For these reasons the instrument of a declaration was opted for and a special procedure for supervision was decided upon.

In the case of the European Communities the Code of Conduct is addressed to the multinational enterprises with headquarters in any of the Member States. It could therefore very well have been given the form of a Council decision, taken within the framework of the common commercial policy, with binding effect for the addressees and supervised as to its implementation through the regular Community procedures. However, the Member States were not prepared to take such a binding decision and opted rather for a recommendation adopted by the Ministers of the Member States not in their capacity as members of the Council.

The OECD gave its Guidelines for Multinational Enterprises the form of an annex to the Declaration on International Investment and Multinational Enterprises, which formally speaking is not an act of the OECD Council. Here again, the main reason was that the acts of the Council can be addressed to States only, whereas the Declaration starts with a joint recommendation of the OECD Members to multinational enterprises operating in their territories to observe the Guidelines. As a consequence the Declaration was issued by the representatives of the governments and not by the Council as such, but a direct link with the OECD was created by a Council decision entrusting to OECD the implementation of the Guidelines.[302] This in fact integrated the Guidelines in the consultation mechanism of the OECD. By way of contrast, the OECD Recommendation of the Council concerning Action against Restrictive Business Practice Affecting International Trade, including those involving Multinational Enterprises,[303] is addressed to the Member States only and was indeed adopted by the Council.

In the context of the United Nations the Codes have taken and will take various forms. The drafting of most of the Codes was not and is not the direct responsibility of the UN organs but rather was done and is being done by Conferences and bodies linked to the UN. The Code of Conduct for Liner Conferences is embodied in a convention drafted by a Conference of Plenipotentiaries and opened for signature by the States. The Principles and Rules for the Control of Restrictive Business Practices were adopted by the General Assembly after approval by the UN Conference on Restrictive Business Practices. The Agreement on Illicit Payments was prepared by an *ad hoc* Intergovernmental Working Group. A draft of the Code of Conduct on the Transfer of Technology has been prepared by the Conference on an International Code of Conduct on the Transfer of Technology. The Code of Conduct for Transnational Corporations, finally, is being prepared by the UN Commission on Transnational Corporations which reports to ECOSOC.

As to the legally binding character it can be said that none of the decisions adopting the various Codes was of such a character that it conferred legally binding force on any of them. Those Codes which have been embodied in a treaty or convention will eventually become binding after their ratification. The other ones are of a recommendatory character. In most cases this is expressly stated in the relevant texts or implied in their wording. Thus, paragraph 10 of the Preamble of the UN Principles for the Control of Restrictive Business Practices states that these Principles 'take the form of recommendations' and paragraph 6 of the Preamble of the OECD Guidelines stresses that the Guidelines are 'voluntary and not legally enforceable', while the ILO Tripartite Declaration, in paragraph 10 of its Preamble, '*invites* the governments [etc. . . .] to observe the principles embodied therein'. For some of the Codes which are still in the process of preparation, it has not yet been agreed whether they will take the form of a treaty or of guidelines. The 'Vredeling Proposal' will, if adopted, have the form of a EEC Directive, which is indeed legally binding. Finally, the Codes adopted by non-governmental organisations are not of a legally binding character for the very reason that these institutions are not endowed with legislative power outside their internal affairs.

As has been repeatedly stated in the preceding chapters, however, principles and rules which do not derive legally binding force from the acts in which they are embodied or the constitution on which they are based, can nevertheless be restatements of existing legally binding principles and rules or can become legally binding by virtue of their acceptance as binding by the States in one way or another. This is also true of the Codes. Even in those cases where it is expressly stated or clearly implied that the participating States – and any non-governmental groups involved – do not wish the Code to be legally binding, it may still contain certain provisions which already form part of international law. Moreover, even if a principle or rule contained in a Code is not legally binding, it may still be subject to a certain supervisory procedure, which in its turn may enhance the normative character of that principle or rule, particularly because it may lead to its further specification and interpretation and thus pave the way for a broader and more genuine acceptance and for a direct or indirect application by national judicial and non-judicial bodies. As was stated by Norbert Horn on the basis of the experience with OECD Guidelines during the first three years:

> Perhaps we can learn from this that, where a code's rules really respond to a need for regulation and where there is an implementation procedure available, conflicts will be settled with due regard to these rules; these settlements will contribute to the precision of the rules and their gradual acceptance by all concerned. Voluntary codes and guidelines can thus be a starting point for binding rules on the level both of public international law and of the law of private (non-governmental) transnational business transactions.[304]

In the case of the Codes of Conduct, like other instruments the exact legal character of which is not totally clear, an important element determining their normative value, and thus the likelihood of their implementation, is the consensus as to their purposes, their contents and the ways and means of their implementation. And since the Codes are not directed towards governments only but also, directly or indirectly, address non-governmental entities, the consensus should exist between all the parties concerned, including the employers' associations, as representing the interest of the MNEs, and the labour unions, which have a direct interest in the activities of the MNEs. It is not to be expected, of course, that full agreement can at once be reached among all these parties on all details – for that the interests as perceived by the various parties involved are still too divergent – but a minimum of consensus is necessary if the Code is ever to become effective. The interesting thing to be noticed in this respect is that in relation to all the Codes thus far adopted, such a minimum of consensus could be achieved mainly[305] due to the fact that these Codes do not contain legally binding obligations for the MNEs themselves – the Codes laid down in treaties will become legally binding after ratification but do not contain direct obligations for the MNEs, only for the States – while at the same time the consensus thus reached will be instrumental in enhancing the normative value and the effectiveness of the Codes concerned and may ultimately lead to their acceptance as legally binding norms.

For this purpose it is important that the consensus continues after the adoption of the Code, and is reinforced by State practice and the practice of the MNEs. Supervision of that practice may perform an important function in this respect, both through its review and correction function but even more so through its creative function, provided that all the parties involved, both governmental and non-governmental, are given full opportunity to participate in this process.

Among the criteria on the basis of which the original measure of consensus as to the purposes, contents, and ways and means of implementation of a certain Code and its separate provisions can be determined are to be mentioned, here again,[306] the *travaux préparatoires,* including any statements made by delegates of the participating States and by representatives of the other interested parties, the wording of the final text and especially the degree of specificity of the language used, the exact legal terminology and its conformity with existing legal principles and rules, the circumstances of adoption such as the voting pattern, supporting statements by State representatives and expressed support on the part of the other interested groups, and any other accompanying or following unilateral or collective declarations or practice indicating the opinion of the States and other parties concerned as to purposes, interpretation and implementation.

Later developments concerning this consensus can be deduced from subsequent unilateral or collective statements and from subsequent practice; practice both at the national and at the international level and practice on the part of both governmental and non-governmental entities. Among these are to be mentioned: active participation in the institutional context of the Code by all parties involved, especially in relation to its supervision and follow-up, home and host government policy towards MNEs, attitude of the MNEs in respect of the Code provisions, and incorporation of the provisions in domestic law and their application by the national courts. We also include here the practice of MNEs, although, outside the exceptional tripartite structure of the ILO organs, non-governmental entities do not participate directly in international norm-creation and consequently their practice cannot directly contribute to the normative value of the Codes. It is clear, however, that their practice can be of great importance for the interpretation, further specifications and effective implementation of the Codes and thus may substantially affect the consensus among the States. At the same time, the encouragement of MNEs' guideline compliance by the home government in response to representations by the host government constitutes an indication of consensus between those two governments and may contribute to the development of the guideline concerned into a rule of international law.[307]

6.3. Some of the legal effects of Codes of Conduct that are not legally binding

Despite the fact that, at the present time, most of the Codes or provisions thereof are not legally binding, they may still have clear legal effects. Taking as a starting point the excellent study by Baade on the subject, the following potential effects should be mentioned.[308]

6.3.1. The legitimation effect

When States enter into mutual commitments on a certain matter – however 'soft' these commitments may be from the point of view of being legally binding – they can no longer claim that the matter is solely within their jurisdiction. Other States which have adopted the same commitments may not attack as inherently unlawful or improper any action by the former States taken in order to implement these commitments, unless that action is in violation of any of the State's international legal obligations.[309] As long as bilateral or multilateral treaties remain in force, they prevail over the provisions of a Code not itself embodied in a treaty,[310] leaving apart the improbable case that a Code would contain a *ius cogens* provision. The same holds true in principle for provisions of customary international law, but there the ensuing obligation must be well-defined and unambiguous in order to prevail over a clear commitment under the Code. Equally, States may not grant diplomatic protection to a MNE for the sole reason that the host State has taken measures in fulfilment of its commitments under the Code, unless these measures are arbitrary or disproportionate. Moreover, the commitments entered into will justify attempts by the State to renegotiate treaties and other agreements concluded with the other States, if these renegotiations are meant to achieve conformity with the Code provisions.

6.3.2. The effect of 'legitimate expectations'

The acceptance by a State of a Code of Conduct creates a legitimate expectation with the other States and with the interested non-governmental entities that it will fulfil the engagements contained therein. Although this expectation will not be legally enforceable, it may lead to justifiable pressure and even retorsions. Thus, 'soft' law may be accompanied by 'soft' sanctions, which in their turn may be instrumental in changing 'soft' law into 'hard' law.[311]

6.3.3. The 'good faith' effect

The legitimate expectations and good faith are two sides of the same coin. A State which adheres to a certain norm of behaviour may be expected to act in good faith in order to implement that norm and cannot subsequently act in contravention of it unless it is bound to do so in virtue of a higher norm. If it does act in contravention of the norm, other States having accepted the same norm of behaviour will no longer be bound to comply with it in their relations with the non-conforming State or its nationals, including the MNEs.[312]

6.3.4. The effect as 'lex mercatoria'

Notwithstanding the fact that they are not legally binding, the Codes will derive from the mere fact of their adoption and from the subsequent international practice the character of a 'source' of law for national and international authorities, who can rely on and utilise the Codes as a developing new *lex mercatoria* to fill gaps in the relevant laws and regulations.

> In this manner, the Code[s] may become a springboard for legally creative action by national courts and other authorities, and even by the transnational corporations themselves, to the extent that the latter may help to shape pertinent legal principles through their continuous practice.[313]

In the same way they are relevant to the interpretation of prior instruments in force between the parties concerned, including treaty provisions and other regulations that are of a general or ambiguous nature.

768

6.4. Supervisory procedures with respect to the Codes of Conduct

As has briefly been indicated in the foregoing section, some Codes of Conduct have been integrated in the supervisory mechanism of the organisation which issued them, while for others special procedures have been provided.

In relation to the Code of Conduct for Liner Conferencees, Chapter VI of the Convention contains provisions concerning the establishment and functioning of a machinery for the settlement of disputes. The disputes referred to are those which relate to the application or operation of the provisions of the Code and which have arisen between the following parties: (a) a conference and a shipping line; (b) the shipping lines members of a conference; (c) a conference or a shipping line member thereof and a shippers' organisation or representatives of shippers or shippers; or (d) two or 'more conferences. According to Article 23, para. 3, the parties to a dispute must first attempt to settle it by an exchange of views or direct negotiations with the intention of finding a mutually satisfactory solution. The fourth paragraph of the same article prescribes for certain categories of disputes that they shall, at the request of any of the parties to the dispute, be referred to international mandatory conciliation, if they have not been resolved through an exchange of views or direct negotiations. It is apparent from Article 38 that this means that the method of settlement is mandatory, not that the proceedings lead to a binding decision. The recommendations of the conciliators are binding only if the parties have agreed so in advance or have accepted them. To the Convention are annexed the 'Model rules of procedure for international mandatory conciliation'. Article 25, however, allows the parties to agree on other procedures for the solution of these disputes. Contrary to what is the general rule in case of disputes between States or of an international action of a private party against a State, *viz.* that domestic remedies in the respondent State's legal system have to be exhausted first, Article 25, para. 3, grants precedence to the conciliation proceedings over remedies available under national law. The State may participate in the conciliation proceedings in support of the party which is its national. All contracting States must recognise a recommendation of the conciliators as binding between the parties which have accepted it and must enforce it at the request of any such party as if it were a final judgment of any of their national courts. Disputes between the contracting States or between a State and a conference or shipping line relating to the interpretation or application of the Code are not dealt with therein. To these the general procedures for the settlement of inter-state disputes and of diplomatic protection are applicable. Article 52, finally, provides for a Review Conference to be convened five years from the date of the entry into force of the Convention or, if the Convention has not entered into force five years from the date of the adoption of the Final Act, at that moment, at the request of one-third of the States entitled to become parties to the Convention. The Registrar to be appointed by the UN Secretary-General in relation to the conciliation procedure will, under Article 46, para. 2(e), make available information of a non-confidential nature on completed conciliation cases, and without attribution to the parties concerned, for the purposes of preparation of material for the Review Conference.

With regard to the ILO Tripartite Declaration the Governing Body, during its 209th session, decided that the Member States must report before its next session on the basis of a questionnaire and that the reports would be examined by a tripartite committee in order to identify problems and make recommendations for the follow-up.[314] Two years later this procedure was further defined by the adoption of the 'Procedures concerning the Effect Given to the Tripartite Declaration etc.', which provide *inter alia* that the employers' and workers' organisations must be consulted before the reports are finalised and that these organisations can submit their own observations. Moreover, both these organisations and the governments are given the opportunity to submit requests for interpretation of the Declaration to the Governing body, which will answer the requests after preparation by its Standing Committee.[315]

The Set of Multilaterally Agreed Equitable Principles and Rules for the Control of Restrictive Business Practices provides for an Inter-governmental Group of Experts on Restrictive Business Practices operating within UNCTAD which, besides the undertaking and dissemination of studies and research on restrictive business practices, has the following functions:

(a) to provide a forum and modalities for multilateral consultations, discussions and exchange of views between States on matters related to the Set of Principles and Rules, in particular its operation and the experience arising therefrom;

(b) to collect and disseminate information on matters relating to the Set of Principles and Rules, to the over-all attainment of its goals and to the appropriate steps States have taken at the national or regional levels to promote an effective Set of Principles and Rules, including its objectives and principles; and

(c) to make appropriate reports and recommendations to States on matters within its competence, including the application and implementation of the Set of Principles and Rules.

In relation to these functions the following provision has been included:

> In the performance of its functions, neither the Inter-governmental Group nor its subsidiary organs shall act like a tribunal or otherwise pass judgment on the activities or conduct of individual Governments or of individual enterprises in connection with a specific business transaction. The Inter-governmental Group or its subsidiary organs should avoid becoming involved when enterprises to a specific business transaction are in dispute.

In addition, a review procedure has been provided for in the form of a Conference to be convened five years after the adoption of the Set of Principles and Rules – *i.e.* in 1985 – for the purpose of reviewing all its aspects. To this end, the Inter-governmental Group is to make proposals to the Conference for the improvement and further development of the Set of Principles and Rules. Finally, the Set contains several principles and rules concerning measures to be taken by the States at national, regional and subregional levels and at the international level. Among these measures are the following:

(a) the institution and improvement of procedures for obtaining information from enterprises, including transnational corporations, necessary for their effective control of restrictive business practices;

(b) the sharing, by States with greater expertise in the operation of systems for the control of restrictive business practices, of their experience with other States wishing to develop or improve such systems;

(c) the annual communication to the Secretary-General of UNCTAD of appropriate information on steps taken to meet their commitment to the Set of Principles and Rules; and

(d) the holding of consultations where a State, particularly a developing State, believes that a consultation with another State or States is appropriate in regard to an issue concerning control of restrictive business practices with a view to finding a mutually acceptable solution.

Within the facilities of UNCTAD experts should be provided to assist developing countries, at their request, in formulating or improving restrictive business practices legislation and procedures, and the officials involved in administering restrictive practices legislation should be trained.

The draft International Code of Conduct on the Transfer of Technology and the draft Code of Conduct for Transnational Corporations contain provisions which are comparable to the ones described in the preceding paragraph. The first-mentioned draft proposes to entrust the Committee on Transfer of Technology with the function of providing a consultation forum and of undertaking and disseminating studies and research, collecting and disseminating information and clarifying the provisions of the Code, or to establish a Special Committee on the Code with UNCTAD for that purpose. The draft Code on TNCs refers to the Commission on Transnational Corporations and to the UN Centre on Transnational Corporations in that respect. The provision – within brackets – that 'Representatives of trade unions, business, consumer organisations and other relevant groups may express their views on matters relating to the Code through the non-governmental organisations represented in the Commission' implies that the composition of the Commission, at least in the view of some delegations in the negotiating process, is not intended to be exclusively inter-governmental. The TOT draft Code contains the provision that the Committee may not act like a tribunal, which is framed in almost the same words as the quotation given in the preceding paragraph, while the TNC draft Code states more briefly that: 'In clarifying the provisions of the Code, the Commission shall not draw conclusions concerning the conduct of the parties involved in the situation which led to the request for clarification'. The TOT draft Code provides for a Conference to be convened four or six years after the adoption of the Code for the purpose of reviewing all the aspects of the Code including its legal nature.[316] The TNC draft Code leaves it to the Commission to make recommendations to the General Assembly for the purpose of reviewing the Code and provides that the first review shall take place not later than six years after the adoption of the Code.

The draft International Agreement on Illicit Payments in International Commercial Transactions contains the provision that the contracting States shall submit to the Centre on Transnational Corporations annual reports concerning their implementation of the Agreement. The Centre shall analyse and study the information provided, review the implementation of the Agreement in the previous year, and prepare annually an analytical report for the contracting States. It shall also organise periodically, or at the request of a contracting State, an exchange of views on issues relating to the implementation of the Agreement. The draft also stipulates that any dispute between contracting States concerning the interpretation or application of the Agreement shall be settled by bilateral consultations unless other peaceful methods are agreed upon. It is still a matter of debate whether or not a provision on the final submission of disputes to an *ad hoc* arbitral tribunal should also be included.

The Andean Code designates in Article 52 the Board of the Agreement of Cartagena as the body which shall:

(a) insure the application and compliance with the common régime for treatment of foreign capitals and of marks, patents, licenses and royalties established by the decision of the Andean Commission;

(b) centralise the statistics, accounting and other relevant information obtained from member countries;

(c) compile economic and legal information on foreign investments and transfer of technology and supply it to the member countries; and

(d) propose to the Commission whatever measures and regulations are necessary for the better application of the régime.

The review concerning the OECD Guidelines is regulated by a decision of 1976 of the Council on Inter-governmental Consultation Procedures on the Guidelines for Multinational Enterprises, which decision was revised on the occasion of the review of the OECD Guidelines in 1979. It provides that the Committee on International Investment and Multinational Enterprises shall periodically or at the request of a Member State hold an exchange of views on matters related to the Guidelines and the experience gained in their application. The same Committee is also made responsible for clarification of the Guidelines if required. It shall periodically invite the Business and Industry Advisory Committee (BIAC) and the Trade Union Advisory Committee (TUAC) to express their views on matters related to the Guidelines. Exchange of views on these matters may also be held upon request by these advisory bodies. The Committee must take account of these views in its reports to the Council. In its workings, the Committee also welcomes the presentation of views by an involved enterprise.[317] It is also expressly stated that the Committee shall not reach conclusions on the conduct of individual enterprises. The Member States may request that consultations be held in the Committee on any problem arising from the fact that multinational enterprises are made subject to conflicting requirements. The governments have further agreed to co-operate in good faith with a view to resolving such problems, either within the Committee or through other mutually acceptable arrangements. In the two other decisions of the

Council accompanying the Declaration and also revised in 1979 – the Decision on National Treatment and the Decision on International Investment Incentives and Disincentives – more or less the same provisions with regard to the periodical review by the Committee and the expression of views by the BIAC and the TUAC are included. The Decision on National Treatment further contains provisions about the obligation of Member States to provide to the Committee all relevant information concerning measures pertaining to the application of 'National Treatment' and exceptions thereto, while the other Decision provides for consultations in the framework of the Committee at the request of a Member State which considers that its interests may be adversely affected by the impact on its flow of international direct investments by measures taken by another Member State in that field. Under that consultation procedure the States must supply all permissible relevant information.

The EC Code of Conduct for Companies with Interests in South Africa provides, in relation to its implementation, that parent companies to which the Code is addressed should publish each year a detailed and fully documented report on the progress made in applying the Code, with a specification of the number of Black Africans employed in the undertaking. A copy of each company's report should be submitted to their national government. The governments of the EC Member States will review annually progress made in implementing the Code. The 'Vredeling Proposal' will, as a Directive, contain legal obligations for the Member States which form the subject of the regular supervisory mechanisms of the EEC Treaty

6.5. Some concluding remarks

On the basis of this short survey the following observations may be made:

(a) The fact that most Codes of Conduct have been embodied in instruments which as such are not legally binding, is not only understandable under the present circumstances but would seem to be the most appropriate intermediate approach. Not only do they deal with subject-matters on which opinions still differ quite substantially among the participating governments and between these governments and the economic and social parties involved; a situation which demands compromises between opposing desires to retain freedom of action and to reap the benefits on international economic co-operation.[318] In addition, while the behaviour of private enterprises is the primary object of regulation in the Codes, most international organisations do not have the power to directly bind these enterprises by their regulatory acts. On the other hand, the form of a treaty, which only binds governments, or of a binding decision addressed to the Member States, if possible at all, in most cases would provide no adequate solution, since harmonisation of national legislation and other implementation measures by the individual States are insufficient to effectively control the transnational activities of the MNEs. In that situation a growing consensus on the necessity of international norms and a growing preparedness, on a voluntary basis, to create and further develop these norms and to participate in their implementation and supervision, are the best that one may hope for at the moment, and may ultimately lead to results which do not differ from the results which can be expected to be achieved under legally binding norms. Indeed, the flexibility of a norm that is not legally binding may very well be found to leave more room for creative interpretation and constructive development than norms petrified in a treaty.[319]

From the foregoing it should not be inferred, of course, that there are main legal obstacles to the adoption of international rules which are legally binding also for private enterprises. If the organisation concerned lacks the power to make such rules, the States can either confer such power on the organisation or include the desired rules in a treaty. Equally, there are no main legal obstacles to the imposition of direct international responsibility on private enterprises. This again requires express legislation by the organisation concerned or by treaty, as the case may be. After several years of experience with the Codes in their present form time may be ripe for such direct international legal obligations and responsibility for the MNEs. But then again, such legally binding rules can be effective only if the consensus on which they are based includes that of the MNEs. This requires direct participation on their part in the formulation of the rules and in the supervision of their implementation. The argument that the lack of full international personality would bar the MNEs from such direct participation in international rule-making, appears to us to be utterly unconvincing. It does not bar the trade unions and employers organisations from participation in the international legislation by the ILO through their representatives, and would not form any obstacle if the Member States of the EEC were to decide to grant legislative power to the Economic and Social Committee. It is up to the States to decide on which entities to confer international personality and what the scope is of the ensuing powers.

(b) The supervision provided for is a very moderate kind of supervision, in accordance with the recommendatory character of most of the Codes. Review procedures have been provided for in all cases, but they consist mainly of data collection, studies and reports on implementation, clarification of the provisions of the Codes, recommendations as to the improvements of the implementation and/or the revision of the provisions of the Codes. The procedures do not result in a binding decision as to the conformity of State behaviour or the activities of MNEs with the provisions of the Codes; in the OECD Code and the UNCTAD Codes any power of the supervisory body to that effect has been expressly excluded. This is only different in those cases where a procedure of dispute settlement by conciliation or arbitration has been provided for and the parties in the dispute have agreed on the binding character of the recommendations of the conciliators or arbitrators. This applies in the case of the Code of Conduct for Liner Conferences and may become the situation under the Agreement on Illicit Payments. However, as the practice under the OECD Code shows, the power of the reviewing body to clarify the provisions of a Code may in actual fact have the same impact as a binding decision, depending on the procedure followed, the information gathered and the exact formulation used by the body. In particular, the provision that individual enterprises will be given the opportunity to express their views either orally or in writing on issues concerning the Guidelines involving their interests leads in fact to a quasi-judicial investigation of concrete cases rather than to a discussion of abstract issues by the Committee, be it that the Committee is not an independent body and its clarifications are not public pronouncements in the real sense.[320]

It is of essential importance for the effectiveness of the Codes that such clarification procedures, which derive their authority from the composition of the body concerned and from the direct participation of all the parties involved, both governmental and non-governmental, are provided for in all the Codes. They will enhance the consensus among the parties involved, create international practice and guide national practice, and may pave the way for legally binding Codes. It is, therefore, to be regretted that no agreement has yet been reached on the inclusion of a provision to that effect in the draft Code on TNCs and that the clause concerning the competence of transnational business, trade unions, consumer organisations and other interested parties to request clarification has been deleted in the most recent draft.

(c) The information on which the supervision is based comes from different sources. Periodical State reports form the main source, except in the EC Code, where the emphasis is fully on the yearly reports which the parent companies must provide. Another source of information is the non-governmental entities narrowly involved in the application of the Codes. The ILO Code, in conformity with the tripartite tradition of the Organisation, prescribes prior consultation with employers' and workers' organisations by the States when drafting their reports and gives these organisations the right also to supply independently information to the tripartite committee. In the case of the OECD, too, these organisations are important sources of information, through the BIAC and the TUAC. In the draft Code on TNCs there is the provision that the non-governmental organisations represented in the Commission on TNCs may provide information as a basis for periodical assessment of the implementation. Finally, the international supervisory bodies themselves collect information, prepare studies, reports and statistical surveys and request information from the governments, international organisations and enterprises. In particular, the UNCTAD Codes and the Andean Code provide for this. Consequently, what has been said in the preceding chapter on the required expertise and the necessity of sufficient support by a qualified staff is equally applicable here.[321]

(d) The UNCTAD Code on Restrictive Business Practices pays special attention to the problems States may experience in obtaining the necessary information from enterprises. It is obvious that similar problems may arise in the case of the other Codes and there too will be an issue in the reporting and in the further discussion. In this respect Articles 44–46 of the UN draft Code on TNCs concerning disclosure of information by the enterprises, on which provisions agreement has been reached, could be instrumental in helping to solve this problem after their adoption and general application.

This in combination with Article 51 of the draft Code dealing with safeguards to protect the confidentiality of information furnished by the enterprises.

(e) The UNCTAD Codes expressly recognise the necessity of assistance and technical advice to developing countries in relation to the implementation of the Codes and their participation in the supervisory procedure. For this we refer to our discussion of similar needs, *supra* in chapter V.[322]

(f) Like the NIEO documents discussed in chapter IV, some of the Codes, especially the UNCTAD Codes and OECD Code, provide for review conferences to discuss the results of the application of the Codes and their improvement and further development. In the case of the OECD Guidelines the first such review meeting actually resulted in important refinements and clarifications of the Code, thanks mainly to the prior clarification activities of the Committee on International Investment and Multinational Enterprises. In the Code of Conduct for Liner Conferences it is also anticipated that the results of the supervisory and dispute-settlement procedures may provide pertinent guidance to the discussions during the Review Conference. The same may hold good for the other Codes, dependent on how much opportunity for action will be given to the supervisory bodies by the interested parties and in how dynamic a way they will be prepared to interpret and perform their functions.

(g) In the Codes, as in the regular supervisory mechanisms, consultations between the States within the framework of the organisation play an important role. Express provisions to that effect are included in the Code on Restrictive Business Practices, the Code on TNCs and the OECD Decision on Inter-governmental Consultation Procedures, but it is obvious that the use of this device for the settlement of disputes and the solution of other difficulties experienced in relation to the Codes will not be limited to these Codes.

(h) The most striking feature of the procedures discussed above is that their function is almost exclusively restricted to the review function and the creative function. Apart from the corrective and preventive effect of consultations and clarifications, there is little room for the correction function, given the fact that most of the Codes are not legally binding and that they are a new phenomenon in international rule-making, with which the governments and other parties concerned have to become acquainted. Precisely for these reasons the creative function is of vital importance. It may clarify and further develop the provisions of the Code, adapt them to unforeseen problems and situations, and strengthen their normative value. As was stated in the 1979 Review Report of the OECD Committee on International Investment and Multinational Enterprises:

> It is, indeed, important that the Guidelines should be seen as setting a framework for a continuing follow-up process under the aegis of the IME Committee, to which other bodies of the OECD have a contribution to make.[323]

In view of their common features this applies in a way to all the Codes. The experience under the OECD Code with the dynamic approach taken by the CIME will not be fully transferable to the other Codes which have to operate in a politically and economically less homogeneous environment, but nevertheless may inspire the bodies charged with comparable functions under the respective Codes and may enhance the confidence of both the governments and the MNEs and other interested parties in supervisory mechanisms like the one set-up under the OECD Code. It may even be that the texts of the several Codes and their interpretation have a supplementary effect one on another, as was exemplified by the *Hertz Rent a Car* case, where the CIME in fact filled a loophole in the OECD Guidelines by applying the relevant principle embodied in the ILO Tripartite Declaration.[324]

(i) Now that the preparation of the Codes of Conduct has been, and is still being, carried out by several international organisations, while there is a considerable degree of overlapping in their contents, the issue of close co-operation and co-ordination between the various institutions involved arises.[325] This certainly also holds good with respect to the supervisory activities; although each provision will have to be interpreted and applied within its own legal and institutional context, diverging and, even more, conflicting interpretations and applications should be avoided to the maximum extent possible in order not to undermine the normative effect of international and national practice.[326]

VII. SOME CONCLUDING OBSERVATIONS: FURTHER NEED FOR DEVELOPMENT FROM POWER-ORIENTED TOWARDS RULE-ORIENTED STRUCTURES

7.1. Introduction

The difference between power-oriented and rule-oriented techniques of conducting international policy and of international dispute settlement has been described in a very clarifying way by John Jackson in two articles in the *Journal of World Trade Law,* on which the following introductory remarks are mainly based.

When using a power-oriented technique, the diplomat or other governmental representative will assert the power of the State he represents. The technique will in general consist of negotiations, because these are best suited for bringing to bear that power in order to win advantage over the other party. A rule-oriented technique of conducting international policy, by way of contrast, aims at the formulation of rules for the common benefit of all States concerned and towards the development of institutions to insure the highest possible degree of adherence to that rule. Equally, in the field of the settlement of international disputes, the power-oriented approach will make use of procedures that focus more on the relative power of the disputants than on the determination of whether a rule has been breached by one of them. On the other hand, a rule-oriented approach is more directed towards settling the dispute by reference to the relevant rules and their application to the respective claims of the disputants.[327] And the same categorisation could be made in relation to supervisory techniques in general. In fact, the ultimate possibility of supervision by an organ which settles a dispute – or assess the rule-conformity of State behaviour in general – independently of the States concerned, is the core test of the rule-oriented approach. As Jackson rightly submits:

> The mere existence of the rules, however, is not enough. When the issue is the application or interpretation of those rules . . . it is necessary for the parties to believe that if their negotiations reach an impasse the settlement mechanisms which take over for the parties will be designed to fairly apply or interpret the rules. If no such system exists, then the parties are left basically to rely upon their respective 'power positions', tempered (it is hoped) by the good will and good faith of the more powerful party (cognisant of his long range interests).[328]

It is obvious that the power-oriented techniques serve the interests of the large and powerful countries best, whereas small and less powerful countries in general may expect a more favourable outcome from the rule-oriented techniques because they cannot bring any counterbalancing threat or inducement into the negotiations. It may well be, however, that this difference of interests exists in the short-term only. In the long term the economies of both categories of countries may profit most from the rule-oriented approach. Indeed, in international economic relations, as in all international relations, there is the necessity for a certain minimum of stability and predictability of these relations. Not only for the governments but even more so for private business and other decentralised decision-makers who for their policy-making must be able to rely on the stability and predictability of the policy and activities of the governments of the countries in which they operate.[329] This requires regulation of these economic relations by agreed principles and rules, and a mechanism which ensures a fair and reasonable interpretation and application of these principles and rules irrespective of the power positions of the States involved; in short, a rule-oriented approach.[330] Therefore, although power-oriented techniques will continue to play a role in international economic relations as they will in human relations, further development towards rule-oriented structures in the international economic order is not only in the interest of the developing countries but of all participants in that order.

The developing countries, however, have the most immediate and urgent need for such structures: rule-oriented approaches towards rule-formulation in which the common interests of the international community are the guiding criteria and not merely or disproportionally the interests of the economically powerful States; rule-oriented decision-making procedures and distribution of voting-power, which assure an equitable representation of the economic interests of the developing countries; rule-oriented procedures for dispute settlement and international supervision which must guarantee a fair and reasonable interpretation and application by and *vis-à-vis* all States, in such a way that not the relative power of the States concerned but the measure of conformity of the State behaviour with the applicable rules is decisive for the outcome. In view of what has been said in chapter III of this Part,[331] 'rule-oriented' should in fact be supplemented by 'principle-oriented' as a reference to the fundamental principles on which a fair and equitable international economic order has to be based: freedom (sovereignty), (substantive) equality, solidarity, equity and respect for human rights.[332]

The following concluding observations concerning supervisory mechanisms are formulated in the perspective of a further need of a development towards rule-oriented structures.

7.2. The existing international economic organisations as the legal régimes within which the required changes can take place

There are several ways and several gradations in which the development towards more rule-oriented structures in the international economic relations can take place. Most of them can be realised within the framework of existing international economic organisations, whereas others could only take place outside of that framework. In the General Introduction we assumed that it was unlikely that a totally new international economic order will be set up on the ruins of the existing order.[333] In the following remarks we hope to further substantiate that assumption.

(a) A first step towards a more rule-oriented structure would be to develop a stronger consensus in relation to the existing principles and rules of the organisation, both among the States and between the States and private interested parties such as enterprises and trade unions. Various instruments could be used for that purpose, like bilateral and multilateral consultation and negotiation; political debate inside and outside the forum of the organisation; 'confidence-building' measures and practice of the organisation and its Member States, including international and national 'case-law'; training of diplomats, civil servants, politicians, managers and union officials; and informing and educating the people who, at least in democracies, need to support this consensus. To be sure, ultimately it is self-interest that motivates States and other units to comply with the rules of the organisation. However, the instruments just mentioned, and for that matter the mere existence of the organisation's 'régime'[334] and the interdependence it symbolises, may give to the notion of self-interest a broader and more durable meaning by developing a 'community of purposes'[335] based upon an agreed 'social purpose'[336] of the organisation. Such a 'new' consensus could pave the way to norm-governed changes in the organisation's policy that would meet justified Third World claims with the support of the industrialised nations. 'For then the decline of hegemony would not necessarily lead to a collapse of régimes, provided that shared purposes are held constant'.[337] The social purpose of the organisation is determined by the common goals and principles of the organisation, but at the same time constitutes the term of reference for the interpretation of these goals and principles, and of the rules, thus shaping the common expectations and making these a function of the self-interest of the individual units.

(b) To the extent that the rules of the organisation are no longer adequate, not even if interpreted in a dynamic way, to reflect the 'new' consensus, a second step would be the adoption of new rules through the existing procedures for rule-making. As has been stressed again and again above, these rules do not have to be legally binding. Depending on the measure of consensus reached and on the subject-matter to be dealt with, not legally binding rules might be the best solution for the time being, provided that they are linked to implementation and follow-up procedures. This may also require the development of *suigeneris* instruments next to the organisation's traditional rule-making instruments.

(c) A further step might be the adoption of new procedures for rule-making in order to better guarantee consensus.[338] Among other issues, this raises the complex relationship between equitable voting procedures and effective rule-making. We need not here go into the extensive discussions about this relationship and the various proposals made concerning devices for weighing of votes. This much is clear, that the developing countries will pursue their claim for a fair – and fairer – share of the voting power, also in the specialised economic organisations. It is equally evident, however, that, as Jackson put it, 'there is virtually no chance of significant rule-making authority developing in any international body today which bases its procedures on the one-nation one-vote system; the major powerful countries simply will not delegate to such a body any meaningful authority'.[339] Both facts stress the need for further negotiation, within each separate organisation, about the issue of what is a 'fair share' and for further development and refinement of the consensus procedure as a decision-making device.[340]

(d) As was argued above, rule-oriented structures can only be said really to exist if effective rule-oriented procedures for dispute settlement and for supervision of the implementation of the rules are provided for. Therefore, another step is the strengthening of the consensus on and effective participation in these procedures, and the adaption of these procedures or introduction of new procedures where circumstances make this desirable and feasible. As is clear from the individual studies in Parts II–IX, in most of the organisations the distance between the supervisory mechanisms provided for in the constitutive treaty and the supervisory practice is staggering. This could mean that the mechanisms as such are no longer adequate. It may also indicate that the way these mechanisms function needs improvement to make them more effective. Several elements of effective supervision have been outlined in detail in chapter V of the Part on this basis of a comparative analysis of certain aspects of the existing mechanisms and need no repetition here. Let us just briefly list some of the core elements.

7.2.1. Dispute—settlement procedures

First of all, each organisation should develop supervisory devices with a preventive effect to avoid disputes as much as possible. The procedures of general supervision, which will be discussed later on, may have such a preventive effect. So may regular consultations and discussions concerning international economic issues, both within the organisation and between Member States. In addition, one could think of the requirement of prior approval of, or consultation with, the organisation before a certain measure is taken. In general, such an *a priori* approach is to be preferred over an *a posteriori* approach.[341] However, the practice under GATT proves that this approach is only effective if the organisation and/or individual Member States are prepared to react if the prior approval or consultation requirement is not complied with.[342]

Disputants should be encouraged to settle their dispute among themselves, since if this can be achieved there is the best guarantee of an effective solution. However, this requires an unambiguous definition of the situations in which, the moment at which, and the procedure by which consultations must start, in order to avoid additional disputes, inordinate delays and the confrontation of one of the disputants with a *fait accompli*. Moreover, right from the beginning there must be the understanding that any unsettled dispute will ultimately be resolved by impartial third party judgment based on the rules, so that both sides will be negotiating with reference to their respective predictions as to the outcome of that judgment and not with reference to their respective power-positions.[343] Under that condition there still may be room for retaliations or the threat thereof, waivers, pay-offs with privileges or aids etc., since the other party then always has the possibility of a check and balance. The organisation should provide the forum and necessary facilities for the consultations, and its secretariat should give technical and administrative assistance. In cases where one of the disputants is a private party or is in actual fact standing up for a private party's interests, the requirement of prior negotiations include the requirement of the exhaustion of local remedies.[344]

Negotiations and consultations often turn out to be more successful if they are combined with good offices, mediation and conciliation. This still leaves the ultimate solution in the hands of the disputants but may bring into their discussions certain abstractions, impartial third-party views, solutions not yet taken into consideration, and the persuasive force of authority and reasonableness.[345] The third party could be the President of one of the organs of the organisation, the Secretary-General, a person or panel appointed by either one of them, or any other person or committee. The organisation and its secretariat should continue to provide their services.

Failing a settlement, a rule-oriented approach requires as the next step submission of the dispute to an independent expert body which will give an opinion on those issues which relate to the interpretation and application of one or more rules of the organisation. This body may be of an *ad hoc* or of a permanent character but must in any case be representative in its composition. In order to build-up sufficient authority and enjoy the parties' confidence, it has to pursue a method of interpretation which is not extensive beyond the point of consensus but at the same time does justice to what was called above the social purpose of the organisation. The question of whether this body of experts should be in permanent session invokes the dilemma between on the one hand the necessity to find experts able to spend enough time for the function, and on the other hand the desirability that these experts keep in touch with the political and economic life at the national level through other responsibilities. Moreover, there may not be enough 'business' for a permanent body, which could be one of the arguments for either selecting the experts from the secretariat or creating a common body of experts for two or more organisations. However, if a combination of functions is desirable and/or necessary, it is of the utmost importance that the other function is compatible with the impartiality required from the experts, as is revealed by the panel system in GATT.[346]

Jackson, in his proposal of a legal system for resolving governmental disputes in international trade relations, submits that the function of deciding on the interpretation or application of the rule and the function of – as he calls it – rule or policy formulation, and of deciding on or recommending sanctions or other measures should be kept separated.[347] We agree as far as policy formulation and sanctions are concerned. But the possibility exists that the independent experts, in the context of the interpretation and application of a certain rule, reach the stage where they have to specify, modify or supplement that rule to such an extent that in fact this amounts to an express or implied formulation of a new rule. International courts do that frequently, even if they are supposed only to interpret and apply existing rules. And the clarifications of the OECD Committee on International Investment and Multinational Enterprises (which, of course, is not independent but has a comparable function) may have the same results. Particularly in the eyes of the national judicial and other authorities these 'judge-made' rules may very well have a higher normative value than the rules of the formal rule-making bodies, be it that the codification of the former rules into the rules of the organisation will indeed require a decision by these rule-making bodies. It is admitted, however, that this rule formulation by independent experts is feasible only, if sufficient consensus exists about their contents.

As to the recommendation of measures, the experts who, due to their examination of the case are well-informed about the legal and factual situation in the country concerned, would seem to be in the right position to make such recommendations. Of course, they will need the support of the political organ of the organisation.[348] And such an organ alone can take a binding decision on measures or sanctions; even judgments of international courts are as a rule declaratory only.[349]

As far as publicity is concerned, we refer to our earlier observations on the matter.[350] It may be advisable that the procedure as such or parts of it take place *in camera,* but the final outcome should be made public, at least all findings as to the interpretation and application of the rules. Without this kind of publicity the supervision cannot play its preventive, corrective and creative role.[351]

Settlement procedures should be as uniform as possible, first of all within a particular organisation, but also between the organisations. Jackson has given several reasons for this, which we summarise as follows: (1) economy in costs and personnel; (2) building-up of experience among governmental officials and development of a career cadre of persons who can serve the system; (3) surveyability of the system and accessibility of the documents as a condition for the development of prestige and trust; (4) avoidance of forum-shopping manipulations by disputants; (5) development of procedural precedents which will limit disputes about the procedures.[352]

7.2.2. *Procedures of general supervision*

Even if dispute-settlement procedures – and other procedures of specific supervision, like complaint procedures, petitions and representations, to which *mutatis mutandis* the same applies – are provided for and are functioning effectively, there is still need for general supervision. Specific supervision is of an incidental character and not performed in a systematic and continuous way. It concerns certain elements of the relevant State behaviour only, *viz.* those acts or failures to act which affect other parties in such a negative way that they react by initiating a procedure. These acts or failures to act are not necessarily the most relevant behaviour from the point of view of the purposes of the organisation concerned. But even more important is, that those negatively affected by such acts or failures to act will not, or even cannot, in all cases initiate a procedure. Private parties in most instances depend for that on the initiative of their national States, which are then left with a broad discretion as to whether or not to act. And even in cases where States are directly affected themselves, they will rarely start a formal procedure against another State, since political or economic reasons, or special links of alliance, may make them hesitant to do so, while in many cases they will not have 'clean hands' themselves and therefore be reluctant to initiate a precedent which may backfire. Altogether this means that specific supervision may provide satisfactory results for the States directly concerned, but it leaves many loopholes for the legal order established or aimed at by the organisation. These loopholes can and should be covered by general supervision.

An additional argument for supplementary general supervision derives from the fact that specific supervision is as a rule performed under heavy political pressure, because at least one of the parties involved feels accused and mobilises its defence. In the case of general supervision all the Member States are equally subject to supervision, without there being a concrete reason for checking specific elements, whereas specific supervision is focusing on one particular State in consequence of an inter-state dispute or a dispute between the State and the international organisation concerned, a complaint by a State or another interested party, or information which the organisation has collected itself. Equal subjection to supervision also requires uniformity in the interpretation and application of the rules and symmetry in the conduct of the procedures, because, as Gold rightly puts it, 'the surrender of some freedom by each member is a concession of authority to other members'.[353]

Although other procedures of general supervision exist – take, *e.g.,* the permanent and structural supervision exercised by the Commission of the European Communities – the reporting procedure is the most commonly institutionalised one. On the basis of the effectiveness of its functioning in organisations such as the OECD, but also in organisations with a world-wide membership like the International Labour Organisation,[354] we are of the

783

view that the introduction of the reporting procedure in all international economic organisations as a supplementary supervisory mechanism would be an important and feasible step towards a more rule-oriented approach. That such a step would be feasible can, in our opinion, be concluded from the fact that all States, developed as well as developing, and also the socialist States, have been prepared in the past to accept this procedure, even in the sensitive field of the international protection of human rights.[355]

However, in order to be an effective tool of rule-oriented supervision and still generally acceptable for the States concerned, the reporting procedure has to meet certain requirements. The most important of these are, in our view, the following ones:

The periodicity of the reports must be well established and must not allow for too broad intervals. This periodicity should enable the supervisory body to assess whether the necessary measures have been taken. It should also put the State concerned under pressure to accept the improvements agreed upon or recommended during the last reporting procedure. This also means that the examination and discussion of the report should take place shortly after the submission of the report. This will put pressure upon the States to prepare their reports in time, and avoid the discussion of moot issues.

It must be clear to the State concerned what kind of information must be supplied. A detailed questionnaire can be instrumental in this respect in order to assure that the relevant data will be provided and that the information contained in the individual reports of the Member States is comparable, so that general conclusions may be drawn from it in addition to the conclusions with respect to each individual State.

To the extent that the date supplied by the States are classified by them as data which they want kept secret by reasons of economic policy, guarantees for confidentiality have to be provided.

The organisation concerned must create optimal conditions for the States for collecting and supplying the required information. Thus, *e.g.*, expert advice and technical assistance should be provided to those governments in need of it. At the same time, the questionnaires and other requests for information should not be more complicated than is strictly necessary. These questionnaires should also, as far as possible, be of the same structure in the successive reporting rounds so that the responsible bodies gain a certain experience in collecting the data and can rely to a large extent on earlier reports. Moreover, the reporting procedures of the different international organisations should be co-ordinated in such a way that the information supplied to the one organisation could at the same time serve as part of the report for another organisation concerning the same field of economic activity.

Regulations have to be made, both at the national level and within the international organisation, in consultation with the representatives of private business and other interested private parties, concerning the co-operation between the latter and the governments in collecting the relevant information on private economic activities.

Since the governments will not necessarily always provide the most relevant information on their own conduct and on the situation in their countries, and, also, are not impartial informants, the reporting procedure should contain devices for verifying and supplementing the data contained in the reports. The following such devices are conceivable:

(i) The competence of the supervisory body to ask for additional information. Logical as such a competence may seem to be, international practice shows that an express provision to that extent is advisable.

(ii) The competence of the supervisory body when examining the reports, to take into consideration any other relevant information it may have at its disposal on the basis of the personal expertise and knowledge of its members and/or on the basis of the information it has received from other sources, *e.g.* from national rapporteurs. This is also a competence which is not self-evident under international law and deserves express regulation.

(iii) The competence of the supervisory body or the secretariat of the organisation to send the reports, or parts of them, for comments to other organisations within whose field of competence the issues concerned also fall.[356]

(iv) The opportunity for other governments to submit observations and comments concerning the information contained in the report.

(v) The same opportunity for international and national non-governmental interested parties in relation to those parts of the reports which directly concern them.[357]

(vi) The competence of the supervisory body or the secretariat of the organisation to hold inspections *in loco,* if indispensable for verification, and the obligation for the government concerned to consent to, and co-operate in such a mission in good faith.[358]

The information should, in the first instance, be examined by a group of persons who are experts on the subject-matters concerned. The complexity of the issues involved and the differences among the national legal, economic and social systems make a thorough examination by the representatives of the States in the competent organs of the organisations almost impossible; even more so since they would have to combine this task with their other responsibilities. Since efficiency in discussion and reporting requires that the body of experts be of a limited composition, it must be representative of the main legal systems and economic groups of the world.[359] The experts should be guided exclusively by the rules of the organisation and by their expertise concerning the interpretation and application of these rules and the concrete political and economic situations to which they have to be applied. Therefore, it is necessary for a rule-oriented supervision that this examination is performed by experts who are independent from the governments. In order to give a really independent evaluation, it is also required that they have no conflicting other responsibilities.[360]

The procedure should result in an evaluation of a State's behaviour as to its conformity with the principles and rules of the organisation. This evaluation should be binding or at least be supported by a decision or recommendation of the highest organ of the organisation to give it optimal authority. It should be sufficiently specific in its conclusions and be followed by a decision or recommendation on the measures to be taken by the State concerned in the field of its policy, legislation or practice, and on possible measures to be taken by the organisation in adapting its rules to a change of circumstances revealed by the examination of the report (the creative function). As has been said above in relation to dispute-settlement procedures, the final conclusions and recommendations may be prepared and proposed by the experts, but need endorsement by the policy-making and rule-making organ of the organisation.

The final evaluations, conclusions, decisions and recommendations should be published in order to strengthen the pressure upon the government concerned to execute the decisions and recommendations, and to enhance the preventive and creative function of the supervisory procedure. However, as long as the discussion, and the mediation and conciliation efforts are still going on, confidentiality may be necessary to obtain concessions or reach a compromise.

A follow-up should be provided for to investigate and, if necessary, promote by renewed pressure the implementation of the decisions and/or recommendations made. The next round of reporting is such a follow-up. However, if more than one year lies between these rounds, it may be advisable that the competent organ, during its intermediate sessions, should discuss the most important aspects of the decisions and/or recommendations and take new action if necessary.

All the organisations discussed in this study represent several of the listed institutional and procedural elements in their supervisory mechanisms but there is ample room for improvement of the way these elements operate and for supplementing them to full-grown rule-oriented mechanisms. Of course, institutionalisation can never be a solution for any problems unless it is itself the expression of the consensus of the States concerned on the required solution.[361] It is submitted, however, that better organised and institutionalised supervisory procedures – with adequate guarantees for both impartiality and political realism – will eventually strengthen the confidence of the governments in these procedures and improve their participation. This will support the development towards more rule-oriented structures of the organisation.

The measures and developments mentioned so far can be effectuated within the existing legal régime of the international economic organisations. They may result in a change of the rules and procedures of the organisation but will leave the purposes and main principles of the organisation intact. Now, in the NIEO debates and in other international fora, the developing countries – supported by the socialist countries and some developed countries – claim that these purposes and principles have to change, too, for the establishment of a more just and equitable international economic order. In their opinion, the principles of redistribution and equity, which should constitute the basis of the new international economic order, find insufficient support in the present purposes and principles of the various organisations. Most of the developed countries, by way of contrast, take the view that redistribution and preferential treatment do not replace the more traditional principles of equal treatment and Most-Favoured-Nation treatment, but constitute a temporal variation of them. As soon as, and to the extent that the developing countries become more developed, the original principles will apply again.[362] In our view neither position is correct. The former seems to neglect the fact that the existing purposes and principles may well be, and to a large extent have already proved to be, sufficiently dynamic for adaptation to a different international economic environment, or rather to changing views on the requirements of that environment.[363] The latter would seem to be unrealistic in assuming that the States will eventually become equal in economic development and power in a measure which would justify the full application of the purposes and principles in their original 'Bretton Woods' form. It is our submission, based also on the comparative analysis of these purposes and principles made by VerLoren van Themaat,[364] that the principles of freedom and equity, which have traditionally formed the fundamental principles of international economic organisations, have been interpreted and developed in such a way as to create room for the principle of preferential treatment without losing their own fundamental character. And these two principles together, as VerLoren van Themaat says, 'form the drive towards the principle of substantive equality in its different variations'.[365] In particular, the principle of equality 'has turned out to be a self-radicalising legal principle'.[366] With the principle of substantive equality, the principle of equity has found expression in changing rules and procedures, especially where substantive equality is not possible or not yet feasible.[367] Moreover, there have been the first signs of a legal recognition of the principle of solidarity, mainly under the influence of the growing interdependence in international economic relations.[368] Finally, the principle of respect for human rights, although it has so far found little express formulation in the rules of the organisations, certainly does not conflict with the principles of freedom and equality in their 'modernised' interpretation. It is our view that the existing international organisations have the institutional, procedural and substantive means at their disposal to further develop the principles of substantive equality, equity, solidarity and respect for human rights. Other such means can be created, if and where necessary, without the need for these organisations to fundamentally change their purposes and principles. This comes down to an evolutionary rather than a revolutionary change.[369]

But even if one would take the view that the present purposes and principles are formulated in such a way that they block further restructuring towards a more just and equitable international economic order, even a fundamental change of these purposes and principles can take place within the existing international organisations. In both cases – (1) structural changes through existing or newly created institutional, procedural and substantive means, and (2) structural changes through a change of the purposes and principles – the supervisory mechanisms may play a vital role in signalling, further defining and effectuating the necessary changes, especially through their creative function. They can equally contribute to a strengthening of the consensus among the States on the required structural changes and on the ways and means of their realisation. In fact, not the present structure of the organisations but the lack of this consensus forms the real hindrance towards a restructuring of the international economic order. The extreme positions taken by both sides in the NIEO discussions, as manifestations of the power-oriented technique employed by the developed countries and the new power-oriented technique on the part of the developing countries, have created a cleavage of distrust which is difficult to bridge. Retreat to a more gradual, technical approach which focuses on the institutional, procedural and substantive means of the existing organisations for development towards rule-oriented structures and thus towards a more just and equitable international economic order, would seem to offer more prospect for a genuine consensus.

7.3. Regionalism as a possible catalyst of structural changes

The concept of a new international economic order is that of a *global* order; an order in which all States participate, and participate in an equal position. Does that allow for a special role to be played by regional organisations and other organisations of restricted membership, or do these organisations, on the contrary, by their mere existence and their functioning, symbolise the imperfection of the international economic order and the remoteness of the ideal of equality?

Our research included two organisations of limited membership – the Western OECD and the Socialist CMEA – while the European Economic Community was also taken into consideration. A study of these organisations and their impact on the position of developing countries reveals that, although the OECD and the EEC do not have developing countries among their members, their activities are more beneficial to that category of countries than those of the CMEA which does have developing countries as members. In the OECD this concerns mainly the promotion, co-ordination and review activities of the Development Assistance Committee (including a review of the performance of donor States as to the quantity and quality of the development aid) and the activities of the Development Centre as 'the OECD window to the Third World'.[370] For the EEC the relations with developing countries are chiefly regulated and institutionalised in the Second Lomé Convention of October 31, 1979,[371] which almost constitutes a legal order of its own. Next to the EEC and its 10 Member States, 63 so called ACP-countries (developing African, Caribbean and Pacific countries) are parties to the Convention. The Convention provides for permanent and flexible possibilities for dialogue between the EEC Member States and the ACP States in the framework of the ACP-EEC Council of Ministers, the ACP-EEC Committee of Ambassadors and the ACP-EEC Consultative Assembly. The substantive provisions concern trade co-operation, stabilisation of export earnings (stabex), insurance and development of mineral production, and industrial, agricultural, financial and technical co-operation. They grant many preferences to the ACP countries with a certain priority for the least-developed, island and land-locked countries. Accession is open to States whose economic structure and production are comparable to those of the ACP States.[372] The CMEA has adopted specific rules in favour of those of its Member States which have a developing economy.[373] However, in fact the States concerned derive the benefits mainly from bilateral relations and not from the CMEA as such. From these facts one may conclude that the question of formal membership is not the decisive factor as to the beneficial effects which a developing country may expect from a certain organisation. If within a regional organisation consensus can be reached on a common development policy that contributes to more just and equitable international economic relations for the developing countries, the loss in terms of real participation in the decision-making process may well be outweighed by the gain in real preferences. Besides, the Lomé Convention shows that membership of the organisation is not a condition for participation in the regulation and administration of the economic relations concerned. This may not be a satisfactory final solution, but should be taken into consideration when intermediate solutions have to be looked for.

Indeed, for some issues of the international economic relations, though in itself of global dimensions, time may not yet be ripe for an effective solution in a world-wide framework.[374] The world organisation may in these cases be instrumental in helping to define the issues and bringing to light the positions of the several States and groups of States with respect to them, but effective regulations are more likely to result from the co-operation of a relatively small group of homogeneous States. The regulation of development assistance accompanied by supervision over the donor States in the OECD, mentioned above,[375] may be given as an example, as well as the 'implementation' of the Guidelines for Multinational Enterprises within that organisation as compared with the stagnation in even the adoption of a Code of Conduct for Transnational Corporations in the UN.[376] Third States may profit from these regional arrangements in two ways. First, they may have a direct impact on their own situation as is clearly the case for developing countries in the first example given, and for host States of MNEs which have an OECD member as home State. In the second place there may be an indirect profit in that the regional arrangement may pave the way for a strong enough consensus to adopt and implement a similar regulation on a world-wide scale. The latter is reminiscent of the 'pilot project' concept mentioned by Claude:

> According to this view, regional organisations do not expand or coalesce into a world system but rather provide working models and serve as training grounds for organisation on a world scale. They invent techniques, conduct experiments in advanced forms of international collaboration, and develop among their participants habits and attitudes which prepare the way for successful organisation of the globe.[377]

Although, indeed, 'regional arrangements can never be a substitute for world organisation',[378] they may through their functioning as an intermediate alternative perform the role of catalyst towards world organisation with a genuine participation on the part of all States.

Precisely the recognition of this fact, *viz.*, that in the field of international economic co-operation greater progress might be made on a regional basis, where the economic homogeneity would lessen the barriers to such co-operation, resulted in the establishment of regional economic commissions within the structure of the United Nations Economic and Social Council, the Economic Commission for Europe (ECE), the Economic Commission for Latin America (ECLA), the Economic Commission for Africa (ECA), the Economic Commission for Western Asia (ECWA), and the Economic and Social Commission for Asia and the Pacific (ESCAP). The present functionings of these regional commissions differ and so does their impact on economic co-operation, but it can be said to be not spectacular in any of the cases.[379] Nevertheless, their possible future role as regional 'nuclei' which might operate as preliminaries to world structures deserves, in our view, further study and discussion. The ECE is unique, because it is the only international institution in which there exists general economic co-operation between Western European and Eastern European countries. The other four commissions may become effective in stimulating regional economic co-operation between developing countries and channelling (part of) the economic co-operation between developed countries and the developing countries of the region concerned. The latter may have more confidence in 'their' regional commission and a sense of greater identification with it than with the central administration of the UN.[380] So, ultimately, may (again?) the General Assembly's statement in 1952 hold true that:

> the regional economic commissions have become effective instruments of international economic co-operation and, for that reason, should continue to play an important part in the work of stimulating co-ordinated economic development in their respective regions and should co-operate in the efforts of the countries to that end.[381]

Procedures for dispute settlement and of general supervision should then be provided for in relation to the field of activities of the commissions along the lines set out above.

Since 1945, several initiatives have been taken for regional economic integration in the Third World, especially in Latin America and in Africa.[382] In many cases the efforts were given up as abruptly as they had started, or the organisation continued on paper without the existence of any solid legal and economic structure. In some cases, however, the legal structures of the organisations are of a more durable character, like those of the Latin American Free Trade Association and the Andean Common Market.[383] There too, however, the results in terms of economic integration or even co-operation have been rather meagre, due to a lack of co-ordination of policies of the participating countries. Some of the Regional Development Banks are more successful, but this is said to be due mainly to the fact that they include one or more developed States in their membership, which evidently hold a predominant position.[384] Also successful are some producers' organisations like OPEC.[385]

Apart from its role as a catalyst of world-wide international economic integration, regionalism may serve another purpose, *viz.,* the furthering of economic self-reliance of the States concerned. As for the future, it is evident, as was stated in Part VII of the Programme of Action on the Establishment of a New International Economic Order, that: 'Collective self-reliance and growing co-operation among developing countries will further strengthen their role in the new international economic order'. The co-operation is – as the UN Director-General for Development and International Economic Co-operation put it – 'at one and the same time a major objective of that order and one of the major instruments for its attainment'.[386] The Brandt Commission argued in favour of regionalism in the following words:

> Now that the political, economic and institutional requirements are better understood, sub-regional integration and other forms of close co-operation offer a viable strategy for accelerated development and structural transformation in many contiguous developing countries. Particularly for very small States, such efforts towards regionalisation deserve the strong support of the international community.[387]

And indeed, UNCTAD has from the beginning promoted regional co-operation among developing countries. In fact, its medium-term plan for 1980 to 1983 contained a strategy for consolidating the regional groupings by means of aid granted to their secretariats and there have been technical assistance projects for them prepared by UNCTAD and financed by UNDP.[388] Other global and regional institutions should also support this important emancipatory process. But most importantly, the developing countries themselves should spend at least as much time, money and energy for defining their individual and collective problems and looking for possibilities of co-operation to solve them, as they spend for formulating and pushing their claims *vis-à-vis* the developed countries. A convincing demonstration by the former of their mutual co-operation and planning is the most likely key to support from the latter, just as after the Second World War the American Government made its aid to Europe conditional on a common recovery programme of the participating European nations.

Since many of the problems which the developing countries are facing are of a comparable character and, therefore, may require a comparable solution, close co-operation between the various regional groups should be a matter of course and could make their functioning more efficient, their policies more coherent and comprehensive, their claims more authoritative and their negotiating power stronger.[389] Besides, such co-operation would strengthen the collective self-reliance of the developing countries.

This raises the question of the desirability and feasibility of an international secretariat or other global Third World institution, co-ordinating and supporting the work of regional and sub-regional groups of developing countries. The establishment of such an institution has been suggested several times.[390] To a certain extent, the UNCTAD Secretariat has tried to perform such a co-ordinating and supporting function. However, although UNCTAD is primarily a creation of the Third World, it is not a Third World institution. It is precisely the 'trade-union mentality' of the UNCTAD Secretariat in support of the Group of 77 which has reinforced the negative attitude of some Western countries towards the Secretariat and towards UNCTAD as a whole. The establishment of a Third World secretariat would, therefore, have the additional advantage of freeing UNCTAD from this image. An effective, separate, Third World institution could be very instrumental in preparing the negotiating positions and strategies of the developing countries. Thus it might counterbalance, to a certain extent, the services which an organisation like the OECD renders to the Western countries. In general, a stable structure of well-prepared and cohesive groups facilitates negotiations, since the positions are clearer and the possibilities for, and scope of, any compromises more predictable. The same holds good for international supervision. Collective support of, and a collective approach towards, supervisory mechanisms by the Third World will make it more difficult for the Western countries to rely on their political and economic power and circumvent the international supervision of its behaviour. At the same time, it will enhance the trust of the Third World – as, most likely, that of the Western countries – in these mechanisms, thus contributing to a more rule-oriented structure of the international economic order.

7.4. A new approach towards consensus?

Since the NIEO debates in the General Assembly, and the resolutions and programmes adopted there, have had little practical result thus far, because of lack of consensus concerning their implementation, is there any hope for a new approach that *will* lead to such consensus? Is it true – as was argued by Aurelio Peccei, the founder and President of the 'Club of Rome' – that:

> Despite the serious state of discord prevailing internationally, the necessary factual, intellectual and psychological elements exist for the world polity and public opinion to approach these crucial . . . North-South issues with a good chance of establishing a working agenda to liberate humankind from the self-imposed shackles of non-governability.[391]

If this is true, how then can these elements be activated and mobilised? And how can a working agenda be established to convert the restructuring of the international economic order from a political manifesto into a functioning reality?

Gregg has outlined three possible scenarios: (1) acquiescence by the developed States in the conversion of the UN into a world development authority, making concessions demanded of them by the developing States' majority; (2) transformation of the UN into a negotiating forum in such a way that it will facilitate synthesis of the opposing positions of developed and developing countries; and (3) negotiations on various issues, if and when they are ripe for such negotiations, not in the UN but in such other fora as offer the best prospects for synthesis of the positions.[392] Gregg indicates that, since the first scenario is 'patently unrealistic' and the third shifts the negotiations to fora where the developed countries have greater leverage than they have in the UN, the developing countries promote the second scenario. He also concludes, however, that in practice changes in the international economic system have occurred along the – decentralised – lines of the third scenario.[393] From the character of the UN, and the composition and powers of its competent organs, we cannot reach a conclusion other than that the third scenario is the only one offering any real perspective for results in the near future, with the UN continuing to play its role as a forum for general debate and global negotiation.

Crucial in the third scenario is the determination of which issues are ripe for negotiation and in what forum. This requires a deep insight in the actual situation and trends of both the international economic relations and national economies. In our opinion, the establishment for that purpose of a new 'Brandt Commission', more or less along the lines of the creation of the 'High-level Monitoring Body' proposed by the Brandt Commission itself,[394] deserves serious consideration. Such a commission of independent experts who enjoy the confidence of all the parties concerned, both at governmental and at private level, could make an inventory of such issues and their appropriate fora. For that purpose it should collect the opinions, demands, expectations, rebukes and suggestions of the governments and private interest groups in order to determine the level of consensus, both with respect to the norms and with respect to how they should be implemented and how that implementation should be supervised. At regular intervals the commission should report its conclusions to a committee of high-ranking governmental experts for further political discussion and negotiation. That committee should, in our view, be of relatively small but sufficiently representative composition. It should, in its turn, submit its conclusions and the results of its general negotiations to the General Assembly of the UN and to the international economic organisations concerned. The General Assembly could discuss the reports of the committee and express its agreement or disagreement with the submitted conclusions, but the responsibility to act upon the political compromises reached within the committee would rest with the economic organisation(s) concerned. The reports of both the independent commission and the inter-governmental committee should be made public to make the levels of discussion as broad as possible.

This leads us to state a few final remarks regarding the role of public opinion in the North-South dialogue and in consensus-building. The Brandt Commission addressed the issue in the following words:

> The Commission considers it essential that the educational aspects of improved North-South relations be given much more attention in the future. It is imperative that ordinary citizens understand the implications for themselves of global interdependence and identify with international organisations that are meant to manage it. It is no accident that those countries in the North which score high in official development assistance also provide an outward-looking education to their people and particularly to the younger generation.
>
> Also, international institutions need to communicate to an audience wider than the community of persons which participates in their discussions and negotiations. Resolutions and declarations will only be effective if they influence the public at large. Youth and their organisations should be among the more important non-governmental organisations with which international institutions should intensify contacts.[395]

Public opinion may operate as a strong and very effective drive towards bringing about consensus among nations. Depending on the measure of democratic structures in the societies concerned, public opinion can influence, steer and correct governmental policies and actions in many ways, directly and indirectly. But even in societies that are not democracies, governments are confronted with public opinion, if not on the part of their own peoples, then from the outside, through such spokesmen as foreign and international parliamentary institutions, foreign and international trade-union associations, foreign and international communication agencies, and other non-governmental organisations and private persons. Ethics, while absent in governmental policy considerations,[396] may, and often do, play an important role in the formation of public opinion and thus may indirectly influence governmental policy by introducing elements which are inspired by the principles of equity, solidarity and respect for human rights. But, in general, public opinion may to a certain extent counterbalance the narrow and short-run concept of self-interest upon which governments hold and base their policy.

However, public opinion can perform this function only if the public at large is sufficiently informed and educated. The fact that consensus is so seriously lacking between and among the governments of the developed and developing countries, indicates that the impact of public opinion is either lacking or works in different directions. And indeed, it is clear that there is no *communis opinio* among the peoples of the world on the lines along which the international economic relations should develop. In the Western countries, the 'outward look' mentioned by the Brandt Commission seems to turn inside more and more under the influence of the economic recession. An observer from the Third World described this attitude as follows: 'A big hurdle now is the sceptical, if not indifferent, attitude of the electorate in Western democracies – an electorate which mistakenly equates North-South economic co-operation with its own immediate economic "sacrifices" in terms of jobs, incomes and standards of living'.[397] With respect to the peoples of the Third World this same observer warns against impatience, radicalisation and over-demanding, and tells them 'to be convinced that a continued dialogue with the industrial countries is the safest and most assured – if not the most efficient or fastest – mechanism for building a better and healthier world'.[398]

Public apathy and even opposition towards even a gradual restructuring of the international economic order, based as these attitudes may be on insufficient information about the overall benefits which such a restructuring will produce in the long run, may easily discourage their governments from supporting a development in that direction. Likewise, demands on the part of the people for fundamental changes of the international structures, based as they may be on insufficient information about the realities of the existing structures, may demotivate their governments from constructively participating in the technical negotiations about separate issues in a step-by-step approach. Consequently, there is an enormous task for national and international governmental and non-governmental institutions to deepen the insight of the peoples in their own concepts and attitudes and in those of other peoples in order to bring about mutual understanding and appreciation

794

and thus to pave the way for a broader consensus and combined aspirations and efforts. And this final outcome need not be based upon idealism; it can be based upon the realistic understanding that a more just and equitable international economic order is ultimately in the interests of all countries as a prerequisite for global peace and prosperity. It opens a perspective to collective and individual self-reliance of the Third World. This will enable them to fulfil the basic needs of their people themselves and become stable, reliable and profitable economic partners.[399] Thomas Jones speaks in this context of a 'reconceptualisation of self-interest'.[400]

What is the role of international supervision in this new approach towards consensus? It is evident that in the decentralised scenario lined out above, the supervisory mechanisms of the individual organisations concerned may be instrumental in indicating which issues are ripe for further negotiation and in preparing these negotiations by clarifying the issues and pointing to the defects of the existing rules and procedures. If and when consensus is reached on new rules and, if necessary, on new procedures, this will in its turn require supervision, and the effectiveness of the supervision will be determined by the measure of consensus and its scope. Thus, here again, we meet with the mutual relationship between the normative value of the rules and the effectiveness of supervision. And the same holds good for the information and education of the people. The outcome of supervisory procedures, if made generally public, provides a great amount of relevant information and deepens the insight in international economic relations. At the same time, the support of a well-informed, rule-oriented public opinion for international supervision will encourage governments to participate in the supervisory procedures and thus will enhance their effectiveness.

NOTES

1. On this, with further references, P. van Dijk, 'De Rechtsvergelijking en het Recht der Internationale Organisaties; Enige Methodologische Notities' (Comparative Law and the Law of International Organisations; Some Methodological Notes), in: *In Orde; Liber Amicorum Pieter VerLoren van Themaat* (Deventer, 1982), pp. 77–98 at p. 90.
2. See Karl P. Sauvant, 'The Origins of the NIEO Discussions', in: Karl P. Sauvant, ed., *Changing Priorities on the International Agenda; The New International Economic Order* (Oxford/New York etc., 1981), pp. 7–40.
3. Ervin Laszlo, 'The Objectives of the New International Economic Order in Historical and Global Perspective', in *idem*, ed., *The Objectives of the New International Economic Order* (New York etc., 1978), p. XVII.
4. J. Meyer, D. Seul & K. H. Klingner, *Die Zweite Entwicklungsdekade der Vereinten Nationen* (Düsseldorf, 1971), p. 18.
5. Philippe de Seynes, Under-Secretary for Economic and Social Affairs of the UN, quoted by Marthinus G. Erasmus, *The New International Economic Order and International Organizations; Towards a Special Status for Developing Countries?* (Frankfurt/Main, 1979), p. 61.
6. UNCTAD I, Final Act, *Proceedings*, Vol. I, pp. 10–11 and 18–65. See P. J. G. Kapteyn, *De Verenigde Naties en de Internationale Economische Orde (The United Nations and the International Economic Order)* (The Hague, 1977), pp. 103–112.
7. See *supra*, Part II, pp. 163–164.
8. GA Res: 2029 (XX) and 2688 (XXV).
9. GA Res. 2152 (XXI).
10. GA Res. 2542 (XXIV) and 2543 (XXIV).
11. GA Res. 2626 (XXV).
12. *Idem*, Nos. 13, 14, 42 and 43.
13. *Idem*, No. 79.
14. Ervin Laszlo, *loc. cit.*, note 3, p. XIX.
15. UN Doc. A/9541, February 5, 1974.
16. See Marthinus G. Erasmus, *op. cit.*, note 5, p. 66.
17. GA Res. 3201 (S-VI) and GA Res. 3202 (S-VI), May 1, 1974.
18. Sixth Special Session, *Official Records*, 2229th–2231st plenary meeting. See Karen Hudes, 'Towards a New International Economic Order', *Yale Studies in World Public Order* (1975), pp. 88–181 at pp. 103–117.
19. See Branislav Gosovic & John G. Ruggie, 'On the Creation of a New International Economic Order: Issue Linkage and the Seventh Special Session of the UN General Assembly' (1976) 30 *International Organization* 309 at 314; P. K. G. Kapteyn, *De Nieuwe Internationale Economische Orde (The New International Economic Order)*, Mededelingen van de Nederlandse Vereniging voor Internationaal Recht No. 75 (Deventer, 1977), p. 16.
20. Resolution 45 (III).
21. UN Doc. A/PV 2315, p. 67.
22. See Andreas Rozental, 'The Charter of Economic Rights and Duties of States and the New International Economic Order' (1976) 16 *Virginia Journal of International Law,* 317–318; P. J. G. Kapteyn, *op. cit.*, note 19, p. 17.
23. See Gosovic & Ruggie, *loc. cit.*, note 19, pp. 319–327.
24. Catherine B. Gwin, 'The Seventh Special Session: Towards a New Phase of Relations Between the Developed and the Developing States?', in: Karl P. Sauvant & Hajo Hasenpflug, eds., *The New International Economic Order* (London, 1977), p. 97.
25. *Ibidem*, p. 113.
26. *Ibidem*.
27. See the analysis of Jahangir Amuzegar, 'A Requiem for the North South Conference' (1977–78) 56 *Foreign Affairs,* 136–159.
28. Robert W. Gregg, 'Negotiating a New International Economic Order: The Issue of Venue', in: Rüdiger Jütte & Annemarie Grosse-Jütte, eds., *The Future of International Organizations* (London, 1981), p. 51 at p. 56.
29. GA Res. 32/174 of December 19, 1977. See also *supra*, General Introduction, Chapter II.
30. *Idem*, para. 4.
31. See Press Release GA/E/21 of September 8, 1978.
32. See Robert Gregg, 'Un Decision-Making Structures and the Implementation of the NIEO', in: Ervin Laszlo & Joel Kurtzman, *Political and Institutional Issues of the New International Economic Order* (New York etc., 1981), p. 103 at pp. 114–115.
33. See GA Res. 34/138 of December 14, 1979.

34. See the Report of the Ad Hoc Commission, A/S-11/25.
35. At the moment of writing, during the 38th session of the General Assembly, informal consultations are being held within the framework of the Second Committee to define the issues with respect to which there is any prospect of fruitful discussions during a NRGN.
36. GA Res. 35/56 of December 5, 1980, para. 179.
37. *Ibidem*, para. 180.
38. See also P. VerLoren van Themaat, *The Changing Structure of International Economic Law* (The Hague etc., 1981), pp. 232–233, 239–247, 346–353 and 363–365.
39. GA Res. 2625 (XXV), October 24, 1970.
40. See Bengt Broms, *The Doctrine of Equality of States as Applied in International Organizations* (Vammala, 1959), esp. pp. 154–271.
41. *Cf.* E. W. Vierdag, *The Concept of Discrimination in International Law* (The Hague, 1973), pp. 7–18.
42. P. VerLoren van Themaat, *op. cit.*, note 38, p. 232.
43. Cited in: J. F. Dorsey, 'Preferential Treatment: A New Standard for International Economic Relations' (1977) 18 *Harvard International Law Journal* 109 at 113.
44. *Op. cit.*, note 38, p. 233.
45. Permanent Court of International Justice, The diversion of water from the Meuse, judgment of June 28, 1937, *Series A/B*, No. 70, p. 77.
46. Thus also the International Court of Justice in the North Sea Continental Shelf Case, judgment of February 20, 1969, *ICJ Reports* (1969), p. 3 at p. 50.
47. See Tawfique Nawaz, 'Equity and the New International Economic Order: A Note', in: Kamal Hassain, ed., *Legal Aspects of the New International Economic Order* (London, 1980), p. 113 at p. 114.
48. *Ibidem*, p. 116.
49. See Norbert Horn, 'Normative Problems and a New International Economic Order' (1982) 16 *Journal of World Trade Law* 338 at 344: "No new (or old) international economic order is conceivable with unlimited use of sovereign rights as the only commonly accepted norm. Instead, economic co-operation based on the equalit⁊ of nations and on mutual respect requires a careful and elaborate extension of international law rules'.
50. P. VerLoren van Themaat, *op. cit.*, note 38, p. 241. See also the proposal for the drafting of the Charter of Economic Rights and Duties of States, made by President Echeverría, 'removing economic co-operation from the realm of good will and rooting it in the field of law by transferring consecrated principles of solidarity among men to the sphere of relation among nations'; *UN Doc. A/PV 2315*.
51. *Ibidem*, pp. 240–241.
52. CHR Res. 4 (XXXIII), para. 4.
53. CHR Res. 5 (XXXV); GA Res. 34/46. The UN Commission, in its resolution, added the following words: 'Equality of opportunity for development is as much a prerogative of nations as of individuals within nations'.
54. Pieter van Dijk, Wil D. Verwey, Karel de Vey Mestdagh & Paul J. I. M. de Waart, *The Right to Development as a Legal Phenomenon* (not yet published), para. 28.
55. *Ibidem*, pp. 9–15 of the provisional publication.
56. Ervin Laslo *et al.*, *The Objectives of the New International Economic Order* (New York etc., 1978).
57. *Ibidem*, Part I, pp. 3–186.
58. *Cf.* P. van Dijk, 'The Final Act of Helsinki – Basic for Pan-European System?' (1980) 11 *Netherlands Yearbook of International Law* 97 at 110.
59. S. Azadon Tiewul, 'The United Nations Charter of Economic Rights and Duties of States' (1975) 10 *Journal of International Law and Economics* 645 at 687. See also Maurice Mendelson, 'The Legal Character of General Assembly Resolutions: Some Consideration of Principle', in: Kamal Hossain, *op. cit.*, note 47, p. 95 at pp. 105–106.
60. For a short survey of the legal history of this fact and also for possible exceptions, see Maurice Mendelson, *loc. cit.* (note 59), pp. 95–96. See also the separate opinion of Judge Lauterpacht in: South-West Africa—Voting Procedure, Advisory Opinion of June 7, 1955: *I.C.J. Reports* (1955), p. 67 at pp. 118–120.
61. Article 2, para. 1, of the Vienna Convention of the Law of Treaties (1969) 8 *International Legal Materials* 679, only says that it has to be a written form, and it is not at all certain that even that is a general requirement, also outside the context of that Convention. See Manfred Rotter, 'Die Abgrenzung zwischen völkerrechtlichem Vertrag und ausserrechtlicher zwischenstaatlicher Abmachung', in: René Marcic *et al.*, eds., *Internationale Festschrift für Alfred Verdross* (Munich etc., 1971), p. 413 at p. 424.

797

62. See the leading study by Anthony d'Amato, *The Concept of Custom in International Law* (Ithaca/London, 1971). See also G. J. H. van Hoof, *Rethinking the Sources of International Law* (Deventer, 1983), pp. 85–113.

63. See Maurice Mendelson, *loc. cit.*, note 59, pp. 99–100.

64. See, among others, Bin Cheng, *General Principles of Law as Applied by International Courts and Tribunals* (London, 1953); Maarten Bos, 'The Recognized Manifestations of International Law; A New Theory of "Sources"' (1977) 20 *German Yearbook of International Law* 9 at 33–42; G. J. H. van Hoof, *op. cit.*, note 62, pp. 131–167.

65. Thus, *e.g.*, G. J. H. van Hoof, *op. cit.* note 62, pp. 139–151; Clive Parry, *The Sources and Evidences of International Law* (Manchester, 1965), p. 91; J. H. W. Verzijl, *International Law in Historical Perspective*, Vol. I, General Subjects (Leyden, 1968), p. 62.

66. Maarten Bos, *loc. cit.*, note 64, pp. 24–25; A. J. P. Tammes, 'Decisions of International Organs as a Source of International Law', *Recueil des Cours de l'Académie de Droit International* (1958–II), pp. 265 *et seq.*

67. Maarten Bos, *ibidem*, p. 71.

68. Nuclear Tests (Australia v. France), Judgment of December 20, 1974, *I.C.J. Reports* (1974), p. 253 at p. 267.

69. Case concerning the Temple of Preak Vihear (Cambodia v. Thailand), Preliminary Objections, Judgement of May 26, 1961, *I.C.J. Reports* (1961), p. 17 at pp. 31–32. See also H. Meyers, 'How is International Law Made?—The Stages of Growth of International Law and the Use of its Customary Rules' (1978) 9 *Netherlands Yearbook of International Law* 3 at 20: 'The manifestation of the will to create law must occur in such a manner that it is sufficiently perceptible for all potential subjects of that law'. For the complex question whether a declaration or other act can create something like an estoppel preventing the State concerned from denying the assertion made, if another State relies on it, see M. Mendelson, *loc. cit.*, note 59, pp. 96–97.

70. For a further elaboration, see G. J. H. van Hoof, *op. cit.*, note 62, pp. 215–279.

71. For special complications raised in this respect by the consensus-procedure, see *ibidem*, pp. 227–234.

72. On this, see Subrata Roy Chowdhury, "Legal Status of the Charter of Economic Rights and Duties of States' in: Kamal Hossain, *op. cit.*, note 47, p. 79 at pp. 81–82.

73. We share the opinion on this and the arguments for it as put forward by G. J. H. van Hoof, *op. cit.*, note 62, pp. 195–203.

74. Kamal Hossain, *op. cit.*, note 47, p. 6.

75. See, among others, F. Blaine Sloan, 'The Binding Force of a "Recommendation" of the General Assembly of the United Nations' (1948) 25 *British Year Book of International Law* 1 at 31; M. Virally, "La valeur juridique des recommandations des organisations internationales' (1956) *Annuaire Français de Droit International*, 66 at 78–90; *idem*, 'La deuxième décennie des Nations Unies pour le développement; essai d'interprétation para-juridique' (1970) *Annuaire Français de Droit International* 9 at 28–32; Castañeda, *Legal Effects of United Nations Resolutions* (New York, 1969), p. 11.

76. South-West Africa—Voting Procedure, Advisory Opinion of June 7, 1955, *I.C.J. Reports* (1955), p. 67 at p. 120. See also the separate opinion of Judge Klaestad, *ibidem*, p. 88.

77. Norbert Horn, *loc. cit.*, note 49, p. 351.

78. On the creative function, see *supra*, pp. 11–14.

79. In this context, see Art. 13 of the UN Charter stating as one of the functions of the General Assembly, to 'initiate studies and make recommendations for the purpose of . . . encouraging the progressive development of international law and its codification'.

80. For efforts by UNITAR to make an inventory of the principles and norms relating to the NIEO concept, see: 'Progressive Development of the Principles and Norms of International Law Relating to the New International Economic Order; The Compendium', UNITAR/DS/4, September 25, 1981. For subsequent analytical papers and analyses of texts and relevant instruments, see UNITAR/DS/5, August 15, 1982, and UNITAR/DS/6, October 12, 1983.

81. *Loc. cit.*, note 76, pp. 120–121.

82. See *supra*, pp. 695–696.

83. GA Res. 3486 (XXX), para. 3.

84. Apart from the provision in chatper I, section 7, concerning the obligation for developed countries of consultation and multilateral surveillance in case of any departure of the standstill provisions regarding imports from developing countries.

85. GA Res. 3506 (XXX).

86. *Idem*, para. 3.

87. GA Res. 32/174.

88. *Supra,* p. 699.
89. GA Res. 37/202 of December 20, 1982, para. 5.
90. GA Res. 35/166 of January 29, 1981.
91. The studies prepared by UNITAR thus far (see note 80) have met with strong criticism in the Sixth Committee of the General Assembly.
92. See Robert I. McLaren, 'The UN system and its quixotic quest for co-ordination' (1980) 34 *International Organization,* 139 at 147–148.
93. See P. J. G. Kapteyn, *op. cit.,* note 6, pp. 52–53.
94. See J. N. Judge, 'International Organizations Networks: A complementary perspective', in: P. Taylor & A. J. R. Groan, eds., *International Organization: A conceptual approach* (London, 1978), pp. 381–413.
95. See, *inter alia,* the 'Jackson Report' of 1969: *A Study of the capacity of the UN Development System* (DP/5), and the study by a group of experts in 1975: *A New United Nations Structure for Global Economic Co-operation,* (E/AC.62/9).
96. See E. Luard, *International Agencies* (London, 1977), pp. 264–287; R. J. Meltzer, 'Restructuring the UN System' (1978) *International Organization,* 993–1018.
97. For the connection between this infrastructure and the instruments and function of the organisation, see P. VerLoren van Themaat, *op. cit.,* note 38, pp. 155–157.
98. For more details and further references, see P. van Dijk, *loc. cit.,* note 1, p. 88.
99. For examples, see *supra,* pp. 229 and 236.
100. For a definition of these functions, see *supra,* pp. 11–14.
101. *Supra,* p. 11.
102. *Supra,* p. 713.
103. *Supra,* pp. 708–713.
104. *Supra,* pp. 707–708. For the impact of the character of the norm on the instruments and functions of supervision, see *infra,* pp. 757–761.
105. *Cf.* the definition of a Directive in Article 189 of the EEC Treaty.
106. *Supra,* pp. 707–713.
107. On this, see Van Hoof, *op. cit.,* note 62, pp. 270–275.
108. This should be one of the elements of the study undertaken by UNITAR; see *supra,* note 80.
109. See *supra,* pp. 62, 69–70 and 108. The Multi-Fibre Arrangement is discussed in Part III, *supra.*
110. See *supra,* p. 63.
111. *Supra,* p. 297.
112. On the legal character of stand-by arrangements and letters of intent, see Joseph Gold, *The Stand-By Arrangements of the International Monetary Fund* (Washington, D.C., 1970), pp. 44–51. See, however, for a somewhat different view, *supra,* pp. 389–390.
113. *Supra,* pp. 418–421.
114. *Supra,* pp. 424–425.
115. *Supra,* p. 499.
116. Art. 6, para. 3, of the OECD Convention.
117. *Supra,* pp. 544, 553–554 and 562; *infra,* p. 763 *et seq.*
118. *Supra,* pp. 624–634.
119. *Cf.* the opinion expressed *supra,* pp. 27–32.
120. See *supra,* pp. 21–22.
121. *Supra,* p. 447.
122. See Joseph Gold, 'The "Sanctions" of the International Monetary Fund' (1972) 66 *American Journal of International Law* 737 at 744–751.
123. *Supra,* pp. 656 and 659–660.
124. *Supra,* pp. 532–533 and 585–587. See, however, pp. 572–573.
125. *Supra,* p. 508 and note 104.
126. For the Bank, see *supra,* pp. 449 and 457; for the IMF, see *supra,* pp. 386–388; for the OECD, see *supra,* pp. 537, 552, 553, 567 and 571–572; for the IAEA, see *supra,* pp. 503–504.
127. For GATT, see *supra,* pp. 196–197; for the TSB, see *supra,* pp. 235–236; for UNCTAD, see *supra,* p. 300; for the CMEA, see *supra,* pp. 647–649 and 660.
128. See the several 'evaluations' in Part II, *supra;* see, *e.g.,* pp. 143, 189 and 196–197.
129. *Supra,* pp. 332–334.
130. *Supra,* pp. 659–660.
131. For the Bank, see *supra,* pp. 440–441 and 449; for the IMF, see *supra,* pp. 386–388 and 392; for the OECD, see *supra,* p. 533.
132. *Supra,* pp. 250–251.

133. *Supra,* pp. 196–197.
134. *Supra,* pp. 312 and 318–319.
135. *Supra,* p. 636.
136. See: Set of Principles and Rules for Control of Restrictive Business Practice; Code of Conduct for Liner Conferences; Code of Conduct for Transfer of Technology, *et al.; infra,* p. 776.
137. Section C, paras. 44 *et seq.*; E/C.10/1983/S/5/Rev. 1, pp. 20–22.
138. *Supra,* p. 88.
139. *Supra,* p. 111.
140. *Supra,* pp. 321 and 329.
141. GA Res. 35/56, para. 172.
142. *Supra,* pp. 323 and 333.
143. For the IAEA, see *supra,* pp. 503–504. For Euratom, see Art. 81 Euratom Treaty.
144. See G. Fischer & D. Vignes, eds., *L'inspection internationale* (Brussels, 1976), pp. 248–385. See also note 126.
145. On this, see N. Valticos, 'The international protection of economic and social rights', in: P. van Dijk, ed., *Rechten van de Mens in Mundiaal en Europees Perspectief* (Human Rights from a Global and European Perspective), (2nd ed., Utrecht, 1981), p. 109, at p. 127.
146. See *ibidem.* Other examples are the several independent supervisory bodies in the field of human rights.
147. See also *supra,* p. 196, where the problem is mentioned that it may not always be easy to find experts who are willing to break out of their normal work for a rather limited function.
148. See also *infra,* p. 784.
149. See *supra,* pp. 250–251.
150. *Supra,* pp. 455–456.
151. *Supra,* p. 387.
152. *Supra,* p. 197.
153. John H. Jackson, 'The Crumbling Institutions of the Liberal Trade System' (1978) 12 *Journal of World Trade Law* 93 at 96.
154. *Supra,* p. 334.
155. *Supra,* pp. 507–508.
156. *Supra,* pp. 584–585.
157. *Supra,* pp. 636–637 and 648–649.
158. *Cf.* A. J. P. Tammes, *Hoofdstukken van Internationale Organisatie* (Chapters of International Organisation) (The Hague, 1951), p. 175.
159. See Th. Meron, *The United Nations Secretariat; The rule and practice* (Lexington, Mass., 1977), especially pp. 27–45 and 122–128. See also H. J. Michelmann, 'Multinational staffing and organizational functioning of the Commission of the European Communities' (1978) 32 *International Organization* 477–496; H. Hahn & A. Weber, *Die OECD Organisation für Wirtschaft* (Baden-Baden, 1976), pp. 168–182; H. Getz & H. Jüttner, *Personal in internationalen Organisationen* (Baden-Baden, 1972), pp. 379–495.
160. *Report of the Secretary-General of the United Nations on the Work of the Organization* (New York, 1982), pp. 4–5.
161. See Th. Meron, *op. cit.* (note 159), pp. 103–115. See also the Report of the Panel on International Trade Policy and Institutions, *op. cit., supra,* note 9 of the General Introduction, p. 32.
162. See the 1982 *Report of the Secretary-General of the United Nations on the Work of the Organization* (New York, 1982), p. 2.
163. See N. Lateef, 'Parliamentary Diplomacy and the North-South Dialogue' (1981) *Georgia Journal of International and Comparative Law* 1 at 16.
164. I. Seidl-Hohenveldern, *Das Recht der Internationalen Organisationen einschlieszlich der Supranationalen Gemeinschaften* (3rd ed., Köln, 1979), pp. 121–122.
165. On this, see H. G. Schermers, *International Institutional Law* (2nd ed., Alphen a/d Rijn, 1980), pp. 286–293; I. Seidl-Hohenveldern, *op. cit.,* note 164, pp. 122 and 135.
166. International Court of Justice, 'Reparation for injuries suffered in the service of the United Nations', Advisory Opinion of April 11, 1949, *I.C.J. Reports* (1949), p. 174 at p. 183. See also: *Report of the Secretary-General on the respect for the privileges and immunities of officials of the United Nations and Specialized Agencies* (A/C.5/36/31).
167. See H. G. Schermers, *Integratie van internationale organisaties* (Integration of international organisations) (inaugural address, Deventer, 1978).
168. *Supra,* p. 11.
169. *Supra,* p. 720.

170. *Supra*, p. 335.
171. *Supra*, pp. 384–386 and 393.
172. See P. J. G. Kapteyn & P. VerLoren van Themaat, *Introduction to the Law of the European Communities* (London etc., 1973), pp. 77–78.
173. See, *e.g.* the OECD 'Interfutures' report: *Facing the Future; Mastering the Probable and Managing the Unpredictable* (Paris, 1979). Reference could also be made to numerous UNCTAD Studies.
174. *Supra*, pp. 96–97 and 198–199.
175. *Supra*, pp. 255–256.
176. See the observations on the correction function, *supra*, p. 657.
177. *Supra*, pp. 455–456.
178. Especially Art. 88, para. 3, ECSC Treaty. The power of the Commission under Art. 169 EEC Treaty and Art. 141 Euratom Treaty to take the case before the Court of Justice if the State does not comply with its obligations within the period set by the Commission in its 'reasoned opinion', may also be considered as a decision with corrective or preventive effect. See H. A. H. Audretsch, *Supervision in European Community Law* (Amsterdam, 1977), pp. 29–30 and 80–82.
179. *Ibidem*, pp. 74–80.
180. Treaty creating the Court of Justice of the Cartagena Agreement, May 28, 1979, (1979) 18 *International Legal Materials* 1203–1210.
181. Inis L. Claude, *The Changing United Nations* (New York, 1967), p. 73.
182. *Supra*, pp. 94, 101 and 103, 129 and 174.
183. *Supra*, pp. 532–533.
184. For an indication of sensitiveness on the part of States with respect to publication, see *supra*, p. 337. For a possible counter-productive effect, see *supra*, p. 255.
185. See *supra*, pp. 588–589.
186. Thus, *e.g.*, Art. 2 of the Treaty Establishing a Single Council and a Single Commission of the European Communities; Art. 14 of the Statute of the Council of Europe.
187. *E.g.* the Ministerial Meeting of GATT; the Session of the Council of the CMEA (prime minister; at important meetings the party leader); the yearly Council meetings at ministerial level of OECD.
188. *Supra*, pp. 661–662.
189. See *supra*, pp. 9–10.
190. Including the recognition of certain exceptions, *viz.*, individual and collective self-defence (Art. 51 UN Charter) and collective enforcement action by the Security Council, and by regional organisations with the permission of the Security Council.
191. See, *e.g.*, Arts. 33–38 UN Charter, especially Art. 36, para. 3, stipulating that legal disputes should as a general rule be referred by the parties to the International Court of Justice.
192. Art. 219 EEC Treaty, *e.g.*, provides: 'Member States undertake not to submit a dispute concerning the interpretation or application of this treaty to any method of settlement other than those provided for therein'.
193. See, *e.g.*, Art. 7, para. 2, of the Mandate concerning South West Africa, cited in *I.C.J. Reports* (1962), p. 335. See also the judgment of August 30, 1924, of the Permanent Court of International Justice in the Mavrommatis Palestine Concessions Case, *Publ.P.C.I.J.*, Series A, No. 2 (1924), p. 15, where the Court, quite generally, spoke of 'the rule laying down that only disputes which cannot be settled by negotiation should be brought before it'.
194. See, *e.g.*, Art XXXII of the Pact of Bogotá, 30 *UNTS*, p. 84 at p. 94.
195. This would seem to be the position taken by the Court of Justice of the European Communities: judgment of November 13, 1964, in the Dairy Products Case, *European Court Reports* (1964), p. 625 at p. 631. H. G. Schermers, *op. cit.*, note 165, p. 739, submits that this is or ought to be the general rule in the case of international organisations.
196. Thus, *e.g.*, P. J. G. Kapteyn & P. VerLoren van Themaat, *op. cit.*, note 172, p. 27. See also H. A. H. Audretsch, *op. cit.*, note 178, p. 82 who suggests that in the case of the EEC such reprisals should be taken upon the authorisation by the Council only.
197. See, *e.g.*, Art. 41 of the UN Charter and Art. XXIII, para. 2, of the GATT. See also Art. 39, para. 2, of the European Convention for the Peaceful Settlement of Disputes of 1962, 444 *UNTS*, p. 48, and Art. 32, para. 2, of the European Convention on Human Rights.
198. In general, see J. H. W. Verzijl, *International Law in Historical Perspective*, Vol. VIII: Inter-State Disputes and their Settlement (Leyden, 1976). On judicial and non-judicial procedures in international organisations, see H. G. Schermers, *op. cit.*, note 165, pp. 667–678. On arbitration, see L. B. Sohn, 'The Function of International Arbitration' (1963-I) 108 *Recueil des Cours de l'Académie de Droit International* 1–113.

199. *Supra,* pp. 33–35.
200. See *ibidem* and *cf.* H. G. Schermers, *op. cit.,* note 165, pp. 667–668.
201. See, however, Art. 38, para. 2, of the Statute of the International Court of Justice empowering the Court to decide a case *ex aequo et bono,* if the parties agree thereto.
202. In this context see, however, Art. 26, para. 1, of the Statute and Arts. 16–18 of the Rules of Court of the International Court of Justice concerning the establishment of Chambers for specific cases.
203. Art. 29 of the Convention of the World Meteorological Organisation ('unless the parties concerned agree on another mode of settlement').
204. Art. 44 of the Treaty establishing the Benelux Economic Union.
205. Art. XVII of the Constitution of the Food and Agriculture Organisation of the United Nations ('or to such other body as the Conference may determine'); Art. 56 of the Convention on the Inter-Governmental Maritime Consultative Organisation ('for an advisory opinion').
206. Art. 84 of the Convention on Civil Aviation ('appeal from the decision of the Council').
207. *Supra,* pp. 386–388.
208. *Supra,* pp. 388–391. See also Joseph Gold, *loc. cit.,* note 122, pp. 744–751.
209. *Supra,* pp. 87–88.
210. Thus, *inter alia,* consultations concerning import restrictions for balance-of-payment problems; see *supra,* pp. 126–129. More in general, see *supra,* pp. 195 and 198.
211. See *supra,* pp. 325–326 and 315 respectively. See also *infra,* p. 771.
212. *Supra,* pp. 538, 542 and 553.
213. *Supra,* pp. 648–649.
214. *Supra,* pp. 94–97. For the power-oriented and rule-oriented approaches, see *infra,* pp. 777–779.
215. *Supra,* pp. 255 and 261–262.
216. For this, see H. A. H. Audretsch, *op. cit.,* note 178, pp. 16–19.
217. See P. van Dijk & G. J. H. van Hoof, *Theory and Practice of the European Convention on Human Rights* (Deventer, 1984), Chapter 2, section 3.2.
218. *Infra,* pp. 781–783.
219. *Supra,* pp. 37–38.
220. Security Council Resolutions 232 (1966) and 253 (1968) concerning economic sanctions against Rhodesia, and Security Council Resolution 418 (1977) concerning an arms boycott against South Africa are the only instances, with dubious effect.
221. *Supra,* p. 458.
222. *Supra,* pp. 372–373. See also Joseph Gold, *loc. cit.,* note 122, pp. 744–751.
223. *Supra,* p. 538.
224. *Supra,* pp. 662–663.
225. *Supra,* pp. 83–87, 88–93 and 198–200.
226. *Supra,* p. 508.
227. *Supra,* pp. 11–14.
228. *Cf.* G. J. H. van Hoof, *op. cit.,* note 62, pp. 274–275.
229. Art. 31 of the Convention.
230. *Cf.* Art. 32 of the same Convention.
231. *Supra,* pp. 27–32 and 39. The term 'consent' used in Part I has been altered here into 'acceptance', because the term 'consent' usually refers to the act through which a State concludes with other States an agreement or adheres to an existing agreement, whereas 'acceptance' can occur tacitly or can be implied.
232. *Supra,* pp. 693–694.
233. *Supra,* p. 606.
234. *Cf.* the observations made above with respect to the World Bank, *supra,* pp. 467–470.
235. *Supra,* pp. 191–194.
236. *Supra,* pp. 200–201.
237. On this, see *supra,* pp. 293–294.
238. *Supra,* pp. 337–338.
239. *Cf.* dissenting opinion of M. Alvarez in: 'Reservations to the Convention on the Prevention and Punishment of the Crime of Genocide', Advisory Opinion of May 28, 1951, *I.C.J. Reports* (1951), p. 15 and p. 53.
240. *Supra,* pp. 98–103.
241. *Supra,* pp. 200 and 237.
242. *Supra,* pp. 648–649.
243. See Part IV of the Final Act, *The Department of State Bulletin,* September 1, 1975.

244. See, *e.g.*, Art. XVII of the Articles of Agreement of the IMF, on which the important amendments of 1968 and 1978 were based, creative both as to procedures and as to rules.
245. *Supra*, p. 499.
246. *Supra*, pp. 302–305.
247. GA Res. 35/56 of December 5, 1980, para. 176. In GA Res. 37/202 of December 20, 1982, para. 5, the General Assembly decided to establish such a committee to carry out the review and appraisal concerned and report to the General Assembly through ECOSOC.
248. *Supra*, p. 316 and *infra*, p. 771.
249. *Supra*, pp. 319–321 and *infra*, p. 770.
250. *Supra*, p. 329 and *infra*, p. 772.
251. *Supra*, p. 322.
252. *Supra*, p. 546 and *infra*, p. 772.
253. *Supra*, p. 730.
254. *Supra*, p. 735.
255. *Supra*, p. 589.
256. *Supra*, pp. 636–637 and 647–648.
257. *Supra*, p. 730.
258. *Supra*, pp. 386–388 and 455–456.
259. *Supra*, notes 152 and 153.
260. *Infra*, p. 792.
261. *Supra*, p. 339.
262. *Supra*, pp. 732–733.
263. See, *e.g.*, Sir Hersch Lauterpacht, *The Development of International Law by the International Court* (London, 1958). For a compact survey, see J. J. G. Syatauw, *Decisions of the International Court of Justice* (Leyden, 1962).
264. See Clouis C. Morrisson, *The dynamics of development in the European Human Rights Convention System* (The Hague etc., 1981).
265. See, *e.g.*, Andrew Wilson Green, *Political Integration by Jurisprudence; The Work of the Court of Justice of the European Communities in European Political Integration* (Leyden, 1969), and C. W. A. Timmermans, *Het recht als multiplier in het Europese integratieproces* (*The law as a multiplier in the European integration process*) (Deventer, 1978). See also Gerhard Bebr, *Development of Judicial Control of the European Communities* (The Hague etc., 1981), esp. pp. 9–13; Anna Bredimas, *Methods of Interpretation and Community Law* (Amsterdam etc., 1978); Jean Boulois, 'A propos de la fonction normative de la jurisprudence; Remarques sur l'oeuvre jurisprudentielle de la Cour de Justice des Communautés', in: *Le juge et le droit public*, Mélanges offerts à Marcel Waline, Vol. I (Paris, 1974), pp. 149–162.
266. See *supra*, pp. 28–30.
267. See R. P. Anand, *Compulsory Jurisdiction of the International Court of Justice* (London, 1961), pp. 60–71.
268. Rudolf L. Bindschedler, 'To which Extent and for which Questions is it Advisable to Provide for the Settlement of International Legal Disputes by other Organs than Permanent Courts?', in: Max Planck Institute for Comparative Public Law and International Law, *Judicial Settlement of International Disputes* (Berlin etc., 1974), p. 131 at p. 143.
269. *Cf.* F. Roessler, 'Law, De Facto Agreements and Declarations of Principle in International Economic Relations' (1978) 21 *German Yearbook of International Law* 27 at 56.
270. See (1979) 18 *International Legal Materials* 561.
271. See for the Principles: *Proceedings of the first session*, Vol. I, pp. 18 ff., and for the Generalised System of Preferences, *TD/332*, 1970.
272. *Supra*, pp. 296–297.
273. See also *supra*, pp. 31–32, where the different levels of consensus are discussed.
274. *Supra*, pp. 379 ff.
275. *Supra*, pp. 565–569.
276. *Supra*, pp. 168–173.
277. *Supra*, pp. 87–88.
278. *Supra*, p. 363.
279. See the listing by P. VerLoren van Themaat, *op. cit.*, note 38, pp. 146–147.
280. For a more elaborated description of this development, see *supra*, pp. 384–391.
281. See Hans W. Baade, 'Codes of Conduct for Multinational Enterprises: An Introductory Survey', in: Norbert Horn, ed., *Legal Problems of Codes of Conduct for Multinational Enterprises* (Deventer, 1980), p. 408, with further references. This definition is rather broad and vague but so are other proposed definitions. Agreement upon a common definition has not yet been reached. For a comprehensive discussion of the definition, see Cynthia Day Wallace,

Legal Control of the Multinational Enterprise (The Hague, 1983), pp. 9–22. *Cf.* also: Commission on Transnational Corporations, *Working Paper No. 13*, March 20, 1980, para. 12.

282. On the question whether and to what extent the MNE evade host-State control, see Cynthia Day Wallace, *op. cit.*, note 281, pp. 33–37 and *passim*. See also the provisions on jurisdiction in the UN Draft Code of Conduct on Transnational Corporations, on which the States still greatly disagree; *infra*, note 292, Arts. 55–58.

283. See Communication of the Commission of the European Communities to the Council, entitled 'Multinational Undertakings and the Community', *Bulletin of the EC*, Supplement 15/73, pp. 7 and 9–12.

284. See, as an example, the impact of the US Voluntary Capital Restraint Program of 1965 on Canadian economy and Canada's response; Hans W. Baade, *loc. cit.*, note 281, pp. 409–410.

285. See, *e.g.*, Section V of the Programme of Action on the Establishment of a NIEO: 'All efforts should be made to formulate, adopt and implement an international code of conduct for transnational corporations'.

286. Reference is made here to the excellent survey of Hans W. Baade, *loc. cit.*, note 281, pp. 407–441.

287. UNCTAD, *United Nations Conference of Plenipotentiaries on a Code of Conduct for Liner Conferences*, Vol. II: *Final Act (including the Convention and resolutions) and tonnage requirements* (New York, 1975).

288. 17 *International Legal Materials* (1978), p. 422.

289. UNCTAD, *TD/RBP/CONF/10/Rev. 1* (New York, 1981).

290. E/AC.67/L.3/Add. 1, May 17, 1979.

291. TD/CODE TOT/33, April 10, 1981, and TD/CODE TOT/38, August 11, 1983.

292. United Nations, *Doc. E/C.10/1983/S/5/Rev. 1*.

293. Decision of the Andean Commission concerning Treatment of Foreign Capital; 10 *International Legal Materials* (1971), p. 152.

294. 15 *International Legal Materials* (1976), p. 969, and 18 *International Legal Materials* (1979), p. 986.

295. *Cmnd.* 7233 (1978), pp. 5–7.

296. *Bulletin of the EC*, Supplement 2/83.

297. Published by the ICC in 1974.

298. Published by the ICC in 1974.

299. ICFTU, *Doc. D/1976/0403/13*, p. 17.

300. 17 *International Legal Materials* (1978), p. 417.

301. See Hans Günther, 'The Tripartite Declaration of Principles (ILO): Standards and Follow-Up', in: Norbert Horn, ed., *op. cit.*, note 281, p. 155 at p. 157.

302. Decision on Inter-Governmental Consultation Procedures on the Guidelines for Multinational Enterprises.

303. C (78) 113, August 9, 1978; 17 *International Legal Materials* (1978), p. 1527.

304. Norbert Horn, 'Codes of Conduct for MNEs and Transnational Lex Mercatoria: An International Process of Learning and Law Making', in: Norbert Horn, ed., *Legal Problems of Codes of Conduct for Multinational Enterprises* (Deventer, 1980), p. 45 at p. 52.

305. Another factor undoubtedly has been the moderate and balanced language of the Codes and the 'carrot and stick' policy followed in certain instances by making the Code part of a package deal. See, *e.g.*, the positive language recognising the important role of MNEs in the OECD Declaration on International Investment and Multinational Enterprises, and the Decision of the OECD Council on National Treatment which is in favour of the TNEs and which formed part of the 'package'.

306. See also *supra*, pp. 710–711. See also Matthijs van Bonzel, *The Movement towards Codes of Conduct for Transnational Corporations and its Impact on International Law* (Seminar Paper, University of Michigan Law School, July 1981 (not yet published)).

307. See Hans W. Baade, 'The Legal Effects of Codes of Conduct for Multinational Enterprises', in: Norbert Horn, ed., *op. cit.*, note 281, p. 3 at p. 11.

308. *Loc. cit.*, note 307. See also Matthijs van Bonzel's paper mentioned in note 306.

309. See UN Commission on Transnational Corporations, 'Certain Modalities for Implementation of a Code of Conduct in Relation to its Possible Legal Nature', Doc. E/C.10/AC.2/, December 22, 1978, p. 7.

310. See the express provision to that effect in section 7 of the ILO Tripartite Declaration.

311. See I. Seidl-Hohenveldern, 'International Economic "Soft Law"', (1979-II), 163 *Recueil des Cours de l'Académie de Droit International* , pp. 169–238 at pp. 205–209. *Cf.* also Sir K. Bailey, 'Making International Law in the United Nations' (1967) *Proc. Am. Society Int'l. L.*

804

233 at 239: 'It is to be remembered that propaganda can create pressure; that pressure can create practice; and that practice can create law'.
312. See the advisory opinion of the International Court of Justice of June 21, 1971, on Legal Consequences for States of the Continued Presence of South Africa in Namibia (South West Africa) notwithstanding Security Council Resolution 276 (1970), *I.C.J. Reports* (1971), p. 16 at p. 46. *Cf.* also Art. 60 of the Vienna Convention on the Law of Treaties.
313. 'Modalities Paper', *loc. cit.*, note 309, para. 23. Thus also Pieter Sanders, 'Codes of Conduct as sources of law', in: *Le droit des relations économiques internationales; Études offertes à Berthold Goldman* (Paris, 1982), p. 281 at pp. 297–298. On the character and contents of the *lex mercatoria*, see Norbert Horn, *loc. cit.*, note 304, pp. 59–78. On the significance of the 'customs of the trade' for national case-law, see I. Seidl-Hohenveldern, *loc. cit.*, note 311, pp. 197–198.
314. ILO, *Official Bulletin*, Vol. LXII (1979), Series A, pp. 118–119. See also *idem*, Vol. LXIII (1980), Series A, p. 120.
315. ILO, *Official Bulletin*, Vol. LXIV (1981), pp. 89–90, especially Article I(c).
316. The exact wording has not yet been agreed upon. The Group of 77 has proposed the words 'with a view to bringing about its universal application as a legally binding instrument'.
317. See the *1979 Review Report* of the Committee, para. 85.
318. This holds good even for a more or less coherent group of States like OECD: Theo W. Vogelaar, 'The OECD Guidelines: Their Philosophy, History, Negotiation, Form, Legal Nature, Follow-Up Procedures and Review', in: Norbert Horn, ed., *Legal Problems of Codes of Conduct for Multinational Enterprises* (Deventer, 1980), p. 127 at p. 129.
319. *Cf.* P. van Dijk, 'The Final Act of Helsinki—Basis for a Pan-European System?' (1980) 11 *Netherlands Yearbook of International Law* 97 at 115–118. See also R. Baxter, 'International Law in "her infinite variety"' (1980) 29 *International and Comparative Law Quarierly* 549 at 565; Norbert Horn, *loc. cit.*, note 304, p. 52; I. Seidl-Hohenveldern, *loc. cit.*, note 311, p. 209: 'Such a "soft procedure" combined with the "softness" of the rules concerned has allowed solutions which might not have been possible under strict law'.
320. On this, see Pieter Sanders, *loc. cit.*, note 313, pp. 285–288 and 291–293. In more detail R. Blanpain, *The OECD Guidelines for Multinational Enterprises and Labour Relations 1976– 1979; Experience and Review* (Deventer, 1979), pp. 123–235.
321. See *supra*, p. 732.
322. See *supra*, pp. 728–729.
323. 'Review of the 1976 Declaration and Decisions on International Investment and Multinational Enterprises', *Doc. C (79) 102 (Final)*, June 5, 1979, para. 9; reprinted in (1979) 18 *International Legal Materials* 986.
324. See R. Blanpain, *op. cit.*, note 320, pp. 226 and 228. The Guidelines have been supplemented in this respect at the occasion of the 1979 revision. In the UN Code on Transnational Corporations express reference will be made to the ILO Tripartite Declaration as applicable in the field of employment, training, conditions of work and life and industrial relations; *loc. cit.*, note 292, p. 27.
325. See UN Doc. A/CN.9/171, May 2, 1979. See also International Law Association, International Committee on Legal Aspects of a New International Economic Order, Second Report, *Report of the Sixtieth Conference* (London, 1982), p. 206.
326. See I. Seidl-Hohenveldern, *loc. cit.*, note 311, pp. 214–216, where he discusses the issue of 'conflict of soft law', and pp. 217–224 on diverging interpretations.
327. John H. Jackson, 'The Crumbling Institutions of the Liberal Trade System', (1978) 12 *Journal of World Trade Law* 93 at 98–99.
328. John H. Jackson, 'Governmental Disputes in International Trade Relations: A Proposal in the Context of GATT' (1979) 13 *Journal of World Trade Law* 1 at 4.
329. John H. Jackson, *loc. cit.*, note 327, p. 101.
330. See also the study by Puchala & Hopkins, mentioned *infra* in note 369, p. 250: '"Fairer" régimes are likely to last longer, as are those that call for side payments to disadvantaged participants'.
331. *Supra*, pp. 708–712.
332. *Supra*, pp. 700–705.
333. *Supra*, General Introduction, Chapter III.
334. For 'international régimes', see the Spring 1982 issue of *International Organization*, edited by Stephen D. Krasner, where international régime is defined as 'principles, norms, rules, and decision-making procedures around which actor expectations converge in a given issue-area' (p. 185).

335. See Charles Lipson, 'The transformation of trade: the sources and effects of régime change' (1982) 36 *International Organization* 417 at 434.

336. On 'legitimate social purpose', see John Gerard Ruggie, 'International régimes, transactions, and change: embedded liberalism in the postwar economic order', *ibidem* 379 at 382 and 404.

337. *Idem*, 404.

338. On this, see also J. Tinbergen, coord., *Reshaping the International Order; a Report to the Club of Rome* (New York, 1976), p. 82.

339. John H. Jackson, *loc. cit.*, note 327, p. 102.

340. On the consensus procedure in general, see E. Suy, 'The Meaning of Consensus in Multilateral Diplomacy', in: R. Akkerman *et al.*, eds., *Liber Röling, Declarations on Principles; A Quest for Universal Peace* (Leyden, 1977), pp. 247–257.

241. See Joseph Gold, 'Strengthening the Soft International Law of Exchange Arrangements' (1983) 77 *American Journal of International Law* 443 and 461–462, who also discusses efforts to introduce the *a priori* approach into the IMF Articles of Agreement.

342. See *supra*, p. 197; see also note 128.

343. Thus John H. Jackson, *loc. cit.*, note 328, p. 4.

344. On this, see P. van Dijk, *Judicial Review of Governmental Action and the Requirement of an Interest to Sue,* (Alphen a/d Rijn, 1980), pp. 381–391. On the requirement of prior negotiations, see *ibidem*, pp. 391–395.

345. On these procedures, see the references in note 198 *supra*.

346. *Supra*, pp. 96–97 and 743.

347. John H. Jackson, *loc. cit.*, note 328, pp. 8–9.

348. See Joseph Gold, *loc. cit.*, note 341, p. 464: 'Only an organ composed of persons appointed or elected by members can apply the pressure, because governments assume that these persons are stating the views of other governments'.

349. For an exception, see Art. 88 of the European Coal and Steel Community Treaty.

350. *Supra*, pp. 736–737.

351. See also Joseph Gold, *loc. cit.*, note 341, p. 485.

352. John H. Jackson, *loc. cit.*, note 328, pp. 11–12.

353. Joseph Gold, *loc. cit.*, note 341, p. 480.

354. For an account of this effectiveness, see E. A. Landy, *The Effectiveness of International Supervision; thirty years of I.L.O. experience* (London, 1966).

355. See Art. 16 of the International Covenant on Economic, Social and Cultural Rights; Art. 40 of the International Covenant on Civil and Political Rights; and Art. 9 of the International Convention on the Elimination of All forms of Racial Discrimination.

356. *Cf.* Article 18 of the International Covenant on Economic, Social and Cultural Rights and Article 40, para. 3, of the International Covenant on Civil and Political Rights.

357. *Cf.* Article 23, para. 2, of the Constitution of the International Labour Organisation which stipulates that the States shall communicate to the representative employers' and workers' associations copies of the reports submitted to the International Labour Office.

358. On the various aspects of the inspections *in loco*, see Georges Fischer & Daniel Vignes, 'Existe-t-il une fonction d'inspection dans la société internationale?', in *idem*, eds., *L'inspection internationale* (Bruxelles, 1976), pp. 7–21. See especially pp. 16–21 on the requirement of the visited State's consent.

359. *Cf.* Article 9 of the Statute of the International Court of Justice.

360. *Supra*, p. 743.

361. See P. van Dijk, *loc. cit.*, note 319, pp. 97–98.

362. See Stephan D. Krasner, 'Structural causes and régime consequences: régimes and intervening variables' (1982) 36 *International Organization* 185 at 188.

363. Ruggie, *loc. cit.*, note 336, p. 384, speaks in this context of 'adaptive restorations of prior sets of norms in the context of a new and different international economic environment'.

364. See the General Introduction, *supra*, and P. VerLoren van Themaat, *op. cit.*, note 38, especially pp. 239–247.

365. *Ibidem*, p. 239.

366. *Ibidem*, p. 240.

367. See *supra*, pp. 702–703.

368. P. VerLoren van Themaat, *supra*, note 38, pp. 241–242.

369. On this, see David J. Puchala & Raymond F. Hopkins, 'International régimes; lessons from inductive analysis' (1982) 36 *International Organization* 245 at 249–250.

370. *Supra*, pp. 553–555, where there is also reference to the Sahel Club.

371. *Official Journal of the EC* (1980), L347/1.

372. See K. R. Simmonds, 'The Second Lomé Convention: the Innovative Features' (1980) 17 *Common Market Law Review* 415–435. See also *idem*, 'The Lomé Convention and the New International Economic Order' (1976) 13 *Common Market Law Review* 315–334.
373. Section 2 of the Comprehensive Program for the Intensification and Improvement of Cooperation and the Development of Socialist Economic Integration of Comecon Member Countries; William E. Butler, *A Source Book on Socialist International Organizations* (Alphen a/d Rij, 1978), pp. 41–44.
374. *Cf.* Edward H. Carr, *Nationalism and After* (London, 1945), p. 45. See, however, Inis L. Claude, *Swords into Plowshares; The Problems and Progress of International Organization* (4th ed., New York, 1971), p. 104, who warns that the assumption that more effective collaboration is possible on the regional level 'should not go unchallenged'. But at p. 105 he admits that this is indeed the case where 'the cultivation of intensive co-operation among states' is concerned.
375. *Supra*, p. 788.
376. *Supra*, pp. 772–773.
377. Inis L. Claude, *op. cit.*, note 374, p. 107. See also pp. 108–112, where the author in discussing the 'pilot' function of the European Communities, unjustly discusses their institutional features only.
378. Trygve Lie, former Secretary-General of the United Nations, quoted by D. W. Bowett, *The Law of International Institutions* (4th ed., New York/London, 1982), p. 167.
379. See W. R. Malinowski, 'Centralisation and Decentralisation in the United Nations Economic and Social Activities' (1962) 16 *International Organization* 521–541.
380. See *idem*, p. 540.
381. GA Resolution 627(VII), December 21, 1952.
382. See the enumeration in Appendix I to: Davidson Nicol, Luis Echeverría & Aurelio Peccei, eds., *Regionalism and the New International Economic Order* (New York etc., 1981).
383. See Alicia Puyana, 'Latin-America: Lessons of the Strength and Weakness of Regional Co-operation', *op. cit.*, note 382, pp. 49–74. For regional organisations in Africa, see B. W. Mutharika, 'A Case Study of Regionalism in Africa', *ibidem*, pp. 91–113.
384. On the difference in this respect between the Inter-American Development Bank and the Asean Development Bank on the one hand, and the African Development Bank on the other, see: R. Barents, 'De Regionale Ontwikkelingsbanken' (The Regional Development Banks), in P. VerLoren van Themaat, *Studies over Internationaal Economisch Recht* (Studies on International Economic Law), vol. I.3(b) (The Hague, 1977), pp. 107–109. See also J. Sys, *International Development Banks* (Leyden, 1974). For a 'NIEO evaluation', see A. K. Bhattacharya & Michael Hudson, 'A Regional Strategy to Finance the New International Economic Order', *op. cit.*, note 382, pp. 299–317.
385. See Abdul Amir O. Kubbak, *OPEC* (Vienna, 1974).
386. Kenneth K. S. Dadzie, 'Aspects of Regionalism', *op. cit.*, note 382, p. xi at p. xii.
387. *North-South; A Program for Survival*, The Report of the Independent Commission on International Development Issues under the Chairmanship of Willy Brandt (Cambridge, Mass./London, 1980), pp. 135–136.
388. See Mario Bettati & Gérard Timsit, 'The Regional Institutional Requirements of the NIEO', in: Ervin Laszlo & Joel Kurtzman, *Political and Institutional Issues of the New International Economic Order* (New York etc., 1981), p. 93 at p. 95.
389. See Luis Echeverría in his introduction to *op. cit.*, note 382, p. xxv; 'As long as Third World countries act independently and not in mutual solidarity, their voice is not going to be heard as it should be'.
390. See, *e.g.*, the Brandt Commission's Report, *op. cit.*, note 387, pp. 138–139; Miguel Wionczek, 'The NIEO: A Diagnosis of Failure and Prospects', in: Ervin Laszlo & Joel Kurtzman, *Structure of the World Economy and the New International Economic Order* (New York etc., 1980); Mario Bettati & Gerald Timsit, 'The Regional Institutional Requisites of the NIEO', in: *op. cit.*, note 382, p. 318 at pp. 318–320. The suggestion of 'co-operative self-reliance' and the establishment of a Third World secretariat was also put forward by Michael Manley, former Prime Minister of Jamaica, in a lecture on a strategy for the Third World in the 1980s, given in Amsterdam on June 26, 1982.
391. Aurelio Peccei, Introduction, in: *op. cit.*, note 382, p. xxix at p. xxxiii.
392. Robert Gregg, *loc. cit.*, note 32, pp. 118–119.
393. *Ibidem*, p. 119.
394. *Op. cit.*, note 387, pp. 261–262.
395. *Op. cit.*, note 387, p. 259.
396. See *supra*, p. 703.
397. Jahangir Amuzegar, *loc. cit.*, note 27, p. 156.

398. *Ibidem*, p. 158.
399. For an analysis of the arguments which form the basis of public opposition in the West, and the common-interests conviction which can turn this opposition into support, see Thomas E. Jones, 'Regionalism: The Problem of Public Support', in: *op. cit.*, note 382, pp. 318–232.
400. *Ibidem*, p. 229.